Management
Accounting

Fourth Canadian Edition

Management Accounting

Fourth Canadian Edition

Charles T. Horngren
Stanford University

Gary L. Sundem
University of Washington - Seattle

William O. Stratton
University of Southern Colorado

Howard D. Teall
Wilfrid Laurier University

Toronto

Canadian Cataloguing in Publication Data

Management accounting

4th Canadian ed.
First Canadian ed. by Charles T. Horngren, Gary L. Sundem, Howard D. Teall with Frank H. Selto.
Includes index.
ISBN 0-13-031389-0

1. Managerial accounting. I. Horngren, Charles T., 1926- .

HF5657.4.H67 2002   658.15'11   C2001-930452-6

0-13-031389-0

Vice President, Editorial Director: Michael Young
Senior Acquisitions Editor: Samantha Scully
Marketing Manager: Cas Shields
Developmental Editor: Paul Donnelly
Production Editor: Gillian Scobie
Copy Editor: Karen Hunter
Production Coordinator: Deborah Starks
Page Layout: ArtPlus Limited
Permissions/Photo Research: Susan Wallace-Cox
Art Director: Mary Opper
Interior Design: Julia Hall
Cover Design: Gillian Tsintziras
Cover Image: Stone

5   06 05

Printed and bound in Canada.

To Joan, Scott, Mary, Susie, Cathy, Liz
Garth and Jens
Norma, Gina and Adam
Luanne, Katrina, Tanya, Vanessa, and Adam

Charles T. Horngren is the Edmund W. Littlefield Professor of Accounting at Stanford University. A graduate of Marquette University, he received his MBA from Harvard and his PhD from the University of Chicago. He is also the recipient of honorary doctorates from Marquette as well as De Paul University.

A Certified Public Accountant, Horngren has served on the Accounting Principles Board, the Financial Accounting Standards Board Advisory Council, the Council of the American Institute of Certified Public Accountants, and as a trustee of the Financial Accounting Foundation.

A member of the American Accounting Association, Horngren has been its President and its Director of Research. He received the Outstanding Accounting Educator Award in 1973. The California Certified Public Accountants Foundation gave Horngren its Faculty Excellence Award in 1975 and its Distinguished Professor Award in 1983. In 1985 the AICPA presented its first Outstanding Accounting Educator to Horngren. In 1990 he was elected to the Accounting Hall of Fame.

Professor Horngren is also a member of the National Association of Accountants. He was a member of the Board of Regents, Institute of Certified Management Accountants, which administers the CMA examinations.

Horngren is the co-author of four other books published by Prentice Hall: *Cost Accounting: A Managerial Emphasis,* Ninth Edition, 1997 (with George Foster); *Introduction to Financial Accounting,* Seventh Edition, 1999 (with Gary L. Sundem and John A. Elliott); *Accounting,* Fourth Edition, 1999 (with Walter T. Harrison, Jr. and Linda Smith Bamber), and *Financial Accounting,* Revised Third Edition, 1998 (also with Harrison). In addition he is the Consulting Editor for the Prentice Hall Series in Accounting.

Gary L. Sundem is Associate Dean and Professor of Accounting at the University of Washington, Seattle. He received his BA degree from Carleton College and his MBA and PhD degrees from Stanford University.

Professor Sundem was the 1992-93 President of the American Accounting Association. He had served as Editor of *The Accounting Review,* 1982-86.

A member of the National Association of Accountants, Sundem is past president of the Seattle chapter. He has served on NAA's national Board of Directors, the Committee on Academic Relations, and the Research Committee.

Professor Sundem has numerous publications in accounting and finance journals including *Issues in Accounting Education, The Accounting Review, Journal of Accounting Research,* and *The Journal of Finance.* He received an award for the most notable contribution to accounting literature in 1978; that same year he was selected Outstanding Accounting Educator by the Washington Society of CPAs. He has made more than 100 presentations at universities in the United States and abroad.

William O. Stratton is Department Chairman and Associate Professor of Accounting at the University of Southern Colorado. He received BS degrees from Florida State University and Pennsylvania State University, his MBA from Boston University, and his PhD from the Claremont Graduate School.

A Certified Management Accountant, Stratton has lectured extensively at management accounting conferences in North America and Europe. He has developed and delivered workshops on activity-based management to manufacturing and service organizations throughout the United States. In 1993, Professor Stratton was awarded the Boeing Competition prize for classroom innovation.

Stratton has numerous publications in accounting and international business journals including *Management Accounting, Decision Sciences, IIE Transaction, and Synergie.*

Howard Teall is a Professor in the School of Business and Economics at Wilfrid Laurier University, where he has previously held the positions of Acting Dean, Associate Dean of Business, and Accounting Area Head. He received HBA, MBA, and Ph.D. degrees from the Ivey School of Business Administration at the University of Western Ontario. He obtained a CA designation while employed with Price-Waterhouse and has been awarded an FCA by the Institute of Chartered Accountants of Ontario.

Previous university positions have been held at the Graduate School of Business, Marseille, France, the Helsinki School of Economics and Business Administration, INSEAD (The European Institute of Business Administration), the International University of Japan, and the University of Western Ontario.

Professor Teall has been a consultant and has provided management training programs for IBM Canada Ltd., Equifax Canada, Rockwell Automation Canada Ltd., Tiger Brand Knitting Factory Co., Woodbridge Limited, Lear Corporation Canada Ltd., Centra Gas Corporation, Challenger Motor Freight Inc., Ontario Hydro, B.F. Goodrich Canada Limited, Petro-Canada, General Motors of Canada Limited, General Motors Corporation, the Federal Business Development Bank, the Canadian Department of Industry, Science and Technology Canada, The Liquor Control Board of Ontario, The Banff Centre for Management, Polysar Rubber Corporation, Royal Bank of Trinidad and Tobago and professional qualification programs for PricewaterhouseCoopers, Deloitte & Touche, the Chartered Accountants Students' Association of Ontario, the Institute of Chartered Accountants of Ontario, the Atlantic Provinces Association of Chartered Accountants and CMA Canada.

Brief Contents

Contents

2 COST BEHAVIOUR AND COST-VOLUME RELATIONSHIPS 39

3 MEASUREMENT OF COST BEHAVIOUR 86

4   COST MANAGEMENT SYSTEMS   132

PART TWO

MANAGEMENT DECISIONS

8   RELEVANT INFORMATION AND DECISION MAKING: MARKETING DECISIONS   320

9 RELEVANT INFORMATION AND DECISION MAKING: PRODUCTION DECISIONS   388

PART THREE   MANAGEMENT ACCOUNTING FOR PLANNING AND CONTROL

12   THE MASTER BUDGET   514

13   FLEXIBLE BUDGETS AND STANDARDS FOR CONTROL   563

15 MANAGEMENT CONTROL IN DECENTRALIZED ORGANIZATIONS 686

Preface

Management Accounting, Fourth Canadian Edition, focuses on the use of accounting, financial, and other types of information by managers of organizations. Managers of all organizations, whether in manufacturing, wholesale, service, e-commerce, non-profit or government, must make decisions in an increasingly complex and changing environment. Information is used by managers to assess the relative merits of alternative courses of action for any given decision. Management accounting involves generating and using this information.

Based upon feedback from students and faculty, this Fourth Edition has been reorganized to present the material in a framework that reflects the use of management accounting by managers. Part One, **Management Accounting, Information and Decisions,** describes how managers make decisions. The relationship between management accounting and other business fields is discussed so students understand the subject within the context of the field of management education. Part One also deals with the generation of management accounting information used by managers, and covers various cost classifications and cost systems that managers use to generate information. A common objective of this information is to indicate the effect of a decision on the organization's profits or goals. Without a firm understanding of the costs, a manager is unable to fully understand and evaluate the impact of alternative courses of action. Part Two, **Management Decisions,** considers marketing and production decisions that are common to many organizations. In addition, it considers decisions that have long-term strategic implications and require more significant capital investments. These decisions require an understanding of management issues that are covered in other subject areas. However, students are provided with sufficient information to use management accounting information to make a decision in a real-world context. These chapters focus on making decisions that will maximize shareholder value. Part Three, **Management Accounting for Planning and Control,** recognizes that a potential conflict exists between the goals of managers and the organizations' shareholders. To assess the performance of an organization and its managers, planning and control systems are needed to establish plans and goals and to reward successful performance. Part Four, **Financial Statement Analysis,** considers the use of financial information that is reported to external shareholders. This part does not deal with the preparation of this information but rather its use by decision-makers such as analysts, creditors, and investors. The four parts can be covered in sequence. However, some may prefer an alternative sequence and this book has been written to accommodate this flexibility by reorganizing the parts as modules of the subject of management accounting.

The four parts are presented as segments to the book, but they are interrelated. Part One helps managers use the information generated by various techniques and systems within the decision process outlined. Part Two provides students an opportunity to make decisions that enhance the value of the organization. Part Three provides various means of assessing the success of these decisions and of rewarding managers. Part Four considers the impact on external shareholders when organizations successfully use management accounting information and decision processes, as outlined throughout this book.

As noted in the acknowledgments, senior managers of a number of leading Canadian companies have reviewed chapters of the book to ensure that the material reflects the issues that exist in a globally competitive world. Their comments and suggestions have been incorporated to ensure that students are exposed to current and relevant material. In addition, the book includes Company Strategies, which have been written by managers to provide an example of the application of the material to an issue faced by their organization. The Perspectives On Decision Making boxes have been selected to further illustrate the application of management accounting to actual business problems.

The assignments have been selected and organized to enhance the use of the book in a variety of applications. **Questions** address conceptual and discussion-oriented material and are generally used to engage the student to understand the issues in the context of management decisions. **Problems** involve assignments that are primarily quantitative and have directed requirements. Spreadsheets are available for problems flagged with a spreadsheet logo. (See our Companion Website for further details.) A Collaborative Learning Exercise has also been provided in each chapter to encourage team building and group learning skills. **Cases** require a management decision. Thus, the cases provide students with the opportunity to apply the concepts in practical situations faced by managers of organizations. Many cases are provided by professional accounting organization such as CMA-Canada, the Institute of Chartered Accountants of Ontario, and the Certified General Accountants of Canada, and are designated by the filefolder logo.

The book has been used successfully as either an introductory or advanced course in management accounting at both the graduate and undergraduate levels. Some may use the cases in introductory courses in both MBA and undergraduate programs where students are interested in the subject as part of their business education, and likely do not plan to undertake a career in accounting. The book has also been used for accounting students in an introductory course, which uses the questions and problems, and in an advanced course which uses the case assignments. The book is also appropriate for management and executive development programs given its focus on management decision making.

Features of the Fourth Canadian Edition

Assignment materials: Collaborative Learning Exercises have been created for this edition to encourage group problem-solving skills. More questions, problems, and cases have been added to the end-of-chapter assignment materials and existing assignments have been updated. The colour band at the edge of the page now makes it easy to identify assignment pages in the text.

Shorter, more concise text: By reorganizing the cost systems material from the Third Canadian Edition, we've reduced the number of chapters from 17 to 16, producing a slimmer, more focused book.

On-the-spot key term definitions: Key terms with definitions are placed in the margins opposite the text that introduces the concepts, while within the text key terms are bolded for easy reference. This feature helps students reinforce their understanding of new concepts as they are introduced, while the Accounting Vocabulary list at the end of the chapter (with page references) facilitates review of the new terminology. In the Subject Index, the pages on which key terms are defined have been printed in bold, sending students back to the original context whenever they look up a term.

Internet connections: Weblinks in the margins give students access to Internet resources for companies and organizations discussed in the text, enhancing their understanding of real-world issues. The Destinations section of the book's Companion Website provides hyperlinks and regular updating of the URLs for all Weblinks (see **www.pearsoned.ca/horngren**).

Videos for accounting students: Our supplements package includes CBC videos, based on *Venture* episodes that illustrate current issues in Canadian business.

Real-world insights 1: New **Perspectives on Decision-Making** boxes have been included throughout the text. These boxes present the latest issues and decisions from Canadian companies, from "New Tools–New Mindsets for Management Accountants" in Chapter 1 to such topical issues as "Marketing in the Cost Competitive Airline Industry" in Chapter 8 and "Aligning IT Investments with Business Strategy" in Chapter 15.

Real-world insights 2: **Company Strategies** boxes continue our presentation of the real-world application of concepts and techniques presented in each chapter.

Alternative Ways of Using This Book

Instructors tend to disagree markedly about the sequence of topics in a course in management accounting. Criticisms of *any* sequence in a textbook are inevitable. Consequently, this book tries to provide a **modular approach** that permits hopping and skipping back and forth with minimal inconvenience. In a nutshell, our rationale is to provide a loosely constrained sequence to ease diverse approaches to teaching. Content is of primary importance; sequence is secondary.

Teaching is highly personal and is heavily influenced by the backgrounds and interests of assorted students in various settings. To satisfy this audience, a book must be a pliable tool, not a straitjacket.

As the authors, we prefer to assign the chapters in the sequence provided in the book. But we are not enslaved by this sequence. We have assigned an assortment of sequences, depending on the readers' backgrounds.

Part One, "Management Accounting, Information and Decisions," provides a bedrock introduction, so we assign it in its entirety. If there is time in the course for students to become more familiar with budgeting and standard costing, Chapters 12 and 13 can be assigned immediately after Chapter 5. Furthermore, there is a logical appeal to studying the chapters on capital budgeting (Chapters 10 and 11) immediately after the chapters on planning and control (Chapters 12 through 15). However, we have avoided placing these chapters there because of tradition and because of their link to relevant costing. Moreover, the Fourth Canadian Edition has maintained coverage of capital budgeting over two chapters to ensure comprehensive attention to issues such as risk and rate of return at schools where these topics are not covered in compulsory related courses. In addition, because the master budget is often covered in finance courses, Chapter 12 is frequently skipped in accounting courses.

Part Four introduces financial statement analysis. This chapter covers basic financial statement analysis in capsule form with heavy stress on interpretation of financial statements, and little attention given to the accumulation of the information.

Chapter 16 may be skipped entirely or may be used in a variety of ways:

1. In courses or executive programs where the students have no accounting background but where the main emphasis is on management rather than financial accounting.
2. In courses where this chapter may be used as a quick review by students who have had some financial statement analysis.

Moreover, some teachers may want to use this chapter to teach the fundamentals of financial statement analysis to students with no prior background. Classroom testing has shown that such teaching can be done successfully.

Supplementary Material

The following items are available to supplement the text:

Instructor's Solutions Manual: Includes solutions to all questions, problems, and cases in text. All solutions were prepared by the authors and technically checked by a professional accountant. ISBN 0-13-060797-5

Instructor's Resource Manual: Includes a sample lesson plan, chapter overview, chapter outline (linked to learning objectives and quiz questions), quiz/demonstration exercises, and suggested readings. ISBN 0-13-060798-3

Test Item File: Every chapter has an average of 15 true/false, 60 multiple choice, and 15 short answer questions, for a total of over 1600 questions. Answers, difficulty ratings, and page references to the text accompany each question. ISBN 0-13-060790-8

WIN PH Custom Test: Prentice Hall's computerized test file uses a state-of-the-art software program to provide fast, simple, and error-free test generation in Windows. Entire tests can be previewed on screen before printing. PH Custom Test can print multiple variations of the same test by scrambling the order of questions and multiple choice answers. ISBN 0-13-060801-7

Transparency Resource Package: This package includes 100 slides of key figures from the text, prepared for electronic presentation in PowerPoint 4.0, plus black-and-white masters that can be duplicated for distribution in class. ISBN 0-13-031389-0

Solutions Acetates: When producing a test with such a rich support package as *Management Accounting,* it is important that we consider the environmental and production costs that result when instructors use only a few transparencies. In response to concerns about these costs, we are offering a special package that contains an unbound copy of the *Instructor's Solutions Manual,* a set of dividers, and a supply of 300 clear acetates. Thus, instructors who adopt the test are provided with the opportunity to organize and produce transparencies for the specific solutions that they choose to show in their classroom. We hope you find this a creative response to concerns about waste and the environment. ISBN 0-13-060803-3

Prentice Hall/CBC Video Library: In an exclusive partnership, the CBC and Pearson Education Canada have worked together to develop an exciting video package consisting of six segments from the prestigious series *Venture.* At an average of seven minutes in length, these segments show students how real Canadian companies are affected by current issues in accounting. Case write-ups with teaching notes and questions will be posted on the book's Companion Website. (Please contact your Pearson Education Canada sales representative for details. These videos are subject to availability and terms negotiated upon adoption of the text.)

Companion Website with Online Study Guide and Excel Templates: Our exciting new Website includes a comprehensive online study guide that presents students with numerous review exercises and research tools. There is a detailed review of key concepts for every chapter and practice tests with true/false and multiple choice questions, completion exercises, and accounting problems. Students obtain instant feedback for questions and exercises, and they may view full solutions to problems. A page reference to the text is supplied with every answer, while Destinations (hyperlinks to the text's Weblinks) and search tools facilitate further research into key organizations and topics discussed in the text. The Companion Website also provides Excel templates for all problems flagged in the text with the spreadsheet disk icon, as well as a syllabus builder for instructors, CBC video case updates, and more. See **www.pearsoned.ca/horngren** and explore.

Pearson Education Canada is also proud to introduce **Accounting Central**, a dynamic, online resource centre for instructors and students. Be sure to bookmark this site at www.pearsoned.ca/accounting.

For the Student:

Student Solutions Manual: Designed for student use, this supplement contains fully worked-out solutions for all even-numbered questions, problems, and cases in the textbook. The *Student Solutions Manual* may be purchased with the instructor's permission. ISBN 0-13-060804-1

Charles T. Horngren
Gary L. Sundem
William O. Stratton
Howard D. Teall

Acknowledgments (Canadian edition)

I have received assistance from many people who have contributed to this book.

I am grateful for the assistance and support provided by Wilfrid Laurier University.

My appreciation is also extended to the Canadian Institute of Chartered Accountants (CICA), the Institute of Chartered Accountants of Ontario (ICAO), the Society of Management Accountants of Canada (SMAC), the Certified General Accountants' Association of Canada (CGAC), and to the other sources as indicated for their generous permission to use or adapt problems from their publications.

I would like to thank the reviewers of this text for their insights and suggestions, especially:

Ibrahim M. Aly, Concordia University
Ann Clarke-Okah, Carleton University
Patricia Corkum, Acadia University
Johan de Rooy, University of British Columbia
Craig Emby, Simon Fraser University
Amin Mawani, York University
Pamela Quon, Athabasca University
Catherine Sequin, University of Toronto
J. Roderick Tilley, Mount Saint Vincent University
Shu-Lun Wong, Memorial University of Newfoundland

Special gratitude is extended to all of the Canadian managers who contributed their time and comments in order that this book reflect today's Canadian environment:

Hugh Atkin, Foster's Brewing Group
John Baeck, Esso Resources Canada Limited
John Carney and Larry Wozniak, J.M. Schneider Inc.
Frank Currie, Budd Canada Inc.
Joe Doolan, PanCanadian Petroleum Ltd.
Robin Hamilton Harding, Bell Canada
David LeNeveu, Procter & Gamble Canada Inc.
Stuart Macdonnell, B.F. Goodrich Canada Inc.
Mick Mast, Jack O'Donnell, and Pat Bandura, RMS Machinery Division Uniroyal Goodrich Canada Inc.
Richard Michalski, The Society of Management Accountants of Canada
John Patterson, Canadian Occidental Petroleum Ltd.
Jeff Pennock, Liquor Control Board of Ontario
John Richardson, Boreal Laboratories Ltd.
Randy Royer and Kirk Morgan, Bayco Hotels & Resorts Ltd.
Randy White, Arriscraft Corporation

This book was based upon the U.S. eleventh edition by Charles T. Horngren, Gary L. Sundem, and William O. Stratton. I appreciate their willingness to share their work with me. This book has certainly benefited from their experience and contribution.

My thanks also go to the following people at Pearson Education Canada Inc. who worked with me on this project: Gillian Scobie, Production Editor; Deborah Starks, Production Co-ordinator; Paul Donnelly, Developmental Editor; and Samantha Scully, Acquisitions Editor. Thanks also to Sarah Weber and Eva Chan for compiling the numerous Weblinks for the text and to Ian Farmer for his detailed technical check.

Finally, special recognition is given to my wife, Luanne, and my children, Katrina, Tanya, Vanessa, and Adam for their constant understanding of the demands of my work.

Comments are most welcome.

Howard D. Teall

Testimonial

In light of the need for accuracy in accounting textbooks, all solutions have been checked.

As requested, I have read the proof copy of the above noted book consisting of chapters 1 to 16 and have checked the arithmetic and logic in all of the worked examples and exhibits in that proof as well as ensuring that references to those examples and exhibits within the text were accurate.

Ian Farmer, C.A.

Your Internet companion to the most exciting, state-of-the-art educational tools on the Web!

The Pearson Education Canada Companion Website is easy to navigate and is organized to correspond to the chapters in this textbook. The Companion Website comprises these distinct, functional features:

Customized Online Resources

Online Interactive Study Guide

Interactivities

Communication

Explore these areas in this Companion Website. Students and distance learners will discover resources for indepth study, research, and communication, empowering them in their quest for greater knowledge and maximizing their potential for success in the course.

A NEW WAY TO DELIVER EDUCATIONAL CONTENT

Course Management

Our Companion Websites provide instructors and students with the ability to access, exchange, and interact with material specially created for our individual textbooks.

- **Syllabus Manager** provides instructors with the option of creating online classes and constructing an online syllabus linked to specific modules in the Companion Website.

- **Grader** allows the student to take a test that is automatically marked by the program. The results of the test can be e-mailed to the instructor and then added to the student's record.

- **Help** includes an evaluation of the user's system and a tune-up area that makes updating browsers and plug-ins easier. This new feature will facilitate the use of our Companion Websites.

Instructor Resources

This section features modules with additional teaching material organized by chapter for instructors. Downloadable PowerPoint Presentations, Electronic Transparencies, and an Instructor's Manual are just some of the materials that may be available in this section. Where appropriate, this section will be password protected. To get a password, simply contact your Pearson Education Canada representative or call Faculty Sales and Services at 1-800-850-5813.

General Resources

This section contains information that is related to the entire book and that will be of interest to all users of the site. A Table of Contents and a Glossary are just two examples of the kind of information you may find in this section.

The General Resources section may also feature *Communication facilities* that provide a key element for distributed learning environments:

- **Message Board** – This module takes advantage of browser technology to provide the users of each Companion Website with a national newsgroup to post and reply to relevant course topics.

- **Chat Room** – This module enables instructors to lead group activities in real time. Using our chat client, instructors can display website content while students participate in the discussion.

Visit www.pearsoned.ca/horngren for great student resources

Pearson Education Canada

Want some practice before an exam?

The Student Resources section contains the modules that form the core of the student learning experience in the Companion Website. The modules presented in this section may include the following:

- Learning Objectives
- Multiple-Choice Questions
- True/False Questions
- Completion Exercises
- Problems
- Destinations
- Net Search
- PowerPoint Presentations

The question modules provide students with the ability to send answers to our grader and receive instant feedback on their progress through our Results Reporter. Coaching comments and references to the textbook may be available to ensure that students take advantage of all available resources to enhance their learning experience.

chapter 1

Student Resources

Objectives

Key Concepts

Multiple Choice

True/False

Completion

Problems

Extras

Destinations

CBC Videos

Net News

Net Search

PowerPoint Presentations

Instructor Resources

Instructor's resource Manual

Instructor's solutions Manual

Syllabus Builder

General Resources

Feedback

Site Search

Help

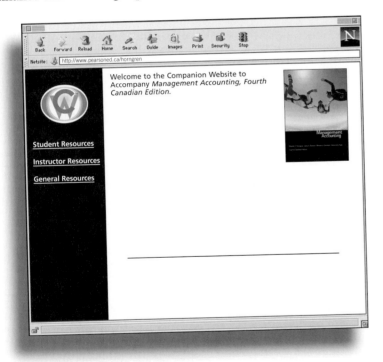

PEARSON EDUCATION CANADA

26 Prince Andrew Place
Toronto, Ontario M3C 2T8

To order:
Call: 1-800-567-3800
Fax: 1-800-263-7733

For samples:
Call: 1-800-850-5813
Fax: (416) 299-2539
E-mail:
phabinfo_pubcanada@pearsoned.com

Companion Websites are currently available for:

- Horngren: *Introduction to Financial Accounting*
- Horngren: *Cost Accounting*
- Revsine: *Financial Reporting and Analysis*
- Arens: *Auditing and Other Assurance Services*

Note: Companion Website content will vary slightly from site to site depending on discipline requirements.

The Companion Website for this text can be found at:

www.pearsoned.ca/horngren

Management Accounting and Management Decisions

Management
Management

LEARNING OBJECTIVES

After studying this chapter, you will be able to

1. Describe the role of management accounting in today's organizations.

2. Explain the role of the management accountant.

3. Identify the characteristics of service organizations that distinguish them from manufacturing organizations.

4. Explain the role of accountants in an organization's value chain functions.

5. Distinguish between the line and staff roles in an organization.

6. Contrast the functions of controllers and treasurers.

7. Describe the two major themes of this book: cost-benefit and behavioural implications.

8. Identify the major distinctions between management accounting and financial accounting.

9. Identify the most important areas of ethical conduct by management accountants.

MANAGEMENT ACCOUNTING FOR MANAGERS

Management accounting exists because managers require information to make decisions; therefore *management accounting is user-driven not data-driven.* The subject of management accounting goes far beyond the issues of generating and disseminating facts, and while these tasks may be part of management accounting, they are not the essence of management accounting. There is a subtle but important difference between the word "data" and the word "information," in that information is data that have been used. Simply stated, to generate records of facts that are not used in a decision is to generate data. However, once the data have been used by a manager, then they become information. It is important for students of management accounting to appreciate the fact that an integral part of the subject deals with information systems and not data systems. In other words, *accounting information systems are the means, and better decisions are the ends.*

The management accounting information system provides information to numerous user groups for a variety of purposes. While some of these user groups are external to the organization, the focus of management accounting is on the needs of users within the organization. For example, information is required for technical and operating decisions such as those concerning quality control and scheduling. Also, managers in an organization's personnel department require information in order to make decisions when monitoring absenteeism and during labour negotiations. The generation of financial statements for external investors and creditors is also a primary requirement of the information system. (In fact, it has been argued that the external reporting needs have inappropriately become the dominant user of accounting information systems.) Finally, the management accounting information system must also provide the information required for product costing, pricing, and evaluation of segment profitability. In summary, management accounting does not exist to generate data, but it exists because managers require information for decisions.

In any organization, whether it is profit-oriented, not-for-profit, a manufacturing firm, a service organization, or government sector, numerous decisions are made each day. Because of the variety of decisions made in any one day, management accounting is similarly diverse. This diversity makes it difficult for students to organize the subject of management accounting. When a subject is organized within a framework, it is then easier to identify a situation as having certain characteristics, rather than attempting to learn the subject as a list of loosely related topics. To help make this diversity comprehensive, the study of management accounting has been organized into frameworks—two of which are presented here.

The first framework focuses on the types of decisions that must be made and categorizes those decisions into "operational control," "management control," or "strategic planning."[1] Operational control decisions ensure that specific tasks are carried out effectively and efficiently. Management control decisions make sure that the resources are used effectively and efficiently by the managers of the organization. Strategic planning decisions focus on the objectives of the organization and the manner in which resources are acquired and employed.

The second framework focuses on the characteristics of decisions.[2] It places decisions on a continuum between structured decisions and unstructured decisions.

---

[1] R.N. Anthony, *Planning and Control Systems: A Framework for Analysis,* Boston: Graduate School of Business Administration, Harvard University, 1965.

[2] H.A. Simon, *The New Science of Management Decision,* New York: Harper and Row, 1960.

Structured decisions are those that are routine and normal, where the information requirements and decision processes are relatively well understood. Unstructured decisions are unique and uncommon and thus the information and decision processes need to be developed for that decision. Exhibit 1-1 provides examples of decisions that have been classified within the two, in this case, complementary frameworks.

EXHIBIT 1-1	OPERATIONAL CONTROL	MANAGEMENT CONTROL	STRATEGIC PLANNING
Structured	Accounts receivable	Budget analysis	Tanker fleet mix
	Order entry	Short-term forecasting	Warehouse and factory location
	Inventory reordering	Engineered costs	
	Inventory control	Variance analysis	Mergers and acquisitions
Semi-Structured	Production scheduling	Overall budget	Capital acquisition analysis
	Bond trading	Budget preparation	New product planning
	Cash management		
Unstructured	PERT COST systems	Sales and production	R and D planning

Frameworks for Management Accounting[3]

A MANAGEMENT DECISION PROCESS

This discussion of management accounting frameworks can be expanded substantially, but these two frameworks provide an initial basis for students to organize the subject of management accounting. These two frameworks also highlight another important point: to practise management accounting it is necessary to make decisions and to understand the role of information in the decision-making process. It is important for management accountants to understand the decision requirements of the information provided to be able to advise senior managers and to be able to make decisions themselves as active managers of an organization. Making good decisions requires a process that is logical and rational. The decision process depicted in Exhibit 1-2 is sufficiently generic to be useful in most situations, but is not the only effective decision process.

As Exhibit 1-2 shows, the first step is to clearly identify the problem or issue. The next step is to ask yourself the following two questions: What information do I need to develop a solution to the problem? What analysis will provide me with the information that I require?

The answers to these questions will result in a list of possible analyses that will often address both quantitative and qualitative issues. It is important not to limit your analysis to only the numerical aspects of the problem because your analysis will no doubt miss important dimensions of the issue. After concluding the necessary analysis, the third step is to identify alternative solutions to the problem. Alternative solutions must exist because if there were only one correct solution,

---

[3] Reprinted from "A Framework for Management Information Systems," by G.A. Garry and M.S. Scott Morton, *Sloan Management Review* Fall, 1970, p. 62. Copyright 1993 by the Sloan Management Review Association. All Rights Reserved.

EXHIBIT 1-2

A Management
Decision Process

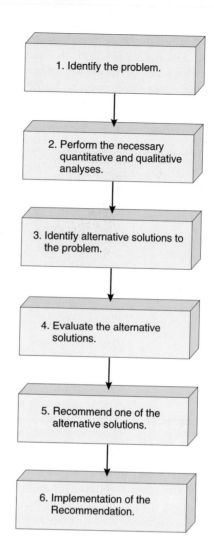

1. Identify the problem.

2. Perform the necessary quantitative and qualitative analyses.

3. Identify alternative solutions to the problem.

4. Evaluate the alternative solutions.

5. Recommend one of the alternative solutions.

6. Implementation of the Recommendation.

the situation did not require a decision. Each alternative solution must have the potential to resolve the identified problem. The fourth step then is to analyze each alternative solution in terms of its advantages/disadvantages, costs/benefits, and pros/cons. After a thorough analysis of the possible courses, a decision can be recommended. The rationale for the decision should focus on its advantages and you should be ready to explain why the disadvantages are not significant or how they can be managed. Finally, the implementation of the recommendation may be the most difficult step as it may depend upon the ability of the manager to effectively change the way an organization operates.

OBJECTIVE 2

Explain the role of the management accountant.

Managers must have a decision process that is both flexible and effective. The decision process must be flexible because it has to adapt to the numerous situations that a manager faces, and effective because it has to enable the manager to reach a decision.

EXHIBIT 1-3

Management

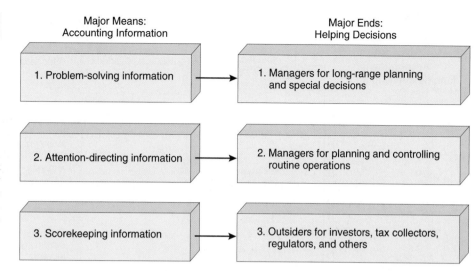

Major Means: Accounting Information

Major Ends: Helping Decisions

1. Problem-solving information → 1. Managers for long-range planning and special decisions

2. Attention-directing information → 2. Managers for planning and controlling routine operations

3. Scorekeeping information → 3. Outsiders for investors, tax collectors, regulators, and others

Problem-Solving.
Aspect of accounting that quantifies the likely results of possible courses of action and often recommends the best course of action to follow.

Attention-Directing.
Reporting and interpreting of information that helps managers to focus on operating problems, imperfections, inefficiencies, and opportunities.

Scorekeeping.
The accumulation and classification of data.

1. **Problem-solving.** This aspect of accounting involves the concise quantification of the relative merits of possible courses of action, often with recommendations as to the best procedure. Problem-solving is commonly associated with nonrecurring decisions—situations that require special accounting analyses or reports.

2. **Attention-directing.** The reporting and interpreting of information that helps managers to focus on operating problems, imperfections, inefficiencies, and opportunities. This aspect of accounting helps managers to concentrate on important aspects of operations promptly enough for effective action. Attention directing is commonly associated with current planning and control and with the analysis and investigation of recurring routine internal accounting reports.

3. **Scorekeeping.** The accumulation of information. This aspect of accounting enables both internal and external parties to evaluate organizational performance and position.

THE MANAGEMENT ACCOUNTANT'S ROLE

Management Accounting.
The process of identifying, measuring, accumulating, analyzing, preparing, interpreting, and communicating information that helps managers fulfill organizational objectives.

Given the importance of information to the subject of management accounting, **management accounting** can be described as the process of identification, measurement, accumulation, analysis, preparation, interpretation, and communication of information that assists managers in making decisions. The management accountant ensures that this process is effective. The management accountant's role involves scorekeeping, attention-directing, and problem-solving as described in Exhibit 1-3. While descriptions of the tasks do overlap or merge, it is necessary to recognize the importance of planning and controlling to the management accountant's role.

The Nature of Planning and Controlling

Exhibit 1-4 demonstrates the division of management accounting into the two processes of planning and controlling.

Planning (the top box) means setting objectives and outlining the means for their attainment. Planning provides the answers to three questions: What is desired? When and how is it to be accomplished? How is success to be evaluated? Controlling (the two boxes labelled "Action" and "Evaluation") entails implementing plans and using feedback to attain objectives. The feedback loop is the central facet of control, and timely, systematic measurement is the chief means of providing useful feedback. Planning and controlling are so intertwined that it is difficult to separate them; yet at times we will find it useful to concentrate on one or the other phase of the planning control cycle.

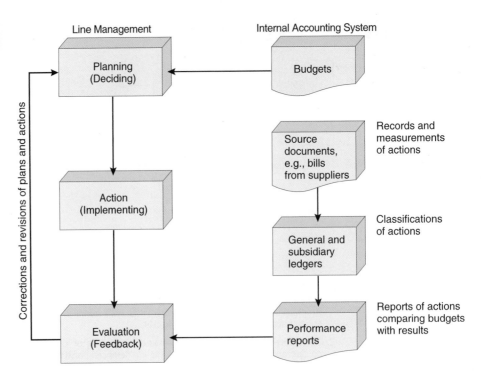

EXHIBIT 1-4

Management
Accounting for
Planning and Control

Management by Exception

Budget. A quantitative expression of a plan of action as an aid to co-ordinating and implementing the plan.

Performance Reports. Feedback provided by comparing results with plans and by highlighting variances.

Management by Exception. Concentrating on areas that deserve attention and ignoring areas that are presumed to be running smoothly.

The right side of Exhibit 1-4 shows that accounting formalizes plans by expressing them in the language of figures as budgets. A **budget** quantitatively expresses a plan of action and aids the coordination and implementation of that plan. Accounting formalizes control as **performance reports** (the last box), which provide feedback by comparing results with plans and by highlighting variances (i.e., deviations from plans). The accounting system records, measures, and classifies actions in order to produce performance reports.

Exhibit 1-5 shows a simple performance report form for a law firm. Such reports spur investigation of exceptions—when actual amounts differ significantly from budgeted amounts. Operations are then brought into conformity with the plans, or the plans are revised. This is an example of management by exception. **Management by exception** is the practice of concentrating on areas that deviate from the plan and ignoring areas that are presumed to be running smoothly. Management should not ordinarily be concerned with results that conform closely to plans. However, well-conceived plans should incorporate enough discretion or flexibility so that the manager may feel free to pursue any unforeseen opportunities. In other words, the definition of control does not mean that managers should blindly cling to a pre-existing plan when unfolding events call for actions that were not specifically authorized in the original plan.

EXHIBIT 1-5

Performance Report

	BUDGETED AMOUNTS	ACTUAL AMOUNTS	DEVIATIONS OR VARIANCES	EXPLANATION
Revenue from fees	xxx	xxx	xx	—
Various expenses	xxx	xxx	xx	—
Net income	xxx	xxx	xx	—

Material (detailed by type: metal stampings, motors, etc.)	$ 68,000
Assembly labour (detailed by job classification, number of workers, etc.)	43,000
Other labour (managers, inspectors)	12,000
Utilities, maintenance, etc.	7,500
Supplies (small tools, lubricants, etc.)	2,500
Total	$133,000

Illustration of the Budget and the Performance Report

An assembly department constructs electric fans. The assembly of the parts and the installation of the electric motor are basically manual operations. Each fan is inspected before being transferred to the painting department. In light of the present sales forecast, a production schedule of 4,000 window fans and 6,000 table fans is planned for the coming month. The Assembly Department Budget in Exhibit 1-6 shows cost classifications.

The operating plan, in the form of a department budget for the coming month, is prepared in conferences attended by the department manager, the manager's supervisor, and an accountant. Each of the costs subject to the manager's control is scrutinized. Its average amount for the past few months is often used as a guide, especially if past performance has been reasonably efficient. However, the budget is a *forecast* of costs. Each cost is projected in light of trends, price changes, alterations in product mix, specifications, labour methods, and changes in production volume from month to month. The budget is then formulated, and it becomes the manager's target for the month.

	BUDGET	ACTUAL	VARIANCE
Material (detailed by type: metal stampings, motors, etc.	$ 68,000	$ 69,000	$1,000 U
Assembly labour (detailed by job classification, number of workers, etc.)	43,000	44,300	1,300 U
Other labour (managers, inspectors)	12,000	11,200	800 F
Utilities, maintenance, etc.	7,500	7,400	100 F
Supplies (small tools, lubricants, etc.)	2,500	2,600	100 U
Total	$133,000	$134,500	$1,500 U

U = Unfavourable
F = Favourable

As actual factory costs are incurred during the month, the accounting system collects them and classifies them by departments. At the end of the month (or perhaps weekly, or even daily for such key items as materials or assembly labour), the accounting department prepares an Assembly Department Performance Report (Exhibit 1-7). In practice, this report may be very detailed and contain explanations of variances from the budget.

Department heads and their superiors use this report to help appraise performance. The spotlight is cast on the **variance**—the deviations from the budget. When managers investigate these variances, they may discover better

Variance. Deviations from plans.

New Tools—New Mindsets for Management Accountants

Mastering the new role of finance requires more than learning a new skill or computer program. It will entail a change in mindset, away from the traditional control and transaction orientation to one that focuses on active participation in a company's ongoing pursuit of competitive excellence.

In becoming business partners, management accountants must build the culture of continuous improvement and value creation into the very fibre of new financial systems and methods. The key to these efforts is the development of dynamic, flexible accounting and decision-support systems that can aid managers throughout the organization in understanding, creating and using reliable and relevant financial information.

Management accounting in the coming millennium will be embedded in the cycle of learning created by the continuous improvement paradigm (see figure below). This paradigm, and the tools it has created or recreated, are at the heart of the race to gain and sustain a global competitive advantage.

These new tools, and others like them, are the means by which management accountants can understand—hence know—what needs to be done to meet ongoing organizational and competitive challenges. The knowing—or art of management accounting—is understanding what tool should be used, when it should be used, and why, as well as being able to implement this knowledge, first hand, or through others.

Source: Reprinted from an article appearing in *CMA Management* by C.J. McNair, February 1997, with permission of the Society of Management Accountants of Canada.

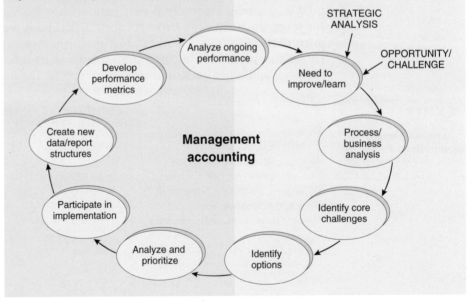

Accounting System. A formal mechanism for gathering, organizing, and communicating information about an organization's activities.

ways of doing things. The budget is the tool that aids planning; the performance report is the tool that aids controlling. The **accounting system** thus helps to direct managerial attention to the exceptions. Exhibit 1-4 shows that accounting does not do the controlling. Controlling consists of actions performed by the managers and their subordinates and of the evaluation that follows the actions. Accounting assists the managerial control function by providing prompt measurements of actions and by systematically pinpointing trouble spots. This management-by-exception approach frees managers from needless concern with those phases of operations that are adhering to plans.

MANAGEMENT ACCOUNTING AND SERVICE ORGANIZATIONS

OBJECTIVE 3

Identify the characteristics of service organizations that distinguish them from manufacturing organizations.

The basic ideas of management accounting were developed in manufacturing organizations. However, these ideas have evolved so that they are applicable to all types of organizations, including service organizations. Service organizations or industries are defined in various ways. For our purposes, they are organizations that do not make or sell tangible goods. Examples are public accounting firms, law firms, management consultants, real estate firms, transportation companies, banks, insurance companies, and hotels. Almost all nonprofit organizations are service industries. Examples are hospitals, schools, libraries, museums, and government departments.

The characteristics of service organizations include the following:

1. *Labour is intensive*. For example, the highest proportion of expenses in schools and law firms are wages, salaries, and payroll-related costs, not costs relating to the use of machinery, equipment, and extensive physical facilities.
2. *Output is usually difficult to define*. For example, the output of a university might be defined as the number of degrees granted, but many critics would maintain that the real output is "what is contained in the students' brains." The output of schools and hospitals is often idealized; attempts to measure output are normally considered impossible.
3. *Major inputs and outputs cannot be stored*. For example, although raw materials and retail merchandise may be stored, a hotel's available labour force and rooms are either used or unused as each day occurs.
4. *Product diversity*. For example, a hospital provides many related services from essentially the same capacity and therefore management of the portfolio of products is very important.

A study of the United States economy, which was cross-checked to industries in Canada, Europe, and Japan, found that the economy is changing from manufacturing-based industries to those whose primary components are knowledge and innovation.[4] It has been reported that Canadian factory jobs fell from 23.5 percent of total employment in the mid-1960s to 15.2 percent in the early 1990s.[5] While some of the growth industries of today are technology-based, many are service-oriented. For example, in terms of the number of employees, the U.S. motion picture industry is larger than the automotive parts industry and the travel service industry is larger than the petroleum and steel industries combined.

Applicability To Non-profit Organizations

This book is aimed at a variety of readers, including students who aspire to become either managers or professional accountants. The focus will be on profit-seeking organizations. However, the fundamental ideas for profit-seeking organizations also apply to non-profit organizations, also referred to as not-for-profit organizations.

---

[4] "Tilting at Smokestacks," *The Globe and Mail*, July 20, 1991.
[5] "How the 'jobless' recovery could have a happy ending," *The Globe and Mail*, February 13, 1993.

Managers and accountants in various settings such as hospitals, universities, and government agencies have much in common with their counterparts in profit-seeking organizations. Money must be raised and spent. Budgets must be prepared, and control systems must be designed and implemented. There is an obligation to use resources wisely. If used intelligently, accounting contributes to efficient operations.

The overlap of government and business is everywhere. Government administrators and politicians are much better equipped to deal with problems inside and outside their organizations if they understand accounting. For example, a knowledge of accounting is crucial for decisions regarding research contracts, government contracts, and loan guarantees.

Key Success Factors

Key Success Factors. The factors that must be managed successfully to achieve organizational success.

While management accounting is relevant to all organizations, whether they are manufacturing-oriented, service-oriented, or non-profit, what does vary are the factors that must be managed effectively if the organization is to be successful. Managers are required to make many decisions that vary in their degree of importance. Errors in decisions of lesser importance, while not desirable, are not critical to the success of the organization. However, errors in some key decisions are critical to the organization's success. Factors that must be managed successfully are called **key success factors**. While this term has also been used to refer to industry factors, the reference here is to organization-specific factors. Management accountants should be well aware of the key success factors of their organization, as these factors must remain the focus of their decisions. Some management accountants fall into the trap of being overwhelmed with developing the perfect information system. It is, however, much more efficient and effective to concentrate on servicing the needs of the key success factors when developing the information system. This perspective will assist the management accountant in maintaining a balance between the demand for complexity and the need for simplicity.

PLANNING AND CONTROL FOR PRODUCT LIFE CYCLES AND THE VALUE CHAIN

Product Life Cycle. The various stages through which a product passes, from conception and development through introduction into the market through maturation and, finally, withdrawal from the market.

Many management decisions relate to a single good or service, or to a group of related products. To effectively plan for and control production of such goods or services, accountants and other managers must consider the product's life cycle. **Product life cycle** refers to the various stages through which a product passes, from conception and development through introduction into the market through maturation and, finally, withdrawal from the market. At each stage, managers face differing costs and potential returns. Exhibit 1-8 shows a typical product life cycle.

Product life cycles range from a few months (for fashion clothing or faddish toys) to many years (for automobiles or refrigerators). Some products, such as

EXHIBIT 1-8

Typical Product Life Cycle

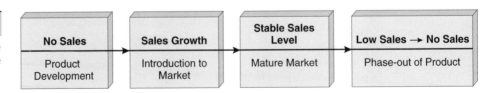

many computer software packages, have long development stages and relatively short market lives. Others, such as Boeing 777 airplanes, have market lives many times longer than their development stage.

In the planning process, managers must recognize revenues and costs over the entire life cycle—however long or short. Accounting needs to track actual costs and revenues throughout the life cycle, too. Periodic comparisons between *planned* costs and revenues and *actual* costs and revenues allow managers to assess the current profitability of a product, determine its current product life-cycle stage, and make any needed changes in strategy.

For example, suppose a pharmaceutical company is developing a new drug to reduce high blood pressure. The budget for the product should plan for costs without revenues in the product development stage. Most of the revenues come in the introduction and mature-market stages, and a pricing strategy should recognize the need for revenues to cover both development and phase-out costs, as well as the direct costs of producing the drug. During phase-out, costs of producing the drug must be balanced with both the revenue generated and the need to keep the drug on the market for those who have come to rely on it.

The Value Chain

Value Chain. A set of business functions that add value to the product or service of an organization.

How does a company actually create the goods or services that it sells? Whether we are making donuts in a shopping mall or making $50-million airplanes, all organizations try to create goods or services that are valued by their customers. The **value chain** is the set of business functions that add value to the products or services of an organization. As shown in Exhibit 1-9, these functions are as follows:

- Research and development—the generation of, and experimentation with, ideas related to new products, services, or processes.
- Design of products, services, or processes—the detail engineering of products.
- Production—the coordination and assembly of resources to produce a product or deliver a service.

EXHIBIT 1-9

The Value Chain of Business Functions

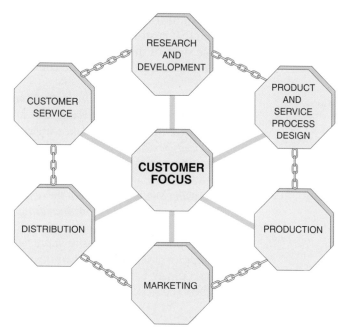

- Marketing—the manner by which individuals or groups learn about the value and features of products or services.
- Distribution—the mechanism by which products or services are delivered to the customer.
- Customer service—the support activities provided to the customer.

Not all of these functions are important to the success of a company. Senior management must decide which of these functions enables the company to gain and maintain a competitive edge. For example, Dell Computers considers the *design* function a key success factor. The features designed into Dell's computers create higher quality. In addition, the design of efficient processes used to make and deliver computers lowers costs and speeds up delivery to its customers. Of course, Dell also performs the other value-chain functions, but it concentrates on being the best process designer in the computer market.

Accountants play a key role in all value-chain functions. Providing estimated revenue and cost data during research and development and design stages (especially the design stage) of the value chain enables managers and engineers to reduce the life-cycle costs of products or services more than in any other value-chain function. Using computer-based planning software, accountants can give managers rapid feedback on ideas for costs reduction long before a commitment must be made to purchase expensive equipment. Then, during the production stage, accountants help track the effects of continuous improvement programs. Accountants also play a central role in cost planning and control through the use of budgets and performance reporting as described in the previous section. Marketing decisions have a significant impact on sales but the cost of promotional programs is also significant. The trade-off between increased costs and revenues is analyzed by accountants. Distributing products or services to customers is a complex function. Should a company sell its products directly to a chain of retail stores, or should it sell to a wholesaler? What transportation system should be used—trucks or trains? What are the costs of each alternative? Finally, accountants provide cost data for customer service activities, such as warranty and repair costs and the costs of goods returned. As you can see, cost management is very important throughout the value chain as is the role of accounting.

Note that customer focus is at the centre of Exhibit 1-9. Successful businesses never lose sight of the importance of maintaining a focus on the needs of its customers. For example, consider the comments of the following business leaders.

Customers, by the choices they make, grant companies a future or condemn them to extinction. We will continuously strive to achieve total customer satisfaction....We will seek to truly understand the complexity of our customers' needs, not push our own ideas or technology.
PHILIP CONDIT, CHAIRMAN AND CHIEF EXECUTIVE OFFICER, BOEING COMPANY

Improving comparable sales in the competitive U.S. market means selling more food. So, our emphasis is on increasing customer visits. In the U.S., we'll do that by concentrating on our customers: re-energizing and focusing our marketing efforts, being aggressive in providing maximum price value, continuing to improve service in our restaurants and enhancing food taste.
MIKE CONLEY, EXECUTIVE VICE PRESIDENT AND CHIEF FINANCIAL OFFICER, MCDONALD'S CORPORATION

The value chain and the concepts of adding value and focusing on the customer are extremely important to companies, and they are becoming more so every day. Therefore, we will return to the value chain and use it as a focus for discussion throughout the book.

THE ROLE OF THE ACCOUNTANT IN THE ORGANIZATION

Line and Staff Authority

The organization chart in Exhibit 1-10 shows how many manufacturing companies are divided into subunits. In particular, consider the distinction between line

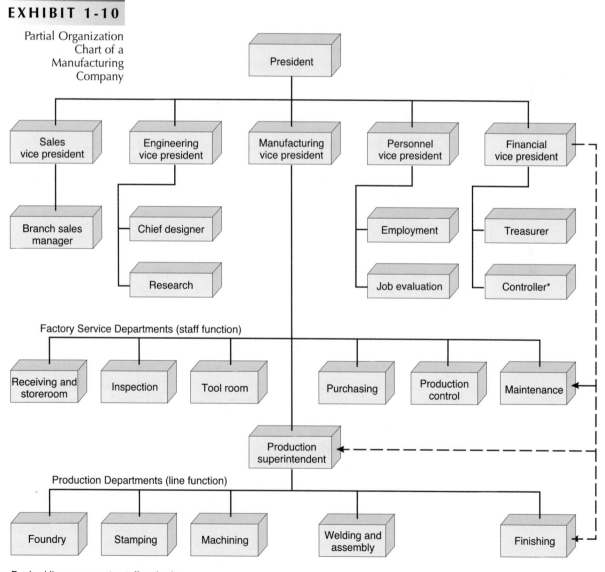

EXHIBIT 1-10

Partial Organization Chart of a Manufacturing Company

Dashed line represents staff authority.
*For detailed organization of a controller's department, see Exhibit 1-11.

Line Authority. Authority exerted downward over subordinates.

Staff Authority. Authority to advise but not command. It may be exerted downward, laterally, or upward.

and staff authority. **Line authority** is exerted downward over subordinates. **Staff authority** is the authority to advise but not to command; it may be exerted downward, laterally, or upward.

Most organizations specify certain activities as their basic mission, such as the production and sale of goods or services. All subunits of the organization that are *directly* responsible for conducting these basic activities are called *line* departments. The others are called *staff* departments because their principal task is to support or service the line departments. Thus, *staff* activities are *indirectly* related to the basic activities of the organization. For instance, Exhibit 1-10 shows a series of factory-service departments that perform the staff functions of supporting the line functions carried out by the production departments.

The controller fills a staff role, in contrast to the line roles of sales and production executives. The accounting department is responsible for providing other managers with specialized services, including advice and help in budgeting, analyzing variances, pricing, and making special decisions. The accounting department does not exercise direct authority over line departments; its authority to prescribe uniform accounting and reporting methods is delegated to the controller by top-line management. The uniform accounting procedure is authorized by the company president and is installed by the controller. When the controller prescribes the line department's role in supplying accounting information, the controller is not speaking as a staff person, but is speaking for top-line management.

OBJECTIVE 5

Distinguish between line and staff roles in an organization.

Theoretically, the controller's decisions regarding the best accounting procedures to be followed by line people are transmitted to the president. In turn, the president communicates these procedures through a manual of instructions, which comes down through the line chain of command to all people affected by the procedures. The controller usually holds delegated authority from top-line management over such matters.

Exhibit 1-11 shows how a controller's department may be organized. In particular, note the distinctions among the scorekeeping, attention-directing, and problem-solving roles. Unless some internal accountants are given the last two roles as their primary responsibilities, the scorekeeping tasks tend to dominate, making the system less helpful to management's decision making.

The Controller

The controller position varies in stature and duties from company to company. In some firms the controller is little more than a glorified bookkeeper who compiles data, primarily for external reporting purposes. In other companies the controller is a key executive who aids managerial planning and control across the company's subdivisions. In most firms controllers belong somewhere between these two extremes. For example, their opinions on the tax implications of certain management decisions may be carefully weighed, yet their opinions on other aspects of these decisions (such as human resource or marketing issues) may not be sought. In this book, **controller** (sometimes called **comptroller**, derived from the French *compte*, for "account") refers to the financial executive who has primary responsibility for both management accounting and financial accounting. We have already seen that the modern controller does not do any controlling in terms of line authority except over his or her own department. Yet the modern concept of controllership maintains that, in a special sense, the *controller does control*: by reporting and interpreting relevant data, the controller

Controller (Comptroller). The top accounting officer of an organization.

EXHIBIT 1-11

Organization Chart of a
Controller's Department

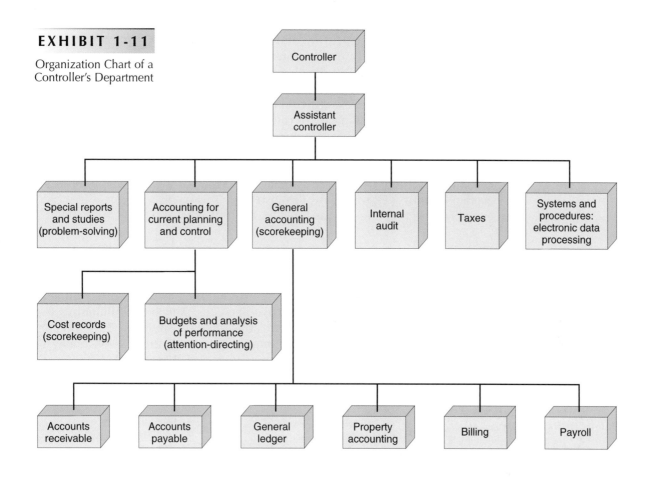

exerts a force or influence, or projects an attitude, that impels management toward logical decisions that are consistent with the company's financial objectives.

Distinctions between Controller and Treasurer

OBJECTIVE 6

Contrast the functions of controllers and treasurers.

Many people confuse the offices of controller and treasurer. The Financial Executives Institute, an association of corporate treasurers and controllers, distinguishes the functions as follows:

Controllership	Treasurership
1. Planning for control	1. Provision of capital
2. Reporting and interpreting	2. Investor relations
3. Evaluating and consulting	3. Short-term financing
4. Tax administration	4. Banking and custody
5. Government reporting	5. Credits and collections
6. Protection of assets	6. Investments
7. Economic appraisal	7. Insurance

Note that management accounting is the controller's primary *means* of implementing the first three functions of controllership.

We shall not dwell at length on the treasurer's functions. As the seven points indicate, the treasurer is concerned mainly with financial rather than operating problems. The exact division of various accounting and financial duties obviously varies from company to company.

The controller has been compared to the ship's navigator. The navigator, with the help of his or her specialized training, assists the captain. Without the navigator, the ship may flounder on reefs or miss its destination entirely, but the captain exerts his or her right to command. The navigator guides and informs the captain on how well the ship is being steered. This navigator's role is especially evident in the first three points listed for controllership.

TWO MAJOR THEMES

OBJECTIVE 7

Describe the two major themes of this book: cost-benefit and behavioural implications.

We have already seen that management accounting is concerned with how accounting systems help make collective decisions. This book emphasizes two major themes, philosophies, or problems regarding the design of these systems: (1) cost-benefit and (2) behavioural implications. Both themes will briefly be described, and will be mentioned often in succeeding chapters.

Cost-Benefit Theme

Cost-Benefit Theme. The primary consideration in choosing among accounting systems and methods: how well they achieve management goals in relation to their costs.

The **cost-benefit theme** (or call it a philosophy or state of mind if you prefer) is our primary criterion for choosing among accounting systems and accounting methods: how well they help achieve management goals in relation to their costs. The cost-benefit theme will dominate this book. Accounting systems and methods are economic goods that are available at various costs. Which system does a manager want to buy? A simple file drawer for amassing receipts and cancelled cheques? An elaborate budgeting system based on computerized descriptive models of the organization and its subunits? Or something in between?

The answer depends on the buyer's perceptions of the expected incremental (additional) benefits in relation to the incremental costs. For example, a hospital administrator may contemplate the installation of a computerized system for controlling hospital operations. Such a system uses a single document of original entry for automatic accumulation of data for financial records, medical records, costs by departments, nurse staffing requirements, drug administration, billings for patients, revenue generated by physicians, and so forth. This system leads to higher efficiency, less waste, and fewer errors. But the system costs $14 million. Thus, the system is not good or bad by itself. It must meet the tests of the economics of information—its value must exceed its cost.

Steak and butter may be "good buys" for many people at fifty cents per kilogram, but they may become "bad buys" at $10 per kilogram. Similarly, a particular accounting system may be a wise investment in the eyes of the buyer if it generates a sufficiently better set of decisions to justify its added cost. However, an existing *accounting system is only one source of information* for decision making. In many organizations it may be more economical to gather information by one-shot special efforts than by a ponderous system that repetitively gathers information that is rarely used.

The cost-benefit theme appeals to both the hard-headed manager and the theoretician. Managers have been employing the cost-benefit test for years, even though they may not have expressed it as such. Instead, they may have referred to the theme as "having to be practical." But the cost-benefit theme has an exceedingly rich underlying theory of information economics. It is a good theory that can supply the missing rationale for many management practices.

Behavioural Theme

Financial accounting is often looked upon as a cold, objective discipline because it is perceived to represent only the reporting of financial information. But management accounting is not; it is wrapped in behavioural ramifications. The buyer of an accounting system should be concerned with how it will affect the decisions (behaviour) of the affected managers. Earlier we saw how budgets and performance reports may play a key role in helping management. An emphasis on the future is an important feature of management accounting; it is less important in financial accounting. Budgets are the chief devices for compelling and disciplining management planning. Without budgets, planning may not get the front-and-centre attention that it usually deserves.

Performance reports are widely used to judge decisions, subunits, and managers and have enormous influence on the behaviour of the affected individuals. Performance reports not only provide feedback for improving future economic decisions but may also provide desirable or undesirable motivation. The choices of the content, format, timing, and distribution of performance reports are heavily influenced by their probable impact on motivation.

In a nutshell, management accounting can best be understood by using a cost-benefit theme coupled with an awareness of the importance of behavioural effects. Even more than financial accounting, management accounting spills over into related disciplines, such as economics, the decision sciences (e.g., operations management and production), and the behavioural sciences.

MANAGEMENT ACCOUNTING AND FINANCIAL ACCOUNTING

Freedom of Choice

Financial Accounting. The field of accounting that serves external decision makers such as shareholders, suppliers, banks, and government regulatory agencies.

Financial accounting and management accounting would be better labelled as external accounting and internal accounting. **Financial accounting** emphasizes the preparation of reports of an organization for external users such as banks and the investing public. Management accounting emphasizes the preparation of reports of an organization for its internal users such as company presidents, university deans, and chief physicians.

The same basic accounting system compiles the fundamental data for both financial accounting and management accounting. Furthermore, external forces (for example, income tax authorities and regulatory bodies, such as the Ontario Securities Commission and the National Energy Board) often limit management's choices of accounting methods. Organizations frequently limp along with

OBJECTIVE 8

Identify the major
distinctions between
management
accounting and
financial accounting.

a system that has been developed in response to the legal requirements imposed by external parties. In short, many existing systems are externally oriented and neglect the needs of internal users.

Consider our cost-benefit theme that accounting systems are commodities like steak or butter. Generally accepted accounting standards or principles affect both internal and external accounting. However, change in internal accounting is not inhibited by generally accepted financial accounting standards. Managers can create any kind of internal accounting system they want—as long as they are willing to pay the price. For instance, for its own management purposes, a hospital, a manufacturer, or a university can account for its assets on the basis of *current values*, as measured by estimates of replacement costs. No outside agency can prohibit such accounting. There are no "generally accepted management accounting principles" that forbid particular measurements. Indeed, the cost-benefit theme refrains from stating that any given accounting is good or bad. *Instead, the theme says that any accounting system or method (no matter how crazy it appears at first glance) is desirable as long as it brings incremental benefits in excess of incremental costs.*

Of course, satisfying internal demands for data as well as external demands means that organizations may have to keep more than one set of records. In North America, there is nothing immoral or unethical about having many sets of books for different users—but they are expensive. The cost-benefit test says that their perceived increases in benefits must exceed their perceived increases in costs. Ultimately, benefits are measured by whether decisions result in increased net cost savings or profit (or, in the case of many nonprofit institutions, increased quality or quantity of service rendered for each dollar spent).

The major distinctions between management accounting and financial accounting are briefly enumerated in Exhibit 1-12. These points will be expanded upon in succeeding chapters.

EXHIBIT 1-12

Distinctions between
Management
Accounting and
Financial Accounting

	MANAGEMENT ACCOUNTING	FINANCIAL ACCOUNTING
1. Primary users	Organization managers at various levels.	Outside parties such as investors and government agencies but also organization managers.
2. Freedom of choice	No constraints other than costs in relation to benefits of improved management decisions.	Constrained by generally accepted accounting principles (GAAP).
3. Behavioural implications	Concern about how measurements and reports will influence managers' daily behaviour.	Concern about how to measure and communicate economic phenomena. Behavioural impact is secondary.
4. Time focus	Future orientation: formal use of budgets as well as historical records. Example: 2001 budget versus 2001 actual performance.	Past orientation: historical evaluation. Example: 2001 actual financial or operational results versus 2000 actual performance.
5. Time span	Flexible, varying from hourly to 10 or 15 years.	Less flexible. Usually one year or one quarter.
6. Reports	Detailed reports: concern about details of parts of the entity, products, departments, territories, etc.	Summary reports: concern primarily with entity as a whole.
7. Delineation of activities	Field is less sharply defined. Heavier use of economics, decision sciences, and behavioural sciences.	Field is more sharply defined. Lighter use of related disciplines.

Career Opportunities

Society of Management Accountants of Canada
www.cma-canada.org

Canadian Institute of Chartered Accountants
www.cica.ca

Certified General Accountants' Association of Canada
www.cga-canada.org

Management Accounting
www.accounting.
rutgers.edu

Society of Management Accountants of Canada (SMAC). An organization of professional accountants, Certified Management Accountants whose primary interest is in management accounting.

Certified Management Accountant (CMA). A professional accountant who is a member of the Society of Management Accountants of Canada.

Accounting deals with all facets of a complex organization and provides an excellent opportunity for gaining a broad range of knowledge. Senior accountants or controllers in a corporation are sometimes chosen as production or marketing executives. Why? Because they may have impressed other executives as having acquired the necessary general management skills. Accounting must embrace all management functions, including purchasing, manufacturing, wholesaling, retailing, and a variety of marketing and transportation activities. A number of recent surveys have indicated that more chief executive officers began their careers in an accounting position than in any other area, such as marketing, production, or engineering.

In Canada, three professional accounting organizations exist. Education is a provincial jurisdiction, so accounting students register with the provincial organization, and then qualify for admission after successfully completing a national examination. While management accounting is a component of each of the three education programs, the extent of coverage of the subject varies.

The **Society of Management Accountants of Canada (SMAC) also known as CMA Canada** offers the **CMA (Certified Management Accountant)** designation; its education program focuses on management accounting and its role in Canadian business. The **Canadian Institute of Chartered Accountants (CICA)** confers the **CA (Chartered Accountant)** designation. The CA education program focuses on external financial reports and in particular the auditing of those reports. The **Certified General Accountants' Association of Canada (CGAAC)** provides the **CGA (Certified General Accountant)** designation, and provides a broad-based education program in accounting and financial management that is somewhat unique in its focus on the use of the computer as a management accounting tool.

ADAPTING TO CHANGE

Canadian Institute of Chartered Accountants (CICA). An organization of professional accountants, Chartered Accountants.

Chartered Accountant (CA). A professional accountant who is a member of the CICA.

Certified General Accountants' Association of Canada (CGAAC). An organization of professional accountants, Certified General Accountants.

Certified General Accountant (CGA). A professional accountant who is a member of the CGAAC.

The growing interest in management accounting also stems from its ability to help managers adapt to change. Indeed, the one constant in the world of business is change. Accountants must adapt their systems to the changes in management practices and technology. A system that produces valuable information in one setting may be valueless in another. Information that was relevant for management decisions yesterday may be out-of-date tomorrow or even today.

Accountants have not always been responsive to the need to change. A decade ago many managers complained about the irrelevance of accounting information. Why? Because their decision environment had changed but accounting systems had not. However, most progressive companies have not changed their accounting systems to recognize the realities of today's complex, technical, and global business environment. Instead of being irrelevant, accountants in such companies are adding more value than ever. For example, *Management Accounting* (September, 1994) reported on a Champion International Corporation paper mill that made major changes in its accounting system. By working with managers to produce the information considered relevant for their decisions, accountants became regarded as "business partners." Previously, managers had considered accountants as a "financial police department." Instead of merely pointing out problems, the accountants became part of the solution.

BRIAN SCOTT, CMA
Manager of Finance and Administration
St. John's Port Corporation
St. John's, Newfoundland

Brian Scott, CMA, says his decision to become a management accountant was based on a careful investigation of potential career options and a decision that an accounting designation would lead to more opportunities in the future.

Scott joined the St. John's Port Corporation 15 years ago as an accountant, and moved into his current job as manager of finance and administration after earning his CMA. He is accountable to the Port's CEO, and his main duties involve coordinating the strategic planning process, conducting financial analysis, and ensuring that accurate, timely, and relevant financial information is presented.

The Port of St. John's is the major intermodal gateway for Newfoundland and Labrador. Like any business, the process of operating a port has changed dramatically in recent years. The port exists to help its customers enhance their competitive position and, in today's world, companies gain and maintain their competitive advantage on the basis of time and cost. "In that respect, the port must efficiently and effectively link different modes of transportation," he says. "Our role is to help users reduce the time and cost it takes for them to move their products."

MARISA FABIANO, CMA
Financial Analyst of Manufacturing
Coca–Cola Beverages Ltd.
Toronto, Ontario

Coca-Cola
www.coca-cola.com

Even before she entered York University's business school, Marisa Fabiano, CMA, knew that she wanted to become an accountant. Originally, however, she thought she wanted to become a financial accountant.

When she graduated from the Toronto-area university with a bachelor degree in business administration in 1989, she immediately went to work in a firm of chartered accountants. But, while in public practice, she realized that auditing was not for her.

She decided to take a year off to start a family and re-evaluate her career goals. It was after this that Marisa decided to pursue the CMA designation.

At almost exactly that time, she was interviewed for a job at Coca-Cola Beverages Ltd. "During my interview, it was obvious they were excited about the fact that I was planning to become a CMA," she says. She was hired by Coca-Cola Beverages Ltd. in August 1991.

In October 1994, Fabiano was promoted to her current job. Reporting to the vice-president of manufacturing, her job involves a variety of duties—many of which are still evolving. Primarily, Fabiano is responsible for variance and expense analysis and management reporting for Coca-Cola's eight manufacturing facilities across Canada. Besides the ongoing monitoring of the manufacturing activities, Marisa is involved in the budgeting process and measurements of productivity, and currently she is assisting with the implementation of a new distribution system and ISO 9002.

"There are a lot of new projects on the go in my new job, and they're all quite exciting. And I'm confident I can handle the challenges, particularly now that I have the added dimension of a CMA designation behind my name."

Three major factors are causing changes in management accounting today:

1. The shift from a manufacturing-based to a service-based economy.
2. Increased global competition.
3. Technological advances.

Each of these factors will affect your study of management accounting.

The service sector now accounts for an increasing proportion of total employment. Service industries are becoming increasingly competitive, and their use of accounting information is growing. Basic accounting principles are applied to service organizations throughout this book.

Global competition has increased in recent years as many international barriers to trade, such as tariffs and duties, have been lowered. In addition, there has been a worldwide trend toward deregulation. The result has been a shift in the balance of economic power in the world. To regain their competitive edge, many companies are redesigning their accounting systems to provide more accurate and timely information about the cost of activities, products, or services. To be competitive, managers must understand the effects of their decisions on costs, and accountants must help managers predict such effects.

By far the most dominant influence on management accounting over the past decade has been technological change. This change has affected both the production and use of accounting information. The increasing capabilities and decreasing cost of computers has changed how accountants gather, store,

PERSPECTIVES ON DECISION-MAKING

E-Commerce Success Stories

Boeing Company
www.boeing.com

One of the early adopters of e-commerce was the Boeing Company. In 1996, Boeing launched its "Boeing PART Page" providing airlines and maintenance organizations with a direct link to half a million different types of spare parts stored in Boeing distibution centres. At the end of 1999, the Web site was processing more than 18,000 transactions each day. Almost 85 percent of all Boeing's spare parts are ordered electronically. According to Tom DiMarco, director of spares systems at Boeing, "In retrospect, it was one of the best steps we've ever taken. It saves time, simplifies business processes for our customers and reduces paperwork, and has improved the productivity of our work force."

In early 2000, Boeing announced the formation of the Global Trading Exchange, an e-commerce alliance with other key businesses in the aerospace and defense industry, with the goal of creating a single e-commerce site for the entire industry. According to Harry Stonecipher, president and chief operating officer. "Transactions, from order placement to shipping and billing, can be completed electronically, reducing intergration costs significantly."

Champion Exposition Services, a $55 million company, provides national trade show and convention decorating services. Champion uses e-commerce to speed up the order-taking process. Salespeople take orders, invoice customers, and receive payments in real time. The company expects to double its growth and increase accounting department productivity by 50 percent as a result of using Business to Customers e-commerce.

Source: New releases, The Boeing Company, January 20, 1999 and March 28, 2000: "Is E-Business for You" *Strategic Finance*, March 1999, pp. 74–77.

DuPont
www.dupont.com

manipulate, and report data. Frequently, the result is faster information at a lower cost. For example, J.M. Schneider Inc. of Kitchener, Ontario, switched from a minicomputer to a PC, and found that an operation that previously took seven hours now required only 15 minutes.[6] Most accounting systems, even small ones, are automated. In addition, computers enable managers to access data directly and to generate their own reports and analyses in many cases. For example, as a result of an assessment of its information systems, DuPont Canada's "... managers no longer have to wait several weeks for reports. Up-to-the-minute information is available on-line and managers can generate reports themselves at any given time."[7] By using spreadsheet software and graphics packages, managers can use accounting information directly in their decision process. All managers need a better understanding of accounting information than they may have needed in the past. And accountants need to create databases that can be readily understood by managers.

Technological change has also dramatically altered the manufacturing environment for many companies, causing changes in how accounting information is used. Manufacturing processes are increasingly automated and automated manufacturing processes make extensive use of robots and other computer-controlled equipment and less use of human labour for direct production activities. Many early accounting systems were designed primarily to measure and report the cost of labour. Why? Because human labour was the largest cost in producing many products and services. Also, a primary objective of an accounting system was to trace costs of essentially mass-production processes. Clearly, such systems are not appropriate in automated environments. Accountants in such settings have had to change their systems to produce information for decisions about how to acquire and efficiently use materials and automated equipment.

Standard Aero
www.standardaero.ca

Just-in-Time Philosophy and Computer-Integrated Manufacturing

Just-In-Time (JIT) Philosophy. A philosophy to eliminate waste by reducing the time products spend in the production process and eliminating the time that products spend in activities that do not add value.

Computer-Integrated Manufacturing (CIM) Systems. Systems that use computer-aided design and computer-aided manufacturing, together with robots and computer-controlled machines.

Changes in management philosophy have accompanied technological change. The most important recent change leading to increased efficiency in factories has been the adoption of a **just-in-time (JIT) philosophy**. The essence of the philosophy is to eliminate waste. Managers try to (1) reduce the time that employees spend in the production process and (2) eliminate the time that employees spend on activities that do not add value (such as inspection and waiting time). For instance, Standard Aero of Winnipeg, Manitoba, a company dedicated to repairing and overhauling airplane engines, has sought to cut down overhaul time from two months to 15 days by eliminating inefficient activities and waiting time.[8]

Process time can be reduced by redesigning and simplifying the production process. Companies can use *computer-aided design (CAD)* to design products that can be manufactured efficiently. Even small changes in design often lead to large manufacturing cost savings. Companies can also use *computer-aided manufacturing (CAM)*, in which computers direct and control production equipment. CAM often leads to a smoother, more efficient flow of production with fewer delays.

Systems that use CAD and CAM together with robots and computer-controlled machines are called **computer-integrated manufacturing (CIM) systems**.

---

[6] "PC networks take bulk out of computing," *The Globe and Mail*, March 18, 1992.
[7] "Bringing quality to accounting," *CMA Management*, July-August, 1992, p. 26.
[8] "World class productivity at Standard Aero," *CMA Management*, April 1991, p. 7.

Companies that install full CIM system use very little labour. Robots and computer-controlled machines perform the routine jobs that were previously done by assembly-line workers. In addition, well-designed systems provide greater flexibility because design changes only require alterations in computer programs, not the retraining of an entire workforce.

Time spent on activities that do not add value to the product can be eliminated or reduced by focusing on quality, improving plant layout, and cross-training workers. Achieving zero production defects ("doing it right the first time") reduces inspection time and eliminates rework time. One factory saved more time by redesigning its plant layout so that the distance products travelled from one operation to the next during production was reduced from 422 metres to 107 metres. Another company reduced setup time on a machine from 45 minutes to one minute by storing the required tools nearby and training the machine operator to do the setup. A British company reduced the time required to manufacture a vacuum pump from three weeks to six minutes by switching from long assembly lines to manufacturing cells that allowed them to accomplish the entire task in quick succession.

Originally, JIT referred only to an inventory system that minimized inventories by arranging for materials and subcomponents to arrive just as they were needed and for goods to be made just in time to be shipped to customers—no sooner and no later. But JIT has become the cornerstone of a broad management philosophy. It originated in Japanese companies such as Toyota and Kawasaki, and has been adopted by many large companies, including Hewlett-Packard and Xerox. Many small firms have also embraced JIT.

Implications for the Study of Management Accounting

As you read this book, remember that accounting systems change as the world changes. The techniques presented here are being applied in organizations today. But tomorrow may be different. To adapt to changes, you must understand why the techniques are being used, not just how they are used. We urge you to resist the temptation to simply memorize rules and techniques. Instead, develop your understanding of the underlying concepts and principles. These will continue to be useful in developing and understanding new techniques for changing environments.

Professional Ethics

OBJECTIVE 9

Identify the most important areas of ethical conduct by management accountants.

Public-opinion surveys have consistently ranked accountants highly in terms of their professional ethics. Professional accountants adhere to codes of conduct regarding competence, confidentiality, integrity, and objectivity. Exhibit 1-13 contains the Code of Professional Ethics for Management Accountants. Professional accounting organizations have procedures for reviewing alleged behaviour that is not consistent with the Code.

External and internal financial reports are primarily the responsibility of line managers. However, management accountants are also responsible for these reports. Accounting systems, procedures, and compilations should be reliable and free of manipulation.

EXHIBIT 1-13

Code of Professional
Ethics

All Members shall adhere to the following "Code of Professional Ethics" of the Society:

(a) A Member shall act at all times with,
   (i) responsibility for and fidelity to public needs;
   (ii) fairness and loyalty to his associates, clients and employers; and
   (iii) competence through devotion to high ideals of personal honour and professional integrity;

(b) A Member shall

   (i) maintain at all times independence of thought and action;
   (ii) not express his opinion on financial statements without first assessing his relationship with his client to determine whether he might expect his opinion to be considered independent, objective and unbiased by one who has knowledge of all the facts; and
   (iii) when preparing financial statements or expressing an opinion on financial statements which are intended to inform management only, disclose all material facts known to him in order not to make such financial statements misleading, acquire sufficient information to warrant an expression of opinion and report all material misstatements or departures from generally accepted accounting principles;

(c) A Member shall

   (i) not disclose or use any confidential information concerning the affairs of his employer or client unless acting in the course of his duties or except when such information is required to be disclosed in the course of any defence of himself or any associate or employee in any lawsuit or other legal proceeding or against alleged professional misconduct by order of lawful authority or the Board or any committee of the Society in the proper exercise of their duties but only to the extent necessary for such purpose;
   (ii) inform his employer or client of any business connections or interests of which his employer or client would reasonably expect to be informed;
   (iii) not, in the course of exercising his duties on behalf of his employer or client, hold, receive, bargain for or acquire any fee, remuneration or benefit without his employer's or client's knowledge and consent; and
   (iv) take all reasonable steps, in arranging any engagement as a consultant, to establish a clear understanding of the scope and objectives of the work before it is commenced and shall furnish the client with an estimate of cost, preferably before the engagement is commenced, but in any event as soon as possible thereafter.

(d) A Member shall

   (i) conduct himself toward other Members with courtesy and good faith;
   (ii) not commit an act discreditable to the profession;
   (iii) not engage in or counsel any business or occupation which, in the opinion of the Society, is incompatible with the professional ethics of a management accountant;
   (iv) not accept any engagement to review the work of another Member for the same employer except with the knowledge of that Member, or except where the connection of that Member with the work has been terminated, unless the Member reviews the work of others as a normal part of his responsibilities;
   (v) not attempt to gain an advantage over other Members by paying or accepting a commission in securing management accounting work;
   (vi) uphold the principle of adequate compensation for management accounting work; and
   (vii) not act maliciously or in any other way which may adversely reflect on the public or professional reputation or business of another Member.

EXHIBIT 1-13

Code of Professional
Ethics
continued

(e) A Member shall

  (i) at all times maintain the standards of competence expressed by the academic and experience requirements for admission to the Society and for continuation as a Member;

  (ii) disseminate the knowledge upon which the profession of management accounting is based to others within the profession and generally promote the advancement of the profession;

  (iii) undertake only such work as he is competent to perform by virtue of his training and experience and shall, where it would be in the best interests of an employer or client, engage, or advise the employer or client to engage, other specialists;

  (iv) expose before the proper tribunals of the Society any incompetent, unethical, illegal or unfair conduct or practice of a Member which involves the reputation, dignity or honour of the Society; and

  (v) endeavour to ensure that a professional partnership or company, with which he is associated as a partner, principal, director or officer abides by the Code of Professional Ethics and the rules of professional conduct established by the Society.

Source: *Management Accounting Handbook: Bylaw 20* (The Society of Management Accountants of Ontario).

Ethical Dilemmas

What makes an action by an accountant unethical? An unethical act is one that violates the ethical standards of the profession. However, the standards leave much room for individual interpretation and judgment. When one action is clearly unethical and another alternative is clearly ethical, managers and accountants should have no difficulty choosing between them. Unfortunately, most ethical dilemmas are not clear-cut. The most difficult situations arise when there is strong pressure to take an action that is "borderline" or when two ethical standards conflict.

Suppose you are an accountant who has been asked to supply the company's banker with a profit forecast for the coming year. A badly needed bank loan rides on the prediction. The company president is absolutely convinced that profits will be at least $500,000. Anything less than that and the loan is not likely to be approved.

Your analysis shows that if the planned introduction of a new product goes extraordinarily well, profits will exceed $500,000. But the most likely outcome is for a modestly successful introduction and a $100,000 profit. If the product fails, the company stands to lose $600,000. Without the loan, the new product cannot be taken to the market, and there is no way the company can avoid a loss for the year. Bankruptcy is even a possibility. What forecast would you make? There is no easy answer. A forecast of less than $500,000 seems to guarantee financial problems, perhaps even bankruptcy. Shareholders, management, employees, suppliers, and customers may all be hurt. But a forecast of $500,000 may not be fair and objective. The bank may be misled by it. Still, the president apparently thinks a $500,000 forecast is reasonable, and you know that there is some chance it will be achieved. Perhaps the potential benefit to the company of an overly optimistic forecast is greater than the possible cost to the bank. There is no right answer to this dilemma. The important thing is to recognize the ethical dimensions and weigh them when forming your judgment.

Ethics at General Motors

The importance of ethics to management accountants was emphasized when *Management Accounting*, the journal of the Institute of Management Accountants, put out a special issue on ethics in June 1990. Two thrusts ran through the articles in the issue: (1) business schools must make students aware of the ethical dimension of the decisions they will face in the business world, and (2) business firms must recognize that establishing standards of ethical conduct for their employees is important to financial success. As a followup, *Management Accounting* instituted a regular column on ethics. A recent column presented a case on the ethics of planned obsolescence of products. Many readers submitted solutions to the case, some of which were published in *Management Accounting*, showing that ethical dilemmas generate a great deal of interest.

Roger B. Smith, former Chairman and Chief Executive Officer of General Motors, stated that "ethical practice is, quite simply, good business." Since 1977 GM has had a policy on personal integrity. But GM recognizes that making ethical decisions is not always easy. Because the world is complex, there are often competing obligations to shareholders, customers, suppliers, fellow managers, society, and self and family. As Smith says, "It is easy to do what is right; it is hard to know what is right." A basic rule used by GM is that employees "should never do anything (they) would be ashamed to explain to (their) families or be afraid to see on the front page of the local newspaper."

General Motors is not alone in promoting ethical conduct. Over half of the large companies in the United States have a "Corporate Code of Conduct." These codes provide support to employees who feel pressured to make decisions they believe to be unethical. They also provide training in the types of behaviour expected of employees.

Sources: Roger B. Smith, "Ethics in Business: An Essential Element of Success," *Management Accounting*, Special Issue on Ethics in Corporate America June 1990, p. 50, Robert B. Sweeney and Howard L. Siers, "Ethics in America," *Management Accounting*, Special Issue on Ethics in Corporate America June 1990, pp. 34–40, and James A. Heely and Roy L. Nersesian, "The Case of Planned Obsolescence," *Management Accounting* February 1994, pp. 67–68.

General Motors
www.gm.com

Professional Ethics
Resources
www.ethics.ubc.ca/
resources/professional

The tone set by top management can have a great influence on managers' ethics. Complete integrity and outspoken support for ethical standards by senior managers is the single greatest motivator of ethical behaviour throughout an organization. But in the final analysis, ethical standards are personal and depend on the values of the individual.

SUMMARY

Accounting information is useful to internal managers for making short-term planning and control decisions and for making nonroutine decisions and formulating overall policies and long-range plans. The accounting information answers scorekeeping, attention-directing, and problem-solving questions. Management accounting focuses on information for internal decision makers (managers) and financial accounting focuses on information for external parties.

Many management accounting techniques were developed in profit-seeking manufacturing companies because such companies often had a greater need for sophisticated accounting information. However, there is increasing application of management accounting in service and nonprofit organizations.

Management accounting systems exist for the benefit of managers. Systems should be judged by a cost-benefit criterion—the benefits of better decisions should exceed the cost of the system. The benefit of a system will be affected by behavioural factors—how the system affects managers and their decisions.

An essential tool for performance evaluation is a budget. A performance report compares actual results to the budget. To appropriately interpret accounting information about a particular product, it is often important to recognize the product's competitive strengths and weaknesses.

Accountants are staff employees who provide information and advice for line managers. The head of accounting is often called the controller. Unlike the treasurer, who is concerned primarily with financial matters, the controller measures and reports on operating performance. The future worth of an accounting system will be affected by how easily the system can adapt to change. A changing business environment may require the accounting system to collect and report new data and discontinue reporting information that is no longer needed. Changes affecting accounting systems include growth in the service sector of the economy, increased global competition, and advances in technology. Organizations that adopt a just-in-time philosophy or use computer-aided design and manufacturing systems have different needs for information than do more traditional firms.

Finally, both external and internal accountants are expected to adhere to standards of ethical conduct. However, many ethical dilemmas require value judgments, not simple application of standards.

HIGHLIGHTS TO REMEMBER

This section appears at the end of each chapter. It briefly recapitulates some key ideas, suggestions, comments, or terms that might otherwise be overlooked or misunderstood.

1. This book stresses two major themes: cost-behavioural implications. The choice of a system or method should be based on weighing the value of the system against its cost. This entails making predictions of how individuals acting as members of an organization's workforce behave under one system versus another. Therefore, the behavioural impact of alternatives is given ample attention throughout this book.
2. Most managers become stronger managers when they attain an understanding of management accounting. Furthermore, their performance and their rewards are often heavily affected by how accounting measurements are made. Consequently, regardless of the size or goals of their organization, managers have a natural self-interest in learning about accounting.

SUMMARY PROBLEMS FOR YOUR REVIEW

Try to solve these problems before examining the solutions that follow.

Problem One

The scorekeeping, attention-directing, and problem-solving duties of the accountant have been described in this chapter. The accountant's usefulness to management is said to be directly influenced by how good an attention director and problem solver he or she is.

Evaluate this contention by specifically relating the accountant's duties to the duties of operating management.

Solution

Operating managers may have to be good scorekeepers, but their major duties are to concentrate on the day-to-day problems that most need attention, to make longer-range plans, and to arrive at special decisions. Accordingly, because managers are concerned mainly with attention-directing and problem-solving, they will obtain the most benefit from the alert internal accountant who is a useful attention director and problem solver.

Problem Two

Starbucks Coffee Company is the leading roaster and retailer of specialty coffee in North America with annual sales revenue of $1 billion. For each of the following activities, indicate the value-chain function that is being performed.

> **a.** Process engineers investigate methods to reduce the time to roast coffee beans and to better preserve their flavour.
> **b.** A direct-to-your-home mail order system is established to sell custom coffees.
> **c.** Arabica coffee beans are purchased and transported to company processing plants.
> **d.** Focus groups investigate the feasibility of a new line of Frappuccino drinks.
> **e.** A hot line is established for mail-order customers to call with comments on the quality and speed of delivery.
> **f.** Each company-owned retail store provides information to customers about the processes used to make its coffee products.

Solution

> **a.** Design
> **b.** Distribution
> **c.** Production
> **d.** Research and development
> **e.** Customer service
> **f.** Marketing

Problem Three

Using the organization charts in this chapter (Exhibits 1-10 and 1-11), answer the following questions.

> **1.** Which of the following have line or staff authority over the machining manager: maintenance manager, manufacturing vice president, production superintendent, purchasing agent, storekeeper, personnel vice president, president, chief budgetary accountant, chief internal auditor?
> **2.** What is the general role of service departments in an organization? How are they distinguished from operating or production departments?
> **3.** Does the controller have line or staff authority over the cost accountants? The accounts receivable clerks?

4. What is probably the major duty (scorekeeping, attention directing, or problem solving) of the following:

Payroll clerk	Cost analyst
Accounts receivable clerk	Head of internal auditing
Cost record clerk	Head of special reports and studies
Head of general accounting	Head of accounting for planning and
Head of taxes	control
Budgetary accountant	Controller

Solution

1. The only executives that have line authority over the machining manager are the president, the manufacturing vice president, and the production superintendent.
2. A typical company's major purpose is to produce and sell goods or services. Unless a department is directly concerned with producing or selling, it is called a service or staff department. Service departments exist only to help the production and sales departments with their most important functions: the efficient production and sale of goods or services.
3. The controller has line authority over all members of his or her own department, all those shown in the controller's organization chart (Exhibit 1-11).
4. The major duty of the first five—through the head of taxes—is typically scorekeeping. Attention directing is probably the major responsibility of the next three. Problem solving is probably the primary duty of the head of special reports and studies. The head of accounting for planning and control and the controller should be concerned with all three duties: scorekeeping, attention directing, and problem solving. However, there is a perpetual danger that day-to-day pressures will emphasize scorekeeping. Therefore, accountants and managers should ensure that attention directing and problem solving are also stressed. Otherwise the major management benefits of an accounting system may be lost.

Problem Four

Yang Electronics Company (YEC) developed a high-speed, low-cost copying machine. It marketed the machine primarily for home use. However, as YEC customers learned how easy and inexpensive it was to make copies with the YEC machine, its use by small businesses grew. Sales soared as some businesses ordered large numbers of the copiers. However, the heavier use of these companies caused a certain component of the equipment to break down. The copiers were warrantied for two years, regardless of the amount of usage. Consequently, YEC experienced high costs for replacing the damaged components.

As the quarterly meeting of the Board of Directors of YEC approached, Mark Chua, assistant controller, was asked to prepare a report on the situation. Unfortunately, it was hard to predict the exact effects. However, it seemed that many business customers were starting to switch to more expensive copiers sold by competitors. And it was clear that the increased maintenance costs would significantly affect YEC's profitability. Mark summarized the situation the best he could for the Board.

Alice Martinez, the controller of YEC, was concerned about the impact of the report on the Board. She did not disagree with the analysis, but thought it made management look bad and might even have led the Board to discontinue the product. She was convinced from conversations with the head of engineering that the copier could be slightly redesigned to meet the needs of high-volume users, so discontinuing it might have passed up a potentially profitable opportunity.

Martinez called Chua into her office and asked him to delete the part of his report dealing with the component failures. She said it was all right to mention this orally to the Board, noting that engineering is nearing a solution to the problem. However, Chua feels strongly that such a revision in his report would mislead the Board about a potentially significant negative impact on the company's earnings.

Required: Explain why Martinez's request to Chua is unethical. How should Chua resolve this situation?

Solution

According to the standards of Ethical Conduct for Management Accountants in Exhibit 1-13, Martinez's request violates requirements for competence, fairness, and independence. It violates competence because she is asking Chua to prepare a report that is not complete and clear—one that omits potentially relevant information. Therefore, the Board will not have all the information it should to make a decision about the component failure problem.

The request violates the fairness requirement because the revised report may subvert the attainment of the organization's objectives in order to achieve Martinez's objectives. Management accountants are specifically responsible for communicating unfavourable as well as favourable information.

Finally, the revised report would not be independent. It would not disclose all relevant information that could be expected to influence the Board's understanding of operations and therefore their decisions.

Chua's responsibility is to discuss this issue with increasingly higher levels of authority within YEC. First, he should let Martinez know about his misgivings. Possibly the issue can be resolved by her withdrawing the request. If not, he should inform her that he intends to take up the matter with her superior and then approach higher levels of authority, even to the Board, if necessary, until the issue is resolved. So that Chua does not violate the standard of confidentiality, he should not discuss the matter with persons outside of YEC.

ACCOUNTING VOCABULARY

Vocabulary is an essential and often troublesome phase of the learning process. A fuzzy understanding of terms hampers the learning of concepts and the ability to solve accounting problems.

Before proceeding to the assignment material or to the next chapter, be sure you understand the listed words or terms. Their meaning is explained in the margin notes in the chapter.

accounting system *p. 8*
attention-directing *p. 5*
budget *p. 6*

Canadian Institute of Chartered
    Accountants (CICA) *p. 19*
Certified General Accountant (CGA) *p. 19*

Certified General Accountants Association of Canada (CGAAC) *p. 19*
Certified Management Accountant (CMA) *p. 19*
Chartered Accountant (CA) *p. 19*
comptroller *p. 14*
computer-integrated manufacturing (CIM) systems *p. 22*
controller *p. 14*
cost-benefit theme *p. 16*
financial accounting *p. 17*
just-in-time (JIT) philosophy *p. 22*
key success factors *p. 10*

line authority *p. 14*
management accounting *p. 5*
management by exception *p. 6*
performance reports *p. 6*
problem-solving *p. 5*
product life cycle *p. 10*
scorekeeping *p. 5*
Society of Management Accountants of Canada (SMAC) *p. 19*
staff authority *p. 14*
value chain *p. 11*
variance *p. 7*

ASSIGNMENT MATERIAL

The assignment material for each chapter is divided into three sections: *questions, problems,* and *cases*. The questions are intended to clarify concepts and definitions. The problems require students to exhibit an understanding of the issues that need further thought and analysis. Cases are selected that require students to apply a decision process in recommending a solution to the problem, which may or may not be explicitly stated in the case.

QUESTIONS

Q1-1 What two major themes will be emphasized in succeeding chapters?

Q1-2 What are the three broad purposes of an accounting system?

Q1-3 "The emphases of financial accounting and management accounting differ." Explain.

Q1-4 Distinguish among scorekeeping, attention directing, and problem solving.

Q1-5 Give examples of special nonrecurring decisions and of long-range planning.

Q1-6 "Planning is much more vital than control." Do you agree? Explain.

Q1-7 Distinguish among a budget, a performance report, and a variance.

Q1-8 "Management by exception means abdicating management responsibility for planning and control." Do you agree? Explain.

Q1-9 "Good accounting provides automatic control of operations." Do you agree? Explain.

Q1-10 Explain the term "key success factors" and why it is important to identify them for a company.

Q1-11 Name the six business functions that comprise the value chain.

Q1-12 "The controller does control in a special sense." Explain.

Q1-13 Give three examples of service organizations. What distinguishes them from other types of organizations?

Q1-14 "The accounting system is intertwined with operating management. Business operations would be a hopeless tangle without the paper work that is so often regarded with disdain." Do you agree? Explain, giving examples.

Q1-15 What is the essence of the JIT philosophy?

Q1-16 Why is it important for management accountants to abide by a Code of Ethics?

PROBLEMS

P1-1 **MANAGEMENT AND FINANCIAL ACCOUNTING.** Jan Harvi, an able mechanical engineer, was informed that she would be promoted to assistant factory manager. Jan was pleased but uncomfortable. She knew little about accounting and she had taken only one course in "financial" accounting.

Jan planned to enrol in a management accounting course as soon as possible. Meanwhile she asked Harland Young, a cost accountant, to state three or four of the principal distinctions between financial and management accounting.

Prepare Harland's written response to Jan.

P1-2 **MANAGEMENT ACCOUNTING IN UNIVERSITIES.** Historically, Canadian universities were funded primarily on a per student basis in the form of tuitions and government grants. More recently there has been increased use of program-specific grants, and ceilings have been placed on the number of students that the government will fund at any one university.

How might these changes alter the management accounting practices of universities? Relate your answer to the decisions of senior university administrators.

P1-3 **SCOREKEEPING, ATTENTION-DIRECTING AND PROBLEM-SOLVING.** For each of the activities listed below, identify the major function (scorekeeping, attention-directing, or problem-solving). Also state whether the departments mentioned are production or service departments.

1. Analyzing, for a Ford production superintendent, the impact on costs of some new drill presses.
2. Preparing a scrap report for the finishing department of a Honda parts factory.
3. Preparing the budget for the maintenance department of St. Jude's Hospital.
4. Interpreting why a Springfield foundry did not adhere to its production schedule.
5. Explaining the stamping department's performance report.
6. Preparing a monthly statement of European sales for the Ford marketing vice-president.
7. Preparing, for the manager of production control of a Dofasco plant, a cost comparison of two computerized manufacturing control systems.
8. Interpreting variances on the University of Alberta purchasing department's performance report.
9. Analyzing, for a Honda international manufacturing manager, the desirability of having some auto parts made in Korea.
10. Preparing a schedule of depreciation for forklift trucks in the receiving department of a General Electric factory in Scotland.

P1-4 **MANAGEMENT BY EXCEPTION.** A fraternity held a homecoming party. The fraternity expected attendance of 80 persons and prepared the following budget:

Room rental	$150
Food	800
Entertainment	600
Decorations	220
Total	$1,770

After all bills for the party were paid, the total cost came to $1,948, or $178 over budget. Details are $150 for room rental; $1,013 for food; $600 for entertainment; and $185 for decorations. Ninety-five persons attended the party.

1. Prepare a performance report for the party that shows how actual costs differed from the budget. That is, include in your report the budget amounts, actual amounts, and variances.
2. Suppose the fraternity uses a management-by-exception rule. Which costs deserve further examination? Why?

P1-5 **ACCOUNTING'S POSITION IN ORGANIZATION**: Controller and Treasurer. For each of the following activities, indicate whether it is most likely to be performed by the controller (C) or treasurer (T). Explain each answer.

1. Prepare credit checks on customers
2. Help managers prepare budgets
3. Advise which alternative action is least costly
4. Prepare divisional financial statements
5. Arrange short-term financing
6. Prepare tax returns
7. Arrange insurance coverage
8. Meet with financial analysts from Bay Street

P1-6 **COSTS AND BENEFITS.** Marks & Spencer, a huge retailer in the United Kingdom, was troubled by its paper bureaucracy. Looked at in isolation, each form seemed reasonable, but overall a researcher reported that there was substantial effort in each department to verify the information. Basically, the effort seemed out of proportion to any value received, and, eventually, many of the documents were simplified or eliminated.

Describe the rationale that should govern systems design.

P1-7 **FOCUS ON FINANCIAL DATA.** A news story reported:

John Anderson, a veteran of Rockwell's automotive operations, recalls that when he sat in on meetings at the company's North American Aircraft Operations twenty years ago, "there'd be 60 or 70 guys talking technical problems, with never a word on profits." Such inattention to financial management helped Rockwell lose the F-15 fighter to McDonnell Douglas, Pentagon sources say. Anderson brought in profit-oriented executives, and he has now transformed North American's staff meetings to the point that "you seldom hear talk of technical problems any more," he says. "It's all financial."

What is your reaction to Anderson's comments? Are his comments related to management accounting?

P1-8 **CHANGES IN ACCOUNTING SYSTEMS.** In the early 1990s, the Boeing Company undertook a large-scale study of its accounting system. The study led to several significant changes. None of these changes was required for reporting to external parties. However, management thought that the new system gave more accurate costs of the airplanes and other products.

1. Boeing had been a very successful company using their old accounting system. What might have motivated it to change the system?
2. When Boeing changed its system, what criteria might its managers have used to decide whether to invest in the new system?

3. Is a change to a system that provides more accurate product costs always a good change? Why or why not?

P1-9 VALUE CHAIN. Nike is an Oregon-based company that focuses on the design, development, and worldwide marketing of high quality footwear, apparel, equipment, and accessory products. Nike is the largest seller of athletic footwear and athletic apparel in the world. The Company sells its products to approximately 19,700 retail accounts in the United States and through a mix of independent distributors, licensees, and subsidiaries in approximately 110 countries around the world. Virtually all of the Company's products are manufactured by independent contractors. Most footwear products are produced outside North America, while apparel products are produced both in North America and abroad.

1. Identify one decision that Nike managers make in each of the six value chain functions.
2. For each decision in the above question, identify one piece of accounting information that would aid the manager's decision.

P1-10 ROLE OF CONTROLLER. Juanita Palencia, newly hired controller of Braxton Industries, had been lured away from a competitor to revitalize the Controller's department. Her first day on the job proved to be an eye-opener. One of her first interviews was with Bill Belton, production supervisor in the Alberta factory. Belton commented: "I really don't want to talk to anyone from the controller's office. The only time we see those accountants is when our costs go over their budget. They wave what they call a 'performance report', but it's actually just a bunch of numbers they make up. It has nothing to do with what happens on the shop floor. Besides, my staff can't afford the time to fill out all the paperwork those accountants want, so I just plug in some numbers and send it back. Now, if you'll let me go back to important matters...." Palencia left quickly, but she was already planning for her next visit with Belton.

1. Identify some of the problems in the relationship between the Controller's department and the production departments (assuming that the Alberta factory is representative of the production departments).
2. What should Juanita Palencia do next?

P1-11 LINE AND STAFF AUTHORITY (CMA ADAPTED). Electronic Equipment Leasing Company (EEL) leases office equipment to a variety of customers. The company's organization chart follows:

The four positions highlighted in the chart are described below:

- Ralph Biddle, assistant controller, special projects. Biddle works on projects assigned to him by the controller. The most recent project was to design a new accounts payable system.
- Betty Kelly, leasing contracts manager. Kelly coordinates and implements leasing transactions. Her department handles everything after the sales department gets a signed contract. This includes requisitioning equipment from the purchasing department, maintaining appropriate insurance, delivering equipment, issuing billing statements, and seeking renewal of leases.
- Larry Dukes, chief accountant. Dukes supervises all the accounting functions. He produces reports for the four supervisors in the functional areas.

- Janice Sefcik, director of human resources. Sefcik works with all departments of EEL in hiring personnel. Her department advertises all positions and screens candidates, but the individual departments conduct interviews and make hiring decisions. Sefcik also coordinates employee evaluations and administers the company's salary schedule and employee-benefit program.

1. Distinguish between line and staff positions in an organization and discuss why conflicts might arise between line and staff managers.
2. For each of the four managers described, identify whether their position is a line or staff position and explain why you classified it that way. Also, indicate any potential conflicts that might arise with other managers in the organization.

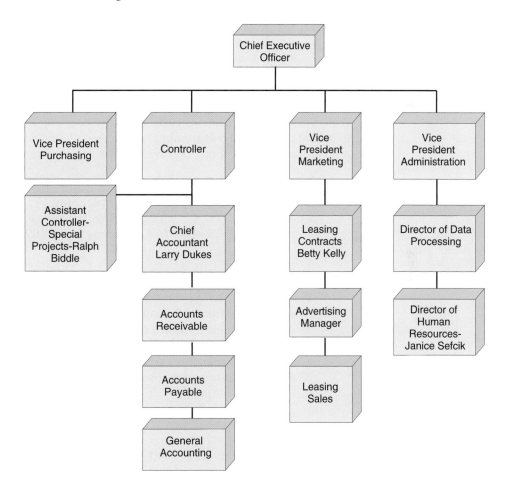

P1-12 ETHICAL ISSUES. Suppose you are controller of a medium-sized oil exploration company in Calgary. You adhere to the standards of ethical conduct for management accountants. How would those standards affect your behaviour in each of the following situations:

1. Late one Friday afternoon you receive a geologist's report on a newly purchased property. It indicates a much higher probability of oil than had previously been expected. You are the only one to read the report

that day. At a party on Saturday night, a friend asks about the prospects for the property.

2. An oil industry stock analyst invites you and your spouse to spend a week in Hawaii free of charge. All she wants in return is to be the first to know about any financial information your company is about to announce to the public.

3. It is time to make a forecast of the company's annual earnings. You know that some additional losses will be recognized before the final statements are prepared. The company's president has asked you to ignore these losses in making your prediction because a lower-than-expected earnings forecast could adversely affect the chances of obtaining a loan that is being negotiated and will be completed before actual earnings are announced.

4. You do not know whether a particular expense is deductible for income tax purposes. You are debating whether to research the tax laws or to simply assume that the item is deductible. After all, if you are not audited, no one will ever know the difference. And, if you are audited, you can plead ignorance of the law.

P1-13 **COLLABORATIVE LEARNING EXERCISE: THE FUTURE MANAGEMENT ACCOUNTANT.** Form groups of four to six students each. Half of each group should read the first of the following articles and half should read the second article. (Alternatively, this exercise can be done as a total class, with half of the class reading each article.)

1) Kulesza, C., and G. Siegel, "It's Not Your Father's Management Accounting," *Management Accounting* (May 1997), pp. 56–59.
2) Siegel, G., and C. Kulesza, "The Practice Analysis of Management Accounting," *Management Accounting* (April 1996), pp. 20–28.

1. Individually write down the three most important lessons you learned from the article you read.
2. As a group, list all the lessons identified in question 1. Combine those that are essentially the same.
3. Prioritize the list you developed in question 2 in terms of their importance to one considering a career in management accounting.
4. Discuss whether this exercise has changed your impression of management accounting and, if so, how your impression has changed.

CASES

C1-1 **PROFESSIONAL ETHICS AND TOXIC WASTE.** Yukon Mining Company extracts and processes a variety of ores and minerals. One of its operations is a coal cleaning plant that produces toxic wastes. For many years the wastes have been properly disposed of through National Disposal, a company experienced in disposing of such items. However, disposal of the toxic waste was becoming an economic hardship because increasing government regulations had caused the cost of such disposal to quadruple in the last six years.

Rebecca Long, director of financial reporting for Yukon Mining, was preparing the company's financial statements for the year ended June 30, 1998. In researching the material needed for preparing a footnote on environmental contingencies, Rebecca found the following note scribbled in pencil at the bottom of a memo to the general manager of the coal-cleaning plant. The body of the memo gave details on the increases in the cost of toxic waste disposals:

> Ralph—We've got to keep these costs down or we won't meet budget. Can we mix more of these wastes with the shipments of refuse to the Oak Hill landfill? Nobody seems to notice the coal-cleaning fluids when we mix it in well.

Rebecca was bothered by the note. She considered ignoring it, pretending that she had not seen it. But, after a couple of hours, her conscience would not let her do it. Therefore, she pondered the following three alternative courses of action:

- Seek the advice of her boss, the vice president, finance of Yukon.
- Anonymously release the information to the local newspaper.
- Give the information to an outside member of the board of directors of Yukon whom she knows because he lives in her neighbourhood.

Required:

1. Discuss why Rebecca Long has an ethical responsibility to take some action about her suspicion of illegal dumping of toxic wastes.
2. For each of the three alternative courses of action, explain whether the action is appropriate.
3. Assume that Rebecca sought the advice of the vice president, finance and discovered that he knew about and approved of the dumping of toxic wastes. What steps should she take to resolve the conflict in this situation?

C1-2 ETHICS AND ACCOUNTING PERSONNEL. Mercury Shoe Company has an equal employment opportunity policy. This policy has the full support of the company's president, Beverly Watson, and is included in all advertisements for open positions.

Hiring in the accounting department is done by the controller, Dwight Laughton. The assistant controller, Jack Smith, also interviews candidates, but Laughton makes all decisions. In the last year, the department hired five new persons. There were 175 applications for the open positions. From this set, 13 had been interviewed, including four minority candidates. The five people who were hired included three sons of close friends of Laughton and no minorities. Smith had felt that at least two of the minority candidates were very well qualified and that the three sons of friends were definitely not among the most qualified.

When Smith questioned Laughton concerning his reservations about the hiring practices, he was told that these decisions were Laughton's and not his, so he should not question them.

Required:

1. Explain why Laughton's hiring practices were unethical.
2. What should Smith do about this situation?

C1-3 CASE ON KEY SUCCESS FACTORS. (CICA)[9] Earthstone Clays Ltd. began as a small pottery studio, selling pottery made by the owners and by other local craftspeople. Gradually, other kinds of crafts and supplies were added, until the company became both a retailer of finished crafts and a supplier to the craftspeople. For example, the

---

[9] Reprinted, with permission, from Uniform Final Examination, Paper III, Q#2, 1983, © 1993, The Canadian Institute of Chartered Accountants, Toronto Canada. Any changes to the original material are the sole responsibility of the Authors and have not been reviewed or endorsed by the CICA.

company sells the raw clay, the glaze materials, and the wheels and kilns used to make pottery, as well as selling finished pottery.

Over the years, the company has expanded to become a major regional supplier of craft raw materials and equipment. Although the retail business has grown, most of Earthstone's revenue comes from wholesale sales to craftspeople. The company now has four outlets, each of which has combined wholesale and retail operations. The company mixes most of its clay and glazes and performs other manufacturing and assembly work in a shop attached to its central warehouse.

In the past, essentially all the retail sales and a large portion of the wholesale sales were for cash. Therefore, the company has had low receivables. Recently, however, the company has tried to maintain its sales level by allowing more credit to wholesale customers.

Wholesale inventories have always been high in dollar value, particularly for larger pieces of equipment, and have been slow to turn over. Due to the nature of the crafts business, it is necessary to carry a wide variety of inventory items.

Retail merchandise quantities are maintained at a high level. Most of this merchandise is held on consignment, and the remainder consists of items purchased from a few well-established craftspeople or produced in the company's shop.

Much of the wholesale inventory is imported from the United States and Japan. The company's margins have been severely squeezed because of recent currency fluctuations and because the recession has prevented recovery of cost increases. Crafts are considered a luxury good, so the company's retail sales and those to its wholesale customers have been hard-hit. In spite of significant price reductions, sales volume has generally fallen.

Recently, cash flow has been a problem. The company exceeded its credit limit and the bank expressed concern about the company's financial state and inability to determine its cash requirements. In an effort to alleviate the problem, several cost-cutting measures were implemented and advertising expenditures were increased to try to encourage sales. However, the company's position continued to deteriorate. The president then considered the following courses of action: the reduction of inventory levels; the elimination of product lines; the shift of emphasis from wholesale to retail sales; and further price reductions. However, the president was unable to evaluate any of these possibilities since the accounting system did not generate the necessary information.

Required:
1. Identify the key success factors for Earthstone Clays Ltd. and identify how they have changed since the company's initial operation.
2. What information is required by the president to manage Earthstone Clays successfully?

Cost Behaviour and Cost-Volume Relationships

LEARNING OBJECTIVES

After studying this chapter, you will be able to

1. Explain how cost drivers affect cost behaviour.

2. Show how changes in cost-driver activity level affect variable and fixed costs.

3. Calculate break-even sales volume in total dollars and total units.

4. Construct a cost-volume-profit graph.

5. Identify the limiting assumptions that underlie cost-volume-profit analysis.

6. Calculate sales volume in total dollars and total units to reach a target profit.

7. Explain the effects of sales mix on profits.

8. Compute cost-volume-profit relationships on an after-tax basis.

9. Distinguish between contribution margin and gross margin.

How do the costs and revenues of a hospital change as one more patient is admitted for a four-day stay? How are the costs and revenues of an airline affected when one more passenger is boarded at the last moment, or when another flight is added to the schedule? How should the budget request by a university be affected by the addition of a new program? These questions have a common theme: What will happen to financial results if a specified level of activity or volume fluctuates? Answering this question is the first step in analyzing **cost behaviour**—how the activities of an organization affect its costs. A knowledge of patterns of cost behaviour offers valuable insights in planning and controlling short- and long-run operations. This important lesson is emphasized throughout this book. In this chapter, however, our goal is to provide perspective rather than to impart an intimate knowledge of the complexities of cost behaviour.

Cost Behaviour. How the activities of an organization affect its costs.

COST DRIVERS

OBJECTIVE 1

Explain how cost drivers affect cost behaviour.

Cost Drivers. Activities that affect costs.

Activities that affect costs are often called **cost drivers**. An organization may have many cost drivers. Consider the costs of running a warehouse that receives and stores material and supplies. The costs of operating the warehouse may be driven by the total dollar value of items handled, the weight of the items handled, the number of different orders received, the number of different items handled, the number of different suppliers, the fragility of the items handled, and possibly several other cost drivers. A major task in specifying cost behaviour is to identify the cost drivers—that is, to determine the activities that cause costs to be incurred.

An organization has many cost drivers across its value chain. Exhibit 2-1 lists examples of costs and potential cost drivers for each of the value-chain functions. How well the accountant does at identifying the most appropriate cost drivers determines how well managers understand cost behaviour and how well costs are controlled.

EXHIBIT 2-1

Examples of Value-Chain Functions, Costs, and Cost Drivers

VALUE-CHAIN FUNCTION AND EXAMPLE COSTS	EXAMPLE COST DRIVERS
Research and development • Salaries of marketing-research personnel, costs of market surveys • Salaries of product and process engineers	Number of new product proposals Complexity of proposed products
Design of products, services, and processes • Salaries of product and process engineers • Cost of computer-aided design equipment, cost to develop prototype of product for testing	Number of engineering hours Number of parts per product
Production • Labour wages • Supervisory salaries • Maintenance wages • Amortization of plant and machinery, supplies • Energy	Labour hours Number of people supervised Number of mechanic hours Number of machine hours Kilowatt hours
Marketing • Cost of advertisements • Salaries of marketing personnel, travel costs, entertainment costs	Number of advertisements Sales dollars
Distribution • Wages of shipping personnel • Transportation costs including depreciation of vehicles and fuel	Labour hours Weight of items delivered
Customer service • Salaries of service personnel • Costs of supplies, travel	Hours spent serving products Number of service calls

To examine cost behaviour without going into much detail, this chapter will focus on *volume-related cost drivers*. Later chapters will introduce cost drivers that are not related to volume. Volume-related cost drivers include the number of orders processed, the number of items billed in a billing department, the number of admissions to a theatre, the number of kilograms handled in a warehouse, the hours of labour worked in an assembly department, the number of rides in an amusement park, the seat-miles on an airline, and the dollar sales in a retail business. All of these cost drivers can serve either directly or indirectly as a measure of the volume of output of goods or services. Of course, when only one product is being produced, the units of production is the most obvious volume-related cost driver for production-related costs.

Utopia Fabricating Ltd. of Winnipeg, Manitoba, converts old oil into reusable replacement diesel fuel using a relatively new method. Traditional oil recovery processes require large volumes of old oil to be trucked to large refineries. While trucking distances and capital costs would be significant cost drivers, traditional cost systems would have focused on the volumes of old oil being processed. By focusing on the more significant cost drivers of trucking distances and capital costs, Utopia's process uses a small refinery that requires substantially smaller volumes. By reducing the trucking expenses, the capital costs of a number of small refineries can then be justified.[1]

COMPARISON OF VARIABLE AND FIXED COSTS

OBJECTIVE 2

Show how changes in cost-driver activity levels affect variable and fixed costs.

Variable Cost. A cost that changes in direct proportion to changes in the cost driver.

Fixed Cost. A cost that is not immediately affected by changes in the cost driver.

A key to understanding cost behaviour is distinguishing *variable costs* from *fixed costs*. Costs are classified as variable or fixed depending on how much they change as the level of a particular cost driver changes. A **variable cost** is a cost that changes in direct proportion to changes in the cost driver. In contrast, a **fixed cost** is not immediately affected by changes in the cost driver. Suppose units of production is the cost driver of interest. A 10 percent increase in the units of production would produce a 10 percent increase in variable costs. However, the fixed costs would remain unchanged.

Some examples may clarify the differences between fixed and variable costs. The costs of most merchandise, materials, parts, supplies, commissions, and many types of labour are generally variable with respect to most volume-related cost drivers. Real estate taxes, real estate insurance, many executive salaries, and space rentals tend to be fixed with respect to any volume-related cost driver.

Consider some variable costs. Suppose Watkins Products pays its door-to-door sales personnel a 40 percent straight commission on their sales. The total cost of sales commissions to Watkins is 40 percent of sales dollars. Thus sales commissions is a variable cost with respect to sales revenues. Or suppose Dan's Bait Shop buys bags of fish bait for $2 each. The total cost of fish bait is $2 times the number of bags purchased. Thus fish bait is a variable cost with respect to units (number of bags) purchased. Notice that variable costs are the same *per unit*, but that their *total* fluctuates in direct proportion to the cost driver activity. Exhibit 2-2 graphically depicts these relationships between cost and cost-driver activity.

Now consider a fixed cost. Suppose Sony rents a factory to produce picture tubes for colour television sets for $500,000 per year. The *total cost* of $500,000 is

Sony
www.sony.com

---

[1] "Utopia finds small solution for used oil," *The Globe and Mail*, March 25, 1992.

EXHIBIT 2-2

Variable-Cost Behaviour

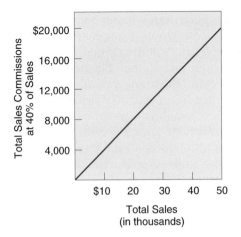

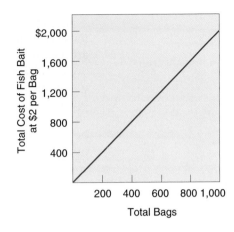

not affected by the number of picture tubes produced. However, the *unit cost* of rent applicable to each tube does depend on the total number of tubes produced. If 100,000 tubes are produced, the unit cost will be $500,000 ÷ 100,000 = $5. If 50,000 tubes are produced, the unit cost will be $500,000 ÷ 50,000 = $10. Therefore, a fixed cost does not change *in total*, but it becomes progressively smaller on a *per unit* basis as the volume increases.

It is important to note from these examples that the "variable" or "fixed" characteristic of a cost relates to its *total dollar amount* and not to its per unit amount. The following table summarizes these relationships.

TYPE OF COST	IF COST-DRIVER ACTIVITY LEVEL INCREASES (OR DECREASES):	
	TOTAL COST	COST PER UNIT*
Fixed costs	No change	Decrease (or increase)
Variable costs	Increase (or decrease)	No change

*Per unit activity volume, for example, product units, passenger-miles, sales dollars.

When predicting costs, two rules-of-thumb are useful:

1. Think of fixed costs as a *total*. Total fixed costs remain unchanged regardless of changes in cost-driver activity.
2. Think of variable costs on a *per unit* basis. The per unit variable cost remains unchanged regardless of changes in cost-driver activity.

Relevant Range

Relevant Range. The limits of cost-driver activity within which a specific realtionship between costs and the cost driver is valid.

Although we have just described fixed costs as unchanging regardless of cost-driver activity, this rule-of-thumb holds true only within reasonable limits. For example, rent costs will rise if increased production requires a larger or additional building—or if the landlord decides to raise the rent. Conversely, rent costs may go down if decreased production causes the company to move to a smaller plant. The **relevant range** is the limits of cost-driver activity within which a specific relationship between costs and the cost driver is valid. In addition, remember that even within the relevant range, a fixed cost remains fixed only over a given time period—usually the budget period. Fixed costs may change from budget year to budget year solely because of changes in insurance and property tax rates, executive salary levels, or rent levels. But these items are unlikely to change within a given year.

For example, in Exhibit 2-3 assume that a General Electric plant has a relevant range of between 40,000 and 85,000 cases of light bulbs per month and that total monthly fixed costs within the relevant range are $100,000. Within the relevant range, fixed costs will remain the same. If production falls below 40,000 cases, changes in personnel and salaries would reduce fixed costs to $60,000. If operations rise above 85,000 cases, increases in personnel and salaries would boost fixed costs to $115,000.

These assumptions—a given time period and a given activity range—are shown graphically at the top of Exhibit 2-3. However, it is highly unusual for monthly operations to be outside the relevant range. Therefore, the three-level refinement at the top of Exhibit 2-3 is usually not graphed. Instead, a single horizontal line is typically extended through the plotted activity levels, as at the bottom of the exhibit. A dashed line is often used outside the relevant range.

EXHIBIT 2-3

Fixed Costs and the
Relevant Range

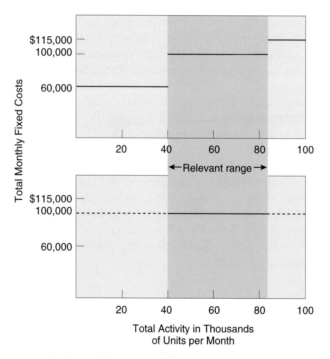

The basic idea of a relevant range also applies to variable costs. That is, outside a relevant range, some variable costs, such as fuel consumed, may behave differently per unit of cost-driver activity. For example, the efficiency of motors is affected if they are used too much or too little.

Difficulties in Classifying Costs

As you may suspect, it is often difficult to classify a cost as exactly variable or exactly fixed. Many complications arise, including the possibility of costs behaving in some nonlinear way (not behaving as a straight line). For example, as tax preparers learn to process the new year's tax forms, their productivity rises. This means that total costs may actually behave like this:

but not like this

Moreover, costs may simultaneously be affected by more than one cost driver. For example, the costs of shipping labour may be affected by *both* the weight and the number of units handled. We shall investigate various facets of this problem in succeeding chapters; for now, we shall assume that any cost may be classified as either variable or fixed. We assume also that a given variable cost is associated with *only one* volume-related cost driver, and that relationship is *linear*.

Finally, in the real world, classifying costs as fixed or variable depends on the decision situation. More costs are fixed and fewer are variable when decisions involve very short time spans and very small increases in activities. Suppose an Air Canada plane is scheduled to depart in two minutes. A potential passenger is running down a corridor bearing a transferable ticket from a competing airline. Unless the airline is held for an extra 30 seconds, the passenger will miss the departure and will not switch to Air Canada for the planned trip. What are the variable costs to Air Canada of delaying the departure and placing one more passenger in an otherwise empty seat? Variable costs (for example, one more meal) are negligible. Virtually all the costs in that decision situation are fixed. Now in contrast, suppose Air Canada's decision is whether to add another flight, or acquire another gate, or add another destination to its routes, or acquire another airplane. Many more costs would be regarded as variable and fewer as fixed.

These examples underscore the importance of how the decision affects the analysis of cost behaviour. Whether costs are really "fixed" depends heavily on the relevant range, the length of the planning period in question, and the specific decision situation.

COST-VOLUME-PROFIT ANALYSIS

Managers often classify costs as fixed or variable when making decisions that affect the volume of output. The managers want to know how such decisions will affect costs and revenues. They realize that many factors in addition to the volume of output will affect costs. Yet, a useful starting point in their decision process is to specify the relationship between the volume of output and the costs and revenues.

The managers of profit-seeking organizations usually study the effects of output volume on revenue (sales), expenses (costs), and net income (net profit). This study is commonly called **cost-volume-profit (CVP) analysis**. The managers of nonprofit organizations also benefit from the study of cost-volume-profit relationships. Why? No organization has unlimited resources, and knowledge of how costs fluctuate as volume changes helps managers to understand how to

Cost-Volume-Profit (CVP) Analysis. The study of the effects of output volume on revenue (sales), expenses (costs), and net income (net profit).

control costs. For example, administrators of nonprofit hospitals are constantly concerned about the behaviour of costs as the volume of patients fluctuates.

To apply CVP analysis, managers resort to some simplifying assumptions. A major assumption is to classify costs as either variable or fixed with respect to a single measure of the volume of output activity. This chapter assumes such a simplified relationship.

Cost Analysis for Ginseng Farming

When ginseng was selling for about $60 a pound, scores of B.C. farmers tilled their hay land and began growing the exotic root. Now, as prices are hovering around $30 a pound, these farmers are growing nervous—and with good reason. Most of the crop is sold at the farm gate to buyers from Hong Kong, the main distribution point. After grading for colour, sizes, and taste, the buyers funnel the dried roots to China where only a few families control the market. It is a system plagued by distribution woes, problems that are exacerbated by uncertainties surrounding the transfer of Hong Kong to Chinese rule July 1. "We know the problem is not a supply-and-demand one," says Allen Smith, president of Associated Ginseng Growers of B.C. The problem is "the movement of the root from the farm gate to the marketplace and a breakdown between the people who are buying it and the people who are distributing it on the retail end," adds Mr. Smith, who grows about 100 acres of the plant at his Gold Valley Farm in Vernon. Low price is not the only problem facing B.C.'s 125 ginseng growers. One major concern is federal regulation controlling the sale of herbal remedies. However, Al Oliver, provincial ginseng specialist with the B.C. Ministry of Agriculture, Food and Fisheries, in Kamloops, says such regulation is unlikely to affect the industry. Ginseng, which is said to invigorate, combat high blood pressure, and increase sex drive, is basically untouchable because it is considered a food supplement, not a medicinal product. Another industry problem is misinformation spread by environmentalists. "Naysayers say ginseng robs the soil of all nutrients," complains Mr. Smith. "Actually ginseng is very conservative in what it requires." Mild fungicides are used sparingly to control disease. "However, we are closely monitored by Agriculture Canada. They take samples of the plants to be sure we're following the government guidelines with regard to chemical use." It is estimated that 1.25 million pounds of ginseng was harvested in B.C. in 1996. Black shade cloths now cover 2,800 acres in the Thompson, Nicola, and Fraser Valleys— dry areas considered ideal for growing top-quality crops. "Our growers are quite competitive because of our high yields," observes Mr. Smith. "We don't have to use as much chemical as our competitors in Ontario or Wisconsin, who each grow about 4,000 acres. Also, we're able to offer our buyers a four-year-old crop. Our competitors have to harvest in three years." Less disease stress due to a drier climate allows the one-year-longer growing term in B.C., and while it would seem to be advantageous to get the crop to market a year earlier, in ginseng older is better. The additional year produces a heavier and more profitable harvest. Using the industry yield of 2,600 pounds per acre, and calculating sales at the current price of $30 a pound, farmers can still realize a gross income of $78,000 an acre. **Fixed costs** are estimated at $60,000 an acre, resulting in a profit of $18,000. However, these figures do not include land, management, interest, or equipment costs. A first planting costs $15,000 an acre for shade cloth and $5,000 an acre for seed. Barring a dramatic price increase, ginseng will never be a get-rich-crop. But the long-term prognosis is good, says Mr. Smith. "We all want higher prices but, in a way, the lower prices are good for us. It's a natural way to level off production."

Source: Alice De Marni, "Uncertainly grows over ginseng: the Hong Kong handover may add to distribution woes for B.C. farmers," *British Columbia Report*, June 30, 1997, pp. 16–17.

CVP Scenario

Amy Winston, the manager of food services for a university's food services department, is trying to decide whether to rent a line of food vending machines. Although individual snack items have various acquisition costs and selling prices, Winston has decided that an average selling price of $.50 per unit and an average acquisition of $.40 per unit will suffice for purposes of this analysis. She predicts the following revenue and expense relationships:

	PER UNIT	PERCENT OF SALES
Selling price	$ .50	100%
Variable cost of each item	.40	80%
Selling price less variable cost	$ .10	20%
Monthly fixed expenses		
Rent	$1,000	
Wages for replenishing and servicing	4,500	
Other fixed expenses	500	
Total fixed expenses per month	$6,000	

We will next use these data to illustrate several applications of cost-volume-profit analysis.

Break-Even Point—Contribution Margin and Equation Techniques

OBJECTIVE 3

Calculate sales volume in total dollars and total units to break even.

Break-Even Point. The level of sales at which revenue equals expenses, and income is zero.

Break-Even Analysis. The study of cost-profit-volume relationships.

Margin of Safety. Equal to the planned unit sales less the breakeven unit sales; it shows how far sales can fall below the planned level before losses occur.

Contribution Margin. The sales price minus all the variable expenses.

The most basic CVP analysis computes the monthly break-even point in number of units and in dollar sales. The **break-even point** is the level of sales at which revenue equals expenses and net income is zero.

The study of cost-volume-profit relationships is often called **break-even analysis**. This term may be misleading, because finding the break-even point is just the first step in a planning decision. Managers need to concentrate on how the decision will affect sales, costs, and net income.

However, one direct use of the break-even point is to assess possible risks. By comparing planned sales with the break-even point, managers can determine a **margin of safety**.

margin of safety = planned unit sales – break-even unit sales

The margin of safety shows how far sales can fall below the planned level before losses occur.

There are two basic techniques for computing a break-even point: contribution margin and equation.

Contribution-Margin Technique

Consider the following commonsense arithmetic approach. Every unit sold generates a **contribution margin** or **marginal income**, which is the sales price minus the variable costs per unit. For the vending machine snack items:

Unit sales price		$.50
Unit variable cost		.40
Unit contribution margin to fixed costs and net income		$.10

When is the break-even point reached? When enough units have been sold to generate a total contribution margin equal to the total fixed costs. Divide the $6,000 in fixed costs by the $.10 unit contribution margin. The number of units that must be sold to break even is $6,000 ÷ $.10 = 60,000 units. The sales revenue at the break-even point is 60,000 units × $.50 per unit, or $30,000.

Think about the contribution margin of the snack items. Each unit purchased and sold generated *extra* revenue of $.50 and *extra* cost of $.40. Fixed costs are unaffected. Therefore, profit increases by $.10 for each unit purchased and sold. If zero units were sold, a loss equal to the fixed cost of $6,000 would be incurred. Each unit reduces the loss by $.10 until sales reach the break-even point of 60,000 units. After that point, each unit adds (or *contributes*) $.10 to profit.

The condensed income statement at the break-even point is

		PER UNIT	PERCENTAGE
Units	60,000		
Sales	$30,000	$ .50	100%
Variable costs	24,000	.40	80%
Contribution			
margin	$6,000	$ .10	20%
Fixed costs	6,000		
Net income	$0		

Sometimes the unit price and unit variable costs are not known. This situation is common at companies that sell more than one product because no single price or variable cost applies to all products at many different prices. A break-even point *in overall units* sold by the store would not be meaningful. In such cases, you must work with total sales and total variable costs and calculate variable costs as a *percentage of each sales dollar*.

Consider our vending machine example:

Sales price	100%
Variable expenses as a percentage of dollar sales	80%
Contribution-margin percentage	20%

Therefore, 20 percent of each sales dollar is available for the recovery of fixed expenses and the making of net income: $6,000 ÷ 20 percent = $30,000 sales needed to break even. The contribution margin percentage you can compute is based on dollar sales without determining the break-even point in units.

COMPANY ⦾ STRATEGIES

PROCTER & GAMBLE CANADA INC.: THE SCOPE EXAMPLE

Procter & Gamble was founded over 150 years ago when soapmaker James Gamble and candlemaker William Procter decided to join forces in Cincinnati, Ohio. The company concentrated on the consumer products market, focusing its effort on quality and consumer satisfaction. One of P&G's historic strengths is its ability to develop truly innovative products to meet consumers' needs. Today, Procter & Gamble is one of the most successful consumer goods companies in the world and its products can be found in nine out of ten Canadian homes. It operates in 54 countries and had sales of more than $27 billion and net earnings of $1.8 billion in 1991. The Canadian subsidiary contributed $1.3 billion in sales and $54 million in net earnings in 1991. The Canadian subsidiary was recognized as the leader in the Canadian packaged goods industry, and its consumer brands lead in most of the categories in which the company operates.

One such brand is Scope, which is part of Procter & Gamble's Health Care Division. Scope was launched in the mid-1960s as the first brand that provided both effective protection against bad breath and a better taste than other mouthwashes. Lines from their advertising included, "Scope fights bad breath" and "Don't let the good taste fool you." Very quickly it became the market leader.

The following analysis indicates the difference between contribution margin and gross margin and provides a break-even volume calculation for the Scope brand. (The numbers are fictitious to protect the confidentiality of P&G's actual cost data.)

	$ thousands	$ product cost/case	$ variable cost/case
Net Sales	$16,860	$38.32	$38.32
Expenses:			
Ingredients	3,337	7.58	7.58
Packaging	2,088	4.74	4.74
Manufacturing	2,861	6.50	3.25
Delivery	1,081	2.46	2.46
Miscellaneous	467	1.06	0.78
Cost of goods sold	9,834	22.34	
Variable costs			18.81
Gross Margin	$ 7,026	$15.98	
Contribution Margin			$19.51

Break-even volume = Fixed costs of $1,554,000/Contribution margin of $19.51= 79,651 cases

Source: Adapted from a case "Gwen Hearst's Dilemma." Written by Franklin Ramsoomair, Wilfrid Laurier University, and David LeNeveau, Mike Wingert and Colleen Jay, Procter & Gamble Canada.

Equation Technique

Procter & Gamble
www.pg.com

The equation technique is the most general form of analysis—the one that may be adapted to any conceivable cost-volume-profit situation. You are familiar with a typical income statement. Any income statement can be expressed in equation form, a mathematical model, as follows:

$$\text{sales} - \text{variable expenses} - \text{fixed expenses} = \text{net income} \quad (1)$$

That is

$$\left(\begin{array}{c}\text{unit}\\\text{sales}\\\text{price}\end{array}\times\begin{array}{c}\text{number}\\\text{of}\\\text{units}\end{array}\right)-\left(\begin{array}{c}\text{unit}\\\text{variable}\\\text{cost}\end{array}\times\begin{array}{c}\text{number}\\\text{of}\\\text{units}\end{array}\right)-\begin{array}{c}\text{fixed}\\\text{expenses}\end{array}=\begin{array}{c}\text{net}\\\text{income}\end{array}$$

At the break-even point net income is zero:

$$\text{sales} - \text{variable expenses} - \text{fixed expenses} = 0$$

Let N = number of units to be sold to break even. Then

$$\$.50N - \$.40N - \$6,000 = 0$$
$$\$.10N = \$6,000$$
$$N = \frac{\$6,000}{\$.10}$$
$$N = 60,000 \text{ units}$$

Total sales in the equation is a price-times-quantity relationship, which was expressed in our example as $.50N. To find the *dollar* sales, multiply 60,000 *units* by $.50, which would yield the break-even dollar sales of $30,000.

You can also solve the equation for sales dollars without computing the unit break-even point by using the relationship of variable costs and profits as a *percentage* of sales:

$$\text{variable-cost ratio or percentage} = \frac{\text{variable cost per unit}}{\text{sales price per unit}}$$
$$= \frac{\$.40}{\$.50}$$
$$= .80 \text{ or } 80\%$$

Let S = sales in dollars needed to break even. Then

$$S - .80S - \$6,000 = 0$$
$$.20S = \$6,000$$
$$S = \frac{\$6,000}{.20}$$
$$S = \$30,000$$

Relationship between the Two Techniques

You may have noticed that the contribution-margin technique is merely a short-cut of the equation technique. Look at the last three lines in the two solutions given for Equation 1. They read

BREAK-EVEN VOLUME	
In Units	**In Dollars**
$.10N = $6,000	.20S = $6,000
$N = \dfrac{\$6,000}{\$.10}$	$S = \dfrac{\$6,000}{.20}$
N = 60,000 units	S = $30,000

From these equations we can derive the general shortcut formulas:

$$\frac{\text{break-even volume}}{\text{in units}} = \frac{\text{fixed expenses}}{\text{contribution margin per unit}} \qquad (2)$$

$$\frac{\text{break-even volume}}{\text{in dollars}} = \frac{\text{fixed expenses}}{\text{contribution margin ratio}} \qquad (3)$$

You may use either the equation or the contribution-margin technique. The choice is a matter of personal preference or convenience for each particular case.

Break-Even Point—Graphical Techniques

OBJECTIVE 4

Construct a cost-volume-profit graph.

Exhibit 2-4 shows the cost-volume-profit relationships in our vending machine example. Study the graph as you read the procedure for constructing it.

Step 1: Draw the axes. The horizontal axis is the sales volume, and the vertical axis is dollars of cost and revenue.

Step 2: Plot sales volume. Select a convenient sales volume, say, 100,000 units, and plot point A for total sales dollars at that volume: 100,000 × 50¢ = $50,000. Draw the revenue (i.e., sales) line from point A to the origin, point 0.

Step 3: Plot fixed expenses. Draw the line showing the $6,000 fixed portion of expenses. It should be a horizontal line intersecting the vertical axis at $6,000, point B.

Step 4: Determine the variable portion of expenses at a convenient level of activity: 100,000 units × $.40 = $40,000. Add this to the fixed expenses $40,000 + $6,000 = $46,000. Plot point C for 100,000 units and $46,000. Then draw a line between this point and point B. This is the total expenses line.

EXHIBIT 2-4

Cost-Volume-Profit Graph

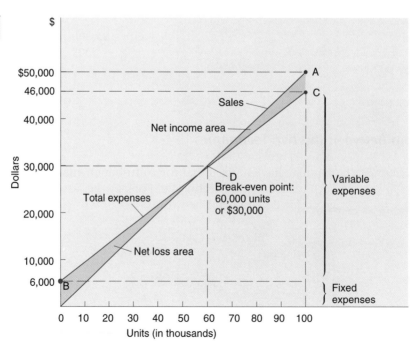

Step 5: Locate the break-even point. The break-even point is where the total expenses line crosses the sales line, 60,000 units or $30,000, namely, where total sales revenues exactly equal total costs, point D.

The break-even point is only one facet of this cost-volume-profit graph. More generally, the graph shows the profit or loss at *any* rate of activity. At any given volume, the vertical distance between the sales line and the total expenses line measures the new income or net loss.

Managers often use break-even graphs because they show potential profits over a wide range of volume more easily than numerical exhibits. Whether graphs or other types of exhibits are used depends largely on management's preference.

Note that the concept of a relevant range applies to the entire break-even graph. Almost all break-even graphs show revenue and cost lines extending back to the vertical axis as shown in Exhibit 2-5(A). This approach is misleading because the relationships depicted in such graphs are valid only within the relevant range that underlies the construction of the graph. Exhibit 2-5(B), a modification of the conventional break-even graph, partially demonstrates the multitude of assumptions that must be made in constructing the typical break-even graph. Some of these assumptions follow.

EXHIBIT 2-5

Conventional and Modified Break-Even Graphs

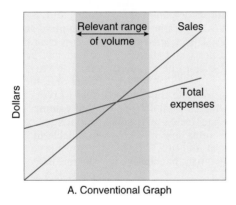

A. Conventional Graph

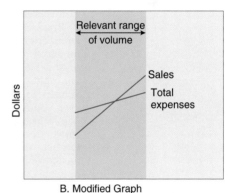

B. Modified Graph

Break-Even Point Assumptions

1. Expenses may be classified into variable and fixed categories. Total variable expenses vary directly with volume. Total fixed expenses do not change with volume.
2. The behaviour of revenues and expenses is accurately portrayed and is linear over the relevant range. The principal differences between the accountant's break-even chart and the economist's chart are that (a) the accountant's sales line is drawn on the assumption that selling prices do not change with production or sales, and the economist assumes that reduced selling prices are normally associated with increased sales volume; (b) the accountant usually assumes a constant variable expense per unit, and the economist assumes that the variable expense per unit changes with production levels. Within the relevant range, the accountant's and the economist's sales and expense lines are usually close to one another, although the lines may diverge greatly outside the range.
3. Efficiency and productivity will be unchanged.

Sales Mix. The relative proportions or combinations of quantities of products that comprise total sales.

4. Sales mix will be constant. The **sales mix** is the relative proportions or combinations of quantities of products that comprise total sales.
5. The difference in inventory levels at the beginning and at the end of a period is insignificant. Otherwise the number of units sold will be significantly different from the number of units produced.

PERSPECTIVES ON P O D M DECISION-MAKING

Break Even in the Auto Industry

Increased worldwide competition in the automobile industry has made many companies acutely aware of their break-even points. In the early 1990s, most auto companies were losing money. With dim prospects for large increases in volume of sales, profitability would result only if they could decrease their break-even points. That is exactly what most companies did.

Break-even points vary greatly for different auto companies. The larger companies have high fixed costs and therefore must achieve higher sales to break even. For example, Chrysler must sell 1.6 million vehicles to break even. While the break-even volume has decreased from 1.9 million vehicles in the late 1980s, it is still above the number of units sold in 1993. Further, the reduction of 16% in the break-even point is less than that achieved by some competitors.

Saab, a Swedish company, has focused on bringing down the number of production hours per car. A reduction from 120 hours to 45 hours has reduced the break-even volume from 125,000 vehicles to 83,000. This is still above 1993 sales of 73,605 cars, but well below the 135,000 vehicles projected for the mid-1990s.

The assembly operations for Jaguar, located 100 miles north of London, have had a dual focus: quality and production time. Quality improvements were expected to increase sales, and this appears to be working. Warranty costs in the U.S. alone are down 60 percent and sales are up. Production improvement were intended to reduce the break-even volume. Since 1990, Jaguar has cut 54 percent from the time required to build a car. This has cut the break-even point from between 50,000 and 60,000 vehicles to 30,000 per year.

Another British company, Rolls-Royce, sells far fewer cars. In fact, sales dropped from 3,300 Rolls-Royces and Bentleys in 1990 to 1,360 in 1993. At a break-even volume of about 2,600 cars, the company was profitable in 1990. However, the company faced serious difficulty as sales plunged to 1,480 in 1991 and further to 1,360 by 1993. Yet, by trimming its worldwide staff from 5,000 to 2,300 people, Rolls-Royce reduced its break-even volume to 1,300 cars by 1993, providing a small profit after two years of losses.

It is clear that break-even volumes differ greatly across automobile companies; Rolls-Royce can generate a profit at a sales level of 1,300 vehicles, but Saab, Jaguar, and Chrysler would go out of business at that volume. Similarly, Chrysler could not survive selling at volumes that are highly profitable to Saab and Jaguar. Each company must compute its own break-even volume based on its own fixed and variable costs. If a company's sales fall below its break-even point, it must either find a way to get more sales or it must restructure its production operations to reduce its break-even point.

Sources: Paul A. Eisenstein, "Jaguar Ledgers to Feature Black, Not Red, Ink Next Year," *The Washington Times* September 16, 1994, p. D3; Mary Beth Vander Schaaf, "Saab Counts on V-6 to Boost 9000," *Automotive News* September 26, 1994, p. 37; "GM's Saab Unit Climbs Back Into Black," *Investor's Business Daily* September 27, 1994, p. A4; James Bennet, "Chrysler's Chief's World View: Place to Sell, Not Build, Cars," *The New York Times* September 30, 1994, p. D1; Christopher Jensen, "Jaguar's Renaissance: Ford Helps Its British Acquisition Make Quality Job One," *The Plain Dealer* October 9, 1994, p. 1H; Dan Jedlicka, "Rebounding Rolls Needs a Partner," *Chicago Sun-Times* October 17, 1994, p. 47.

Saab
www.saabcanada.com

Jaguar Cars
www.jaguarcars.com

Rolls-Royce
www.rolls-royce.com

Changes in Fixed Expenses

Changes in fixed expenses cause changes in the break-even point. For example, if the $1,000 monthly rent for the vending machines were doubled, what would the monthly break-even point be in number of units and in dollar sales?

The fixed expenses would increase from $6,000 to $7,000, so

$$\frac{\text{break-even volume}}{\text{in units}} = \frac{\text{fixed expenses}}{\text{contribution margin per unit}} = \frac{\$7,000}{\$.10} = 70,000 \text{ units} \qquad (2)$$

$$\frac{\text{break-even volume}}{\text{in dollars}} = \frac{\text{fixed expenses}}{\text{contribution margin ratio}} = \frac{\$7,000}{.20} = \$35,000 \qquad (3)$$

Note that a one-sixth increase in fixed expenses altered the break-even point by one-sixth: from 60,000 to 70,000 units and from $30,000 to $35,000. This type of relationship always exists between fixed expenses and the break-even point, if everything else remains constant.

Companies frequently lower their break-even points by reducing their total fixed costs. For example, closing or selling factories decreases property taxes, insurance, depreciation, and managers' salaries. Further, it is, of course, also possible to reduce a break-even point by reducing variable costs per unit or by increasing the selling price per unit.

Changes in Contribution Margin per Unit

Changes in variable costs also cause the break-even point to shift. Companies also reduce their break-even points by increasing their contribution margins per unit of product through either increases in sales prices or decreases in unit-variable costs, or both. For example, assume that the fixed rent is still $1,000. (1) If the owner is paid $.01 rental per unit in addition to the fixed rent, find the monthly break-even point in number of units and in dollar sales. (2) If the selling price falls from $.50 to $.45 per unit, and the original variable expenses per unit are unchanged, find the monthly break-even point in number of units and in dollar sales.

1. The variable expenses would increase from $.40 to $.41, the unit contribution margin would decline from $.10 to $.09, and the contribution-margin ratio would become .18 ($.09 ÷ $.50).

   The original fixed expenses of $6,000 would be unaffected, but the denominators would change from those previously used. Thus,

   $$\text{break-even point in units} = \frac{\$6,000}{\$.09} = 66,667 \text{ units} \qquad (2)$$

   $$\text{break-even point in dollars} = \frac{\$6,000}{.18} = \$33,333 \qquad (3)$$

2. If the selling price fell from $.50 to $.45, and the original variable expenses were unchanged, the unit contribution would be reduced from $.10 to $.05 (i.e., $.45 − $.40) and the break-even point would

soar to 120,000 units ($6,000 ÷ $.05). The break-even point, in dollars, would be $54,000 (120,000 units × $.45) or, using the formula:

$$\text{break-even point in units} = \frac{\$6,000}{\$.05} = 120,000 \text{ units} \quad (2)$$

$$\text{break-even point in dollars} = \frac{\$6,000}{.1111^*} = \$54,000 \quad (3)$$

$$^* \ \$.05/\$.45$$

Target Net Profit and an Incremental Approach

OBJECTIVE 6

Calculate sales volume in total dollars and total units to reach a target profit.

Managers can also use CVP analysis to determine the total sales and/or units needed to reach a target profit. For example, in our vending machine example, suppose Winston considers $480 per month the minimum acceptable net income. How many units will have to be sold to justify the adoption of the vending machine plan? How does this figure "translate" into dollar sales?

The method for computing desired or target sales volume in units and the desired or target net income is the same as we used in our earlier break-even computations. However, now the targets are expressed in the following equations:

$$\text{target sales} - \text{variable expenses} - \text{fixed expenses} = \text{target net income}$$

$$\text{target sales volume in units} = \frac{\text{fixed expenses} + \text{target net income}}{\text{contribution margin per unit}} \quad (4)$$

$$= \frac{\$6,000 + \$480}{\$.10}$$

$$= 64,800 \text{ units} \quad (5)$$

Incremental Approach. The change in total results (such as revenue, expenses, or income) under a new condition in comparison with some given or known condition.

Another way of getting the same answer is to use your knowledge of the break-even point and adopt an **incremental approach**. The term incremental is widely used in accounting. It refers to the change in total results (such as revenue, expenses, or income) under a new condition in comparison with some given or known condition.

In this instance, the given condition is assumed to be the 60,000 unit break-even point. All expenses would be recovered at that volume. Therefore the *change* or *increment* in net income for every unit *beyond* 60,000 would be equal to the contribution margin of $.50 – $.40 = $.10. If $480 were the target net profit, $480 ÷ $.10 would show that the target volume must exceed the break-even volume by 4,800 units; it would therefore be 60,000 + 4,800 = 64,800 units. To find the answer in terms of *dollar* sales, multiply 64,800 units by $.50 or use the formula:

$$\text{target sales volume in dollars} = \frac{\text{fixed expenses} + \text{target net income}}{\text{contribution margin ratio}} \quad (6)$$

$$= \frac{\$6,000 + \$480}{.20} = \$32,400$$

To solve directly for sales dollars with the alternative incremental approach, we would start at the break-even point in dollar sales of $30,000. Every sales dollar beyond that point contributes $.20 to net profit. Divide $480 by .20. Dollar sales must exceed the break-even volume by $2,400 to produce a net profit of $480; thus the total dollar sales would be $30,000 + $2,400 = $32,400.

The following table summarizes these assumptions:

	BREAK-EVEN POINT	INCREMENT	NEW CONDITION
Volume in units	60,000	4,800	64,800
Sales	$30,000	$2,400	$32,400
Variable expenses	24,000	1,920	25,920
Contribution margin	6,000	480	6,480
Fixed expenses	6,000	—	6,000
Net Income	$ 0	$ 480	$ 480

Multiple Changes in the Key Factors

So far we have seen changes in one CVP factor at a time. In the real world, managers often must make decisions about the probable effects of multiple factor changes. For instance, suppose that after the vending machines have been in place a while, Winston is considering locking them from 6:00 p.m. to 6:00 a.m., which she estimates will save $820 in wages monthly. The cutback from 24-hour service would hurt volume substantially because many night-time employees use the machines. However, employees could find food elsewhere, so not too many complaints are expected.[2] Should the machines remain available 24 hours per day? Assume that monthly sales would decline by 10,000 units from current sales. We will perform the analysis using two different levels of current sales volume: (a) 62,000 units and (b) 90,000 units.

Consider two approaches. One approach is to construct and solve equations for conditions that prevail under each alternative and select the volume level that yields the highest net income.

Regardless of the current volume level, be it 62,000 or 90,000 units, if we accept the prediction that sales will decline by 10,000 units as accurate, closing from 6:00 p.m. to 6:00 a.m. will decrease net income by $180:

	DECLINE FROM 62,000 TO 52,000 UNITS		DECLINE FROM 90,000 TO 80,000 UNITS	
Units	62,000	52,000	90,000	80,000
Sales	$31,000	$26,000	$45,000	$40,000
Variable expenses	24,800	20,800	36,000	32,000
Contribution margin	6,200	5,200	9,000	8,000
Fixed expenses	6,000	5,180	6,000	5,180
Net Income	$ 200	$ 20	$ 3,000	$ 2,820
Change in net income	($180)		($180)	

---

[2] The quality of overall working conditions might affect these decisions even though such factors are difficult to quantify. In particular, if costs or profits do not differ much between alternatives, the nonquantifiable subjective aspects may be the deciding factors.

A second approach—an incremental approach—is quicker and simpler. Simplicity is important to managers because it keeps the analysis from being cluttered by irrelevant and potentially confusing data.

What does the insightful manager see in this situation? First, whether 62,000 or 90,000 units are being sold is irrelevant to the decision at hand. The issue is the decline in volume, which would be 10,000 units in either case. The essence of this decision is whether the prospective savings in cost exceed the prospective loss in total contribution margin dollars:

Lost total contribution margin, 10,000 units @ $.10	$1,000
Savings in fixed expenses	820
Prospective decline in net income	$ 180

Locking the vending machines from 6:00 p.m. to 6:00 a.m. would cause a $180 decrease in monthly net income. Whichever way you analyze it, locking the machines is not a sound financial decision.

CVP Analysis in the Computer Age

As we have seen, cost-volume-profit analysis is based on a mathematical model, the equation

$$\text{sales} - \text{variable expenses} - \text{fixed expenses} = \text{net income}$$

The CVP model is widely used in planning. Managers in a variety of organizations use a personal computer and a CVP modelling program to study combinations of changes in selling prices, unit variable costs, fixed costs, and desired profits. Many nonprofit organizations also use computerized CVP modelling. For example, some universities have models that help measure how decisions such as raising tuition, adding programs, and decreases in government grants will affect financial results. The computer quickly calculates the results of changes.

Exhibit 2-6 is a sample spreadsheet that shows what the sales level would have to be at three different fixed expense levels and three different variable expense levels to reach three different income levels. The computer calculates the 27 different sales levels rapidly and without error. Managers can insert any numbers they want for fixed expenses (column A), variable expenses percentage (column B), target net income (row 3 of columns C, D, and E) or combinations thereof, and the computer will compute the required sales level.

In addition to speed and convenience, computers allow a more sophisticated approach to CVP analysis than the one illustrated in this chapter. The assumptions listed in Objective 5 are necessary to simplify the analysis enough for most managers to construct a CVP model by hand. But computer analysts can construct a model that does not require all the simplifications. Computer models can include multiple cost drivers, nonlinear relationships between costs and cost drivers, varying sales mixes, and analyses that need not be restricted to a relevant range.

EXHIBIT 2-6

Spreadsheet Analysis of
CVP Relationship

	A	B	C	D	E
1			SALES REQUIRED @ $50 PER UNIT TO EARN		
2	FIXED	VARIABLE	ANNUAL NET INCOME OF		
3	EXPENSES	EXPENSES %	$2,000	$4,000	$6,000
4					
5	$4,000	0.40	$10,000*	$13,333	$16,667
6	$4,000	0.44	$10,714*	$14,286	$17,857
7	$4,000	0.48	$11,538*	$15,385	$19,231
8	$6,000	0.40	$13,333	$16,667	$20,000
9	$6,000	0.44	$14,286	$17,857	$21,429
10	$6,000	0.48	$15,385	$19,231	$23,077
11	$8,000	0.40	$16,667	$20,000	$23,333
12	$8,000	0.44	$17,857	$21,429	$25,000
13	$8,000	0.48	$19,231	$23,077	$26,923
14					
15					
16	*(A5+C3)/(1-B5)=($4,000+$2,000)/(1-$.40)				
17	(A6+C3)/(1-B6)=($4,000+$2,000)/(1-$.44)				
18	(A7+C3)/(1-B7)=($4,000+$2,000)/(1-$.48)				
19	Etc.				

Use of computer models is a cost/benefit issue. Sometimes the costs of modelling are exceeded by the value of better decisions made using the models. However, the reliability of these models depends on the accuracy of their underlying assumptions about how revenues and costs will actually be affected. Moreover, in small organizations, simplified CVP models are often accurate enough that more sophisticated modelling is unwarranted.

SALES MIX ANALYSIS

OBJECTIVE 7

Explain the effects of
sales mix on profits.

Sales Mix. The relative proportions or combinations of quantities of products that comprise total sales.

To emphasize fundamental ideas, the cost-volume-profit analysis in this chapter has focused on a single product. But nearly all companies sell more than one product. **Sales mix** is defined as the relative proportions or combinations of quantities of products that comprise total sales. If the proportions of the mix change, the cost-volume-profit relationships also change.

Suppose Ramos Company has two products, wallets (W) and key cases (K). The income budget follows:

	WALLETS (W)	KEY CASES (K)	TOTAL
Sales in units	300,000	75,000	375,000
Sales @ $8 and $5	$2,400,000	$375,000	$2,775,000
Variable expenses @ $7 and $3	2,100,000	225,000	2,325,000
Contribution margins @ $1 and $2	$ 300,000	$150,000	$ 450,000
Fixed expenses			180,000
Net income			$ 270,000

For simplicity, ignore income taxes. What would be the break-even point? The typical answer assumes a constant mix of four units of W for every unit of K.

$$K = \text{number of units of product K to break even}$$
$$4K = \text{number of units of product W to break even}$$
$$\text{sales} - \text{variable expenses} - \text{fixed expenses} = \text{zero net income}$$
$$\$8(4K) + \$5(K) - \$7(4K) - \$3(K) - \$180,000 = 0$$
$$\$32K + \$5K - \$28K - \$3K - \$180,000 = 0$$
$$\$6K = \$180,000$$
$$K = 30,000$$
$$4K = 120,000 = W$$

The break-even point is 30,000K + 120,000W = 150,000 units.

This is the only break-even point for a sales mix of four wallets for every key case. Clearly, there are other break-even points for other sales mixes. For instance, suppose only key cases were sold, fixed expenses being unchanged:

$$\text{break-even point} = \frac{\text{fixed expenses}}{\text{contribution margin per unit}}$$
$$= \frac{\$180,000}{\$2}$$
$$= 90,000 \text{ key cases}$$

If only wallets were sold:

$$\text{break-even point} = \frac{\$180,000}{\$1}$$
$$= 180,000 \text{ wallets}$$

Managers are not primarily interested in the break-even point for its own sake. Instead, they want to know how changes in a planned sales mix will affect net income. When the sales mix changes, the break-even point and the expected net income at various sales levels are altered. For example, suppose overall actual total sales were equal to the budget of 375,000 units. However, if only 50,000 key cases were sold:

	WALLETS (W)	KEY CASES (K)	TOTAL
Sales in units	325,000	50,000	375,000
Sales @ $8 and $5	$2,600,000	$250,000	$2,850,000
Variable expenses @ $7 and $3	2,275,000	150,000	2,425,000
Contribution margins @ $1 and $2	$ 325,000	$100,000	$ 425,000
Fixed expenses			180,000
Net income			$ 245,000

The change in sales mix has resulted in a $245,000 actual net income rather than the $270,000 budgeted net income—an unfavourable difference of $25,000. The budgeted and actual sales in number of units were identical, but the proportion of sales of the product bearing the higher unit contribution margin declined.

Different advertising strategies may also affect the sales mix. Clearly, if a sales budget is not actually attained, the budgeted net income will be affected by the individual sales volumes of each product. The fewer the units sold, the lower the profit, and vice versa. All other things being equal, the higher the proportion of the more profitable products, the higher the profit. For any given level of total sales, the greater the proportion of the key cases, the greater the total profit.

Managers usually want to maximize the sales of all their products. However, faced with limited resources and time, executives prefer to generate the most profitable sales mix achievable. For example, consider a recent annual report of Deere & Co., a manufacturer of farm equipment. "The increase in the ratio of cost of goods sold to net sales resulted from higher production costs, a less favourable mix of products sold, and sales incentive programs."

Profitability of a given product helps guide executives who must decide to emphasize or de-emphasize particular products. For example, given limited production facilities or limited time of sales personnel, should we emphasize brand A or brand B fertilizer? These decisions may be affected by other factors beyond the contribution margin per unit of product. Chapter 8 explores some of these factors, including the importance of the amount of contribution per *unit of time* rather than per *unit of product*.

Deere & Co.
www.deere.com

IMPACT OF INCOME TAXES

OBJECTIVE 8

Compute cost-volume-profit relationships on an after-tax basis.

Thus far we have (as so many people would like to) ignored income taxes. However, in most nations, private enterprises are subject to income taxes. Reconsider the vending machine example. In Objective 6, as part of our CVP analysis, we discussed the sales necessary to achieve a target income before income taxes of $480. If an income tax were levied at 40 percent, the new results would be:

Income before income tax:	$480	100%
Income tax	192	40%
Net income	$288	60%

Note that:

net income = income before income taxes − .40 (income before income taxes)
net income = .60 (income before income taxes)

$$\text{income before income taxes} = \frac{\text{net income}}{.60}$$

$$\text{target income before income taxes} = \frac{\text{target after-tax net income}}{1 - \text{tax rate}}$$

$$\text{target income before income taxes} = \frac{\$288}{1 - .40} = \frac{\$288}{.60} = \$480$$

Suppose the target net income after taxes was $288. The only change in the general equation approach would be on the right-hand side of the following equation:

$$\text{target sales} - \text{variable expenses} - \text{fixed expenses} = \frac{\text{target after-tax net income}}{1 - \text{tax rate}}$$

Thus, letting N be the number of units to be sold at $.50 each with a variable cost of $.40 each and total fixed costs of $6,000:

$$\$.50N - \$.40N - \$6,000 = \frac{\$288}{1 - .40}$$

$$\$.10N = \$6,000 + \frac{\$288}{.60}$$

$$\$.06N = \$3,600 + \$288$$

$$N = \$3,888 \div \$ .06$$

$$N = 64,800 \text{ units}$$

Sales of 64,800 units produce an *after-tax profit* of $288 as shown here and a *before-tax profit* of $480.

Suppose the target net income after taxes was $480. The volume needed would rise to 68,000 units as follows:

$$\$.50N - \$.40N - \$6,000 = \frac{\$480}{1 - .40}$$

$$\$.10N = \$6,000 + \frac{\$480}{.60}$$

$$\$.06N = \$3,600 + \$480$$

$$N = \$4,080 \div \$ .06$$

$$N = 68,000 \text{ units}$$

As a shortcut to computing the effects of volume on the change in after-tax income, use the formula:

$$\frac{\text{change in}}{\text{net income}} = \left(\begin{array}{c}\text{change in volume}\\ \text{in units}\end{array}\right) \times \left(\begin{array}{c}\text{contribution margin}\\ \text{per unit}\end{array}\right) \times (1 - \text{tax rate})$$

In our example, suppose operations were at a level of 64,800 units and $288 after-tax net income. The manager is wondering how much after-tax net income would increase if sales became 68,000 units:

$$\begin{aligned}\text{change in net income} &= (68,000 - 64,800) \times \$.10 \times (1 - .4)\\ &= 3,200 \times \$.10 \times .60 = 3,200 \times \$.06\\ &= \$192\end{aligned}$$

In brief, each unit beyond the break-even point adds to after-tax net profit at the unit contribution margin multiplied by (1 – income tax rate).

Throughout our illustration, the break-even point itself does not change. Why? *Because there is no income tax at a level of zero profits.*

USES AND LIMITATIONS OF COST-VOLUME ANALYSIS

Best Combination of Factors

The analysis of cost-volume-profit relationships is an important management responsibility. Managers try to obtain the most profitable combination of variable- and fixed-cost factors. For example, one Canadian bread manufacturer handles and distributes its products to grocery stores by using independent commissioned agents. Agents are assigned a territory and are responsible for delivering the product. Alternatively, most companies use a sales and distribution staff that are employed by the company. This bread manufacturer has shifted a substantially fixed cost of salaries to a substantially variable cost in commissions.

Generally, companies that spend heavily for advertising are willing to do so because they have high contribution-margin percentages (airlines, cigarette, and cosmetic companies). Conversely, companies with low contribution-margin percentages usually spend less for advertising and promotion (manufacturers of industrial equipment). Obviously, two companies with the same unit sales volumes at the same unit prices could have different attitudes toward risking an advertising outlay. Assume the following:

	PERFUME COMPANY	JANITORIAL SERVICE
Unit sales volume	100,000 bottles	100,000 square feet
Dollar sales at $20 per unit	$2,000,000	$2,000,000
Variable costs	200,000	1,700,000
Contribution margin	$1,800,000	$ 300,000
Contribution-margin percentage	90%	15%

Suppose each company wants to increase sales volume by 10 percent:

	PERFUME COMPANY	JANITORIAL SERVICE
Increase in sales volume, 10,000 × $20	$200,000	$200,000
Increase in contribution margin, 90%, 15%	$180,000	$ 30,000

The perfume company would be inclined to increase advertising considerably to boost contribution margin by $180,000. In contrast, it would be riskier for the janitorial service to spend large amounts to increase contribution margin by $30,000.

Note that when the contribution-margin percentage of sales is low, great increases in volume are necessary before significant increases in net profits can occur. As sales exceed the break-even point, a high contribution-margin percentage increases profits faster than does a small contribution-margin percentage.

Operating Leverage

Operating Leverage. A firm's ratio of fixed and variable costs.

In addition to weighing the varied effects of changes in fixed and variable costs, managers need to consider their firms' ratio of fixed and variable costs called **operating leverage**. In highly leveraged companies—those with high

Lowering the Break-Even Point

One way that companies cope with hard economic times is to lower their break-even point. *Business Week* suggested that investors look for such firms "because efficiency gains at companies that have pared fixed costs as well as variable ones should be deep and lasting."

Why is lowering the break-even point important? Because a company that maintains its profitability in times of low sales is poised to take off when the economy improves. Baldwin, the piano maker, actually improved its profits in a time of decreasing sales by successfully cutting costs—especially fixed costs. If it maintains its new cost structure as sales rebound, profits will soar. Lowering fixed costs is especially important because these costs will not necessarily increase as production increases to meet renewed demand for sales.

Chrysler is another example of a company that pared its fixed costs in the slow sales period in the early 1990s. According to *Business Week*, it became "close to being the low-cost producer among the Big Three . . . (and) will benefit most if an auto turnaround comes soon."

Source: "Lots of Companies Are Lean, But Which Are Mean?" *Business Week*, February 3, 1992, p. 84.

Baldwin Piano Company
www.baldwinpiano.com

Chrysler
www.chrysler.com

fixed costs and low variable costs—small changes in sales volume result in large changes in net income. Companies with less leverage (that is, lower fixed costs and higher variable costs) are not affected as much by changes in sales volume.

Exhibit 2-7 shows cost behaviour relationships at two firms—one highly leveraged and one with low leverage. The firm with higher leverage has fixed costs of $14,000 and variable cost per unit of $.10. The firm with lower leverage

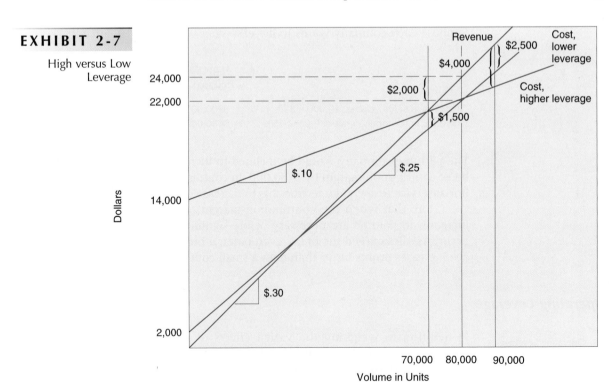

EXHIBIT 2-7

High versus Low Leverage

has fixed costs of only $2,000 but variable costs of $.25 per unit. Expected sales at both companies are 80,000 units at $.30 per unit. At this sales level, both firms would have net incomes of $2,000. If sales fall short of 80,000 units, profits *drop* more sharply for the highly leveraged business. But if sales exceed 80,000 units, profits *increase* more sharply for the highly leveraged concern.

The highly levered alternative is more risky. Why? Because it provides the higher possible net income, and the higher possible losses. In other words, net income is highly variable, depending on the actual level of sales. The low leverage alternative is less risky because variations in sales lead to only small variability in net income. At sales of 90,000 units, net income is $4,000 for the higher leveraged firm but only $2,500 for the lower leveraged firm.

Contribution Margin and Gross Margin

OBJECTIVE 9

Distinguish between contribution margin and gross margin.

Contribution margin. The sales price minus all the variable expenses.

Variable-Cost Ratio (Variable-Cost Percentage). All variable costs divided by sales.

Gross Margin (Gross Profit). The excess of sales over the total cost of goods sold.

Cost of Goods Sold. The cost of the merchandise that is acquired or manufactured and resold.

Contribution margin may be expressed as a *total* absolute amount, a *unit* absolute amount, a *ratio*, and a *percentage*. The **variable-cost ratio** or **variable-cost percentage** is defined as all variable costs divided by sales. Thus a contribution-margin ratio of 20 percent means that the variable-cost ratio is 80 percent.

Too often people confuse the terms contribution margin and gross margin. **Gross margin** (which is also called **gross profit**) is the excess of sales over the **cost of goods sold** (that is, the cost of the merchandise that is acquired or manufactured and resold). It is a widely used concept, particularly in the retailing industry.

Compare the gross margin with the contribution margin:

$$\text{gross margin} = \text{sales price} - \text{cost of goods sold}$$
$$\text{contribution margin} = \text{sales price} - \text{all variable expenses}$$

The following comparisons from our vending machine illustration show the similarities and differences between the contribution margin and the gross margin in a retail store:

Sales	$.50
Variable costs: acquisition cost of unit sold	.40
Contribution margin and gross margin are equal	$.10

Thus the original data resulted in no difference between the measure of contribution margin and gross margin. There *would* be a difference if the firm had to pay a commission of one cent per unit for the use of the machines.

	CONTRIBUTION MARGIN	GROSS MARGIN
Sales	$.50	$.50
Acquisition cost of unit sold	$.40	.40
Variable commission	.01	
Total variable expense	.41	
Contribution margin	$.09	
Gross margin		$.10

As the preceding tabulation indicates, contribution margin and gross margin are not the same concepts. Contribution margin focuses on sales in relation to *all variable* costs, whereas gross margin focuses on sales in relation to cost of goods sold.

NON-PROFIT APPLICATION

Consider how cost-volume-profit relationships apply to non-profit organizations. Suppose a city has a $100,000 lump-sum budget appropriation from a government agency to conduct a counselling program for drug addicts. The variable costs for drug prescriptions are $400 per patient per year. Fixed costs are $60,000 in the relevant range of 50 to 150 patients. If all of the budget appropriation is spent, how many patients can be served in a year? We can use the break-even equation to solve this problem.

Let N be the number of patients.

$$\text{revenue} - \text{variable expenses} - \text{fixed expenses} = 0 \text{ if budget is completely spent}$$
$$\$100,000 \text{ lump sum} - \$400N - \$60,000 = 0$$
$$\$400N = \$100,000 - \$60,000$$
$$N = \$40,000 \div \$400$$
$$N = 100 \text{ patients}$$

Suppose the total budget for the following year is cut by 10 percent. Fixed costs will be unaffected, but service will decline.

$$\text{revenue} - \text{variable expenses} - \text{fixed expenses} = 0$$
$$\$90,000 - \$400N - \$60,000 = 0$$
$$\$400N = \$90,000 - \$60,000$$
$$N = 30,000 \div 400$$
$$N = 75$$

The percentage reduction in service is more than the 10 percent reduction in the budget. Unless the city restructured its operations, the service volume must be reduced 25 percent (from 100 to 75 patients) to stay within budget. Note that lump-sum revenue is a horizontal line on the graph:

EXHIBIT 2-8

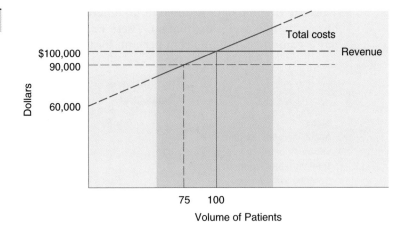

HIGHLIGHTS TO REMEMBER

Understanding cost-behaviour patterns and cost-volume-profit relationships can help guide a manager's decisions. The first step in assessing cost behaviour is to identify cost drivers. Variable costs and fixed costs have contrasting behaviour patterns with respect to a particular cost driver—variable costs change in proportion to changes in the cost driver while fixed costs are unaffected by cost driver activity.

CVP analysis (sometimes called break-even analysis) can be approached graphically or with equations. Managers use CVP analysis to compute a break-even point, to compute a target net income, or to examine the effects on income of changes in factors such as fixed costs, variable costs, or volume. CVP analysis is used in nonprofit organizations as well as in profit-seeking companies.

Be sure to recognize the limitations of CVP analysis. Most important, it relies on the ability to separate costs into fixed and variable categories. Therefore, it applies only to a relevant range of activity. In addition, it assumes constant efficiency, sales mix, and inventory levels.

The contribution margin is an important concept—the difference between sales price and variable costs. Do not confuse it with gross margin—the difference between sales price and cost of goods sold.

SUMMARY PROBLEMS FOR YOUR REVIEW

Problem One

The budgeted income statement of Port Williams Gift Shop is summarized as follows:

Net revenue	$800,000
Less: expenses, including $400,000 of fixed	
expenses	880,000
Net loss	$ (80,000)

The manager believes that an increase of $200,000 in advertising outlays will increase sales substantially.

1. At what sales volume will the store break even after spending $200,000 in advertising?
2. What sales volume will result in a net profit of $40,000?

Solution

1. Note that all data are expressed in dollars. No unit data are given. Most companies have many products, so the overall break-even analysis deals with dollar sales units. The variable expenses are $880,000 – $400,000, or $480,000. The variable expense ratio is $480,000 ÷ $800,000 or .60. Therefore, the contribution-margin is .40.

Let S = break-even sales in dollars, then

$$S - \text{variable expenses} - \text{fixed expenses} = \text{net profit}$$
$$S - .60S - (\$400,000 + \$200,000) = 0$$
$$.40S = \$600,000$$
$$S = \frac{\$600,000}{.40} = \frac{\text{fixed expenses}}{\text{contribution-margin ratio}}$$
$$S = \$1,500,000$$

2. $$\text{required sales} = \frac{\text{fixed expenses} + \text{target net profit}}{\text{contribution-margin ratio}}$$
$$\text{required sales} = \frac{\$600,000 + \$40,000}{.40} = \frac{\$640,000}{.40}$$
$$\text{required sales} = \$1,600,000$$

Alternatively, we can use an incremental approach and reason that all dollar sales beyond the $1.5-million break-even point will result in a 40 percent contribution to net profit. Divide $40,000 by .40. Sales must therefore be $100,000 beyond the $1.5-million break-even point to produce a net profit of $40,000.

Problem Two

Hospitals measure their volume in terms of patient-days, which are defined as the number of patients multiplied by the number of days that the patients are hospitalized. Suppose a large hospital has fixed costs of $48 million per year and variable costs of $600 per patient-day. Daily revenues vary among classes of patients. For simplicity, assume that there are two classes: (1) private-plan patients (P) who are the responsibility of insurance companies and who pay an average of $1,000 per day and (2) government-plan patients (G) who are the responsibility of government agencies and who pay an average of $800 per day. Twenty percent of the patients are private-plan.

Required:

1. Compute the break-even point in patient-days, assuming that the planned mix of patients is maintained.
2. Suppose that 200,000 patient-days were acheived but that 25% of the patient-days were private-plan (instead of 20%). Compute the net income. Compute the break-even point.

Solution

1. Let P = number of private-plan patients (P)
    4P = number of government-plan patients (G)
$$\$1,000P + \$800(4P) - \$600P - \$600(4P) - \$48,000,000 = 0$$
$$\$1,000P + \$3,200P - \$600P - \$2,400P = \$48,000,000$$
$$\$1,200P = \$48,000,000$$
$$P = 40,000$$
$$4P = 160,000 = G$$

The break-even point is 40,000 private-plan patient days plus 40,000 × 4 = 160 patient days, a grand total of 200,000 patient days.

2. Contribution Margins:
P = \$1,000 − \$600 = \$400 per patient day
G = \$ 800 − \$600 = \$200 per patient day

Patient days:
P = .25 × 200,000 = 50,000
G = .75 × 200,000 = 150,000

Net income = 50,000(\$400) + 150,000(\$200) − \$48,000,000
= \$20,000,000 + \$30,000,000 − \$48,000,000 = \$2,000,000

Let P = number of private-plan patients (P)
3P = number of government-plan patients (G)
\$1,000P + \$800(3P) − \$600P − \$600(3P) − \$48,000,000 = 0
\$1,000P + \$2,400P − \$600P − \$1,800P = \$48,000,000
\$1,000P = \$48,000,000
P = 48,000
3P = 144,000 = G

The break-even point is now lower (192,000 patient days instead of 200,00 patient days). The more profitable mix produces a net income of \$2,000,000 at the 200,000 patient-day level.

ACCOUNTING VOCABULARY

break-even analysis *p. 46*
break-even point *p. 46*
contribution margin *pp. 46, 63*
cost behaviour *p. 40*
cost drivers *p. 40*
cost of goods sold *p. 63*
cost-volume-profit (CVP)
analysis *p. 44*
   fixed cost *p. 41*

gross margin *p. 63*
gross profit *p. 63*
incremental approach *p. 54*
margin of safety *p. 46*
operating leverage *p. 61*
relevant range *p. 42*
sales mix *pp. 57*
variable cost *p. 41*
variable-cost percentage *p. 63*
variable-cost ratio *p. 63*

ASSIGNMENT MATERIAL

QUESTIONS

Q2-1 "Cost behaviour is simply identification of cost drivers and their relationships to costs." Comment.

Q2-2 Give three examples of variable costs and fixed costs.

Q2-3 "Fixed costs decline as volume increases." Do you agree? Explain.

Q2-4 "It is confusing to think of fixed costs on a per unit basis." Do you agree? Why or why not?

Q2-5 "All costs are either fixed or variable. The only difficulty in cost analysis is determining which of the two categories each cost belongs to." Do you agree? Explain.

Q2-6 "The relevant range pertains to fixed costs, not variable costs." Do you agree? Explain.

Q2-7 Identify two simplifying assumptions that underlie CVP analysis.

Q2-8 "Classification of costs into variable and fixed categories depends on the decision situation." Explain.

Q2-9 "Contribution margin is the excess of sales over fixed costs." Do you agree? Explain.

Q2-10 Why is "break-even analysis" a misnomer?

Q2-11 "Companies in the same industry generally have about the same break-even point." Do you agree? Explain.

Q2-12 "It is essential to choose the right CVP technique—equation, contribution margin, or graphical. If you pick the wrong one, your analysis will be faulty." Do you agree? Explain.

Q2-13 Describe three ways of lowering a break-even point.

Q2-14 "Incremental analysis is quicker, but it has no other advantage over an analysis of all costs and revenues associated with each alternative." Do you agree? Why or why not?

Q2-15 Explain operating leverage and why a highly leveraged company is risky.

Q2-16 "The contribution margin and gross margin are always equal." Do you agree? Explain.

Q2-17 "CVP relationships are unimportant in nonprofit organizations." Do you agree? Explain.

Q2-18 "Two products were sold. Total budgeted and actual total sales in number of units were identical. Unit variable costs and sales prices were the same. Actual contribution margin was lower." What could be the reason for the lower contribution margin?

Q2-19 Present the CVP formula for computing the target income before income taxes.

Q2-20 Present the CVP formula for computing the effects of a change in volume on after-tax income.

PROBLEMS

P2-1 NATURE OF VARIABLE AND FIXED COSTS. "As I understand it, costs such as the salary of the vice president of transportation operations are variable because the more traffic you handle, the less your unit cost. In contrast, costs such as fuel are fixed because each tonne-kilometre should entail consumption of the same amount of fuel and hence bear the same unit cost." Do you agree? Explain.

P2-2 BASIC REVIEW EXERCISES. Fill in the blanks for each of the following independent cases (ignore income taxes):

	SALES	VARIABLE EXPENSES	CONTRIBUTION MARGIN	FIXED EXPENSES	NET INCOME
1.	$900,000	$500,000	$ —	$350,000	$ —
2.	$800,000	—	$350,000	—	$80,000
3.	—	$600,000	$340,000	$250,000	—

P2-3 BASIC REVIEW EXERCISES. Fill in the blanks for each of the following independent cases:

CASE	(A) SELLING PRICE PER UNIT	(B) VARIABLE COST PER UNIT	(C) TOTAL UNITS SOLD	(D) TOTAL CONTRIBUTION MARGIN	(E) TOTAL FIXED COSTS	(F) NET INCOME
1.	$30	—	120,000	$720,000	$640,000	$ —
2.	10	$ 6	100,000	—	320,000	—
3.	20	15	—	100,000	—	15,000
4.	30	20	70,000	—	—	12,000
5.	—	9	80,000	160,000	120,000	—

P2-4 HOSPITAL COSTS AND PRICING. A hospital has overall variable costs of 20 percent of total revenue and fixed costs of $40 million per year.

   1. Compute the break-even point expressed in total revenue.
   2. A patient-day is often used to measure the volume of a hospital. Suppose there are going to be 40,000 patient-days next year. Compute the average daily revenue per patient necessary to break even.

P2-5 MOTEL RENTALS. The Holiday Motel has annual fixed costs applicable to its rooms of $1.6 million for its 200-room motel, average daily room rents of $50, and average variable costs of $10 for each room rented. It operates 365 days per year.

   1. How much net income on rooms will be generated (a) if the motel is completely full throughout the entire year? and (b) if the motel is half full?
   2. Compute the break-even point in number of rooms rented. What percentage occupancy for the year is needed to break even?

P2-6 BASIC RELATIONSHIPS, HOTEL. The Pippin Hotel in Vancouver has 400 rooms, with a fixed cost of $350,000 per month during the peak season. Room rates average $65 per day with variable costs of $15 per rented room per day. Assume a 30-day month.

   1. How many rooms must be occupied per day to break even?
   2. How many rooms must be occupied per month to make a monthly profit of $120,000?
   3. Assume that the Pippin Hotel has these average contribution margins per month from use of space in its hotel:

Leased shops in hotel	$70,000
Meals served, conventions	40,000
Dining room and coffee shop	32,400
Bar and cocktail lounge	30,000

Also assume that the Pippin Hotel averages 80 percent occupancy per day. What average rate per day per rented room must the hotel charge to make a profit of $120,000 per month?

P2-7 SALES MIX ANALYSIS. Nakata Farms produces strawberries and raspberries. Annual fixed costs are $14,400. The cost driver for variable costs is litre of fruit produced. The variable cost is $.65 per litre of strawberries and $.85 per litre of raspberries. Strawberries sell for $1.00 per litre, raspberries for $1.35 per litre. Two litres of strawberries are produced for every litre of raspberries.

1. Compute the number of litres of strawberries and the number of litre of raspberries produced and sold at the break-even point.
2. Suppose only strawberries are produced and sold. Compute the break-even point in litres.
3. Suppose only raspberries are produced and sold. Compute the break-even point in litres.

P2-8 COST-VOLUME-PROFIT RELATIONSHIPS. The Global United Moving Company specializes in hauling heavy goods over long distances. The company's revenues and expenses depend on revenue kilometres, a measure that combines both weights and mileage. Summarized budget data for next year are based on predicted total revenue kilometres of 800,000.

	Per Revenue Kilometre
Average Selling Price (revenue)	$1.50
Average variable expenses	1.30
Fixed expenses, $120,000	

1. Compute the budgeted net income. Ignore income taxes.
2. Management is trying to decide how various possible conditions or decisions might affext net income. Compue the new net income for each of the following changes. Consider each case independently.
   a. A 10% increase in revenue kilometre
   b. A 10% increase in sales price
   c. A 10% increase in variable expenses
   d. A 10% increase in fixed expenses
   e. An average decrease in selling price of 3¢ per kilometre and a 5% increase in revenue kilometre. Refer to the original data
   f. An average increase in selling price of 5% and a 10% decrease in revenue kilometres
   g. A 10% increase in fixed expenses in the form of more advertising and a 5% increase in revenue kilometres

P2-9 BASIC COST-VOLUME-PROFIT ANALYSIS. Carmen Guerrero opened Carmen's Corner, a small day care facility, just over two years ago. After a rocky start, Carmen's has been thriving. Guerrero is now preparing a budget for November 2002.

Monthly fixed costs for Carmen's are

Rent	$ 800
Saleries	1,500
Other fixed costs	100
Total fixed costs	$2,400

The salary is for Ann Penilla, the only employee, who works with Carmen in caring for the children. Guerrero does not pay herself a salary, but she receives the excess of revenues over costs each month.

The cost driver for variable costs is "child-days." One child-day is one day in day care for one child, and the variable cost is $10 per child-day. The facilty is open 6:00 A.M. to 6:00 P.M. weekdays (that is, Monday through Friday), and there are 22 weekdays in November 2002. An average day has 8 children attending Carmen's Corner. Provincial law prohibits Carmen's from having more than 14 children, a limit it has never reached. Guerrero charges $30 per day per child, regardless of how long the child is at the facility.

1. Suppose attendance for November 2002 is equal to the average, resulting in 22 x 8=176 child-days. What amount will Guerero have left after paying all her expenses.

2. Suppose both costs and attendance are difficult to predict. Compute the amount Guerrero will have left after paying all her expenses for each of the following situations. Consider each case independently.

   a. Average attendance is 9 children per day instead of 8, generating 198 child-days.
   b. Variable costs increase to $11 per child-day.
   c. Rent is increased by $200 per month.
   d. Guerrero spends $300 on advertising (a fixed cost) in November, which increases average daily attendance to 9.5 children.
   e. Guerrero begins charging $33 per day on November 1, and average daily attendance slips to 7 children.

P2-10 INCOME TAXES AND COST-VOLUME-PROFIT ANALYSIS. Suppose Merla Security Company has a 40 percent income tax rate, a contribution-margin ratio of 30 percent, and fixed costs of $440,000. How many sales are necessary to achieve an after-tax income of $42,000?

P2-11 FIXED COSTS AND RELEVANT RANGE. Boulder Systems Group (BSG) has a substantial year-to-year fluctuation in billings to clients. Top management has the following policy regarding the employment of key personnel:

IF GROSS ANNUAL BILLINGS ARE	NUMBER OF PERSONS TO BE EMPLOYED	ANNUAL SALARIES AND RELATED EXPENSES
$2,000,000 or less	10	$1,200,000
$2,000,001 – 2,400,000	11	1,320,000
$2,400,001 – 2,800,000	12	1,440,000

Top management believes that at least 10 individuals should be retained for a year or more even if billings drop drastically below $2 million.

For the past five years, gross annual billings for BSG have fluctuated between $2,020,000 and $2,380,000. Expectations for next year are that gross billings will be between $2,100,000 and $2,300,000. What amount should be budgeted for key professional personnel? Graph the relationships on an annual basis, using the two approaches illustrated in Exhibit 2-3. Indicate the relevant range on each graph. You need not use graph paper; simply approximate the graphical relationships.

P2-12   MOVIE MANAGER.   Malia Mertz is the manager of Lakehead's traditional Sunday Flicks. Each Sunday a film has two showings. The admission price is deliberately set at a very low $3. A maximum of 500 tickets is sold for each showing. The rental of the auditorium is $330 and labour is $400, including $90 for Mertz. Mertz must pay the film distributor a guarantee, ranging from $300 to $900 or 50 percent of gross admission receipts whichever is higher.

Before and during the show, refreshments are sold; these sales average 12 percent of gross admission receipts, and yield a contribution margin of 40 percent.

1. On June 3, Mertz showed *Canadian Bacon*. The film grossed $2,250. The guarantee to the distributor was $750, or 50 percent of gross admission receipts, whichever is higher. What operating income was produced for the Students Association, which sponsored the showings?
2. Recompute the results if the film grossed $1,350.
3. The "four-wall" concept is increasingly being adopted by movie producers. In this situation the movie's producer pays a fixed rental to the theatre owner for, say, a week's showing of a movie. As a theatre owner, how would you evaluate a "four-wall" offer?

P2-13   BASIC RELATIONSHIPS, RESTAURANT.   Genevieve Giraud owns and operates a restaurant. Her fixed costs are $21,000 per month. Luncheons and dinners are served. The average total bill (excluding tax and tip) is $18 per customer. Giraud's present variable costs average $9.60 per meal.

1. How many meals must be served to attain a profit before taxes of $8,400 per month?
2. What is the break-even point in number of meals served per month?
3. Giraud's rent and other fixed costs rise to a total of $29,400 per month. Assume that variable costs also rise to $11.50 per meal. If Giraud increases her average price to $22, how many meals must she now serve to make $8,400 profit per month?
4. Giraud's accountant tells her she may lose 10 percent of her customers if she increases her prices to a $22 average price. If this happens, what would be Giraud's profit per month? Assume that the restaurant had been serving 3,500 customers per month.
5. To help offset the anticipated 10 percent loss of customers, Giraud hires a pianist to perform for four hours each night for $2,000 per month. Assume that this would increase the total monthly meals from 3,150 to 3,450. Would Giraud's total profit change? By how much?

P2-14   COST-VOLUME-PROFIT ANALYSIS AND BARBERING.   Andre's Hair Styling in Singapore has five barbers. (Andre is not one of them.) Each barber is paid $9.90 per hour and works a 40-hour week and a 50-week year. Rent and other fixed expenses are $1,750 per month. Assume that cutting hair is the only service performed and has a unit price of $12.

1. Find the contribution margin per haircut. Assume that the barbers' compensation is a fixed cost.
2. Determine the annual break-even point, in number of haircuts.
3. What will the operating income be if 20,000 haircuts are sold?
4. Suppose Andre revises the compensation method. The barbers will receive $4 per hour plus $6 for each haircut. What is the new

contribution margin per haircut? What is the annual break-even point (in number of haircuts)?

5. Ignore requirements 3 and 4 and assume that the barbers cease to be paid by the hour but receive $7 for each haircut. What is the new contribution margin per haircut? What is the annual break-even point (in number of haircuts)?

6. Refer to requirement 5. What would be the operating income if 20,000 haircuts are sold? Compare your answer with the answer in requirement 3.

7. Refer to requirement 5. If 20,000 haircuts are sold, at what rate of commission would Andre earn the same operating income as he earned in requirement 3?

P2-15 BINGO AND LEVERAGE. An Ontario law permits a game of chance called Bingo when it is offered by specific non-profit institutions, including churches. Reverend Jill Bond, the pastor of a new parish in suburban Mississauga, is investigating the desirability of conducting weekly Bingo nights. The parish has no hall, but a local hotel would be willing to commit its hall for a lump-sum rental of $800 per night. The rent would include cleaning, setting up and taking down the tables and chairs, and so on.

1. Bingo cards would be provided by a local printer in return for free advertising therein. Door prizes would be donated by local merchants. The services of clerks, callers, a security force, and others would be donated by volunteers. Admission would be $4.00 per person, entitling the player to one card; extra cards would be $1.50 each. Reverend Bond also learns that many people buy extra cards, so there would be an average of four cards played per person. What is the maximum in total cash prizes that the church may award and still break even if 200 persons attend each weekly session?

2. Suppose the total cash prizes are $900. What will be the church's operating income if 100 persons attend? If 200 persons attend? If 300 persons attend? Briefly explain the effects of the cost behaviour on income.

3. After operating for 10 months, Reverend Bond is considering negotiating a different rental arrangement but keeping the prize money unchanged at $900. Suppose the rent is $400 weekly plus $2 per person. Compute the operating income for attendance of 100, 200, and 300 persons, respectively. Explain why the results differ from those in requirement 2.

P2-16 PROMOTION OF A ROCK CONCERT. NLR Productions, Ltd., is promoting a rock concert in London. The bands will receive a flat fee of £8 million in cash. The concert will be shown worldwide on closed-circuit television. NLR will collect 100 percent of the receipts and will return 30 percent to the individual local closed-circuit theatre managers. NLR expects to sell 1.1 million seats at a net average price of £13 each. NLR will also receive £300,000 from the London arena (which has sold out its 19,500 seats, ranging from £150 for box seats down to £25 for general admission, for a gross revenue of £1.25 million); NLR will not share the £300,000 with the local promoters.

1. The general manager of NLR Productions is trying to decide what amount to spend for advertising. What is the most NLR could spend and still break even on overall operations, assuming sales of 1.1 million tickets?

2. If NLR desired an operating income of £500,00, how many seats would have to be sold? Assume that the average price was £13 and the total fixed costs were £9 million.

P2-17 ADDING A PRODUCT.   Andy's Ale House, a pub located in a university community, serves as a gathering place for the university's more social scholars. Andy sells beer on draft and all brands of bottled beer at a contribution margin of $.60 a beer.

Andy is considering also selling hamburgers during selected hours. His reasons are twofold. First, hamburgers would attract daytime customers. A hamburger and a beer are a quick lunch. Second, he has to compete with other local bars, some of which provide more extensive menus.

Andy analyzed the costs as follows:

Monthly fixed expenses:	
Wages of part-time cook	$1,200
Other	360
Total	$1,560
Variable expenses per hamburger	
Rolls	$.12
Meat @ $2.80 per kilogram	
(7 hamburgers per kilogram)	.40
Other	.18
Total	$ .70

Andy planned a selling price of $1.10 per hamburger to lure many customers. For all questions, assume a 30-day month.

1. What are the monthly and daily break-even points, in number of hamburgers?
2. What are the monthly and daily break-even points, in dollar sales?
3. At the end of two months, Andy finds he has sold 3,600 hamburgers. What is the operating profit per month on hamburgers?
4. Andy thinks that at least 60 extra beers are sold per day because he sells hamburgers. This means that 60 extra people come to the bar or that 60 buy an extra beer because they are attracted by the hamburgers. How does this affect Andy's monthly operating income?
5. Refer to requirement 3. How many extra beers would have to be sold per day so that the overall effects of the hamburger sales on monthly operating income would be zero?

P2-18 COST-VOLUME-PROFIT RELATIONSHIPS AND A RACE TRACK.   The Western Race Track is a horse-racing track. Its revenue is derived mainly from attendance and a fixed percentage of the betting. Its expenses for a 90-day season are

Wages of cashiers and ticket takers	$160,000
Commissioner's salary	20,000
Maintenance (repairs, etc.)	20,000
Utilities	30,000
Other expenses (depreciation, insurance, advertising, etc.)	90,000
Purses: Total prizes paid to winning racers	810,000

The track made a contract with A.P. Inc. to park cars. A.P. charged the track $6 per car. A survey revealed that on the average, three people arrived in each car and half the attendees arrived by private automobiles. The others arrived by taxi and public buses.

The track's sources of revenue are

Rights for concession and vending	$50,000
Admission charge (deliberately low)	$1 per person
Percentage of the amount of bets placed	10%

1. Assuming that each person bets $27 a night:
   a. How many persons have to be admitted for the track to break even for the season?
   b. What is the total contribution margin at the break-even point?
   c. If the desired operating profit for the year is $270,000, how many people would have to attend?
2. If a policy of free admission brought a 20 percent increase in attendance, what would be the new level of operating profit? Assume that the previous level of attendance was 600,000 people.
3. If the purses were doubled in an attempt to attract better horses and thus increase attendance, what would be the new break-even point? Refer to the original data and assume that each person bets $27 a night.

P2-19 COST-VOLUME-PROFITS AND VENDING MACHINES. Cola Food Services operates and services soft-drink vending machines located in restaurants, gas stations, factories, etc. The machines are rented from the manufacturer. In addition, Cola must rent the space occupied by its machines. The following expense and revenue relationships pertain to a contemplated expansion program of 20 machines.

Machine rental: 20 machines @ $43.50	$870
Space rental: 20 locations @ $28.80	576
Part-time wages to service the additional 20 machines	1,454
Other fixed costs	100
Total monthly fixed costs	$3,000

Other data follows:

	PER UNIT	PER $100 OF SALES
Selling price	$1.00	100%
Cost of snack	.80	80%
Contribution margin	$.20	20%

These questions relate to the above data unless otherwise noted. **Consider each question independently**.

1. What is the monthly break-even point in number of units? In dollar sales?
2. If 18,000 units were sold, what would be the company's net income?

3. If the space rental cost were doubled, what would be the monthly break-even point in number of units? In dollar sales?
4. If, in addition to the fixed rent, Cola Food Services Company paid the vending machine manufacturer $.01 per unit sold, what would be the monthly break-even point in number of units? In dollar sales? Refer to the original data.
5. If, in addition to the fixed rent, Cola paid the machine manufacturer $.02 for each unit sold in excess of the break-even point, what would be the new net income if 18,000 units were sold? Refer to the original data.

P2-20 **TRAVELLING EXPENSES.** Yuko Nomo is a travelling inspector for Environment Canada. She uses her own car and the department reimburses her at $.23 per kilometre. Yuko claims she needs $.27 per kilometre just to break even. Shaun McHale, the district manager, looks into the matter and compiles the following information about Yuko expenses:

Oil change every 3,000 kilometres	$ 30
Maintenance (other than oil) every 6,000 kilometres	240
Yearly insurance	700
Auto cost $13,500 with an average cash trade-in value of $6,000; has a useful life of three years.	
Gasoline is approximately $.60 per litre and Yuko averages 6 kilometres per litre.	

When Yuko is on the road, she averages 120 kilometres a day. McHale knows that Yuko does not work Saturdays or Sundays, has 10 working days' vacation and six holidays, and spends approximately 15 working days in the office.

1. How many kilometres per year would Yuko have to travel to break even at the current rate of reimbursement?
2. What would be an equitable per-kilometre rate?

P2-21 **GOVERNMENTAL ORGANIZATION.** A social welfare agency has a government budget appropriation for 2001 of $900,000. The agency's major mission is to help disabled persons who are unable to hold jobs. On the average, the agency supplements each person's other income by $5,000 annually. The agency's fixed costs are $290,000. There are no other costs.

1. How many disabled persons are helped during 2001?
2. For 2002, the agency's budget appropriation has been reduced by 15 percent. If the agency continues the same level of monetary support per person, how many disabled people will be helped in 2002? Compute the percentage decline in the number of persons helped.
3. Assume a budget reduction of 15 percent, as in requirement 2. The manager of the agency has discretion as to how much to supplement each disabled person's income. She does not want to reduce the number of persons served. On the average, what is the amount of the supplement that can be given to each person? Compute the percentage decline in the annual supplement.

P2-22 CVP AND FINANCIAL STATEMENTS. ConAgra, Inc. is an Omaha-based company that produces food products under brand names such as Healthy Choice, Armour, and Banquet. In 1997 the company's sales increased by 10 percent and its 1997 income statement showed the following (in millions):

Net sales	$24,002
Cost of goods sold	20,442
Selling, administrative, and general expense	2,265
Interest expense	277
Operating income (before tax)	$ 1,018

Suppose that the cost of goods sold is the only variable cost; selling, administrative, general, and interest expenses are fixed with respect to sales. Assume that ConAgra had another 10 percent increase in sales in 1998 and that there was no change in costs except for increases associated with the higher volume of sales. Compute the predicted 1998 operating profit for ConAgra and the percentage increase in operating profit. Explain why the percentage increase in profit differs from the percentage increase in sales.

P2-23 GROSS MARGIN AND CONTRIBUTION MARGIN. Eastman Kodak Company produces and sells cameras, film, and other imaging products. A condensed 1996 income statement follows (in millions):

Sales	$15,968
Cost of goods sold	8,326
Gross margin	7,642
Other operating expenses	6,086
Operating income	$ 1,556

Assume that $1,800 million of the cost of goods sold is a fixed cost representing depreciation and other production costs that do not change with the volume of production. In addition, $4,000 million of the other operating expenses is fixed.

1. Compute the total contribution margin for 1996 and the contribution margin percentage. Explain why the contribution margin differs from the gross margin.
2. Suppose that sales for Eastman Kodak were predicted to increase by 10 percent in 1997 and that the cost behaviour was expected to continue in 1997 as it had been in 1996. Compute the predicted operating income for 1997. By what percentage did this predicted 1997 operating income exceed the 1996 operating income?
3. What assumptions were necessary to compute the predicted 1997 operating income in requirement 2?

P2-24 CHOOSING EQUIPMENT FOR DIFFERENT VOLUMES. Multiplex Cinema owns and operates a nationwide chain of movie theatres. The 500 properties in the Multiplex chain vary from low-volume, small-town, single-screen theatres to high-volume, big-city, multiscreen theatres.

The management is considering installing machines that will make popcorn on the premises. These machines would allow the theatres to sell popcorn that would be freshly popped daily rather than the prepopped corn that is currently purchased in large bags. This proposed feature would be properly advertised and is intended to increase patronage at the company's theatres.

The machines can be purchased in several different sizes. The annual rental costs and the operating costs vary with the size of the machines. The machine capacities and costs are

	POPPER MODEL		
	Economy	Regular	Super
Annual capacity	50,000 boxes	120,000 boxes	300,000 boxes
Costs:			
Annual machine rental	$8,000	$11,200	$20,200
Popcorn cost per box	.14	.14	.14
Cost of each box	.09	.09	.09
Other variable costs per box	.22	.14	.05

1. Calculate the volume level in boxes at which the Economy Popper and Regular Popper would earn the same operating profit (loss).
2. The management can estimate the number of boxes to be sold at each of its theatres. Present a decision rule that would enable Multiplex's management to select the most profitable machine without having to make a separate cost calculation for each theatre. That is, at what anticipated range of unit sales should the Economy model be used? The Regular model? The Super model?
3. Could the management use the average number of boxes sold per seat for the entire chain and the capacity of each theatre to develop this decision rule? Explain your answer.

P2-25 **SALES-MIX ANALYSIS.** The Pacific Catering Company specializes in preparing tasty main courses that are frozen and shipped to the finer restaurants in the Montreal area. When a diner orders the item, the restaurant heats and serves it. The budget data for 2001 are:

	PRODUCT	
	Chicken Cordon Bleu	Veal Marsala
Selling price to restaurants	$7	$9
Variable expenses	$4	$5
Contribution margin	$3	$4
Number of units	250,000	125,000

The items are prepared in the same kitchens, delivered in the same trucks, and so forth. Therefore, the fixed costs of $1,320,000 are unaffected by the specific products.

1. Compute the planned net income for 2001.
2. Compute the break-even point in units, assuming that the planned sales mix is maintained.

3. Compute the break-even point in units if only veal were sold and if only chicken were sold.

4. Suppose 99,000 units of veal and 297,000 units of chicken were sold. Compute the net income. Compute the new break-even point if these relationships persisted in 2001. What is the major lesson of this problem?

P2-26 INCOME TAXES ON HOTELS. The Grove Hotel has annual fixed costs applicable to rooms of $10 million for its 600-room hotel, average daily room rates of $105, and average variable costs of $25 for each room rented. It operates 365 days per year. The hotel is subject to an income tax rate of 40 percent.

1. How many rooms must the hotel rent to earn a net income after taxes of $720,000? of $360,000?

2. Compute the break-even point in number of rooms rented. What percentage occupancy for the year is needed to break even?

3. Assume that the volume level of rooms sold is 150,000. The manager is wondering how much income could be generated by adding sales of 15,000 rooms. Compute the additional net income after taxes.

P2-27 HOSPITAL COSTS. The Metropolitan City Hospital is unionized. In 2001, nurses received an average annual salary of $45,000. The hospital administrator is considering how the contract with nurses should be changed for 2002. In turn, charging nursing costs to each department might also be changed.

Each department is accountable for its financial performance. Revenues and expenses are allocated to departments. Consider the expenses of the obstetrics department in 2001:

Variable expenses (based on 2001 patient-days) are

Meals	$ 510,000
Laundry	260,000
Laboratory	900,000
Pharmacy	800,000
Maintenance	150,000
Other	530,000
Total	$3,150,000

Fixed expenses (based on number of beds) are

Rent	$3,000,000
General administrative services	2,100,000
Janitorial	200,000
Maintenance	150,000
Other	450,000
Total	$5,900,000

Nurses are assigned to departments on the basis of annual patient-days, as follows:

VOLUME LEVEL INPATIENT-DAYS	NUMBER OF NURSES
10,000 – 12,000	30
12,001 – 16,000	35

Total patient-days are the number of patients multiplied by the number of days they are hospitalized. Each department is charged for the salaries of the nurses assigned to it.

During 2001 the obstetrics department had a capacity of 60 beds, billed insurance and government agencies an average of $800 per day for each patient, and had revenues of $12 million.

1. Compute the 2001 volume of activity in patient-days.
2. Compute the 2001 patient-days that would have been necessary for the obstetrics department to recoup all fixed expenses except nursing expenses.
3. Compute the 2001 patient-days that would have been necessary for the obstetrics department to break even, including nurses' salaries as a fixed cost.
4. Suppose Obstetrics must pay $200 per patient-day for nursing services. This plan would replace the two-level fixed-cost system employed in 2001. Compute what the break-even point in patient-days would have been in 2001 under this plan.

P2-28 **MULTIPRODUCT BREAK-EVEN IN A RESTAURANT.** An article in *Washington Business* included an income statement for La Brasserie, a French restaurant. A simplified version of the statement follows:

Revenues	$2,098,400
Cost of sales, all variable	1,246,500
Gross profit	$ 851,900
Operating expenses	
Variable	222,380
Fixed	170,700
Administrative expenses, all fixed	451,500
Net income	$ 7,320

The average dinner tab at La Brasserie is $40, and the average lunch tab is $20. Assume that the variable cost of preparing and serving dinner is also twice that of a lunch. The restaurant serves twice as many lunches as dinners. Assume that the restaurant is open 305 days a year.

1. Compute the daily break-even volume in lunches and dinners for La Brasserie. Compare this to the actual volume reflected in the income statement.
2. Suppose that an extra annual advertising expenditure of $15,000 would increase the average daily volume by three dinners and six lunches, and that there is plenty of capacity to accommodate the extra business. Prepare an analysis for the management of La Brasserie explaining whether this would be desirable.
3. La Brasserie uses only premium food, and the cost of food makes up 25 percent of the restaurant's total variable costs. Use of average rather than premium ingredients could cut the food cost by 20 percent. Assume that La Brasserie uses average-quality ingredients and does not change its prices. How much of a drop-off in volume could it endure and still maintain the same net income? What factors in addition to

revenue and costs would influence the decision about the quality of food to use?

P2-29 CVP AND PREDICTION OF INCOME.   According to an article in *Business Week*, T.J. Izzo had a great idea after a bad back almost forced him to give up golf. His problem was carrying a golf bag, not swinging a club. So he designed a harness-like golf bag strap that distributed the weight equally on both shoulders. In April 1992, he formed Izzo Systems Inc. In 1993, Izzo made an operating income of $12,000 on revenue of $1 million from selling 75,000 straps. In 1994, Izzo expected to sell 92,000 straps for $1.7 million.

1. Suppose that variable costs per strap are $10. Compute total fixed and total variable costs for 1993.
2. Suppose the cost behaviour in 1994 was the same as in 1993. Estimate Izzo's operating income for 1994 (a) with sales at the predicted 92,000, (b) with sales 10 percent above the predicted level, and (c) with sales 10 percent below the predicted level.
3. Explain why the predicted 1994 operating income was so much greater than the 1993 operating income.

P2-30 CVP IN A MODERN MANUFACTURING ENVIRONMENT.   A division of Hewlett-Packard Company changed its production operations from one where a large labour force assembled electronic components to an automated production facility dominated by computer-controlled robots. The change was necessary because of fierce competitive pressures. Improvements in quality, reliability, and flexibility of production schedules were necessary just to match the competition. As a result of the change, variable costs fell and fixed costs increased, as shown in the following assumed budgets:

	OLD PRODUCTION OPERATION	NEW PRODUCTION OPERATION
Unit variable cost		
Material	$ .88	$ .88
Labour	1.22	.22
Total per unit	$2.10	$1.10
Monthly fixed costs		
Rent and depreciation	$450,000	$875,000
Supervisory labour	85,000	175,000
Other	50,000	90,000
Total per month	$585,000	$1,140,000

Expected volume is 600,000 units per month, with each unit selling for $3.10. Capacity is 800,000 units.

1. Compute the budgeted profit at the expected volume of 600,000 units under both the old and the new production environments.
2. Compute the budgeted break-even point under both the old and the new production environments.
3. Discuss the effect on profits if volume falls to 500,000 units under both the old and the new production environments.

4. Discuss the effect on profits if volume increases to 700,000 units under both the old and the new production environments.
5. Comment on the riskiness of the new operation versus the old operation.

P2-31 AIRLINE CVP. Airline companies regularly provide operating statistics with their financial statements. In 1996 Continental Airlines reported that it had approximately 61,000-million seat-kilometres available, of which 68.1 percent were filled. (A seat-kilometre is one seat travelling one kilometre. For example, if an airplane with 100 seats travelled 400 kilometres, capacity would have been 100 x 400 = 40,000 seat-kilometres.) The average revenue was $.1310 per revenue-passenger-kilometre, where a revenue passenger-kilometre is one seat occupied by a passenger travelling one kilometre. In 1995, approximately the same number of seat-kilometres were available, but only 65.6 percent of them were filled at an average revenue of $.1251 per filled seat-kilometre. Continental calls the percentage of seat-kilometres available that are filled with passengers their load factor.

1. Compute Continental's passenger revenue for 1996 and 1995.
2. Assume that Continental's variable costs were $.05 per revenue-passenger-kilometre in both 1995 and 1996 and that fixed costs are $3,000 million per year each year.
   a. Compute Continental's break-even point at the 1995 level of revenue per passenger-kilometre. Express it in both revenue-passenger-kilometres and as a load factor (that is, as a percentage of available capacity used).
   b. Compute Continental's break-even point at the 1996 level of revenue per passenger-kilometre. Express it in both revenue-passenger-kilometres and as a load factor (that is, as a percentage of available capacity used).
3. Suppose Continental maintained the same level of seat-kilometres available in 1997, had revenue of $.13 per revenue-passenger-kilometre, and maintained the same level of fixed and variable costs as in the previous two years. Compute the load factor necessary to achieve an operating income of $400 million.

P2-32 BOEING BREAKS EVEN. Boeing is the largest commercial airplane manufacturer in the world. In 1999 it began development of the 757-300, a 240 passenger plane with a range up to 4,010 miles. First deliveries will take place in 2002, and the price will be about $70 million per plane.

Assume that Boeing's annual fixed costs for the 757-300 are $950 million, and its variable cost per airplane is $45 million.

1. Compute Boeing's break-even point in number of 757-300 airplanes and in dollars of sales.
2. Suppose Boeing plans to sell forty-two 757-300 airplanes in 2002. Compute Boeing's projected operating profit.
3. Suppose Boeing increased its fixed costs by $84 million and reduced variable costs per airplane by $2 million. Compute its operating profit if forty-two 757-300 airplanes are sold. Compute the break-even point. Comment on your results.

4. Ignore requirement 3. Suppose fixed costs do not change but variable costs increase by 10 percent before deliveries of 757-300 airplanes begin in 2002. Compute the new break-even point. What strategies might Boeing use to help assure profitable operations in light of increases in variable cost?

P2-33 COLLABORATIVE LEARNING EXERCISE: CVP FOR A SMALL BUSINESS. Form a group of two to six students. Each group should select a very simple business, one with a single product or one with approximately the same contribution margin percentage for all products. Some possibilities are:

A child's lemonade stand
A retail video rental store
An espresso cart
A retail store selling compact disks
An athletic-shoe store
A cookie stand in a mall

However, you are encouraged to use your imagination rather than just select one of these examples.

The following tasks might be split up among the group members:

1. Make a list of all fixed costs associated with running the business you selected. Estimate the amount of each fixed cost per month (or per day or per year, if one of them is more appropriate for your business).
2. Make a list of all variable costs associated with making or obtaining the product or service your company is selling. Estimate the cost per unit for each variable cost.
3. Given the fixed and variable costs you have identified, compute the break-even point for your business in either units or dollar sales.
4. Assess the prospects of your business making a profit.

CASES

C2-1 EFFECTS OF CHANGES IN COSTS, INCLUDING TAX EFFECTS. Friendly Candy Company is a wholesale distributor of candy. The company services grocery, convenience, and drug stores in a large metropolitan area.

Small but steady growth in sales has been achieved by the Friendly Candy Company over the past few years while candy prices have been increasing. The company is formulating its plans for the coming fiscal year. Presented below are the data used to project the current year's after-tax net income of $110,400.

Average selling price per box	$	5.00
Average variable costs per box:		
Cost of candy	$	2.50
Selling expenses		.50
Total	$	3.00
Annual fixed costs		
Selling	$	200,000
Administrative		350,000
Total	$	550,000
Expected annual sales volume		
(390,000 boxes)		$1,950,000
Tax rate		40%

Manufacturers of candy have announced that they will increase prices of their products an average of 15 percent in the coming year, owing to increases in raw material (sugar, cocoa, peanuts, etc.) and labour costs. Friendly Candy Company expects that all other costs will remain at the same rates or levels as in the current year.

Required:

1. What is Friendly Candy Company's break-even point in boxes of candy for the current year?
2. What selling price per box must Friendly charge to cover the 15 percent increase in the cost of candy and still maintain the current contribution-margin ratio?
3. What volume of sales in dollars must Friendly achieve in the coming year to maintain the same net income after taxes as projected for the current year if the selling price of candy remains at $5 per box and the cost of candy increases 15 percent?
4. What strategies might Friendly use to maintain the same net income after taxes as projected for the current year?

C2-2 **INCREMENTAL APPROACH ANALYSIS.** (ICAO) Ontario Electronics Corporation (OEC) has three divisions. One of the divisions experienced serious difficulties in 2000 because a modernization program encountered equipment failure. You have been engaged by the owners to calculate the loss suffered by OEC so that a claim can be filed against the supplier of the new (but defective) machinery that was to have been an integral part of the modernization. The machinery supplier has agreed to pay for "reasonable losses suffered" because the contract signed by OEC guaranteed performance of the machinery; the payment will be on or about June 30, 2002 if the supplier is satisfied with OEC's calculation of the losses.

OEC's divisional plan was to have the old machinery dismantled and disposed of in the last week of June 2000, and to have the new machinery installed and operating by the end of the first week of July 2000. The old and new machinery produced four variations of the same product, which was the only product of the division. Unfortunately, the new machinery was not working by the end of the first week of July 2000. Breakdowns and faulty products were so common that alternative replacement machinery had to be ordered. The replacement machinery could not be installed until December 2000. By January 1, 2001 the replacement machinery, obtained from a different manufacturer, was functioning well and production commenced. The defective machinery was returned to the manufacturer.

OEC had accepted orders for their product through July 2000, but after the end of July orders had to be turned away because the inventory on hand in late June 2000 was expected to be depleted by mid-August, and the new equipment had proved to be incapable of producing the product. The division began accepting orders once again in January 2001. By the middle of 2001, the division manager believed that the company was "getting back to normal."

You have been able to gather the following information about the OEC division:

1. The old machinery could be sold for $10,000, but was traded in on the machinery that proved to be defective.
2. The new machinery (that proved to be defective) cost $1,200,000 cash plus the old machinery. The machinery was paid for at the beginning of July 2000; a bank loan for $1,200,000 at 13 percent interest per annum over five years was arranged to finance the purchase.
3. The replacement machinery was delivered and installed in December 2000 and cost $1,500,000, with payment on delivery. Another bank loan had to be arranged over several years at 14 percent per annum because the $1,200,000 had not yet been repaid on the defective machinery that was returned.
4. Divisional income statements for 2000 and 2001 for the relevant division are shown in Exhibit 2A-1.

Required: Determine the loss from the defective machinery. Explain how you are calculating the loss, and the strengths and weaknesses of your method. Clearly state any assumptions that you make.

EXHIBIT 2A-1

ONTARIO ELECTRONICS CORPORATION
Divisional Income Statement
(000 Omitted)

| | Years Ended December 31 | | | |
| | 2000 | | 2001 | |
	Jan. - June	July - Dec.	Jan. - June	July - Dec.
Revenue	$4,250	$ 920	$2,020	$4,400
Cost of goods sold:				
Material	1,800	385	890	1,850
Labour	670	145	315	690
Overhead:				
Fixed	600	620	640	650
Variable	550	120	310	555
	3,620	1,270	2,155	3,745
Gross profit (loss)	630	(350)	(135)	655
Expenses:				
Selling	235	245*	295*	250
Office	120	130	135	140
Depreciation	45	45	45	45
Loss on disposal of machinery	65	-	-	-
Interest on machinery loans	-	80	185	185
	465	500	660	620
Income (loss) before income tax	$ 165	$ (850)	$ (795)	$ 35

* Included $120,000 of advertising in December 2000 and $170,000 in January 2001 to inform customers that products were again available.

3

Measurement of Cost Behaviour

Chapter 2 demonstrated the importance of understanding relationships between an organization's activities and its costs, revenues, and profits. This chapter focuses on *measuring cost behaviour*, which means understanding and *quantifying* how activities of an organization affect levels of costs. Recall that the activities that affect costs are called *cost drivers*. Understanding relationships between costs and their cost drivers allows managers in all types of organizations—profit-seeking, non-profit, and government—to:

- Evaluate new manufacturing methods or service practices (Chapter 5)
- Make proper short-run decisions (Chapters 8 and 9)
- Plan or budget the effects of future activities (Chapters 12 and 13)
- Design effective management control systems (Chapters 14 and 15)
- Make proper long-run decisions (Chapters 10 and 11)
- Design accurate and useful product costing systems (Chapters 5, 6, 7)

As you can see, understanding cost behaviour is fundamental to management accounting. There are numerous real-world cases where managers have made very poor decisions to drop product lines, close manufacturing plants, or bid too high or too low on jobs because they used erroneous cost-behaviour information. This chapter, therefore, deserves careful study.

COST DRIVERS AND COST BEHAVIOUR

Linear-Cost Behaviour. Activity that can be graphed with a straight line when a cost changes proportionately with changes in a cost driver.

Accountants and managers usually assume that cost behaviour is *linear* over some *relevant range* of activities or cost drivers. **Linear-cost behaviour** can be graphed with a straight line when a cost changes proportionately with changes in a cost driver. Recall that the *relevant range* specifies the limits of cost driver activity within which a specific relationship between a cost and its cost driver will be valid. Managers usually define the relevant range based on their previous experience with different levels of activity and cost.

Many activities influence costs, but for some costs, *volume* of a product produced or service provided is the primary driver. These costs are easy to identify with or trace to products or services. Examples of volume-driven costs include the costs of printing labour, paper, ink, and binding to produce this textbook. The number of copies printed obviously affects the total printing labour, paper, ink, and binding costs. Equally important, we could relatively easily *trace* the use of these resources to the copies of the text printed. Schedules, payroll records, and other documents show how much of each was used to produce the copies of this text.

Other costs are more affected by activities *not* directly related to volume and often have *multiple* cost drivers. Such costs are not easy to identify with or trace to outputs. Examples of costs that are difficult to trace include the wages and salaries of the editorial staff of the publisher of this textbook. These editorial personnel produce many different textbooks, and it would be very difficult to determine exactly what portion of their costs went into a specific book, such as *Introduction to Management Accounting*.

Understanding and measuring costs that are difficult to trace to outputs can be especially challenging. In practice, many organizations use single cost drivers to describe each cost even though many have multiple causes. This approach is easier and less expensive than using nonlinear relationships and/or multiple cost drivers. *Careful* use of linear cost behaviour with a single cost driver often provides cost estimates that are accurate enough for most decisions. Linear cost behaviour with a single cost driver may seem at odds with reality and economic theory, but *the added benefit of understanding "true" cost behaviour may be less than the cost of determining "true" cost behaviour.*

For ease of communication and understanding, accountants usually describe cost behaviour in visual or graphical terms. Exhibit 3-1 shows linear cost behaviour, the relevant range, and a cost driver. Note the similarity to the CVP charts of Chapter 2.

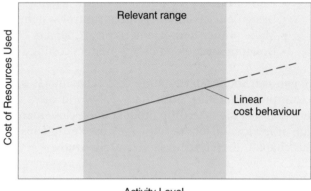

Types of Cost Behaviour

OBJECTIVE 1

Explain step- and mixed-cost behaviour.

Chapter 2 describes two patterns of cost behaviour: *variable* and *fixed* costs. Recall that a purely variable cost varies in proportion to the selected cost driver, while a purely fixed cost is not affected by the cost driver activity. In addition to these pure versions of cost, two additional types of costs combine characteristics of both fixed and variable cost behaviour. There are *step* costs and *mixed* costs.

Step costs

Step Costs. Costs that change abruptly at intervals of activity because the resources and their costs come in indivisible chunks.

Step costs change abruptly at intervals of activity because the resources and their costs are incurred in indivisible chunks. If the individual chunks of cost are relatively large and apply to a specific, broad range of activity, the cost is considered a fixed cost over that range of activity. An example is in Exhibit 3-2 (panel A), which shows the cost of leasing oil and gas drilling equipment. When oil and gas exploration activity reaches a certain level in a given region, an additional rig must be leased. However, one level of oil and gas rig leasing will support all volumes of exploration activity within a relevant range of drilling. Within each relevant range, this step cost behaves as a *fixed cost*. The total step cost at a level of activity is the amount of fixed cost appropriate for the range containing that activity level.

In contrast, accountants describe step costs as variable when the individual chunks of cost are relatively small and apply to a narrow range of activity. Exhibit 3-2 (panel B) shows the wage cost of cashiers at a supermarket. Suppose one cashier can serve an average of 20 shoppers per hour and that within the relevant range of shopping activity, the number of shoppers can range from 40 per hour to

EXHIBIT 3-2

Step-Cost Behaviour

Panel A: Lease Cost

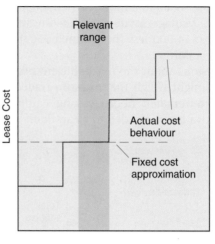

Panel B: Supermarket Checker Wage Cost

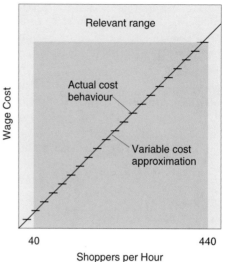

440 per hour. The corresponding number of cashiers would range between two and 22. Because the steps are relatively small, this step cost behaves much like a variable cost, and could be used as such for planning with little loss of accuracy.

Mixed Costs

Mixed Costs. Costs that contain elements of both fixed and variable-cost behaviour.

Mixed costs contain elements of both fixed- and variable-cost behaviour. As with step costs, the fixed element is determined by the planned *range* of activity level. Unlike step costs, however, usually in a mixed cost there is only one relevant range of activity and one level of fixed cost. The variable-cost element of the mixed cost is a purely variable cost that varies proportionately with activity within the single relevant range. In a mixed cost, the variable cost is incurred in addition to the fixed cost: the total mixed cost is the sum of the fixed cost plus the variable cost.

Many costs are mixed costs. For example, consider the monthly facilities maintenance department cost of the Parkview Medical Centre, shown in Exhibit 3-3. Salaries of the maintenance personnel and costs of equipment are fixed at $10,000 per month. In addition, cleaning supplies and repair materials may vary at a rate of $5 per patient-day delivered by the hospital.

An administrator at Parkview Medical Centre could use knowledge of the facilities maintenance department cost behaviour to:

1. Plan costs. Suppose the hospital expects to service 4,000 patient-days[1] next month. The month's predicted facilities maintenance department costs are $10,000 fixed plus the variable cost that equals 4,000 patient-days times $5 per patient-day, for a total of $30,000.

---

[1] A patient-day is one patient spending one day in the hospital—one patient spending five days is five patient-days of service.

2. Provide feedback to managers. Suppose actual facilities maintenance costs were $34,000 in a month when 4,000 patient-days were serviced as planned. Managers would want to know why the hospital overspent by $4,000 ($34,000 less the planned $30,000) so that they could take corrective action.

3. Make decisions about the most efficient use of resources. For example, managers might weigh the long-run tradeoffs of increased fixed costs of highly automated floor-cleaning equipment against the variable costs of extra hours needed to clean floors manually.

B.F. Goodrich
www.bfgoodrich.com

EXHIBIT 3-3

Mixed-Cost Behaviour

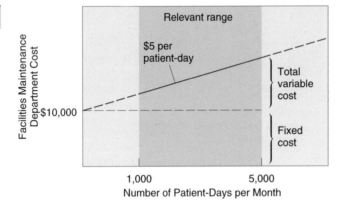

UNDERSTANDING COST BEHAVIOUR AT B.F. GOODRICH CANADA INC.

B.F. Goodrich Canada Inc. produces and sells polyvinyl chloride (PVC) resins and compounds. PVC resin is the second-largest volume thermoplastic sold in the world. In North America, the market approximates 5-billion kilograms and Canada is slightly less than 10 percent of this total. Traditional applications for vinyl have included construction products (such as pipe and house siding), wire-and-cable covering and window frames. In recent years, the market has expanded to include appliance parts and business machine components, among other applications.

The PVC industry is very capital-intensive and is becoming more so; the traditional applications for vinyl that use large volumes of PVC resins are very price-competitive and are marketed as "commodities." Typically, North American purchasers of PVC resin buy by the truckload or railcar. Off-shore orders are usually for volumes in the range of millions of kilograms. In many instances, an order is won or lost based on pricing of a mere one-tenth of a cent.

As a result of the commodity nature of the PVC resin market and the desire on the part of producers to keep their plants running at capacity (shutdowns are extremely costly and do not result in any ability to reduce fixed costs in the short term), prices tend to drift downward in weak markets—eventually settling out at the variable cost of the incremental producer.

It is therefore critical that B.F. Goodrich understand its cost structure in detail. Variable selling and manufacturing costs are precisely identified by resin type using recipes and current purchased material costs. To the extent that costs are variable within the range of volume being negotiated, the variable component is split out from the fixed component.

continued . . .

	A	B
Net Unit Selling Price	26.0¢	20.5¢
Variable Selling & Manufacturing Costs		
Freight	2.1	-
Duty	0.6	-
Raw materials	17.1	17.1
Utilities	3.5	3.5
Packaging (material and labour)	-	1.1
Export Allowance	(1.5)	(2.5)
Selling	0.6	0.1
Total Variable Costs	22.4	19.3
Incremental Contribution (per kilogram)	3.6	1.2
Fixed Costs (per unit)		
Manufacturing - overhead	3.2	3.2
- depreciation	1.8	1.8
Selling and administration	1.6	0.5
Total Fixed Costs	6.6	5.5
Operating Income/(Loss)	(3.0)¢	(4.3)¢

The major focus on large export orders (where the pricing will not have any negative impacts on domestic pricing) is "Incremental Contribution per kilogram." In many cases, orders will be accepted with Incremental Contributions of one cent per kilogram or less. Raw material suppliers for these export orders will be approached to determine their desire to provide an "Export Allowance" in order to obtain an order; these approaches will usually result in negotiation as to the amount of the "Export Allowance" required to obtain the order and the willingness of the supplier to accept it.

A typical analysis of the profitability of two proposed sales is demonstrated above. Note that variable costs are clearly separated from fixed costs. A positive "Incremental Contribution" will result in the order being accepted rather than rejected even though it will result in an operating loss. The contribution to fixed costs is a better result than the alternative where a greater total operating loss will result.

Source: Written by Stuart J. Macdonnell, Corporate Controller & Chief Administrative Officer, B.F. Goodrich Canada Inc.

MANAGEMENT'S INFLUENCE ON COST FUNCTIONS

OBJECTIVE 2

Explain management's influence on cost behaviour.

In addition to measuring and evaluating current cost behaviour, managers can influence cost behaviour through decisions about such factors as *product* or *service attributes, capacity, technology*, and policies to create *incentives to control costs*.

Product and Service Decisions

Budget Rent-a-Car
www.budgetrentacar.com

Perhaps the greatest influences on product and service costs are a manager's choices of product mix, design, performance, quality, features, distribution, and so on. Each of these decisions contributes to the organization's performance and should be made in a cost/benefit framework. For example, Budget Rent-a-Car, would add a feature to its services only if the cost of the feature (for example, free mileage) could be justified (more than recovered by increased business).

Capacity Decisions

Ford
www.ford.com

Mazda
www.mazda.com

Strategic decisions about the scale and scope of an organization's activities generally result in fixed levels of *capacity costs*. **Capacity costs** are the fixed costs of being able to achieve a desired level of production or to provide a desired level of service, while maintaining product or service attributes, such as quality. Companies in industries with long-term variations in demand must exercise caution when making capacity decisions. Fixed-capacity costs can not be recovered when demand falls during an economic downturn. Consider the dilemma facing Ford. In the mid-1980s, Ford was operating at full capacity. To meet demand, workers worked overtime and Ford even contracted with Mazda to produce some of its Probe cars. Ford had to choose between building new plants and assembly lines or continuing to pay premiums for overtime and outside production. Building new plants would enable Ford to produce cars at less cost but the fixed capacity costs would not be controllable. Overtime and outsourcing production to Mazda was expensive but Ford could control these variable costs much more easily during any business downturn. What did Ford do? According to executives at Ford,

> We know in 1986 and 1987 we lost some sales. We could have probably had a higher market share. But we felt it was worth it to keep our costs under control....sooner or later there's going to be a downturn and we'll be running down days and short weeks even with the capacity we have.

During the business downturn in the early 1990s, Ford was able to exercise more control over its costs. Again, in the mid-1990s, Ford faced the same strategic decision concerning scale and scope of operations.

Committed Fixed Costs

Every organization has some costs to which it is committed perhaps for quite a few years. **Committed fixed costs** usually arise from the possession of facilities, equipment, and a basic organization. These are large, indivisible chunks of cost that the organization is obligated to incur or usually would not consider avoiding. Committed fixed costs include mortgage or lease payments, interest payments on long-term debt, property taxes, insurance, and salaries of key personnel. Only major changes in the philosophy, scale, or scope of operations could change these committed fixed costs in future periods. Recall the example of the facilities maintenance department for the Parkview Medical Centre. The capacity of the facilities maintenance department was a management decision, and in this case that decision determined the magnitude of the equipment cost. Suppose Parkview Medical Centre were to increase permanently its patient-days per month beyond the relevant range of 5,000 patient-days. Because more capacity would be needed, the committed equipment cost would rise to a new level per month.

Discretionary Fixed Costs

Some costs are fixed at certain levels only because management decided that these levels of cost should be incurred in order to meet the organization's goals. These **discretionary fixed costs** have no obvious relationship to levels of output activity, but are determined as part of the periodic planning process. Each planning period, management will determine how much to spend on discretionary items such as advertising and promotion costs, public relations and research and development costs, charitable donations, employee training programs, and purchased management consulting services.

Unlike committed fixed costs, managers can alter discretionary fixed costs easily—up or down—even within a budget period, if they decide that different levels of spending are desirable. Conceivably, managers could reduce such discretionary costs almost entirely for a given year in dire times, whereas they could not reduce committed costs. Discretionary fixed costs may be essential to the long-run achievement of the organization's goals, but managers can vary spending levels broadly in the short run.

Sometimes managers plan discretionary fixed costs, such as advertising or research and development, as a percentage of planned sales revenue. Of course, managers would not contract for advertising or conduct research and development only as current revenues are received. Rather, this planning is needed if the organization is to be able to pay for discretionary fixed costs.

Consider Marietta's Corporation, which is experiencing financial difficulties. Sales for its major products are down, and Marietta's management is considering cutting back on costs *temporarily*. Marietta's management must determine which of the following fixed costs to reduce or eliminate, and how much money each would save:

COSTS	PLANNED AMOUNTS
Advertising and Promotion	$ 30,000
Amortization	400,000
Employee Training	100,000
Management Salaries	800,000
Mortgage Payment	250,000
Property Taxes	600,000
Research and Development	1,500,000
Total	$3,680,000

Can Marietta reduce or eliminate any of these fixed costs? The answer depends on Marietta's long-run outlook. Marietta could reduce costs but also greatly reduce its ability to compete in the future, if it cuts carelessly. Rearranging these costs by categories of committed and discretionary costs yields the following analysis:

FIXED COSTS	PLANNED AMOUNTS
Committed:	
Amortization	$ 400,000
Mortgage Payment	250,000
Property Taxes	600,000
Total Committed	$1,250,000
Discretionary (Potential Savings):	
Advertising and Promotion	30,000
Employee Training	100,000
Management Salaries	800,000
Research and Development	1,500,000
Total Discretionary	$2,430,000
Total Committed and Discretionary	$3,680,000

Eliminating all discretionary fixed costs would save Marietta $2,430,000 per year. As is clear from Chapter 2, reducing fixed costs lowers the break-even point or increases the profit at a given level of sales, which might benefit Marietta at this time. Marietta would be unwise to arbitrarily eliminate all of these costs. Nevertheless, distinguishing committed and discretionary fixed costs would be the company's first step to identifying where costs *could* be reduced.

Technology Decisions

One of the most critical decisions that managers make is the type of technology that the organization will use to produce its products and/or deliver its services. Choice of technology (for example, labour-intensive versus robotic manufacturing, or traditional banking services versus automatic tellers) positions the organization to meet its current goals and to respond to changes in the environment (for example, changes in customer needs or actions by competitors). Not surprisingly, technology may have a great impact on the costs of products and services.

Cost Control Incentives

Finally, future costs may be affected by the *incentives* that management creates for employees to control costs. Managers use their knowledge of cost behaviour to set cost expectations, and employees may receive compensation or other rewards that are tied to meeting these expectations. For example, the administrator of Parkview Medical Centre may give the supervisor of the facilities maintenance department a favourable evaluation if the supervisor maintained quality of service *and* kept department costs below the expected amount for the level of patient-days serviced. This strong form of feedback could cause the supervisor to carefully watch department costs and to find ways to reduce costs without reducing quality of service.

MEASURING COST BEHAVIOUR

OBJECTIVE 3

Measure cost functions and use them to predict costs.

Measuring Cost Behaviour (Cost Measurement). Understanding and quantifying how activities of an organizations affect levels of cost.

The decision-making, planning, and control activities of management accounting require accurate and useful estimates of future fixed and variable costs. The first step in estimating or predicting costs is **measuring cost behaviour (cost measurement)** as a function of appropriate cost drivers. The second step is to use these cost measures to estimate future costs at expected, future levels of cost-driver activity.

It is usually easy to measure costs that are obviously linked with a volume-related cost driver. Why? Because you can trace such costs to particular cost drivers, and measurement simply requires a system for identifying the costs. For example, *systems* for controlling inventories measure the amount of materials issued for a particular product or service. Similarly, payroll systems that use labour records or time cards may detail the amount of time each worker spends on a particular product or service.

In contrast it is usually difficult to measure costs without obvious links to cost drivers, or those with multiple cost drivers. *Assumed* relationships between costs and cost drivers often are used because an observable link is not present.

Cost Functions

In order to describe the relationship between a cost and its cost driver(s), managers often use an algebraic equation called a **cost function**. When there is only one cost driver, the cost function is similar to the algebraic CVP relationships discussed in Chapter 2. Consider the mixed cost graphed in Exhibit 3-3, facilities maintenance department cost:

$$\begin{aligned} \text{total facilities maintenance} \atop \text{department cost} &= {\text{total fixed} \atop \text{maintenance cost}} + {\text{variable} \atop \text{maintenance cost}} \\ &= {\text{fixed maintenance} \atop \text{cost per month}} + \left({\text{variable cost} \atop \text{per patient-day}} \times {\text{number of} \atop \text{patient-days}} \right) \end{aligned}$$

Let

Y = total (facilities maintenance department) cost
F = fixed (maintenance) cost
V = the variable cost (per patient-day)
X = the cost driver (number of patient-days)

We can rewrite the mixed-cost function as:

$$Y = F + VX, \text{ or}$$
$$Y = \$10,000 + \$5.00 \, X$$

This mixed-cost function has the familiar form of a straight line—it is called a *linear* cost function. When graphing a cost function, F is the *intercept*, the point on the vertical axis where the cost function begins. In Exhibit 3-3 the intercept is the $10,000 fixed cost per month. V, the variable cost per unit of activity, is the *slope* of the cost function. In Exhibit 3-3 the cost function slopes upwards at the rate of $5.00 for each additional patient-day.

Criteria for Choosing Functions

Managers should apply two principles to obtain accurate and useful cost functions: plausibility and reliability.

1. The cost function must be plausible or believable. Personal observation of costs and activities, when it is possible, provides the best evidence of a plausible relationship between a cost and its driver. Some cost relationships, by nature, are not directly observable, so the cost analyst must be confident that the proposed relationship is sound. Many costs may move together with a number of cost drivers, but no cause-and-effect relationships may exist. A cause-and-effect relationship (that is, X causes Y) is necessary for cost functions to be accurate and useful.

2. In addition to being plausible, a cost function's estimates of costs at actual levels of activity must reliably conform with actually observed costs. Reliability can be assessed in terms of "goodness of fit"—how well the cost function explains past cost behaviour. If the fit is good and conditions do not change, the cost function should be a reliable predictor of future costs.

Note especially that managers use these criteria *together* in choosing a cost function: each is a check on the other. Knowledge of operations and how costs are recorded is helpful in choosing a plausible and reliable cost function that links cause and effect. For example, maintenance is often performed when output is low, because that is when machines can be taken out of service. However, lower output does not *cause* increased maintenance costs, nor does increased output cause *lower* maintenance costs. The timing of maintenance is somewhat discretionary. A more plausible explanation is that over a longer period of time increased output causes higher maintenance costs, but daily or weekly recording of maintenance costs may make it appear otherwise. Understanding the nature of maintenance costs should lead to a reliable, long-run cost function.

Choosing Cost Drivers: Activity Analysis

OBJECTIVE 4

Describe the importance of activity analysis for measuring cost functions.

Activity Analysis. The process of identifying appropriate cost drivers and their effects on the costs of making a product or providing a service.

Incorrect assumptions about cost behaviour may cause incorrect decisions. The remedy is a careful examination of cost behaviour. To aid such an examination, managers apply **activity analysis**, which identifies appropriate cost drivers and their effects on the costs of making a product or providing a service. The final product or service may have a number of cost drivers because a number of separate activities may be involved. The greatest benefit of activity analysis is that it directs management accountants to the appropriate cost drivers for each cost.

Activity analysis is especially important for measuring and predicting costs for which cost drivers are not obvious. Earlier in this chapter we said that a cost is fixed or variable *with respect to a specific cost driver*. A cost that appears fixed in relation to one cost driver could in fact be variable in relation to another cost driver. For example, suppose the Jupiter automobile plant uses automated painting equipment. The cost of adjusting this equipment may be fixed with regard to the total *number* of automobiles produced; that is, there is no discernible cost relationship between these support costs and the number of automobiles produced. However, this same cost may vary dramatically with the number of different *colours* and *types of finishes* of automobiles produced. Activity analysis examines various potential cost drivers for plausibility and reliability. As always, the expected benefits of improved decision making from using more accurate cost behaviour should exceed the expected costs of the cost-driver search.

Identifying the appropriate cost drivers is the most critical aspect of any method for measuring cost behaviour. For many years, most organizations used only one cost driver: the amount of labour used. In essence, they assumed that the only activity affecting costs was the use of labour. But in the past decade we have learned that previously "hidden" activities greatly influence cost behaviour. Often analysts in both manufacturing and service companies find that activities related to the complexity of performing tasks affect costs more directly than labour usage or other cost drivers that are related to the volume of output activity.

Consider Northern Computers, which makes two products for personal computers: a plug-in music board ("Mozart-Plus") and a hard disk drive ("Powerdrive"). When most of the work on Northern's products was done by hand, most costs, other than the cost of materials, were related to (driven by) labour cost. However, the use of computer-controlled assembly equipment has increased the costs of support activities and has reduced labour cost. Labour cost is now only 5 percent of the total costs at Northern. Furthermore, activity analysis has shown that the majority of today's support costs are driven by the

Northern Computers Inc.
www.nciaccess.com

number of components added to products (a measure of product complexity), not by labour cost.

On average, support costs were twice as much as labour costs. Suppose Northern wants to assess how much support cost is incurred in producing one Mozart-Plus and how much for one Powerdrive. Using the old cost driver, labour cost, support costs would be

	MOZART-PLUS	POWERDRIVE
Labour Cost	$ 8.50	$130.00
Support Cost:		
2 × Direct Labour Cost	$17.00	$260.00

Using the more appropriate cost driver, the *number of components added to products*, the support costs are

	MOZART-PLUS	POWERDRIVE
Support Cost:		
at $20 per component		
$20 × 5 components	$100.00	
$20 × 9 components		$180.00
Difference in Support Cost:		
	$ 83.00	$ 80.00
	higher	lower

By using an appropriate cost driver, Northern can measure its support costs on a much more meaningful basis. Managers will make better decisions with this revised information. For example, prices charged for products can be more closely related to the costs of production.

METHODS OF MEASURING COST FUNCTIONS

Once managers have determined the most plausible drivers behind different costs, they can choose from a broad selection of methods of approximating cost functions, including (1) engineering analysis, (2) account analysis, (3) high-low analysis, (4) visual fit analysis, and (5) least squares regression. These methods are not mutually exclusive; managers frequently use two or more together to avoid major errors in measuring cost behaviour. Some organizations use each of these methods in succession over the years as the need for more accurate measures becomes evident and more hard evidence becomes available. The first two methods may rely only on logical analysis, while the last three involve analysis of past costs.

Activity Analysis at Hughes Aircraft Company

Hughes Aircraft Company
www.raytheon.com

The regulatory and competitive environment of Hughes Aircraft Company has changed dramatically over the past several years. Government agencies demand better cost estimates, and shrinking defence spending means more competition among government contractors. Hughes Aircraft found that its 50-year-old financial reporting system provided irrelevant and inaccurate measures of cost behaviour for management decision making. These cost measures were based on labour usage, which is no longer a relevant cost driver at Hughes.

Managers at Hughes spent considerable time and money analyzing the firm's service and manufacturing activities to find more appropriate cost drivers than labour usage. Among other things, they found that human resource service costs are driven in part by the number of new hires and the number of training hours rather than total direct labour usage. In fact, very few of Hughes' major activities were found to be driven by labour usage.

Managers also had to convince Hughes' employees, managers, auditors, and customers (primarily the U.S. government) that the new activity analysis produces plausible and reliable cost estimates. Toward that end, Hughes conducted pilot studies at a few sites before moving to company-wide implementation of activity analysis for cost measurement. These pilot studies demonstrated that activity analysis greatly improved cost predictions and also streamlined the cost-impact studies required by government agencies.

Source: Adapted from Jack Haedicke and David Feil, "Hughes Aircraft Sets the Standard for ABC," *Management Accounting,* February 1991, pp. 29–33.

Engineering Analysis

Engineering Analysis. The systematic review of materials, supplies, labour, support services, and facilities needed for products and services; measuring cost behaviour according to what cost should be, not by what costs have been.

The first method, **engineering analysis**, measures cost behaviour according to what costs *should be*, not by what costs *have been*. It entails a systematic review of materials, supplies, labour, support services, and facilities needed for products and services. Analysts can even use engineering analysis successfully for new products and services, as long as the organization has had experience with similar costs. Why? Because measures can be based on information from personnel who are directly involved with the product or service. In addition to actual experience, analysts learn about new costs from experiments with prototypes, accounting and industrial engineering literature, the experience of competitors, and the advice of management consultants. From this information, cost analysts determine what future costs should be. If the cost analysts are experienced and understand the activities of the organization, then their engineering cost predictions may be quite reliable and useful for decision making. The disadvantages of engineering cost analysis are that the efforts are costly and often not timely.

Weyerhaeuser Company, producer of wood products, used engineering analysis to determine the cost functions for its 14 corporate service departments. These cost functions are used to measure the cost of corporate services used by three main business groups. For example, accounts payable costs for each division are a function of three cost drivers: the number of hours spent on each division, the number of documents, and the number of invoices. This approach to measuring cost behaviour could also be used by nearly any service organization.

At Parkview Medical Centre, an assistant to the hospital administrator interviewed facilities maintenance personnel and observed their activities on several

Weyerhaeuser Canada
www.abforestprod.org/
weyerpulp.html

random days for a month. From data she collected, she confirmed that the most plausible cost driver for facilities maintenance cost is the number of patient-days. She also estimated from current department salaries and equipment charges that monthly fixed costs approximated $10,000 per month. From interviews and supplies usage during the month she observed, she estimated that variable costs are $5 per patient-day. She communicated this information to the hospital administrator, but cautioned that her cost measures may be in error because:

1. The month she observed may be abnormal.
2. The facilities maintenance personnel may have altered their normal work habits because she was observing them.
3. The facilities maintenance personnel may have not told the complete truth about their activities because of their concerns about the use of the information they revealed.

However, if we assume the observed and estimated information is correct, facilities maintenance cost in any month could be predicted by first forecasting that month's expected patient-days and then entering that figure into the following algebraic, mixed-cost function:

$$Y = \$10,000 \text{ per month} + \$5 \times \text{patient-days}$$

For example, if the administrator expects 4,000 patient-days next month, she will predict facilities maintenance costs to be:

$$Y = \$10,000 + \$5 \times 4,000 \text{ patient-days} = \underline{\underline{\$30,000}}$$

Account Analysis

In contrast to engineering analysis, users of **account analysis** look to the accounting system for information about cost behaviour. The simplest method of *account analysis* selects a volume-related cost driver and classifies each account as a variable cost or as a fixed cost. The cost analyst then looks at each cost account balance and estimates either the variable cost per unit of cost-driver activity or the periodic fixed cost.

To illustrate this approach to account analysis, let's return to the facilities maintenance department at Parkview Medical Centre and analyze costs for January, 2001. Recall that the most plausible driver for these costs is the number of patient-days serviced per month. The table below shows costs recorded in a month with 3,700 patient-days:

COST	JANUARY, 2001 AMOUNT
Supervisor's salary and benefits	$ 3,800
Hourly workers' wages and benefits	14,674
Equipment amortization and rentals	5,873
Equipment repairs	5,604
Cleaning supplies	7,472
Total facilities maintenance cost	$37,423

Next, the analyst determines how much of each cost may be fixed and how much may be variable. Assume that the analyst has made the following judgments:

COST	JANUARY 2001 AMOUNT	FIXED/ MONTH	VARIABLE
Supervisor's salary and benefits	$ 3,800	$3,800	
Hourly workers' wages and benefits	14,674		$14,674
Equipment amortization and rentals	5,873	5,873	
Equipment repairs	5,604		5,604
Cleaning supplies	7,472		7,472
Totals	$37,423	$9,673	$27,750

Measuring total facilities maintenance cost behaviour, then, requires only simple arithmetic. Add all the fixed costs to get the total fixed cost per month. Divide the total variable costs by the units of cost-driver activity to get the variable costs per unit of cost driver.

$$\text{fixed cost per month} = \$9,673$$
$$\text{variable cost per patient-day} = \$27,750 \div 3,700 \text{ patient-days}$$
$$= \$7.50 \text{ per patient-day}$$

The algebraic, mixed cost function, measured by account analysis is

$$Y = \$9,673 \text{ per month} + \$7.50 \times (\text{patient-days})$$

Account analysis methods are less expensive to conduct than engineering analysis, but they require recording of relevant cost accounts and cost drivers. In addition, account analysis is subjective because the analyst decides whether each cost is variable or fixed based on judgment.

High-Low, Visual Fit, and Least Squares Methods

When enough cost data are available, we can use historical data to measure the cost function mathematically. Three popular historical-cost methods are the high-low, visual fit, and least squares methods.

These three methods are more objective than the engineering analysis method because each is based on hard evidence as well as on judgment. They can also be more objective than account analysis because they use more than one period's cost and activity information. However, because these methods require more past cost data, account analysis—and especially engineering analysis—probably will remain primary methods of measuring cost behaviour. Products, services, technologies, and organizations are changing rapidly in response to increased global competition. *In some cases, by the time enough historical data are collected to support these analyses, the data are obsolete*—the organization has changed, the production process has changed, or the product has changed. The cost analyst must be careful that the historical data are from a past environment that still closely resembles the future environment for which costs are being predicted. This can be particularly troublesome if data are collected on a monthly basis and they do not capture the operations they are being used to model. Another concern is that historical data may hide past inefficiencies that could be reduced if they are identified. Further, one must ensure that the high and low points are representative of the full set of points and do not significantly change the analysis if, for example, the second highest and lowest points were selected.

Data for Illustration

In discussing the high-low, visual fit, and least squares regression methods, we will use Parkview Medical Centre's facilities maintenance department costs as our example. The table below shows monthly data collected on facilities maintenance department costs and on the number of patient-days serviced in the year 2001:

Facilities Maintenance Department Data, 2001

MONTH	FACILITIES MAINTENANCE DEPARTMENT COST (Y)	NUMBER OF PATIENT-DAYS (X)
January	$37,000	3,700
February	23,000	1,600
March	37,000	4,100
April	47,000	4,900
May	33,000	3,300
June	39,000	4,400
July	32,000	3,500
August	33,000	4,000
September	17,000	1,200
October	18,000	1,300
November	22,000	1,800
December	20,000	1,600

High-low Method

High-Low Method. A simple method for measuring a linear cost function from past cost data, focusing on the highest-activity and lowest-activity points and fitting a line through these two points.

When sufficient cost data are available, the cost analyst may use historical data to measure the cost function mathematically. A simple method to measure a linear cost function from past cost data is the **high-low method** shown in Exhibit 3-4.

The first step in analyzing historical data is to plot the data points on a graph. This visual display helps the analyst see whether there are obvious errors in the data. Even though many points are plotted, the high-low method focuses on the highest-activity and lowest-activity points. Normally, the next step is for the analyst to fit a line through these two points. However, if one of these points is an "outlier" that seems in error or nonrepresentative of normal operations, the analyst will use the next-highest or next-lowest activity point. For example, you should not use a point from a time period with abnormally low activity caused by a labour strike or fire. Why? Because that point is not representative of a normal relationship between the cost and the cost driver.

After selecting the representative high and low points, the analyst can draw a line between them, extending the line to the vertical (Y) axis of the graph. Note that this extension in Exhibit 3-4 is a dashed line as a reminder that costs may

EXHIBIT 3-4

High-Low Method

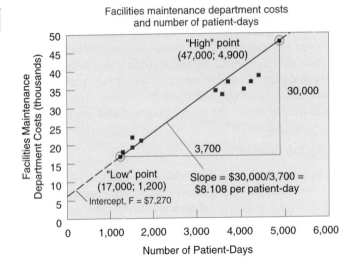

Facilities maintenance department costs and number of patient-days

not be linear outside the relevant range. Also, managers usually are concerned with how costs behave within the relevant range, not with how they behave either at zero activity or at impossibly high activity (given current capacity). Measurements of costs within the relevant range probably are not reliable measures or predictors of costs *outside* the relevant range.

The point at which the line intersects the Y-axis is the intercept, F, or estimate of fixed cost. The slope of the line measures the variable cost, V, per patient-day. The clearest way to measure the intercept and slope with the high-low method is to use algebra:

MONTH	FACILITIES MAINTENANCE DEPARTMENT COST (Y)	NUMBER OF PATIENT-DAYS (X)
High: April	$47,000	4,900
Low: September	17,000	1,200
Difference	$30,000	3,700

Variable cost per patient-day,

$$V = \frac{\text{change in costs}}{\text{change in activity}} = \frac{\$47,000 - \$17,000}{4,900 - 1,200 \text{ patient-days}}$$

$$V = \frac{\$30,000}{3,700} = \underline{\$8.108} \text{ per patient-day}$$

Fixed cost per month, F = Total mixed cost less total variable cost

$$
\begin{aligned}
\text{at X (high): } F &= \$47,000 - \$8.108(4,900) \\
&= \$47,000 - \$39,730 \\
&= \underline{\$7,270} \text{ per month}
\end{aligned}
$$

$$
\begin{aligned}
\text{at X (low): } F &= \$17,000 - \$8.108(1,200) \\
&= \$17,000 - \$9,730 \\
&= \underline{\$7,270} \text{ per month}
\end{aligned}
$$

Therefore, the facilities maintenance department algebraic, total mixed-cost function, measured by the high-low method, is:

$$Y = \$7{,}270 \text{ per month} + \$8.108 \times (\text{patient-days})$$

The high-low method is easy to use and illustrates mathematically how a change in a cost driver can change total cost. The cost function that resulted in this case is *plausible*. However, it depends entirely upon the selected high and low points. Without further information—for example, about whether either of the points represents a typical month—this method may be *unreliable*. Before the widespread availability of computers, managers often used the high-low method to quickly measure a cost function. Today, however, the high-low method is not often used in practice because of its unreliability and because it makes inefficient use of information, using only two periods' cost experience, regardless of how many relevant data have been collected. Other methods that we now consider can use all the available data.

Visual Fit Method

Visual Fit Method. A method in which the cost analysis visually fits a straight line through a plot for all the available data, not just between the high and low points, making it more reliable than the high-low method.

The **visual fit method** is more reliable than the high-low method because it can use all the available data instead of just two points. In the visual fit method, the cost analyst visually fits a straight line through a plot of all the available data, not just between the high point and the low point. If the cost function for the data is linear, it is possible to visualize a straight line through the scattered points that comes reasonably close to most of them and thus captures the general tendency of the data. The analyst extends that line back until it intersects the vertical axis of the graph.

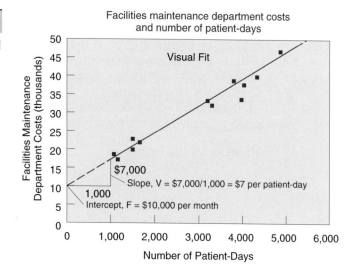

Exhibit 3-5 shows this method applied to the facilities maintenance department cost data for the past 12 months. By measuring where the line intersects the cost axis, the analyst can estimate the monthly fixed cost—in this case, about $10,000 per month. To find the variable cost per patient-day, select any activity level (say 1,000 patient-days) and find the total cost at that activity level ($17,000). Then divide the variable cost (which is total cost less fixed cost) by the units of activity:

$$\text{variable cost per patient-day} = (\$17,000 - \$10,000)/1,000$$
$$= \$7 \text{ per patient-day}$$

The linear cost function measured by the visual fit method is:

$$Y = \$10,000 \text{ per month} + \$7 \times \text{(patient-days)}$$

Although the visual fit method can use all the data, the placement of the line and the measurement of the fixed and variable costs are subjective. The method is somewhat unreliable because it depends on the skill of an analyst who must "eyeball" a straight line by visually "averaging" the fit through the data. As with the high-low method, different analysts could easily find different measures of cost behaviour. This subjectivity is the primary reason why the visual fit method is now rarely used in practice, even though using computers to plot data and draw lines has made the method easier to implement. This method is a good introduction to what least squares regression accomplishes with statistics.

Least Squares Regression Method

Least Squares Regression (Regression Analysis). Measuring a cost function objectively by using statistics to fit a cost function to all the data.

Least squares regression measures a cost function more objectively (with statistics rather than human eyesight) using the same data. Least squares **regression analysis** (or simply, regression analysis) uses statistics to fit a cost function to all the data. Regression analysis that uses one cost driver to measure a cost function is called simple regression. The use of multiple cost drivers for a single cost is called multiple regression. Only a basic discussion of simple regression analysis is presented in this section of the chapter. Some statistical properties of regression and using computer regression software are discussed in the Appendix to Chapter 3.

Regression analysis usually measures cost behaviour more reliably than other cost measurement methods. In addition, regression analysis yields important statistical information about the reliability of cost estimates, so analysts can assess confidence in the cost measures and select the best cost driver. One such measure of reliability, or goodness of fit, is the **coefficient of determination, R^2** (or R-squared), which measures how much of the fluctuation of a cost is explained by changes in the cost driver. Appendix 3 explains R^2 and discusses how to use it to select the best cost driver.

Coefficient of Determination. A measurement of how much of the fluctuation of a cost is explained by changes in the cost driver.

Exhibit 3-6 shows the linear, mixed-cost function for facilities maintenance costs as measured by simple regression analysis.

EXHIBIT 3-6

Least Squares Regression Method

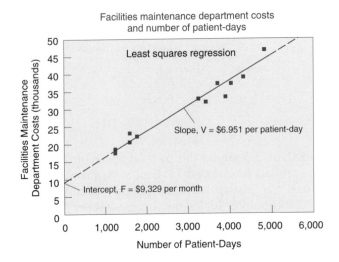

Facilities maintenance department costs and number of patient-days

1. The fixed cost measure is $9,329 per month. The variable cost measure is $6.951 per patient-day. The linear cost function is:

facilities maintenance department cost = $9,329 per month
+ $6.951 per patient-day

or

$$Y = \$9,329 + \$6.951 \times \text{(patient-days)}$$

Compare the cost measures produced by each of the five approaches:

METHOD	FIXED COST PER MONTH	VARIABLE COST PER PATIENT DAY
Engineering Analysis	$10,000	$5.000
Account Analysis	9,673	7.500
High-Low	7,270	8.108
Visual Fit	10,000	7.000
Regression	9,329	6.951

To see the differences in results between methods, we will use account analysis and regression analysis measures to predict total facilities maintenance department costs at 1,000 and 5,000 patient-days, the approximate limits of the relevant range.

	ACCOUNT ANALYSIS	REGRESSION ANALYSIS	DIFFERENCE
1,000 Patient-days:			
Fixed Cost	$ 9,673	$ 9,329	$ 344
Variable Costs			
$7.500 (1,000)	7,500		
$6.951 (1,000)		6,951	549
Predicted Total Cost	$17,173	$16,280	$ 893
5,000 Patient-days:			
Fixed Cost	$ 9,673	$ 9,329	$ 344
Variable Costs			
$7.500 (5,000)	37,500		
$6.951 (5,000)		34,755	2,745
Predicted Total Cost	$47,173	$44,084	$3,089

At lower levels of patient-day activity, both methods yield similar cost predictions. At higher levels of patient-day activity, however, the account analysis cost function predicts much higher facilities maintenance department costs. The difference between the predicted total costs is primarily due to the higher variable cost per patient-day (approximately $0.55 more) measured by account analysis, which increases the difference in predicted total variable costs proportionately as the number of planned patient-days increases. Because of their grounding in statistical analysis, the regression cost measures are probably more reliable than are the other methods. Managers would feel more confidence in cost predictions from the regression cost function.

Measuring Cost Behaviour at Hewlett-Packard

**Hewlett-Packard
www.hp.com**

Consider how Hewlett-Packard (HP), the computer manufacturer, measured cost behaviour as part of its company-wide implementation of activity-based costing. HP used detailed engineering analysis to revise its accounting system at many of its manufacturing sites. The old cost system at HP used labour cost as the cost driver for all nonmaterial costs, regardless of the actual cost drivers. On average, labour costs were only 2 percent of total costs, so it was unlikely that they were the major cause of most other costs. The result of using labour cost was significant cost distortion—products with higher labour costs were overcosted whereas products with lower labour costs were undercosted. Managers did not have confidence in the product cost predictions using this labour-based system.

Cost analysts spent several years talking with managers and engineers and carefully observing facilities maintenance, manufacturing support, and other activities to identify more appropriate cost drivers and their relationships to cost behaviour.

At HP's Surface Mount Center in Boise, the ABC system has been fully operational since early in 1993. This facility manufactures about 50 different electronic circuit boards for internal customers within HP. The selection of cost drivers at the Center resulted from an "intense analysis of the production process and cost behaviour patterns by the accounting production, and engineering staffs." This combination of account analysis and engineering analysis resulted in 10 different cost drivers.

One interesting aspect of the ABC system is the continuous involvement of managers and engineers in improving the system. "An almost daily dialogue goes on among production, engineering, and the accountants about how the ABC cost system could be improved to reflect product costs more accurately."

A series of simple-linear regressions between overhead dollars and cost driver volumes was conducted to test the statistical validity of the cost drivers. For example, one of the regressions was "all automatic placement overhead costs" versus the cost-driver "number of automatic placements," which had a coefficient of determination (R-Squared) of 92 percent. Another regression measured the relationship between "material procurement overhead costs" and the cost-driver "number of distinct parts" (R-Squared of 91 percent). The regression analyses tended to confirm that the cost drivers selected indeed were correlated with overhead costs.

Source: Mike Merz and Arlene Hardy, "ABC Puts Accounting on Design Team at HP," *Management Accounting*, September 1993, pp. 22–27.

HIGHLIGHTS TO REMEMBER

Cost behaviour refers to how costs change as levels of an organization's activities change. Costs can behave as fixed, variable, step, or mixed costs. Fixed costs may behave in a step manner and may be committed or discretionary. Committed fixed costs cannot be changed easily, but discretionary fixed costs may be changed at nearly any time as management sees fit. Management may also influence fixed- and variable-cost behaviour by its choices of product or service attributes, capacity, technology, and cost control incentives.

Cost measurement quantifies the behaviour of costs into fixed and variable components. This behaviour is measured with respect to appropriate cost drivers within the relevant range of cost-driver activity. Fixed costs are usually estimated per time period. Variable costs are estimated per unit of cost driver. One of the most important aspects of cost measurement is activity analysis, or determining the proper cost driver.

A cost function is the mathematical expression of cost behaviour. The typical linear cost function is of the form:

$$Y = F + VX$$

where

F = fixed cost per time period
V = variable cost per unit of cost driver
X = the most plausible cost driver

Three major approaches to measuring cost functions are engineering analysis, account analysis, and least squares regression analysis methods. All these methods require expert judgment. Engineering analysis may be performed for new or revised processes, but account and regression analyses require historical cost data. All analyses may be combined. The most objective method is usually least squares regression analysis, but this analysis requires considerable past data and statistical sophistication on the part of the analyst. The reliability of all methods may be improved if the analyst has relevant experience with similar costs and activities.

SUMMARY PROBLEMS FOR YOUR REVIEW

Problem One

The Reetz Company has its own photocopying department. Reetz's photocopying costs include costs of copy machines, operators, paper, toner, utilities, and so on. We have the following cost and activity data:

MONTH	TOTAL PHOTOCOPYING COST	NUMBER COPIES
1	$25,000	320,000
2	29,000	390,000
3	24,000	300,000
4	23,000	310,000
5	28,000	400,000

1. Use the high-low method to measure the cost behaviour of the photocopy department in formula form.
2. What are the benefits and disadvantages of using the high-low method for measuring cost behaviour?

Solution

1. The lowest and highest activity levels are in months three (300,000 copies) and five (400,000 copies).

$$\text{variable cost per copy} = \frac{\text{change in cost}}{\text{change in activity}} = \frac{\$28,000 - \$24,000}{400,000 - 300,000}$$

$$= \frac{\$4,000}{\$100,000} = \underline{\$.04} \text{ per copy}$$

fixed cost per month = total cost less variable cost

at 400,000 copies: $28,000 − $.04(400,000) = $12,000 per month

at 300,000 copies: $24,000 − $.04(300,000) = $12,000 per month

Therefore, the photocopy cost function is:

$$Y \text{ (total cost)} = \$12,000 \text{ per month} + \$.04 \times \text{(number of copies)}$$

2. The benefits of using the high-low method are:

- The method is easy to use.
- Not many data are needed.

The disadvantages of using the high-low method are:

- The choice of the high and low points is subjective.
- The method does not use all available data.
- The method may not be reliable.

Problem Two

The Reliable Insurance Company processes a variety of insurance claims for losses, accidents, thefts, and so on. Account analysis has estimated the variable cost of processing each claim at 0.5 percent (.005) of the dollar value of the claim. This estimate seemed reasonable since higher claims often involve more analysis before settlement. To better control processing costs, however, Reliable Insurance conducted an activity analysis of claims processing. The analysis suggested that more appropriate cost drivers and behaviour for automobile accident claims are:

0.2 percent of Reliable Insurance policyholders' property claims
0.6 percent of other parties' property claims
0.8 percent of total personal injury claims

Below are data from two recent automobile accident claims.

	AUTOMOBILE CLAIM #607788	AUTOMOBILE CLAIM #607991
Total Claim Amount	$16,900	$27,000
Policyholder Claim	$ 4,500	$23,600
Other Party Claim	0	3,400
Personal Injury Claim	12,400	0

1. Estimate the cost of processing each claim using data from the account analysis and the activity analysis.
2. How would you recommend that Reliable Insurance estimate the cost of processing claims?

Solution

	AUTOMOBILE CLAIM #607788	AUTOMOBILE CLAIM #607991
Using account analysis:		
Total claim amount	$ 16,900.00	$ 27,000.00
Estimated processing cost at 0.5 percent	$ 84.50	$135.00
Using activity analysis:		
Policyholder claim	$ 4,500.00	$ 23,600.00
Estimated processing cost at 0.2 percent	9.00	47.20
Other party claim	0	3,400.00
Estimated processing cost at 0.6 percent	0	20.40
Personal injury claim	$ 12,400.00	0
Estimated processing cost at 0.8 percent	99.20	0
Total estimated processing cost	$ 108.20	$ 67.60

2. The activity analysis estimates of processing costs are considerably different from those using cost account analysis. If the activity analyses are reliable, then automobile claims that include personal injury losses are considerably more costly to process than property damage claims. If these estimates are relatively inexpensive to keep current and to use, then it seems reasonable to adopt the activity analysis approach. Reliable Insurance will have more accurate cost estimates and will be better able to plan its claims processing activities. However, Reliable Insurance processes many different types of claims. Extending activity analysis to all types of claims would result in a complicated system for predicting costs—much more complex (and costly) than simply using the total dollar value of claims. Whether to adopt the activity approach overall depends on cost-benefit considerations that may be estimated by first adopting activity analysis for one type of claim and assessing the usefulness and cost of the more accurate information.

APPENDIX 3: USE AND INTERPRETATION OF LEAST SQUARES REGRESSION ANALYSIS

Regression analysis of historical cost data can be accomplished with no more than a simple calculator. It would be unusual, however, to find cost analysts doing regression analysis by hand—computers are much faster and less prone to error. Therefore, we focus on using a computer to perform regression analysis and on interpretation of the results.

This appendix should not be considered a substitute for a good statistics class or for self-taught statistics. More properly, this appendix should be seen as a motivator for studying statistics so that analysts can provide and managers can interpret top-quality cost estimates.

Assume that there are two potential cost drivers for the costs of the facilities maintenance department in Parkview Medical Centre: (1) number of patient-days and (2) total value of hospital room charges. Regression analysis helps to determine which activity is the better cost driver. The following table shows the past 12 months' cost and cost driver data for the facilities maintenance department.

MONTH	FACILITIES MAINTENANCE COST (Y)	NUMBER OF PATIENT-DAYS (X_1)	VALUE OF ROOM CHARGES (X_2)
January	$37,000	3,700	$2,983,000
February	23,000	1,600	3,535,000
March	37,000	4,100	3,766,000
April	47,000	4,900	3,646,000
May	33,000	3,300	3,767,000
June	39,000	4,400	3,780,000
July	32,000	3,500	3,823,000
August	33,000	4,000	3,152,000
September	17,000	1,200	2,625,000
October	18,000	1,300	2,315,000
November	22,000	1,800	2,347,000
December	20,000	1,600	2,917,000

Regression Analysis Procedures

Very good statistical software is available for both mainframe and personal computers. Most spreadsheet software available for personal computers offers basic regression analysis in the "data" analysis or "tools" commands. We illustrate elements of these spreadsheet commands because many readers will be familiar with other aspects of spreadsheet software from work experience and from academic applications—*not* because spreadsheets are the best software to use for regression analysis. In general, sophisticated regression analysis, beyond what spreadsheets can offer, is easier with more specialized statistical software.

Entering Data

First create a spreadsheet with the historical cost data in rows and columns. Each row should be data from one time period. Each column should be a cost category or a cost driver. For ease of analysis, all the potential cost drivers should be in adjacent columns. Each row and column should be complete (no missing data) and without errors.

Plotting Data

There are two main reasons why the first step in regression analysis should be to plot the cost against each of the potential cost drivers: (1) Plots may show obvious nonlinear trends in the data; if so, linear regression analysis may not be appropriate for the entire range of the data. (2) Plots help identify "outliers"—costs that are in error or are otherwise obviously inappropriate. There is little agreement about what to do with any outliers that are not the result of data entry errors or nonrepresentative cost and activity levels (e.g., periods of labour strikes, natural catastrophes). After all, if the data are not in error and are representative, the process that is being studied generated them. Even so, some analysts might recommend removing outliers from the data set. Leaving these outliers in the data makes regression analysis statistically less appealing, since data far removed from the rest of the data set will not fit the line well. The most conservative action is to leave all data in the data set unless uncorrectable errors are detected or unless the data are known to be nonrepresentative of the process.

Plotting with spreadsheets uses "graph" commands on the columns of cost and cost driver data. These graph commands typically offer many optional graph types (such as bar charts and pie charts), but the most useful plot for regression analysis is usually called the XY graph. This graph is the type shown earlier in this chapter—the X-axis is the cost driver, and the Y-axis is the cost. The XY graph should be displayed without lines drawn between the data points (called data symbols)—an optional command. (Consult your spreadsheet manual for details, because each spreadsheet program is different.)

Regression Output

The regression output is generated by commands that are unique to each software package but they identify the cost to be explained ("dependent variable") and the cost driver(s) ("independent variable[s]").

Producing regression output with spreadsheets is simple: just select the "regression" command, specify (or "highlight") the X-dimension (the cost driver) and specify the Y-dimension or "series" (the cost). Next specify a blank area on the spreadsheet where the output will be displayed, and select "go." Below is a regression analysis of facilities maintenance department costs using one of the two possible cost drivers, number of patient-days, X1. Note that this output can be modified somewhat by the analyst, and the values in the output can be used elsewhere in the spreadsheet.

FACILITIES MAINTENANCE DEPARTMENT COST
EXPLAINED BY
NUMBER OF PATIENT-DAYS

REGRESSION OUTPUT:

Constant	$9,329
Standard Error of Y Estimate	$2,145.875
R-Squared	0.9546625
No. of Observations	12
Degrees of Freedom	10
X Coefficient(s)	$6.9506726
Standard Error of Coefficient	0.478994

Interpreting Regression Output

The fixed cost measure is labelled "Constant" or "Intercept" and is $9,329 per month. The variable cost measure is labelled "X Coefficient(s)" (or something similar in other spreadsheets) and is $6.9506726 per patient-day. The linear cost function (after rounding) is:

$$Y = \$9,329 \text{ per month} + \$6.951 \times \text{(patient-days)}$$

Typically, the computer output gives a number of statistical measures that indicate how well each cost driver explains the cost and how reliable the cost predictions are likely to be. A full explanation of the output is beyond the scope of this text. One of the most important statistics, the coefficient of determination or R^2 (or R-squared), is very important to assessing the goodness of fit of the cost function to the actual cost data.

What the visual fit method tried to do with eyesight, regression analysis has accomplished more reliably. In general, the better a cost driver is at explaining a cost, the closer the data points will lie to the line, and the higher the R^2, which varies between 0 and 1. An R^2 of 0 would mean that the cost driver does not explain the cost at all, while an R^2 of 1 means that the cost driver explains the cost perfectly. The R^2 of the relationship measured with number of patient-days as the cost driver is 0.955, which is quite high. This value indicates that number of patient-days explains facilities maintenance department cost extremely well, and can be interpreted as meaning that number of patient-days explains 95.5 percent of the past fluctuation in facilities maintenance department cost.

In contrast, performing a regression analysis on the relationship between facilities maintenance department cost and value of hospital room charges produces the following results:

FACILITIES MAINTENANCE DEPARTMENT COST EXPLAINED BY VALUE OF HOSPITAL ROOM CHARGES

REGRESSION OUTPUT:

Constant	$ – 8,627.01
Standard Error of Y Estimate	$ 7,045.371
R-Squared	0.511284
No. of Observations	12
Degrees of Freedom	10
X Coefficient(s)	0.011939
Standard Error of Coefficient	0.003691

The R^2 value, 0.511, indicates that the cost function using value of hospital room charges does not fit facilities maintenance department cost as well as the cost function using number of patient-days.

To fully use the information generated by regression analysis, an analyst must understand the meaning of the statistics and must be able to determine whether the statistical assumptions of regression are satisfied by the cost data. Indeed, one of the major reasons why cost analysts study statistics is to better understand the assumptions of regression analysis. With this understanding, analysts can provide their organizations with top-quality estimates of cost behaviour.

SUMMARY PROBLEM FOR YOUR REVIEW

Problem One

Contell, Inc. makes computer peripherals (disk drives, tape drives, and printers). Until recently, production scheduling and control (PSC) costs were predicted to vary in proportion to labour costs according to the following cost function:

$$\text{PSC costs, } Y = 2 \times (\text{labour cost}) \text{ (or 200 percent of labour)}$$

Because PSC costs have been growing at the same time that labour cost has been shrinking, Contell is concerned that its cost estimates are neither plausible nor reliable. Contell's controller has just completed activity analysis to determine the most appropriate drivers of PSC costs. She obtained two cost functions using different cost drivers:

$$Y = 2 \times (\text{labour cost})$$
$$R^2 = 0.233$$

and

$$Y = \$10,000/\text{month} + 11 \times (\text{number of components used})$$
$$R^2 = 0.782$$

1. What would be good tests of which cost function better predicts PSC costs?
2. During a subsequent month, labour costs were $12,000 and 2,000 product components were used. Actual PSC costs were $31,460. Using each of the above cost functions, prepare reports that show predicted and actual PSC costs and the difference or variance between the two.
3. What is the meaning and importance of each cost variance?

Solution

1. A statistical test of which function better explains past PSC costs compares the R^2 of each function. The second function, using Number of Components Used, has a considerably higher R^2, so it better explains the past PSC costs. If the environment is essentially unchanged in the future, the second function will probably predict future PSC costs better than the first, too.

   A useful predictive test would be to compare the cost predictions of each cost function with actual costs for several months that were not used to measure the cost functions. The function that more closely predicted actual costs is probably the more reliable function.

2. Note that more actual cost data would be desirable for a better test, but the procedure would be the same.

   PSC cost predicted on the basis of:

	predicted cost	actual cost	variance
labour cost	2($12,000) = $24,000	$31,460	$7,460 underestimate
components	$10,000 + $11(2,000) = $32,000	$31,460	$540 overestimate

3. The cost function that relies on labour cost underestimated PSC cost by $7,460. The cost function that uses number of components closely predicted actual PSC costs (off by $540). Planning and control decisions would have been based on more accurate information using this prediction than using the labour cost-based prediction. An issue is whether the benefits of collecting data on the number of components used exceed the added cost of so doing.

ACCOUNTING VOCABULARY

account analysis *p. 99*
activity analysis *p. 96*
capacity costs *p. 92*
coefficient of determination *p. 104*
committed fixed costs *p. 92*
cost function *p. 95*
discretionary fixed costs *p. 92*
engineering analysis *p. 98*
high-low method *p. 101*

least squares regression *p. 104*
linear-cost behaviour *p. 87*
measuring cost behaviour
   (cost measurement) *p. 94*
mixed costs *p. 89*
regression analysis *p. 104*
step costs *p. 88*
visual fit method *p. 103*

ASSIGNMENT MATERIAL

QUESTIONS

Q3-1 What is a cost driver? Give three examples of costs and their possible cost drivers.

Q3-2 What is the "relevant range?" Why is it important?

Q3-3 Explain linear-cost behaviour.

Q3-4 "Variable costs should fluctuate directly in proportion to sales." Do you agree? Explain.

Q3-5 Why are fixed costs also called capacity costs?

Q3-6 "Step costs can be fixed or variable depending on your perspective." Explain.

Q3-7 Explain how mixed costs are related to both fixed and variable costs.

Q3-8 What are the benefits of using "cost functions" to describe cost behaviour?

Q3-9 How do management's product and service choices affect cost behaviour?

Q3-10 How do committed fixed costs differ from discretionary fixed costs?

Q3-11 Why are committed fixed costs the most difficult to change of the fixed costs?

Q3-12 What are the primary determinants of the level of committed costs? Discretionary costs?

Q3-13 "Planning is far more important than day-to-day control of discretionary costs." Do you agree? Explain.

Q3-14 How can a company's choice of technology affect its costs?

Q3-15 Explain the use of incentives to control cost.

Q3-16 Describe the methods for measuring cost functions using past cost data.

Q3-17 Explain "plausibility" and "reliability" of cost functions. Which is preferred? Explain.

Q3-18 What is activity analysis?

Q3-19 What is engineering analysis? Account analysis?

Q3-20 How could account analysis be combined with engineering analysis?

Q3-21 Explain the strengths and weaknesses of the high-low method and the visual fit method.

Q3-22 Why is regression analysis usually preferred to the high-low method?

Q3-23 "You never know how good your fixed and variable cost measures are if you use account analysis or if you visually fit a line on a data plot. That's why I like least squares regression analysis." Explain.

Q3-24 At a conference, a consultant stated, "Before you can control, you must measure." An executive complained, "Why bother to measure when work rules and guaranteed employment provisions in labour contracts prevent discharging workers, using part-time employees, and using overtime." Evaluate these comments. Summarize your personal attitudes toward the usefulness of engineering analysis.

PROBLEMS

P3-1   VARIOUS COST-BEHAVIOUR PATTERNS.   In practice, there is often a tendency to simplify approximations of cost behaviour patterns, even though the "true" underlying behaviour is not simple. Choose from the accompanying graphs A through H (shown below) the one that matches the numbered items. Indicate by letter which graph best fits each of the situations described. Next to each number-letter pair, identify a likely cost driver for that cost.

   The vertical axes of the graphs represent total dollars of costs incurred, and the horizontal axes represent levels of cost driver activity *during a particular time period*. The graphs may be used more than once.

1. Availability of quantity discounts, where the cost per unit falls as each price break is reached.
2. Price of an increasingly scarce raw material as the quantity used increases.
3. Guaranteed annual wage plan, whereby workers get paid for 40 hours of work per week even at zero or low levels of production that require working only a few hours weekly.
4. Water bill, which entails a flat fee for the first 10,000 litres used and then an increasing unit cost for every additional 10,000 litres used.

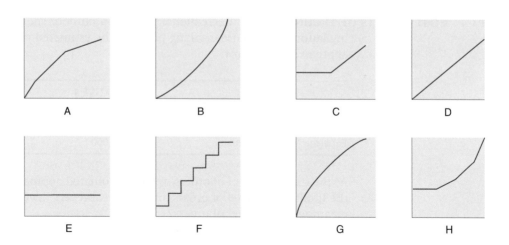

5. Cost of machining labour that tends to decrease as workers gain experience.
6. Amortization of office equipment.
7. Cost of sheet steel for a manufacturer of farm implements.
8. Salaries of supervisors, where one supervisor is added for every 12 phone solicitors.
9. Natural gas bill consisting of a fixed component, plus a constant variable cost per thousand cubic metres after a specified number of cubic metres are used.

P3-2 PREDICTING COSTS. Given the following cost behaviours and expected levels of cost driver activity, predict total costs:

1. Fuel costs of driving vehicles, $.20 per kilometre driven; at 15,000 kilometres per month.
2. Equipment rental cost, $6,000 per piece of equipment per month; at seven pieces for three months.
3. Ambulance personnel cost for a soccer tournament, $1,100 for each 250 tournament participants; the tournament is expecting 2,400 participants.
4. Purchasing department cost, $7,500 per month plus $4 per material order processed; at 4,000 orders in one month.

P3-3 IDENTIFYING DISCRETIONARY AND COMMITTED FIXED COSTS. Identify and compute total monthly discretionary and total committed fixed costs from the following list prepared by the accounting supervisor for Nicholas Inc.:

Advertising	$20,000
Amortization	47,000
Company health insurance	15,000
Management salaries	85,000
Payment on long-term debt	50,000
Property tax	32,000
Grounds maintenance	9,000
Office remodelling	21,000
Research and development	36,000

P3-4 COST EFFECTS OF TECHNOLOGY. Recreational Sports, an outdoor sports retailer, is considering automating its order-taking process. The estimated costs of two alternative approaches are below:

	ALTERNATIVE 1	ALTERNATIVE 2
Annual Fixed Cost	$200,000	$400,000
Variable Cost per Order	$8.00	$4.00
Expected Number of Orders	70,000	70,000

At the expected level of orders, which automated approach is preferred? What is the indifference level of orders, or the "break-even" level of orders? What is the meaning of this level of orders?

P3-5   MIXED-COST, CHOOSING COST DRIVERS, HIGH-LOW AND VISUAL FIT METHODS.   Wheatown Implement Company produces farm implements for various large vehicles used for farming. Wheatown is in the process of measuring its manufacturing costs and is particularly interested in the costs of the manufacturing maintenance activity since maintenance is a significant mixed cost. Activity analysis indicates that maintenance activity consists primarily of maintenance labour setting up machines using certain supplies. A setup consists of preparing the necessary machines for a particular production run of a product. During setup, machines must still be running, which consumes energy. Thus, the costs associated with maintenance include labour, supplies, and energy. Unfortunately, Wheatown's cost accounting system does not trace these costs to maintenance activity separately. Wheatown employs two full-time maintenance mechanics to perform maintenance. The annual salary of a maintenance mechanic is $25,000 and is considered a fixed cost. Two plausible cost drivers have been suggested—units produced and number of setups.

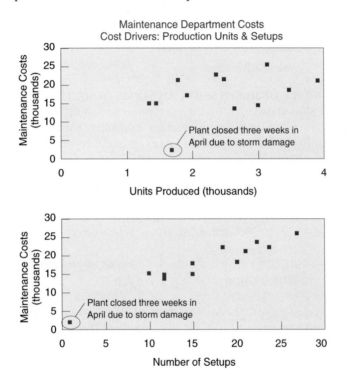

Data had been collected for the past 12 months and a plot made for the cost driver—units of production. The maintenance cost figures collected include estimates for labour, supplies, and energy. Toby Hatcher, controller at Wheatown, recently attended an activity-based costing seminar where she learned that some types of activities are performed each time a batch of goods is produced rather than each time a unit is produced. Based on this concept, she has gathered data on the number of setups performed over the past 12 months. The plot of monthly maintenance costs versus the two potential cost drivers is given below.

1. Find monthly fixed maintenance cost and the variable maintenance cost per driver unit using the visual-fit method based on each potential cost driver. Explain how you treated the April data.

2. Find the monthly fixed maintenance cost and the variable maintenance cost per driver unit using the high-low method based on each potential cost driver.

3. Which cost driver best meets the criteria for choosing cost functions? Explain.

P3-6 ACCOUNT ANALYSIS. From the following costs of a recent month, compute the total cost function and total cost for the month. Genial Computers, Inc. is a company started by two university students to market and assemble personal computers to faculty and students. The company operates out of the garage of one of the student's homes.

• Phone	$ 50	fixed
• Utilities	260	25 percent attributable to the garage, 75 percent to the house
• Advertising	75	fixed
• Insurance	80	fixed
• Materials	7,500	variable, for five computers
• Labour	1,800	$1,300 fixed plus $500 for hourly help for assembling five computers

P3-7 ECONOMIC PLAUSIBILITY OF REGRESSION ANALYSIS RESULTS. The head of the Warehousing Division of the Lackton Co. was concerned about some cost-behaviour information given to her by the new assistant controller, who was hired because of his recent training in cost analysis. His first assignment was to apply regression analysis to various costs in the department. One of the results was presented as follows:

A regression on monthly data was run to explain building maintenance cost as a function of direct labour hours as the cost driver. The results are

$$Y = \$6,810 - \$.47 \times \text{direct labour hours}$$

I suggest that we use the building as intensively as possible to keep the maintenance costs down.

The department head was puzzled. How could increased use cause decreased maintenance cost? Explain this counter-intuitive result to the department head. What step(s) did the assistant controller probably omit in applying and interpreting the regression analysis?

P3-8 LINEAR COST FUNCTIONS. Let Y=total costs, X_1=production volume, and X_2=number of setups. Which of the following are linear cost functions? Which are mixed cost functions?

a. $Y = \$1,000$
b. $Y = \$8X_1$
c. $Y = \$5,00 + \$4X_1$
d. $Y = \$3,00 + \$6X_1 + \$30X^2$
e. $Y = \$9,000 + \$3X_1 \times \$2X_2$
f. $Y = \$8,000 + \$1.50X_1^2$

P3-9 HIGH-LOW METHOD. Southampton Foundry produced 45,000 tonnes in March at a cost of £1,100,000. In April, 35,000 tonnes were produced at a cost of £900,000. Using only these two data points, determine the cost function for Southampton.

P3-10 TYPES OF COST BEHAVIOUR   Identify the following planned costs as (a) purely variable costs, (b) discretionary fixed costs, (c) committed fixed costs, (d) mixed costs, or (e) step costs. For purely variable costs and mixed costs, indicate the most likely cost driver.

1. Total repairs and maintenance of a school building.
2. Sales commission based on revenue dollars. Payments to be made to advertising salespersons employed by a radio station.
3. Jet fuel costs of Air Canada.
4. Total costs of renting trucks by the city of Vancouver. Charge is a lump sum of $300 per month plus $.20 per kilometre.
5. Straight-line amortization on desks in the office of an attorney.
6. Advertising costs, a lump sum planned by ABC, Inc.
7. Rental payment by the federal government on a five-year lease for office space in a private office building.
8. Advertising allowance granted to wholesalers by Pepsi Bottling on a per-case basis.
9. Compensation of lawyers employed internally by Microsoft.
10. Crew supervisor in a Lands' End, Inc., mail-order house. A new supervisor is added for every 12 workers employed.
11. Public relations employee compensation to be paid by Imperial Oil.

P3-11 ACTIVITY ANALYSIS.   Evergreen Signs makes customized wooden signs for businesses and residences. These signs are made of wood, which the owner glues and carves by hand or with power tools. After carving the signs, he paints them or applies a natural finish. He has a good sense of his labour and materials cost behaviour, but he is concerned that he does not have good measures of other support costs. Currently, he predicts support costs to be 60 percent of the cost of materials. close investigation of the business reveals that $40 times the number of power tool operations is more plausible and reliable support cost relationship.

Consider estimated support costs of the following two signs that Evergreen Signs is making:

	SIGN A	SIGN B
Material cost	$300	$150
Number of power tool operations	3	6
Support cost	?	?

Required:

1. Prepare a report showing the support costs of both signs using each cost driver and showing the differences between the two.
2. What advice would you give Evergreen Signs about predicting support costs?

P3-12 ACTIVITY ANALYSIS.   NewWave Technology, a manufacturer of printed circuit boards, has always costed its circuit boards with a 100 percent "mark-up" over its material costs to cover its manufacturing support costs (which include labour). An activity analysis suggests that support costs are driven primarily by the number of manual operations performed on each board, estimated at $4 per manual operation. Compute the estimated support costs of two typical circuit boards below using the traditional mark-up and the activity analysis results:

	BOARD Z15	BOARD Q52
Material cost	$30	$55
Manual operations	16	7

Why are the cost estimates different?

P3-13 **DIVISION OF MIXED COSTS INTO VARIABLE AND FIXED COMPONENTS.** The president and the controller of Monterrey Transformer Company (Mexico) have agreed that refinement of the company's cost measurements will aid planning and control decisions. They have asked you to measure the function for mixed-cost behaviour of repairs and maintenance from the following sparse data. Currency is the Mexican peso (P).

MONTHLY ACTIVITY IN MACHINE HOURS	MONTLY REPAIR AND MAINTENANCE COST
8,000	P190,000,000
12,000	P260,000,000

P3-14 **CONTROLLING RISK, CAPACITY DECISIONS, TECHNOLOGY DECISIONS.** Consider the discussion of Ford Motor on page 92 of the text. Ford had been outsourcing production to Mazda and using overtime for as much as 20 percent of production—Ford's plants and assembly lines were running at 100 percent of capacity and demand was sufficient for an additional 20 percent. Ford had considered building new highly automated assembly lines and plants to earn more profits since overtime premiums and outsourcing were costly. However, the investment in high technology and capacity expansion was rejected.

Assume that all material and labour costs are variable with respect to the level of production and that all overhead costs are fixed. Consider one of Ford's plants that makes Probes. The cost to convert the plant to use fully automated assembly lines is $20 million. The resulting labour costs would be significantly reduced. The costs, in millions of dollars, of the build option and the outsource/overtime option are given in the table below.

	BUILD OPTION		
Percent of Capacity	60%	100%	120%
Material Costs	$18	$30	$36
Labour Costs	6	10	12
Overhead Costs	40	40	40
Total Costs	$64	$80	$88

	OUTSOURCE/OVERTIME OPTION		
Percent of Capacity	60%	100%	120%
Material Costs	$18	$30	$ 36
Labour Costs	18	30	44
Overhead Costs	20	20	20
Total Costs	$56	$80	$100

1. Prepare a line-graph showing total costs for the two options—build new assembly lines, and continue to use overtime and outsource production of Probes. Give an explanation of the cost behaviour of the two options.
2. Which option enables Ford management to control risk better? Explain. Assess the cost/benefit associated with each option.
3. A solid understanding of cost behaviour is an important prerequisite to effective managerial control of costs. Suppose you are an executive at Ford and currently the production (and sales) level is approaching the 100 percent-level of capacity and the economy is expected to remain strong for at least one year. While sales and profits are good now, you are aware of the cyclical nature of the automobile business. Would you recommend committing Ford to building automated assembly lines in order to service potential near term increases in demand or would you recommend against building, looking to the likely future downturn in business? Discuss your reasoning.

P3-15 **ACTIVITY ANALYSIS.** Violet Blossom Technology develops and markets computer software for the agriculture industry. Since support costs comprise a large portion of the cost of software development, the director of cost operations of Violet Blossom, Shirley Donko, is especially concerned with understanding the effects of support cost behaviour. Donko has completed a preliminary activity analysis of one of its primary software products: Ferti Mix (software to manage fertilizer mixing). This product is a software "template" that is customized for specific customers, who are charged for the basic product plus customizing costs. The activity analysis is based on the number of customized lines of Ferti Mix code. Currently, support cost estimates are based on a fixed rate of 50 percent of the basic cost. Data are shown below for two recent customers:

	CUSTOMER	
	WEST ACRES PLANT	BEAUTIFUL BLOOM
Basic cost of Ferti Mix	$12,000	$12,000
Lines of customized code	490	180
Estimated cost per line of customized code	$ 23	$ 23

1. Compute the support cost of customizing Ferti Mix for each customer using each cost estimating approach.
2. If the activity analysis is reliable, what are the pros and cons of adopting it for all of Violet Blossom's software products?

P3-16 **SEPARATION OF DRUG-TESTING LABORATORY MIXED COSTS INTO VARIABLE AND FIXED COMPONENTS.** A staff meeting has been called at Sports Lab, a drug-testing facility retained by several professional and university sport leagues and associations. The chief of testing, Dr. Mueller has demanded an across-the-board increase in prices for a particular test due to the increased testing and precision that is now required.

The administrator of the laboratory has asked you to measure the mixed-cost behaviour of this particular testing department and to prepare a short report that she can present to Dr. Mueller. Consider the limited data below:

	AVERAGE TEST PROCEDURES PER MONTH	AVERAGE MONTHLY COST OF TEST PROCEDURES
Monthly averages, 2000	500	$ 60,000
Monthly averages, 2001	600	70,000
Monthly averages, 2002	700	144,000

P3-17 **HIGH-LOW, REGRESSION ANALYSIS.** On November 15, 2001, Sandra Cook, a newly hired cost analyst at Demgren Company, was asked to predict overhead costs for the company's operations in 2002, when 500 units are expected to be produced. She collected the following quarterly data:

QUARTER	PRODUCTION IN UNITS	OVERHEAD COSTS
1/1998	76	$ 721
2/1998	79	715
3/1998	72	655
4/1998	136	1,131
1/1999	125	1,001
2/1999	128	1,111
3/1999	125	1,119
4/1999	133	$1,042
1/2000	124	997
2/2000	129	1,066
3/2000	115	996
4/2000	84	957
1/2001	84	835
2/2001	122	1,050
3/2001	90	991

1. Using the high-low method to estimate costs, prepare a prediction of overhead costs for 2002.
2. Sandra ran a regression analysis using the data she collected. The result was:

$$Y = \$337 + \$5.75X$$

Using this cost function, predict costs for 2002.
3. Which prediction do you prefer? Why?

P3-18 **INTERPRETATION OF REGRESSION ANALYSES.** Elliott Bay Tarp and Tent (EBTT) Company has difficulty controlling its use of supplies. The company has traditionally regarded supplies as a purely variable cost. But nearly every time production was above average, EBTT spent less than predicted for supplies; when production was below average, EBTT spent more than predicted. This pattern suggested to Kerry Kane, the new controller, that part of the supplies cost was probably not related to production volume, or was fixed.

She decided to use regression analysis to explore this issue. After consulting with production personnel, she considered two cost drivers for supplies cost: (1) number of tents and tarps produced, and (2) square metres of material used. She obtained the following results based on monthly data:

	COST DRIVER	
	NUMBER OF TENTS AND TARPS	SQUARE METRES OF MATERIAL USED
Constant	2,200	1,900
Variable Coefficient	.033	.072
R^2	.220	.686

1. Which is the preferred cost function? Explain.
2. What percentage of supplies cost depends on square metres of materials? Do fluctuations in supplies cost depend on anything other than square metres of materials? What proportion of the fluctuations are not explained by square metres of materials?

P3-19 STEP COSTS. Atlantic jail requires a staff of at least one guard for every four prisoners. The jail will hold 48 prisoners. Atlantic has a beach that attracts numerous tourists and transients in the spring and summer. However, the region is rather sedate in the fall and winter. The fall/winter population of the jail is generally between 12 and 16 prisoners. The numbers in the spring and summer can fluctuate from 12 to 48, depending on the weather, among other factors (including phases of the moon, according to some longtime residents).

Atlantic has four permanent guards hired on a year-round basis at an annual salary of $36,000 each. When additional guards are needed, they are hired on a weekly basis at a rate of $600 per week. (For simplicity, assume that each month has exactly four weeks.)

1. Prepare a graph with the weekly planned cost of jail guards on the vertical axis and the number of prisoners on the horizontal axis.
2. What would be the amount planned for jail guards for the month of January? Would this be a fixed cost or a variable cost?
3. Suppose the jail population of each of the four weeks in July was 25, 38, 26, and 43, respectively. The actual amount paid for jail guards in June was $19,800. Prepare a report comparing the actual amount paid for jail guards with the amount that would be expected with efficient scheduling and hiring.
4. Suppose Atlantic treated jail-guard salaries for nonpermanent guards as a variable expense of $150 per week per prisoner. This variable cost was applied to the number of prisoners in excess of 16. Therefore, the weekly cost function was

Weekly jail-guard cost = $3,000 + $150 × (total prisoners − 16)

Explain how this cost function was determined.
5. Prepare a report similar to that in step three above except that the cost function in step four should be used to calculate the expected amount of jail-guard salaries. Which report, this one or the one in step three, is more accurate? Is accuracy the only concern?

P3-20 REGRESSION ANALYSIS. See Appendix 3. Liao, Inc., a manufacturer of fine china and stoneware, is troubled by fluctuations in productivity and wants to compute how much manufacturing support costs are related to the various sizes of batches of output. The following data show the results of a random sample of 10 batches of one pattern of stoneware:

SAMPLE	BATCH SIZE, X	SUPPORT COSTS, Y
1	15	$180
2	12	140
3	20	230
4	17	190
5	12	160
6	25	300
7	22	270
8	9	110
9	18	240
10	30	320

1. Plot support costs versus batch size.
2. Using regression analysis, measure the cost function of support costs and batch size.
3. Predict the support costs for a batch size of 30.
4. Using the high-low method, repeat step two and three above. Should the manager use the high-low method or the regression method? Explain.

P3-21 **DIVISION OF MIXED-COSTS INTO VARIABLE AND FIXED COMPONENTS.** Martina Fernandez, the president of Fernandez Tool Co., has asked for information about the cost behaviour of manufacturing support costs. Specifically, she wants to know how much support cost is fixed and how much is variable. The following data are the only records available:

MONTH	MACHINE HOURS	SUPPORT COSTS
May	850	$ 9,000
June	1,400	12,500
July	1,000	7,900
August	1,250	11,000
September	1,750	13,500

1. Find the monthly fixed support cost and the variable support cost per machine hour by the high-low method.
2. A least squares regression analysis gave the following output:

Regression equation: Y = $1,500 + 6.80X

What recommendations would you give the president based on this analysis?

P3-22 **COLLABORATIVE LEARNING EXERCISE: COST BEHAVIOUR EXAMPLES.** Select about 10 students to participate in a "cost-behaviour bee." The game proceeds like a spelling bee—when a participant is unable to come up with a correct answer, he or she is eliminated from the game. The last one in the game is the winner.

The object of the game is to identify a type of cost that fits a particular cost-behaviour pattern. The first player rolls a die.[1] If a 1 or 6 comes up, the die passes

[1] Instead of rolling a die, players could draw one of the four cost categories out of a hat (or similar container) or from a deck of four 3x5 cards. This eliminates the chance element that can let some players proceed to a later round without having to give an example of a particular cost behaviour. However, the chance element can add to the enjoyment of the game.

to the next player (and the roller makes it to the next round). If a 2, 3, 4, or 5 comes up, the player has to identify one of the following types of costs:

If a 2 is rolled, identify a variable cost.
If a 3 is rolled, identify a fixed cost.
If a 4 is rolled, identify a mixed cost.
If a 5 is rolled, identify a step cost.

A scribe should label four columns on the board, one for each type of cost, and list the costs that are mentioned for each category. Once a particular cost has been used, it cannot be used again.

Each played has a time limit of 10 seconds to produce an example. (For a tougher game, make the time limit 5 seconds.) The instructor is the referee, judging if a particular example is acceptable. It is legitimate for the referee to ask a player to explain why he or she thinks the cost mentioned fits the category before making a judgment.

After each player has had a turn, a second round begins with the remaining players taking a turn in the same order as in the first round. The game continues through additional rounds until all but one player has failed to give an acceptable answer within the time limit. The remaining player is the winner.

CASES

C3-1 **GOVERNMENT HEALTH COST BEHAVIOUR.** Dr. Maxine Black, the chief administrator of a community mental health agency, is concerned about the dilemma of coping with reduced budgets next year and into the foreseeable future while facing increasing demand for services. In order to plan for reduced budgets, she must first identify where costs can be cut or reduced and still keep the agency functioning. Below are some data from the past year.

PROGRAM AREA	COSTS
Administration	
Salaries	
Administrator	$60,000
Assistant	30,000
Two secretaries	42,000
Supplies	35,000
Advertising and Promotion	9,000
Professional Meetings, Dues, and Literature	14,000
Purchased Services	
Accounting and Billing	15,000
Custodial and Maintenance	13,000
Security	12,000
Consulting	10,000
Community Mental Health Activities	
Salaries (Two social workers)	46,000
Transportation	10,000
Out-Patient Mental Health Treatment	
Salaries	
Psychiatrist	85,000
Two social workers	70,000

1. Identify which costs you feel are likely to be discretionary costs or committed costs.
2. One possibility is to eliminate all discretionary costs. How much would be saved? What do you think of this recommendation?
3. How would you advise Dr. Black to prepare for reduced budgets?

C3-2 ACTIVITY ANALYSIS. The costs of the Systems Support (SS) department (and other service departments) of Northwest Wood Products, have always been charged to the three business divisions (Forest Resources, Lumber Products, and Paper Products) based on the *number of employees* in each division. This measure is easy to obtain and update, and until recently none of the divisions has complained about the charges. The Paper Products division has recently automated many of its operations and has reduced the number of its employees. At the same time, however, in order to monitor its new process, Paper Products has increased its requests for various reports provided by the SS department. The other divisions have begun to complain that they are being charged more than their fair share of SS department costs. Based on activity analysis of possible cost drivers, cost analysts have suggested using the number of reports prepared as a means of charging for SS costs and have gathered the following information:

	FOREST MANAGEMENT	LUMBER PRODUCTS	PAPER PRODUCTS
2000 Number of Employees	762	457	502
2000 Number of Reports	410	445	377
2000 SS Costs: $300,000			
2001 Number of Employees	751	413	131
2001 Number of Reports	412	432	712
2001 SS Costs: $385,000			

Required:

1. Discuss the *plausibility* and probable *reliability* of each of the cost drivers—number of employees or number of reports.
2. What are the 2000 and 2001 SS costs per unit of cost driver for each division using each cost driver? Do the Forest Management and Lumber Products divisions have legitimate complaints? Explain.
3. What are the *incentives* that are implied by each cost driver?
4. Which cost driver should Northwest Wood Products use to charge its divisions for SS services? For other services? Why?

C3-3 CHOICE OF COST DRIVER. See Appendix 3. Richard Ellis, the director of cost operations of Micro Devices Company, wishes to develop the most accurate cost function to explain and predict support costs in the company's printed circuit board assembly operation. Mr. Ellis has read about activity-based costing and is concerned that the cost function that he currently uses—based on direct labour costs—is not accurate enough for proper planning and control of support costs. Mr. Ellis directed one of his financial analysts to obtain a random sample of 25 weeks of support costs and three possible cost drivers in the circuit board assembly department: direct labour cost, number of boards assembled, average cycle time of boards assembled. Average cycle time is the average time between start and certified completion after quality testing of boards assembled during a week. Much of the effort in this assembly operation is devoted to testing for quality and reworking defective boards, all of which increase the average cycle time in any period. Therefore, Mr. Ellis believes that average cycle time will be the best support cost driver. Mr. Ellis wants his analyst to use regression analysis to demonstrate which cost driver best explains support costs.

SAMPLE NUMBER	CIRCUIT BOARD ASSEMBLY SUPPORT COSTS	DIRECT LABOUR HOURS	NUMBER OF BOARDS COMPLETED	AVERAGE CYCLE TIME (HOURS)
1	$66,402	7,619	2,983	186.44
2	56,943	7,678	2,830	139.14
3	60,337	7,816	2,413	151.13
4	50,096	7,659	2,221	138.39
5	64,241	7,646	2,701	158.63
6	60,846	7,765	2,656	148.71
7	43,119	7,685	2,495	105.85
8	63,412	7,962	2,128	174.02
9	59,283	7,793	2,127	155.30
10	60,070	7,732	2,127	162.20
11	53,345	7,771	2,338	142.97
12	65,027	7,842	2,685	176.08
13	58,220	7,940	2,602	150.19
14	65,406	7,750	2,029	194.06
15	35,268	7,954	2,136	100.51
16	46,394	7,768	2,046	137.47
17	71,877	7,764	2,786	197.44
18	61,903	7,635	2,822	164.69
19	50,009	7,849	2,178	141.95
20	49,327	7,869	2,244	123.37
21	44,703	7,576	2,195	128.25
22	45,582	7,557	2,370	106.16
23	43,818	7,569	2,016	131.41
24	62,122	7,672	2,515	154.88
25	52,403	7,653	2,942	140.07

Required:

1. Plot support costs versus each of the possible cost drivers.
2. Use regression analysis to measure cost functions using each of the cost drivers.
3. Interpret the economic meaning of the best cost function.
4. According to the criteria of plausibility and reliability, which is the best cost driver for support costs in the circuit board assembly department?

C3-4 **USE OF COST FUNCTIONS FOR PRICING.** Read the previous case. If you worked through this case, use your measured cost functions. If you did not work the previous problem, assume the following measured cost functions:

$$Y = \$9,000/wk + \$6 \times (\text{direct labour hours}); R^2 = .10$$
$$Y = \$20,000/wk + \$14 \times (\text{number of boards completed}); R^2 = .40$$
$$Y = \$5,000/wk + \$350 \times (\text{average cycle time}); R^2 = .80$$

1. Which of the above cost functions would you expect to be the most reliable for explaining and predicting support costs? Why?
2. Micro Devices prices its products by adding a percentage markup to its product costs. Product costs include assembly labour, components, and support costs. Using each of the cost functions, compute the circuit board portion of the support cost of an order that used the following resources:
   a. Effectively utilized the capacity of the assembly department for three weeks.
   b. Assembly labour hours: 20,000
   c. Number of boards 6,000 hours
   d. Average cycle time: 180
3. Which cost would you recommend that Micro Devices use? Why?
4. Assume that the market for this product is extremely cost-competitive. What do you think of Micro Devices' pricing method?

C3-5 IDENTIFYING RELEVANT DATA. Super Byte Company manufactures palm-sized, portable computers. Because these very small computers compete with larger portable computers that have more functions and flexibility, understanding and using cost behaviour is critical to Super Byte's profitability. Super Byte's controller, Kelly Hudsa, has kept meticulous files on various cost categories and possible cost drivers for most of the important functions and activities of Super Byte. Because most of the manufacturing at Super Byte is automated, labour cost is relatively fixed. Other support costs comprise most of Super Byte's costs. Below are partial data that Hudsa has collected on one of these support costs, logistics operations (materials purchasing, receiving, warehousing, and shipping), over the past 25 weeks.

WEEK	LOGISTICS COST	NUMBER OF ORDERS
1	$23,907	1,357
2	18,265	1,077
3	24,208	1,383
4	23,578	1,486
5	22,211	1,292
6	22,862	1,425
7	23,303	1,306
8	24,507	1,373
9	17,878	1,031
10	18,306	1,020
11	20,807	1,097
12	19,707	1,069
13	23,020	1,444
14	20,407	733
15	20,370	413
16	20,678	633
17	21,145	711
18	20,775	228
19	20,532	488
20	20,659	655
21	20,430	722
22	20,713	373
23	20,256	391
24	21,196	734
25	20,406	256

Required:

1. Plot logistics cost versus number of orders. What cost behaviour is evident? What do you think happened in week 14?

2. What is your recommendation to Kelly Hudsa regarding the relevance of the past 25 weeks of logistics cost and number of orders data for measuring logistics cost behaviour?

3. Hudsa remarks that one of the improvements that Super Byte has made in the past several months was to negotiate just-in-time deliveries from its suppliers. This was made possible by substituting an automated ordering system for the previous manual (labour-intensive) system. Though fixed costs increased, the variable cost of placing an order was expected to drop greatly. Do the data support this expectation? Do you believe that the change to the automated ordering system was justified? Why or why not?

C3-6 REGRESSION ANALYSIS (CGAC). Berengar Ltd. is a small manufacturing company that produces a variety of products using a number of different processes in different-sized job lots. For example, some products will be ordered in lots of 10 or less, while others are produced in batches of up to 1,000 units.

Berengar will modify products as required by customer order and, thus, there is little product standardization. Despite the high level of product differentiation, Berengar has, up until now, used a single factory-wide overhead rate based upon direct labour hours. The company president, J.P. Blomer, believes that this over-simplified way of applying overhead has led to the loss of several contracts for long production runs (that is, large job lots) of two of Berengar's most popular products.

Blomer has consulted with the operations staff in the machining department to see whether they have any suggestions for alternate overhead bases (other than direct labour hours for their department). Because of the recent addition to five numerically controlled machines, the supervisor of scheduling has noticed that direct labour hours in the department have declined considerably. The chief production engineer for machining believes that, with the new machine environment, production overhead probably varies more with machine hours per batch and set-up time than it does with the current overhead application base, direct labour hours.

Blomer asked the controller to run four regressions to assist in predicting overhead cost in the machining department. The four regressions were based on:

1. direct labour hours
2. machine hours
3. set-up hours
4. machine hours and set-up hours

One problem that the controller had to deal with was that approximately 35 percent of departmental overhead consisted of various lump-sum monthly charges for central services such as personnel and power. The controller decided that these charges were justifiably an expense of running the machining department and left them in for the regression analyses.

The results of the regressions (using the most recent 24 weeks of data shown below) are given in Exhibit 3A–1.

BERENGAR LTD.
MACHINE DEPARTMENT
DATA FOR REGRESSION ANALYSIS
MOST RECENT 24 WEEKS

WEEK	OVERHEAD COST (OH COST)	DIRECT LABOUR HOURS (DL HRS)	MACHINE HOURS (MACH HRS)	SET-UP HOURS (SET-UP HRS)
1	$72,892	2,036	379	98
2	76,451	2,125	385	101
3	75,930	2,012	378	110
4	78,591	1,900	390	112
5	77,870	1,934	401	108
6	75,420	2,095	376	110
7	73,529	1,966	365	95
8	78,210	1,924	387	103
9	85,620	1,865	464	130
10	84,322	1,912	451	110
11	89,621	1,901	496	125
12	79,739	1,864	401	101
13	81,221	1,850	425	95
14	85,130	1,812	456	102
15	83,550	1,800	446	110
16	79,985	1,712	398	114
17	87,870	1,718	485	135
18	90,565	1,741	502	129
19	89,032	1,622	491	142
20	87,979	1,639	487	110
21	86,646	1,641	479	124
22	90,772	1,628	516	99
23	85,542	1,598	472	125
24	90,159	1,597	508	160

Required:

a. From the results of the regression output of overhead cost with machine hours and set-up hours (Exhibit 3A-1, regression 4), identify the following:
i) the independent variables
ii) the marginal cost of an additional set-up hour
iii) the regression equation

b. Using the information provided in Exhibit 3A-1, evaluate the results of the regressions, based upon the coefficient of determination (R^2).

Regression 1
Regression Output: Overhead cost with direct labour hours

Constant		135479.2
Std Err of Y Est		3523.623
R-Squared		0.642200
No. of Observations		24
Degrees of Freedom		22
X Coefficient(s)	−28.8174	
Std Err of Coef.	4.585940	
t-statistic	−6.28387	

Regression 2

Regression Output: Overhead cost with machine hours

Constant		33310.56
Std Err of Y Est		1010.593
R-Squared		0.970568
No. of Observations		24
Degrees of Freedom		22
X Coefficient(s)	112.6582	
Std Err of Coef.	4.182588	
t-statistic	26.93505	

Regression 3

Regression Output: Overhead cost with set-up hours

Constant		56802.56
Std Err of Y Est		4524.324
R-Squared		0.410114
No. of Observations		24
Degrees of Freedom		22
X Coefficient(s)	226.8502	
Std Err of Coef.	58.00416	
t-statistic	3.910930	

Regression 4

Regression Output: Overhead cost with machine hours and set-up hours

Constant		32898.746
Std Err of Y Est		1453.4722
R-Squared		0.9391202
No. of Observations		24
Degrees of Freedom		22
X Coefficient(s)-Machine Hours	110.6029	
Std Err of Coef.	5.482857	
t-statistic	20.17249	
X Coefficient(s)-Set up hours	10.0621	
Std Err of Coef.	16.984198	
t-statistic	0.592	

4

Cost Management Systems

After studying this chapter, you will be able to

1. Define the following terms and explain how they are related: cost, cost objective, cost accumulation, and cost allocation.

2. Distinguish between direct and indirect costs.

3. Define and identify examples of each of the three major categories of manufacturing costs.

4. Differentiate between product costs and period costs, and identify examples of each.

5. Explain how the financial statements of merchandisers and manufacturers differ because of the types of goods they sell.

6. Compare income statements of a manufacturing company in both the absorption format and the contribution format.

7. Identify the basic feature that distinguishes the variable costing approach from the absorption costing approach.

8. Construct an income statement using the variable costing approach.

9. Construct an income statement using the absorption costing approach.

10. Explain why a company might prefer to use a variable costing approach.

Managers rely on accountants to measure the cost of the goods or services the company produces. Consider the case of Mark Controls Company, a valve manufacturer that relies on strict financial controls to protect its profit margins. The company had been relying on broad averages of product costs to make manufacturing and pricing decisions. According to one report: "The company set up a computerized costing system that calculated the precise cost and profit margin for each of the 15,000 products the company sold. Since then, about 15 percent of those products have been dropped from the company's line because they were insufficiently profitable." Similarly, Sears just recently installed a cost system capable of judging the profitability (or unprofitability) of the products it sells. Even non-profit organizations such as hospitals and universities are finding it necessary to develop accurate costs for the different types of services they provide.

All kinds of organizations—manufacturing firms, service companies, and non-profit organizations—need some form of **cost accounting**, that part of the accounting system that measures costs for the purposes of management decision making and financial reporting. Because it is the most general case, embracing production, marketing, and general administration functions, we will focus on cost accounting in a manufacturing setting. Bear in mind, though, that you can apply this framework to any organization.

In this chapter we will introduce the concepts of cost and management accounting appropriate to any manufacturing company. Manufacturing companies are in the midst of great changes. The need to compete in global markets has changed the types of information useful to managers. At the same time technology has changed both the manufacturing processes and information processing capabilities. While the basic concepts of management accounting have not changed, their *application* is significantly different in many companies than it was a decade ago. Management accountants today must be able to develop systems to support globally oriented, technology-intensive companies, often called *world-class manufacturing companies*.

Cost Accounting. That part of the accounting system that measures costs for the purpose of management decision making and financial reporting.

CLASSIFICATION OF COSTS

Costs may be classified in many ways—far too many to be covered in a single chapter. We have already seen costs classified by their behaviour—fixed, variable, step, and mixed. This section concentrates on how costs are accumulated and classified.

Cost Objectives

Cost. A sacrifice or giving up of resources for a particular purpose, frequently measured by the monetary units that must be paid for goods and services.

A **cost** may be defined as a sacrifice or giving up of resources for a particular purpose. Costs are frequently measured by the monetary units (for example, dollars or francs) that must be paid for goods and services. Costs are initially recorded in elementary form (for example, repairs or advertising). These costs are then grouped in different ways to help managers make decisions, such as evaluating subordinates and subunits of the organization, expanding or deleting products or territories, and replacing equipment.

Cost Objective (Cost Object). Any activity for which a separate measurement of costs is desired.

To aid decisions, managers want the cost of something. This "something" is called a **cost objective** or **cost object**, defined as any activity for which a separate measurement of costs is desired. Examples of cost objects include departments, products, territories, kilometres driven, patients seen, students taught, and tax bills sent. Costs are then assigned or allocated to one or more cost objectives.

Define the following
terms and explain
how they are related:
cost, cost objective,
cost accumulation,
and cost allocation.

Exhibit 4-1 illustrates these processes. In it, the costs of all raw materials are *accumulated*. They are then *charged* to the departments that use them and further to the specific items made by these departments. The total raw materials cost of a particular product is the sum of the raw materials costs charged to it in the various departments.

To make intelligent decisions, managers want reliable measurements. When A&P ran into profit difficulties, it began retrenching by closing many stores. Management's lack of adequate cost information about individual store operations made the closing program a hit-or-miss affair. A news story reported:

> Because of the absence of detailed profit-and-loss statements, and a cost-allocation system that did not reflect true costs, A&P's strategists could not be sure whether an individual store was really unprofitable. For example, distribution costs were shared equally among all the stores in a marketing area without regard to such factors as a store's distance from the warehouse. Says one close observer of the company: "When they wanted to close a store, they had to wing it. They could not make rational decisions, because they did not have a fact basis."

Direct and Indirect Costs

Direct Costs. Costs that can be identified specifically and exclusively with a given cost objective in an economically feasible way.

Indirect Costs. Costs that cannot be identified specifically and exclusively with a given cost objective in an economically feasible way.

A major feature of costs in both manufacturing and nonmanufacturing activities is whether the costs have a direct or an indirect relationship to a particular cost objective. **Direct costs** can be identified specifically and exclusively with a given cost objective in an economically feasible way. Thus, direct costs can be assigned specifically to a cost objective. **Indirect costs**, in contrast, cannot be identified specifically and exclusively with a given cost objective in an economically feasible way. Thus, indirect costs can only be charged to a cost objective by means of allocating the costs on some basis.

The use of terms for assigning costs or allocating costs to a cost objective tend to be interchangeable. However, students may find it helpful to think of direct costs being *assigned* to a cost objective and indirect costs being *allocated* to a cost objective. This distinction will become clearer as we proceed through the study of cost systems.

Whenever it is "economically feasible," managers prefer to classify costs as direct rather than indirect. In this way, managers have greater confidence in the reported costs of products and services. But, "economically feasible" means "cost effective" in the sense that managers do not want cost accounting to be too expensive in relation to expected benefits. For example, it may be economically feasible to trace the exact cost of steel and fabric (direct costs) to a specific lot of desk chairs, but it may be economically infeasible to trace the exact cost of rivets or thread (indirect costs) to the chairs.

Other factors also influence whether a cost is considered direct or indirect. The key is the particular cost objective. For example, consider a supervisor's salary in a maintenance department of a telephone company. If the cost objective is the department, the supervisor's salary is a direct cost. In contrast, if the cost objective is a service (the "product" of the company) such as a telephone call, the supervisor's salary is an indirect cost. In general, many more costs are direct when a department is the cost objective than when a service (a telephone call) or a physical product (a razor blade) is the cost objective.

EXHIBIT 4-1

Cost Accumulation and Assignment

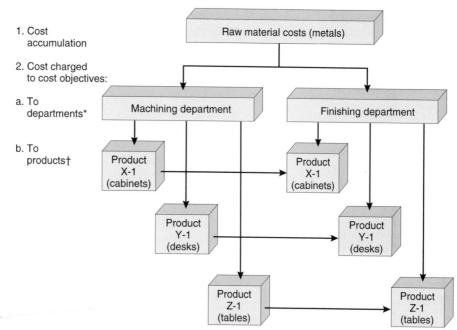

1. Cost accumulation

2. Cost charged to cost objectives:

a. To departments*

b. To products†

*Purpose: to evaluate performance of manufacturing departments.
†Purpose: to obtain costs of various products for valuing inventory, determining income, and judging product profitability.

Managers want to know both the costs of running departments and the costs of products and services; costs are inevitably charged to more than one cost objective. Thus, a particular cost may simultaneously be direct and indirect. As you have just seen, a supervisor's salary can be both direct (with respect to his or her department) and indirect (with respect to the department's individual products or services).

Categories of Manufacturing Costs

OBJECTIVE 3

Define and identify examples of the three major categories of manufacturing costs.

Any raw material, labour, or other input, used by an organization could, in theory, be identified as a direct or indirect cost, depending on the cost objective. In manufacturing, the transformation of materials into other goods through the use of labour and factory facilities products are frequently the cost objective. As a result, manufacturing costs are most often divided into three major categories: (1) direct materials, (2) direct labour, and (3) factory overhead.

Direct-Materials Costs. The acquisition costs of all materials that are physically identified as a part of manufactured goods and that may be traced to manufactured goods in an economically feasible way.

1. **Direct-materials costs** include the acquisition costs of all materials that are physically identified as a part of the manufactured goods and that may be traced to the manufactured goods in an economically feasible way. Examples are iron castings, lumber, aluminum sheets, and subassemblies. Direct materials often do not include minor items such as tacks or glue because the costs of tracing these items are greater than the possible benefits of having more precise product costs. Such items are usually called *supplies* or *indirect materials* and are classified as a part of the factory overhead described in this list.

2. **Direct-labour costs** include the wages of all labour that can be traced specifically and exclusively to the manufactured goods in an economically feasible way. Examples are the wages of machine operators and of assemblers. Much labour, such as that of janitors, fork-lift truck operators, plant guards, and storeroom clerks, is considered to be indirect labour because it is impossible or economically infeasible to trace such activity to specific products. Such indirect labour is generally classified as a part of factory overhead. In highly automated factories there may be no direct labour costs. Why? Because it may be economically infeasible to physically trace any labour cost directly to specific products.

3. **Factory overhead costs** include all costs other than direct material or direct labour that are associated with the manufacturing process. Other terms that are used to describe this category are **indirect manufacturing costs, factory burden,** and **manufacturing overhead**. Examples are power, supplies, indirect labour, supervisory salaries, property taxes, rent, insurance, and amortization.

In traditional accounting systems, all manufacturing overhead costs are considered to be indirect. However, computers have allowed modern systems to physically trace many overhead costs to products in an economically feasible manner. For example, meters wired to computers can monitor the electricity used to produce each product, and the costs of setting up a batch production run can be traced to the items produced in the run. In general, the more overhead costs that can be traced directly to products, the more complete and accurate the product cost.

Prime Costs, Conversion Costs, and Direct-Labour Category

Exhibit 4-2 shows that direct labour is sometimes combined with one of the other types of manufacturing costs. The combined categories are **prime costs**— direct labour plus direct materials—and **conversion costs**—direct labour plus factory overhead.

The twofold categorization—direct materials and conversion costs—has replaced the threefold categorization—direct materials, direct labour, and factory overhead, in many modern automated manufacturing companies. Why? Because direct labour is increasingly a small part of costs and not worth tracing directly to the products. In fact, some companies call their two categories direct materials and factory overhead and simply include direct labour costs in the factory overhead category.

Why so many different systems? As mentioned earlier, accountants and managers weigh the costs and benefits of additional categories when they design their cost accounting systems. Where the costs of any single category or item become relatively insignificant, separate tracking may no longer be desirable. For example, in highly automated factories, direct labour may be less than five percent of total manufacturing costs. In such cases, it may make economic sense to combine direct-labour costs with one of the other major cost categories. For example in a Canadian automotive parts manufacturer, automation on some lines eliminated the need for almost all of the direct labour.

EXHIBIT 4-2

Relationships of Key
Categories of
Manufacturing Costs for
Product-Costing
Purposes

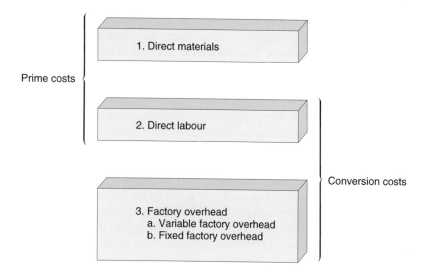

To recap, the three major categories for manufacturing product costs are direct material, direct labour, and factory overhead. However, some companies have only two categories: direct materials and conversion costs. As information technology improves, some companies may have four or more. For instance, a company might have direct materials, direct labour, other direct costs (such as specifically metered power), and factory overhead.

In addition to direct-materials, direct-labour, and factory-overhead costs, all manufacturing companies also incur selling and administrative costs. These costs are accumulated by departments such as research and development, advertising, and sales departments. As you will see later in this chapter, most firm's financial statements do not allocate these costs to the physical units produced. In short, these costs do not become a part of the inventory cost of the manufactured products. However, to aid in decisions, managers may want to know all the costs associated with each product line. Therefore, management reports sometimes include such costs as product costs.

COST ACCOUNTING FOR FINANCIAL REPORTING

Regardless of the type of cost management system used, the resulting costs are used in a company's financial statements. This section discusses how financial reporting requirements influence the design of cost management systems.

Product Costs and Period Costs

Product Costs. Costs identified with goods produced or purchased for resale.

Period Costs. Costs that are deducted as expenses during the current period without going through an inventory stage.

When preparing income statements and balance sheets, accountants frequently distinguish between product costs and period costs. **Product costs** are costs identified with goods produced or purchased for resale. Product costs are initially identified as part of the inventory on hand. These product costs (inventoriable costs) become expenses (in the form of cost of goods sold) only when the inventory is sold. In contrast, **period costs** are costs that are deducted as expenses during the current period without going through an inventory stage.

OBJECTIVE 4

Differentiate between
product costs and
period costs, and
identify examples of
each.

For example, look at the top half of Exhibit 4-3. A merchandising company (retailer or wholesaler) acquires goods for resale without changing their basic form. The only product cost is the purchase of the merchandise. Unsold goods are held as merchandise inventory cost and are shown as an asset on a balance sheet. As the goods are sold, their costs become expenses in the form of "cost of goods sold."

A merchandising company also has a variety of selling and administrative expenses. These costs are period costs because they are deducted from revenue as expenses without ever being regarded as a part of inventory.

The bottom half of Exhibit 4-3 illustrates product and period costs in a manufacturing firm. Note that direct materials are transformed into saleable form with the help of direct labour and factory overhead. All these costs are product costs because they are allocated to inventory until the goods are sold. As in merchandising accounting, the selling and administrative expenses are not regarded as product costs but are treated as period costs.

Be sure you are clear on the differences between merchandising accounting and manufacturing accounting for such costs as insurance, amortization, and wages. In merchandising accounting, all such items are period costs (expenses of the current period). In manufacturing accounting, many of these items are related to production activities and thus, as factory overhead, are product costs (become expenses in the form of cost of goods sold as the inventory is sold).

In both merchandising and manufacturing accounting, selling and general administrative costs are period costs. Thus, the inventory costs of a manufactured product excludes sales salaries, sales commissions, advertising, legal, public relations, and the president's salary. Manufacturing overhead is traditionally regarded as a part of finished-goods inventory cost, whereas selling expenses and general administrative expenses are not.

Balance Sheet Presentation

OBJECTIVE 5

Explain how the
financial statements of
merchandisers and
manufacturers differ
because of the types
of goods they sell.

Examining both halves of Exhibit 4-3 together, you can see that the balance sheets of manufacturers and merchandisers differ with respect to inventories. In a manufacturing company, the "inventory account" is segmented into three inventory classes that help managers trace all product costs through the production process to the time of sales. These classes are:

- *Direct-materials inventory:* Materials on hand and awaiting use in the production process.
- *Work-in-process inventory:* Goods undergoing the production process but not yet fully completed. Costs include appropriate amounts of the three major manufacturing costs (direct materials, direct labour, and factory overhead).
- *Finished-goods inventory:* Goods fully completed but not yet sold.

The only essential difference between the structure of the balance sheet of a manufacturer and that of a retailer or wholesaler would appear in their respective current asset sections.

EXHIBIT 4-3

Relationship of Product Costs and Period Costs

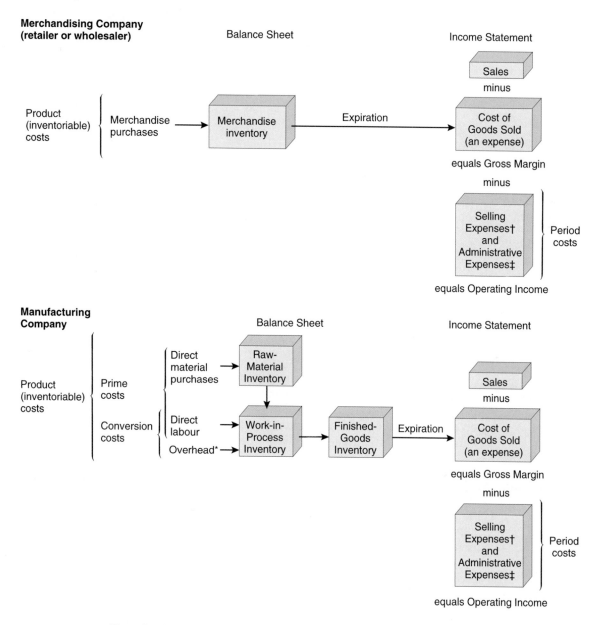

*Examples: indirect labour, factory supplies, insurance, and amortization on plant.
†Examples: insurance on salespersons' cars, amortization on salespersons' cars, salespersons' salaries.
‡Examples: insurance on corporate headquartes building, amortization on office equipment, clerical salaries.
    Note particularly that where insurance and amortization relate to the manufacturing function, they are inventoriable, but where they relate to selling and administration, they are not inventoriable.

Current Asset Sections of Balance Sheets ($ millions)	TOYOTA MOTOR CORPORATION MARCH 31, 2001 (MILLIONS OF YEN)		LOBLAW COMPANIES LIMITED JANUARY 2, 2001 ($ MILLIONS)
Cash	$1,226,550		$672.0
Accounts receivable	1,169,982		345.0
Short-term investments	541,747		345.0
Inventories – raw materials & supplies	110,943	– merchandise	1,141.0
– work in process	101,239		
– finished goods	523,247		
Prepaid expenses and other assets	699,479		84.0
Taxes recoverable	–		7.0
	4,373,187		2,249.0

Unit Cost for Product Costing

Reporting cost of goods sold or inventory values requires costs to be assigned to units of product. Assume the following:

Total cost of goods manufactured	$40,000,000
Total units manufactured	10,000,000
Unit cost of product for inventory purposes ($40,000,000 ÷ 10,000,000)	$4

If some of the 10-million units manufactured are still unsold at the end of the period, a part of the $40-million cost of goods manufactured will be "held back" as a cost of the ending inventory of finished goods (and shown as an asset on a balance sheet). The remainder becomes "cost of goods sold" for the current period and is shown as an expense on the income statement.

Costs and Income Statements

In income statements, the detailed reporting of selling and administrative expenses is typically the same for manufacturing and merchandising organizations, but the cost of goods sold is different.

Consider the *additional assumed* details as they are presented in the model income statement of a manufacturing company in Exhibit 4-4. The $40-million cost of goods manufactured is subdivided into the major components of direct materials, direct labour, and factory overhead. In contrast, a wholesale or retail company would replace the entire "cost of goods manufactured" section with a single line, "cost of goods purchased."

The terms "costs" and "expenses" are often used loosely by accountants and managers. "Expenses" denote all costs deducted from (matched against) revenue in a given period. On the other hand, "costs" is a much broader term and is used, for example, to describe both an asset (the cost of inventory) and an expense (the cost of goods sold). Thus, manufacturing costs are funnelled into an income statement as an expense (in the form of cost of goods sold) via the multistep inventory procedure shown earlier in Exhibit 4-3. In contrast, selling and general administrative costs are commonly deemed expenses immediately as they are incurred.

EXHIBIT 4-4

Model Income
Statement,
Manufacturing
Company

Sales (8,000,000 units @ $10)			$80,000,000
Cost of goods manufactured and sold:			
Beginning finished-goods inventory		$ —0—	
Cost of goods manufactured:			
Direct materials used	$20,000,000		
Direct labour	12,000,000		
Factory overhead	8,000,000	40,000,000	
Cost of goods available for sale		$40,000,000	
Ending finished-goods inventory			
2,000,000 units @ $4		8,000,000	
Cost of goods sold (an expense)			32,000,000
Gross margin or gross profit			$48,000,000
Less: Other expenses			
Selling expenses		$30,000,000	
General and administrative expenses		$ 8,000,000	$38,000,000
Operating income*			$10,000,000

* Also net income in this example since interest and income taxes are ignored here for simplicity.
Manufacturer: Manufacturing cost of goods produced and then sold, usually composed of three major
    categories of cost: direct materials, direct labour, and factory overhead.
Retailer or Wholesaler: Merchandise cost of goods sold, usually composed of the purchase cost of items,
    including freight in, that are acquired and then resold.

Transactions Affecting Inventories

The three manufacturing inventory accounts are affected by the following transactions:

- Direct-Materials Inventory:
  Increased by purchases of direct materials
  Decreased by use of direct materials
- Work-In-Process Inventory:
  Increased by use of direct materials, direct labour, or factory overhead
  Decreased by transfers to completed-goods inventory
- Finished-Goods Inventory:
  Increased by transfers of completed goods from work-in-process inventory
  Decreased by amount of cost of goods sold at time of sale

Direct labour and factory overhead are used at the same time they are acquired. Therefore, they are entered directly into work-in-process inventory and have no separate inventory account. In contrast, direct materials are often purchased in advance of their use and held in inventory for some time.

Exhibit 4-5 traces the effects of these transactions. It uses the dollar amounts from Exhibit 4-4, with one exception. Purchases of direct materials totalled $30 million, with $20 million used in production (as shown in Exhibit 4-4) and $10 million left in inventory at the end of the period. As the bottom of Exhibit 4-5 indicates, the ending balance sheet amounts would be:

Direct-Materials Inventory	$10,000,000
Work-In-Process Inventory	0
Finished-Goods Inventory	8,000,000
Total Inventories	$18,000,000

EXHIBIT 4-5

Industry Transactions

TRANSACTION	DIRECT-MATERIALS INVENTORY	WORK-IN-PROCESS INVENTORY	FINISHED-GOODS INVENTORY
Beginning Balance	$ 0	$ 0	$ 0
Purchase direct materials	+30	—	—
Use direct materials	−20	+20	—
Acquire and use direct labour	—	+12	—
Acquire and use factory overhead	—	+8	—
Complete production	—	−40	+40
Sell goods and record cost of goods sold	—	—	−32
Ending Balance	$ 10	$ 0	$ 8

COST BEHAVIOUR AND INCOME STATEMENTS

OBJECTIVE 6

Compare income statements of a manufacturing company created in both the absorption and contribution formats.

In addition to differences between manufacturing and merchandising firms in their external financial reporting, manufacturers differ among themselves in accounting for costs on internal income statements, with some favouring an absorption approach and others using a contribution approach. To highlight the different effects of these approaches, we will assume that in 2002 the Samson Company has direct-materials costs of $7 million and direct-labour costs of $4 million. Assume also that the company incurred the factory overhead illustrated in Exhibit 4-6 and the selling and administrative expenses illustrated in Exhibit 4-7. Total sales were $20 million. Finally, assume that the units produced are equal to the units sold. That is, there is no change in inventory levels.

Note that Exhibits 4-6 and 4-7 subdivide costs as variable or fixed. Many companies do not make such subdivisions in their income statements. Furthermore, when these subdivisions are made, sometimes arbitrary decisions are necessary as to whether a given cost is variable or fixed or partially fixed (for example, repairs). Nevertheless, to aid decision making, many companies are attempting to report the extent to which their costs are approximately variable or fixed.

EXHIBIT 4-6

SAMSON COMPANY
Schedules of Manufacturing Overhead (which are product costs) for the Year Ended December 31, 2002 (in thousands of dollars)

SCHEDULE 1: VARIABLE COSTS		
Supplies (lubricants, expendable tools, coolants, sandpaper)	$ 150	
Material-handling labour (forklift operators)	700	
Repairs	100	
Power	50	$1,000
SCHEDULE 2: FIXED COSTS		
Managers' salaries	$ 200	
Employee training	90	
Factory picnic and holiday party	10	
Supervisory salaries, except foremen's salaries	700	
Amortization, plant and equipment	1,800	
Property taxes	150	
Insurance	50	3,000
Total manufacturing overhead		$4,000

EXHIBIT 4-7

SAMSON COMPANY
Schedules of Selling
and Administrative
Expenses (which are
period costs) for the
Year Ended
December 31, 2002
(in thousands of dollars)

SCHEDULE 3: SELLING EXPENSES

Variable:		
Sales commissions	$ 700	
Shipping expenses for products sold	300	$1,000
Fixed:		
Advertising	$ 700	
Sales salaries	1,000	
Other	300	2,000
Total selling expenses		$3,000

SCHEDULE 4: ADMINISTRATIVE EXPENSES

Variable:		
Some clerical wages	$ 80	
Computer time rented	20	$ 100
Fixed:		
Office salaries	$ 100	
Other salaries	200	
Amortization on office facilities	100	
Public-accounting fees	40	
Legal fees	100	
Other	360	900
Total administrative expenses		$1,000

Absorption Approach

Absorption Approach. A costing approach that considers all factory overhead (both variable and fixed) to be product (inventoriable) costs that become an expense in the form of manufacturing cost of goods sold only as sales occur.

Exhibit 4-8 presents Samson's income statement using the **absorption approach** (variable costing) (*absorption costing*)—the approach used by most companies. Firms that take this approach consider all factory overhead (both variable and fixed) to be product (inventoriable) costs that become an expense in the form of manufacturing cost of goods sold only as sales occur.

Take a moment to compare Exhibits 4-4 and 4-8. Note that gross profit or gross margin is the difference between sales and the *manufacturing* cost of goods sold. Note, too, that the *primary classifications* of costs on the income statement are by three major management *functions*: manufacturing, selling, and administrative.

Contribution Approach

Contribution Approach. A method of internal (management accounting) reporting that emphasizes the distinction between variable and fixed costs for the purpose of better decision making.

In contrast, Exhibit 4-9 uses the **contribution approach** (variable costing) to present Samson's income statement. The contribution approach is generally not allowed for external financial reporting. However, many companies use this approach for internal (management accounting) purposes and an absorption format for external purposes, because they expect the benefits of making better decisions to exceed the extra costs of using different reporting systems simultaneously.

For decision purposes, the major difference between the contribution approach and the absorption approach is that the former emphasizes the distinction between variable and fixed costs. Its primary classifications of costs are by variable and fixed *cost behaviour patterns*, not by *business functions*.

The contribution income statement provides a *contribution margin*, which is computed after deducting all variable costs, including variable selling and administrative costs. This approach makes it easier to see the impact of changes in sales demand on operating income. It also dovetails neatly with the cost-volume-profit analysis illustrated in Chapter 2.

VARIABLE VERSUS ABSORPTION COSTING: A COMPANY PRESIDENT'S PERSPECTIVE

To properly understand the difference between variable cost accounting and absorption cost accounting to today's manufacturers, the individual must understand that the environment in which the manufacturer operates and the concerns of the manager of such an operation have changed with time.

Priorities are now product quality, which includes all aspects of design, service, and price. A common definition of quality is "that which the customer wants, at a competitive price."

The accounting system must provide the correct data to make informed decisions about these quality issues. The absorption-costing system was developed by accountants whose objective was to match revenue and expenses for financial statement presentation. It was developed during times of high set-up costs and long runs of identical products. There is no mention in these objectives of customer or quality.

Consider the environment in which decisions are presently being made:

- The whole world is the market and the whole world is the competitor. This market cares only about product quality. Competitors are interested only in what they can do better than the competition. Manufacturers must ensure that no such opportunity exists or they will lose competitive position.
- Niche Marketing. Meaning specific products aimed at particular markets or market segments. Customer needs do vary, which means the manufacturer must be in a position to continually make decisions as to the costs associated with making the changes requested and required by the individual customer.
- Flexible Manufacturing. Being capable of setting up quickly and changing or modifying products quickly to meet the demands of the niche market.
- Continuous Improvement. Everyone in the operation, from the President to the floor sweeper, must continually strive to find better methods to do what they do. If they do not do so, they can be assured that a competitor somewhere will be doing such, and the organization will lose competitive advantage.

None of the above refers to short-term profit presentation, financial statement ratios, or current share prices—the issues around which absorption costing was developed.

Since managers are now looking at numerous customized orders and specialized markets, their decisions in this environment cannot be made on the basis of an arbitrary allocation of overhead costs.

Rather, the managers must know what costs will vary with any particular decision and how the costs will vary with volume. The manager must look at the price that can be obtained for the product in question and at the contribution margin generated by that product during the plant time absorbed to produce the product. The manager must investigate the overheads to ensure that in fact these will not vary as a result of taking a particular order (or entering a particular market). The manager must compare the value of that order against other possible orders that cannot be accepted because they would require the same production time slot.

The manager can then consider all aspects of an order (or market segment) and its effect on the overall marketing plans of the organization, including such subjective items as corporate image and market share and the long-term effect on customers and markets.

A manager who follows this procedure will be in a position to truly maximize real profits. Real profits are the cash generated over time, not the short-term results reported in audited financial statements in any particular year.

Variable costs are important not only to managers but to all levels of the manufacturing organization. The people on the floor are involved in making recommendations and improvements in the organization. As such, they have access to and are using costs to calculate the return on investment of proposed improvements. Such decisions must be made on the basis of cash flow, not financial statement profit and loss. Only variable costing systems provide the correct information.

Continued

Absorption costing is meant to match revenue with costs. If used by managers to make operating decisions about quality or competitive position, it will distort the decisions. These are the decisions that affect the customers and the markets. It must be understood that the key to the success of the manufacturer is the customer; it is not an accountant's view of profit and loss.

The absorption costing system adds nothing of value to the manager's operating decisions, therefore, nothing of value to the product or the customer. If the important decisions within the company are being based upon variable costs, does it not follow that eventually the outside investor will want to make their decisions on a similar basis? Perhaps absorption costing will go the way of the large, inflexible manufacturer and the dinosaur.

Arriscraft International
www.arriscraft.com

Source: Written by Randy White, President, Arriscraft Corporation.

EXHIBIT 4-8

SAMSON COMPANY
Absorption Income Statement for the Year Ended December 31, 2002 (in thousands of dollars)

Sales		$20,000
Less: Manufacturing costs of goods sold:		
Direct material	$7,000	
Direct labour	4,000	
Factory overhead (Schedules 1 and 2)	4,000	15,000
Gross margin or gross profit		$ 5,000
Selling expenses (Schedule 3)	$3,000	
Administrative expenses (Schedule 4)	1,000	
Total selling and administrative expenses		4,000
Operating income		$1,000

Note: Schedules 1 and 2 are in Exhibit 4-6. Schedules 3 and 4 are in Exhibit 4-7.

EXHIBIT 4-9

SAMSON COMPANY
Contribution Income Statement for the Year Ended December 31, 2002 (in thousands of dollars)

Sales		$20,000
Less: Variable expenses:		
Direct material	$ 7,000	
Direct labour	4,000	
Variable manufacturing overhead costs (Schedule 1)	1,000	
Total variable manufacturing cost of goods sold	12,000	
Variable selling expenses (Schedule 3)	1,000	
Variable administrative expenses (Schedule 4)	100	
Total variable expenses		13,100
Contribution margin		$ 6,900
Less: Fixed expenses:		
Manufacturing overhead (Schedule 2)	$ 3,000	
Selling (Schedule 3)	2,000	
Administrative (Schedule 4)	900	5,900
Operating income		$ 1,000

Note: Schedules 1 and 2 are in Exhibit 4-6. Schedules 3 and 4 are in Exhibit 4-7.

The contribution approach stresses the lump-sum amount of fixed costs to be recouped before net income emerges. This highlighting of total fixed costs focuses management attention on fixed-cost behaviour and control in making both short-run and long-run plans. Keep in mind that advocates of the contribution approach do not maintain that fixed costs are unimportant or irrelevant. However, they do stress that the distinctions between behaviours of variable and fixed costs are crucial for certain decisions.

The difference between the gross margin (from the absorption approach) and the contribution margin (from the contribution approach) is striking in manufacturing companies. Why? Because fixed manufacturing costs are regarded as

<table>
<tr><td colspan="2">PERSPECTIVES ON</td><td>P O D M</td><td colspan="2">DECISION-MAKING</td></tr>
</table>

Dabbling in E-Commerce

A survey finds that many Canadian companies are still not putting e-commerce high on their list of priorities. More than 70 percent of Canadian companies do not consider electronic commerce to be a high business priority according to a study released by Andersen Consulting. Even though 84 percent of senior business leaders interviewed agree that their companies will rely more on e-commerce within five years, few in Canada are readying to compete and thrive in the electronic economy.

Only 20 percent of the more than 250 major Canadian companies surveyed were identified as e-commerce "Leaders," while 41 percent were characterized as "Dabblers" and the remaining percent demonstrated attitudes and behaviours associated with "Side-line Observers."

However, 90 percent of Canadian business leaders said their organization plans to spend more money on developing e-commerce capabilities in the next one to two years. And, companies that are already doing business on-line expect revenues from e-commerce to increase by nearly four times by 2001, according to the survey.

"E-commerce is not only changing the way business is conducted, it is changing the fundamental economic assumptions on which business is based. Canadian executives must take action now to survive and succeed during this shift from an industrial economy to an electronic econ-omy," says Rudy Puryear, global managing partner of e-commerce for Andersen.

The study found that the top five business priorities among Canadian senior executives are: improving customer service (78 percent); Y2K readiness (76 percent); increasing customer loyalty (68 percent); attracting new customers (65 percent), and cost reduction (62 percent). At 29 percent, exploiting the full potential of the Internet and developing e-commerce initiatives was ranked last in terms of the business priorities surveyed.

"E-commerce strategies can deliver strong results on four of the top five business priorities cited by Canadian business leaders," noted Puryear. "Winning in the e-economy requires more than creating Web sites and virtual channels, or automating customer service and building new skills. Organizations must continuously evaluate their entire business in the context of the e-economy."

The *Andersen Consulting 1999 E-Commerce Survey of Canadian Business* is the first in an annual series of reports designed to measure the evolution of e-commerce. The study, conducted by Northstar Research Partners, surveyed the opinions of business leaders from March to April 1999

Source: "Dabbling in E-Commerce," *CMA Management*, November 1999, p. 63.

E-COMMERCE REVENUE PROJECTIONS

% of revenue from	Current	next 1-2 Years
1-9% of revenue	27	13
10-15%	7	13
20-29%	3	13
Over 30%	4	13
None	44	8
Don't know	15	31
Average	5.4	19.6

a part of cost of goods sold, and these fixed costs reduce the gross margin accordingly. However, *fixed* manufacturing costs do not reduce the contribution margin, which is affected solely by revenues and *variable* costs.

VARIABLE VERSUS ABSORPTION COSTING

Accounting for Fixed Manufacturing Overhead

OBJECTIVE 7

Identify the basic feature that distinguishes the variable costing approach from the absorption costing approach.

Two major methods of product costing are compared in this chapter: *variable costing* (the contribution approach) and *absorption costing* (the functional, full-costing, or traditional approach). These methods differ in one primary conceptual respect: fixed manufacturing overhead is excluded from the cost of products under *variable costing* but is included in the cost of products under *absorption costing*. In other words, variable costing signifies that fixed factory overhead is not inventoried. In contrast, absorption costing indicates that inventory values include fixed factory overhead.

As Exhibit 4-10 shows, a variable costing system treats fixed manufacturing overhead (fixed factory overhead) as an expired cost to be immediately charged against sales—not as an unexpired cost to be held back as inventory and charged against sales later as part of cost of goods sold.

Variable costing is commonly called *direct costing*. However, this is a misnomer because the inventorying of costs is not confined to only "direct" materials and labour; it also includes an "indirect" cost—the *variable* manufacturing overhead. Such confusion is unfortunate but apparently unavoidable in a field such as management accounting, where new analytical ideas or approaches arise in isolated fashion. Newly coined terms, which may not be accurately descriptive, often become embedded too deeply to be supplanted later.

Consider Exhibit 4-10. Note that the primary difference between variable and absorption costing is the accounting for fixed manufacturing overhead.

Absorption costing is more widely used than variable costing. However the growing use of the contribution approach in performance measurement and cost analysis has led to increasing use of variable costing for internal reporting purposes. Many major firms use variable costing for some internal reporting, and nearly 25 percent of firms use it as the primary internal format.

For external purposes, the use of variable costing is much more restricted. The *CICA Handbook* states that cost of inventories should include "the laid-down cost of material plus the cost of direct labour applied to the product and the applicable share of overhead expense properly chargeable to production."[1] Thus, the *CICA Handbook* advocates absorption costing. However, Revenue Canada's position is somewhat more flexible as noted in the following:

> Either direct costing, which allocates variable overheads to inventory or absorption costing, which allocates both variable and fixed overheads to inventory, will be accepted by the Department as a method of costing inventory, but if overhead is included in inventory on an acceptable basis for financial statement purposes, the method of valuation used for tax purposes must not be inconsistent with the method used for financial statement purposes.[2]

CICA Handbook
http://handbook.cica.ca/
main.cica_hb.cfm

Revenue Canada
www.ccra-adrc.gc.ca

---

[1] *CICA Handbook*, section 3030, paragraph .06.
[2] Revenue Canada, Taxation, "Interpretation Bulletin No. 473," paragraph 8.

EXHIBIT 4-10

Comparison of Flow of Costs

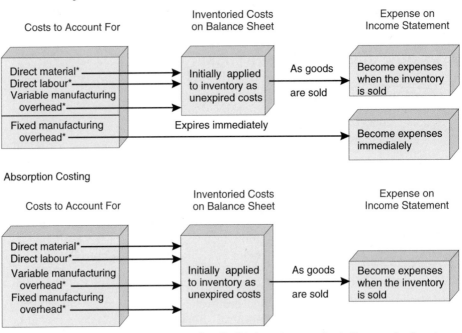

*As goods are manufactured, the costs are "applied" to inventory usually via the use of unit costs.

Until the last decade or two, use of variable costing for internal reporting has been expensive. It requires information to be processed two ways—one for external reporting and one for internal reporting. The increasing use and decreasing cost of computers has reduced the added cost of a variable costing system. Most managers no longer face the question of whether to invest in a separate variable costing *system*. Rather, they simply choose a variable costing or absorption costing *format* for reports. Many well-designed accounting systems used today can produce either format.

Facts for Illustration

To make these ideas more concrete, consider the following example. In 2001 and 2002, the Greenberg Company had the following costs for production of its single product:

BASIC PRODUCTION DATA AT STANDARD COST	
Direct material	$1.30
Direct labour	1.50
Variable manufacturing overhead	.20
Variable costs per unit	$3.00

Fixed manufacturing overhead (fixed factory overhead) was budgeted at $150,000. Expected (or budgeted) production in each year is 150,000 units, and the sales price is $5 per unit. For simplicity, we will assume that there is a $.20 per unit variable manufacturing overhead and that both budgeted and actual selling and administrative expenses are fixed at $65,000 yearly, except for sales commissions at 5 percent of dollar sales. Actual product quantities are:

	2001	2002
In units:		
Opening inventory	—	30,000
Production	170,000	140,000
Sales	140,000	160,000
Ending inventory	30,000	10,000

We will also assume that the standard variable manufacturing costs, and fixed manufacturing overhead were incurred as budgeted.

Based on this information, we can

1. Prepare income statements for 2001 and 2002 under variable costing.
2. Prepare income statements for 2001 and 2002 under absorption costing.
3. Show a reconciliation of the difference in operating income for 2001, 2002, and the two years as a whole.

Variable Costing Method

OBJECTIVE 8

Construct an income statement using the variable costing approach.

We begin by preparing income statements under variable costing. The variable costing statement shown in Exhibit 4-11 has the same format that was introduced earlier. The only new characteristic of Exhibit 4-11 is the presence of a detailed calculation of cost of goods sold, which is affected by changes in the beginning and ending inventories.

The costs of the product are accounted for by applying all *variable* manufacturing costs to the goods produced at a rate of $3 per unit; thus inventories are valued at the total variable costs. In contrast, fixed manufacturing cost are not applied to any products but are regarded as expenses in the period they are incurred.

EXHIBIT 4-11

Variable Costing
GREENBERG COMPANY
Comparative Income Statements (in thousands of dollars) For the Years 2001 and 2002

		2001		2002	
Sales, 140,000 and 160,000 units, respectively	(1)		$700		$800
Variable expenses:					
Variable manufacturing cost of goods sold					
Opening inventory, at standard variable costs of $3		$ —		$ 90	
Add: Variable cost of goods manufactured at standard, 170,000 and 140,000 units, respectively		510		420	
Available for sale, 170,000 units in each year		$510		$510	
Deduct: Ending inventory, at standard variable cost of $3		90*		30†	
Variable manufacturing cost of goods sold		$420		$480	
Variable selling expenses, at 5% of dollar sales		35		40	
Total variable expenses	(2)		455		520
Contribution margin	(3) = (1) – (2)		$245		$280
Fixed expenses:					
Fixed factory overhead		150		150	
Fixed selling and administrative expenses		65		65	
Total fixed expenses	(4)		215		215
Operating income	(3) – (4)		$ 30		$ 65

*30,000 units x $3 = $90,000.
†10,000 units x $3 = $30,000.

Before reading on, be sure to trace the facts from the illustrative problem to the presentation in Exhibit 4-11, step by step. Note that both variable cost of goods sold and variable selling and administrative expense are deducted in computing the contribution margin. However, variable selling and administrative expense is not inventoriable. It is affected only by the level of sales, not by changes in inventory.

Absorption Costing Method

Fixed Overhead Rate. The amount of fixed manufacturing overhead applied to each unit of production. It is determined by dividing the budgeted fixed overhead by the expected volume of production for the budget period.

Production Volume Variance. A variance that appears whenever actual production deviates from the expected volume of production used in computing the fixed-overhead rate. It is calculated as (actual volume − expected volume) × fixed-overhead rate.

Exhibit 4-12 shows the absorption costing framework. As you can see, it differs from the variable costing format in three ways.

First, the unit product cost used for computing cost of goods sold is $4, not $3. Why? Because fixed manufacturing overhead of $1 is added to the $3 variable manufacturing cost. The $1 of fixed manufacturing overhead applied to each unit is the **fixed overhead rate**. It is determined by dividing the budgeted fixed overhead by the expected volume of production for the budget period:

$$\text{fixed overhead rate} = \frac{\text{budgeted fixed manufacturing overhead}}{\text{expected volume of production}} = \frac{\$150,000}{150,000 \text{ units}} = \$1$$

Second, fixed factory overhead does not appear as a separate line in an absorption costing income statement. Instead, the fixed factory overhead is included in two places: as part of the cost of goods sold and as a *production volume variance*. A **production volume variance** (which is explained in more detail later) appears whenever actual production deviates from the expected volume of production used in computing the fixed overhead rate:

$$\text{production volume variance} = (\text{actual volume} - \text{expected volume}) \times \text{fixed-overhead rate}$$

Finally, the format for an absorption costing income statement separates costs into the major categories of *manufacturing* and *nonmanufacturing*. In contrast, a variable costing income statement separates costs into the major categories of *fixed* and *variable*. In an absorption costing statement, revenue less *manufacturing* cost (both fixed and variable) is *gross profit* or *gross margin*. In a variable costing statement, revenue less all *variable* costs (both manufacturing and nonmanufacturing) is the *contribution margin*. This difference is illustrated by a condensed comparison of 2002 income statements (in thousands of dollars):

VARIABLE COSTING		ABSORPTION COSTING	
Revenue	$800	Revenue	$800
All variable costs	520	All manufacturing costs*	650
Contribution margin	280	Gross margin	150
All fixed costs	215	All nonmanufacturing costs	105
Operating income	$ 65	Operating income	$ 45

* Absorption cost of goods sold plus production volume variance.

Despite the importance of such differences in most industries, more and more firms are not concerned with the choice between variable and absorption costing. Why? Because they have implemented just-in-time production methods and sharply reduced inventory levels. There is no difference between variable costing and absorption costing income if the inventory level does not change, and companies with little inventory generally experience only insignificant *changes* in inventory.

EXHIBIT 4-12

Absorption Costing
**GREENBERG
COMPANY**
Comparative Income
Statements (in thousands of dollars) For the
Years 2001 and 2002

		2001		2002
Sales		$700		$800
Cost of goods sold:				
Opening inventory, at absorption cost of $4*	$—		$120	
Cost of goods manufactured at $4	680		560	
Available for sale	680		680	
Deduct: Ending inventory at absorption cost of $4*	120		40	
Cost of goods sold		560		640
Gross profit		$140		$160
Production volume variance†		20 F		10 U
Gross margin or gross profit, at "actual"		160		150
Selling and administrative expenses		100		105
Operating income		$60		$45

* Variable cost $3
 Fixed cost ($150,000 ÷ 150,000) 1
 Absorption cost $4

† Computation of productive volume variance based on expected volume of production of 150,000 units:

2001	$20,000 F	(170,000 − 150,000) × $1	
2002	10,000 U	(140,000 − 150,000) × $1	
Two years together	$10,000 F	(310,000 − 300,000) × $1	

U = Unfavourable. F = Favourable.

Reconciliation of Variable Costing and Absorption Costing

Exhibit 4-13 reconciles the operating incomes shown in Exhibits 4-11 and 4-12. The difference in those two earlier exhibits is explained by multiplying the fixed-overhead product-costing rate by the *change* in the total units in the beginning and ending inventories. Consider 2002: the change in units was 20,000, so the difference in net income would be 20,000 units multiplied by $1 = $20,000.

The difference in income also equals the difference in the total amount of fixed manufacturing overhead charged as expense during a given year. (See Exhibits 4-14 and 4-15.) The $150,000 fixed manufacturing overhead incurred in 2002 is automatically the amount recognized as an expense on a variable costing income statement.

	2001	2002	TOGETHER
Operating income under			
Absorption costing (see Exhibit 4-12)	$60,000	$ 45,000	$105,000
Variable costing (see Exhibit 4-11)	−30,000	−65,000	−95,000
Difference to be explained	$30,000	$ −20,000	$ 10,000
The difference can be reconciled by multiplying the fixed-overhead rate by the change in the total inventory units:			
Fixed-overhead rate	$1	$1	$1
Change in inventory units:			
Opening inventory	—	30,000	—
Ending inventory	30,000	10,000	10,000
Change	30,000	−20,000	10,000
Difference in operating income explained	$30,000	$ −20,000	$ 10,000

EXHIBIT 4-14

Flow of Fixed Manufacturing Costs During 2002 (Format Derived from Exhibit 4-10)

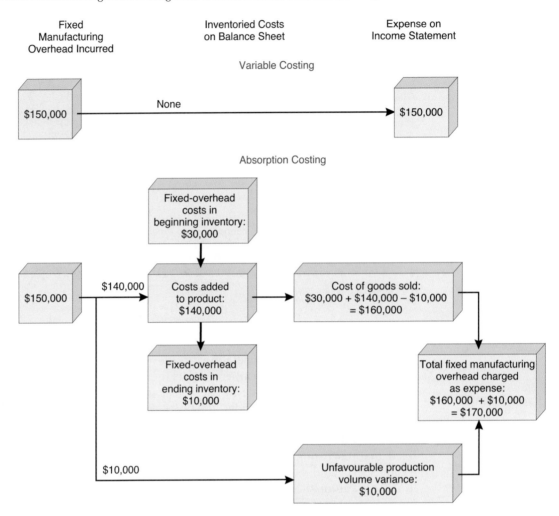

Under absorption costing, fixed manufacturing overhead appears in two places: cost of goods sold and production volume variance. Note that $30,000 of these fixed costs were incurred before 2002 and held over in the beginning inventory. During 2002, $140,000 of fixed manufacturing overhead was added to inventory, and $10,000 was still lodged in the ending inventory of 2002. Thus, the fixed manufacturing overhead included in cost of goods sold for 2002 was $30,000 + $140,000 − $10,000 = $160,000. In addition, the production-volume variance is $10,000 unfavourable. The total fixed manufacturing overhead charged as expenses under absorption costing is $170,000, or $20,000 more than the $150,000 charged under variable costing. Therefore, 2002 variable-costing income is higher by $20,000.

Remember that it is the relationship between sales and production that determines the difference between variable costing and absorption costing income. Whenever sales exceed production, that is, when inventory decreases, variable costing income is greater than absorption costing income.

EXHIBIT 4-15

	INVENTORY		EXPENSE
VARIABLE COSTING			
No fixed overhead carried over from 2001			
Fixed overhead actually incurred in 2002	$150,000	⟶	$150,000

ABSORPTION COSTING		UNITS	DOLLARS	
Fixed overhead in beginning inventory	$ 30,000	30,000	$ 30,000	
Fixed overhead incurred in 2002	150,000			
To account for:	$180,000			
Applied to product, 140,000 @ $1		140,000	140,000	
Available for sale		170,000	$170,000	
Contained in cost of goods sold	$160,000	160,000	160,000 →	$160,000
In ending inventory	10,000	10,000	$ 10,000	
Not applied, so becomes unfavourable				
production volume variance	10,000		⟶	10,000
Fixed factory overhead charged				
against 2002 operations				$170,000
Accounted for, as above	$180,000			
Difference in operating income				
occurs because $170,000 expires				
rather than $150,000				$ 20,000

Why Use Variable Costing?

OBJECTIVE 10

Explain why a
company might prefer
to use a variable
costing approach.

Why do many companies use variable costing for internal statements? One reason is that absorption costing income is affected by production volume while variable costing income is not. Consider the 2002 absorption costing statement in Exhibit 4-12 which shows operating income of $45,000. Suppose a manager decides to produce 10,000 additional units in December 2002 even though they will remain unsold. Will this affect operating income? First, note that the gross profit will not change. Why? Because it is based on sales, not production. However, the production volume variance will change:

$$\text{If production} = 140{,}000 \text{ units}$$
$$\text{Production volume variance} = (150{,}000 - 140{,}000) \times \$1 = \$10{,}000 \text{ U}$$
$$\text{If production} = 150{,}000 \text{ units}$$
$$\text{Production volume variance} = (150{,}000 - 150{,}000) \times \$1 = 0$$

Because there is no production volume variance when 150,000 units are produced, the new operating income equals gross profit less selling and administrative expenses, $160,000 − $105,000 = $55,000. Therefore, increasing *production* by 10,000 units without any increase in *sales* increases absorption costing operating income by $10,000, from $45,000 to $55,000.

How will such an increase in production affect the variable costing statement in Exhibit 4-11? Nothing will change. Production does not affect operating income under variable costing.

Suppose the evaluation of a manager's performance is based heavily on operating income. If the company uses the absorption costing approach, a manager might be tempted to produce unneeded units just to increase reported operating income as the increase in inventory would absorb some of the overhead costs rather than being expensed. No such temptation exists with variable costing.

Companies also choose variable or absorption costing based on which system they believe gives a better signal about performance. A sales-oriented company may prefer variable costing because its income is affected primarily by the level of sales. In contrast, a production oriented company (for example a company that can easily sell all the units it produces), might prefer absorption costing. Why? Because additional production increases the operating income with absorption costing but not with variable costing.

HIGHLIGHTS TO REMEMBER

Cost accounting systems are designed to provide cost information about various types of objectives—products, customers, activities, and so on. To do this, resource costs are first accumulated by natural classifications such as materials, labour, and energy. Then costs are traced to cost objectives, either directly or indirectly through allocations.

Direct costs can be identified specifically and exclusively with a cost object in an economically feasible way. When this is not possible, costs must be allocated to cost objectives using a cost driver. Such costs are called indirect costs. The greater the proportion of direct costs, the greater the accuracy of the cost system. When the proportion of indirect costs is significant, care must be taken to find the most appropriate cost drivers.

The primary difference between the financial statements of a merchandiser and a manufacturer is the reporting of inventories. A merchandiser has only one type of inventory whereas a manufacturer has three types of inventory: raw material, work-in-process, and finished goods.

The major difference between the absorption and contribution formats for the income statement is that cost behaviour (fixed and variable) is reported in the contribution format whereas the focus of the absorption format is in reporting costs by business functions. The contribution approach makes it easier for managers to evaluate the effects of changes in demand on income and thus it is better for planning and control purposes.

Cost-accounting systems are usually designed to satisfy *control* and *product-costing* purposes simultaneously. Many varieties of product costing are in use. For years, manufacturing companies have regularly used absorption costing, which includes fixed factory overhead as a part of the cost of the product based on some predetermined application rate (variances are not inventories). In contrast, variable costing charges fixed factory overhead to the period immediately—that is, fixed overhead is altogether excluded from inventories. Absorption costing continues to be much more widely used than variable costing, although the growing use of the contribution approach in performance measurement has led to increasing use of variable costing for internal purposes.

The production volume variance is linked with absorption costing, not variable costing. It arises from the conflict between the control-budget purpose and the product-costing purpose of cost accounting. The production volume variance is measured by the predetermined fixed-overhead rate multiplied by the difference between expected production volume and actual production volume.

SUMMARY PROBLEMS FOR YOUR REVIEW

Problem One

1. Review the illustrations in Exhibits 4-6 through 4-9. Suppose that all variable costs fluctuate in direct proportion to units produced and sold and

that all fixed costs are unaffected over a wide range of production and sales. What would operating income have been if sales (at normal selling prices) had been $20.9 million instead of $20.0 million? Which statement—the absorption income statement or the contribution income statement—did you use as a framework for your answer? Why?

2. Suppose employee training (Exhibit 4-6) was regarded as a variable rather than a fixed cost at a rate of $90,000 per 1,000,000 units, or $0.09 per unit. How would your answer in part 1 change?

Solution

1. Operating income would increase from $1,000,000 to $1,310,500, computed as follows:

Increase in revenue	$ 900,000
Ratio in total contribution income statement	
(Exhibit 4-9) is $6,900,000 ÷ $20,000,000 = .345	
Ratio times revenue increase is .345 × $900,000	$ 310,500
Increase in fixed expenses	— 0 —
Operating income before increase	1,000,000
New operating income	$1,310,500

Computations are easily made by using data from the contribution income statement. In contrast, the traditional absorption costing income statement must be analyzed and divided into variable and fixed categories before the effect on operating income can be estimated.

2. The contribution-margin ratio would be lower because the variable costs would be higher by $.09 per unit:

$$(\$6,900,000 - \$90,000) \div \$20,000,000 = .3405$$

	GIVEN LEVEL	HIGHER LEVEL	DIFFERENCE
Revenue	$20,000,000	$20,900,000	$900,000
Variable expenses ($13,100,000 + $90,000)	13,190,000	13,783,550	593,550
Contribution margin at .3405	$ 6,810,000	$ 7,116,450	$306,450
Fixed expenses ($5,900,000 − $90,000)	5,810,000	5,810,000	–
Operating income	$ 1,000,000	$ 1,306,450	$306,450

Problem Two

1. Reconsider Exhibits 4-11 and 4-12. Suppose production in 2002 was 145,000 units instead of 140,000 units, but sales were 160,000 units. Assume that the net variances for all variable manufacturing costs were $37,000, unfavourable. Regard these variances as adjustments to the cost of goods sold. Also assume that actual fixed costs were $157,000. Prepare income statements for 2002 under variable costing and under absorption costing.

2. Explain why operating income was different under variable costing and absorption costing. Show your calculations.

3. Without regard to requirement 1, would variable costing or absorption costing give a manager more leeway in influencing short-run operating income through production-scheduling decisions? Why?

Solution

1. See Exhibits 4-16 and 4-17 below. Note that the ending inventory will be 15,000 units instead of 10,000 units.

2. Decline in inventory levels is 30,000 – 15,000, or 15,000 units. The fixed-overhead rate per unit in absorption costing is $1. Therefore $15,000 more fixed overhead was charged against operations under absorption costing than under variable costing. The variable costing statement shows fixed factory overhead of $157,000, whereas the absorption costing statement includes fixed factory overhead in three places: $160,000 in cost of goods sold, $7,000 U in fixed factory overhead flexible-budget variances, and $5,000 U as a production volume variance, for a total of $172,000. Generally, when inventories decline, absorption costing will show less income than variable costing; when inventories rise, absorption costing will show more income than variable costing.

3. Some version of absorption costing will give a manager more leeway in influencing operating income via production scheduling. Operating income will fluctuate in harmony with changes in net sales under variable costing, but it is influenced by both production and sales under absorption costing. For example, compare variable costing in Exhibits 4-11 and 4-16. As the second note to Exhibit 4-16 indicates, the operating income may be affected by assorted variances (but not the production-volume variance) under variable costing, but production scheduling *per se* will have no effect on operating income.

EXHIBIT 4-16			
GREENBERG COMPANY Income Statement (Variable Costing) For the Year 2002 (in thousands of dollars)			

Sales			$800
Opening inventory, at variable cost of $3	$ 90		
Add: Variable cost of goods manufactured	435		
Available for sale	$525		
Deduct: Ending inventory, at variable cost of $3	45		
Variable cost of goods sold		$480	
Net variances for all variable costs, unfavourable		37	
Variable cost of goods sold, at actual		$517	
Variable selling expenses, at 5% of dollar sales		40	
Total variable costs charged against sales			557
Contribution margin			$243
Fixed factory overhead		$157*	
Fixed selling and administrative expenses		65	
Total fixed expenses			222
Operating income			$ 21†

* This could be shown in two lines, $150,000 budget plus $7,000 variance.
† The difference between this and the $65,000 operating income in Exhibit 4-11 occurs because of the $37,000 unfavourable variable-cost variances and the $7,000 unfavourable fixed-cost variance.

EXHIBIT 4-17

Greenberg Company
Income Statement
(Absorption Costing)
For the Year 2002
(in thousands of dollars)

Sales		$800
Opening inventory, at cost of $4	$120	
Cost of goods manufactured	580	
Available for sale	$700	
Deduct: Ending inventory	60	
Cost of goods sold	$640	
Net flexible-budget variances for all variable manufacturing costs, unfavourable	$37	
Fixed factory overhead flexible-budget variance, unfavourable	7	
Production volume variance, unfavourable	5*	
Total variances	49	
Cost of goods sold, at actual		689
Gross profit, at "actual"		$111
Selling and administrative expenses:		
Variable	40	
Fixed	65	105
Operating income		$ 6

* Production volume variance is $1 × (150,000 denominator volume − 145,000 actual production).

As the third note to Exhibit 4-17 explains, production scheduling as well as sales influence operating income. Production was 145,000 rather than 140,000 units. So, $5,000 of fixed overhead became a part of ending inventory (an asset) instead of part of the production volume variance (an expense)—that is, the production volume variance is $5,000 lower and the ending inventory contains $5,000 more fixed overhead. The manager adds $1 to 2002 operating income with each unit of production under absorption costing, even if the unit is not sold.

APPENDIX 4: MORE ON LABOUR COSTS

Classifications of Labour Costs

The terms used to classify labour costs are often confusing. Each organization seems to develop its own interpretation of various labour-cost classifications. We begin by considering some commonly encountered labour-cost terms:

- Direct labour (already defined)
- Factory overhead (examples of prominent labour components of these indirect manufacturing costs follow):
    Indirect labour (wages):
        Forklift truck operators (internal handling of materials)
        Maintenance
        Production set-up
        Expediting (overseeing special and rush orders)
        Janitors
        Plant guards
        Rework labour (time spent by direct labourers redoing defective work)

Overtime premium paid to all factory workers
Idle time
Managers' salaries
Employee benefit costs (for example, health care premiums, pension costs)

Indirect Labour. All factory labour wages, other than those for direct labour and managers' salaries.

All factory labour wages, other than those for direct labour and managers' salaries, are usually classified as **indirect labour** costs—a major component of factory overhead. The term *indirect labour* is usually divided into many subsidiary classifications. The wages of forklift truck operators are generally not combined with janitors' salaries, for example, although both are regarded as indirect labour.

Costs are classified in a detailed fashion primarily to associate a specific cost with its specific cost driver. Two classes of indirect labour deserve special mention: overtime premium and idle time.

Overtime Premium. An indirect labour cost, consisting of the wages paid to all factory workers in excess of their straight-time wage rates.

Overtime premium paid to all factory workers is usually considered a part of overhead. If a lathe operator earns $8 per hour for straight time and time and a half for overtime, the premium is $4 per overtime hour. If the operator works 44 hours, including four overtime hours, in one week, the gross earnings are classified as follows:

Direct labour: 44 hours × $8	$352
Overtime premium (factory overhead): 4 hours × $4	16
Total earnings for 44 hours	$368

Why is overtime premium considered an indirect cost rather than direct? After all, it can usually be traced to specific batches of work. It is usually not considered a direct charge because the scheduling of production jobs is generally random. Suppose that at 8:00 a.m. you bring your automobile to a shop for repair. Through random scheduling, your auto is repaired between 5 p.m and 6 p.m., when the mechanics receive overtime pay. When you come to get your car, you learn that all the overtime premium had been added to your bill. You probably would not be overjoyed.

Thus, in most companies, the overtime premium is not allocated to any specific job. Instead, the overtime premium is considered to be attributable to the heavy overall volume of work, and its cost is thus regarded as part of the indirect manufacturing costs because it happened to be worked on during the overtime hours.

Idle Time. An indirect labour cost consisting of wages paid for unproductive time caused by machine breakdowns, material shortages, and sloppy scheduling.

Another subsidiary classification of indirect-labour costs is **idle time**. This cost typically represents wages paid for unproductive time caused by machine breakdowns, material shortages, sloppy production scheduling, and the like. For example, if the same lathe operator's machine broke down for three hours during the week, the operator's earnings would be classified as follows:

Direct labour: 41 hours × $8	$328
Overtime premium (factory overhead): 4 hours × $4	16
Idle time (factory overhead): 3 hours × $8	24
Total earnings for 44 hours	$368

Managers' salaries usually are not classified as a part of indirect labour. Instead, the compensation of supervisors, department heads, and all others who are regarded as part of manufacturing management are placed in a separate classification of factory overhead.

Employee Benefit Costs.
Employer contributions to employee benefits such as Canada Pension, unemployment insurance, life insurance, health insurance, and pensions.

A type of labour cost growing in importance is **employee benefit costs** (e.g., employer contributions to employee benefits such as Canada Pension Plan, employment insurance, life insurance, health insurance, and pensions). Historically, these costs were referred to as fringe benefits; but today, for most organizations, these costs are too substantial to be referred to as "fringe" costs. Most companies classify these as factory overhead. In some companies, however, employee benefits related to direct labour are charged as an additional direct-labour cost. For instance, a direct labourer, such as a lathe operator or an auto mechanic whose gross wages are computed on the basis of $10 an hour, may enjoy fringe benefits totalling $4 per hour. Most companies classify the $10 as direct-labour cost and the $4 as factory overhead. Other companies classify the entire $14 as direct-labour cost. The latter approach is conceptually preferable because these costs are a fundamental part of acquiring labour services.

Accountants and managers need to pinpoint exactly what direct labour includes and excludes. Such clarity may avoid disputes regarding cost reimbursement contracts, income tax payments, and labour union matters. For example, some countries offer substantial income tax savings to companies that locate factories there. To qualify, these companies' "direct labour" in that country must equal at least a specified percentage of the total manufacturing costs of their products. Disputes have arisen regarding how to calculate the direct-labour percentage for qualifying for such tax relief. For instance, are employee benefits on direct labour an integral part of direct labour, or are they a part of factory overhead? Depending on how companies classify costs, you can readily see that two firms may show different percentages of total manufacturing costs. Consider a company with $10,000 of payroll fringe costs (figures are assumed):

CLASSIFICATION A			CLASSIFICATION B		
Direct materials	$ 80,000	40%	Direct materials	$ 80,000	40%
Direct labour	40,000	20%	Direct labour	50,000	25%
Factory overhead	80,000	40%	Factory overhead	70,000	35%
Total manufacturing costs	$200,000	100%	Total manufacturing costs	$200,000	100%

Classification A assumes that employee benefit costs are part of factory overhead. In contrast, Classification B assumes that employee benefit costs are part of direct labour.

ACCOUNTING VOCABULARY

absorption approach *p. 143*
contribution approach *p. 143*
conversion costs *p. 136*
cost *p. 133*
cost accounting *p. 133*
cost objective *p. 133*
direct costs *p. 134*
direct-labour costs *p. 136*
direct-materials costs *p. 135*
employee benefit costs *p. 159*
factory burden *p. 136*
factory overhead costs *p. 136*

fixed overhead rate *p. 150*
idle time *p. 158*
indirect costs *p. 134*
indirect labour *p. 158*
indirect manufacturing costs *p. 136*
manufacturing overhead *p. 136*
overtime premium *p. 158*
period costs *p. 137*
prime costs *p. 136*
product costs *p. 137*
production volume variance *p. 150*

ASSIGNMENT MATERIAL

QUESTIONS

Q4-1 Name four cost objectives or cost objects.

Q4-2 What is the major purpose of detailed cost accounting systems?

Q4-3 "Departments are not cost objects or objects of costing." Do you agree? Explain.

Q4-4 "The same cost can be direct and indirect." Do you agree? Explain.

Q4-5 "Economic feasibility is an important guideline in designing cost accounting systems." Do you agree? Explain.

Q4-6 How does the idea of economic feasibility relate to the distinction between direct and indirect costs?

Q4-7 "The typical accounting system does not allocate selling and administrative costs to units produced." Do you agree? Explain.

Q4-8 Distinguish between the two prime costs.

Q4-9 "For a furniture manufacturer, glue and tacks become an integral part of the finished product, so they would be direct material." Do you agree? Explain.

Q4-10 Many cost accounting systems have a twofold instead of a threefold category of manufacturing costs. What is a common name for the second item in the twofold category?

Q4-11 "Amortization is an expense for financial statement purposes." Do you agree? Explain.

Q4-12 Distinguish between "costs" and "expenses."

Q4-13 "Unexpired costs are always inventory costs." Do you agree? Explain.

Q4-14 Why is there no Direct Labour Inventory account on a manufacturing company's balance sheet?

Q4-15 What is the advantage of the contribution approach as compared with the absorption approach?

Q4-16 Distinguish between manufacturing and merchandising.

Q4-17 "The primary classifications of costs are by variable- and fixed-cost behaviour patterns, not by business functions." Name three commonly used terms that describe this type of income statement.

Q4-18 "With variable costing, only direct material and direct labour are inventoried." Do you agree? Why?

Q4-19 "Absorption costing regards more categories of costs as product costs." Explain. Be specific.

Q4-20 "An increasing number of companies should not be using variable costing in their corporate annual reports." Do you agree? Explain.

Q4-21 Why is variable costing used only for internal reporting and not for external financial reporting?

Q4-22 Compare the contribution margin with the gross margin.

Q4-23 How is fixed overhead applied to products?

Q4-24 Name the three ways that an absorption costing format differs from a variable costing format.

Q4-25 "Variable costing is consistent with cost-volume-profit analysis." Explain.

PROBLEMS

P4-1   MEANING OF TECHNICAL TERMS.   Refer to Exhibit 4-4. Give the amounts of the following with respect to the cost of goods available for sale: (1) prime costs, (2) conversion costs, (3) factory burden, and (4) indirect manufacturing costs.

P4-2   PRESENCE OF ENDING WORK IN PROCESS.   Refer to Exhibits 4-4 and 4-5. Suppose manufacturing costs were the same, but there was an ending work-in-process inventory of $3 million. The cost of the completed goods would therefore be $37 million instead of $40 million. Suppose also that the cost of goods sold is unchanged.

   1. Recast the income statement of Exhibit 4-4.
   2. What lines and ending balances would change in Exhibit 4-5 and by how much?

P4-3   RELATING COSTS TO COST OBJECTIVES.   A company uses an absorption cost system. Prepare headings for two columns: (1) assembly department costs, and (2) products assembled. Fill in the two columns for each of the costs below. If a specific cost is direct to the department but indirect to the product, place a D in column 1 and an I in column 2. The costs are materials used, supplies used, assembly labour, material-handling labour (transporting materials between and within departments), depreciation—building, assembly supervisor's salary, and the building and grounds supervisor's salary.

P4-4   CLASSIFICATION OF MANUFACTURING COSTS.   Classify each of the following as direct or indirect (D or I) with respect to traceability to product and as variable or fixed (V or F) with respect to whether the cost fluctuates in total as activity or volume changes over wide ranges of activity. You will have two answers, D or I and V or F, for each of the 10 items.

   1. Supervisor training program
   2. Abrasives (sandpaper, etc.)
   3. Cutting bits in a machinery department
   4. Food for a factory cafeteria
   5. Factory rent
   6. Salary of a factory storeroom clerk
   7. Workers' compensation insurance in a factory
   8. Cement for a roadbuilder
   9. Steel scrap for a blast furnace
   10. Paper towels for a factory washroom

P4-5   INVENTORY TRANSACTIONS.   Review Exhibit 4-5. Assume that the Slider Company had no beginning inventories. The following transactions occurred in 2002 (in thousands):

1. Purchase of direct materials	$350
2. Direct materials used	300
3. Acquire direct labour	160
4. Acquire factory overhead	200
5. Complete all goods that were started	??
6. Cost of goods sold (half of the goods completed were sold)	??

Prepare an analysis similar to Exhibit 4-5. What are the ending balances of direct materials, work-in-process, and finished goods inventory?

P4-6 INVENTORY TRANSACTIONS.   Refer to the preceding problem. Suppose some goods were still in process that cost $100,000. Half the goods completed were sold. What are the balances of all the accounts in the ending balance sheet?

P4-7 STRAIGHTFORWARD ABSORPTION STATEMENT.   The Pierce Company had the following data (in thousands) for a given period:

Sales	$700
Direct materials	210
Direct labour	150
Indirect manufacturing costs	170
Selling and administrative expenses	150

There were no beginning or ending inventories. Compute the (1) manufacturing cost of goods sold, (2) gross profit, (3) operating income, (4) prime cost, and (5) conversion cost.

P4-8 STRAIGHTFORWARD CONTRIBUTION INCOME STATEMENT.   Yoko Trucks Ltd. had the following data (in millions of Yen) for a given period:

Sales	¥770
Direct materials	290
Direct labour	140
Variable factory overhead	60
Variable selling and administrative expenses	100
Fixed factory overhead	120
Fixed selling and administrative expenses	45

There were no beginning or ending inventories. Compute the (1) variable manufacturing cost of goods sold, (2) contribution margin, and (3) operating income.

P4-9 STRAIGHTFORWARD ABSORPTION AND CONTRIBUTION STATEMENT.   Anzola Company had the following data (in millions) for a recent period. Fill in the blanks. There were no beginning or ending inventories.

a. Sales	$920
b. Direct materials used	350
c. Direct labour	210
Factory overhead:	
d. Variable	100
e. Fixed	50
f. Variable manufacturing cost of goods sold	—
g. Manufacturing cost of goods sold	—
Selling and Administrative expenses:	
h. Variable	90
i. Fixed	80
j. Gross profit	—
k. Contribution margin	—
l. Prime costs	—
m. Conversion costs	—
n. Operating income	—

P4-10 ABSORPTION STATEMENT.   Raynard's Jewellery had the following data (in thousands) for a given period. Assume there are no inventories. Fill in the blanks.

Sales	$ – *900*
Direct materials	370
Direct labour	– *230*
Factory overhead	– *180*
Manufacturing cost of goods sold	780
Gross margin	120
Selling and administrative expense	– *100*
Operating income	20
Conversion cost	– *910*
Prime cost	600

P4-11 CONTRIBUTION INCOME STATEMENT.   Marlinski had the following data (in thousands) for a given period. Assume there are no inventories.

Direct labour	$170
Direct materials	210
Variable factory overhead	110
Contribution margin	200
Fixed selling and administrative expenses	100
Operating income	10
Sales	970

Compute the (1) variable manufacturing cost of goods sold, (2) variable selling and administrative expenses, and (3) fixed factory overhead.

P4-12 FINANCIAL STATEMENTS FOR MANUFACTURING AND MERCHANDISING COMPANIES.
Outdoor Equipment Company (OEC) and Mountain Supplies Inc. (MSI) sell tents. OEC purchases its tents from a manufacturer for $90 each and sells them for $120. It purchased 10,000 tents in 2002.

MSI produces its own tents. In 2002 MSI produced 10,000 tents. Costs were

Direct materials purchased		$ 535,000
Direct materials used		$ 520,000
Direct labour		260,000
Factory overhead:		
Amortization	$40,000	
Indirect labour	50,000	
Other	30,000	120,000
Total cost of production		$ 900,000

Assume that MSI had no beginning inventory of direct materials. There was no beginning inventory of finished tents, but ending inventory consisted of 1,000 finished tents. Ending work-in-process inventory was negligible.

Each company sold 9,000 tents for $1,080,000 in 2002 and incurred the following selling and administrative costs:

Sales salaries and commissions	$ 90,000
Depreciation on retail store	30,000
Advertising	20,000
Other	10,000
Total selling and administrative cost	$150,000

1. Prepare the inventories section of the balance sheet for December 31, 2002 for OEC.
2. Prepare the inventories section of the balance sheet for December 31, 2002 for MSI.
3. Using Exhibit 4-4 as a model, prepare an income statement for the year 2002 for OEC.
4. Using Exhibit 4-4 as a model, prepare an income statement for the year 2002 for MSI.
5. Summarize the differences between the financial statements of OEC, a merchandiser, and MSI, a manufacturer.

P4-13 **VARIABLE COSTS AND FIXED COSTS; MANUFACTURING AND OTHER COSTS.** For each of the numbered items, choose the appropriate classifications for a manufacturing company. If in doubt about whether the cost behaviour is basically variable or fixed, decide on the basis of whether the total cost will fluctuate substantially over a wide range of volume. Most items have two answers among the following possibilities with respect to the cost of a particular job:

a. Selling cost
b. Manufacturing costs, direct
c. Manufacturing costs, indirect
d. General and administrative cost
e. Fixed cost
f. Variable cost
g. Other (specify)

Sample answers are

Direct material	e,f
President's salary	d,e
Bond interest expense	e,g (financial expense)

Items for your consideration:

1. Factory power for machines
2. Salespersons' commissions
3. Salespersons' salaries
4. Welding supplies
5. Fire loss
6. Sandpaper
7. Supervisory salaries, production control
8. Supervisory salaries, assembly department
9. Supervisory salaries, factory storeroom
10. Company picnic costs
11. Overtime premium, punch press

12. Idle time, assembly
13. Freight out
14. Property taxes
15. Paint for finished products
16. Heating and air conditioning, factory
17. Material-handling labour
18. Straight-line amortization, salespersons' automobiles

P4-14 CONTRIBUTION AND ABSORPTION INCOME STATEMENTS. The following information is taken from the records of the Kingland Company for the year ending December 31, 2002. There were no beginning or ending inventories.

Sales	$ 10,000,000	Long-term rent, factory	$ 100,000
Sales commissions	500,000	Factory superintendent's	
Advertising	200,000	salary	30,000
Shipping expenses	300,000	Supervisors' salaries	100,000
Administrative executive		Direct material used	4,000,000
salaries	100,000	Direct labour	2,000,000
Administrative clerical		Cutting bits used	60,000
salaries (variable)	400,000	Factory methods research	40,000
Fire insurance on		Abrasives for machining	100,000
factory equipment	2,000	Indirect labour	800,000
Property taxes on		Depreciation on	
factory equipment	10,000	equipment	300,000

1. Prepare a contribution income statement and an absorption income statement. If you are in doubt about any cost-behaviour pattern, decide on the basis of whether the total cost in question will fluctuate substantially over a wide range of volume. Prepare a separate support schedule of indirect manufacturing costs subdivided between variable and fixed costs.
2. Suppose that all variable costs fluctuate directly in proportion to sales, and that fixed costs are unaffected over a wide range of sales. What would operating income have been if sales had been $10.5 million instead of $10.0 million? Which income statement did you use to help get your answer? Why?

P4-15 SIMPLE COMPARISON OF VARIABLE AND ABSORPTION COSTING. Ithalid Company began business on January 1, 2001, with assets of $150,000 cash and equity of $150,000 capital stock. In 2001 it manufactured some inventory at a cost of $60,000, including $12,000 for factory rent and other fixed factory overhead. In 2002 it manufactured nothing and sold half of its inventory for $42,000 cash. In 2003 it manufactured nothing and sold the remaining half for another $42,000 cash. It had no fixed expenses in 2002 or 2003. There are no other transactions of any kind. Ignore income taxes.

Prepare an ending balance sheet plus an income statement for 2001, 2002, and 2003 under (1) absorption costing and (2) variable costing.

P4-16 **COMPARISONS OVER FOUR YEARS.** The Balakrishnan Corporation began business on January 1, 2000, to produce and sell a single product. Reported operating income figures under both absorption and variable costing for the first four years of operation are

YEAR	VARIABLE COSTING	ABSORPTION COSTING
2000	$70,000	$50,000
2001	70,000	60,000
2002	50,000	50,000
2003	40,000	70,000

Standard production costs per unit, sales prices, application (absorption) rates, and expected-volume levels were the same each year. There were no cost variances in any year. All nonmanufacturing expenses were fixed, and there were no nonmanufacturing cost variances in any year.

1. In what year(s) did "units produced" equal "units sold"?
2. In what year(s) did "units produced" exceed "units sold"?
3. What is the dollar amount of the December 31, 2003, finished-goods inventory? (Give absorption costing value.)
4. What is the difference between "units produced" and "units sold" in 2003, if you know that the absorption-costing fixed-manufacturing-overhead application rate is $3 per unit? (Give answer in units.)

P4-17 **VARIABLE AND ABSORPTION COSTING.** Chan Company data for 2001 are as follows:

Sales: 12,000 units at $17 each	
Actual production	15,000 units
Expected volume of production	18,000 units
Manufacturing costs incurred:	
Variable	$105,000
Fixed	63,000
Nonmanufacturing costs incurred:	
Variable	$ 24,000
Fixed	18,000

1. Determine operating income for 2001, assuming the firm uses the variable costing approach to product costing. (Do not prepare a statement.)
2. Assume that there is no January 1, 2001, inventory; no variances are allocated to inventory; and the firm uses a "full absorption" approach to product costing. Compute (a) the cost assigned to December 31, 2001, inventory; and (b) operating income for the year ended December 31, 2001. (Do not prepare a statement.)

P4-18 **COMPUTE PRODUCTION VOLUME VARIANCE.** Osaka Manufacturing Company budgeted its 2001 variable overhead at ¥14,100,000 and its fixed overhead at ¥25,620,000. Expected 2001 volume was 6,100 units. Actual costs for production of 5,800 units during 2001 were

Variable overhead	¥14,160,000
Fixed overhead	25,620,000
Total overhead	¥39,780,000

Compute the production volume variance. Be sure to label it favourable or unfavourable.

P4-19 **RECONCILING VARIABLE COSTING AND ABSORPTION COSTING OPERATING INCOME.**
Blackstone Tools produced 12,000 electric drills during 2001, although expected production was only 10,500 drills. The company's fixed overhead rate is $7 per drill. Absorption-costing operating income for the year is $18,000, based on sales of 11,000 drills.

1. Compute: (a) Budgeted fixed overhead
   (b) Production volume variance
   (c) Variable costing operating income
2. Reconcile absorption costing operating income and variable-costing operating income. Include the amount of the difference between the two and an explanation for the difference.

P4-20 **COMPARING VARIABLE COSTING AND ABSORPTION COSTING.** Simple numbers are used in this problem to highlight the concepts covered in the chapter.

Assume that the Canberra Company produces one product—a bath mat—that sells for $10. Canberra uses a standard-cost system. Total standard variable costs of production are $4 per mat, fixed manufacturing costs are $1,500 per year, and selling and administrative expenses are $300 per year, all fixed. Expected production volume is 500 mats per year.

1. For each of the following nine combinations of actual sales and production (*in units*) for 2000, prepare condensed income statements under variable costing and under absorption costing.

	(1)	(2)	(3)	(4)	(5)	(6)	(7)	(8)	(9)
Sales units	300	400	500	400	500	600	500	600	700
Production units	400	400	400	500	500	500	600	600	600

Use the following formats:

VARIABLE COSTING		ABSORPTION COSTING	
Revenue	$ aa	Revenue	$ aa
Cost of goods sold	(bb)	Cost of goods sold	(uu)
Contribution margin	$ cc	Gross profit at standard	$ vv
Fixed manufacturing costs	(dd)	Favourable (unfavourable)	
Fixed selling and adminis-		production-volume variance	ww
trative expenses	(ee)	Gross profit at "actual"	$ xx
		Selling and administrative	
		expenses	(yy)
Operating income	$ ff	Operating income	$ zz

2. a. In which of the nine combinations is variable-costing income greater than absorption-costing income? In which is it lower? The same?

b. In which of the nine combinations is the production volume variance unfavourable? Favourable?

c. How much profit is added by selling one more unit under variable costing? Under absorption costing?

d. How much profit is added by producing one more unit under variable costing? Under absorption costing?

e. Suppose sales, rather than production, is the critical factor in determining the success of Canberra Company. Which format, variable costing or absorption costing, provides the better measure of performance?

P4-21 ALL-FIXED COSTS. The Marple Company has built a massive water-desalting factory next to an ocean. The factory is completely automated. It has its own source of power, light, heat, and so on. The salt water costs nothing. All producing and other operating costs are fixed; they do not vary with output because the volume is governed by adjusting a few dials on a control panel. The employees have flat annual salaries.

The desalted water is not sold to household consumers. It has a special taste that appeals to local breweries, distilleries, and soft-drink manufacturers. The price, $.50 per litre, is expected to remain unchanged for quite some time.

The following are data regarding the first two years of operations:

	IN LITRES		COSTS (ALL FIXED)	
	SALES	PRODUCTION	MANUFACTURING	OTHER
2001	1,500,000	3,000,000	$600,000	$200,000
2002	1,500,000	0	600,000	200,000

Orders can be processed in four hours, so management decided, in early 2002, to gear production strictly to sales.

1. Prepare three-column income statements for 2001, for 2002, and for the two years together using (a) variable costing and (b) absorption costing.

2. What is the break-even point under (a) variable costing and (b) absorption costing?

3. What inventory costs would be carried on the balance sheets on December 31, 2001 and 2002, under each method?

4. Comment on your answers in requirements 1 and 2. Which costing method appears more useful?

P4-22 SEMIFIXED COSTS. The Carley Company differs from the Marple Company (described in Problem 4-21) in only one respect: it has both variable and fixed manufacturing costs. Its variable costs are $.14 per litre and its fixed *manufacturing* costs are $325,000 per year.

1. Using the same data as in the preceding problem, except for the change in production-cost behaviour, prepare three-column income statements for 2001, for 2002 and for the two years together using (a) variable costing and (b) absorption costing.

2. What inventory costs would be carried on the balance sheets on December 31, 2001 and 2002, under each method?

P4-23 **ABSORPTION AND VARIABLE COSTING.** The Trapani Company had the following actual data for 2001 and 2002:

	2001	2002
Units of finished goods:		
Opening inventory	—	2,000
Production	15,000	13,000
Sales	13,000	14,000
Ending inventory	2,000	1,000

The basic production data at standard unit costs for the two years were

Direct materials	$22
Direct labour	18
Variable factory overhead	4
Standard variable costs per unit	$44

Fixed factory overhead was budgeted at $98,000 per year. The expected volume of production was 14,000 units, so the fixed overhead rate was $98,000 ÷ 14,000 = $7 per unit.

Budgeted sales price was $75 per unit. Selling and administrative expenses were budgeted at variable, *$9 per unit sold*, and fixed, $80,000 per year.

Assume that there were absolutely no variances from any standard variable costs, budgeted selling prices or budgeted fixed costs in 2001.

There were no beginning or ending inventories of work in process.

1. For 2001, prepare income statements based on variable costing and absorption costing. (The next problem deals with 2002.)
2. Explain why operating income differs between variable costing and absorption costing. Be specific.

P4-24 **ABSORPTION AND VARIABLE COSTING.** Assume the same facts as in the preceding problem. In addition, consider the following actual data for 2002:

Direct materials	$285,000
Direct labour	174,200
Variable factory overhead	36,000
Fixed factory overhead	95,000
Selling and administrative costs:	
Variable	118,400
Fixed	80,000
Sales	1,068,000

1. For 2002, prepare income statements based on variable costing and absorption costing. Arrange your income statements in the following general format:
   Sales (at budgeted prices)
   Cost of goods sold
   Gross profit
   Selling and administrative costs
   Operating income before variances

Variances (list in detail)

Operating income

2. Explain why operating income differs between variable costing and absorption costing. Be specific.

P4-25 EMPLOYEE BENEFIT COSTS. Appendix 4. Direct labour is often accounted for at the gross wage rate, and the related "benefit costs" such as employer payroll taxes and employer contributions to health care plans are accounted for as part of overhead. Suppose Amy O'Keefe, a direct labourer, works 40 hours during a particular week as an auditor for a public accounting firm. She receives $18 gross pay per hour plus related benefit costs of $10 per hour.

1. What would be the cost of O'Keefe's direct labour? Of related general overhead?
2. Suppose O'Keefe works 30 hours for Client A and 10 hours for Client B, and the firm allocates costs to each client. What would be the cost of O'Keefe's direct labour on the Client A job? The Client B job?
3. How would you allocate general overhead to the Client A job? The Client B job?
4. Suppose O'Keefe works a total of 50 hours (30 for A and 20 for B), 10 of which are paid on the basis of time-and-one-half. What would be the cost of O'Keefe's "direct labour" on the Client A job? The Client B job? The addition to general overhead?

P4-26 REVIEW OF CHAPTERS 2 THROUGH 4. The Gumey Hosiery Company provides you with the following miscellaneous data regarding operations in 2001.

Gross profit	$ 20,000
Net profit (loss)	(5,000)
Sales	100,000
Direct material used	35,000
Direct labour	25,000
Fixed manufacturing overhead	15,000
Fixed selling and administrative expenses	10,000

There are no beginning or ending inventories.

Compute the (1) variable selling and administrative expenses, (2) contribution margin in dollars, (3) variable manufacturing overhead, (4) break-even point in sales dollars, and (5) manufacturing cost of goods sold.

P4-27 REVIEW OF CHAPTERS 2 THROUGH 4. Stephenson Corporation provides you with the following miscellaneous data regarding operations for 2001:

Break-even point (in sales dollars)	$ 66,667
Direct materials used	24,000
Gross profit	25,000
Contribution margin	30,000
Direct labour	28,000
Sales	100,000
Variable manufacturing overhead	5,000

There are no beginning or ending inventories.

Compute the (1) fixed manufacturing overhead, (2) variable selling and administrative expenses, and (3) fixed selling and administrative expenses.

P4-28 REVIEW OF CHAPTERS 2 THROUGH 4. U. Grant Company manufactured and sold 1,000 sabres during November. Selected data for November follow:

Sales	$100,000
Direct materials used	26,000
Direct labour	16,000
Variable manufacturing overhead	13,000
Fixed manufacturing overhead	14,000
Variable selling and administrative expenses	?
Fixed selling and administrative expenses	?
Contribution margin	40,000
Operating income	22,000

There were no beginning or ending inventories.

1. What were the variable selling and administrative expenses for November?
2. What were the fixed selling and administrative expenses for November?
3. What was the cost of goods sold during November?
4. Without prejudice to your earlier answers, assume that the fixed selling and administrative expenses for November amounted to $14,000.
   a. What was the break-even point in units for November?
   b. How many units must be sold to earn a target operating income of $12,000?
   c. What would the selling price per unit have to be if the company wanted to earn an operating income of $17,000 on the sale of 900 units?

P4-29 COLLABORATIVE LEARNING PROBLEM: INTERNET RESEARCH AND COST MANAGEMENT SYSTEM. Form groups of three to five persons each. Each member of the group should pick one of the following industry types:

- Manufacturing
- Insurance
- Healthcare
- Government
- Service

Each person should explore the Internet for an example of an organization that has changed its cost management practices. Prepare and give a briefing for your group. Do this by completing the following:

1. Describe the company and its business.
2. What was the scope of the cost systems project?
3. What were the goals for the cost systems project?
4. Summarize the results of the project.

After each person has briefed the group on his/her company, discuss within your group the commonalities between the cost management systems.

P4-30 **COLLABORATIVE LEARNING EXERCISE: VARIABLE AND ABSORPTION COSTING.** Form groups of four persons each. Each person should select one of the following four roles (if groups have between four and eight persons, two persons can play any of the roles in the exercise):

> Bernard Schwartz, President
> Ramona Sanchez, Controller
> Leonard Swanson, Marketing Manager
> Kate Cheung, Treasurer

Each of the four should prepare a justification for the type of financial statements, variable or absorption costing, that he or she favours. The setting is explained in the case, "Boylston Company," that follows.

Bernard Schwartz took over as president of Boylston Company in mid-May, 2002. The company's operating income for May was $4,000, and Schwartz was determined that June would be a better month. But when he received the following income statements for May and June, he was shocked:

Boylston Company

	MAY	JUNE
Sales	$280,000	$340,000
Cost of sales	150,000	180,000
Gross margin	130,000	160,000
Variances:		
Labour	6,000F	4,000F
Material	5,000U	3,000U
Overhead:		
Volume	1,000F	27,000U
Spending	2,000U	1,000U
Selling & administrative	126,000	136,000
Operating income (loss)	$ 4,000	$ (3,000)

He called Ramona Sanchez, the company's controller, and asked, "Sales were up by $60,000 in June. How could operating income possibly have decreased by $7,000? There must be something wrong with your numbers."

Sanchez replied, "The numbers are right. I agree with you they don't make sense, but since our production was down in June, operating income suffered." Schwartz wasn't satisfied with that explanation. "If your accounting numbers don't give a good signal about performance, what good are they?"

Sanchez had anticipated this reaction. She suggested charging the fixed manufacturing costs as a period cost instead of including them in the product cost. Her reworked income statement was as follows:

	MAY	JUNE
Sales	$280,000	$340,000
Cost of sales	102,000	125,000
Gross margin	178,000	215,000
Fixed overhead	66,000	67,000

	MAY	JUNE
Variances		
Labour	6,000F	4,000F
Material	5,000U	3,000U
Overhead spending	2,000U	1,000U
Selling & administrative	126,000	136,000
Operating income (loss)	$ (15,000)	$ 12,000

Sanchez also called on Leonard Swanson, the marketing manager, to support her new statements. Swanson pointed out that the current accounting system did not provide the right incentives to his sales force. For example, he pointed to two products, A and B, with the following price and costs:

PRODUCT	PRICE	COST OF SALES	MARGIN	% OF SALES
A	$1.90	$1.10	$ .80	42.1
B	2.30	1.30	1.00	43.5

The sales force would be inclined to focus on Product B because of its higher margin as a percent of sales. However, he believed the following figures, based on the controller's new product costs, was a better measure of the relative profitability of the products:

PRODUCT	PRICE	COST OF SALES	MARGIN	% OF SALES
A	$1.90	$ .50	$1.40	73.7
B	2.30	1.00	1.30	56.5

After some discussion, Schwartz brought in Kate Cheung, corporate treasurer, who was skeptical about the new system. She maintained that "the sales force will start cutting prices if we leave fixed costs out of our product costs. They will try for the same margin over the reduced costs, and we will not be able to cover our fixed costs. Further, it's lack of control of long-run costs, not short-run variable costs that can destroy a company. In the short-run, things constantly change and we don't make much of a commitment. But if long-run costs get out of control, there isn't much we can do about it."

Cheung was not finished. "And what about taxes? The government won't let us use your new system. And what about the balance sheet? Inventories that we now show at about $520,000 would have to be shown at about $365,000 if the fixed costs are not considered product costs. That sure doesn't make us look better to investors."

Although Schwartz liked the June profit shown by the revised statements, he thought there was some truth in all of the comments made. He wasn't sure how to proceed.

C4-1 ANALYSIS WITH CONTRIBUTION INCOME STATEMENT. The following data have been condensed from Chateau Corporation's report of 2001 operations (in millions of French francs [FF]):

	VARIABLE	FIXED	TOTAL
Manufacturing cost of goods sold	FF420	FF200	FF620
Selling and administrative expenses	150	70	220
Sales			950

Required:

1. Prepare the 2001 income statement in contribution form, ignoring income taxes.
2. Chauteau's operations have been fairly stable from year to year. In planning for the future, top management is considering several options for changing the annual pattern of operations. You are asked to perform an analysis of their estimated effects. Use your contribution income statement as a framework to compute the estimated operating income (in millions) under each of the following separate and unrelated assumptions:
   a. Assume that a 10 percent reduction in selling prices would cause a 30 percent increase in the physical volume of goods manufactured and sold.
   b. Assume that an annual expenditure of FF30 million for a special sales promotion campaign would enable the company to increase its physical volume by 10 percent with no change in selling prices.
   c. Assume that a basic redesign of manufacturing operations would increase annual fixed manufacturing costs by FF80 million and decrease variable manufacturing costs by 15 percent per product unit, but with no effect on physical volume or selling prices.
   d. Assume that a basic redesign of selling and administrative operations would double the annual fixed expenses for selling and administration and increase the variable selling and administrative expenses by 25 percent per product unit, but would also increase physical volume by 20 percent. Selling prices would be increased by 5 percent.
   e. Would you prefer to use the absorption form of income statement for the above analyses? Explain.
3. Discuss the desirability of alternatives a through d in requirement 2. If only one alternative could be selected, which would you choose? Explain.

C4-2 CANADIAN OIL SPILL. (CICA) Two years ago, a ship owned by a foreign company ran aground during a severe storm and sank at the entrance of a Canadian harbour. The vessel blocked the entrance to the harbour and spilled considerable amounts of oil. Under federal legislation, the Canadian government is required to clean up an oil spill immediately and render the harbour's entrance safe for other vessels. The legislation states that costs are to be compiled in accordance with "accepted Canadian financial and cost accounting practices," and that they are to be charged to the shipping company and/or its insurers.

Neal & Co., Chartered Accountants, has been approached by a federal government department and asked for assistance in supporting its claim against the shipping company. The partner considering acceptance of this engagement has asked you, CA,

addressed in determining whether the Cost Schedule has been prepared in accordance with "accepted Canadian financial and cost accounting practices."

Currently, there is a lack of agreement between the shipping company and the government. Therefore, the report will also be filed with the court if a lawsuit by the federal government becomes essential. No amount has been paid by the shipping company, although the first invoice was rendered one year ago. Government policy is to charge 10 percent interest on all unpaid amounts.

In the discussion of these issues, CA has been asked to indicate what arguments Neal & Co. can provide in testimony in court. These arguments should include:

1. A defence of the logic of the procedures that were applied in the preparation of the Cost Schedule; and
2. A rebuttal of possible objections to the procedures used in the preparation of the Cost Schedule that might be raised by accountants and lawyers for the shipping company.

Your review of the Cost Schedule and discussions with government employees provided the following information:

1. The $14.5 million is made up of the following cost categories:

Direct contract costs	$ 6,200,000
Government ships and helicopters assigned to clean up and salvage	4,500,000
Government supervisory ships assigned to general duty	2,000,000
Shore facilities—to support ships and helicopters	950,000
Administration—government departments involved in clean-up and salvage	850,000
	$14,500,000

2. The "direct contract costs" represent the costs charged by various companies and government groups contracted by the government department for clean-up and salvage. Invoices are available to support the $6.2 million and have been signed by government officials to indicate that the services were provided. Included in the $6.2 million are invoices for $800,000, representing one-half of the $1.6 million billed by one supplier. The other half, $800,000, was charged to a government account and represented improvements to the harbour entrance.
3. The "government ships and helicopters" charge of $4.5 million represents the cost of ships and helicopters specifically assigned to the clean-up. They would normally be performing defence and limited commercial duties elsewhere. Therefore, the ships and helicopter were taken from specific assignments to perform the clean-up and salvage quickly. The $4.5 million is made up of

Wages and benefits of crews	$2,500,000*
Fuel for ships and helicopters	1,050,000
Supplies for ships and helicopters	500,000
Direct maintenance of ships during clean-up period	150,000
Amortization of ships during clean-up period	300,000
	$4,500,000

* Includes pension costs of $250,000 and personal life insurance costs of $90,000. All crew members were employed by the armed forces of Canada.

4. The "government supervisory ships" charge of $2 million represents the cost of ships that were needed to coordinate the clean-up and direct commercial ships safely through the harbour. They also served to keep sightseeing vessels and other groups away from the wreck. These ships would have been assigned to general civilian rescue and coast-guard duties if they had not been at the location of the clean-up and salvage. The $2 million is made up of

Wages and benefits of crews	$1,200,000*
Fuel for ship	270,000
Crew meals and related supplies	80,000
Overtime pay to crews for clean-up period	300,000
Direct maintenance of ships during clean-up period	50,000
Amortization of ships during clean-up	100,000
	$2,000,000

* Includes vacation pay of $80,000, pension costs of $70,000, and insurance and other fringe benefits of $50,000. All crew members are government employees.

5. The "shore facilities" cost of $950,000 is primarily for the refuelling of ships and aircraft:

Fuel used by direct-contract ships (not included in the $6,200,000)	$600,000
Labour to service direct-contract ships	175,000
Labour to fuel government ships and helicopters	75,000
Supplies used by government ships	100,000
	$950,000

6. "Administration" costs of $850,000 include

Armed forces personnel taken from other duties and assigned to shore duties related to the clean-up	$475,000*
Estimated cost of telecommunications equipment used for clean-up—(at commercial rates)	225,000
Cost of assembling the cost data, for invoicing to the shipping company; estimated, using commercial rates for accounting services	100,000
Legal advice on invoicing the shipping company	50,000
	$850,000

* Includes accrued vacation pay of $30,000, pension costs of $45,000 and other fringe benefits of $40,000. These personnel would otherwise have been assigned to general duties.

Required: Prepare the memorandum to the partner by discussing the relevance of each of these costs. In your memorandum, determine an amount that you think should be claimed against the shipping company.

5

Cost Allocation and Activity-Based Costing Systems

After studying this chapter, you will be able to

1. Explain the major purposes for allocating costs.

2. Explain the relationship between activities, resources, costs, and cost drivers.

3. Use recommended guidelines to charge the variable and fixed costs of service departments to other organizational units.

4. Identify methods for allocating the central costs of an organization.

5. Use the direct, step-down, and reciprocal allocation methods to allocate service department costs to user departments.

6. Describe the general approach to allocating costs to products or services.

7. Use the physical units and relative-sales-value methods to allocate joint costs to products.

8. Use activity-based costing to allocate costs to products or services.

9. Identify the steps involved in the design and implementation of activity-based costing systems.

10. Calculate activity-based costs for cost objects.

11. Explain why activity-based costing systems are being adopted.

12. Explain how just-in-time systems can reduce non-value-added activities

A university's computer is used for teaching and for government-funded research. How much of its cost should be assigned to each task? A city creates a special police unit to investigate a series of related assaults. What is the total cost of the effort? A company uses a machine to make two different products. How much of the cost of the machine belongs to each product? These are all problems of cost allocation, the subject of this chapter. University presidents, city managers, corporate executives, and others all face problems of cost allocation.

Cost Accounting System. The techniques used to determine the cost of a product or service by collecting and classifying costs and assigning them to cost objects.

This is the first of three chapters on **cost accounting systems**—the techniques used to determine the cost of a product or service. A cost accounting system collects and classifies costs and assigns them to cost objects. The goal of a cost accounting system is to measure the cost of designing, developing, producing (or purchasing), selling, distributing, and servicing particular products or services. Cost allocation is at the heart of most cost accounting systems.

The first part of this chapter describes general approaches to cost allocation. Although we present some factors to consider in selecting cost-allocation methods, there are no easy answers. Recent attempts to improve cost-allocation methods have focused on activity-based costing, the subject of the last part of this chapter.

COST ALLOCATION IN GENERAL

As Chapter 4 pointed out, cost allocation is fundamentally a problem of linking (1) some cost or groups of costs with (2) one or more *cost objectives*, such as products, departments, and divisions. Ideally, costs should be assigned to the cost objective that *caused* it. In short, cost allocation tries to identify (1) with (2) via some function representing causation.

Cost-Allocation Base. A cost driver when it is used for allocating costs.

Cost Pool. A group of individual costs that is allocated to cost objectives using a single cost driver.

Linking costs with cost objectives is accomplished by selecting cost drivers. When used for allocating costs, a cost driver is often called a **cost-allocation base**. Major costs, such as newsprint for a newspaper and direct professional labour for a law firm, may each be allocated to departments, jobs, and projects on an item-by-item basis, using obvious cost drivers such as tonnes of newsprint consumed or direct-labour-hours used. Other costs, taken one at a time, are not important enough to justify being allocated individually. These costs are *pooled* and then allocated together. A **cost pool** is a group of individual costs that is allocated to *cost objectives* using a single cost driver. For example, building rent, utilities cost, and janitorial services may be in the same cost pool because all are allocated on the basis of square metres of space occupied. Or a university could pool all the operating costs of its registrar's office and allocate them to its colleges on the basis of the number of students in each faculty. In summary, all costs in a given cost pool should be caused by the same factor. That factor is the cost driver.

Many different terms are used by companies to describe cost allocation in practice. You may encounter terms such as *allocate, attribute, reallocate, trace, assign, distribute, redistribute, load, burden, apportion,* and *reapportion,* which can be used interchangeably to describe the allocation of costs to cost objectives.

Three Purposes of Allocation

Managers within an organizational unit should be aware of all the consequences of their decisions, even consequences outside of their unit. Examples are the addition of a new course in a university that causes additional work in the registrar's office, the addition of a new flight or an additional passenger on an airline that requires reservation and booking services, and the addition of a new specialty in a medical clinic that produces more work for the medical records department.

In each of these situations, it is important to *assign* to the organizational unit the *direct* incremental costs of the decision. Using the distinction noted in Chapter 4, managers assign direct costs without using allocated costs. The allocation of costs is necessary when the linkage between the costs and the cost objective is indirect. In this case, a basis for the allocation, such as direct-labour-hours or tonnes of raw material, is used even though its selection is arbitrary.

A cost allocation base has been described as *incorrigible*, since it is impossible to objectively determine which base perfectly describes the link between the cost and the cost objective. Given this subjectivity in the selection of a cost-allocation base, it has always been difficult for managers to determine "When should costs be allocated?" and "On what basis should costs be allocated?" The answers to these questions depend on the principal purpose or purposes of the cost allocation.

Costs are allocated for three main purposes:

1. *To obtain desired motivation.* Cost allocations are sometimes made to influence management behaviour and thus promote goal congruence and managerial effort. Consequently, in some organizations there is no cost allocation for legal or internal auditing services or internal management consulting services because top management wants to encourage their use. In other organizations there is a cost allocation for such items to spur managers to make sure the benefits of the specified services exceed the costs.

2. *To compute income and asset valuations.* Costs are allocated to products and projects to measure inventory costs and cost of goods sold. These allocations frequently service financial accounting purposes. However, the resulting costs are also often used by managers in planning, performance evaluation, and to motivate managers, as described above.

3. *To justify costs or obtain reimbursement.* Sometimes prices are based directly on costs, or it may be necessary to justify an accepted bid. For example, government contracts often specify a price that includes reimbursement for costs plus some profit margin. In these instances, cost allocations become substitutes for the usual working of the marketplace in setting prices.

The first purpose specifies planning and control uses for allocation. The second and third show how cost allocations may differ for inventory costing (and cost of goods sold) and for setting prices. Moreover, different allocations of costs to products may be made for various purposes. Thus, full costs may guide pricing decisions, manufacturing costs may be appropriate for asset valuations, and some "in-between" costs may be negotiated for a government contract.

Ideally, all three purposes would be served simultaneously by a single cost allocation. But thousands of managers and accountants will testify that for most costs, this ideal is rarely achieved. Instead, cost allocations are often a source of discontent and confusion for the affected parties. Allocating fixed costs usually causes the greatest problems. When all three purposes cannot be attained simultaneously, the manager and the accountant should start attacking a cost allocation problem by trying to identify which of the purposes should dominate in the particular situation at hand.

Often inventory-costing purposes dominate by default because they are externally imposed. When allocated costs are used in decision making and performance evaluation, managers should consider adjusting the allocations used to satisfy inventory-costing purposes. Often the added benefit of using separate allocations for planning and control and inventory-costing purposes is much greater than the added cost.

Three Types of Allocations

As Exhibit 5-1 shows, there are three basic types of cost allocations:

1. *Allocation of joint costs to the appropriate responsibility centres.* Costs that are used jointly by more than one unit are allocated based on cost-driver activity in the units. Examples are allocating rent to departments based on floor space occupied, allocating amortization on jointly used machinery based on machine-hours, and allocating general administrative expense based on total direct cost.

2. *Reallocation of costs from one responsibility centre to another.* When one unit provides products or services to another, the costs are transferred along with the products or services. Some units, called **service departments**, exist only to support other departments, and their costs are totally reallocated. Examples include personnel departments, laundry departments in hospitals, and legal departments in industrial firms.

3. *Allocation of costs of a particular organizational unit to its outputs of products or services.* The paediatrics department of a medical clinic allocates its costs to patient visits, the assembly department of a manufacturing firm to units assembled, and the tax department of a CA firm to clients served. The costs allocated to products or services include those allocated to the organizational unit in allocation types 1 and 2.

Service Departments. Units that exist only to serve other departments.

All three types of allocations are fundamentally similar. Let us look first at how service department costs are allocated to production departments.

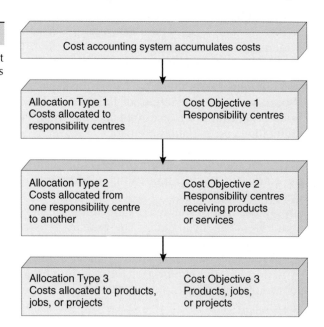

ALLOCATION OF SERVICE DEPARTMENT COSTS

OBJECTIVE 2

Explain the relationship between activities, resources, costs, and cost drivers.

What causes costs? Organizations incur costs to produce goods and services and to provide the support services required for that production. Essentially, costs are caused by the very same activities that are usually chosen as cost objectives. Examples are products produced, patients seen, personnel records processed, and legal advice given. The ultimate *effects* of these activities are various costs. It is important to understand how cost behaviour relates to activities and the consumption of resources. To perform activities, resources are required. These resources have costs. Some costs vary in direct proportion to the consumption of resources. Examples could be materials, labour, energy, and supplies. Other costs do not directly vary (in the short run) with resource usage. Examples of their indirect costs could be amortization, supervisory salaries, and rent. So we say that activities consume resources and the costs of these resources follow various behavioural patterns. Therefore, the manager and the accountant should search for some cost driver that establishes a convincing relationship between the cause (activity being performed) and the effect (consumption of resources and related costs) and that permits *reliable predictions* of how costs will be affected by decisions regarding the activities.

To illustrate this important principle, we will consider allocation of service department costs. Service departments typically provide a service to a broad range of functions and products within an organization, and thus the allocation of costs becomes more difficult. The preferred guidelines for allocating service department costs are:

1. *Evaluate performance using budgets* for each service (staff) department, just as is done for each production or operating (line) department. The performance of a service department is evaluated by comparing actual costs with a budget, regardless of how the costs are later allocated. From the budget, variable-cost pools and fixed-cost pools can be identified.
2. *Charge variable-and fixed-cost pools separately* (sometimes called the dual method of allocation). Note that one service department (such as a computer department) can contain multiple cost pools if more than one cost driver causes the department's costs. At a minimum, there should be a variable-cost pool and a fixed-cost pool.
3. *Establish part of all of the details regarding cost allocation in advance* of rendering the service, rather than after the fact. This approach establishes the "rules of the game" so that all departments can plan appropriately.

Consider a simplified example of a computer department of a university that serves two major users: the School of Business and the School of Engineering. The computer mainframe was acquired on a five-year lease that is not cancellable unless prohibitive cost penalties are paid.

How should costs be charged to the user departments? Suppose there are two major purposes for the information: (1) predicting economic effects of the use of the computer and (2) motivating departments and individuals to use its capabilities more fully.

To apply the first of the above guidelines, we need to analyze the costs of the computer department in detail. The primary activity performed is computer processing. Resources consumed include processing time, operator time, consulting time, energy, materials, and building space. Suppose cost behaviour analysis has been performed and the budget formula for the forthcoming fiscal year is $100,000 monthly fixed costs plus $200 variable cost per hour of computer time used. We will apply guidelines two and three in the next two sections.

COST ALLOCATIONS AT BOREAL LABORATORIES LTD.

Boreal Laboratories
www.boreal.com

Boreal is Canada's largest supplier of science supplies and apparatus to Canadian schools. The product line is diverse and thus product costing is complex.

A recent project included revisiting our inventory costing. In order to determine the inventory cost, many allocations have had to be made.

A combination of all the costing techniques listed in Chapter 13 have been used since there are several different production departments and the production activities vary for each commodity.

In making allocations, three guidelines should be kept in mind.

1. The allocation must be fair.
2. The allocation must be rational and verifiable.
3. The impact on the people who use or work with this information must be known.

These guidelines provide a useful reference since there may be ramifications beyond just the immediate task or project, for which the initially intended allocation calculation was made.

Recently, the Inventory Costing System was revised to reflect current input costs and to reflect the change in operating costs and procedures as a result of moving to a new facility. When this inventory information was updated, the above three guidelines were considered when it came time to make allocations of costs.

This proved to be very beneficial since there have been many other applications of these calculations than those originally made for inventory purposes. Some of the additional uses of this information have been:

- Used to re-calculate selling prices in our catalogue to reflect the fact that our costs have changed.
- Used to calculate a selling price on several special orders that involve different quantities and mixture of products.
- Assisted in determining if Boreal would continue to produce a product in-house or to buy elsewhere.
- Useful for accounting taxation purposes.
- A useful calculation in determining a profit-share amount since each department manager's work is based upon performance.

Based upon the number and varying uses of an allocation, we can see how important allocations are in business. Furthermore, we should be aware that allocations may be used for more than one intended use.

Source: Written by John Richardson, Controller, Boreal Laboratories Ltd.

Variable-Cost Pool

OBJECTIVE 3

Use recommended guidelines to charge the variable and fixed costs of service departments to other organizational units.

The cost driver for the variable-cost pool is *hours of computer time used*. Therefore, variable costs should be assigned as follows:

$$\text{budgeted unit rate} \times \text{actual hours of computer time used}$$

The cause-and-effect relationship is direct and clear: the heavier the usage, the higher the total costs. In this example, the rate used would be the budgeted rate of $200 per hour.

The use of *budgeted* cost rates rather than *actual* cost rates for allocating variable costs of service departments protects the using departments from intervening price fluctuations and also often protects them from inefficiencies in the service departments. When an organization allocates *actual* total service department cost, it holds user-department managers responsible for costs beyond their control and provides less incentive for service departments to be efficient. Both effects are undesirable.

Consider the charging of *variable* costs to a department that uses 600 hours of computer time. Suppose inefficiencies in the computer department caused the variable costs to be $140,000 instead of the 600 hours times $200, or $120,000 budgeted. A good cost-accounting scheme would charge only the $120,000 to the consuming departments and would let the $20,000 remain as an unfavourable budget variance of the computer department. This scheme holds computer department managers responsible for the $20,000 variance and reduces the resentment of user managers. User-department managers sometimes complain more vigorously about uncertainty over allocations and the poor management of a service department than about the choice of a cost driver (such as direct-labour dollars or number of employees). Such complaints are less likely if the service department managers have budget responsibility and the user departments are protected from short-run price fluctuations and inefficiencies.

Most consumers prefer to know the total price in advance. They become nervous when an automobile mechanic or contractor undertakes a job without specifying prices. As a minimum, they like to know the hourly rates that they must bear. Therefore, predetermined unit prices (at least) should be used. Where feasible, predetermined total prices should be used for various kinds of work based on budgets and standards.

To illustrate, consider an automobile repair and maintenance department for a provincial government. Agencies who use the department's service should receive firm prices for various services. Imagine the reaction of an agency manager who had an agency automobile repaired and was told, "Normally your repair would have taken five hours, but we had a new employee work on it, and the job took ten hours. Therefore, we must charge you for ten hours of labour time."

Fixed-Cost Pool

The cost driver for the fixed-cost pool is the amount of capacity required when the computer facilities were acquired. Therefore, fixed costs could be allocated as follows:

budgeted fraction of capacity available for use × total budgeted fixed costs

Consider again our example of the university computer department. Suppose the dean had originally predicted the following long-run average monthly usage: Business, 210 hours, and Engineering, 490 hours, for a total of 700 hours. The fixed-cost pool would be allocated as follows:

	BUSINESS	ENGINEERING
Fixed costs per month:		
210/700, or 30% of $100,000	$30,000	
490/700, or 70% of $100,000		$70,000

This predetermined lump-sum approach is based on the long-run capacity *available* to the user, regardless of actual usage from month to month. The reasoning is that the level of fixed costs is affected by long-range planning regarding the overall level of service and the *relative expected* usage, not by *short-run* fluctuations in service levels and relative *actual* usage.

A major strength of using capacity *available* rather than capacity used when allocating *budgeted* fixed costs is that short-run allocations to user departments are not affected by the *actual* user departments. Such a budgeted lump-sum approach is more likely to have the desired motivational effects with respect to the ordering of services in both the short run and the long run.

In practice, fixed-cost pools are often inappropriately allocated on the basis of capacity used, not capacity available. Suppose the computer department allocated the total actual costs after the fact. At the end of the month, total *actual* would be allocated in proportion to the *actual* hours used by the consuming departments. Compare the costs borne by the two schools when Business uses 200 hours and Engineering 400 hours:

Total costs incurred, $100,000 + 600($200) = $220,000	
Business: 200/600 x $220,000 =	$ 73,333
Engineering: 400/600 x $220,000 =	146,667
Total cost allocated	$220,000

What happens if Business uses only 100 hours during the following month while Engineering still uses 400 hours?

Total costs incurred, $100,000 + 500(200) = $200,000	
Business: 100/500 x $200,000 =	$ 40,000
Engineering: 400/500 x $200,000 =	160,000
Total cost allocated	$200,000

Engineering has done nothing differently, but it must bear higher costs of $13,333, an increase of 9 percent. Its short-run costs depend on what *other* consumers have used, not solely on its own actions. This phenomenon is caused by a faulty allocation method for the *fixed* portion of the total costs, a method whereby the allocations are highly sensitive to fluctuations in the actual volumes used by the various consuming departments. This weakness is avoided by using a predetermined lump-sum allocation of fixed costs, based on budgeted usage.

Consider the automobile repair shop example introduced above. You would not be happy if you came to get your car and were told, "Our daily fixed overhead is $1,000. Yours was the only car in our shop today, so we are charging you the full $1,000. If we had processed 100 cars today, your charge would have been only $10."

Troubles with Using Lump Sums

There are problems with using lump-sum allocations. If fixed costs are allocated on the basis of long-range plans, there is a natural tendency on the part of consumers to underestimate their planned usage and thus obtain a smaller fraction of the cost allocation. Top management can counteract these tendencies by monitoring predictions and by following up and using feedback to keep future predictions more honest.

In some organizations there are even rewards in the form of salary increases for managers who make accurate predictions. Moreover, some cost-allocation methods provide for penalties for underpredictions. For example, suppose a manager predicts usage of 210 hours and then demands 300 hours. The manager either doesn't get the hours or pays a price for every hour beyond 210.

Allocating Central Costs

J.C. Penney
www.jcpenney.com

Business Week **Online**
www.businessweek.com

The need to allocate central costs is a manifestation of a widespread, deep-seated belief that all costs must somehow be fully allocated to the revenue-producing (operating) parts of the organization. Such allocations are neither necessary from an accounting viewpoint nor useful as management information. However, most managers accept them as a fact of life—as long as all managers are treated alike.

Whenever possible, the preferred cost driver for central services is usage, either actual or estimated. But the costs of such services as public relations, top corporate-management overhead, real estate departments, and corporate-planning departments are the least likely to be allocated on the basis of usage. Data processing, advertising, and operations research are the most likely to choose usage as a cost driver.

Companies that allocate central costs by usage tend to generate less resentment. Consider the experience of J.C. Penney Co. as reported in *Business Week*:

> The controller's office wanted subsidiaries such as Thrift Drug Co. and the insurance operations to base their share of corporate personnel, legal, and auditing costs on their revenues. The subsidiaries contended that they maintained their own personnel and legal departments, and should be assessed far less.
>
> The subcommittee addressed the issue by asking the corporate departments to approximate the time and costs involved in servicing the subsidiaries. The final allocation plan, based on these studies, cost the divisions less than they were initially assessed but more than they had wanted to pay. Nonetheless, the plan was implemented easily.

Usage is not always an economically viable way to allocate central costs, however. Also, many central costs, such as the president's salary and related expenses, public relations, legal services, income tax planning, company-wide advertising, and basic research, are difficult to allocate on the basis of cause and effect. As a result, some companies use cost drivers such as the revenue of each division, the cost of goods sold by each division, the total assets of each division, or the total costs of each division (before allocation of the central costs) to allocate central costs.

The use of the foregoing cost drivers might provide a *rough* indication of cause-and-effect relationship. Basically, however, they represent an "ability to bear" philosophy of cost allocation. For example, the costs of company-wide advertising, such as the goodwill sponsorship of a program on a non-commercial television station, might be allocated to all products and divisions on the basis of the dollar sales in each. But such costs precede sales. They are discretionary costs as determined by management policies, not by sales results. Although 60 percent of the companies in a large survey treat sales revenue as a cost driver for cost allocation purposes, it is not truly a cost driver in the sense of being an activity that *causes* the costs.

If the costs of central services are to be allocated based on sales even though the costs do not vary in proportion to sales, the use of *budgeted* sales is preferable to the use of *actual* sales. At least this method means that the short-run costs of a given consuming department will not be affected by the fortunes of other consuming departments.

For example, suppose $100 of fixed central advertising costs were allocated on the basis of potential sales in two territories:

	TERRITORIES			
	A	B	TOTAL	PERCENT
Budgeted sales	$500	$500	$1,000	100%
Central advertising allocated	$ 50	$ 50	$ 100	10%

Consider the possible differences in allocations when actual sales become known:

	TERRITORIES	
	A	B
Actual Sales	$300	$600
Central advertising:		
1. Allocated on basis of budgeted sales	$ 50	$ 50
or		
2. Allocated on basis of actual sales	$ 33	$ 67

Compare allocation 1 with 2. Allocation 1 is preferable. It indicates a low ratio of sales to advertising in territory A. It directs attention where it is deserved. In contrast, allocation 2 soaks territory B with more advertising cost because of the *achieved* results and relieves territory A despite its lower success. This is another example of the analytical confusion that can arise when cost allocations to one consuming department depend on the activity of other consuming departments.

Reciprocal Services

Service departments often support other service departments as well as supporting producing departments. Consider a manufacturing company with two producing departments—moulding and finishing—and two service departments, facilities management (rent, heat, light, janitorial services, etc.) and personnel. All costs in a given service department are assumed to be caused by, and therefore vary in proportion to, a single cost driver. The company has decided that the best cost driver for facilities management costs is square metres occupied and the best cost drivers for personnel is the number of employees. Exhibit 5-2 shows the direct costs, square metres occupied, and number of employees for each department. Note that facilities management provides services for the personnel department in addition to providing services for the producing departments, and that personnel aids employees in facilities management as well as those in production departments.

EXHIBIT 5-2

Cost Drivers

	SERVICE DEPARTMENTS		PRODUCTION DEPARTMENTS	
	FACILITIES MANAGEMENT	PERSONNEL	MOULDING	FINISHING
Direct department costs	$126,000	$24,000	$100,000	$160,000
Square metres	3,000	9,000	15,000	3,000
Number of employees	20	30	80	320
Direct labour hours			2,100	10,000
Machine-hours			30,000	5,400

There are three popular methods for allocating service department costs in such cases: the direct method, the step-down method, and the reciprocal allocation method.

Direct Method

Direct Method. Ignores other service departments when any given service department's costs are allocated to the revenue-producing departments.

As its name implies, the **direct method** ignores other service departments when any given service department's costs are allocated to the revenue-producing (operating) departments. In other words, the fact that facilities management provides services for personnel is ignored, as is the support that personnel provides to facilities management. Facilities management costs are allocated based on the relative square metres *occupied by the production departments only*:

- Total square metres in production departments:
  15,000 + 3,000 = 18,000
- Facilities management cost allocated to moulding
  = (15,000 ÷ 18,000) × $126,000 = $105,000
- Facilities management cost allocated to finishing
  = (3,000 ÷ 18,000) × $126,000 = $21,000

Likewise, personnel department costs are allocated *only to the production departments* on the basis of the relative number of employees in the production departments:

- Total employees in production departments
  = 80 + 320 = 400
- Personnel costs allocated to moulding
  = (80 ÷ 400) × $24,000 = $4,800
- Personnel costs allocated to finishing
  = (320 ÷ 400) × $24,000 = $19,200

Step-Down Method

Step-Down Method. Recognizes that some service departments support the activities in other service departments as well as those in production departments.

The **step-down method** recognizes that some service departments support the activities in other service departments as well as those in production departments. A sequence of allocations is chosen, usually by starting with the service department that renders the greatest service (as measured by costs) to the greatest number of other service departments. The last service department in the sequence is the one that renders the least service to the least number of other service departments. Once a department's costs are allocated to other departments, no subsequent service department costs are allocated back to it.

In our example, facilities management costs are allocated first. Why? Because facilities management renders more support to personnel than personnel provides for facilities management.[1] Examine Exhibit 5-3. After facilities management costs are allocated, no costs are allocated back to facilities management, even though personnel does provide some services for facilities management. The personnel costs to be allocated to the production departments include the amount allocated to personnel from facilities management ($42,000) in addition to the direct personnel department costs of $24,000.

---

[1] How should we determine which of the two service departments provides the most service to the other? One way is to carry out step one of the step-down method with facilities management allocated first, and then repeat it assuming personnel is allocated first. With facilities management allocated first, $42,000 is allocated to personnel, as shown in Exhibit 5-3. If personnel had been allocated first, (20/420) × $24,000 = $1,143 would have been allocated to facilities management. Because $1,143 is smaller than $42,000, facilities management is allocated first.

EXHIBIT 5-3

Step-Down Allocation

	FACILITIES MANAGEMENT	PERSONNEL	MOULDING	FINISHING	TOTAL
Direct department costs before allocation	$126,000	$24,000	$100,000	$160,000	$410,000
Step 1:					
Facilities management	$(126,000)	(9 ÷ 27) x $126,000 = $42,000	(15 ÷ 27) x $126,000 = $70,000	(3 ÷ 27) x $126,000 = $14,000	0
Step 2:					
Personnel		$(66,000)	(80 ÷ 400) x $66,000 = $13,200	(320 ÷ 400) x $66,000 = $52,800	0
Total cost after allocation	$ 0	$ 0	$183,200	$226,800	$410,000

EXHIBIT 5-4

Reciprocal Allocation Method

	FACILITIES MANAGEMENT	PERSONNEL	MOULDING	FINISHING	TOTAL
Direct department costs before allocation	$126,000	$24,000	$100,000	$160,000	$410,000
Allocation of facilities management	$(129,220)	(9 ÷ 27) x $129,220 = $43,073	(15 ÷ 27) x $129,220 = $71,789	(3 ÷ 27) x $129,220 = $14,358	0
Allocation of personnel	(20 ÷ 420) x $67,030 = $3,192	$(67,030)	(80 ÷ 450) x $67,030 = $12,768	(320 ÷ 450) x $67,030 = $51,070	0
Total cost after allocation	$(28)*	$ 43*	$184,557	$225,428	$410,000

* due rounding

EXHIBIT 5-5

Direct versus Step-Down Method

	MOULDING			FINISHING		
	DIRECT	STEP-DOWN	RECIPROCAL	DIRECT	STEP-DOWN	RECIPROCAL
Direct department costs	$100,000	$100,000	$100,000	$160,000	$160,000	$160,000
Allocated from facilities management	105,000	70,000	71,789	21,000	14,000	14,358
Allocated from personnel	4,800	13,200	12,768	19,200	52,800	51,070
Total costs	$209,800	$183,200	$184,557	$200,200	$226,800	$225,428

Examine the last column of Exhibit 5-3. Before allocation, the four departments incurred costs of $410,000. In step 1, $126,000 was deducted from facilities management and added to the other three departments. There was no net effect on the total cost. In step 2, $66,000 was deducted from personnel and added to the remaining two departments. Again, total cost was unaffected. After allocation, all $410,000 remains, but it is all in moulding and finishing. None was left in facilities management or personnel.

Reciprocal Allocation Method

Reciprocal Allocation Method. Allocates costs by recognizing that the service departments provide services to each other as well as to the production departments.

The **reciprocal allocation method** allocates costs by recognizing that the service departments provide services to each other as well as to the production departments. This method is generally viewed as being the most theoretically correct as it enables us to cost the interdepartmental relationships fully into the service department cost allocations. In our example, the facilities management cost is allocated to the personnel department and the personnel cost is allocated to the facilities management department before the costs of the service departments are allocated to the production departments.

First, we must allocate the costs of the services provided between the two service departments. We do this using the following two equations in which the facilities management costs are defined as FM and the personnel costs as P.

$$FM = \$126,000 + 20/420 \ P = \$126,000 + .048 \ P$$

$$P = \$24,000 + 9/27 \ FM = \$24,000 + .333 \ FM$$

Then we solve the two simultaneous equations to determine the total amount of costs for each service department.

$$FM = \$126,000 + (.048 \ [\$24,000 + .333 \ FM])$$

$$FM = \$126,000 + \$1,152 + .016 \ FM$$

$$.984 \ FM = \$127,152$$

$$FM = \$129,220$$

$$P = \$24,000 + .333 \ (\$129,220)$$

$$P = \$24,000 + \$43,030$$

$$P = \$67,030$$

Thus, the total costs to be allocated for facilities management is $129,220 and for personnel is $67,030. Exhibit 5-4 provides the details of the allocations of the costs for these two service departments to the two production department. Note that the total of the costs allocated is still $410,000 (after minor adjustments due to rounding errors).

Compare the costs of the production departments under direct, step-down and reciprocal allocation methods as shown in Exhibit 5-5.

Note that the method of allocation can greatly affect the costs. Moulding appears to be a much more expensive operation to a manager using the direct method than to one using the step-down or reciprocal allocation method. Conversely, finishing seems more expensive to a manager using the non-direct method.

Which method is better? It is sometimes difficult to say. An advantage of the step-down method is that it recognizes the effects of the most significant support provided by service departments to other service departments. In our example, the direct method does not make any assumptions about the following possible cause-effect link: if the cost of facilities management is caused by the space used, then the space used by personnel causes $42,000 of facilities management costs. If the space used in personnel is caused by the number of production-department employees supported, then the number of production-department employees, not the square metres, causes $42,000 of the facilities management cost. The producing department with the most employees, not the one with the most square metres, should bear this cost.

The greatest virtue of the direct method is its simplicity. If the three methods do not produce significantly different results, many companies opt for the direct method because it is easier for managers to understand.

ALLOCATING COSTS TO OUTPUTS

Cost Application. The allocation of total departmental costs to the revenue-producing products or services.

Up to this point, we have concentrated on cost allocation to divisions, departments, and similar segments of a company. Cost allocation is often carried one step further—to the outputs of these departments, however defined. Examples are *products*, such as automobiles, furniture, and newspapers, and *services*, such as banking, health care, and education. Sometimes the allocation of total departmental costs to the revenue-producing products or services is called **cost application** or *cost attribution*.

General Approach

OBJECTIVE 6

Describe the general approach to allocating costs to products or services.

The general approach to allocating costs to final products or services is as follows:

1. Allocate production-related costs to the operating (line), production, or revenue-producing departments. This includes allocating service department costs to the production departments following the guidelines listed on page 182. The production departments then contain all the costs: their direct department costs and the service department costs.

2. Select one or more cost drivers in each production department. Historically, most companies have used only one cost driver per department. Recently, a large number of companies have started using multiple costs pools and multiple cost drivers within a department. For example, a portion of the departmental costs may be allocated on the basis of direct-labour hours, another portion on the basis of machine hours, and the remainder on the basis of the number of machine setups.

3. Allocate (assign) the total costs accumulated in step 1 to products or services that are the outputs of the operating departments using the cost drivers specified in step 2. If only one cost driver is used, two cost pools should be maintained, one for variable costs and one for fixed costs. Variable costs should be assigned on the basis of actual cost driver activity. Fixed costs should either remain unallocated or be allocated on the basis of budgeted cost driver activity.

Consider our manufacturing example, and assume that the step-down method was used to allocate service department costs. Exhibit 5-3 shows total costs of $183,200 accumulated in moulding and $226,800 in finishing. Note that all $410,000 total manufacturing costs reside in the production departments. To allocate these costs to the products produced, cost drivers must be selected for each department. We will use a single cost driver for each department and assume that all costs are caused by that cost driver. Suppose machine hours is the best measure of what causes costs in the moulding department, and direct-labour hours measures causation in finishing. Exhibit 5-2 showed 30,000 total machine-hours used in moulding and 10,000 direct labour hours in finishing. Therefore, costs are allocated to products as follows:

Moulding: $183,200 ÷ 30,000 machine-hours = $6.11 per machine-hour
Finishing: $226,800 ÷ 10,000 direct labour hours = $22.68 per direct labour hours

A product that takes four machine-hours in moulding and two direct labour hours in finishing would have a cost of

$$(4 \times \$6.11) + (2 \times \$22.68) = \$24.44 + \$45.36 = \$69.80$$

PERSPECTIVES ON P O D M DECISION-MAKING

Phone Carriers Battle Over Accounting Methods

Bell Canada
www.bell.ca

Unitel
www.unitelcom.com

Canadian Radio-television and Telecommunications Commission
www.crtc.gc.ca

The battle between **Bell Canada** and long-distance rival **Unitel Communications Inc.** moved into the accounting field yesterday on the issue of how monthly phone rates break down.

The Canadian Radio-television and Telecommunications Commission will hold hearings in May on the so-called "split rate base" — the separation of a phone company's costs for long-distance competitive services from local monopoly services.

Competitors charge that Bell and others misallocate costs of providing competitive services to the monopoly costs. That allows for lower long-distance rates and hurts rival companies that have to beat those prices, driving up the subsidy competitors pay to the local business.

Both sides will be offering their versions of "benchmarks" — the per-minute cost comparisons between Canadian and U.S. carriers. Unitel has charged that the Canadian carriers' costs are 40 percent to 50 percent lower than U.S. counterparts in the most competitive market in the world.

Bell said Andersen Consulting Canada undertook a cost comparison study on behalf of provincial telephone companies.

It found Bell's costs were 2.8¢ lower per minute than U.S. giant AT&T. The difference was attributed to AT&T's higher marketing and customer service costs, and higher corporate operations.

Unitel said that using CRTC Phase III accounting methods, long-distance costs for U.S. carriers are 12.3¢ per minute, while costs for Canadian carriers average about 8.1¢ — a 52 percent difference.

One of the problems is that telephone companies often make use of the same personnel and equipment for both local and long-distance business. Unitel cites customer billing as an example of when both monopoly and competitive services are charged on the same bill, jointly incurring the costs.

Source: Joanne Chianello, "Phone carriers battle over accounting methods," *The Financial Post*, (February 1, 1995), p. 7.

ALLOCATING JOINT COSTS AND BY-PRODUCT COSTS

OBJECTIVE 7

Use the physical units and relative-sales-value methods to allocate joint costs to products.

Joint Costs

Joint Costs. Costs of inputs added to a process before individual products are separated.

Dow Chemical
www.dow.com

Joint costs and by-product costs create especially difficult cost allocation problems. By definition, such costs relate to more than one product but cannot be separately identified with an individual product.

So far we have assumed that cost drivers could be identified with an individual product. For example, if costs are being allocated to products or services on the basis of machine hours, we have assumed that each machine hour is used on a single final product or service. However, sometimes inputs are added to the production process before individual products are separately identifiable (that is, before the *split-off point*). Such costs are called **joint costs**. Joint costs include all inputs of material, labour, and overhead costs that are incurred before the split-off point.

Suppose a department has more than one product and some costs are joint costs. How should such joint costs be allocated to the products? Allocation of joint costs should not affect decisions about the individual products. Nevertheless, joint product costs are routinely allocated to products for purposes of *inventory valuation* and *income determination*.

Assume a department in Dow Chemical Company produces two chemicals, X and Y. The joint cost is $100,000, and production is 1,000,000 litres of X and 500,000 litres of Y. Product X can be sold for $.09 per litre and Y for $.06 per litre. Ordinarily, some part of the $100,000 joint cost will be allocated to the inventory of X and the rest to the inventory of Y. Such allocations are useful for inventory purposes only. Joint cost allocations should be ignored for decisions such as selling a joint product or processing it further.

Two conventional ways of allocating joint costs to products are widely used: *physical units* and *relative sales values*. If physical units were used, the joint costs would be allocated as follows:

	LITRES	WEIGHTING	ALLOCATION OF JOINT COSTS	SALES VALUE AT SPLIT-OFF
X	1,000,000	10/15 x $100,000	$ 66,667	$ 90,000
Y	500,000	5/15 x $100,000	33,333	30,000
	1,500,000		$100,000	$120,000

This approach shows that the $33,333 joint cost of producing Y exceeds its $30,000 sales value at split-off, which seems to indicate that Y should not be produced. However, such an allocation is not helpful in making production decisions. Neither of the two products could be produced separately.

A decision to produce Y must be a decision to produce X *and* Y. Because total revenue of $120,000 exceeds the total joint cost of $100,000, both will be produced. The allocation was not useful for this decision.

The physical units method requires a common physical unit for measuring the output of each product. For example, board feet is a common unit for a variety of products in the lumber industry. However, sometimes such a common denominator is lacking. Consider the production of meat and hides from butchering a steer. You might use kilograms as a common denominator, but kilograms is not a good measure of the output of hides. As an alternative, many companies use the *relative sales value method* for allocating joint costs. The following allocation results from applying the relative sales value method to the Dow Chemical department:

	RELATIVE SALES VALUE AT SPLIT-OFF	WEIGHTING	ALLOCATION OF JOINT COSTS
X	$ 90,000	90/120 x $100,000	$ 75,000
Y	30,000	30/120 x $100,000	25,000
	$120,000		$100,000

The weighting is based on the sales values of the individual products. Because the sales value of X at split-off is $90,000 and total sales value at split-off is $120,000, X is allocated 90/120 of the joint cost.

Now each product would be assigned a joint cost portion that is less than its sales value at split-off. Note how the allocation of a cost to a particular product such as Y depends not only on the sales value of Y but also on the sales value of X. For example, suppose you were the product manager for Y. You planned to sell your 500,000 litres for $30,000, achieving a profit of $30,000 − $25,000 = $5,000. Everything went as expected except that the price of X fell to $.07 per litre for revenue of $70,000 rather than $90,000. Instead of 30/120 of the joint cost, Y received 30/100 × $100,000 = $30,000 and had a profit of $0. Despite the fact that Y operations were exactly as planned, the cost-allocation method caused the profit on Y to be $5,000 below plan.

The relative sales value method can also be used when one or more of the joint products cannot be sold at the split-off point. To apply the method, we approximate the sales value at split-off as follows:

$$\text{sales value at split-off} = \text{final sales value} - \text{separate costs}$$

For example, suppose the 500,000 litres of Y requires $20,000 of processing beyond the split-off point, after which it can be sold for $.10 per litre. The sales value at split-off would be $.10 × 500,000 − $20,000 = $50,000 − $20,000 = $30,000.

By-Product Costs

By-Product. A product that, like a joint product, is not individually identifiable until manufacturing reaches a split-off point, but has relatively insignificant total sales value.

By-products are similar to joint products. A **by-product** is a product that, like a joint product, is not individually identifiable until manufacturing reaches a split-off point. By-products differ from joint products because they have relatively insignificant total sales value in comparison with the other products emerging at split-off. Joint products have relatively significant total sales values at split-off in comparison with the other jointly produced items. Examples of by-products are glycerine from soap-making and mill ends of cloth and carpets.

If an item is accounted for as a by-product, only separable costs are assigned to it. All joint costs are allocated to main products. Any revenues from by-products, less their separable costs, are deducted from the cost of the main products.

Consider a lumber company that sells sawdust generated in the production of lumber to companies making particle board. Suppose the company regards the sawdust as a by-product. In 2001, sales of sawdust totalled $30,000, and the cost of loading and shipping the sawdust (that is, costs incurred beyond the split-off point) was $20,000. The inventory cost of the sawdust would consist of only the $20,000 separable cost. None of the joint cost of producing lumber and sawdust would be allocated to the sawdust. The difference between the revenue and separable cost, $30,000 − $20,000 = $10,000, would be deducted from the cost of the lumber produced.

ACTIVITY-BASED COSTING (ABC)

OBJECTIVE 8

Use activity-based costing to allocate costs to products or services.

In the past, the vast majority of departments used direct labour hours as the only cost driver for applying costs to products. But direct labour hours is not a very good measure of the cause of costs in modern, highly automated departments. Labour-related costs in an automated system may be only 5 percent to 10 percent of the total manufacturing costs and often are not related to the causes of most manufacturing overhead costs. Therefore, many companies are beginning to use machine-hours as their cost-allocation base. However, some managers in modern manufacturing firms and automated service companies believe it is inappropriate to allocate all costs based on measures of volume. Using direct labour hours or cost—or even machine hours—as the only cost driver seldom meets the cause/effect criterion desired in cost allocation. If many costs are caused by non-volume-based cost drivers, **Activity-Based Costing (ABC)** should be considered.

C O M P A N Y ⓢ S T R A T E G I E S

J.M. Schneider
www.jmschneider.com

ACTIVITY-BASED COSTING AT J. M. SCHNEIDER INC.

Schneider Corporation is one of Canada's largest producers of premium-quality food products. The company's mission statement, which provides a common focus to all activities within the corporation, is:

To generate profitable growth by providing high-quality food products of superior value in specific market segments while maintaining our status as a financially secure, well-managed, ethical company.

The majority of the Corporation's meat processing is done through its subsidiary, J. M. Schneider Inc.

In the late 1980s the Canadian meat-packing industry, in which the company's core business operated, was in critical condition. Red meat consumption levels were declining at an alarming rate, as consumers adopted changing lifestyles and eating habits. Meat producers and food retailers rationalized into a handful of participants engaged in intense price competition. This development resulted in a sharp decline in profitability for Schneider.

In the absence of significant market growth opportunities, Schneider launched an initiative to internally generate efficiencies and cost reductions in order to improve profit margins. The vehicle chosen to drive these improvements was the implementation of a broadly based continuous improvement program.[2]

This program, in order to be successful, required the support of a more up-to-date and relevant cost system. Up until this time, Schneider had used a standard cost system to meet the requirements of measuring the success of its labour and materials yield productivity program. This program measured productivity gains by comparing actual results to costs in the standard cost system.[3]

Continued

There were a number of shortcomings with the company's conventional standard cost system, however:

1. The focus was on minimizing costs within each department. Consequently, actions would be taken in one department that would reduce their costs, but would create additional costs in downstream departments.
2. Targets were limited to material yield and direct labour productivity. Opportunities to better control and manage a number of other manufacturing costs and overheads were not measured.
3. Comparisons were made to standards that incorporated allowances for waste and non-value-added activity. Although meeting the standard costs satisfied management, it resulted in "satisfactory" costs rather than "minimum" costs.

Schneider realized that the primary emphasis of its cost system should be to provide relevant and reliable information for management decision making rather than focusing only on financial reporting requirements.

Under continuous improvement, the focus on minimizing costs broadened from control of yields and direct labour productivity to better understanding and managing the entire business cycle. Continuous improvement initiatives were launched to address just-in-time, productive maintenance, total quality control, quick changeover techniques, cycle time, identification and elimination of non-value-added activities. The standard cost system was unable to accurately measure and report the true costs of these activities, and was in need of an overhaul.

In order to better measure and, in turn, understand production cost behaviour, Schneider decided to implement Activity-Based Costing (ABC). ABC systems are designed on the premise that products require "activities" and that these activities, in turn, consume "resources," i.e., incur costs. Non-value-added activities and waste are more clearly highlighted and therefore better managed. Non-financial measures have also been recognized as key yardsticks in measuring operational performance (i.e., tonnage throughput, machine downtime hours, process cycle time, etc.).

The information generated by this updated management accounting system will be supportive of the firm's continuous improvement and cost reduction programs, providing relevant and reliable decision-making information.

[2] Dodds, Douglas W., "MAKING IT BETTER....and better," *CMA MAGAZINE*, February 1992, pp. 16–21.
[3] For a more complete discussion of the standard cost system, see Armitage, H.M., and A. A. Atkinson, "The Choice of Productivity Measures in Organizations: A Field Study of Practice in Seven Canadian Firms." Society of Management Accountants of Canada, Hamilton, Ontario, 1990.

CMA Magazine
www.cma-canada.org

Source: Written by John Carney, Manager Accounting Services and Larry Wozniak, Senior Cost Analyst, J. M. Schneider Inc.

Activity-Based Costing

Activity-Based Costing (ABC). A system that first accumulates overhead costs for each of the activities of an organization, and then assigns the costs of activities to the products, services, or other cost objects that caused that activity.

Activity-based costing (ABC) systems first accumulate overhead costs for each of the activities of an organization, and then assign the costs of activities to the products, services, or other cost objects that caused that activity. To establish a cause-effect relationship between an activity and a cost object, cost drivers are identified for each activity. Consider the following activities and *cost drivers* for the Belmont manufacturing plant department of a major appliance producer:

ACTIVITY	COST DRIVER
Production set-up	Number of production runs
Production control	Number of production process changes
Engineering	Number of engineering change orders
Maintenance	Number of machine hours
Power	Number of kilowatt hours

Outsourcing

Most organizations are now realizing that to succeed they must focus on a few core competencies, things they uniquely do very well. For example, Compaq defines itself as a "platform integrator" developing and marketing products whose components are largely manufactured by others. Such organizations realize that they should not seek to do activities for which they do not have competitive advantage.

Traditionally, outsourcing started with narrow, low-risk activities such as payroll processing, data centre management, and catering. Now much more strategic activities are starting to be outsourced, including financial management, human resource management, supply chain management and even customer management processes. Also, the scope of the outsourcing relationships is much broader; for example, outsourcing of accounting used to consist primarily of accounts receivable collection and payroll. Now, organizations are outsourcing their entire financial transaction processing, recognizing that their own competencies are in the use of financial information, not its creation.

An important change in the outsourcing environment is the rapid emergence of e-business, which is making it far more possible, and necessary, for organizations to implement new business models, with extensive outsourcing of processes to third parties. Organizations such as Cisco have demonstrated that they can dominate the value chain while outsourcing many processes, including manufacturing, to other organizations.

Future outlook

The outsourcing market will change quite dramatically over the next few years towards a new relationship characterized by the following factors:
- a broadening of the scope of outsourcing relationships;
- significant investment by the service provider, particularly in information technology infrastructure to support service delivery;
- use of e-business to implement new and highly innovative outsourcing relationships; and
- sharing of risks and rewards associated with the outsourcing.

The outsourcing market move towards highly strategic partnering arrangements addresses such broad processes as: financial transaction processing; human resource administration; supply chain management; document and print management; and customer service.

Several of the most progressive global organizations will seek outsourcing partnerships that focus on enhancing shareholder value and enabling organizations to be more focused and flexible.

Global research findings

PricewaterhouseCoopers commissioned a study of outsourcing trends amongst 300 of the largest global companies, including 26 large Canadian organizations. The research, conducted by an independent market research organization, highlighted some interesting issues and trends amongst the Canadian participants.
- Seventy-three percent of the organizations have outsourced at least one activity or process. The main reasons for outsourcing are: to enable a focus on core competencies; enhance profitability and share-holder value; and avoid the investment in technology required to enhance efficiency.
- The most commonly outsourced activities and those most likely to be outsourced in the near future are: benefits administration payroll processing; logistics; real estate management, and internal audits.
- About half of the respondents believe outsourcing to be more important to their organizations then was the case three years ago, ninety-five percent were somewhat or very satisfied with their outsourcing to date, while sixty three percent achieved at least the cost savings expected from outsourcing.

Source: John Simke, "Emerging Trends in Outsourcing", *CMA Management*, February 2000, pp. 26–27.

Cost-driver activity is measured by the number of transactions involved in the activity. For example, in this case, engineering costs are caused by change orders (a document detailing a production change that requires the attention of the engineering department). Therefore, engineering costs are assigned to products in proportion to the number of engineering change orders issued for each product. If the production of microwave ovens caused 18 percent of the engineering change orders, then the ovens should bear 18 percent of the costs of engineering. Because transactions are often used for assigning costs of activities to cost objects, activity-based costing is also called **transaction-based accounting** or **transaction costing**.

Transaction-Based Accounting (Transaction Costing). See **Activity-Based Costing.**

Consider the Belmont manufacturing plant of a major appliance producer. Exhibit 5-6 contrasts the traditional costing system with an ABC system. In the traditional cost system, the portion of total overhead allocated to a product depends on the proportion of total direct labour hours consumed in making the product. In the ABC system, significant overhead activities (machining, assembly, quality inspection, etc.) and related resources are separately identified and traced to products using cost drivers—machine hours, number of parts, number of inspections, etc. In the ABC system, the amount of overhead costs allocated to a product depends on the proportion of total machine hours, total parts, total inspections, etc. consumed in making the product. One large overhead cost pool has been broken into several pools, each associated with a key activity. We now consider a more in-depth illustration of the design of an ABC system.

EXHIBIT 5-6

Traditional and Activity-Based Cost Systems

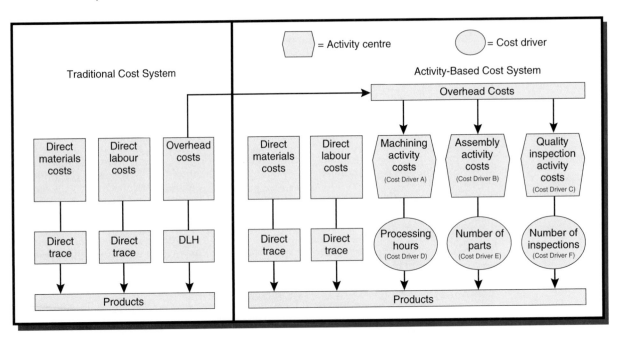

Illustration of Activity-Based Costing[4]

Consider the Billing Department at Pacific Power Company (PPC), an electric utility. The Billing Department (BD) at PPC provides account inquiry and bill printing services for two major classes of customers—residential and commercial. Currently, the Billing Department services 120,000 residential and 20,000 commercial customer accounts.

Two factors are having a significant impact on PPC's profitability. First, deregulation of the power industry has led to increased competition and lower rates, so PPC must find ways of reducing its operating costs. Second, the demand for power in PPC's area will increase due to the addition of a large housing development and a shopping centre. The marketing department estimates that residential demand will increase by almost 50 percent and commercial demand will increase by 10 percent during the next year. Since the BD is currently operating at full capacity, it needs to find ways to create capacity to service the expected increase in demand. A local service bureau has offered to take over the BD functions at an attractive lower cost (compared to the current cost). The service bureau's proposal is to provide all the functions of the BD at $3.50 per residential account and $8.50 per commercial account.

Exhibit 5-7 depicts the residential and commercial customer classes (cost objects) and the resources used to support the BD. The costs associated with the BD are all indirect—they cannot be identified specifically and exclusively with either customer class in an economically feasible way. The BD used a traditional costing system that allocated all support costs based on the number of account inquiries of the two customer classes. Exhibit 5-7 shows that the cost of the resources used in the BD last month was $565,340. BC received 23,000 account inquiries during the month, so the indirect cost per inquiry was $565,340 ÷ 23,000 = $24.58. There were 18,000 residential account inquiries, about 78 percent of the total. Thus, residential accounts were charged with 78 percent of the support costs while commercial accounts were charged with 22 percent. The resulting cost per account is $3.69 and $6.15 for residential and commercial accounts, respectively.

Based on the costs provided by the traditional cost system, the BD management would be motivated to accept the service bureau's proposal to service all residential accounts because of the apparent savings of $.19 ($3.69 − $3.50) per account. The BD would continue to service its commercial accounts because its costs are $2.35 ($8.50 − $6.15), less than the service bureau's bid.

However, management believed that the actual consumption of support resources was much greater than 22 percent for commercial accounts because of their complexity. For example, commercial accounts average 50 lines per bill compared with only 12 for residential accounts. Management was also concerned about activities such as correspondence (and supporting labour) resulting from customer inquiries because these activities are costly but do not add value to PPC's services from the customer's perspective. However, management wanted a more thorough understanding of key BD activities and their interrelationships

---

[4] Much of the discussion in this section is based on an illustration used in Implementing Activity-Based Costing—The Model Approach, a workshop sponsored by the Institute of Management Accounting and Sapling Corporation.

Step 1. Determine cost objectives, key activities centres, resources, and related cost drivers.
Step 2. Develop a process-based map representing the flow of activities, resources, and their interrelationships.
Step 3. Collect relevant data concerning costs and the physical flow of cost-driver units among activities.
Step 4. Calculate and interpret the new activity-based information.

before making important decisions that would affect PPC's profitability. The company decided to perform a study of the BD, using activity-based costing. The following is a description of the study and its results.

The activity-based-costing study was performed by a team of managers from the BD and the chief financial officer from PPC. The team followed a four-step procedure to conduct the study.

Step 1. *Determine cost objectives, key activities centres, resources, and related cost drivers.* Management had set the objective for the study—determine the BD cost per account for each customer class. The team identified the following activities, resources, and related cost drivers for the BD through interviews with appropriate personnel.

ACTIVITY CENTRES	COST DRIVERS
Account Billing	Number of Lines
Account Verification	Number of Accounts
Account Inquiry	Number of Labour Hours
Correspondence	Number of Letters

The four key BD activity centres are account billing, bill verification, account inquiry, and correspondence. The resources shown in Exhibit 5-7 support these major activity centres. Cost drivers were selected based on two criteria.

1. There had to be a reasonable assumption of a cause-effect relationship between the driver unit and the consumption of resources and/or the occurrence of supporting activities.
2. Data on the cost-driver units had to be available.

Step 2. *Develop a process-based map representing the flow of activities, resources, and their interrelationships.* An important phase of any activity-based analysis is identifying the interrelationships between key activities and the resources consumed. This is typically done by interviewing key personnel. Once the linkage between activities and resources is identified, a process map is drawn that provides a visual representation of the operations of the BD.

Exhibit 5-8 is a process map that depicts the flow of activities and resources at the BD.[5] Note that there are no costs on Exhibit 5-8. BD first focused on understanding business processes. Costs were not considered until Step 3, after the key interrelationships of the business are understood.

Consider residential accounts. Three key activities support these accounts—account billing, account inquiry, and correspondence. Bill printing activity consumes printing machine time, paper, computer transaction time, billing labour time, and supervisory time. This activity also takes up significant occupancy space. Account inquiry activity consumes labour time and requires correspondence for some inquiries. Account inquiry labour, in turn, uses the telecommunication, computer, supervisory resources, and also occupies a significant amount of occupancy space. Finally, the correspondence activity requires supervision and inquiry labour. The costs of each of the resources consumed were determined during Step 3—data collection.

---

[5] This example illustrates the process-based modelling approach to activity-based costing. For a more detailed description of the process modelling approach, see Raef A. Lawson, "Beyond ABC: Process-Based Costing," *Journal of Cost Management*, Volume 8, No. 3 (Fall 1994), pp. 33–43. Also, for a discussion of how one major firm used process-based costing to implement ABC in its billing centre, see T. Hobdy, J. Thomson, and P. Sharman, "Activity-Based Management at AT&T," *Management Accounting* (April 1994), pp. 35–39.

EXHIBIT 5-7

Pacific Power
Company—Billing
Department

Current Costing Based on One Overall Rate
Total Indirect Cost: $565,340

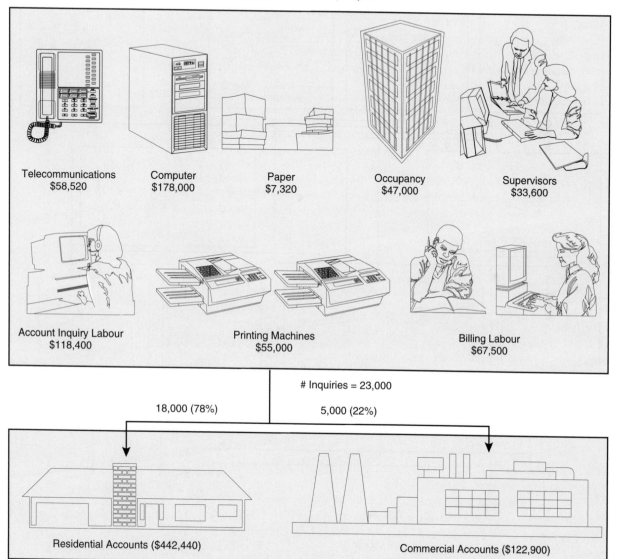

	Cost/Inquiry $565,340/23,000 (1)	#Inquiries (2)	#Accounts (3)	Cost/Account (1)X(2)/(3)
Residential	$24.58	18,000	120,000	$3.69
Commercial	$24.58	5,000	20,000	$6.15

EXHIBIT 5-8

Process Map of Billing Department Activities

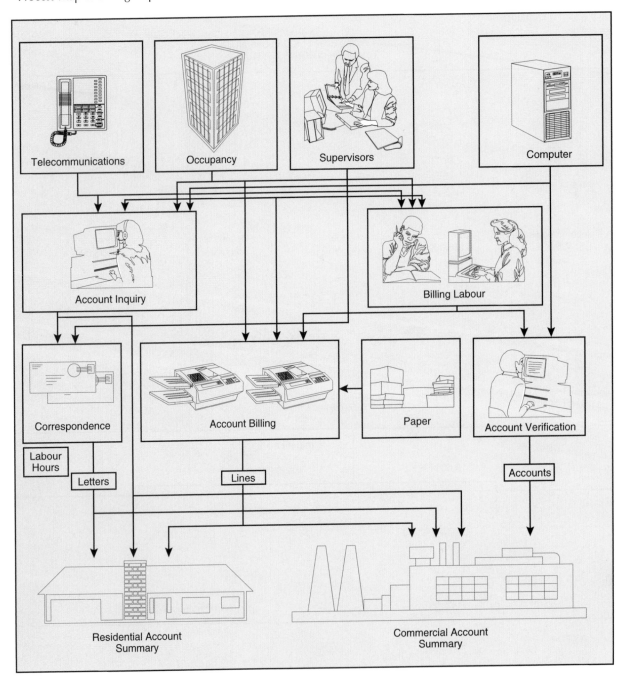

Step 3. *Collect relevant data concerning costs and the physical flow of cost-driver units among resources and activities.* Using the process map as a guide, BD accountants collected the required cost and operational data by further interviews with relevant personnel. Sources of data include the accounting records, special studies, and sometimes "best estimates of managers."

Exhibit 5-9 is a graphical representation of the data collected for the four activity centres identified in Step 1. For each activity centre, data collected included traceable costs and the physical flow of cost-driver units. For example, Exhibit 5-9 shows traceable costs of $235,777 for the account billing activity. Traceable costs include the costs of the printing machines ($55,000 from Exhibit 5-7) plus portions of the costs of all other resources that support the billing activity (paper, occupancy, computer, and billing labour). Notice that the total traceable costs of $205,332 + $35,384 + $235,777 + $88,847 = $565,340 in Exhibit 5-9 equals the total indirect costs in Exhibit 5-7. Next, the physical flow of cost-driver units was determined for each activity or cost object. For each activity centre, the traceable costs were divided by the sum of the physical flows to establish a cost per cost-driver unit.

Step 4.   *Calculate and interpret the new activity-based information.* The activity-based cost per account for each customer class can be determined from the data in Step 3. Exhibit 5-10 shows the computations.

EXHIBIT 5-9

ABC System

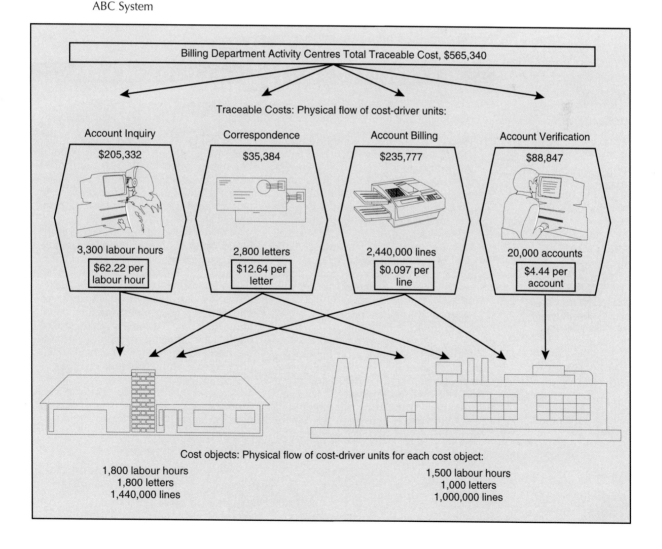

Examine the last two items in Exhibit 5-10. Notice that traditional costing indicated higher costs for the high-volume residential accounts and substantially lower costs for the low-volume commercial accounts. The ABC cost per account for residential accounts is $2.28, which is $1.41 less than the $3.69 cost generated by the traditional costing system. The cost per account for commercial accounts is $14.57, which is $8.42 more than the $6.15 cost from the traditional cost system. Management's belief that traditional costing was undercosting commercial accounts was supported. PPC's management now has the cost information that they think is preferred for planning and decision-making purposes.

These results are common when companies perform activity-based costing studies—high-volume cost objects with simple processes are overcosted when only one volume-based cost driver is used. In the BD, this volume-based cost-driver was the number of inquiries. Which system makes more sense—the traditional allocation system that "spreads" all support costs to customer classes based solely on the number of inquiries, or the activity-based-costing system that identifies key activities and assigns costs based on the consumption of units of cost drivers chosen for each key activity? For PPC, the probable benefits of the new activity-based-costing system may outweigh the costs of implementing and maintaining the new cost system. However, the cost-benefit balance must be assessed on a case-by-case basis.

PERSPECTIVES ON P O D M DECISION-MAKING

The ABCs of Profitability

Activity-Based Costing
www.abctech.com

Today, many organizations are using Activity Based Costing (ABC) to make strategy changes and to cut costs, and the process may end up affecting a broad range of operations: simple ones, like the way a truck delivery is unloaded at a store, or major ones, such as whether to outsource direct store deliveries. ABC shows the individual impact of each decision, and the impact of one decision on another. A company may even discover that changing the way deliveries are processed makes outsourcing them uneconomical.

ABC can produce results. Here are some examples:

• A mining company needed to reduce logistics costs and to assess the bottom-line impact of some proposed capital investments. It conducted an ABC pilot project which focused on customer service and distribution. The study found enough "quick hit" improvements to pay for the cost of the pilot project. Management used

the model to justify several strategic initiatives, which led to even greater bottom-line improvements. ABC was then rolled out to the mining and milling processes. Today, strategic planning, budgeting, and performance measurement have all been upgraded.

• A food processor and wholesale distribution company needed to understand the economics of its processing and logistics activities. Management suspected that some customer groups, products, and delivery routes were losing money. As it turned out, all products contributed to the bottom line, but some customers were indeed unprofitable. The improvement opportunities that ABC discovered amounted to ten times the cost of the pilot project.

Source: Henry Kolisnik, "The ABCs of Profitability," *Canadian Transportation Logistics,* March 1995, p. 50.

Summary of Activity-Based Costing

Activity-based accounting systems can turn many indirect manufacturing overhead costs into direct costs—costs identified specifically with given cost objectives. Appropriate selection of activities and cost drivers allows managers to trace many manufacturing overhead costs to cost objectives just as specifically as they have traced direct material and direct labour costs. Because activity-based accounting systems classify more costs as direct than do traditional systems, managers have greater confidence in the costs of products and services reported by activity-based systems.

Because activity-based accounting systems are more complex and costly than traditional systems, not all companies use them. But more and more organizations in both manufacturing and non-manufacturing industries are adopting activity-based systems for a variety of reasons:

OBJECTIVE 11

Explain why activity-based costing systems are being adopted.

- Fierce competitive pressure has resulted in shrinking margins. Companies may know their overall margin, but they often do not believe in the accuracy of the margins for *individual* products or services.
- Business complexity has increased, which results in greater diversity in the types of products and services as well as customer classes. Therefore, the consumption of a company's shared resources also varies substantially across products and customers.
- New production techniques have increased the proportion of indirect costs—that is, indirect costs are far more important in today's world-class manufacturing environment. In many industries direct labour is being replaced by automated equipment. Indirect costs are sometimes over 50 percent of total cost.
- The rapid pace of technology change has shortened product life-cycles. Hence, companies do not have time to make price or cost adjustments once errors are discovered.
- Computer technology has reduced the costs of developing and operating cost systems that track many activities.

EXHIBIT 5-10

Key Results of Activity-Based Costing Study

DRIVER COSTS

Activity/Resource (Driver Units)	Traceable Costs (From Exhibit 5-9) (1)	Total Physical Flow of Driver Units (From Exhibit 5-9) (2)	Cost Per Driver Unit (1) ÷ (2)
Account Inquiry (Labour Hours)	$205,332	3,300 Hours	$62.22
Correspondence (Letters)	$ 35,384	2,800 Letters	$12.64
Account Billing (Lines)	$235,777	2,440,000 Lines	$ 0.097
Account Verification (Accounts)	$ 88,847	20,000 Accounts	$ 4.44

COST PER CUSTOMER CLASS

	Cost Per Driver Unit	Residential		Commercial	
		Physical Flow of Driver Units	Cost	Physical Flow of Driver Units	Cost
Account Inquiry	$62.22	1,800 Hrs.	$111,999	1,500 Hrs.	$ 93,333
Correspondence	$12.64	1,800 Ltrs.	$ 22,747	1,000 Ltrs.	$ 12,638
Account Billing	$0.097	1,440,000 Lines	$139,147	1,000,000 Lines	$ 96,629
Account Verification	$4.44	0	$ 0	20,000 Accts.	$ 88,847
Total Cost			$273,893		$291,447
Number of Accounts			120,000		20,000
Cost per Account			$ 2.28		$ 14.57
Cost per Account (Traditional System)			$ 3.69		$ 6.15

Note: Some differences may exist due to rounding.

Identifying Activities, Resources, and Cost Drivers

Arkansas Blue Cross Blue Shield (ABCBS) is the largest health insurer in Arkansas with annual revenue of more than $450 million. Recently, ABCBS implemented activity-based management. The identification of key activities, resources, and cost drivers was one of the early steps performed.

• A pilot study was performed on one area of the firm—information management. The criteria for selection of a pilot area included significant costs, the possibility of improving the existing cost allocation system, access to data, and a receptive staff.

• The cost objectives were defined—the internal customers of information management.

• Activities, resources, and cost drivers were identified based on meetings with managers. Examples of key activities are Production (job scheduling, production control), Electronic Media Claims Processing, Printing, and Mail Processing. Resources include Systems Programmers, Mail Labour, Print Labour, Tape Labour, Data Base Administrators, 3080 CPU, 3090 CPU, LSM (robotic cartridge system), DASD (hard disk storage), and Telecommunications, Cost drivers included CPU minutes, single-density volumes (DASD), number of tape/cartridge mounts (LSM), number of jobs, and number of CRTs (telecommunications).

• Once the key activities, resources, and drivers were identified, the project team developed a process map of the operations of the information management function. This map reflected the flow of activities and resources in support of the cost centres. The map also identified the data that needed to be collected to complete the study. (Note that the process map is very similar to Exhibit 4-12 in appearance.)

• Once the ABC model was built and validated, the results were interpreted and recommendations for improvement were made.

As a result of the ABC study, the following actions were taken by management:

• A separate utility meter was placed on the computer room.

• CRT purchases are now charged directly to the user. Maintenance costs for CRTs are now assigned based on CRT count.

• Three new cost centres were created—EMC Systems, Change Control, and Production Control.

• CPU was upgraded.

ABCBS is now in the process of expanding the new ABM system corporate-wide to include purchasing, actuarial, advertising, and claims processing. The company is also using the new ABM system for activity-based budgeting.

Source: "Implementing Activity-Based Costing—The Model Approach," Institute of Management Accountants and Sapling Corporation, Orlando (November, 1994).

Institute of Management Accountants
www.imanet.org

Sapling: Software Aided Planning
www.sapling.com

Cost Management Systems

Cost Management System. Identifies how management's decisions affect costs, by first measuring the resources used in performing the organization's activities and then assessing the effects on costs of changes in those activities.

To better support managers' decisions, accountants go beyond simply determining the cost of products and services. They develop cost management systems. A **cost management system** identifies how management's decisions affect costs. To do so, it first measures the resources used in performing the organization's activities and then assesses the effects on costs of changes in those activities.

Activity-Based Management

Recall that managers' day-to-day focus is on managing activities, not costs. So, because ABC systems also focus on activities, they are very useful in cost management. Using an activity-based costing system to improve the operations of an organization is **activity-based management (ABM)**. In the broadest terms, activity-based management aims to improve the value received by customers and to improve profits by providing this value.

The cornerstone of ABM is distinguishing between value-added costs and non-value-added costs. A **value-added cost** is the cost of an activity that cannot be eliminated without affecting a product's value to the customer. Value-added costs are necessary (as long as the activity that drives such costs is performed efficiently). In contrast, companies try to minimize **non-value-added costs**—costs that can be eliminated without affecting a product's value to the customer. Activities such as handling and storing inventories, transporting partly finished products from one part of the plant to another, and changing the set-up of production line operations to produce a different model of the product are all non-value-added activities that can be reduced, if not eliminated, by careful redesign of the plant layout and the production process.

Let us return now to Pacific Power Company to see how the billing department could use the ABC system to improve its operation. Recall that the BD needed to find a way to increase its capacity to handle accounts due to an expected large increase in demand from a new housing development and shopping centre. BD managers also were interested (as always is the case) in reducing the operating costs of the department while not impairing the quality of the service it provided to its customers. To do so, they used the ABC information from Exhibit 5-10 to identify non-value-added activities that had significant costs. Account inquiry and bill verification activities are non-value-added and costly, so management asked for ideas cost reductions. The new information provided by the ABC system generated the following ideas for improvement:

- Use the service bureau for commercial accounts because of the significant cost savings. From Exhibit 5-10, the service bureau's bid is for $8.50 per account compared to the BD's activity-based cost of $14.57, a difference of more than $6 per account! The freed-up capacity can be used to meet the expected increase in residential demand. Bill verification, a non-value-added activity, would also be eliminated because only commercial bills are verified.
- Exhibit 5-10 indicates that account inquiry activity is very costly, accounting for a significant portion of total BD costs. One idea is to make bills more descriptive in order to reduce the number of inquiries. Doing so would add lines to each bill, resulting in higher billing-activity costs, but the number of inquiries would be reduced, thus reducing a significant non-value-added cost. Whether this idea would result in a net cost reduction needs to be evaluated by the accountants with the help of the new ABC system.

Just-in-Time (JIT) Systems

Attempts to minimize non-value-added costs have led many organizations to adopt just-in-time systems to eliminate waste and improve quality. In a **just-in-time (JIT) production system**, an organization purchases materials and parts and produces components just when they are needed in the production process. Goods are not produced until it is time for them to be shipped to a customer. The goal is to have zero inventory, because holding inventory is a non-value-added activity.

JIT companies are customer-oriented because customer orders drive the production process. An order triggers the immediate delivery of materials, followed by production and delivery of the goods. Instead of producing inventory

Explain how JIT
systems can reduce
non-value-added
activities.

Production Cycle Time. The
time from initiating pro-
duction to delivering the
goods to the
customer.

and hoping an order will come, a JIT system produces products directly for received orders. Several factors are crucial to the success of JIT systems:

1. Focus on quality. JIT companies try to involve all employees in controlling quality. While any system can seek quality improvements, JIT systems emphasize *total quality control (TQC)* and *continuous improvement in quality*. If all employees strive for zero defects, non-value-added activities such as inspection and rework of defective items are minimized.

2. Short **production cycle time**. The time from initiating production to delivery of goods to the customer. Keeping production cycle times short allows timely response to customer orders and reduces the level of inventories. Many JIT companies have achieved remarkable reductions in production cycle times. For example, applying JIT methods in one IBM division in Bromont, Quebec cut process lead times from 30 to 40 days to seven days on a ceramic substrate product.

3. Smooth flow of production. Fluctuations in production rates inevitably lead to delays in delivery to customers and excess inventories. To achieve smooth production flow, JIT companies simplify the production process to reduce the possibilities of delay, to develop close relationships with suppliers to assure timely delivery and high quality of purchased materials, and to perform routine maintenance on equipment to prevent costly breakdowns. For example, Omark, a chain-saw manufacturer in Guelph, Ontario reduced production flow distance from 806 to 53 metres.

4. Flexible production operations. Two dimensions are important: facilities flexibility and employee flexibility. Facilities should be able to produce a variety of components and products to provide extra capacity when a particular product is in high demand and to avoid shutdown when a unique facility breaks down. Facilities should also require short set-up times—the time it takes to switch from producing one product to another. Cross-training employees—training employees to do a variety of jobs—provides further flexibility. Multiskilled workers can fill in when a particular operation is overloaded, and can reduce set-up time. One company reported a reduction in set-up time from 45 minutes to one minute by training production workers to perform the set-up operations.

Many companies help achieve these objectives by improving the physical layout of their plants. In conventional manufacturing, similar machines (lathes, molding machines, drilling machines, etc.) are grouped together. Workers specialize on only one machine operation (operating either the moulding or the drilling machine). There are at least two negative effects of such a layout. First, products must be moved from one area of the plant to another for required processing. This increases material handling costs and results in work-in-process inventories that can be substantial. These are non-value-added activities and costs. Second, the specialized labour resource is often idle—waiting for work-in-process. This wasted resource—labour time—is also non-value-added.

Cellular Manufacturing. In
a JIT production system,
the process of organizing
machines into cells
according to the specific
requirements of the
product family.

In a JIT production system, machines are often organized in cells according to the specific requirements of a product family. This process is called **cellular manufacturing**. Only the machines that are needed for the product family are in the cell, and these machines are located as close to each other as possible. Workers are trained to use all the cellular machines. Each cell (often shaped in the form of a "U") is a mini-factory or focused factory. Both of the problems associated with the conventional production layout are eliminated in cellular manufacturing.

Work-in-process inventories are reduced or eliminated because there is no need for moving and storing inventory. Idle time is reduced or eliminated because workers are capable of moving from idle machine activity to needed activities. As a result, cycle times are reduced.

Accounting for a JIT system is often simpler than for other systems. Most cost accounting systems focus on determining product costs for inventory valuation. But JIT systems have minimal inventories, so there is less benefit from an elaborate inventory costing system. In JIT systems, materials, labour, and overhead costs could potentially be charged directly to cost of goods sold because inventories are small enough to be ignored. All costs of production are assumed to apply to products that have already been sold.

HIGHLIGHTS TO REMEMBER

Costs are allocated for three major purposes: (1) motivation, (2) income and asset measurement, and (3) cost justification or cost-plus contracts.

Costs to be allocated are traced to cost pools, preferably keeping variable costs and fixed costs in separate pools. Fixed costs of service departments should be allocated using predetermined monthly lump sums for providing a basic capacity to serve. Variable costs should be assigned by using a predetermined standard unit rate for the services actually used. Often it is best to allocate only those central costs of an organization for which measures of usage by departments are available. Service department costs can be allocated using either the direct method or the step-down method.

Joint costs are often allocated to products for inventory valuation and income determination using the physical-units or relative-sales-value method. However, such allocations should not effect decisions.

Activity-based costing is growing in popularity. It first assigns costs to the activities of an organization. Then costs are traced to products or services based on cost drivers that measure the causes of the costs of a particular activity.

Designing and implementing an activity-based costing system involves four steps. First, managers determine the cost objectives, key activities, and resources used. Cost drivers (output measures) are also identified for each resource and activity. Second, a process-based map is drawn that represents the flow of activities and resources that support the cost objects. The third is collecting cost and operating data. The last step is to calculate and interpret the new activity-based information. Often, this last step requires the use of a computer due to the complexity of many ABC systems. Using ABC information to improve operations is called activity-based management.

Just in time (JIT) production systems are used to improve profitability of companies by eliminating waste and improving quality. JIT systems focus on quality, short production cycles, reducing inventory, and flexible use of operating assets and human resources. Each of these factors is associated with nonvalue-added activities and thus improvements result in reduced operating costs and improved proftability.

SUMMARY PROBLEMS FOR YOUR REVIEW

Problem One

Non-manufacturing organizations often find it useful to trace costs to final products or services. Consider a hospital. The output of a hospital is not as easy to define as the output of a factory. Assume the following measures of output in three revenue-producing departments:

DEPARTMENT	MEASURES OF OUTPUT*
Radiology	X-ray films processed
Laboratory	Tests administered
Daily Patient Services**	Patient-days of care (that is, the number of patients multiplied by the number of days of each patient's stay)

* These become the "product" cost objectives, the various revenue-producing activities of a hospital.

** There would be many of these departments, such as obstetrics, pediatrics, and orthopedics. Moreover, there may be both in-patient and out-patient care.

Budgeted output for 2002 is 60,000 X-ray films processed in Radiology, 50,000 tests administered in the Laboratory, and 30,000 patients-days in Daily Patient Services.

In addition to the revenue-producing departments, the hospital has three main service departments: Administrative and Fiscal Services, Plant Operations and Maintenance, and Laundry. (Of course, real hospitals have more than three revenue-producing departments and more than three service departments. This problem is simplified to keep the data manageable.)

The hospital has decided that the cost driver for Administrative and Fiscal Services costs is the direct department costs of the other departments. The cost driver for Plant Operations and Maintenance is square metres occupied and for Laundry, kilograms of laundry. The pertinent budget data for 2002 are as follows:

	DIRECT DEPARTMENT COSTS	SQUARE METRES OCCUPIED	KILOGRAMS OF LAUNDRY
Administrative and Fiscal Services	$1,000,000	1,000	—
Plant Operations and Maintenance	800,000	2,000	—
Laundry	200,000	5,000	—
Radiology	1,000,000	12,000	80,000
Laboratory	400,000	3,000	20,000
Daily Patient Services	$1,600,000	80,000	300,000
Total	$5,000,000	103,000	400,000

1. Allocate service department costs using the direct method.
2. Allocate service department costs using the step-down method. Allocate Administrative and Fiscal Services first, Plant Operations and maintenance second, and Laundry third.

3. Compute the cost per unit of output in each of the revenue-producing departments using the costs determined using (a) the direct method for allocating service department costs (requirement 1) and (b) the costs determined using the step-down method for allocating service department costs (requirement 2).

Solution

1. The solutions to all three requirements are shown in Exhibit 5-11. The direct method is presented first. Note that no service department costs are allocated to another cost driver in the revenue-producing department only. For example, in allocating Plant Operations and Maintenance, square metres occupied by the service departments is ignored. The cost driver is the 95,000 square metres occupied by the revenue-producing departments.

EXHIBIT 5-11

Allocation of Service-Department Costs: Two Methods

	ADMINISTRATIVE AND FISCAL SERVICES	PLANT OPERATIONS AND MAINTENANCE	LAUNDRY	RADIOLOGY	LABORATORY	DAILY PATIENT SERVICES
Allocation base	Accumulated costs	Sq metres	Kilograms			
1. **Direct Method**						
Direct department costs before allocation	$1,000,000	$ 800,000	$200,000	$1,000,000	$400,000	$1,600,000
Administrative and Fiscal Services	(1,000,000)	—	—	333,333*	133,333	533,334
Plant Operations and Maintenance		(800,000)	—	101,052†	25,263	673,685
Laundry			(200,000)	40,000††	10,000	150,000
Total costs after allocation				$1,474,385	$568,596	$2,957,019
Product output in films, tests, and patient-days, respectively				60,000	50,000	30,000
3a. Cost per unit of output				$ 24.573	$ 11.372	$ 98.567
2. **Step-Down Method**						
Direct department costs before allocation	$1,000,000	$ 800,000	$200,000	1,000,000	$400,000	$1,600,000
Administrative and Fiscal Services	(1,000,000)	200,000§	50,000	250,000	100,000	400,000
Plant Operations and Maintenance		(1,000,000)	50,000¶	120,000	30,000	800,000
Laundry			(300,000)	60,000#	15,000	225,000
Total costs after allocation				$1,430,000	$545,000	$3,025,000
Product output in films, tests, and patient-days, respectively				60,000	50,000	30,000
3b. Cost per unit of output				$ 23.833	$ 10.900	$ 100.833

* $1,000,000 ÷ ($1,000,000 + $400,000 + $1,600,000) = 33 1/3%; 33 1/3% × $1,000,000 = $333,333; etc.
† $800,000 ÷ (12,000 + 3,000 + 80,000) = $8.4210526; $8.4210526 × 12,000 sq. metres = $101,052; etc.
†† $200,000 ÷ (80,000 + 20,000 + 300,000) = $.50; $.50 × 80,000 = $40,000; etc.
§ $1,000,000 ÷ ($800,000 + $200,000 + $1,000,000 + $400,000 + $1,600,000) = $0.25; $0.25 × $800,000 = $200,000; etc.
¶ $1,000,000 ÷ (5,000 + 12,000 + 3,000 + 80,000) = $10.00; $10.00 x 5,000 sq. metres = $50,000; etc.
# $300,000 ÷ (80,000 + 20,000 + 300,000) = $.75; $.75 × 80,000 = $60,000; etc.

Note that the total cost of the revenue-producing departments after allocation, $1,474,385 + $568,596 + $2,957,019 = $5,000,000, is equal to the total of the direct department costs in all six departments before allocation.

2. The step-down method is shown in the lower half of Exhibit 5-11. The costs of Administrative and Fiscal Services are allocated to all five other departments. Because a department's own costs are not allocated to itself, the cost driver consists of the $4,000,000 direct department costs in the five departments excluding Administrative and Fiscal Services.

Plant Operations and Maintenance is allocated second on the basis of square metres occupied. No cost will be allocated to itself or back to Administrative and Fiscal Services. Therefore, the square metres used for allocation is the 100,000 square metres occupied by the other four departments.

Laundry is allocated third. No cost would be allocated back to the first two departments, even if they had used laundry services.

As in the direct method, note that the total costs of the revenue-producing departments after allocation, $1,430,000 + $545,000 + $3,025,000 = $5,000,000, equal the total of the direct department costs before allocation.

3. The solutions are labelled 3a and 3b in Exhibit 5-11. Compare the unit costs derived from the direct method with those of the step-down method. In many instances, the final product costs may not differ enough to warrant investing in a cost-allocation method that is any fancier than the direct method. But sometimes even small differences may be significant to a government agency or anybody paying for a large volume of services based on costs. For example, in Exhibit 5-11, the "cost" of an "average" laboratory test is either $11.37 or $10.90. This may be significant for the fiscal committee of the hospital's board of trustees, who must decide on hospital prices. Thus cost allocation is often a technique that helps answer the vital question, "Who should pay for what, and how much?"

Problem Two

Last year, TCY Company's demand for product H17 was 14,000 units. At a recent meeting, the sales manager asked the controller about the expected cost for the sales-order activity for the current year. A new ABC system had been installed, and the controller had provided the sketch of the order-processing activity to the sales manager (see Exhibit 5-12). The sales manager wanted to know how the order-processing activity affects costs. The average sales order is for 20 units. The order-processing activity shown in Exhibit 5-12 requires a computer, processing labour, and telecommunications. The computer is leased at a cost of $2,000 per period. Salaries are $7,000, and telecommunication charges are $1.60 per minute.

1. How many labour hours does it take to process each order? How much telecommunication time does each order take?
2. What is the total cost formula for the order processing activity? What is the total and unit cost for demand of 14,000 units?
3. The sales manager calculated the cost per order to be $32.06 based on the expected demand of 14,000 units of H17. Because he believed that

this year's demand for H17 may be only 12,000 units, he then calculated the total cost of processing 600 orders as $19,236 = 600 \times \$32.06$. Comment on the validity of the sales manager's analysis.

Solution

1. It takes .1 hours or 6 minutes of labour time and 12 minutes of telecommunications time to process an order.
2. The total cost formula for order processing activity is:

Total Cost = Fixed Costs + Variable Costs

= Lease Cost + Labour Cost + Telecom. cost/min. $\times$ min./order $\times$ no. of orders

= $2,000 + $7,000 + $1.60 \times 12 \times$ Number of Orders

= $9,000 + $19.20 \times$ Number of Orders

For 14,000 units, there will be 700 orders processed. The total cost to process these orders is:

Total Cost = $9,000 + ($19.20 \times 700) = $22,440$ and the unit cost is $32.06 (22,440/700).

3. The sales manager has fallen into the trap of ignoring cost behaviour. His calculation assumes that unit fixed costs will not change with changes in demand or the cost driver. The correct prediction of total cost for a demand of 12,000 units (or 600 orders) is:

Total Cost = $9,000 + $19.20 \times 600 = $20,520$

This problem illustrates why it is important to take cost behaviour into consideration when using any costing system for planning purposes.

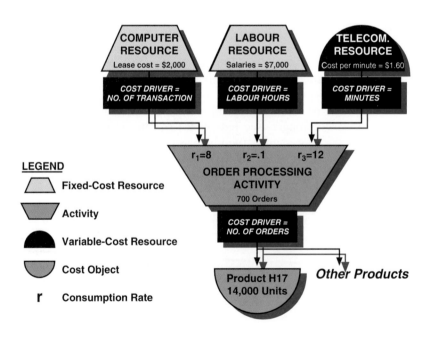

EXHIBIT 5-12

TCY's Order-Processing Activity

LEGEND

△ Fixed-Cost Resource

▽ Activity

◗ Variable-Cost Resource

◖ Cost Object

r Consumption Rate

ACCOUNTING VOCABULARY

ASSIGNMENT MATERIAL

QUESTIONS

Q5-1 What is the purpose of a cost accounting system?

Q5-2 "A cost pool is a group of costs that is physically traced to the appropriate cost objective." Do you agree? Explain.

Q5-3 Give five terms that are sometimes used as substitutes for the term "allocate."

Q5-4 What are the three purposes of cost allocation?

Q5-5 What are the three types of allocations?

Q5-6 Give three guides for the allocation of service department costs.

Q5-7 Why should budgeted-cost rates, rather than actual-cost rates, be used for assigning the variable costs of service departments?

Q5-8 Why do many companies allocate fixed costs separately from variable costs?

Q5-9 "We used a lump-sum allocation method for fixed costs a few years ago, but we gave it up because managers always predicted usage below what they actually used." Is this a common problem? How might it be prevented?

Q5-10 "A commonly misused basis for allocation is dollar sales." Explain.

Q5-11 How could national advertising costs be allocated to territories?

Q5-12 Briefly describe the two popular methods for allocating service-department costs.

Q5-13 "The step-down method allocates more costs to the producing departments than does the direct method." Do you agree? Explain.

Q5-14 How does the term *cost application* differ from *cost allocation*?

Q5-15 What is a non-volume-related cost driver? Give two examples.

Q5-16 How are costs of various overhead resources allocated to products, services, or customers in an ABC system?

Q5-17 Briefly explain each of the two conventional ways of allocating joint costs to products.

Q5-18 What are by-products and how do we account for them?

Q5-19 Give four examples of activities and related cost drivers that can be used in an ABC system to allocate costs to products, series, or customers.

Q5-20 "Activity-based costing is useful for product costing but not for planning and control." Do you agree? Explain.

Q5-21 Refer to Exhibit 5-6. Suppose the appliance maker has two plants—the Salem plant and the Youngstown plant. The Youngstown plant produces only three appliances that are very similar in material and production requirements. The Salem plant produces a wide variety of appliances with diverse material and production requirements. Which type of costing system would you recommend for each plant (traditional or ABC)? Explain.

Q5-22 Name four steps in the design and implementation of an activity-based costing system.

Q5-23 Refer to the Pacific Power illustration. Which resource costs depicted in Exhibit 5-7 could have variable cost behaviour?

Q5-24 Why do organizations adopt activity-based costing systems?

Q5-25 Why do managers want to distinguish between value-added activities and non-value-added activities?

Q5-26 Name four factors crucial to the success of just-in-time production systems.

Q5-27 "ABC and JIT are alternative techniques for achieving competitiveness." Do you agree?

PROBLEMS

P5-1 FIXED- AND VARIABLE-COST POOLS. The city of Castle Rock signed a lease for a photocopy machine at $2,500 per month and $.02 per copy. Operating costs for toner, paper, operator salary, etc. are all variable at $.03 per copy. Departments had projected a need for 100,000 copies a month. The City Planning Department predicted its usage at 36,000 copies a month. It made 42,000 copies in August.

1. Suppose one predetermined rate per copy was used for all photocopy costs. What rate would be used and how much cost would be allocated to the City Planning Department in August?
2. Suppose fixed- and variable-cost pools were charged separately. Specify how each pool should be charged. Compute the cost charged to the City Planning Department in August.
3. Which method, the one in requirement 1 or the one in requirement 2, do you prefer? Explain.

P5-2 SALES-BASED ALLOCATIONS. Pioneer Markets has three grocery stores in the metropolitan area. Central costs are allocated using sales as the cost driver. The following are budgeted and actual sales during November:

	SUNNYVILLE	WEDGEWOOD	CAPITAL
Budgeted sales	$600,000	$1,000,000	$400,000
Actual sales	600,000	700,000	500,000

Central costs of $200,000 are to be allocated in November.

1. Compute the central costs allocated to each store with *budgeted* sales as the cost driver.
2. Compute the central costs allocated to each store with *actual* sales as the cost driver.

3. What advantages are there to using budgeted rather than actual sales for allocating the central costs?

P5-3 DIRECT AND STEP-DOWN ALLOCATIONS. Bulter Home Products has two producing departments, machining and assembly, and two service departments, personnel and custodial. The company's budget's for April, 2001 is:

	SERVICE DEPARTMENT		PRODUCTION DEPARTMENTS	
	PERSONNEL	CUSTODIAL	MACHINING	ASSEMBLY
Direct department costs	$32,000	$70,000	$600,000	$800,000
Square metres	2,000	1,000	10,000	25,000
Number of employees	15	30	200	250

Bulter allocates personnel costs on the basis of number of employees and custodial costs on the basis of square metres.

14222.22   17777.78

1. Allocate personnel and custodial costs to the producing departments using the direct method. *2000   13333.33 16666.67*

2. Allocate personnel and custodial costs to the producing departments using the step-down method. Allocate personnel costs first.

P5-4 JOINT COSTS. Robinson Company's production process for two of its solvents can be diagrammed as follows:

Joint input = 30,000 litres

Split-off point

Solvent A = 20,000 litres

Solvent B =10,000 litres

The cost of the joint inputs, including processing costs before the split-off point, is $400,000. Solvent A can be sold at split-off for $10 per litre and Solvent B for $30 per litre.

1. Allocate the $400,000 joint cost to Solvents A and B by the physical-units method.

2. Allocate the $400,000 joint cost to Solvents A and B by the relative-sales-value method.

P5-5 JOINT PRODUCTS. Millbank Milling buys oats at $.60 per kilogram and produces MM Oat Flour, MM Oat Flakes, and MM Oat Bran. The process of separating the oats into oat flour and oat bran costs $.30 per kilogram. The oat flour can be sold for $1.50 per kilogram, the oat bran for $2.00 per kilogram. Each kilogram of oats has .2 kilograms of oat bran and .8 kilograms of oat flour. A kilogram of oat flour can be made into oat flakes for a fixed cost of $240,000 plus a variable cost of $.60 per kilogram. Millbank Milling plans to process one-million kilograms of oats in 2001, at a purchase price of $600,000.

1. Allocate all the joint costs to oat flour and oat bran using the physical-units method.

2. Allocate all the joint costs to oat flour and oat bran using the relative-sales-value method.
3. Suppose there was no market for oat flour. Instead, it must be made into oat flakes to be sold. Oat flakes sell for $2.90 per kilogram. Allocate the joint cost to oat bran and oat flakes using the relative-sales-value method.

P5-6 BY-PRODUCT COSTING. The Wenatchee Company buys apples from local orchards and presses them to produce apple juice. The pulp that remains after pressing is sold to farmers as livestock food. This livestock food is accounted for as a by-product.

During the 2001 fiscal year, the company paid $1,000,000 to purchase eight-million kilograms of apples. After processing, one-million kilograms of pulp remained. Jones spent $35,000 to package and ship the pulp, which was sold for $50,000.

1. How much of the joint cost of the apples is allocated to the pulp?
2. Compute the total inventory cost (and therefore the cost of goods sold) for the pulp.
3. Assume that $130,000 was spent to press the apples and $150,000 was spent to filter, pasteurize, and pack the apple juice. Compute the total inventory cost of the apple juice produced.

P5-7 JIT AND NON-VALUE-ADDED ACTIVITIES. A motorcycle manufacturer was concerned with declining market share because of foreign competition. To become more efficient, the company was considering changing to a just-in-time (JIT) production system. As a first step in analyzing the feasibility of the change, the company identified its major activities. Among the 120 activities were the following:

Materials receiving and inspection
Production scheduling
Production set-up
Rear-wheel assembly
Move engine from fabrication to assembly building
Assemble handlebars
Paint inspection
Rework defective brake assemblies
Instal speedometer
Put completed motorcycle in finished goods storage

1. From the list of 10 activities given above, prepare two lists—one of value-added activities and one of non-value-added activities.
2. For each non-value-added activity, explain how a JIT production system might eliminate, or at least reduce, the cost of the activity.

P5-8 COST ASSIGNMENT AND ALLOCATION. Hwang Manufacturing Company has two departments—machining and finishing. For a given period, the following costs were incurred by the company as a whole: direct materials, $120,000; direct labour, $60,000; and manufacturing overhead, $78,000. The total costs were $258,000.

The machining department incurred 80 percent of the direct-materials costs, but only 20 percent of the direct-labour costs. As is commonplace, manufacturing overhead incurred by each department was allocated to products in proportion to the direct-labour costs of products within the departments.

Three products were produced:

PRODUCT	DIRECT MATERIALS	DIRECT LABOUR
X-1	50%	33⅓%
Y-1	25	33⅓
Z-1	25	33⅓
Total for the machining department	100%	100%
X-1	33⅓%	40%
Y-1	33⅓	40
Z-1	33⅓	20
Total added by finishing department	100%	100%

The manufacturing overhead incurred by the machining department and allocated to all products therein amounted to the following: machining, $36,000; finishing, $42,000.

1. Compute the total costs incurred by the machining department and added by the finishing department.
2. Compute the total costs of each product that would be shown as finished goods inventory if all the products were transferred to finished stock upon completion.

P5-9 COST ALLOCATION AND ACTIVITY-BASED ACCOUNTING. The cordless phone manufacturing division of a consumer electronics company uses activity-based accounting. For simplicity, assume that its accountants have identified only the following three activities and related cost drivers for manufacturing overhead:

ACTIVITY	COST DRIVER
Materials handling	Direct materials cost
Engineering	Engineering change orders
Power	Kilowatt hours

Three types of cordless phones are produced: SA2, SA5, and SA9. Direct costs and cost-driver activity for each product for a recent month are:

	SA2	SA5	SA9
Direct materials cost	$25,000 (12.5%)	$50,000 (25%)	$125,000 (62.5%)
Direct labour cost	$4,000 (50%)	$1,000 (12.5%)	$3,000 (37.5%)
Kilowatt hours	50,000 (12.5%)	200,000 (50%)	150,000 (37.5%)
Engineering change orders	13 (65%)	5 (25%)	2 (10%)

Manufacturing overhead for the month was

Materials handling	$ 8,000
Engineering	20,000
Power	16,000
Total manufacturing overhead	$44,000

1. Compute the manufacturing overhead allocated to each product with the activity-based accounting system.
2. Suppose all manufacturing overhead costs have been allocated to products in proportion to their direct labour costs. Compute the manufacturing overhead allocated to each product.
3. In which product costs—those in requirement 1 or those in requirement 2—do you have the most confidence? Why?

P5-10 **HOSPITAL ALLOCATION BASE.** Jade Soon, the administrator of Saint Jude Hospital, is interested in obtaining more accurate cost allocations on the basis of cause and effect. The $180,000 of laundry costs had been allocated on the basis of 600,000 kilograms processed for all departments, or $.30 per kilogram.

Soon is concerned that government health-care officials will require weighted statistics to be used for cost allocation. She asks you, "Please develop a revised base for allocating laundry costs. It should be better than our present base, but should not be overly complex either."

You study the situation and find that the laundry processes a large volume of uniforms for student nurses and physicians, and for dietary, housekeeping, and other personnel. In particular, the coats or jackets worn by personnel in the radiology department require unusual handwork.

A special study of laundry for radiology revealed that 7,500 of the 15,000 kilograms were jackets and coats that were five times more expensive to process than regular laundry items. A number of reasons explained the difference, but it was principally because of handwork involved.

Ignore the special requirements of the departments other than radiology. Revise the cost-allocation base and compute the new cost-allocation rate. Compute the total cost charged to radiology using kilograms and using the new base.

P5-11 **COST OF PASSENGER TRAFFIC.** Northern Pacific Railroad (NP) has a commuter operation that services passengers along a route between San Jose and San Francisco. Problems of cost allocation were highlighted in a news story about NP's application to the Public Utilities Commission (PUC) for a rate increase. The PUC staff claimed that the "avoidable annual cost" of running the operation was $700,000, in contrast to NP officials' claim of a loss of $9 million. PUC's estimate was based on what NP would be able to save if it shut down the commuter operations.

The NP loss estimate was based on a "full-allocation-of-costs" method, which allocates a share of common maintenance and overhead costs to the passenger service.

If the PUC accepted its own estimate, a 25 percent fare increase would have been justified, whereas NP sought a 96 percent fare increase.

The PUC stressed that commuter costs represent less than 1 percent of the systemwide costs of NP and that 57 percent of the commuter costs are derived from some type of allocation method—sharing the costs of other operations.

NP's representative stated that "avoidable cost" is not an appropriate way to allocate costs for calculating rates. He said that "it is not fair to include just so-called above-the-rail costs" because there are other real costs associated with commuter service. Examples are maintaining smoother connections and making more frequent track inspections.

1. As Public Utilities Commissioner, what approach toward cost allocation would you favour for making decisions regarding fares? Explain.

2. How would fluctuations in freight traffic affect commuter costs under the NP method?

P5-12 ALLOCATING AUTOMOBILE COSTS. The motor pool of a Megalopolis provides automobiles for the use of various city departments. Currently, the motor pool has 50 autos. A recent study showed that it costs $3,600 of annual fixed cost per automobile plus $.10 per kilometre variable cost to own, operate, and maintain autos such as those provided by the motor pool.

Each month, the costs of the motor pool are charged to the user departments on the basis of kilometres driven. On average, each auto is driven 24,000 kilometres annually, although wide month-to-month variations occur. In April 2001, the 50 autos were driven a total of 50,000 kilometres. The motor pool's total costs for April were $24,000.

The chief planner for the city always seemed concerned about her auto costs. She was especially upset in April when she was charged $7,200 for the 15,000 kilometres driven in the department's five autos. This is the normal monthly mileage in the department. Her memo to the head of the motor pool stated, "I can certainly get autos at less than the $.48 per kilometre you charged in April." The response was, "I am under instructions to allocate the motor-pool costs to the user departments. Your department was responsible for 30 percent of the April usage (15,000 kilometres ÷ 50,000 kilometres), so I allocated 30 percent of the motor pool's April costs to you (.30 × $24,000). That just seems fair."

1. Calculate the city's average annual cost per kilometre for owning, maintaining, and operating an auto.
2. Explain why the allocated cost in April ($.48 per kilometre) exceeds the average in requirement 1 above.
3. Describe any undesirable behavioural effects of the cost-allocation method used.
4. How would you improve the cost-allocation method?

P5-13 ALLOCATION OF COSTS. The Pegasus Trucking Company has one service department and two regional operating departments. The budgeted cost behaviour pattern of the service department is $750,000 monthly in fixed costs plus $.80 per 1,000 tonne-kilometres operated in the East and West regions. (Tonne-kilometres are the number of metric tonnes carried times the number of kilometres travelled.) The actual monthly costs of the service department are allocated using tonne-kilometres operated as the cost driver.

1. Pegasus processed 500-million tonne-kilometres of traffic in April, half for each operating region. The actual costs of the services department were exactly equal to those predicted by the budget for 500-million tonne-kilometres. Compute the costs that would be allocated to each operation region.
2. Suppose the East region was plagued by strikes, so that the freight handled was much lower than originally anticipated. East moved only 150-million tonne-kilometres of traffic. The West region handled 250-million tonne-kilometres of traffic. The actual costs were exactly as budgeted for this lower level of activity. Compute the costs that would be allocated to East and West. Note that the total costs will be lower.

3. Refer to the facts in requirement 1 above. Various inefficiencies caused the service department to incur costs of $1,275,000. Compute the costs to be allocated to East and West. Are the allocations justified? If not, what improvement do you suggest?

4. Refer to the facts in requirement 2 above. Assume that assorted investment outlays for equipment and space in the service department were made to provide a basic maximum capacity to serve the East Region at a level of 360-million tonne-kilometres and the West region at a level of 240-million tonne-kilometres. Suppose fixed costs are allocated on the basis of this capacity to serve. Variable costs are assigned by using a predetermined standard rate per 1,000 tonne-kilometres. Compute the costs to be allocated to each department. What are the advantages of this method over other methods?

P5-14 HOSPITAL EQUIPMENT. Many provinces have a hospital regulatory board that must approve the acquisition of specified medical equipment before the hospitals in the province can qualify for cost-based reimbursement related to that equipment. That is, hospitals cannot bill government agencies for the later use of the equipment unless the board originally authorized the acquisition.

Two hospitals in one such province proposed the acquisition and sharing of some expensive X-ray equipment to be used for unusual cases. The amortization and related fixed costs of operating the equipment were predicted at $12,000 per month. The variable costs were predicted at $30 per patient procedure.

The board asked each hospital to predict its usage of the equipment over its expected useful life of five years. Premier Hospital predicted an average usage of 75 X-rays per month, and St. Mary's Hospital predicted 50 X-rays per month. The commission regarded this information as critical to the size and degree of sophistication that would be justified. That is, if the number of X-rays exceeded a certain quantity per month, a different configuration of space, equipment, and personnel would be required, which would mean higher fixed costs per month.

1. Suppose fixed costs are allocated on the basis of the hospitals' predicted average use per month. Variable costs are assigned on the basis of $30 per X-ray, the budgeted variable-cost rate for the current fiscal year. In October, Premier Hospital had 50 X-rays and St. Mary's Hospital had 50 X-rays. Compute the total costs allocated to Premier Hospital and St. Mary's Hospital.

2. Suppose the manager of the equipment had various operating inefficiencies so that the total October costs were $16,500. Would you change your answers in requirement 1? Why?

3. A traditional method of cost allocation does not use the method in requirement 1. Instead, an allocation rate depends on the actual costs and actual volume encountered. The actual costs are totalled for the month and divided by the actual number of X-rays during the month. Suppose the actual costs agreed exactly with the budget for a total of 100 actual X-rays. Compute the total costs allocated to Premier Hospital and St. Mary's Hospital. Compare the results with those in requirement 1. What is the major weakness in this traditional method? What are some of its possible behavioural effects?

4. Describe any undesirable behavioural effects of the method described in requirement 1. How would you counteract any tendencies toward deliberate false predictions of long-run usage?

P5-15 DIRECT METHOD FOR SERVICE DEPARTMENT ALLOCATION. Wheelock Controls Company has two producing departments, Mechanical Instruments and Electronic Instruments. In addition, there are two service departments, Building Services and Materials Receiving and Handling. The company purchases a variety of component parts from which the departments assemble instruments for sale in domestic and international markets.

The Electronic Instruments division is highly automated. The manufacturing costs depend primarily on the number of subcomponents in each instrument. In contrast, the Mechanical Instruments division relies primarily on a large labour force to hand-assemble instruments. Its costs depend on direct labour hours.

The cost of Building Services depend primarily on the square metres occupied. The costs of Materials Receiving and Handling depend primarily on the total number of components handled.

Instruments M1 and M2 are produced in the Mechanical Instruments department, and E1 and E2 are produced in the Electronic Instruments department. Information about these products is as follows:

	DIRECT MATERIALS COST	NUMBER OF COMPONENTS	DIRECT LABOUR HOURS
M1	$74	25	4.0
M2	86	21	8.0
E1	63	10	1.5
E2	91	15	1.0

Budget figures for 2002 include:

	BUILDING SERVICES	MATERIALS RECEIVING AND HANDLING	MECHANICAL INSTRUMENTS	ELECTRONIC INSTRUMENTS
Direct department costs (excluding direct materials cost)	$150,000	$120,000	$680,000	$548,000
Square metres occupied		5,000	50,000	25,000
Number of final instruments produced			8,000	10,000
Average number of components per instrument			10	16
Direct labour hours			30,000	8,000

1. Allocate the costs of the service departments using the direct method.
2. Using the results of requirement 1, compute the cost per comonent in the Electronic Instruments department.
3. Using the results of requirement 2, compute the cost per unit of roduct for insruments M1, M2, E1, and E2

P5-16 STEP-DOWN METHOD FOR SERVICE DEPARTMENT ALLOCATION. Refer to the data in Problem 5-15.

1. Allocate the costs of the service departments using the step-down method.
2. Using the results of requirement 1, compute the cost per direct-labour hour in the Mechanical Instruments department and the cost per component in the Electronic Instruments department.
3. Using the results of requirement 2, compute the cost per unit of product for instruments M1, M2, E1, and E2.

P5-17 ACTIVITY-BASED COSTING. Reliable Machining Products (RMP) is an automotive component supplier. RMP has been approached by Chrysler with a proposal to significantly increase production of Part T151A to a total annual quantity of 100,000. Chrysler believes that by increasing the volume of production of Part T151A, RMP should realize the benefits of economies of scale and hence should accept a lower price than the current $6 per unit. Currently, RMP's gross margin on Part T151A is 3.3 percent, computed as follows:

The 400 percent overhead allocation rate is based on $3,300,000 annual factory overhead divided by $825,000 annual direct labour.

	TOTAL	PER UNIT (÷100,000)
Direct materials	$150,000	$1.50
Direct labour	86,000	.86
Factory overhead [400% × direct labour]	344,000	3.44
Total cost	$580,000	$5.80
Sales price		6.00
Gross margin		$ .20
Gross margin percentage		3.3%

Activity Centre: Cost Drivers	Annual Cost Driver Quantity
Quality: No. of pieces scrapped	10,000
Production Scheduling and Set-up:	
No. of set-ups	500
Shipping: No. of containers shipped	60,000
Shipping Administration: No. of shipments	1,000
Production: No. of machine hours	10,000

Part T151A seems to be a marginal profit product. If additional volume of production of Part T151A is to be added, RMP management believes that the sales price must be increased, not reduced as requested by Chrysler. The management of RMP sees this quoting situation as an excellent opportunity to examine the effectiveness of their traditional costing system versus an activity-based costing system. Data have been collected by a team consisting of accounting and engineering analysts.

Activity Centre	Traceable Factor Overhead Costs (Annual)
Quality	$800,000
Production Scheduling	50,000
Set-Up	600,000
Shipping	300,000
Shipping Administration	50,000
Production	1,500,000
Total costs	$3,300,000

The accounting and engineering team has provided the following cost-driver consumption estimates for the production of 100,000 units of Part T151A:

Cost Driver	Cost-Driver Consumption
Pieces scrapped	1,000
Set-ups	12
Containers shipped	500
Shipments	100
Machine hours	500

1. Prepare a schedule calculating the unit cost and gross margin of Part T151A using the activity-based costing approach.
2. Based on the ABC results, what course of action would you recommend regarding the proposal by Chrysler? List the benefits and costs associated with implementing an activity-based costing system at RMP.

P5-18   DIRECT AND STEP-DOWN METHODS OF ALLOCATION.   General Textiles Company has prepared departmental overhead budgets for normal activity levels before reapportionments, as follows:

Building and grounds	$ 20,000
Personnel	1,200
General factory administration*	28,020
Cafeteria operating loss	1,430
Storeroom	2,750
Machining	35,100
Assembly	56,500
	$145,000

*To be reapportioned before cafeteria.

Management has decided that the most sensible product costs are achieved by using departmental overhead rates. These rates are developed after appropriate service department costs are allocated to production departments.

Cost drivers for allocation are to be selected from the following data:

DEPARTMENT	DIRECT LABOUR HOURS	NUMBER OF EMPLOYEES	SQUARE METRES OF FLOOR SPACE OCCUPIED	TOTAL LABOUR HOURS	NUMBER OF REQUISITIONS
Building and grounds	—	—	—	—	—
Personnel*	—	—	2,000	—	—
General factory administration	—	35	7,000	—	—
Cafeteria operating loss	—	10	4,000	1,000	—
Storeroom	—	5	7,000	1,000	—
Machining	5,000	50	30,000	8,000	3,000
Assembly	15,000	100	50,000	17,000	1,500
	20,000	200	100,000	27,000	4,500

* Basis used is number of employees.

1. Allocate service-department costs by the step-down method. Develop overhead rates per direct labour hour for machining and assembly.
2. Same as requirement 1, using the direct method.
3. What would be the blanket plantwide factory-overhead application rate, assuming that direct labour hours are used as a cost driver?
4. Using the following information about Job K10 and Job K11, prepare three different total overhead costs for each job, using rates developed in requirements 1, 2, and 3.

	DIRECT LABOUR HOURS	
	MACHINING	ASSEMBLY
Job K10	19	2
Job K12	3	18

P5-19 JOINT COSTS AND DECISIONS.   A chemical company has a batch process that takes 1,000 litres of a raw material and transforms it into 80 kilograms of X-1 and 400 kilograms of X-2. Although the joint costs of their production are $1,200, both products are worthless at their split-off point. Additional separable costs of $350 are necessary to give X-1 a sales value of $1,000 as Product A. Similarly, additional separable costs of $200 are necessary to give X-2 a sales value of $1,000 as Product B.

You are in charge of the batch process and the marketing of both products. (Show your computations for each answer.)

1. a. Assuming that you believe in assigning joint costs on a physical basis, allocate the total profit of $250 per batch to Products A and B.
   b. Would you stop processing one of the products? Why?
2. a. Assuming that you believe in assigning joint costs on a net-realizable-value (relative-sales-value) basis, allocate the total operating profit of $250 per batch to Products A and B. If there is no market for X-1 and X-2 at their split-off point, a net realizable value is usually imputed by taking the ultimate sales value at the point of sale and working backward to obtain approximated "synthetic" relative sales values at the split-off point. These synthetic values are then used as weights for allocating the joint costs to the products.

b. You have internal product-profitability reports in which joint costs are assigned on a net-realizable-value basis. Your chief engineer says that, after seeing these reports, she has developed a method of obtaining more of Product B and correspondingly less of Product A from each batch, without changing the per-kilogram cost factors. Would you approve this new method? Why? What would the overall operating profit be if 40 kilograms more of B were produced and 40 kilograms less of A?

P5-20 **ALLOCATION, DEPARTMENT RATES, AND DIRECT LABOUR HOURS VERSUS MACHINE-HOURS.** The Manning Manufacturing company has two producing departments, machining and assembly. Mr. Manning recently automated the machining department. The installation of a computer-aided manufacturing (CAM) system, together with robotic workstations, drastically reduced the amount of direct labour required. Meanwhile the assembly department remained labour-intensive.

The company had always used one firmwide rate based on direct labour hours as the cost driver for applying all costs (except direct materials) to the final products. Mr. Manning was considering two alternatives: (1) continue using direct labour hours as the only cost driver, but use different rates in machining and assembly, and (2) use machine-hours as the cost driver in the machining department while continuing with direct labour hours in assembly.

Budgeted data for 2001 are:

	MACHINING	ASSEMBLY	TOTAL
Total cost (except direct materials), after allocating service department costs	$630,000	$450,000	$1,080,000
Machine hours	105,000	*	105,000
Direct labour hours	15,000	30,000	45,000

*Not applicable

	MACHINE-HOURS OF MACHINING	DIRECT LABOUR HOURS IN MACHINING	DIRECT LABOUR HOURS IN ASSEMBLY
Product A	10.0	1.0	14.0
Product B	17.0	1.5	3.0
Product C	14.0	1.3	8.0

1. Suppose Manning continued to use one firmwide rate based on direct labour hours to apply all manufacturing costs (except direct materials) to the final products. Compute the cost-application rate that would be used.
2. Suppose Manning continued to use direct labour hours as the only cost driver but used different rates on machining and assembly:
   a. Compute the cost-application rate for machining.
   b. Compute the cost-application rate for assembly.
3. Suppose Manning changed the cost accounting system to use machine-hours as the cost driver in machining and direct labour hours in assembly:
   a. Compute the cost-application rate for machining.
   b. Compute the cost-application rate for assembly.
4. Three products use the following machine-hours and direct labour hours:

a. Compute the manufacturing cost of each product (excluding direct materials) using one firmwide rate based on direct labour hours.

b. Compute the manufacturing cost of each product (excluding direct materials) using direct labour hours as the cost driver, but with different cost-application rates in machining and assembly.

c. Compute the manufacturing cost of each product (excluding direct materials) using a cost-application rate based on direct labour hours in assembly and machine-hours in machining.

d. Compare and explain the result in requirements 4a, 4b, and 4c.

P5-21 MULTIPLE ALLOCATION BASES. The Glasgow Electronics Company produces three types of circuit boards; L, M, and N. The cost accounting system used by Glasgow until 1999 applied all costs except direct materials to the products using direct labour hours as the only cost driver. In 1999 the company undertook a cost study. The study determined that there were six main factors causing costs to be incurred. A new system was designed with a separate cost pool for each of the six factors. The factors and the costs associated with each are as follows:

1. Direct labour hours—direct labour cost and related fringe benefits and payroll taxes.
2. Machine-hours—amortization and repairs and maintenance costs.
3. Kilograms of materials—materials receiving, handling, and storage costs.
4. Number of production setups—labour used to change machinery and computer configurations for a new production batch.
5. Number of production orders—costs of production scheduling and order processing.
6. Number of orders shipped—all packaging and shipping expenses.

The company is now preparing a budget for 2001. The budget includes the following predictions:

	BOARD L	BOARD M	BOARD N
Units to be produced	10,000	800	5,000
Direct material cost	£66/unit	£88/unit	£45/unit
Direct labour hours	4/unit	18/unit	9/unit
Machine hours	7/unit	15/unit	7/unit
Kilograms of materials	3/unit	4/unit	2/unit
Number of production setups	100	50	50
Number of production orders	300	200	70
Number of orders shipped	1,000	800	2,000

The total budgeted cost for 2001 is £3,712,250, of which £955,400 was direct materials cost, and the amount in each of the six pools defined above is:

COST POOL	COST
1	£1,391,600
2	936,000
3	129,600
4	160,000
5	25,650
6	114,000
Total	£2,756,850

1. Prepare a budget that shows the total budgeted cost and the unit cost for each circuit board. Use the new system with six cost pools (plus a separate direct application of direct materials cost).
2. Compute the budgeted total and unit costs of each circuit board if the old direct labour hour-based system had been used.
3. How would you judge whether the new system is better than the old one?

P5-22 ALLOCATING CENTRAL COSTS. The Central Railroad allocates all central corporate overhead costs to its divisions. Some costs, such as specified internal auditing and legal costs, are identified on the basis of time spent. However, other costs are harder to allocate, so the revenue achieved by each division is used as an allocation base. Examples of such costs were executive salaries, travel, secretarial, utilities, rent, amortization, donations, corporate planning, and general marketing costs.

Allocations on the basis of revenue for 2001 were (in millions):

DIVISION	REVENUE	ALLOCATED COSTS
Northern	$120	$ 7
Mesa	240	14
Plains	240	14
Total	$600	$35

In 2002, Northern's revenue remained unchanged. However, Plains' revenue soared to $280 million because of unusually bountiful crops. The latter are troublesome to forecast because unpredictable weather has a pronounced influence on volume. Mesa had expected a sharp rise in revenue, but severe competitive conditions resulted in a decline to $200 million. The total cost allocated on the basis of revenue was again $35 million, despite rises in other costs. The president was pleased that central costs did not rise for the year.

1. Compute the allocations of costs to each division for 2002.
2. How would each division manager probably feel about the cost allocation in 2002 as compared with 2001? What are the weaknesses of using revenue as a basis for cost allocation?
3. Suppose the budgeted revenues for 2002 were $120 million, $240, and $280, respectively, and the budgeted revenues were used as a cost driver for allocation. Compute the allocations of costs to each division for 2002. Do you prefer this method to the one used in requirement 1? Why?
4. Many accountants and managers oppose allocating any central costs. Why?

P5-23 ALLOCATION OF SERVICE-DEPARTMENT COSTS. Chief Cleaning, Inc., provides cleaning services for a variety of clients. The company has two producing divisions, Residential and Commercial, and two service-departments, Personnel and Administrative. The company has decided to allocate all service-department costs to the producing departments: Personnel, on the basis of number of employees, and Administrative, on the basis of direct department costs. The budget for 2002 shows the following:

	PERSONNEL	ADMINISTRATIVE	RESIDENTIAL	COMMERCIAL
Direct department costs	$70,000	$90,000	$ 240,000	$ 400,000
Number of employees	3	5	12	18
Direct labour hours			24,000	36,000
Square metres cleaned			4,500,000	9,970,000

1. Allocate service-department costs using the direct method.
2. Allocate service-department costs using the step-down method. The Personnel Department costs should be allocated first.
3. Suppose the company prices by the hour in the Residential Department and by the square metre cleaned in Commercial. Using the results of the step-down allocations in requirement 2,
   a. Compute the cost of providing one direct labour hour of service in the Residential Department.
   b. Compute the cost of cleaning one square metre of space in the Commercial Department.

P5-24 ACTIVITY-BASED COSTING. Yamaguchi Company makes printed circuit boards in a suburb of Kyoto. The production process is automated with computer-controlled robotic machines assembling each circuit board from a supply of parts. Yamaguchi has identified four activities:

ACTIVITY	COST DRIVER	RATE
Materials handling	Cost of direct materials	5% of materials cost
Assembly	Number of parts used	¥50 per part
Soldering	Number of circuit boards	¥1,500 per board
Quality assurance	Minutes of testing	¥400 per minute

Yamaguchi makes three types of circuit boards, Model A, Model B, and Model C. Requirements for production of 100 circuit boards are as follows:

	MODEL A	MODEL B	MODEL C
Direct materials cost	¥4,000	¥6,000	¥8,000
Number of parts used	60	40	20
Minutes of testing	5	3	2

1. Compute the cost of production of 100 of the three types of circuit boards and the cost per circuit board for each type.
2. Suppose the design of Model A could be simplified so that it required only 30 parts (instead of 60) and took only three minutes of testing time (instead of five). Compute the cost of 100 Model A circuit boards and the cost per circuit board.

P5-25 **ACTIVITY-BASED COSTING.**   The Maori Novelty company makes a variety of souvenirs for visitors to New Zealand. The Otago Division manufactures stuffed kiwi birds using a highly automated operation. A recently installed activity-based costing system has four activities:

ACTIVITY	COST DRIVER	RATE
Materials receiving and handling	Kilograms of materials	$1.20 per kilogram
Production setup	Number of setups	$60 per setup
Cutting, sewing, and assembly	Number of units	$0.40 per unit
Packing and shipping	Number of orders	$10 per order

Two products are called "Standard Kiwi" and "Giant Kiwi." They require .20 and .40 kilograms of materials, respectively, at a materials cost of $1.30 for Standard Kiwis and $2.20 for Giant Kiwis. One computer-controlled assembly line makes all products. When a production run of a different product is started, a setup procedure is required to reprogram the computers and make other changes in the process. Normally, 600 Standard Kiwis are produced per setup, but only 240 Giant Kiwis. Products are packed and shipped separately, so a request from a customer for, say, three different products is considered three different orders.

Ausiland Waterfront Market just placed an order for 100 Standard Kiwis and 50 Giant Kiwis.

1. Compute the cost of products shipped to Ausiland Waterfront Market.
2. Suppose the products made for Ausiland Waterfront required "AWM" to be printed on each kiwi. Because of the automated process, printing the initials takes no extra time or materials, but it requires a special production setup for each product. Compute the cost of products shipped to the Ausiland Waterfront Market.
3. Explain how the activity-based costing system helps Maori Novelty to measure costs of individual products or orders better than a traditional system that allocates all non-materials costs based on direct labour.

P5-26 **ACTIVITY-BASED ALLOCATIONS.**   Winnipeg Wholesaler Distributors uses an activity-based costing system to determine the cost of handling its products. One important activity is the receiving of shipments in the warehouse. Three resources support that activity: recording and record-keeping; labour; and inspection.

Recording and record-keeping is a cost driven by number of shipments received. The cost per shipment is $16.50.

Labour is driven by kilograms of merchandise received. Because labour is hired in shifts, it is fixed for large ranges of volume. Currently, labour costs are running $23,000 per month for handling 460,000 kilograms. This same cost would apply to all volumes between 300,000 kilograms and 550,000 kilograms.

Finally, inspection is a cost driven by the number of boxes received. Inspection costs are $2.75 per box.

One product distributed by Winnipeg Wholesale Distributors is candy. There is a wide variety of types of candy, so many different shipments are handled in the warehouse. In July the warehouse received 550 shipments, consisting of 4,000 boxes weighing a total of 80,000 kilograms.

1. Compute the cost of receiving shipments during July.
2. Management is considering elimination of brands of candy that have small sales levels. This would reduce the warehouse volume to 220 shipments, consisting of 2,500 boxes weighing a total of 60,000 kilograms. Compute the amount of savings from eliminating the small-sales-level brands.
3. Suppose receiving costs were estimated on a per kilogram basis. What was the total receiving cost per kilogram of candy received in July? If management had used this cost to estimate the effect of eliminating the 20,000 kilograms of candy, what mistake might be made?

P5-27 COLLABORATIVE LEARNING EXERCISE: LIBRARY RESEARCH ON ABC. Form groups of three to six students. Each student should choose a different article about activity-based costing (ABC) or activity-based management (ABM) from the current literature. The article should include evidence about at least one company's application of ABC. Such articles are available in a variety of sources. You might try bibliographic searches for "activity-based costing" or "activity-based management." Journals that will have articles on ABC and ABM include:

Management (CMA Magazine) (Canada)
Management Accounting (USA)
Management Accounting (United Kingdom)
Journal of Cost Management

1. After reading the article, note the following (if given in the article) for one company:
   a. The benefits of ABC or ABM
   b. The problems encountered in implementing ABC or ABM
   c. Suggestions by the author(s) about employing ABC or ABM
2. As a group, using the collective wisdom garnered from the articles, respond to the following:
   a. What kinds of companies can benefit from ABC or ABM?
   b. What kinds of companies have little to gain from ABC or ABM?
   c. What steps should be taken to ensure successful implementation of ABC or ABM?
   d. What potential pitfalls are there to avoid in implementing ABC or ABM?

CASES

C5-1 IDENTIFYING ACTIVITIES, RESOURCES, AND COST DRIVERS IN MANUFACTURING. Extrusion Plastics is a multinational, diversified organization. One of its manufacturing divisions, Northeast Plastics Division, has become less profitable due to increased competition. The division produces three major lines of plastic products within its single plant. Product Line A is high-volume, simple pieces produced in large batches. Product Line B is medium-volume, more complex pieces. Product Line C is low-volume, small-order, highly complex pieces.

Currently, the division allocates indirect manufacturing costs based on direct labour. The vp manufacturing is uncomfortable using the traditional cost figures. He thinks the company is under-pricing the more complex products. He decides to conduct an activity-based costing analysis of the business.

Interviews were conducted with the key managers in order to identify activities, resources, cost drivers, and their interrelationships.

Interviewee: production manager

Q1: What activities are carried out in your area?

A1: *All products are manufactured using three similar, complex, and expensive molding machines. Each molding machine can be used in the production of the three product lines. Each setup takes about the same time irrespective of the product.*

Q2: Who works in your area?

A2: *Last year, we employed thirty machine operators, two maintenance mechanics, and two supervisors.*

Q3: How are the operators used in the molding process?

A3: *It requires nine operators to support a machine during the actual production process.*

Q4: What do the maintenance mechanics do?

A4: *Their primary function is to perform machine setups. However, they were also required to provide machine maintenance during the molding process.*

Q5: Where do the supervisors spend their time?

A5: *They provide supervision for the machine operators and the maintenance mechanics. For the most part, the supervisors appear to spend the same amount of time with each of the employees that they supervise.*

Q6: What other resources are used to support manufacturing?

A6: *The molding machines use energy during the molding process and during the setups. We put meters on the molding machines to get a better understanding of their energy consumption. We discovered that for each hour that a machine ran, it used 6.3 kilowatts of energy. The machines also require consumable shop suppliers (e.g., lubricants, hoses, etc.). We have found a direct correlation between the amount of suppliers used and the actual processing time.*

Q7: How is the building used, and what costs are associated with it?

A7: *We have a 100,000-square-metre building. The total rent and insurance costs for the year were $675,000. These costs are allocated to production, sales, and administration based on square metres.*

Required:

1. Identified the activities, resources, and cost drivers for the division.
2. For each resource identified in requirement 1, indicate its cost behaviour with respect to the activities it supports (assume a planning period of 1 month).

C5-2   CASE OF ALLOCATION OF DATA-PROCESSING COSTS.   (CMA, adapted) Independent Outside Underwriters Co. (IOU) established a Systems Department two years ago to implement and operate its own data-processing systems. IOU believed that its own system would be more cost effective than the service bureau it had been using.

IOU's three departments—Claims, Records, and Finance—have different requirements with respect to hardware and other capacity-related resources and operating resources. The system was designed to recognize these differing needs. In addition, the system was designed to meet IOU's long-term capacity needs. The excess capacity designed into the system would be sold to outside users until needed by IOU. The estimated resource requirements used to design and implement the system are shown in the following schedule.

	HARDWARE AND OTHER CAPACITY-RELATED RESOURCES	OPERATING RESOURCES
Records	25%	60%
Claims	50	15
Finance	20	20
Expansion (outside use)	5	5
Total	100%	100%

IOU currently sells the equivalent of its expansion capacity to a few outside clients. At the time the system became operational, management decided to redistribute total expenses of the Systems Department to the user departments based on actual computer time used. The actual costs for the first quarter of the current fiscal year were distributed to the user departments as follows:

DEPARTMENT	PERCENTAGE UTILIZATION	AMOUNT
Records	60%	$330,000
Claims	15	82,500
Finance	20	110,000
Outside	5	27,500
Total	100%	$550,000

The three user departments have complained about the cost distribution method since the Systems Department was established. The Records Department's monthly costs have been as much as three times the costs experienced with the service bureau. The Finance Department is concerned about the costs distributed to the outside-user category because these allocated costs form the basis for the fees billed to the outside clients.

Jerry Owens, IOU's controller, decided to review the cost-allocation method. The additional information he gathered for his review is reported in Exhibits 5A-1, 5A-2, and 5A-3.

Owens has concluded that the method of cost allocation should be changed. He believes that the hardware and capacity-related costs should be allocated to the user departments in proportion to the planned long-term needs. Any difference between actual and budgeted hardware costs would not be allocated to the departments but remain with the Systems Department.

The costs for software development and operations would be charged to the user departments based on actual hours used. A pre-determined hourly rate based on the annual budget data would be used. The hourly rates that would be used for the current fiscal year are as follows:

FUNCTION	HOURLY RATE
Software development	$ 30
Operations:	
Computer related	200
Input/output related	10

Systems-Department Costs and Activity Levels

| | ANNUAL BUDGET | | FIRST QUARTER | | | |
| | | | BUDGET | | ACTUAL | |
	HOURS	DOLLARS	HOURS	DOLLARS	HOURS	DOLLARS
Hardware and other capacity-related costs	—	$ 600,000	—	$150,000	—	$155,000
Software development	18,750	562,500	4,725	141,750	4,250	130,000
Operations:						
Computer related	3,750	750,000	945	189,000	920	187,000
Input/output related	30,000	300,000	7,560	75,600	7,900	78,000
		$2,212,500		$556,350		$550,000

Historical Usage

| DEPARTMENT | HARDWARE AND OTHER CAPACITY NEEDS | DEVELOPMENT | | OPERATIONS | | | |
| | | | | COMPUTER | | INPUT/OUTPUT | |
		RANGE	AVERAGE	RANGE	AVERAGE	RANGE	AVERAGE
Records	25%	0-30%	15%	55-65%	60%	10-30%	15%
Claims	50	15-60	40	10-25	15	60-80	75
Finance	20	25-75	40	10-25	20	3-10	5
Outside	5	0-25	5	3-8	5	3-10	5
	100%		100%		100%		100%

Usage of Systems Department's Services First Quarter (in hours)

| | SOFTWARE DEVELOPMENT | OPERATIONS | |
		COMPUTER RELATED	INPUT/OUTPUT
Records	450	540	1,540
Claims	1,800	194	5,540
Finance	1,600	126	410
Outside	400	60	410
Total	4,250	920	7,900

Owens plans to use first-quarter activity and cost data to illustrate his recommendations. The recommendations will be presented to the Systems Department and the user departments for their comments and reaction. He then expects to present his recommendations to management for approval.

Required:

1. Calculate the amount of data-processing costs that would be included in the Claims Department's first-quarter budget according to the method Jerry Owens has recommended.

2. Prepare a schedule to show how the actual first-quarter costs of the Systems Department would be charged to the users if Owens' recommended method were adopted.
3. Explain whether Owens' recommended system for charging costs to the user departments will
   a. improve cost control in the Systems Department, or
   b. improve planning and cost control in the user departments.

C5-3 COST DRIVERS AND PRICING DECISIONS. (SMAC) The Eastclock Corporation (EC) manufactures timing devices that are used in industrial settings. Recently, profits have fallen and management is seeking your advice as an outside consultant on changes which should be made.

During its 60-year history, EC has developed a strong and loyal customer base due largely to its reputation for quality timing devices. Significant investments in new computer-designed products and automated tooling have reduced operating costs and enabled EC to maintain its competitive edge. However, during the past three years, sales of its two major products have declined or have become stagnant. Had it not been for increased sales of its "custom" timing devices, EC would have incurred losses.

EC's basic product line consists of the "standard" model and the "deluxe" model. The "standard" model requires $8 in direct materials and requires one hour of direct labour (0.4 hours of machining and 0.6 hours of assembly). The "deluxe" model requires an additional $4 worth of direct materials and requires a total of 1.5 hours of direct labour (0.5 hours of machining and one hour of assembly). The standard labour rate is $12 per hour.

In addition to the basic product line, the company manufactures custom timing devices. The average direct material and direct labour costs for a custom timing device are approximately $20 and $30 per unit respectively. Each custom unit requires 2.5 hours of direct labour (0.8 hours of machining and 1.7 hours of assembly).

Indirect manufacturing overhead costs are significant and totalled $1,700,000 in 2001. Variable overhead costs include small tools, lubricants, and indirect labour charges. Fixed overhead costs consist of the following: Engineering (design and estimating) $80,000; Quality Control (set-up time and materials) $130,000; Amortization on buildings and equipment $690,000; and other costs such as property taxes, maintenance and supervisory salaries of $200,000. A complete income statement for 2001 is shown in Exhibit 5B-1 of this case.

As an outside consultant, you begin your analysis of the current situation by meeting with the controller, Jack Downie, in early January, 2002. Jack, who has no formal training in accounting, is nonetheless proud of the internal accounting system and the changes that he has introduced during the past five years. "We've spent a lot of time converting to the contribution format. We've carefully analyzed the variable and fixed costs using our little microcomputer and some pretty powerful software. I'm really confident that we've got an accurate handle on how costs behave as volume rises and falls in the various product lines. Because the volume of 'custom' orders has increased during the past three years, we have charged relatively more overhead to this line on each of the semi-annual statements. The 5 percent sales commission is tacked on to the analysis of each of the product lines and we charge out the fixed selling and administrative expenses based on the volume of orders processed."

	STANDARD	DELUXE	CUSTOM	TOTAL
Volume (units)	50,000	25,000	5,000	80,000
Revenue	$2,100,000	$1,575,000	$525,000	$4,200,000
VARIABLE COSTS:				
Material	400,000	300,000	100,000	800,000
Labour	600,000	450,000	150,000	1,200,000
Overhead[1]	300,000	225,000	75,000	600,000
Commission	105,000	78,750	26,250	210,000
Total variable costs	1,405,000	1,053,750	351,250	2,810,000
Contribution margin	695,000	521,250	173,750	1,390,000
FIXED COSTS:				
Engineering[2]	40,000	30,000	10,000	80,000
Quality control[2]	65,000	48,750	16,250	130,000
Amortization[2]	345,000	258,750	86,250	690,000
Other manufacturing[3]	125,000	62,500	12,500	200,000
Selling & administrative[3]	78,125	39,063	7,812	125,000
Total fixed costs	653,125	439,063	132,812	1,225,000
Net income	$ 41,875	$ 82,187	$ 40,938	$ 165,000

NOTES:

1. It has been reliably determined that variable overhead is a function of direct labour dollars.

2. Fixed manufacturing overhead (Engineering, Quality Control, and Amortization) is allocated to products based on their relative proportion of total direct labour dollars.

3. Other fixed manufacturing overhead and fixed selling and administrative expenses are allocated to products based on the relative volume of units sold.

Further discussions took place with the production people, including representatives of engineering, quality control, and the machining and assembly departments. Interviews also took place with representatives of the marketing and administrative departments. A summary of the highlights of these discussions follows:

Karl Bechtold (Engineering Department): "Our new computer-assisted design system has really changed the way we do things around here. When an order comes in, it is tagged as being either standard, deluxe, or custom. I'd guess that 75 percent of our time is spent on the custom orders as they usually require significant adaptations. I've pointed this out to the accounting people on several occasions, but they seem pretty tied up lately with their new computer. The standard model requires our attention from time to time but I'd guess that it's only about 5 percent. Revisions to the deluxe model are a little more complicated and take up the remainder of our efforts during the average month. If we were to return to more normal levels of production for the three products, I'd guess that we would spend about half of our time on the custom orders and split the remaining hours between the other two lines."

Harvey Ramsoomair (Quality Control): "Nothing leaves this plant that isn't strictly to our customers' specifications. It may not be what they wanted but it's guaranteed to be what they ordered. This sort of quality assurance is only possible by carefully monitoring the quality of our raw materials and the production process. We check the output of the work centres when they begin each job and monitor outputs randomly. Given that the standard and deluxe models are produced in large batches, I'd guess that they each currently take about 20 percent of our time on a monthly basis. I couldn't be much more accurate than that because we only get official information on production volumes twice a year. If the volume of standard sales returned to its normal level, I'm sure that the amount of time for the two basic products would increase to about 30 percent per product. Whatever happens, the remaining time goes to the custom work, which really keeps us on our toes."

Fran Sprocket (Supervisor Machining & Assembly): "This new computer-aided manufacturing equipment has really changed our manufacturing procedures. I can remember just a few years ago how we had to carefully monitor each operation. Now, once we get the thing set up, all we have to do is monitor the output. This machinery is very expensive. The annual depreciation on the machinery is $230,000 for each of the product lines. I've never understood why the accounting system charges so little depreciation to the custom line given that we invested a lot in the machinery to accommodate these special orders for customers. The costs that are labelled as "other manufacturing" in the accounting reports seem to relate mostly to the volume of goods produced and sold. My biggest problem is scheduling the assembling hours. The physical layout of the plant restricts the amount of assembly space and, therefore, the number of hours that I can schedule. The maximum number of assembly hours is 70,000 and nothing can be done to increase this in the next 12 months."

Steve Wong (Marketing): "I don't feel that there is any problem with the costing system as far as marketing expenses are concerned. The amount of time, energy, and expense devoted to each of the product lines seems to depend on the volume of orders sold. The big problem I hear about from the salespeople centres around our prices. We're running about $5 above our competitors on the standard model and this is really cutting into our volume. If we could justify a more competitive price, I expect sales would jump to a more normal level of 74,000 units per year. We currently base all of our prices on a 50 percent mark-up over variable costs and then round off to the nearest dollar.

"My people are glad to see those custom orders rolling in. It's hard to find out what our competitors are charging for similar work but there is some evidence to suggest that our prices are way out of line compared to our competition. The strategy of the company is to market the standard and deluxe models and offer the custom model as a service to regular customers at a premium price. As a result, we would normally sell about 1,000 custom units per year, which is the level we operated at several years ago. With respect to the deluxe model, I feel that the current price is more or less correct and, thus, we expect that volume will remain at current levels for the foreseeable future."

Toni Anderson (Vice President): "We've got to turn this situation around or we'll have to sell out. The boss says he's been getting some pretty attractive offers from some American tool-and-die firms. I'd hate to see us sell out without a fight because I think we've got a responsibility to our employees— some of whom have been with us since high school. The bottom line is each product should cover its own costs and earn at least a profit margin of 10 percent before taxes this year."

Required: Assume the role of the outside consultant. Prepare a report addressed to the management of Eastclock Corporation that clearly identifies and analyzes the issues it faces, and make specific recommendations for improvement. Also include a pro forma income statement for 2002 that incorporates your recommendations.

C5-4 COST ALLOCATION AND CONTRIBUTION MARGIN.   (R. Anderson, adapted) An analogy helps to understand the treatment of costs incident to various types of operations. Consider the following conversation between a restaurant owner (Joe) and his Accountant-Efficiency-Expert (Eff Ex) about adding a rack of peanuts to the counter in an effort to pick up additional profit in the usual course of business. Some people may consider this conversation an oversimplification, but the analogy highlights some central issues in cost allocation.

Eff Ex: Joe, you said you put in these peanuts because some people ask for them, but do you realize what this rack of peanuts is *costing* you?

Joe: It isn't going to cost. It's going to be a profit. Sure, I had to pay $250 for a fancy rack to hold the bags, but the peanuts cost $.60 a bag and I will sell them for $1. I figure if I sell 50 bags a week to start, it'll take 121/2 weeks to cover the cost of the rack. After that I am going to clear a profit of $.40 a bag. The more I sell, the more I make.

Eff Ex: That is an antiquated and completely unrealistic approach, Joe. Fortunately, modern accounting procedures permit a more accurate picture, which reveals the complexities involved.

Joe: Huh?

Eff Ex: To be precise, those peanuts must be integrated into your entire operation and be allocated their appropriate share of business overhead. They must share a proportionate part of your expenditure for rent, heat, light, equipment amortization, decorating, salaries for your waitresses, cook ——

Joe: The *cook*? What does he have to do with the peanuts? He doesn't even have them!

Eff Ex: Look Joe, the cook is in the kitchen, the kitchen prepares the food, the food is what brings people in here, and the people ask to buy peanuts. That's why you must charge a portion of the cook's wages as well as part of your own salary to peanut sales. This sheet contains a carefully calculated cost analysis, which indicates that the peanut operation should pay exactly $12,780 per year toward these general overhead costs.

Joe: The peanuts? $12,780 a year for overhead? The nuts?

Eff Ex: It's really a little more than that. You also spend money each week to have the windows washed, have the place swept out in the mornings, keep soap in the washroom, and provide free soft drinks to the police. That raises the total to $13,130 per year.

Joe: [Thoughtfully] But the peanut salesman said that I would make money . . . put them on the end of the counter, he said . . . and get $.40 a bag profit . . .

Eff Ex: [With a sniff] He's not an accountant. Do you actually know what the portion of the counter occupied by the peanut rack is worth to you?

Joe: It's not worth anything . . . no stool there . . . just a dead spot at the end.

Eff Ex:	The modern cost picture permits no dead spots. Your counter contains 20 square metres and your counter business grosses $150,000 a year. Consequently, the square metres of space occupied by the peanut rack is worth $2,500 per year. Since you have taken that area away from general counter use, you must charge the value of the space to the occupant.
Joe:	You mean I have to add $2,500 a year more to the peanuts?
Eff Ex:	Right. That raises their share of the general operating costs to a grand total of $15,630 per year. Now then, if you sell 50 bags of peanuts per week for 52 weeks, these allocated costs will amount to approximately $6 per bag.
Joe:	*What*?
Eff Ex:	Obviously, to that must be added your purchase price of $.60 per bag, which brings the total to $6.60. So you see by selling peanuts at $1 per bag, you are losing $5.60 on every sale.
Joe:	Something is crazy!
Eff Ex:	Not at all! Here are the *figures*. They *prove* your peanuts operation cannot stand on its own feet.
Joe:	[Brightening] Suppose I sell *lots* of peanuts . . . say a thousand bags a week instead of fifty.
Eff Ex:	[Tolerantly] Joe, you don't understand the problem. If the volume of peanuts sales increases, our operating costs will go up . . . you'll have to handle more bags with more time, more amortization, more everything. The basic principle of accounting is firm on that subject: "The Bigger the Operation, the More General Overhead Costs That Must Be Allocated." No, increasing the volume of sales won't help.
Joe:	Okay, if you're so smart, *you* tell *me* what I have to do.
Eff Ex:	[Condescendingly] Well . . . you could first reduce operating costs.
Joe:	How?
Eff Ex:	Move to a building with cheaper rent. Cut salaries. Wash the windows bi-weekly. Have the floor swept only on Thursday. Remove the soap from the washrooms. Decrease the square-metre value of your counter. For example, if you can cut your costs 50 percent, that will reduce the amount allocated to peanuts from $15,630 to $7,815 per year, reducing the cost to $3.60 per bag.
Joe:	[Slowly] That's better?
Eff Ex:	Much, much better. However, even then you would lose $2.60 per bag if you charge only $1. Therefore, you must also raise your selling price. If you want an income of $.40 per bag you would have to charge $4.00.
Joe:	[Flabbergasted] You mean even after I cut operating costs by 50 percent I still have to charge $4 for a $1 bag of peanuts? Nobody's that nuts about nuts! Who would buy them?

Eff Ex:	That's a secondary consideration. The point is, at $4 you'd be selling at a price based upon a true and proper evaluation of your then reduced costs.
Joe:	[Eagerly] Look! I have a better idea. Why don't I just throw the nuts out?
Eff Ex:	Can you afford it?
Joe:	Sure. All I have is about 50 bags of peanuts . . . which cost about $30 . . . and I would lose $250 on the rack, but I would be out of this nut business with no more grief.
Eff Ex:	[Shaking head] Joe it isn't that simple. You are in the peanut business! The minute you throw those peanuts out you are adding $15,630 of annual overhead to the rest of your operation. Joe . . . be realistic . . . *can you afford to do that*?
Joe:	[Completely crushed] It's unbelievable! Last week I was making money. Now I'm in trouble . . . just because I think peanuts on the counter is going to bring in some extra profit . . . just because I believe 50 bags of peanuts a week is easy.
Eff Ex:	[With raised eyebrow] That is the object of modern cost studies, Joe . . . to dispel those false illusions.

Required:

1. Is Joe losing $5.60 on every sale of peanuts? Explain.
2. Do you agree that if the volume of peanut sales is increased, operating losses will increase? Explain.
3. Do you agree with the Efficiency Expert that, in order to make the peanut operation profitable, the operating costs in the restaurant should be decreased and the selling price of the peanuts should be increased? Give reasons.
4. Do you think that Joe can afford to get out of the peanut business? Give reasons.
5. Do you think that Joe should eliminate his peanut operations? Why or why not?

6

Job-Costing Systems

Job-Costing
Systems

LEARNING OBJECTIVES

After studying this chapter, you will be able to

1. Distinguish between job-order costing and process-costing systems.
2. Prepare summary journal entries for the typical transactions of a job-costing system.
3. Compute budgeted factory-overhead rates and factory overhead applied to production.
4. Use appropriate cost drivers for overhead application.
5. Identify the meaning and purpose of normalized overhead rates.
6. Use an activity-based costing system in a job-order environment.
7. Show how job costing is used in service organizations.

Accountants compute product costs for both decision-making and financial-reporting purposes. They supply product costs to managers for setting prices and evaluating product lines. For example, Ford managers need to know the cost of each kind of car being produced to set prices, to determine marketing and production strategies for various models, and to evaluate production operations. At the same time, product costs appear as cost of goods sold in income statements and as finished-goods inventory values in balance sheets. Although it would be possible to have two product-costing systems, one for management decision making and one for financial reporting, seldom do the benefits of two systems exceed the costs. Therefore, both decision-making and financial-reporting needs influence the design of product-costing systems.

In this chapter, we will focus on one type of product-costing system, the job-order-costing system, and will look at the elements of such systems and how they track the flow of costs. This system focuses on costs involved in the *production* of goods and services. Selling, administrative, distribution, and other non-manufacturing costs are period costs, not *product* costs of product for inventory valuation and other external reporting purposes.

DISTINCTION BETWEEN JOB COSTING AND PROCESS COSTING

OBJECTIVE 1

Distinguish between job-order costing and process-costing systems.

Job-Order Costing (Job Costing). The method of allocating costs to products that are readily identified by individual units or batches, each of which receives varying degrees of attention and skill.

Process Costing. The method of allocating costs to products by averaging costs over large numbers of nearly identical products.

Two fundamental types of product costing are *job-order costing* and *process costing*. **Job-order costing** (or simply **job costing**) allocates costs to products that are readily identified by individual units or batches, each of which receives varying degrees of attention and skill. Industries that commonly use job-order methods include construction, printing, aircraft, furniture, special-purpose machinery, and any manufacturer of tailor-made or unique goods.

Process costing averages costs over large numbers of nearly identical products. It is most often found in such industries as chemicals, oil, textiles, plastics, paints, flour, canneries, rubber, lumber, food processing, glass, mining, cement, and meat packing. These industries involve mass production of like units, which usually pass in continuous fashion through a series of uniform production steps called *productions* or *processors*.

The distinction between the job-cost and the process-cost methods centres largely on how product costing is accomplished. Job costing applies costs to specific jobs that may consist of either a single physical unit (such as a custom sofa) or a few like units (such as a dozen tables) in a distinct batch or job lot. In contrast, process costing deals with great masses of like units and broad averages of unit costs.

The most important point is that product costing is an *averaging* process. The unit cost used for inventory purposes is the result of taking some accumulated cost that has been allocated to production departments and dividing it by some measure of production. The basic distinction between job-order costing and process costing is the breadth of the denominator: in job-order costing, it is small (for example, one painting, 100 advertising circulars, or one special packaging machine); but in process costing, it is large (for example, thousands of kilograms, litres, or board feet).

Job costing and process costing are extremes along a continuum of potential costing systems. Each company designs its own accounting system to fit its underlying production activities. Some companies use hybrid costing systems, which are blends of ideas from both job costing and process costing. Chapter 7 describes process costing and hybrid costing.

Tredegar Molded Products
www.tredegar.com

Implementing Activity-Based Costing in a Job-Order and Process-Manufacturing Environment: Tredegar Molded Products

Tredegar Molded Products Company, a subsidiary of Tredegar Industries, Inc., is a diversified custom-injection moulder of plastics and metal products. Tredegar has six injection moulding plants and one tooling facility and uses both job- and process-production and cost-accounting systems.

JOB-ORDER PRODUCTION	**PROCESS PRODUCTION**
Steel Molds	Deodorant Canisters
Medical Devices	Lip Balm Closures (Various Sizes)
	Plugs and Fitments

Recently, Tredegar began implementing activity-based costing at three of its plants. The business issues leading to the implementation of ABC included the need for

- more accurate product costing
- better understanding of key business processes
- better utilization of resources.

Specific applications of the new ABC information include
- activity-based budgeting
- support for process improvement
- new product pricing
- capital spending justification.

Future uses of ABC at Tredegar include
- make-or buy-decisions
- pricing of existing products.

Source: "Beyond the Pilot at Tredegar," Janet B. Wynn, NetProphet User Conference (September 1994), Sapling Corporation, Toronto.

ILLUSTRATION OF JOB-ORDER COSTING

Job costing is best learned by example. But first we will examine the basic records used in a job-costing system.

Basic Records

Job-Cost Record (Job-Cost Sheet, Job Order). A document that shows all costs for a particular products, service, or batch of products.

The centrepiece of a job-costing system is the **job-cost record** (also called a **job-cost sheet** or **job order**), shown in Exhibit 6-1. All costs for a particular product, service, or batch of products are recorded on the job-cost record. A file of job-cost records for partially completed jobs provides supporting details for the Work-In-Process-Inventory account, often simply called Work in Process (WIP). A file of completed job-cost records comprises the Finished-Goods-Inventory account.

As Exhibit 6-1 shows, the job-cost record summarizes information contained on source documents such as *materials requisitions* and *labour time tickets*. **Materials requisitions** are records of materials issued to particular jobs. **Labour time tickets** (or *time cards*) record the time a particular direct labourer spends on each job.

Materials Requisitions. Records of materials issued to particular jobs.

Labour Time Tickets. The record of the time a particular direct labourer spends on each job.

Today job-cost records and source documents are likely to be computer files, not paper records. In fact, with on-line data entry, bar coding, and optical scanning, much of the information needed for such records enters the computer without ever being written on paper. Nevertheless, whether records are on paper or in computer files, the accounting system must collect and maintain the same basic information.

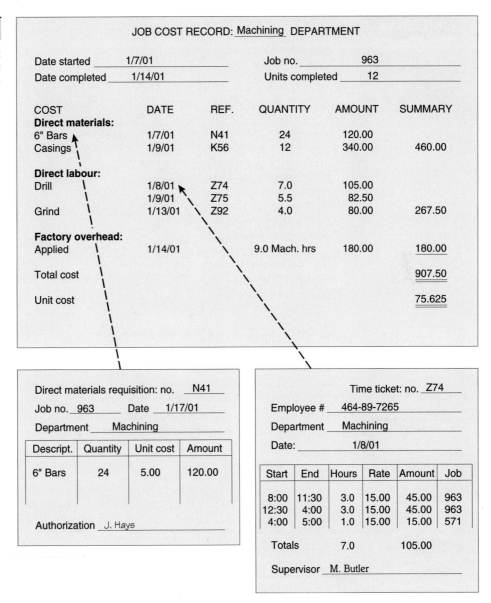

EXHIBIT 6-1

Completed Job-Cost Record and Sample Source Documents

JOB COST RECORD: <u>Machining</u> DEPARTMENT

Date started _____ 1/7/01 _____   Job no. _____ 963 _____
Date completed _____ 1/14/01 _____   Units completed _____ 12 _____

COST	DATE	REF.	QUANTITY	AMOUNT	SUMMARY
Direct materials:					
6" Bars	1/7/01	N41	24	120.00	
Casings	1/9/01	K56	12	340.00	460.00
Direct labour:					
Drill	1/8/01	Z74	7.0	105.00	
	1/9/01	Z75	5.5	82.50	
Grind	1/13/01	Z92	4.0	80.00	267.50
Factory overhead:					
Applied	1/14/01		9.0 Mach. hrs	180.00	180.00
Total cost					907.50
Unit cost					75.625

Direct materials requisition: no. _____ N41 _____

Job no. _961_   Date _1/17/01_

Department _____ Machining _____

Descript.	Quantity	Unit cost	Amount
6" Bars	24	5.00	120.00

Authorization _J. Hays_

Time ticket: no. _Z74_

Employee # _____ 464-89-7265 _____

Department _____ Machining _____

Date: _____ 1/8/01 _____

Start	End	Hours	Rate	Amount	Job
8:00	11:30	3.0	15.00	45.00	963
12:30	4:00	3.0	15.00	45.00	963
4:00	5:00	1.0	15.00	15.00	571
Totals		7.0		105.00	

Supervisor _M. Butler_

As each job begins, a job-cost record is prepared. As units are worked on, entries are made on the job-cost record. Three classes of costs are applied to the units as they pass through the departments: material requisitions are the source of direct material costs, time tickets provide direct labour costs, and budgeted overhead rates are used to apply factory overhead to products. The computation of these budgeted rates will be described later in this chapter.

Data for Illustration

To illustrate the functioning of a job-order costing system, we will use a job-costing system, including the basic records and journal entries of the Martinez Electronics Company. On December 31, 2001 the firm had the following inventories:

OBJECTIVE 2

Prepare summary
journal entries for the
typical transactions of
a job-costing system.

Direct materials (12 types)	$110,000
Work in process	—
Finished goods (unsold units from two jobs)	12,000

The following is a summary of pertinent transactions for 2002:

	MACHINING	ASSEMBLY	TOTAL
1. Direct materials purchased on account	—	—	$1,900,000
2. Direct materials requisitioned for manufacturing	$1,000,000	$890,000	1,890,000
3. Direct labour costs incurred	200,000	190,000	390,000
4a. Factory overhead incurred	290,000	102,000	392,000
4b. Factory overhead applied	280,000	95,000	375,000
5. Cost of goods completed and transferred to finished-goods inventory	—	—	2,500,000
6a. Sales on account	—	—	4,000,000
6b. Cost of goods sold	—	—	2,480,000

We will explain the notion of *factory overhead applied* later in this chapter. First, however, we need to consider the accounting for these transactions.

Exhibit 6-2 is an overview of the general flow of costs through the Martinez Electronics Company's job-order-costing system. The exhibit summarizes the effects of transactions on the key manufacturing accounts in the firm's books. As you proceed through the detailed explanation of transactions, keep checking each explanation against the overview in Exhibit 6-2.

Explanation of Transactions

The following transaction-by-transaction summary analysis will explain how product costing is achieved. Entries are usually made as transactions occur. However, to obtain a sweeping overview, our illustration uses a summary for the entire year 2002.

---

1. Transaction: Direct materials purchased, $1,900,000
    Analysis: The asset Direct Materials Inventory is increased. The liability Accounts Payable is increased.
       Entry: In the journal (explanation omitted):

Direct materials inventory	1,900,000	
Accounts payable		1,900,000

2. Transaction: Direct materials requisitioned, $1,890,000
    Analysis: The asset Work in Process (Inventory) is increased. The asset Direct Materials Inventory is decreased.
       Entry: In the journal:

Work in process	1,890,000	
Direct materials inventory		1,890,000

3. Transaction: Direct labour cost incurred, $390,000.
    Analysis: The asset Work in Process (Inventory) is increased. The liability Accrued Payroll is increased.
       Entry: In the journal:

Work in progress	390,000	
Accrued payroll		390,000

4a. Transaction: Factory overhead incurred, $392,000.

Analysis: These actual costs are first charged to departmental overhead accounts, which may be regarded as assets until their amounts are later "cleared" or transferred to other accounts. Each department has detailed overhead accounts such as indirect labour, utilities, repairs, depreciation, insurance, and property taxes. These details support a summary factory department overhead control account. The managers are responsible for regulating these costs, item by item. As these costs are charged to the departments, the other accounts affected will be assorted assets and liabilities. Examples include cash, accounts payable, accrued payables, and accumulated depreciation.

Entry: In the journal:

Factory department overhead   392,000

    Cash, accounts payable, and various

        other balance sheet accounts   392,000

4b. Transaction: Factory overhead applied, $95,000 + $280,000 = $375,000.

Analysis: The asset Work in Process (Inventory) is increased. The asset Factory Department Overhead Control is decreased. (A fuller explanation occurs later in this chapter.)

Entry: In the journal:

Work in process   375,000

    Factory department overhead   375,000

5. Transaction: Cost of goods completed, $2,500,000.

Analysis: The asset Finished Goods (Inventory) is increased. The asset Work in Process (Inventory) is decreased.

Entry: In the journal:

Finished goods   2,500,000

    Work in process   2,500,000

6a. Transaction: Sales on account, $4,000,000.

Analysis: The asset Accounts Receivable is increased. The revenue account Sales is increased.

Entry: In the journal:

Accounts receivable   4,000,000

    Sales   4,000,000

6b. Transaction: Cost of goods sold, $2,480,000.

Analysis: The expense Cost of Goods Sold is increased. The asset Finished Goods is decreased.

Entry: In the journal:

Cost of goods sold   2,480,000

    Finished goods   2,480,000

Summary of Transactions

Exhibit 6-2 summarizes the Martinez transactions for the year, focusing on the inventory accounts. Work in process receives central attention. The costs of direct material used, direct labour, and factory overhead applied to products are brought into work in process. In turn, the cost of completed goods are transferred from work in process to finished goods. As goods are sold, their costs become expense in the form of cost of goods sold. The year-end accounting for the $17,000 of underapplied overhead is explained later.

EXHIBIT 6-2

Job-Order Costing, General Flow of Costs (in thousands)

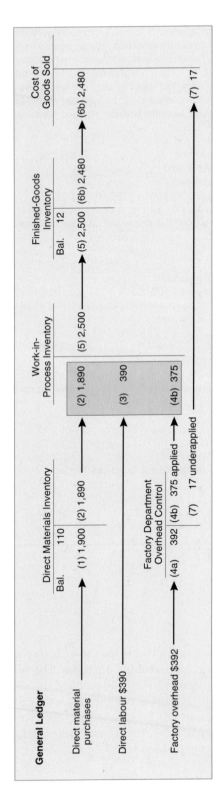

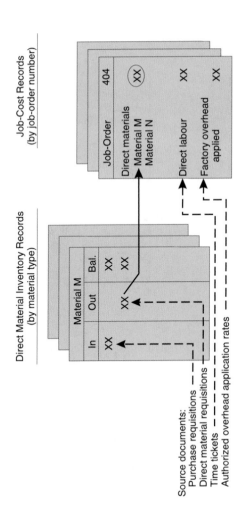

JOB COSTING AT RMS MACHINERY DIVISION OF UNIROYAL GOODRICH CANADA INC.

The RMS Machinery Division is a unique business located in Kitchener, Ontario. From its humble beginnings as a mould shop 75 years ago, the business has diversified and grown to the point where its products are sold worldwide. Today, RMS is a designer and manufacturer of industrial machinery whose primary role continues to be the development and supply of proprietary tire-building equipment to the Uniroyal Goodrich Michelin plants. In addition, RMS rubber extrusion products are used by the world's major tire companies. As well, several other industries (automotive, rubber, paper, metals, and plastics) also rely on RMS for the design and manufacture of their equipment.

B.F. Goodrich
www.bfgoodrich.com

Michelin
www.michelin.com

Sales Orders

It is very important to understand the time lag from the time of the quote, to the order, engineering drawings, letting out of purchase orders, to production and final shipping of a product. In some cases final settlements are contingent on the successful installation of the equipment at the customer's plant. Thus, jobs may linger on accounting records for months past the shipping date. Due to each job's complexity, a project engineer is assigned to monitor and be responsible for the project—acting as liaison with the customer and the job floor.

In general the machinery manufactured is very intricate in design and usually weighs a great deal, and so it is very important that the engineering drawings produced for the shop floor be extremely accurate. If parts are incorrectly machined, a new casting or further machining may be required, resulting in additional costs and valuable time lost, which may result in not meeting the customer's delivery expectation.

Job-Cost Tracking System

In order to provide a vehicle for the project engineer and management to monitor the progress of a job, as well as to identify whether it is on schedule to meet financial estimates and the customer's promised date, a detailed job-cost tracking system is mandatory to capture and report data on a very timely and dependable (accurate) basis.

A detailed estimate is entered on the job-cost system for the job-master and sub jobs for various major stages of the project. Sequence numbers further break down the sub-jobs by particular sub components. A specialized purchasing group uses the information to let out purchase orders for material or the sub contracting of parts. This also provides manufacturing with a map for machining and assembly scheduling, given the material arrival schedule.

Application of Burden

Two cost drivers are currently in use for developing applied burden rates.

    A. Direct Labour Dollars
    B. Material and Outside Contracts.

A single rate for each cost driver is used for machining and assembly. The two cost drivers are used to assign burden to jobs, which by their nature or by management's decision may have a high content of outside labour (subcontracts) versus utilization of inside staff.

Over/under applied burden is treated as a period cost to operations and not allocated to every job. The objective is to keep this amount in check by changing the cost-driver rates if business conditions change favourably or unfavourably, keeping in mind that normal monthly fluctuations do occur and are offset by year-end.

The primary objective is to assign a commensurate amount of burden to each and every job, enabling management to track profitability of a job during the work-in-process stage and at completion.

Progress Billings

Issuing progress billings by its nature causes unique accounting complications in the assignment of costs (material, labour and burden) to the cost of sales for that particular job resulting in an "anticipated" profit margin. Normal conservatism rules apply to this rate, which is usually worked out from the estimate/quote for the project. Accounting personnel need to monitor jobs closely in order not to be embarrassed by over- or underestimated profit once jobs are completed. Keeping track of this type of activity becomes very important and requires knowledgeable experience about the operation and constant contact with all team members.

Source: Written by Nick Mask, Accounting Manager, Jack O'Donnell, General Manager, and Pat Bandura, Accounting, RMS Machinery Division, Uniroyal Goodrich Canada Inc.

ACCOUNTING FOR FACTORY OVERHEAD

In the Martinez Company example, factory overhead of $375,000 was applied to the work-in-process account. This section describes how to determine the amount of applied factory overhead.

Few companies wait until the actual factory overhead is finally known before computing the costs of products. Instead, they compute a budgeted (pre-determined) overhead rate at the beginning of a fiscal year and use it to apply overhead costs as products are manufactured. Most managers want a close approximation of the costs of various products continuously, not just at the end of a year. Managers desire those costs for various ongoing uses, including choosing which products to emphasize or de-emphasize, pricing products, producing interim financial statements, and managing inventories.

Budgeted Overhead Application Rates

OBJECTIVE 3

Compute budgeted factory overhead rates and factory overhead applied to production.

Budgeted Factory Overhead Rate. The budgeted total overhead divided by the budgeted cost-driver activity.

The following steps summarize how to account for factory overhead:

1. Select one or more cost drivers to serve as a base for applying overhead costs. Examples include direct labour hours, direct labour costs, machine hours, and production setups. The cost driver should be an activity that is the common denominator for systematically relating a cost or group of costs, such as factory overhead, with products. The cost driver or drivers should be the best available measure of the cause-and-effect relationships between overhead costs and production volume.
2. Prepare a factory-overhead budget for the planning period, ordinarily a year. The two key items are (a) budgeted overhead and (b) budgeted volume of the cost driver.
3. Compute the **budgeted factory overhead rate** by dividing the budgeted total overhead by the budgeted cost driver. There could be a separate budgeted overhead rate for each cost component of the total overhead.
4. Obtain actual cost-driver data (such as machine-hours) as the year unfolds.
5. Apply the budgeted overhead to the jobs by multiplying the budgeted rate times the actual cost-driver data.
6. At the end of the year, account for any differences between the amount of overhead actually incurred and overhead applied to products.

Illustration of Overhead Application

To understand how to apply factory overhead to jobs, consider the Martinez illustration again.

The following manufacturing overhead budget has been prepared for the coming year, 2003:

	MACHINING	ASSEMBLY
Indirect labour	$ 75,600	$ 36,800
Supplies	8,400	2,400
Utilities	20,000	7,000
Repairs	10,000	3,000
Factory rent	10,000	6,800
Supervision	42,600	35,400
Amortization on equipment	104,000	9,400
Insurance, property taxes, etc.	7,200	2,400
	$277,800	$103,200

As products are worked on, Martinez applies the factory overhead to the jobs. A budgeted overhead rate is used, computed as follows:

$$\text{budgeted overhead application rate} = \frac{\text{total budgeted factory overhead}}{\text{total budgeted amount of cost driver}}$$

Suppose machine-hours are chosen as the only cost driver in the machining department and direct labour cost is chosen in the assembly department. The overhead rates are as follows:

| | YEAR 2003 | |
	MACHINING	ASSEMBLY
Budgeted manufacturing overhead	$277,800	$103,200
Budgeted machine-hours	69,450	
Budgeted direct labour cost		206,400
Budgeted overhead rate, per machine-hour: $277,800 ÷ 69,450 =	$4	
Budgeted overhead rate, per direct labour dollar: $103,200 ÷ $206,400 =		$0.50

Note that the overhead rates are budgeted; they are estimates. These rates are then used to apply overhead based on *actual* events. That is, the total overhead applied in our illustration is the result of multiplying *actual* machine-hours or labour cost by the *budgeted* overhead rates:

Machining: Actual machine-hours of 70,000 x $4 = $280,000
Assembly: Actual direct labour of $190,000 x .50 =   95,000
Total factory overhead applied $375,000

The summary journal entry for the application (entry 4b) is:

4b. Work in process   375,000
        Factory department overhead   375,000

E-Accounting
Why do we Need E-Accounting?

The Internet environment mandates that organizations "do routine things differently." Every organization faces major challenges in technologies, markets, employees, competitors, and customers. And the challenges are instantaneous. The speed and intensity of change is causing organizations all over the world to rethink their core accounting operations and transaction processing models. Consequently, many organizations find they need to re-create their accounting operations from the ground up in order to compete. The very thought of having to do so give most executives that same "I think I'm gonna be sick" feeling we so much enjoyed on our last roller coaster ride.

Organizations also recognize the benefits that an e-accounting function can yield. The successful organizations understand how to deploy these new processes and manage the risks associated with implementing enhanced accounting technologies. Today's accountant must have an appreciation of the benefits, risks, and the constraints of new technology to provide both effective direction and adequate control.

What will we need to climb on board?

The rapid development of the Internet provides an organization's financial management with many opportunities to implement improved accounting services. To take advantage of these opportunities, we must recognize the importance of planning our e-accounting function, and how to implement processes that will assist our management in better meeting the organization's business objectives.

An e-accounting plan should include processes that are integrated into current needs as well as the future direction of the organization. Your focus must be on the information and services you will provide and the technology required to accomplish your plan. Deploying an e-accounting plan must be prioritized within the framework of your key business strategies. For example do the components of your e-accounting function include:

- your organization's business direction and any future changes that are anticipated? Have you considered any new product launches, emerging delivery channels, or alternate business scenarios?
- changes to your legal and regulatory framework? Can you anticipate the impact of these changes and include them in your planning process?
- changes in your competitive environment and the corresponding challenges and opportunities, such as third party alliances through deployment of inter-organizational systems?
- key business strategies and their related information technology support requirements?
- service-level requirements of the accounting function in terms of security (information availability, integrity, and confidentiality), response times (particularly during peak periods), and data accessibility, storage, and archiving requirements?

The scope of your e-accounting function will have a major impact on the effort required to deploy it, as well as your ultimate success.

Source: Preston Cameron, "The Need for Speed: Are you ready for the e-accounting roller coaster?", *CMA Management*, June 2000, pp. 50–51.

Choosing Cost Drivers

Factory overhead is a conglomeration of manufacturing costs that, unlike direct material or direct labour, cannot conveniently be applied on an individual job basis. But such overhead is an integral part of a product's total cost. Therefore it is applied indirectly, using as a base a cost driver that is common to all jobs worked on and is the best available index of the product's relative use of, or benefits from, the overhead items. In other words, there should be a strong cause-and-effect relationship between the factory overhead incurred (the effect) and the cost driver chosen for its application.

As we have noted earlier in this text, no one cost driver is right for all situations. The goal is to find the driver that best links cause and effect. In the Martinez machining department, two or more machines can often be operated simultaneously by a single direct labourer. Use of machines causes most overhead cost in the machining department, for example, depreciation and repairs. Therefore machine hours is the cost driver and the appropriate base for applying overhead costs. Thus Martinez must keep track of the machine-hours used for each job, creating an added data-collection cost. That is, both direct labour costs and machine-hours must be accumulated for each job.

In contrast, direct labour is a principal cost driver in the Martinez assembly department. It is an accurate reflection of the relative attention and effort devoted to various jobs. The workers are paid equal hourly rates. Therefore all that is needed is to apply the 50 percent overhead rate to the cost of direct labour already entered on the job-cost records. No separate job records have to be kept of the labour hours. If the hourly labour rates differ greatly for individuals performing identical tasks, the hours of labour, rather than the dollars spent for labour, might be used as a base. Otherwise a $9-per-hour worker would cause more overhead applied than an $8-per-hour worker, even though the same time would probably be taken and the same facilities used by each employee for the same work.

Sometimes direct labour cost is the best overhead cost driver even if wage rates vary within a department. Survey after survey has indicated that over 90 percent of the companies use direct labour cost or direct labour hours as their single cost driver for overhead application. For example, higher-skilled labour may use more costly equipment and have more indirect labour support. Moreover, many factory-overhead costs include costly labour fringe benefits such as pensions and payroll taxes. The latter are often more closely driven by direct labour cost than by direct labour hours.

If a department identifies more than one cost driver for overhead costs, these costs ideally should be put into as many cost pools as there are cost drivers. In practice, such a system is too costly for many organizations. Instead, these organizations select a small number of cost drivers (often only one) to serve as a basis for allocating overhead costs.

The selected cost driver or cost drivers should be the ones that cause most of the overhead costs. For example, suppose machine hours cause 70 percent of the overhead costs in a particular department, number of component parts cause 20 percent, and five assorted cost drivers cause the other 10 percent. Instead of using seven cost pools allocated on the basis of the seven cost drivers, most managers would use one cost driver—machine-hours—to allocate all overhead costs. Others would assign all cost to two cost pools, one allocated on the basis of machine-hours and one on the basis of number of component parts.

No matter which cost drivers are chosen, the overhead rates are applied day after day throughout the year to cost the various jobs worked on by each department. All overhead is applied to all jobs worked on during the year on the appropriate basis of machine hours of direct labour costs of each job. Suppose management predictions coincide exactly with actual amounts (an extremely unlikely situation). Then the total overhead applied to the year's jobs via these budgeted rates would be equal to the total overhead costs actually incurred.

PROBLEMS OF OVERHEAD APPLICATION

Normalized Overhead Rates

OBJECTIVE 5

Identify the meaning and purpose of normalized overhead rates.

Basically, our illustration has demonstrated the normal costing approach. Why the term "normal?" Because an annual average overhead rate is used consistently throughout the year for product costing, *without altering it from day to day and from month to month*. The resultant "normal" product costs include an average or normalized chunk of overhead.

As actual overhead costs are incurred by departments from month to month, they are charged to the departments. On a weekly or monthly basis, these actual costs are then compared with budgeted costs to obtain budget variances for performance evaluation. This *control* process is distinct from the *product-costing* process of applying overhead to specific jobs.

During the year and at year-end, the actual overhead amount incurred will rarely equal the amount applied. This variance between incurred and applied can be analyzed. The most common—and most important—contributor to this variance is operating at a different level of volume than the level used as a denominator in calculating the budgeted overhead rate (e.g., using 100,000 budgeted direct labour hours as the denominator and then actually working only 80,000 hours). Other frequent contributory causes include poor forecasting, inefficient use of overhead items, price changes in individual overhead items, erratic behaviour of individual overhead items (e.g., repairs made only during slack time), and calendar variations (e.g., 20 work days in one month, 22 in the next).

All these peculiarities of overhead are mingled in an *annual* overhead pool. Thus, an annual rate is budgeted and used regardless of the month-to-month peculiarities of specific overhead costs. Such an approach is more defensible than, say, applying the actual overhead for *each month*. Why? Because a *normal* product cost is more useful for decisions, and more representative for inventory-costing purposes, than an "actual" product cost that is distorted by month-to-month fluctuations in production volume and by the erratic behaviour of many overhead costs. For example, the employees of a gypsum plant using an "actual"

	ACTUAL OVERHEAD			DIRECT LABOUR HOURS	ACTUAL OVERHEAD APPLICATION RATE* PER DIRECT LABOUR HOUR
	VARIABLE	FIXED	TOTAL		
Peak-volume month	$60,000	$40,000	$100,000	100,000	$1.00
Low-volume month	30,000	40,000	70,000	50,000	$1.40

*Divide total overhead by direct labour hours. Note that the presence of fixed overhead causes the fluctuation in unit costs from $1.00 to $1.40. The variable component is $.60 an hour in both months, but the fixed component is $.40 in the peak-volume month ($40,000 ÷ 100,000), and $.80 in the low-volume month ($40,000 ÷ 50,000).

product cost system had the privilege of buying company-made items "at cost." Employees joked about the benefits of buying "at cost" during high-volume months when unit costs were lower because volume was higher.

Disposition of Underapplied and Overapplied Overhead

Our Martinez illustration contained the following data:

Transaction		
4a.	Factory overhead incurred	$392,000
4b.	Factory overhead applied	375,000
	Underapplied factory overhead	$ 17,000

Total costs of $392,000 must eventually be charged to expense in some way. The $375,000 will become part of the Cost-of-Goods-Sold expense when the products to which it is applied are sold. The remaining $17,000 must also become expense by some method.

When budgeted rates are used, the difference between incurred and applied overhead is typically allowed to accumulate during the year. When the amount applied to product *exceeds* the amount incurred by the departments, the difference is called **overapplied overhead**; when the amount applied is *less than* incurred, the difference is called **underapplied overhead**. At year-end, the difference ($17,000 in our illustration) is disposed of either through a write-off or through proration.

Overapplied Overhead. The excess of overhead applied to products over actual overhead incurred.

Underapplied Overhead. The excess of actual overhead over the overhead applied to products.

Immediate Write-off

Under this method, the $17,000 is regarded as a reduction in current income by adding the underapplied overhead to the cost of goods sold. The same logic is followed for overapplied overhead except that the result would be an addition to current income because cost of goods sold would be decreased.

The theory underlying the direct write-off is that most of the goods worked on have been sold, and a more elaborate method of disposition is not worth the extra trouble. Another justification is that the extra overhead costs represented by underapplied overhead do not qualify as part of ending inventory costs because they do not represent assets. They should be written off because they largely represent inefficiency or the underutilization of available facilities in the current period.

The immediate write-off eliminates the $17,000 difference with a simple journal entry, labelled as transaction 7 in Exhibit 6-2:

7.	Cost of goods sold (or a separate		
	charge against revenue)	17,000	
	Factory department overhead		17,000
	To close ending underapplied		
	overhead directly to cost of goods sold.		

Pro-ration among Inventories

This method pro-rates over- or underapplied overhead among WIP, finished goods, and cost of goods sold. Theoretically, if the objective is to obtain as

	(1) UNADJUSTED BALANCE, END OF 2002*	(2) PRORATION OF UNDERAPPLIED OVERHEAD		(3) ADJUSTED BALANCE, END OF 2002
Work in Process	$ 155,000	155/2,667 × 17,000 = $	988	$ 155,988
Finished Goods	32,000	32/2,667 × 17,000 =	204	32,204
Cost of Goods Sold	2,480,000	2,480/2,667 × 17,000 =	15,808	2,495,808
	$2,667,000		$17,000	

accurate a cost allocation as possible, all the overhead costs of the individual jobs worked on should be recomputed, using the actual rather than the budgeted rates. This approach is rarely feasible, so a practical attack is to prorate on the basis of the ending balances in each of three accounts (Work-in-process, $155,000; finished goods, $32,000; and cost of goods sold, $2,480,000).

The journal entry for the proration follows:

Work-in-process	988	
Finished goods	204	
Cost of goods sold.	15,808	
Factory department overhead		17,000
To pro-rate ending underapplied overhead among three accounts.		

EXHIBIT 6-3

Year-end Disposition of Underapplied Factory Overhead

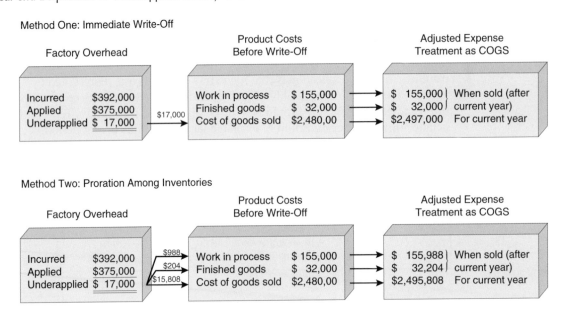

The amounts prorated to inventories here are not significant. In actual practices, prorating is done only when inventory valuations would be materially affected. Exhibit 6-3 provides a schematic comparison of the two major methods of disposing of underapplied (or overapplied) factory overhead.

The Use of Variable and Fixed Application Rates

As we have seen, overhead application is the most troublesome aspect of product costing. The presence of fixed costs is a major reason for the costing difficulties. Most companies have made no distinction between variable- and fixed-cost behaviour in the design of their accounting systems. For instance, the machining department at Martinez Electronics Company developed the following rate:

$$\text{budgeted overhead application rate} = \frac{\text{budgeted total overhead}}{\text{budgeted machine-hours}}$$

$$= \frac{\$277,800}{69,450} = \$4 \text{ per machine-hour}$$

Some companies distinguish between variable overhead and fixed overhead for product costing as well as for control purposes. If the machining department had made this distinction, then rent, supervision, depreciation, and insurance would have been considered the fixed portion of the total manufacturing overhead, and two rates would have been developed:

$$\text{budgeted variable-overhead application rate} = \frac{\text{budgeted total variable overhead}}{\text{budgeted machine-hours}}$$

$$= \frac{\$114,000}{69,450}$$

$$= \$1.64 \text{ per machine-hour}$$

$$\text{budgeted fixed-overhead application rate} = \frac{\text{budgeted total fixed overhead}}{\text{budgeted machine-hours}}$$

$$= \frac{\$163,800}{69,450}$$

$$= \$2.36 \text{ per machine-hour}$$

Such rates can be used for product costing. Distinctions between variable- and fixed-overhead can also be made for control purposes.

Actual Costing versus Normal Costing

Normal Costing System. The cost system in which overhead is applied on an average or normalized basis in order to get representative or normal inventory valuations.

The overall system we have just described is sometimes called an *actual costing system* because every effort is made to trace the *actual* costs, as incurred, to the physical units benefitted. However, it is only partly an actual system because overhead, by definition, cannot be traced to physical products. Instead, overhead is applied on an average or normalized basis, in order to get representative or normal inventory valuations. Hence we shall label the system a **normal costing system**. The cost of the manufactured product is composed of *actual* direct material, *actual* direct labour, and *normal* applied overhead.

The two job-order costing approaches may be compared as follows:

	ACTUAL COSTING	NORMAL COSTING
Direct materials	Actual	Actual
Direct labour	Actual	Actual
Manufacturing overhead	Actual	Budgeted rates*

*Actual inputs (such as direct labour hours or direct labour costs) multiplied by budgeted overhead rates (computed by dividing total budgeted manufacturing overhead by a budgeted cost driver such as direct labour hours).

In a true actual costing system, overhead would not be applied as jobs were worked on but only after all overhead costs for the year were known. Then, using an "actual" average rate(s) instead of a budgeted rate(s), costs would be applied to all jobs that had been worked on throughout the year. All costs incurred would be exactly offset by costs applied to the Work-in-process inventory. However, increased accuracy would be obtained at the sacrifice of timeliness in using costs for measuring operating efficiency, determining selling prices, and producing interim financial statements.

Normal costing has replaced actual costing in many organizations precisely because the latter approach fails to provide costs of products as they are worked on during the year. It is possible to use a normal-costing system plus year-end adjustments to produce final results that closely approximate the results under actual costing. To do so in our illustration, the underapplied overhead is pro-rated among work in process, finished goods, and cost of goods sold, as shown in Exhibit 6-3.

ACTIVITY-BASED COSTING IN A JOB-ORDER ENVIRONMENT

OBJECTIVE 6

Use an activity-based costing system in a job-order environment.

Regardless of the nature of a company's production system, there will always be resources that are shared among different products. The costs of these resources are part of overhead and must be accounted for in the company's cost accounting system. In most cases, the magnitude of overhead is large enough to justify investing in a cost system that provides accurate cost information. Whether this cost information is being used for inventory reporting, to cost jobs, or for cost planning and control, most often the benefits of more accurate costs exceed the costs of installing and maintaining the cost system. As we have seen, activity-based costing usually increases costing accuracy because it focuses on the cause-effect relationship between work performed (activities) and the consumption of resources (costs).

Illustration of Activity-Based Costing in a Job-Order Environment

Dell Computers
www.dell.com

We illustrate an activity-based costing (ABC) system in a job-order environment by considering Dell Computer Corporation. What motivated Dell to adopt activity-based costing? Company managers cite two reasons: 1) the aggressive cost reduction targets set by top management and 2) the need to understand product-line profitability. As is the case with any business, understanding profitability means understanding the cost structure of the entire business. One of the key advantages of an ABC system is its focus on understanding how work (activities) is related to the consumption of resources (costs). So, an ABC system was a logical choice for Dell. Of course, once Dell's managers understand the company's cost structure, cost reduction through activity-based management will be much easier.

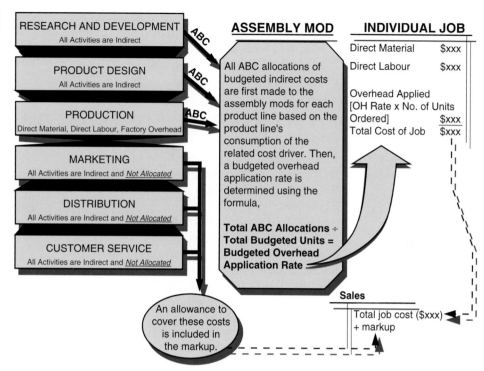

EXHIBIT 6-4

Dell Computer Corporation's Value Chain and ABC System

| RESEARCH AND DEVELOPMENT |
| All Activities are Indirect |

| PRODUCT DESIGN |
| All Activities are Indirect |

| PRODUCTION |
| Direct Material, Direct Labour, Factory Overhead |

| MARKETING |
| All Activities are Indirect and *Not Allocated* |

| DISTRIBUTION |
| All Activities are Indirect and *Not Allocated* |

| CUSTOMER SERVICE |
| All Activities are Indirect and *Not Allocated* |

ASSEMBLY MOD

All ABC allocations of budgeted indirect costs are first made to the assembly mods for each product line based on the product line's consumption of the related cost driver. Then, a budgeted overhead application rate is determined using the formula,

Total ABC Allocations ÷ Total Budgeted Units = Budgeted Overhead Application Rate

An allowance to cover these costs is included in the markup.

INDIVIDUAL JOB

Direct Material	$xxx
Direct Labour	$xxx
Overhead Applied [OH Rate x No. of Units Ordered]	$xxx
Total Cost of Job	$xxx

Sales

| Total job cost ($xxx) + markup |

Dell began developing its ABC system by viewing its business from a value chain perspective. Exhibit 6-4 shows the functions (or core processes) that add value to the company's products and how the costs of these functions are assigned to an individual job under the current ABC system.

To understand product-line profitability, Dell mangers first identified key activities for the research and development, product design, and production functions. Then, they used appropriate cost drivers to allocate activity costs to the assembly mods that produced product lines. While each of the functions shown in Exhibit 6-4 is important, we will focus on the product design and production functions. Product designs is one of Dell's most important value-adding functions. The role of design is to provide a defect-free computer product that is easy to manufacture and reliable to the customer. Engineering costs (primarily salaries and CAD equipment amortization) account for most of the design costs. These costs are indirect and, thus, must be allocated to assembly mods using a cost driver.

The production costs include direct material, direct labour, and factory overhead. Factory overhead consists of six activity centres and related cost pools: receiving, preparation, assembly, testing, packaging, and shipping. Facility costs (plant amortization, insurance, taxes) are considered part of the production function and are allocated to each activity centre based on the square feet occupied by the function.

At Dell, there is a different assembly mod for each product line. Thus, the total annual budgeted indirect cost allocated to an assembly mod is divided by the total budgeted units produced to find a budgeted overhead rate. This rate, which is adjusted periodically to reflect changes in the budget, is used to cost individual jobs.

Notice in Exhibit 6-4 that the costs of the marketing, distribution, and customer-service functions are not allocated to the assembly mod. How does Dell account for the indirect costs of marketing, distribution, and customer-service functions? The costs of these functions are estimated during the budgeting process and included in the markup used to price a job. That is, Dell uses cost-plus pricing based on total assembly mod costs. The markup includes an allowance for all unallocated costs and the desired profits. As Dell expands its ABC system, these functions will also be broken down by activities, increasing the overall accuracy of the job-costing system.

PRODUCT COSTING IN SERVICE AND NON-PROFIT ORGANIZATIONS

OBJECTIVE 7

Show how job costing is used in service organizations.

This chapter has concentrated on how to apply costs to manufactured products. However, the job-costing approach is used in nonmanufacturing situations too. For example, universities have research "projects," airlines have repair and overhaul "jobs," and public accountants have audit "engagements." In such situations, the focus shifts from the costs of products to the costs of services.

In non-profit organizations, the "product" is usually not called a "job order." Instead, it may be called a program or a class of service. A "program" is an identifiable group of activities that frequently produces outputs in the form of services rather than goods. Examples include a safety program, an education program, or a family-counselling program. Costs or revenues may be traced to individual hospital patients, individual social welfare cases, and individual university research projects. However, departments often work simultaneously on many programs, so the "job-order" costing challenge is to "apply" the various department costs to the various programs. Only then can managers make wiser decisions regarding the allocation of limited resources among competing programs.

In service industries—such as repairing, consulting, legal, and accounting services—each customer order is a different job with a special account or order number. Sometimes only costs are traced directly to the job, sometimes only revenue is traced, and sometimes both. For example, automobile repair shops typically have a repair order for each car worked on, with space for allocating materials and labour costs. Customers are permitted to see only a copy showing the retail prices of the materials, parts, and labour billed to their orders. If the repair manager wants cost data, a system may be designed so that the "actual" parts and labour costs of each order are traced to a duplicate copy of the repair order. That is why you often see auto mechanics "punching in" and "punching out" their starting and stopping times on "time tickets" as each new order is worked on.

Budgets and Control of Engagements

In many service organizations and some manufacturing organizations, job orders are used primarily for product costing but also for planning and control purposes. For example, a public accounting firm might have a condensed budget for 2001 as follows:

Revenue	$10,000,000	100%
Direct labour (for professional hours charged to engagements)	2,500,000	25
Contribution to overhead and operating income	$ 7,500,000	75
Overhead (all other costs)	6,500,000	65
Operating income	$ 1,000,000	10%

In this illustration:

$$\text{budgeted overhead rate} = \frac{\text{budgeted overhead}}{\text{budgeted direct labour}}$$
$$= \frac{\$6,500,000}{\$2,500,000} = 260\%$$

As each engagement is budgeted, the partner in charge of the audit predicts the expected number of necessary direct professional hours. Direct professional hours are those worked by partners, managers, and subordinate auditors to complete the engagement. The budgeted direct labour cost is the pertinent hourly labour costs multiplied by the budgeted hours. Partners' time is charged to the engagement at much higher rates than subordinates' time.

How is overhead applied? Accounting firms usually use either direct labour cost or direct labour hours as the cost driver for overhead application. In our example, the firm uses direct labour cost. Such a practice implies that partners require proportionately more overhead support for each of their hours charged.

The budgeted total cost of an engagement is the direct labour cost plus applied overhead (260 percent of direct labour cost in this illustration) plus any other direct costs.

The engagement partner uses a budget for a specific audit that includes detailed scope and steps. For instance, the budget for auditing cash or receivables would specify the exact work to be done, the number of hours, and the necessary hours of partner time, manager time, and subordinate time. The partner monitors progress by comparing the hours logged to date with the original budget and with the estimated hours remaining on the engagement. Obviously, if a fixed audit fee has been quoted, the profitability of an engagement depends on whether the audit can be accomplished within the budgeted time limits.

Accuracy of Costs of Engagements

Suppose the accounting firm has costs on an auditing engagement as follows:

Direct professional labour	$ 50,000
Applied overhead, 260%	130,000
Total costs excluding travel costs	$180,000
Travel costs	14,000
Total costs of engagement	$194,000

Two direct costs—professional labour and travel costs—are traced to the jobs. But only direct professional labour is a cost driver for overhead. (Note that costs reimbursed by the client—such as travel costs—do not add to overhead costs and normally would not be subject to any markups in the setting of fees.)

Managers of service firms, such as auditing and consulting firms, frequently use either the budgeted or "actual" costs of engagements as guides to pricing and to allocating effort among particular services or customers. Hence the accuracy of costs of various engagements may affect decisions.

Activity-Based Costing in Service and Non-profit Organizations

Our accounting firm example described a widely used, relatively simple job-costing system. Only two direct cost items (direct professional labour and travel costs) are used and only a single overhead application rate is used.

In recent years, to obtain more accurate costs, many professional service firms such as manufacturing firms have refined their data-processing systems and adopted activity-based costing. Computers help accumulate information that is far more detailed than was feasible a few years ago. As noted in earlier chapters, firms that used activity-based costing generally shift costs from being classified as overhead to being classified as direct costs. Using our previously assumed numbers for direct labour ($50,000) and travel ($14,000), we recast the costs of our audit engagement as follows:

Direct professional labour	$ 50,000
Direct support labour, such as secretarial costs	10,000
Employee benefits for all direct labour*	24,000
Telephone calls	1,000
Photocopying	2,000
Computer time	7,000
Total direct costs	94,000
Applied overhead**	103,400
Total costs excluding travel costs	$197,400
Travel costs	14,000
Total costs of engagement	$211,400

* 40% assumed rate multiplied by ($50,000 + $10,000) = $24,000

** 110% assumed rate multiplied by total direct costs of $94,000 = $103,400.

In an ABC system, costs such as direct support labour, telephone calls, photocopying, computer time, and travel costs are applied by directly measuring their usage on each engagement. The remaining costs to be allocated are assigned to cost pools based on their cause. The cost driver for fringe benefits is labour cost and for other overhead is total direct costs.

The more detailed approach of activity-based costing will nearly always produce total costs that differ from the total costs in the general approach shown earlier: $211,400 compared with $194,000. Of course, any positive or negative difference is attributable to having more types of costs traced directly to the engagement.

Effects of Classifications on Overhead Rates

There are two reasons why the activity-based costing approach also has a lower overhead application rate, assumed at 110 percent of total direct costs instead of the 260 percent of direct labour used in the first example. First, there are fewer overhead costs because more costs are traced directly. Second, the application base is broader, including all direct costs rather than only direct labour.

Even with activity-based costing, some firms may prefer to continue to apply their overhead based on direct labour costs rather than total direct costs. Why? Because the partners believe that overhead is greatly affected by the amount of direct labour costs rather than other direct costs such as telephone calls. But at least the activity-based costing firm has made an explicit decision that direct labour costs are the best cost driver.

Whether the overhead cost driver should be total direct costs, direct professional labour costs or hours, or some other cost driver is a knotty problem for many firms, including most professional service firms. Ideally, activity analysis should uncover the principal cost drivers and they should all be used for overhead application. In practice, only one or two cost drivers are usually used.

HIGHLIGHTS TO REMEMBER

Accounting systems are designed to help satisfy control and product-costing purposes simultaneously. Costs are initially charged to departments; then they are applied to products to get inventory costs for balance sheets and income statements, to guide prices, and to evaluate product performance.

Product costing is an averaging process. Process costing deals with broad averages and great masses of like units. Job costing deals with narrow averages and a unique unit or small batches of like units. The job-cost sheet summarizes the costs of a particular job and holds the underlying detail for the work-in-process inventory account.

Indirect manufacturing costs (factory overhead) are often applied to products using budgeted overhead rates. The rates are computed by dividing total budgeted overhead by a measure of cost-driver activity such as expected labour hours or machine-hours. These rates are usually annual averages. The resulting product costs are normal costs, consisting of actual direct material plus actual direct labour plus applied overhead using budgeted rates. When actual overhead differs from applied overhead, overapplied or underapplied overhead arises, which is either written off at the end of the year or pro-rated to the inventory accounts.

The job-costing approach is used in nonmanufacturing as well as in manufacturing. Examples include costs of services such as auto repair, consulting, and auditing. For example, the job order is a key device for planning and controlling an audit engagement by a public accounting firm.

SUMMARY PROBLEM FOR YOUR REVIEW

Problem

Review the Martinez illustration, especially Exhibits 6-2 and 6-3. Prepare an income statement for 2002 through the gross-profit line. Use the immediate write-off method for overapplied overhead.

Solution

Exhibit 6-5 recapitulates the final effect of the Martinez illustration on the financial statements. Note how the immediate write-off means that the $17,000 is added to the cost of goods sold. As you study Exhibit 6-5, trace the three major elements of cost (direct material, direct labour, and factory overhead) through the accounts.

EXHIBIT 6-5

Relation of Costs of Financial Statements

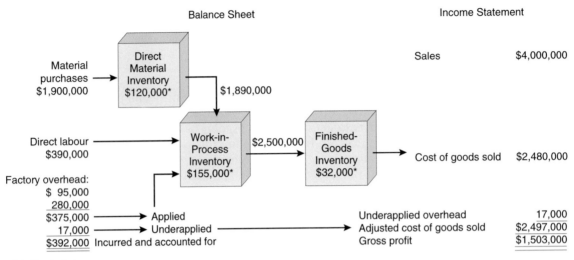

*Ending balance.

ACCOUNTING VOCABULARY

budgeted factory overhead rate *p. 250*
job costing *p. 243*
job-cost record *p. 244*
job-cost sheet *p. 244*
job order *p. 244*
job-order costing *p. 243*

labour time tickets *p. 244*
materials requisitions *p. 244*
normal costing system *p. 257*
overapplied overhead *p. 255*
process costing *p. 243*
underapplied overhead *p. 255*

ASSIGNMENT MATERIAL

QUESTIONS

Q6-1 "There are different product costs for different purposes." Name at least two purposes.

Q6-2 "Job costs are accumulated for purposes of inventory valuation and income determination." State two other purposes.

Q6-3 Distinguish between job costing and process costing.

Q6-4 "The basic distinction between job-order costing and process costing is the breadth of the denominator." Explain.

Q6-5 How does hybrid costing relate to job costing and process costing?

Q6-6 Describe the supporting details for work in process in a job-cost system.

Q6-7 What types of source documents provide information for job-cost record?

Q6-8 Suppose a company uses machine-hours as a cost driver for factory overhead. How does the company compute a budgeted overhead application rate? How does it compute the amount of factory overhead applied to a particular job?

Q6-9 Explain the role of the factory department overhead control account in a job-cost system.

Q6-10 "Each department must choose one cost driver to be used for cost application." Do you agree? Explain.

Q6-11 "There should be a strong relationship between the factory overhead incurred and the cost driver chosen for its application." Why?

Q6-12 "Sometimes direct labour cost is the best cost driver for overhead allocation even if wage rates vary within a department." Do you agree? Explain.

Q6-13 Identify four cost drivers that a manufacturing company might use to apply factory overhead costs to jobs.

Q6-14 What are some reasons for differences between the amounts of *incurred* and *applied* overhead?

Q6-15 "Under actual overhead application, unit costs soar as volume increases, and vice versa." Do you agree? Explain.

Q6-16 Define *normal* costing.

Q6-17 What is the best theoretical method of allocating underapplied or over-applied overhead, assuming that the objective is to obtain as accurate a cost application as possible?

Q6-18 State three examples of service industries that use the job-costing approach.

Q6-19 "Service firms trace only direct labour costs to jobs. All other costs are applied as a percentage of direct labour cost." Do you agree? Explain.

Q6-20 "As data processing becomes more economical, more costs than just direct material and direct labour will be classified as direct costs wherever feasible." Give three examples of such costs.

PROBLEMS

P6-1 DIRECT MATERIALS. For each of the following independent cases, fill in the blanks (in millions of dollars):

	1	2	3	4
Direct materials inventory, Dec. 31, 2001	8	8	5	—
Purchased	5	9	—	8
Used	7	—	7	3
Direct materials inventory, Dec. 31, 2002	—	6	8	7

P6-2 DIRECT MATERIALS. Genesis Athletic Shoes had an ending inventory of direct materials of $9 million. During the year the company had acquired $15 million of additional direct materials and had used $12 million. Compute the beginning inventory.

P6-3 USING THE WORK-IN-PROCESS INVENTORY ACCOUNT. September production resulted in the following activity in a key account of Colebury Costing Company (in thousands):

WORK-IN-PROCESS INVENTORY			
September 1 balance	12		
Direct material used	50		
Direct labour charged to jobs	25		
Factory overhead applied to jobs	55		

Job Order 13N and 37Q, with total costs of $70 and $54 thousand, respectively, were completed in September.

1. Journalize the completed production for September.
2. Compute the balance in work-in-Process inventory, September 30, after recording the completed production.
3. Journalize the credit sale of Job 13N for $101,000.

P6-4 JOB-COST RECORD. East University uses job-cost records for various research projects. A major reason for such records is to justify requests for reimbursement for costs on projects sponsored by the federal government.

Consider the following summarized data regarding Project No. 76 conducted by a group of physicists:

- Jan. 5   Direct materials, various metals, $925
- Jan. 7   Direct materials, various chemicals, $780
- Jan. 5-12   Direct labour, research associates, 120 hours
- Jan. 7-12   Direct labour, research assistants, 180 hours

Research associates receive $32 per hour; assistants, $19. The overhead rate is 70 percent of direct labour cost.

Sketch a job-cost record. Post all the data to the project-cost record. Compute the total cost of the project through January 12.

P6-5 ANALYZING JOB-COST DATA. Job-cost records for Naomi's Remodelling Ltd. contained the following data:

JOB NO.	DATES			TOTAL COST OF JOB AT MAY 31
	STARTED	FINISHED	SOLD	
1	April 19	May 14	May 15	$3,200
2	April 26	May 22	May 25	8,800
3	May 2	June 6	June 8	6,500
4	May 9	May 29	June 5	8,100
5	May 14	June 14	June 16	3,900

Compute Naomi's (1) work-in-process inventory at May 31, (2) finished-goods inventory at May 31, and (3) cost of goods sold for May.

P6-6 ANALYZING JOB-COST DATA. The Cortez Construction Company constructs houses on speculation. That is, the houses are begun before any buyer is known. Even if the buyer agrees to purchase a house under construction, no sales are recorded until the house is completed and accepted for delivery. The job-cost records contained the following (in thousands):

JOB NO.	DATES STARTED	DATES FINISHED	SOLD	TOTAL COST OF JOB AT SEPT. 30	TOTAL CONSTRUCTION COST ADDED IN OCT.
43	4/26	9/7	9/8	$180	
51	5/17	9/14	9/17	170	
52	5/20	9/30	10/4	150	
53	5/28	10/14	10/18	200	$50
61	6/3	10/20	11/24	115	20
62	6/9	10/21	10/27	180	25
71	7/7	11/6	11/22	118	36
81	8/7	11/24	12/24	106	48

1. Compute Cortez's cost of (a) construction-in-process inventory at September 30 and October 31, (b) finished-houses inventory at September 30 and October 31, and (c) cost of houses sold for September and October.
2. Prepare summary journal entries for the transfer of completed houses from construction in process to finished houses for September and October.
3. Record the cash sale and cost of house sold of Job 53 for $345,000.

P6-7 **BASIC JOURNAL ENTRIES.** The following data (in thousands) summarize the factory operations of the Lewis Manufacturing Co. for the year 2002, its first year in business:

a. Direct materials purchased for cash	$450
b. Direct materials issued and used	420
c. Labour used directly on production	125
d1. Indirect labour	80
d2. Amortization of plant and equipment	55
d3. Miscellaneous factory overhead (ordinarily would be detailed)	40
e. Overhead applied: 180% of direct labour	?
f. Cost of production completed	705
g. Cost of goods sold	460

1. Prepare summary journal entries. Omit explanations. For purposes of this problem, combine the items in *d* as "overhead incurred."
2. Show the T-accounts for all inventories, Cost of Goods Sold, and Factory Department Overhead. Compute the ending balances of the inventories. Do not adjust for underapplied or overapplied factory overhead.

P6-8 **FINDING UNKNOWNS.** DeMond Chemicals has the following balances at December 31, 2002. All amounts are in millions:

Factory overhead applied	$200
Cost of goods sold	500
Factory overhead incurred	210
Direct materials inventory	30
Finished-goods inventory	160
Work-in-process inventory	120

The cost of goods completed was $420. The cost of direct materials requisitioned for production during 2002 was $210. The cost of direct materials purchased was $225. Factory overhead was applied to production at a rate of 160 percent of direct labour cost.

Compute the beginning inventory balances of direct materials, work in process, and finished goods. Make these computations before considering any possible adjustments for overapplied or underapplied overhead.

P6-9 FINDING UNKNOWNS. The Chickadee Company has the following balances (in millions) as of December 31, 2001:

Work-in-process inventory	$ 14
Finished-goods inventory	205
Direct materials inventory	65
Factory overhead incurred	180
Factory overhead applied at 150%	
of direct labour cost	150
Cost of goods sold	350

The cost of direct materials purchased during 2001 was $305. The cost of direct materials requisitioned for production during 2001 was $265. The cost of goods completed was $523, all in millions.

Before considering any year-end adjustments for overapplied or underapplied overhead, compute the beginning inventory balances of direct materials, work in process, and finished goods.

P6-10 JOURNAL ENTRIES FOR OVERHEAD. Consider the following summarized data regarding 2002:

	BUDGET	ACTUAL
Indirect labour	$ 290,000	$ 305,000
Supplies	35,000	30,000
Repairs	80,000	75,000
Utilities	130,000	123,000
Factory rent	125,000	125,000
Supervision	60,000	75,000
Depreciation, equipment	220,000	220,000
Insurance, property taxes, etc.	40,000	42,000
a. Total factory overhead	$ 980,000	$ 995,000
b. Direct materials used	$1,650,000	$1,605,000
c. Direct labour	$1,225,000	$1,200,000

Omit explanations for journal entries.

1. Prepare a summary for journal entry for the actual overhead incurred for 2002.
2. Prepare summary journal entries for direct materials used and direct labour.
3. Factory overhead was applied by using a budgeted rate based on budgeted direct labour costs. Compute the rate. Prepare a summary journal entry for the application of overhead to products.
4. Post the journal entries to the T-accounts for work in process and factory department overhead.

5. Suppose overapplied or underapplied factory overhead is written off as an adjustment to cost of goods sold. Prepare the journal entry. Post the overhead to the overhead T-account.

P6-11 RELATIONSHIPS AMONG OVERHEAD ITEMS. Fill in the unknowns:

	CASE A	CASE B	CASE C
Budgeted factory overhead	$3,400,000	?	$1,750,000
Budgeted cost drivers:			
Direct labour cost	$2,000,000		
Direct labour hours		450,000	
Machine-hours			250,000
Overhead application rate	?	$5	?

P6-12 RELATIONSHIP AMONG OVERHEAD ITEMS. Fill in the unknowns:

	CASE 1	CASE 2
a. Budgeted factory overhead	$750,000	$420,000
b. Cost driver, budgeted		
direct labour cost	500,000	? 350,000
c. Budgeted factory overhead rate	? 1.5	120%
d. Direct labour cost incurred	570,000	? 325
e. Factory overhead incurred	825,000	415,000
f. Factory overhead applied	? 855	? 390
g. Underapplied (overapplied)		
factory overhead	? (30)	25,000

P6-13 UNDERAPPLIED AND OVERAPPLIED OVERHEAD. Wosepka Welding Company applied factory overhead at a rate of $8.50 per direct labour hour. Selected data for 2001 operations are (in thousands).

	CASE 1	CASE 2
Direct labour hours	30	36
Direct labour cost	$220	$245
Indirect labour cost	32	40
Sales commissions	20	15
Amortization, manufacturing equipment	22	32
Direct material cost	230	250
Factory fuel costs	35	47
Amortization, finished-goods warehouse	5	17
Cost of goods sold	420	510
All other factory costs	138	214

Compute for both cases:

1. Factory overhead applied.
2. Total factory overhead incurred.
3. Amount of underapplied or overapplied factory overhead.

P6-14   DISPOSITION OF OVERHEAD.   Assuming the following at the end of 2002 (in thousands):

Cost of goods sold	$300
Direct materials inventory	70
Work in process	50
Finished goods	150
Factory department overhead control	60 cr.

1. Assume that the underapplied or overapplied overhead is regarded as an adjustment to cost of goods sold. Prepare the journal entry.
2. Assume that the underapplied or overapplied overhead is prorated among the appropriate accounts in proportion to their ending unadjusted balances. Show computations and prepare the journal entry.
3. Which adjustment, the one in requirement 1 or 2, would result in the higher gross profit? Explain, indicating the amount of the difference.

P6-15   DISPOSITION OF OVERHEAD.   A Paris manufacturer uses a job-order system. At the end of 2002 the following balances existed (in millions of French francs):

Cost of goods sold	FF150
Finished goods	120
Work in process	30
Factory overhead (actual)	70
Factory overhead (applied)	60

1. Prepare journal entries for two different ways to dispose of the underapplied overhead.
2. Gross profit, before considering the effects of requirement 1, was FF43 million. What is the adjusted gross profit under the two methods demonstrated?

P6-16   DISPOSITION OF YEAR-END OVERAPPLIED OVERHEAD.   Gloria Cosmetics uses a normal cost system and has the following balances at the end of its first year's operations:

Work-in-process inventory	$200,000
Finished-goods inventory	200,000
Cost of goods sold	400,000
Actual factory overhead	409,000
Factory overhead applied	457,000

Prepare journal entries for two different ways to dispose of the year-end overhead balances. By how much would gross profit differ?

P6-17   RELATIONSHIPS OF MANUFACTURING COSTS.   Selected data concerning the past fiscal year's operations of the Woodson Manufacturing Company are as follows (in thousands):

	INVENTORIES	
	BEGINNING	**ENDING**
Raw materials	$55	$ 75
Work in process	75	35
Finished goods	90	110
Other data:		
Raw materials used		$455
Total manufacturing costs charged to production during the year (includes raw materials, direct labour, and factory overhead applied at a rate of 80% of direct labour cost)		851
Cost of goods available for sale		1,026
Selling and general expenses		50

1. Compute the cost of raw materials purchased during the year.
2. Compute the direct labour costs charged to production during the year.
3. Compute the cost of goods manufactured during the year.
4. Compute the cost of goods sold during the year.

P6-18 **BASIC JOURNAL ENTRIES.** Consider the following data for Oxford Printing Company (in thousands):

Inventories, December 31, 2001	
Direct materials	£18
Work in process	25
Finished goods	100

Summarized transactions for 2002:

a. Purchase of direct materials	£112
b. Direct materials used	98
c. Direct labour	105
d. Factory overhead incurred	90
e. Factory overhead applied, 80 percent of direct labour	?
f. Cost of goods completed and transferred to finished goods	280
g. Cost of goods sold	350
h. Sales on account	600

1. Prepare summary journal entries for 2002 transaction. Omit explanations.
2. Show the T-accounts for all inventories, cost of goods sold, and factory department overhead control. compute the ending balances of the inventories. Do not adjust for underapplied or overapplied factory overhead.

P6-19 **DISPOSITION OF OVERHEAD.** MacLachlan Mfg. Co. had overapplied overhead of $20,000 in 2002. Before adjusting for overapplied or underapplied overhead, the ending inventories for direct materials, WIP, and finished goods were $75,000, $100,000, and $150,000, respectively. Unadjusted cost of goods sold was $250,000.

1. Assume that the $20,000 was written off solely as an adjustment to cost of goods sold. Prepare the journal entry.
2. Management has decided to prorate the $20,000 to the appropriate accounts (using the unadjusted ending balances) instead of writing it off solely as an adjustment of cost of goods sold. Prepare the journal entry. Would gross profit be higher or lower than in requirement 1? by how much?

P6-20 APPLICATION OF OVERHEAD USING BUDGETED RATES. The Bellevue Clinic computes cost of treating each patient. It allocates costs to departments and then applies departmental overhead costs to individual patients using a different budgeted overhead rate in each department. Consider the following predicted 2001 data for two of Bellevue's departments:

	PHARMACY	MEDICAL RECORDS
Department overhead cost	$225,000	$300,000
Number of prescriptions filled	90,000	
Number of patient visits		60,000

The cost driver for overhead in Pharmacy is *number of prescriptions filled*; in Medical Records it is *number of patient visits*.

In June 2001, David Li paid two visits to the clinic and had four prescriptions filled at the pharmacy.

1. Compute departmental overhead rates for the two departments.
2. Compute the overhead costs applied to the patient David Li in June 2001.
3. At the end of 2001, actual overhead costs were:

Pharmacy	$217,000
Medical records	$325,000

The pharmacy filled 85,000 prescriptions, and the clinic had 63,000 patient visits during 2001. Compute the overapplied or underapplied overhead in each department.

P6-21 RELATIONSHIP OF SUBSIDIARY AND GENERAL LEDGERS, JOURNAL ENTRIES. The following summarized data are available on three job-cost records of Weeks Company, a manufacturer of packaging equipment:

	412		413		414
	APRIL	MAY	APRIL	MAY	MAY
Direct materials	$9,000	$2,500	$12,000	—	$13,000
Direct labour	4,000	1,500	5,000	2,500	2,000
Factory overhead applied	8,000	?	10,000	?	?

The company's fiscal year ends on May 31. Factory overhead is applied as a percentage of direct-labour costs. The balances in selected accounts on April 30 were direct materials inventory, $19,000; and finished-goods inventory, $18,000.

Job 412 was completed during May and transferred to finished goods. Job 413 was still in process at the end of May as was Job 414, which had begun on May 24. These were the only jobs worked on during April and May.

Job 412 was sold along with other finished goods by May 30. The total cost of goods sold during May was $33,000. The balance in Cost of Goods Sold on April 30 was $450,000.

1. Prepare a schedule showing the balance of the work-in-process inventory, April 30. This schedule should show the total costs of each job record. Taken together, the job-cost records are the subsidiary ledger supporting the general-ledger balance of work in process.

2. What is the overhead application rate?
3. Prepare summary general-journal entries for all costs added to Work in Process during May. Also prepare entries for all costs transferred from work in process to finished goods and from finished goods to cost of goods sold. Post to the appropriate T-accounts.
4. Prepare a schedule showing the balance of the work-in-process inventory, May 31.

P6-22 STRAIGHTFORWARD JOB COSTING. The Scott Furniture Company has two departments. Data for 2002 include the following:

Direct materials (30 types)	$65,000
Work in process (in assembly)	50,000
Finished goods	40,000

Manufacturing overhead budget for 2003:

	MACHINING	ASSEMBLY
Indirect labour	$250,000	$ 410,000
Supplies	45,000	40,000
Utilities	110,000	75,000
Repairs	140,000	110,000
Supervision	130,000	215,000
Factory rent	95,000	75,000
Amortization on equipment	160,000	105,000
Insurance, property taxes, etc.	60,000	70,000
	$990,000	$1,100,000

Budgeted machine-hours were 90,000; budgeted direct labour cost in Assembly was $2,200,000. Manufacturing overhead was applied using budgeted rates on the basis of machine-hours in Machining and on the basis of direct labour cost in Assembly.

Following is a summary of actual events for the year:

	MACHINING	ASSEMBLY	TOTAL
a. Direct materials purchased			$ 1,900,000
b. Direct materials requisitioned	$ 1,100,000	$ 750,000	1,850,000
c. Direct labour costs incurred	900,000	2,800,000	3,700,000
d1. Factory overhead incurred	1,100,000	1,100,000	2,200,000
d2. Factory overhead applied	880,000	?	?
e. Cost of goods completed	—	—	7,820,000
f1. Sales	—	—	13,000,000
f2. Cost of goods sold	—	—	7,800,000

The ending work in process (all in Assembly) was $60,000.

1. Compute the budgeted overhead rates.
2. Compute the amount of the machine-hours actually worked.
3. Compute the amount of factory overhead applied in the Assembly Department.

4. Prepare general journal entries for transactions *a* through *f*. Work solely with the total amounts, not the details for Machining and Assembly. Explanations are not required. Show data in thousands of dollars. Present T-accounts, including ending inventory balances, for direct materials, work in process, and finished goods.
5. Prepare a partial income statement similar to the one illustrated in Exhibit 6-5. Overapplied or underapplied overhead is written off as an adjustment of current cost of goods sold.

P6-23 **NON-PROFIT JOB COSTING.** Job-order costing is usually identified with manufacturing companies. However, service industries and non-profit organizations also use the method. Suppose a social service agency has a cost accounting system that tracks cost by department (for example, family counselling, general welfare, and foster children) and by case. In this way, the manager of the agency is better able to determine how its limited resources (mostly professional social workers) should be allocated. Furthermore, the manager's interactions with superiors and various politicians are more fruitful when they can cite the costs of various types of cases.

The condensed line-item budgeted for the general welfare department of the agency for 2001 showed

Professional salaries:		
Level 12	5 @ $35,000 = $175,000	
Level 10	21 @ $26,000 = 546,000	
Level 8	34 @ $18,000 = 612,000	$1,333,000
Other costs		533,200
Total costs		$1,866,200

For costing various cases, the manager favoured using a single overhead application rate based on the ratio of total overhead to direct labour. The latter was defined as those professional salaries assigned to specific cases.

The professional workers filled out a weekly "case time" report, which approximated the hours spent for each case.

The instructions on the report were: "Indicate how much time (in hours) you spent on each case. Unassigned time should be listed separately." About 20 percent of available time was unassigned to specific cases. It was used for professional development (for example, continuing-education programs). "Unassigned time" became a part of "overhead," as distinguished from the direct labour.

1. Compute the "overhead rate" as a percentage of direct labour (that is, the assignable professional salaries).
2. Suppose that last week a welfare case, Client No. 273, required two hours of Level-12 time, four hours of Level-10 time, and nine hours of Level-8 time. How much job cost should be allocated to Client No. 273 for the week? Assume that all professional employees work an 1,800-hour year.

P6-24 **JOB COSTING IN A CONSULTING FIRM.** Link Engineering Consultants is a firm of professional civil engineers. It mostly has surveying jobs for the heavy-construction industry throughout Western Canada. The firm obtains its jobs by giving fixed-price quotations, so profitability depends on the ability to predict the time required for the various subtasks on the job. (This situation is similar to that in the auditing profession, where time is budgeted for such audit steps as reconciling cash and confirming accounts receivable.)

A client may be served by various professional staff, who hold positions in the hierarchy from partners to managers to senior engineers to assistants. In addition, there are secretaries and other employees.

Link Engineering has the following budget for 2003:

Compensation of professional staff	$3,600,000
Other costs	1,449,000
Total budgeted costs	$5,049,000

Each professional staff member must submit a weekly time report, which is used for charging hours to a client job-order record. The time report has seven columns, one for each day of the week. Its rows are as follows:

- Chargeable hours:
  Client 156
  Client 183
  Etc.

- Nonchargeable hours:
  Attending seminar on new equipment
  Unassigned time
  Etc.

In turn, these time reports are used for charging hours and costs to the client job-order records. The managing partner regards these job records as absolutely essential for measuring the profitability of various jobs and for providing an "experience base for improving predictions on future jobs."

1. This firm applies overhead to jobs at a budgeted percentage of the professional compensation charged directly to the job ("direct labour"). For all categories of professional personnel, chargeable hours average 85 percent of available hours. Non-chargeable hours are regarded as additional overhead. What is the overhead rate as a percentage of "direct labour," the chargeable professional compensation cost?

2. A senior engineer works 48 weeks per year, 40 hours per week. His compensation is $60,000. He has worked on two jobs during the past week, devoting 10 hours to Job 156 and 30 hours to Job 183. How much cost should be charged to Job 156 because of his work there?

P6-25 CHOOSING COST DRIVERS IN AN ACCOUNTING FIRM. The managing partner of Brenda McCoy Accounting is considering the desirability of tracing more costs to jobs than just direct labour. In this way, the firm will be better able to justify billings to clients.

Last year's costs were

Direct professional labour	$ 5,000,000
Overhead	10,000,000
Total costs	$15,000,000

The following costs were included in overhead:

Computer time	$ 750,000
Secretarial costs	700,000
Photocopying	250,000
Fringe benefits to direct labour	800,000
Phone call time with clients	
(estimated but not tabulated)	500,000
Total	$3,000,000

The firm's data-processing techniques now make it feasible to document and trace these costs to individual jobs.

As an experiment in December, Brenda McCoy arranged to trace these costs to six audit engagements. Two job records showed the following:

	ENGAGEMENT	
	EAGLEDALE COMPANY	FIRST VALLEY BANK
Direct professional labour	$15,000	$15,000
Fringe benefits to direct labour	3,000	3,000
Phone call time with clients	1,500	500
Computer time	3,000	700
Secretarial costs	2,000	1,500
Photocopying	500	300
Total direct costs	$25,000	$21,000

1. Compute the overhead application rate based on last year's costs.
2. Suppose last year's costs were reclassified so that $3 million would be regarded as direct costs instead of overhead. Compute the overhead application rate as a percentage of direct labour and as a percentage of total direct costs.
3. Using the three rates computed in requirements 1 and 2, compute the total costs of engagements for Eagledale Company and First Valley Bank.
4. Suppose that client billing was based on a 30 percent markup of total job costs. Compute the billings that would be forthcoming in requirement 3.
5. Which method of job costing and overhead application do you favour? Explain.

P6-26 RECONSTRUCTION OF TRANSACTIONS. You are asked to bring the following incomplete accounts of a printing plant acquired in a merger up to date through January 31, 2001. Also consider the data that appear following the T-accounts.

Direct Materials Inventory			Accrued Factory Payroll	
12/31/00				1/31/01
Balance	20,000			Balance 5,000

Work in Process			Factory Department Overhead Control	
			Total January charges 55,000	

Finished Goods			Cost of Goods Sold	
12/31/00				
Balance	25,000			

Additional information:

a. The overhead is applied using a budgeted rate that is set every December by forecasting the following year's overhead and relating it to forecast direct labour costs. The budget for 2001 called for $640,000 of direct labour and $800,000 of factory overhead.

b. The only job unfinished on January 31, 2001, was No. 419 on which total labour charges were $3,000 (200 direct labour hours). Total direct material charges were $21,000.

c. Total materials placed into production during January totalled $140,000.

d. Cost of goods completed during January was $260,000.

e. January 31 balances of direct materials totalled $27,000.

f. Finished-goods inventory as of January 31 was $35,000.

g. All factory workers earn the same rate of pay. Direct labour hours for January totalled 3,000. Indirect labour and supervision totalled $12,000.

h. The gross factory payroll paid on January paydays totalled $55,000. Ignore withholdings.

i. All "actual" factory overhead incurred during January has already been posted.

Compute:

1. Direct materials purchased during January.

2. Cost of goods sold during January.

3. Direct labour costs incurred during January.

4. Overhead applied during January.

5. Balance, Accrued Factory Payroll, December 31, 2000.

6. Balance, Work in Process, December 31, 2000.

7. Balance, Work in Process, January 31, 2001.

8. Overapplied or underapplied overhead of January.

P6-27   ACCOUNTING FOR OVERHEAD, BUDGETED RATES.   Donald Aeronautics Co. uses a budgeted overhead rate in applying overhead to individual job orders on a *machine-hour* basis for Department A and on a *direct-labour-hour* basis for Department B. At the beginning of 2000, the company's management made the following budget predictions:

	DEPT. A	DEPT. B
Direct labour cost	1,500,000	1,200,000
Factory overhead	2,170,000	1,000,000
Direct labour hours	90,000	125,000
Machine-hours	350,000	20,000

Cost records of recent months show the following accumulations for Job Order No. M89:

	DEPT. A	DEPT. B
Material placed in production	12,000	32,000
Direct labour cost	10,800	10,000
Direct labour hours	900	1,250
Machine-hours	3,500	150

1. What is the budgeted overhead rate that should be applied in Department A? In Department B?
2. What is the *total overhead cost* of Job Order No. M89?
3. If Job Order No. M89 consists of 200 units of product, what is the unit cost of this job?
4. At the end of 2000, actual results for the year's operations were as follows:

	DEPT. A	DEPT. B
Actual overhead costs incurred	1,600,000	1,200,000
Actual direct labour hours	80,000	120,000
Actual machine-hours	300,000	25,000

Find the underapplied or overapplied overhead for each department and for the factory as a whole.

P6-28   JOB COSTING AT DELL COMPUTER.   Dell Computer Company's manufacturing process at its Austin, Texas facility consists of assembly, functional testing, and quality control of the company's computer systems. The company's build-to-order manufacturing process is designed to allow the company to quickly produce customized computer systems. For example, the company contracts with various suppliers to manufacture unconfigured base Latitude notebook computers and then custom configures these systems for shipment to customers. Quality control is maintained through the testing of components, parts, and suvassemblies at various stages in the manufacturing process.

Dell Computer Company
www.dell.com

Describe how Dell might set up a job-costing system to determine the costs of its computers. What is a "job" to Dell? How might the costs of components, assembly, testing, and quality control be allocated to each "job"?

P6-29   COLLABORATIVE LEARNING EXERCISE: ACCOUNTING FOR OVERHEAD.   Form groups of four to six persons. Each group should identify a management accountant at a local company to interview. The interviewee could be the top financial officer of a small company, but a division controller or cost analyst might be more appropriate for a large company. The essential factor is that the person understand how overhead costs are allocated to products or services in the company.

Set up an interview with the cost accountant, and explore the following issues. Be prepared with follow-up questions if your first question receives a superficial answer. Your goal should be to get as much operational detail as possible about the procedures used for allocating overhead costs at the company. If the company is large, you may want to focus on one department, one product line, or some other subdivision of the company.

The issues to explore are:

a. What types of costs are included in overhead? How large is overhead compared with direct material and labour costs?

b. What types of overhead cost pools exist? Are there different pools by department? By activity? By cost driver? By fixed or variable cost? Be prepared to explain what you mean by these terms, because terminology varies widely.

c. How is overhead applied to final products or services? What cost drivers are used?

After the interview, draw a diagram of the cost allocation system in as much detail as possible. Be prepared to share this with the entire class, using it to explain the overhead-cost-allocation system at the company your group studied.

CASES

C6-1 **MULTIPLE OVERHEAD RATES AND ACTIVITY-BASED COSTING.** A division of Hewlett-Packard assembles and tests printed circuit (PC) boards. The division has many different products. Some are high volume, others are low volume. For years, manufacturing overhead was applied to products using a single overhead rate based on direct labour dollars. However, direct labour had shrunk to 6 percent of total manufacturing costs.

Managers decided to refine the division's product-costing system. Without using a direct labour category, they included all manufacturing labour as a part of factory overhead. They also identified several activities and the appropriate cost driver for each. The cost driver for the first activity, the start station, was the number of raw PC boards. The application rate was computed as follows:

$$\begin{aligned} \text{application rate} \\ \text{for start station} \\ \text{activity} \end{aligned} = \frac{\text{budgeted total factory overhead at the activity}}{\text{budgeted raw PC boards for the year}}$$

$$= \frac{\$150{,}000}{125{,}000} = \$1.20$$

Each time a raw PC board passes through the start station activity, $1.20 is added to the cost of a product. The product cost is the sum of costs directly traced to the product plus the indirect costs (factory overhead) accumulated at each of the manufacturing activities undergone.

Using assumed numbers, consider the following data regarding PC Board 37:

Direct materials	$55.00
Factory overhead applied	?
Total manufacturing product sold	?

The activities involved in the production of PC Board 37 and the related cost drivers chosen were

ACTIVITY	COST DRIVER	FACTORY-OVERHEAD COSTS APPLIED FOR EACH ACTIVITY
1. Start station	No. of raw PC boards	1 x $ 1.20 = $1.20
2. Axial insertion	No. of axial insertions	39 x .07 =　?
3. Dip insertion	No. of dip insertions	? x .20 =　5.60
4. Manual insertion	No. of manual insertions	15 x ? =　6.00
5. Wave solder	No. of boards soldered	1 x 3.20 =　3.20
6. Backload	No. of backload insertions	8 x .60 =　4.80
7. Test	Standard time board is in test activity	.15 x 80.00 =　?
8. Defect analysis	Standard time for defect analysis and repair	.05 x ? = $4.50
Total		$?

Required:

1. Fill in the blanks.
2. How is direct labour identified with products under this product-costing system?
3. As a manager, what would be your assessment of the multiple-overhead rate, activity-costing system as compared to the older system?

C6-2 **ONE OR TWO COST DRIVERS.** The Matterhorn Instruments Co. in Geneva, Switzerland, has the following 2002 budget for its two departments in Swiss francs (SF):

	MACHINING	FINISHING	TOTAL
Direct labour	SF 300,000	SF 800,000	SF 1,100,000
Factory overhead	SF 960,000	SF 800,000	SF 1,760,000
Machine-hours	60,000	20,000	80,000

In the past, the company has used a single plantwide overhead application rate based on direct labour cost. However, as its product line has expanded and as competition has intensified, Hans Volkert, the company president, has questioned the accuracy of the profits or losses shown on various products. Volkert makes custom tools on special orders from customers. To be competitive and still make a reasonable profit, it is essential that the firm measure the cost of each customer order. Volkert has focused on overhead allocation as a potential problem. He knows that changes in costs are more heavily affected by machine-hours in the first department and by direct labour costs in the second department. As company controller, you have gathered the following data regarding two typical customer orders:

	ORDER NUMBER	
	K102	K156
Machining		
Direct materials	SF 4,000	SF 4,000
Direct labour	SF 3,000	SF 1,500
Machine-hours	1,200	100
Finishing		
Direct labour	SF 1,500	SF 3,000
Machine-hours	120	120

1. Compute six factory overhead application rates, three based on direct-labour cost and three based on machine-hours for machining, finishing, and for the plant as a whole.
2. Use the application rates to compute the total costs of orders K102 and K156 as follows: (a) plantwide rate based on direct-labour cost and (b) machining based on machine-hours and finishing based on direct-labour cost.
3. Evaluate your answers in requirement 2. Which set of job costs do you prefer? Why?

C6-3 JOB-COSTING SYSTEM ANALYSIS.   (SMAC) Wayne Andrews, the president and major shareholder of Walnut Furniture Limited (Walnut), was reviewing the 2000 and 2001 comparative income statements (Exhibit 6A-1) and was wondering why, despite all his efforts, profits had not improved. Walnut manufactured and installed fitted furniture and fixtures in new buildings on a contract basis.

Walnut's operations were organized into three departments: fabricating, finishing, and installing. Each department was treated as a cost centre. The total hourly operating costs, including labour of each department were determined each month and charged to each job on the basis of the hours it was in process in each department (Exhibit 6A-2). The departmental operating costs per hour were compared to those of the previous year for cost control. Wayne attempted to keep his workers employed on a steady full-time basis which sometimes required workers to be transferred from one department to another. Therefore, he regarded labour costs as being fixed.

Wayne has been very satisfied with the cost accounting system since its introduction, and felt it gave him good cost control and a basis for submitting bids for contracts. However, Wayne had two recurring problems: winning contracts to fill capacity, and controlling rejects. Bids were based on estimates of processing time required in each department costed at the most recent month's departmental processing costs per hour. Wayne and the estimator discussed how much should be added for profit for each bid; normally, the target profit rate of 10 percent of total estimated costs was used as a starting point in deciding the final bid amount to submit.

Walnut competed for contracts in two distinct market segments, both involving the manufacture of furniture and fixtures in the plant, and then

	2001	2000
Sales	$940,000	$925,000
Cost of sales:		
Materials	127,800	123,000
Labour	493,000	486,000
Amortization	36,000	36,000
Heat, light and power	25,800	21,400
Maintenance	24,200	20,200
Rejects - departmental	17,150	37,000
- corporate	72,050	50,200
Total cost of sales	796,000	773,800
Gross profit	144,000	151,200
Selling and administration expenses	49,000	46,500
Net income before taxes	95,000	104,700
Income taxes	23,800	26,200
Net income	$ 71,200	$ 78,500

EXHIBIT 6A-1

WALNUT FURNITURE LIMITED
Income Statement For the Years Ended December 31

EXHIBIT 6A-2

WALNUT FURNITURE
LIMITED
Department Operating
Statement For the Month
of December, 2001

	FABRICATING	FINISHING	INSTALLING	TOTAL
Labour	$24,000	$4,500	$11,250	$39,750
Amortization	1,900	600	500	3,000
Heat, light & power[1]	1,200	750	150	2,100
Maintenance[1]	1,400	550	100	2,050
Material	8,575	900	300	9,775
Processing costs	37,075	7,300	12,300	56,675
Rejects - Departmental[2]	556	110	734	1,400
Total processing costs	$37,631	$7,410	$13,034	$58,075
Operating hours[3]	160	100	150	
Processing cost per hour: 2001	$ 235	$ 74	$ 87	
2000	$ 225	$ 72	$ 85	
Number of persons at $15/hour	10	3	5	

[1]About 90% of these costs are fixed.
[2]A majority of the reject costs charged to the fabricating and finishing departments are directly attributable to the regularly scheduled 5% overproduction for standard contracts. A majority of the reject costs charged to the installing department are directly attributable to customized contracts.
[3]Operating hours include reprocessing time as well as normal processing time.

installation on site. The first segment involved large contracts for standard units to be installed in multiunit apartment buildings and franchised, fast-food outlets. Wayne devoted a great deal of time pursuing this type of contract since the large quantities involved would fill capacity. He had succeeded in increasing the number of bids won in this segment, but not to the extent he had hoped to achieve. The second segment involved smaller contracts for luxury apartments requiring high-quality work and material, often customized for each apartment. Most of Walnut's contracts had been won in the second segment. Wayne had asked his estimator to prepare a schedule of data on two recent bids (Exhibit 6A-3) and a summary of bids submitted and won in 2000 and 2001 (Exhibit 6A-4).

Wayne's second cost-control problem was difficult to analyze. Rejects might be identified either during production or at final inspection by the contractor-customer. In either event, an attempt was made to charge the responsible department with the cost of the reprocessing work. If the responsibility could not be identified, the reprocessing cost was charged to the corporate reject-reprocessing account. In processing large volume contracts, rejects were normally not a major problem and production scheduling provided for 5 percent overproduction to replace rejects. In processing the high-priced, low-volume customized contracts, it was not economically feasible to overproduce, so supervisors were urged to emphasize quality work; nevertheless, the reject rate at the final inspection by customers was over 15 percent. Rejects found after installation usually required replacement. Since Wayne had made a point of severely reprimanding each supervisor for any rejects on his or her monthly operating statements, departmental reject charges had significantly declined for each department except the installing department. Much bitterness resulted from attempting to identify responsibility for rejects. Meanwhile, the total reject expense increased slightly.

Wayne was not overly concerned about the reject problem since the cost was incorporated into Walnut's bids. The corporate reject cost percentage of the total processing cost was determined and added to the bids as part of the corporate overhead charge. However, he wondered whether the answer to the reject problem might not be to subcontract installation. Wayne would have liked to spend more time on the reject problem, but felt that this time was better spent on the road soliciting orders.

Upon reviewing the 2001 financial statements with Wayne, Walnut's banker was also concerned that profits had not improved and, therefore, requested that a budget be prepared for 2002. Wayne argued that budgets simply were not feasible in his business because production and sales were a function of bids won and could not be predicted accurately.

On his banker's advice, Wayne engaged a management-accounting consultant to study the operations and problems of Walnut, and to submit a report on his findings. Wayne asked the consultant to include an analysis of the following in his report:

1. Walnut's management-accounting system.
2. The feasibility of budgeting for Walnut.
3. Control of rejects.
4. The bidding process.

Required: As the management-accounting consultant engaged by Wayne Andrews, prepare the requested report on Walnut's operations and problems.

EXHIBIT 6A-3

WALNUT FURNITURE LIMITED
Data on Recent Bids

	BID #SX5-19 100 STD. APTMTS. BATHROOM FIXTS.		BID #CX5-4 40 CUSTOMIZED APTMTS. BUILT-IN CUPBOARDS		
	EST. HOURS	BID AMOUNTS	EST. HOURS	ACTUAL HOURS	BID AMOUNTS
Processing costs:					
Fabricating ($235/hrs.)	120	$28,200	78	80	$18,330
Finishing ($74/hr.)	60	4,440	62	70	4,588
Installing ($87/hr.)	100	8,700	100	110	8,700
		41,340			31,618
Corporate overhead (17%)[1]		7,028			5,375
Total processing costs		48,368			36,993
Profit (10%)		4,837			3,699
Estimated bid amount		$53,205			$40,692
Actual bid amount		$53,000			$41,000
Won/Lost		Lost			Won
Successful bid amount		$49,000			$41,000
Next lowest bid		n/a			$45,000

[1]A standard adjustment of 7% to cover head-office expenses and an adjustment of 10% to cover reject costs (not including identified departmental reject costs) are added to total costs.
Other Information: The actual hours on standard contracts were usually close to the estimated hours.

EXHIBIT 6A-4

Summary of Bids Submitted and Won

	STANDARD				CUSTOMIZED			
	2001		2000		2001		2000	
$	#	(000)	#	(000)	#	(000)	#	(000)
Submitted	90	$3,950	80	$4,410	29	$1,135	35	$1,200
Won	7	350	4	210	15	590	21	715
% Won	8%		5%		52%		60%	

7

Process-Costing Systems

Cost accounting systems fulfil two major purposes: (1) they allocate costs to departments for *planning and control*, and (2) they apply costs to units of product for *product costing*. This chapter concentrates on a basic type of product costing called process costing and includes discussion of an adaptation of process costing called *backflush costing*. Appendix 7 describes hybrid-costing systems by illustrating operation costing.

The first part of this chapter presents the basic ideas of process costing. This coverage is sufficient for someone who wants just a general understanding of such systems. The second part introduces the complications arising from consideration of beginning inventories, which is important in applying process costing. The last part discusses backflush costing, a simplified version of process costing used by many companies that have adopted a just-in-time inventory system.

INTRODUCTION TO PROCESS COSTING

As noted in Chapter 6, all product costing uses averaging to determine costs per unit of production. The average unit cost may be relatively narrow, as in the production of a particular printing order in job-order costing. In contrast, the average may be broad, as in the production of beverages in process costing. *Process-costing systems* apply costs to like products that are usually mass-produced in continuous fashion through a series of production processes. These processes are often organized as separate departments, although a single department sometimes contains more than one process.

Process Costing Compared to Job Costing

OBJECTIVE 1

Explain the basic ideas underlying process costing and how those ideas differ from job costing.

Job costing and process costing are used for different types of products. Firms in industries such as printing, construction, and furniture manufacturing, where each unit or batch (job) of product is unique and easily identifiable, use job-order costing. Process costing is used where there is mass production through a sequence of several processes, such as mixing and cooking. Examples include chemicals, flour, glass, and toothpaste.

Exhibit 7-1 shows the major differences between job-order costing and process costing. Process costing requires several work-in-process accounts, one for each process or department. As goods move from process to process, their costs are transferred accordingly. Process manufacturing systems vary in design. The design shown in panel B of Exhibit 7-1 is *sequential*—units pass from process A to process B and so on until the product is finished. Many other designs are found in practice—each tailored to meet specific product requirements. For example, processes can be operated in *parallel* until final assembly. In this case Process A and Process B might occur at the same time to produce different parts of the finished product. Whatever the specific layout, the basic principles of process costing are the same.

The process-costing approach does not distinguish among individual units of product. Instead, accumulated costs for a period are divided by quantities produced during that period to get broad, average unit costs. Process costing is applied to nonmanufacturing activities as well as manufacturing activities. Examples include dividing the costs of giving provincial automobile driver's licence tests by the number of tests given and dividing the costs of a post office sorting department by the number of items sorted.

EXHIBIT 7-1

Comparison of Job-
Order and Process
Costing

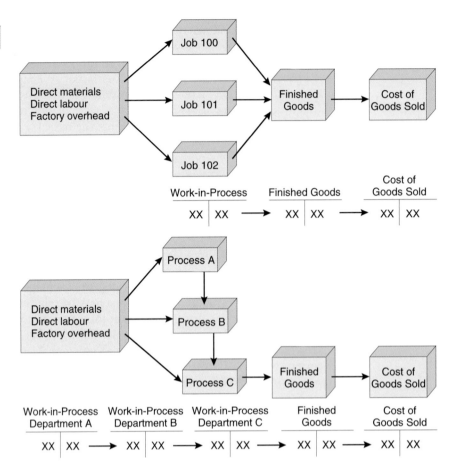

Process-costing systems are usually simpler and less expensive than job-order costing. Individual jobs do not exist. There are no job-cost records. The unit cost for inventory purposes is calculated by accumulating the costs of each processing department and dividing the total cost by an appropriate measure of output.

To get a feel for process costing, consider Magneta Midget Frozen Vegetables. It quick-cooks tiny carrots, beans, and so on before freezing them. As the following T-accounts show, its cooking costs (in millions of dollars)—divided by the kilograms of vegetables processed—are transferred to the freezing department:

Work-in-Process—Cooking				Work-in-Process—Freezing			
Direct materials	14	Transfer cost of		Cost		Transfer cost	
Direct labour	4	goods completed		transferred		of goods	
Factory overhead	8	to next		in from		completed to	
	26	department	24 →	cooking	24	finished	
				Additional		goods	25
				costs	3		
					27		
Ending inventory	2						
				Ending			
				inventory	2		

The journal entries for process-costing systems are similar to those for the job-order costing system. That is, direct materials, direct labour, and factory overhead are accounted for as before. However, now there is more than a single work-in-process account for all units being manufactured. There is one work-in-process account for each processing department, work-in-process—Cooking and work-in-process—Freezing, in our example. The foregoing data would be journalized as follows:

1. Work-in-process—Cooking	14	
Direct-materials inventory		14
To record direct materials used		
2. Work-in-process—Cooking	4	
Accrued payroll		4
To record direct labour		
3. Work-in-process—Cooking	8	
Factory overhead		8
To record factory overhead applied to product		
4. Work-in-process—Freezing	24	
Work-in-process—Cooking		24
To transfer goods from the cooking process		
5. Work-in-process—Freezing	3	
Accrued payroll		1
Factory overhead		2
To record direct labour and factory overhead applied to product		
6. Finished goods	25	
Work-in-process—Freezing		25
To transfer goods from the freezing process		

The central product-costing problem is how each department should compute the cost of goods transferred out and the cost of goods remaining in the department. If the same amount of work was done on each unit transferred and on each unit in ending inventory, the solution is easy. Total costs are simply divided by total units. However, if the units in the inventory are each partially completed, the product-costing system must distinguish between the costs of fully completed units transferred out and the costs of partially completed units not yet transferred.

APPLYING PROCESS COSTING

Consider another illustration. Suppose Parker Wooden Toys, Inc. buys wood as a direct material for its Forming Department. The department processes only one type of toy: marionettes. The marionettes are transferred to the Finishing Department, where hand shaping, strings, paint, and clothing are added.

The Forming Department manufactured 25,000 identical units during April, and its costs that month were as follows:

Direct materials		$ 70,000
Conversion costs		
Direct labour	$10,625	
Factory overhead	31,875	42,500
Costs to account for		$112,500

The unit cost of goods completed would simply be $112,500 \div 25,000 = \$4.50$. An itemization would show:

Direct materials, $70,000\div25,000	$2.80
Conversion costs, $42,500\div25,000	1.70
Unit cost of a whole completed marionette	$4.50

But what if not all 25,000 marionettes were completed during April? For example, assume that 5,000 were still in process at the end of April—only 20,000 were started and fully completed. All direct materials had been placed in process, but on average only 25 percent of the conversion costs had been applied to the 5,000 marionettes. How should the Forming Department calculate the cost of goods transferred and the cost of goods remaining in the ending work-in-process inventory? The answer lies in the following five key steps:

- **Step 1:** Summarize the flow of physical equivalent units.
- **Step 2:** Calculate output in terms of equivalent units.
- **Step 3:** Summarize the total costs to account for, which are the total debits in work in process (that is, the costs applied to work in process).
- **Step 4:** Calculate unit costs.
- **Step 5:** Apply costs to units completed and to units in the ending work in process.

Physical Units and Equivalent Units (Steps 1 and 2)

Step 1, as the first column in Exhibit 7-2 shows, tracks the physical units of production. How should the output for April be measured? Not as 25,000 units. Instead, the output was 20,000 fully completed units and 5,000 partially completed units. A partially completed unit is not a perfect substitute for a fully completed unit. Accordingly, output is usually stated in *equivalent units*, not physical units.

Equivalent Units. The number of completed units that could have been produced from the inputs applied.

Equivalent units are the number of completed units that could have been produced from the inputs applied. For example, four units, each one-half completed represent two equivalent units. If each unit had been one-fourth completed, the four units would have represented one equivalent unit. So, equivalent units are determined by multiplying physical units by the percent of completion.

EXHIBIT 7-2

Forming Department Output in Equivalent Units for the month ended April 30, 2001

| | (STEP 1) | (STEP 2) EQUIVALENT UNITS | |
FLOW OF PRODUCTION	PHYSICAL UNITS	DIRECT MATERIALS	CONVERSION COSTS
Started and completed	20,000	20,000	20,000
Work-in-process, ending inventory	5,000	5,000	1,250*
Units accounted for	25,000		
Work done to date		25,000	21,250

* 5,000 physical units x .25 degree of completion of conversion costs.

In our example, as Step 2 in Exhibit 7-2 shows, the output would be measured as 25,000 equivalent units of direct-materials cost but only 21,250 equivalent units of *conversion costs*. Conversion costs include all manufacturing costs other than direct materials. Why only 21,250 equivalent units of conversion costs but 25,000 of direct-material cost? Because direct materials had been added to all 25,000 units. In contrast, the direct materials had been added to all 5,000 units, which are 25 percent partially completed and would have been sufficient to complete 1,250 units in addition to the 20,000 units that were actually completed.

Of course, to compute equivalent units you need to estimate how much of a given resource was applied to units in process, which is not always an easy task. Some estimates are easier to make than others. For example, estimating the amount of direct materials used is fairly easy. However, how do you measure how much energy, maintenance labour, or supervision was used on a given unit? Conversion costs can involve a number of these hard-to-measure resources, which really leave you estimating both how much effort it takes to complete a unit and how much of that effort has been put into the units in process. Coming up with accurate estimates is further complicated in industries such as textiles, where there is a great deal of work in process at all time. To simplify estimation, some companies have decided that all work in process must be deemed either one-third, one-half, or two-thirds complete. In cases where continuous processing leaves roughly the same amount in process at the end of every month, work in process is ignored altogether and monthly production costs are assigned only to units completed and transferred out.

Measures in equivalent units are not confined to manufacturing situations. Such measures are a popular way of expressing workloads in terms of a common denominator. For example, radiology departments measure their output in terms of weight unit. Various X-ray procedures are ranked in terms of the time, supplies, and related costs devoted to each. A simple chest X-ray may receive a weight of one. But a skull X-ray may receive a weight of three because it uses three times the resources (for example, technicians' time) as a procedure with a weight of one. Another example is the expression by universities of students enroled in terms of full-time enrolment equivalents.

Calculation of Product Costs (Steps 3, 4, and 5)

Exhibit 7-3 is a production-cost report. It shows Steps 3, 4, and 5 of process costing. Step 3 summarizes the total costs to account for (that is, the total costs in, or debits to, work in process—Forming). Step 4 obtains unit costs by dividing total costs by the appropriate measures of equivalent units. The unit cost of a completed unit—material cost plus conversion costs—is $2.80 + $2.00 = $4.80.[1] Step 5 then uses these unit costs to apply costs to products.

From Exhibit 7-3, determine how the costs are applied to obtain an ending work in process of $16,500. The 5,000 physical units in process are fully completed in terms of direct materials. Therefore, the direct materials applied to work in process are 5,000 equivalent units times $2.80, or $14,000. In contrast, the

---

[1] Why is the unit cost $4.80 instead of the $4.50 calculated earlier in this chapter? Because the $42,500 conversion cost is spread over 21,250 units instead of 25,000 units.

			DETAILS	
			---	---
		TOTAL COSTS	**DIRECT MATERIALS**	**CONVERSION COSTS**
(Step 3)	Costs to account for	$112,500	$70,000	$42,500
(Step 4)	Divide by equivalent units		÷ 25,000	÷ 21,250
	Unit costs	$ 4.80	$ 2.80	$ 2.00
(Step 5)	Application of costs:			
	To units completed and transferred to the Finishing Department, 20,000 units ($4.80)	$ 96,000		
	To units not completed and still in process, April 30, 5,000 units:			
	Direct materials	$ 14,000	5,000 ($2.80)	
	Conversion costs	2,500		1,250 ($2.00)
	Work-in-process, April 30	$ 16,500		
	Total costs accounted for	$112,500		

5,000 physical units are 25 percent completed in terms of conversion costs. Therefore, the conversion costs applied to work-in-process are 1,250 equivalent units (25 percent of 5,000 physical units) times $2 or $2,500.

Journal entries for the data in our illustration are as follows:

1.	Work-in-process—Forming	70,000	
	Direct materials inventory		70,000
	Materials added to production in April		
2.	Work-in-process—Forming	10,625	
	Accrued payroll		10,625
	Direct labour in April		
3.	Work-in-process—Forming	31,875	
	Factory overhead		31,875
	Factory overhead applied in April		
4.	Work-in-process—Finishing	96,000	
	Work-in-process—Forming		96,000
	Cost of goods completed and transferred in April from Forming to Assembly		

The $112,500 added to the work-in-process—Forming account less the $96,000 transferred out leaves an ending balance of $16,500:

Work-in-Process—Forming			
1. Direct materials	$ 70,000	4. Transferred out to finishing	96,000
2. Direct labour	10,625		
3. Factory overhead	31,875		
Costs to account for	112,500		
Bal. April 30	$ 16,500		

PROCESS-COSTING SYSTEMS: A LOOK AT MOLSON BREWERIES

Molson Breweries
www.molson.com

Molson uses a hybrid cost accounting system, which has evolved from the many business pressures facing its management today, as well as certain unique aspects of Molson's operations.

Following is an outline of certain aspects of Molson's cost accounting system and certain complexities that arise in Molson's cost accounting system as a result of business issues and aspects unique to Molson and/or the brewing industry in Canada.

Inventory valuation:

Molson uses a weighted-average inventory valuation.

In practice, operating costs can often experience unusual fluctuations due to accounting corrections or operating abnormalities. To smooth out these peaks and valleys, Molson actually uses a three-month moving average. To accommodate time pressures, we apply the three-month moving average one month in arrears. For example, the January inventory will be valued at the weighted average of production costs for the months of October, November, and December.

Equivalent units:

The concept of equivalent units is not practical for Molson's cost accounting system.

In the packaging department, hundreds of units are completed, from start to finish, each minute. Thus, the cost difference between a fully complete unit and a partially complete unit, extended by the small number of partially complete units at any point in time, is not material enough to warrant the cost of accounting for equivalent units.

In the brewing department, most materials are added at (or near) the beginning of the brewing process and most of the brewing process (in terms of time) involves fermentation and storage with little labour being applied. Thus, it is not considered a material misstatement to value the physical inventory rather than equivalent units.

Though the concept of equivalent units is not significant to the Molson cost accounting system, the critical role of the monthly inventory reconciliation must be stressed. Central to Molson's cost accounting system is a tremendously detailed inventory reconciliation that starts at the first dip measurement in the brewing department and tracks every inventory movement until the beer reaches the customer. This inventory reconciliation includes several physical verifications throughout the production and distribution stages and accounts for every unit along the way. This is considered the single most important aspect of Molson's cost accounting system and the month-end cycle would stall if this reconciliation could not be accurately completed.

Factory overhead:

Brewery overhead (excluding administration) is inventoried in Molson's finished goods and WIP; however, this is not done as part of the monthly cost accounting system.

Year-over-year inventory levels and overhead costs are either stable or predictable. Thus, except for manageable variations, the overhead in inventory is relatively consistent from year to year and overhead costs expensed approximate overhead costs incurred. In addition, management finds it easier to monitor and control overhead costs when they're reported as period items in the P&L. Thus, Molson finds it more efficient to calculate overheads in inventory once a year (though forecasted inventory levels and overhead rates are monitored so there are no surprises).

Added complexities:

One complexity results from having multiple plants that supply a single finished goods inventory and market in certain provinces. This results in having to apply a weighted-average inventory value that averages the costs of multiple plants as well as multiple production periods (as discussed above).

continued

Another complexity results from Molson's substantial export business. Export brands often have a significantly different cost structure and, thus, an inventory value that averages domestic and export production can yield significant misstatements. Thus, Molson maintains separate cost accounting systems for domestic and export beer.

In addition, substantially different cost structures for our three packaging types (bottles, cans and kegs) require separate cost accounting systems.

Molson maintains separate profit and loss reports for each division. Often beer is produced in one division for sale in another. Thus, the cost accounting system of each division is designed to accommodate the inventoried value and cost of sales of imported beer.

Source: Written by Hugh Atkin, Vice President, Operations/Business Systems, Molson Breweries.

SUMMARY PROBLEM FOR YOUR REVIEW

Problem One

Taylor Plastics makes a variety of plastic products. Its Extruding Department had the following output and costs:

> Units:
>   Started and completed, 30,000 units
>   Started and still in process, 10,000 units, 100% completed for direct materials
>   but 60% completed for conversion costs
> Costs applied:
>   Total, $81,600; direct materials of $60,000 plus conversion costs of $21,600

Compute the cost of work completed and the cost of the ending inventory of work-in-process.

Solution

| | | | (STEP 2) EQUIVALENT UNITS | |
| | | (STEP 1) | | |
FLOW OF PRODUCTION	PHYSICAL UNITS	DIRECT MATERIALS	CONVERSION
Started and completed	30,000	30,000	30,000
Ending work-in-process	10,000	10,000*	6,000*
Units accounted for	40,000		
Work done to date		40,000	36,000

* 10,000 x 100% = 10,000; 10,000 × 60% = 6,000.

		TOTAL COSTS	DETAILS DIRECT MATERIALS	DETAILS CONVERSION COSTS
(Step 3)	Costs to account for	$81,600	$60,000	$21,600
(Step 4)	Divide by equivalent units		÷ 40,000	÷ 36,000
	Unit costs	$ 2.10*	$ 1.50	$ .60
(Step 5)	Application costs:			
	To units completed and transferred, 30,000 units ($2.10)	$63,000		
	To ending work-in-process, 10,000 units			
	Direct materials	$15,000	10,000($1.50)	
	Conversion costs	3,600		6,000($.60)
	Work-in-process, ending inventory	$18,600		
	Total costs accounted for	$81,600		

* Unit cost ($2.10) = Direct materials costs ($1.50) + Conversion costs ($.60).

EFFECTS OF BEGINNING INVENTORIES

OBJECTIVE 4

Demonstrate how the presence of beginning inventories affects the computations of unit costs under the weighted-average method.

When beginning inventories are present, product costing becomes more complicated. Suppose Parker Wooden Toys had 3,000 marionettes in work in process in its Forming Department on March 31. All direct materials had been placed in process, but on the average only 40 percent of the conversion costs had been applied to the 3,000 units. Because 25,000 units were worked on during April (20,000 units completed plus 5,000 still in process at the end of the month), and because there were 3,000 units in beginning inventory, 22,000 units must have been started in production during April.

The following table presents the data we use in our illustrations:

Units:
  Work-in-process, March 31, 3,000 units, 100% completed for
    materials but only 40% completed for conversion costs.
  Units started in April, 22,000.
  Units completed in April, 20,000.
  Work-in-process, April 30, 5,000 units, 100% completed for
    materials but only 25% completed for conversion costs.

Costs:		
Work-in-process, March 31:		
Direct materials	$7,500	
Conversion costs	2,125	$ 9,625
Direct materials added during April		70,000
Conversion costs added during April ($10,625 + $31,875)		42,500
Total costs to account for		$122,125

Note that the $122,125 total costs to account for include the $9,625 of beginning inventory in addition to the $112,500 added during April.

In the next section, we will discuss common inventory methods: the weight-average method and the first-in, first-out method. The five-step approach is recommended for both methods.

Weighted-Average Method

Weighted-Average (WA) Process-Costing Method. A process-costing method that adds the cost of (1) all work done in the current period to (2) the work done in the preceding period on the current period's beginning inventory of work in process and divides the total by the equivalent units of work done to date.

The **weighted-average (WA) process-costing method** determines total costs by adding the cost of (1) all work done in the current period to (2) the work done in the preceding period on the current period's beginning inventory of work in process. This total is divided by the equivalent units of work done to date, whether that work was done in the current period or previously.

Why is the term *weighted-average* method used to describe this method? Primarily because the unit costs used for applying costs to products are affected by the total costs incurred to date, regardless of whether those costs were incurred during or before the current period.

Exhibit 7-4 shows the first two steps in this method—the computation of physical units and equivalent units. Note that this illustration differs from the previous illustration in only one major respect, the presence of beginning work-in-process.

EXHIBIT 7-4

Forming Department Output in Equivalent Units for the month ended April 30, 2001 (Weighted-Average Method)

FLOW OF PRODUCTION	(STEP 1) PHYSICAL UNITS	(STEP 2) EQUIVALENT UNITS DIRECT MATERIALS	(STEP 2) EQUIVALENT UNITS CONVERSION COSTS
Work-in-process, March 31	3,000 (40%)*		
Started in April	22,000		
To account for	25,000		
Completed and transferred out during current period	20,000	20,000	20,000
Work-in-process, April 30	5,000 (25%)	5,000	1,250†
Units accounted for	25,000		
Work done to date		25,000	21,250

* Degrees of completion for conversion costs at the dates of inventories.
† .25 × 5,000 = 1,250.

The computation of equivalent units ignores whether all 25,000 units to account for came from beginning work in process, or were started in April, or some combination thereof. Exhibits 7-2 and 7-4 show the total work done to date, 25,000 equivalent units of direct materials and 21,250 units of conversion costs. The equivalent units for work done to date, which is the divisor for unit costs, is unaffected by whether all work was done in April or some before April on the March 31 inventory of work in process.

Exhibit 7-5 presents a production-cost report. Its pattern is similar to that in Exhibit 7-3. That is, the report summarizes Steps 3, 4, and 5 regarding computations of product costs.

The unit costs in Exhibit 7-5 are higher than those in Exhibit 7-3. Why? Because the equivalent units are the same, but the total costs include the costs incurred before April on the units in beginning inventory as well as those costs added during April.

The following recaps what we have learned so far in this chapter:

1. In the first simple example, we assumed no beginning or ending inventories of work-in-process. Thus, when the $112,500 of costs incurred during April were applied to the 25,000 units worked on and fully completed during April, the unit cost was $2.80 + $1.70 = $4.50.
2. However, in the next example, we assumed that some of the units were not fully completed by the end of the month. This reduced the equivalent units and thus increased the unit cost (Exhibit 15-3) to $2.80 + $2.00 = $4.80.
3. Then, in the latest example, we assumed that some of the units had also been worked on before April. The costs of that work are carried in work-in-process inventory, March 31. The addition of these costs (with no change in the equivalent units) increased the unit cost of work completed in April to $3.10 + $2.10 = $5.20.

EXHIBIT 7-5

Forming Department Production-Cost Report for the month ended April 30, 2001 (Weighted-Average Method)

		TOTALS	DETAILS DIRECT MATERIALS	DETAILS CONVERSION COSTS
(Step 3)	Work-in-process, March 31	$ 9,625	$ 7,500	$ 2,125
	Costs added currently	112,500	70,000	42,500
	Total costs to account for	$122,125	$77,500	$44,625
(Step 4)	Divisor, equivalent units			
	for work done to date		÷ 25,000	÷ 21,250
	Unit costs (weighted averages)	$ 5.20	$ 3.10	$ 2.10
(Step 5)	Application of costs:			
	Completed and transferred, 20,000			
	units ($5.20)	$104,000		
	Work-in-process, April 30, 5,000 units:			
	Direct materials	$ 15,500	5,000 ($3.10)	
	Conversion costs	2,625		1,250* ($2.10)
	Total work-in-process	$ 18,125		
	Total costs accounted for	$122,125		

* Equivalent units of work done. For more details, see Exhibit 7-4.

First-In, First-Out Method (FIFO)

First-In, First-Out (FIFO) Process-Costing Method. A process-costing method that sharply distinguishes the current work done from the previous work done on the beginning inventory of work-in-process.

The **first-in, first-out (FIFO) process-costing method** makes a sharp distinction between the current work done and the previous work done on the beginning inventory of work-in-process. The calculation of equivalent units is confined to the work done in the current period (April in this illustration).

Exhibit 7-6 presents Steps 1 and 2. The easiest way to compute equivalent units under the FIFO method is, first, to compute the costs associated with work done to date. Exhibit 7-6 shows these computations, which are exactly the same as in Exhibit 7-4. Second, deduct the work done *before* the current period. The remainder is the work done *during* the current period, which is the key to computing the unit costs by the FIFO method.

Exhibit 7-7 is the production-cost report. It presents Steps 3, 4, and 5. The $9,439 beginning inventory balance is kept separate from current costs. The calculations of equivalent unit costs are confined to costs added in April only.

EXHIBIT 7-6

Forming Department
Output in Equivalent
Units for the Month
Ended April 30, 2001
(FIFO Method)

SAME AS EXHIBIT 7-4 ▼ FLOW OF PRODUCTION	(STEP 1) PHYSICAL UNITS	(STEP 2) EQUIVALENT UNITS DIRECT MATERIALS	CONVERSION COSTS
Work-in-process, March 31	3,000 (40%)		
Started in April	22,000		
To account for	25,000		
Completed and transferred out	20,000	20,000	20,000
Work-in-process, April 30	5,000 (25%)*	5,000	1,250[†]
Units accounted for	25,000		
Work done to date		25,000	21,250
Less: Equivalent units of work from previous periods included in beginning inventory		3,000[††]	1,200[§]
Work done in current period only		22,000	20,050

*Degrees of completion for conversion costs at the dates of inventories.
[†] 5,000 x .25 = 1,250.
[††] 3,000 x 1.00 = 3,000.
[§] 3,000 x .40 = 1,200.

EXHIBIT 7-7

Forming Department
Production-Cost Report
for the Month Ended
April 30, 2001
(FIFO Method)

		TOTALS	DETAILS DIRECT MATERIALS	CONVERSION COSTS
(Step 3)	Work-in-process, March 31	$ 9,439	(work done before April)	
	Costs added currently	112,686	$70,180	$42,506
	Total costs to account for	$122,125		
(Step 4)	Divisor, equivalent units of work done in April only		22,000*	20,050*
	Unit costs (for FIFO basis)	$ 5.31	$ 3.19	$ 2.12
(Step 5)	Application of costs:			
	Work-in-process, April 30:			
	Direct materials	$ 15,950	5,000 ($3.19)	
	Conversion costs	2,650		1,250*($2.12)
	Total work-in-process	18,600		
	(5,000 units)			
	Completed and transferred out			
	(20,000 units),			
	$122,125 – $18,600	103,525[†]		
	Total costs accounted for	$122,125		

* Equivalent units of work done. See Exhibit 7-6 for more details.
[†] Check: work in process, March 31 $ 9,439
      Additional costs to complete, conversion costs of
        60% of 3,000 × $2.12 =   3,816
      Started and completed, 22,000 – 5,000 = 17,000;
        17,000 × $5.31 =   90,270
      Total cost transferred $103,525
      Unit cost transferred, $103,525 ÷ 20,000 = $5.17625

OBJECTIVE 5

Demonstrate how the
presence of beginning
inventories affects the
computation of unit
costs under the first-in,
first-out method.

The bottom half of Exhibit 7-7 shows two ways to compute the cost of goods completed and transferred out. The first and fastest way is to compute the $18,600 ending work-in-process and then deduct it from the $122,125 total costs to account for, obtaining $103,525. To check for accuracy, it is advisable to use a second way as well: compute the cost of goods transferred in the detailed manner displayed in the footnote in Exhibit 7-7.

Differences Between FIFO and Weighted-Average Methods

The key difference between FIFO and weighted-average methods is the calculation of equivalent units:

- FIFO—Equivalent units are based on the work done in the current period only.
- Weighted-average—Equivalent units are the work done to date, including the earlier work done on the current period's beginning inventory of work in process.

These differences in equivalent units lead to differences in unit costs. Accordingly, there are differences in costs applied to goods completed and still in process. In our example, the FIFO method results in a larger work-in-process inventory on April 30, and a smaller April cost of goods transferred out:

	WEIGHTED AVERAGE*	FIFO†
Cost of goods transferred out	$104,000	$103,525
Ending work in process	18,125	18,600
Total costs accounted for	$122,125	$122,125

* From Exhibit 7-5.
† From Exhibit 7-7.

Differences in unit costs between FIFO and weighted-average methods are normally insignificant because (a) changes in prices of material, labour wage rates, and other manufacturing costs from month to month tend to be small, and (b) changes in the volume of production and inventory levels also tend to be small.

The FIFO method involves more detailed computations than the weighted-average method. That is why FIFO is almost never used in practice in process costing *for product-costing purposes*. However, the FIFO *equivalent units* for current work done are essential *for planning and control purposes*. Why? Because they isolate the output for one particular period. Consider our example. The FIFO computations of equivalent units help managers to measure the efficiency of April's performance independently from March's performance. Thus budgets or standards for each month's departmental costs can be compared against actual results in light of the actual work done during any given month.

Transferred-in Costs

Transferred-In Costs. The costs of the items a department receives from another department.

Many companies that use process costing have sequential production processes. For example, Parker Wooden Toys transfers the items completed in its Forming Department to the Finishing Department. The Finishing Department would call the costs of the items it receives **transferred-in costs**—costs incurred in a previous department for items that have been received by a subsequent department. They are similar to, but not identical to, additional direct materials costs. Because transferred-in costs are a combination of all types of costs (direct materials and conversion costs) incurred in previous departments, they should not be called a direct material cost in a subsequent department.

We account for transferred-in costs in the same manner as when we account for direct materials, with one exception: they are kept separate from the direct materials added in the department. Therefore, reports such as Exhibits 7-5 and 7-7 will include three columns of costs instead of two: transferred-in costs, direct materials costs, and conversion costs. The total unit cost will be the sum of all three types of unit costs.

SUMMARY PROBLEM FOR YOUR REVIEW

Problem Two

Consider the Cooking Department of Middleton Foods, a British food-processing company. Compute the cost of work completed and the cost of the ending inventory of work-in-process, using the (1) weighted-average (WA) method and (2) FIFO method.

Units:
  Beginning work-in-process, 5,000 units, 100% completed for materials, 40% completed for conversion costs.
  Started during month, 28,000 units
  Completed during month, 31,000 units
  Ending work-in-process, 2,000 units, 100% completed for materials, 50% for conversion costs.

Costs:

Beginning work-in-process:		
Direct materials	£8,060	
Conversion costs	1,300	£ 9,360
Direct materials added in current month		41,440
Conversion costs added in current month		14,700
Total cost to account for		£65,500

Solution

	(STEP 1)	(STEP 2) EQUIVALENT UNITS	
FLOW OF PRODUCTION	PHYSICAL UNITS	MATERIAL	CONVERSION COSTS
Completed and transferred out	31,000	31,000	31,000
Ending work-in-process	2,000	2,000*	1,000*
1. Equivalent units, WA	33,000	33,000	32,000
Less: Beginning work-in-process	5,000	5,000†	2,000†
2. Equivalent units, FIFO	28,000	28,000	30,000

* 2,000 × 100% = 2,000; 2,000 × 50% = 1,000
† 5,000 × 100% = 5,000; 5,000 × 40% = 2,000

Note especially that the work done to date is the basis for computing the equivalent units under the weighted-average method. In contrast, the basis for computing the equivalent units under the FIFO method is the work done in the current period only.

1.

WEIGHTED-AVERAGE METHOD	TOTAL COST	DIRECT MATERIALS	CONVERSION COSTS
Beginning work-in-process	£ 9,360	£ 8,060	£ 1,300
Costs added currently	56,140	41,440	14,700
Total cost to account for	£65,500	£49,500	£16,000
Equivalent units		÷ 33,000	÷ 32,000
Unit costs	£ 2.00	£ 1.50	£ 0.50
Transferred out, 31,000 x £2.00	£62,000		
Ending work-in-process:			
Direct materials	£ 3,000	2,000(£1.50)	
Conversion cost	500		1,000(£.50)
Total work-in-process	£ 3,500		
Total costs accounted for	£65,500		

2.

FIFO METHOD			
Beginning work-in-process	£ 9,360	(work done before month)	
Costs added currently	56,140	£41,440	£14,700
Total costs to account for	£65,500		
Equivalent units		÷ 28,000	÷ 30,000
Unit costs	£ 1.97	£ 1.48	£ 0.49
Ending work-in-process:			
Direct materials	£ 2,960	2,000(£1.48)	
Conversion cost	490		1,000(£.49)
Total work-in-process	£ 3,450		
Transferred out, £65,500 - £3,450	62,050*		
Total costs accounted for	£65,500		

* Check:

Beginning work-in-process	£ 9,360
Costs to complete, 60% x 5,000 x £.49	1,470
Started and completed,	
(31,000 - 5,000)(£1.48 + £.49)	51,220
Total cost transferred	£62,050

Unit cost transferred, £62,050 ÷ 31,000 = £2.00161

PROCESS COSTING IN A JUST-IN-TIME SYSTEM: BACKFLUSH COSTING

Backflush Costing. An accounting system that applies costs to products only when the production is complete.

Tracking costs through various stages of inventory—raw materials, work in process, and finished goods inventory—makes accounting systems complex. If there were no inventories, all costs would be charged directly to cost of goods sold, and accounting systems would be much simpler. Organizations using just-in-time production systems usually have very small inventories, and they may not want to bear the expense of a system that traces costs through all the inventory accounts. Such firms can use **backflush costing**, an accounting system that applies costs to products only when the production is complete.

Principles of Backflush Costing

OBJECTIVE 6

Use backflush costing with a just-in-time production system.

Backflush costing has only two categories of costs: materials and conversion costs. Its unique feature is an absence of a work-in-process account. Actual material costs are entered into a *material inventory account*, and actual labour and overhead costs are entered into a *conversion costs account*. Costs are transferred from these two temporary accounts directly into finished goods inventories. Some backflush systems even eliminate the finished goods inventory account and transfer costs directly to cost of goods sold, if goods are not kept in inventory but are shipped immediately upon completion. Backflush systems assume that production follows so soon after the application of conversion activities that balances in the conversion costs accounts always should remain near zero. Thus, costs are transferred out almost immediately after being initially recorded.

Example of Backflush Costing

Speaker Technology Inc. (STI) produces speakers for automobile stereo systems. STI recently introduced a just-in-time production system and backflush costing. Consider the July production for speaker model AX27. The standard material cost per unit of AX27 is $14, and the standard unit conversion cost is $21. During July, STI purchased materials for $5,600, incurred conversion costs of $8,400, which included all labour costs and manufacturing overhead, and completed and sold 400 units of AX27.

Backflush costing is accomplished in three steps:

1. Record actual materials and conversion costs. For simplicity, we assume for now that actual materials and conversion costs were identical to the standard costs. As materials are purchased, backflush systems add their cost to the materials inventory account:

Materials inventory	5,600	
Accounts payable (or cash)		5,600
To record material purchases		

Similarly, as direct labour and manufacturing overhead costs are incurred, they are added to the conversion costs account.

Conversion costs	8,400	
Accrued wages and other accounts		8,400
To record conversion costs incurred		

2. Apply costs to completed units. When production is complete, costs from materials inventory and conversion costs accounts are transferred directly to finished goods based on the number of units completed and a standard cost of each unit:

Finished goods inventory (400 x $35)	14,000	
Materials inventory		5,600
Conversion costs		8,400
To record costs of completed production		

Because of short production cycle times, there is little lag between additions to the conversion costs account and transfers to finished goods. The conversion costs account, therefore, remains near zero.

3. Record cost of goods sold during the period. The standard cost of the items sold is transferred from finished goods inventory to cost of goods sold:

Cost of goods sold	14,000	
Finished goods inventory		14,000
To record cost of 400 units sold @ $35 per unit		

Suppose completed units are delivered immediately to customers, so that finished goods inventories are negligible. Steps 2 and 3 can then be combined and the finished goods inventory account eliminated:

Cost of goods sold	14,000	
Material inventories		5,600
Conversion costs		8,400

What if actual costs added to the conversion costs accounts do not equal the standard amounts that are transferred to finished goods inventory? Variances are treated like overapplied or underapplied overhead. Backflush systems assume that conversion costs account balances should be approximately zero at all times. Any remaining balance in the account at the end of an accounting period is charged to cost of goods sold. Suppose actual conversion costs for July had been $8,600 and the amount transferred to finished goods (that is, applied to the product) was $8,400. The $200 balance in the conversion costs account at the end of the month would be written off to cost of goods sold:

Cost of goods sold	200	
Conversion costs		200
To recognize underapplied conversion costs		

SUMMARY PROBLEM FOR YOUR REVIEW

Problem Three

The most extreme (and simplest) version of backflush costing makes product costing entries at only one point. Suppose Speaker Technology Inc. (STI) had no materials inventory account (in addition to no work in process inventory account). Materials are not "purchased" until they are needed for production. Therefore, STI enters both materials and conversion costs directly into its finished goods inventory account.

Prepare journal entries (without explanation) and T-accounts for July's production of 400 units. Material purchases totalled $5,600, and conversion costs were $8,400. Why might a company use this extreme type of backflush costing?

Solution

In one step, material and conversion costs are applied to finished goods inventories:

Finished goods inventories	14,000	
Accounts payable		5,600
Wages payable and other accounts		8,400

Finished Goods Inventories		Accounts Payable, Wages Payable, and Other Accounts	
Materials	5,600		5,600
Conversion costs	8,400		8,400

This example of backflush costing illustrates a system that is simple and inexpensive. It provides reasonably accurate product costs if (1) material inventories are low (most likely because of just-in-time delivery schedules), and (2) production cycle times are short so that at any time only inconsequential amounts of material costs or conversion costs have been incurred for products that are not yet complete.

HIGHLIGHTS TO REMEMBER

Process costing is used for inventory costing when there is continuous mass production of like units. The key concept in process costing is that of equivalent units—the number of fully completed units that could have been produced from the inputs applied. The concept of equivalent units applies to both manufacturing and nonmanufacturing settings.

Five basic steps may be used to solve process-cost problems.

1. Summarize the flow of physical units.
2. Calculate output in terms of equivalent units.
3. Summarize the total costs to account for.
4. Calculate unit costs.
5. Apply costs to units completed and to units in the ending work in process.

Process costing is complicated by the presence of beginning inventories. Two process-costing methods can be used when these complications arise: first-in, first-out (FIFO) and weighted-average (WA). The first-in, first-out method focuses on the work done only in the current period, while the weighted-average method focuses on the work done in previous periods on the current period's beginning inventory in addition to work done in the current period.

Many companies with just-in-time production systems use backflush costing. Such systems have no work-in-process inventory account and apply costs to products only after the production process is complete.

APPENDIX 7: HYBRID SYSTEMS—OPERATION COSTING

Hybrid-Costing System.
An accounting system that is a blend of ideas from job costing and process costing.

Job costing and process costing are extremes along a continuum of potential costing systems. Each company designs its own accounting system to fit its underlying production activities. Many companies use **hybrid-costing systems**, which are blends of ideas from both job costing and process costing. This appendix discusses one of many possible hybrid costing systems, *operation costing*.

Nature of Operation Costing

OBJECTIVE 7

Generate costs using an operation-costing system.

Operation Costing. A hybrid-costing system often used in the batch or group manufacturing of goods that have some common characteristics plus some individual characteristics.

Operation costing is a hybrid-costing system often used in batch or group manufacturing that have some common characteristics plus some individual characteristics. Examples of such goods include personal computers, clothing, and semiconductors. Such products are specifically identified by work orders. The goods are often variations of a single design but require a varying sequence of standardized operations. For instance, men's suits may differ, requiring various materials and hand operations. Similarly, a textile manufacturer may apply special chemical treatments (such as waterproofing) to some fabrics but not to others.

Operation costing may entail mass production, but there is sufficient product variety to have products scheduled in different batches or groups, each requiring a particular sequence of operations.

An *operation* is a standardized method or technique that is repetitively performed, regardless of the distinguishing features of the finished product. Examples include cutting, planing, sanding, painting, and chemical treating. Products proceed through the various operations in groups as specified by work orders or production orders. These work orders list the necessary direct materials and the step-by-step operations required to make the finished product.

Suppose a clothing manufacturer produces two lines of blazers. The wool blazers use better materials and undergo more operations than the polyester blazers, as follows:

	WORK ORDER A	WORK ORDER B
Direct materials	Wool Satin lining Bone buttons	Polyester Rayon lining Plastic buttons

Operations	1. Cutting cloth
	2. Checking edges
	3. Sewing body
	4. Checking seams
	5. —
	
	6. Sewing collars and
	  and lapels by hand
		1. Cutting cloth
		2. —
		3. Sewing body
		4. —
		5. Sewing collars and lapels
		  by machine
		6. —

The costs of the blazers are compiled by work order. As in job costing, the direct materials—different for each work order—are specifically identified with the appropriate order. Conversion costs—direct labour plus factory overhead—are initially compiled for each operation. A cost driver, such as the number of units processed or minutes or seconds used, is identified for each operation, and a conversion cost per unit of cost-driver activity is computed. Then conversion costs are applied to products in a manner similar to the application of factory overhead in a job-cost system.

Example of Operation Costing Entries

Suppose our manufacturer has two work orders, one for 100 wool blazers and the other for 200 polyester blazers as follows:

	WORK ORDER A	WORK ORDER B
Number of blazers	100	200
Direct materials	$2,500	$3,100
Conversion costs:		
1. Cutting cloth	600	1,200
2. Checking edges	300	—
3. Sewing body	500	1,000
4. Checking seams	600	—
5. Sewing collars and lapels by machine	—	800
6. Sewing collars and lapels by hand	700	—
Total manufacturing costs	$5,200	$6,100

Direct labour and factory overhead vanish as separate classifications in an operation-costing system. The sum of these costs is most frequently called conversion cost. The conversion cost is applied to products based on the company's budgeted rate for performing each operation. For example, suppose the conversion costs of Operation 1, cutting cloth, are driven by machine hours and are budgeted for the year as follows:

$$\text{budgeted rate for applying conversion costs for cutting cloth to product} = \frac{\text{budgeted conversion cost for cutting cloth for the year (direct labour, power, repairs, supplies, other factory overhead of this operation)}}{\text{budgeted machine-hours for the year for cutting cloth}}$$

$$\text{rate per machine-hour} = \frac{\$150,000 + \$450,000}{20,000 \text{ hours}} = \$30 \text{ per machine-hour}$$

As goods are manufactured, conversion costs are applied to the work orders by multiplying the $30 hourly rate times the number of machine hours used for cutting cloth.

If 20 machine hours are needed to cut the cloth for the 100 wool blazers, then the conversion cost involved is $600 (20 hours × $30 per hour). For the 200 polyester blazers, the conversion cost for cutting the cloth is twice as much, $1,200 (40 hours × $30), because each blazer takes the same cutting time and there are twice as many polyester blazers.

Summary journal entries for applying costs to the polyester blazers follow. (Entries for the wool blazers would be similar.)

The journal entry for the requisition of direct materials for the 200 polyester blazers is as follows:

Work-in-process inventory (polyester blazers) . . .	3,100	
Direct materials inventory		3,100

Direct labour and factory overhead are subparts of a conversion costs account in an operation-costing system. Suppose actual conversion costs of $3,150 were entered into the conversion costs account:

Conversion costs	3,150	
Accrued payroll, accumulated amortization, accounts payable etc.		3,150

The application of conversion costs to products in operation costing is similar to the application of factory overhead in job-order costing. A budgeted rate per unit of cost-driver activity is used. To apply conversion costs to the 200 polyester blazers, the following summary entry is made for Operations 1, 3, and 5 (cutting cloth, sewing body, and sewing collars and lapels by machine):

Work-in-process inventory (polyester blazers) . . .	3,000	
Conversion costs, cutting cloth		1,200
Conversion costs, sewing body		1,000
Conversion costs, sewing collars and lapels		
by machine		800

After posting, work-in-process inventory has the following debit balance:

Work-in-Process Inventory (polyester blazers)		
Direct materials	3,100	
Conversion costs applied	3,000	
Balance	6,100	

As the blazers are completed, their cost is transferred to finished-goods inventory in the usual manner.

Any overapplication or underapplication of conversion costs is disposed of at the end of the year in the same manner as overapplied or underapplied overhead in a job-order costing system. In this case, conversion costs has been debited for actual cost of $3,150 and credited for costs applied of $3,000. The debit balance of $150 indicates that conversion costs are underapplied.

ACCOUNTING VOCABULARY

backflush costing *p. 299*
equivalent units *p. 288*
first-in, first-out (FIFO)
    process-costing method *p. 295*
hybrid-costing systems *p. 302*

operation costing *p. 303*
transferred-in costs *p. 297*
weighted-average(WA)
    process-costing method *p. 294*

ASSIGNMENT MATERIAL

QUESTIONS

Q7-1   Give three examples of industries where process-costing systems are probably used.

Q7-2   Give three examples of non-profit organizations where process-costing systems are probably used.

Q7-3   What is the central product-costing problem in process costing?

Q7-4   "There are five key steps in process-cost accounting." What are they?

Q7-5   Identify the major distinction between the first two and the final three steps of the five major steps in accounting for process costs.

Q7-6 Suppose a university has 10,000 full-time students and 5,000 half-time students. Using the concept of equivalent units, compute the number of "full-time equivalent" students.

Q7-7 "Equivalent units are the work done to date." What method of process costing is being described?

Q7-8 Present an equation that describes the physical flow in process costing, where there are beginning inventories in work-in-process.

Q7-9 "The beginning inventory is regarded as if it were a batch of goods separate *and* distinct from the goods started and completed by a process during the current period." What method of process costing is being described?

Q7-10 Why is "work done in the current period only" a key measurement of equivalent units?

Q7-11 "The total conversion costs are divided by the equivalent units for the work done to date." Does this quotation describe the weighted-average method or does it describe FIFO?

Q7-12 "Ordinarily, the differences in unit costs under FIFO and weighted-average methods are insignificant." Do you agree? Explain.

Q7-13 "FIFO process costing is helpful for planning and control even if it is not used for product costing." Do you agree? Explain.

Q7-14 How are transferred-in costs similar to direct materials costs? How are they different?

Q7-15 "Backflush costing systems only work for companies using a just-in-time production system." Do you agree? Explain.

Q7-16 Explain what happens in a backflush costing system when the amount of actual conversion cost in a period exceeds the amount applied to the products completed that period.

Q7-17 Give three examples of industries that probably use operation costing.

Q7-18 "In operation costing or activity costing, average conversion costs are applied to products in a manner similar to the application of factory overhead in a job-cost system." Do you agree? Explain.

PROBLEMS

P7-1 BASIC PROCESS COSTING. A department of Jamestown Textiles produces cotton fabric. All direct materials are introduced at the start of the process. Conversion costs are incurred uniformly throughout the process.

In April there was no beginning inventory. Units started, completed, and transferred, 650,000. Units in process, April 30, 220,000. Each unit in ending work in process was 60 percent converted. Costs incurred during April: direct materials, $3,741,000; conversion costs, $860,200.

1. Compute the total work done in equivalent units and the unit cost for April.
2. Compute the cost of units completed and transferred. Also compute the cost of units in ending work in process.

P7-2 UNEVEN FLOW. One department of Wamego Technology Company manufactures basic hand-held calculators. Various materials are added at different stages of the process. The outer front sheet and the carrying case, which represent 10 percent of the total material cost, are added at the final step of the assembly process. All other materials are considered to be "in process" by the time the calculator reaches a 50 percent stage of completion.

During 2001, 74,000 calculators were started in production. At year-end, 6,000 calculators were in various stages of completion, but all of them were beyond the 50 percent stage and on the average they were regarded as being 70 percent completed.

The following costs were incurred during the year: direct materials, $205,520; conversion costs, $397,100.

1. Prepare a schedule of physical units and equivalent units.
2. Tabulate the unit costs, cost of goods completed, and cost of ending work in process.

P7-3   BASIC PROCESS COSTING.   Celltel Ltd. produces cellular phones in large quantities. For simplicity, assume that the company has two departments, Assembly and Testing. The manufacturing costs in the Assembly Department during February were

Direct materials added		$ 57,000
Conversion costs		
Direct labour	$50,000	
Factory overhead	40,000	90,000
Assembly costs to account for		$147,000

There was no beginning inventory of work-in-process. Suppose work on 19,000 phones was begun in the Assembly Department during February, but only 17,000 phones were fully completed. All the parts had been made or placed in process, but only half the labour had been completed for each of the phones still in process.

1. Compute the equivalent units and unit costs for February.
2. Compute the costs of units completed and transferred to the Testing Department. Also compute the cost of the ending work-in-process.
3. Prepare summary journal entries for the use of direct materials, direct labour, and factory overhead applied. Also prepare a journal entry for the transfer of goods completed and transferred. Show the postings to the work-in-process account.

P7-4   BASIC PROCESS COSTING.   Hasoon Company produces digital watches in large quantities. The manufacturing costs of the Assembly Department were:

Direct materials added		$ 1,620,000
Conversion costs		
Direct labour	$475,000	
Factory overhead	275,000	750,000
Assembly costs to account for		$2,370,000

For simplicity, assume that this is a two-department company—assembly and finishing. There was no beginning work-in-process.

Suppose 900,000 units were begun in the Assembly Department. There were 600,000 units completed and transferred to the Finishing Department. The

300,000 units in ending work in process were fully completed regarding direct materials but half completed regarding conversion costs.

1. Compute the equivalent units and unit costs in the Assembly Department.
2. Compute the costs of units completed and transferred to the Finishing Department. Also compute the cost of the ending work-in-process in the Assembly Department.
3. Prepare summary journal entries for the use of direct materials, direct labour, and factory overhead applied. Also prepare a journal entry for the transfer of goods completed and transferred. Show the postings to the work-in-process—Assembly Department account.

P7-5 PHYSICAL UNITS. Fill in the unknowns in physical units:

	CASE	
FLOW OF PRODUCTION	**A**	**B**
Work-in-process, beginning inventory	1,500	4,000
Started	6,500	? 7300
Completed and transferred	? 6 000	8,000
Work-in-process, ending inventory	2,000	3,300

P7-6 FLOW OF PRODUCTION, FIFO. Fill in the unknowns in physical or equivalent units:

		EQUIVALENT UNITS	
	PHYSICAL	**DIRECT**	**CONVERSION**
FLOW OF PRODUCTION	**UNITS**	**MATERIALS**	**COSTS**
Beginning work-in-process	1,000 (50%)		
Started	?		
To account for	36,000		
Completed and transferred out	33,000	33,000	33,000
Ending work-in-process	? (40%)*	?	?
Units accounted for	?		
Work done to date		?	?
Equivalent units in beginning inventory		?	?
Work done in current period only		?	?

* Degree of completion of conversion costs at dates of inventory. Assume that all materials are added at the beginning of the process.

P7-7 EQUIVALENT UNITS. The production department of Garcia Paints Inc. had the following flow of litres of latex paint for the month of April:

Litres completed:	
From work-in-process on April 1	5,000
From April production	25,000
	30,000

Direct materials are added at the beginning of the process. Units of work-in-process at April 30 were 10,000. The work in process at April 1 was 30 percent complete regarding conversion costs, and the work-in-process at April 30 was 50 percent complete regarding conversion costs. What are the equivalent units (litres) of production for (a) direct materials and (b) conversion costs for the month of April using the FIFO method?

P7-8 EQUIVALENT UNITS. Fill in the unknowns.

| | (STEP 1) PHYSICAL UNITS | (STEP 2) EQUIVALENT UNITS | |
FLOW OF PRODUCTION IN UNITS		DIRECT MATERIALS	CONVERSION COSTS
Work-in-process, beginning inventory	20,000*		
Started	45,000		
To account for	65,000		
Completed and transferred out	?	?	?
Work-in-process, ending inventory	2,000†	?	?
Units accounted for	65,000		
Work done to date		?	?
Less: Equivalent units of work from previous periods included in beginning inventory		?	?
Work done in current period only (FIFO method)		?	?

* Degree of completion: direct materials, 80%; conversion costs 40%.
† Degree of completion: direct materials, 40%; conversion costs, 10%.

P7-9 COMPUTE EQUIVALENT UNITS. Consider the following data for 2002:

	PHYSICAL UNITS
Started in 2002	80,000
Completed in 2002	90,000
Ending inventory, work-in-process	10,000
Beginning inventory, work-in-process	20,000

The beginning inventory was 80 percent complete regarding direct materials and 40 percent complete regarding conversion costs. The ending inventory was 20 percent complete regarding direct materials and 30 percent complete regarding conversion costs.

Prepare a schedule of equivalent units for the work done to date and the work done during 2002 only.

P7-10 FIFO AND UNIT DIRECT MATERIAL COSTS. The Fujita Company uses the FIFO process-cost method. Consider the following for July:

- Beginning inventory, 15,000 units, 70 percent completed regarding direct materials, which cost ¥89,250,000.
- Units completed, 80,000.
- Cost of materials placed in process during July, ¥580,000,000.
- Ending inventory, 5,000 units, 60 percent completed regarding materials.

Compute the direct-material cost per equivalent unit for the work done in July only.

P7-11 FIFO METHOD, CONVERSION COST. Given the following information, compute the unit conversion cost for the month of February for the Benjamin Company, using the FIFO process-cost method. Show details of your calculations.

- Units completed, 45,000.
- Conversion cost in beginning inventory, $30,000
- Beginning inventory, 10,000 units with 75 percent of conversion cost.
- Ending inventory, 15,000 units with 30 percent of conversion cost.
- Conversion costs put into production in February, $222,600.

P7-12 WEIGHTED-AVERAGE PROCESS-COSTING METHOD. The Rainbow Paint Co. uses a process-cost system. Materials are added at the beginning of a particular process, and conversion costs are incurred uniformly. Work-in-process at the beginning of the month is 40 percent complete; at the end, 20 percent. One litre of material makes one litre of product. Data are as follows:

Beginning inventory	550 litres
Direct material added	7,150 litres
Ending inventory	400 litres
Conversion costs incurred	$34,986
Cost of direct materials added	$65,340
Conversion costs, beginning inventory	$ 1,914
Cost of direct materials, beginning inventory	$ 3,190

1. Use the weighted-average method. Prepare a schedule of output in equivalent units and a schedule of application of costs to products. Show the cost of goods completed and of ending work in process.
2. Prepare summary journal entries for the use of direct materials and conversion costs. Also prepare a journal entry for the transfer of goods completed, assuming that the goods are transferred to another department.

P7-13 FIFO COMPUTATIONS. Refer to the preceding problem, P7-12. Using FIFO, answer the same questions.

P7-14 WEIGHTED-AVERAGE PROCESS COSTING METHOD. The Magnotta Company manufactures electric drills. Material is introduced at the beginning of the process in the Assembly Department. Conversion costs are applied uniformly throughout the process. As the process is completed, goods are immediately transferred to the Finishing Department.

Data for the Assembly Department for the month of July 2002 follow:

Work-in-process, June 30, 100% completed for direct materials, but only 25% completed for conversion costs, $175,500 (consisting of $138,000 materials and $37,500 conversion costs)	10,000 units
Units started during July	80,000 units
Units completed during July	70,000 units
Work-in-process, July 31, 100% completed for direct materials, but only 50% completed for conversion costs:	20,000 units
Direct materials added during July	$852,000
Conversion costs added during July	$634,500

1. Compute the total cost of goods transferred out of the department during July. Compute the total costs of the ending work-in-process. Prepare a production-cost report or a similar orderly tabulation of your work. Assume weighted-average product costing.
2. Prepare summary journal entries of the use of direct materials and conversion costs. Also prepare a journal entry for the transfer of the goods completed and transferred from the Assembly Department to the Finishing Department.

P7-15 FIFO METHOD.   Refer to problem P7-14. Using FIFO costing, answer the same questions.

P7-16 NON-PROFIT PROCESS COSTING.   Canada Customs and Revenue Agency must process millions of income tax returns yearly. When the taxpayer sends in a return, documents such as withholding statements and cheques are matched against the data. Then various other inspections of the data are conducted. Of course, some returns are more complicated than others, so the expected time allowed to process a return is geared to an "average" return.

Some work-measurement experts have been closely monitoring the processing at a particular branch. They are seeking ways to improve productivity.

Suppose three-million returns were received on April 30. On May 17, the work-measurement teams discovered that all supplies (punched cards, inspection check sheets, and so on) had been affixed to the returns, but 40 percent of the returns still had to undergo a final inspection. The other returns were fully completed.

1. Suppose the final inspection represents 25 percent of the overall processing time in this process. Compute the total work done in terms of equivalent units.
2. The materials and supplies consumed were $600,000. For these calculations, materials and supplies are regarded just like direct materials. The conversion costs were $4,725,000. Compute the unit costs of materials and supplies and of conversion.
3. Compute the cost of the tax returns not yet completely processed.

P7-17 PROCESS VERSUS ACTIVITY-BASED.   Consider the potato chip production process at a company such as Frito-Lay. Frito-Lay uses a continuous-flow technology that is suited for high volumes of product. At the Plano, Texas, facility, between six- and seven-thousand pounds of potato chips are produced each hour. The plant operates 24 hours a day. It takes 30 minutes to completely produce a bag of potato chips from the raw potato to the packed end-product.

1. What product and process characteristics of potato chips dictate the cost accounting system used? Describe the costing system best suited to Frito-Lay.
2. What product and process characteristics dictate the use of an activity-based costing system? What implications does this have for Frito-Lay?
3. When beginning inventories are present, product costing becomes more complicated. Estimate the relative magnitude of beginning

inventories at Frito-Lay compared to total production. What implication does this have on the costing system?

P7-18 **PROCESS COSTING AT NALLY AND GIBSON.** Nally and Gibson produces crushed limestone used in highway construction, among other products. To produce the crushed limestone, the company starts with limestone rocks from its quarry in Georgetown, Kentucky and puts the rocks through a crushing process. Suppose that on May 1, Nally and Gibson has 24 tonnes of rock (75 percent complete) in the crushing process. The cost of that beginning work-in-process inventory was $6,000. During May, the company added 288 tonnes of rock from its quarry, and at the end of the month, 15 tonnes remained in process, on average one-third complete. The cost of rocks from the quarry for the last five months has been $120 per tonne. Labour and overhead cost during May in the rock crushing process were $40,670. Nally and Gibson uses weighted-average process costing.

1. Compute the cost per tonne of crushed rock for production in May.
2. Compute the cost of the work-in-process inventory at the end of May.
3. Suppose the flexible budget for labour and overhead was $16,000 plus $80 per tonne. Evaluate the control of overhead and labour costs during May.

P7-19 **TWO MATERIALS.** The following data pertain to the Blending Department at Fasten Chemicals for April:

Units:	
Work-in-process, March 31	0
Units started	60,000
Completed and transferred to finishing department	40,000
Costs:	
Materials:	
Plastic compound	$300,000
Softening compound	$ 80,000
Conversion costs	$240,000

The plastic compound is introduced at the start of the process, while the softening compound is added when the product reaches an 80 percent stage of completion. Conversion costs are incurred uniformly throughout the process.

The ending work in process is 40 percent completed for conversion costs.

1. Compute the equivalent units and unit costs for April.
2. Compute the total cost of units completed and transferred to finished goods. Also compute the cost of the ending work in process.

P7-20 **MATERIALS AND CARTONS.** A Birmingham, England company manufactures and sells small portable tape recorders. Business is booming. Various materials are added at various stages in the assembly department. Costs are accounted for on a process-cost basis. The end of the process involves conducting a final inspection and adding a cardboard carton.

The final inspection requires 5 percent of the total processing time. All materials except the carton are added by the time the recorders reach an 80 percent stage of completion of conversion.

There were no beginning inventories. During 2001, 150,000 recorders were started in production. At the end of the year, which was not a busy time, 5,000 recorders were in various stages of completion. All the ending units in work-in-process were at the 95 percent stage. They awaited final inspection and being placed in cartons.

Total direct materials consumed in production, except for cartons, cost £2,250,000. Cartons used cost £290,000. Total conversion costs were £1,198,000.

1. Present a schedule of physical units, equivalent units, and unit costs of direct materials, cartons, and conversion costs.
2. Present a summary of the cost of goods completed and the cost of ending work-in-process.

P7-21 BACKFLUSH COSTING. Adirondak Meter Company manufactures a variety of measuring instruments. One product is an altimeter used by hikers and mountain climbers. Adironack adopted a just-in-time philosophy with an automated, computer-controlled, robotic production system. Production is scheduled after an order is received, materials and parts arrive just as they are needed, the production cycle time for altimeters is less than one day, and completed units are packaged and shipped as part of the production cycle.

Adironack's backflush costing system has only three accounts related to production of altimeters: materials and parts inventory, conversion costs, and finished goods inventory. At the beginning of April (as at the beginning of every month) each of the three accounts had a balance of zero. Following are the April transactions related to the production of altimeters:

Materials and parts purchased	$287,000
Conversion costs incurred	$ 92,000
Altimeters produced	11,500 units

The budgeted (or standard) cost for one altimeter is $24 for materials and parts and $8 for conversion costs.

1. Prepare summary journal entries for the production of altimeters in April.
2. Compute the cost of goods sold for April. Explain any assumptions you make.
3. Suppose the actual conversion costs incurred during April were $94,600 instead of $92,000, and all other facts were as given. Prepare the additional journal entry that would be required at the end of April. Explain why the entry was necessary.

P7-22 BACKFLUSH COSTING. Digital Controls Inc. makes electric thermostats for homes and offices. The Westplains Division makes one product, Autotherm, that has a standard cost of $37, consisting of $22 of materials and $15 of conversion costs. In January, actual purchases of materials totalled $46,000, labour payroll costs were $11,000, and manufacturing overhead was $19,000. Completed output was 2,000 units.

The Westplains Division uses a backflush costing system that records costs in materials inventory and conversion costs accounts and applies costs to products at the time production is completed. There were no finished goods inventories on January 1 and 20 units on January 31.

1. Prepare journal entries (without explanations) to record January's costs for the Westplains Division. Include the purchase of materials, incurrence of labour and manufacturing overhead costs, application of product costs, and recognition of cost of goods sold.
2. Suppose January's actual manufacturing overhead costs had been $21,000 instead of $19,000. Prepare the journal entry to recognize underapplied conversion costs at the end of January.

P7-23 BACKFLUSH COSTING. Audio Components Ltd. recently installed a backflush costing system. One department makes ten-centimetre speakers with a standard cost as follows:

Materials	$10.00
Conversion costs	4.20
Total	$14.20

Speakers are scheduled for production only after orders are received, and products are shipped to customers immediately upon completion. Therefore, no finished goods inventories are kept, and product costs are applied directly to cost of goods sold.

In October, 1,500 speakers were produced and shipped to customers. Materials were purchased at a cost of $16,000, and actual conversion costs (labour plus manufacturing overhead) of $6,300 were recorded.

1. Prepare journal entries to record October's costs for the production of ten-centimetre speakers.
2. Suppose October's actual conversion costs had been $5,900 instead of $6,300. Prepare a journal entry to recognize overapplied conversion costs.

P7-24 BASIC OPERATION COSTING. Study Appendix 7. Oak Furniture Co. manufactures a variety of wooden chairs. The company's manufacturing operations and costs applied to products for June were

	CUTTING	ASSEMBLY	FINISHING
Direct labour	$60,000	$30,000	$96,000
Factory overhead	115,500	37,500	156,000

Three styles of chairs were produced in June. The quantities and direct material cost were

STYLE	QUANTITY	DIRECT MATERIALS
Standard	6,000	$108,000
Deluxe	4,500	171,000
Unfinished	3,000	66,000

Each unit, regardless of style, required the same cutting and assembly operations. The unfinished chairs, as the name implies, had no finishing operations whatsoever. Standard and deluxe styles required the same finishing operations.

1. Tabulate the total conversion costs of each operation, the total units produced, and the conversion cost per unit.
2. Tabulate the total costs, the units produced, and the cost per unit.

P7-25 **OPERATION COSTING WITH ENDING WORK-IN-PROCESS.** Study Appendix 7. Sonor Instruments Co. uses three operations in sequence to make two models of its depth finders for sport fishing. Consider the following:

	PRODUCTION ORDERS	
	FOR 1,000 STANDARD DEPTH FINDERS	FOR 1,000 DELUXE DEPTH FINDERS
Direct materials (actual costs applied)	$57,000	$100,000
Conversion costs (predetermined costs applied on the basis of machine-hours used):		
Operation 1	19,000	19,000
Operation 2	?	?
Operation 3	—	15,000
Total manufacturing costs applied	$?	$?

1. Operation 2 was highly automated. Product costs depended on a budgeted application rate for conversion costs based on machine-hours. The budgeted costs for 2001 were $220,000 direct labour and $580,000 factory overhead. Budgeted machine-hours were 20,000. Each depth finder required six minutes of time in Operation 2. Compute the costs of processing 1,000 depth finders in Operation 2.

2. Compute the total manufacturing costs of 1,000 depth finders and the cost per standard depth finder and per deluxe depth finder.

3. Suppose that at the end of the year, 500 standard depth finders were in process through Operation 1 only and 600 deluxe depth finders were in process through Operation 2 only. Compute the cost of the ending work-in-process inventory. Assume that no direct materials are applied in Operation 2, but that $10,000 of the $100,000 direct-materials cost of the deluxe depth finders are applied to each 1,000 depth finders processed in Operation 3.

P7-26 **COLLABORATIVE LEARNING EXERCISE: JOB, PROCESS, AND HYBRID COSTING.** Form groups of three to six students. For each of the following production processes, assess whether a job-cost, process-cost, or hybrid-cost system is most likely to be used to determine the cost of the product or service. Also, explain why you think that system is most logical. (This can be done by individuals, but it is a much richer experience when done as a group, because the knowledge and judgment of several interact to produce a much better analysis than can a single student.)

a. Production of Cheerios by General Mills.
b. Production of a sport utility vehicle by Toyota.
c. Processing an application for life insurance by Clarica.
d. Production of a couch by Krug.
e. Building of a bridge by Kiewit Construction Co.
f. Production of gasoline by Petro Canada.
g. Production of 200 copies of a 140-page course packet by Kinkos.
h. Production of a superferry by Todd Shipyards.

C7-1 **PROCESS/JOB PRICING.** In February 2001, Randy White, President of Arriscraft Corporation (Arriscraft), had just received two requests for a price on two of their marble products. The first request was from a nearby city for 140,000 square feet, or approximately 2,000 tonnes, of paving stones. The second request was from a construction firm in Ohio, which requested a price on 3,000 tonnes of window sills of varying sizes. While White was confident that a price of $300 a tonne for the paving stones and $500 a tonne for the window sills would result in Arriscraft receiving the orders, he was unsure that these prices would result in a reasonable profit.

Arriscraft
www.arriscraft.com

COMPANY BACKGROUND

Arriscraft was established in Cambridge, Ontario, in 1949 by E.B. Ratcliffe, a Chemical Engineer, to produce precast stones. In 1956, he developed a unique worldwide process that compressed sand into stone without the use of cement. The result was a stone that was more durable than the normal clay bricks or other masonry products and that could be formed into a variety of shapes, sizes, colours, and textures.

In 1962, Arriscraft added a second product line that involved the cutting of limestone blocks from a quarry near Wiarton, Ontario, and the production of marble hearth slabs and window sills in Cambridge. In 1980, additional marble products, of paving stones and building stones, were added to the line. These marble products are sold under the trade name of Adair Marble.

As of 2001, the company was the only producer of the manufactured stones in the world and was Canada's largest producer of marble products, with only one smaller competitor located in Winnipeg, Manitoba. Recently Arriscraft had been successful in obtaining some significant contracts that included supplying the marble stone for the Canadian Chancery in Washington, the Ontario Court House and Registry Office in Ottawa, and the reconstruction of the Rideau Canal locks. With these and other contracts, Arriscraft had established a reputation among architects and contractors as a leading producer of unique and top-quality stone products.

White had been with the company for nine years, after graduating from Queen's University with a degree in commerce and obtaining his Chartered Accountants designation. During his nine years, White held the positions of controller, executive vice president, and president. With this experience, he was fully aware of both the financial and technical implications of the various alternatives that he faced. In particular, he was acutely aware that the variability of the yields and product mix significantly complicated any analyses of product line profitability.

PRODUCTION PROCESS

As the decisions facing White concerned marble products, only the production process related to these products will be described. Exhibit 7-1A illustrates the following description of this process.

First, limestone blocks are drilled and cut from a quarry. The top surface of the quarry is the side of the block, the dimensions are 75 centimetres by 210 centimetres. The depth of the block will vary depending upon the natural bed depth of the quarry, but lengths vary from one to three metres. The net result are limestone blocks that vary in size from four to 12 metric tonnes, with an average size being approximately eight tonnes. These limestone blocks are then trucked to Arriscraft's plant. The total direct cost of the limestone blocks is approximately $50 per tonne, which includes the removal and transportation costs.

At the plant, each limestone block is positioned in front of a saw, which first cuts off two sides. These cuts will remove approximately one tonne of waste from an average eight-tonne block, leaving seven tonnes. Next, the saw operator must make a series of critical judgment calls as he or she cuts the limestone block into slices called product blocks. The saw operator must examine the face of the stone for cracks, pits, or other faults. If any are found, a cut approximately 20 centimetres wide will be made and the product block will be further processed into paving stones. If the limestone block is reasonably clear of faults, then a 15 centimetre cut will be made and the product block will be produced into window sills. If the stone is of highest quality, then cuts varying from six to 75 centimetres will be made to produce specialized products and hearth slabs. A fourth product line is referred to as larger units, where the quality may be low and these sections would otherwise be used for paving stones. However, if a wider cut is made, the stone can be used in place of some top-quality large pieces for some specific applications. The skill of the saw operator is extremely important as a limestone block will normally produce many grades of products, and thus a judgment call is required after each cut is made. The cutting of the limestone block into product blocks results in an 80 percent yield of the seven tonnes, and the cutting costs per tonne of product block vary for each of the four product lines as follows:

paving stones	$14 per tonne
window sills	$15 per tonne
hearth slabs	$10 per tonne
large units	$12 per tonne

While a variance of 10 to 15 percent exists, it is expected that 10 percent of the product block tonnage will be in paving stones, 40 percent in window sills, 40 percent in hearth slabs, and 10 percent in large units.

The processing of the product blocks into their designated final products first involves some additional sawing and splitting. Then, depending upon the quality of the final product, the stones are honed (smoothed) to produce the marble product. The extent of the processing varies by product line and the ultimate yield will also vary by product line. The paving stones have a 50 percent yield and the processing costs total $115 per tonne of finished product. The window sills have a yield of 48 percent with a processing cost of $180 per tonne of finished product. The waste from the window sills can be used for paving stones, and after a further processing cost of $65 per tonne of finished product, a yield of 21 percent of the waste is obtained. The hearth slabs are processed for a cost of $150 per tonne of finished product, which is a 65 percent yield of the product blocks. The large units result in a yield of 70 percent for a processing cost of $75 per finished tonne.

The above description is the typical production process, however, it is possible to produce paving stones and window sills from higher-grade material. While the cutting and processing costs for the paving stones and window sills

EXHIBIT 7-1A

ARRISCRAFT
CORPORATION
Normal Production
Process for Marble
Products

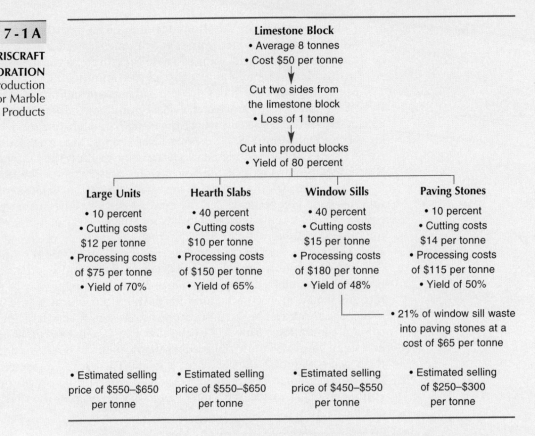

Limestone Block
- Average 8 tonnes
- Cost $50 per tonne

Cut two sides from
the limestone block
- Loss of 1 tonne

Cut into product blocks
- Yield of 80 percent

Large Units	**Hearth Slabs**	**Window Sills**	**Paving Stones**
• 10 percent	• 40 percent	• 40 percent	• 10 percent
• Cutting costs $12 per tonne	• Cutting costs $10 per tonne	• Cutting costs $15 per tonne	• Cutting costs $14 per tonne
• Processing costs of $75 per tonne	• Processing costs of $150 per tonne	• Processing costs of $180 per tonne	• Processing costs of $115 per tonne
• Yield of 70%	• Yield of 65%	• Yield of 48%	• Yield of 50%

- 21% of window sill waste into paving stones at a cost of $65 per tonne

| • Estimated selling price of $550–$650 per tonne | • Estimated selling price of $550–$650 per tonne | • Estimated selling price of $450–$550 per tonne | • Estimated selling of $250–$300 per tonne |

would remain the same, the yields would increase as follows. Window sills may be cut from the material that would normally be used for hearth slabs and large units and the yields would increase by 10 percentage points to 75 percent and 80 percent respectively. Similarly, paving stones may be cut from window-sill, hearth-slab, and large-unit materials with a 15 percentage point increase in yields to 63 percent, 80 percent, and 85 percent respectively. In addition, the cutting of paving stones from window sill waste would increase to 31 percent. White was, however, concerned that this alternate production process would not yield satisfactory profit margins.

SITUATION SUMMARY

White had been faced many times with similar situations like those before him now. If 2,000 tonnes of paving stones are produced by means of the normal production process, more than the required quantities of window sills must also be produced. Furthermore, product blocks that will eventually be produced into hearth slabs and large units must also be cut even though they are not currently required. However, if the limestone blocks were cut into only paving stones, only window sills, or both paving stones and window sills, the higher-quality material would be used where lower-quality material would meet the customer requirements. The market for these marble products was somewhat unpredictable as the orders tended to be large and depended essentially upon the preferences of an architect or contractor. While Arriscraft did not have any direct competition, the small amount of competition came from less expensive alternative building products. For example, the paving stones will cost the city $4.29 a square foot, whereas, interlocking brick (an alternative cement-based product) would cost $1 to $2 a square metre. The issue is essentially how much more is the market willing to pay for a marble product than a more common alternative. Given the common costs of the limestone block and the cutting, White again wondered whether a price of $300 per tonne of paving stones and $500 per tonne of window sills would generate sufficient profits. As a rule of thumb, the company has historically attempted to attain a markup of 100 percent on the direct product costs. Typically, a markup of less than 70 percent was viewed as unprofitable. However, in a situation such as this, the measurement of the direct costs by product line are not straightforward. Furthermore, the unsold product, both finished and unfinished, had always presented a problem when costing the inventory for Arriscraft's annual financial report. Depending upon the approach adopted, the costing of the inventory could have a material effect on the net income.

Required: As Randy White, would you bid on both of the orders and, if so, at what price? Explain your reasoning.

8

Relevant Information and Decision Making: Marketing Decisions

LEARNING OBJECTIVES

After studying this chapter, you will be able to

1. Discriminate between relevant and irrelevant information for making decisions.

2. Diagram the relationships among the main elements of the decision process.

3. Analyze data by the contribution approach to support a decision for accepting or rejecting a special sales order.

4. Explain the potential pitfalls of using a unit-cost approach for predicting the effect of a special order on operating income.

5. Analyze data by the relevant-information approach to support a decision for adding or deleting a product line.

6. Compute a measure of product profitability when production is constrained by a scarce resource.

7. Identify the role of costs in pricing decisions in perfect and imperfect markets.

8. Discuss the factors that influence pricing decisions.

9. Compute a target sales price by various approaches and identify their advantages and disadvantages.

10. Use target costing to decide whether to add a new product or service.

What price should Loblaws stores charge for a kilogram of hamburger? What should Boeing charge for a 767 airplane? Should a clothing manufacturer accept a special order from Zellers at a price lower than that generally charged? Should an appliance manufacturer add a new product, say an automatic bread maker, to its product line? Or should an existing product be dropped? Which product makes best use of a particular limited resource? All these questions relate to the marketing strategy of a firm, and accounting information can play an important role in each of them.

At the start of this book, we emphasized that the purpose of management accounting is to provide information that enables managers to make sound decisions. In this segment of the book, we will focus on identifying *relevant information* for particular management decisions. This chapter focuses primarily on marketing decisions.[1] Although the word "relevant" has been much overworked in recent years, the ability to separate relevant from irrelevant information is often the difference between success and failure in modern business.

THE MEANING OF RELEVANCE: THE MAJOR CONCEPTUAL LESSON

OBJECTIVE 1

Discriminate between relevant and irrelevant information for making decisions.

Relevant Information. The predicted future costs and revenues that will differ among alternative courses of action.

What information is relevant depends on the decision being made. As described in Chapter 1, decision making is essentially choosing among several courses of action. The available actions are determined by an often time-consuming formal or informal search and screening process, perhaps carried on by a company team that includes engineers, accountants, and operating executives.

The decision is based on the difference in the effect of each alternative on future performance. The key question is, What difference will the choice make? **Relevant information** is the predicted future costs and revenues that will differ among the alternatives.

Note that relevant information is a prediction of the future, not a summary of the past. Historical (past) data have no *direct* bearing on a decision. Such data can have an *indirect* bearing on a decision because they may help in predicting the future. But past figures, in themselves, are irrelevant to the decision itself. Why? Because the decision cannot affect past data. Decisions affect the future. Nothing can alter what has already happened.

Of the expected future data, only those that will differ from alternative to alternative are relevant to the decision. Any item that will remain the same regardless of the alternative selected is irrelevant. For instance, if a department manager's salary will be the same regardless of the products stocked, the salary is irrelevant to the selection of products.

Accuracy and Relevance

In the best of all possible worlds, information used for decision making would be both relevant and accurate. However, in reality, the cost of such information often exceeds its benefit. Accountants often trade-off relevance for accuracy. Of course, relevant information must be reasonably accurate, but not precisely so.

---

[1] Throughout this and the next chapter, in order to concentrate on the fundamental ideas we shall ignore the time value of money (discussed in Chapter 10) and income taxes (discussed in Chapter 11).

Precise but irrelevant information is worthless for decision making. For example, a company president's salary may be $140,000 per year, to the penny, but may have no bearing on the question of whether to buy or rent data processing equipment. On the other hand, imprecise but relevant information can be useful. For example, sales predictions for a new product may be subject to great error, but they still are helpful in deciding whether to manufacture the product.

The degree to which information is relevant and/or precise often depends on the degree to which it is *qualitative* and/or *quantitative*. Qualitative aspects are those for which measurement in dollars and cents is difficult and imprecise; quantitative aspects are those for which measurement is easier and more precise. Accountants, statisticians, and mathematicians try to express as many decision factors as feasible in quantitative terms, since this approach reduces the number of qualitative factors to be judged. Just as we noted that relevance is more crucial than precision in decision making, so a qualitative aspect may easily carry more weight than a measurable (quantitative) financial impact in many decisions. For example, the opposition of a militant union to new labour-saving machinery may cause a manager to defer or even reject completely the contemplated installation even if it would save money. Or, to avoid a long-run dependence on a particular supplier, a company may pass up the opportunity to purchase a component from the supplier at a price below the cost of producing it.

On the other hand, managers sometimes introduce new technology (for example, advanced computer systems or automated equipment) even though the expected quantitative results seem unattractive. Managers defend such decisions on the grounds that failure to keep abreast of new technology will surely bring unfavourable financial results sooner or later.

Examples of Relevance

The following examples will help you clarify the sharp distinctions needed to discriminate between relevant and irrelevant information.

Suppose you always buy gasoline from either of two nearby gasoline stations. Yesterday you noticed that one station was selling gasoline at $.70 per litre; the other, at $.65 per litre. Your automobile needs gasoline, and in making your choice of stations, you *assume* that these prices have not been changed. The relevant costs are $.70 and $.65, the expected future costs that will differ between the alternatives. You use your past experience (i.e., what you observed yesterday) for predicting today's price. Note that the relevant cost is not what you paid in the past, or what you observed yesterday, but what you *expect to pay* when you drive in to get gasoline. This cost meets our two criteria: (1) it is the expected future cost, and (2) it differs between the alternatives.

You may also plan to have your car lubricated. The recent price at each station was $19, and this is what you expect to pay. This expected future cost is irrelevant because it will be the same under either alternative. It does not meet our second criterion.

On a business level, consider the following decision. A manufacturer is thinking of using aluminum instead of copper in a product line. The cost of direct material will decrease from $.30 to $.20 The analysis in a nutshell is

	ALUMINUM	COPPER	DIFFERENCE
Direct materials	$.20	$.30	$.10

The cost of copper used for this comparison probably came from historical-cost records on the amount paid most recently for copper, but the *relevant* costs in the foregoing analysis are the *expected future* costs of copper compared to the *expected future* cost of aluminum.

The direct-labour cost will continue to be $.70 per unit regardless of the material used. It is irrelevant because our second criterion—an element of difference between the alternatives—is not met:

	ALUMINUM	COPPER	DIFFERENCE
Direct materials	$.20	$.30	$.10
Direct labour	.70	.70	—

Therefore, we can safely exclude direct labour from the comparison of the alternative. There is no harm in including irrelevant items in a formal analysis, provided that they are included properly. However, confining reports to the relevant items only provides greater clarity and time-savings for managers.

OBJECTIVE 2

Diagram the relationships among the main elements of the decision process.

Decision Model. Any method for making a choice, sometimes requiring elaborate quantitative procedures.

Exhibit 8-1 provides a more elaborate view than is necessary for this simple decision, but it serves to show the appropriate framework for more complex decisions. Box 1(a) represents historical data from the accounting system. Box 1(b) represents other data, such as price indices or industry statistics, gathered from outside the accounting system. Regardless of their source, the data in Step 1 help the formulation of *predictions* in Step 2. (Remember that while historical data may act as a guide to predicting, they are irrelevant to the decision itself.)

In Step 3 the predictions become inputs to the *decision model*. A **decision model** is defined as *any* method for making a choice. Such models often require elaborate quantitative procedures, such as a petroleum refinery's mathematical method for choosing which products to manufacture for any given day or week. But a decision model may also be simple. It may be confined to a single comparison of costs for choosing between two materials. In this instance, our decision model is to compare the predicted unit costs and select the alternative with the lesser cost.

Above all, note the commonality of the relevant-information approach to the various special decisions explored in this and the next chapter. Managers should focus on predictions for future outcomes, not dwell on past outcomes. The major difficulty is predicting how revenues and costs will be affected under each alternative. No matter what the decision situation, the key question to ask is, What difference will it make?

THE SPECIAL SALES ORDER

The first decision for which we will examine relevant information is the special sales order.

Illustrative Example

Exhibit 8-2 illustrates the primary data for the Samson Company from Exhibits 4-8 and 4-9—two very important exhibits. As you can see, the two income statements differ somewhat in format. The difference in format may be unimportant if

EXHIBIT 8-1

Decision Process and
Role of Information

The decision is whether to use aluminum instead of copper.
The objective is to minimize costs.

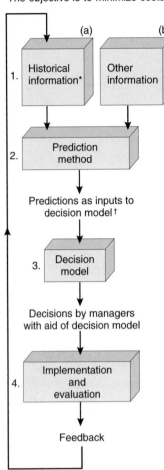

(a)   (b)

1. Historical information*

1. Other information

2. Prediction method

Predictions as inputs to
decision model†

3. Decision model

Decisions by managers
with aid of decision model

4. Implementation
and
evaluation

Feedback

1. Historical direct material costs were $.30 per unit.
   Direct labour costs were $.70 per unit and will not be
   affected by the switch in materials.

2. Use the information as a basis for predicting the future
   costs of direct material and direct labour. Direct material unit costs are expected to be $.20 and $.30 for aluminum and copper, respectively.

3.

COST COMPARISON PER UNIT

	Aluminum	Copper	Difference
Direct material	$.20	$.30	$.10

The expected future costs are the outputs of the prediction method and are inputs of the decision model
together with other quantitative and qualitative information.

4. The chosen action is implemented and the evaluation
   of performance becomes a principal source of feedback. This can update historical information and
   improve the prediction method, the decision model,
   and the implementation of the decision.

* Note that historical data may be relevant for prediction methods.
† Historical data are never relevant *per se* for decision models. Only those expected future data that differ
between alternatives are really relevant. For instance, in this example, direct material makes a difference
and direct labour does not. Therefore, *under our definition here*, direct labour is irrelevant.

OBJECTIVE 3

Analyze data by the
contribution approach
to support a decision
for accepting or
rejecting a special
sales order.

the accompanying cost analysis leads to the same set of decisions. But these two
approaches sometimes lead to different *unit* costs that must be interpreted warily.

In our illustration, suppose one million units of product were made and sold.
Under the absorption-costing approach, the unit manufacturing cost would be
$15,000,000 ÷ 1,000,000 units, or $15 per unit. Suppose a mail-order house near
year-end offered Samson $13 per unit for a 100,000-unit special order that (1)
would not affect Samson's regular business in any way, (2) would not raise any
issues concerning price discrimination, (3) would not affect total fixed costs, (4)
would not require any additional variable selling and administrative expenses,
and (5) would use some otherwise idle manufacturing capacity. Should Samson
accept the order? Perhaps the question should be stated more sharply. What is the
difference in the short-run financial results between not accepting and accepting?
As usual, the key question is, What difference will it make?

EXHIBIT 8-2

Samson Company
Absorption and
Contribution Forms of
the Income Statement
for the Year Ended
December 31, 2002 (in
thousands of dollars)

ABSORPTION FORM		CONTRIBUTION FORM		
Sales	$20,000	Sales		$20,000
Less: Manufacturing cost of		Less: Variable expenses:		
goods sold	15,000	Manufacturing	$12,000	
Gross margin or gross profit	5,000	Selling and administrative	1,100	13,100
Less: Selling and		Contribution margin		$ 6,900
administrative expenses	4,000			
Operating income	$ 1,000	Less: Fixed expenses:		
		Manufacturing	$ 3,000	
		Selling and		
		administrative	2,900	5,900
		Operating income		$ 1,000

Correct Analysis

The correct analysis employs the contribution approach and concentrates on the final *overall* results. As Exhibit 8-3 shows, only variable manufacturing costs are affected by the particular order, at a rate of $12 per unit. All other variable costs and all fixed costs are unaffected so a manager may safely ignore them in making this special-order decision. Note how the contribution approach's distinction between variable- and fixed-cost-behaviour patterns indicates that both contribution margin and operating income will increase by $100,000 if the order is accepted—despite the fact that the unit selling price of $13 is less than the absorption manufacturing cost of $15.

Exhibit 8-3 shows total fixed expenses in the first and last columns. There is no harm in including such irrelevant items in an analysis as long as they are included under every alternative at hand.

A fixed-cost element of an identical amount that is common among all alternatives is essentially irrelevant. Whether irrelevant items should be included in an analysis is a matter of taste, not a matter of right or wrong. However, if irrelevant items are included in an analysis, they should be inserted in a correct manner.

EXHIBIT 8-3

Samson Company
Comparative Predicted
Income Statement,
Contribution Approach
for the Year Ended
December 31, 2002

	WITHOUT SPECIAL ORDER 1,000,000 UNITS	EFFECT OF SPECIAL ORDER 100,000 UNITS		WITH SPECIAL ORDER 1,100,000 UNITS
		TOTAL	PER UNIT	
Sales	$20,000,000	$1,300,000	$13	$21,300,000
Less: Variable expenses:				
Manufacturing	12,000,000	1,200,000	12	13,200,000
Selling and administrative	1,100,000	—	—	1,100,000
Total variable expenses	13,100,000	1,200,000	12	14,300,000
Contribution margin	6,900,000	100,000	1	7,000,000
Less: Fixed expenses:				
Manufacturing	3,000,000	—	—	3,000,000
Selling and administrative	2,900,000	—	—	2,900,000
Total fixed expenses	5,900,000	—	—	5,900,000
Operating income	$ 1,000,000	$ 100,000	$ 1	$ 1,100,000

Incorrect Analysis

OBJECTIVE 4

Explain the potential pitfalls of using a unit-cost approach for predicting the effect of a special order on operating income.

Faulty cost analysis sometimes occurs because of misinterpretating unit fixed costs. Managers might erroneously use the $15 absorption manufacturing cost per unit to make the following prediction for the year.

	WITHOUT SPECIAL ORDER	INCORRECT EFFECT OF SPECIAL ORDER	WITH SPECIAL ORDER
	1,000,000 UNITS	100,000 UNITS	1,100,000 UNITS
Sales	$20,000,000	$1,300,000	$21,300,000
Less: Manufacturing cost of goods sold @ $15	15,000,000	1,500,000	16,500,000
Gross margin	5,000,000	(200,000)	4,800,000
Selling and administrative expenses	4,000,000	—	4,000,000
Operating income	$ 1,000,000	$ (200,000)	$ 800,000

The $1.5-million increase in costs results from multiplying $15 times 100,000 units. Of course, the fallacy in this approach is that it treats a fixed cost (fixed manufacturing cost) as if it were variable. Avoid the assumption that unit costs may be used indiscriminately as a basis for predicting how total costs will behave. Unit costs are useful for predicting variable costs, but often are misleading when used to predict fixed costs.

Confusion of Variable and Fixed Costs

Consider the relationship between total fixed manufacturing costs and a fixed manufacturing cost per unit of product:.

$$\text{fixed cost per unit of product} = \frac{\text{total fixed manufacturing costs}}{\text{some selected volume level used as the denominator}}$$

$$= \frac{\$3,000,000}{1,000,000 \text{ units}} = \$3 \text{ per unit}$$

As noted in Chapter 2, the typical cost accounting system serves two purposes simultaneously: *planning and control* and *product costing*. The total fixed cost for *budgetary planning* and *control purposes* can be graphed as a lump sum:

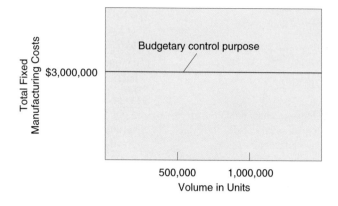

For *product-costing purposes*, however, the absorption-costing approach implies that these *fixed* costs have a *variable*-cost behaviour pattern:

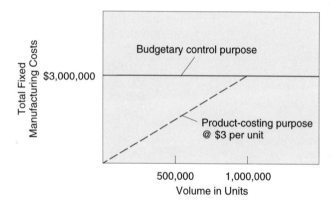

The addition of 100,000 units will *not* add any *total* fixed costs as long as total output is within the relevant range. However, incorrect analysis includes $100,000 \times \$3 = \$300,000$ of fixed cost in the predictions of increases in total costs.

In short, the increase in manufacturing costs should be computed by multiplying 100,000 units by $12, not by $15. The $15 includes a $3 component that will not affect the total manufacturing costs as volume changes.

Spreading Fixed Costs

As we have just seen, the unit cost-total cost distinction can become particularly troublesome when analyzing fixed-cost behaviour. Assume the same facts concerning the special order as before, except that the order was for 250,000 units at a selling price of $11.50. The analytical pitfalls of unit-cost analysis can be avoided by using the contribution approach and concentrating on totals (in thousands of dollars) instead of units:

	WITHOUT SPECIAL ORDER	EFFECT OF SPECIAL ORDER	WITH SPECIAL ORDER
	1,000,000 UNITS	250,000 UNITS	1,250,000 UNITS
Sales	$20,000	$2,875*	$22,875
Variable manufacturing costs	12,000	3,000†	15,000
Other variable costs	1,100	—	1,100
Total variable costs	13,100	3,000	16,100
Contribution margin	$ 6,900	$ (125)‡	$ 6,775

* 250,000 × $11.50 selling price of special order.
† 250,000 × $12.00 variable manufacturing cost per unit of special order.
‡ 250,000 × $.50 negative contribution margin per unit of special order.

Short-run income will fall by $125,000 (that is, 250,000 units × $.50) if the special order is accepted. No matter how the fixed manufacturing costs are "unitized" and "spread" over the units produced, their total of $3 million will be *unchanged* by the special order (in thousands of dollars):

	WITHOUT SPECIAL ORDER	EFFECT OF SPECIAL ORDER	WITH SPECIAL ORDER
	1,000,000 UNITS	250,000 UNITS	1,250,000 UNITS
Contribution margin (as above)	$6,900	$ (125)	$6,775
Total fixed costs:			
At an average rate of $3.00*:			
1,000,000 × $3.00	3,000		
At an average rate of $2.40†:			
1,250,000 × $2.40		—	3,000
Contribution to other fixed costs and operating income	$3,900	$ (125)	$3,775

* $3,000,000 ÷ 1,000,000 units.
† $3,000,000 ÷ 1,250,000 units.

No matter how fixed costs are spread for *unit* product-costing purposes, *total* fixed costs are unchanged, even though fixed costs *per unit* fall from $3.00 to $2.40.

The lesson here is important. Do not be deceived. Follow Robert McNamara's First Law of Analysis when he was U.S. secretary of defense: "Always start by looking at the grand total. Whatever problem you are studying, back off and look at it in the large." In this context, that law means, "Beware of unit costs. When in doubt, convert all unit costs into the total costs under each alternative to get the big picture." In particular, beware of unit costs when analyzing fixed costs. Think in terms of totals instead.

Multiple Cost Drivers and Special Orders

To identify costs affected by a special order (or by other special decisions) more and more firms are going a step beyond simply identifying fixed and variable costs. As pointed out in Chapter 3, many different cost drivers may cause companies to incur costs. Firms that have identified all their significant cost drivers can predict the effects of special orders more accurately.

Suppose Samson Company examined its $12 million of variable costs very closely and identified two significant cost drivers: $9 million that varies directly with *units produced* at a rate of $9 per unit and $3 million that varies with the *number of production set-ups*. Normally, for production of 1,000,000 units, Samson has 500 set-ups at a cost of $6,000 per set-up, with an average of 2,000 units produced for each set-up. Additional sales generally require a proportional increase in the number of set-ups.

Now suppose the special order is for 100,000 units that vary only slightly in production specifications. Instead of the normal 50 setups, Samson will need only five set-ups. To produce 100,000 units, $930,000 of additional variable costs will be required.

Additional unit-based variable cost 100,000 × $9	$900,000
Additional set-up-based variable cost 50 × $6000	30,000
Total additional variable cost	$930,000

Instead of the original estimate of 100,000 × $12 = $1,200,000 additional variable-cost, the special order will cause only $930,000, or $270,000 less than the original estimate. Therefore, the special order is $270,000 more profitable than predicted from the simple, unit-based assessment of variable cost.

A special order may also be more costly than predicted by a simple fixed/variable-cost analysis. Suppose the 100,000-unit special order called for a variety of models and colours delivered at various times, so that 100 set-ups are required. The variable cost of the special order would be $1.5 million:

Additional unit-based variable cost, 100,000 × $9	$ 900,000
Additional set-up-based variable cost, 100 × $6,000	600,000
Total additional variable cost	$1,500,000

SUMMARY PROBLEM FOR YOUR REVIEW

Problem One

1. Return to the basic illustration in Exhibit 8-3. Suppose a special order like the one described in conjunction with Exhibit 8-3 had the following terms: selling price would be $13.50 instead of $13.00, but a manufacturer's agent who had obtained the potential order would have to be paid a flat fee of $40,000 if the order were accepted. What would be the new special-order difference in operating income if the order were accepted?
2. Assume the original facts concerning the special order, except that the order was for 250,000 units at a selling price of $11.50. Some managers have been known to argue for acceptance of such an order as follows: "Of course, we will lose $.50 each on the variable manufacturing costs, but we will gain $.60 per unit by spreading our fixed manufacturing costs over 1.25 million units instead of one million units. Consequently, we should take the offer because it represents an advantage of $.10 per unit."

Old fixed manufacturing cost per unit, $3,000,000 ÷ 1,000,000		$3.00
New fixed manufacturing cost per unit, $3,000,000 ÷ 1,250,000		2.40
"Saving" in fixed manufacturing cost per unit		$ .60
Loss on variable manufacturing cost per unit, $11.50 − $12.00		.50
Net saving per unit in manufacturing cost		$ .10

Explain why this is faulty thinking.

Solution

1. Focus on the *differences* in revenues and costs. In this problem, in addition to the difference in variable costs, there is a difference in fixed costs between the two alternatives.

Additional revenue, 100,000 units @ $13.50 per unit	$1,350,000
Less additional costs:	
Variable costs, 100,000 units @ $12 per unit	1,200,000
Fixed costs, agent's fee	40,000
Increase in operating income from special order	$ 110,000

2. The faulty thinking comes from attributing a "savings" to the decrease in unit fixed costs. Regardless of how the fixed manufacturing costs are "unitized" or "spread" over the units produced, their total of $3 million will be *unchanged* by the special order. As the tabulation on page 181 indicates, short-run income will fall by 250,000 units × ($12.00 − $11.50) = $125,000 if the special order is accepted.

DELETING OR ADDING PRODUCTS OR DEPARTMENTS

The same principles of relevance applied to special orders apply—albeit in slightly different ways—to decisions about adding or deleting products for departments. Consider a discount department store that has three major departments: groceries, general merchandise, and drugs. Management is considering dropping groceries, which have consistently shown a net loss. The following table (in thousands of dollars) reports the present annual net income.

		DEPARTMENTS		
	TOTAL	GROCERIES	GENERAL MERCHANDISE	DRUGS
Sales	$1,900	$1,000	$ 800	$100
Variable cost of goods sold and expenses*	1,420	800	560	60
Contribution margin	$ 480 (25%)	$ 200 (20%)	$ 240 (30%)	$ 40 (40%)
Fixed expenses (salaries, depreciation, insurance, property taxes, etc.):				
Avoidable	$ 265	$ 150	$ 100	$ 15
Unavoidable	180	60	100	20
Total fixed expenses	$ 445	$ 210	$ 200	$ 35
Operating income	$ 35	$ (10)	$ 40	$ 5

* Examples of variable expenses include paper bags and sales commissions.

OBJECTIVE 5

Analyze data by the
relevant-information
approach to support a
decision for adding and
deleting a product line.

Avoidable Costs. Costs that
will not continue if an
ongoing operation is
changed or deleted.

Unavoidable Costs. Costs
that continue even if an
operation is halted.

Common Costs. The costs
of facilities and
services that are shared
by users.

Notice that the fixed expenses are divided into two categories, *avoidable* and *unavoidable*. **Avoidable costs**—costs that will *not* continue if an ongoing operation is changed or deleted—are relevant. Avoidable costs include department salaries and other costs that could be eliminated by not operating the specific department. **Unavoidable costs**—costs that continue even if an operation is halted—are not relevant because they are not affected by a decision to delete the department. Unavoidable costs include many **common costs**, which are defined as those costs of facilities and services that are shared by users. Examples are store depreciation, heating, air conditioning, and general management expenses.[2]

Assume first that the only alternatives to be considered are dropping or continuing the grocery department. Assume further that the total assets invested would be unaffected by the decision. The vacated space would be idle, and the unavoidable costs would continue. Which alternative would you recommend? An analysis (in thousands of dollars) as follows:

The preceding analysis shows that matters would be worse, rather than better, if groceries were dropped and the vacated facilities left idle. In short, as the income statement shows, groceries bring in a contribution margin of $200,000, which is $50,000 more than the $150,000 fixed expenses that would be saved by closing the grocery department.

	STORE AS A WHOLE		
	TOTAL BEFORE CHANGE (A)	DROP GROCERIES (B)	TOTAL AFTER CHANGE (A)–(B)
Sales	$1,900	$1,000	$ 900
Variable expenses	1,420	800	620
Contribution margin	$ 480	$ 200	$ 280
Avoidable fixed expenses	265	150	115
Profit contribution to common space and other unavoidable costs	$ 215	$ 50	$ 165
Common space and other unavoidable costs	180	—	180
Operating income	$ 35	$ 50	$ (15)

Assume now that the space made available by the dropping of groceries could be used to expand the general merchandise department. The space would be occupied by merchandise that would increase sales by $500,000 generate a 30 percent contribution-margin percentage, and have avoidable fixed costs of $70,000. The $80,000 increase in operating income of general merchandise more than offsets the $50,000 decline from eliminating groceries and provides an overall increase in operating income of $65,000 – $35,000 = $30,000:

---

[2] The concept of avoidable cost is used by government regulators as well as business executives. For example, Amtrak divides its costs into avoidable—costs that would "cease if the route were eliminated"—and fixed—costs that would "remain relatively constant if a single route were discontinued." The U.S. Interstate Commerce Commission then considers the avoidable costs when considering approval of a railroad's request to abandon a route. Similarly, the Canadian government looks at the avoidable cost when determining the amount of subsidy to give to the country's passenger-rail system. The *Montreal Gazette* reported in 1993 revenues covered only 35 percent of the "$7 million in avoidable costs (costs that wouldn't exist if the train disappeared tomorrow— things like staff salaries, food, fuel, and upkeep of train stations."

(IN THOUSANDS OF DOLLARS)	TOTAL BEFORE CHANGE (A)	DROP GROCERIES (B)	EXPAND GENERAL MERCHANDISE (C)	TOTAL AFTER CHANGE (A)-(B)+(C)
Sales	$1,900	$1,000	$ 500	$1,400
Variable expenses	1,420	800	350	970
Contribution margin	$ 480	$ 200	150	$ 430
Avoidable fixed expenses	265	150	70	185
Profit contribution to common space and other unavoidable costs	$ 215	$ 50	$ 80	$ 245
Common space and other unavoidable costs*	180	—	—	180
Operating income	$ 35	$ 50	$ 80	$ 65

* Includes the $60,000 of former grocery fixed costs, which were allocations of unavoidable common costs that will continue regardless of how the space is occupied.

As the following summary analysis demonstrates, the objective is to obtain, from a given amount of space or capacity, the maximum contribution to the payment of those unavoidable costs that remain unaffected by the nature of the product sold (in thousands of dollars):

	PROFIT CONTRIBUTION OF GIVEN SPACE		
	GROCERIES	EXPANSION OF GENERAL MERCHANDISE	DIFFERENCE
Sales	$1,000	$ 500	$500 U
Variables expenses	800	350	450 F
Contribution margin	$ 200	$ 150	$ 50 U
Avoidable fixed expenses	150	70	80 F
Contribution to common space and other unavoidable costs	$ 50	$ 80	$ 30 F

F = Favourable difference resulting from replacing groceries with general merchandise.
U = Unfavourable difference.

In this case, the general merchandise will not achieve the dollar sales volume that groceries will, but the higher contribution margin percentage and the lower wage costs (mostly because of the diminished need for stocking and checkout clerks) will bring more favourable net results.

This illustration provides another lesson. Avoid the idea that relevant-cost analysis merely says, "Consider all variable costs, and ignore all fixed costs." In this case, fixed costs are relevant because they differ under each alternative.

OPTIMAL USE OF LIMITED RESOURCES

When a multiple-product plant is being operated at capacity, managers often must decide which orders to accept. The contribution approach also applies here, because

OBJECTIVE 6

Compute a measure of
product profitability
when production is
constrained by a
scarce resource.

**Limiting Factor (Scarce
Resource).** The item that
restricts or constrains the
production or sale of a
product or service.

the product to be emphasized or the order to be accepted is the one that makes the biggest total profit contribution per unit of the limiting factor. A **limiting factor** or **scarce resource** is that item that restricts or constrains the production or sale of a product or service. Limiting factors include labour-hours and machine-hours that limit production and hence sales in manufacturing firms; and square metres of floor space or cubic metres of display space that limit sales in department stores.

The contribution approach must be used wisely, however. Managers sometimes mistakenly favour those products with the biggest contribution margin or gross margin per sales dollar, without regard to scarce resources.

Assume that a company has two products: a plain portable heater and a fancier heater with many special features. Unit data follow:

	PLAIN HEATER	FANCY HEATER
Selling price	$20	$30
Variable costs	16	21
Contribution margin	$ 4	$ 9
Contribution-margin ratio	20%	30%

Which product is more profitable? On which should the firm spend its resources? The correct answer is, "It depends." If sales are restricted by demand for only a limited *number* of heaters, fancy heaters are more profitable. Why? Because the sale of a plain heater contributes $4 to profit; the sale of a fancy heater contributes $9. If the limiting factor is *units* of sales, the more profitable product is the one with the higher contribution *per unit*.

But suppose annual demand for heaters of both types is more than the company can produce in the next year. Now productive capacity is the limiting factor. If 10,000 hours of capacity are available, and three plain heaters can be produced per hour in contrast to one fancy heater, the plain heater is more profitable. Why? Because it contributes more profit *per hour*:

	PLAIN HEATER	FANCY HEATER
1. Units per hour	3	1
2. Contribution margin per unit	$ 4	$ 9
Contribution margin per hour (1) × (2)	$12	$ 9
Total contribution for 10,000 hours	$120,000	$90,000

The criterion for maximizing profits when one factor limits sales is to *obtain the greatest possible contribution to profit for each unit of the limiting or scarce factor*. The product that is most profitable when one particular factor limits sales may be the least profitable if a different factor restricts sales.

When capacity is limited, the conventional contribution-margin or gross-margin-per-sales-dollar ratios provide an insufficient clue to profitability. Consider an example of two department stores. The conventional gross profit percentage (gross profit ÷ selling price) is an insufficient clue to profitability because profits also depend on the space occupied and the **inventory turnover** (number of times the average inventory is sold per year).

Inventory Turnover. The
average number of times
the inventory is sold
per year.

Wal-Mart
www.walmart.com

Zellers
www.zellers.com

Discount department stores such as Wal-Mart and Zellers have succeeded, while using lower markups than other department stores, because they have been able to increase turnover and thus increase the contribution to profit per unit of space. The following illustrates the same product, taking up the same amount of space, in each of two stores. The contribution margins per unit and per sales dollar are less in the discount store, but faster turnover makes the same product a more profitable use of space in the discount store.

	REGULAR DEPARTMENT STORE	DISCOUNT DEPARTMENT STORE
Retail price	$4.00	$3.50
Cost of merchandise and other variable costs	3.00	3.00
Contribution to profit per unit	$1.00 (25%)	$ .50 (14+%)
Units sold per year	10,000	22,000
Total contribution to profit, assuming the same space allotment in both stores	$10,000	$11,000

Notice that throughout this discussion, fixed costs have been ignored. They are irrelevant unless their total is affected by the choices.

PRICING DECISIONS

One of the major decisions managers face is pricing. Actually, pricing can take many forms. Among the many pricing decisions to be made are

1. Setting the price of a new product
2. Setting the price of products sold under private labels
3. Responding to a new price of a competitor
4. Pricing bids in both sealed- and open-bidding situations

The pricing decision is extensively covered in the literature of economics and marketing. Our purpose here is not to provide a comprehensive review of that literature, but simply to highlight a few important points that help define the role of costs in pricing.

Economic Theory and Pricing

OBJECTIVE 7

Identify the role of costs in pricing decisions in perfect and imperfect markets.

Pricing decisions depend on the characteristics of the market a firm faces. In **perfect competition**, a firm can sell as much of a product as it can produce, all at a single market price. If it charges more, no customer will buy. If it charges less, it sacrifices profits. Therefore, every firm in such a market will charge the market price, and the only decision for managers is how much to produce.

Although costs do not directly influence prices in perfect competition, they affect the production decision. Consider the *marginal cost curve* in Exhibit 8-4. The **marginal cost** is the additional cost resulting from producing and selling one additional unit. The marginal cost often decreases as production increases up to a point because efficiencies are possible with larger production amounts. But, at some point, marginal costs begin to rise with increases in production because facilities begin to be overcrowded, resulting in inefficiencies.

Perfect Competition. A market in which a firm can sell as much of a product as it can produce, all at a single market price. If it charges more, no customer will buy; if it charges less, it sacrifices profits.

Exhibit 8-4 also includes a *marginal revenue curve*. The **marginal revenue** is the additional revenue resulting from the sale of an additional unit. In perfect competition, the marginal revenue curve is a horizontal line equal to the price per unit at all volumes of sales.

As long as the marginal cost is less than the price, additional production and sales are profitable. But when marginal costs exceed price, the firm loses money on each additional unit. Therefore, the profit maximizing volume is the quantity at which marginal cost equals price. In Exhibit 8-4, the firm should produce V_0 units. Producing fewer units passes up profitable opportunities; producing more units reduces profit for each additional unit.

EXHIBIT 8-4

Marginal Revenue and Cost in Perfect Competition

Marginal Cost. The additional cost resulting from producing and selling one additional unit.

Marginal Revenue. The additional revenue resulting from the sale of an additional unit.

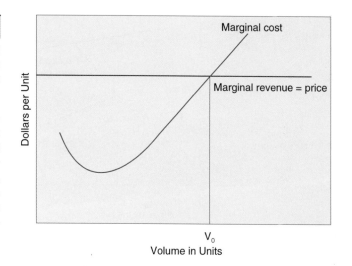

Imperfect Competition. A market in which a firm's price will influence the quantity it sells; at some point, price reductions are necessary to generate additional sales.

In **imperfect competition**, a firm's price will influence the quantity it sells. At some point, price reductions are necessary to generate additional sales. Exhibit 8-5 contains a demand curve (also called the average revenue curve) for imperfect competition that shows the volume of sales at each possible price. To sell additional units, the price of *all units sold* must be reduced. Therefore, the marginal revenue curve, also shown in Exhibit 8-5, is below the demand curve. That is, the marginal revenue for selling one additional unit is less than the price at which it is sold because the price of all other units falls as well. For example, suppose 10 units can be sold for $50 per unit. The price must be dropped to $49 per unit to sell 11 units, to $48 to sell 12 units, and to $47 to sell 13 units. The fourth column of Exhibit 8-6 shows the marginal revenue for units 11 through 13. Notice that the marginal revenue decreases as volume increases.

Price Elasticity. The effect of price changes on sales volume.

To estimate marginal revenue, managers must predict the effect of price changes on volume, which is called **price elasticity**. If small price increases cause large volume declines, demand is *elastic*. If prices have little or no effect on volume, demand is *inelastic*.

Now suppose the marginal cost of the units is as shown in the fifth column of Exhibit 8-6. The optimal production and sales level would be 12 units. The last column illustrates that the 11th unit adds $4 to profit, the 12th adds $1, but production and sale of the 13th unit would *decrease* profit by $2. In general, firms should produce and sell units until the marginal revenue equals the marginal cost, represented by volume V_0 in Exhibit 8-5.

Notice that in economic theory the cost that is relevant for pricing decisions is the *marginal cost*. The accountant's approximation to marginal cost is *variable cost*. What is the major difference between the economist's marginal cost and the accountant's variable cost? Variable cost is assumed to be constant within a relevant range of volume, while marginal cost increases with each unit produced. However, within large ranges of production volume, increases in marginal cost are often small. Therefore, using variable cost can be a reasonable approximation to marginal cost in many situations.

EXHIBIT 8-5

Marginal Revenue and Cost in Imperfect Competition

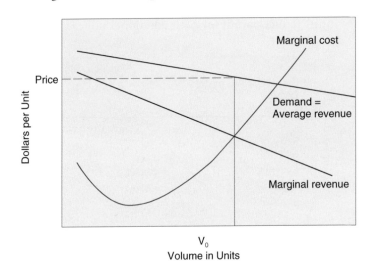

EXHIBIT 8-6

Profit Maximization in Imperfect Competition

UNITS SOLD	PRICE/ UNIT	TOTAL REVENUE	MARGINAL REVENUE	MARGINAL COST	PROFIT FROM PRODUCTION AND SALE OF ADDITIONAL UNIT
10	$50	10 × $50 = $500			
11	49	11 × 49 = 539	$539 − 500 = $39	$35	$4
12	48	12 × 48 = 576	576 − 539 = 37	36	1
13	47	13 × 47 = 611	611 − 576 = 35	37	(2)

Maximizing Total Contribution

Managers seldom compute marginal revenue curves and marginal cost curves. Instead, they use estimates based on judgment to predict the effects of additional production and sales on profits. In addition, they examine selected volumes, not the whole range of possible volumes. Such simplifications are justified because the cost of a more sophisticated analysis would exceed the benefits.

Consider a division of General Electric (GE) that makes microwave ovens. Suppose market researchers estimate that 700,000 ovens can be sold if priced at $200 per unit, but 1,000,000 could be sold at $180. The variable cost of production is $130 per unit at production levels of both 700,000 and 1,000,000. Both volumes are also within the relevant range so that fixed costs are unaffected by the changes in volume. Which price should be charged?

The GE manager could compute the additional revenue and additional costs of the 300,000 additional units of sales at the $180 price:

Additional revenue: (1,000,000 × $180) −(700,000 × $200)= $40,000,000
Additional costs: 300,000 × $130   = 39,000,000
Additional profit: $ 1,000,000

Alternatively, the manager could compare the total contribution for each alternative:

Contribution at $180: ($180 − $130) × 1,000,000= $50,000,000
Contribution at $200: ($200 − $130) × 700,000 = 49,000,000
Difference $ 1,000,000

Notice that comparing the total contributions is essentially the same as computing the additional revenues and costs. Further, both approaches correctly ignore fixed costs, which are unaffected by this pricing decision.

INFLUENCES ON PRICING IN PRACTICE

A number of factors interact to shape the environment in which managers make pricing decisions. Legal requirements, competitors' actions, costs, and customer demands all influence pricing.

Legal Requirements

Pricing decisions must be made within constraints imposed by laws. In addition to prohibiting out-and-out collusion in setting prices, laws generally prohibit prices that are *predatory* or *discriminatory*.

Predatory pricing is establishing prices so low that competitors are driven out of the market so that the predatory pricer then has no significant competition and can raise prices dramatically. Courts have generally ruled that pricing is predatory only if companies set prices below average variable cost.

Discriminatory pricing is charging different prices to different customers for the same product or service. However, pricing is not discriminatory if it reflects a cost differential incurred in providing the good or service.

Closely related to the issues of predatory and discriminatory pricing is the practice of *dumping*. **Dumping** refers to the selling of goods in a foreign country at a price that is below the full cost of the product and below the selling price in the domestic market. International laws prohibit this practice because it would allow large foreign competitors to force smaller domestic producers out of business.

Businesses can defend themselves against charges of predatory, discriminatory, or dumping pricing-practices by citing their costs as a basis for their prices. Therefore, a good understanding of the cost of a product or service— especially the activities that cause additional costs to be incurred— is useful in avoiding legal pitfalls. Our discussion here assumes that pricing practices do not violate legal constraints.

Marketing in the Cost Competitive Airline Industry

Boeing
www.boeing.com

Bombardier
www.bombardier.com

Over the next two decades, the airlines industry will need 16,000 new airplanes worth over $1 trillion. How will Boeing maintain their competitive edge and profitability? With increased competition, they know that profits can be improved more by controlling (reducing) costs than by increasing prices to customers. So, should they build bigger airplanes or more of the existing size but with improvements in features and efficiencies that will lower customers' costs? Which alternative has lower costs for their customers? To answer these questions, Bombardier and Boeing had to understand their own costs, as well as the costs of their customers. The real question is: What do their customers value in return for a price tag of $50+ million per airplane?

A case in point is the Boeing 747-X. In 1992, the company began their research and development program for this huge 500-passenger airplane. An important part of their research was the assessment of their customers' costs—both of operating their existing fleet of planes and of the reduced costs of the new 747-X planes. It formed a working group with 19 airline customers (for example, United and American Airlines and British Airways) to look at their requirements in the 500+ seat market. By 1996, the company had completed the design of the new airplane and was faced with the final decision to launch. A decision to launch would involve a huge immediate investment in costly plant and equipment resources. In order to pay for these assets and make a profit, they had to be confident that their customers would demand the new plane.

The key question was whether customers wanted the latest, largest, and most costly airplane or one with the highest value. In 1997, Boeing made the final decision. According to Philip Condit, Chairman and Chief Executive Officer, "The prospective market for airplanes with over 500 seats was limited. We were at last in a position of balancing the significant cost of the program against the limited size of the market." Most of the company's customers needed more airplanes for the expected increase in the number of nonstop routes. In short, customers said, "We would rather have two new 250-seat airplanes that are more *cost efficient* than one 500-seat super airplane." So, the 747-X program was stopped. Instead, the company is concentrating on upgrading their existing aircraft. For example, the new model of the existing 747 will offer 16 percent more seats and up to 10 percent lower "seat-mile" costs.

Montreal-based Bombardier Inc. demonstrated how strategic planning and marketing have produced a "potential gold mine." Building on the reputation of the Dash 8, Bombardier designed a new 78-seat Dash 8-400 at a cost of $600 million. This fast and efficient aircraft is targeted at the niche market of the busy short runs between cities, distances of less than 650 kilometres, that are required in northern Europe and Asia. Using market survey information, Bombardier calculated that airlines will spend $26 billion (U.S.) on propeller-driven aircraft in the 60 to 90-seat category over the next 20 years. A month before the first flight, 63 Dash 8-400 planes had been sold at a list price of $24.2 million, one third of the amount needed to break even. This $1.5 billion in gross sales will keep Toronto's de Havilland Inc. plant busy for almost two years.

Niche marketing has been one of Bombardier's strengths. The 500th Dash 8 regional airliner was recently delivered. The Dash 8-200 is a 37-seat version of the Dash 8 with more powerful engines for use in mountainous terrain. Building on their success, the sales team spent years studying the airline market before committing themselves to the 400 model and feel they are well ahead of the competition.

Sources: Adapted from O. Bertin, "Bombardier sells 26 Dash 8 airliners," *The Globe and Mail* (November 22, 1997), p. B5 and O. Bertin, "Bombardier targets new niche," *The Globe and Mail* (November 24, 1997), p. B8.

Competitors' Actions

Dumping. Refers to the selling of goods in a foreign country at a price that is below the full cost of the product and below the selling price in the domestic market.

Competitors usually react to the price changes of their rivals. Tinkering with prices is often most heavily affected by the price-setter's expectations of competitors' reactions and of the overall effects on the total industry demand for the good or service in question. For example, an airline might cut prices even if it expects price cuts from its rivals. A justification for the price cut may be the prediction that total customer demand for the tickets of all airlines will increase sufficiently to offset the reduction in the price per ticket.

Competition is becoming increasingly international. Overcapacity in some countries often causes aggressive pricing policies, particularly for a company's exported goods.

Knowledge of a competitor's costs can be useful. Therefore many companies will gather information regarding a rival's capacity, technology, and operating policies. In this way, managers make more informed predictions of competitors' reactions to a company's prices.

Costs

Costs influence the deliberate setting of prices in some industries, but not in others. Frequently, the market price is regarded as a given. Examples include the prices of metals and agricultural commodities. Consider gold. A mining company sells at the established market prices. Whether profits or losses are forthcoming depends on how well the company controls its costs and volume. Here cost data help managers decide on the level and mix of outputs.

The influence of costs on the setting of prices is often overstated. Nevertheless, many managers say that their prices are set by cost-plus pricing. For example, consider the automobile and construction industries. Their executives describe the procedure as computing an average unit cost and then adding a "reasonable" **markup** (that is, the amount by which price exceeds cost) that will generate a target return on investment. But the key is the "plus" in cost-plus. It is rarely an unalterable markup. Its magnitude depends on the behaviour of competitors and customers.

Markup. The amount by which price exceeds cost.

Prices are mostly directly related to costs in industries where revenue is based on cost reimbursement. A prime example is defence contracting. Cost-reimbursement contracts generally specify how costs should be measured and what costs are allowable.

In short, the market sets prices after all. Why? Because the price as set by a cost-plus formula is inevitably adjusted "in light of market conditions." The maximum price that may be charged is the one that does not drive the customer away. The minimum price is zero. Indeed, companies may give out free samples to gain entry into a market. A more practical guide is that, in the short run, the minimum price to be quoted, *subject to consideration of long-run effects*, should be equal to the costs that may be avoided by not landing the order—often all variable costs of producing, selling, and distributing the good or service. And, in the long run, the price must be high enough to cover all costs, including fixed costs.

Customer Demands and Target Costing

More than ever before, managers are recognizing the needs of customers. Pricing is no exception. If customers believe a price is too high, they may turn to other sources for the product or service, substitute a different product, or decide to produce the item themselves.

Target Costing. A product strategy in which companies first determine the price at which they can sell a new product and then design a product that can be produced at a low enough cost to provide an adequate profit margin.

Most companies have traditionally started with costs and added a markup to get prices. However, a growing number of companies are turning the equation around and developing costs based on prices. Companies that use **target costing** first determine the price at which they can sell a new product and then design a product that can be produced at a low enough cost to provide an adequate profit margin. Product designers thus become aware of the cost impacts of the design of both the product itself and the process used to produce it.

For example, market research may indicate that Toyota could sell 100,000 units of one model of a sports car annually at a list price of $35,000. The engineers who design the product might consider several different combinations of features bearing different costs. If the total product cost is sufficiently low, the product may be launched. Conversely, if the total product cost is too high, the product may be unjustified. Of course, the point here is that the customer helps determine the price. The product designers and the management accountants work together to see if an attractive product can be developed at a target cost that will provide room for an attractive profit.

Whether a company sets prices based on costs or costs based on prices, it is inevitable that prices and costs interact. If the focus is on prices that are influenced primarily on market forces, managers must make sure that all costs can be covered in the long run. If prices are based on a markup of costs, managers must examine the actions of customers and competitors to assure that products or services can be sold at the determined prices.

Target Pricing

OBJECTIVE 9

Compute a target sales price by various approaches and identify their advantages and disadvantages.

Cost plus is often the basis for target prices. The size of the "plus" depends on target (desired) operating incomes, which, in turn, frequently depend on the target return on investment for a division, a product line, or a product. Chapter 15 discusses return on investment. For simplicity here, we work with a target operating income.

Target prices can be based on a host of different markups based on a host of different definitions of cost. Thus, there are many ways to arrive at *the same target price*. They simply reflect different arrangements of the components of the same income statement.

Exhibit 8-7 displays the relationships of costs to target selling prices, assuming a target operating income of $1 million. The percentages there represent four popular markup formulas for pricing: (1) as a percentage of variable manufacturing costs, (2) as a percentage of total variable costs, (3) as a percentage of full costs, and (4) as a percentage of absorption costs. Of course, the percentages differ. For instance, the markup on variable manufacturing costs is 66.67 percent and on absorption costs is 33.33 percent. Regardless of the formula used, the pricing decision maker will be led toward the *same* target price. For a volume of one million units, assume that the target selling price is $20 per unit. If the decision maker is unable to obtain such a price consistently, the company will not achieve its $1 million operating income objective.

The history of accounting reveals that most companies' systems have gathered costs via some form of full-cost system. In recent years, when systems are changed, variable costs and fixed costs are often identified. But managers have regarded this change as an addition to the existing full-cost system. That is, many managers insist on having information regarding *both* variable costs per unit and the allocated fixed costs per unit before setting selling prices. If the accounting system routinely gathers data regarding both variable and fixed costs, such data can readily be provided. However, most absorption-costing systems in practice do

Target Costing, ABC, and Service Companies

Many companies use target costing together with an activity-based costing (ABC) system. Target costing requires a company to first determine what a customer will pay for a product and then work backwards to design the product and production process that will generate a desired level of profit. ABC provides data on the costs of the various activities needed to produce the product. Knowing the costs of activities allows product and production process designers to assess the potential impacts of their designs on the product's cost. Target costing can be used with activity-based costs.

For example, Culp, Inc., a North Carolina textile manufacturer, uses target costing and ABC to elevate cost management into one of the most strategically imperative areas of the firm. Culp found that 80 percent of its product costs are predetermined at the design stage, but earlier cost control efforts had focused only on the other 20 percent. By shifting cost management efforts to the design stage and by determining the costs of the various activities involved in production, cost management became an integral part of the strategic decisions of the firm.

Cost management at Culp evolved into a process of cutting costs when a product is being designed, not identifying costs that are out of line after the production is complete.

A basic goal of target costing is to reduce costs before they occur. After all, once costs have been incurred, they cannot be changed. Such a strategy is especially important if product life cycles are short—and, since most product life cycles are shrinking, use of target costing is expanding. Target costing focuses on reducing costs in the product design and development stages—when costs can really be affected. For example, Chrysler's design of the low-priced Neon was heavily influenced by the company's use of target costing, and Procter and Gamble's

CEO credits target costing for helping eliminate costs that could lead products to be priced too high for the market.

Target costing has traditionally been applied in manufacturing companies. However, its use in service and nonprofit companies is growing. For example, a process nearly identical to target costing is being used in some hospitals. Development of treatment protocols, the preferred treatment steps for a patient with a particular diagnosis, is the "product design" phase for a hospital. Treatment protocols have short life cycles because of rapid advances in medical technology and knowledge. Therefore, with increased attention to cost containment in health care, it is important to consider the costs of the various activities in a treatment protocol at the time of designing the protocol.

Measuring the costs of a particular treatment protocol after it is in use was the best that could be done until recently, even in the most cost-conscious hospitals. But identifying cost overruns after the fact, although better than never measuring them, did not lead to good cost control. By using target costing techniques, that is, identifying the maximum amount that would be paid for a treatment, protocols can be designed to point out potential cost overruns before a treatment begins. This focuses cost containment on the patient level, where most decisions are made, not at the department level, where identifying the causes of cost overruns is more difficult.

Sources: J. Bohn, "Chrysler Cuts Costs by Nurturing Links with Suppliers," *Automotive Age* (January 17, 1994), p. 18; J. Brausch, "Target Costing for Profit Enhancement," *Management Accounting* (November 1994), pp. 45–49; G. Hoffman, "Future Vision," *Grocery Marketing* (March 1994), p. 6; D. Young, "Managing the Stages of Hospital Cost Accounting," *Healthcare Financial Management* (April 1993), p. 58.

Culp
www.culp.com

not organize their data collection so as to distinguish between variable and fixed costs. As a result, special studies or special analysis must be used to designate costs as variable and fixed.

EXHIBIT 8-7

Relationships of Costs
to Same Target Selling
Prices

ALTERNATIVE MARKUP PERCENTAGES TO ACHIEVE SAME TARGET SALES (DOLLARS IN THOUSANDS)

Target sales	$20,000,000	
Variable costs:		
Manufacturing	$12,000,000	($20,000 − $12,000) ÷ $12,000 = 66.7%
Selling and administrative	1,100,000	
Total variable costs	$13,100,000	($20,000 − $13,100) ÷ $13,100 = 52.67%
Fixed costs:		
Manufacturing	$ 3,000,000*	
Selling and administrative	2,900,000	
Total fixed costs	$ 5,900,000	
Full costs:	$19,000,000	($20,000 − $19,000) ÷ $19,000 = 5.26%
Target operating income	$ 1,000,000	

* A frequently used formula is based on absorption costs:
[$20,000 − ($12,000 + $3,000)] ÷ $15,000 = 33.33%.

ADVANTAGES OF VARIOUS APPROACHES TO PRICING DECISIONS

Contribution Approach Provides Detailed Information

When it is used intelligently, the contribution approach has some advantages over the absorption-costing approach, or the full-cost approach, because the latter often fails to highlight different cost-behaviour patterns.

Obviously, the contribution approach offers more detailed information because it displays variable- and fixed-cost-behaviour patterns separately. Since the contribution approach is sensitive to cost-volume-profit relationships, it is a helpful basis for developing pricing formulas. The contribution approach emphasizes cost-volume-profit relationships. Consequently, the approach makes it easier for managers to prepare price schedules at different volume levels.

The correct analysis in Exhibit 8-8 shows how changes in volume affect operating income. The contribution approach helps managers with pricing decisions

EXHIBIT 8-8

Analyses of Effects of Changes in Volume on Operating Income

	CORRECT ANALYSIS			INCORRECT ANALYSIS		
Volume in units	900,000	1,000,000	1,100,000	900,000	1,000,000	1,100,000
Sales @ $20.00	$18,000,000	$20,000,000	$22,000,000	$18,000,000	$20,000,000	$22,000,000
Total variable costs @ $13.10	11,790,000	13,100,000	14,410,000			
Contribution margin	6,210,000	6,900,000	7,590,000			
Fixed costs[†]	5,900,000	5,900,000	5,900,000			
Full costs @ $19.00				17,100,000	19,000,000	20,900,000
Operating income	$ 310,000	$ 1,000,000	$ 1,690,000	$ 900,000	$ 1,000,000	$ 1,100,000

[†] Fixed manufacturing costs	$3,000,000
Fixed selling and administrative costs	2,900,000
Total fixed costs	$5,900,000

because it readily displays the interrelationships among variable costs, fixed costs, and potential changes in selling prices.

In contrast, target pricing with absorption costing or full costing presumes a given volume level. When volume changes, the unit cost used at the original planned volume may mislead managers. As indicated earlier, there have been actual cases where managers have erroneously assumed that the change in total costs may be computed by multiplying any change in volume by the full unit cost.

The incorrect analysis in Exhibit 8-8 shows how managers may be misled if the $19 full cost per unit is used to predict effects of volume changes on operating income. Suppose a manager uses the $19 figure to predict an operating income of $900,000 if the company sells 900,000 instead of 1,000,000 units. If actual operating income is $310,000 instead, as the correct analysis predicts, that manager may be stunned—and may have to look for a new job.

Other Advantages of Contribution Approach

Two other advantages of the contribution approach deserve mention. First, a normal or target-pricing formula can be as easily developed by the contribution approach as by absorption-costing or full-costing approaches, as shown in Exhibit 8-7.

Second, the contribution approach offers insight into the short-run versus long-run effects of cutting prices on special orders. For example, assume the same cost-behaviour patterns as at the Samson Co. (Exhibit 8-3). The 100,000-unit order added $100,000 to operating income at a selling price of $13, which was $7 below the target selling price of $20 and $2 below the absorption manufacturing cost of $15. Given all the stated assumptions, accepting the order appeared to be the better choice. No general answer can be given, but the relevant information was more easily generated by the contribution approach:

	CONTRIBUTION APPROACH	ABSORPTION COSTING APPROACH
Sales, 100,000 units @ $13	$1,300,000	$1,300,000
Variable manufacturing costs @ $12	1,200,000	
Absorption manufacturing costs @ $15		1,500,000
Apparent change in operating income	$ 100,000	$ −200,000

Under the absorption approach, the decision maker has no direct knowledge of cost-volume-profit relationships. The decision maker makes the decision by hunch. On the surface, the offer is definitely unattractive because the price of $13 is $2 below absorption costs.

Under the contribution approach, the decision maker sees a short-run advantage of $100,000 from accepting the offer. Fixed costs will be unaffected by whatever decision is made and operating income will increase by $100,000. Still, there are often long-run effects to consider. Will acceptance to the offer undermine the long-run price structure? In other words, is the short-run advantage of $100,000 more than offset by highly probable long-run financial disadvantages? The decision maker may think so and may reject the offer. But—and this is important—by doing so the decision-maker is, in effect, foregoing $100,000 now in order to protect long-run market advantages. Generally, the decision maker can assess problems of this sort by asking whether the probability of long-run benefits is worth an "investment" equal to the foregone contribution margin ($100,000 in this case). Under absorption approaches, the decision maker must ordinarily conduct a special study to find the immediate effects. Under the contribution approach, the manager has a system that will routinely and more surely provide such information.

The contribution approach is being advocated in the Canadian grocery industry. The approach known as "Management Product Performance Cost" focuses on the relevant variable costs of providing a product to the consumer under various conditions. This varies from an absorption costing approach known as "Direct Product Profitability," which attempts to include every cost, both fixed and variable, that is associated with the entire business of running a grocery chain.

> In management product performance costing, each product is assigned a true, standardized cost — the cost of delivering the shelf-ready product from the vendor to the store during a non-promotional period. In grocery departments, for example, the true performance cost equals the vendor list price, plus freight charges, plus any direct variable cost (e.g., warehousing) — all numbers that are readily available.

> During non-promotional periods, the merchandising margin would be "normal retail price" less "normal cost." To figure the "true cost" during the promotion period, the merchandising margin would be "the promotion retail" less "normal cost" less the matching promotion allowance.

> By always considering this management product performance cost, managers will be less inclined to stock shelves with enormous quantities of promotional goods — and automatically assume all margins are being made.[3]

Advantages of Absorption-Cost or Full-Cost Approaches

Our general theme of focusing on relevant information also extends into the area of pricing. To say that either a contribution approach or an absorption-cost approach or a full-cost approach provides the "best" guide to pricing decisions is a dangerous oversimplification of one of the most perplexing problems in business. Lack of understanding and judgment can lead to unprofitable pricing regardless of the kind of cost data available or cost accounting system used.

Frequently, managers do not employ a contribution approach because they fear that variable costs will be substituted indiscriminately for full costs and will therefore lead to suicidal price cutting. This problem should *not* arise if the data are used wisely. However, if top managers perceive a pronounced danger of under-pricing when variable-cost data are revealed, they may justifiably prefer an absorption-costing approach or a full-cost approach for guiding pricing decisions.

Cost-plus pricing based on absorption costs or full costs entails circular reasoning. That is, price, which influences sales volume, is often based on an average absorption cost per unit, which in turn is partly determined by the underlying volume of sales.

---

[3] Scott D. Myers, "Technology: New Tools that Bind," *Canadian Grocer*, December, 1990, p. 22.

Despite these criticisms, absorption costs or full costs are far more widely used in practice than is the contribution approach. Why? In addition to the reasons already mentioned, the following have been offered:

1. In the long run, all costs must be recovered to stay in business. Sooner or later fixed costs do indeed fluctuate as volume changes. Therefore it is prudent to assume that all costs are variable (even if some are fixed in the short run).
2. Computing target prices based on cost-plus may indicate what competitors might charge, especially if they have approximately the same level of efficiency as you and also aim at recovering all costs in the long run.
3. Absorption-cost or full-cost formula pricing meets the cost-benefit test. It is too expensive to conduct individual cost-volume tests for the many products (sometimes thousands) that a company offers.
4. There is much uncertainty about the shape of the demand curves and the correct price-output decisions. Absorption-cost or full-cost pricing copes with this uncertainty by not encouraging managers to take too much marginal business.
5. Absorption-cost or full-cost pricing tends to promote price stability. Managers prefer price stability because it eases their professional lives, primarily because planning is more dependable.
6. Absorption-cost pricing or full-cost pricing provides the most defensible basis for justifying prices to all interested parties, including government antitrust investigators.
7. Absorption-cost or full-cost pricing provides convenient reference (target) points to simplify hundreds or thousands of pricing decisions.

EXHIBIT 8-9		
Quote Sheet for Pricing	Direct materials, at cost	$25,000
	Direct labour and variable manufacturing overhead, 600 direct-labour-hours x $30 =	18,000
	Sales commission (varies with job)	2,000
	Total variable costs—minimum price*	45,000
	Add fixed costs allocated to job, 600 direct-labour-hours x $20	12,000
	Total costs	57,000
	Add desired markup	30,000
	Selling price—maximum price that you think you can obtain*	$87,000

* This sheet shows two prices, maximum and minimum. Any amount you can get above the minimum price is a contribution margin.

Advantages of Using a Variety of Approaches

No single method of pricing is always best. An interview study of executives reported use of *both* full-cost and variable-cost information in pricing decisions: "The full- versus variable-cost pricing controversy is not one of either black or white. The companies we studied used both approaches."[4]

---

[4] T. Bruegelmann, G. Haessly, C. Wolfangel, and M. Schiff, "How Variable Costing is Used in Pricing Decisions," *Management Accounting*, Vol. 65, No. 10, p. 65.

Cost-Based Pricing for International Telephone Calls

Accounting has a direct effect on the revenue of many government contractors because prices are often simply costs plus a profit margin. Accounting costs also can directly affect the revenues of other companies, especially those subject to regulation.

An intriguing area of cost-based pricing is international telephone calls. When a customer in the United States calls someone (or receives a call from someone) in another country, the revenue from the call must be split between the telephone companies in the two countries. Under international agreements, revenues should be shared according to the costs of the two telephone companies, so that there is an equitable division of profits.

In the early 1990s the U.S. Federal Communications Commission (FCC) proposed changing the way revenues on international calls are shared among companies. Under current rules, U.S. firms pay foreign carriers about $.75 out of every dollar collected on overseas calls. The FCC suspected that payments above the foreign carriers' costs amounted to an overpayment of $1 billion a year. To assure equitable revenues for U.S. telephone companies, the FCC wanted "to learn about the true costs, levels of profits, and how those costs and profits are shared among U.S. telephone companies and foreign telecommunications authorities."

At least two factors make the FCC's task difficult. First, it has no authority over foreign companies. Only U.S. companies must meet reporting requirements specified by the FCC. Second, accounting systems differ by country. For example, many South American countries explicitly adjust their accounting numbers for inflation, but U.S. companies do not. International cost comparisons will not be easy, but if cost-based pricing is to be used for international telephone calls, some method of comparison is necessary. This type of situation is leading many authorities to support more standardization of accounting measurement and reporting rules throughout the world.

Source: Adapted from "Accounting Changes on International Calls Proposed by the FCC," *The Wall Street Journal*, July 13, 1990, p. A2.

U.S. Federal Communications Commission
www.fcc.gov

Managers are especially reluctant to focus on variable costs and ignore allocated fixed costs when their performance evaluations, and possibly their bonuses, are based on income shown in published financial statements. Why? Because such statements are based on absorption costing and thus are affected by allocations of fixed costs.

Formats for Pricing

Exhibit 8-7 showed how to compute alternative general markup percentages that would produce the same selling prices if used day after day. In practice, the format and arithmetic of quote sheets, job proposals, or similar records vary considerably.

Exhibit 8-9 is from an actual quote sheet used by the manager of a small job shop that bids on welding machinery orders in a highly competitive industry. The Exhibit 8-9 approach is a tool for informed pricing decisions. Notice that the minimum price is the total variable cost.

Of course, the manager will rarely bid the minimum price. To do so regularly would virtually ensure eventual bankruptcy. Still, the manager wants to know the effect of a job on the company's total variable costs. Occasionally, a bid near that minimum total may be justified because of idle capacity or the desire to establish a presence in new markets or with a new customer.

Note that Exhibit 8-9 classifies costs especially for the pricing task. Pricing decisions may be made by more than one person. The accountant's responsibility is to prepare an understandable format that involves a minimum of computations. Exhibit 8-9 combines direct labour and variable manufacturing overhead. All fixed costs, whether manufacturing, selling, or administrative, are lumped together and applied to the job using a single fixed-overhead rate per direct-labour-hour. Obviously, if more accuracy is desired, many more detailed cost items and overhead rates could be formulated.

Some managers, particularly in construction and service industries such as auto repair, compile separate categories of costs of (1) direct materials, parts, and supplies, and (2) direct labour. These managers then use different markup rates for each category. These rates are developed to provide revenue for both related overhead costs and operating profit. For example, an automobile repair shop might have the following format for each job:

	BILLED TO CUSTOMERS
Auto parts ($200 cost plus 40% markup)	$280
Direct labour (Cost is $20 per hour. Bill at 300% to recover overhead and provide for operating profit. Billing rate is $20 × 300% = $60 per hour. Total billed for 10 hours is $60 × 10 = $600)	600
Total billed to customer	$880

Another example is an Italian printing company in Milan that wants to price its jobs so that each one generates a margin of 28 percent of revenues—14 percent to cover selling and administrative expenses and 14 percent for profit. To achieve this, the manager uses a pricing formula of 140 percent times predicted material cost plus 25,000 Italian Lira (abbreviated Lit.) per hour of production time. The latter covers labour and overhead costs of Lit.18,000 per hour. For a product with Lit. 400,000 of materials cost and 30 hours of production time, the price would be Lit.1,310,000:

	COST	PRICE	PROFIT
Materials	Lit. 400,000	Lit. 560,000	Lit. 160,000
Labour and overhead	540,000	750,000	210,000
Total	Lit. 940,000	Lit. 1,310,000	Lit. 370,000

The profit of Lit. 370,000 is approximately 40 percent of the cost of Lit. 940,000 and 28 percent of the price of Lit. 1,310,000.

Thus, there is a jumble of ways to compute selling prices. However, some general words of caution are appropriate here. Managers are better able to understand their options and the effects of their decisions on profits if they know their costs. That is, it is more informative to pinpoint costs first, before adding markups, than to have a variety of markups already embedded in the "costs" used as guides for setting selling prices. For example, if materials cost $1,000, they should be shown on a price quotation guide at $1,000, not at, say, a marked-up $1,400 because that is what the seller hopes to get.

TARGET COSTING

OBJECTIVE 10

Use target costing to decide whether to add a new product or service.

As we have seen, both prices and costs are affected by the actions of the company and market conditions. However, the degree to which each can be affected by company actions determines the approach companies use to plan operations. Cost-plus pricing is used for products where company actions (for example, advertising) can influence the market. The focus in this case is on marketing and the revenue side of the profit equation.

Target Costing and New Product Development

Consider a situation in which a company is deciding whether or not to develop and market a new product. The ability to achieve a profit on this new product is determined by the difference between the market price and the cost.

But what if the market conditions are such that the company cannot influence prices? If the desired profit is to be achieved, the company must then focus on the product's cost. Target costing is a tool for making cost a key throughout the life of a product. A desired, or target, cost is set before the product is created or even designed. Managers must then try to control costs so that the product's cost does not exceed its target cost. The emphasis of target costing is on proactive, up-front planning throughout every activity of the new product development process. However, it is most effective at reducing costs during the product design phase, when the vast majority of costs are committed. For example, the costs of resources such as new machinery, materials, parts, and even future refinements are largely determined by the design of the product and the associated production processes. These costs are not easily reduced once production begins.

Marketing might appear to have a limited role in target costing because the price is set by competitive market conditions. Actually, market research from the marketing departments at the beginning of the target costing activity guides the whole product development process by supplying information on customer-required product functions. In fact, one of the key characteristics of successful target costing is a strong emphasis on understanding customer needs.

ITT Automotive
www.ittautomotive.com

Compaq
www.compaq.com

Mercedes-Benz
www.mercedes-benz.com

For example, consider the target costing system used by ITT Automotive— one of the world's largest automotive suppliers. The company designs, develops, and manufactures a broad range of products including brake system, electric motors, and lamps. Also, the company is the worldwide market leader in anti-lock braking systems (ABS), producing 20,000 such systems a day. Because these ABS are computerized, ITT Automotive actually ships 30 percent more computers daily than does Compaq!

What pricing approach does ITT Automotive use for the ABS? The pricing process starts when one of ITT's customers, say Mercedes-Benz, sends an invitation to bid. The market for brake systems is so competitive that very little variance exists in the price companies can ask (bid). A cost targeting group is formed and charged with determining whether the price and costs allow for enough of a profit margin. This group is made up of engineers, cost accountants, and sales personnel. Factors considered in determining the feasibility of earning the desired target profit margin include competitor pricing, inflation rates, interest rates, and potential cost reductions during both the design and production stages of the ABS product life. Many of the component parts the make up the ABS are purchased from the company's suppliers. Thus, the cost targeting group works closely with suppliers during the target costing process. After product and process design improvements are made and commitments from suppliers are received, the company has the cost information needed for deciding whether or not to make a bid.

The target costing seems to be working well at ITT Automotive. The company's bid for the ABS resulted in Mercedes-Benz U.S. International selecting ITT Automotive as the developer and supplier of major vehicle performance system (including the ABS) for the automaker's M-Class All-Activity Vehicle.[5]

Target Costing and Cost-Plus Pricing Compared

It is important for companies to understand the market in which they operate and to use the most appropriate pricing approach. To see how target costing and cost-plus pricing can lead to different decisions, suppose that ITT Automotive receives an invitation to bid from Ford on the ABS to be used in a new model car.

Assume the following data apply:

- the specifications contained in Ford's invitation lead to an estimated current manufacturing cost (component parts, direct labour, and manufacturing overhead) of $170,
- ITT Automotive had a desired gross margin rate of 30 percent on sales, which means that actual costs should make up 70 percent of the price.
- highly competitive market conditions exist and have established a sales price of $200 per unit.

If cost-plus pricing is used to bid on the ABS, the bid price would be $243 ($170 ÷ 70 percent). This bid would most likely be rejected by Ford because the market price is only $200. ITT Automotive's pricing approach would lead to a lost opportunity.

Suppose that ITT Automotive recognizes that the market conditions dictate a set price of $200. If a target-costing system is used, what would the pricing decision be? The target cost is $140 (70 percent × $200), so a required cost reduction of $30 per unit is necessary. The target costing group would work with product and process engineers and suppliers to determine if the average unit cost could be reduced by $30 over the product's life. Note that it is not necessary to get costs down to the $140 target cost before production begins. The initial unit cost will likely be higher, say $150. Continuous improvement over the product's life will result in the final $10 of cost reduction. Assuming that the required commitments for cost reductions are received, the decision is to make a bid for $200 per unit. Note that if the bid is accepted, ITT Automotive must carry through with its focus on cost management through out the life of the product.

Target costing originated in Japan, but now it is used by many companies worldwide, including Chrysler, Mercedes-Benz, Procter & Gamble, Caterpillar, and ITT Automotive. Even some hospitals use target costing.

Why the increasing popularity of target costing? With increased global competition in many industries, companies are more and more limited in influencing market prices. Cost management then becomes the key to profitability.

---

[5] *Sources:* G. Schmeize, R. Grier, and E. Buttross, "Target Costing at ITT Automotive," *Management Accounting*, December 1996, pp. 26–30; News release, ITT Automotive, August 6, 1996, Auburn Hills, Mich.

The Six Sigma Program at Bombardier

Bombardier
www.bombardier.com

In today's business world, all good companies are committed to continuous improvement. Whatever the techniques used, the goal is the same: to produce better products at lower cost.

In this environment, simply improving our costs or quality on an annual basis is not good enough. We must ensure that our rate of improvement is better than the competition's.

To meet this challenge, Bombardier is undertaking the Six Sigma initiative, as it provides the means of achieving the highest level of customer-defined quality at the lowest cost, thereby increasing profit margins and enhancing Bombardier's competitive position.

A highly disciplined initiative, it aims at virtually eliminating defects in products as well as in the processes through which they are produced. It is based on the principle that the best way to reduce costs and improve cycle time and customer satisfaction is to reduce and eventually eliminate defects the first time around in engineering, procurement, production, and administrative systems. At a level of Six Sigma, there are only 3.4 defects per million opportunities, virtual perfection!

A focus on quality is not new to Bombardier. A number of important quality initiatives have already been successfully implemented.

How will Six Sigma help Bombardier improve its performance?

- It establishes a rigorous problem-solving process that flows from a clear understanding of customer needs.
- It develops the skills of, and provides the tools for, statistical reasoning that helps to achieve new breakthroughs in product and process performance.
- Six Sigma methodology and tools not only improve the Corporation's ability to control its processes, but also its ability to design products that can be made without defects.
- Six Sigma emphasizes practical, focused projects that have customer and business impact.
- The Six Sigma effort is linked to Bombardier's business priorities and strategies and is supported by top management and full-time, well-trained

resources that help to get improvement under way.
- By providing a common set of tools and techniques, Six Sigma will ensure that Bombardier has a common quality language that allows easy transfer of best practices.
- The measurable stretch goal of Six Sigma, 3.4 defects per million opportunities (DPMO), forces the search for new, innovative solutions.

The Six Sigma program requires a major training effort. Every agent is provided with four weeks of training in advanced techniques to identify and eliminate defects before they are assigned to practical and focused projects. As projects are completed, quality and costs results are carefully tracked and best practices are shared in a systematic fashion.

During the next two years, over 400 full-time Six Sigma Agents will be developed across Bombardier. Ultimately, Six Sigma methodologies will become a standard part of every manager's "tool kit" and to this end, Bombardier will offer managers an intense two-week training program.

Launched last year at Bombardier Aerospace, Six Sigma projects are already yielding concrete results. Annual savings of several million dollars will be captured by eliminating defects in manufacturing and administrative processes.

As an example, a team involved in a recent Six Sigma project at Bombardier Aerospace looked at customer and Transport Canada requirements pertaining to documentary evidence and traceability. The project objective was to reduce documentation errors by 80 percent. Actual improvements to date are in the order of 90 percent, and savings are expected to approximate $200,000 per year.

Improvements were made through standardization of criteria, better document format, training, and improved feedback.

Another Bombardier Aerospace project brought together a cross-functional project team from Toronto and Montreal facilities in an effort to reduce defects within the experimental and ground testing design process. The team identified changes that can potentially provide a tenfold reduction

continued...

in defects and continues to study further possibilities to reduce defects. Potential net savings in design, manufacturing, and assembly are estimated at $1 million over four years.

In addition to improving Bombardier's performance, Six Sigma will provide many opportunities to identify and develop a large number of young future leaders within the organization.

Six Sigma is one of the most ambitious quality and productivity improvement programs undertaken by Bombardier. Six Sigma will contribute to Bombardier's success by increasing both its operating margins and the quality of its products, even in an environment of stable or declining prices.

Source: "Six Sigma" Bombardier Inc., 1998 Annual Report, p. 3.

HIGHLIGHTS TO REMEMBER

The accountant's responsibility in business is to assist the manager in using relevant data as guidance for decisions. Accountants and managers must have a clear understanding of relevant information, especially costs.

To be relevant to a particular decision, a cost must meet two criteria: (1) it must be an expected *future* cost, and (2) it must be an element of *difference* among the alternatives. All *past (historical or sunk)* costs are in themselves irrelevant to any *decision* about the future, although they often provide the best available basis for the *prediction* of expected future data.

The combination of the relevant-costing and contribution approaches provides a commonality of approach, a fundamental framework, based on economic analysis, that applies to a vast range of problems.

The following generalizations apply to a variety of decisions:

1. Wherever feasible, think in terms of total costs rather than unit costs. Too often, unit costs are regarded as an adequate basis for predicting changes in total costs. This assumption is satisfactory when analyzing variable costs, but it is frequently misleading when analyzing fixed costs.

2. A common error is to regard all unit costs indiscriminately, as if all costs were variable costs. In the short run, changes in volume will affect *total* variable costs but not *total* fixed costs. The danger then is to predict total costs assuming that all unit costs are variable. The correct relationships are:

	BEHAVIOUR AS VOLUME FLUCTUATES	
	VARIABLE COST	FIXED COST
Cost per unit	No change	Change
Total cost	Change	No change

Decisions to accept or reject a special sales order should focus on the *additional* revenues and *additional* costs of the order. Decisions on whether to delete a department or a product require analysis of the revenues foregone and the costs saved from the deletion. The key to obtaining the maximum profit from a given capacity is to obtain the greatest possible contribution to profit per unit of the limiting or scarce factor.

Pricing decisions are influenced by economics, the law, customers, competitors, and costs. Profit markups can be added to a variety of cost bases, including variable manufacturing costs, all variable costs, absorption (full manufacturing) cost, or all costs. The contribution approach to pricing has the advantage of providing detailed information that is consistent with cost-volume-profit analysis.

Target costing is used to reduce costs when the market sets the price for new products or services. The desired profit margin is subtracted from the market price to determine the target cost.

SUMMARY PROBLEM FOR YOUR REVIEW

Problem One appeared earlier in the chapter.

Problem Two

Custom Graphics is a printing company that bids on a wide variety of design and printing jobs. The owner of the company, Janet Solomon, prepares the bids for most jobs. She has budgeted the following costs for 2001:

Materials		$ 350,000
Labour		250,000
Overhead:		
Variable	300,000	
Fixed	150,000	450,000
Total production cost of jobs		1,050,000
Selling and administrative expenses:		
Variable	75,000	
Fixed	125,000	200,000
Total costs		$1,250,000

Solomon has a target profit of $250,000 for 2001.

Compute the average target profit percentage for setting prices as a percentage of:

1. Prime costs (materials plus labour)
2. Variable production cost of jobs
3. Total production cost of jobs
4. All variable costs
5. All costs

Solution

The purpose of this problem is to emphasize that many different approaches to pricing might be used that, if properly employed, would achieve the *same* target selling prices. To achieve $250,000 of profit, the desired revenue for 2001 is $1,250,000 + $250,000 = $1,500,000. The target markup percentages are:

1. Percent of prime cost $= \dfrac{(\$1,500,000 - \$600,000)}{(\$600,000)} = 150\%$

2. Percent of variable production cost of jobs $= \dfrac{(\$1,500,000 - \$900,000)}{(\$900,000)} = 66.7\%$

3. Percent of total production cost of jobs $= \dfrac{(\$1,500,000 - \$1,050,000)}{(\$1,050,000)} = 42.9\%$

$$4. \text{ Percent of all variable costs} = \frac{(\$1,500,000 - \$975,000)}{(\$975,000)} = 53.8\%$$

$$5. \text{ Percent of all costs} = \frac{(\$1,500,000 - \$1,250,000)}{(\$1,250,000)} = 20\%$$

ACCOUNTING VOCABULARY

avoidable costs *p. 331*

common costs *p. 331*

decision model *p. 323*

discriminatory pricing *p. 337*

dumping *p. 339*

imperfect competition *p. 335*

inventory turnover *p. 333*

limiting factor *p. 333*

marginal cost *p. 335*

marginal revenue *p. 335*

markup *p. 339*

perfect competition *p. 335*

predatory pricing *p. 337*

price elasticity *p. 335*

relevant information *p. 321*

scarce resource *p. 333*

target costing *p. 340*

unavoidable costs *p. 331*

ASSIGNMENT MATERIAL

QUESTIONS

Q8-1 "The distinction between precision and relevance should be kept in mind." Explain.

Q8-2 Distinguish between the quantitative and qualitative aspects of decisions.

Q8-3 Describe the accountant's role in decision making.

Q8-4 "Any future cost is relevant." Do you agree? Explain.

Q8-5 Why are historical or past data irrelevant to special decisions?

Q8-6 Describe the role of past or historical costs in the decision process. That is, how do these costs relate to the prediction method and the decision model?

Q8-7 "There is a commonality of approach to various special decisions." Explain.

Q8-8 "In relevant-cost analysis, beware of unit costs." Explain.

Q8-9 "Increasing sales will decrease fixed costs because it spreads them over more units." Do you agree? Explain.

Q8-10 "The key decisions to delete a product or department is identifying avoidable costs." Do you agree? Explain.

Q8-11 "Avoidable costs are variable costs." Do you agree? Explain.

Q8-12 Give four examples of limiting or scarce factors.

Q8-13 Compare and contrast *marginal cost* and *variable cost*.

Q8-14 Describe the major factors that influence pricing decisions.

Q8-15 Why are customers one of the factors influencing price decisions?

Q8-16 "In target costing, prices determine costs rather than vice versa." Explain.

Q8-17 "Basing pricing on only the variable costs of a job results in suicidal underpricing?" Do you agree? Why?

Q8-18 Provide three examples of pricing decisions other than the special order.

Q8-19 List four popular mark-up formulas for pricing.

Q8-20 Describe two long-run effects that may lead to managers rejecting opportunities to cut prices and obtain increases in short-run profits.

Q8-21 Give two reasons why full costs are far more widely used than variable costs for guiding pricing.

Q8-22 Why do most executives use both full-cost and variable-cost information for pricing decisions?

PROBLEMS

P8-1 PINPOINTING OF RELEVANT COSTS. Today you are planning to see a movie and you can attend either of two theatres. You have only a small budget for entertainment, so prices are important. You have attended both theatres recently. One charged $6 for admission; the other charged $7. You habitually buy popcorn in the theatre—each theatre charges $2. The movies now being shown are equally attractive to you, but you are virtually certain that you will never see the motion picture that you reject today.

Identify the relevant costs. Explain your answer.

P8-2 INFORMATION AND DECISIONS. Suppose the historical costs for the manufacture of a calculator were as follows: direct materials, $5 per unit; direct labour, $3 per unit. Management is trying to decide whether to replace some materials with different materials. The replacement should cut material costs by 5 percent per unit. However, direct-labour time will increase by 5 percent per unit. Moreover, direct-labour rates will be affected by a recent 10 percent wage increase.

Prepare an exhibit like Exhibit 8-1 (page 324), showing where and how he data about direct material and direct labour fit in the decision process.

P8-3 IDENTIFYING RELEVANT COSTS. Sonkar and Raji Ramaswamy were trying to decide whether to go to the symphony or the baseball game. They already have two nonrefundable tickets to "Pops Night at the Symphony" that cost $40 each. This is the only concert of the season they considered attending because it is the only one with the type of music they enjoy. The baseball game is the last one of the season and it will decide the league championship. They can purchase tickets for $20 each.

They will drive a 50-kilometre round-trip to either event. Variable costs for operating their auto are $.14 per kilometre, and fixed costs average $.13 per kilometre for the 20,000 kilometres they drive annually. Parking at the symphony is free, but it costs $6 at the baseball game.

To attend either event, Sonkar and Raji will hire a babysitter at $4 per hour. They expect to be gone five hours to attend the baseball game but only four hours to attend the symphony.

Compare the cost of attending the baseball game to the cost of attending the symphony. Focus on relevant costs. Compute the difference in cost, and indicate which alternative is most costly to the Ramaswamys.

P8-4 SPECIAL-ORDER DECISION. Belltown Athletic Supply (BAS) makes game jerseys for athletic teams. The F.C. Strikers soccer club has offered to buy 100 jerseys for the teams in its league for $15 per jersey. The team price for such jerseys is normally $18, an 80 percent markup over BAS's purchase price of $10 per jersey. BAS adds a name and number to each jersey at a variable cost of $2 per jersey. The annual fixed cost of equipment used in the printing process is $6,000 and other fixed costs allocated to jerseys is $2,000. BAS produces about 2,000 jerseys per year, making the fixed cost $4 per jersey. The equipment is used only for printing jerseys, and stands idle 75 percent of the usable time.

The manager of BAS turned down the offer, saying, "If we sell at $15 and our cost is $16, we lose money on each jersey we sell. We would like to help your league, but we can't afford to lose money on the sale."

1. Compute the amount by which the operating income of BAS would change if the F.C. Strikers' offer were accepted.
2. Suppose you were the manager of BAS. Would you accept the offer? In addition to considering the quantitative impact computed in Requirement 1, list two qualitative considerations that would influence your decision—one qualitative factor supporting acceptance of the offer and one supporting rejection.

P8-5 SPECIAL ORDER. Consider the following details of the income statement of the Pocket Calculator Division (PCD) of the Kim Electronics Company for the year ended December 31, 2001:

Sales	$10,000,000
Less manufacturing cost of goods sold	6,000,000
Gross margin or gross profit	$ 4,000,000
Less selling and administrative expenses	3,300,000
Operating income	$ 700,000

PCD's fixed manufacturing costs were $2.4 million and its fixed selling and administrative costs were $2.5 million. Sales commissions of 3 percent of sales are included in selling and administrative expenses.

The company had sold two million calculators. Near the end of the year, Pizza Hut Corporation had offered to buy 150,000 calculators on a special order. To fill the order, a logo bearing the Pizza Hut emblem would have had to be added to each calculator. Pizza Hut intended to use the calculators in special promotions in an eastern city during early 2002.

Even though PCD had some idle plant capacity, the president rejected the Pizza Hut offer of $660,000 for the 150,000 calculators. He said: "The Pizza Hut offer is too low. We'd avoid paying sales commissions, but we'd have to incur an extra cost of 20¢ per calculator to add the logo. If PCD sells below its regular selling prices, it will begin a chain reaction of competitors price-cutting and of customers wanting special deals. I believe in pricing at no lower than 8 percent above our full costs of $9,300,000 ÷ 2,000,000 units = $4.65 per unit plus the extra 20¢ less the savings in commissions."

1. Using the contribution approach, prepare an analysis similar to that in Exhibit 8-3. Use three columns: without the special order, the special order (total and per unit), and totals with the special order.
2. By what percentage would operating income increase or decrease if the order had been accepted? Do you agree with the president's decision? Why?

P8-6 VARIETY OF COST TERMS.   Consider the following data:

Variable selling and administrative costs per unit	$ 3.00
Total fixed selling and administrative costs	$2,900,000
Total fixed manufacturing costs	$3,000,000
Variable manufacturing costs per unit	$ 10.00
Units produced and sold	500,000

1. Compute the following per unit of product: (a) total variable costs, (b) absorption cost, (c) full cost.
2. Give a synonym for full cost.

P8-7 PROFIT PER UNIT OF SPACE.

1. Several successful chains of warehouse stores such Costco have merchandising policies that differ considerably from those of traditional department stores. Name some characteristics of these warehouse sores that have contributed to their success.
2. Food chains such as Loblaw Company have typically regarded approximately 20 percent of selling price as an average target gross profit on canned goods and similar grocery items. What are the limitations of such an approach? Be specific.

P8-8 CHOOSING PRODUCTS.   The Ibunez Tool Company has two products: a plain circular saw and a fancy circular saw. The plain circular saw sells for $66 and has a variable cost of $50. The fancy circular saw sells for $100 and has a variable cost of $70.

1. Compute the contribution margin and contribution margin ratios for plain and fancy circular saws.
2. The demand is for more units than the company can produce. There are only 20,000 machine hours of manufacturing capacity available. Two plain circular saws can be produced in the same average time (one hour) needed to produce one fancy circular saws. Compute the total contribution margin for 20,000 hours for plain circular saws only and for fancy circular saws only.
3. In two or three sentences, state the major lesson of this problem.

P8-9 FORMULAS FOR PRICING.   Randy Azarski, a building contractor, constructs houses in tracts, often building as many as 20 homes simultaneously. The president of the corporation has budgeted costs for an expected number of houses in 2002 as follows:

Direct materials	$3,500,000
Direct labour	1,000,000
Job construction overhead	1,500,000
Cost of jobs	$6,000,000
Selling and administrative costs	1,500,000
Total costs	$7,500,000

The job construction overhead includes approximately $600,000 of fixed costs, such as the salaries of supervisors and depreciation on equipment. The selling and administrative costs include $300,000 of variable costs, such as sales commissions and bonuses that depend fundamentally on overall profitability. Azarski wants an operating income of $1.5 million for 2002.

Compute the average target profit percentage for setting prices as a percentage of:

1. Prime costs (direct materials plus direct labour).
2. The full "cost of jobs."
3. The variable "cost of jobs."
4. The full "cost of jobs" plus selling and administrative costs.
5. The variable "cost of jobs" plus variable selling and administrative costs.

P8-10 SPECIAL ORDER, TERMINOLOGY, AND UNIT COSTS. The following is the income statement of a manufacturer of blue jeans:

HUNTER COMPANY
Income Statement
for the Year Ended
December 31, 2001

	TOTAL	PER UNIT
Sales	$40,000,000	$20.00
Less manufacturing cost of goods sold	24,000,000	12.00
Gross margin	$16,000,000	8.00
Less selling and administrative expenses	14,000,000	7.00
Operating income	$ 2,000,000	$ 1.00

Hunter had manufactured two million units, which had been sold to various clothing wholesalers and department stores. In early 2002, the president, Rosemary Munoy, died of a stroke. Her son, Hector, became the new president. Hector had worked for 15 years in the marketing departments of the business. He knew very little about accounting and manufacturing, which were his mother's strengths. Hector has several questions for you, including inquiries regarding the pricing of special orders.

1. To prepare better answers, you decide to recast the income statement in contribution form. Variable manufacturing cost was $19 million. Variable selling and administrative expenses, which were mostly sales commissions, shipping expenses, and advertising allowances, paid to customers based on units sold, were $9 million.
2. Hector asks, "I can't understand financial statements until I know the meaning of various terms. In scanning my mother's assorted notes, I found the following pertaining to both total and unit costs: *absorption cost, full manufacturing cost, variable cost, full cost, fully allocated cost, gross margin, contribution margin.* Using our data for 2001, please give me a list of these costs, their total amounts, and their per-unit amounts."
3. "Near the end of 2001 I brought in a special order from The Bay for 100,000 pairs of jeans at $17 each. I said I'd accept a flat $20,000 sales commission instead of the usual 6 percent of selling price, but my mother refused the order. She usually upheld a relatively rigid pricing policy, saying that it was bad business to accept orders that did not at least generate full manufacturing cost plus 80 percent.
   "That policy bothered me. We had idle capacity. The way I figured, our manufacturing costs would go up by 100,000 × $12 = $1,200,000, but our selling and administrative expenses would only go up by $20,000. That would mean additional operating income of 100,000 × ($17 −$12) minus 20,000, or $500,000 minus $20,000 or $480,000. That's too much money to give up just to maintain a general pricing policy. Was my analysis of the impact on operating income correct? If not, please show me the correct additional operating income."

4. After receiving the explanations offered in requirements 2 and 3, Hector said: "Forget that I had The Bay order. I had an even bigger order from Wal-Mart. It was for 500,000 units and would have filled the plant completely. I told my mother I'd settle for no commission. There would have been no selling and administrative costs whatsoever because Wal-Mart would pay for the shipping and would not get any advertising allowances.

"Wal-Mart offered $9.20 per unit. Our fixed manufacturing costs would have been spread over 2.5-million instead of 2-million units. Wouldn't it have been advantageous to accept the offer? Our old fixed manufacturing costs were $2.50 per unit. The added volume would reduce that cost more than our loss on our variable costs per unit.

"Am I correct? What would have been the impact on total operating income if we had accepted the order?"

P8-11 UNIT COSTS AND CAPACITY. Fargo Manufacturing Company produces two industrial solvents for which the following data have been tabulated. Fixed manufacturing cost is applied to product at a rate of $1 per machine-hour.

The sales manager has had a $160,000 increase in her budget allotment for advertising and wants to apply the money to the most profitable product. The solvents are not substitutes for one another in the eyes of the company's customers.

PER UNIT	XY-7	BD-4
Selling price	$6.00	$4.00
Variable manufacturing cost	3.00	1.50
Fixed manufacturing cost	.80	.20
Variable selling cost	2.00	2.00

1. How many machine hours does it take to produce one XY-7? To produce one BD-4? (Hint: Focus on applied fixed manufacturing cost.)
2. Suppose Fargo has only 100,000 machine-hours that can be made available to produce XY-7 and BD-4. If the potential increase in sales units for either product resulting from advertising is far in excess of these production capabilities, which product should be produced and advertised and what is the estimated increase in contribution margin earned?

P8-12 DROPPING A PRODUCT LINE. Hambley's Toy Store is on Regent Street in London. It has a magic department near the main door. Management is considering dropping the magic department, which has consistently shown an operating loss. The predicted income statements, in thousands of pounds (£), follow (for ease of analysis, only three product lines are shown):

	TOTAL	GENERAL MERCHANDISE	ELECTRONIC PRODUCTS	MAGIC DEPARTMENT
Sales	£6,000	£5,000	£400	£ 600
Variable expenses	4,090	3,500	200	390
Contribution margin	£1,910 (32%)	£1,500 (30%)	£200 (50%)	£ 210 (35%)
Fixed expenses (compensation, amortization, property taxes, insurance, etc.)	1,110	750	50	310
Operating income	£ 800	£ 750	£150	£(100)

The £310,000 of fixed expenses include the compensation of magic department employees of £100,000. These employees will be released if the magic department is abandoned. All equipment is fully amortized, so none of the £310,000 pertains to such items. Furthermore, disposal values of the equipment will be exactly offset by the costs of removal and remodelling.

If the magic department is dropped, the manager will use the vacated space for either more general merchandise or more electronic products. The expansion of general merchandise would not entail hiring any additional salaried help, but more electronic products would require an additional person at an annual cost of £25,000. The manager thinks that sales of general merchandise would increase by £300,000; electronic products, by £200,000. The manager's modest predictions are partially based on the fact that she thinks the magic department has helped lure customers to the store and thus improved overall sales. If the magic department is closed, that lure would be gone.

Should the magic department be closed? Explain, showing computations.

P8-13 DELETE A PRODUCT LINE. Zurich Day School is a private elementary school. In addition to regular classes, after-school care is provided between 3:00 p.m. and 6:00 p.m. at SF 12 per child per hour. Financial results for the after-school care for a representative month are shown on the next page, in Swiss Francs.

The director of Zurich Day School is considering discontinuing the after-school care services because it is not fair to the other students to subsidize the after-school care program. He thinks that eliminating the program will free up SF 400 a month to be used in the regular classes.

Revenue, 600 hours @ SF12 per hour		SF 7,200
Less:		
Teacher salaries	SF 5,200	
Supplies	800	
Amortization	1,300	
Sanitary engineering	100	
Other fixed costs	200	7,600
Operating income (loss)		SF (400)

1. Compute the financial impact on Zurich Day School from discontinuing the after-school care program.
2. List three qualitative factors that would influence your decision.

P8-14 ACCEPTING A LOW BID. The Velasquez Company, a maker of a variety of metal and plastic products, is in the midst of a business downturn and is saddled with many idle facilities. The National Hospital Supply Company has approached Velasquez to produce 300,000 nonslide serving trays. National will pay $1.30 each.

Velasquez predicts that its variable costs will be $1.40 each. However, its fixed costs, which had been averaging $1 per unit on a variety of other products, will now be spread over twice as much volume. The president commented, "Sure, we'll lose $.10 each on the variable costs, but we'll gain $.50 per unit by spreading our fixed costs. Therefore, we should take the offer, because it represents an advantage of $.40 per unit."

Do you agree with the president? Why? Suppose the regular business had a current volume of 300,000 units, sales of $600,000, variable costs of $420,000, and fixed costs of $300,000.

P8-15 PRICING BY AUTO DEALERS.   Many automobile dealers have an operating pattern similar to that of City Motors. Each month, City initially aims at a unit volume quota that approximates a break-even point. Until the break-even point is reached, City has a policy of relatively lofty pricing, whereby the "minimum deal" must contain a sufficiently high markup to ensure a contribution to profit of no less than $400. After the break-even point is attained, City tends to quote lower prices for the rest of the month.

What is your opinion of this policy? As a prospective customer, how would you react to this policy?

P8-16 TARGET SELLING PRICES.   Consider the following data from Klastorin Company's budgeted income statement (in thousands of dollars):

Target sales	$60,000
Variable costs:	
Manufacturing	30,000
Selling and administrative	6,000
Total variable costs	36,000
Fixed costs:	
Manufacturing	8,000
Selling and administrative	6,000
Total fixed costs	14,000
Total all costs	50,000
Operating income	$10,000

Compute the following markup formulas that would be used for obtaining the same target selling prices as a percentage of (1) total variable costs, (2) full costs, (3) variable manufacturing costs, and (4) absorption costs.

P8-17 COMPETITIVE BIDS.   Griffey, Rodriguez and Martinez, a CA firm, is preparing to bid for a consulting job. Although Alice Griffey will use her judgment about the market in finalizing the bid, she has asked you to prepare a cost analysis to help in the bidding. You have estimated the following costs for the consulting job:

Materials and supplies, at cost	$ 28,000
Hourly pay for consultants, 2,000 hours @ $36 per hour	72,000
Fringe benefits for consultants, 2,000 hours @ $12 per hour	24,000
Total variable costs	124,000
Fixed costs allocated to the job:	
Based on labour, 2,000 hours @ $10.30 per hour	21,600
Based on materials and supplies, 80% of 28,000	22,400
Total cost	$168,000

Of the $44,000 allocated fixed costs, $35,000 will be incurred even if the job is not undertaken.

Alice normally bids jobs at 150 percent of the estimated materials and supplies cost plus $80 per estimated labour hour.

1. Prepare a bid using the normal formula.
2. Prepare a minimum bid equal to the additional costs expected to be incurred to complete the job.
3. Prepare a bid that will cover full costs plus a markup for profit equal to 20 percent of full cost.

P8-18 PRICING AND CONTRIBUTION APPROACH. The Transnational Transportation Company has the following operating results to date for 2001:

Operating revenues	$50,000,000
Operating costs	40,000,000
Operating income	$ 10,000,000

A large Toronto manufacturer has inquired about whether Transnational would be interested in trucking a large order of its parts to Vancouver. Steven Minkler, operations manager, investigated the situation and estimated that the "fully allocated" costs of servicing the order would be $40,000. Using his general pricing formula, he quoted a price of $50,000. The manufacturer replied: "We'll give you $37,000, take it or leave it. If you do not want our business, we'll truck it ourselves or go elsewhere."

A cost analyst had recently been conducting studies of how Transnational's operating costs tended to behave. She found that $32 million of the $40 million could be characterized as variable costs. Minkler discussed the matter with her and decided that this order would probably generate cost behaviour little different from Transnational's general operations.

1. Using a contribution format, prepare an analysis for Minkler.
2. Should Transnational accept the order? Explain.

P8-19 PRICING AT THE GRAND CANYON RAILWAY. Suppose a tour guide approached the general manager of The Grand Canyon Railway with a proposal to offer a special guided tour to the agent's clients. The tour would occur 20 times each summer and be part of a larger itinerary that the agent is putting together. The agent presented two options: (1) a special 65-kilometre tour with the agent's 30 clients as the only passengers on the train, or (2) adding a car to an existing train to accommodate the 30 clients on the 65-kilometre tour.

Under either option Grand Canyon would hire a tour guide for $150 for the trip. Grand Canyon has extra cars in its switching yard, and it would cost $40 to move a car to the main track and hook it up. The extra fuel cost to pull one extra car is $.20 per kilometre. To run an engine and a passenger car on the trip would cost $2.20 per kilometre, and an engineer would be paid $400 for the trip.

Amortization on passenger cars is $5,000 per year, and amortization on engines is $20,000 per year. Each passenger car and each engine travels about 50,000 kilometres a year. They are replaced every eight years.

The agent offered to pay $30 per passenger for the special tour and $15 per passenger for simply adding an extra car.

1. Which of the two options is more profitable for Grand Canyon? Comment on which costs are irrelevant to this decision.
2. Should Grand Canyon accept the proposal for the option you found best in requirement 1? Comment on what costs are relevant for this decision but not for the decision in requirement 1.

P8-20 CHOICE OF PRODUCTS. West Coast Fashions sells both designer and moderately priced women's wear in Vancouver. Profits have been volatile. Top management is trying to decide which product line to drop. Accountants have reported the following data:

	PER ITEM	
	DESIGNER	MODERATELY PRICED
Average selling price	$240	$150
Average variable expenses	120	85
Average contribution-margin	$120	$ 65
Average contribution-margin percentage	50%	43%

The store has 8,000 square metres of floor space. If moderately priced goods are sold exclusively, 400 items can be displayed. If designer goods are sold exclusively, only 300 items can be displayed. Moreover, the rate of sale (turnover) of the designer items will be two-thirds the rate of moderately priced goods.

1. Prepare an analysis to show which product to drop.
2. What other considerations might affect your decision in requirement 1?

P8-21 COST ANALYSIS AND PRICING. The budget for the University Printing Company for 2002 follows.

Sales		£1,100,000
Direct material	£280,000	
Direct labour	320,000	
Overhead	400,000	1,000,000
Net income		£ 100,000

The company typically uses a so-called cost-plus pricing system. Direct material and direct labour are computed, overhead is added at a rate of 125 percent of direct labour, and 10 percent of the total cost is added to obtain the selling price.

The sales manager has placed a £22,000 bid on a particularly large order with a cost of £5,600 direct material and £6,400 direct labour. The customer informs him that he can have the business for £19,800, take it or leave it. If University accepted the order, total sales for 2002 will be £1,119,800.

The sales manager refuses the order, saying: "I sell on a cost-plus basis. It is bad policy to accept orders at below cost. I would lose £200 on the job." The company's annual fixed overhead is £160,000.

1. What would net income have been with the order? Without the order? Show your computations.
2. Give a short description of a contribution approach to pricing that University might follow. Include a stipulation of the pricing formula that University should routinely use if he hopes to obtain a target net income of £100,000.

P8-22 PRICING OF EDUCATION. You are the director of continuing education programs for a well-known university. Courses for executives are especially popular, and you have developed an extensive menu of one-day and two-day courses that are presented in various locations throughout the country. The performance of these courses for the current fiscal year, excluding the final course, which is scheduled for next Saturday, is as follows:

Tuition revenue	$2,000,000
Costs of courses	800,000
Contribution margin	1,200,000
General administrative expenses	400,000
Operating income	$ 800,000

The costs of the courses include fees for instructors, rentals of classrooms, advertising, and any other items, such as travel, that can be easily and exclusively identified as being caused by a particular course.

The general administrative expenses include your salary, your secretary's compensation, and related expenses, such as a lump-sum payment to the university's central offices as a share of university overhead.

The enrolment for your final course of the year is 30 students, who have paid $200 each. Two days before the course is to begin, a city manager phones your office. "Do you offer discounts to non-profit institutions?" he asks. "If so, we'll send 10 managers. But our budget will not justify spending more than $100 per person." The extra cost of including these 10 managers would entail lunches at $20 each and course materials at $40 each.

1. Prepare a tabulation of the performance for the full year, including the final course. Assume that the costs of the final course for the 40 enrollees' instruction, travel, advertising, rental of hotel classroom, lunches, and course materials would be $4,000. Show a tabulation in four columns: before final course, final course with 30 registrants, effect of 10 more registrants, and grand totals.
2. What major considerations would probably influence the pricing policies for these courses? For setting regular university tuition in private universities?

P8-23 UTILIZATION OF PASSENGER JETS. In a recent year, National Air Lines, Inc., filled 50 percent of the available seats on its flights, a record about 15 percentage points below the national average.

National could have eliminated about 4 percent of its runs and raised its average load considerably. But the improved load factor would have reduced profits. Give reasons for or against this elimination. What factors should influence an airline's scheduling policies?

When you answer this question, suppose that National had a basic package of 3,000 flights per month that had an average of 100 seats available per flight. Also suppose that 52 percent of the seats were filled at an average ticket price of $200 per flight. Variable costs are about 70 percent of revenue.

National also had a marginal package of 120 flights per month that had an average of 100 seats available per flight. Suppose that only 20 percent of the seats were filled at an average ticket price of $100 per flight. Variable costs are about 50 percent of this revenue. Prepare a tabulation of the basic package, marginal package, and total package, showing percentage of seats filled, revenue, variable expenses, and contribution margin.

P8-24 EFFECTS OF VOLUME ON OPERATING INCOME. The Wittred Division of Victoria Sports Company manufactures boomerangs, which are sold to wholesalers and retailers. The division manager has set a target of 250,000 boomerangs for next month's production and sales. However, the manager has prepared an analysis of the effects on operating income of deviations from the target:

Volume in units	200,000	250,000	300,000
Sales @ $3.00	$600,000	$750,000	$900,000
Full costs @ $2.50	500,000	625,000	750,000
Operating income	$100,000	$125,000	$150,000

The costs have the following characteristics. Variable manufacturing costs are $1 per boomerang; variable selling costs are $.20 per boomerang. Fixed manufacturing costs per month are $300,000; fixed selling and administrative costs, $50,000.

1. Prepare a correct analysis of the changes in volume on operating income. Prepare a tabulated set of income statements at levels of 200,000, 250,000, and 300,000 boomerangs. Also show percentages of operating income in relation to sales.
2. Compare your tabulation with the manager's tabulation. Why is the manager's tabulation incorrect?

P8-25 PRICING A SPECIAL ORDER. The Drosselmeier Corporation, which makes Christmas nut-crackers, has an annual plant capacity of 2,400 product units. Its predicted operating results (in German Marks) for the year are

Production and sales of 2,000 units, total sales	DM 180,000
Manufacturing costs:	
Fixed (total)	DM 60,000
Variable (per unit)	DM 26
Selling and administrative expenses:	
Fixed (total)	DM 30,000
Variable (per unit)	DM 10

Compute, ignoring income taxes:

1. If the company accepted a special order for 300 units at a selling price of DM 40 each, how would the *total* predicted net income for the year be affected, assuming no effect on regular sales at regular prices?
2. Without decreasing its total net income, what is the lowest *unit price* for which the Drosselmeier Corporation could sell an additional 100 units not subject to any variable selling and administrative expenses, assuming no effect on regular sales at regular prices?
3. In solving requirement 2 above, list the numbers given in the problem that are irrelevant (not relevant).
4. Compute the expected annual net income (with no special orders) if plant capacity can be doubled by adding additional facilities at a cost of DM 500,000. Assume that these facilities have an estimated life of five years with no residual scrap value and that the current unit selling price can be maintained for all sales. Total sales are expected to equal the new plant capacity each year. No changes are expected in variable costs per unit or in total fixed costs except for amortization.

P8-26 PRICING AND CONFUSING VARIABLE AND FIXED COSTS. Diaz Telecom had a fixed factory overhead budget for 2002 of $1 million. The company planned to make and sell 200,000 units of the product—a communications device. All variable manufacturing costs per unit were $10. The budgeted income statement contained the following:

Sales	$4,000,000
Manufacturing cost of goods sold	3,000,000
Gross margin	1,000,000
Selling and administrative expenses	400,000
Operating income	$ 600,000

For simplicity, assume that the actual variable costs per unit and the total fixed costs were exactly as budgeted.

1. Compute Diaz's budgeted fixed factory overhead per unit.
2. Near the end of 2002, a large computer manufacturer offered to buy 10,000 units for $120,000 on a one-time special order. The president of Diaz stated: "The offer is a bad deal. It's foolish to sell below full manufacturing costs per unit. I realize that this order will have only a modest effect on selling and administrative costs. They will increase by a $1,000 fee paid to our sales agent." Compute the effect on operating income if the offer is accepted.
3. What factors should the president of Diaz consider before finally deciding whether to accept the offer?
4. Suppose the original budget for fixed manufacturing costs was $1 million, but budgeted units of product were one million. How would your answers to requirements 1 and 2 change? Be specific.

P8-27 DEMAND ANALYSIS. (SMA adapted.) Zimmerman Manufacturing Limited produces and sells flags. During 2001, the company manufactured and sold 50,000 flags at $24 each. Existing production capacity is 60,000 flags per year.

In formulating the 2002 budget, management is faced with a number of decisions concerning product pricing and output. The following information is available:

1. A market survey shows that the sales volume depends largely on the selling price. For each $1 drop in selling price, sales volume would increase by 10,000 flags.
2. The company's expected cost structure for 2002 is as follows:
   (a) Fixed cost (regardless of production or sales activities), $360,000
   (b) Variable costs per flag (including production, selling, and administrative expenses), $16.
3. To increase annual capacity from the present 60,000 to 90,000 flags, additional investment for plant, building, equipment, and the like, of $200,000 would be necessary. The estimated average life of the additional investment would be 10 years, so the fixed costs would increase by an average of $20,000 per year. (Expansion of less than 30,000 additional units of capacity would cost only slightly less than $200,000.)

Indicate, with reasons, what the level of production and the selling price should be for the coming year. Also, indicate whether the company should approve the plant expansion. Show your calculations. Ignore income tax considerations and the time value of money.

P8-28 ANALYSIS OF UNIT COSTS. The Home Appliance Company manufactures small appliances, such as electric can openers, toasters, food mixers, and irons. The peak season is at hand, and the president is trying to decide whether to produce more of the company's standard line of can openers or its premium line that includes a built-in knife sharpener, a better finish, and a higher-quality motor. The unit data follow:

	PRODUCT	
	STANDARD	PREMIUM
Selling price	$28	$38
Direct material	$ 8	$13
Direct labour	2	1
Variable factory overhead	4	6
Fixed factory overhead	6	9
Total cost of goods sold	$20	$29
Gross profit per unit	$ 8	$10

The sales outlook is very encouraging. The plant could operate at full capacity by producing either or both products. Both the standard and the premium products are processed through the same departments. Selling and administrative costs will not be affected by this decision, so they may be ignored.

Many of the parts are produced on automatic machinery. The factory overhead is allocated to products by developing separate rates per machine-hour for variable and fixed overhead. For example, the total fixed overhead is divided by the total machine-hours to determine a rate per hour. Thus the amount of overhead allocated to product depends on the number of machine-hours allocated to the product. It takes one hour of machine time to produce one unit of the standard product.

Direct labour may not be proportionate with overhead because many workers operate two or more machines simultaneously. Which product should be produced? If more than one should be produced, indicate the proportions of each. Show computations. Explain your answer briefly.

P8-29 TARGET COSTING. Belleville Electrical Inc. makes small electric motors for a variety of home appliances. Belleville sells the motors to appliance makers, which assemble and sell the appliances to retail outlets. Although Belleville makes dozens of different motors, it does not currently make one to be used in garage door openers. The company's market research department has discovered a market for such a motor.

The market research department has indicated that a motor for garage door openers would likely sell for $25. A similar motor currently being produced has the following manufacturing costs:

Direct materials	$13.00
Direct labour	6.00
Overhead	8.00
Total	$27.00

Belleville desires a gross margin of 15 percent of the manufacturing cost.

1. Suppose Belleville used cost-plus pricing, setting the price 15 percent above the manufacturing cost. What price would be charged for the motor? Would you produce such a motor if you were a manager at Belleville? Explain.
2. Suppose Belleville uses target costing. What price would the company charge for a garage-door-opener motor? What is the highest acceptable manufacturing cost for which Belleville would be willing to produce the motor?
3. As a user of target costing, what steps would Belleville managers take to try to make production of this market feasible?

P8-30 **PRICING, ETHICS, AND THE LAW.** Great Lakes Pharmaceuticals, Inc. (GLPI) produces both pre-scription and over-the-counter medications. In January, GLPI introduces a new prescription drug, Capestan, to relieve the pain of arthritis. The company spent more than $50 million over the last five years developing the drug, and adver-tising alone during the first year of introduction will exceed $10 million. Production cost for a bottle of 100 tables is approximately $12. Sales in the first three years are predicted to be 500,000, 750,000, and 1,000,000 bottles, respec-tively. To achieve these sales, GLPI plans to distribute the medicine through three sources: directly from physicians, through hospital pharmacies, and through retail pharmacies. Initially, the bottles will be given free to physicians to give to patients, hospital pharmacies will pay $25 per bottle, and retail pharmacies will pay $40 per bottle. In the second and third year, the company plans to phase out the free distributions to physicians and move all other customers toward a $50 per bottle sales price.

Comment on the pricing and promotion policies of GLPI. Pay particular attention to the legal and ethical issues involved.

P8-31 **PRICING TO MAXIMIZE CONTRIBUTION.** Reynolds Company produces and sells picture frames. One particular frame for 8 × 10 photos was an instant success in the mar-ket, but recently competitors have come out with comparable frames. Reynolds has been charging $12 wholesale for the frames, and sales have fallen from 10,000 units last year to 7,000 units this year. The product manager in charge of this frame is considering lowering the price to $10 per frame. He believes sales will rebound to 10,000 units at the lower price, but they will fall to 6,000 units at the $12 price. The unit variable cost of producing and selling the frames is $6, and $40,000 of fixed cost is assigned to the frames.

1. Assuming that the only prices under consideration are $10 and $12 per frame, which price will lead to the largest profit for Reynolds? Explain why?
2. What subjective consideration might affect your pricing decision?

P8-32 **VIDEOTAPE SALES AND RENTAL MARKETS.** Is it more profitable to sell your product for $50 or $15? This is a difficult question for many movie studio executives. Consider a movie that cost $60 million to produce and required another $40 million to pro-mote. After its theatre release, the studio must determine whether to sell video-tapes directly to the public at a wholesale price of about $15 per tape or to sell to video rental store distributors for about $50 per tape. The distributors will then sell to about 14,000 video rental stores in North America.

Assume that the variable cost to produce and ship one videotape is $2.00.

1. Suppose each video rental store would purchase 10 tapes of this movie. How many tapes would need to be sold directly to customers to make direct sales a more profitable option than sales to video store distributors?
2. How does the cost of producing and promoting the movie affect this decision?
3. Disney elected to sell *The Lion King* directly to consumers, and it sold 30 million copies at an average price of $15 per tape. How many tapes would each video rental store have to purchase to provide Disney as much profit as the company received from direct sales? Assume that Disney would receive $50 per tape from the distributors.

P8-33 **USE OF AVAILABLE FACILITIES.** The Oahu Company manufactures electronic subcomponents that can be sold directly or can be processed further into "plug-in" assemblies for a variety of intricate electronic equipment. The entire output of subcomponents can be sold at a market price of $2.20 per unit. The plug-in assemblies have been generating a sales price of $5.30 for three years, but the price has recently fallen to $5.10 on assorted orders.

Janet Oh, the vice-president of marketing, has analyzed the markets and the costs. She thinks that production of plug-in assemblies should be dropped whenever the price falls below $4.70 per unit. However, at the current price of $5.10, the total available capacity should currently be devoted to producing plug-in assemblies. She has cited the data below.

Direct-materials and direct-labour costs are variable. The total overhead is fixed; it is allocated to units produced by predicting the total overhead for the coming year and dividing this total by the total hours of capacity available.

The total hours available are 600,000. It takes one hour to make 60 subcomponents and two hours of additional processing and testing to make 60 plug-in assemblies.

OAHO AUDIO COMPANY PRODUCT PROFITABILITY DATA		
		SUBCOMPONENTS
Selling price, after deducting relevant selling costs		$2.20
Direct material	$1.10	
Direct labour	.30	
Manufacturing overhead	.60	
Cost per unit		2.00
Operating profit		$ .20
		PLUG-IN ASSEMBLIES
Selling price, after deducting relevant selling costs		$5.30
Transferred-in variable cost for subcomponents	$1.40	
Additional direct materials	1.45	
Direct labour	.45	
Manufacturing overhead	1.20*	
Cost per unit		4.50
Operating profit		$ .80

*For additional processing to make and test plug-in assemblies.

1. If the price of plug-in assemblies for the coming year is going to be $5.30, should sales of subcomponents be dropped and all facilities devoted to the production of plug-in assembles? Show computations.
2. Prepare a report for the vice-president of marketing to show the lowest possible price for plug-in assembles that would be acceptable.
3. Suppose 40 percent of the manufacturing overhead is variable with respect to processing and testing time. Repeat requirements 1 and 2. Do your answers change? If so, how?

P8-34 TARGET COSTING OVER PRODUCT LIFE CYCLE. Western Equipment, Inc. makes a variety of motor-driven products for the home and small businesses. The market research department recently identified power lawn mowers as a potentially lucrative market. As a first entry into this market Western is considering a riding lawn mower that is smaller and less expensive than those of most of the competition. Market research indicates that such a lawn mower would sell for about $995 at retail and $800 wholesale. At that price, Western expects life cycle sales as follows:

2001	1,000
2002	5,000
2003	10,000
2004	10,000
2005	8,000
2006	6,000
2007	4,000

The production department has estimated that the variable cost of production will be $475 per lawn mower, and annual costs will be $900,000 per year for each of the seven years. Variable selling costs will be $25 per lawn mower and fixed selling costs will be $50,000 per year. In addition, the product development department estimates that $5 million of development costs will be necessary to design the lawn mower and the production process for it.

1. Compute the expected profit over the entire product life cycle of the proposed riding lawn mower.
2. Suppose Western expects pretax profits equal to 10 percent of sales on new products. Would the company undertake production and selling of the riding lawn mower?
3. Western Equipment uses a target costing approach to new products. What steps would management take to try to make a profitable product of the riding lawn mower?

P8-35 REVIEW PROBLEM. The Disposable Camera Division of Saari Optics Co. has the following cost-behaviour patterns:

Production range in units	0–5,000	5,001–10,000	10,001–15,000	15,001–20,000
Fixed costs	$15,000	$22,000	$25,000	$27,000

Maximum production capacity is 20,000 units per year. Variable costs per units are $5 at all production levels.

Each situation described below is to be considered independently.

1. Production and sales are expected to be 11,000 units for the year. The sales price is $7 per unit. How many additional units need to be sold, in an unrelated market, at $6 per unit to show a total overall net income of $900 per year?

2. The company has orders for 23,000 units at $7. If it wanted to make a minimum overall net income of $14,500 on these 23,000 units, what unit purchase price would it be willing to pay a subcontractor for 3,000 units? Assume that the subcontractor would act as Saari's agent, deliver the units to customers directly, and bear all related costs of manufacture, delivery, etc. The customers, however, would pay Saari directly as goods were delivered.

3. Production is currently expected to be 7,000 units for the year at a selling price of $7. By how much may advertising or special promotion costs be increased to bring production up to 14,500 units and still earn a total net income of two percent of dollar sales?

4. Net income is currently $12,500. Nonvariable costs are $25,000. However, competitive pressures are mounting. A five percent decrease in price will not affect sales volume but will decrease net income by $4,750. What is the present volume, in units? Refer to the original data.

P8-36   **REVIEW PROBLEM.**   The Natural Water Company is a processor of mineral water. Sales are made principally in litre bottles to grocery stores throughout the country.

The company's income statements for the past year and the coming year are being analyzed by top management.

Consider each requirement independently.

Unless otherwise stated, assume that all unit costs of inputs such as material and labour are unchanged. Also, assume that efficiency is unchanged—that is, the labour and quantity of material consumed per unit of output are unchanged. Unless otherwise stated, assume that there are no changes in fixed costs.

1. The president has just returned from a management conference at a local university, where he heard an accounting professor criticize conventional income statements. The professor had asserted that knowledge of cost-behaviour patterns was of key importance in determining managerial strategies. The president now feels that the income statement should be recast to harmonize with cost-volume-profit analysis—that is, the statement should have three major sections: sales, variable costs, and fixed costs. Using the 2001 data, prepare such a statement, showing the contribution margin as well as operating income.

2. Comment on the changes in each item in the 2002 income statement. What are the most likely causes for each increase? For example, have selling prices been changed for 2002? How do sales commissions fluctuate in relation to units sold or in relation to dollar sales?

3. The president is unimpressed with the 2002 budget: "We need to take a fresh look in order to begin moving toward profitable operations. Let's tear up the 2002 budget, concentrate on 2001 results, and prepare a new comparative 2002 budget under each of the following assumptions:
   a. A 5 percent average price cut will increase unit sales by 20 percent.
   b. A 5 percent average price increase will decrease unit sales by 10 percent.

	FOR THE YEAR 2001 JUST ENDED		FOR THE YEAR 2002 TENTATIVE BUDGET	
Sales 1,500,000 litres in 2001		$900,000		$1,000,000
Cost of goods sold:				
Direct materials	$450,000		$495,000	
Direct labour	90,000		99,000	
Factory overhead:				
Variable	18,000		19,800	
Fixed	50,000	608,000	50,000	663,800
Gross margin		$292,000		$ 336,200
Selling expenses:				
Variable:				
Sales commissions				
(based on dollar sales)	$ 45,000		$ 50,000	
Shipping and other	90,000		99,000	
Fixed:				
Salaries, advertising, etc.	110,000		138,000	
Administrative expenses:				
Variable	12,000		13,200	
Fixed	40,000	297,000	40,000	340,200
Operating income		$ (5,000)		$ (4,000)

c. A sales commission rate of 10 percent and a 3.33 percent price increase will boost unit sales by 10 percent."

Prepare the budgets for 2002, using a contribution-margin format and three columns. Assume that there are no changes in fixed costs.

4. The advertising manager maintains that the advertising budget should be increased by $130,000 and that prices should be increased by 10 percent. Resulting unit sales will soar by 25 percent. What would be the expected operating income under such circumstances?

5. A nearby distillery has offered to buy 300,000 litres in 2002 if the unit price is low enough. The Natural Water Company would not have to incur sales commissions or shipping costs on this special order, and regular business would be undisturbed. Assuming that 2002's regular operations will be exactly like 2001's, what unit price should be quoted in order for the Natural Water Company to earn an operating income of $10,000 in 2002?

6. The company chemist wants to add a special ingredient, an exotic flavouring that will add $.03 per litre to the mineral water. Assuming no other changes in cost behaviour, how many units must be sold to earn an operating income of $10,000 in 2002?

P8-37 **COLLABORATIVE LEARNING EXERCISE: UNDERSTANDING PRICING DECISIONS.** Form a group of three to six students. Each team should contact and meet with a manager responsible for pricing in a company in your area. This could be a product manager or brand manager for a large company or a vice-president of marketing or sales for a smaller company.

Explore with the manager how his or her company sets prices. Among the questions you might ask are:

- How do costs influence your price? Do you set prices by adding a markup to costs? If so, what measure of costs do you use? How do you determine the appropriate markup?
- How do you adjust prices to meet market competition? How do you measure the effects of price on sales level?
- Do you use target costing? That is, do you find out what a product will sell for and then try to design the product and production process to make a desired profit on the product?
- What is your goal in setting prices? Do you try to maximize revenue, market penetration, contribution margin, gross margin, or some combination of these, or do you have other goals when setting prices?

After each team has its interview, it would be desirable, if time permits, to get together as a class and share your findings. How many different pricing policies did the groups find? Can you explain why policies differ across companies? Are there characteristics of different industries or difficult management philosophies that explain the different pricing policies?

CASES

C8-1   PRICING STRATEGY.   (SMAC) Banyan Industries Limited (Banyan) manufactures various models of alternators, mainly for the North American automobile industry. The company, located in Canada, has grown steadily over the past 15 years and, two years ago, installed a computer automated manufacturing system that significantly increased manufacturing capacity. Sales over the past few years have not grown at the rate predicted; therefore, the plant has been operating at well below capacity. The president is very concerned about this situation and has put the objective of increasing sales volume at the top of his list of priorities.

Banyan sells alternators in three main markets: (1) North American automobile manufacturers, (2) North American automotive replacement-parts distributors, and (3) foreign automobile manufacturers and replacement-part distributors. Sales are made to automobile manufacturers through a contract bidding process and contracts are generally long term. Bids are prepared by the accounting department and are then reviewed and approved by the president before submission to the potential customer. No sales commissions are paid for sales to automobile manufacturers.

Sales to replacement-parts distributors are made by sales staff who use a standard price list for standard models of alternators. Sales staff are each paid a base salary plus a 5 percent commission on the gross value of orders received from the salesperson's designated territory. Sales staff have some discretion to deviate from listed prices; however, for orders of more than 2,000 units, any deviations from listed prices must be approved by head office.

Banyan currently has sales commitments that would utilize 60 percent of its capacity over the 2002 year. From past experience, it can expect additional short-term sales during 2002 that would require 10 percent of its capacity. Four potential contracts awaiting renewal and approval by the president are as follows:

1. Ovlov Motors is open for tenders on a contract for 50,000 alternators during 2002. The standard bid proposal prepared by the accounting department is shown in Exhibit 8A-1.

2. National Auto Parts has requested a 20 percent discount on the list price for a large order of 20,000 model Z-20 alternators for delivery at staggered times during 2002 (see Exhibit 8A-2). National Auto Parts is a retail distributor and an important customer of Banyan.

3. A Pacific Rim exporter has approached Banyan to supply 100,000 alternators to its specifications at a price well below the normal list price (see Exhibit 8A-3). The specifications are well below acceptable standards for North American automobile manufacturers. Although the alternators would not bear the Banyan logo, the president suspects that they would be packaged by the exporter to resemble brand-name products for sale in the replacement parts market both in North America and abroad.

EXHIBIT 8A-1

Ovlov Motors
Contract for 50,000
Alternators

	COST PER UNIT
Direct materials	$ 25.00
Direct labour	5.00
Factory overhead (10 machine hours @ $4/hr.)	40.00
Total manufacturing cost	70.00
Target markup (20%)	14.00
Target sales price	$ 84.00
Standard bid for 50,000 units	$4,200,000
Proposed bid	$4,000,000

EXHIBIT 8A-2

National Auto Parts
Order for 20,000
Model Z-20 Alternators

	COST PER UNIT
Direct materials	$ 24.00
Direct labour	5.00
Factory overhead (10 machine hours @ $4/hr.)	40.00
Total manufacturing cost	69.00
Target markup (30%)	20.70
Target sales price	$ 89.70
Standard price for 20,000 units	$1,794,000
Sales commission	$ 89,700
Discount requested by National Auto Parts (20%)	$ 358,800

NOTE: National Auto Parts has indicated that it could obtain the required alternators from an offshore supplier at the $71.76 per unit discounted price, but, because it has dealt with Banyan for a long time, it wanted to give Banyan a chance to match this price.

EXHIBIT 8A-3

Pacific Rim Exporter
Order for 100,000
Alternators

	COST ESTIMATE PER UNIT
Direct material	$ 19.00
Direct labour	3.00
Factory overhead (6 machine hours @ $4/hr.)	24.00
Total manufacturing cost	$ 46.00
Price offered by Pacific Rim exporter	$6,500,000
Sales commission	$ 325,000

	COST PER UNIT
Direct material	$ 21.00
Direct labour	20.00
Factory overhead (15 machine hours @ $.80/hr.)	12.00
Total manufacturing cost	$ 53.00
Book carrying cost of 5,000 units	$265,000
Price offered by British firm	$200,000

NOTE: These units were manufactured three years ago, before the plant was fully automated. The overhead rate at that time was 50 percent fixed.

4. A British firm has offered to buy 5,000 modified alternators that have been in Banyan's inventory for three years (see Exhibit 8A-4). These alternators were left over from a special order from a customer who had declared bankruptcy before the alternators were delivered.

Banyan uses a standard cost system under which total overhead is charged at a standard rate based on the plant's previous year's expected activity. The standards for 2002 were based on the expected 2001 activity of 3,750,000 machine hours, which is about 75 percent of capacity. With the new automated equipment, about 80 percent of the overhead rate for 2002 represented the fixed costs.

Required:

1. Assuming that Banyan has sufficient capacity to handle all four potential contracts, analyze and propose a pricing strategy for each of the four contracts. Include in your analysis a discussion of all considerations and implications involved in making a decision regarding the approval of each potential contract.
2. Assume that, for 2002, Banyan has idle capacity of only 600,000 machine hours available for the four potential contracts. Indicate how your answers to requirement 1 would change given this new assumption.
3. Evaluate Banyan's current pricing strategy.

C8-2 **PRICING WITH REBATES.** (Braithwaite) "I wonder if we can afford these larger rebates," commented John Wiley, president of Lakeview Beverage Products Limited (LBP) of Oshawa, Ontario. It was May 10, 2001 and John was meeting with his business partners to discuss a number of recent requests from customers for increases in the rebates they receive on dairy products. The requests were in response to higher rebates on dairy products announced recently by their major competitor, Ault Foods, a subsidiary of John Labatt Ltd. If LBP were to meet the competition in this area, they would have to increase the total rebates paid out by 15 percent.

General Background

LBP was established 11 years ago, as a partnership of three individuals: John and Marie Wiley, and Paul Lawrence. Share ownership was 50 percent, one percent, and 49 percent, respectively, and all three individuals were active in the management of the company. John Wiley started in the beverage business as a distributor for the Bev-a-ready line of convenience-type drinks, a "just-add-water" product suitable for offices and schools. John Wiley had expanded his business to include the distribution of snack foods and the vending of soft drinks. Paul Lawrence bought into the company, after being employed by John for one year.

The partners further expanded the operation by increasing the size of the vending enterprise, and by starting to distribute office coffee services and milk to schools. LBP had evolved over the years to the point where the company was a major independent distributor of dairy products for Beatrice Foods. This activity accounted for over 80 percent of sales. The company divested itself of the vending operation in 1983, but had four other enterprises that comprised the balance of the sales.

Product Mix and Marketing

LBP distributed 810 products across five different enterprises: dairy, ice cream, coffee, soft drinks and juice, and paper products.

LBP's total trading area extended across Central Ontario but was centred in the Oshawa-Pickering area. The size of the dairy trading area was restricted to a radius of 50 kilometres in each direction, by the presence of Beatrice Dairy Divisions in Barrie, Oakville, and Peterborough. Customers of the other enterprises were spread throughout the south central region of the province.

LBP was a full-line distributor for Beatrice Foods Canada since 1992 and worked in close association with Oakwood Dairy Division, a Peterborough-based profit centre of Beatrice. In 2001, LBP signed a formal written agreement stating that the company would solely distribute Beatrice dairy and ice-cream products. All products were perishable and included milk, cream, butter, eggs, and dairy by-products, such as sour cream and cheeses. This enterprise accounted for 82 percent of gross sales (see Exhibit 8A-5). Beatrice provided sales support in the Oshawa-Pickering area and promotional support to LBP in the form of point-of-purchase displays and special pricing.

LBP was a full-line distributor of Beatrice Ice Cream and Good Humour Novelties. All products required constant freezing and had a shelf life of approximately three to four months. This product line accounted for approximately 9 percent of gross sales. Beatrice provided sales and promotional support for the full product line, the same as for the dairy enterprise.

Over 50 different products were distributed including coffee, tea, and other hot drinks. The bulk of these sales were office coffee services, where LBP provided a drip coffee-maker to clients in exchange for the right to sell the coffee and complementary items at that site. The coffee enterprise accounted for 3.5 percent of gross sales. One employee was responsible for servicing all the coffee accounts, but there never had been any formal sales effort on the part of LBP to secure new accounts. Most accounts had been serviced by LBP for many years.

This enterprise had its roots in the vending operation, and had evolved over the years to a point where the juice products comprised the majority of the sales. On the whole it accounted for just under 2 percent of gross sales. In 2002, LBP entered into a distribution agreement with Dew Drop Juice Co., a full-line juice and fruit-drink manufacturer. Under the terms of the agreement, Dew Drop provided sales and promotional support.

LBP sold a variety of food items within this enterprise. The sale of products such as snack foods, soups, condiments, and candy represented just under 4 percent of the total sales revenue. Most of these sales were to schools and caterers.

This accounted for less than 1 percent of the sales and functioned mainly as a complementary enterprise to the coffee enterprise. The product line included cups, plates, plastic utensils, serviettes, etc. No sales or promotional effort existed for this product line.

Description of Clientele

More than 1,200 customers were on file across all of the enterprises. Deliveries to customers varied from six times per week to several times in a year. In 2002 there were approximately 5,400 deliveries made per month. An analysis of customer numbers revealed the following breakdown of customer types:

Restaurants	34%
Institutional Kitchens or Cafeterias	29%
Variety Stores	16%
Donut Shops	8%
Caterers/Vendors	7%
Grocery Stores	6%

The higher-volume customers tended to be institutional kitchens and cafeterias, donut shops, and grocery stores.

In addition to their own COD and credit customers, LBP serviced buyback customers. Buybacks were customers of Oakwood Dairy Division from whom LBP provided only a delivery function. The company was paid a commission on the dollar volume of product delivered.

MONTHLY DELIVERY	BUYBACK COMMISSION
> $20,000	5%
$1,400–$20,000	7%
< $1,400	10%

Billing and payment collection was the responsibility of Oakwood. Within the dairy and ice-cream enterprises (the majority of the total customers) it was an even three-way split among COD, charge, and buyback customers.

Financial Situation

Unaudited financial statements are included in Exhibit 8A-6 and cost information is included in Exhibit 8A-7 for the last three fiscal years, and for nine months of 2002.

Over the last few years, the owners had observed that the cost structure of LBP had changed considerably. The cost of goods sold to sales ratio had been reduced substantially, due to increases in the buyback commission received, but during the same time period this improvement had been almost entirely offset by increases in the rebate to sales ratio. Nevertheless, net income had tripled over the period 1998 to 2002.

Company Operations

LBP had 20 people on the payroll besides the owners. The office operations were directed by Mr. Lawrence, the company vice president, and the duties were performed by four full-time employees and one part-time employee. Marie Wiley, the secretary-treasurer, kept the books, looked after the payroll and accounts payable, and headed up the credit department. John Wiley was company president, and directed the warehouse operations. Under his authority were 12 full-time delivery people, a full-time warehouse coordinator, and two part-time utility people who could fill in in several different capacities.

A delivery fleet of 15 leased trucks was employed. Twelve of the trucks were van trucks with a refrigerated box and were equipped with an automatic transmission. This was in contrast to the large tandem trucks and tractor trailer units utilized by other distributors. There were also two standard vans, and a large straight truck with a freezer compartment. Six of the trucks had been converted to run on natural gas. The balance of the fleet was either gas-, diesel-, or propane-fuelled. Beatrice provided free decaling of their logo for the refrigerated trucks, under the distribution agreement.

The delivery process began in the office where orders were taken by phone for delivery the next working day. The orders were entered into a computer that, at the end of the day, produced a priced invoice for each delivery, a route load sheet for each of the 12 routes, and a master load sheet that listed the total amount of each product that was to be shipped the next day. The route load sheet was used by warehouse staff the next morning to build the specific route loads, while the master load sheet was used that evening in conjunction with stock figures to order dairy products from Oakwood for delivery the next morning.

Dairy products arrived daily at 4 a.m. from Oakwood in palletized loads. The product was then put into the route loads by LBP staff. The first loaded truck left LBP at approximately 4:45 a.m., the last one at approximately 8 a.m. It was common for a delivery truck to go out in the afternoon to accommodate late orders or specials. The actual process of breaking down the arriving stock into the individual route loads was labour-intensive, and did not lend itself to mechanization due to physical constraints and product variability.

More lead time was associated with the acquisition of other products handled by LBP. Ice cream had to be ordered 24 hours in advance of delivery, while products in other enterprises could have had a one-week lead time.

Description of Competition and the Industry

In the 1980s and early 1990s, the provincial dairy-processing industry was consolidated due to the acquisition of smaller regional dairies by large national companies. The market in the south of the province was primarily served by five large processors: Ault, Neilsons, Beckers, Heritage Farms, and Beatrice.

The main competitors of LBP in its dairy trading area were Ault Foods and Neilsons Dairy. Ault was a subsidiary of John Labatt Ltd. of London, and through acquisitions had gained 40 percent of the province's dairy product market. Ault Foods had purchased Runnymede Dairy, a long-time Oshawa-based company that enjoyed great loyalty amongst its customers. Very little processing was performed in Aults' Oshawa plant since the acquisition; it was used primarily as a distribution centre.

Two characteristics are specific to the dairy industry: buyback customers (discussed above) and price rebates. With price rebates, customers receive a check-off on their invoice, equivalent to a set percentage of their invoice total. Historically, the rebate percentage had been tied directly to volume purchased, but more recently it had become a tool used by the dairies to attract customers, and was not truly reflective of the volume purchased. Among LBP's customers, rebates ranged from zero percent to 30 percent, with little correlation to volume purchased.

Competitive Advantage

Over the years LBP had developed a reputation for excellent service. This had proven to be the main reason that the company survived and had become profitable. LBP's ability to provide fast and dependable service, and management's willingness to "bend over backward" to keep the customer happy had allowed the company to secure a market niche. Beatrice had recognized this, and decided to turn over to LBP all accounts that were not big enough to service with a tractor-trailer unit.

LBP differentiated itself from all of the competition through its policy of providing a net price to its customer by taking off the rebate directly on each sales invoice. The competition sent out month-end cheques to customers based on the monthly sales total.

The Decision

LBP's owners realized that it was only recently, after some tough times, that the business has started to show some profit. Their reputation for providing excellent service had placed them in good standing with Beatrice, and with a large core group of their clientele. The partners decided they had three alternatives:

1. They could hold at their present rebate levels and rely on their service reputation to maintain a large client base.
2. The company could give the customers 50 percent of the requested increases and attempt to compensate by reducing the level of service and cutting costs.
3. The company could give the customers the rebates requested, remain competitive, and attempt to compensate by cutting costs and service.

The company was obligated to provide the customers with a reply within the next week.

Required: | As John Wiley, what is your recommendation? Why?

EXHIBIT 8A-5

Lakeview Beverage Products Limited
Schedule of Sales
9 Months Ended
April 30, 2001

	CURRENT MONTH	CURRENT YEAR	PRIOR YEAR
Dairy	$230,101	$2,060,418	$1,588,572
Buyback Commission	27,835	197,913	120,479
Ice Cream	27,004	180,344	142,234
Snacks	11,907	92,841	54,880
Coffee	10,870	110,150	97,985
Pop/Juice	5,444	41,133	39,375
Paper	1,623	14,307	10,904
Total	$314,784	$2,697,106	$2,054,429

	1998	1999	2000	2001*
Gross Sales	$2,144,569	$2,410,134	$2,886,757	$2,697,106
Rebates	(126,850)	(221,692)	(335,250)	(358,122)
Cost of Sales	(1,478,017)	(1,614,960)	(1,819,911)	(1,655,084)
Gross Profit	539,702	573,482	731,596	683,900
Variable Operating				
Expenses	(345,683)	(405,694)	(493,431)	(479,471)
Fixed Expenses	(172,905)	(167,650)	(183,439)	(124,734)
Income from				
Operations	21,114	138	54,726	79,695
Other Income	7,383	5,943	10,048	4,672
Provision for				
Income Taxes	(4,367)	—	(7,169)	—
Tax Deductible				
Business Loss	4,367	—	—	—
Net Income	$ 28,497	$ 6,081	$ 57,605	$ 84,367

* Figures for nine months ended April 30, 2001.

	1998	1999	2000	2001*
Assets				
Current Assets				
Cash	$ 4,368	$ —	$ 5,379	$ 19,576
Accts. Receivable	102,306	122,290	140,804	168,018
Inventory	44,436	34,157	53,527	77,763
Prepaid Expenses	8,138	10,288	12,850	25,072
	159,248	166,735	212,560	290,429
Equipment	66,361	58,148	55,337	78,817
Cash Surrender Value				
of Life Insurance	14,522	18,265	22,299	24,999
Total Assets	$240,131	$243,148	$290,196	$394,245
Liabilities				
Current Liabilities				
Bank Debt	$ 48,000	$ 40,161	$ —	$ —
Accounts Payable				
and Accrued Liabilities	173,068	184,965	236,656	257,140
Current Portion of				
Long-Term Debt	9,500	6,550	812	546
Long-Term Debt	34,519	30,347	13,998	13,462
Total Liabilities	265,087	262,023	251,466	271,148
Share Capital				
Common Shares	299	299	299	299
Retained Earnings				
(Deficit)	(25,255)	(19,174)	38,431	122,798
Total Liabilities and				
Share Capital	$240,131	$243,148	$290,196	$394,245

* Figures for nine months ended April 30, 2001.

EXHIBIT 8A-7

Variable and Fixed
Operating Expenses

	1998	1999	2000	2001*
Variable				
Bad Debt	$ 6,106	$ 7,744	$ 8,548	$ 13,734
Canada Pension Plan	3,985	4,480	5,275	5,228
Delivery	158	691	339	961
Employee Benefits	4,674	4,488	5,804	12,648
Office and Postage	7,765	9,050	8,525	6,905
Repairs – General	5,852	4,970	10,923	8,507
Sundry	2,765	5,493	6,495	6,376
Telephone	3,518	3,828	4,061	4,364
Truck Operation	64,451	72,489	89,450	65,686
Truck Lease	46,915	50,382	67,081	74,449
Employment Insurance	5,256	6,390	7,760	7,839
Uniforms	2,554	148	1,668	1,771
Wages	190,019	232,639	273,712	268,303
Workers' Compensation	1,665	2,902	3,790	2,700
Total	$345,683	$405,694	$493,431	$479,471

* Figures for nine months ended April 30, 2001.

EXHIBIT 8A-7 (cont'd)

Variable and Fixed
Operating Expenses

	1998	1999	2000	2001*
Fixed				
Advertising/Promotion	$ 1,960	$ 438	$ 1,949	$ 2,962
Auto Lease	8,075	7,832	7,242	2,271
Bank Charges	1,972	2,684	2,265	1,653
Amortization	21,752	18,852	15,223	9,168
Equipment Lease	7,109	2,593	2,733	3,573
Insurance	3,852	4,282	4,698	5,793
Interest	8,544	10,534	7,585	1,566
Management Salaries	72,185	73,763	93,631	60,761
Municipal Taxes	2,565	2,842	3,697	4,025
Professional Fees	6,770	7,670	6,975	5,200
Rent	24,118	24,156	24,156	18,117
Utilities	14,003	12,004	13,285	9,645
Total	$172,905	$167,650	$183,439	$124,734

* Figures for nine months ended April 30, 2001.

C8-3 **PRICING WITH CONSTRAINTS.** (SMAC) Milt Pearson, the president of Supergrip Corporation Limited (SCL), is concerned with the results achieved by SCL for the fiscal year ended May 31, 2001, and has called a meeting of the Executive Committee. Present are the vice president of manufacturing, the vice president of sales, and Diane Crombie, CMA, who has just been hired as the corporate controller.

SCL is a large centralized manufacturer of pliers. The pliers are cast, finished and assembled in the company's plant and are distributed to wholesalers for sale to retail outlets, automotive service shops, and general manufacturing companies. Included in the product line are four different grades and sizes of locking pliers and a special chain plier that is used for many purposes including removing oil filters from engines.

President: "I'm not very happy with our 2001 results, and the budget for next year doesn't show any improvement (see Exhibit 8A-8). The trend of declining profits that we've experienced over the past few years must be reversed. Diane, your first task was to prepare an analysis of last year's results. Please summarize the results of your analysis."

Controller: "My analysis indicated that actual manufacturing costs were equal to standard last year and that the main problems were with the selling prices and mix of sales. I'll need more information before I can identify the cause of each problem."

President: "Can either of you provide the information Diane requires?"

VP Sales: "Yes. Although the products with the smallest market volumes are selling well, we've been losing ground on the products with the higher-market volumes. This is mainly because we can't match the prices of our two main competitors. Halfway through last year, we had to drop our prices for both the economy and 15-centimetre pliers just to keep our largest customers. We'll have to do the same this year or risk losing 20 percent of our sales volume for these two products. For Diane's benefit, I've brought along the standard pricing and cost report that Joe, Diane's predecessor, and I had put together when planning for this year's budget (see Exhibit 8A-9). This report explains our standard pricing policy."

Controller: "From what I've seen of Joe's work, I'm sure the standard costs used in the budget and costing reports are accurate. I'll need some additional data to properly assess the situation."

President: "What can be done to achieve at least a 10 percent profit margin?"

VP Sales: "The budgeted sales volumes are the best we can expect using the budgeted sales prices. Our market research indicates that we should bring our prices more in line with our two main competitors. Here are the projected sales volumes which we can expect to achieve if we match our competitor's prices (see Exhibit 8A-10)."

President: "But we'll lose money on the 15-centimetre pliers and may only break even on the economy pliers unless we cut down the production costs."

VP Manufacturing: "I don't think there's any way that we can reduce costs further. We've about finished automating the production end of operations. We acquired a lot of computer-aided manufacturing equipment which has virtually eliminated wastage and spoiled units. Direct labour costs have been cut by 20 percent per year for the last five years. We've been working at our capacity of approximately 200,000 machine hours and costs have been right on target. Scheduling of work on machines is becoming increasingly difficult because of the uncertainty in sales volume. We've just managed to keep up with the sales orders, but, with an increase in sales, we'll end up with back orders."

VP Sales: "There is something else we may want to look at. I met with my senior salespeople and they suggested that we introduce a set of high-quality wrenches to the product line. They say the wrenches will make money, but cost and profit projections don't look very good (see Exhibit 8A-11)."

VP Manufacturing: "Milt, in order to help solve our capacity problems, especially if the wrench set is added to the product line, my staff has made a proposal to lease additional casting machinery. The addition of this new machinery will increase the overall production capacity by 5,000 machine hours per year and it is expected that there will be no change in variable production costs per unit. The net fixed cost to lease this machinery will be $60,000 per year."

President: "Diane, please analyze our situation and report back to me next week."

Supergrip Corporation Limited
Operating Budget for the Year Ending May 31, 2002

	CUSTOM PLIERS	ECONOMY PLIERS	15 CM PLIERS	20 CM PLIERS	CHAIN PLIERS
Price per unit	$9.00	$7.50	$11.25	$14.50	$35.75
Sales volume (in units)	20,000	100,000	300,000	70,000	10,000
Required machine hours per unit	1/2	1/4	1/4	1	3

		BUDGET
Revenue		$5,677,500
Manufacturing costs:		
Direct materials	$1,285,500	
Direct labour	327,500	
Overhead*	3,275,000	
		4,888,000
Gross margin		789,500
Selling & administrative:		
Variable**	299,000	
Fixed	195,000	494,000
Operating income		$ 295,500

* Manufacturing overhead is 90 percent fixed.

** Variable selling and administrative costs are composed entirely of sales commissions.

Supergrip Corporation Limited
Standard Pricing and Unit Cost Summary for the Year Ending May 31, 2002

	CUSTOM PLIERS	ECONOMY PLIERS	15 CM PLIERS	20 CM PLIERS	CHAIN PLIERS
Standard unit costs:					
Direct materials	$2.13	$1.10	$ 2.75	$ 3.35	$ 7.34
Direct labour	.47	.50	.65	.75	2.06
Overhead*	4.70	5.00	6.50	7.50	20.60
Total manufacturing cost	7.30	6.60	9.90	11.60	30.00
Sales commissions**	.55	.35	.55	1.10	1.10
Fixed selling administrative costs***	.17	.26	.40	.46	1.20
Total cost	$8.02	$7.21	$10.85	$13.16	$32.30
Standard price****	$9.00	$7.50	$11.25	$14.50	$35.75

* Manufacturing overhead is allocated to products using the following formula:

$$\frac{\text{Budgeted overhead \$}}{\text{Budgeted direct labour \$}} \times \text{Actual direct labour \$}$$

= $3,275,000/$327,500 × Actual direct labour $

= ten times direct labour $

Ninety percent of total overhead is composed of amortization, fixed production related salaries and other fixed manufacturing costs.

** These unit costs represent flat commission amounts per unit for each product which were negotiated with the salespeople two years ago.

*** Fixed selling and administrative costs are allocated to products using the following formula:

$$\frac{\text{Budgeted fixed selling and administrative costs}}{\text{Budgeted total manufacturing costs}} \times \text{Total product manufacturing cost}$$

= $195,000/$4,888,000 × Total product manufacturing cost

= .04 times total product manufacturing cost.

**** Normally, standard selling prices are determined by multiplying total cost by 1.1 and rounding up to the nearest quarter (i.e., $.25). Due to current market conditions, the standard prices for economy and 15cm pliers have been adjusted downward.

EXHIBIT 8A-10

Date: May 31, 2001
To: Milt Pearson,
President
From:
Vice President, Sales
Subject: Product Pricing

Our competitive position in the pliers market has been steadily decreasing over the past few years. Market research indicates that the prices for all of our products should be brought into line with those of our two main competitors which are as follows:

	CUSTOM PLIERS	ECONOMY PLIERS	15 CM PLIERS	20 CM PLIERS	CHAIN PLIERS
Competitor A	$12.25	$6.90	$9.00	$24.50	$67.00
Competitor B	$13.00	$7.40	$9.50	$23.00	$65.00

With competitive pricing, sales for the fiscal year ending May 31, 2002, are expected to be as follows:

	CUSTOM PLIERS	ECONOMY PLIERS	15CM PLIERS	20CM PLIERS	CHAIN PLIERS
Expected unit sales	4,000	120,000	480,000	39,000	3,000

After the meeting, Diane returned to her office and determined that she would have to consider at least the following six issues:

1. cost allocation
2. product prices
3. the proposal to introduce a set of wrenches to the product line
4. the option to increase capacity by leasing machinery
5. production mix planning
6. management reporting system

Required:

Assuming the role of Diane Crombie, prepare a report to Milt Pearson. Include in the report your analysis of and recommendations on the six issues above as well as any other issues you feel should be addressed. Also, include a projected income statement for the fiscal year ending May 31, 2002, which reflects the effects of your recommendations.

Estimated annual sales volume = 36,000 to 56,000 sets		
Machine hours required per set = 1/4		
Wholesale price per set		$14.00
Costs per set:		
Direct materials	$ 4.00	
Direct labour	1.00	
Overhead*	10.00	
Commission	1.10	
Fixed selling and administrative costs**	.52	
Total costs		16.62
Profit (loss) per set		$ (2.62)

* Overhead costs = 10 × Estimated direct labour costs
= 10 × $1 = $10

** The only increase in annual fixed selling and administrative costs would be $18,550 for advertising. The cost per set was calculated as follows:
Advertising/Minimum sales volume
= $18,550/36,000 sets
= $.52 per set

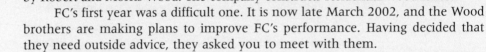

C8-4 PRICING. (CICA) Fence Company Ltd. (FC) was incorporated in March 2001, and is equally owned by Robert and Morris Wood. The company constructs residential wood fences.

FC's first year was a difficult one. It is now late March 2002, and the Wood brothers are making plans to improve FC's performance. Having decided that they need outside advice, they asked you to meet with them.

At the meeting, you asked the brothers to describe their operations and to highlight their major concerns. The following paragraphs are your notes from the meeting.

- FC lost business last year because it could not meet its promised installation dates during the peak period. The owners consider, however, that their biggest problem last year was caused by the need to repair fences. They guarantee their work, and they had to go back and change broken boards and clean up work sites, which cost them money and did nothing for their reputation.
- The owners project that FC will construct 50,000 linear metres of fence this year. To achieve this target, they think that one work team will be needed during the 12 weeks of April, October and November, and three teams during the 20 weeks from May through September. Their projection assumes an eight-hour day and a regular five-day week. Last year they found that a good work team consisting of three people could build a 100-linear-metre fence in an eight-hour day.
- The average labour cost including benefits last year was $5 per hour. Labour and material costs are expected to increase 10 percent in 2002. Last year there was little control over the amount of wood used on projects; the owners want to change this situation.
- The brothers recognize that fence building is not a year-round activity and are willing to cover any cash deficiency as long as there are prospects of profitability.
- The owners need to take out at least $15,000 each per year. In addition, they intend to hire a full-time receptionist to start on April 1 and to employ this person year-round. They expect that the salary will be about $12,000 a year but think that the cost will be worth it to ensure continuity and maintain the company's image.
- A truck will have to be rented for each work team, at $500 per month. Robert Wood thinks that they should keep two of the trucks from December to March for snow removal. He and Morris could do the work and lay off everyone except the receptionist.
- FC will also need to rent a machine for $600 a month to dig holes. In addition, it will cost approximately $120 to move the machine from one work site to another.
- The company spent $8,000 on gas and maintenance and $1,200 on telephone last year. The owners expect to hold the line on these costs this year.
- Morris Wood estimates that their costs last year were approximately $6 per linear metre for wood and $1 for nails and stain.
- The standard selling price last year was $11 per linear metre. Robert Wood thinks that they should try for $13 this year. FC's salesperson complained last year because he could not discount the price. The brothers think that it might be a good idea to allow the salesperson to go down to $12 if forced to do so in order not to lose the sale. They

are considering offering a special in April — perhaps 4 percent off — to get things rolling. They may also offer a 10 percent discount on group orders for fences for four or more houses. This discount offer worked well last year.

- According to the owners, a good incentive for their salesperson is crucial to increased sales. Last year, they paid the salesperson 5 percent of gross revenue for a basic one-house order for a fence of about 100 linear metres. For a two- or three-house order, they paid 6 percent and for a four-house order, which is about 400 linear metres, they paid 8 percent. They believe that the incentive was responsible for the fact that FC had a lot of two-house orders last year.
- Starting in April, FC will pay $2,500 a month to rent a warehouse for storing wood and equipment for the year. The landlord wants a security deposit of one month's rent. The company also has to buy new tools that cost at least $3,000, since the work teams either stole or broke all the tools used last year.

Required: Draft a report to the Wood brothers that presents your analysis of the issues and your recommendations.

C8-5 RELEVANT COSTS. (CGAC) Shepton Specialty Products Ltd. is a manufacturer of surgical instruments. Given the changes in surgical technology, Shepton has had to invest heavily in maintaining and upgrading its state-of-the-art product line. Shepton has become noted for the high quality of its product and the reasonableness of its prices.

Shepton is currently evaluating the design and production of its neurosurgical line of products. They want to know what the current quality costs are and how much it would cost to improve quality. Currently, the company has an expected spoilage rate in the neurosurgical line of one unit for every 200 units produced. It costs $2,000 per week plus $.10 per unit to inspect this product. With the current inspection policy and production specifications, the company experiences a return and warranty claim of one unit for every 500 units produced. Such a return normally costs the company the cost of the replacement unit and creates the potential for lost customers. Shepton estimates that every warranty claim loses five unit sales for the company.

Shepton has looked at revamping its quality control system. Using a new computer-assisted design and manufacturing system (that can be leased for $200,000 per year) the company could reduce the spoilage rate to one unit for every 350 units produced and reduce variable inspection costs to $.065 per unit. As well, product returns are expected to drop to one unit for every 900 units produced. Average unit cost for the neurosurgical line is shown below.

SHEPTON LABS
NEUROSURGICAL PRODUCT LINE
AVERAGE UNIT COST[1]
FOR THE YEAR 2001

Material	$5.00
Labour	6.50
Variable overhead	6.00
Fixed overhead[2]	5.00
	$22.50

[1] Excludes inspection costs
[2] Based on estimated production of 5,000,000 good units of production in 2001.

The average selling price is $33 per unit and variable selling costs are 15 percent of the selling price.

Required:

Given Shepton's interest in quality control, determine whether they should lease the computer system.

C8-6 USE OF CAPACITY. (CMA, adapted.) St. Tropez manufactures several different styles of jewellery cases in southern France. Management estimates that during the second quarter of 2002 the company will be operating at 80 percent of normal capacity. Because the company desires a higher utilization of plant capacity, it will consider a special order.

St. Tropez has received special-order inquires from two companies. The first is from Lyon, Inc., which would like to market a jewellery case similar to one of St. Tropez's cases. The Lyon jewellery case would be marketed under Lyon's own label. Lyon, Inc., has offered St. Tropez FF67.5 per case for 20,000 cases to be shipped by July 1, 2002. The cost data for the St. Tropez case, which would be similar to the specifications of the Lyon special order, are as follows:

Regular selling price per unit	FF100
Costs per unit:	
Raw materials	FF35
Direct labour .5 hr @ FF60	30
Overhead .25 machine-hr @ FF40	10
Total costs	FF75

According to the specifications provided by Lyon, Inc., the special-order case requires less expensive raw materials, which will cost only FF32.5 per case. Management has estimated that the remaining costs, labour time, and machine time will be the same as those for the St. Tropez case.

The second special order was submitted by the Avignon Co. for 7,500 cases at FF85 per case. These cases would be marketed under the Avignon label and would have to be shipped by July 1, 2002. The Avignon case is different from any case in the St. Tropez line; its estimated per-unit costs are as follows:

Raw materials	FF42.5
Direct labour .5 @ FF60	30.0
Overhead .5 machine-hr @ FF40	20.0
Total costs	FF92.5

In addition, St. Tropez will incur FF15,000 in additional setup costs and will have to purchase a FF25,000 special device to manufacture these cases; this device will be discarded once the special order is completed.

The St. Tropez manufacturing capabilities are limited by the total machine-hours available. The plant capacity under normal operations is 90,000 machine-hours per year, or 7,500 machine-hours per month. The budgeted fixed overhead for 2002 amounts to FF2.16 million, or FF24 per hour. All manufacturing overhead costs are applied to production on the basis of machine-hours at FF40 per hour.

St. Tropez will have the entire second quarter to work on the special orders. Management does not expect any repeat sales to be generated from either special order. Company practice precludes St. Tropez from subcontracting any portion of an order when special orders are not expected to generate repeat sales.

Required: Should St. Tropez accept either special order? Justify your answer and show your calculations.

(Hint: Distinguish between variable and fixed overhead.)

9

Relevant Information and Decision Making: Production Decisions

Should Ford make the tires it mounts on its cars, or should Ford buy them from suppliers? Should General Mills sell the flour it mills, or should it use the flour to make more breakfast cereal? Should Air Canada add routes to use idle air-planes, or should it sell the planes? Successful managers can discriminate between relevant and irrelevant information in making decisions such as these.

In the preceding chapter we provided a framework for identifying relevant costs and applied the framework to various decisions. In this chapter we extend the analysis by introducing the concepts of opportunity cost and differential costs and by examining additional decisions: make or buy, sell or process further, and replace equipment.

This chapter and the preceding one illustrate relevant costs for many types of decisions. Does this mean that each decision requires a different approach to identifying relevant costs? No. *The fundamental principle in all decision situations is that relevant costs are future costs that differ among alternatives.* The principle is simple, but its application is not always straightforward. Because it is so important to be able to apply this principle, we present multiple examples.

OPPORTUNITY, OUTLAY, AND DIFFERENTIAL COSTS

OBJECTIVE 1

Use opportunity cost to analyze the income effects of a given alternative.

Opportunity Cost. The maximum available contribution to profit forgone (rejected) by using limited resources for a particular purpose.

Outlay Cost. A cost that requires a cash disbursement.

The concept of opportunity cost is often used by decision makers. An **opportunity cost** is the maximum available contribution to profit forgone by using limited resources for a particular purpose. This definition indicates that opportunity cost is not the usual **outlay cost** recorded in financial accounting ledgers. An outlay cost that will eventually require a cash disbursement is the typical of cost recorded by accountants.

An example of an opportunity cost is the salary forgone by a person who quits a job to start a business. Consider Maria Morales, a chartered accountant employed by a large accounting firm at $60,000 per year who yearns to have her own practice.

Maria's alternatives may be framed in more than one way. A straightforward comparison follows.

	ALTERNATIVES UNDER CONSIDERATION		
	REMAIN AS AN EMPLOYEE	OPEN AN INDEPENDENT PRACTICE	DIFFERENCE
Revenues	$60,000	$200,000	$140,000
Outlay costs (operating expenses)	—	120,000	120,000
Income effects per year	$60,000	$ 80,000	$ 20,000

The annual difference of $20,000 favours Maria's choosing independent practice.

This tabulation is sometimes called a *differential analysis*. The *differential revenue* is $140,000, the *differential cost* is $120,000, and the *differential income* is $20,000. Each amount is the difference between the corresponding items under each alternative being considered. **Differential cost** and **incremental cost** are widely used synonyms. They are defined as the difference in total cost between two alternatives. For instance, the differential costs or incremental costs of

Differential Cost (Incremental Cost). The difference in total cost between two alternatives.

increasing production from 1,000 automobiles to 1,200 automobiles per week would be the added costs of producing an additional 200 automobiles each week. In the reverse situation, the decline in costs caused by reducing production from 1,200 to 1,000 automobiles per week would often be called differential or incremental savings.

Focus on the meaning of opportunity cost. What is the contribution to profit of the best of the rejected alternatives available to Maria Morales? Independent practice has an opportunity cost of $60,000, the forgone annual salary.

These same facts may also be presented as follows:

		ALTERNATIVE CHOSEN: INDEPENDENT PRACTICE
Revenue		$200,000
Expenses:		
Outlay costs (operating expenses)	$120,000	
Opportunity cost of employee salary	60,000	180,000
Income effects per year		$ 20,000

Ponder the two preceding tabulations. Each produces the correct key difference between the alternatives, $20,000. The first tabulation does not mention opportunity cost because the economic impacts (in the form of revenues and outlay costs) are individually measured for each of the alternatives (two in this case). Neither alternative has been excluded from consideration. The second tabulation mentions opportunity cost because the $60,000 annual economic impact of the *best excluded* alternative is included as a cost of the chosen alternative. The failure to recognize opportunity cost in the second tabulation will misstate the difference between alternatives.

Suppose Morales prefers less risk and chooses to stay on as an employee:

		ALTERNATIVE CHOSEN: REMAIN AS EMPLOYEE
Revenue		$ 60,000
Expenses:		
Outlay costs	$ 0	
Opportunity cost of independent practice	80,000	80,000
Decrease in income per year		$(20,000)

If the employee alternative is selected, the key difference in favour of independent practice is again $20,000. The opportunity cost is $80,000, the annual operating income forgone by rejecting the best excluded alternative. Morales is sacrificing $20,000 annually to avoid the risks of an independent practice. In sum, the opportunity cost is the contribution of the best alternative that is excluded from consideration.

RELEVANT INFORMATION AND DECISION MAKING AT ROYCO HOTELS & RESORTS

Royco Hotels and Resorts is a hotel-management company whose head office is located in Calgary, Alberta. Royco currently manages 27 properties (25 hotels and two resorts) throughout Canada. Included among the properties managed are the Relax Hotel and Inn chain and recent franchises of the Travelodge chain. The company just entered into an agreement with Forte Hotels through its U.S. subsidiary located in San Diego. In the near future, it is anticipated that additional management contracts will be gained across Canada.

The structure of the management is such that there is centralized accounting and associated functions. This allows uniformity and consistency in the production of financial information and analysis. Additional benefits of centralized accounting are economies of scale and the synergy from the efforts of the accounting team.

In our business environment, an ongoing analysis of the optimal pricing strategy for our hotel properties is critical. In pricing decisions, all the relevant information is taken into account without losing the focus of the pricing issue, by ensuring that costs or revenues that are not affected by the decision are not considered. An example of the analytical process used in pricing decisions is as follows:

1. Determine the purpose of the pricing decision. Is it a special promotion, one-time price, or is it the standard price? The relevant costs are significantly different in each of these cases.
2. Competitive analysis. It is important that we take into account the position of the competitors in our marketplace and our niche within the market. Pricing decisions can have competitive reactions that need to be considered.
3. Costs. While cost controls are a critical component to ensure long-term success of the organization, costs play a relatively small role in pricing decisions, due to our competitive environment.
4. Profit maximization. For the long-term success of our company and all the stakeholders (owners, suppliers, creditors, and employees), it is imperative that the company remains profitable. In this regard, the maximization of contribution is the core of the analysis. In this we must take into account both the Price (Average room rate), Variable Costs, and Volume (Occupancy rate). Together these factors provide a Yield calculation which enables us to determine the optimal price.

Source: Written by Kirk Morgan, Corporate Controller, Royco Hotels & Resorts Ltd.

MAKE-OR-BUY DECISIONS

OBJECTIVE 2

Decide whether to make or buy certain parts or products.

Travelodge Hotels
www.travelodge.com

Forte Hotels
www.forte-hotels.co.uk

Managers apply relevant cost analysis to a variety of make-or-buy decisions, including:

- A pump manufacturer's decision to produce all the components of the pump or purchase some of the components from suppliers.
- IBM's decision whether to develop its own operating system for a new computer or to buy it from a software vendor.
- A university's decision whether to use its own personnel or hire a consulting firm to design and implement a new computerized accounting system.

Make-or-Buy and Idle Facilities

To focus on basic principles, we will examine relatively straightforward make-or-buy decisions. Consider manufacturers who must often decide whether to make or buy a product. For example, should a firm manufacture its own parts and subassemblies or buy them from vendors? Sometimes qualitative factors dominate quantitative assessments of costs. Some manufacturers always make parts because they want to control quality, others because they possess special know-how—usually skilled labour or rare materials needed in production. Alternatively, some companies always purchase parts to protect long-run relationships with their suppliers. These companies may deliberately avoid the practice of making their parts during slack times to avoid difficulties in obtaining needed parts during boom times, when there may well be shortages of material and workers but no shortage of sales orders.

What factors are relevant to the decision of whether to make or buy? The answer, again, depends on the situation. A key factor is whether there are idle facilities. Many companies make parts only when their facilities cannot be used to better advantage.

General Electric
www.ge.com

Assume that the following costs are reported for General Electric Company (GE) for Part No. 900:

	TOTAL COST FOR 20,000 UNITS	COST PER UNIT
Direct material	$ 20,000	$ 1
Direct labour	80,000	4
Variable factory overhead	40,000	2
Fixed factory overhead	80,000	4
Total costs	$220,000	$11

Another manufacturer offers to sell GE the same part for $10. Should GE make or buy the part?

Although the $11 unit cost seems to indicate that the company should buy, the answer is rarely so obvious. The essential question is the difference in expected future costs between the alternatives. If the $4 fixed overhead per unit consists of costs that will continue regardless of the decision, the entire $4 becomes irrelevant. Examples of such costs include depreciation, property taxes, insurance, and allocated executive salaries.

Again, are only the variable costs relevant? No. Perhaps $20,000 of the fixed costs will be eliminated if the parts are bought instead of made. For example, a supervisor with a $20,000 salary might be released. In other words, fixed costs that may be avoided in the future are relevant.

For the moment, suppose the capacity now used to make parts will become idle if the parts are purchased and the $20,000 supervisor's salary is the only fixed cost that would be saved. The relevant computations follow:

	MAKE		BUY	
	TOTAL	PER UNIT	TOTAL	PER UNIT
Direct material	$ 20,000	$1		
Direct labour	80,000	4		
Variable factory overhead	40,000	2		
Fixed factory overhead that can be avoided by not making (supervisor's salary)	20,000*	1*		
Total relevant costs	$160,000	$8	$200,000	$10
Difference in favour of making	$ 40,000	$2		

*Note that fixed costs of $80,000 − $20,000 = $60,000 are irrelevant. Thus, the irrelevant costs per unit are $4 − $1 = $3.

The key to make-or-buy decisions is identifying the *additional costs* for making (or the *costs avoided* by buying) a part or subcomponent. Activity analysis, described in Chapter 3, helps identify these costs. Production of a product requires a set of activities. A company with accurate measurements of the costs of its various activities can better estimate the additional costs incurred to produce an item. GE's activities for production of part number 900 were measured by two cost drivers, units of production of $8 per unit and supervision at a $20,000 fixed cost. Sometimes identification and measurement of additional cost drivers, especially non-volume-related cost drivers, can improve the predictions of the additional cost to produce a part or subcomponent.

Make-or-Buy and the Utilization of Facilities

Make-or-buy decisions are rarely as simple as is the one in our GE example. As we said earlier, the use of facilities is a key to the make-or-buy decision. For simplicity we assumed that the GE facilities would remain idle if the company chose to buy the product. Of course, in most cases companies will not leave their facilities idle. Instead, idle facilities will often be put to some other use, and the financial outcomes of these uses must be considered when choosing to make or buy.

Suppose the released facilities can be used advantageously in some other manufacturing activity (to produce a contribution to profits of, say, $55,000) or can be rented out (say, for $35,000).

We now have four alternatives to consider (figures are in thousands):

	MAKE	BUY AND LEAVE FACILITIES IDLE	BUY AND RENT	BUY AND USE FACILITIES FOR OTHER PRODUCTS
Rent revenue	$ —	$ —	$ 35	$ —
Contribution from other products	—	—	—	55
Obtaining of parts	(160)	(200)	(200)	(200)
Net relevant costs	$(160)	$(200)	$(165)	$(145)

The final column indicates that buying the parts and using the vacated facilities for the production of other products would yield the lowest net costs in this case.

In sum, the make-or-buy decision should focus on relevant costs in a particular decision situation. In all cases, companies should relate make-or-buy decisions to the long-run policies for the use of capacity.

To illustrate, suppose a company uses its facilities, *on average*, 80 percent of the time. However, because of seasonal changes in the demand for its product, the actual demand for the facilities varies from 60 percent in the off season to over 100 percent in the peak season. During the off season, the company may decide to perform special projects for other manufacturers (on a subcontract). There is profit on these projects but not enough to justify expanding the capacity of the facilities. During the peak season, the company meets the high volume by purchasing parts. Again, the cost of purchased parts is higher than the cost to make them in the company's own facilities, but the additional cost is less than it would be if new equipment were used only part of the time.

JOINT PRODUCT COSTS

Nature of Joint Products

When two or more manufactured products (1) have relatively significant sales values and (2) are not separately identifiable as individual products until their split-off point, they are called **joint products**. The **split-off point** is that juncture of manufacturing where the joint products become individually identifiable. Any costs beyond that stage are called **separable costs** because they are not part of the joint process and can be exclusively identified with individual products. The costs of manufacturing joint products prior to the

Joint Products. Two or more manufactured products that (1) have relatively significant sales values and (2) are not identifiable as individual products until their split-off point.

Split-Off Point. The juncture in manufacturing where the joint products become individually identifiable.

Separable Costs. Any costs beyond the split-off point in a joint product production process.

Electronic Data Systems
www.eds.com

Kodak
www.kodak.com

J.P. Morgan & Co.
www.jpmorgan.com

Unilever
www.unilever.com

Modular Industrial
Computers
www.mic.com

Chevron
www.chevron.com

Sun Microsystems
www.sun.com

PERSPECTIVES ON DECISION-MAKING

An Example of Make or Buy: Outsourcing

Make-or-buy decisions apply to services as well as to products. One type of make-or-buy decision faced by many companies in the 1990s was whether to buy data-processing and computer-network services or to provide them internally. Many companies eliminated their internal departments and "outsourced" (or bought) data-processing services and network services from companies such as Electronic Data Systems, a General Motors subsidiary.

One of the first major companies to outsource its data processing was Eastman Kodak. By hiring IBM and Digital Equipment, Kodak was able to eliminate 1,000 jobs and avoid huge capital investments. Another example is J.P. Morgan & Co., which hired BT North America to link 26 Morgan offices in 14 countries. The five-year, $20-million contract is expected to save Morgan $12.5 million. Other outsourcing agreements include Sprint running Unilever's network, MIC handling Sun Microsystem's Pacific Rim network, AT&T working on Chevron's network, and GE Information Services operating the Vatican's global data network. Some companies, such as Sun Microsystems, outsource everything except their core technologies. Sun focuses on hardware and software design and outsources nearly everything else. Its employees do not actually produce any of the products that bear the company's name.

The driving forces behind most outsourcing decisions are access to technology and cost savings. As the complexity of data processing and especially networking has grown, companies have found it harder and harder to keep current with the technology. Instead of investing hugh sums in personnel and equipment and diverting attention from the value-added activities of their own businesses, many firms have found outsourcing attractive from a financial standpoint. The big stumbling block has been subjective factors, such as control. To make outsourcing attractive, the services must be reliable, be available when needed, and be flexible enough to adapt to changing conditions. Companies that have successful outsourcing arrangements have been careful to include the subjective factors in their decisions.

Sources: Adapted from "Telecommunications: More Firms 'Outsource' Data Networks," *The Wall Street Journal*, March 11, 1992, p. B1; R. Suh, "Guaranteeing that Outsourcing Serves Your Business Strategy," *Information Strategy: The Executive's Journal*, Spring 1992, pp. 39–42; R. Zahler, "Identifying the Key Issues for Assessing Outsourcing," *Network World*, March 30, 1992, pp. 21, 23; J. Radigan, "All Wired Up at Morgan," *Bank Systems & Technology*, March 1992, pp. 25, 27; R.E. Ortina, "The Outsourcing Decision," *Management Accounting*, March 1994, pp. 56–62, and M.F. Corbett, "Outsourcing: Redefining the Corporation of the Future," *Fortune*, December 12, 1994, pp. 51–92.

Joint Costs. The costs of manufacturing joint products prior to the split-off point.

split-off point are called **joint costs**, a popular synonym is "common costs." Examples of joint products include chemicals, lumber, flour, and the products of petroleum-refining and meat-packing. A meat-packing company cannot kill a sirloin steak; it has to slaughter a steer, which supplies various cuts of dressed meat, hides, and trimmings.

To illustrate joint costs, suppose Dow Chemical Company produces two chemical products, X and Y, as a result of a particular joint process. The joint processing cost is $100,000. This includes raw-material costs and the cost of processing to the point where X and Y go their separate ways. Both products are sold to the petroleum industry to be used as ingredients of gasoline. The relationships follow:

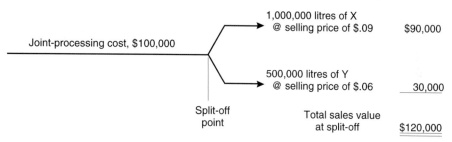

Sell or Process Further

Management frequently faces decisions of whether to sell joint products as split-off or to process some or all products further. Suppose the 500,000 litres of Y can be processed further and sold to the plastics industry as product YA—an ingredient for plastic sheeting—the additional processing cost would be $.08 per litre for manufacturing and distribution, a total of $40,000. The net sales price of YA would be $.16 per litre, a total of $80,000 for 500,000 litres.

Product X cannot be processed further and will be sold at the split-off point, but management is undecided about Product Y. Should Y be sold or should it be processed into YA? To answer this question we need to find the relevant costs involved. Because the joint costs must be incurred to reach the split-off point, they might seem relevant. However, they cannot affect anything beyond the split-off point. Therefore, they do not differ between alternatives and are completely irrelevant to the question of whether to sell or process further. The only approach that will yield valid results is to concentrate on the separable costs and revenue *beyond* split-off, as shown in the following table. This analysis shows that it would be $10,000 more profitable to process Y beyond split-off than to sell Y at split-off. Briefly, it is profitable to extend processing or to incur additional distribution costs on a joint product *if* the additional revenue exceeds the additional expenses.

	SELL AT SPLIT-OFF AS Y	PROCESS FURTHER AS YA	DIFFERENCE
Revenues	$30,000	$80,000	$50,000
Separable costs beyond split-off @ $.08	—	40,000	40,000
Income effects	$30,000	$40,000	$10,000

For decisions regarding whether to sell or process further, the most straightforward analysis is shown above. An alternative opportunity cost format is shown on the next page.

	PROCESS FURTHER
Revenue	$80,000
Outlay cost: separable cost beyond split-off, @ $.08	$40,000
Opportunity cost: sales value of Y at split-off	30,000 70,000
Income effects	$10,000

This format is merely a different way of recognizing another alternative (sell Y at split-off) when considering the decision to process further.

When decision alternatives are properly analyzed, they may be compared either (1) by excluding the idea of opportunity costs altogether, or (2) by including opportunity costs, derived from the best excluded alternative, as is shown here. The key difference, $10,000, is generated either way. Exhibit 9-1 illustrates still another way to compare the alternatives of (1) selling Y at the split-off point and (2) processing Y beyond split-off. It includes the joint costs, which are the same for each alternative and therefore do not affect the difference.

Earlier discussions in this and the preceding chapter have emphasized the desirability of concentrating on totals and being wary of unit costs and allocations of fixed costs. Similarly, the allocation of joint product costs to units of product is fraught with analytical perils.

The allocation of joint costs would not affect the decision, as Exhibit 9-1 demonstrates. The joint costs are not allocated in the exhibit, but no matter how they might be allocated, the total income effects would be unchanged. Additional coverage of joint costs and inventory valuation is in Chapter 13.

EXHIBIT 9-1

Firm as a Whole

	(1) ALTERNATIVE ONE			(2) ALTERNATIVE TWO			(3) DIFFERENTIAL EFFECTS
	X	Y	TOTAL	X	YA	TOTAL	
Revenues	$90,000	$30,000	$120,000	$90,000	$80,000	$170,000	$50,000
Joint costs			$100,000		—	$100,000	—
Separable costs			—		$40,000	40,000	40,000
Total costs			$100,000			$140,000	$40,000
Income effects			$ 20,000			$ 30,000	$10,000

IRRELEVANCE OF PAST COSTS

The ability to recognize and thereby ignore irrelevant costs is sometimes just as important to decision makers as identifying relevant costs. How do we know that past costs are irrelevant in decision making? Consider such past costs as obsolete inventory and the book value of old equipment and why they are irrelevant to decisions.

Obsolete Inventory

General Dynamics
www.gdls.com

Suppose General Dynamics has 100 obsolete aircraft parts that it is carrying in its inventory. The original manufacturing cost of these parts was $100,000. General Dynamics can (1) remachine the parts for $30,000 and then sell them for $50,000 or (2) scrap them for $5,000. Which should it do?

This is an unfortunate situation; yet the $100,000 past cost is irrelevant to the decision to remachine or scrap. The only relevant factors are the expected future revenue and costs:

	REMACHINE	SCRAP	DIFFERENCE
Expected future revenue	$ 50,000	$ 5,000	$45,000
Expected future costs	30,000	—	30,000
Relevant excess of revenue over costs	$ 20,000	$ 5,000	$15,000
Accumulated historical inventory cost*	100,000	100,000	—
Net overall loss on project	$(80,000)	$(95,000)	$15,000

* Irrelevant because it is unaffected by the decision.

We can completely ignore the $100,000 historical cost and still arrive at the $15,000 difference, the key figure in the analysis.

Book Value of Old Equipment

Amortization (Depreciation). The periodic cost of plant and equipment which is spread over (or charged to) the future periods in which the plant and equipment are expected to be used.

Like obsolete parts, the book value of equipment is not a relevant consideration in deciding whether to replace such equipment. When equipment is purchased, its cost is spread over (or charged to) the future periods in which the equipment is expected to be used. This periodic cost is called **amortization** or **depreciation**. The equipment's **book value** (or **net book value**) is the original cost less **accumulated depreciation**, which is the summation of depreciation charged to past periods. For example, suppose a $10,000 machine with a 10-year life has depreciation of $1,000 per year. At the end of six years, accumulated depreciation is 6 × $1,000 = $6,000, and the book value is $10,000 − $6,000 = $4,000.

Book Value (Net Book Value). The orginal cost of equipment less accumulated amortization, which is the summation of amortization charged to past periods.

Consider the following data for a decision whether to replace an old machine:

Accumulated Amortization. The summation of amortization charged to past periods.

	OLD MACHINE	REPLACEMENT MACHINE
Original cost	$10,000	$8,000
Useful life in years	10	4
Current age in years	6	0
Useful life remaining in years	4	4
Accumulated amortization	$ 6,000	0
Book value	$ 4,000	Not acquired yet
Disposal value (in cash) now	$ 2,500	Not acquired yet
Disposal value in 4 years	0	0
Annual cash operating costs (maintenance, power, repairs, coolants, etc.)	$ 5,000	$3,000

Sunk Cost. A cost that has already been incurred and, therefore, is irrelevant to the decision-making process.

We have been asked to prepare a comparative analysis of the two alternatives. Before proceeding, consider some important concepts. The most widely misunderstood facet of replacement decision making is the role of the book value of the old equipment in the decision. The book value, in this context, is sometimes called a **sunk cost**, which is really just another term for historical or past cost. A cost that has already been incurred and, therefore, is irrelevant to the decision. At one time or another, we all try to soothe the wounded pride arising from having made a bad purchase decision by using an item instead of replacing it. But it is a serious mistake to think that a current or future action can influence the long-run impact of a past outlay. All past costs are down the drain. Nothing can change what has already happened.

The irrelevance of past costs for decisions does not mean that knowledge of past costs is useless. Often managers use past costs to help predict future costs. But the past cost itself is not relevant. The only relevant cost is the predicted future cost.

In deciding whether to replace or keep using equipment, four commonly encountered items differ in relevance.[1]

- *Book value of old equipment.* Irrelevant, because it is a past (historical) cost. Therefore depreciation on old equipment is irrelevant.
- *Disposal value of old equipment.* Relevant (ordinarily), because it is an expected future inflow that usually differs among alternatives.
- *Gain or loss on disposal.* This is the algebraic difference between book value and disposal value. It is therefore a meaningless combination of book value, which is always irrelevant, and relevant items. The combination form, *loss* (or *gain*) *on disposal* blurs the distinction between the irrelevant book value and the relevant disposal value. Consequently, it is best to think of each separately.
- *Cost of new equipment.* Relevant, because it is an expected future outflow that will differ among alternatives. Therefore, depreciation on new equipment is relevant.

Exhibit 9-2 deserves close study because it should clarify the foregoing assertions. Book value of old equipment is irrelevant regardless of the decision-making technique used. The "difference" column in Exhibit 9-2 shows that the $4,000 book value of the *old* equipment does not differ between alternatives. It should be completely ignored for decision-making purposes.

The $4,000 appears in the income statement either as a $4,000 deduction from the $2,500 cash proceeds received to obtain a $1,500 loss on disposal in one year or as a $1,000 depreciation in each of four years. But how it appears is irrelevant to the replacement decision. In contrast, the $2,000 annual depreciation on the new equipment is relevant because the total $8,000 depreciation is a future cost that may be avoided by not replacing.

Examining Alternatives over the Long Run

Exhibit 9-2 is the first example that looks beyond one year. Examining the alternatives over the entire life ensures that peculiar nonrecurring items (such as loss on disposal) will not obstruct the long-run view vital to many managerial decisions.

Exhibit 9-3 concentrates on relevant items only: the cash operating costs, the disposal value of the old equipment, and the depreciation on the new equipment. To demonstrate that the amount of the book value will not affect the answer, suppose the book value of the old equipment is $500,000 rather than $4,000. Your final answer will not change. The cumulative advantage of replacement is still $2,500. (If you are in doubt, rework this example, using $500,000 as the book value.)

---

[1] For simplicity, we ignore income tax considerations and the effects of the interest value of money in this chapter. Book value is irrelevant even if income taxes are considered because the relevant item is then the tax cash flow, not the book value. For elaboration, see Chapter 11.

EXHIBIT 9-2

Cost Comparison—
Replacement of
Equipment Including
Relevant and
Irrelevant Items

	FOUR YEARS TOGETHER		
	KEEP	REPLACE	DIFFERENCE
Cash operating costs	$20,000	$12,000	$8,000
Old equipment (book value):			
Periodic write-off as amortization	4,000	—	—
or			
Lump-sum write-off		4,000*	
Disposal value	—	−2,500	2,500
New machine acquisition cost	—	8,000†	−8,000
Total costs	$24,000	$21,500	$2,500

The advantage of replacement is $2,500 for the four years together.

- In a formal income statement, these two items would be combined as "loss on disposal" of $4,000 −$2,500 = $1,500.
- † In a formal income statement, written off as straight-line depreciation of $8,000 ÷ 4 = $2,000 for each of four years.

EXHIBIT 9-3

Cost Comparison—
Replacement of
Equipment, Relevant
Items Only

	FOUR YEARS TOGETHER		
	KEEP	REPLACE	DIFFERENCE
Cash operating costs	$20,000	$12,000	$8,000
Disposal value of old machine	—	−2,500	2,500
New machine, acquisition cost	—	8,000	−8,000
Total relevant costs	$20,000	$17,500	$2,500

IRRELEVANCE OF FUTURE COSTS THAT WILL NOT DIFFER

In addition to past costs, some *future* costs may be irrelevant because they will be the same under all feasible alternatives. These, too, may be safely ignored for a particular decision. The salaries of many members of top management are examples of expected future costs that will be unaffected by the decision at hand.

Other irrelevant future costs include fixed costs that will be unchanged by such considerations as whether Machine X or Machine Y is selected. However, it is not merely a case of saying that fixed costs are irrelevant and variable costs are relevant. Variable costs can be irrelevant and fixed costs can be relevant. For instance, sales commissions might be paid on an order regardless of whether the order was filled from Plant G or Plant H. Variable costs are irrelevant whenever they do not differ among the alternatives at hand. Fixed costs are relevant whenever they differ under the alternatives at hand.

The key issue again is to identify which costs will differ between alternatives and by how much.

BEWARE OF UNIT COSTS

The pricing illustration in the preceding chapter showed that unit costs should be analyzed with care in decision making. There are two ways one can go wrong in decision making: (1) the inclusion of irrelevant costs, such as the $3 allocation of unavoidable fixed costs in the make-or-buy example (page 392), which would result in a unit cost of $11 instead of the relevant unit cost of $8, and (2) comparisons of unit costs not computed on the same volume basis, as the following example demonstrates. Generally, be wary of unit fixed costs. Use total costs rather than unit costs. Then, if desired, the totals may be unitized. Machinery sales personnel, for example, often brag about the low unit costs of using the new machines. Sometimes they neglect to point out that the unit costs are based on outputs far in excess of the volume of activity of their prospective customer.

Assume that a new machine can produce 100,000 units a year at a variable cost of $1 per unit, as opposed to a variable cost per unit of $1.50 with an old machine. The new machine can be rented for $20,000 per year. A sales representative claims that it will reduce cost by $.30 per unit. Is the new machine a worthwhile acquisition?

The new machine is attractive at first glance. If the customer's expected volume is 100,000 units, unit-cost comparisons are valid, provided that the new rent is also considered. Assume that the disposal value of the old equipment is zero. The rent on the new machine is relevant because the new machine entails a *future* cost that can be avoided by not acquiring it:

	OLD MACHINE	NEW MACHINE
Units	100,000	100,000
Variable costs	$150,000	$100,000
Rent	—	20,000
Total relevant costs	$150,000	$120,000
Unit relevant costs	$1.50	$1.20

Apparently, the sales representative is correct. However, if the customer's expected volume is only 30,000 units per year, the unit costs change in favour of the old machine:

	OLD MACHINE	NEW MACHINE
Units	30,000	30,000
Variable costs	$45,000	$30,000
Rent	—	20,000
Total relevant costs	$45,000	$50,000
Unit relevant costs	$1.50	$1.67

The allocation of the $20,000 rent fixed cost to a unit-cost basis leads to an analysis that distorts the actual differential costs.

CONFLICTS BETWEEN DECISION MAKING AND PERFORMANCE EVALUATION

We have focused on using relevant information in decision making. To motivate people to make optimal decisions, methods of performance evaluation should be consistent with the decision analysis.

Consider the replacement decision shown in Exhibit 9-3, where replacing the machine had a $2,500 advantage over keeping it. To motivate managers to make the right choice, the method used to evaluate performance should be consistent with the decision model. That is, it should show better performance when managers replace the machine than when they keep it. Because performance is often measured by accounting income, consider the accounting income in the first year after replacement compared to that in Years 2, 3, and 4:

	YEAR 1		YEARS 2, 3, AND 4	
	KEEP	**REPLACE**	**KEEP**	**REPLACE**
Cash operating costs	$5,000	$3,000	$5,000	$3,000
Amortization	1,000	2,000	1,000	2,000
Loss on disposal ($4,000–$2,500)	—	1,500	—	—
Total charges against revenue	$6,000	$6,500	$6,000	$5,000

If the machine is kept rather than replaced, first-year expenses will be $6,500 – $6,000 = $500 lower, and first-year income will be $500 higher. Because managers naturally want to make decisions that maximize the measure of their performance, they may be inclined to keep the machine. This is an example of a conflict between the analysis for decision making and the method used to evaluate performance.

The conflict is especially severe if managers jump from one position to another. Why? Because the $500 first-year advantage will be offset by a $1,000 advantage of replacing in Years 2, 3, and 4. (Note that the net difference of $2,500 in favour of replacement over the four years together is the same as in Exhibit 9-3.) But a manager who moves to a new position after the first year bears the entire loss on disposal without reaping the benefits of lower operating costs in Years 2, 3, and 4.

The decision to replace a machine earlier than planned also reveals that the original decision to purchase the machine may have been flawed. The old machine was bought six years ago for $10,000; its expected life was 10 years. However, if a better machine is now available, then the useful life of the old machine was really six years, not 10. This feedback on the actual life of the old machine has two possible effects: the first good and the second bad. First, managers might learn from the earlier mistake. If the useful life of the old machine was over-estimated, how believable is the prediction that the new machine will have a four-year life? Feedback can help avoid repeating past mistakes. Second, another mistake might be made to cover up the earlier one. A "loss on disposal" could alert superiors to the incorrect economic-life prediction used in the earlier decision. By avoiding replacement, the $4,000 remaining book value is spread over the future as "amortization"—a more appealing term than "loss on disposal." The superiors may never find out about the incorrect prediction of economic life. The accounting income approach to performance evaluation mixes the financial effects of various decisions, hiding both the earlier mis-estimation of useful life and the current failure to replace.

The conflict between decision making and performance evaluation is a widespread problem in practice. Unfortunately, there are no easy solutions. In theory, accountants could evaluate performance in a manner consistent with decision making. In our equipment example, this would mean predicting year-by-year income effects over the planning horizon for four years, noting that the first year would be poor, and evaluating actual performance against the predictions.

Canadian Government Inventory Control

Office of the Auditor General (Canada)
www.oag-bvg.gc.ca

Bedford Institute of Oceanography
www.mar.dfo-mpo.gc.ca/e/s_bio.html

Royal Canadian Mounted Police
www.rcmp-grc.gc.ca

The federal government's inventory control systems are out of control and costing tax-payers between $2 billion and $2.5 billion every year, federal Auditor General Denis Desautels has told Parliament.

The government buys $8 billion worth of material every year, Desautels says in his annual report. But because there is too much of it, departments tend to forget over time what they own, or watch as it becomes obsolete or deteriorates.

One of the worst examples uncovered by Desautel's eight-person audit team was at the Bedford Institute of Oceanography in Halifax, where scientific equipment was stored outside for so long it had trees and vegetation sprouting through it.

The auditors also discovered that the RCMP has almost 4,000 extra dress hats, a three-year supply, stashed in a warehouse, the product of a seriously flawed forecasting system.

Desautels estimated that the government has about $10 billion in assets and materials stockpiled in warehouses. Apparently, it is unaware of the existence of much of it because of faulty record-keeping.

One department found it had $1.7 billion more in inventory than it will need for the next four years.

The cost of holding all that equipment could reach $2.5 billion based on an esti-

mated annual carrying cost of 25 per cent of the purchase price.

Defence officials estimate the annual cost of maintaining their $8.5 billion inventory is almost $568 million.

Desautels's office audited six departments and organizations that account for about 60 per cent of the annual federal expenditure on materials.

The audit team said about 17,000 federal workers are employed in trying to manage the $10 billion inventories they have acquired.

Desautels recalled that his office conducted a government-wide audit of material management in 1980 and found serious problems in the acquisition and handling of supplies.

Sixteen years later, he observes that "this audit has confirmed that many of these deficiencies still exist in the government's current material management practices."

Nevertheless, Desautels praised the serious, and sometimes, major efforts that some departments are making to bring inventories under control.

But he harbours some doubts about the outcome of initiatives over time.

Source: Rennie MacKenzie, "Ottawa's inventory system out of control, AG says," *The Bottom Line*, December 1996, p. 16.

The trouble is that evaluating performance, decision by decision, is a costly procedure. Therefore, aggregate measures are used. For example, an income statement shows the results of many decisions, not just the single decision of buying a machine. Consequently, in many cases like our equipment example, managers may be most heavily influenced by the first-year effects on the income statement. Thus, managers refrain from taking the longer view that would benefit the company.

Conflicts between decision making and performance evaluation are commonly referred to as problems of "goal congruency." These issues will be examined in more detail in Chapters 14 and 15.

HIGHLIGHTS TO REMEMBER

Chapters 8 and 9 have focused on identifying relevant information for a variety of decisions. Relevant costs are future costs that differ among alternatives. Past costs are not relevant, but they might help to predict future costs.

Sometimes the notion of an opportunity cost is helpful in cost analysis. An opportunity cost is the maximum sacrifice in rejecting an alternative; it is the maximum earnings that might have been obtained if the productive good, service, or capacity had been applied to some alternative use. The opportunity-cost approach does not affect the important final differences between the courses of action, but the format of the analysis differs. This chapter also introduced differential costs or incremental costs, which are the differences in the total costs under each alternative.

Some generalizations about the decisions in this chapter follow:

- Make-or-buy decisions are, fundamentally, examples of obtaining the most profitable utilization of given facilities.
- Joint product costs are irrelevant in decisions about whether to sell at split-off or process further.
- The book value of old equipment is always irrelevant in replacement decisions. This cost is often called a sunk cost. Disposal value, however, is generally relevant.
- Generally, use total costs, rather than unit costs, in cost analysis.

Also, be aware that managers are often motivated to reject desirable economic decisions because of a conflict between the measures used in the decision making and those used in performance evaluation.

SUMMARY PROBLEM FOR YOUR REVIEW

Problem

Block Company makes industrial power drills. The data on the following page show the costs of the plastic housing separately from the costs of the electrical and mechanical components.

1. During the year, a prospective customer in an unrelated market offered $82,000 for 1,000 finished units. The latter would be in addition to the 100,000 units sold. The regular sales commission rate would have been paid. The president rejected the order because "it was below our costs of $97 per unit." What would operating income have been if the order had been accepted?

2. A supplier offered to manufacture the year's supply of 100,000 plastic housings for $13.50 each. What would be the effect on operating income if the Block Company purchased rather than made the plastic housings? Assume that $350,000 of the separable fixed costs assigned to plastic housings would have been avoided if the parts were purchased.

3. The company could have purchased their entire supply of the plastic housings for $13.50 each and used the vacated space for the manufacture of a deluxe version of its drill. Assume that 20,000 deluxe units could have been made (and sold in addition to the 100,000 regular units) at a unit variable cost of $90, exclusive of plastic housings and exclusive of the 10 percent sales commission. The 20,000 extra plastic housings could also be purchased for $13.50 each. The sales price

	A ELECTRICAL & MECHANICAL COMPONENTS*	B PLASTIC HOUSING	A + B INDUSTRIAL DRILLS
Sales: 100,000 units, @ $100			$10,000,000
Variable costs:			
Direct materials	$4,400,000	$ 500,000	$ 4,900,000
Direct labour	400,000	300,000	700,000
Variable factory overhead	100,000	200,000	300,000
Other variable costs	100,000	—	100,000
Sales commissions, @ 10%of sales	1,000,000	—	1,000,000
Total variable costs	$6,000,000	$1,000,000	$ 7,000,000
Contribution margin			$ 3,000,000
Separable fixed costs	$1,900,000	$ 400,000	$ 2,300,000
Common fixed costs	320,000	80,000	400,000
Total fixed costs	$2,220,000	$ 480,000	$ 2,700,000
Operating income			$ 300,000

* Not including the costs of parts (Column B).

would have been $130. All the fixed costs pertaining to the plastic housings would have continued, because these costs related primarily to the manufacturing facilities used. What would operating income have been if Block had bought the necessary plastic housings and made and sold the deluxe units?

Solution

1. Costs of filling the special order:

Direct materials	$49,000
Direct labour	7,000
Variable factory overhead	3,000
Other variable costs	1,000
Sales commission @ 10% of $82,000	8,200
Total variable costs	$68,200
Selling price	82,000
Contribution margin	$13,800

Operating income would have been $300,000 + $13,800, or $313,800, if the order had been accepted. In a sense, the decision to reject the offer implies that the Block Company is willing to invest $13,800 in immediate gains forgone (an opportunity cost) in order to preserve the long-run selling-price structure.

2. Assuming that $350,000 of the fixed costs could have been avoided by not making the plastic housings and that the other fixed costs would have been continued, the alternatives can be summarized as follows:

	MAKE	BUY
Purchase cost		$1,350,000
Variable costs	$1,000,000	
Avoidable fixed costs	350,000	
Total relevant costs	$1,350,000	$1,350,000

If the facilities used for plastic housings became idle, the Block Company would be indifferent as to whether to make or buy. Operating income would be unaffected.

3. The effect of purchasing the plastic housings and using the vacated facilities by the manufacture of a deluxe version of its main product is

Sales would increase by 20,000 units @ $130		$2,600,000
Variable costs exclusive of housing would increase		
by 20,000 units @ $90	$1,800,000	
Plus: Sales commission, 10% of		
$2,600,000	260,000	2,060,000
Contribution margin on 200,000 units		$ 540,000
Plastic Housings: 120,000 rather than 100,000 would		
be needed		
Buy 120,000 @ $13.50	$1,620,000	
Make 100,000 @ $10 (only the variable costs		
are relevant)	1,000,000	
Excess cost of outside purchase		620,000
Fixed costs, unchanged		—
Disadvantage of making deluxe units		$ (80,000)

Operating income would decline to $220,000 ($300,000 – $80,000, the disadvantage of selling the deluxe units). The deluxe units bring in a contribution margin of $540,000, but the additional costs of buying rather than making plastic housings is $620,000, leading to a net disadvantage of $80,000.

It is also necessary to consider other more qualitative considerations in addition to the above analysis. For example, what are the implications of the above decisions in terms of developing and maintaining a long-term relationship with your existing customers? Further, could one argue that there may be ethical concerns, for example in the first scenario, of accepting a lower-than-normal price?

ACCOUNTING VOCABULARY

ASSIGNMENT MATERIAL

QUESTIONS

Q9-1 Distinguish between an opportunity cost and an outlay cost.

Q9-2 "I had a chance to rent my summer home for two weeks for $800. But I chose to leave it empty. I didn't want strangers living in my summer house." What term in this chapter describes the $800? Why?

Q9-3 "Accountants do not ordinarily record opportunity costs in the formal accounting records." Why?

Q9-4 Distinguish between an incremental cost and a differential cost.

Q9-5 "Incremental cost is the addition to costs from the manufacture of one unit." Do you agree? Explain.

Q9-6 "The differential costs or incremental costs of increasing production from 1,000 automobiles to 1,200 automobiles per week would be the additional costs of producing the additional 200 automobiles." If production were reduced from 1,200 to 1,000 automobiles per week, what would the decline in costs be called?

Q9-7 "Qualitative factors generally favour making over buying a component." Do you agree? Explain.

Q9-8 "Choices are often mislabelled as simply *make-or-buy*." Do you agree? Explain.

Q9-9 What is the split-off point and why is it important in analyzing joint costs?

Q9-10 "No technique used to assign the joint cost to individual products should be used for management decisions regarding whether a product should be sold at the split-off point or processed further." Do you agree? Explain.

Q9-11 "Inventory that was purchased for $5,000 should not be sold for less than $5,000 because such a sale would result in a loss." Do you agree? Explain.

Q9-12 "Recovering sunk costs is a major objective when replacing equipment." Do you agree? Explain.

Q9-13 "Past costs are indeed relevant in most instances because they provide the point of departure for the entire decision process." Do you agree? Why?

Q9-14 Which of the following items are relevant to replacement decisions? Explain.
a. Book value of old equipment
b. Disposal value of old equipment
c. Cost of new equipment

Q9-15 "Some expected future costs may be irrelevant." Do you agree? Explain.

Q9-16 "Variable costs are irrelevant whenever they do not differ among the alternatives at hand." Do you agree? Explain.

Q9-17 There are two major reasons why unit costs should be analyzed with care in decision making. What are they?

Q9-18 "Machinery sales personnel sometimes erroneously brag about the low unit costs of using their machines." Identify one source of an error concerning the estimation of unit costs.

Q9-19 Give an example of a situation where the performance evaluation model is not consistent with the decision model.

Q9-20 "Evaluating performance, decision by decision, is costly. Aggregate measures, like the income statement, are frequently used." How might the wide use of income statements affect managers' decisions about buying equipment?

PROBLEMS

P9-1 UNIT COSTS. Brandon Company produces and sells a product that has variable costs of $9 per unit and fixed costs of $110,000 per year.

1. Compute the unit cost at a production and sales level of 10,000 units per year.
2. Compute the unit cost at a production and sales level of 20,000 units per year.
3. Which of these unit costs is more accurate? Explain.

P9-2 WEAK DIVISION. Lake Forest Electronics Company paid $7 million in cash four years ago to acquire a company that manufactures CD-ROMS. This company operates as a division of Lake Forest and has lost $500,000 each year since its acquisition.

The minimum desired return for this division is that, when a new product is fully developed, it should return a net profit of $500,000 per year for the fore-seeable future.

Recently the IBM Corporation offered to purchase the division from Lake Forest for $4 million. The president of Lake Forest commented, "I've got an investment of $9 million to recoup ($7 million plus losses of $500,000 for each of four years). I have finally got this situation turned around, so I oppose selling the division now."

Prepare a response to the president's remarks. Indicate how to make this decision. Be as specific as possible.

P9-3 MAKE OR BUY. A BMW executive in Germany is trying to decide whether the company should continue to manufacture an engine component or purchase it from Hanover Corporation for 50 deutsche marks (DM) each. Demand for the coming year is expected to be the same as for the current year, 200,000 units. Data for the current year follow:

Direct material	DM 5,000,000
Direct labour	1,900,000
Factory overhead, variable	1,100,000
Factory overhead, fixed	2,500,000
Total costs	DM 10,500,000

If BMW makes the components, the unit costs of direct material will increase 10 percent. If BMW buys the components, 40 percent of the fixed costs will be avoided. The other 60 percent will continue regardless of whether the components are manufactured or purchased. Assume that variable overhead varies with output volume.

1. Tabulate a comparison of the make-and-buy alternatives. Show totals and amounts per unit. Compute the numerical difference between making and buying. Assume that the capacity now used to make the components will become idle if the components are purchased.
2. Assume also that the BMW capacity in question can be rented to a local electronics firm for DM, 250,000 for the coming year. Tabulate a comparison of the net relevant costs of the three alternatives: make, buy and leave capacity idle, buy and rent. Which is the most favourable alternative? By how much in total?

P9-4 HOSPITAL OPPORTUNITY COST. An administrator at Sacred Heart Hospital is considering how to use some space made available when the outpatient clinic moved to a new building. She has narrowed her choices as follows:

   a. Use the space to expand laboratory testing. Expected future annual revenue would be $320,000; future costs, $290,000.

   b. Use the space to expand the eye clinic. Expected future annual revenue would be $500,000; future costs, $480,000.

   c. The gift shop is rented by an independent retailer who wants to expand into the vacated space. The retailer has offered an $11,000 early rental for the space. All operating expenses will be borne by the retailer.

The administrator's planning horizon is unsettled. However, she has decided that the yearly data given will suffice for guiding her decision.

Tabulate the total relevant data regarding the decision alternatives. Omit the concept of opportunity cost in one tabulation, but use the concept in a second tabulation. As the administrator, which tabulation would you prefer if you could receive only one?

P9-5 JOINT PRODUCTS: SELL OR PROCESS FURTHER. Mussina Chemical Company produced three joint products at a joint cost of $117,000. These products were processed further and sold as follows:

CHEMICAL PRODUCT	SALES	ADDITIONAL PROCESSING COSTS
A	$230,000	$190,000
B	330,000	300,000
C	175,000	100,000

The company has had an opportunity to sell at split-off directly to other processors. If that alternative had been selected, sales would have been: A, $56,000; B, $28,000; and C, $54,000.

The company expects to operate at the same level of production and sales in the forthcoming year.

Consider all the available information, and assume that all costs incurred after split-offs are variable.

   1. Could the company increase operating income by altering its processing decisions? If so, what would be the expected overall operating income?

   2. Which products should be processed further and which should be sold at split-off?

P9-6 MAKE OR BUY. Assume that a division of Sony, Inc. makes an electronic component for its speakers. Its manufacturing process for the component is a highly automated part of a just-in-time production system. All labour is considered to be an overhead cost, and all overhead is regarded as fixed with respect to output volume. Production costs for 100,000 units of the component are:

Direct materials		$300,000
Factory overhead:		
Indirect labour	$80,000	
Supplies	30,000	
Allocated occupancy cost	40,000	150,000
Total cost		$450,000

A small, local company has offered to supply the components at a price of $3.45 each. If the division discontinued its production of the component, it would save two-thirds of the supplies cost and $30,000 of indirect labour cost. All other overhead costs would continue.

The division manager recently attended a seminar on cost behaviour and learned about fixed and variable costs. He wants to continue to make the component because the variable cost of $3.00 is below the $3.45 bid.

1. Compute the relevant costs of (a) making, and (b) purchasing the component. Which alternative is less costly and by how much?
2. What qualitative factors might influence the decision about whether to make or buy the component?

P9-7   REPLACING OLD EQUIPMENT.   Consider these data regarding Douglas County's photocopying requirements:

	OLD EQUIPMENT	PROPOSED REPLACEMENT EQUIPMENT
Useful life, in years	5	3
Current age, in years	2	0
Useful life remaining, in year	3	3
Original cost	$32,000	$15,000
Accumulated amortization	12,000	0
Book value	18,000	Not acquired yet
Disposal value (in cash) now	3,000	Not acquired yet
Disposal value in two years	0	0
Annual cash operating costs for power maintenance, toner, and supplies	14,000	7,500

The county administrator is trying to decide whether to replace the old equipment. Because of rapid changes in technology, she expects the replacement equipment to have only a three-year useful life. Ignore the effects of taxes.

1. Tabulate a cost comparison that includes both relevant and irrelevant items for the next three years together.
2. Tabulate a cost comparison of all relevant items for the next three years together. Which tabulation is clearer, this one or the one in requirement 1.
3. Prepare a simple "shortcut" or direct analysis to support your choice of alternatives.

P9-8 DECISIONS AND PERFORMANCE MODELS. Refer to the preceding problem. (9-7)

1. Suppose the "decision model" favoured by top management consisted of a comparison of a three-year accumulation of cash under each alternative. As the manager of office operations, which alternative would you choose? Why?
2. Suppose the "performance evaluation model" emphasized the minimization of overall costs of photocopying operations for the first year. Which alternative would you choose?

P9-9 OPPORTUNITY COSTS. Martina Bridgeman is a lawyer employed by a large law firm at $90,000 per year. She is considering whether to become a sole practitioner, which would probably generate annually $320,000 in operating revenues and $220,000 in operating expenses.

1. Present two tabulations of the annual income effects of these alternatives. The second tabulation should include the opportunity cost of Bridgeman's compensation as an employee.
2. Suppose Bridgeman prefers less risk and chooses to remain at the law firm. Show a tabulation of the income effects of rejecting the opportunity of independent practice.

P9-10 OPPORTUNITY COST OF HOME OWNERSHIP. Oliver Kemp has just made the final payment on his mortgage. He could continue to live in the home; cash expenses for repairs and maintenance (after any tax effects) would be $500 monthly. Alternatively, he could sell the home for $200,000, invest the proceeds in 8 percent bonds, and rent an apartment for $18,000 annually. The landlord would then pay for repairs and maintenance.

Prepare two analysis of alternatives, one showing no explicit opportunity cost and the second showing the explicit opportunity cost of the decision to hold the present home.

P9-11 MAKE OR BUY. Sunshine State Fruit Company sells premium-quality oranges and other citrus fruits by mail-order. Protecting the fruit during shipping is important, so the company has designed and produces special shipping boxes. The annual cost of 80,000 boxes is:

Materials	$120,000
Labour	20,000
Overhead	
Variable	16,000
Fixed	60,000
Total	$216,000

Therefore, the cost per box averages $2.70.

Suppose National Boxes Inc. submits a bid to supply Sunshine State with boxes for $2.40 per box. Sunshine State must give National Boxes Inc. the box design specifications, and the boxes will be made according to those specifications.

1. How much, if any, would Sunshine State save by buying the boxes from National Boxes Inc.?

2. What subjective factors should affect Sunshine State's decision whether to make or buy the boxes?
3. Suppose all the fixed costs represent amortization on equipment that was purchased for $600,000 and is just about at the end of its 10-year life. New replacement equipment will cost $1 million and is also expected to last ten years. In this case, how much, if any, would Sunshine State save by buying from National Boxes Inc.?

P9-12 OPPORTUNITY COST. Renee Behr, MD, is a psychiatrist who is in heavy demand. Even though she has raised her fees considerably during the past five years, Dr. Behr still cannot accommodate all the patients who wish to see her.

Behr has conducted six hours of appointments a day, six days a week, for 48 weeks a year. Her fee averages $140 per hour.

Her variable costs are negligible and may be ignored for decision purposes. Ignore income taxes.

1. Behr is weary from working a six-day week. She is considering taking every other Saturday off. What would be her annual income (a) if she worked every Saturday and (b) if she worked every other Saturday?
2. What would be her opportunity cost for the year of not working every other Saturday?
3. Assume that Dr. Behr has definitely decided to take every other Saturday off. She loves to repair her sports car by doing the work herself. If she works on her car during half a Saturday when she otherwise would not see patients, what is her opportunity cost?

P9-13 SELL OR PROCESS FURTHER. A petrochemical factory produces two products, L and M, as a result of a joint process. Both products are sold to manufacturers as ingredients for assorted chemical products.

Product L sells at split-off for $.25 per litre; M, for $.30 per litre. Data for April follow:

Joint processing cost	$1,600,000
Litres produced and sold:	
L	4,000,000
M	2,500,000

Suppose that in April the 2,500,000 litres of M could have been processed further into Super M at an additional cost of $225,000. The Super M output would be sold for $.38 per litre. Product L would be sold at split-off in any event.

Should M have been processed further in April and sold as Super M? Show computations.

P9-14 OBSOLETE INVENTORY. The local book store bought more Wealthy Barber calendars than it could sell. It was nearly June and 200 calendars remained in stock. The store paid $4.50 each for the calendars and normally sold them for $8.95. Since February, they had been on sale for $6, and two weeks ago the price was dropped to $5. Still, few calendars were being sold. The book store manager felt it was no longer worthwhile using shelf space for the calendars.

The proprietor of Mac's Collectibles offered to buy all 200 calendars for $250. He intended to store them a few years, then sell them as novelty items.

The book store manager was not sure she wanted to sell for $1.25 calendars that cost $4.50. But the only alternative was to scrap them because the publisher would not take them back.

1. Compute the difference in profit between accepting the $250 offer and scrapping the calendars.
2. Describe how the $4.50 × 200 = $900 paid for the calendars affects your decision.

P9-15 **REPLACE OLD EQUIPMENT.** Three years ago the Oak Street TCBY bought a frozen-yogurt machine for $8,000. A salesperson has just suggested to the manager that she replace the machine with a new $12,500 machine. The manager has gathered the following data:

	OLD MACHINE	NEW MACHINE
Original cost	$8,000	$12,500
Useful life in years	8	5
Current age in years	3	0
Useful life remaining in years	5	5
Accumulated amortization	$3,000	Not acquired yet
Book value	$5,000	Not acquired yet
Disposal value (in cash) now	$2,000	Not acquired yet
Disposal value in 5 years	0	0
Annual cash operating cost	$22,500	$10,000

1. Compute the difference in total costs over the next five years under both alternatives, that is, keeping the original machine or replacing it with the new machine. Ignore taxes.
2. The manager replaces the original machine. Compute the "loss on disposal" of the original machine. How does this amount affect your computation in requirement 1? Explain.

P9-16 **HOTEL ROOMS AND OPPORTUNITY COSTS.** International Hotels operates many hotels throughout the world. One of its hotels is facing difficult times because several new competing hotels are opening.

To accommodate its flight personnel, Air Canada has offered International a contract for the coming year that provides a rate of $50 per night per room for a minimum of 50 rooms for 365 nights. This contract would assure International of selling 50 rooms of space nightly, even if some of the rooms are vacant on some nights.

The International manager has mixed feelings about the contract. On several peak nights during the year, the hotel could sell the same space for $100 per room.

1. Suppose the contract is signed. What is the opportunity cost of the 50 rooms on October 20, the night of a big convention of retailers when every midtown hotel room is occupied? What is the opportunity cost on December 28, when only 10 of these rooms would be expected to be rented at an average rate of $80?
2. If the year-round rate per room averaged $90, what percentage of occupancy of the 50 rooms in question would have to be rented to make International indifferent about accepting the offer?

P9-17 EXTENSION OF PRECEDING PROBLEM.   Assume the same facts as in the preceding problem. However, also assume that the variable costs per room per day are $10.

1. Suppose the best estimate is a 53 percent general occupancy rate at an average $90 room rate for the next year. Should International accept the contract?
2. What percentage of occupancy of the 50 rooms in question would have to make International indifferent about accepting the offer?

P9-18 IRRELEVANCE OF PAST COSTS AT STARBUCKS.   Starbucks purchases and roasts high-quality whole bean coffees and sells them, along with other coffee-related products, primarily through its company-operated retail stores. The company is known for its high-quality coffees.

Suppose that the quality control manager at Starbucks discovered a 1,000-kilogram batch of roasted beans that did not meet the company's quality standards. Company policy would not allow such beans to be sold with the Starbucks name on it. However, it could be reprocessed, at which time it could be sold by Starbucks' retail stores, or it could be sold as-is on the wholesale coffee-been market.

Assume that the beans were initially purchased for $2,000, and the total cost of roasting the batch was $1,500, including $500 of variable cost and $1,000 of fixed costs (primarily depreciation on the equipment).

The wholesale price at which Starbucks could sell the beans was $2.75 per kilogram. Purchasers would pay the shipping costs from the Starbucks plant to their warehouse.

If the beans were reprocessed, the processing cost would be $600 because other beans would not require as much processing as new beans. All $600 would be additional costs, that is, costs that would not be incurred without the reprocessing. The beans would be sold to the retail stores for $3.70 per kilogram, and Starbucks would have to pay an average of $.20 per kilogram to ship the beans to the stores.

1. Should Starbucks sell the beans on the market as-is for $2.75 per kilogram, or should the company reprocess the beans and sell them through its own retail stores? Why?
2. Compute the amount of extra profit Starbucks earns from the alternative you selected in requirement 1 compared to what it would earn from the other alternative.
3. What cost numbers in the problem were irrelevant to your analysis? Explain why they were irrelevant.

P9-19 HOTEL PRICING AND DISCOUNTS.   A growing corporation in a large city has offered a 200-room hotel a one-year contract to rent 40 rooms at reduced rates of $50 per room instead of the regular rate of $85 per room. The corporation will sign the contract for 365-day occupancy because its visiting manufacturing and marketing personnel are virtually certain to use all the space each night.

Each room occupied has a variable cost of $10 per night (for cleaning, laundry, lost linens, and extra electricity).

The hotel manager expects an 85 percent occupancy rate for the year, so she is reluctant to sign the contract. If the contract is signed, the occupancy rate on the remaining 160 rooms will be 95 percent.

1. Compute the total contribution margin for the year with and without the contract.
2. Compute the lowest room rate that the hotel should accept on the contract so that the total contribution margin would be the same with or without the contract.

P9-20 **SPECIAL AIR FARES.** The manager of operations of Air Canada is trying to decide whether to adopt a new discount fare. Focus on one 134-seat airplane now operating at a 56 percent load factor. That is, on the average the airplane has .56 × 134 = 75 passengers. The regular fares produce an average revenue of $.12 per passenger-kilometre.

Suppose an average 40 percent fare discount (which is subject to restrictions regarding time of departure and length of stay) will produce three new additional passengers. Also suppose that three of the previously committed passengers accept the restrictions and switch to the discount fare from the regular fare.

1. Compute the total revenue per airplane kilometre with and without the discount fares.
2. Suppose the maximum allowed allocation to new discount fares is 50 seats. These will be filled. As before, some previously committed passengers will accept the restrictions and switch to the discount fare from the regular fare. How many will have to switch so that the total revenue per mile will be the same either with or without the discount plan?

P9-21 **JOINT COSTS AND INCREMENTAL ANALYSIS.** (CMA) Jacque de Paris, a high-fashion women's dress manufacturer, is planning to market a new cocktail dress for the coming season. Jacque de Paris supplies retailers in Europe.

Four metres of material are required to lay out the dress pattern. Some material remains after cutting, which can be sold as remnants.

The leftover material could also be used to manufacture a matching cape and handbag. However, if the leftover material is to be used for the cape and handbag, more care will be required in the cutting, which will increase the cutting costs.

The company expected to sell 1,250 dresses if no matching cape or handbag were available. Market research reveals that dress sales will be 20 percent higher if a matching cape and handbag are available. The market research indicates that the cape and/or handbag will not be sold individually but only as accessories with the dress. The various combinations of dresses, capes, and handbags that are expected to be sold by retailers are as follows:

	PERCENT OF TOTAL
Complete sets of dress, cape and handbag	70%
Dress and cape	6
Dress and handbag	15
Dress only	9
Total	100%

The material used in the dress costs FF75 per metre, or FF300 for each dress. The cost of cutting the dress if the cape and handbag are not manufactured is estimated at FF100 a dress, and the resulting remnants can be sold for FF25 for each dress cut out. If the cape and handbag are to be manufactured, the cutting costs will be increased by FF36 per dress. There will be no saleable remnants if the capes and handbags are manufactured in the quantities estimated.

The selling prices and the costs to complete the three items once they are cut are

	SELLING PRICE PER UNIT	UNIT COST TO COMPLETE (EXCLUDES COST OF MATERIAL AND CUTTING OPERATION)
Dress	FF1,050	FF400
Cape	140	100
Handbag	50	30

1. Calculate the incremental profit or loss to Jacque de Paris from manufacturing the capes and handbags in conjunction with the dresses.
2. Identify any nonquantitative factors that could influence the company's management in its decision to manufacture the capes and handbags that match the dress.

P9-22 MAKE OR BUY. Hayes-Dana Corporation manufactures automobile parts. It frequently subcontracts work to other manufacturers, depending on whether Hayes-Dana's facilities are fully occupied. Hayes-Dana is about to make some final decisions regarding the use of its manufacturing facilities for the coming year.

The following are the costs of making part EC113, a key component of an emission-control system:

	TOTAL COST FOR 50,000 UNITS	COST PER UNIT
Direct materials	$ 400,000	$ 8
Direct labour	300,000	6
Variable factory overhead	150,000	3
Fixed factory overhead	300,000	6
Total manufacturing costs	$1,150,000	$23

Another manufacturer has offered to sell the same part to Hayes-Dana for $21 each. The fixed overhead consists of amortization, property taxes, insurance, and supervisory salaries.

All the fixed overhead would continue if Hayes-Dana bought the component except that the costs of $100,000 pertaining to some supervisory and custodial personnel could be avoided.

1. Assume that the capacity now used to make parts will become idle if the parts are purchased. Should the parts be made or bought? Show computations.
2. Assume that the capacity now used to make parts will either (a) be rented to a nearby manufacturer for $65,000 for the year or (b) be used to make oil filters that will yield a profit contribution of $200,000. Should part EC113 be made or bought? Show computations.

P9-23 **RELEVANT COST AND SPECIAL ORDER.** Antonio Company's *unit* costs of manufacturing and selling a given item at a planned activity level of 10,000 units per *month* are as follows:

Manufacturing costs:	
Direct materials	$4.10
Direct labour	.60
Variable overhead	0.70
Fixed overhead	0.80
Selling expenses	
Variable	3.00
Fixed	1.10

Ignore income taxes in all requirements. These four parts have no connection with each other.

1. Compute the planned *annual* operating income at a selling price of $12 per unit.
2. Compute the expected *annual* operating income if the volume can be increased by 20 percent when the selling price is reduced to $11. Assume the implied cost-behaviour patterns are correct.
3. The company desires to seek an order for 5,000 units from a foreign customer. The variable selling expenses for the order will be 40 percent less than usual, but the fixed costs for obtaining the order will be $6,000. Domestic sales will not be affected. Compute the minimum break-even price per unit to be considered.
4. The company has an inventory of 2,000 units of this item left over from last year's model. These must be sold through *regular channels* at reduced prices. The inventory will be valueless unless sold this way. What unit cost is relevant for establishing the minimum selling price of these 2,000 units?

P9-24 **NEW MACHINE.** A new $300,000 machine is expected to have a five-year life and terminal value of zero. It can produce 40,000 units a year at a variable cost of $4 per unit. The variable cost is $6 per unit with an old machine, which has a book value of $100,000. It is being amortized on a straight-line basis at $20,000 per year. It too is expected to have a terminal value of zero. Its current disposal value is also zero because it is highly specialized equipment.

The salesman of the new machine prepared the following comparison:

	NEW MACHINE	OLD MACHINE
Units	40,000	40,000
Variable costs	$160,000	$240,000
Straight-line amortization	60,000	20,000
Total cost	$220,000	$260,000
Unit cost	$5.50	$6.50

He said, "The new machine is obviously a worthwhile acquisition. You will save $1 for every unit you produce."

1. Do you agree with the salesman's analysis? If not, how would you change it? Be specific. Ignore taxes.

2. Prepare an analysis of total and unit costs if the annual volume is 20,000 units.
3. At what annual volume would both the old and new machines have the same total relevant costs?

P9-25 ROLE OF OLD EQUIPMENT REPLACEMENT.   On January 2, 2001, the S.H. Park company installed a brand new $87,000 special molding machine for producing a new product. The product and the machine have an expected life of three years. The machine's expected disposal value at the end of three years is zero.

On January 3, 2001, Kimiyo Lee, a star salesperson for a machine tool manufacturer, tells Mr. Park: "I wish I had known earlier of your purchase plans. I can supply you with a technically superior machine for $99,000. The machine you just purchased can be sold for $16,000. I guarantee that our machine will save $35,000 per year in cash operating costs, although it too will have no disposal value at the end of three years."

Park examines some technical data. Although he has confidence in Lee's claims, Park contends: "I'm locked in now. My alternatives are clear: (a) disposal will result in a loss, (b) keeping and using the 'old' equipment avoids such a loss, I have brains enough to avoid a loss when my other alternative is recognizing a loss. We've got to use that equipment until we get our money out of it."

The annual operating costs of the old machine are expected to be $60,000, exclusive of amortization. Sales, all in cash, will be $910,000 per year. Other annual cash expenses will be $810,000 regardless of this decision. Assume that the equipment in question is the company's only fixed asset.

Ignore income taxes and the time value of money.

1. Prepare statements of cash receipts and disbursements as the would appear in each of the next three years under both alternatives. What is the total cumulative increase or decrease in cash for the three years?
2. Prepare income statements as they would appear in each of the next three years under both alternatives. Assume straight-line amortization. What is the cumulative increase or decrease in net income for the three years?
3. Assume that the cost of the "old" equipment was $1 million rather than $87,000. Would the net difference computed in requirements 1 and 2 change? Explain.
4. As Kimiyo Lee, reply to Mr. Park's contentions.
5. What are the irrelevant items in each of your presentations for requirements 1 and 2? Why are they irrelevant?

P9-26 DECISION AND PERFORMANCE MODELS.   Refer back to the preceding problem P9-25.

1. Suppose the "decision model" favoured by top management consisted of a comparison of a three-year accumulation of wealth under each alternative. Which alternative would you choose? Why? (Accumulation of wealth means cumulative increase in cash.)
2. Suppose the "performance evaluation model" emphasized the net income of a subunit (such as a division) each year rather than considering each project, one by one. Which alternative would you expect a manager to choose? Why?
3. Suppose the same quantitative data existed, but the "enterprise" was a city and the "machine" was a computer in the treasurer's department. Would your answers to the first two parts change? Why?

P9-27 BOOK VALUE OF OLD EQUIPMENT. Consider the following data:

	OLD EQUIPMENT	PROPOSED NEW EQUIPMENT
Original cost	$24,000	$12,000
Useful life, in years	8	3
Current age, in years	5	0
Useful life remaining, in year	3	3
Accumulated amortization	15,000	0
Book value	9,000	Not acquired yet
Disposal value (in cash) now	3,000	Not acquired yet
Annual cash operating costs (maintenance, power, repairs, lubricants, etc.)	$10,000	$ 6,000

1. Prepare a cost comparison of all relevant items for the next three years together. Ignore taxes.
2. Prepare a cost comparison that includes both relevant and irrelevant items.
3. Prepare a comparative statement of the total charges against revenue for the first year. Would the manager be inclined to buy the new equipment? Explain.

P9-28 CONCEPTUAL APPROACH. A large automobile-parts plant was constructed four years ago in an Ontario city served by two railroads. The PC Railroad purchased 40 specialized 20-metre freight cars as a direct result of the additional traffic generated by the new plant. The investment was based on an estimated useful life of 20 years.

Now the competing railroad has offered to service the plant with new 29-metre freight cars, which would enable more efficient shipping operations at the plant. The automobile company has threatened to switch carriers unless PC Railroad buys 10 new 29-metre freight cars.

The PC marketing management wants to buy the new cars, but PC operating management says. "The new investment is undesirable. It really consists of the new outlay plus the loss on the old freight cars. The old cars must be written down to a low salvage value if they cannot be used as originally intended.

Evaluate the comments. What is the correct conceptual approach to the quantitative analysis in this decision?

P9-29 RELEVANT-COST ANALYSIS. Following are the unit costs of making and selling a single product at a normal level of 5,000 units per month and a current unit selling price of $90:

Manufacturing costs:	
Direct materials	$35
Direct labour	12
Variable overhead	8
Fixed overhead (total for the year, $300,000)	5
Selling and administrative expenses:	
Variable	15
Fixed (total for the year, $480,000)	8

Consider each requirement separately. Label all computations, and present your solutions in a form that will be comprehensible to the company president.

1. This product is usually sold at a rate of 60,000 units per year. It is predicted that a rise in price to $98 will decrease volume by 10 percent. How much may advertising be increased under this plan without having annual operating income fall below the current level?

2. The company has received a proposal from an outside supplier to make and ship this item directly to the company's customers as sales orders are forwarded. Variable selling and administrative costs would fall 40 percent. If the supplier's proposal is accepted, the company will use its own plant to produce a new product. The new product would be sold through manufacturer's agents at a 10 percent commission based on a selling price of $40 each. The cost characteristics per unit of this product, based on predicted yearly normal volume, are as follows:

Direct materials	$ 6
Direct labour	12
Variable overhead	8
Fixed overhead	6
Manufacturing costs	$32
Selling and administrative expenses:	
Variable	10% of selling price
Fixed	$2

What is the maximum price per unit that the company can afford to pay to the supplier for subcontracting the entire old product? This is not easy. Assume the following:

- Total fixed factory overhead and total fixed selling expenses will not change if the new product line is added.
- The supplier's proposal will not be considered unless the present annual net income can be maintained.
- Selling price of the old product will remain unchanged.
- All $300,000 of fixed overhead will be assigned to the new product.

P9-30 SELL OR PROCESS FURTHER. ConAgra Inc. produces meat products with brand names such as Swift, Armour, and Butterball. Suppose one of the company's plants process beef cattle into various products. For simplicity, assume that there are only three products: steak, hamburger, and hides, and that the average steer costs $700. The three products emerge from a process that costs $100 per cow to run, and output can be sold for the following net amounts:

Steak (100 kilograms)	$400
Hamburger (500 kilograms)	600
Hides (120 kilograms)	100
Total	$1,100

Assume that each of these three products can be sold immediately or processed further in another ConAgra plant. The steak can be the main course in frozen dinners sold under the Healthy Choice label. The vegetables and desserts in the 400 dinners produced from the 100 kilograms of steak would cost $120, and production, sales, and other costs for the 400 meals would total $350. Each meal would be sold wholesale for $2.15.

The hamburger could be made into frozen Salisbury Steak patties sold under the Armour label. The only additional cost would be a $200 processing cost for the 500 kilograms of hamburger. Frozen Salisbury Steaks sell wholesale for $1.70 per kilogram.

The hides can be sold before or after tanning. The cost of tanning one hide is $80, and a tanned hide can be sold for $175.

1. Compute the total profit if all three products are sold at the split-off point.
2. Compute the total profit if all three products are processed further before being sold.
3. Which products should be sold at the split-off point? Which should be processed further?
4. Compute the total profit if your plan in requirement 3 is followed.

P9-31 **RELEVANT COSTS.** A cable television network is considering cancelling the program "Toronto Lawyer" because it is watched by only 2.3 percent of the audience in its Monday evening time slot. It would be replaced by "Hawaiian Surfers," a new show being created from the same formula as the popular "Baywatch." Market research indicates that "Hawaiian Surfers" would be watched by four percent of the audience in the same time slot. For audiences between 1.5 percent and 5 percent, the network believes each 1 percent of the audience in this time slot results in additional advertising revenue of $40,000 per week (including beneficial effects on other programs, both present and future). Replacement would come halfway through the 30-week season.

The network's accounting staff has prepared the following financial information to be used in making the decision:

- Developmental expenses for "Toronto Lawyer" were $600,000, and these are being amortized over the originally projected complete season (30 programs).
- Developmental expenses for "Hawaiian Surfers" were $900,000. If "Hawaiian Surfers" is shown for the second half of this season, the entire development cost must be amortized over those 15 programs. If it is not aired until next season, amortization will take place over 30 programs.
- The cost of a script for one program of "Toronto Lawyer" is $20,000 and for "Hawaiian Surfers" is $24,000. No contract for scripts for "Hawaiian Surfers" has yet been signed, but a contract for 20 programs of "Toronto Lawyer" was signed and the $400,000 was already paid.
- The star of "Toronto Lawyer" is under contract to the network for the entire season at $240,000. If "Toronto Lawyer" is cancelled, the star will do one special in the spring; if "Toronto Lawyer" continues, he will not do the special. If the star does not do the special, another

person (with completely equivalent audience appeal) will be hired for $40,000 to do the special.

- The star of "Hawaiian Surfers" has been hired for the next season for $180,000. If she does 15 shows this season, she will have to forgo a part in a movie. Consequently, she must be paid $120,000 for 15 shows this season.
- Investment in the set for "Toronto Lawyer" was $100,000, which was immediately expenses. Additional expense for the set averages $10,000 per show. If "Toronto Lawyer" cancelled, the set can be sold for $20,000. Another alternative use of the set is for a TV movie that the network is planning. Additional set expenses for the movie would be $50,000, but building a completely new set would cost $80,000.
- "Hawaiian Surfers" is filmed on location; thus, there is no investment required for a set. However, $20,000 per show is required to make the location suitable for filming.
- The production crew of "Toronto Lawyer" (including actors other than the star) receive $50,000 per show. Most of these people could be used profitably in other operations at the network. However, two actors must be fired if the show is cancelled, and the actors' union requires severance pay of $4,000 each.
- There will be a large start-up cost of production for "Hawaiian Surfers" because of suddenly needing it six months ahead of schedule. This will amount to $150,000, only $60,000 of which would be necessary if it were not aired until next season. The production crew is very important to "Hawaiian Surfers," and they receive $80,000 per show.
- The network allocates corporate overhead to each show by a complex formula. Each program of "Toronto Lawyer" was allocated $20,000 of overhead; each program of "Hawaiian Surfers" will be allocated $30,000 of overhead. The only corporate overhead expense that would change if "Toronto Lawyer" replaced "Hawaiian Surfers" is the consultation time that corporate management spends with the production staff. This averages 10 percent of the total production crew expense.
- This decision is to be made by top management, who will invest about $20,000 of their time and effort in it. In addition, a consultant will be paid $4,000 to review the decision.

Should the network cancel "Toronto Lawyer" and replace it with "Hawaiian Surfers" immediately? Explain. Be sure to describe the information that was relevant to this decision and compute the monetary advantage or disadvantage to switching from "Toronto Lawyer" to "Hawaiian Surfers."

P9-32 **RELEVANT COSTS ON BROADWAY.** The *New York Times* reported that Neil Simon planned to open his play, "London Suite," off Broadway. Why? For financial reasons. Producer Emanuel Azenberg predicted the following costs before the play even opens:

	ON BROADWAY	OFF BROADWAY
Sets, costumes, lights	$ 357,000	$ 87,000
Loading in (building set, etc.)	175,000	8,000
Rehearsal salaries	102,000	63,000

Director and designer fees	126,000	61,000
Advertising	300,000	121,000
Administration	235,000	100,000
Total	$1,295,000	$440,000

Broadway ticket prices average $55, and theatres can seat about 1,000 persons per show. Off-Broadway prices average $40, and the theatres seat only 500. Normally, plays run eight times a week, both on and off Broadway. Weekly operating expenses off Broadway average $82,000; they average a weekly $206,000 on Broadway.

1. Suppose 400 persons attended each show, whether on or off Broadway. Compare the weekly financial results from a Broadway production to one produced off Broadway.
2. Suppose attendance averaged 75 percent of capacity, whether on or off Broadway. Compare the weekly financial results from a Broadway production to one produced off Broadway.
3. Compute the attendance per show required to just cover weekly expenses a) on Broadway, and b) off Broadway.
4. Suppose average attendance on Broadway was 600 per show and off Broadway was 400. Compute the total net profit for a 26-week run a) on Broadway, and b) off Broadway.
5. Repeat requirement 4 for a 100-week run.
6. Using attendance figures from requirements 4 and 5, compute a) the number of weeks a Broadway production must run before it breaks even, and b) the number of weeks an off-Broadway production must run before it breaks even.
7. Using attendance figures from requirements 4 and 5, determine how long a play must run before the profit from a Broadway production exceeds that of an off-Broadway production.
8. If you were Neil Simon, would you prefer "London Suite" to play on Broadway or off Broadway? Explain.

P9-33 **MAKE OR BUY, OPPORTUNITY COSTS, AND ETHICS.** Agribiz Food Products, Inc. produces a wide variety of food and related products. The company's tomato canning operation relies partly on tomatoes grown on Aribiz's own farms and partly on tomatoes bought from other growers.

Agribiz's tomato farm is on the edge of Sharpestown, a fast-growing and medium-sized city. It produces eight-million kilograms of tomatoes a year and employs 55 persons. The annual costs of tomatoes grown on this farm are:

Variable production costs	$ 550,000
Fixed production costs	1,200,000
Shipping costs (all variable)	200,000
Total costs	$1,950,000

Fixed production costs include amortization on machinery and equipment, but not on land because land should not be amortized. Agribiz owns the land, which was purchased for $600,000 many years ago. A recent appraisal placed the value of the land at $15 million because it was prime land for development of an industrial park and shopping centre.

Agribiz could purchase all the tomatoes it needs on the market for $25 per kilogram delivered to its factory. If it did this, it would sell the farmland and shut down the operations in Sharpestown. If the farm were sold, $300,000 of the annual fixed costs would be saved. Agribiz can invest excess cash and earn an annual rate of 10 percent.

1. How much does it cost Agribiz annually for the land used by the tomato farm?
2. How much would Agibiz save annually if it closed the tomato farm? Is this more or less than would be paid to purchase the tomatoes on the market?
3. What ethical issues are involved with the decision of whether to shut down the tomato farm?

P9-34 COLLABORATIVE LEARNING EXERCISE: OUTSOURCING. A popular term for make-or-buy decisions is "outsourcing" decisions. There are many examples of outsourcing, from Nike's outsourcing of nearly all its production activities, to small firms outsourcing of their payroll activities. Especially popular outsourcing activities are warehousing and computer systems.

The purpose of this exercise is to share information on different types of outsourcing decisions. It can be done in small groups or as an entire class. Each student should pick an article from the literature that tells about a particular company's outsourcing decision. There are many such articles; a recent electronic search of the business literature turned up more than 4,000 articles. An easy way to find such an article is to search an electronic database of business literature. Magazines that have had outsourcing articles include *Canadian Business, CMA Magazine (Management), Fortune, Forbes, Business Week*, and *Management Accounting*. Many business sections of newspapers also have published such articles.

1. List as many details about the outsourcing decision as you can. Include the type of activity that is being outsourced, the size of the outsourcing, and the type of company providing the outsourcing service.
2. Explain why the company decided to outsource the activity. If reasons are not given in the article, prepare a list of reasons that you think influenced the decision.
3. What disadvantages are there to outsourcing the activity?
4. Be prepared to make a three- to five-minute presentation to the rest of the group or to the class covering your answers to requirements 1, 2, and 3.

CASES

C9-1 MAKE OR BUY. The Minnetonka Corporation, which produces and sells a highly successful line of water skis, has decided to diversify to stabilize sales throughout the year. The company is considering the production of cross-country skis.

After considerable research, a cross-country ski line has been developed. However, because of the conservative nature of the company management, Minnetonka's president has decided to introduce only one of the new skis for this coming winter. If the product is a success, further expansion in future years will be initiated.

The cross-country skis will be sold to wholesalers for $80 per pair. Because of available capacity, no additional fixed charges will be incurred to produce the skis. However, a $100,000 fixed charge will be absorbed by the skis to allocate a fair share of the company's present fixed costs to the new product.

Using the estimated sales and production of 10,000 pairs of skis as the expected volume, the accounting department has developed the following costs per pair:

Direct labour	$35
Direct material	30
Total overhead	15
Total	$80

Minnetonka has approached a subcontractor to discuss the possibility of purchasing the bindings. The purchase price of the bindings would be $5.25 per binding or $10.50 per pair. If the Minnetonka Corporation accepts the purchase proposal, it is predicted that direct-labour and variable-overhead costs would be reduced by 10 percent and direct-material costs would be reduced by 20 percent.

Required:

1. Should the Minnetonka Corporation make or buy the bindings? Show calculations to support your answer.
2. What would be the maximum purchase price acceptable to Minnetonka for the bindings? Support your answer with an appropriate explanation.
3. Instead of sales of 10,000 pairs of skis, revised estimates show sales volume at 12,500 pairs. At this new volume, additional equipment, at an annual rental of $10,000, must be acquired to manufacture the bindings. However, this incremental cost would be the only additional fixed cost required even if sales increased to 30,000 pairs. (The 30,000 level is the goal for the third year of production.) Under these circumstances, should the Minnetonka Corporation make or buy the bindings? Show calculations to support your answer.
4. The company has the option of making and buying at the same time. What would be your answer to requirement 3 if this alternative were considered? Show calculations to support your answer.
5. What nonquantifiable factors should the Minnetonka Corporation consider in determining whether they should make or buy the bindings?

C9-2 MAKE OR BUY. The Rohr Company's old equipment for making subassemblies is worn out. The company is considering two courses of action: (a) completely replacing the old equipment with new equipment or (b) buying subassemblies from a reliable outside supplier, who has quoted a unit price of $1 on a seven-year contract for a minimum of 50,000 units per year.

Production was 60,000 units in each of the past two years. Future needs for the next seven years are not expected to fluctuate beyond 50,000 to 70,000 units per year. Cost records for the past two years reveal the following unit costs of manufacturing the subassembly:

Direct materials	$ .30
Direct labour	.35
Variable overhead	.10
Fixed overhead (including $.10 depreciation and	
$.10 for direct departmental fixed overhead)	.25
	$1.00

The new equipment will cost $188,000 cash, will last seven years, and will have a disposal value of $20,000. The current disposal value of the old equipment is $10,000.

The salesperson for the new equipment has summarized her position as follows: the increase in machine speeds will reduce direct labour and variable overhead by $.35 per unit. Consider last year's experience of one of your major competitors with identical equipment. They produced 100,000 units under operating conditions very comparable to yours and showed the following unit costs:

Direct materials	$ .30
Direct labour	.05
Variable overhead	.05
Fixed overhead (including depreciation of $.24)	.40
	$ .80

For purposes of this case, assume that any idle facilities cannot be put to alternative use. Also assume that five cents of the old Rohr unit cost is allocated fixed overhead that will be unaffected by the decision.

Required:

1. The president asks you to compare the alternatives on a total-annual-cost basis and on a per-unit basis for annual needs of 60,000 units. Which alternative seems more attractive?
2. Would your answer to requirement 1 change if the needs were 50,000 units? 70,000 units? At what volume level would Rohr be indifferent between make and buy? Show your computations.
3. What factors, other than those above, should the accountant bring to the attention of management to assist them in making their decision? Include the considerations that might be applied to the outside supplier.

C9-3 **HOTEL PRICING.** (Braithwaite) "I will give you my decision in about a week," said Georges Villedary, directeur general of the Le Centre Sheraton, Montreal, as he put down the phone and looked pensively at the letter before him. The letter, dated March 15, 1994, was from Alitalia requesting a one-year contract for 40 rooms at $42 per night. In addition, the hotel would have to provide a crew allowance of $25,000 per day. Bills are to be paid within seven days of receipt of statement on a weekly basis. The problem facing Georges was a simple one: does he take Alitalia and fill the 40 rooms for 365 days at $42 or does he refuse the business and hope that he can sell the rooms at the full rack rate of $105.00? Last year he had 115 nights sold out.

General Background of the Hotel

Le Centre Sheraton was located in the downtown area of Montreal. It was viewed as a corporate/convention hotel. In 1987 the hotel was named winner of the Canadian Automobile Association "Four Diamond Award" and the "Four Star Award" from the *Mobil Travel Guide*. The hotel had 824 rooms including the Sheraton Towers—a prestigious five-storey hotel within a hotel. The Towers had its own check-in facilities, lounge, and special amenities. It contained 131 rooms including 16 suites. The balance of the hotel offered a choice of king, queen, and double beds with an additional 24 suites and six rooms specially equipped for people with disabilities. All rooms were equipped with a pay-TV system.

The hotel operated three restaurants. Le Point de Vue on the 37th floor offered gourmet French cuisine and an exceptional wine list. It had a seating capacity of 84. Le Boulevard on the third floor was open for breakfast, lunch, and dinner and had a seating capacity of 259. La Musette was a European-style "express" restaurant on the promenade level for people in a hurry. It had a seating capacity of 60. In addition to the restaurants, the hotel had five lounges and 14 function rooms, including a ballroom that would accommodate 1,100 people for banquets and 2,600 people for receptions. Other features of the hotel included a five-storey glassed-in atrium, a glass-enclosed year-round pool and a health club with gymnasium, sauna, whirlpool, and masseuse. There was indoor parking for 500 cars and boutiques and specialty shops on the promenade level. Other services included multilingual staff, and audio-visual services. All meeting rooms had cable-TV outlets, audio-visual facilities, and telephone jacks.

Competition

For airline crews, all hotels in the Montreal area were Sheraton's competitors because airlines choose hotels based on price. Nevertheless, for Alitalia, the criteria for selecting a hotel were slightly different. They preferred four-star hotels located near shopping and entertainment facilities. Hence, the competition was limited to about 10 hotels located in the downtown area. Since all 10 hotels met the Alitalia criteria, the decision would be made on the basis of price and service. Georges was well aware that a number of his competitors had expressed interest in the Alitalia business. He was also aware that if he took the contract and satisfied the Alitalia crew, then he would have more negotiating power when the contract came up for renewal next year (i.e., the room rate could be increased). In the hotel business, it was always easier to renew existing room contracts than to solicit new ones.

The Proposal

Sheraton's target market included all forms of corporate groups, professional associations, and conventions. The Alitalia proposal appeared to be a good opportunity for the Le Centre Sheraton because it guaranteed 40 rooms per night for the entire year plus potential clients from their flights. The contract, if accepted, would require the hotel to have clean rooms immediately upon check-in; to have on hand $25,000 every day as an allowance for crews and to distribute the allowance as instructed; and to control the crew's wake-up calls. These services were standard tasks for the Sheraton Centre; however, because of the late departure of aircraft to Europe, check-out time for Alitalia would be between 04:00 p.m. and 06:00 p.m. while the other crews would be arriving sometime between 09:00 p.m. and 10:00 p.m. the same night. This meant the hotel had to keep extra maids on duty to have these rooms ready within two to four hours. In addition, when flight schedules were changed, there would be changes in wake-up calls and in the distribution of the allowances. This extra service to the crews would be at the expense of the other guests who were paying the full rack rate.

Experience with other airlines had shown that airline crews spend less during their stay at a hotel than a regular guest. This was because their usual stay was only one night. If they were grounded for several days, they preferred to explore the city of Montreal, hence food and beverage purchases were often made outside the hotel.

Sales and Cost Data

Georges knew he would have to work fast on this proposal so he called in his assistant Marie Alfieri and asked her to collect all the data required to estimate the additional revenue and costs that would be involved if the hotel decided to accept the Alitalia offer.

She began with an analysis of room statistics for the previous year, which showed that if the proposal had been in place, then the number of regular guest rooms lost was equivalent to 115 sold-out nights. An analysis of food and beverage statistics for the previous year showed average food revenue (not including banquets) of $17 per occupied room and average beverage revenue (not including banquets) of $13 per occupied room. The hotel's standard cost percentage was 36 percent for food and 32 percent for beverage.

In analyzing the probable effect on operating costs, Marie found that during the period when the hotel was not full they would require the equivalent of one additional front-desk clerk to handle the Alitalia crew. The average hourly wage for this job was $9.20 per hour. Fringe benefits were calculated at 35 percent of wage cost. In addition to this cost, Marie estimated the following variable costs per occupied room:

1. Housekeeping—one half-hour per room. Housekeepers were paid $8.60 per hour.
2. Laundry and linen—$.75 per occupied room
3. Utilities—$1.00 per occupied room
4. Amenities—$2.25 per occupied room

With this information in hand, she turned it over to Georges for final analysis and a decision. As Georges sat in his office with the new information supplied by Marie, he remembered a discussion at the recent meeting of general managers of all Sheraton hotels where they were told that one of the Company's objectives for the coming fiscal year was a 12 percent return on investment. He was also very aware of the serious cash-flow problem facing the hotel at that time. Cash flow for the last fiscal year was negative by over $2 million and with a $50-million long-term mortgage at a floating interest rate and $4.2 million in annual municipal taxes to pay, the Alitalia business promised a steady and certain cash flow every week.

Required: | As Georges Villedary, what is your decision? Why?

C9-4 MAKE OR BUY. (ICAO) Maxim Auto Parts Ltd. has operated three automobile parts manufacturing plants in Ontario for many years. Two produce engine parts, and the third makes seats ("the seat division"). In recent years, the seat division's plant has been operating at well below capacity as a result of the loss of a major contract. The operating results of the seat division for the past three years are as follows:

| | YEARS ENDED APRIL 30 | | |
	2001	2000	1999
Revenue	$9,000,000	$9,000,000	$9,000,000
Variable cost of goods sold	7,580,000	7,490,000	7,380,000
Gross margin	1,420,000	1,510,000	1,620,000
Expenses:			
Amortization	130,000	130,000	130,000
Interest on bank loan (10% rate)	520,000	500,000	475,000
Sales commissions	900,000	900,000	900,000
Other selling expenses	115,000	110,000	105,000
Head office allocation	280,000	270,000	270,000
Factory overhead	200,000	200,000	200,000
Capital investment charge	220,000	210,000	205,000
Total Expenses	2,365,000	2,320,000	2,285,000
Net	$ (945,000)	$ (810,000)	$ (665,000)

All revenue is from one sales contract with a large automobile manufacturer. Amortization is calculated on a straight-line basis on each of the division's assets: building, machinery and equipment, and vehicles. Interest is based on a $5.2-million bank loan made directly to the seat division. Sales commissions are based on revenue and are payable to the agent who negotiated the sales contract several years ago. Other selling expenses consist primarily of transportation expenses (approximately one percent of revenue) plus other non-transportation costs to service the automobile manufacturer's needs. The head office allocation is a charge for the use of the head office staff and is based on relative sales revenue of the three divisions. Factory overhead is for non-variable costs of manufacturing the seats. The capital investment charge is for imputed interest on the current replacement cost of the division's land, building, inventories, and other assets (net of divisional debt).

The seat division has received an offer to lease its land and building for five years at $1,000,000 per annum, receivable at the beginning of each year with an agreement to sell the building and land at the end of the five years for $5,000,000. The prospective lessee has agreed to pay for all operating expenses of the building, such as property taxes, insurance, heating, and water. If Maxim does not enter into the lease and sale agreement, the net realizable value of the land is expected to increase at least enough to offset any decline in the value of the building over the next five years.

The machinery and equipment has a replacement cost of $3 million. Management estimates that it could be sold now for about $500,000. The machinery and equipment will be worth only about $100,000 in scrap value in another five years.

Seat-division management has determined that another auto parts manufacturer would be willing to produce the seats for the five years that remain on the contract with the automobile manufacturer. The contract cannot be cancelled without incurring heavy penalties. The seat division is required to manufacture exactly 100,000 seats. The other manufacturer will charge $95 per seat for the entire five-year period, and will deliver them at no cost to Maxim.

If the seat division is closed, sales commissions would still have to be paid by Maxim, as would $150,000 of head office allocation that is currently being charged to the seat division. In addition, 25 percent of the "factory overhead" would still have to be paid if the seat division were closed or if the land and building were leased. The non-transportation portion of "other selling expenses" would not be incurred if the division is sold.

No other long-term liabilities exist in the seat division, other than the bank loan at 10 percent interest per annum.

You have been requested by Maxim's management to prepare a report on the course of action they should follow. Management wants you to include in your report the analysis supporting your recommendations.

Required: Write the report requested by Maxim's management. (Ignore income taxes and the time value of money.)

C9-5 **MAKE OR BUY.**

(ICAO) Pandagan Vacuums Limited (PVL) is a worldwide leader in the manufacturing of industrial vacuums. The company is located in Thorold, Ontario. PVL sells vacuums to distributors in North America, Europe, and Asia. Over the last 10 years, PVL has seen its sales and market share deteriorate due to foreign competition. While PVL is considered a leader in product development and quality, the company has been unable to secure large contracts due to its higher-than-average selling prices. Management attributes this to the high cost of labour in Canada.

PVL has two divisions—the vacuum-assembly division and the components-production division. Currently, PVL manufactures seven standard industrial-vacuum models in its vacuum-assembly division (see Exhibit 9A-1). This division also manufactures special order models for its customers when its standard models are unsuitable. The vacuum-assembly division also has a service department that repairs vacuums under warranty or, when the warranty has expired, for a service fee. PVL's distributors also provide warranty service on PVL's behalf. PVL's components-production division currently produces about 60 percent of the components used in the manufacturing of its vacuums. The other 40 percent is purchased from external suppliers by the vacuum-assembly division. Components are sold from the components-production division to the vacuum-assembly division using a negotiated transfer price, which approximates market value.

Recently, PVL was approached by a Korean manufacturing company, Engine Tech Limited (ETL). ETL specializes in manufacturing small engines. ETL has proposed an arrangement whereby it would produce engine model P12, which PVL currently uses in two of its standard vacuum models. PVL currently produces these engines in its components division. ETL has agreed to provide P12 engines for a five-year period at a cost of 130,000 Korean Won per unit. At current exchange rates, this would amount to $2,200 Canadian per unit. Duty and freight would cost approximately $300 Canadian per unit for a total of $2,500 Canadian per unit. PVL would agree to purchase a minimum of 5,000 units per year during the five-year term of the contract. If PVL failed to purchase the minimum amount, it would be required to pay a penalty of 30,000 Korean Won (currently $500 Canadian) per unit of shortfall from the minimum. This penalty payment would be due at the end of the year in which the shortfall occurs.

PVL is considering modifying two of its existing models so that they use the P12 engine. The model 3 unit could be modified to use the P12 engine instead of its existing engine, the P10, which is a less powerful engine than the P12. If this occurs, the cost of the engine to the vacuum-assembly division would increase by

$1,000 per unit. All other costs would remain the same. Annual sales of the Model 3 would be expected to rise by 20 percent if this modification was made. PVL is also considering modifying the Model 4A to use the P12 engine instead of its existing engine, the P14, which is more powerful engine than the P12. If this occurs, the cost of the engine to the vacuum-assembly division would decrease by $1,000 per unit. All other costs would remain the same. Annual sales of the Model 4A would be expected to decrease by 20 percent if this modification was made.

You are the assistant controller of PVL. The controller of PVL has asked you to prepare a report to her on whether the offer from ETL should be accepted. She would also like you to discuss whether the P12 engine should be used in Models 3 and 4A. In order to assist you in your analysis, she has asked the accounting and marketing departments of the vacuum-assembly division to prepare information on expected sales and costs for the seven standard models that PVL produces (Exhibit I). This information represents management's best estimate of average selling prices and costs for the five-year term of the contract proposed by ETL. Costs and selling prices are not expected to change substantially over the five-year term of the contract. The controller has also had the accounting department of the component production division provide you with the expected costs of producing the P12 engine (Exhibit 9A-2). These costs are not expected to change substantially over the five-year term of the proposed contract with ETL either. The controller has instructed you to provide a quantitative analysis of the decisions in your report. She would also like your report to address the qualitative aspects of these decisions.

Required: | Prepare the report requested by the controller.

EXHIBIT 9A-1

PANADAGAN VACUUMS LIMITED
INFORMATION ON STANDARD MODELS

MODEL	SELLING PRICE	ESTIMATED (1) ANNUAL SALES VOLUME (UNITS)	ENGINE MODEL USED	ENGINE SOURCE
3	$20,000	4,000	P10	External vendor
3A	$25,000	2,000	P12	Components division
4	$40,000	2,000	P12	Components division
4A	$50,000	1,500	P14	External vendor
5	$70,000	500	P16	External vendor
6	$80,000	500	S4	Components division
7	$95,000	200	S8	Components division

Note 1: Estimated sales amount were prepared by the marketing department of PVL. Historically, the marketing department's estimates have been reasonably accurate.

Current Production Costs
(in dollars)

MODEL	3	3A	4	4A	5	6	7
LABOUR	$5,000	$7,000	$11,000	$15,000	$20,000	$25,000	$30,000

DIVISIONAL OVERHEAD (1)	1,000	1,400	2,200	3,000	4,000	5,000	6,000
COMPONENTS							
ENGINE	3,000	4,000	4,000	5,000	7,000	10,000	15,000
HOUSING	2,000	2,500	3,000	3,500	4,000	6,000	7,000
OTHER	6,000	6,100	9,000	18,400	20,200	20,200	28,000
TOTAL COST	$17,000	$21,000	$29,200	$44,900	$55,200	$66,200	$86,000

Note 1: Division overhead has been applied at a rate of 20 percent of direct labour. Division overhead includes purchasing costs, management salaries, rent, utilities, warranty service costs, and administrative costs.

EXHIBIT 9A-2

PANADAGAN VACUUMS LIMITED
INFORMATION ON CURRENT COST OF PRODUCING P12 ENGINE

Process Description

The divisions purchasing department purchases all of the subcomponents needed to produce the engine. These subcomponents are then inspected. The engine is then assembled and inspected before being transferred to the vacuum-assembly division.

Production Costs per Unit:

Materials and subcomponents	$1,200.00	
Direct Labour (including employee benefits):		
Subcomponent inspection	100.00	(1)
Assembly	500.00	(2)
Testing	150.00	(3)
Identifiable overhead:		
Amortization of equipment	300.00	(4)
Management salaries	240.00	(5)
Rent	200.00	(6)
Repairs and maintenance of equipment	200.00	(7)
Other	300.00	(8)
Allocated divisional overhead	300.00	(9)
$3,490.00		

Note 1. Costs consist of a supervisor and a team of inspection workers. One inspection worker can, in one year, inspect the components needed to assemble 500 engines. Each inspector's yearly salary and benefits costs $40,000. One supervisor is needed who can supervise up to 20 inspection workers.

Based on annual production of 4,000 units, expected costs are:

Inspection workers

4,000 units/500 units per worker × $40,000	$320,000
Supervisor's salary and benefits	80,000
	$400,000
Annual production	4,000
Cost per unit	$ 100.00

Note 2. Assembly is conducted by production teams. Each team can assemble up to 500 units per year. Each team consists of 10 workers and a supervisor. Total salaries and benefits per team averages $250,000 per year.

Cost per team	$250,000
Production per team	500
Cost per unit	$ 500.00

Note 3. Costs consist of quality control inspectors, who each receive an annual salary and benefits of $75,000 per year. Each can inspect a maximum of 500 units per year.

Cost per inspector	$ 75,000
Units inspected	500
Cost per unit	$ 150.00

Note 4. Amortization is calculated based on the percentage of use of the component production division's machines. Currently, these machines are being used at 70 percent of their full capacity. All of these machines are required for the production of components other than the P12. Cost is determined as follows:

Cost per hour of machine usage	$ 9,000
Units produced per hour	30
Charge per hour	$ 300.00

Note 5. Management salaries of the salaries for 14 managers who work exclusively on the P12. These costs are not expected to increase if the volume of P12 engines produced changes.

Annual costs	$960,000
Units produced	4,000
Cost per unit	$ 240.00

Note 6. Rent relates to space used exclusively in the plant for the production of the P12 engine. The space currently being used would allow the component production division to produce up to 90,000 units per year without any increase in costs. If the P12 engine was no longer manufactured, PVL could sublease the space currently used for manufacturing this component. However, it would only be able to recover 50 percent of the cost it is currently incurring.

Annual cost	$800,000
Units produced	4,000
Cost per unit	$ 200.00

Note 7. Repairs and maintenance costs (like amotization) are also allocated based on machine usage. The actual amount of repairs and maintenance costs incurred during a year has been found to be directly related to the number of machine hours used.

Rate per hour of usage	$ 6,000
Units produced per hour	30
Costs per unit	$200.00

Note 8. Other overhead consists of utilities, training and other administrative costs. Approximately 50% of these costs are dependent upon the volume of units produced. The other 50 percent of these costs is not dependent on the volume of units produced.

Expected annual cost based on 4,000 units produced	$1,200,000
Annual volume	4,000
Cost per unit	$ 300.00

Note 9. Divisional overhead costs consist of costs that cannot be specifically attributed to a particular component. Divisional overhead costs are allocated based on the direct labour costs attributable to each component. Based on past results, a rate of 40 percent of direct labour is used to allocate divisional overhead. These costs are expected to remain the same regardless of the volume of P12 engines produced.

Capital Budgeting Decisions: An Introduction

LEARNING OBJECTIVES

After studying this chapter, you will be able to

1. Compute a project's net present value (NPV).

2. Compute a project's internal rate of return (IRR).

3. Identify the assumptions of the two discounted-cash-flow (DCF) models.

4. Apply the decision rules for the DCF models.

5. Use both the total project and differential approaches to determine the NPV difference between two projects.

6. Identify relevant cash flows for DCF analysis.

7. Use the payback model and the accounting rate-of-return model and compare them with DCF models.

8. Identify the methods for reconciling the conflict between using a DCF model for making a decision and using accounting income for evaluating the related performance.

Should the Waterloo County Board of Education purchase new photocopy equipment? Should partners of Stone, Goldberg, and Gomez (a law firm) buy personal computers for the staff? Should Boeing begin production of a proposed new airplane? Should Procter & Gamble introduce a new mouthwash?

Capital-Budgeting Decisions. Decisions that have significant financial effects beyond the current year.

Such decisions, which have significant financial effects beyond the current year, are called capital-budgeting decisions. **Capital-budgeting decisions** are faced by managers in all types of organizations, including religious, medical, and government enterprises.

Capital budgeting has three phases: (1) identifying potential investments, (2) selecting the investments to undertake (including the gathering of data to aid the decision), and (3) follow-up monitoring or "postaudit," of investments. Accountants are sometimes involved in the first phase, and play important roles in phases 2 and 3.

Managers use many different capital-budgeting models in *selecting* investments. Each model summarizes facts and forecasts about an investment in a way that provides information for a decision maker. Accountants contribute to this choice process in their problem-solving role. In this chapter we compare the uses and limitations of various capital-budgeting models, with particular attention to relevant-cost analysis. Accountants' score-keeping is important to the *postaudit* of investments, discussed later in the chapter.

FOCUS ON PROGRAMS OR PROJECTS

In planning and controlling, operations managers typically focus on a particular *time period*. For example, the chief administrator of a university will be concerned with all activities for a given academic year. But the administrator will also be concerned with individual *programs* or *projects* that have a longer-range focus. Examples are new programs in educational administration or health care education, joint law-management programs, new athletic facilities, new trucks, or new parking lots. In fact, many organizations may be perceived as a collection of individual investment projects.

This chapter concentrates on the planning and controlling of those programs or projects that affect more than one year's financial results. Such decisions require investments of resources that are often called capital outlays. Hence, the term *capital budgeting* has arisen to describe the long-term planning for making and financing such outlays.

All capital outlays involve risk. The organization must commit funds to the project or program but cannot be sure what—if any—returns this investment will yield later on. Many factors affecting future returns are unknown, but well-managed organizations try to gather and quantify as many known or predictable factors as possible before making a decision. Capital-budgeting models facilitate this process.

Most large organizations use more than one capital-budgeting model. Why? Because each model summarizes information in a different way and reveals various useful perspectives on investments. There are three general types of capital-budgeting models: discounted-cash-flow models, payback models, and rate-of-return models. We will look at each of these model types in turn in this chapter.

Investing in Ferries: Western Canada

**Laidlaw
www.laidlaw.com**

**B.C. Ferries
www.bcferries.bc.ca**

**Nanaimo Chamber of Commerce
www.nanaimochamber.bc.ca**

Due to its proximity to Vancouver, Nanaimo has become the transportation hub for Vancouver Island. With a population of 70,000, it is less than a quarter the size of Greater Victoria, yet its port has become the island's largest export centre. The growth in marine traffic has been forced through a ferry terminal at Departure Bay that is too small and in the wrong place. Traffic is often backed up into Nanaimo's downtown, a distance of nearly two miles. Weary travellers hope those day will be gone with the June 10 opening of a new $42-million terminal at Duke Point, nine miles south of city hall.

The change is long overdue, says Nanaimo Mayor Gary Korpan. "We've needed it for 10 years." Not everybody is excited. In particular, residents of Gabriola Island and truckers needing direct access to Vancouver resent the changes being forced on them. But traffic between Vancouver and Victoria will experience an enormous improvement.

Previously, drivers had to work through the town's 23 stoplights before getting to Departure Bay, but soon they will be able to connect to the new terminal via a new four-lane expressway. Admittedly, drivers approaching the terminal from the north will have farther to go, but the added distance should not add too much time due to the new Nanaimo Parkway that bypasses downtown. Duke Point is expected to handle 1.5-million passengers and 600,000 vehicles its first year. Eventually, it will handle all commercial traffic, something that Nanaimo Chamber of Commerce manager Jane Hutchins says will ease the burden on the city's crowded core. "It will be much easier to do business in Nanaimo," she says.

The terminal itself offers something most do not: a room with a view. Its most notable characteristics may be the floor-to-ceiling glass windows and the half-acre lawn, both of which allow waiting passengers to look out over the water to Gabriola Island. The facility is also compact, which means "for your 60-year-old granny, it's about a one-minute walk [to the ship]," says Duke Point's proud manager, Don Cheshire. "It's probably the best ferry facility in the world." Others aren't impressed.

Pedestrians will find Duke Point hard to access because the city's transit service plans send out only three buses per day, meaning many foot passengers leaving on Tsawwassen's eight daily sailings to Duke Point will have lengthy waits at both ends. Seeking to take advantage of the situation, busing giant Laidlaw Transit Inc. has applied for permission to operate a shuttle service. Most truck traffic already passes through Tsawwassen, but some truckers are worried that the new terminal means that in a few years they will no longer be able to opt instead for the B.C. Ferries run between Nanaimo and Horseshoe Bay in West Vancouver.

Current plans are that by 1999, high-speed catamarans—unequipped to carry commercial vehicles—will be the only ferries on the Departure Bay-Horseshoe Bay route. Mr. Cheshire says it is possible a commercial run will be added from Duke Point to Horseshoe Bay to meet the demand, but nothing is certain. Meanwhile, residents of Gabriola Island are disgruntled over rumours that their ferry, which has docked downtown for more than 80 years, will soon be switched to Duke Point.

B.C. Ferries, worried over the Gabriola ferry's annual loss of $600,000, has proposed the change as a money saver, but Gabriola resident Fred Apstein argues that landing at Duke Point would discomfit some 300 high-school students who must travel to Nanaimo every day. The extra time to Duke Point would preclude many of them from after-school activities. Furthermore, many of the several hundred people who commute to the city for work would lose the luxury of leaving their cars at home. "Gabriola's life is tied to downtown Nanaimo," says Mr. Apstein, who thinks the island's 3,000 residents would be willing to raise fares to keep the ferry docking downtown.

Fearful of Duke Point's effect, Gabriolans have opened up an old debate about building a bridge to Nanaimo. B.C. Ferries has said it wants the Gabriola route to break even within five years. Rather than raise fares or move the run to Duke Point, suggests island resident Jeremy Baker, why not scrap the whole thing and have private interests build a

B.C. Report
www.axionet.com/bcreport

toll bridge? According to Mr. Baker, developers such as Strait Crossing—the company that built the Confederation Bridge to P.E.I.—would jump at the chance to span the gap. He would like to see a referendum on the idea.

"I'm saying, don't waste the taxpayers' money anymore, until you have pre-

sented to the population of Gabriola the option of building a bridge and doing away with the ferry service altogether."

Source: Derek DeCloet, "New terminal, new problems: Duke Point will eliminate Nanaimo traffic jams," *British Columbia Report*, (June 23, 1997) pp. 16–17.

DISCOUNTED-CASH-FLOW MODELS

Discounted-Cash-Flow (DCF) Model. A capital-budgeting model that focuses on cash inflows and outflows and the time value of money.

Financial Post
www.financialpost.com

According to a list of *Financial Post* 500 industries, **discounted-cash-flow (DCF) models**, conceptually the most attractive models, are used by over 65 percent of industries and are the best measures of the financial effects of an investment. They are based on the old adage that a bird in the hand is worth two in the bush—that a dollar in the hand today is worth more than a dollar to be received (or spent) five years from today. This adage applies because the use of money has a cost, and we call that cost interest. Because the discounted-cash-flow model focuses on a project's cash inflows and outflows and explicitly and systematically incorporates the time value of money, it is the best method to use for capital-budgeting decisions.

Major Aspects of DCF

DCF models focus on expected *cash* inflows and outflows rather than on *net income*. Companies invest cash today to receive cash in future periods. DCF compares the value of the cash outflows with the cash inflows.

There are two main variations of DCF: (a) net present value (NPV) and (b) internal rate of return (IRR). Both variations are based on the theory of compound interest. A brief summary of the tables and formulas used is included in Appendix B at the end of this book. Before reading on, examine Appendix B to be sure you understand the concept of compound interest and how to use Table 1 on page 776 and Table 2 on page 777. The mechanics of compound interest may appear formidable to those readers who are encountering them for the first time. However, a little practice with the interest tables should easily clarify the mechanical aspect.

Example

Throughout the rest of this section, we will use the following example to illustrate the major concepts: A buildings and grounds manager of a university is contemplating the purchase of some lawn-maintenance equipment that is expected to increase efficiency and produce cash operating savings of $2,000 per year. The useful life of the equipment is four years, after which it will have a net disposal value of zero. The equipment will cost $6,075 now and the minimum desired rate of return is 10 percent per year.

Net Present Value (NPV)

OBJECTIVE 1

Compute a project's net present value (NPV).

Net Present Value (NPV) Method. A discounted-cash-flow approach to capital budgeting that discounts all expected future cash flows to the present using a minimum desired rate of return.

Required Rate of Return (Hurdle Rate, Discount Rate, Cost of Capital). The minimum desired rate of return.

The **net present value (NPV) method** is a discounted-cash-flow approach to capital budgeting that discounts all expected future cash flows to the present using a minimum desired rate of return. To apply the net present value (NPV) method to a proposed investment project, a manager first determines some minimum desired rate of return. The rate depends on the risk of a proposed project—the higher the risk, the higher the minimum desired rate of return. The minimum rate is often called the **required rate of return, hurdle rate, discount rate, or cost of capital**. Managers then determine the present values of all expected cash flows from the project, using this minimum desired rate. If the sum of the present values of the cash flow is positive, the project is desirable. If the sum is negative, the project is undesirable. Why? A positive NPV means that accepting the project will increase the value of the firm because the present value of the project's cash inflows exceeds the present value of its cash outflows. (If by some chance, the NPV is exactly zero, a decision maker would be indifferent between accepting and rejecting the project.) When choosing among several investments, the one with the greatest net present value is the most desirable from a financial perspective.

The NPV method is applied in three steps, which are shown in Exhibit 10-1 and outlined below.

1. Prepare a diagram of relevant expected cash inflows and outflows including the outflow at time zero, the date of acquisition. The right-hand side of Exhibit 10-1 shows how these cash flows are sketched. Outflows are in parentheses. Although a sketch is not essential, it clarifies thought.
2. Find the present value of each expected cash inflow or outflow. Examine Table 1 on page 776 in Appendix B. Find the discount factor from the correct row and column of the table. Multiply each expected cash inflow or outflow by the appropriate discount factor. For example, the $2,000 cash savings that will occur two years hence is worth $2,000 × .8264 = $1,653 today.
3. Sum the individual present values. Accept a project whose total is positive and reject a project whose total is negative.

Exhibit 10-1 shows a positive net present value of $265, so the investment is desirable. The value today (that is, at time zero) of the four $2,000 cash inflows is $6,340. The manager pays only $6,075 to obtain these cash inflows. Thus a favourable difference can be achieved at time zero of $265 ($6,340 − $6,075). The minimum desired rate of return can have a large effect on net present values. The higher the minimum desired rate of return, the lower the present value of each future cash inflow and thus the lower the net present value of the project. At a rate of 16 percent, the net present value of the project in Exhibit 10-1 would be a negative of $479 (i.e., $2,000 × 2.7982 = $5,596, which is $479 less than the required investment of $6,075), instead of the +$265 computed with a 10 percent rate. (Present-value factor 2.7982 is taken from Table 2 on page 777 in Appendix B.) When the desired rate of return is 16 percent rather than 10 percent, the project is undesirable at a price of $6,075.

EXHIBIT 10-1

Net Present Value Technique

Original investment, $6,075. Useful life, four years. Annual cash inflow from operations, $2,000. Minimum desired rate of return, 10 percent. Cash outflows are in parentheses; cash inflows are not. Total present values are rounded to the nearest dollar.

	PRESENT VALUE OF $1, DISCOUNTED AT 10%	TOTAL PRESENT VALUE	SKETCH OF CASH FLOWS AT END OF YEAR				
			0	1	2	3	4
APPROACH 1: DISCOUNTING EACH YEAR'S CASH INFLOW SEPARATELY*							
Cash flows:							
Annual savings	.9091	$1,818	←	$2,000			
	.8264	1,653	←		$2,000		
	.7513	1,503	←			$2,000	
	.6830	1,366	←				$2,000
Present value of future inflows		$6,340					
Initial outlay	1.0000	(6,075)	$(6,075)				
Net present value		$ 265					
APPROACH 2: USING ANNUITY TABLE†							
Annual savings	3.1699	$6,340	←	$2,000	$2,000	$2,000	$2,000
Initial outlay	1.0000	(6,075)	$(6,075)				
Net present value		$ 265					

* Present values from Table 1, Appendix B, page 776. (You may wish to put a paper clip on this page).
† Present values of annuity from Table 2, Appendix B, page 777. (Incidently, hand-held programmable calculators may give slightly different answers than tables due to rounding differences.)

439

Choosing the Correct Table

Exhibit 10-1 also shows another way to calculate NVP, shown here as "Approach 2." The basic steps are the same as for "Approach 1." The only difference is that Approach 2 uses Table 2 in Appendix B instead of Table 1. Table 2 is an annuity table that provides a shortcut to reduce hand calculations. That is, it gives discount factors for computing the present value of a *series* of *equal* cash flows at equal intervals at the same desired rate of return. Because the series of four cash flows in our example are all equal, you can use Table 2 to make one present value computation instead of four individual computations. Table 2 is merely a summation of the pertinent present-value factors of Table 1.[1]

$$.9091 + .8264 + .7513 + .6830 = 3.1698$$

In this example, Table 2 accomplishes in one computation what Table 1 accomplishes in four multiplications and one summation.

Beware of using the wrong table. Table 1 should be used for discounting *individual* amounts; Table 2 for a *series* of equal amounts. Of course, Table 1 is the fundamental table. If shortcuts are not desired or if there are changes in the amount of the annual cash flows or in the desired rate of return in some future years, then Table 1 must be used. Table 1 can be used for all present-value calculations.

The use of Tables 1 and 2 can be avoided entirely by those with a present-value function on their hand-held calculator or those who use the present-value function on a spreadsheet program on their personal computer. However, we encourage you to use the tables when learning the net present value method. Using the tables leads to an understanding of the process that does not come if calculators or computers are used exclusively. After you are comfortable with the method, you can take advantage of the speed and convenience of calculators and computers.

Internal Rate of Return (IRR)

Another way to decide whether to make a capital outlay is to calculate a project's **internal rate of return (IRR),** which is the discount rate that makes the net present value of the project equal to zero. Expressed another way, the internal rate of return is the discount rate that makes the present value of a project's expected cash inflows equal to the present value of the expected cash outflows, including the investment in the project.

The three steps in calculating IRR are shown in Exhibit 10-2:

1. Prepare a diagram of the expected cash inflows and outflows exactly as you did in calculating the NPV (see Exhibit 10-1).
2. Find an interest rate that equates the present value of the cash inflows to the present value of the cash outflows, that is, produces an NPV of zero. Approach 1 uses Table 1 in Appendix B and can be used with any

---

[1] Rounding error causes a .0001 difference between the Table 2 factor and the summation of Table 1 factors.

EXHIBIT 10-2

Two Proofs of Internal Rate of Return

Original investment, $6,075. Useful life, four years. Annual cash inflow from operations, $2,000. Internal rate of return (selected by trial-and-error methods), 12 percent. Total present values are rounded to the nearest dollar.

	PRESENT VALUE OF $1, DISCOUNTED AT 12%	TOTAL PRESENT VALUE	SKETCH OF CASH FLOWS AT END OF YEAR				
			0	1	2	3	4
APPROACH 1: DISCOUNTING EACH YEAR'S CASH INFLOW SEPARATELY*							
Cash flows:							
Annual savings	.8929	$1,786	←	$2,000			
	.7972	1,594	←		$2,000		
	.7118	1,424	←			$2,000	
	.6355	1,271	←				$2,000
Present value of future inflows		$6,075					
Initial outlay	1.0000	(6,075)	$(6,075)				
Net present value (the zero difference proves that the rate of return is 12%)		$ 0					
APPROACH 2: USING ANNUITY TABLE†							
Annual savings	3.0373	$6,075	←	$2,000	$2,000	$2,000	$2,000
Initial outlay	1.0000	(6,075)	$(6,075)				
Net present value		$ 0					

* Present values from Table 1, Appendix B.

† Present values of annuity from Table 2, Appendix B.

set of cash flows. If one outflow is followed by a series of equal outflows, you can use the following equation:

initial investment = annual cash flow × annuity PV factor (F)

$$\$6,075 = \$2,000 \times F$$

$$F = \frac{\$6,075}{\$2,000} = 3.0375$$

In Table 2 of Appendix B, scan the row that represents the relevant life of the project, row 4 in our example. Select the column with an entry closest to the annuity PV factor that was calculated. The factor closest to 3.0375 is 3.0373 in the 12 percent column. Because these factors are extremely close, the IRR is almost exactly 12 percent. Approach 2 shows that an interest rate of 12 percent indeed produces an NPV of zero.

3. Compare the IRR with the minimum desired rate of return. If the IRR is equal to or greater than the minimum desired rate, the project should be accepted. Otherwise it should be rejected.

Interpolation and Trial and Error

Not all IRR calculations work out exactly. Suppose the expected cash inflow in step 1 were $1,800 instead of $2,000. The equation in step 2 would produce

$$\$6,075 = \$1,800 \times F$$

$$F = \frac{\$6,075}{\$1,800} = 3.3750$$

On the period 4 line of Table 2, the column closest to 3.3750 is 7 percent, which may be close enough for most purposes. To obtain a more accurate rate, interpolation is needed: the factor 3.3750 is between the 7 percent factor (3.3872) and the 8 percent factor (3.3121).

	PRESENT-VALUE FACTORS	
7%	3.3872	3.3872
True rate		3.3750
8%	3.3121	
Difference	.0751	.0122

$$\text{true rate} = 7\% + \frac{.0122}{.0751}\,(1\%) = 7.16\%$$

These hand computations become even more complex when the cash inflows and outflows are not uniform. Then trial-and-error methods are needed. See Appendix 10, page 462 for examples. Of course, in practice, managers today use computer programs and spreadsheets to greatly simplify trial-and-error procedures.

Meaning of Internal Rate

Exhibit 10-2 shows that the present value of four annual cash inflows of $2,000 each is $6,075, assuming a rate of return of 12 percent. That is, 12 percent is the rate that equates the amount invested ($6,075) with the present value of the cash inflows ($2,000 per year for four years). Exhibit 10-3 shows that, if money were obtained at an effective interest rate of 12 percent, the cash inflow produced by the project would exactly repay the principal plus the interest over the four years. If money is available at less than 12 percent, the organization will have cash left over after repaying the principal and interest.

Exhibit 10-3 highlights how the internal rate of return is computed on the basis of the investment tied up in the project from period to period instead of solely on the initial investment. The internal rate is 12 percent of the capital invested during each year. The $2,000 inflow is composed of two parts, as analyzed in columns 3 and 4. Consider Year 1. Column 3 shows the interest on the $6,075 invested capital as $.12 \times \$6,075 = \$729$. Column 4 shows that the amount of investment recovered at the end of the year is $2,000 - \$729 = \$1,271$. By the end of Year 4, the series of four cash inflows exactly recovers the initial investment plus annual interest at a rate of 12 percent on the as yet unrecovered capital.

EXHIBIT 10-3

Rationale Underlying
Internal Rate-of-Return
Model
(Same data as in
Exhibit 11-2)

Original investment, $6,075. Useful life, 4 years. Annual cash savings from operations, $2,000. Internal rate of return, 12 percent. Amounts are rounded to the nearest dollar.

	(1)	(2)	(3)	(4)	(5)
				AMOUNT OF INVESTMENT	UNRECOVERED
	UNRECOVERED INVESTMENT AT BEGINNING	ANNUAL CASH	INTEREST AT 12% PER YEAR	RECOVERED AT END OF YEAR	INVESTMENT AT END OF YEAR
YEAR	OF YEAR	SAVINGS	(1) X 12%	(2) - (3)	(1) - (4)
1	$6,075	$2,000	$729	$1,271	$4,804
2	4,804	2,000	576	1,424	3,380
3	3,380	2,000	406	1,594	1,786
4	1,786	2,000	214	1,786	0

Assumptions: Unrecovered investment at the beginning of each year earns interest for a whole year. Annual cash inflows are received at the end of each year. For simplicity in the use of tables, all operating cash inflows are assumed to take place at the end of the years in question. This is unrealistic because such cash flows ordinarily occur uniformly throughout the given year, rather than in lump sums at the end of the year. Compound interest tables especially tailored for these more stringent conditions are available, but we shall not consider them here.

Exhibit 10-3 can be interpreted from either the borrower's or the lender's vantage point. Suppose the university borrowed $6,075 from a bank at an interest rate of 12 percent per annum, invested in the project, and repaid the loan with the $2,000 saved each year. Each $2,000 payment would represent interest of 12 percent plus a repayment of the loan. At a rate of 12 percent, the borrower would end up with an accumulated wealth of zero. Obviously, if the borrower could borrow at 12 percent, and the project could generate cash at more than the 12 percent rate (that is, in excess of $2,000 annually), the borrower would be able to keep some cash—and the internal rate of return, by definition, would exceed 12 percent. Again the internal rate of return is the discount rate that would provide a net present value of zero (no more, no less).

Assumptions of DCF Models

OBJECTIVE 3

Identify the assumptions of the two discounted-cash-flow models.

While both DCF models are good, neither is perfect. Two major assumptions underlie DCF models. First, we assume a world of certainty. That is, we act as if the predicted cash inflows and outflows are certain to occur at the times specified. Second, we assume perfect capital markets. That is, if we have extra cash at any time, we can borrow or lend money at the same interest rate. This rate is our minimum desired rate of return for the NPV model and the internal rate of return for the IRR model. If these assumptions are met, no model could possibly be better than a DCF model.

Unfortunately, our world has neither certainty nor perfect capital markets.

Nevertheless, the DCF model is usually preferred to other models. The assumptions of most other models are even less realistic. The DCF model is not perfect, but it generally meets our cost-benefit criterion. The payoff from better decisions is greater than the cost of applying the DCF model. More sophisticated models often do not improve decisions enough to be worth their cost.

USING DCF MODELS

Managers must keep in mind the limitations of the two DCF models. Using such models is also complicated by the difficulties of determining a desired rate of return.

PERSPECTIVES ON P O D M DECISION-MAKING

Property Valuation and DCF

The use of discounted-cash-flow analysis (DCF) began to be widely applied in industrial firms in the 1950s. By the 1970s most large companies used DCF. In the 1980s, real estate appraisers began using DCF to estimate the value of commercial properties. By the mid-1990s, lenders of all types (including appraisers, banks, insurance companies, pension funds, etc.) routinely used DCF to value properties for purposes such as determining offering prices for properties for sale, establishing limits on loans for which property was used as collateral, and for estimating market prices for portfolios that include real estate.

In addition to using DCF to value specific properties, most corporations acquiring another firm used DCF to establish an appropriate bid price. E.L. Morris, president of Fortune Finance Inc., a St. Louis investment banking firm, indicates that buyers find DCF "indisputably superior" to less sophisticated valuation methods.

For example, consider TeleWest, a British cable television company. When it made plans for being listed on both U.S. and U.K. stock markets in 1995, discounted cash flow was used to estimate its market value. The securities house of Kleinwort Benson computed net present values of £1.379 billion using a 17 percent rate and £1.667 billion using a rate of 15 percent. Kleinwort Benson also estimated the net present value of a single cable subscriber. Using a rate of 16 percent, each cable subscriber is worth £876. Using this figure, investors could use their own estimates of population, cable penetration rates, and churn rates (rates at which current subscribers cancel their subscriptions) to predict TeleWest's market value.

Despite its widespread use, not everyone is convinced that DCF is superior to other valuation methods. A recent controversy in Britain was prompted by the failure of the Queens Moat chain of hotels. Two different appraisers came up with estimates of the value of the chain's assets that diverged by more than £1 billion. The British Association of Hotel

TeleWest Communications
www.telewest.co.uk

Accountants supported a valuation based on DCF, while the Royal Institute of Chartered Surveyors (RICS) backed a method based on applying a multiple to the company's accounting earnings. RICS believes an earnings-based valuation is more objective because it is based on "achieved" profits, not simply on cash-flow estimates. Supporters of DCF would argue that estimates based on "best predictions" of cash flow are more accurate than those based on current earnings. After all, earnings are based on costs such as depreciation, which may have little relation to the current values of the assets being used.

Sources: R.J. Okaneski, "Present Values: A Useful Underwriting Tool?", *Appraisal Journal*, October 1994, p. 609; "TeleWest is Good Four-Way Bet, Says Kleinwort Benson," *New Media Markets*, October 27, 1994; S. London, "Facts and Forecasts: The Paucity of Credible Market Analysis," *Financial Times*, September 23, 1994, p. 12.

Choosing the Minimum Desired Rate

There are two key aspects of capital budgeting: investment decisions and financing decisions. *Investment decisions* focus on whether to acquire an asset, a project, a company, a product line, and so on. *Financing decisions* focus on whether to raise the required funds via some form of debt or equity or both. This textbook concentrates on the investment decision. Finance textbooks provide ample discussions of financing decisions.

A common mistake occurs when students do not clearly make this distinction between the investment decision and the financing decision. The faulty logic occurs when students include the interest payments as a cash outflow and then proceed to perform a DCF analysis on the cash flows. Remember that we employ DCF analysis to incorporate the time value of money—the interest—into the analysis. Thus, if interest payments are included in a DCF analysis, the interest has been incorrectly included twice. Remember, do not include the financing costs in the DCF analysis of an investment decision. How a project is financed may affect the desired rate of return, but it should not alter the amount of the cash flows.

Depending on a project's risk (that is, the probability that the expected cash inflows will not be achieved) and what alternative investments are available, investors usually have some notion of a minimum rate of return that would make various projects desirable investments. The problem of choosing this required rate of return is complex and is really more a problem of finance than of accounting. In general, the higher the risk, the higher the required rate of return. In this book we shall assume that the minimum acceptable rate of return is given to the accountant by management. It represents the rate that can be earned by the best alternative investments of similar risk.

Note too that the minimum desired rate is not affected by whether the *specific project* is financed by all debt, all ownership capital, or some of each. Thus the cost of capital is not "interest expense" on borrowed money as the accountant ordinarily conceives it. For example, a mortgage-free home still has a cost of capital—the maximum amount that could be earned with the proceeds if the home were sold.

Avoid a piecemeal approach. It is nearsighted to think that the required rate is the interest expense on any financing associated with a specific project. Under this faulty approach, a project will be accepted as long as its expected internal rate of return exceeds the interest rate on funds that might be borrowed to finance the project. Thus, a project would be desirable if it has an expected internal rate of 11 percent and a borrowing rate of 9 percent. The trouble here is that a series of such decisions will lead to a staggering debt that will cause the borrowing rate to skyrocket or will result in an inability to borrow at all. Conceivably, during the next year, some other project might have an expected internal rate of 16 percent and will have to be rejected, even though it is the most profitable in the series, because the heavy debt permits no further borrowing.

Amortization and Discounted Cash Flow

Accounting students are sometimes mystified by the apparent exclusion of amortization from discounted-cash-flow computations. A common error is to deduct depreciation or amortization from cash inflows. This is a misunderstanding of one of the basic ideas involved in the concept of the discounting. Because the discounted-cash-flow approach is fundamentally based on inflows and outflows of cash and not on the accounting concepts of revenues and expenses, no adjustments should be made to the cash flows for amortization expense (which is not a cash flow).[2] In the discounted-cash-flow approach, the entire cost of an asset is typically a *lump-sum* outflow of cash at time zero. Therefore, it is wrong to also deduct depreciation from operating cash inflows. To deduct periodic amortization would be a double-counting of a cost that has already been considered as a lump-sum outflow.

Use of DCF Models by Non-profit Organizations

Religious, educational, healthcare, governmental, and other non-profit organizations face a variety of capital-budgeting decisions. Examples include investments in buildings, equipment, national defence systems, and research programs. Thus, even when no revenue is involved, organizations try to choose projects with the least cost for any given set of objectives.

The unsettled question of the appropriate discount rate plagues all types of organizations, profit-seeking and non-profit. One thing is certain: as all cash-strapped organizations soon discover, capital is not cost-free. A discussion of the appropriate required rate is beyond the scope of this book. But typically long-term debt rates are used. It represents a crude approximation of the opportunity cost to the economy of having investments made by public agencies instead of by private organizations.

Progress in management practices and in the use of sophisticated techniques has generally tended to be faster in profit-seeking organizations. Thus, in

---

[2] Throughout this and the next chapter, our examples assume that revenues are in cash and that all expenses (except for amortization) are in cash. Of course, if the revenues and expenses are accounted for on the accrual basis of accounting, there will be leads and lags of cash inflows and cash outflows that a precise DCF model must recognize. For example, a $10,000 sale on credit may be recorded as revenue in one period, but the related cash inflow would not be recognized in a DCF model until collected, which may be in a second period. Such refinements are not made in this chapter.

general, managers have more opportunities in non-profit than in profit-seeking organizations to contribute to improved decision making by introducing newer management-decision models such as DCF.

Review of Decision Rules

Apply the decision rules for the DCF models.

Before proceeding, take time to review the basic ideas of discounted cash flow. The decision maker in our example cannot readily compare an immediate out-flow of $6,075 with a series of future inflows of $2,000 each because the outflows and inflows do not occur simultaneously. The net present value model expresses all amounts in equivalent terms, that is, in today's monetary units (for example, dollars, francs, marks, yen) at time zero. An interest rate measures the decision maker's preference for receiving money sooner rather than later. At a rate of 12 percent, the comparison would be:

Outflow in today's dollars	$(6,075)
Inflow equivalent in today's dollars @ 12%	6,075
Net present value	$ 0

Therefore, at a time preference for money of 12 percent, the decision maker is indifferent between having $6,075 now or having a stream of four annual inflows of $2,000 each. If the interest rate were 16 percent, the decision maker would find the project unattractive because the net present value would be negative:

Outflow	$(6,075)
Inflow equivalent in today's dollars @ 16% =	
$2,000 x 2.7982 (from Table 2) =	5,596
Net present value	$ (479)

At 10 percent, the NPV is positive, and the project is desirable:

Outflow	$(6,075)
Inflow equivalent in today's dollars @ 10% =	
$2,000 x 3.1699 from Table 2 =	6,340
Net present value	$ 265

We can summarize the decision rules offered by these two models as follows:

NET PRESENT VALUE (NPV) MODEL	**INTERNAL RATE-OF-RETURN (IRR) MODEL**
1. Calculate the net present value, using the minimum desired rate of return as the discount rate.	1. Using present-value tables, compute the internal rate of return by trial and error.
2. If the net present value is positive, accept the project; if negative, reject the project.	2. If this rate equals or exceeds the minimum desired rate of return, accept the project; if not, reject the project.

CAPITAL EXPANSION AT TRANSCANADA PIPELINES LTD.

Capital projects may have significant financial and strategic impacts on a company as the following newspaper article excerpt describes.[3]

TransCanada Pipelines
www.transcanada.com

National Energy Board
www.neb-one.gc.ca/

TransCanada Pipelines Ltd. is planning a $500-million expansion of its natural gas pipeline system. This follows hard on the heels of $2.4-billion of work in progress and a recent request for a further $390 million in construction.

The Calgary-based company's bullish proposals are based on growing markets in Central Canada and the United States, with much of the gas destined for electrical generation plants in both countries.

In the $500-million application filed Friday with the National Energy Board, TransCanada has sought permission to build 366 kilometres of pipeline looping near its existing cross-country line in Saskatchewan, Manitoba and Ontario, adding 227 million cubic feet of new daily capacity.

"If it's approved, the work will be substantially done in 1993 and 1994," said spokesman Frank Dabbs.

This new proposal comes as the company awaits NEB approval of a $390-million construction plan for this year and next. In that application, TransCanada asked to add 150 kilometres and 150 million cubic feet of daily capacity to its system. The NEB decision is expected later this spring.

That application was scaled back from an original forecast of $1 billion in construction work when the recession dampened customers' demand for natural gas.

The most recent application will return spending plans close to that level, but Mr. Dabbs said he is uncertain whether it indicates the economy is recovering.

"What we're seeing isn't just simple structural recession recovery. What we're seeing in our business is industrial restructuring," he said.

He emphasized, however, that the expansion work is being proposed because customers have asked for additional capacity.

"We are balancing the long-term requirements of our customers and we are balancing that with the cycles in the economy," he said.

Just over 100-million cubic feet of gas a day is destined for Canadian markets under the new proposal. And of that, 60 per cent is destined for co-generation projects in Ontario.

The remainder of the natural gas—about 125 million cubic feet a day—is to be shipped to the United States, Mr. Dabbs said, with the bulk of it finding end markets down the recently opened Iroquois Pipeline through New York state.

The application continues a period of heavy spending by TransCanada. It is about midway through its largest expansion project, with about $1.2 billion to be spent in 1992 on the $2.4-billion project, which is expected to be completed late this year.

[3] *Source:* "TCPL planning pipeline expansion worth $500 million," *The Globe and Mail*, April 7, 1992. Reprinted with permission from *The Globe and Mail*.

A report in *Business Week* provided an example of using a net present value model:

Eaton
www.eaton.com

Cutler-Hammer
www.ch.culler-hammer.com

Like many of the amounts being paid in big acquisitions of the last year, the $350 million that Eaton Corp. will have paid this January to acquire Cutler-Hammer, Inc., appears to be a stiff price. ... Eaton is justifying the price in large part by using an old but increasingly popular financial tool: discounted cash flow analysis (DCF). To set the price, Eaton projected the future cash flows it expects from Cutler over the next five to 10 years and then discounted them, using a rate that reflects the risks involved in the investment and the time value of the money used. Eaton figures that, based on DCF, Cutler will return at least 12 percent on its $350-million outlay.

Cash Flows for Investments in Technology

Many capital budgeting decisions compare a possible investment with a continuation of the status quo. One such decision is an investment in a highly automated production system to replace a traditional system.

Cash flows predicted for the automated system should be compared to those *predicted for continuation of the present system into the future. The latter are not necessarily the cash flows currently being experienced.* Why? Because the competitive environment is changing. If others invest in automated systems, failure to invest may cause a decline in market share and therefore lower revenues. The future without an automated system might be a continual decline in revenues and a non-competitive cost structure.

There are two ways to deal with hard-to-predict revenue and cost effects. First, they can be quantified as best as possible and included in an NPV analysis. Second, they can be recognized subjectively. For example, investment in a an automated system may have a *negative* NPV of $500,000 without considering subjective effects. A manager must then decide whether the potential losses in contribution margin from a decline in competitiveness—plus possible non-quantified cost savings—exceed $500,000. If so, the automated system is a desirable investment, despite its negative NPV.

THE NET PRESENT VALUE COMPARISON OF TWO PROJECTS

Managers are seldom asked to perform analysis on a single option. More often, managers want to compare several alternatives.

Total Project versus Differential Approach

OBJECTIVE 5

Use both the total project and differential approaches to determine the NPV difference between two projects.

Total Project Approach. An approach that compares two or more alternatives by computing the total impact on cash flows of each and then converting these total cash flows to their present values.

Differential Approach. An approach that compares two alternatives by computing the differences in cash flows between them and then converting these differences to their present values.

Two common methods for comparing alternatives are (1) the total project approach and (2) the differential approach.

The **total project approach** compares two or more alternatives by computing the total effect of each alternative on cash flows and then converting these total cash flows to their present values. It is the most popular approach and can be used for any number of alternatives. The alternative with the largest NPV of total cash flows is preferred.

The **differential approach** compares two alternatives by computing the differences in cash flows between alternatives and then converting these differences in cash flows to their present values. Its use is restricted to cases where only two alternatives are being examined.

To compare these approaches, suppose a company owns a packaging machine that it purchased three years ago for $56,000. The machine has a remaining useful life of five years but will require a major overhaul at the end of two more years at a cost of $10,000. Its disposal value now is $20,000. In five years its disposal value is expected to be $8,000, assuming that the $10,000 major overhaul will be done on schedule. The cash operating costs of this machine are expected to be $40,000 annually. A sales representative has offered a substitute machine for $51,000, or for $31,000 plus the old machine. The new machine will reduce annual cash operating costs by $10,000, will not require any overhauls, will have a useful life of five years, and will have a disposal value of $3,000. If the minimum desired rate of return is 14 percent, what should the company do? (Try to solve this problem yourself before examining the solution that follows.)

A difficult part of long-range decision making is the structuring of the data. We want to see the effects of each alternative on future cash inflows and outflows. The following steps apply to either the total project or the differential approach, and are illustrated in Exhibit 10-4.

Step 1. Arrange the relevant cash flows by project, so that a sharp distinction is made between total project flows and differential flows. The differential flows are merely algebraic differences between two alternatives. There are always at least two alternatives. One is the status quo—i.e., doing nothing.

Step 2. Total Project Approach: Determine the net present value of the cash flows for each individual project. Choose the project with the largest positive present value (i.e., largest benefit) or smallest negative present value (i.e., smallest cost).

Differential Approach: Compute the differential cash flows; that is, subtract the cash flows for project B from the cash flow from project A for each year. Calculate the present value of the differential cash flows. If this present value is positive, choose project A; if it is negative, choose project B.

Which approach you use when there are only two alternatives is a matter of preference. (The total project approach is necessary when analyzing three or more alternatives simultaneously.) However, to develop confidence in this area, you should work with both at the start. One approach can serve as proof of the accuracy of the other. In this example, the $8,429 net difference in favour of replacement is the result under either approach.

Analysis of Typical Items under Discounted Cash Flow

When you array the relevant cash flows, be sure to consider four types of inflows and outflows: 1) initial cash inflows and outflows at time zero, 2) investments in receivables and inventories, 3) future disposal values, and 4) operating cash flows.

1. *Initial cash inflows and outflows at time zero.* These cash flows include both outflows for the purchases and installation of equipment and other items required by the new project and either inflows or outflows from disposal of any items that are replaced. In Exhibit 10-4 the $20,000 received from selling the old machine was offset against the $51,000 purchase price of the new machine; the net cash outflow of $31,000 was shown. If the old machine could not be sold, any cost incurred to dismantle and discard it would be added to the purchase price of the new machine.

2. *Investments in receivables and inventories.* Investments in receivables, inventories, and intangible assets are basically no different from investments in plant and equipment. In the discounted-cash-flow model, the initial outlays are entered in the sketch of cash flows at time zero. At the end of the useful life of the project, the original outlays for machines may not be recouped at all or may be partially recouped in

EXHIBIT 10-4

Total Project versus Differential Approach to Net Present Value

	PRESENT VALUE DISCOUNT FACTOR AT 14%	TOTAL PRESENT VALUE	SKETCH OF CASH FLOWS AT END OF YEAR					
			0	1	2	3	4	5
I. TOTAL PROJECT APPROACH								
A. REPLACE								
Recurring cash operating costs, using an annuity table*	3.4331	$(102,993)		($30,000)	($30,000)	($30,000)	($30,000)	($30,000)
Disposal value, end of year 5	.5194	1,558						3,000
Initial required investment	1.0000	(31,000)	($31,000)					
Present value of net cash outflows		$(132,435)						
B. KEEP								
Recurring cash operating costs, using an annuity table*	3.4331	$(137,324)		(40,000)	(40,000)	(40,000)	(40,000)	(40,000)
Overhaul, end of year 2	.7695	(7,695)			(10,000)			
Disposal value, end of year 5	.5194	4,155						8,000
Present value of net cash outflows		$(140,864)						
Difference in favour of replacement		$ 8,429						
II. DIFFERENTIAL APPROACH								
A—B. ANALYSIS CONFINED TO DIFFERENCES								
Recurring cash operating savings, using an annuity table*	3.4331	$ 34,331		$10,000	$10,000	$10,000	$10,000	$10,000
Overhaul avoided, end of year 2	.7695	7,695			$10,000			
Disposal values, end of year 5	.5194	(2,597)						(5,000)
Incremental initial investment	1.0000	(31,000)	($31,000)					
Net present value of replacement		$ 8,429						

* Table 2, Appendix B.

the amount of the salvage values. In contrast, the entire original investments in all initial investments are typically regarded as outflows at time zero, and their terminal disposal values, if any, are regarded as inflows at the end of the project's useful life.

The example in Exhibit 10-4 required no additional investment in inventory or receivables. However, the expansion of a retail store, for example, entails an additional investment in a building and fixtures plus inventories. Such investments would be shown in the format of Exhibit 10-4 as follows (numbers assumed):

		SKETCH OF CASH FLOWS			
End of year	0	1	2 . . . 19		20
Investment in building and fixtures	(10)				
Investment in working capital (inventories)	(6)				6

As the sketch shows, the residual value of the building and fixtures might be small. However, the entire investment in inventories would ordinarily be recouped when the venture is terminated.

The difference between the initial outlay for working capital (mostly receivables and inventories) and the present value of its recovery is the present value of the cost of using working capital in the project. Working capital is constantly revolving in a cycle from cash to inventories to receivables and back to cash throughout the life of the project. But to be sustained, the project required that money be tied up in the cycle until the project ends.

3. *Future disposal values.* The disposal value at the end of a project is an increase in the cash inflow in the year of disposal. Errors in forecasting terminal disposal values are usually not crucial because the present value is usually small.

4. *Operating cash flows.* The major purpose of most investments is to affect revenues or costs (or both). The cash inflows and outflows associated with most of these effects are easy to identify, but three points deserve special mention. First, in relevant-cost analysis, the only pertinent overhead costs are those that will differ among alternatives. Fixed overhead under the available alternatives needs careful study. In practice, this is an extremely difficult phase of cost analysis, because it is hard to relate the individual costs to any single project. Second, amortization and book values should be ignored. The cost of assets is recognized by the initial outlay (point one in this section), not by amortization as computed under accrual accounting. Third, a reduction in a cash outflow is treated the same as a cash inflow. Both signify increases in value.

Complications

The foregoing material has been an *introduction* to the area of capital budgeting. In practice, a variety of factors complicate the analysis, including the following:

1. *Income taxes.* Comparison between alternatives is best made after considering tax effects, because the tax impact may alter the picture. The effects of income taxes are considered in Chapter 11.
2. *Inflation.* Predictions of cash flows and discount rates should be based on consistent inflation assumptions. This is explained in more detail in Chapter 11.
3. *Mutually exclusive projects.* When the projects are mutually exclusive, so that the acceptance of one automatically entails the rejection of the other (e.g., buying Toyota or Ford trucks), the project that has the largest net present value should be undertaken.
4. *Unequal lives.* What if alternative projects have unequal lives? Comparisons may be made over the useful life of either the longer-lived project or the shorter-lived one. For our purposes, we will use the life of the longer-lived project. To provide comparability, we assume reinvestment in the shorter-lived project at the end of its life and give it credit for any residual value at the time the longer-lived project ends. The important consideration is what would be done in the time interval between the termination dates of the shorter-lived and longer-lived projects.

OTHER MODELS FOR ANALYZING LONG-RANGE DECISIONS

Although the use of discounted-cash-flow models for business decisions has increased steadily over the past four decades, simpler models are also used. Often managers use them in *addition* to DCF analysis.

These models, which we are about to explain, are conceptually inferior to discounted-cash-flow approaches. Then why do we bother studying them? First, because changes in business practice occur slowly. Many businesses still use the simpler models. Second, because where simpler models are in use, they should be used properly, even if better models are available. Third, the simpler models might provide some useful information to supplement the DCF analysis.

In 1985, 208 companies from the 1985 *Financial Post* listing of the largest 500 Canadian industrial companies responded to a survey on capital budgeting.[4] The following table reveals that DCF methods are the primary methods used and that their use is gradually increasing. However, other simpler methods such as payback and accounting rate-of-return are still widely used. Of course, as always, the accountant and manager face a cost-and-value-of-information decision when they choose a decision model. Reluctance to use discounted-cash-flow models may be justified if the more familiar payback model or other simple models lead to the same investment decisions.

One existing technique may be called the emergency-persuasion method. No formal planning is used. Fixed assets are operated until they crumble, product lines are carried until they are obliterated by competition, and requests by

---

[4] Reprinted from an article in *CMA Management*, by J.D. Blazouske, I. Carlin, and S.H. Kim, "Current capital budgeting techniques in Canada," March 1988 issue, by permission of the Society of Management Accountants of Canada.

managers for authorization of capital outlays are judged on the basis of their ability to convince top management that the investment is necessary. These approaches to capital budgeting are examples of the unscientific management that often leads to bankruptcy.

In contrast, both the payback and the accounting rate-of-return models, while flawed, are attempts to approach capital budgeting systematically.

| | CAPITAL BUDGETING TECHNIQUES | | | |
| | PRIMARY METHOD | | SECONDARY METHOD | |
TECHNIQUE	1980	1985	1980	1985
Payback	25%	19%	41%	44%
Average accounting rate of return	11	9	10	9
Net present value	22	25	10	11
Internal rate of return	38	40	7	13
Other method	1	4	1	3
No method used	3	3	31	20
Total	100%	100%	100%	100%

Payback Model

Payback Time (Payback Period). The measure of the time it will take to recoup, in the form of cash inflows from operations, the initial dollars of outlay.

Payback time or **payback period** is the measure of the time it will take to recoup, in the form of cash inflows from operations, the initial dollars of outlay. Assume that $12,000 is spent for a machine with an estimated useful life of eight years. Annual savings of $4,000 in cash outflow are expected from operations. Amortization is ignored. The payback of three years is calculated as follows:

$$\text{payback time} = \frac{\text{initial incremental amount invested}}{\text{equal annual incremental cash inflow from operations}}$$

$$P = \frac{I}{O} = \frac{\$12,000}{\$4,000} = 3 \text{ years}$$

The payback model merely measures how quickly investment dollars may be recouped; it does not measure profitability. This is its major weakness. A project with a shorter payback time is not necessarily preferable to one with a longer payback time. On the other hand, the payback time might provide a rough estimate of riskiness, especially in decisions involving rapid technological change.

Assume that an alternative to the $12,000 machine is a $10,000 machine whose operation will also result in a reduction of $4,000 annually in cash outflow. Then

$$P_1 = \frac{\$12,000}{\$4,000} = 3.0 \text{ years}$$

$$P_2 = \frac{\$10,000}{\$4,000} = 2.5 \text{ years}$$

The $10,000 machine has a shorter payback time, and therefore it may appear more desirable. However, one fact about the $10,000 machine has been purposely withheld. What if its useful life is only 2.5 years? Ignoring the impact of compound interest for the moment, the $10,000 machine results in zero benefit, while the $12,000 machine (useful life eight years) generates cash inflows for five years beyond its payback period.

The main objective in investing is profit, not the recapturing of the initial outlay. If a company wants to recover its outlay fast, it need not spend in the first place, then no waiting time is necessary; the payback time is zero.

When a wealthy investor was assured by the promoter of a risky oil venture that he would have his money back within two years, the investor replied, "I already have my money."

The formula $P = I \div O$ can be used with assurance only when there are equal annual cash inflows from operations. When annual cash inflows are not equal, the payback computation must take a cumulative form—that is, each year's net cash flows are accumulated until the initial investment is recouped:

	INITIAL	NET CASH INFLOWS	
0	$31,000	—	—
1	—	$10,000	$10,000
2	—	20,000	30,000
2.1	—	1,000	31,000

In this situation, the payback time is slightly beyond the second year. Straight-line interpolation within the third year reveals that the final $1,000 needed to recoup the investment would be forthcoming in 2.1 years:

$$2 \text{ years} + \frac{\$1,000}{\$10,000} \times 1 \text{ year} = 2.1 \text{ years}$$

Accounting Rate-of-Return Model

Accounting Rate of Return (ARR). A non-discounted-cash-flow capital-budgeting model expressed as the increase in expected average annual operating income divided by the initial increase in required investment.

Another non-DCF capital-budgeting model is the **accounting rate-of-return (ARR)** model:

$$\text{accounting rate of return (ARR)} = \frac{\text{increase in expected average annual operating income}}{\text{initial required investment}}$$

$$\text{ARR} = \frac{O - D}{I}$$

where ARR is the average annual accounting rate of return on initial additional investment, O is the average annual incremental cash inflow from operations, D is the incremental average annual amortization, and I is the initial incremental amount invested. The *accounting rate-of-return model* is also known as the *accrual accounting rate-of-return model* (a more accurate description), the *unadjusted rate-of-return model,* and the *book-value model.* Its computations dovetail most closely with conventional accounting models of calculating income and required investment and show the effect of an investment in an organization's financial statements.

Assume the same facts as in Exhibit 10-1: investment is $6,075, useful life is four years, estimated disposal value is zero, and expected annual cash inflow from operations is $2,000. Annual amortization would be $6,075 ÷ 4 = $1,518.75, rounded to $1,519. Substitute these values in the accounting rate-of-return equation:

$$\text{ARR} = \frac{\$2,000 - \$1,519}{\$6,075} = 7.9\%$$

If the denominator is the "average" investment, which is often assumed for equipment as being the average book value over the useful life, or $6,075 ÷ 2 = $3,037.5, rounded to $3,038, the rate would be doubled:[5]

$$\text{R} = \frac{\$2,000 - \$1,519}{\$3,038} = 15.8\%$$

Defects of Accounting Rate-of-Return Model

The *accounting rate-of-return* model is based on the familiar financial statements prepared under accrual accounting. Unlike the payback model, the accounting model at least has profitability as an objective. Nevertheless, it has a major drawback. The accounting model ignores the time value of money. Expected future dollars are erroneously regarded as equal to present dollars. The discounted-cash-flow model explicitly allows for the force of interest and the timing of cash flows. In contrast, the accounting model is based on *annual averages*.

EXHIBIT 10-5 Comparison of Accounting Rates of Return and Internal Rates of Return	EXPANSION OF EXISTING GASOLINE STATION	INVESTMENT IN AN OIL WELL	PURCHASE OF NEW GASOLINE STATION
Initial investment	$ 90,000	$ 90,000	$ 90,000
Cash inflows from operations:			
Year 1	$ 40,000	$ 80,000	$ 20,000
Year 2	40,000	30,000	40,000
Year 3	40,000	10,000	60,000
Totals	$120,000	$120,000	$120,000
Average annual cash inflow	$ 40,000	$ 40,000	$ 40,000
Less: Average annual amortization			
($90,000 ÷ 3)	30,000	30,000	30,000
Increase in average annual net income	$ 10,000	$ 10,000	$ 10,000
Accounting rate of return on initial investment	11.1%	11.1%	11.1%
Internal rate of return, using discounted-cash-flow techniques	16.0%*	23.2%*	13.4%*

* Computed by trial-and-error approaches using Tables 1 and 2, pages 776 and 777. See Appendix 10, page 462, for a detailed explanation.

---

[5] The measure of the investment recovered in the example above is $1,519 per year, the amount of the annual amortization. Consequently, the average investment committed to the project would decline at a rate of $1,519 per year from $6,075 to zero; hence the average investment would be the beginning balance plus the ending balance ($6,075) divided by 2, or $3,038. Note that when the ending balance is not zero, the average investment will not be half the initial investment.

The accounting model uses concepts of investment and income that were originally designed for the quite different purpose of accounting for periodic income and financial position. The resulting *accounting* rate of return may differ greatly from the project's *internal* rate of return.

To illustrate, consider a petroleum company with three potential projects to choose from: an expansion of an existing gasoline station, an investment in an oil well, and the purchase of a new gasoline station. To simplify the calculations, assume a three-year life for each project. Exhibit 10-5 summarizes the comparisons. The projects differ only in the timing of the cash inflows. Note that the accounting rate of return would indicate that all three projects are equally desirable and that the internal rate of return properly discriminates in favour of earlier cash inflows.

PERFORMANCE EVALUATION

Potential Conflict

Many managers are reluctant to accept DCF models as the best way to make capital-budgeting decisions. Their reluctance stems from the wide usage of the accrual accounting model for evaluating performance. That is, managers become frustrated if they are instructed to use a DCF model for making decisions that are evaluated later by a non-DCF model, such as the typical accrual accounting rate-of-return model.

To illustrate, consider the potential conflict that might arise in the example of Exhibit 10-1. Recall that the internal rate of return was 12 percent, based on an outlay of $6,075 that would generate cash savings of $2,000 for each of four years and no terminal disposal value. Under accrual accounting, using straight-line depreciation, the evaluation of performance for years one through four would be

	YEAR 1	YEAR 2	YEAR 3	YEAR 4
Cash operating savings	$2,000	$2,000	$2,000	$2,000
Straight-line amortization, $6,075 ÷ 4	1,519	1,519	1,519	1,519*
Effect on operating income	481	481	481	481
Book value at beginning of year	6,075	4,556	3,037	1,518
Accounting rate of return	7.9%	10.6%	15.8%	31.7%

* Total amortization of 4 × $1,519 = $6,076 differs from $6,075 due to rounding error.

Many managers would be reluctant to replace equipment, despite the internal rate of 12 percent, if their performance were evaluated by accrual accounting models. They might be especially reluctant if they were likely to be transferred to new positions every year or two. This accrual accounting system understates the return in early years.

As Chapter 9 indicated, the reluctance to replace is reinforced if a heavy book loss on old equipment would appear in Year 1's accrual income statement even though such a loss would be irrelevant in a properly constructed decision model.

Thus, performance evaluation based on typical accounting measures can cause rejection of major, long-term projects such as investment in technologically advanced production systems. This pattern may help explain why many North American firms seem to be excessively short-term oriented.

Reconciliation of Conflict

How can the foregoing conflict be reconciled? An obvious solution would be to use the same model for decisions and for evaluating performance. The accrual accounting model is often dominant for evaluating all sorts of performance; that is why many organizations use it for both purposes and do not use a DCF model at all. Critics claim that not using DCF may lead to many instances of poor capital-budgeting decisions.

Another obvious solution would be to use DCF for both capital-budgeting decisions and performance evaluation. A survey showed that most large companies conduct a follow-up evaluation of at least some capital-budgeting decisions, often called a **postaudit**. The survey of Canadian companies revealed that all of the sample companies compared the actual investment cash flows to the budgeted figures, but only about one-half postaudited the operating cash flows.[6] The purposes of postaudits include the following:

Postaudit. A follow-up evaluation of capital-budgeting decisions.

1. To see that investment expenditures are proceeding on time and within budget.
2. To compare actual cash flows with those originally predicted, in order to motivate careful and honest predictions.
3. To provide information for improving future predictions of cash flows.
4. To evaluate the continuation of the project.

By focusing the postaudit on actual versus predicted *cash flows*, the evaluation is consistent with the decision process.

However, postauditing of all capital-budgeting decisions is costly. Most accounting systems are designed to evaluate operating performances of products, departments, divisions, territories, and so on, year by year. In contrast, capital-budgeting decisions frequently deal with individual *projects*, not the collection of projects that are usually being managed simultaneously by divisional or department managers. Therefore, usually only selected capital-budgeting decisions are audited.

The conflicts between the longstanding, pervasive accrual accounting model and various formal decision models represent one of the most serious unsolved problems in the design of management control systems. Top management cannot expect goal congruence if it favours the use of one type of model for decisions and the use of another type for performance evaluation.

HIGHLIGHTS TO REMEMBER

Capital budgeting is long-term planning for proposed capital outlays and their financing. Because the discounted-cash-flow model explicitly and automatically weighs the time value of money, it is the best method to use for long-range decisions. The overriding goal is maximum long-run net cash inflows.

The discounted-cash-flow model has two variations: internal rate of return and net present value. Both models take into account the timing of cash flows and are thus superior to other methods. Common errors in DCF analysis include deducting amortization from operating cash inflows, using the wrong present-value table, ignoring disposal values on old equipment or future disposal values

---

[6] Boersema, *Capital Budgeting Practices Including the Impact of Inflation*, CICA, 1978.

on new equipment, and incorrectly analyzing investments in working capital (for example, inventories).

Frequently, the optimal decision under discounted cash flow will not produce good accounting income in the early years. Heavy amortization charges and the expensing rather than capitalizing of development costs will hurt reported income for the first year. Postaudits help to limit the effect of this conflict.

The payback model is a popular approach to capital-spending decisions. It is simple and easily understood, but it neglects profitability.

The accounting rate-of-return model is also widely used in capital budgeting, although it is conceptually inferior to discounted-cash-flow models. It fails to recognize explicitly the time value of money. Instead, the accounting model depends on averaging techniques that may yield inaccurate answers, particularly when cash flows are not uniform through the life of a project.

Performance evaluation using accrual accounting can conflict with the DCF analysis used for decisions.

SUMMARY PROBLEMS FOR YOUR REVIEW

Problem One

Use the appropriate interest table to compute the following:

1. It is your sixty-fifth birthday. You plan to work five more years before retiring. Then you want to take $10,000 for a round-the-world tour. What lump sum do you have to invest now in order to accumulate the $10,000? Assume that your minimum desired rate of return is
   (a) 4 percent, compounded annually
   (b) 10 percent, compounded annually
   (c) 20 percent, compounded annually
2. You want to spend $2,000 on a vacation at the end of each of the next five years. What lump sum do you have to invest now in order to take the five vacations? Assume that your minimum desired rate of return is
   (a) 4 percent, compounded annually
   (b) 10 percent, compounded annually
   (c) 20 percent, compounded annually
3. At age sixty, you find that your employer is moving to another location. You receive termination pay of $50,000. You have some savings and wonder whether to retire now.
   (a) If you invest the $50,000 now at 4 percent, compounded annually, how much money can you withdraw from your account each year so that at the end of five years there will be a zero balance?
   (b) If you invest it at 10 percent?
4. At 16 percent, compounded annually, which of the following plans is more desirable in terms of present values? Show computations to support your answer.

YEAR	ANNUAL CASH INFLOWS	
	MINING	FARMING
1	$10,000	$ 2,000
2	8,000	4,000
3	6,000	6,000
4	4,000	8,000
5	2,000	10,000
	$30,000	$30,000

Solution

The general approach to these exercises centres on one fundamental question: Which of the two basic tables am I dealing with? No calculations should be made until after this question is answered with assurance. If you made any errors, it is possible that you used the wrong table.

1. From Table 1, page 776
   (a) $8,219
   (b) $6,209
   (c) $4,019

The $10,000 is an *amount of future worth*. You want the present value of that amount:

$$PV = \frac{S}{(1 + i)^n}$$

The conversion factor, $1/(1 + i)^n$, is on line 5 of Table 1. Substituting:

PV = $10,000 (.8219) = $8,219 (1)
PV = $10,000 (.6209) = $6,209 (2)
PV = $10,000 (.4019) = $4,019 (3)

Note that the higher the interest rate, the lower the present value.

2. From Table 2, page 777:
   (a) $8,903.60
   (b) $7,581.60
   (c) $5,981.20

The $2,000 withdrawal is a uniform annual amount, an annuity. You need to find the present value of an annuity for five years:

PV_A = annual withdrawal × F, where F is the conversion factor.

Substituting:

PV_A = $2,000 (4.4518) = $8,903.60 (1)
PV_A = $2,000 (3.7908) = $7,581.60 (2)
PV_A = $2,000 (2.9906) = $5,981.20 (3)

3. From Table 2:
   (a) $11,231.41
   (b) $13,189.83

You have $50,000, the present value of your contemplated annuity. You must find the annuity that will just exhaust the invested principal in five years:

$$PV_A = \text{annual withdrawal} \times F(1)$$

$$\$50,000 = \text{annual withdrawal } (4.4518)$$
$$\text{annual withdrawal} = \$50,000 \div 4.4518$$
$$= \$11,231.41$$

$$\$50,000 = \text{annual withdrawal } (3.7908)(2)$$
$$\text{annual withdrawal} = \$50,000 \div 3.7908$$
$$= \$13,189.83$$

4. From Table 1: Mining is preferable; its present value exceeds that of farming by $21,572 − $17,720 = $3,852. Note that the nearer dollars are more valuable than the distant dollars.

YEAR	PRESENT VALUE @ 16% FROM TABLE 1	PRESENT VALUE OF MINING	PRESENT VALUE OF FARMING
1	.8621	$ 8,621	$ 1,724
2	.7432	5,946	2,973
3	.6407	3,844	3,844
4	.5523	2,209	4,418
5	.4761	952	4,761
		$21,572	$17,720

Problem Two

Review the problem and solution shown in Exhibit 10-4. Conduct a sensitivity analysis as indicated below. Consider each requirement as independent of other requirements.

1. Compute the net present value if the minimum desired rate of return was 20 percent.
2. Compute the net present value if predicted cash operating costs was $35,000 instead of $30,000, using the 14 percent discount rate.
3. By how much may the cash operating savings fall before reaching the point of indifference, the point where the net present value of the project is zero, using the original discount rate of 14 percent?

Solution

1. Either the total project approach or the differential approach could be used. The differential approach would show:

	TOTAL PRESENT VALUE
Recurring cash operating savings, using an annuity table (Table 2):	
2.9906 × $10,000 =	$29,906
Overhaul avoided: .6944 × $10,000 =	6,944
Difference in disposal values:	
.4019 × $5,000 =	(2,010)
Incremental initial investment	(31,000)
Net present value of replacement	$ 3,840
2. Net present value in Exhibit 10-4	$ 8,429
Present value of additional $5,000 annual operating costs,	
3.4331 × $5,000	17,166
New net present value	$ (8,737)

3. Let X = annual cash operating savings and find the value of X such that NPV = 0. Then

$$0 = 3.4331(X) + \$7,695 - \$2,597 - \$31,000$$
$$3.4331X = \$25,902$$
$$X = \$7,545$$

(Note that $7,695, $2,597, and $31,000 are at the bottom of Exhibit 10-4.) If the annual savings fall from $10,000 to $7,545, a decrease of $2,455 or almost 25 percent, the point of indifference will be reached.

An alternative way to obtain the same answer would be to divide the net present value of $8,429 (see bottom of Exhibit 11-4) by 3.4331, obtaining $2,455, the amount of the annual difference in savings that will eliminate the $8,429 of net present value.

APPENDIX 10: CALCULATIONS OF INTERNAL RATES OF RETURN

This appendix shows how to compute internal rates of return. It uses data from Exhibit 10-5.

Expansion of an Existing Gasoline Station

The formula from page 442 can be used to compute the IRR of the expansion of the existing gas station:

$90,000 = present value of annuity of $40,000 at X percent for three years, or what factor F in the table of the present values of an annuity will satisfy the following equation:

$$\$90,000 = \$40,000 \ F$$
$$F = \$90,000 \div \$40,000 = 2.2500$$

Now, on the Year 3 line of Table 2, page 777, find the column that is closest to 2.2500. You will find that 2.2500 is extremely close to a rate of return of 16 percent—so close that straight-line interpolation is unnecessary between 14 percent and 16 percent. Therefore, the internal rate of return is 16 percent.

Investment in an Oil Well

Trial-and-error methods must be used to calculate the rate of return that will equate the future cash flows with the $90,000 initial investment. As a start, note that the 16 percent rate was applicable to a uniform annual cash inflow. But now use Table 1, page 776 because the flows are not uniform, and try a higher rate, 22 percent, because you know that the cash inflows are coming in more quickly than under the uniform inflow:

YEAR	CASH INFLOWS	TRIAL AT 22%		TRIAL AT 24%	
		PRESENT-VALUE FACTOR	TOTAL PRESENT VALUE	PRESENT-VALUE FACTOR	TOTAL PRESENT VALUE
1	$80,000	.8197	$65,576	.8065	$64,520
2	30,000	.6719	20,157	.6504	19,512
3	10,000	.5507	5,507	.5245	5,245
			$91,240		$89,277

Because $91,240 is greater than $90,000, the true rate must be greater than 22 percent. Try 24 percent. Now $89,277 is less than $90,000 so the true rate lies somewhere between 22 percent ad 24 percent. It can be approximated by interpolation:

INTERPOLATION	TOTAL PRESENT VALUES	
22%	$91,240	$91,240
True rate		90,000
24%	89,277	
Difference	$ 1,963	$ 1,240

Therefore:

$$\text{true rate} = 22\% + \frac{1,240}{1,963} \times 2\%$$
$$= 22\% + 1.3\% = 23.3\%$$

Purchase of a New Gasoline Station

In contrast to the oil-well project, this venture will have slowly increasing cash inflows. The trial rate should be much lower than the 16 percent rate applicable to the expansion project. Let us try 12 percent:

YEAR	CASH INFLOWS	TRIAL AT 12% PRESENT-VALUE FACTOR	TRIAL AT 12% TOTAL PRESENT VALUE	TRIAL AT 14% PRESENT-VALUE FACTOR	TRIAL AT 14% TOTAL PRESENT VALUE
1	$20,000	.8929	$17,858	.8772	$17,544
2	40,000	.7972	31,888	.7695	30,780
3	60,000	.7118	42,708	.6750	40,500
			$92,454		$88,824

Because $92,454 is greater than $90,000, try 14 percent, and then interpolate a rate between 12 percent and 14 percent.

INTERPOLATION	TOTAL PRESENT VALUES	
12%	$92,454	$92,454
True rate		90,000
14%	88,824	
Difference	$ 3,630	$ 2,454

$$\text{true rate} = 12\% + \frac{2,454}{3,630} \times 2\%$$
$$= 12\% + 1.4\% = 13.4\%$$

Special Note: Ignore income taxes in the Questions, Problems, and Cases. The effects of income taxes are considered in the next chapter.

ACCOUNTING VOCABULARY

accounting rate of return (ARR) *p. 455*
capital-budgeting decisions *p. 435*
cost of capital *p. 438*
differential approach *p. 449*
discount rate *p. 438*
discounted-cash-flow (DCF) model *p. 437*
hurdle rate *p. 438*
internal rate of return (IRR) *p. 440*

net-present-value (NPV) method *p. 438*
payback period *p. 454*
payback time *p. 454*
postaudit *p. 458*
required rate of return *p. 438*
total project approach *p. 449*

ASSIGNMENT MATERIAL

QUESTIONS

Q10-1 Capital budgeting has three phases: 1) identification of potential investments, 2) selection of investments, and 3) postaudit of investments. What is the accountant's role in each phase?

Q10-2 Why is discounted cash flow a superior method for capital budgeting?

Q10-3 Distinguish between simple interest and compound interest.

Q10-4 Can net present value ever be negative? Why?

Q10-5 Define DCF, NPV, and IRR.

Q10-6 "The higher the minimum rate of return desired, the higher the price that a company will be willing to pay for cost-saving equipment." Do you agree? Explain.

Q10-7 "The DCF model assumes certainty and perfect capital markets. Thus it is impractical to use it in most real-world situations." Do you agree? Explain.

Q10-8 "Double-counting occurs if amortization is separately considered in discounted-cash-flow analysis." Do you agree? Explain.

Q10-9 "Nonprofit organizations do not use DCF because their cost of capital is zero." Do you agree? Explain.

Q10-10 Why should the differential approach to alternatives always lead to the same decision as the total project approach?

Q10-11 "The higher the interest rate, the less I worry about errors in predicting terminal values." Do you agree? Explain.

Q10-12 "The NPV model should not be used for investment decisions about advanced technology such as computer-integrated manufacturing systems." Do you agree? Explain.

Q10-13 "Discounted-cash-flow approaches will not work if the competing projects have unequal lives." Do you agree? Explain.

Q10-14 "It is important that a firm use one and only one capital-budgeting model. Using multiple models may cause confusion." Do you agree? Explain.

Q10-15 "If discounted-cash-flow approaches are superior to the payback and the accounting rate-of-return methods, why should we bother to learn the others? All it does is confuse things." Answer this contention.

Q10-16 What is the basic flaw in the payback model?

Q10-17 Compare the accounting rate-of-return approach and the discounted-cash-flow approach with reference to the time value of money.

Q10-18 Explain how a conflict can arise between capital-budgeting decision models and performance-evaluation methods.

PROBLEMS

P10-1 EXERCISES IN COMPOUND INTEREST. Use the appropriate table to compute the following:

1. You have always dreamed of taking a trip to the Great Barrier Reef. What lump sum do you have to invest today to have the $12,000 needed for the trip in three years? Assume that you can invest the money at
   (a) 5 percent, compounded annually
   (b) 10 percent, compounded annually
   (c) 18 percent, compounded annually

2. You are considering partial retirement. To do so you need to use part of your savings to supplement your income for the next five years. Suppose you need an extra $15,000 per year. What lump sum do you have to invest now in order to supplement your income for five years? Assume that your minimum desired rate of return is
   (a) 5 percent, compounded annually
   (b) 10 percent, compounded annually
   (c) 18 percent, compounded annually

3. You just won a lump sum of $400,000 in a local lottery. You have decided to invest the winnings and withdraw an equal amount each

year for 10 years. How much can you withdraw each year and have a zero balance left at the end of 10 years if you invest at
(a) 6 percent, compounded annually
(b) 10 percent, compounded annually

4. A professional athlete is offered the choice of two four-year salary contracts: contract A for $1.4 million and contract B for $1.3 million:

	CONTRACT A	CONTRACT B
End of Year 1	$ 200,000	$ 450,000
End of Year 2	300,000	350,000
End of Year 3	400,000	300,000
End of Year 4	500,000	200,000
	$1,400,000	$1,300,000

Which contract has the higher present value at 14 percent compounded annually? Show computations to support your answer.

P10-2 NPV, IRR, ARR, AND PAYBACK. Sally's Subs is considering a proposal to invest in a speaker system that would allow its employees to service drive-through customers. The cost of the system (including installation of special windows and driveway modifications) is $60,000. Sally Holding, manager of Sally's Subs, expects the drive-through operations to increase annual sales by $50,000, with a 40 percent contribution margin ratio. Assume that the system has an economic life of six years, at which time it will have no disposal value. The required rate of return is 14 percent.

1. Compute the payback period. Is this a good measure of profitability?
2. Compute the net present value (NPV). Should Holding accept the proposal? Why or why not?
3. Compute the internal rate of return (IRR). How should the IRR be used to decide whether to accept or reject the proposal?
4. Using the accounting rate of return model, compute the rate of return on the initial investment.

P10-3 EXERCISE IN COMPOUND INTEREST. Rhonda Reynolds wishes to purchase a $250,000 house. She has accumulated a $50,000 down payment, but she wishes to borrow $200,000 on a 25-year mortgage. For simplicity, assume annual mortgage payments at the end of each year and no loan fees.

1. What are Reynolds's annual payments if her interest rate is (a) 8 percent, (b) 10 percent, and (c) 12 percent, compounded annually?
2. Repeat requirement 1 for a 15-year mortgage.
3. Suppose Reynolds had to choose between a 25-year and a 15-year mortgage, either one at a 10 percent interest rate. Compute the total payments and total interest paid on (a) a 25-year mortgage, and (b) a 15-year mortgage.

P10-4 EXERCISE IN COMPOUND INTEREST. Suppose General Electric (GE) wishes to borrow money from The Canadian Bank. An annual rate of 12 percent is agreed upon.

1. Suppose GE agrees to repay $400 million at the end of five years. How much will The Canadian Bank lend GE?

2. Suppose GE agrees to repay a total of $400 million at a rate of $100 million at the end of each of the next four years. How much will The Canadian Bank lend GE?

P10-5 EXERCISE IN COMPOUND INTEREST.

1. First National Bank offers depositors a lump-sum payment of $30,000 six years hence. If you desire an interest rate of 8 percent compounded annually, how much would you be willing to deposit now? At an interest rate of 16 percent?
2. Repeat requirement 1, but assume that the interest rates are compounded semi-annually.

P10-6 EXERCISE IN COMPOUND INTEREST. A building contractor has asked you for a loan. You are pondering various proposals for repayment:

1. Lump sum of $600,000 four years hence. How much will you lend if your desired rate of return is (a) 12 percent compounded annually, (b) 20 percent compounded annually?
2. Repeat requirement 1, but assume that the interest rates are compounded semi-annually.
3. Suppose the loan is to be paid in full by equal payments of $150,000 at the end of each of the next four years. How much will you lend if your desired rate of return is (a) 12 percent compounded annually, (b) 20 percent compounded annually?

P10-7 BASIC RELATIONSHIPS IN INTEREST.

1. Suppose you borrow $80,000 now at 14 percent interest compounded annually. The borrowed amount plus interest will be repaid in a lump sum at the end of eight years. How much must be repaid? Use Table 1 (p. 776) and the basic equation: PV = Future amount × Conversion factor.
2. Assume the same facts as above except that the loan will be repaid in equal installments at the end of each of eight years. How much must be repaid each year? Use Table 2 (p. 777) and the basic equation PVA = Future annual amounts × Conversion factor.

P10-8 DEFERRED ANNUITY EXERCISE. It is your twentieth birthday. On your twenty-fifth birthday, and on three successive birthdays thereafter, you intend to spend exactly $1,000 for a birthday celebration. What lump sum do you have to invest now in order to have the four celebrations? Assume that the money will earn interest, compounded annually, of 12 percent.

P10-9 PRESENT VALUE AND SPORTS SALARIES. Because of a salary cap, National Basketball Association teams are not allowed to exceed a certain annual limit in total player salaries. Suppose the Chicago Bulls had scheduled salaries exactly equal to their cap of $16 million for 1997. Michael Pippin, a star player, was scheduled to receive $3 million in 1997. To free up money to pay a prize rookie, Pippin agreed to defer $1 million of his salary for two years, by which time the salary cap will have been increased. His contract called for salary payments of $3 million in 1997, $3.5 million in 1998, and $4 million in 1999. Now he will receive $2 million in 1997, still $3.5 million in 2001, and $5 million in 1999. For simplicity, assume that all salaries are paid on July 1 of the year they are scheduled. Pippin's minimum desired rate of return is 12 percent.

Did the deferral of salary cost Pippin anything? If so, how much? Compute the present value of the sacrifice on July 1, 1997. Explain your findings.

P10-10 INTERNAL RATE OF RETURN. Fill in the blanks:

	NUMBER OF YEARS		
	10	**20**	**30**
Amount of annual cash inflow*	$ 5,000	$ _____	$10,000
Required initial investment	$19,615	$22,000	$ _____
Internal rate of return	_____ %	16%	20%

* To be received at the end of each year

P10-11 INTERNAL RATE AND NPV. Fill in the blanks:

	NUMBER OF YEARS		
	8	**18**	**28**
Amount of annual cash inflow*	$10,000	$ _____	$ 7,000
Required initial investment	$ _____	$80,000	$29,099
Internal rate of return	18%	16%	_____ %
Minimum desired rate of return	14%	_____ %	26%
Net present value	$ _____	($13,835)	$ _____

* To be received at the end of each year

P10-12 ILLUSTRATION OF TRIAL-AND-ERROR METHOD OF COMPUTING RATE OF RETURN. Study Exhibit 10-2. Suppose the annual cash inflow will be $2,500 rather than $2,000. What is the internal rate of return?

P10-13 NEW EQUIPMENT. The Office Equipment Company has offered to sell some new packaging equipment to the Diaz Company. The list price is $42,000, but Office Equipment has agreed to accept some old equipment in trade. A trade-in allowance of $9,000 was agreed upon. The old equipment was carried at a book value of $7,700 and could be sold outright for $6,000 cash. Cash operating savings are expected to be $5,000 annually for the next 12 years. The minimum desired rate of return is 12 percent. The old equipment has a remaining useful life of 12 years. Both the old and the new equipment will have zero disposal values 12 years from now.

Should Diaz buy the new equipment? Show your computations, using the net present value method. Ignore income taxes.

P10-14 PRESENT VALUES OF CASH INFLOWS. Nouvenu Office Products has just been established. Operating plans indicate the following expected cash flows:

	OUTFLOWS	INFLOWS
Initial investment now	$210,000	$—
End of year: One	150,000	200,000
Two	200,000	250,000
Three	250,000	300,000
Four	300,000	400,000
Five	350,000	450,000

1. Compute the net present value for all of these cash flows. This should be a single amount. Use a discount rate of 14 percent.
2. Is the internal rate of return more than 14 percent or less than 14 percent? Explain.

P10-15 CAPITAL BUDGETING WITH UNEVEN CASH FLOWS.   The University of Toronto Faculty of Applied Science and Engineering is considering the purchase of a special-purpose machine for $60,000. It is expected to have a useful life of three years with no terminal salvage value. The university's controller estimates the following savings in cash operating costs:

YEAR	AMOUNT
1	$28,000
2	26,000
3	24,000

Compute:

1. Payback period
2. Net present value if the required rate of return is 12 percent
3. Internal rate of return
4. Accounting rate of return (a) on the initial investment and (b) on the "average" investment.

P10-16 RATIONALE OF NPV MODEL.   Evergreen Outdoor School (EOS) has a chance to invest $10,000 in a project that is certain to pay $4,500 at the end of each of the next three years. The minimum desired rate of return is 10 percent.

1. What is the project's net present value?
2. Show that EOS would be equally well off undertaking the project as having its present value in cash. Do this by calculating the cash available at the end of three years if (a) $10,000 is borrowed at 10 percent, with interest paid at the end of each year, and the investment is made, or (b) cash equal to the project's NPV is invested at 10 percent compounded annually for three years. Use the following formats. Year 1 for the first alternative is completed for you.

P10-17 REPLACEMENT OF EQUIPMENT.   Assume that new equipment will cost $100,000 in cash and that the old machine cost $84,000 and can be sold now for $16,000 cash. Annual cash savings of $15,000 are expected for 10 years.

1. Compute the net present value of the replacement alternative, assuming that the minimum desired rate of return is 10 percent.

	ALTERNATIVE (A)—INVEST IN PROJECT				
	(1)	**(2)**	**(3)**	**(4)**	**(5)**
					(3) – (4)
	LOAN		**(1) + (2)**		**LOAN**
	BALANCE AT	**INTEREST**	**ACCUMULATED**	**CASH FOR**	**BALANCE**
	BEGINNING	**AT 10%**	**AMOUNT AT**	**REPAYMENT**	**AT END**
YEAR	**OF YEAR**	**PER YEAR**	**END OF YEAR**	**OF LOAN**	**OF YEAR**
1	$10,000	$1,000	$11,000	$4,500	$6,500
2					
3					

	ALTERNATIVE (B)—KEEP CASH		
	(1)	**(2)**	**(3)**
	INVESTMENT		**(1) + (2)**
	BALANCE	**INTEREST**	**ACCUMULATED**
	AT BEGINNING	**AT 10%**	**AMOUNT AT**
YEAR	**OF YEAR**	**PER YEAR**	**END OF YEAR**
1			
2			
3			

2. What will be the internal rate of return?
3. How long is the payback period on the incremental investment?

P10-18 **INVESTMENT IN SOLAR WATER HEATER.** A brochure entitled *A Guide to Buying a Solar Water Heater* contained an example showing how a homeowner could save $14 more than the cost of a solar water heater over seven years. The total purchase price of the water heater, after all tax effects, was $1,575. Savings of $168 were predicted for the first year. The amount saved increased by 10 percent each year because the cost of heating water was expected to increase at a 10 percent annual rate. Therefore, the seven-year savings were $168 + $185 + $203 + $223 + $245 + $269 + $296 = $1,589. (Note that $185 = 1.1 × $168, $203 = 1.1 × $185, etc.) Assume that the cost of capital for investing in a solar water heater is 8 percent.

    1. Do you agree that a homeowner could save a net amount of $14 during the seven years by purchasing a solar water heater? Explain.
    2. Assume that a homeowner bought a solar water heater for a net outlay of $1,575 and received the savings promised in the brochure. What was the net present value of the purchase of the heater at the time it was acquired? Assume that all savings occur at the end of the year.

P10-19 **REPLACING OFFICE EQUIPMENT.** Simon Fraser University is considering replacing some Xerox copies with faster copiers purchased from Kodak. The administration is very concerned about the rising costs of operations during the last decade.

In order to convert to Kodak, two operators would have to be retrained. Required training and remodelling would cost $2,000.

Simon Fraser's three Xerox machines were purchased for $10,000 each, five years ago. Their expected life was 10 years. Their resale value is now $2,000 each and will be zero in five more years. The total cost of the new Kodak equipment will be $49,000; it will have zero disposal value in five years.

The three Xerox operators are paid $8 an hour each. They usually work a 40-hour week. Machine breakdowns occur monthly on each machine, resulting in repair costs of $50 per month and overtime of four hours, at time-and-one-half, per machine per month, to complete the normal monthly workload. Toner, supplies, etc., cost $100 a month for each Xerox copier.

The Kodak system will require only two regular operators, on a regular work-week of 40 hours each, to do the same work. Rates are $10 an hour, and no over-time is expected. Toner, supplies, etc., will cost $3,300 annually. Maintenance and repairs are fully serviced by Kodak for $1,050 annually. (Assume a 52-week year.)

1. Using discounted-cash-flow techniques, compute the present value of all relevant cash flows, under both alternatives, for the five-year period discounted at 12 percent. As a not-for-profit organization, Simon Fraser University does not pay income taxes.
2. Should Simon Fraser keep the Xerox copiers or replace them if the decision is based solely on the given data?
3. What other considerations might affect the decision?

P10-20   REPLACEMENT DECISION FOR RAILWAY EQUIPMENT.   The Wabash Railroad is considering replacement of a Kalamazoo Power Jack Tamper, used for maintenance of track, with a new automatic raising device that can be attached to a production tamper.

The present power jack tamper cost $18,000 five years ago and has an esti-mated life of 12 years. A year from now the machine will require a major over-haul estimated to cost $5,000. It can be disposed of now via an outright cash sale for $3,500. There will be no value at the end of 12 years.

The automatic raising attachment has a delivered selling price of $72,000 and an estimated life of 12 years. Because of anticipated future developments in combined maintenance machines, it is felt that the machine should be disposed of at the end of the seventh year to take advantage of newly developed machines. Estimated sales value at the end of seven years is $5,000.

Tests have shown that the automatic raising machine will produce a more uniform surface on the track than the power jack tamper now in use. The new equipment will eliminate one labourer whose annual compensation, including fringe benefits, is $30,000.

Track maintenance work is seasonal, and the equipment normally works from May 1 to October 31 each year. Machine operators and labourers are trans-ferred to other work after October 31, at the same rate of pay.

The salesperson claims that the annual normal maintenance of the new machine will run about $1,000 per year. Because the automatic raising machine is more complicated than the manually operated machine, it is felt that it will require a thorough overhaul at the end of the fourth year at an estimated cost of $7,000.

Records show the annual normal maintenance of the Kalamazoo machine to be $1,200. Fuel consumption of the two machines is equal. Should the Wabash keep or replace the Kalamazoo Power Jack Tamper? A 10 percent rate of return is desired. Compute present values. Ignore income taxes.

P10-21   DISCOUNTED CASH FLOW, UNEVEN REVENUE STREAM, RELEVANT COSTS.   Anika Paar, the owner of a nine-hole golf course on the outskirts of a large city, is consider-ing the proposal that the course be illuminated and operated at night. Ms. Paar purchased the course early last year for $90,000. Her receipts from operations during the 28-week season were $24,000. Total disbursements for the year, for all purposes, were $16,500.

The required investment in lighting this course is estimated at $20,000. The system will require 150 lamps of 1,000 watts each. Electricity costs $.032 per kilowatt-hour. The expected average hours of operation per night is five. Because of occasional bad weather and the probable curtailment of night operation at the beginning and end of the season, it is estimated that there will be only 130 nights of operation per year. Labour for keeping the course open at night will cost $15 per night. Lamp renewals are estimated at $300 per year; other maintenance and repairs, per year, will amount to 4 percent of the initial cost of the lighting system. Property taxes on this equipment will be about 2 percent of its initial cost. It is estimated that the average revenue, per night of operation, will be $90 for the first two years.

Considering the probability of competition from the illumination of other golf courses, Ms. Paar decides that she will not make the investment unless she can make at least 10 percent per annum on her investment. Because of anticipated competition, revenue is expected to drop to $60 per night for Years 3 through 5. It is estimated that the lighting equipment will have a salvage value of $7,000 at the end of the five-year period.

Using discounted-cash-flow techniques, determine whether Ms. Paar should install the lighting system.

P10-22 **MINIMIZING TRANSPORTATION COSTS.** The Luxon Company produces industrial and residential lighting fixtures at its manufacturing facility located in Calgary. Shipment of company products to an eastern warehouse is presently handled by common carriers at a rate of $.25 per kilogram of fixtures. The warehouse is located 2,500 kilometres from Calgary.

The treasurer of Luxon Company is presently considering whether to purchase a truck for transporting products to the eastern warehouse. The following data on the truck are available:

Purchase price	$35,000
Useful life	5 years
Salvage value after 5 years	zero
Capacity of truck	10,000 kilograms
Cash costs of operating truck	$.90 per kilometre

Luxon feels that an investment in this truck is particularly attractive because of their successful negotiation with Retro Company to back-haul Retro's products from the warehouses to Calgary on every return trip from the warehouse. Retro has agreed to pay Luxon $2,400 per load of Retro's products hauled from the warehouse to Calgary up to and including 100 loads per year.

Luxon's marketing manager has estimated that 500,000 kilograms of fixtures will have to be shipped to the eastern warehouse each year for the next five years. The truck will be fully loaded on each round trip.

Ignore income taxes.

1. Assume that Luxon requires a minimum rate of return of 20 percent. Should the truck be purchased? Show computations to support your answer.

2. What is the minimum number of trips that must be guaranteed by the Retro Company to make the deal acceptable to Luxon, based on the foregoing numbers alone?

3. What qualitative factors might influence your decision? Be specific.

P10-23 INVESTMENT IN MACHINE AND WORKING CAPITAL.   The Glasgow Company has an old machine with a net disposal value of £15,000 now and £4,000 five years from now. A new Rapido machine is offered for £62,000 cash or £47,000 with a trade-in. The new machine will result in an annual operating cash outflow of £40,000 as compared with the old machine's annual outflow of £50,000. The disposal value of the new machine five years hence will be £4,000.

Because the new machine will produce output more rapidly, the average investment in inventories by using the new machine will be £160,000 instead of £200,000.

The minimum desired rate of return is 20 percent. The company uses discounted-cash-flow techniques to guide these decisions.

Should the Rapido machine be acquired? Show your calculations. Company procedures require the computing of the present value of each alternative. The most desirable alternative is the one with the least cost. Assume that the PV of £1 at 20 percent for five years is £.40; the PV of an annuity of £1 at 20 percent for five years is £3.

P10-24 COMPARISON OF INVESTMENT MODELS.   Dominique's Frozen Food Company makes frozen dinners and sells them to retail outlets near London. Dominique has just inherited £10,000 and has decided to invest it in the business. She is trying to decide between:

Alternative a: Buy a £10,000 contract, payable immediately, from a local reputable sales promotion agency. The agency would provide various advertising services, as specified in the contract, over the next 10 years. Dominique is convinced that the sales promotion would increase net cash inflow from operations, through increased volume, by £2,000 per year for the first five years, and by £1,000 per year thereafter. There would be no effect after the 10 years had elapsed.

Alternative b: Buy new mixing and packaging equipment, at a cost of £10,000, which would reduce operating cash outflows by £1,500 per year for the next 10 years. The equipment would have zero salvage value at the end of the 10 years.

Ignore any tax effect.

1. Compute the rates of return on initial investment by the accounting model for both alternatives.

2. Compute the rates of return by the discounted-cash-flow model for both alternatives.

3. Are the rates of return different under the discounted-cash-flow model? Explain.

P10-25 FIXED AND CURRENT ASSETS; EVALUATION OF PERFORMANCE.   Metro Hospital has been under pressure to keep costs down. Indeed, the hospital administrator has been managing various revenue-producing centres to maximize contributions to the recovery of the operating costs of the hospital as a whole. The administrator has been considering whether to buy a special-purpose X-ray machine for $193,000. Its unique characteristics would generate additional cash operating income of $50,000 per year for the hospital as a whole.

The machine is expected to have a useful life of six years and a terminal salvage value of $22,000.

The machine is delicate. It requires a constant inventory of various supplies and spare parts. When these items can no longer be used, they are instantly replaced, so an investment of $15,000 must be maintained at all times. However, this investment is fully recoverable at the end of the useful life of the machine.

1. Compute the net present value if the required rate of return is 14 percent.
2. Compute the internal rate of return (to the nearest whole percentage).
3. Compute the accounting rate of return on (a) the initial investment and (b) the "average" investment.
4. Why might the administrator be reluctant to base her decision on the DCF model?

P10-26 INVESTMENT IN CAD/CAM. The Gustav Borg Manufacturing Company is considering the installation of a computer-aided design/computer-aided manufacturing (CAD/CAM) system. The current proposal calls for implementation of only the CAD portion of the system. Bergit Olsson, the manager in charge of production design and planning, has estimated that the CAD portion of CAD/CAM could do the work of five designers, who are each paid Skr 260,000 per year (52 weeks × 40 hours × Skr 125/hour), where Skr is the symbol for the Swedish kroner.

The CAD/CAM system can be purchased for Skr 1,600,000. (The CAD portion cannot be purchased separately.) The annual out-of-pocket costs of running the CAD portion of the system are Skr 900,000. The system is expected to be used for eight years. The company's minimum desired rate of return is 12 percent.

1. Compute the NPV and IRR of the investment in the CAD/CAM system. Should the system be purchased? Explain.
2. Suppose Olsson was not certain about her predictions of savings and economic life. Possibly only four designers will be replaced, but if everything works out well, as many as six might be replaced. If better systems become available, the CAD/CAM system might be used only five years, but it might last as long as 10 years. Prepare pessimistic, most likely, and optimistic predictions of NPV. Would this analysis make you more confident or less confident in your decision in requirement 1? Explain.
3. What subjective factors might influence your decision?

P10-27 CAFETERIA FACILITIES. The cafeteria in Haekon Towers, an office building in downtown Oslo, is open 250 days a year. It offers typical cafeteria-line service. At the noon meal (open to the public), serving-line facilities can accommodate 200 people per hour for the two-hour serving period. The average customer has a 30-minute lunch period. Serving facilities are unable to handle the overflow of noon-hour customers with the result that, each day, 20 dissatisfied customers who do not wish to stand in line choose to eat elsewhere. Projected over a year, this results in a considerable loss to the cafeteria.

To tap this excess demand, the cafeteria is considering two alternatives: (a) installing two vending machines, at a cost of NK 25,000 apiece (NK means Norwegian kroner), or (b) completely revamping present serving-line facilities with new equipment, at a cost of NK 150,000. The vending machines and serving-line equipment have a useful life of 10 years and will be amortized on a straight-line basis. The minimum desired rate of return for the cafeteria is 10 percent. The average sale is NK 15, with a contribution margin of 30 percent. This will remain the same if new serving-line facilities are installed.

Data for alternative (a) vending machines are as follows:

- Service cost per year is NK 2,000; salvage value of each machine at the end of 10 years is NK 5,000.
- Contribution margin is 20 percent. It is estimated that 60 percent of the dissatisfied customers will use the vending machines and spend an average of NK 15. The estimated salvage value of the present equipment will net NK 20,000 at the end of the 10-year period.

Data for alternative (b) new serving-line facilities are as follows:

- Yearly salary for an extra part-time cashier is NK 8,000; salvage value of old equipment is NK 50,000; salvage value of new equipment, at the end of ten years, is NK 50,000; cost of dismantling old equipment is NK 5,000. It is estimated that all the previously dissatisfied customers will use the new facilities.

All other costs are the same under both alternatives and need not be considered.

Using the net present value model, which is the better alternative?

P10-28 COLLABORATIVE LEARNING EXERCISE.   James LaGrande had recently been appointed controller of the Breakfast Cereals Division of a major food company. The division manager, Renee Osterland, was known as a hard-driving, intelligent, non-compromising manager. She had been very successful, and was rumoured to be on the fast-track to corporate top management, maybe even in line for the company presidency. One of Jim's first assignments was to prepare the financial analysis for a new cold cereal, Krispie Krinkles. This product was especially important to Ms. Osterland because she was convinced that it would be a success and thereby a springboard for her ascent to top management.

Mr. LaGrande discussed the product with the food lab that had designed it, with the market research department that had tested it, and with the finance people who would have to fund its introduction. After putting together all the information, he developed the following optimistic and pessimistic sales projections:

	OPTIMISTIC	PESSIMISTIC
Year 1	$1,600,000	$800,000
Year 2	3,600,000	1,200,000
Year 3	5,000,000	1,000,000
Year 4	8,000,000	800,000
Year 5	10,000,000	400,000

The optimistic predictions assume a successful introduction of a popular product. The pessimistic predictions assume that the product is introduced but does not gain wide acceptance and is terminated after five years. LaGrande thinks the most likely results are halfway between the optimistic and pessimistic predictions.

LaGrande learned from finance that this type of product introduction requires a predicted rate of return of 16 percent before top management will authorize funds for its introduction. He also determined that the contribution margin should be about 50 percent on the product, but could be as low as 42 percent or as high at 58 percent. Initial investment would include $3 million for production facilities, $2.5 million for advertising and other product introduction expenses, and $500,000 for working capital (inventory, etc.). The production facilities would have a value of $800,000 after five years.

Based on his preliminary analysis, LaGrande recommended to Osterland that the product not be launched. Osterland was not pleased with the recommendation. She claimed that LaGrande was much too pessimistic and asked him to redo his numbers so that she could justify the product to top management.

LaGrande carried out further analysis, but his predictions came out no differently. In fact, he became even more convinced that his projections were accurate. Yet, he was certain that if he returned to Osterland with numbers that did not support introduction of the product, he would incur her wrath. And, in fact, she could be right—that is, there is so much uncertainty in the forecasts that he could easily come up with believable numbers that would support going forward with the product. He would not believe them, but he thinks he could convince top management that they are accurate.

This role-play could be done as an entire class or in teams of three to six persons. It will be explained here as if being done by a team. Choose one member of the team to be James LaGrande and one to be Renee Osterland.

1. With the help of the entire team except the person chosen to be Osterland, LaGrande should prepare the capital-budgeting analysis used for his first meeting with Osterland.
2. Next, LaGrande should meet again with Osterland. They should try to agree on the analysis to take forward to top management. As they discuss the issues and try to come to an agreement, the remaining team members should record all the ethical judgements each discussant makes.
3. After LaGrande and Osterland have completed their role-play assignment, the entire team should assess the ethical judgements made by each and recommend an appropriate position for LaGrande to take in this situation.

CASES

C10-1 **INVESTMENT IN TECHNOLOGY.** Terwilliger Company is considering installation of a computer-integrated manufacturing (CIM) system as part of its implementation of a just-in-time philosophy. Roy Terwilliger, company president, is convinced that the new system is necessary, but he needs the numbers to convince the board of directors. This is a major move for the company, and approval at board level is required.

Jennifer Terwilliger, Roy's daughter, has been assigned the task of justifying the investment. She is a business-school graduate and understands the use of net present value for capital budgeting decisions. To identify relevant costs, she developed the following information.

Terwilliger Company produces and sells a variety of small, electronic components sold to final equipment manufacturers. It has a 40 percent market share, with the following condensed results expected for 2000:

Sales		$12,000,000
Cost of goods sold:		
Variable	$4,000,000	
Fixed	4,300,000	8,300,000
Selling & administrative expenses:		
Variable	$2,000,000	
Fixed	400,000	2,400,000
Operating income		$ 1,300,000

Installation of the CIM system will cost $6 million, and the system is expected to have a useful life of six years with no salvage value. In 2001, the training costs for personnel will exceed any cost savings by $400,000. In years 2002 through 2006, variable cost of goods sold will decrease by 40 percent, an annual savings of $1.6 million. There will be no savings in fixed cost of goods sold—in fact, it will increase by the amount of the straight-line amortization on the new system. Selling and administrative expenses will not be affected. The required rate of return is 12 percent. Assume that all cash flows occur at the end of the year, and the initial investment, which occurs at the beginning of 2001.

Required:

1. Suppose Jennifer Terwilliger assumes that production and sales would continue for the next 10 years as they were in 2000 in the absence of investment in the CIM. Compute the NPV of investing in the CIM.

2. Now suppose Jennifer predicts that it will be difficult to compete if the CIM is not installed. In fact, she has undertaken market research that estimates a drop in market share of three percentage points a year starting in 2001 in the absence of investment in the CIM. (That is, market share will be 37 percent in 2001, 34 percent in 2002, 31 percent in 2003, etc.) Her study also showed that the total market sales level will stay the same and market prices are not expected to change. Compute the NPV of investing in the CIM.

3. Prepare an explanation from Jennifer Terwilliger to the board of directors of Terwilliger Company explaining why the analysis in Requirement 2 is appropriate and why analysis such as that in Requirement 1 cause companies to underinvest in high-technology projects. Include an explanation of qualitative factors that are not included in the NPV calculation.

C10-2 **INVESTMENT IN QUALITY.** The Woolongong Manufacturing Company produces a single model of a CD player that is sold to Australian manufacturers of sound systems. Each CD player is sold for $210, resulting in a contribution margin of $70 before considering any costs of inspection, correction of product defects, or refunds to customers.

In 2000, top management at Woolongong is contemplating a change in its quality control system. Currently, $40,000 is spent annually on quality control inspections. Woolongong produces and ships 50,000 CD players a year. In producing those CD players, an average of 2,000 defective units are produced. Of these, 1,500 are identified by the inspection process, and an average of $85 is spent on each to correct the defects. The other 500 players are shipped to customers. when a customer discovers a defective CD player, Woolongong refunds the $210 purchase price.

As more and more customers change to JIT inventory systems and automated production processes, the receipt of defective goods poses greater and greater problems for them. Sometimes a defective CD player causes them to

	PREDICTED SALES VOLUME IN UNITS WITHOUT QUALITY CONTROL PROGRAM	PREDICTED SALES VOLUME IN UNITS WITH QUALITY CONTOL PROGRAM
2001	50,000	50,000
2002	45,000	50,000
2003	40,000	50,000
2004	35,000	50,000

delay their whole production line while the CD player is being replaced. Companies competing with Woolongong recognize this situation, and most have already begun extensive quality control programs. If Woolongong does no improve quality, sales volume is expected to fall by 5,000 CD players a year beginning in 2001.

The proposed quality control program has two elements. First, Woolongong would spend $900,000 immediately to train workers to recognize and correct defects at the time they occur. This is expected to cut the number of defective CD players produced from 2,000 to 500 without incurring additional manufacturing costs. Second, an earlier inspection point would replace the current inspection. This would require purchase of an x-ray machine at a cost of $200,000 plus additional annual operating costs of $50,000 more than the current inspection costs. Early detection of defects would reduce the average amount spent to correct defects from $85 to $50, and only 50 defective CD players would be shipped to customers. To compete, Woolongong would refund one-and-one-half times the purchase price ($315) for defective CD players delivered to customers.

Top management at Woolongong has decided that a four-year planning period is sufficient for analyzing this decision. The minimum required rate of return is 20 percent. For simplicity, assume that under the current quality control system, if the volume of production decreases, the number of defective CD players produced remains at 2,000. Also assume that all annual cash flows occur at the end of the relevant year.

Required: | Should Woolongong Manufacturing Company undertake the new quality control program? Explain, using the NPV model. Ignore income taxes.

C10-3 **FEASIBILITY ANALYSIS.**   (ICAO) Ydeeps Limited was incorporated under the Ontario Business Corporations Act four months ago. The owner of Ydeeps, Mr. M. Sadim, incorporated the company because he believed that he would be investing in an automobile repair franchise. After a delay, Mr. Sadim has been able to assemble the following information about the franchise opportunity:

1. For a payment of $32,000 per year, payable at the beginning of each year, the franchisee would be entitled to exclusive rights in a territory. The franchise rights are non-transferable. Except in unusual circumstances, the payments would be made for five years, and entitle the franchisee to one repair location. In addition to the annual franchise fee, the franchisee would be required to pay an annual royalty of 3 percent of gross revenue.

2. A site is available to construct a repair facility. The land would cost $250,000 and a suitable building would cost $400,000. The building would be capable of handling about $1,500,000 of revenue per year and would have a life of 40 years. A mortgage for about $500,000 could be placed on the property at an interest rate of 12 percent per annum.

3. At the end of 10 years, the repair building and land probably could be sold for $1,300,000 to $1,500,000.

4. The site that Mr. Sadim has an opportunity to invest in is in the middle of a busy region in which two taxi companies compete. Mr. Sadim believes that he would have little difficulty obtaining all of the repair work for one of the taxi companies that has 210 automobiles. Mr. Sadim believes that a two-year contract could be signed to generate revenue of $400,000 to $450,000 per year. In addition, Mr. Sadim believes that he has a good probability of obtaining the following repair revenue from different sources:

First year	$200,000 - $300,000
Thereafter, each year	$450,000 - $555,000

5. In order to generate repair revenue of $900,000 per year, Mr. Sadim believes that Ydeeps' annual expenses probably would be:

Repair parts and supplies	$420,000
Labour and benefits	225,000
Salary to Mr. Sadim (owner-manager)	60,000
Heat, light, water and similar expenses	25,000
Office supplies and other expenses	5,000
Amortization on building	10,000
Amortization on tools and equipment	20,000
Interest on bank loan of $200,000	28,000
Repair shop overhead (variable)	18,000
Mortgage payments	70,000
Royalty - 3% of revenue paid to franchiser	27,000
Advertising	10,000
Franchise payment	32,000

Most of the operating costs would be variable except for Mr. Sadim's salary, advertising, and the franchise fee.

6. The franchiser has provided the following estimates of the investment (except for land and building) that would be required to support a franchisee having repair revenue of roughly $1,000,000 per year:

Equipment and tools	$200,000
Receivables due from customers	150,000
Inventory on hand	60,000
Accounts payable	10,000

7. Mr. Sadim believes that he can obtain repair work of about $300,000 per year from a car rental company, if he gives them a 20 percent discount (from the $375,000 regular price). Variable costs of repairing these cars would be similar to that that would be encountered to earn

the $900,000 of revenue. Mr. Sadim believes that other contracts are possible if discounts are given.

Mr. Sadim would like a return on investment of 40 percent on any of the dollar investments that he personally makes. However, an overall required rate of return is estimated to be 22 percent.

Required: | Mr. Sadim has asked you to prepare a report on the feasibility of operating a repair franchise. If the franchise would not be feasible under the above conditions, explain if and how feasibility could be attained. Recommend what decisions he should make with respect to signing a contract to be a franchisee and to any other alternatives that exist. Income tax effects should be ignored.

C10-4 **CAPITAL PROJECT ANALYSIS.** (ICAO) Joan Staines is the controller of the Tage division of Canam Enterprises Ltd. William Chu, head of plant engineering, has just left Ms. Staines' office after presenting to her three alternatives for submission in the capital expenditure budget for the fiscal year 2002. The budget is due in Windsor in two days and therefore Joan realizes that time is of the essence.

Chu has outlined the following alternatives to replace an outdated milling machine: (1) build a general-purpose milling machine; (2) buy a special-purpose numerically controlled milling machine; (3) buy a general-purpose milling machine. Chu has stated that Tage does not have the expertise to build a numerically controlled milling machine.

Background

Canam Enterprises Ltd. is a well-established company. The company was set up about 25 years ago by brothers Al and Steve Jablonski, in Windsor, Ontario, to produce accessories for the automobile industry. The Alpha division continues to serve the auto industry, and is the largest division in the company with sales of $35 million annually. Al's son now heads this division. Steve is still active in the company and is the chief executive officer (CEO). His office is located in the Alpha division's Windsor factory.

The Monte division supplies seals to the mining and petrochemical industry from a plant in Toronto. This division is only 10 years old and until 1996 was highly profitable. As a result of the downturn in this sector of the economy, sales in 2000 were only $12 million.

The Tage division, located in Scarborough, is the engineering division. Regular product lines include industrial fans, industrial cooling units, and refrigeration units for industrial uses. The division is highly capital-intensive and sales tend to be directly related to general economic conditions.

Each division is run independently and performance is based upon budgeted return on investment. Bonuses are paid if the budget target is achieved. Annually, each division prepares a detailed budget submission to Steve, outlining expected profit performance and capital expenditure requests. The milling machine proposal is part of the capital expenditure request.

The 2001 pro forma income statement for Tage division is set out below:

Sales	$ 22,364,000
Cost of Goods Sold	14,760,240
Gross Profit	7,603,760
Selling and General Administrative Costs	3,578,240
Allocated Costs (based on sales)	1,677,300
	5,255,540
Income before income taxes	$ 2,348,220
Return on Sales	10.5%
Return on Investment	8.5%
Investment (historical cost)	$ 27,626,118

The Proposed Purchase

Chu has pointed out to Ms. Staines that the existing machine is not only out-dated but maintenance costs are becoming prohibitive. The machine has no market or salvage value and he is sure that its book value is now zero. The trouble is that he doesn't know which proposal is best for the company. In addition to the cost and revenue data provided in Exhibit 10A-1, Chu provided comments on each alternative.

1. Build a general-purpose machine.

    This machine can be built by the Tage Division. The division is below capacity at present as a major contract has just been completed. The division could thus produce the machine without affecting revenue producing activity, but it will take six months to complete. The machine is expected to last five years and have no salvage value because removal costs will probably equal selling price.

    Chu believes that the division has the technical expertise to undertake the work. In 2000, the division produced a specialized drilling machine that has proven very successful. Chu pointed out that David Williams, chief engineer, loves the design challenge of new machines.

    Ms. Staines sat down with Chu and produced the following cost estimates:

Material and parts	$ 55,000
Direct labour (DL$)	90,000
Variable overhead (50% of DL$)	45,000
Fixed overhead (25% of DL$)	22,500
	$212,500

    Ms. Staines argues that this job should also bear a proportion of administrative costs; she suggests $12,000.

2. Buy a special-purpose machine.

    The advantage of the special-purpose machine is that only one operator is required and output per hour could increase by 25 percent. In addition, maintenance costs are significantly reduced because microchip circuitry is employed.

    Chu points out that this machine is state-of-the-art and would probably mean that new work could be taken on. A numerically controlled machine requires extensive training of operators. In total, 26 weeks are spent in the supplier's factory located in Minneapolis. While the training is going on, the supplier provides an operator to work the machine without charge. Expected costs of this training period including hotel, per diem, and travel will cost $3,000 per week, excluding operator's labour.

The machine costs $625,000, and the supplier guarantees the salvage value of $25,000 at the end of five years. It is available immediately.

3. Buy a general-purpose machine.

The purchase price of this machine is $295,000 and cost levels associated with the machine are expected to be the same as the general-purpose machine built by the company because the technology is similar. The salvage value of the machine net of removal costs, is estimated to be $5,000 in five years. It can be delivered immediately.

General Comments

The required rate of return for this investment class has been set at 8 percent by Steve Jablonski.

Required: | Prepare a budget submission to Mr. Steve Jablonski, CEO, outlining the qualitative and quantitative analysis required. Ignore income taxes. Outline the assumptions you have employed and your recommended course of actions.

EXHIBIT 10A-1

Cost and Revenue Data on an Annual Basis*

	GENERAL PURPOSE EQUIPMENT	SPECIAL PURPOSE
Supervisor	$20,000	$20,000
Operators - required	2	1
- wages and benefits	$15.00/hour	$15.00/hour
Insurance	$3,000	$5,000
Maintenance	$26,000	$12,000
Capacity (sales)	$195,000	$243,750
Direct Materials	$19,500	$19,500
Variable Overhead	50% of DL$	50% of DL$
Fixed Overhead (including dep'n)	25% of DL$	25% of DL$
Amortization Method	5 years straight line	5 years straight line

* assumes single-shift operation will continue

Capital Budgeting Decisions: Considering Taxes, Inflation, and Risk

LEARNING OBJECTIVES

After studying this chapter, you will be able to

1. Analyze the impact of income taxes on operating cash flows.

2. Analyze the effect of income taxes on capital cash flows and compute the after-tax net present values of projects.

3. Explain the after-tax effect on cash of trade-ins and disposals of assets.

4. Compute the impact of inflation on a capital-budgeting project.

5. Assess the risk in evaluating capital projects.

Nearly all economic decisions affect taxes. As Benjamin Franklin said, "Nothing in this world is certain except death and taxes." Companies certainly recognize this truth as they write large tax cheques to the government. Annual tax bills for some major corporations exceed $1 billion. Income taxes are a significant cash flow and companies need to consider the tax effects when making capital-budgeting decisions. This chapter introduces tax considerations. However, the tax law is exceedingly complex, so qualified advice should be sought when the slightest doubt exists.

Inflation. The decline in the general purchasing power of the monetary unit.

Inflation is nearly as pervasive as taxes. **Inflation** is the decline in the general purchasing power of the monetary unit. For example, a dollar today will buy only half as much as it did in the late 1970s. Although inflation in Canada is well below the double-digit level of a decade or so ago, it still persists. Even a 5 percent annual rate results in a rise of more than 60 percent in average prices over 10 years. In countries such as Brazil and Argentina, triple-digit annual inflation rates (that is, average prices more than doubling each year) are commonplace. Therefore, inflation can greatly influence the cash-flow predictions used in capital-budgeting decisions.

INCOME TAXES AND CAPITAL BUDGETING

General Characteristics

Income taxes are cash disbursements. Income taxes can influence the *amount* and/or the *timing* of cash flows. Their basic role in capital budgeting is no different from that of any other cash disbursement. However, taxes tend to narrow the cash differences between projects.

The Canadian federal and provincial governments raise money through corporate income taxes. Income tax rates differ considerably, and thus, overall corporate income tax rates can vary widely.

Marginal Income Tax Rate. The tax rate paid on additional amounts of pre-tax income.

Income tax rates also depend on the amount of pre-tax income. Larger income is taxed at higher rates. In capital budgeting, the relevant rate is the **marginal income tax rate**, that is, the tax rate paid on additional amounts of pre-tax income. Suppose corporations pay income taxes of 15 percent on the first $50,000 of pre-tax income and 30 percent on pre-tax income over $50,000. What is the *marginal income tax rate* of a company with $75,000 of pre-tax income? It is 30 percent, because 30 percent of any *additional* income will be paid in taxes. In contrast, the company's *average income tax rate* is only 20 percent (i.e., 15 percent × $50,000 + 30 percent × $25,000 = $15,000 of taxes on $75,000 of pre-tax income). When we assess tax effects of capital-budgeting decisions, we will always use the *marginal* tax rate. Why? Because that is the rate applied to the additional cash flows generated by a proposed project.

Organizations that pay income taxes generally report two net incomes—one for reporting to the public and one for reporting to the tax authorities. This is not illegal or immoral; in fact, it is necessary. Tax reporting must follow detailed rules designed to achieve certain social goals. These rules do not lead to financial statements that best measure an organization's financial results and position, so it is more informative to financial-statement users if a separate set of rules is used for financial reporting. In this chapter we are concerned with effects on the cash outflows for taxes. Therefore we focus on the *tax reporting* rules, not those for public financial reporting.

Capital Budgeting for Information Technology

Recent surveys have shown that nearly all large companies use discounted-cash-flow (DCF) methods for their capital budgeting decisions. This is true in most of the developed countries in the world. But even as DCF is becoming dominant, it is being criticized by some for leading to overly cautious investment decisions in information technology (IT). Critics maintain that the benefits of IT investments are difficult to quantify and such investments often lead to unforeseen opportunities. By ignoring some of the potential benefits and opportunities, companies pass up desirable IT investments.

Two ways to rectify this situation have been recently suggested. Both use the basic tenets of DCF analysis but add degrees of sophistication to help identify and value all the benefits of IT investments: (1) use of activity-based costing (ABC) to better define and qualify the benefits of IT investments and (2) use of options pricing models to recognize the value of future options that result for IT investments.

Using ABC to better assess the benefits of an IT investment is simply a refinement measuring the cash flows for a DCF model. Scott Gamster of Grant Thornton's Performance Management Practice suggests that the capital budgeting analysis of IT investments often looks primarily at the direct costs and benefits and ignores many of the savings in indirect costs. Because an ABC system focuses on indirect costs, it can help identify other cost impacts of new IT systems. This attention to activities allows managers to better assess the various impacts on a new IT system. For example, an enterprise resource planning (ERP) system will transform much of the work in many company activities. Examining each activity in light of the potential implementation of an ERP will help managers assess the full impact of the new system.

The other suggestion is to use an options pricing theory for valuing IT investments. This is a refinement of DCF, not an alternative to it. It explicitly recognizes the future opportunities created by a current investment decision, and it uses the complete range of possible outcomes to determine a potential investment's value. It is not our purpose to describe options pricing models; we leave that to the finance textbooks. However, the essence of the models is the impact of the possible future options on the value of a current investment decision. For example, investment today may eliminate the option of making a similar investment in six months when more information is available. Or investment today may create an infrastructure that will allow additional investments in the future that would not be otherwise possible. Limiting or expanding future options by today's investment decision can certainly affect the desirability of the investment.

Criticisms of DCF models for IT investments should lead to refinements of DCF, not rejection of it. Of course, if refinements are not used, managers must use judgment regarding subjective impacts of the investment that are not measured in the DCF analysis

Source: Adapted from S. Gamster, "Using Activity Based Management to Justify ERP Implementations," *Journal of Cost Management* (September/October 1999), pp. 24–33; M. Benaroch and R.J. Kauffman, "A Case for Using Real Options Pricing Analysis to Evaluate Information Technology Project Investments," *Information systems Research* (March 1999), pp. 70–76; and G.C. Arnold and P.D. Aatzopoulos, "The Kingdom," *Journal of Business Finance and Accounting* (June/July 2000), pp. 603–626.

TAX IMPACT ON OPERATING CASH FLOWS

OBJECTIVE 1

Analyze the impact of income taxes on operating cash flows.

Recognizing the impact of income taxes on operating cash flows is straightforward. If a capital proposal results in annual savings of $60,000 and the company has a marginal tax rate of 40 percent, then the company's income taxes will increase by $24,000 ($60,000 × .40). Net annual after-tax savings of $36,000 results. This can be computed by deducting the $24,000 of extra income taxes from the pre-tax annual savings of $60,000. Conversely the $36,000 can be computed by multiplying the $60,000 by (1 minus the tax rate of 40 percent) or 60 percent.

If operating expenses increase by $250,000, and if the company has a 40 percent marginal tax rate, then a net after-tax cost of $150,000 results. The $150,000 is the net of the $100,000 in tax savings of $250,000 multiplied by 40 percent, and the $250,000. The $150,000 can also be computed by multiplying $250,000 by (1 minus the tax rate of 40 percent) or 60 percent.

Thus, to incorporate the impact of income taxes on operating cash flows poses no real difficulty. The difficulty occurs in the recognition of the tax effects of investment expenditures in capital equipment.

TAX IMPACT ON INVESTMENT CASH FLOWS

OBJECTIVE 2

Analyze the effect of income taxes on capital cash flows and compute the after-tax net present values of projects.

Capital Cost Allowance (CCA). A system for the deducting of the capital costs of acquired assets for the purpose of determining income taxes.

In financial reporting, the expenditure on capital equipment results in the recording of the asset and the related depreciation or amortization expense over the asset's useful economic life. Depreciation and amortization rates and policies are determined by the company's management and vary from company to company even for the same asset.

To apply a consistent set of regulations and to provide a means to implement government initiatives, the federal government has implemented its own system of **capital cost allowance (CCA)**. The Income Tax Act (ITA) does not permit a company to deduct amortization expense in determining taxable income but rather a company is allowed to deduct CCA. If you like, CCA is the income tax counterpart to financial reporting amortization.

Capital Cost Allowance—Declining Balance Classes

Federal Income Tax Act Collection
www.cica.ca/cica/
cicawebsite.nsf/
public/41120612

The ITA assigns all capital purchases to a CCA class. (Appendix 11 provides a list of some of the more commonly used CCA classes.) For example, a desk would qualify as a Class 8 asset that includes all furniture and fixtures. Class 8 has a predetermined rate of 20 percent declining balance capital cost allowance. Exhibit 11-1 depicts the calculation of CCA for a desk that costs $10,000.

A number of years ago, a company could deduct a full year's worth of CCA on any asset acquired during the year, as long as the company had been in business the entire year. Thus companies with a December 31 year-end would buy assets on or about December 31 and claim a full year's deduction even though the asset had not really been used to generate the income. To minimize this problem, the government implemented the so-called "half-year rule."

EXHIBIT 11-1

Capital Cost Allowance
Illustration

CCA - CLASS 8 RATE - 20% DECLINING BALANCE (ROUNDED TO THE NEAREST DOLLAR)			
Year 1 (Day 1) Addition	$10,000	Year 13 - UCC	$ 618
CCA - Year 1 (10%)	1,000	CCA - Year 14	124
Year (end) - UCC	9,000	Year 14 - UCC	494
CCA - Year 2 (20%)	1,800	CCA - Year 15	99
Year 2 - UCC	7,200	Year 15 - UCC	395
CCA - Year 3 (20%)	1,440	CCA - Year 16	79
Year 3 - UCC	5,760	Year 16 - UCC	316
CCA - Year 4	1,152	CCA - Year 17	63
Year 4 - UCC	4,608	Year 17 - UCC	253
CCA - Year 5	922	CCA - Year 18	51
Year 5 - UCC	3,686	Year 18 - UCC	202
CCA - Year 6	737	CCA - Year 19	40
Year 6 - UCC	2,949	Year 19 - UCC	162
CCA - Year 7	590	CCA - Year 20	32
Year 7 - UCC	2,359	Year 20 - UCC	130
CCA - Year 8	472	CCA - Year 21	26
Year 8 - UCC	1,887	Year 21 - UCC	104
CCA - Year 9	377	CCA - Year 22	21
Year 9 - UCC	1,510	Year 22 - UCC	83
CCA - Year 10	302	CCA - Year 23	17
Year 10 - UCC	1,208	Year 23 - UCC	66
CCA - Year 11	242	CCA - Year 24	13
Year 11 - UCC	966	Year 24 - UCC	53
CCA - Year 12	193	CCA - Year 25	11
Year 12 - UCC	773	Year 25 - UCC	42
CCA - Year 13	155		

Half-Year Rule. A requirement of the capital cost allowance system that treats all assets as if they were placed in service at the midpoint of the tax year.

Undepreciated Capital Cost (UCC). The balance in the pool of assets after deducting capital cost allowance.

The **half-year rule** assumes that all net additions are purchased in the middle of the year, and thus only one-half of the stated CCA rate is allowed in the first year. Thus in Year 1 of the example in Exhibit 11-1, the CCA is $1,000 or 1/2 times 20 percent multiplied by the $10,000 capital expenditure. This leaves a balance of $9,000 ($10,000 – $1,000), which is known as the **undepreciated capital cost (UCC)**.

In Year 2 and all succeeding years, the rate of 20 percent is applied to the UCC of the previous year. This results in a declining amount of capital cost allowance for each year. Even after the 25 years shown in Exhibit 11-1, a UCC of $42 remains and will require 15 more years to get to a zero balance (which in practice can only be obtained by rounding to the nearest dollar).

The CCA of each year is deducted in the calculation of a company's taxable income. Thus the CCA is not a cash flow. Rather we must multiply the CCA of each year by the company's marginal tax rate to calculate the actual tax savings in each year. In Chapter 10, we recognized the time value of money. Thus, to determine the present value of the tax savings, we would need to multiply the tax savings of each year by the present value factor from Table 1, p. 776, for each year at the company's required rate of return (say 10 percent).

This, as you could well imagine, would be a long and laborious task to perform for each capital proposal. An efficient way to calculate the present value of the tax savings is to use the following **tax shield formula**:

$$\begin{array}{c}\text{Present value} \\ \text{of tax savings}\end{array} = \left(\begin{array}{c}\text{Investment} \times \\ \text{Marginal} \\ \text{tax rate}\end{array}\right) \left(\dfrac{\text{CCA rate}}{\begin{array}{c}\text{CCA rate} + \text{required rate} \\ \text{of return}\end{array}}\right) \left(\dfrac{2 + \begin{array}{c}\text{required} \\ \text{rate of return}\end{array}}{2\left(\begin{array}{c}1 + \text{required} \\ \text{rate of return}\end{array}\right)}\right)$$

In the case of the $10,000 desk, the present value of the tax savings from deducting CCA, commonly referred to as the tax shield, is $2,548, computed as follows assuming a 10 percent required rate of return.

$$\text{tax shield} = (\$10,000 \times 40\%) \left(\frac{20\%}{20\% + 10\%}\right) \left(\frac{2 + 10\%}{2(1 + 10\%)}\right)$$

$$= \$4,000 \times .667 \text{ x } .955$$

$$= \$2,668 \times .955$$

$$= \$2,548$$

Therefore, the net after-tax cost of the desk is $7,452, or $10,000 less $2,548.

A detailed proof of the tax shield formula is not necessary for our purposes, but some explanation will be useful.

The first component of the formula, investment times the marginal tax rate, computes the total tax savings over the life of the asset from the CCA deduction. The $4,000, however, does not incorporate any time value of money considerations.

The second component, namely the CCA rate divided by the sum of the CCA rate plus the required rate of return, calculates the present values of all the annual tax savings assuming the half-year rule did not exist. This is important to note when residual values are discussed later in the chapter.

The third component incorporates an adjustment for the half-year rule. For example in the above scenario, the tax shield was reduced to 95.5 percent of the benefit that existed prior to the introduction of the half-year rule.

Capital Cost Allowance—Other Classes

Most CCA classes use the declining-balance method. However, occasionally the straight-line method is used in which the CCA is the same for each year, except for the first and last years, which have one-half of the CCA due to the half-year rule. For example, for patents, the CCA is computed on a straight-line basis over the legal life of the patent.

Another exception occurs where the CCA rate is varied year by year. For example, Class 39 upon its introduction allowed 40 percent in Year 1 (subject to the half-year rule), 35 percent in Year 2, and 30 percent in the remaining years. Thus the first two years need to be computed separately and then the tax shield formula could be applied to the UCC at the end of Year 2.

Trade-ins and Disposals of Capital Assets

OBJECTIVE 3

Explain the after-tax effect on cash of trade-ins and disposals of assets.

In the case when a capital asset is traded in on another asset or is sold, we do not need to concern ourselves with the net tax book value of the asset.

Assume that a company's Class 8 UCC for all of its furniture and fixtures is $50,000 as shown in Exhibit 11-2, at the end of Year 3. Let us also assume that included in the $50,000 is the remaining UCC on the desk of $5,760.

If in Year 3 the desk was traded in on a new desk, where the price of the new desk is $12,000 and $4,000 was allowed as a trade-in, the CCA Class 8 would increase by $8,000. Note that the CCA system works on a pool basis, in that we are not concerned with the UCC of the specific desk being sold. Rather we are only concerned with the net cash flows. The UCC of the desk that existed prior to the disposal is only reduced by the amount of the cash received. Thus the actual amount of the UCC of the specific asset is irrelevant to the decision. In this example, the net capital expenditure of $8,000 is the relevant cash flow.

Continuing with the example in Exhibit 11-2, the CCA for Year 4 is $10,800. This is a combination of the CCA at the rate of 20 percent on the opening UCC of $50,000 ($10,000) and the CCA at the half-year rule rate of 10 percent on the net addition of $8,000 ($800).

Thus, as shown in Exhibit 11-3A, the net after-tax present value of the cost of the new desk is $5,962. This amount recognizes the fact that the tax shield of $2,038 on the net addition of $8,000 must recognize the half-year rule.

EXHIBIT 11-2

Trade-in of a Capital Asset

CCA CLASS 8	
UCC - Year 3	$50,000
Purchase	12,000
Less trade-in	(4,000)
	8,000
Revised UCC	58,000
Year 4 - CCA	
20% x 50,000	10,000
10% x 8,000	800
	10,800
UCC - Year 4	$47,200

EXHIBIT 11-3

Net Capital Cash Flow of Trade-ins and Disposals

A: Trade-in:	Purchase price	$12,000
Trade-in	(4,000)	
Net cash payment	8,000	
Tax shield[1]	(2,038)	
NPV cash outflow	$5,962	
B: Sale: Selling Price	$4,000	
Lost tax shield[2]	(1,067)	
NPV cash inflow	$2,933	

[1] Includes the half-year adjustment

$$\left(\$8,000 \times 40\%\right) \times \left(\frac{20\%}{20\% + 10\%}\right) \times \left(\frac{2 + 10\%}{2(1 + 10\%)}\right) = \$2,038$$

[2] Excludes the half-year adjustment

$$(\$4,000 \times 40\%) \times \left(\frac{20\%}{20\% + 10\%}\right) = \$1,067$$

If, in the above scenario, a new desk had not been purchased but rather the old desk was sold for $4,000, the CCA would be 20 percent of $46,000 or $9,200. Note the half-year rule does not apply to disposals where no additions have occurred during the year.

From Exhibit 11-3B, we note that the sale of $4,000 reduces the future CCA and results in a lost tax shield of $1,067. Thus, the net after-tax present value of the sale is $2,933.

SIMPLIFYING ASSUMPTIONS

It is useful to note that a number of simplifying assumptions have been made when using the tax shield formula.

1. We have assumed that the company's marginal tax rate will remain the same, (at 40 percent in the above examples). Further, the above examples also assume that the company will have a taxable income each year.
2. While it is uncommon, governments can change the CCA rates that we have assumed to be constant.
3. We have also assumed that all CCA tax savings occur at the year-end. In reality, companies make monthly instalments. However, the additional cost of attempting to be more precise is not warranted, given the degree of uncertainty that already exists in the estimation of the cash flows.

INCOME TAX COMPLICATIONS

In the foregoing illustrations, we deliberately avoided many possible income tax complications. As all taxpaying citizens know, income taxes are affected by many intricacies, including progressive tax rates, loss carrybacks and carryforwards, varying provincial income taxes, capital gains, distinctions between capital assets and other assets, offsets of losses against related gains, exchanges of property of like kind, exempt income, and so forth.

Keep in mind that changes in the tax law occur each year. Always check the current tax law before calculating the tax consequences of a decision.

CONFUSION ABOUT AMORTIZATION

The meaning of amortization or depreciation and book value is widely misunderstood. Pause and consider their role in decisions. Suppose a bank has some printing equipment with a book value of $30,000, an expected terminal disposal value of zero, a current disposal value of $12,000, and a remaining useful life of three years. For simplicity, assume that straight-line amortization of $10,000 yearly will be taken.

In particular, note that the inputs to the decision model are the predicted income tax effects on cash. The book loss of $18,000 or the amortization of $10,000 may be necessary for making *predictions*. By themselves, however, they are not inputs to DCF decision models.

The following points summarize the role of amortization regarding the replacement of equipment:

1. *Initial investment.* The amount paid for (and, hence, amortization on) old equipment is irrelevant except for its effect on tax cash flows. In contrast, the amount paid for new equipment is relevant because it is an expected future cost that will not be incurred if replacement is rejected.
2. *Do not double-count.* The investment in equipment is a one-time outlay at time zero, so it should not be double-counted as an outlay in the form of amortization. Amortization by itself is irrelevant; it is not a cash outlay.

3. *Relation to income tax cash flows.* Relevant quantities were defined in Chapter 4, as expected future data that will differ among alternatives. Given this definition, book values and past amortization are irrelevant in all capital-budgeting decision models. The relevant item is the *income tax cash effect*, not the book value or the amortization. The book value and amortization are essential data for the *prediction method*, but the expected future income tax cash disbursements are the relevant data for the decision model.

SUMMARY PROBLEM FOR YOUR REVIEW

Problem One

Consider the following investment opportunity: original cost of computer, $125,000; five-year economic life; zero terminal salvage value; pre-tax annual cash inflow from operations, $60,000; income tax rate, 40 percent; required after-tax rate of return, 12 percent. Assume that the computer qualifies for CCA Class 10, which has a rate of 30 percent declining balance.

Calculate the net present value (NPV) of the investment.

Further, suppose the equipment was expected to be sold for $20,000 cash immediately after the end of Year 5. Compute the net present value of the investment.

Solution

Cash effects of operations		
$60,000 x (1 − .4) x 3.6048		$129,773
Cash effects of investment		
initial outlay	$125,000	
less tax shield	(33,725)*	91,275
Net present value		$ 38,498

$$*(\$125,000 \times 40\%) \left(\frac{30\%}{30\% + 12\%} \right) \left(\frac{2 + 12\%}{2(1 + 12\%)} \right)$$
$$= \$50,000 \times .71 \times .95 = \$33,725$$

Net present value (above)			$ 38,498
Cash proceeds of sale	$ 20,000		
Less lost tax shield	(5,680)+	14,320 × .5674 = $ 8,125
Net present value			$ 46,623

+($20,000 × 40%) × .71 = $5,680

CAPITAL BUDGETING AND INFLATION

Watch for Consistency

Inflation is the decline in the general purchasing power of the monetary unit. If significant inflation is expected over the life of a project, it should be specifically and consistently analyzed in a capital-budgeting model. Indeed, even a relatively

OBJECTIVE 4

Compute the impact of inflation on a capital-budgeting project.

small inflation rate, say, 3 percent, can have sizable cumulative effects over a number of years.

The key to appropriate consideration of inflation in capital budgeting is *consistent* treatment of the minimum desired rate of return and the predicted cash inflows and outflows. Such consistency can be achieved by including an element for inflation in both the minimum desired rate of return and in the cash inflow and outflow predictions:

Nominal Rates. Quoted market interest rates that include an inflation element.

1. Many firms base their minimum desired rate of return on market interest rates, also called **nominal rates**, that include an inflation element. For example, consider the three components of a 15 percent nominal rate (using assumed percentages):

(a)	Risk-free element—the "pure" rate of interest that is paid on long-term government bonds	6%
(b)	Business-risk element—the "risk" premium that is demanded for taking larger risks	5
(a) + (b)	Often called the "real rate"	11%
(c)	Inflation element—the premium demanded because of expected deterioration of the general purchasing power of the monetary unit	4
(a) + (b) + (c)	Often called the "nominal rate"	15%

Four percentage points out of the 15 percent return compensate an investor for receiving future payments in inflated dollars, that is, dollars with less purchasing power than those invested. Therefore, basing the minimum desired rate of return on quoted market rates automatically includes an inflation element in the rate.

2. Inflation affects many cash inflows and outflows. The predictions used in capital budgeting should include those inflation effects. For example, suppose 1,000 units of a product are expected to be sold in each of the next two years. Assume this year's price is $50 and inflation causes next year's price to be $52.50. This year's predicted cash inflow is 1,000 × $50 = $50,000 and next year's *inflation adjusted* cash inflow is 1,000 × $52.50 = $52,500.

Consider an illustration: the purchase of equipment with a useful life of five years; a pre-tax operating cash savings per year of $83,333 (in Year 0 dollars); and an income tax rate of 40 percent. The after-tax minimum desired rate, based on quoted market rates, is 25 percent. It includes an inflation factor of 10 percent.

Exhibit 11-4 (on page 493) displays correct and incorrect ways to analyze the effects of inflation. The key words are *internal consistency*. The correct analysis (1) uses a minimum desired rate that includes an element attributable to inflation and (2) explicitly adjusts the predicted operating cash flows for the effects of inflation. Note that the correct analysis biases in favour of purchasing the equipment, as the incorrect analysis has a lower net present value.

The analysis in Exhibit 11-4 is inherently inconsistent and thus is technically incorrect. The predicted cash inflows *exclude* adjustments for inflation. Instead, they are stated in Year 0 dollars. However, the discount rate *includes* an element attributable to inflation. Such an analytical flaw may induce an unwise refusal to purchase.

Another correct analysis of inflation uses "real" monetary units (real dollars) exclusively. To be internally consistent, the DCF model would use an inflation-free required rate of return and inflation-free operating cash flows. Using the numbers in Exhibit 11-4, the 25 percent minimum desired rate would be lowered to exclude the 10 percent expected inflation rate, the $50,000 operating cash savings in Year 0 dollars would be used in Year 1, Year 2, Year 3, and Year 4, and the tax savings due to amortization would be reduced to Year 0 dollars. Properly used, this type of analysis would lead to the same net present value as the analysis used in Exhibit 11-4. In this case, the inflation-free minimum desired rate, also called a *real* rate, would be calculated as follows: (1 + market rate) ÷ (1 + inflation rate) = (1 + inflation-free rate), or 1.25 ÷ 1.10 = 1.13636. The inflation-free rate is 1.13636 − 1 = 13.636%. The net present value can be calculated as follows:

(1) AFTER-TAX SAVINGS IN YEAR 0 DOLLARS	(2) PV FACTOR AT 13.636%	(3) PRESENT VALUE (1) X (2)
$50,000	.8800	$ 44,000
50,000	.7744	38,720
50,000	.6815	34,075
50,000	.5997	29,985
50,000	.5277	26,387
	Total present value =	$173,167

This analysis yields a net present value of $173,167, the same as in Exhibit 11-4.

EXHIBIT 11-4

Inflation and Capital Budgeting

DESCRIPTION END OF YEAR		AT 25%	
		PV FACTOR	PRESENT VALUE
Correct Analysis (Be sure the discount rate includes an element attributable to inflation and adjust the predicted cash flows for inflationary effects.)			
Cash operating inflows:			
Pre-tax inflow in Year 0 dollars	$83,333		
Income tax effect at 40%	33,333		
After-tax effect on cash	$50,000		
	Year 1: $55,000* × .8000		$ 44,000
	2: $60,500 × .6400		38,720
	3: $66,550 × .5120		34,074
	4: $73,205 × .4096		29,985
	5: $80,526 × .3277		26,388
			$173,167

* Each year is adjusted for anticipated inflation: $50,000 × 1.10, $50,000 × 1.10², $50,000 × 1.10³, and so on.

Incorrect Analysis (A common error is to include an inflation element in the discount rate as above, but not adjust the predicted cash inflows.)
Cash operating inflows after taxes of 5 years @ $50,000 × 2.6893 = $134,465

Improving Predictions and Feedback

The ability to forecast and cope with changing prices is a valuable management skill, especially when inflation is significant. In other words, price variances become more important. Auditing and feedback should help evaluate management's predictive skills.

The adjustment of the operating cash flows in Exhibit 11-4 uses a *general-price-level* index of 10 percent. However, where feasible use *specific* indexes or tailor-made predictions for price changes in materials, labour, and other items. These predictions may have different percentage changes from year to year.

Confederation Bridge
www.confederation
bridge.com

The Confederation Bridge Monitoring Project
www.pwgsc.gc.ca/rps/
confed/text/pg1e.htm

Confederation Centre of the Arts
www.confederation
centre.com

PERSPECTIVES ON PODM DECISION-MAKING

Investing in Bridges: Eastern Canada

The new bridge to Prince Edward Island is being billed as a wonder of the modern world, but for anybody wondering how much it cost—keep guessing. The 13-kilometre Confederation Bridge opens to traffic on Saturday and Islanders are gearing up for a huge party to celebrate their connection to mainland Canada. The graceful, S-shaped bridge over the Northumberland Strait is an engineering marvel and one of the longest fixed links in the world.

Canadian taxpayers will start paying for it on Monday as the federal government begins the 35-year process of buying it from Strait Crossing Development Inc., the Calgary-based company that designed and built the bridge in a unique public-private partnership. Paul Giannelia, project director of Strait Crossing, told a news conference Thursday the total cost of the link is not the public's business. "The total cost of the project is something that is between ourselves and ourselves," Giannelia said. "It's our nickel and our risk."

Canadians are shouldering what amounts to a mortgage on the bridge with an annual payment of about $42 million. At the end of the 35 years, taxpayers will have paid out at least $1 billion. The company says it will make its profit on tolls. The tolls are flat rates for round trips: $35 for cars, $40 for recreational vehicles, $200 for buses, $14 for motorcycles and $50 for tractor-trailers. "With that toll revenue, we pay our bills and the remaining is our return on investment," Giannelia said. "Our profit is contingent on how many people use the bridge."

Strait Crossing and Ottawa had difficulty agreeing on tolls. Giannelia said the company originally wanted higher rates and settled for the current package with the provision that tolls can be increased annually to a limit of three-quarters the rate of inflation. There were cost overruns on the mega-project. But Giannelia would only say they were within "acceptable" limits.

When the project was launched in 1993, it was estimated construction would cost about $840 million. The company won't say how much it actually cost. But the fine points of financing weren't preoccupying officials and celebrants on Thursday as the hoopla began for Saturday's official opening. "This is the wonder of the modern world," enthused Island Premier Pat Binns. "With the loss of the railway, the cost of air transportation and an uncertain future for our ports, the highway is our primary link and that link just got stronger."

Islanders predict the bridge will forever change life on the tiny province famous for its rich, red earth and pristine, white-sand beaches. Only 135,000 people live on P.E.I., but the annual tourist population is expected to explode to over one million by the year 2000. "There are valuable qualities possessed by this beautiful land of bright soil, rolling hills, and dramatic seascapes that should never and will never change," said Curtis Barlow, director of the Confederation Centre for the Arts in Charlottetown. "What will change, however, is how the world views Canada's smallest province and how Canada's smallest province views the world."

Source: Chris Morris, "Bridge billed as wonder, but final bill will be secret," *Canadian Press Newswire,* May 29, 1997.

SENSITIVITY ANALYSIS AND ASSESSING RISK

Capital investments entail risk. Why? Because the actual cash inflows may differ from what was expected or predicted. When considering a capital-budgeting project, a manger should first determine the riskiness of the investment. Then the inputs to the capital-budgeting model should be adjusted to reflect the risk.

There are three common ways to recognize risk. They can be used alone or in combination:

1. Reduce individual expected cash inflows or increase expected cash outflows by an amount that depends on their riskiness.
2. Reduce the expected life of riskier projects.
3. Increase the minimum desired rate of return for riskier projects.

One method that helps identify the riskiness of a project is sensitivity analysis, a "what-if" technique that indicates how decisions would be affected by changes in the data. Another approach is to compare the results of different capital-budgeting models. A manager can compare the NPV and IRR results with those of simpler measures such as the payback period and accounting rate-of-return (discussed in Chapter 10).

C O M P A N Y (S) S T R A T E G I E S

THE USE OF RISK PREMIUMS—THE CASE OF THE ENERGY FROM WASTE PLANT

In 1982, an Environmental Assessment Hearing examined the feasibility of establishing an Energy from Waste Plant for use by Victoria Hospital in London, Ontario. The Energy from Waste Plant feasibility study involved a range of possible alternatives, each of which had the objective "to define a source of economic energy."

The alternatives ranged from remaining with conventional fuels such as natural gas, oil and electricity to an Energy from Waste Plant. The Energy from Waste Plant had the potential to incinerate both solid waste garbage and sewage sludge from the city to produce a substantial portion of the energy requirements of the hospital.

A hospital requires a continuous and dependable supply of energy for its operating rooms, heart-lung machines, monitoring equipment, etc. Thus, for Victoria Hospital, the decision regarding its source of energy was critical to its effective operations.

The Environmental Assessment Hearing's objectives were to examine the potential environmental concerns that may occur as a result of the operating of the Energy from Waste Plant. But first, prior to considering these environmental issues, it was necessary to establish that the alternatives were technically and financially viable. All the alternatives were found to be technically viable. In terms of financial viability, the Energy from Waste Plant was found to be financially viable using a net present value analysis, when compared to the conventional fuels alternative under many of the scenarios. The Environmental Assessment Hearing then proceeded to examine the many potential environmental concerns that were difficult to evaluate given that the Energy from Waste Plant involved the use of new technology.

Given the subjectivity of the ability to quantify the potential costs of these environmental concerns, another approach would have been to return to the net present value financial analysis and consider altering the discount factor to adjust for the increased risk associated with the uncertainty of using the new technology in the Energy from Waste Plant. In fact, depending upon the assumption used for future inflation rates, a risk

continued

premium of only two percentage points reversed the financial viability analysis to indicate that the conventional fuels alternative represented a lower cost alternative than the Energy from Waste Plant.

Incorporating risk differences into a capital project analysis can have a significant impact on the net present values, particularly in projects where the time span and risk differences are significant.

Source: This material has been summarized and adapted from "Energy from Waste Plant: Victoria Hospital Corporation, London, Ontario. Environment Assessment July 1982" as obtained from the London Public Library.

Sensitivity Analysis

Sensitivity analysis shows the financial consequences that would occur if actual cash inflows and outflows differed from those expected. It can be usefully applied whenever a decision requires predictions. It answers the question: "How will my net present value or internal rate of return be changed if my predictions of useful life or cash flows are inaccurate?"

We examine two types of sensitivity analysis: (1) comparing the optimistic, pessimistic, and most likely predictions and (2) determining the amount of deviation from expected values before a decision is changed.

1. Suppose the forecasts of annual cash inflow could range from the original cash outflow of $6,075 to a low of $1,700 to a high of $2,300 for four years. The pessimistic, most likely, and optimistic NPV predictions at 10 percent are

   Pessimistic: ($1,700 x 3.1699) − $6,075 = $5,389 − $6,075 = − $686
   Most likely: ($2,000 x 3.1699) − $6,075 = $6,340 − $6,075 = $ 265
   Optimistic: ($2,300 x 3.1699) − $6,075 = $7,291 − $6,075 = $1,216

   Although the expected NPV is $265, the actual NPV might turn out to be as low as −$686 or as high as $1,216.

2. A manager would reject a project if its expected NPV were negative. How far below $2,000 must the annual cash inflow drop before the NPV becomes negative? The cash inflow at the point where NPV = 0 is the "break-even" cash flow:

$$NPV = 0$$
$$(3.1699 \times \text{cash flow}) - \$6,075 = 0$$
$$\text{cash flow} = \$6,075 \div 3.1699$$
$$= \$1,916$$

   If the annual cash inflow is less than $1,916, the project should be rejected. Therefore annual cash inflows can drop only $2,000 − $1,916 = $84, or 4 percent, before the manager would change the decision. He or she must decide whether this margin of error is acceptable or whether undertaking the project represents too great a risk.

Sensitivity analysis can also be performed on the useful life prediction. Suppose three years is a pessimistic prediction and five years is optimistic. Using present-value factors from the third, fourth, and fifth rows of the 10 percent column of Table 2, the NPVs are

Pessimistic: (2.4869 x $2,000) – $6,075 = –$1,101
Most likely: (3.1699 x $2,000) – $6,075 = $ 265
Optimistic: (3.7908 x $2,000) – $6,075 = $1,507

If the useful life is even one year less than predicted, the investment will be undesirable.

Sensitivity analysis provides an immediate financial measure of the consequences of possible errors in forecasting. Why is this useful? It helps to identify decisions that may be readily affected by prediction errors. It may be most worthwhile to gather additional information about cash flows or useful life for such decisions.

Adjusting the Required Rate of Return

An alternative to sensitivity analysis to assess the risk of a project is to increase the minimum desired rate of return. In the above breakdown of the three components of a 15 percent nominal rate (p. 492), a risk premium of five percentage points was included. If a company was considering a project with varying degrees of riskiness, the riskiness could be assessed by adjusting the required rate of return.

For example, if annual cash inflows are estimated at $2,000 for four years, a risk premium could be added to the minimum required rate of return as follows, using 10 percent for normal risk and 14 percent for higher risk.

normal risk ($2,000 × 3.1699) – $6,075 = $ 265
higher risk ($2,000 × 2.9137) – $6,075 = $(248)

The NPV is reduced from a positive $265 to a negative $248 after incorporating a risk premium of four additional percentage points.

The following table indicates that most Canadian companies perform subjective adjustments of risk, no doubt by means of varying degrees of sensitivity analysis.[1]

RISK-ADJUSTMENT TECHNIQUES		
TECHNIQUE	2000	2005
No adjustment is made	13%	1%
Adjustment is made subjectively	51	54
Shortened payback period	3	2
Risk-adjusted discount rate	2	2
Certainty equivalent approach	0	0
Two methods are used	12	15
Three methods are used	8	12
Four methods are used	2	2
Other methods	9	12
Total	100%	100%

---

[1] Reprinted from an article appearing in *CMA Management*, by J.D. Blazouske, I. Carlin, and S.H. Kim, "Current capital budgeting techniques in Canada," March 1988 issue, by permission of the Society of Management Accountants of Canada.

HIGHLIGHTS TO REMEMBER

Income taxes can have a significant effect on the desirability of an investment. An outlay for a depreciable asset results in two streams of cash: (a) inflows from operations plus (b) savings in income tax outflows. The after-tax impact of operating cash inflows is obtained by multiplying the inflows by one minus the tax rate. In contrast, savings in income taxes from writing off the depreciable cost on cash flows is obtained by using the tax shield formula.

The correct analysis in capital budgeting provides an internally consistent analysis of inflationary aspects. For example, the required rate of return should include an element attributable to anticipated inflation, and predicted operating cash flows should be adjusted for the effects of anticipated inflation.

Risk is present in almost all capital investments. Sensitivity analysis helps to assess the riskiness of a project. Increases in the minimum required rate of return can also be used to reflect the increased risk of a project.

SUMMARY PROBLEM FOR YOUR REVIEW

Problem One

Problem One appeared earlier in the chapter.

Problem Two

Examine the correct analysis in Exhibit 11-4. Suppose the cash operating inflows persisted for an extra year. Compute the present value of the inflow for the sixth year.

Solution

The cash operating inflow would be $50,000 × 1.7716, or $80,526 × 1.10, or $88,579. Its present value would be $88,579 × .2621, the factor from Table 1 (period 6 row, 25 percent column), or $23,217.

APPENDIX 11: SELECTED CCA CLASSES AND RATES

Class 1	(4%)	Buildings or other structures, including component parts acquired after 1987;
Class 3	(5%)	Buildings or other structures, including component parts acquired before 1988;
Class 8	(20%)	Miscellaneous tangible capital property and machinery or equipment not included in another class;
Class 9	(25%)	Electrical generating equipment, radar and radio equipment, acquired before 1976;
Class 10	(30%)	Automotive equipment and general-purpose electronic data processing equipment with its systems software;
Class 12	(100%)	Tools or utensils costing less than $200, video tape, certified feature films, computer software;
Class 14		Patent, franchise, concession or licence for a limited period (straight-line over legal life);
Class 29		Property used in manufacturing or processing acquired before 1988 (2 years straight-line);
Class 39		Property used in manufacturing or processing acquired after 1987 (1988 - 40%; 1989 - 35%; 1990 - 30%; after 1990 - 25%)

ACCOUNTING VOCABULARY

capital cost allowance (CCA) *p. 486*
half-year rule *p. 487*
inflation *p. 484*
marginal income tax rate *p. 484*

nominal rates *p. 492*
tax shield formula *p. 488*
undepreciated capital cost (UCC) *p. 487*

ASSIGNMENT MATERIAL

QUESTIONS

Q11-1 Distinguish between average and marginal tax rates.

Q11-2 "The government should pass a law forbidding corporations to keep two sets of books." Do you agree? Explain.

Q11-3 "An investment in equipment really buys two streams of cash." Do you agree? Explain.

Q11-4 Why should tax deductions be taken sooner rather than later?

Q11-5 What are the major influences on the present value of a tax deduction?

Q11-6 How much CCA is taken in the first year if a $10,000 asset is amortized on a 20 percent declining-balance schedule? How much in the second year?

Q11-7 What are the three components of market (nominal) interest rates?

Q11-8 Describe how internal consistency is achieved when considering inflation in a capital-budgeting model.

Q11-9 "Capital investments are always more profitable in inflationary times because the cash inflows from operations generally increase with inflation." Comment on this statement.

Q11-10 "We can't use sensitivity analysis because our cash-flow predictions are too inaccurate." Comment.

Q11-11 Name three ways to recognize risk in capital budgeting.

PROBLEMS

P11-1 CAPITAL COST ALLOWANCE AND PRESENT VALUES. The president of a software company is contemplating acquiring some computers used for designing software. The computers will cost $150,000 cash and will have zero terminal salvage value. The recovery period and useful life are both three years. Annual pre-tax cash savings from operations will be $75,000. The income tax rate is 40 percent, and the required after-tax rate of return is 16 percent.

1. Compute the net present value, assuming Class 10, 30 percent declining balance for tax purposes.
2. Suppose the required after-tax rate of return is 12 percent instead of 16 percent. Should the computers be acquired? Show computations.

P11-2 GAINS OR LOSSES ON DISPOSAL.   An asset with an accounting book value of $50,000 was sold for cash on January 1, 2001.

Assume two selling prices: $65,000 and $30,000. For each selling price, prepare a tabulation of the gain or loss, the effect on income taxes, and the total after-tax effect on cash. Assume the asset qualifies for Class 8, 20 percent declining balance and assume a required rate of return of 10 percent. The applicable income tax rate is 30 percent.

P11-3 TAX INCENTIVES FOR CAPITAL INVESTMENT.   Goladen Vineyards is a successful small winery. The owner, Gino Colucchio, is considering an additional line of business: selling wind-generated electricity to the local utility. Tax law requires power utilities to purchase windmill electricity. Gino could put windmills on his current land without disturbing the grape crop. A windmill generates 200,000 kilowatt-hours annually, and the utility would pay $.07 per kilowatt-hour. There are essentially no operating costs.

At the time Gino considered purchasing his first windmill, the cost was $100,000 per windmill. Initially he was discouraged and almost abandoned the idea. But then he learned about two government tax-credit programs that applied to investments in windmills. First, a general investment tax credit of 8 percent could be taken. That is, Goladen's federal income taxes could be immediately reduced by 8 percent of the cost of the windmill. In addition, windmills qualified for a "business energy credit" of 15 percent, reducing federal income taxes by another 15 percent of the cost.

Assume that a windmill's economic life is 20 years. Goladen's required rate of return is 14 percent after taxes, and the marginal income tax rate is 45 percent. Assume windmills qualify for a CCA rate of 25 percent declining balance.

1. Would Gino purchase a windmill without the tax credits? Calculate the net present value.
2. Would Gino purchase a windmill with the tax credits? Calculate the net present value.
3. What is the most that Gino would pay for a windmill, provided the tax credits are available?

P11-4 INCOME TAXES AND INCREMENTAL COSTS.   Yvette Thirdgill has a small sewing and tailoring shop in the basement of her home. She uses the single telephone line into the home for both business and personal calls. She estimates that 50 percent of the phone use is for business. Until 2001 she allocated the basic cost of the telephone line, $20 per month, between business and personal use and charged $10 per month for telephone services on her income statement submitted to the tax authorities.

Assume that beginning in 2001, Canada Customs and Revenue Agency rules that no portion of the first phone line into a residence is allowed as an expense for tax purposes. However, if a second line is installed and used strictly for business purposes, its total cost is allowed as an expense. The phone company charges $20 per month for a second line.

Thirdgill's marginal income tax rate is 40 percent.

1. Under the old tax law (in effect before 2001), how much extra per month (after tax effects) would Thirdgill have paid for a second phone line?

2. Under the new tax law (in effect beginning in 2001), how much extra per month (after tax effects) would Thirdgill pay for a second phone line?

3. How might the new tax law affect the demand for second phone lines?

P11-5 PRODUCT VERSUS PERIOD COSTS AND MINIMIZING TAXES. South Chemicals Corporation was adversely affected by a tax ruling that certain selling and administrative expenses must be treated as product costs instead of period costs for reporting to the tax authorities. (Recall that period costs are charged as expenses in the period they are incurred. Product costs are added to the inventory value of the products and are charged as expenses when the products are sold.)

South is a maker of wax compounds with annual sales of more than $15 million. The company keeps large inventories to be able to respond quickly to customer demands. Suppose in 2002 South's financial reporting system measured the revenue at $15 million, cost of goods sold (a product cost) at $10 million, and selling and administrative expenses (all period costs) at $3 million. Now suppose the tax ruling required $2 million of the $3 million selling and administrative costs to be product, not period, costs. (The remaining $1 million is still a period cost for tax reporting as well as financial reporting.) Of the $2 million additional product cost, $1.5 million was allocated to products that were sold and $.5 million to products remaining in inventory.

1. Compute 2002 income before taxes as reported in the financial statements issued to the public.

2. Compute 2002 income before taxes as reported in the statements prepared for the tax authorities.

P11-6 PRESENT VALUE OF AFTER-TAX CASH FLOWS. Tsumagari Company, an electronics company in Kobe, Japan, is planning to buy new equipment to produce a new product. Estimated data (monetary amounts are in thousands of Japanese yen) are:

Cash cost of new equipment now	¥400,000
Estimated life in years	10
Terminal salvage value	¥50,000
Incremental revenues per year	¥320,000
Incremental expenses per year other than amortization	¥165,000

Assume a 60 percent flat rate for income taxes. All revenues and expenses other than amortization will be received or paid in cash. Use a 14 percent discount rate. Assume a 10-year straight-line amortization for tax purposes. Also assume that the terminal salvage value will affect the amortization per year.

Compute:

1. Amortization expenses per year
2. Anticipated net income per year
3. Annual net cash flow
4. Payback period
5. Accounting rate of return on initial investment
6. Net present value

P11-7 INCOME TAXES AND DISPOSAL OF ASSETS. Assume that income tax rates are 30 percent and that the asset qualifies for a 25 percent declining balance, and the required rate of return is 10 percent.

1. The book value of an old machine is $20,000. It is to be sold for $8,000 cash. What is the effect of this decision on cash flows, after taxes?
2. The book value of an old machine is $20,000. It is to be sold for $30,000 cash. What is the effect on cash flows, after taxes, of this decision?

P11-8 PURCHASE OF EQUIPMENT. The Sea Pines Company is planning to spend $45,000 for modernized production equipment. It will replace equipment that has zero book value and no salvage value, although the old equipment would last another seven years.

The new equipment will save $13,500 in cash operating costs for each of the next seven years, at which time it will be sold for $4,000. A major overhaul costing $5,000 will occur at the end of the fourth year; the old equipment would require no such overhaul. The entire cost of the overhaul is deductible for tax purposes in the fourth year. The equipment is in Class 39 at a rate of 30 percent declining balance for tax purposes.

The minimum desired rate of return after taxes is 12 percent. The applicable income tax rate is 40 percent.

Compute the after-tax net present value. Is the new equipment a desirable investment?

P11-9 MINIMIZING TRANSPORTATION COSTS. The Luxon Company produces industrial and residential lighting fixtures at its manufacturing facility in Calgary. Shipment of company products to an eastern warehouse is presently handled by common carriers at a rate of $.25 per kilogram of fixtures (expressed in year-zero dollars). The warehouse is located 2,500 kilometres from Calgary.

The treasurer of Luxon Company is presently considering whether to purchase a truck for transporting products to the eastern warehouse. The following data on the truck are available:

Purchase price	$40,000
Useful life	5 years
Terminal residual value	Zero
Capacity of truck	10,000 kilogram
Cash costs of operating truck	$.90 per kilometre
	(expressed in year-one dollars)

Luxon believes that an investment in this truck is particularly attractive because of their successful negotiation with Retro Company to back-haul Retro's products from the warehouse to Calgary on every return trip from the warehouse. Retro has agreed to pay Luxon $2,400 per load of Retro's products hauled from the warehouse to Calgary for as many loads as Luxon can accommodate, up to and including 100 loads per year over the next five years.

The Luxon marketing manager has estimated that 500,000 kilograms of fixtures will have to be shipped to the eastern warehouse each year for the next five years. The truck will be fully loaded on each round trip.

Make the following assumptions:

a. Luxon requires a minimum 20 percent after-tax rate of return, which includes a 10 percent element attributable to inflation.
b. A 40 percent tax rate.
c. The truck qualifies for Class 10, 30 percent declining balance.
d. An inflation rate of 10 percent.

1. Should the truck be purchased? Show computations to support your answer.
2. What qualitative factors might influence your decision? Be specific.

P11-10   **INFLATION AND NONPROFIT INSTITUTIONS.**   The city of Bremerton is considering the purchase of a photocopying machine for $7,200 on December 31, 2002, useful life five years, and no residual value. The cash operating savings are expected to be $2,000 annually, measured in 2002 dollars.

The minimum desired rate is 14 percent, which includes an element attributable to anticipated inflation of 6 percent. (Remember that the city pays no income taxes.)

Use the 14 percent minimum desired rate for requirements 1 and 2:

1. Compute the net present value of the project without adjusting the cash operating savings for inflation.
2. Repeat requirement 1, adjusting the cash operating savings upward in accordance with the 6 percent inflation rate.
3. Compare your results in requirements 1 and 2. What generalization seems applicable about the analysis of inflation in capital budgeting?

P11-11   **SENSITIVITY OF CAPITAL BUDGETING TO INFLATION.**   G. Esteban, the president of a Toronto trucking company, is considering whether to invest $410,000 in new semiautomatic loading equipment that will last five years, have zero scrap value, and generate cash operating savings in labour usage of $160,000 annually, using 2001 prices and wage rates. It is December 31, 2001.

The minimum desired rate of return is 18 percent per year after taxes.

1. Compute the net present value of the project. Assume a 40 percent tax rate and that the truck qualifies for Class 10, 30 percent declining balance for tax purposes.
2. Esteban is wondering if the model in requirement 1 provides a correct analysis of the effects of inflation. She maintains that the 18 percent rate embodies an element attributable to anticipated inflation. For purposes of this analysis, she assumes that the existing rate of inflation, 10 percent annually, will persist over the next five years. Repeat requirement 1, adjusting the cash operating savings upward by using the 10 percent inflation rate.
3. Which analysis, the one in requirement 1 or 2, is correct? Why?

P11-12   **INFLATION AND CAPITAL BUDGETING.**   The head of the consulting division of a major firm has proposed investing $300,000 in personal computers for the staff. The useful life of the computers is five years. Computers qualify for Class 10, 30 percent declining balance. There is no terminal salvage value. Labour savings of $125,000 per year (in year-zero dollars) are expected from the purchase. The income tax rate is 45 percent, the after-tax required rate of return is 20 percent, which includes a 4 percent element attributable to inflation.

1. Compute the net present value of the computers. Use the nominal required rate of return and adjust the cash flows for inflation. (For example, year-one cash flow = 1.04 × year-zero cash flow.)
2. Compute the net present value of the computers using the nominal required rate of return without adjusting the cash flows for inflation.
3. Compare your answers in requirements 1 and 2. Which is correct? Would using the incorrect analysis generally lead to overinvestment or underinvestment? Explain.

P11-13 MAKE OR BUY AND REPLACEMENT OF EQUIPMENT.   Toyland Company was one of the original producers of "Transformers." An especially complex part of "Sect-a-con" needs special tools that are not useful for other products. These tools were purchased on November 16, 1998 for $200,000.

It is now July 1, 2002. The manager of the Transformer Division, Ramona Ruiz, is contemplating three alternatives. First, she could continue to produce "Sect-a-con" using the current tools; they will last another five years, at which time they would have zero terminal value. Second, she could sell the tools for $30,000 and purchase the parts from an outside supplier for $1.10 each. Third, she could replace the tools with new, more efficient tools costing $180,000.

Ruiz expects to produce 80,000 units of "Sect-a-con" in each of the next five years. Manufacturing costs for the part have been as follows, and no change in costs is expected:

Direct material	$ .38
Direct labour	.37
Variable overhead	.17
Fixed overhead*	.45
Total unit cost	$1.37

* Amortization accounts for two-thirds of the fixed overhead.

The balance is for other fixed overhead costs of the factory that require cash outlays, 60 percent of which would be saved if production of the parts were eliminated.

The outside supplier offered the $1.10 price as a once-only offer. It is unlikely such a low price would be available later. Toyland would also have to guarantee to purchase at least 70,000 parts for each of the next five years.

The new tools that are available would last for five years with a disposal value of $40,000 at the end of five years. Tools qualify for CCA at 30 percent declining balance for tax purposes. Straight-line amortization is used for book purposes. The sales representative selling the new tools stated, "The new tools will allow direct labour and variable overhead to be reduced by $.21 per unit." Ruiz thinks this estimate is accurate. However, she also knows that a higher quality of materials would be necessary with the new tools. She predicts the following costs with the new tools:

Direct material	$ .40
Direct labour	.25
Variable overhead	.08
Fixed overhead*	.60*
Total unit cost	$1.33

* The increase in fixed overhead is caused by amortization on the new tools.

The company has a 40 percent marginal tax rate and requires a 12 percent after-tax rate of return.

1. Calculate the net present value of each of the three alternatives. Recognize all applicable tax implications. Which alternative should Ruiz select?
2. What are some factors besides the net present value that should influence Ruiz's selection?

P11-14 SENSITIVITY ANALYSIS. Western Power is considering the replacement of an old billing system with new software that should save $5,000 per year in net cash operating costs. The old system has zero disposal value, but it could be used for the next 12 years. The estimated useful life of the new software is 12 years and it will cost $25,000.

1. What is the payback time?
2. Compute the internal rate of return.
3. Management is unsure about the useful life. What would be the internal rate of return if the useful life were (a) six years instead of 12, and (b) 20 years instead of 12?
4. Suppose the life will be 12 years, but the savings will be $3,000 per year instead of $5,000. What would be the rate of return?
5. Suppose the annual savings will be $4,000 for eight years. What would be the rate of return?

CASES

C11-1 CAPITAL BUDGETING. (CICA) Steve Hammer started his contracting business, Hammer Contractors (HC), six years ago and now owns three machines: a bulldozer, an excavator, and a front-end loader. His business is primarily excavating, landscaping, and moving earth. His sole proprietorship has a year-end of December 31. He employs three full-time people and his wife, Judy, does all the bookkeeping and office work on a part-time basis. HC has been quite successful. According to Judy's figures, the business earned $86,000 before amortization in 2001 after deducting $26,000 of "salary" paid to Steve.

Steve and Judy have no training in accounting or financial matters and have approached you, early in 2002, for assistance in deciding whether a new grader should be purchased.

Some of HC's jobs are obtained by sealed tender but others are from repeat customers who like Steve's reliability and ability to offer full service. Steve wants to extend this service by purchasing a grader in time for the spring construction season. He has made the following estimates about the new grader:

Cost of machine	$110,000
Useful life	10 years
Value at the end of 10 years	$ 20,000
Operating costs per hour:	
operator's wage	$ 14.00
fuel	16.00
on-job maintenance	8.00
	$ 38.00

Major repair expenses were predicted by his dealer to be $6,000 in Year four, $20,000 in Year six and $28,000 in Year nine. Insurance on the machine is expected to amount to $2,400 a year.

Steve estimates that on some jobs he can charge $60 per hour for use of this machine. However, other jobs are very competitive and he would like to know how low he can drop his price on the grader before he starts losing money.

Steve estimates about 2,000 hours use from the grader yearly.

Required: Draft a report to Steve Hammer that analyzes the issue and provides your recommendation. Assume a required rate of return of 10 percent, an income tax rate of 35 percent, and a capital cost allowance of 25 percent.

C11-2 CAPITAL BUDGETING. (CICA) Tube and Pipe Ltd. (T & P) was founded in the early seventies and its sales grew very rapidly until the beginning of the eighties. At that time, several competitors expanded their operations, and sales by T & P stabilized.

T & P uses substantial amounts of electricity in its manufacturing process. Therefore, the company had built a power plant that supplies all its electricity needs.

Annual consumption of electricity over the last two years has reached 9,300,000 kilowatt hours (KWH). The annual production cost of electricity was $492,000 as follows:

Fuel	$201,000
Other variable costs	195,000
Property tax	15,000
Manager of the power plant	51,000
Amortization	30,000
Total	$492,000

In June 2001, Regional Hydro Ltd. approached T & P with an offer to supply all of its electricity needs. Regional Hydro will guarantee the supply for the next 20 years, but each party has the option of cancelling the agreement after 10 years.

If T & P signs the contract, it can sell its own power plant for $180,000. The book value of the plant is currently $300,000. In June 2001, the remaining life of the generators in the plant is 20 years. At the end of the tenth year, the generators must be given a major overhaul that would cost $450,000.

According to the proposed agreement, Regional Hydro will transfer the necessary power from its main plant to a secondary station that T & P will build. The secondary station will cost $1,200,000, its estimated life is 20 years, and it will have no salvage value. The firm will receive a 5 percent rebate on the cost of the secondary station from the government. The secondary station will convert the electricity from alternating current into direct current that T & P requires. The cost of electricity will be 1.5 cents per KWH and T & P is required to purchase at least 8,000,000 KWH annually. The maximum amount of electricity it can purchase is 10,000,000 KWH per year. T & P will pay the secondary station operation expenses (excluding amortization) of $30,000 annually.

Management of T & P decided that if it sells its power plant, the manager will be transferred to another department in need of a manager. It estimated that a new manager for the department would cost the company $45,000 a year, but the salary of the manager of the power plant will not change if he is transferred to the other department. Other employees of the power plant will be dismissed (their salaries are included in the "other variable costs" figure above).

Required: For simplification, assume that the CCA rate is 6 percent (Class 2), and all capital assets are in the same class for income tax purposes. Also assume that the corporate tax rate is 40 percent.

Assume that the "after-tax" cost of capital is 12 percent. Prepare a report to the management of T & P advising them whether they should enter into the agreement with Regional Hydro.

C11-3   RELEVANT COST INVESTMENT ANALYSIS.   (ICAO) De Steur Plastics Limited (DPL) manufactures a wide range of household plastic products for kitchens and bathrooms. The company's products are sold primarily to large retailers, including department stores, discount chains, and grocery chains. One of DPL's products is a line of plastic dishware that is sold prepackaged as four-piece place settings. DPL sells the dishes to the retailers at $8 per set, and has in recent years been operating at or near the limited capacity of the equipment, which is approximately 500,000 sets per year.

The costs of producing the dishes have been determined by DPL's bookkeeper as follows:

Material	$2.00 per set
Direct labour	1.60
Factor overheads:	
Assignable variable	.60
Allocated fixed	.40
Equipment amortization	.15
Selling, delivery and administration	.20
Total cost per set	$4.95

The selling, delivery, and administration costs are those that are identifiable with the product, and are essentially variable.

The equipment used for the dishes is old and substantially amortized, and will have to be retired or replaced within the next two years. Its present book value is $130,000, although it would probably fetch only about $15,000 scrap value (or twice that on a trade-in). The equipment has no other uses within DPL.

A major grocery chain that is not a regular customer of DPL approaches the company in late 2001 and offered to buy 700,000 sets per year for at least four years to use in special promotions commencing the following June 2002. The additional sets would be identical to DPL's regular line, except that the packaging would bear the grocery chain's name and teddy bear logo. The chain proposes to buy the special sets for $5 per set. They would be priced in the stores at two-thirds the price of the regular line.

Since DPL does not presently have the capacity to produce the additional sets, they would have to buy additional dish-making capacity if the company decides to accept the order. Rather than supplement the current capacity, DPL proposes to retire the old equipment and to buy new equipment that has triple the capacity of the old. This would allow for possible expansion of the regular line as well as provide the capacity for both the regular and the special dishes.

The DPL plant manager estimates that if the new equipment is purchased, the greater efficiency of the machine would permit a 10 percent savings in material cost and 25 percent savings in labour cost. Amortization, however, would go from $.15 per set to $.40 per set, and there would also be the added cost of the interest on the loan to buy the new equipment. The bookkeeper has also pointed out that the fixed overhead allocation would increase because the allocation is based partially on the cost of the equipment in use. The estimated cost per set to produce the additional 700,000 sets is estimated as follows:

Material	$1.80
Direct labour	1.20
Factor overheads:	
Assignable variable	.50
Allocated fixed	.64
Equipment amortization	.40
Selling, delivery and administration	.10
Interest on loan	.41
Total per set	$5.05

The selling, delivery and administration cost is less per set on the special 700,000 set order, but the cost of servicing the regular line would not change. The interest cost is 12 percent per annum on the $2,400,000 loan that would be required to purchase the new equipment, divided by the 700,000 additional sets. The total cost of the new equipment is $3,000,000.

DPL's cost of capital is 14 percent after income tax. The new equipment would probably be purchased by means of a bank term loan with a five-year term, although DPL would also be willing to consider a long-term lease arrangement through its bank's leasing subsidiary. DPL's fiscal year ends on December 31.

Required:

Perform the necessary calculations to determine whether DPL should accept the offer for the 700,000 additional sets of dishes per year. Indicate what uncertainties exist and what qualitative factors are important in this decision.

Assume a 40 percent tax rate. The new equipment is in Class 39 for CCA. The CCA rate in Class 39 is 30 percent for 2002, dropping to 25 percent for 2003 and later years. The half-year rule applies.

C11-4 **CAPITAL BUDGETING AND INFLATION.** (BRAITHWAITE) In November 2001, Charles Bird, President of Bird Packaging Co., Guelph, Ontario, was trying to decide whether the company should purchase a new scoring-printing machine. The attraction of the new machine was that it would double capacity and also reduce labour costs. However, the relatively large capital outlay and the uncertainty of projected sales concerned Mr. Bird so he was anxious for a thorough and careful analysis of future cash flows.

Bird Packaging is a small firm, which caters to the packaging needs of small and medium-size firms within a 80-kilometre radius of Guelph, including the cities of Hamilton, Kitchener-Waterloo, and Mississauga. Bird Packaging was established about 10 years ago with first-year sales of $120,000. Sales in 2001 were projected to reach $1,900,000. The present workforce comprises 24 employees. Its operations includes cutting, folding, and printing boxes. Bird Packaging stresses service as its main selling point; this includes custom box sizes, printing, and fast delivery. According to Charles Bird, "If a prospective customer just wants boxes, we send him to Domtar or MacMillan-Bloedel." In effect, Bird Packaging has carved out a niche for itself, dealing with customers who require different types of services, along with the actual box.

Although Bird Packaging expected sales of $1.9 million in 2001, Mr. Bird estimated that the sales attributable to the present machine were only $400,000, since this represents its production capacity on a one-shift basis. If the new investment is not undertaken, this sales level would remain constant in real dollar terms, but would grow by the full inflation rate in nominal terms. If the new machine was purchased, Mr. Bird expected sales to increase by $400,000 in real terms, over the next five years but even he admitted that this outcome was far from certain.

Materials were approximately 55 percent of sales, and were expected to remain at the same percentage regardless of sales volume. Mr. Bird estimated that manufacturing overhead was presently 10.7 percent of sales, 80 percent of this overhead (.086 of sales) was fixed, and 20 percent (.021 of sales) was variable. Labour costs were considered 100 percent variable, and were expected to fall from 12 percent of sales to 10 percent of sales. This labour savings results from a decrease in time required for setup and an increase in speed of production runs. Fewer people would be needed to run the new machine at higher production rates.

Selling expenses were presently 10.7 percent of sales, of which 80 percent is fixed and 20 percent is variable (similar to manufacturing overhead). Administrative overhead was budgeted at $33,200 for 2001 and was considered by Mr. Bird to be totally fixed.

Bird Packaging was subject to the small business tax rate of 20 percent and was expected to qualify for this reduced rate over the life of the investment.

The new machine would cost $120,000 plus installation costs of $10,000. The company used five years as the expected life for all equipment purchases. Mr. Bird estimated that the new machine could be sold for $120,000 at the end of the five-year period. The salvage value was expected to remain the same as the purchase price because there are few technological advances in this type of machinery and any amortization on the machine would be offset by price increases due to inflation. The salvage value of the old machine was $17,000. Assume a capital cost allowance rate of 30 percent.

The minimum required rate of return for the firm was estimated between 15 and 20 percent, depending upon the expected future rate of inflation and interest costs selected.

The last federal budget predicted that inflation would peak at 6 percent in 2001 and would then fall continuously to between 3 and 5 percent in 2007.

Mr. Bird prided himself on the company's ability to fill orders much more quickly than competitors. The new machine would enable the company to improve its service in this area. The new machine would also provide a boost to the morale of Bird Packaging's employees, who would benefit from both the change and the increased ease of operation. Workers tended to identify with the company, so when production ran smoothly, job satisfaction was increased.

Required: | Should Mr. Bird buy the new machine?

C11-5 CAPITAL BUDGETING AND SENSITIVITY ANALYSIS. (SMAC) Lemont Electronics Limited (Lemont) is a Canadian public corporation that manufactures special electronic steering systems for various types of vehicles. Lemont's sales have grown steadily since it was incorporated. The draft financial statements for 2002, however, show a net income of $1,685,600, which is a decrease in profits for the first time (see Exhibit 11A-1).

Recently, Lemont was awarded a large contract with DOF Motor Company (DOF), a large North American automobile manufacturer. The contract is for 100,000 electronic steering systems, 40 percent to be delivered to DOF uniformly throughout 2003 and 60 percent to be delivered uniformly throughout 2004. In order to accommodate this contract, Lemont is required to make a capital investment of $5,000,000 for specialized manufacturing equipment. After two years, this equipment can be adapted to the regular production process. Net present value analysis indicates that investment in this equipment is worthwhile. However, Lemont has insufficient cash to pay for the equipment and, since it cannot lease the equipment and DOF is not prepared to advance any funds, Lemont's president decided to meet with the bank manager to arrange the necessary financing.

President: As you know, four years ago you helped to finance a replacement of all of Lemont's manufacturing equipment. Now, we've won a large contract with DOF, a large automobile manufacturer, but, to fill the order, we need to buy some special equipment. Will the bank finance the $5,000,000 we need for the special equipment?

Bank manager: I've seen your 2002 draft financial statements, which indicate that profits are down. Also, your cash position could be better. What are your total sales expectations for 2003?

President: The DOF contract is for $25,000,000 over two years, which is a good start. Other than that, I'm not sure since sales depend on what other contracts we win. Some new foreign competition has invaded the market by undercutting domestic manufacturers. We've had to cut our bids to a minimum in order to compete. That's why our profits dropped for 2002. This new competition is making it increasingly difficult to predict sales. There's simply no way to anticipate which contracts we'll win. All we can do is adjust our bidding policy to try to maximize capacity utilization.

Bank manager: Well, the bank will need a cash budget for at least 2003 before it will consider lending Lemont any more money.

President: The last time we prepared any kind of budget was for you four years ago. You saw how useless that was. Sales turned out to be lower and expenses higher than the budget. That's why we don't have any cash now to finance the new equipment. We even had to reduce dividends to $500,000 in 2002 in order to maintain our $200,000 minimum cash balance.

Bank manager: You'll just have to do your best to estimate sales. Are there any other major factors that would affect cash flow over the next few years?

President: Only a reasonable increase in fixed costs. Under the circumstances, we will continue to pay dividends of $500,000 annually until cash flow has improved. It is doubtful that sales will increase sufficiently to necessitate further capital expenditure other than the $5,000,000 that we need now.

Bank manager: If the loan is approved, the bank would prefer that it be repaid within two years at an interest rate of 12 percent per year payable at the end of each year. Next Monday, I'll expect to see a cash budget to support your loan request.

EXHIBIT 11A-1

Draft (Summarized)
2002 Financial
Statements
**LEMONT
ELECTRONICS
LIMITED**
Balance Sheet As At
December 31, 2002

ASSETS		
Current assets:		
Cash	$ 200,000	
Accounts receivable	10,000,000	
Inventory	10,000,000	$20,200,000
Fixed assets:		
Machinery and equipment	70,000,000	
Less accumulated amortization	(28,000,000)	42,000,000
Total assets		$62,200,000

LIABILITIES AND SHAREHOLDERS' EQUITY			
Current liabilities:			
Accounts payable			$ 2,736,000
Long-term liabilities:			
Bank loan payable (Note 1)			30,000,000
Shareholders' equity:			
Common shares		$12,500,000	
Retained earnings			
- Opening balance	$15,778,400		
- 2002 net income	1,685,600		
- 2002 dividends	(500,000)	16,964,000	29,464,000
Total liabilities and shareholders' equity			$62,200,000

**LEMONT
ELECTRONICS
LIMITED**
Operating Statement
For the Year Ended
December 31, 2002

Sales:		$60,000,000
Manufacturing cost of goods sold:		
Variable manufacturing cost	$30,000,000	
Machinery and equipment amortization	7,000,000	
Fixed manufacturing overhead	8,000,000	45,000,000
Gross margin		15,000,000
Expenses:		
Variable selling and administration expenses	4,200,000	
Interest expense (Note 1)	4,200,000	
Fixed selling and administration expenses	4,500,000	12,900,000
Income before taxes		2,100,000
Income taxes (Note 2)		414,400
Net income		$ 1,685,600

1. In January 1999, the bank loaned Lemont $50,000,000 to help finance replacement of its equipment. The terms of the loan stipulated that a payment of $5,000,000 plus interest be made at the end of each year for 10 years. The annual interest rate was set at 12 percent.
2. Income taxes were calculated as 40 percent times taxable income as follows:

Income before taxes	$2,100,000
Plus amortization	7,000,000
Less CCA (UCC of 40,320,000 × 20%)	8,064,000
Taxable income	1,036,000
Times tax rate	× .40
Income taxes	$ 414,400

The next day, the president asked Lemont's newly appointed controller for his advice on how best to finance the required equipment purchase. After being briefed on the president's meeting with the bank manager, the controller indicated that he would conduct a quick initial analysis and present his preliminary findings within 24 hours.

Back in his office, the controller decided that his initial analysis should consist of the following:

1. Preparation of a draft cash budget for 2003.
2. Analysis of Lemont's general financial planning and control system, and identification of alternatives for improvement.

The controller then gathered some data on which to base his cash budget (see Exhibit 11A-2).

Required: | As Lemont's newly appointed controller, what would you recommend?

EXHIBIT 11A-2

Underlying Data for
2003 Cash Budget

Sales:
  DOF contract, 2003, 40,000 units @ $250/unit = $10,000,000
  Other sales—The president estimated that sales for 2003, other than the DOF contract, would be as follows:

Low	$40,000,000
Most likely	$50,000,000
High	$60,000,000

Manufacturing cost of goods sold:
For all sales, including the DOF contract, the relationship of variable manufacturing cost of goods sold dollars to sales dollars is expected to be the same as for 2002.

If the new equipment is purchased, related fixed manufacturing overhead of $750,000 will be required in 2003. Fixed manufacturing overhead related to current operations for 2003 is expected to be 5 percent greater than for 2002.

Both the existing machinery and equipment and the new special equipment have useful lives of ten years and are amortized on a straight-line basis. The net disposal costs are expected to be zero. The CCA rate for all machinery and equipment owned by Lemont, including the new special equipment, is 20 percent declining balance.

Selling and administration expenses:
For all sales, including the DOF contract, the relationship of variable selling and administration expenses dollars to sales dollars is expected to be the same as for 2002.

If the DOF contract is accepted, related fixed selling and administration expenses of $300,000 will be required in 2003. Fixed selling and administrative expenses related to current operations for 2003 are expected to be 5 percent greater than for 2002.

Working capital:
Sales are made uniformly over the year and all customers, including DOF, pay 60 days after delivery. Lemont's policy is to maintain a minimum cash balance of $200,000 and inventory levels are expected to be maintained at the $10,000,000 level.

The average accounts payable balance will be maintained at 8 percent of the total variable costs (i.e., variable manufacturing, selling and administration costs) incurred during the year. All fixed costs are paid in the year they are incurred.

C11-6 **CAPITAL BUDGETING.** (CGAC) Calgary Pipefitters Ltd. (CPL) is considering the purchase of a new fabricating machine for $40,000. The new machine will replace an old machine that has a book value of $10,000 but can be sold for $7,500. The new machine has an estimated life of five years, after which it would have a salvage value of $5,000. The operating cost of the new machine is estimated at $12,500 per annum. This machine will be in Class 8 (with a 20 percent CCA rate), the firm's marginal tax rate is 30 percent, and the cost of capital is 15 percent.

As an alternative to the new machine, CPL could overhaul the existing machine at a cost of $25,000. With this overhaul, the machine will cost $15,000 per year to operate, will last for five years, and will have zero salvage value at the end of its life. The existing machine is in Class 8 and the firm expects to always have assets in this class.

The new machine may be leased at a cost of $12,000 per year payable in advance. The leasing company will not be responsible for any operating or maintenance costs. Alternatively, CPL can obtain a five-year loan at 10 percent from its bank to finance the new machine.

Should the new machine be acquired? Why?

The Master Budget

Planning is the key to good management. This is true for individuals, small family-owned companies, new high-technology companies, large corporations, government agencies, and nonprofit organizations. For example, most successful students, who earn good grades, finance their education, and finish their degrees in a reasonable amount of time, do so in part because they are able to plan their time, their work, and their recreation. These students are *budgeting* their scarce resources in order to make the best use of their time, money, and energy. Likewise, owners of successful small companies who survive and grow even in difficult economic times carefully plan or budget their inventory purchases and their expansion of facilities so that they do not overextend themselves financially but can still meet customers' needs.

High-technology firms are often started by highly intelligent scientists and engineers who have valuable product ideas, but the high-technology firms that thrive are those whose managers also have superior planning and budgeting skills. Coordinating the use of scarce resources in a large, diverse corporation is an extremely complex and vital activity. Budgeting in these large corporations takes place throughout the year. Taxpayers demand that governments plan for the effective use of their hard-earned dollars, so government budgeting is especially important in difficult economic times, when tax dollars could otherwise have been spent for private purposes. Non-profit organizations must develop more effective plans to achieve their objectives as they compete for scarce donations or grant monies. Not only are budgets critical to good planning in any endeavour, budgets are necessary for evaluation of performance. A **budget**—a formal, quantitative expression of plans (whether for an individual, business, or other organization)—provides a benchmark against which to measure actual performance.

Budget. A quantitative expression of a plan of action, and an aid to coordinating and implementing the plan.

As you will see in this chapter, a budget can be much more than a limit on expenditures. While government agencies too often use a budget merely as a limit on their spending, businesses and other organizations generally use budgets to focus on operating or financial problems early, so that managers can take steps to avoid or remedy the problems. Thus a budget is a tool that helps managers both *plan* and *control* operations. Advocates of budgeting maintain that the process of budgeting *forces a manager to become a better administrator and puts planning in the forefront of the manager's mind*. Indeed, failure to draw up, monitor, and adjust budgets to changing conditions is one of the primary reasons behind the collapse of many businesses.

In this chapter we will look at the uses and benefits and consider the construction of the master budget.

BUDGETS: WHAT THEY ARE AND HOW THEY BENEFIT THE ORGANIZATION

OBJECTIVE 1

Explain the major features and advantages of a master budget.

Another way to describe a budget is as a condensed business plan for the forthcoming year (more or less). Few investors or bank loan officers today will provide funds for the would-be entrepreneur without a credible business plan including a cash-flow budget. Similarly, within a firm, managers need budgets to guide them in allocating resources and maintaining control and to enable them to measure and reward progress.

Types of Budgets

Strategic Plan. A plan that sets the overall goals and objectives of the organization.

There are several different types of budgets used by organizations. The most forward-looking budget is the **strategic plan**, which sets the overall goals and objectives of the organization.

Some business analysts won't classify the strategic plan as an actual budget, though, because it does not deal with a specific time frame, and it does not produce forecasted financial statements. In any case, the strategic plan leads to **long-range planning**, which produces forecasted financial statements for 5- to 10-year periods. The financial statements are estimates of what management would like to see in the company's future financial statements.

Long-Range Planning. Producing forecasted financial statements for five- or ten-year periods.

Decisions made during long-range planning include addition or deletion of product lines, design and location of new plants, acquisitions of buildings and equipment, and other long-term commitments. Long-range plans are coordinated with **capital budgets**, which detail the planned expenditures for facilities, equipment, new products, and other long-term investments. Capital budgeting was covered in Chapters 10 and 11.

Capital Budgets. Budgets that detail the planned expenditures for facilities, equipment, new products, and other long-term investments.

Long-range plans and budgets give the company direction and goals for the future, while short-term plans and budgets guide day-to-day operations. Managers who pay attention to only short-term budgets will quickly lose sight of long-term goals. Similarly, managers who pay attention to only the long-term budget could wind up mismanaging day-to-day operations. There has to be a happy medium that allows managers to pay attention to their short-term budgets while still keeping an eye on long-term plans. The master budget is an extensive analysis of the first year of the long-range plan.

Master Budget. A budget that summarizes the planned activities of all subunits of an organization.

A **master budget** summarizes the planned activities of all subunits of an organization—sales, production, distribution, and finance. The master budget quantifies targets for sales, cost-driver activity, purchases, production, net income, and cash position, and any other objective that management specifies. It expresses these amounts in the form of forecasted financial statements and supporting operating schedules. These supporting schedules provide the information that is too highly detailed to appear in the actual financial statements. *Thus, the master budget is a periodic business plan that includes a coordinated set of detailed operating schedules and financial statements. It includes forecasts of sales, expenses, cash receipts and disbursements, and balance sheets.* Sometimes master budgets are also called **pro forma financial statements**, another term for forecasted financial statements. Management might prepare monthly budgets for the year or perhaps monthly budgets for only the first quarter and quarterly budgets for the three remaining quarters. The master budget is the most detailed budget that is coordinated across the whole organization, but individual managers also may prepare daily or weekly *task-oriented* budgets to help them carry out their particular functions and meet operating and financial goals.

Pro Forma Financial Statements. The planned financial statements based upon the planned activities in the master budget.

Continuous Budget (Rolling Budget). A common form of master budget that adds a month in the future as the month just ended is dropped.

Continuous budgets (rolling budgets) are a very common form of master budgets that add a month in the future as the month just ended is dropped. Continuous budgets compel managers to think specifically about the forthcoming 12 months and thus maintain a stable planning horizon. As they add a new twelfth month to a continuous budget, managers may update the other 11 months as well. Then they can compare actual monthly results with both the original plan and the most recently revised plan.

Components of the Master Budget

OBJECTIVE 2

Distinguish between operating and financial budgets.

The terms used to describe specific budget schedules vary from organization to organization. However, most master budgets have common elements. The usual master budget for a nonmanufacturing company has the following components:

A. Operating budget
   1. Sales budget (and other cost driver budgets as necessary)
   2. Purchases budget
   3. Cost of goods sold budget
   4. Operating expenses budget
   5. Budgeted income statement
B. Financial budget
   1. Capital budget
   2. Cash budget
   3. Budgeted balance sheet

Exhibit 12-1 presents a condensed diagram of the relationships among the various parts of a master budget for a nonmanufacturing company. In addition to these categories, manufacturing companies that maintain physical product inventories prepare ending inventory budgets and additional budgets for each type of resource activity (such as labour, materials, and factory overhead).

Operating Budget (Profit Plan). A major part of a master budget that focuses on the income statement and its support- ing schedules.

The two major parts of a master budget are the **operating budget** and the financial budget. The operating budget focuses on the income statement and its supporting schedules. Though sometimes called the **profit plan**, an operating

---

EXHIBIT 12-1

Preparation of Master Budget for a Nonmanufacturing Company

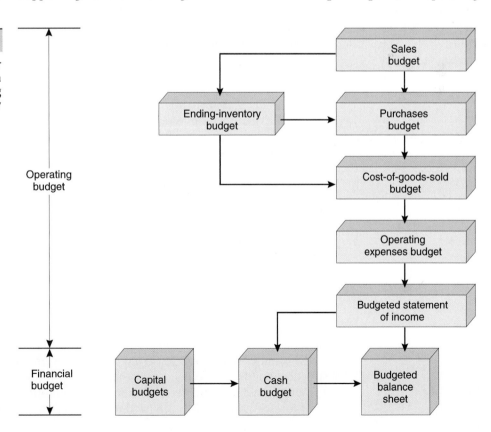

Financial Budget. The part of the master budget that focuses on the effects that the operating budget and other plans (such as capital budgets and repayments of debt) will have on cash flow and the balance sheet.

budget may show a budgeted *loss*, or even be used to budget expenses in an organization or agency with no sales revenues. In contrast, the **financial budget** focuses on the effects that the operating budget and other plans (such as capital budgets and repayments of debt) will have on cash.

In addition to the master budget, there are countless forms of special budgets and related reports. For example, a report might detail goals and objectives for improvements in quality or customer satisfaction during the budget period. This is particularly important if the firm uses non-financial performance measures as well as financial performance measures to evaluate executives.

Advantages of Budgets

OBJECTIVE 3

Identify a budget's major advantages to an organization.

W.R. Grace & Co.
www.grace.com

All managers do some kind of planning or budgeting. Sometimes plans and budgets are unwritten, especially in small organizations. Unwritten plans might work in a small organization but as an organization grows, informal, seat-of-the-pants planning is not enough. A more formal budgetary system becomes a necessity.

Sceptical managers have claimed, "I face too many uncertainties and complications to make budgeting worthwhile for me." Be wary of such claims. Planning and budgeting are especially important in uncertain environments. A budget allows *systematic rather than chaotic reaction to change.* For example, the Natural Resources Group of W.R. Grace & Co. greatly reduced a planned expansion in reaction to a worldwide abundance of oil and gas. A top executive quoted in the company's annual report stated that "management used the business planning process to adjust to changes in operating conditions."

Three major benefits of budgeting are that

1. It compels them to think ahead by formalizing their responsibilities for planning.
2. It provides definite expectations that are the best framework for judging subsequent performance.
3. It aids managers in coordinating their efforts, so that the objectives of the organization as a whole match the objectives of its parts.

Let's look more closely at each of these benefits.

Formalization of Planning

Budgeting forces managers to think ahead—to anticipate and prepare for changing conditions. The budgeting process makes planning an *explicit* management responsibility. Too often, managers operate from day to day, extinguishing one business brush fire after another. They simply have "no time" for any tough-minded thinking beyond the next day's problems. Planning takes a back seat to or is actually obliterated by daily pressures.

The trouble with the day-to-day approach to managing an organization is that objectives are never crystallized. Managers react to current events rather than plan for the future. To prepare a budget, a manager should set goals and objectives and establish policies to aid their achievement. The objectives are the destination points, and budgets are the roadmaps guiding us to those destinations. Without goals and objectives, company operations lack direction; problems are not foreseen; and results are hard to interpret afterward.

Framework for Judging Performance

Nexen Inc.
www.cdnoxy.com

Budgeted goals and performance are generally a better basis for judging actual results than past performance. The news that a company had sales of $100 million this year, as compared with $80 million the previous year, may or may not indicate that the company has been effective and has met company objectives. Perhaps sales should have been $110 million this year. Recognize as well that without the budget, the $110 million of potential sales would not even be assumed. The major drawback of using historical results for judging current performance is that inefficiencies may be concealed in the past performance. Intervening changes in economic conditions, technology, manoeuvres by competitors, personnel, and so forth also limit the usefulness of comparisons with the past.

COMPANY ⟨S⟩ STRATEGIES

BUDGETING AT CANADIAN OCCIDENTAL PETROLEUM LTD.

Canadian Occidental Petroleum Ltd. (CanadianOxy) is a diversified energy and chemicals company. With worldwide operations in the chemicals, oil and gas, and syncrude industries, CanadianOxy requires up-to-date information to manage its activities. Some of the highlights of its budget system are as follows:

(1) Economic parameters such as interest rates, foreign exchange rates, tax horizons, product prices, inflation, etc., are set at the beginning of the process.

(2) The primary divisions (chemical, oil and gas, syncrude, and corporate head office) prepare monthly budgets for one year. Capital projects are identified and segregated into high-risk, medium-risk, and low-risk categories.

(3) The divisional budgets are then assembled using the same reporting system that is used to generate the actual results.

(4) Management then reviews the assembled budget to identify areas of cost reduction, capital programs, levels of financing requirements, etc., with the objective of determining desired targets for cash generation, capital financing, and income.

(5) The final approved budget is then fixed and becomes the plan for the year.

(6) Using the annual budget as a base for year one, a long-range budget is prepared for five years and with a reasonable level of care for 15 to 20 years. These budgets are prepared using a PC-based software modelling package that has been designed for strategic and tax planning.

(7) Each month the entire company reexamines the annual budget. Each of the approximately 300 profit centres prepares a revised outlook, which is entered into the accounting budgeting and reporting system.

(8) The revised outlook and budget is then reported to each area with comparisons to actual results and previous-year results.

(9) Where it is needed, such as in the field estimating system, which forecasts weekly levels of oil and gas production, the budget system can accommodate budgets for shorter than one-month periods.

(10) During periods of rapid price changes for oil and gas, CanadianOxy has the potential to prepare revised budgets based upon the new prices. The revised budgets can be compiled and delivered overnight so that by the next day managers can respond to the new information. For example, following the Gulf Crisis, the decline in oil prices required that managers reexamine the capital and operating budgets to ensure that targets would be achieved despite the dramatic changes occurring within the industry.

Source: Written by John Patterson, vice president and controller, Canadian Occidental Petroleum Ltd.

Communication and Coordination

Budgets tell employees what is expected of them. Nobody likes to drift along, not knowing what "the boss" expects or hopes to achieve. A good budget process communicates from the top down and from the bottom up. Top management makes clear the goals and objectives of the organization in its budgetary directives to middle- and lower-level managers, and increasingly to all employees. Employees and lower-level managers then inform higher-level managers how they plan to achieve the goals and objectives.

Budgets also help managers coordinate objectives. For example, a budget forces purchasing personnel to integrate their plans with production requirements, while production managers use the sales budget and delivery schedule to help them anticipate and plan for the employees and physical facilities they will require. Similarly, financial officers use the sales budget, purchasing requirements, and so forth to anticipate the company's need for cash. Thus the budgetary process obliges managers to visualize the relationship of their department's activities to other departments, and to the company as a whole.

PREPARING THE MASTER BUDGET

Now that you know what budgets are and why they are important, we can return to Exhibit 12-1 and trace the preparation of the master components. *Follow each step carefully and completely*. Although the process may seem largely mechanical, remember that the master-budgeting process generates key decisions regarding pricing, product lines, capital expenditures, research and development, and personnel assignments. Therefore, the first draft of the budget leads to decisions that prompt subsequent drafts before a final budget is chosen. Because budget preparation is somewhat mechanical, many organizations use spreadsheet or modelling software to prepare and modify budget drafts. Appendix 12 discusses using personal computer spreadsheets for budgeting.

Description of Problem

To illustrate the budgeting process, we will use as an example The Cooking Hut Company (CHC), a local retailer of a wide variety of kitchen and dining-room items. The company rents a retail store in a mid-sized community near a large metropolitan area. CHC's management prepares a continuous budget to aid financial and operating decisions. For simplicity in this illustration, the planning horizon is only four months, April through July. In the past, sales have increased during this season. However, the company's collections have always lagged well behind its sales. As a result, the company has often found itself pressed to come up with the cash for purchases, employees wages, and other operating outlays. To help meet this cash squeeze, CHC has used short-term loans from local banks, paying them back when cash comes in. CHC plans to keep on using this system.

Exhibit 12-2 is the closing balance sheet for the fiscal year ending March 31, 2001. Sales in March were $40,000. Monthly sales are forecasted as follows:

April	$50,000
May	$80,000
June	$60,000
July	$50,000
August	$40,000

Management expects future sales collections to follow past experience: 60 percent of the sales should be in cash, and 40 percent on credit. All credit accounts are collected in the month following the sales. The $16,000 or accounts receivable on March 31 represents credit sales made in March (40 percent of $40,000). Uncollectible accounts are negligible and are to be ignored. Also ignore taxes for this illustration.

Because deliveries from suppliers and customer demands are uncertain, at the end of each month CHC wants to have on hand a basic inventory of items valued at $20,000 plus 80 percent of the expected cost of goods sold for the following month. The cost of merchandise sold averages 70 percent of sales. Therefore, the inventory on March 31 is $20,000 + .7(.8 × April sales of $50,000) = $20,000 + $28,000 = $48,000. The purchase terms available to CHC are net, 30 days. It pays for each month's purchases as follows: 50 percent during that month and 50 percent during the next month. Therefore, the accounts payable balance on March 31 is 50 percent of March's purchases, or $33,600 (as explained in step 1c) × .5 = $16,800.

CHC pays wages and commissions semi-monthly, half a month after they are earned. They are divided into two portions: monthly fixed wages of $2,500 and commissions, equal to 15 percent of sales, which we will assume are uniform throughout each month. Therefore, the March 31 balance of accrued wages and commissions payable is (.5 × $2,500) + .5(.15 × $40,000) = $1,250 + $3,000 = $4,250. CHC will pay this amount on April 15.

EXHIBIT 12-2

The Cooking Hut Company
Balance Sheet
March 31, 2001

ASSETS		
Current assets:		
Cash	$10,000	
Accounts receivable, net (.4 × March sales of $40,000)	16,000	
Merchandise inventory, $20,000 + .8 (.7 × April sales of $50,000)	48,000	
Unexpired insurance	1,800	$ 75,800
Plant assets:		
Equipment, fixtures, and other	$37,000	
Accumulated amortization	12,800	24,200
Total assets		$100,000

LIABILITIES AND OWNERS' EQUITY		
Current liabilities:		
Accounts payable (.5 × March purchases of $33,600)	$16,800	
Accrued wages and commissions payable ($1,250 + $3,000)	4,250	$ 21,050
Owners' equity		78,950
Total liabilities and owners' equity		$100,000

In addition to buying new fixtures for $3,000 cash in April, CHC's other monthly expenses are

Miscellaneous expenses	5% of sales, paid as incurred
Rent	$2000, paid as incurred
Insurance	$200 expiration per month
Amortization, including new fixtures	$500 per month

The company wants a minimum of $10,000 as a cash balance at the end of each month. To keep this simple, we will assume that CHC can borrow or repay loans in multiples of $1,000. Management plans to borrow no more cash than necessary and to repay as promptly as possible. Assume that borrowing takes place at the beginning and repayment at the end of the months in question. Interest is paid, under the terms of this credit arrangement, when the related loan is repaid. The interest rate is 18 percent per year.

Steps in Preparing the Master Budget

OBJECTIVE 4

Follow the principal steps in preparing a master budget.

The principal steps in preparing the master budget are:

Operating Budget:
1. Using the data given, prepare the following detailed schedules for each of the months of the planning horizon:
   a. Sales budget
   b. Cash collections from customers
   c. Purchases budget
   d. Disbursements for purchases
   e. Operating expense budget
   f. Disbursements for operating expenses
2. Using these schedules, prepare a budgeted income statement for the four months ending July 31, 2001 (Exhibit 12-3).

Financial Budget:
3. Using the data given and the supporting schedules, prepare the following forecasted financial statements:
   a. Capital budget
   b. Cash budget, including details of borrowings, repayments, and interest for each month of the planning horizon (Exhibit 12-4)
   c. Budgeted balance sheet as of July 31, 2001 (Exhibit 12-5)

You will need schedules a, c, and e to prepare the budgeted income statement (Exhibit 12-3), and schedules b, d, and f to prepare the cash budget (Exhibit 12-4).

Organizations with effective budget systems have specific guidelines for the steps and timing of budget preparation. Although the details differ, the guidelines invariably include the above steps. As we follow these steps to examine the schedules of this illustrative problem, *be sure that you understand the source of each figure in each schedule and budget.*

EXHIBIT 12-3

The Cooking Hut Company
Budgeted Income Statement for the Four Months Ended July 31, 2001

		DATA	SOURCE OF DATA
Sales		$240,000	Schedule a
Costs of goods sold		168,000	Schedule c
Gross margin		$ 72,000	
Operating Expenses:			
Wages and commissions	$46,000		Schedule e
Miscellaneous expenses	12,000		Schedule e
Rent	8,000		Schedule e
Insurance	800		Schedule e
Amortization	2,000	68,800	Schedule e
Income from operations		$ 3,200	
Interest Expense		675	Exhibit 12-4*
Net income		$ 2,525	

* For May, June, and July: $30 + $405 + $240 = $675.

EXHIBIT 12-4

The Cooking Hut Company
Cash Budget for the Four Months Ending July 31, 2001

	APRIL	MAY	JUNE	JULY
Cash balance, beginning	$10,000	$10,550	$10,970	$10,965
Cash receipts:				
Collections from customers (Schedule b)	46,000	68,000	68,000	54,000
w.* Total cash available for needs, before financing	56,000	78,550	78,970	64,965
Cash disbursements:				
Merchandise (Schedule d)	42,700	48,300	40,600	32,900
Operating expenses (Schedule f)	13,750	18,250	18,000	15,250
Fixtures purchase (given)	3,000	—	—	—
x. Total disbursements	59,450	66,550	58,600	48,150
y. Minimum cash balance desired	10,000	10,000	10,000	10,000
Total cash needed	69,450	76,550	68,600	58,150
Excess (deficiency) of total cash available over total cash needed before current financing (w − x − y)	(13,450)	2,000	10,370	6,815
Financing:				
Borrowings (at beginning)	14,000†			
Repayments (at ends)	—	(1,000)	(9,000)	(4,000)
Interest (at 18% per annum)††	—	(30)	(405)	(240)
z. Total cash increase (decrease) from financing	14,000	(1,030)	(9,405)	(4,240)
Cash balance, ending (w − x + z)	$10,550	$10,970	$10,965	$12,575

Note: Expired insurance and amortization do not entail cash outlays.

* Letters are keyed to the explanation in the text.

† Borrowings and repayments of principal are made in multiples of $1,000, at an interest rate of 18% per annum.

†† Interest computations: .18 × $1,000 × 2/12 = $30; .18 × $9,000 × 3/12 = $405; .18 × $4,000 × 4/12 = $240.

ASSETS

Current assets:		
Cash (Exhibit 12-4)	$12,575	
Accounts receivable (.40 x July sales of $50,000) (Schedule a)	20,000	
Merchandise inventory (Schedule c)	42,400	
Unexpired insurance ($1,800 old balance – $800 expired)	1,000	$ 75,975
Plant:		
Equipment, fixtures, and other ($37,000 + truck, $3,000)	$40,000	
Accumulated amortization ($12,800 + $2,000 amortization)	14,800	25,200
Total assets		$101,175

LIABILITIES AND OWNERS' EQUITY

Current liabilities:		
Accounts payable (.5 × July purchases of $29,400) (Schedule d)	$14,700	
Accrued wages and commissions payable (.5 × $10,000)		
(Schedule e)	5,000	$ 19,700
Owners' equity ($78,950 + $2,525 net income)		81,475
Total liabilities and owners' equity		$101,175

Note: Beginning balances were used as a start for the computations of unexpired insurance, plant, and owners' equity.

Step 1: Preparing the Operating Budget

OBJECTIVE 5

Use sales and other
cost drivers in
preparing budgets.

Step 1a: Sales budget

The sales budget (Schedule a in the following table) is the starting point for budgeting because inventory levels, purchases, and operating expenses are geared to the rate of sales activities (and other cost drivers not appropriate in this example). Accurate sales and cost-driver activity forecasting is essential to effective budgeting; sales forecasting is considered in a later section of this chapter. March sales are included in Schedule a because they affect cash collections in April. Trace the final column in Schedule a to the first row of Exhibit 12-3. In non-profit organizations, forecasts of revenue or some level of services are also the focal points for budgeting. Examples are patient revenues and government reimbursement expected by hospitals and donations expected by churches. If no revenues are generated, as in the case of municipal fire protection, a desired level of service is predetermined.

	MARCH	APRIL	MAY	JUNE	JULY	TOTAL APRIL-JULY
Schedule a: Sales Budget						
Credit sales, 40 percent	$16,000	$20,000	$32,000	$24,000	$20,000	
Plus cash sales, 60 percent	24,000	30,000	48,000	36,000	30,000	
Total sales	$40,000	$50,000	$80,000	$60,000	$50,000	$240,000
Schedule b: Cash Collections						
Cash sales this month		$30,000	$48,000	$36,000	$30,000	
Plus 100 percent of last month's credit sales		16,000	20,000	32,000	24,000	
Total collections		$46,000	$68,000	$68,000	$54,000	

Step 1b: Cash collections

It is easiest to prepare Schedule b, cash collections, at the same time as preparing the sales budget. Cash collections include the current month's cash sales plus the previous month's credit sales. We will use total collections in preparing the cash budget—see Exhibit 12-4.

Step 1c: Purchases budget

> **OBJECTIVE 6**
>
> Prepare the operating budget and supporting schedules.

After sales are budgeted, prepare the purchases budget (Schedule c). The total merchandise needed will be the sum of the desired ending inventory plus the amount needed to fulfill budgeted sales demand. The total need will be partially met by the beginning inventory but the remainder must come from planned purchases. These purchases are computed as follows:

budgeted purchases = desired ending inventory + cost of goods sold – beginning inventory

Trace the total purchases figure in the final column of Schedule c to the second row of Exhibit 12-3. (In many organizations, additional budgets would be prepared for other appropriate cost drivers as well.)

	MARCH	APRIL	MAY	JUNE	JULY	TOTAL
Schedule c: Purchases Budget						
Desired ending inventory	$48,000*	$64,800	$ 53,600	$48,000	$42,400	
Plus cost of goods sold	28,000†	35,000	56,000	42,000	35,000	$168,000
Total needed	$76,000	$99,800	$109,600	$90,000	$77,400	
Less beginning inventory	42,400#	48,000	64,800	53,600	48,000	
Purchases	$33,600	$51,800	$ 44,800	$36,400	$29,400	
Schedule d: Disbursements for Purchases						
50 percent of last month's purchases		$16,800	$ 25,900	$22,400	$18,200	
Plus 50 percent of this month's purchases		25,900	22,400	18,200	14,700	
		$42,700	$ 48,300	$40,600	$32,900	

* $20,000 + .8 × April cost of goods sold = $20,000 + .8($35,000) = $48,000
† .7 × March sales of $40,000 = $28,000; .7 × April sales of $50,000 = $35,000, and so on
# $20,000 + .8 × March cost of goods sold of $28,000 = $20,000 + $22,400 = $42,400.

Step 1d: Disbursements for purchases

Schedule d, disbursements for purchases, is based on the purchases budget. Disbursements include 50 percent of the current month's purchases and 50 percent of the previous month's purchases. We will use total disbursements in preparing the cash budget, Exhibit 12-4, for the financial budget.

Step 1e: Operating expense budget

The budgeting of operating expenses depends on several factors. Month-to-month fluctuations in sales volume and other cost-driver activities directly influence many operating expenses. Examples of expenses driven by sales volume include sales commissions and many delivery expenses. Other expenses are not influenced by sales or other cost-driver activity (such as, rent, insurance, depreciation, and salaries) within appropriate relevant ranges and are regarded as fixed. Trace the total operating expenses in the final column of Schedule e, which summarizes these expenses, to the budgeted income statement, Exhibit 12-3.

Step 1f: Disbursements for operating expenses

Disbursements for operating expenses are based on the operating expense budget. Disbursements include 50 percent of last month's and this month's wages and commissions, miscellaneous, and rent expenses. We will use the total of these disbursements in preparing the cash budget, Exhibit 12-4.

	MARCH	APRIL	MAY	JUNE	JULY	TOTAL
Schedule e: Operating Expense Budget						
Wages (fixed)	$2,500	$ 2,500	$ 2,500	$ 2,500	$ 2,500	
Commissions (15 percent						
of current months' sales	6,000	7,500	12,000	9,000	7,500	
Total wages and commissions	$8,500	$10,000	$14,500	$11,500	$10,000	$46,000
Miscellaneous expenses						
(5 percent of current sales)		$ 2,500	$ 4,000	$ 3,000	$ 2,500	$12,000
Rent (fixed)		2,000	2,000	2,000	2,000	8,000
Insurance (fixed)		200	200	200	200	800
Amortization (fixed)		500	500	500	500	2,000
Total Operating Expenses		$15,200	$21,200	$17,200	$15,200	$68,800
Schedule f: Disbursements for Operating Expenses						
Wages and Commissions:						
50 percent of last month's expenses		$ 4,250	$ 5,000	$ 7,250	$ 5,750	
50 percent of this month's expenses		5,000	7,250	5,750	5,000	
Total wages and commissions		$ 9,250	$12,250	$13,000	$10,750	
Miscellaneous expenses		2,500	4,000	3,000	2,500	
Rent		2,000	2,000	2,000	2,000	
Total disbursements		$13,750	$18,250	$18,000	$15,250	

Step 2: Preparing the Budgeted Income Statement

Steps 1a through 1f provide enough information to construct a budgeted income statement *from operations* (Exhibit 12-3). The income statement will be complete after addition of the interest expense, which is computed after the cash budget has been prepared. Budgeted income from operations is often a benchmark for judging management performance.

Step 3: Preparing the Financial Budget

OBJECTIVE 7

Prepare the financial budget.

The second major part of the master budget is the financial budget, which consists of the capital budget, cash budget, and ending balance sheet. In our illustration, the $3,000 purchase of new fixtures would be included in the capital budget.

Step 3a: Capital budget.

See Chapters 10 and 11.

Step 3b: Cash budget

Cash Budget. A statement of planned cash receipts and disbursements.

The **cash budget** is a statement of planned cash receipts and disbursements. The cash budget is heavily affected by the level of operations summarized in the budgeted income statement. The cash budget has the following major sections, where the letters w, x, y, and z refer to the lines in Exhibit 12-4 that summarize the effects of that section:

w. The *total cash available before financing* equals the beginning cash balance plus cash receipts. Cash receipts depend on collections from customers' accounts receivable and cash sales and on other operating income sources. Trace total collections from Schedule b to Exhibit 12-4.

x. *Cash disbursements for:*
1. purchases depend on the credit terms extended by suppliers and the bill-paying habits of the buyer (disbursements for merchandise from Schedule d should be traced to Exhibit 12-4)
2. payroll depends on wage, salary, and commission terms and on payroll dates (wages and commissions from Schedule f should be traced as part of Operating expenses to Exhibit 12-4)
3. some costs and expenses depend on contractual terms for installment payments, mortgage payments, rents, leases, and miscellaneous items (miscellaneous and rent from Schedule f should be traced as part of Operating expenses to Exhibit 12-4)
4. other disbursements include outlays for fixed assets, long-term investments, dividends, and the like (the $3,000 expenditure for new fixtures).

y. Management determines the *minimum cash balance desired* depending on the nature of the business and credit arrangements.

z. *Financing requirements* depend on how the *total cash available*, w in Exhibit 12-4, compares with the *total cash needed*. Needs include the disbursements, x, plus the desired ending cash balance, y. If the total cash available is less than the cash needed, borrowing is necessary (Exhibit 12-4 shows that CHC will borrow $14,000 in April to cover the planned *deficiency*). If there is an *excess*, loans may be repaid—$1,000, $9,000, and $4,000 are repaid in May, June, and July, respectively. The pertinent outlays for interest expenses are usually contained in this section of the cash budget. Trace the calculated interest expense to Exhibit 12-3.

The *ending cash balance* is w − x + z. Financing, z, has either a positive (borrowing) or a negative (repayment) effect on the cash balance. The illustrative cash budget shows the pattern of short-term, "self-liquidating" financing. Seasonal peaks often result in heavy drains on cash—for merchandise purchases and operating expenses—before the sales are made and cash is collected from customers. The resulting loan is "self-liquidating"—that is, the borrowed money is used to acquire merchandise for sale, and the proceeds from sales are used to repay the loan. This "working capital cycle" moves from cash to inventory to receivables and back to cash.

Cash budgets help management to avoid having unnecessary idle cash, on the one hand, and unnecessary cash deficiencies on the other. An astutely mapped financing program keeps cash balances from becoming too large or too small.

Step 3c: Preparing the Budgeted Balance Sheet

The final step in preparing the master budget is to construct the budget balance sheet (Exhibit 12-5) that projects each balance-sheet item in accordance with the business plan as expressed in the previous schedules. Specifically, the beginning balances at March 31 would be increased or decreased in light of the expected cash receipts and cash disbursements in Exhibit 12-4 and in light of the effects of noncash items appearing on the income statement in Exhibit 12-3. For example, unexpired insurance would decrease from its balance of $1,800 on March 31 to $1,000 on July 31, even though it is a noncash item.

When the complete master budget is formulated, management can consider all the major financial statements as a basis for changing the course of events. For example, the initial formulation of the financial statements may prompt management to try new sales strategies to generate more demand. Or management may explore the effects of various adjustments in the timing of receipts and disbursements. The large cash deficiency in April, for example, may lead to an emphasis on cash sales or an attempt to speed up collection of accounts receivable. In any event, the first draft of the master budget is rarely the final draft. As it is reworked, the budgeting process becomes an integral part of the management process itself—budgeting is planning and communicating.

PERSPECTIVES ON **PODM** DECISION-MAKING

The Budgeting Process at Daihatsu

Daihatsu Motor Company
www.ingway.co.jp/
~daihatsu

Daihatsu Motor Company is a Japanese-based mini-car manufacturer owned in part by Toyota. Daihatsu ranks seventh of the nine Japanese automakers in terms of their domestic sales volume. The annual budgeting process (short-term profit planning process) at Daihatsu is the first-year segment of the five-year long-range plan.

Each year, departments prepare six plans that are combined to form an operating profit budget. A brief description of these six plans follows.

Plan 1. Production, Distribution, and Sales Plan.
Plan 2. Projected Parts and Materials Costs.
Plan 3. Plant Rationalization Plan (projected reductions in variable costs).
Plan 4. Personnel Plan (direct labour and service department).
Plan 5. Facility Investment Plan (capital budget).

Plan 6. Fixed Expense Plan (design costs, maintenance costs, advertising, general and administrative costs).

The starting point for each plan is the actual cost performance of the previous year—*actual cost performance of the previous year is used as the* **standard** *for the coming year. The six plans are combined as follows:*

Sales Forecast   Plan 1
Less Expected Variable Costs (standards)
          Plan 1
Contribution Margin
Less Expected Changes in Variable Costs
          Plans 2 and 3
Adjusted Contribution Margin
Less Expected Fixed Costs
          Plans 4, 5, and 6
Budgeted Operating Profit

Source: Y. Monden and John Lee, "How a Japanese Auto Maker Reduces Costs," *Management Accounting* August 1993, pp. 22–26.

DIFFICULTIES OF SALES FORECASTING

OBJECTIVE 8

Understand the difficulties of sales forecasting.

Sales Forecast. A prediction of sales under a given set of conditions.

Sales Budget. The result of decisions to create conditions that will generate a desired level of sales.

As you have seen in the foregoing illustration, the sales budget is the foundation of the entire master budget. The accuracy of estimated purchases budgets, production schedules, and costs depends on the detail and accuracy (in dollars, units, and mix) of the budgeted sales.

Sales forecasting is a key to preparing the sales budget, but a forecast and a budget are not necessarily identical. A **sales forecast** is a *prediction* of sales under a given set of conditions. A **sales budget** is the result of *decisions* to create the conditions that will generate a *desired* level of sales. For example, you may have forecasts of sales at various levels of advertising. The forecast for the one level you decide to implement becomes the budget.

Sales forecasts are usually prepared under the direction of the top sales executive. Important factors considered by sales forecasters include:

1. *Past patterns of sales.* Past experience combined with detailed past sales by product line, geographic region, and type of customer can help predict future sales.
2. *Estimates made by the sales force.* A company's sales force is often the best source of information about the desires and plans of customers.
3. *General economic conditions.* Predictions for many economic indicators, such as gross domestic product and industrial production indexes (local and foreign), are published regularly. Knowledge of how sales relate to these indicators can aid sales forecasting.
4. *Competitors' actions.* Sales depend on the strength and actions of competitors. To forecast sales, a company should consider the likely strategies and reactions of competitors, such as changes in their prices, product quality, or services.
5. *Changes in the firm's prices.* Sales can be increased by decreasing prices, and vice versa. A company should consider the effects of price changes in customer demand.
6. *Changes in product mix.* Changing the mix of products can affect not only sales levels but also overall contribution margin. Identifying the most profitable products and devising methods to increase their sales is a key part of successful management.
7. *Market research studies.* Some companies hire market research experts to gather information about market conditions and customer preferences. Such information is useful to managers making sales forecasts and product mix decisions.
8. *Advertising and sales promotion plans.* Advertising and other promotional costs affect sales levels. A sales forecast should be based on anticipated effects of promotional activities.

Sales forecasting usually combines various techniques. In addition to the opinions of the sales staff, statistical analysis of correlations between sales and economic indicators (prepared by economists and members of the market research staff) provide valuable help. The opinions of line management also heavily influence the final sales forecasts. Ultimately, no matter how many technical experts are used in forecasting, the *sales budget* is the responsibility of line management.

Sales forecasting is still somewhat mystical, but its procedures are becoming more formalized and are being reviewed more seriously because of the intensity of global competitive pressures. Although this book does not include a detailed discussion of the preparation of the sales budget, the importance of an accurate sales forecast cannot be overstressed.

Governments and other non-profit organizations also face a problem similar to sales forecasting. For example, the budget for city revenues may depend on a variety of factors, such as predicted property taxes, traffic fines, parking fees, and licence fees. In turn, property taxes depend on the extent of new construction and, in most localities, general increases in real estate values. Thus, a municipal budget may require forecasting that is just as sophisticated as that required by a private firm.

COMPANY ⓒ STRATEGIES

LIQUOR CONTROL BOARD OF ONTARIO—THE ANNUAL FINANCIAL PLAN PROCESS

The Process The financial planning process at the LCBO is coordinated by the Financial Planning and Analysis department. This process involves sales planning, expense budgeting, capital expenditure budgeting and inventory planning, as well as planning for all other balance-sheet, income-statement and cash-flow items.

Liquor Control Board of Ontario
www.lcbo.com

Sales Plans Sales plans are prepared by both the Retail and Merchandising divisions. The retail sales plan is prepared on a total net sales by store basis by store managers and is approved by District Managers, Regional Directors and the Vice President of Retail. The Merchandising sales plan is prepared by Category Managers (Buyers). Approval for this plan comes from the Vice President of Merchandising. Financial Planning and Analysis ensures that the retail sales plan and merchandising store sales plan are in agreement for total net sales, cost of sales and gross margin.

Financial Planning and Analysis also works with the Distribution division to develop a sales plan for Specialty Services. This plan consists of sales, cost of sales and gross margin for both the Toronto Distribution Depot and Private Ordering operations. This plan is approved by the Vice President of Distribution.

Operating Expense and Capital Expenditure Budgeting Operating expense and capital expenditure guidelines for Head Office departments are prepared and distributed by Financial Planning and Analysis. The Retail division is responsible for preparing and distributing similar guidelines to the retail stores. Store expenditure plans are prepared by Store Managers and are then consolidated by the Retail division to the district, regional and divisional levels. Following approval, the operating and capital budgets are forwarded to Financial Planning and Analysis. Meanwhile, Financial Planning and Analysis provides expenditure planning assistance to all Head Office departments and consolidates all Head Office department operating and capital budgets to the divisional and corporate levels.

Inventory Plans Retail inventory plans are prepared by Financial Planning and Analysis. Warehouse inventory volume plans are prepared by the Category Managers. The warehouse inventory plan is approved by the Vice President of Merchandising.

Income Statement and Balance Sheet Plans Sales, expenditure and inventory plans provide the backbone for the Annual Financial Plan. However, to prepare comprehensive income statement and balance-sheet plans, additional planning information is required (e.g., accounts payable, other income details, etc.) Financial Planning and Analysis coordinates the preparation and consolidation of this additional information with the Controller's department and the Treasury Operations Department. The income statement and balance sheet are approved by the Vice President of Finance and the Executive Vice President before being presented to the Chair and the Board of Directors for final approval.

continued

The 2000-01 Annual Financial Plan Schedule

Task	Date	Responsible
Submit Economic Guidelines to Financial Planning	- November 17	Executive Vice President
Submit Human Resources Guidelines to Financial	- November 17	V.P. Human Resources
Distribute Head Office Budget Guidelines	- January 3	Financial Planning
Send Sales Forecast Worksheets to Merchandising	- January 19	Financial Planning
Finalize Current Year Sales Volume Forecast	- February 2	Merchandising
Submit Preliminary Expense, Capital & Staffing Plans	- February 2	Division Heads
Consolidate Preliminary Expense, Capital, Staffing Plans	- February 9	Financial Planning
Prepare Current Year Financial Statement Forecast	- February 9	Financial Planning
Submit Preliminary Sales and Inventory Plan	- February 9	Merchandising
Submit Preliminary Store Sales Plan	- February 9	Retail
Prepare Preliminary Annual Financial Plan (AFP)	- February 9	Financial Planning
Review Preliminary AFP	- February 14	Executive Vice President
Review Preliminary Sales and Inventory Plan	- February 14	Executive Vice President
Review Preliminary Capital & Staffing Plan	- February 14	Executive Vice President
Submit Final Sales and Inventory Plan	- March 1	Merchandising
Submit Final Expense, Capital & Staffing Plans	- March 8	Division Heads
Consolidate Final Expense, Capital & Staffing Plans	- March 15	Financial Planning
Submit Final Store Sales Plan	- March 15	Retail
Review Final AFP	- March 20	Executive Vice President
Review Final Sales and Inventory Plan	- March 20	Executive Vice President
Review Final Expense, Capital & Staffing	- March 20	Executive Vice President
Send AFP Submission for Approval to Board of Directors	- March 22	Financial Planning
Approve AFP	- March 29	Board of Directors
Prepare Year End Financial Statements	- April 27	Controller
Revise AFP Schedules to include Current Year Actuals	- May 14	Financial Planning
Send AFP Binder for Review to Board of Directors	- May 21	Financial Planning
Distribute Final AFP (Binders) to Management	- May 28	Financial Planning

Source: Jeff Pennock, Director, Financial Planning and Analysis, LCBO

MAKING A BUDGET WORK: ANTICIPATING HUMAN BEHAVIOUR

OBJECTIVE 9

Anticipate problems of human behaviour toward budgets.

No matter how accurate sales forecasts are, if budgets are to benefit an organization, they need the support of all the organization's employees. Lower-level workers and managers' attitudes toward budgets will be heavily influenced by the attitude of top management. But even with the support of top management, budgets—and the managers who implement them—can run into opposition.

Managers often compare actual results with budgets in evaluating subordinates. Few individuals are immediately ecstatic about techniques used to check their performance. Lower-level managers sometimes regard budgets as embodiments of restrictive, negative top-management attitudes. Accountants reinforce this view if they use a budget only to point out managers' failings. Such negative attitudes are even greater when the budget's primary purpose is to limit spending. For example, budgets are generally unpopular in government agencies where their only use is usually to request and authorize funding. To avoid negative attitudes toward budgets, accountants and top management must demonstrate how budgets can *help each manager and employee* achieve better results. Only then will the budget become a positive aid in motivating employees at all levels to work toward goals, set objectives, measure results accurately, and direct attention to the areas that need investigation.

Another serious human relations problem, which may preclude some of these benefits of budgeting, can result if budgets stress one set of performance goals, but employees and managers are rewarded for performance on other dimensions. For example, a budget may concentrate on current costs of production, but managers and employees may be rewarded based on quality of production and on timely delivery of products to customers. These dimensions of performance could be in direct conflict.

The overriding importance of the human aspects of budgeting cannot be overemphasized. Too often, top management and accountants are overly concerned with the mechanics of budgets, ignoring the fact that the effectiveness of any budgeting system depends directly on whether the affected managers and employees understand and accept the budget. Budgets formulated with the active participation of all affected employees are generally more effective than budgets imposed on subordinates. This involvement is usually called **participative budgeting**.

Participative Budgeting. Budgets formulated with the active participation of all affected employees.

FINANCIAL PLANNING MODELS

OBJECTIVE 10

Identify the uses of a financial planning model.

Financial Planning Models. Mathematical models of the master budget that can react to any set of assumptions about sales, costs, or product mix.

Because a well-made master budget considers all aspects of the company (the entire value chain), it serves as an effective model for decision making. For example, managers can use the master budget to predict how various decisions might affect the company in both the long and short run. Using the master budget in this way is a step-by-step process whereby tentative plans are revised as managers exchange views on various aspects of expected activities.

Today, most companies have developed **financial planning models**, mathematical models of the master budget that can react to any set of assumptions about sales, costs, product mix, and so on. For instance, Dow Chemical's model uses 140 separate, constantly revised cost inputs that are based on a number of different cost drivers.

By mathematically describing the relationships among all the operating and financial activities, and among the other major internal and external factors that can affect the results of management decisions, financial planning models allow managers to assess the predicted impacts of various alternatives before final decisions are selected. For example, a manager might want to predict the consequences of changing the mix of products offered for sale to emphasize several products with the highest prospects for growth. A financial planning model would provide budgeted operational and financial budgets well into the future under alternative assumptions about the product mix, sales levels, production constraints, quality levels, scheduling, and so on. Most importantly, managers can get answers to "what if" questions, such as "What if sales are ten percent below forecasts? What if material prices increase eight percent instead of four percent, as expected? What if the new union contract grants a six percent raise in consideration for productivity improvements?" Building models that can help answer "what if" questions is the subject of Appendix 12.

Financial planning models have shortened managers' reaction times dramatically. A revised plan for a large company that took many accountants many days to prepare by hand can be prepared in minutes.

Warning: The use of spreadsheet software on personal computers has put financial planning models within reach of even the smallest organizations. But the ready access to powerful modelling does not guarantee plausible or reliable results. Financial planning models are only as good as the assumptions and the inputs used to build and manipulate them—what computer specialists call GIGO (garbage-in, garbage-out). Nearly every chief financial officer has a horror story to tell about following bad advice from a faulty financial planning model.

HIGHLIGHTS TO REMEMBER

A budget is developed from an organization's objectives and outlines possible steps for achieving them. The budgetary process compels managers to think ahead and to prepare for changing conditions. Budgets are aids in planning, communicating, setting standards of performance, motivating personnel toward goals, measuring results, and directing attention to the areas that need investigation.

Master budgets typically cover relatively short periods of time—usually one month to a year. Long-range plans, however, may extend over a much longer time horizon, up to 10 years ahead. Because the future is uncertain, long-range plans focus on strategic considerations. The master budget is more detailed and offers specific guidance over the immediate budget period. Within the master budget are operating budgets, which detail resource requirements, and financial budgets, which are forecasted financial statements. The steps involved in preparing a master budget vary across organizations but follow the general outline given on page 522. Invariably, the first step is to forecast future sales or service levels, which can be quite difficult. The next step should be to forecast cost-driver activity levels, given expected sales and/or service. From these forecasts and knowledge of cost behaviour, collection patterns, and so on, the operating and financing budgets can be prepared.

One of the most crucial determinants of successful budgeting is how the organization includes and considers the people who are directly affected by the budget. Negative attitudes toward budgets usually prevent realization of many of the benefits of budgeting, and are usually caused by managers who use budgets to force behaviour or to punish substandard performance. Budgets generally are more useful when they are formulated with the willing participation of all affected parties.

Financial planning models are mathematical representations of the organization's master budget. Most large companies use financial planning models, and many small companies are beginning to use them. These models usually are prepared with computer spreadsheet software that allows powerful budget analysis and flexible planning (see Appendix 12).

SUMMARY PROBLEM FOR YOUR REVIEW

Do not attempt to solve this problem until you understand the *step-by-step* illustration in this chapter.

Problem

The Country Store is a retail outlet for a variety of hardware and homewares. The owner of the Country Store is anxious to prepare a budget for the next quarter, which is typically quite busy. She is most concerned with her cash position because she expects that she will have to borrow to finance purchases in anticipation of sales. She has gathered all the data necessary to prepare a simplified budget. Exhibit 12-6 shows these data in tabular form. Review the structure of the example in the chapter and then prepare the Country Store's master budget for the months of April, May, and June. The solution follows after the budget data. Note that there are a few minor differences between this example and the one in the chapter. These are identified in Exhibit 12-6 and in the solution. The primary difference is in the payment of interest on borrowing. Borrowing occurs at the beginning of a month when cash is needed. Repayments (if appropriate) occur at the end of a month when cash is available. Interest also is paid in cash at the end of the month at an annual rate of 12 percent on the amount of note payable outstanding during the previous month.

EXHIBIT 12-6

The Country Store
Budget Data Balance
Sheet as of
March 31, 2001

Assets:		
Cash	$	9,000
Accounts receivable		48,000
Inventory		12,600
Plant and equipment (net)		200,000
Total assets		$269,600
Liabilities and equities:		
Interest payable		0
Note payable		0
Accounts payable		18,300
Share capital		180,000
Retained earnings		71,300
Total liabilities and equities		$269,600

Budgeted expenses (per month):	
Wages and salaries	$ 7,500
Freight out as a % of sales	6%
Advertising	$ 6,000
Amortization	$ 2,000
Other expense as a % of sales	4%
Minimum inventory policy as a % of next month's cost of goods sold	30%
Equipment Purchase:	
April	$19,750
May	0
June	0

Budgeted Sales:	
March (actual)	$60,000
April	70,000
May	85,000
June	90,000
July	50,000

Required cash balance:	$ 8,000

Sales mix, cash/credit:	
Cash sales	20%
Credit sales (collected the following month)	80%
Gross profit rate	40%
Loan interest rate (interest paid in cash monthly)	12%
Inventory paid for in:	
Month purchased	50%
Month after purchase	50%
Dividends to be paid:	
April	$0
May	0
June	4,000

EXHIBIT 12-6 (cont'd)

SCHEDULE A: SALES BUDGET

	APRIL	MAY	JUNE	TOTAL
Credit sales, 80%	$56,000	$68,000	$72,000	$196,000
Cash sales, 20%	14,000	17,000	18,000	49,000
Total sales	$70,000	$85,000	$90,000	$245,000

SCHEDULE B: CASH COLLECTIONS

	APRIL	MAY	JUNE	TOTAL
Cash sales	$14,000	$17,000	$18,000	$ 49,000
Collection from prior month	48,000	56,000	68,000	172,000
Total collections	$62,000	$73,000	$86,000	$221,000

SCHEDULE C: PURCHASES BUDGET

	APRIL	MAY	JUNE	TOTAL
Desired ending inv.	$15,300	$16,200	$ 9,000	$ 40,500
Plus CGS	42,000	51,000	54,000	147,000
Total needed	$57,300	$67,200	$63,000	$187,500
Less beginning inv.	12,600	15,300	16,200	44,100
Total purchases	$44,700	$51,900	$46,800	$143,400

SCHEDULE D: CASH DISBURSEMENTS FOR PURCHASES

	APRIL	MAY	JUNE	TOTAL
For March*	$18,300			$ 18,300
For April	22,350	$22,350		44,700
For May		25,950	$25,950	51,900
For June			23,400	23,400
Total disbursements	$40,650	$48,300	$49,350	$138,300

* The amount payable from the previous month.

SCHEDULES E AND F: OPERATING EXPENSES AND DISBURSEMENTS FOR EXPENSES (EXCEPT INTEREST)

	APRIL	MAY	JUNE	TOTAL
Cash expenses:				
Salaries and wages	$ 7,500	$ 7,500	$ 7,500	$22,500
Freight-out	4,200	5,100	5,400	14,700
Advertising	6,000	6,000	6,000	18,000
Other expenses	2,800	3,400	3,600	9,800
Total disbursements for expenses	$20,500	$22,000	$22,500	$65,000
Noncash expenses:				
Amortization	2,000	2,000	2,000	6,000
Total expenses	$22,500	$24,000	$24,500	$71,000

The Country Store
Cash Budget
April-June, 2001

	APRIL	MAY	JUNE
Beginning cash balance	$ 9,000	$ 8,000	$ 8,000
Cash collections	62,000	73,000	86,000
Total cash available	71,000	81,000	94,000
Cash disbursements:			
Inventory purchases	40,650	48,300	49,350
Operating expenses	20,500	22,000	22,500
Equipment purchases	19,750	0	0
Dividends	0	0	4,000
Interest*	0	179	179
Total disbursements	80,900	70,479	76,029
Minimum cash balance	8,000	8,000	8,000
Total cash needed	$ 88,900	$78,479	$84,029
Cash excess (deficit)	$(17,900)	$ 2,521	$ 9,971
Financing:			
Borrowing†	17,900	0	0
Repayments	0	(2,521)	(9,971)
Total cash from financing	17,900	(2,521)	(9,971)
Ending cash balance	$ 8,000	$ 8,000	$ 8,000

* In this example interest is paid on the loan amounts outstanding during the previous month: May and June: $(0.12/12) \times \$17,900 = \$179$.
† In this example, borrowings are at the beginning of the month in the amounts needed. Repayments also are made at the end of the month as excess cash permits.

The Country Store
Budgeted Income
Statement
April-June, 2001

	APRIL	MAY	JUNE	APRIL-JUNE TOTAL
Sales	$70,000	$85,000	$90,000	$245,000
Cost of goods sold	42,000	51,000	54,000	147,000
Gross margin	28,000	34,000	36,000	98,000
Operating expenses:				
Salaries and wages	7,500	7,500	7,500	22,500
Freight-out	4,200	5,100	5,400	14,700
Advertising	6,000	6,000	6,000	18,000
Other	2,800	3,400	3,600	9,800
Interest*	179	179	154	512
Amortization	2,000	2,000	2,000	6,000
Total expense	$22,679	$24,179	$24,654	$ 71,512
Net operating income	$ 5,321	$ 9,821	$11,346	$ 26,488

* Note that interest expense is the monthly interest rate times the borrowed amount held for the month; April: $(0.12/12) \times \$17,900 = \$179$. Amount is accrued in the month incurred but paid in the following month.

ASSETS	APRIL	MAY	JUNE
Current: assets			
Cash	$ 8,000	$ 8,000	$ 8,000
Accounts receivable	56,000	68,000	72,000
Inventory	15,300	16,200	9,000
Total current assets	79,300	92,200	89,000
Plant, less accum. amort.†	217,750	215,750	213,750
Total assets	$297,050	$307,950	$302,750

LIABILITIES AND EQUITIES			
Liabilities:			
Accounts payable	$ 22,350	$ 25,950	$ 23,400
Interest payable	179	179	154
Notes payable	17,900	15,379	5,408
Total liabilities	40,429	41,508	28,962
Shareholders' equity:			
Capital stock	180,000	180,000	180,000
Retained earnings	76,621	86,442	93,788
Total equities	256,621	266,442	273,788
Total liabilities & equities	$297,050	$307,950	$302,750

* The June 30, 2001 balance sheet is the ending balance sheet for the entire three-month period.

† $200,000 + $19,750 - $2,000 = $217,750.

APPENDIX 12: USING SPREADSHEETS FOR BUDGETING

OBJECTIVE 11

Use a spreadsheet to develop a budget.

Spreadsheet software for personal computers is an extremely powerful and flexible tool for budgeting. An obvious advantage of the spreadsheet is that arithmetic errors are virtually non-existent. The real value of spreadsheets, however, is that they can be used to make a mathematical model (a financial planning model) of the organization. This model can be used repeatedly at very low cost and can be altered to reflect possible changes in expected sales, cost drivers, cost functions, and so on. The objective of this appendix is to illustrate *sensitivity analysis*—one aspect of the power and flexibility of spreadsheet software that has made this software an indispensable budgeting tool. It is necessary to emphasize that the assumptions underlying the spreadsheet first need a careful examination.

Recall the chapter's master budgeting example. Suppose CHC has prepared its master budget using spreadsheet software. In order to simplify making changes to the budget, the relevant forecasts and other budgeting details have been placed in Exhibit 12-7. Note that for simplification, only the data necessary for the purchases budget have been shown here. The full master budget would require a larger table with all the data given in the chapter. Each part of the table can be identified by its column and row intersection or "cell address." For example, the beginning inventory for the budget period can be located with the cell address "D4," which is shown as $48,000.

EXHIBIT 12-7

The Cooking Hut Company Budget Data

	A	B	C	D	E	F	G
1	BUDGET DATA						
2	Sales Forecasts		Other information				
3							
4	March (actual)	$40,000	Beginning inventory	$48,000			
5	April	50,000	Desired ending inventory: Base amount	$20,000			
6	May	80,000	plus percent of next				
7	June	60,000	month's cost of				
8	July	50,000	goods sold	80 percent			
9	August	40,000	Cost of goods sold				
10			as percent of sales	70 percent			

Column and Row labels are given by the spreadsheet.

EXHIBIT 12-8

The Cooking Hut Company
Purchases Budget Formulas

	A	B	C	D	E	F	G
11	SCHEDULE C						
12	Purchases budget			April	May	June	July
13	Desired ending inventory			=D5+D8* D10*B6	+D5+D8* D10*B7	+D5+D8* D10*B8	+D5+D8* D10*B9
14	Plus cost of goods sold			+D10*B5	+D10*B6	+D10*B7	+D10*B8
15							
16	Total needed			+D13+D14	+E13+E14	+F13+F14	+G13+G14
17	Less beginning inventory			+D4	+D13	+E13	+F13
18							
19	Purchases			+D16−D17	+E16−E17	+F16−F17	+G16−G17
20							

EXHIBIT 12-9

The Cooking Hut Company
Purchases Budget

	A	B	C	D	E	F	G
11	Schedule C:						
12	Purchases budget			April	May	June	July
13	Desired ending inventory			$64,800	$53,600	$48,000	$42,000
14	Plus cost of goods sold			35,000	56,000	42,000	35,000
15							
16	Total needed			99,800	109,600	90,000	77,000
17	Less beginning inventory			48,000	64,800	53,600	48,000
18							
19	Purchases			$51,800	$44,800	$36,400	$29,000
20							

By referencing the budget data's cell addresses, you can generate the purchases budget (Exhibit 12-9) within the same spreadsheet by entering *formulas* instead of numbers into the schedule. Consider Exhibit 12-8. Instead of typing $48,000 as April's beginning inventory in the purchases budget at cell D17, type a "formula" with the cell address for the beginning inventory from the preceding *table*, +D4 (the cell address preceded by a "+" sign—a spreadsheet rule to identify a formula (Lotus); some spreadsheets use "=" to indicate a formula (Excel)). Likewise, all the cells of the purchases budget will be composed of formulas containing cell addresses instead of numbers. The *total needed* in April (D16) is +D13 + D14, and purchases in April (D19) are budgeted to be +D16 − D17. The figures for May, June, and July are computed similarly within the respective columns. This approach gives the spreadsheet the most flexibility, because you could change any number in the budget data in Exhibit 12-7 (e.g., a sales forecast), and the software automatically recalculates the formulas in the entire purchases budget. Exhibit 12-8 shows the formulas used for the purchases budget. Exhibit 12-9 is the purchases budget displaying the numbers generated by the formulas in Exhibit 12-8.

Now, what if sales could be 10 percent higher than initially forecasted during April through August? What effect will this alternative forecast have on budgeted purchases? Even to revise this simple purchases budget would require a considerable number of manual recalculations. Merely changing the sales forecasts in spreadsheet Exhibit 12-7, however, results in a nearly instantaneous revision of the purchases budget. Exhibit 12-10 shows the alternative sales forecasts (in boldface type) and other, unchanged data along with the revised purchases budget. We could alter every piece of budget data in the table, and easily view or print out the effects on purchases.

EXHIBIT 12-10

The Cooking Hut Company
Purchases Budget

	A	B	C	D	E	F	G
1	BUDGET DATA						
2	Sales Forecasts		Other information				
3							
4	March (actual)	$40,000	Beginning inventory	$48,000			
5	April	55,000	Desired ending inv.	$20,000			
6	May	88,000	plus percent of next				
7	June	66,000	month's cost of				
8	July	55,000	goods sold	80 percent			
9	August	44,000	Cost of goods sold as				
10			a percent of sales	70 percent			
11	SCHEDULE C:						
12	Purchases Budget			APRIL	MAY	JUNE	JULY
13	Desired ending inventory			$ 69,280	$ 56,960	$50,800	$44,640
14	Cost of goods sold			38,500	61,600	46,200	38,500
15							
16	Total needed			107,780	118,560	97,000	83,140
17	Beginning inv.			48,000	69,280	56,960	50,800
18							
19	Purchases			$ 59,780	$ 49,280	$40,040	$32,340
20							

Sensitivity Analysis. The systematic varying of budget assumptions in order to determine the effects of each change on the budget.

This sort of analysis, assessing the effects of varying one of the budget inputs, up or down, is called *sensitivity analysis*. **Sensitivity analysis** for budgeting is the systematic varying of budget data input in order to determine the effects of each change on the budget. Such "what if" analysis is one of the most powerful uses of spreadsheets for financial planning models. Note, though, that it is generally not a good idea to vary more than one of the types of budget inputs at a time, unless they are obviously related, because doing so makes it difficult to isolate the effect of each change.

Every schedule, operating budget, and financial budget of the master budget can be prepared on the spreadsheet. Each schedule would be linked by the appropriate cell addresses just as the budget input data (Exhibit 12-7) are linked to the purchases budget (Exhibits 12-8 and 12-9). As in the purchases budget, ideally all cells in the master budget are formulas, not numbers. That way, every budget input can be the subject of sensitivity analysis, if desired, by simply changing the budget data in Exhibit 12-7.

Preparing the master budget on a spreadsheet the first time is time-consuming. After that, the time savings and planning capabilities through sensitivity analysis are enormous compared to a manual approach. However, a problem can occur if the master budget model is not well-documented when a person other than the author attempts to modify the spreadsheet model. Any assumptions that are made should be described either within the spreadsheet or in a separate budget preparation document.

ACCOUNTING VOCABULARY

budget *p. 515*

capital budgets *p. 516*

cash budget *p. 527*

continuous budget *p. 516*

financial budget *p. 518*

financial planning models *p. 532*

long-range planning *p. 516*

master budget *p. 516*

operating budget *p. 517*

participative budgeting *p. 532*

profit plan *p. 517*

pro forma financial statements *p. 516*

rolling budget *p. 516*

sales budget *p. 529*

sales forecast *p. 529*

sensitivity analysis *p. 541*

strategic plan *p. 516*

ASSIGNMENT MATERIAL

QUESTIONS

Q12-1 Is budgeting used primarily for scorekeeping, attention directing, or problem solving?

Q12-2 "Budgets are primarily a tool used to limit expenditures." Do you agree? Explain.

Q12-3 How do strategic planning, long-range planning, and budgeting differ?

Q12-4 "Capital budgets are plans for managing long-term debt and common shares." Do you agree? Explain.

Q12-5 "I oppose continuous budgets because they provide a moving target. Managers never know what to aim at." Discuss.

Q12-6 "Pro forma statements are those statements prepared in conjunction with continuous budgets." Do you agree? Explain.

Q12-7 Differentiate between an operating budget and a financial budget.

Q12-8 "Budgets are okay in relatively certain environments. But everything changes so quickly in the electronics industry that budgeting is a waste of time." Comment on this statement.

Q12-9 What are the major benefits of budgeting?

Q12-10 "Budgeting is an unnecessary burden on many managers. It takes time away from important day-to-day problems." Do you agree? Explain.

Q12-11 Why is budgeted performance better than past performance, as a basis for judging actual results?

Q12-12 Why is the sales forecast the starting point for budgeting?

Q12-13 Explain the relationship between the sales (or service) forecast and cost-driver activity.

Q12-14 Distinguish between operating expenses and disbursements for operating expenses.

Q12-15 What is the principal objective of a cash budget?

Q12-16 Differentiate between a sales forecast and a sales budget.

Q12-17 What factors influence the sales forecast?

Q12-18 "Education and salesmanship are key features of budgeting." Explain.

Q12-19 What are financial planning models?

Q12-20 Financial planning models guide managers through the budget process so that managers do not need to really understand budgeting." Do you agree? Explain.

Q12-21 "I cannot be bothered with setting up my monthly budget on a spreadsheet. It just takes too long to be worth the effort." Comment.

Q12-22 How do spreadsheets aid the application of sensitivity analysis?

PROBLEMS

P12-1 SALES BUDGET. Eckart's Runners Inc. has the following data:

- Accounts receivable, May 31: (.3 × May sales of $400,000) = $120,000.
- Monthly forecasted sales: June, $400,000; July, $440,000; August, $500,000; September, $530,000.

Sales consist of 70 percent cash and 30 percent credit. All credit accounts are collected in the month following the sales. Uncollectible accounts are negligible and may be ignored.

Prepare a sales budget schedule and a cash collections budget schedule for June, July, and August.

P12-2 SALES BUDGET. A Tokyo wholesaler was preparing its sales budget for the first quarter of 2002. Forecast sales are (in thousands of yen):

January	¥180,000
February	¥210,000
March	¥240,000

Sales are 20 percent cash and 80 percent on credit. Fifty percent of the credit accounts are collected in the month of sale, 40 percent in the month following the sale, and 10 percent in the following month. No uncollectible accounts are anticipated. Accounts receivable at the beginning of 2002 are ¥96 million (10 percent × November credit sales of ¥180 million and 50 percent of December credit sales of ¥156 million).

Prepare a schedule showing sales and cash collections for January, February, and March, 2002.

P12-3 CASH COLLECTION BUDGET. Pioneer Square Carpets has found that cash collections from customers tend to occur in the following pattern:

Collected within cash discount period in month of sale	50%
Collected within cash discount period in first month after month of sale	10
Collected after cash discount period in first month after month of sale	25
Collected after cash discount period in second month after month of sale	12
Never collected	3
Total sales in any month (before cash discounts)	100%
Cash discount allowable as a percentage of invoice price	1%

Compute the total cash budgeted to be collected in March if sales are predicted as $300,000 for January, $400,000 for February, and $450,000 for March.

P12-4 PURCHASE BUDGET. Fernandez Furniture Mart plans inventory levels (at cost) at the end of each month as follows:

May, $250,000; June, $220,000; July, $270,000; August, $250,000.

Sales are expected to be: June, $440,000; July, $350,000; August, $400,000. Cost of goods sold is 60 percent of sales.

Purchases in April were $250,000; in May, $180,000. A given month's purchases are paid as follows: 10 percent during that month; 80 percent the next month; and the final 10 percent the next month.

Prepare budget schedules for June, July, and August for purchases and for disbursements for purchases.

P12-5 PURCHASE BUDGET. The inventory of the Belfast Appliance Company was £200,000 on May 31. The manager was upset because the inventory was too high. She has adopted the following policies regarding merchandise purchases and inventory. At the end of any month, the inventory should be £15,000 plus 90 percent of the cost of goods to be sold during the following month. The cost of merchandise sold averages 60 percent of sales. Purchase terms are generally net, 30 days. A given month's purchases are paid as follows: 20 percent during that month and 80 percent during the following month.

Purchases in May had been £150,000. Sales are expected to be: June, £300,000; July, £280,000; August, £340,000; and September, £400,000.

1. Compute the amount by which the inventory on May 31 exceeded the manager's policies.
2. Prepare budget schedules for June, July, and August for purchases and for disbursements for purchases.

P12-6 PURCHASES AND COST OF GOODS SOLD. The Northfield Co., a wholesaler of food products, budgeted the following sales for the months shown below:

	JUNE 2002	JULY 2002	AUGUST 2002
Sales on account	$1,800,000	$1,920,000	$2,040,000
Cash sales	240,000	250,000	260,000
Total sales	$2,040,000	$2,170,000	$2,300,000

All merchandise is marked up to sell at its invoice cost plus 25 percent. Merchandise inventories at the beginning of each month are at 30 percent of that month's projected cost of goods sold.

1. Compute the budgeted cost of goods sold for the month of June 2002.
2. Compute the budgeted merchandise purchases for July 2002.

P12-7   PURCHASES AND SALES BUDGETS.   All sales of Dunn's Building Supplies (DBS) are made on credit. Sales are billed twice monthly, on the tenth of the month for the last half of the prior month's sales and on the twentieth of the month for the first half of the current month's sales. The terms of all sales are 2/10, net 30. Based on past experience, the collection experience of accounts receivable is as follows:

Within the discount period	80%
On the 30th day	18%
Uncollectible	2%

The sales value of shipments for May 2002 was $750,000. The forecast sales for the next four months are:

June	$800,000
July	900,000
August	900,000
September	600,000

DBS's average markup on its products is 20 percent of the sales price.

DBS purchases merchandise for resale to meet the current month's sales demand and to maintain a desired monthly ending inventory of 25 percent of the next month's sales. All purchases are on credit with terms of net 30. DBS pays for one-half of a month's purchases in the month of purchase and the other half in the month following the purchase.

All sales and purchases occur uniformly throughout the month.

1. How much cash can DBS plan to collect from accounts receivable collections during July 2002?
2. How much can DBS plan to collect in September from sales made in August 2002?
3. Compute the budgeted dollar value of DBS's inventory on August 31, 2002.
4. How much merchandise should DBS plan to purchase during June 2002?
5. How much should DBS budget in August 2002 for the payment of merchandise?

P12-8   CASH BUDGET.   Consider the following information for the month ending June 30, 2002 for the Johnson Company:

The cash balance, May 31, 2002, is $15,000. Sales proceeds are collected as follows: 80 percent month of sale, 10 percent second month, 10 percent third month.

Accounts receivable are $40,000 on May 31, 2002, consisting of $16,000 from April sales and $24,000 from May sales.

Accounts payable on May 31, 2002, are $145,000. Johnson Company pays 25 percent of purchases during the month of purchase and the remainder during the following month. All operating expenses requiring cash are paid during the month of recognition. However, insurance and property taxes are paid annually in December.

JOHNSON COMPANY		
Budgeted Income Statement for the Month Ended June 30, 2002 (in thousands)		
Sales		$290
Inventory, May 31	$ 50	
Purchases	192	
Available for sale	$242	
Inventory, June 30	40	
Cost of goods sold		202
Gross margin		$ 88
Operating expenses:		
Wages	$ 36	
Utilities	5	
Advertising	10	
Amortization	1	
Office expenses	4	
Insurance and property taxes	3	59
Operating income		$ 29

Prepare a cash budget for June. Confine your analysis to the given data. Ignore income taxes and other possible items that might affect cash.

P12-9   CASH BUDGET.   Catherine O'Shea is the manager of an extremely successful gift shop, Kate's Gifts, which is operated for the benefit of local charities. From the data below, she wants a cash budget showing expected cash receipts and disbursements for the month of April, and the cash balance expected as of April 30, 2003:

- Bank note due April 10: $90,000 plus $4,500 interest
- Amortization for April: $2,100
- Two-year insurance policy due April 14 for renewal: $1,500, to be paid in cash
- Planned cash balance, March 31, 2003: $80,000
- Merchandise purchases for April: $500,000, 40 percent paid in month of purchase, 60 percent paid in next month
- Customer receivables as of March 31: $60,000 from February sales, $450,000 from March sales
- Payrolls due in April: $90,000
- Other expenses for April, payable in April: $45,000
- Accrued taxes for April, payable in June: $7,500
- Sales for April: $1,000,000, half collected in month of sale, 40 percent in next month, 10 percent in third month
- Accounts payable, March 31, 2003: $460,000

Prepare the cash budget.

P12-10   CASH BUDGET.   Prepare a statement of estimated cash receipts and disbursements for October 2002 for the Aquarius Company, which sells one product, herbal soap, by the case. On October 1, 2002, part of the trial balance showed:

Cash	$ 4,800
Accounts receivable	15,600
Allowance for bad debts	1,900
Merchandise inventory	11,500
Accounts payable, merchandise	7,200

The company pay for its purchases within 10 days. Assume that one-third of the purchases of any month are due and paid for in the following month.

The cost of the merchandise purchased is $12 per case. At the end of each month it is desired to have an inventory equal in units to 50 percent of the following month's sales in units.

Sales terms include a 1 percent discount if payment is made by the end of the calendar month. Past experience indicates that 60 percent of the billings will be collected during the month of the sale, 30 percent in the following calendar month, and six percent in the next following calendar month. Four percent will be uncollectible. The company's fiscal year begins August 1.

Unit selling price	$ 20
August actual sales	12,000
September actual sales	36,000
October estimated sales	30,000
November estimated sales	22,000
Total sales expected in the fiscal year	360,000

Exclusive of bad debts, total budgeted selling and general administrative expenses for the fiscal year are estimated at $55,500, of which $18,000 is fixed expense, which includes a $7,200 annual amortization charge. Aquarius incurs these fixed expenses uniformly throughout the year. The balance of the selling and general administrative expenses varies with sales. Expenses are paid as incurred.

P12-11 MASTER BUDGET. Computer Superstores Inc. has a strong belief in using highly decentralized management. You are the new manager of one of its small "computer boutiques." You know a great deal about how to buy, how to display, how to sell, and how to reduce shoplifting. However, you know little about accounting and finance.

Top management is convinced that training for higher management should include the active participation of store managers in the budgeting process. You have been asked to prepare a complete master budget for your store for June, July, and August. You are responsible for its preparation. All accounting is done centrally, so you have no expert help on the premises. In addition, the branch manager and the assistant controller will arrive tomorrow to examine your work; at that time they will assist you in formulating the final budget document. The idea is to have you prepare the budget a few times so that you gain more confidence about accounting matters. You want to make a favourable impression on your superiors, so you gather the following data as of May 31, 2002:

Cash	$ 29,000	Recent and	
Inventory	420,000	Projected Sales	
Accounts receivable	369,000		
Net furniture and fixtures	168,000	April	$300,000
Total assets	$986,000	May	350,000
		June	700,000
Accounts payable	$475,000	July	400,000
Owners' equity	511,000	August	400,000
Total liabilities and owners'		September	300,000
equities	$986,000		

Credit sales are 90 percent of total sales. Credit accounts are collected 80 percent in the month following the sale and 20 percent in the next following month. Assume that bad debts are negligible and can be ignored. The accounts receivable on May 31 are the result of the credit sales for April and May: $(.20 \times .90 \times \$300,000 = \$54,000) + (1.00 \times .90 \times \$350,000 = \$315,000) = \$369,000$. The average gross profit on sales is 40 percent.

The policy is to acquire enough inventory each month to equal the following month's projected sales. All purchases are paid for in the month following purchase.

Salaries, wages, and commissions average 20 percent of sales; all other expenses, excluding amortization, are 4 percent of sales. Fixed expenses for rent, property taxes, and miscellaneous payroll and other items are $55,000 monthly. Assume that these expenses require cash disbursements each month. Amortization is $2,500 monthly.

In June, $55,000 is going to be disbursed for fixtures acquired in May. The May 31 balance of accounts payable includes this amount.

Assume that a minimum cash balance of $25,000 is to be maintained. Also assume that all borrowings are effective at the beginning of the month and all repayments are made at the end of the month of repayment. Interest is paid only at the time principal is repaid. Interest rate is 10 percent per annum; round interest computations to the nearest 10 dollars. All loans and repayments of principal must be made in multiples of a thousand dollars.

1. Prepare a budgeted income statement for the coming quarter, a budgeted statement of monthly cash receipts and disbursements (for the next three months), and a budgeted balance sheet for August 30, 2002. All operations are evaluated on a before-income-tax basis, so income taxes may be ignored here.
2. Explain why there is a need for a bank loan and what operating sources supply cash for repaying the bank loan.

P12-12 MASTER BUDGET. Victoria Kite Company wants a master budget for the next three months, beginning January 1, 2003. It desires an ending minimum cash balance of $5,000 each month. Sales are forecasted at an average selling price of $8 per kite. In January, Victoria Kite is beginning just-in-time deliveries from suppliers, which means that purchases equal expected sales. The December 31 inventory balance will be drawn down to $6,000, which will be the desired ending inventory thereafter. Merchandise costs are $4 per kite. Purchases during any given month are paid in full during the following month. All sales are on credit, payable within 30 days, but experience has shown that 60 percent of current sales is collected in the current month, 30 percent in the next month, and 10 percent in the month thereafter. Bad debts are negligible.

Wages and salaries	$15,000
Insurance expired	125
Amortization	250
Miscellaneous	2,500/month
Rent	250/month + 10% of quarterly sales over $10,000

Cash dividends of $1,500 are to be paid quarterly, beginning January 15, and are declared on the fifteenth of the previous month. All operating expenses are paid as incurred, except insurance, amortization, and rent. Rent of $250 is paid at the beginning of each month and the additional 10 percent of sales is paid quarterly on the tenth of the month following the quarter. The next settlement is due January 10.

The company plans to buy some new fixtures for $3,000 cash in March.

Money can be borrowed and repaid in multiples of $500, at an interest rate of 10 percent per annum. Management wants to minimize borrowing and repay rapidly. Interest is computed and paid when the principal is repaid. Assume that borrowing takes place at the beginning, and repayments at the end, of the months in question. Money is never borrowed at the beginning and repaid at the end of the same month. Compute interest to the nearest dollar.

ASSETS AS OF DECEMBER 31, 2002		LIABILITIES AS OF DECEMBER 31, 2002	
Cash	$ 5,000	Accounts payable (merchandise)	$35,550
Accounts receivable	12,500	Dividends payable	1,500
Inventory*	39,050	Rent payable	7,800
Unexpired insurance	1,500		$44,850
Fixed assets, net	12,500		
	$70,550		

* November 30 inventory balance = $16,000

Recent and forecasted sales:

October	$38,000	December	$25,000	February	$75,000	April	$45,000
November	$25,000	January	$62,000	March	$38,000		

1. Prepare a master budget including a budgeted income statement, balance sheet statement of cash receipts and disbursements, and supporting schedules for the months January through March, 2003.
2. Explain why there is a need for a bank loan and what operating sources provide the cash for the repayment of the bank loan.

P12-13 **BUDGETING AT RITZ-CARLTON.** Suppose Ritz-Carlton has a 300-room hotel in a tropical climate. Management expects occupancy rates to be 95 percent in December, January, February, 85 percent in November, March, and April, and 70 percent the rest of the year. The average room rental is $250 per night. Of this, on average 10 percent is received as a deposit the month before the stay, 60 percent is received in the month of the stay, and 28 percent is collected the month after. The remaining 2 percent is never collected.

Most of the costs of running the hotel are fixed. The variable costs are only $20 per occupied room per night. Fixed salaries (including benefits) run $400,000 per month, amortization is $350,00 a month, other fixed operating costs are $120,000 per month, and interest expense is $500,000 per month. Variable costs and salaries are paid in the month they are incurred, amortization is recorded at the end of each quarter, other fixed operating costs are paid as incurred, and interest is paid each June and December.

1. Prepare a monthly cash budget for this Ritz-Carlton hotel. For simplicity, assume that there are 30 days in each month
2. How much would the hotel's annual profit increase if occupancy rates

increased by five percentage points each month in the off-season (that is, from 70 percent to 75 percent in May through October)?

P12-14 **CASH BUDGETING FOR A HOSPITAL.** (CMA, adapted) Mercy Hospital provides a wide range of health services in its community. Mercy's board of directors has authorized the following capital expenditures:

Interaortic balloon pump	$1,300,000
CT scanner	850,000
X-ray equipment	550,000
Laboratory equipment	1,200,000
	$3,900,000

The expenditures are planned for October 1, 2002, and the board wants to know how much, if anything, the hospital has to borrow. Jill Todd, hospital controller, has gathered the following information to be used to prepare an analysis of future cash flows.

a. Billings, made in the month of service, for the first half of 2003 are:

MONTH	ACTUAL AMOUNT
January	$5,300,000
February	5,300,000
March	5,400,000
April	5,400,000
May	6,000,000
June	6,000,000

Ninety percent of Mercy's billings are made to third parties such as Blue Cross, provincial governments, and private insurance companies. The remaining 10 percent of the billings are made directly to patients. Historical patterns of billing collections are:

	THIRD-PARTY BILLINGS	DIRECT PATIENT BILLINGS
Month of service	20%	10%
Month following service	50	40
Second month following service	20	40
Uncollectible	10	10

Estimated billings for the last six months of 2003 are listed next. Todd expects the same billing and collection patterns that have been experienced during the first six months of 2003 to continue during the last six months of the year.

MONTH	ESTIMATED AMOUNT
July	$5,400,000
August	6,000,000
September	6,600,000
October	6,800,000
November	7,000,000
December	6,600,000

b. The following schedule presents the purchases that have been made during the past three months and the planned purchases for the last six months of 2003.

MONTH	AMOUNT
April	$1,300,000
May	1,450,000
June	1,450,000
July	1,500,000
August	1,800,000
September	2,200,000
October	2,350,000
November	2,700,000
December	2,100,000

All purchases are made on account, and accounts payable are remitted in the month following the purchase.

c. Salaries for each month during the remainder of 2003 are expected to be $1,800,000 per month plus 20 percent of that month's billings. Salaries are paid in the month of service.

d. Mercy's monthly amortization charges are $150,000.

e. Mercy incurs interest expense of $180,000 per month and makes interest payments of $540,000 on the last day of each calendar quarter.

f. Endowment fund income is expected to continue to total $210,000 per month.

g. Mercy has a cash balance of $350,000 on July 1, 2003, and has a policy of maintaining a minimum end-of-month cash balance of 10 percent of the current month's purchases.

h. Mercy Hospital employs a calendar-year reporting period.

1. Prepare a schedule of budgeted cash receipts by month for the third quarter of 2003.

2. Prepare a schedule of budgeted cash disbursements by month for the third quarter of 2003.

3. Determine the amount of borrowing, if any, necessary on October 1, 2003, to acquire the capital items totalling $4,600.000.

P12-15   COMPREHENSIVE BUDGETING FOR A UNIVERSITY.   (CPA, adapted) Suppose you are the controller of Western University. The university president is preparing for her annual fundraising campaign for 2003–04. To set an appropriate target, she has asked you to prepare a budget for the academic year. You have collected the following data for the current year (2002–03). See the following data.

a. For 2003–04, all faculty and staff will receive a six percent salary increase. Undergraduate enrolment is expected to decline by two percent, but graduate enrolment is expected to increase by five percent.

	UNDERGRADUATE DIVISION	GRADUATE DIVISION
Average salary of faculty member	$46,000	$46,000
Average faculty teaching load in semester credit hours per year (eight undergraduate or six graduate courses)	24	18
Average number of students per class	30	20
Total enrolment (full-time and part-time students)	3,600	1,800
Average number of semester credit hours carried each year per student	25	20
Full-time load, semester hours per year	30	24

b. The 2002–03 budget for operation and maintenance of facilities is $500,000, which includes $240,000 for salaries and wages. Experience so far this year indicates that the budget is accurate. Salaries and wages will increase by six percent and other operating costs by $12,000 in 2003–04.

c. The 2002–03 and 2003–04 budgets for the remaining expenditures are:

	2002–03	2003–04
General administrative	$500,000	$525,000
Library:		
Acquisitions	150,000	155,000
Operations	190,000	200,000
Health services	48,000	50,000
Intramural athletics	56,000	60,000
Intercollegiate athletics	240,000	245,000
Insurance and retirement	520,000	560,000
Interest	75,000	75,000

d. Tuition is $70 per credit hour. In addition, the provincial government provides $780 per full-time-equivalent student. (A full-time equivalent is 30 undergraduate semester credit-hours or 24 graduate semester credit-hours.) Tuition scholarships are given to 30 *full-time* undergraduates and 50 *full-time* graduate students.

e. Revenues other than tuition and the government apportionment are:

	2002–03	2003–04
Endowment income	$200,000	$210,000
Net income from auxiliary services	325,000	335,000
Intercollegiate athletic receipts	290,000	300,000

f. The chemistry/physics classroom building needs remodelling during the 2003–04 period. Projected cost is $550,000.

1. Prepare a schedule for 2003–04 that shows, by division, (a) expected enrolment, (b) total credit hours, (c) full-time-equivalent enrolment, and (d) number of faculty members needed. Assume that part-time faculty can be hired at one-half the same salary per credit hour as full-time faculty.

2. Calculate the budget for faculty salaries for 2003–04 by division.

3. Calculate the budget for tuition revenue and government apportionment for 2003–04 by division.

4. Prepare a schedule for the president showing the amount that must be raised by the annual fundraising campaign.

P12-16 **ACTIVITY-BASED BUDGETING.** A recent directive from Helen Prescott, CEO of Comtel, had instructed each department to cut its cost by 10 percent. The traditional budget for the Warehousing Department was as follows:

Salaries, 4 employees @ $42,000	$168,000
Benefit @ 20%	33,600
Amortization, straight-line basis	76,000
Parts and supplies	42,400
Overhead @ 35% of direct costs	112,000
Total	$432,000

Therefore, the Warehousing Division needed to find $43,200 to cut.

Tom Procter, a recent MBA graduate, was asked to pare $43,200 from the Warehousing Department's budget. As a first step, he recast the traditional budget into an activity-based budget:

Receiving, 620,000 kilograms	$ 93,000
Shipping, 402,000 boxes	201,000
Handling, 11,200 moves	112,000
Record-keeping, 65,000 transactions	26,000
Total	$432,000

1. What actions might Procter suggest to attain a $43,200 budget cut? Why would these be the best actions to pursue?
2. Which budget helped you most in answering requirement 1? Explain.

P12-17 **SPREADSHEETS AND SENSITIVITY ANALYSIS OF THE INCOME STATEMENT.** Study Appendix 12. The Speedy-Mart Store has the following budgeted sales, which are uniform throughout the month:

May	$450,000
June	375,000
July	330,000
August	420,000

Cost of goods sold averages 70 percent of sales and is purchased as it is needed. Employees earn fixed salaries of $22,000 (total) monthly and commissions of 10 percent of the current month's sales. Other expenses are rent, $6,000, paid on the first of each month; miscellaneous expenses, six percent of sales, paid as incurred; insurance, $450 per month, from a one-year policy that was paid for on January 2; and amortization, $2,850 per month.

1. Using spreadsheet software, prepare a table of budget data for the Speedy Mart Store.
2. Continue the spreadsheet in requirement 1 to prepare budget schedules for (a) disbursements for operating expenses and (b) operating income for June, July, and August.
3. Adjust the budget data appropriately for each of the following scenarios independently and recompute operating income using the spreadsheet.

a. A sales promotion that will cost $30,000 in May could increase sales in each of the following three months by five percent.

b. Eliminating the sales commissions and increasing employees' salaries to $52,500 per month could decrease sales thereafter by a net of two percent.

P12-18 **SPREADSHEETS AND SENSITIVITY ANALYSIS OF OPERATING EXPENSES.** Study Appendix 12. The CD-ROM Division (CDRD) of Micro Storage, Inc. produces CD-ROM drives for personal computers. The drives are assembled from purchased components. The costs (value) added by CDRD are indirect costs (which include assembly labour), packaging, and shipping. Cost behaviour is as follows:

	FIXED	VARIABLE
Purchased components		
10X drives		$100 per component
5X drives		$40 per component
Indirect costs	$40,000	$16 per component
Packaging	$8,000	$4 per drive
Shipping	$8,000	$2 per drive

Both CD-ROM drives require five components. Therefore, the total cost of components for A100 drives is $500 and for A50 drives is $200. CDRD uses a six-month continuous budget that is revised monthly. Sales forecasts for the next eight months are as follows:

	A100 DRIVES	A50 DRIVES
October	3,200 units	4,000 units
November	2,400	3,000
December	5,600	7,000
January	3,200	4,000
February	3,200	4,000
March	2,400	3,000
April	2,400	3,000
May	2,800	3,500

Treat each event in succession.

1. Use spreadsheet software to prepare a table of budgeting information and an operating expense budget for the CD-ROM Division for October through March. Incorporate the expectation that sales of A50 drives will be 125 percent of A100 drives. Prepare a spreadsheet that can be revised easily for succeeding months.

2. October's actual sales were 2,800 A100 drives and 3,600 A50 drives. This outcome has caused CDRD to revise its sales forecasts downward by 10 percent. Revise the operating expense budget for November through April.

3. At the end of November, CDRD decides that the proportion of A100 drives to A50 drives is changing. Sales of A50 drives are expected to be 150 percent of A100 drive sales. Expected sales of A100 drives are unchanged from requirement 2. Revise the operating expense budget for December through May.

P12-19 **BUDGETING, BEHAVIOUR, AND ETHICS.** Since Stan Legree had become President of Alberta Mining, Ltd., budgets had become a major focus for managers. In fact, making budget was such an important goal that the two managers who had missed their budgets in 2002 (by 2 percent and 4 percent, respectively) had been summarily fired. This caused all managers to be wary when setting their 2003 budgets.

The GSL Copper Division of Alberta Mining had the following results for 2002:

Sales, 1.6 million pounds @ $.95/pound	$1,520,000
Variable costs	880,000
Fixed costs, primarily amortization	450,000
Pretax profit	$190,000

Sheila Masur, General Manager of GSL, received a memo from Legree that contained the following:

"We expect your profit for 2003 to be at least $209,000. Prepare a budget showing how you plan to accomplish this."

Masur was concerned the market for copper had recently softened. Her market-research staff forecast that sales would be at or below the 2002 level and prices would likely be between $.92 and $.94 per pound. Her manufacturing manager reported that most of the fixed costs were committed and there were few efficiencies to be gained in the variable costs. He indicated that perhaps a 2 percent savings might be achievable, but certainly no more.

1. Prepare a budget for Masur to submit to headquarters. What dilemmas does Masur face in preparing this budget?
2. What problems do you see in the budgeting process at Alberta Mining?
3. Suppose Masur submitted a budget showing a $209,000 profit. It is now late in 2003, and she has had a good year. Despite an industry-wide decline in sales, GSL's sales matched last year's 1.6 million kilograms, and the average price per kilogram was $.945, nearly at last year's level and well above that forecast. Variable costs were cut by 2 percent through extensive efforts. Still, profit projections were $9,000 below budget. Masur was concerned for her job, so she approached the controller and requested that amortization schedules be changed. By extending the lives of some equipment for 2 years, $15,000 of amortization could be saved in 2003. Estimating the economic lives of equipment is difficult, and it would be hard to prove that the old lives were better than the new proposed lives. What should the controller do? What ethical issues does this raise?

P12-20 **COLLABORATIVE LEARNING EXERCISE: PERSONAL BUDGETING.** Budgeting is useful to many different types of entities. One is the individual. Consider the entity that you know best, the college or university student. Form a group of two to six students, and pool the information that you have about what it costs to spend a year as a full-time student.

Prepare a revenue and expense budget for an average prospective full-time student at your college or university. Identify possible sources of revenue and the amount to be received from each. Identify the costs a student is likely to incur during the year. You can assume that cash disbursements are make immediately for all expenses, so the budgeted income statement and cash budget are identical.

When all groups have completed their budgets, compare those budgets. What are the differences? What assumptions led to the differences?

CASES

C12-1   BUDGETING FOR EXPANSION.   (ICAO) Tom's Outdoor Experience (TOE) is a sporting goods store owned by Tom Dennison. Tom handles limited product lines. Summer sales centre on bicycles, camping gear, and clothing for both activities. Cross-country skis and related equipment and clothing are the major winter lines. The store is a year-round centre for running enthusiasts because better footwear and clothing for this sporting activity are featured. The store is situated in a small city in Ontario.

Operations began 14 years ago when Tom purchased the building that houses the store. The business provided adequate cash flow to raise a family of three children. Now that the children are grown, Tom's wife has resumed her career. Tom has decided to open a new store in a nearby city as he is certain there is an available market.

Tom has been a close friend of your family for many years. In April 2002, he telephoned to ask your advice about preparing a presentation to his banker so that he could proceed with his expansion plans.

The conversation proceeded as follows:

Tom: I spoke to the bank manager about borrowing $200,000 to buy that building, clean it up a little, and install some equipment. The building, at $175,000, is a good buy according to the real estate agent. I got a $15,000 quote from a contractor to do the renovations it requires. I think that $10,000 is enough to buy a cash register, display racks, and the little pieces of equipment needed to repair bikes and skis.

You: I guess the banker needs some collateral and some indication that you'll be able to repay the loan.

Tom: That's right. And that's where I thought you might be able to help. Tell me what you think he wants and how to put it together.

You: He probably wants to see cash-flow statements and anticipated results for the new location. Do you have financial statements prepared?

Tom: Yes, the January 31, 2002 year-end balance sheet and income statements are done (Exhibits 12A-1 and 12A-2). I also have written a list of things that I expect will happen with the new store (Exhibit 12A-3).

You: Good. Have you borrowed money from this bank before?

Tom: Yes, I have a line of credit with them, and I'm still paying the $386 per month on the mortgage of the old store. The banker says my credit rating is good, and that I could probably get both long- and short-term money at 12 percent. I asked him if a working capital loan of $20,000 for the new store would be possible. He said that he would consider it at the same time as the new building package.

You: You seem to have thought this out thoroughly.

Tom: If I brought over the documentation, could we put something together tonight? I'm seeing the banker tomorrow morning. If you can do the numbers, I can justify the marketing aspects. I'd really like to know what you think about this new venture.

You: Sure Tom. I'll see you about 7:30.

Tom arrived with his documentation and financial statements. He assured you that he could have the presentation typed in the morning before his meeting with the banker.

Required: | Prepare the necessary quantitative and qualitative analysis that would help Tom present his request to his banker. State any assumptions you make.

EXHIBIT 12A-1

Tom's Outdoor Experience
Tom Dennison, Proprietor
Balance Sheet as at January 31, 2002

ASSETS	2002	2001	2000
Current Assets			
Cash	$ 2,570	$ 2,400	$ 1,500
Accounts receivable	840	1,160	950
Inventory	49,130	44,760	38,950
Prepaids	2,010	1,860	1,400
	54,550	50,180	42,800
Fixed Assets			
Equipment	8,500	8,500	6,000
Building	40,000	40,000	40,000
Land	6,000	6,000	6,000
	54,500	54,500	52,000
Less: Accumulated amortization	24,700	21,450	18,200
	29,800	33,050	33,800
Total Assets	$84,350	$83,230	$76,600

LIABILITIES AND OWNER'S EQUITY			
Current liabilities			
Bank indebtedness	$ 7,000	$ 9,300	$ 4,700
Accounts payable	24,410	28,580	27,700
Accrued liabilities	1,450	1,950	1,700
	32,860	39,830	34,100
Mortgage payable	30,830	32,300	33,600
Owner's equity			
Tom Dennison, capital	20,660	11,100	8,900
Total Liabilities and Owner's Equity	$84,350	$83,230	$76,600

EXHIBIT 12A-2

Tom's Outdoor Experience
Tom Dennison, Proprietor
Statement of Income and Owner's Equity for the year ended January 31, 2002

	2002	2001	2000
Sales	$265,360	$233,800	$203,100
Cost of goods sold	171,690	147,360	125,860
Gross profit	93,670	86,440	77,240
Expenses			
Selling and administration	43,120	44,580	35,130
Amortization	3,250	3,250	3,000
Interest on long-term debt	3,160	3,330	3,400
Interest on short-term debt	1,180	980	1,360
	50,710	52,140	42,890
Net income for the year	42,960	34,300	34,350
Owner's equity beginning of year	11,100	8,900	6,400
Drawings	<33,400>	<32,100>	<31,850>
Owner's Equity, end of year	$ 20,660	$ 11,100	$ 8,900

EXHIBIT 12A-3

Basis of projections for
new store prepared by
Tom Dennison

1. The deal for the store will close May 31 if financing is secured. This will allow time for renovations and inventory stocking. Projected opening date: August 1, 2002.
2. Sales in the old store are expected to increase by a minimum of 15 percent per year during the next few years since fitness is becoming an essential part of many life styles.

   Sales in the new store in the first six months will be about 80 percent of the projected results in the old store, then will equal or better the level of the old store. I expect better sales because the new store is in a larger community and the store area is larger.
3. Profit margins in the old store have slipped slightly in past years because of pressure from the chain stores. With two stores, purchasing economies will ensure that my profit margin won't slip more than one percent per year. I am even expecting a slight recovery because we provide excellent service on all equipment. Customers appreciate that and are willing to pay for it.
4. Selling and administration expenses have levelled off because we are using more part-time staff. I expect that in addition to the regular costs, I'll have to pay about $5,000 per year more for one of the staff to act as a manager.
5. Drawings can be reduced to $15,000 per year. My wife's income is more than sufficient for living expenses since our house mortgage has been paid.

C12-2 CASH BUDGETING. (SMAC) George Brown, a self-employed management consultant had just settled down to work when he received a call from Ray Donald, vice president of Software Corporation (SC), a software distributing and consulting firm.

Donald had been through a hectic holiday period and, to some extent, he had let the financial controls slip away. Preoccupied with devoting much of his attention to the customer service side, Donald had suddenly become aware that cash flow was devastated. In December, three suppliers put him on C.O.D. basis and three more threatened to stop supplying. At the end of November, the bank line of credit was $260,000 over limit and the bank had refused to honour any cheques except payroll until SC either reduced the outstanding balance to the limit or renegotiated its bank loan. As a condition of refinancing the bank loan, the bank wanted audited financial statements as support for Donald's claim that business was great.

"Business is great," Donald had said to Brown. "We just don't have any cash! George, I was wondering if you could come over here and help me out. I need you to analyze our cash-flow problem. Specifically, I would like you to prepare a statement of cash flow for each of the last four months of 2003 for me so that I can answer any questions that the bank manager may have when I meet with her."

Brown visited SC two days later to analyze the cash-flow problem. Exhibit 12A-4 presents information gathered by Brown in support of his analysis. Exhibit 12A-5 contains a condensed balance sheet of SC as at August 31, 2003, and December 31, 2003.

Required: | Analyze the cash-flow problem at SC and make recommendations for improvement.

SALES FORECASTS (000s)	
April	$150
May	200
June	275
July	300
Aug.	400
Sept.	450
Oct.	535
Nov.	580
Dec.	690

AGED ACCOUNTS RECEIVABLE TOTALS AT MONTH END (000s)
SEPTEMBER TO DECEMBER, 2003

| | AGE IN DAYS | | | | | | |
	CURRENT	30	60	90	120	OVER 120	TOTAL
September	$540	$480	$405	$380	$350	$ 315	$2,470
October	600	515	460	400	370	520	2,865
November	670	585	475	450	360	825	3,365
December	750	660	555	465	410	1,050	3,890

ANALYSIS OF WORK-IN-PROCESS
AUGUST TO DECEMBER, 2003

| | MONTH (000s) | | | | |
	AUG.	SEPT.	OCT.	NOV.	DEC.
Consulting Work-in-Process at Month End	$310	$375	$460	$575	$675
Consulting Fees Invoiced		240	225	225	100

AGED ACCOUNTS PAYABLE TOTALS AT MONTH END (000s)
SEPTEMBER TO DECEMBER, 2003

| | AGE IN DAYS | | | | | |
	CURRENT	30	60	90	OVER 90	TOTAL
September	$615	$640	$450	$360	–	$2,065
October	750	615	640	450	150	2,605
November	510	750	615	640	200	2,715
December	400	510	750	615	645	2,920

EXHIBIT 12A-5

Information Collected by George Brown Software Corporation Condensed Balance Sheet as at August 31 and December 31, 2003 (Before December Adjustments) (000s)

	AUGUST	DECEMBER
Accounts receivable	$2,055	$3,890
Work-in-process—consulting*	310	675
Fixed assets—net	695	815
	$3,060	$5,380
Bank loan payable	$ 350	$ 615
Accounts payable	1,750	2,920
Shareholders' equity	960	1,845
	$3,060	$5,380

* Obtained from time sheet summaries costed at a regular billing rate.

Other information with respect to SC's cash flows:

1. Bank advances of $80,000 were received in September.
2. Regular operating cash outflows per month are $75,000.
3. Fixed assets of $150,000 were acquired in September for cash.
4. No purchases are paid for in the month in which they are bought.

Part A

Milly Banilli, a successful entrepreneur, is setting up a new division for the manufacture of three new products that will complement her current line of business. Milly is currently involved in the manufacture of motorboats. She believes that overall corporate profits can be enhanced by manufacturing custom boat covers (CBC), waterskis (WS), and boat ladders (BL) in her new division and has asked you to assist her in planning a production schedule for the next month.

The three products will be manufactured in a plant with three departments. As the products proceed through each department, applicable labour and machine time are applied. Each department is composed of specialized machinery and specialized labour skills and accordingly, neither machine time nor labour time can be switched between departments.

The following data have been accumulated by Milly:

	DEPARTMENT		
	1	**2**	**3**
Available machine capacity in machine hours per month	10,000	10,000	10,000
Available direct labour hours per month	15,000	15,000	15,000
UNIT SPECIFICATIONS:			
Product			
CBC — machine hours	3	1	2
CBC — direct labour hours	5	2	3
WS — machine hours	2	2	1
WS — direct labour hours	4	3	1
BL — machine hours	1	2	3
BL — direct labour hours	3	4	5

MONTHLY DEMAND	
CBC	1,000 units
WS	1,500 units
BL	2,000 units

UNIT COSTS			
	PRODUCT		
	CBC	**WS**	**BL**
	$	**$**	**$**
Direct materials	20	30	40
Direct labour:			
Department 1	25	20	15
Department 2	20	30	40
Department 3	15	5	25
Variable overhead	60	95	150
Fixed overhead	40	50	40
Variable selling and administrative	10	20	15
Fixed administration	10	30	10
Unit selling prices	240	300	360

Other information:

Since the business is seasonal and space is limited, Milly has asked you to assume zero inventory and work in progress at the end of each month. Unit fixed costs are based on sufficient monthly production to meet sales demand. Fixed overhead costs for a given product are incurred only if that product is produced.

Required:

1. Prepare a monthly production schedule for one month only that will maximize the division's profit given the above information and prepare a schedule of estimated divisional profit.
2. What steps would you advise Milly to consider for next year in order to further enhance her divisional profit?

Part B

Milly's banker is convinced that only the custom boat covers (CBC) should be manufactured. In order to authorize a long-term bank loan for equipment and an operating line of credit for day-to-day operations, the banker requires a three-month schedule of cash flows that will identify the amount of operating line of credit required and illustrate the division's ability to adhere to the long-term loan repayment schedule and maintain adequate collateral for the operating line of credit.

Milly has provided the following *additional* information in this regard:

a) All of the data described in Part A will be valid for the entire three-month period.
b) Milly will deposit $100,000 into the division's bank account as start-up funds.
c) Direct material for one month's production is ordered in the month prior to production, is delivered on the first day of the month of production and is paid for in the month of production.
d) Fixed costs are paid for in the month of production.
e) Variable selling expenses are paid for in the month of production.
f) Anticipated cash flows from sales are as follows:
20 percent of monthly sales will be cash sales; 80 percent of monthly sales will be credit sales with 30 day net terms; and 10 percent of credit sales are expected to be uncollectible.
g) The division will require a term loan of $120,000 in order to purchase equipment for the production of custom boat covers. The bank has agreed to a 12 percent annual interest rate for 60 months with payments at the end of each month of $2,000 principal, plus interest. The term loan proceeds will be advanced and the equipment will be purchased at the beginning of the first month.
h) The required operating funds (as per the cash-flow statement) will be advanced at the beginning of each month to a maximum of 75 percent of the anticipated collectible receivables as at the end of the month the operating line of credit funds are advanced. Operating line of credit funds are advanced in multiples of $20,000.
i) Interest expense on the operating line of credit funds, charged at an annual rate of 18 percent, is to be minimized subject to a desired minimum cash-on-hand balance of $15,000. Any repayments of operating line of credit funds will be made at the end of the month and can be made only in multiples of $10,000.

Prepare the three-month schedule of cash flows as required by the banker. (Your schedule should include four numeric columns: one column for each of the three months and one column containing the totals for the three months. The columns should only include cash flows pertaining to custom boat covers (CBC). *All* information available relating to custom boat covers (CBC) should be utilized.

C12-4 CASH BUDGETING. (CGAC) Grover Cleveland is trying to decide whether he is going to need to take a loan in January to buy a new microcomputer system for his business. The microcomputer will cost $10,800.

Cleveland has collected the following information about his operations as of December 31:

1) Balances of selected ledger accounts:

Cash	$2,120
Accounts payable	6,667

2) Sales history and forecast (Unit selling price $10):

(Actual)	October	$43,000
(Actual)	November	35,000
(Actual)	December	40,000
(Forecast)	January	50,000

3) All sales are on credit and are due (required to be paid) 30 days after the sale.

4) Fifty percent of a given month's sales are collected one month after the sale (that is, 30 days), 45 percent are collected two months after sales and 5 percent are uncollectible.

5) Inventory is purchased under terms of 2/10 net 30. Cleveland always takes the 2 percent discount, but records purchases at gross cost. Accounts payable (shown above) related solely to inventory purchases. Inventory costs $5 per unit, gross.

6) Other expenses, all paid in cash as required, average about 30 percent of sales dollars. Amortization is part of these expenses and costs $3,000 per month.

7) Cleveland keeps a minimum cash balance of $1,000.

Required: Prepare a cash budget for January, indicating whether Grover will need a loan to finance his computer acquisition.

Flexible Budgets and Standards for Control

LEARNING OBJECTIVES

After studying this chapter, you will be able to

1. Distinguish between flexible budgets and master (static) budgets.

2. Use flexible-budget formulas to construct a flexible budget based on the volume of sales.

3. Prepare an activity-based flexible budget.

4. Understand the performance evaluation relationship between master (static) budgets and flexible budgets.

5. Compute flexible-budget variances and sales activity variances.

6. Distinguish between expectations, standard costs, and standard cost systems.

7. Compute and interpret price and usage variances for inputs based on cost-driver activity.

8. Compute the production-volume variance in the income statement.

9. Identify the differences between the three alternative cost bases of an absorption-costing system: actual, normal, and standard.

10. Identify the two methods for disposing of the standard cost variances at the end of a year and give the rationale for each.

11. Analyze and compare all the major variances in a standard absorption-costing system (Appendix 13).

As we saw in Chapter 12, formal budgeting procedures result in comprehensive operational and financial plans for future periods. These budgets guide managers and employees as they make their daily decisions and as they try to anticipate future problems and opportunities. As the budget period unfolds, it is only natural that employees and managers want to know, "How did we do?" Employees and their supervisors should know how they are doing in meeting their non-financial objectives (such as making on-time deliveries and resolving customer problems) and any applicable financial objectives. Upper-level managers also want to know how the organization is meeting its financial objectives as spelled out in the master budget. Managers obtain feedback on how effectively economic conditions were forecast and how well plans were executed by comparing budgets to actual results. Knowing what went right and what went wrong should help managers plan and manage more effectively in future periods. The accounting system in most organizations is designed to record transactions continuously and report actual financial results at designated intervals. The way budgets and actual results are compared, however, determines the value of financial feedback.

This chapter introduces flexible budgets, which are budgets designed to direct management to areas of actual financial performance that deserve attention. (Managers can apply this same basic process to control of other important areas of performance, such as quality or customer service.) After discussing flexible budgets and basic budget variances that are applicable to all organizations, we take a detailed look at variances for traditional manufacturing inputs such as material, labour, and overhead.

FLEXIBLE BUDGETS: THE BRIDGE BETWEEN STATIC BUDGETS AND ACTUAL RESULTS

Static Budgets

OBJECTIVE 1

Distinguish between flexible budgets and master (static) budgets.

Static budget is really just another name for *master budget*. All the master budgets discussed in Chapter 12 are *static* or inflexible, because even though they may be easily revised, the budgets assume fixed levels of activity. In other words, a master budget is prepared for only one level of a given type of activity. For example, consider a company using a traditional costing system with only one cost driver. The Dominion Company is a one-department firm in Toronto that manufacturers and sells a wheeled, collapsible suitcase carrier that is popular with airline flight crews. Manufacture of this suitcase carrier requires several manual and machine operations. The product has some variations, but may be viewed for our purposes essentially as a single product bearing one selling price. Assume that the cost driver is sales volume (that is, units sold), and the projected level of activity (sales volume) is 9,000 units. All of the budget figures are then based on projected sales of 9,000 units.

All *actual* results could be compared with the original budgeted amounts, even through, for example, sales volume turned out to be only 7,000 units instead of the originally planned 9,000 units.

The master (static) budget for June 2002 included the condensed income statement shown in Exhibit 13-1, column 2. The actual results for June 2002 are in column 1. Differences or variances between actual results and the master budget are in column 3. The master budget called for production and sales of 9,000 units, but only 7,000 units were actually produced and sold. There were no beginning or ending inventories, so the units made in June were sold in June.

The performance report in Exhibit 13-1 compares the actual results with the master budget. *Performance report* is a generic term that usually means a comparison of actual results with some budget. A helpful performance report will include *variances* that direct upper management's attention to significant deviations from expected results, allowing management by exception. Recall that a *variance* is a deviation of an actual amount from the expected or budgeted amount. Each significant variance should cause a manager to ask "Why?" By explaining why a variance occurs, managers are forced to recognize changes that have affected costs and that might affect future decisions. Exhibit 13-1 shows variances of actual results from the master budget; these are called **master (static) budget variances**. Actual *revenues* that *exceed* expected revenues result in *favourable* variances, and vice-versa. Similarly, actual *expenses* that *exceed* expected expenses result in *unfavourable* variances, and vice versa.

Master (Static) Budget Variances. The variances of actual results from the master budget.

Suppose the president of Dominion Company asks you to explain *why* there was an operating loss of $11,570 when a profit of $12,800 was budgeted. Clearly, sales were below expectations, but the favourable variances for the variable costs are misleading. Considering the lower-than-projected level of sales activity, was cost control really satisfactory? The comparison of actual results with a master budget is not much help in answering that question. Master budget variances are not very useful for management by exception.

Flexible Budgets

Flexible Budget (Variable Budget). A budget that adjusts for changes in sales volume and other cost-driver activities.

A more helpful benchmark for analysis is the *flexible budget*. A **flexible budget** (sometimes called **variable budget**) is a budget that adjusts for changes in volume and other cost-driver activities. The flexible budget is identical to the master budget in format, but managers may prepare them for any levels of activity. So, when sales turn out to be 7,000 units instead of 9,000, managers can use the

EXHIBIT 13-1

Dominion Company
Performance Report
Using Master Budget
for the Month Ended
June 30, 2002

	ACTUAL	MASTER BUDGET	MASTER BUDGET VARIANCES
Units	7,000	9,000	2,000
Sales	$217,000	$279,000	$62,000 U
Variable expenses:			
Variable manufacturing expenses	$151,270	$189,000	$37,730 F
Shipping expenses (selling)	5,000	5,400	400 F
Administrative expenses	2,000	1,800	200 U
Total variable expenses	$158,270	$196,200	$37,930 F
Contribution margin	$ 58,730	$ 82,800	$24,070 U
Fixed expenses:			
Fixed manufacturing expenses	$ 37,300	$ 37,000	$ 300 U
Fixed selling and administrative expenses	33,000	33,000	—
Total fixed expenses	$ 70,300	$ 70,000	$ 300 U
Operating income (loss)	$ (11,570)	$ 12,800	$24,370 U

Unfavourable Expense Variances. Variances that occur when actual expenses are more than budgeted expenses.

Favourable Expense Variances. Variances that occur when actual expenses are less than budgeted expenses.

U = **Unfavourable expense variances** occur when actual expenses are more than budgeted expenses.

F = **Favourable expense variances** occur when actual expenses are less than budgeted expenses.

flexible budget to prepare a new budget *based on this new cost-driver level.* We can then see what the total variable expenses should be based on a sales level of 7,000 and compare this amount to the actual result. For performance evaluation, the flexible budget would be prepared at the actual levels of activity. In contrast, the master budget is kept fixed or static to serve as the primary benchmark for evaluating performance. It shows revenues and costs or expenses at only the originally *planned* levels of activity.

The flexible budget approach says, "Give me any activity level you choose, and I'll provide a budget tailored to that particular level." Many companies routinely "flex" their budgets to help evaluate recent financial performance. For example, Procter and Gamble evaluates monthly financial performance of all its business units by comparing actual results to new, flexible budgets that are prepared for actual levels of activity.

Flexible-Budget Formulas

The flexible budget is based on the same assumptions of revenue and cost behaviour (within the relevant range) as is the master budget. It is based on knowledge of cost behaviour with regard to appropriate cost drivers—*cost functions* or *flexible-budget formulas.* The cost functions that you used in Chapter 2 and estimated in Chapter 3 can be used as flexible-budget formulas. Recall that these cost functions had units of volume as the single cost driver. The flexible budget incorporates how each cost and revenue is affected by changes in activity. Exhibits 13-2 and 13-3 show Dominion Company's simple flexible budget, which has a single cost driver, units of output. Dominion Company's cost functions or flexible-budget formulas are believed to be valid within the relevant range of 7,000 to 9,000 units. Be sure that you understand that each column of Exhibit 13-2 (7,000 units, 8,000 units, and 9,000 units) is prepared using the same flexible-budget formulas, and any activity within this range could be used, as shown in the graph in Exhibit 13-3. Note that fixed costs are expected to be constant across this range of activity.

EXHIBIT 13-2

Dominion Company
Flexible Budgets

BUDGET FORMULA PER UNIT		FLEXIBLE BUDGETS FOR VARIOUS LEVELS OF SALES/PRODUCTION ACTIVITY		
Units		7,000	8,000	9,000
Sales	$ 31.00	$217,000	$248,000	$279,000
Variable costs/expenses:				
Variable Manufacturing Costs	$ 21.00	$147,000	$168,000	$189,000
Shipping expenses (selling)	.60	4,200	4,800	5,400
Administrative	.20	1,400	1,600	1,800
Total variable costs/expenses	$ 21.80	$152,600	$174,400	$196,200
Contribution margin	$ 9.20	$ 64,400	$ 73,600	$ 82,800
BUDGET FORMULA PER MONTH				
Fixed costs/expenses:				
Fixed manufacturing costs	$37,000	$ 37,000	$ 37,000	$ 37,000
Fixed selling and administrative				
costs	33,000	33,000	33,000	33,000
Total fixed costs/expenses	$70,000	$ 70,000	$ 70,000	$ 70,000
Operating income (loss)		$ (5,600)	$ 3,600	$ 12,800

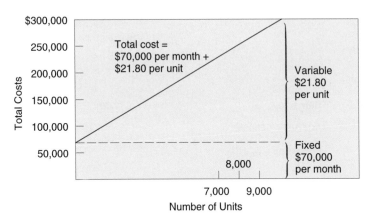

EXHIBIT 13-3

Dominion Company
Graph of Flexible
Budget of Costs

Total cost =
$70,000 per month +
$21.80 per unit

Variable
$21.80
per unit

Fixed
$70,000
per month

PERSPECTIVES ON P O D M DECISION-MAKING

Canada Post Turnaround

Canada Post
www.mailposte.ca

There is pressure for the gigantic Canada Post corporation to become profitable and financially self-sufficient. With 63,000 employees, 20,000 retail outlets and the processing of forty to fifty million units a day, this is a large organization to turn around. Cost controls are essential. But scale is not the only issue. The demands being made on Canada Post are modified by the expectation of retaining a uniform service. At the same time that Canada Post is being asked to become financially sound, it is expected to continue to provide first-class letter service at a single price to the most remote regions of the country. Currently, the short haul routes subsidize the rural and long-distance routes. This fixed price to consumers regardless of the cost of providing the service is not expected of telephone services, freight or air travel, so why should it be for postage?

As the corporation is being pushed toward competition, the environment for communication is changing rapidly. "A number of people suggest that electronic mail will be the death knell of the post office," says Jim Ross, who has spent 22 years as a counter clerk. But many people inside the post office do not agree, believing that the huge amount of electronic shopping on the internet will generate orders for goods that will be delivered through the post office. Some Canadian postal outlets have even joined the electronic age sufficiently to assist their customers in sending e-mail messages.

Managers and employees agree that the corporation has to exploit the business opportunities of the electronic age if Canada Post is become competitive.

Sources: Adapted from M. Grange, "Canada Post's costs the issue, experts say," *The Globe and Mail,* (November 21, 1997), p. A10; S. McCarthy, "Can Canada Post deliver?," *The Globe and Mail* (November 22, 1997), p. B1; R. Campbell, "Canada Post is far from a dead letter," *The Globe and Mail* (November 24, 1997), p. A17.

Activity-based Flexible Budgets

The flexible budget for Dominion Company shown in Exhibit 13-2 is based on a single cost driver—units of product. For companies that use a traditional, volume-based costing system, this is an appropriate approach to flexible budgeting.

Companies that use an activity-based costing system use a more detailed approach. An **activity-based flexible budget** is based on budgeted costs for each activity centre and related cost driver at varying volumes of activity. Exhibit 13-4

EXHIBIT 13-4

Dominion Company
Activity-based Flexible
Budget for the Month
Ended June 30, 2002

	BUDGET FORMULA	Units		
		7,000	8,000	9,000
Sales	$31.00	$217,000	$248,000	$279,000

ACTIVITY CENTRE

Processing

Cost Driver: Number of Machine Hours

	BUDGET FORMULA			
Cost-Driver Level		14,000	16,000	18,000
Variable Costs	$10.50	$147,000	$168,000	$189,000
Fixed Costs	$13,000	13,000	13,000	13,000
Total Costs of Processing Activity		$160,000	$181,000	$202,000

Setup

Cost Driver: Number of Setups

	BUDGET FORMULA			
Cost-Driver Level		21	24	27
Variable Costs	$500	$10,500	$12,000	13,500
Fixed Costs	$12,000	12,000	12,000	12,000
Total Costs of Setup Activity		$22,500	$24,000	$25,500

Marketing

Cost Driver: Number of Orders

	BUDGET FORMULA			
Cost-Driver Level		350	400	450
Variable Costs	$12.00	$4,200	$4,800	$5,400
Fixed Costs	$15,000	15,000	15,000	15,000
Total Costs of Marketing Activity		$19,200	$19,800	$20,400

Administration

Cost Driver: Number of Units

	BUDGET FORMULA			
Cost-Driver Level		7,000	8,000	9,000
Variable Costs	$.20	$1,400	$1,600	$1,800
Fixed Costs	$18,000	18,000	18,000	18,000
Total Costs of Administration Activity		$19,400	$19,600	$19,800
Total Costs		$221,100	$244,400	$267,700
Operating Income (loss)		$(4,100)	$3,600	$11,300

Activity-Based Flexible Budget. A budget based on costs for each activity centre and cost driver at varying volumes of activity.

shows an activity-based flexible budget for the Dominion Company. There are four activity centres: processing, setup, marketing, and administration. Within each activity centre, costs depend on an appropriate cost driver.

Compare the traditional flexible budget (Exhibit 13-2) and the activity-based flexible budget (Exhibit 13-4). The key difference is that some manufacturing costs that are fixed with respect to *units* are variable with respect to more appropriate cost driver *setups*. The fixed manufacturing costs ($37,000) in Exhibit 13-2 include setups costs that are largely fixed with respect to "units produced" but that vary with respect to the "number of setups." An example is the cost of supplies used to set up the production run. Each time a setup is done, supplies are used. Therefore, the cost of supplies varies directly with the number of setups. However, no setup supplies are used during production, so there is little change in the cost of supplies over wide ranges of units produced. This basic difference explains why the total costs differ using the two approaches—activity-based flexible budgets provide more detailed measures of cost behaviour.

When should a company use activity-based flexible budgets? When a significant portion of its costs vary with cost drivers other then units of production. In our Dominion example, the $500 per setup is the only such cost. For the rest of this chapter we will ignore the fact that this cost varies with the number of setups, and go back to assuming that Dominion's operations are simple enough that a traditional flexible budget with a single cost driver is appropriate.

Evaluation of Financial Performance Using the Flexible Budget

OBJECTIVE 4

Understand the performance evaluation relationship between master (static) budgets and flexible budgets.

Comparing the flexible budget to actual results accomplishes an important performance evaluation purpose. There are basically two reasons why actual results might differ from the master budget. One is that sales and cost-driver activities were not the same as originally forecasted. The second is that revenues or variable costs per unit of activity and fixed costs per period were not as expected. Though these reasons may not be completely independent (for example, higher sales prices may have caused lower sales levels), it is useful to separate these effects because different people may be responsible for them, and different management actions may be indicated. The intent of using the flexible budget for performance evaluation is to isolate varied, significant effects on actual results that can be corrected if adverse, or enhanced if beneficial. Because the flexible budget is prepared at the actual levels of activity (in our example, sales volume), any variances between the flexible budget and actual results cannot be due to activity levels (again, assuming cost and revenue functions are valid). These *variances between the flexible budget and actual results are called* **flexible-budget variances** or **efficiency variances** and must be due to *departures of actual costs or revenues from flexible-budget formula amounts*—due to pricing or cost control. In contrast, any differences or *variances between the master budget and the flexible budget are due to activity levels*, not cost control. These differences between the master budget amounts and the amounts in the flexible budget are called **activity-level variances** or **sales volume variances**.

Consider Exhibit 13-5. The flexible budget (column 3) from Exhibit 13-2 (and simplified), provides an explanatory bridge between the master budget (column 5) and the actual results (column 1). The variances for operating income are summarized at the bottom of columns 2 and 4, and are the sum of the sales activity variances and the flexible-budget variances. The difference between actual results and the original master budget can also be divided into two components: the sales activity variances and the flexible-budget variances.

Flexible-Budget Variances (Efficiency Variances). Variances between the flexible budget and the actual results.

Activity-Level Variances (Sales Volume Variances). Variances between the flexible budget and the master budget.

ISOLATING BUDGET VARIANCES AND THEIR CAUSES

Effectiveness. The degree to which a goal, objective, or target is met.

Efficiency. The degree to which inputs are used in relation to a given level of outputs.

Managers use comparisons between actual results, master budgets, and flexible budgets to evaluate organizational performance. When evaluating performance, it is useful to distinguish between **effectiveness**—the degree to which a goal, objective, or target is met—and **efficiency**—the degree to which inputs are used in relation to a given level of outputs.

EXHIBIT 13-5

Dominion Company
Summary of Performance for the Month Ended June 30, 2002

	(1) ACTUAL RESULTS AT ACTUAL ACTIVITY LEVEL*	(2) (1) - (3) FLEXIBLE-BUDGET VARIANCES+	(3) FLEXIBLE BUDGET FOR ACTUAL SALES ACTIVITY++	(4) (3) - (5) SALES ACTIVITY VARIANCES	(5) MASTER BUDGET*
Units	7,000	—	7,000	2,000 U	9,000
Sales	$217,000	—	$217,000	$62,000 U	$279,000
Variable Costs	158,270	5,670 U	152,600	43,600 F	196,200
Contribution Margin	$ 58,730	$5,670 U	$ 64,400	$18,400 U	$ 82,800
Fixed Costs	70,300	300 U	70,000	—	70,000
Operating Income	$ (11,570)	$5,970 U	$ (5,600)	$18,400 U	$ 12,800

Total flexible-budget variances
$5,970 Unfavourable

Total sales activity variances
$18,400 Unfavourable

Total master budget variances, $24,370 Unfavourable

U = Unfavourable. F = Favourable
* Figures are from Exhibit 13-1
+ Figures are shown in more detail in Exhibit 13-6
++ Figures are from the 7,000 unit column in Exhibit 13-2

Performance may be effective, efficient, both, or neither. For example, Dominion Company set a master budget objective of manufacturing and selling 9,000 units. However, only 7,000 units were actually made and sold. Performance, as measured by sales activity variances, was ineffective because the sales objective was not met.

Was Dominion's performance efficient? Managers judge the degree of efficiency by comparing actual outputs achieved (7,000 units) with actual inputs (such as the costs of direct materials and direct labour). *The less input used to produce a given output, the more efficient the operation.* As indicated by the flexible-budget variances, Dominion was inefficient in its use of a number of inputs. Later in this chapter we consider in detail direct material, direct labour, and variable overhead flexible-budget variances.

Flexible-Budget Variances

OBJECTIVE 5

Compute flexible-budget variances and sales activity variances.

Flexible-budget variances measure the efficiency of operations at the actual level of activity. The first three columns of Exhibit 13-5 compare the actual results with the flexible-budget amounts. The flexible-budget variances are the differences between columns 1 and 3, which total $5,970. The results are unfavourable, because:

Total flexible-budget variance = total actual results − total flexible-budget
= ($11,570) − ($5,600)
= ($5,970) or $5,970 unfavourable[1]

---

[1] What if the total flexible-budget results were positive, say, $4,000? The total flexible-budget variance would be ($11,570) + ($4,000) = ($15,570) or $15,570 unfavourable.

SUMMARIZE TO PRIORITIZE

It is generally agreed that we must set priorities in order to ensure that the most important work is completed first. The most important issues must be addressed first. Everyone knows this; however, this simple requirement is too often ignored when developing financial and management reports.

Consider the following example:

A person working for a large retail chain is responsible for the operations of 30 stores. This person (a district manager) has 30 store managers reporting to her.

Every month each store manager receives a financial report (Store Income Statement) showing sales, cost of sales, gross margin, expenses, and net income. Sales details are shown to indicate sales by major product group (what was sold) and sales by customer type (who bought the products). Expense details are shown to indicate amounts for salaries, rent, taxes, stationery, etc. For each line item of information actual results are compared to budget and last year with the variance to budget and last year being shown in dollars and as a percent.

The district manager receives a report similar to that of the store manager that has been consolidated for the district. The report sent to the district manager reflects the financial performance for the entire district. The sales line on the district income statement reflects a sum of sales for all stores in the district; the expenses line reflects a sum of expenses for all stores in the district.

Often, when the district manager receives her report she has questions related to why certain things are happening. For example, why are sales 3 percent below budget and why are expenses $727,000 greater than last year? At the district manager level, questions would typically relate to which stores attribute to the variance. The district manager is accountable for the district's performance. In order to determine why performance is better or worse than expected, she must know which stores are causing the variance.

One suggestion is to send the district manager a copy of all the Store Income Statements for the stores in her district. If she has a question related to one of the lines on her Income Statement, she can simply flip through the individual Store Income Statements to determine which store is causing the variance. This is a common practice in management reporting today and is absolutely unacceptable.

This process is time-consuming and makes it difficult for the sistrict manager to prioritize her time on areas that may require attention. A district manager should not have to flip through 30 Store Income Statements to determine which store is contributing to an unfavourable or favourable variance. Management (and financial) reporting should simplify the job of the field manager (district manager in our example). It should bring attention to problem areas so the manager can focus on these problem areas immediately.

Summarize results (do not simply consolidate) to prioritize work.

A consolidation for the district is useful information to the district manager. This is what she is accountable for and she is indeed interested in a Consolidated Income Statement. Rather than a copy of each Store Income Statement to provide store-specific information, a series of summary reports is much more effective.

Without summary reports, if the district manager notices a 3 percent variance in sales when reviewing the Consolidated District Income Statement, she now must flip through 30 Store Income Statements to see which store is causing the variance. It would be much easier to turn to a one-page summary report showing sales by store compared to last year and budget. The summary report can be sorted in various ways (by store number, by dollar variance in descending order, by percent variance in ascending order, etc.).

A list of summary reports that would be useful to the district manager include

Sales by Store
Gross Margin by Store
Gross Margin as Percent of Sales by Store
Salaries by Store

continued

Stock Shortages by Store
Total Expenses by Store
Total Expenses by Store as Percent of Sales by Store
Net Income by Store
Net Income by Store as Percent of Sales by Store

All reports would compare actual results to budget and to last year. Variance to budget and last year would be shown in dollars and as a percent.

By referring to the summary reports, the district manager can zero in on one line (sales, gross margin, expenses or net income) of her Income Statement at a time. The summary report provides the ability to review, on one page, the performance of all stores in the district. The report allows the district manager to prioritize efforts (follow-up discussions, interviews, etc.) on the store with unfavourable results. Also, stores with above-average performance would stand out; therefore, discussions with these stores may lead to successful ideas being implemented in other stores in the district.

Financial and management reporting must summarize information in an effective manner. This will ensure that management can easily determine problem areas as well as peak performing areas. These reports will enable management to prioritize work in an effective manner to Increase Revenue, Avoid Cost and Improve Service (IRACIS). IRACIS is a common factor considered by management to determine if certain initiatives should be undertaken. By providing useful summary reports to management, information can be used to increase revenue, avoid cost and improve service.

Source: Jeff Pennock, Director, Financial Planning and Analysis, LCBO.

The total flexible-budget variance arises from sales prices received and the variable and fixed costs incurred. Dominion Company had no difference between actual sales price and the flexible-budgeted sales price, so the focus is on the differences between actual costs and flexible-budgeted costs at the actual 7,000-unit level of activity. Without the flexible budget in column 3, we cannot separate these variances from the effects of changes in sales activity. The flexible budget variances indicate whether operations were efficient or not, and may form the basis for periodic performance evaluation. Operations managers are in the best position to explain flexible-budget variances and in many organizations are held accountable for meeting quality and cost targets as expressed in the budget.

Companies that use variances primarily to fix blame often find that managers resort to cheating and subversion to beat the system. Managers of operations usually have more information about those operations than higher-level managers. If that information is used against them, lower-level managers may withhold or misstate valuable information for their own self-protection. For example, one manufacturing firm actually *reduced* the next period's departmental budget by the amount of the department's unfavourable variances in the current period. If a division had a $50,000 budget and experienced a $2,000 unfavourable variance, the following period's budget would be set at $48,000. This system led managers to cheat and to falsify reports to avoid unfavourable variances. We can criticize departmental managers' ethics, but the system was as much at fault as the managers.

Exhibit 13-6 gives an expanded, line-by-line computation of variances for all master budget items at Dominion. Note how most of the costs that had seemingly favourable variances when a master budget was used as a basis for comparison have, in reality, unfavourable variances. Do not conclude automatically

EXHIBIT 13-6

Dominion Company
Cost-Control Performance Report for the Month Ended June 30, 2002

	ACTUAL COSTS INCURRED	FLEXIBLE BUDGET*	FLEXIBLE-BUDGET VARIANCES[+]	EXPLANATION
Units	7,000	7,000	—	
Variable Costs				
Direct material	$ 69,920	$ 70,000	$ 80 F	Lower prices but higher usage
Direct labour	61,500	56,000	5,500 U	Higher wage rates and higher usage
Indirect labour	9,100	11,900	2,800 F	Decreased setup time
Idle time	3,550	2,800	750 U	Excessive machine breakdowns
Cleanup time	2,500	2,100	400 U	Cleanup of spilled solvent
Supplies	4,700	4,200	500 U	Higher prices and higher usage
Variable manufacturing costs	$151,270	$147,000	$4,270 U	
Shipping	5,000	4,200	800 U	Use of air freight to meet delivery
Administration	2,000	1,400	600 U	Excessive copying and long-distance calls
Total variable costs	$158,270	$152,600	$5,670U	
Fixed costs:				
Factory supervision	$ 14,700	$ 14,400	$ 300 U	Salary increase
Factory rent	5,000	5,000	—	
Equipment amortization	15,000	15,000	—	
Other fixed factory costs	2,600	2,600	—	
Fixed manufacturing costs	$ 37,300	$ 37,000	$ 300 U	
Fixed selling and administrative costs	33,000	33,000	—	
Total fixed costs	$ 70,300	$ 70,000	$ 300 U	
Total variable and fixed costs	$228,570	$222,600	$5,970 U	

* From 7,000-unit column of Exhibit 13-2.

[+] This is a line-by-line breakout of the variances in column 2 of Exhibit 13-5.

that favourable flexible-budget variances are good and unfavourable flexible-budget variances are bad. Instead, *interpret all variances as signals that actual operations have not occurred exactly as anticipated* when the flexible-budget formulas were set. Any cost that differs significantly from the flexible budget deserves an explanation. The last column of Exhibit 13-6 gives possible explanations for Dominion Company's variances.

Sales-Activity Variances

Sales-Activity Variances. Variances that measure how effective managers have been in meeting the planned sales objective, calculated as actual unit sales less master-budget unit sales times the budgeted unit-contribution margin.

Sales-activity variances measure how *effective* managers have been in meeting the planned sales objective. In Dominion Company, sales activity fell 2,000 units short of the planned level. The final three columns of Exhibit 13-5 clearly show how the sales-activity variances (totalling $18,400 U) are unaffected by any changes in unit prices or variable costs. Why? Because the same budgeted unit prices and variable costs are used in constructing both the flexible budget and master budget. Therefore, all unit prices and variable costs are held constant in columns 3, 4, and 5.

The total of the sales-activity variances informs the manager that falling short of the sales target by 2,000 units caused operating income to be $18,400 lower than initially budgeted (a $5,600 loss instead of a $12,800 profit). In summary, the shortfall of sales by 2,000 units caused Dominion Company to incur a total sales-activity variance of 2,000 units at a contribution margin of $9.20 per unit (from the first column of Exhibit 13-2).

$$
\begin{aligned}
\text{Total sales activity variance} &= \left(\begin{array}{c} \text{flexible-budget units} - \\ \text{master budget units} \end{array} \right) \times \left(\begin{array}{c} \text{budgeted contribution} \\ \text{margin per unit} \end{array} \right) \\
&= (9,000 - 7,000) \times \$9.20 \\
&= \$18,400 \text{ unfavourable}
\end{aligned}
$$

Who has responsibility for the sales-activity variance? Marketing managers usually have the primary responsibility for reaching the sales level specified in the static budget. Of course, variations in sales may be attributable to many factors. For example it is common to analyze the change in sales-activity variances due to changes in market share and market size. A *market share* variance assumes the market or industry sales volume is on budget, but that the activity variance was due to a change in the company's share of the total industry sales. A *market size* variance assumes that the company's share as a percentage of the total market is on target, and then attributes the sales-activity variance to the change in market sales volume.

Assume that Dominion's planned sales objective of 9,000 units was based on a 40 percent market share of a budget industry sales volume of 22,500 units. If the total market for Dominion's product was 21,000 units, then the actual volume of 7,000 units would represent 33.33 percent of the market. Given these facts the following variances can be computed.

$$
\begin{aligned}
\text{market share variance} &= \left(\begin{array}{c} \text{actual} \\ \text{market share} \\ \text{percentage} \end{array} - \begin{array}{c} \text{budgeted} \\ \text{market share} \\ \text{percentage} \end{array} \right) \times \left(\begin{array}{c} \text{actual} \\ \text{industry sales} \\ \text{volume in units} \end{array} \right) \times \left(\begin{array}{c} \text{budgeted} \\ \text{contribution} \\ \text{margin per unit} \end{array} \right) \\
&= (33.33\% - 40\%) \ 21,000 \text{ units} \times \$9.20 \\
&= (6.6\%) \ 21,000 \times \$9.20 \\
&= 1,400* \text{ units} \times \$9.20 \\
&= \$12,880 \text{ unfavourable}
\end{aligned}
$$

* rounded to the nearest 100 units.

$$
\begin{aligned}
\text{market size variance} &= \begin{array}{c} \text{budgeted} \\ \text{market share} \\ \text{percentage} \end{array} \times \left(\begin{array}{c} \text{actual} \\ \text{industry sales} \\ \text{volume in units} \end{array} - \begin{array}{c} \text{budgeted} \\ \text{industry sales} \\ \text{volume in units} \end{array} \right) \times \left(\begin{array}{c} \text{budgeted} \\ \text{contribution} \\ \text{margin per unit} \end{array} \right) \\
&= 40\% \ (21,000 - 22,500 \text{ units}) \ \$9.20 \\
&= 40\% \ (-1,500) \times \$9.20 \\
&= 600 \text{ units} \times \$9.20 \\
&= \$5,520 \text{ unfavourable}
\end{aligned}
$$

Thus, of the $18,400 unfavourable sales-activity variance, $12,880 is due to a 6.67 percent reduction in market share and $5,520 is the result of a decreased market of 1,500 units.[2]

---

[2] A more advanced treatment of sales-activity variances is covered in Horngren, Foster, Datar, and Teall, *Cost Accounting: A Managerial Emphasis* (Prentice Hall, 2000) pp. 561–566. These sales-activity variances might result from changes in the product, changes in customer demand, effective advertising, and so on.

Expectations, Standard Costs, and Standard Cost Systems

Standard Cost. A carefully determined cost per unit that should be attained.

Standard Cost Systems. Accounting systems that value products according to standard cost only.

Expectations or *standard costs* are the building blocks of a planning and control system and a *standard cost* is the cost that is most likely to be attained. A **standard cost** is a carefully designed cost per unit that *should be* attained. It may be synonymous with expected cost, but this is not necessarily so in a *standard cost system*. Do not confuse having expectations or *standards* with having a *standard cost system*. **Standard cost systems** value products according to standard costs only.[3] These inventory valuation systems simplify financial reporting, but in most companies they are expensive to install and to maintain. Therefore, standard costs may not be revised often enough to be useful for management decision making regarding specific products or services. (Ideally, only one cost system should be necessary in any organization, but in practice many organizations have developed multiple cost systems.) Budgeting links these cost systems and applies expectations for future costs to expected future activity levels. These expectations may also be called standards because they are benchmarks or objectives to be attained. The fact that they are called standards does not imply that one also must have a standard cost system for inventory valuation or that one must use the standard cost system for planning and control.

COMPANY ⓒ STRATEGIES

STANDARD COST SYSTEM AT BUDD CANADA INC.

Budd Canada is an automotive parts manufacturer, specializing in the production of chassis component parts, light truck frames, cold weather starting products, and accessories. Its standard cost system is not their primary vehicle for cost control but rather its primary focus is to facilitate financial reporting and planning. In a unionized environment with practically no opportunity to recover cost increases, the emphasis in the system is on timely upfront operational information, as opposed to after-the-fact cost reporting.

For example:

1. Materials and services are obtained through a computerized hierarchy of approvals.
2. For all capital and major expense expenditures, there are evaluation and pre-approval procedures.
3. Weekly major issue reviews by operating and support personnel of areas such as inventory status, crew rates, overtime requirements, and stakeholder updates of capital and major expenditures ensure that issues are managed quickly.
4. Formal cost-reduction programs are incorporated into short- and long-term financial plans with a quarterly review of performance by senior management.

Budd's cost system represents in part their following commitment to quality:

Strive for total quality management that will promote continuous Planned Quality Improvement and product superiority. Quality management is the job of every employee. An organized approach to quality is necessary in our current and future business environment. We must maintain a quality management plan that is solid enough to be ongoing, flexible enough to handle change, innovative enough to make us leaders, and effective enough to reduce waste of resources.

Source: Written by Frank Currie, Controller, Budd Canada Inc. Material also obtained from the Budd Canada Inc., Annual Report, 1989.

---

[3] Details of standard cost systems for financial reporting are covered in Horngren, Foster, Datar, and Teall, *Cost Accounting: A Managerial Emphasis* (Prentice Hall, 2000), Chapters 7 and 8.

Current Attainability: The Most Widely Used Standard

What standard of expected performance should be used? Should it be so strict that it is rarely, if ever, attained? Should it be attainable 50 percent of the time? Ninety percent? Twenty percent? Individuals who have worked a lifetime setting and evaluating standards for performance disagree, so there is no one single answer to this question.

Perfection Standards. Expressions of the most efficient performance possible under the best conceivable conditions using existing specifications and equipment.

Perfection standards (also called *ideal standards*) are expressions of the most efficient performance possible under the best conceivable conditions, using existing specifications and equipment. No provision is made for waste, spoilage, machine breakdowns, and the like. Those who favour using perfection standards maintain that the resulting unfavourable variances will constantly remind personnel of the continuous need for improvement in all phases of operations. Though concern for continuous improvement is widespread, these standards are not widely used because they have an adverse effect on employee motivation. Employees tend to ignore unreasonable goals, especially if they would not share the gains from meeting imposed perfection standards. Organizations that apply the just-in-time philosophy attempt to achieve continuous improvement from "the bottom up," not by prescribing what should be achieved via perfection standards.

Currently Attainable Standards. Levels of performance that can be achieved by realistic levels of effort.

Currently attainable standards are levels of performance that can be achieved by realistic levels of effort. Allowances are made at normal rates for defects, spoilage, waste, and non-productive time. There are at least two popular interpretations of the meaning of currently attainable standards. The first interpretation has standards set just tightly enough that employees regard their attainment as highly probable if normal effort and diligence are exercised. That is, variances should be random and negligible. Hence, the standards are predictions of what will indeed occur, anticipating some inefficiencies. Managers accept the standards as being reasonable goals. The reasons for setting "reasonable" standards, then, are

1. The resulting standards serve multiple purposes. For example, the same cost can be used for financial budgeting, inventory valuation, and budgeting departmental performance. In contrast, perfection standards cannot be used for inventory valuation or financial budgeting, because the costs are known to be inaccurate.
2. Reasonable standards have a desirable motivational impact on employees, especially when combined with incentives for continuous improvement. The standard represents reasonable future performance, not fanciful goals. Therefore, unfavourable variances direct attention to performance that is not meeting reasonable expectations.

A second interpretation of currently attainable standards is that standards are set tightly. That is, employees regard their fulfilment as possible, though unlikely. Standards can only be achieved by very efficient operations. Variances tend to be unfavourable; nevertheless, employees accept the standards as being tough, but not unreasonable, goals. Is it possible to achieve continuous improvement using currently attainable standards? Yes, but expectations must reflect improved productivity and must be tied to incentive systems that reward continuous improvement.

Tradeoffs Among Variances

Because the operations of organizations are linked, the level of performance in one area of operations will affect performance in other areas. Nearly any combination of effects is possible: improvements in one area could lead to improvements in others, and vice versa. Likewise, substandard performance in one area may be balanced by superior performance in others. For example, a service organization may generate favourable labour variances by hiring less-skilled and thus lower-paid customer representatives, but this favourable variance may lead to unfavourable customer satisfaction and future unfavourable sales activity variances. In another situation, a manufacturer may experience unfavourable materials variances by purchasing higher-quality materials, but this variance will be more than offset by the favourable variances caused by lower inventory handling costs (for example, inspections) and higher-quality products (such as favourable scrap and rework variances).

Because of the many interdependencies among activities, an "unfavourable" or "favourable" label should not lead the manager to jump to conclusions. By themselves, such labels merely raise questions and provide clues to the causes of performance. *They are attention directors, not problem solvers.* Furthermore, the cause of variances might be faulty expectations rather than the execution of plans by managers. One of the first questions a manager should consider when explaining a large variance is whether expectations were valid.

When to Investigate Variances

When should variances be investigated? Frequently the answer is based on subjective judgments, hunches, guesses, and rules of thumb that have proven to be useful. The most troublesome aspect of using the feedback from flexible budgeting is deciding when a variance is large enough to warrant management's attention. The master and flexible budgets imply that the standard cost is the only permissible outcome. Practically speaking, the accountant (and everybody else) realizes that the standard is one of many possible acceptable cost outcomes. Consequently, the accountant expects variances to fluctuate randomly within some normal limits. Of course, an activity that allows wildly fluctuating variances as "normal" may be poorly designed. A random variance from a well-designed activity, by definition, is not caused by controllable actions and calls for no corrective action. In short, a random variance is attributable to chance rather than to management's implementation of plans. Consequently, the more a variance randomly fluctuates, the larger the variance required to make investigation worthwhile. There are two questions: First, what is a large versus a small variance? Second, is a large variance random or controllable? Usually, the second question is answered only after an investigation, so answering the first question is critical.

Managers recognize that, even if everything operates as planned, variances are unlikely to be exactly zero. They predict a range of "normal" variances; this range may be based on economic criteria (that is, how big a variance must be before investigation could be worth the effort) or on statistical criteria (for example, whether a variance is more than one *standard deviation* away from the expected or historical *mean* level of cost). For some critical items, any deviation may prompt a follow-up. For most items, a minimum dollar or percentage deviation from budget may be necessary before investigations are expected to be worthwhile. For example, a 4 percent variance in a $1-million material cost may deserve more attention than a 20 percent variance in a $10,000 repair cost. Because knowing exactly when to investigate is difficult, many organizations have developed such rules of thumb as, "Investigate all variances exceeding $5,000 or 25 percent of expected cost, whichever is lower."

PERSPECTIVES ON PODM DECISION-MAKING

The Need to Adapt Standard Cost Approaches

The use of standard costs and variance analysis came under attack during the last two decades of the twentieth century. Critics maintained that comparing actual costs to predetermined standards is a static approach that does not work well in today's dynamic, fast-paced, just-in-time environment. However, companies continue to use standards and to measure performance against them. Surveys in five different countries have shown that between 65 percent and 86 percent of manufacturing companies use standard costs, with the high level of 86 percent applying to the United States. Companies have apparently adapted the approach to fit their modern environments.

To apply standards in a dynamic environment, how should managers measure and report variances? First, standards should be regularly evaluated. If a company is in a continuous-improvement environment, standards must be constantly revised. Second, standards and variances should measure key strategic variables. The concept of setting a benchmark, comparing actual results to the benchmark, and identifying causes for any differences is universal. It can be applied to many types of measures, such as production quantity or quality, as well as to costs. Finally, variances should not lead to affixing blame. Standards are plans, and things do not always go according to plan—often with no one being at fault.

One company that has adapted standard costs to meets its particular needs is the Brass Products Division (BPD) at Parker Hannifin Corporation. The BPD uses standard costs and variances to pinpoint problem areas that need attention if the division is to meet its goal of continu-

ous improvement. Among the changes that have increased the value of the standard cost information are more timely product cost information, variances computed at more detailed levels, and holding regular meetings to help employees understand their impact on the variances.

The BPD also created three new variances: 1) standard run quantity variance—examines the effect of actual compared to optimal batch size for production runs, 2) material substitution variance—compares material costs to the costs of alternative materials, and 3) method variance—measures costs using actual machines compared to costs using alternative machines. All three variances use the concept of setting a standard and comparing actual results to the standard, but they do not apply the traditional standard cost variance formulas.

It was premature to declare standard costs dead. They are alive and well in many companies. However, there are fewer and fewer environments where traditional variance analysis is useful, and more and more environments where managers and accountants must adapt the standard cost concept to fit the particular needs of a company.

Sources: Adapted from D. Johnsen and P. Sopariwala, "Standard Costing Is Alive and Well at Parker Brass," *Management Accounting Quarterly*, Winter 2000, pp. 12–20; C. B. Cheatham and L. R. Cheatham, "Redesigning Cost Systems: Is Standard Costing Obsolete?", *Accounting Horizons*, December 1996, pp. 23–31; and C. Horngren, G. Foster, and S. Datar, *Cost Accounting: A Managerial Emphasis*, Prentice Hall, 2000, p. 226.

Parker Hannifin Corporation www.parker.com

Comparisons with Prior Period's Results

Some organizations compare the most recent budget period's actual results with last year's results for the same period rather than use flexible budget benchmarks. For example, an organization might compare June 2002's actual results to June 2001's actual results. In general these comparisons are not as useful for evaluating the performance of an organization as comparisons of actual outcomes with planned results for the same period. Why? Because many changes have probably occurred in the environment and in the organization that make a comparison to a prior period invalid. Very few organizations and environments are so stable that the only difference between now and a year ago is merely the passage of time. Even comparisons with last month's actual results may not be as useful as comparisons with flexible budgets. Comparisons over time may be useful for analyzing *trends* in such key variables as sales volume, market share, and product mix, but they do not help answer questions such as "Why did we have a loss of $11,570 in June, when we expected a profit of $12,800?"

FLEXIBLE-BUDGET VARIANCES IN DETAIL

The rest of this chapter probes the analysis in detail. The emphasis is on subdividing labour, material, and overhead cost variances into usage and price or spending components. Note that in companies where direct labour costs are small in relation to total costs (that is, in highly automated companies), direct labour costs may be treated as an overhead cost item, so separate standards, budgets, or variances need not be analyzed.

Variances from Material and Labour Standards

Consider Dominion Company's $10 standard cost of direct materials and $8 standard cost of direct labour. As shown below, these standards per unit are derived from two components, a standard quantity and a standard price:

	STANDARDS		
	STANDARD INPUTS EXPECTED PER UNIT OF OUTPUT	STANDARD PRICE EXPECTED PER UNIT OF INPUT	STANDARD COST EXPECTED PER UNIT OF OUTPUT
Direct Materials	5 kilograms	$ 2.00	$10.00
Direct Labour	1/2 hour	$16.00	$ 8.00

Once standards are set and actual results are observed, we can measure variances from the flexible budget. To show how the analysis of variances can be pursued more fully, we will reconsider Dominion's direct material and direct labour costs, as shown in Exhibit 13-6 and assume that the following actually occurred for the production of 7,000 units of output:

- *Direct material*: 36,800 kilograms of material were purchased and *used* at an actual unit *price* of $1.90 for a total actual cost of $69,920.

- *Direct labour*: 3,750 hours of labour were used at an actual hourly *price* (rate) of $16.40, for a total cost of $61,500.

Note that the flexible-budget variances for direct labour and direct material can be attributed to (1) using more of the resource than planned and (2) spending more for the resource than planned at the actual level of output achieved. These additional data enable us to subdivide the flexible-budget variances (column 3) from Exhibit 13-6 into the separate *usage* and *price* components, which are shown below in columns 4 and 5:

	(1) ACTUAL COSTS	(2) FLEXIBLE BUDGET	(3) FLEXIBLE-BUDGET VARIANCE	(4) PRICE VARIANCE*	(5) USAGE VARIANCE*
Direct Materials	$69,920	$70,000	$ 80 F	$3,680 F	$3,600 U
Direct Labour	61,500	56,000	5,500 U	1,500 U	4,000 U

* Computations to be explained shortly.

The flexible-budget totals for direct materials and direct labour are the amounts that would have been spent with expected efficiency. They are often labelled total *standard costs allowed*, computed as follows:

$$\begin{matrix} \text{flexible} \\ \text{budget or} \\ \text{total standard} \\ \text{cost allowed} \end{matrix} = \begin{matrix} \text{units of good} \\ \text{output} \\ \text{achieved} \end{matrix} \times \begin{matrix} \text{input allowed} \\ \text{per unit of} \\ \text{output} \end{matrix} \times \begin{matrix} \text{standard unit} \\ \text{price of input} \end{matrix}$$

standard direct
materials cost = 7,000 units × 5 kilograms × $2.00 per kilogram = $70,000
allowed

standard direct
labour cost = 7,000 units × ½ hour × $16.00 per hour = $56,000
allowed

Before reading on, note particularly that the flexible-budget amounts (that is, the standard costs allowed) are tied to an initial question: What was the output achieved? Always ask yourself: What was the good output? Then proceed with your computations of the total standard cost allowed for the good output achieved.

Price and Usage Variances

As noted earlier, we computed the flexible-budget amounts using the flexible-budget formulas, or currently attainable standards. Flexible-budget variances measure the relative efficiency of achieving the actual output. Price and usage variances subdivide each flexible-budget variance into two parts:

Price Variance. The difference between actual input prices and expected input prices multiplied by the actual quantity of inputs used.

1. **Price variance**—difference between actual input prices and standard input prices multiplied by the actual quantity of inputs used; and
2. **Usage variance**—difference between the quantity of inputs actually used and the quantity of inputs that should have been used to achieve

General Mills
www.generalmills.com

the actual quantity of output (also called a **quantity variance** or **efficiency variance**) multiplied by the standard price.

When feasible, you should separate the variances that are subject to a manager's direct influence from those that are not. The usual approach is to separate price factors from usage factors. Price factors are less subject to immediate control than are usage factors, principally because of external forces, such as general economic conditions, that can influence prices. Even when price factors are regarded as being outside management control, isolating them helps to focus on the efficient usage of inputs. For example, the commodity prices of wheat, oats, corn, and rice are outside the control of General Mills. By separating price variances from usage variances, the breakfast-cereal maker can focus on whether grain was used efficiently.

Variances themselves do not show why the budgeted operating income was not achieved. But they raise questions, provide clues, and direct attention. For instance, one possible explanation for this set of variances is that a manager might have made a tradeoff—the manager might have purchased at a favourable price some materials that were of substandard quality, saving $3,680 (the materials price variance). Excessive waste might have nearly offset this saving, as indicated by the $3,600 material usage variance and net flexible-budget variance of $80 Favourable. The material waste also might have caused at least part of the excess use of direct labour. Suppose more than $80 of the $4,000 unfavourable direct labour usage variance was caused by reworking units with defective materials. Then the manager's tradeoff was not successful. The cost inefficiencies caused by using substandard materials exceeded the savings from the favourable price.

Price and Usage Variance Computations

Calculation of price and usage variances is a good idea because the system provides control feedback to those responsible for inputs. But these variances should not be the only information used for decision making, control, or evaluation. Exclusive focus on material price variances by purchasing agents or buyers, for example, can work against an organization's just-in-time and total quality management goals. A buyer may be motivated to earn favourable material price variances by buying in large quantities and by buying low-quality material. The result could then be excessive inventory-handling and opportunity costs, and increased manufacturing defects due to faulty material. Similarly, exclusive focus on labour price and usage variances could motivate supervisors to use lower-skilled workers or to rush workers through critical tasks, both of which could impair quality of products and services.

Calculating price and usage variances is not difficult. The objective of these variance calculations is to hold either price or usage constant so that the effect of the other can be isolated. When calculating the price variance, you hold use of inputs constant at the actual level of usage. When calculating the usage variance, you hold price constant at the standard price. For Dominion Company the price variances are computed as follows:

Direct material price variance = (actual price–standard price) × actual quantity
= ($1.90–$2.00) per kilogram × 36,800 kilograms (actual)
= $3,680 Favourable

$$\text{Direct labour price variance} = \text{(actual price–standard price)} \times \text{actual quantity}$$
$$= (\$16.40\!-\!\$16.00) \text{ per hour} \times 3{,}750 \text{ hours}$$
$$\text{(actual)}$$
$$= \$1{,}500 \text{ Unfavourable}$$

The usage variances are computed as:

$$\text{Direct material usage variance} = \text{(actual quantity used–standard quantity}$$
$$\text{allowed)} \times \text{standard price}$$
$$= [(36{,}800\!-\!(7{,}000 \times 5)] \text{ kilograms} \times \$2.00 \text{ per}$$
$$\text{kilogram (standard)}$$
$$= \$3{,}600 \text{ Unfavourable}$$

$$\text{Direct labour usage variance} = \text{(actual quantity used–standard quantity}$$
$$\text{allowed)} \times \text{standard price}$$
$$= [3{,}750\!-\!(7{,}000 \times \tfrac{1}{2})] \text{ hours} \times \$16.00 \text{ per hour}$$
$$\text{(standard)}$$
$$= (3{,}750\!-\!3{,}500) \times \$16.00$$
$$= \$4{,}000 \text{ Unfavourable}$$

Note that the sum of the direct labour price and usage variances equals the direct labour flexible-budget variance. Furthermore, the sum of the direct material price and usage variances equals the total direct material flexible-budget variance.

$$\text{Direct materials flexible-budget variance} = \$80 \text{ Favourable}$$
$$= \$3{,}680 \text{ Favourable} + \$3{,}600 \text{ Unfavourable}$$

$$\text{Direct labour flexible-budget variance} = \$5{,}500 \text{ Unfavourable}$$
$$= \$1{,}500 \text{ Unfavourable} + \$4{,}000 \text{ Unfavourable}$$

To determine whether a variance is favourable or unfavourable, use logic rather than memorizing a formula. A price variance is favourable if the actual price is less than the standard. A usage variance is favourable if the actual quantity used is less than the standard quantity allowed. The opposite relationships imply unfavourable variances.

Exhibit 13-7 shows the price and usage variance computations graphically. The standard cost (or flexible budget) is the standard quantity multiplied by the standard price—the unshaded rectangle. The price variance is the difference between the unit prices, actual and standard, multiplied by actual quantity used—the area of the shaded rectangle on top. The usage variance is the standard price multiplied by the difference between the actual quantity used and the standard quantity allowed for the good output achieved—the area of the shaded rectangle on the lower right. (Note that for clarity the graph portrays only unfavourable variances.)

EXHIBIT 13-7

Dominion Company
Graph of Flexible
Budget of Costs

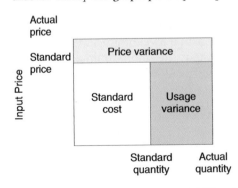

Effects of Inventories

Analysis of Dominion Company was simplified because: (1) there were no finished goods inventories—any units produced were sold in the same period— and (2) there was no direct material inventory—the materials were purchased and used in the same period.

What if production does not equal sales? The sales activity variance then is the difference between the static budget and the flexible budget for the number of units *sold*. In contrast, the flexible-budget cost variances compare actual costs with flexible-budgeted costs for the number of units *produced*.

Generally, managers want quick feedback and want variances to be identified as early is as practical. In the case of direct materials, that time is when the materials are purchased rather than when they are used, which may be much later. Therefore, the material price variance is usually based on the quantity purchased, measured at the time of purchase. The material usage variance remains based on the quantity used. Suppose Dominion Company purchased 40,000 kilograms of material (rather than the 36,800 kilograms used) at $1.90 per kilogram.

EXHIBIT 13-8

General Approach to Analysis of Direct Labour and Direct Material Variances

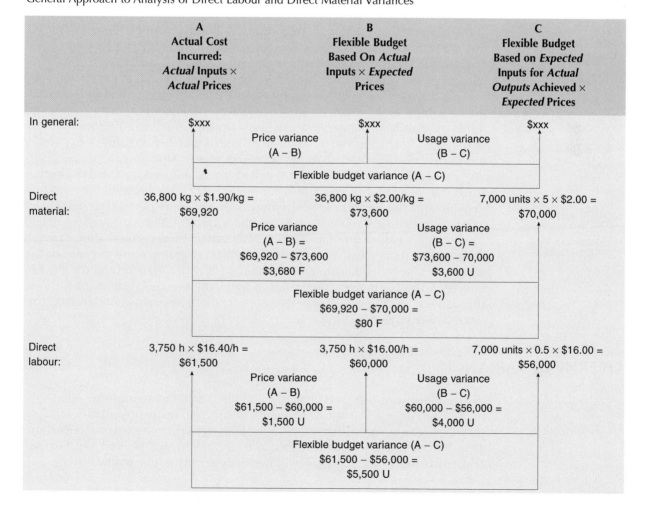

The material price variance would be (actual price - standard price) × material *purchased* = ($1.90 − $2.00) per kilogram × 40,000 kilograms = $4,000 favourable. The material usage variance would remain at $3,600 unfavourable because it is based on the material *used*.

A General Approach

Exhibit 13-8 presents the previous analysis in a format that deserves close study. The general approach is at the top of the exhibit. The specific applications then follow. Even though the exhibit may seem unnecessarily complex at first, its repeated use will solidify your understanding of variance analysis. Of course, the other flexible-budget variances in Exhibit 13-6 could be further analyzed in the same manner in which direct labour and direct material are analyzed in Exhibit 13-8. Such a detailed investigation depends on the manager's perception of whether the extra benefits will exceed the extra costs of the analysis.

Column A of Exhibit 13-8 contains the actual costs incurred for the inputs during the budget period being evaluated. Column B is the flexible-budgeted costs for the inputs *given the actual inputs used*, using expected prices but actual usage. Column C is the flexible budget amount using both expected prices and expected usage for the outputs actually achieved. (This is the flexible-budget amount from Exhibit 13-6 for 7,000 units.) Column B is inserted between A and C by using *expected* prices and *actual* usage. The difference between columns A and B is attributed to changing prices since usage is held constant between A and B at actual levels. The difference between columns B and C is attributed to changing usage since price is held constant between B and C at expected levels.

Note that we can express output activity levels in units of inputs. For example, in Exhibit 13-8 we could use labour hours or kilograms of material as activity levels. This is a common practice. Most organizations manufacture a variety of products. When the variety of units are added together, the sum is frequently a nonsensical number (such as, apples and oranges). Therefore, all units of output are expressed in terms of the standard inputs allowed for their production (such as, kilograms of fruit). Labour hours may also become the common denominator for measuring total output volume. Thus production, instead of being expressed as 12,000 chairs and 3,000 sofas, could be expressed as 20,000 *standard hours allowed* (or more accurately as *standard hours of input allowed for output achieved*). Remember that *standard hours allowed* is a measure of actual *output* achieved. A key idea illustrated in Exhibit 13-8 is the versatility of the flexible budget. A flexible budget is geared to activity volume, and Exhibit 13-8 shows that activity volume can be measured in terms of either *actual inputs allowed* or *actual outputs achieved*.

OVERHEAD VARIANCES

We have just seen that direct material and direct labour variances are often subdivided into price and usage components. In contrast, many organizations believe that it is not worthwhile to monitor individual overhead items to the same extent. Therefore, overhead variances often are not subdivided beyond the flexible-budget variances—the complexity of the analysis may not be worth the effort.

In some cases however, it may be worthwhile to subdivide the flexible-budget overhead variances, for variable overhead. Part of the variable overhead flexible-budget variance is related to changes in the cost driver and part to the control of overhead spending itself. When the actual cost driver varies from the standard amount allowed for the actual output achieved, a **variable overhead efficiency variance** will occur. Suppose that Dominion Company's supplies cost, a variable overhead cost, was driven by direct labour hours. A variable overhead cost rate of $.60 per unit at Dominion would be equal to $1.20 per hour (because one half-hour is allowed per unit of output). Of the $500 unfavourable variance, $300 is due to using 3,750 direct labour hours rather than the 3,500 expected direct labour hours, as calculated below:

Variable overhead
efficiency variance = [3,750(actual) − 3,500(expected)] × $1.20 per hour
  for supplies   = $300 Unfavourable

This $300 excess usage of supplies is attributable to inefficient use of the cost-driver activity, direct labour hours. Whenever actual cost-driver activity exceeds that allowed for the actual output achieved, overhead efficiency variances will be unfavourable, and vice-versa. In essence, this efficiency variance tells management the cost of *not* controlling the use of cost-driver activity. The remainder of the flexible-budget variance measures control of overhead spending itself, given actual cost-driver activity as

Variable overhead
spending variance = $500 U − $300 U
for supplies   = $200 U

That is, the **variable overhead spending variance** is the difference between the actual variable overhead and the amount of variable overhead budgeted for the actual level of cost-driver activity.

As with other variances, the overhead variances by themselves cannot identify causes for results that differ from the static and flexible budgets. The only way for management to discover why overhead performance did not agree with the budget is to investigate possible causes. However, the distinction between spending and usage variances provides a springboard for more investigation.

Exhibit 13-9 summarizes the general approach to overhead variances. The flexible-budget variances for fixed overhead items are not subdivided here. Fixed overhead flexible-budget variances only arise in absorption cost systems, which is explained in more detail in the next section. Note that the sales activity variance for fixed overhead is zero, because as long as activities remain within relevant ranges, the fixed overhead budget is the same at both planned and actual levels of activity.

EXHIBIT 13-9

General Approach to Analysis of Overhead Variances

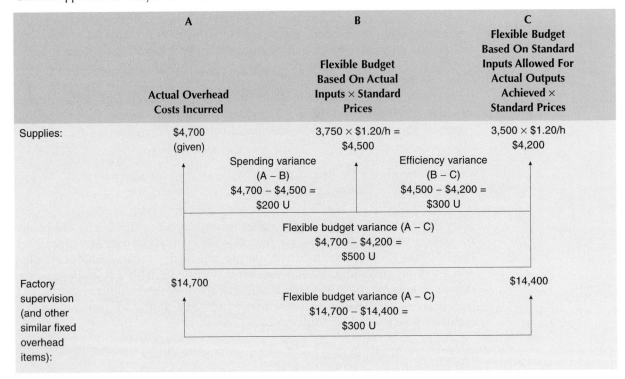

	A Actual Overhead Costs Incurred	B Flexible Budget Based On Actual Inputs × Standard Prices	C Flexible Budget Based On Standard Inputs Allowed For Actual Outputs Achieved × Standard Prices
Supplies:	$4,700 (given)	3,750 × $1.20/h = $4,500	3,500 × $1.20/h $4,200

Spending variance
(A – B)
$4,700 – $4,500 =
$200 U

Efficiency variance
(B – C)
$4,500 – $4,200 =
$300 U

Flexible budget variance (A – C)
$4,700 – $4,200 =
$500 U

Factory supervision (and other similar fixed overhead items): $14,700

Flexible budget variance (A – C)
$14,700 – $14,400 =
$300 U

$14,400

Production-Volume Variance

OBJECTIVE 8

Compute the production-volume variance.

In chapter 4, the *production-volume variance* was introduced and it was calculated as follows:

production-volume variance = applied fixed overhead − budgeted fixed overhead
= (actual volume × fixed-overhead rate)
− (expected volume × fixed-overhead rate)

or

production-volume variance = (actual volume − expected volume) × fixed-overhead rate

Volume Variance. (See Production-Volume Variance)

In practice, the *production-volume variance* is usually called simply the **volume variance**. We use the term *production-volume variance* because it is a more precise description of the fundamental nature of the variance.

A production-volume variance arises when the actual production volume achieved does not coincide with the expected volume of production used as a denominator for computing the fixed-overhead rate for product-costing purposes:

1. When expected production volume and actual production volume are identical, there is no production-volume variance.
2. When actual volume is less than expected volume, the production-volume variance is unfavourable because usage of facilities is less than

expected and fixed overhead is underapplied. It was previously measured in Exhibit 4-12 (page 151) for 2002 as follows:

$$\text{(actual volume – expected volume)} \times \text{budgeted fixed-overhead rate} = \text{production-volume variance}$$

$$(140,000 \text{ hours} - 150,000 \text{ hours}) \times \$1 = -\$10,000 \text{ or } \$10,000 \text{ U}$$

or

$$\text{budgeted minus applied} = \text{production-volume variance}$$
$$\$140,000 - \$150,000 = -\$10,000 \text{ or } \$10,000 \text{ U}$$

The \$10,000 unfavourable production-volume variance increases the manufacturing costs shown on the income statement. Why? Recall that \$150,000 of fixed manufacturing cost was incurred, but only \$140,000 was applied to inventory. Therefore, only \$140,000 will be charged as expense when the inventory is sold. But all \$150,000 must be charged sometime, so the extra \$10,000 is an added expense in the current income statement.

3. Where actual volume exceeds expected volume, as was the case in 2001, the production-volume variance is favourable because the use of facilities is better than expected and fixed overhead is overapplied:

$$\text{production-volume variance} = (170,000 \text{ units} - 150,000 \text{ units}) \times \$1$$
$$= \$20,000 \text{ F}$$

In this case, \$170,000 will be charged through inventory. Because actual costs of only \$150,000 are incurred, future expenses will be overstated by \$20,000. Therefore, current period expenses are reduced by the \$20,000 favourable variance.

The production-volume variance is the conventional measure of the cost of departing from the level of activity originally used to set the fixed-overhead rate.[4] Most companies consider production-volume variances to be beyond immediate control, although on occasion a manager responsible for volume has to do some explaining or investigating. Sometimes failure to reach the expected volume is caused by idleness due to disappointing total sales, poor production scheduling, unusual machine breakdowns, shortages of skilled workers, strikes, storms, and the like.

There is no production-volume variance for variable overhead. The concept of production-volume variance arises for fixed overhead because of the conflict between accounting for control (by flexible budgets) and accounting for product costing (by application rates). Note again that the fixed-overhead budget serves the control purpose, whereas the development of a product-costing rate results in the treatment of fixed overhead as if it were a variable cost.

Above all, bear in mind that fixed costs are simply not divisible as variable costs are. Rather, they come in big chunks and are related to the provision of big chunks of production or sales capability, not to the production or sale of a single unit of product.

---

[4] Do not confuse the production-volume variances described here with the sales-volume variance described earlier in this chapter. Despite similar nomenclature, they are completely different concepts.

Selecting the Expected Volume for Computing the Fixed-Overhead Rate

The fixed-overhead rate in an absorption-costing framework depends on the expected volume level chosen as the denominator in the computation; the higher the level of volume, the lower the rate.

The selection of an appropriate volume for the denominator is a matter of judgment. Management usually wants to apply a single representative standard fixed cost for a unit of product to apply over a period of at least one year, despite month-to-month changes in production volume. Therefore the predicted total fixed cost and the expected volume used in calculating the fixed-overhead rate should cover at least a one-year period. Most managers favour using the budgeted annual volume as the expected volume in the denominator. Others favour using some longer-run (three- to five-year) approximation of "normal" activity to adjust for annual fluctuations in volume. Still others favour using maximum or full capacity (often called **practical capacity**).

Practical Capacity.
Maximum or full capacity.

Although fixed-overhead rates are often important for product costing and long-run pricing, such rates have limited significance for control purposes. At the lower levels of supervision, almost no fixed costs are under direct control. Even at higher levels of supervision, many fixed costs are uncontrollable in the short run within wide ranges of anticipated activity.

Actual, Normal, and Standard Costing

OBJECTIVE 9

Identify the differences between the three alternative cost bases of an absorption-costing system: actual, normal, and standard.

Normal Costing. A cost system that applies actual direct materials and actual direct-labour costs to products or services but uses standards for applying overhead.

Overhead variances are not restricted to standard-costing systems. Many companies apply *actual* direct materials and actual direct labour costs to products or services but use *standards* for applying overhead. Such a procedure is called **normal costing**. The following chart compares normal costing with two other basic ways for applying costs by the absorption-costing method:

	ACTUAL COSTING	NORMAL COSTING	STANDARD COSTING
Direct materials	Actual costs	Actual costs	Budgeted prices or rates x standard inputs allowed for actual output achieved
Direct labour	Actual costs	Actual costs	
Variable factory overhead	Actual costs	Budgeted rates x actual inputs	
Fixed factory overhead			

Dropping fixed factory overhead from this chart produces a comparison of the same three basic ways of applying costs by the variable-costing method.

Both normal absorption costing and standard absorption costing generate production-volume variances. In addition, normal- and standard-costing systems produce all other overhead variances under both variable and absorption formats.

Flexible-Budget Variances

Returning again to the Greenberg Company, from Chapter 4 (summarized below) we will assume some additional facts for 2002 (the second of the two years covered by our example):

Flexible-budget variances:	
Direct material	None
Direct labour	$ 34,000 U
Variable factory overhead	$ 3,000 U
Fixed factory overhead	$ 7,000 U
Supporting data	
Standard direct labour hours allowed for	
140,000 units of output produced	35,000
Standard direct labour rate per hour	$ 6.00
Actual direct labour hours of inputs	40,000
Actual direct labour rate per hour	$ 6.10
Variable manufacturing overhead actually incurred	$ 31,000
Fixed manufacturing overhead actually incurred	$157,000

As explained in this chapter, flexible-budget variances may arise for both variable overhead and fixed overhead. Consider the following:

	ACTUAL AMOUNTS	FLEXIBLE-BUDGET AMOUNTS 140,000 UNITS	FLEXIBLE-BUDGET VARIANCES
Variable factory overhead	$ 31,000	$ 28,000	$3,000 U
Fixed factory overhead	157,000	150,000	7,000 U

Exhibit 13-10 shows the relationship between the fixed-overhead flexible-budget variance and the production-volume variance. The difference between the actual fixed overhead and that applied to products is the underapplied (or overapplied) overhead. Because the actual fixed overhead of $157,000 exceeds the $140,000 applied, fixed overhead is *underapplied* by $17,000, which means that the variance is *unfavourable*. The $17,000 underapplied fixed overhead has two components: (1) a production-volume variance of $10,000 U and (2) a fixed-overhead flexible-budget variance (also called the *fixed-overhead spending variance* or simply the *fixed-overhead budget variance*) of $7,000 U.

All variances other than the production-volume variance are essentially flexible-budget variances. They measure components of the differences between actual amounts and the flexible-budget amounts for the output achieved. Flexible budgets are primarily designed to assist planning and control rather than product costing. The production-volume variance is not a flexible-budget variance. It is designed to aid product costing.

Exhibit 13-11 contains an income statement under absorption costing that incorporates these new facts. These new variances hurt income by $44,000 because, like the production-volume variance, they are all unfavourable variances, which are charged against income in 2002. When variances are favourable, they increase operating income.

EXHIBIT 13-10

Fixed-Overhead
Variances for 2002
(Data were originally
presented in
Exhibit 4-12)

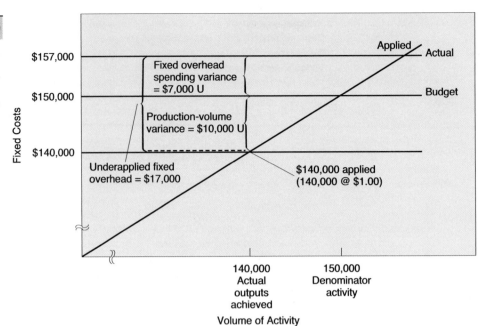

EXHIBIT 13-11

Absorption Costing for
2002 (Modification of
Exhibit 4-12, with addi-
tional data from the text)

	(IN THOUSANDS)	
Sales, 160,000 at $5		$800
Opening inventory at standard, 30,000 at $4	$120	
Cost of goods manufactured at standard, 140,000 at $4	560	
Available for sale, 170,000 at $4	$680	
Deduct ending inventory at standard, 10,000 at $4	40	
Cost of goods sold at standard, 160,000 at $4		640
Gross profit at standard		$160
Flexible-budget variances, both unfavourable:		
Variable manufacturing costs ($34,000 + $3,000)	$ 37	
Fixed factory overhead	7	
Production-volume variance (arises only because of		
fixed overhead), unfavourable	10	
Total variances		54
Gross profit at "actual"		$106
Selling and administrative expenses		105
Operating income		$ 1

Disposition of Standard Cost Variances

OBJECTIVE 10

Identify the two
methods for disposing
of the standard cost
variances at the end of
a year and give the
rationale for each.

Advocates of standard costing contend that variances are generally subject to current control, especially when the standards are viewed as being currently attainable. Therefore variances are not inventoriable and should be considered as adjustments to the income of the period instead of being added to inventories. In this way, inventory valuations will be more representative of desirable and attainable costs.

Others favour assigning the variances to the inventories and cost of goods sold related to the production during the period that the variances arose. This is often called **prorating the variances**. Prorating makes inventory valuations more representative of the "*actual*" costs incurred to obtain the products. In practice, unless variances and inventory levels are significant, the variances are usually not prorated.

Prorating the Variances.
Assigning the variances to the inventories and cost of goods sold related to the production during the period that the variances arose.

Therefore, in practice, all cost variances are typically regarded as adjustments to current income. Where variances appear on the income statement is generally unimportant. Exhibit 13-11 shows variances as a component of the computation of gross profit at "actual." But, variances could appear instead as a completely separate section elsewhere in the income statement. Such placement would help to distinguish between product costing (that is, the cost of goods sold, at standard) and loss recognition (unfavourable variances are "lost" or "expired" costs because they represent waste and inefficiency thereby not qualifying as inventoriable costs; that is, waste is not an asset). The *placement* of the variance does not affect operating income.

SUMMARY

OBJECTIVE 11

Analyze and compare all the major variances in a standard absorption-costing system.

Let us examine the variances in perspective by using the approach originally demonstrated in Exhibit 13-8. The results of the approach appear in Exhibit 13-12, which deserves your careful study, particularly the two notes. Please examine the exhibit before reading on.

Exhibit 13-13 graphically compares the variable- and fixed-overhead costs analyzed in Exhibit 13-12. Note how the control-budget line and the product-costing line (the applied line) are superimposed in the graph for variable overhead but differ in the graph for fixed overhead.

Underapplied or overapplied overhead is always the difference between the actual overhead incurred and the overhead applied. An analysis may then be made:

$$\text{underapplied overhead} = \left(\begin{array}{c}\text{flexible-budget} \\ \text{variance}\end{array}\right) + \left(\begin{array}{c}\text{production-volume} \\ \text{variance}\end{array}\right)$$

$$\text{for variable overhead} = \$3{,}000 + 0 = \$3{,}000$$
$$\text{for fixed overhead} = \$7{,}000 + \$10{,}000 = \$17{,}000$$

EXHIBIT 13-12

Analysis of Variances (Data are from text for 2002)

INPUTS	(A) Cost Incurred: Actual Inputs × Actual Price	(B) Flexible Budget Based On Actual Inputs × Standard Prices	(C) Flexible Budget Based On Standard Inputs Allowed For Actual Outputs Achieved × Standard Prices	(D) Product Costing: Applied To Product
Direct labour:	40,000 × $6.10 = $244,000	40,000 × $6 = $240,000	(35,000 × $6 or 140,000 × $1.50) = $210,000*	(35,000 × $6 or 140,000 × $1.50) = $210,000*
	$210,000*			
Variable factory overhead:	(given) $31,000	40,000 × $.80 = $32,000	(35,000 × $0.80 or 140,000 × $0.20) = $28,000*	$28,000*
Fixed factory overhead:	$157,000	Lump sum, $150,000	Lump sum $150,000†	140,000 × $1.00 = $140,000

Direct labour:
- 40,000 × ($6.10 − 6) = $4,000 U = price variance
- 5,000 × $6 = efficiency variance, $30,000 U
- Flexible-budget variance, $34,000 U
- Never a variance
- Never a variance

Variable factory overhead:
- Spending variance, $1,000 F
- 5,000 × $.80 = efficiency variance, $4,000 U
- Flexible-budget variance, $3,000 U
- Underapplied overhead, $3,000 U
- Never a variance
- Never a variance

Fixed factory overhead:
- Spending variance, $7,000 U
- Never a variance
- Production-volume variance, $10,000 U
- Flexible-budget variance, $7,000 U
- Production-volume variance, $10,000 U
- Underapplied overhead, $17,000 U

U = Unfavourable. F = Favourable.

*Note especially that the flexible budget for variable costs rises and falls in direct proportion to production. Note also that the control-budget purpose and the product-costing purpose harmonize completely; the total costs in the flexible budget will always agree with the standard variable costs applied to the product, because they are based on standard costs per unit multiplied by units produced.

† In contrast to variable costs, the flexible-budget total for fixed costs will always be the same regardless of the units produced. However, the control-budget purpose and the product-costing purpose conflict; whenever actual production differs from denominator production, the standard costs applied to the product will differ from the flexible budget. This difference is the production-volume variance. In this case, the production-volume variance may be computed by multiplying the $1 rate by the difference between the 150,000 denominator volume and the 140,000 units of output achieved.

EXHIBIT 13-13

Comparison of Control and Product-Costing Purposes
Variable Overhead and Fixed Overhead (not to scale)

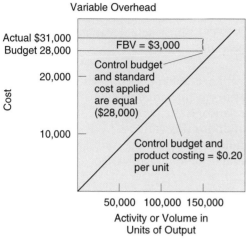

Variable Overhead

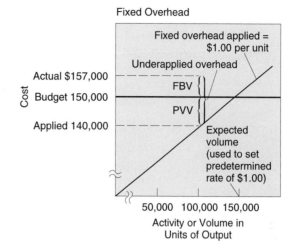

Fixed Overhead

FBV = Flexible-budget variance.
PVV = Production-volume variance.

HIGHLIGHTS TO REMEMBER

Flexible budgets are geared to changing levels of activity rather than to a single, static level of the master budget. Flexible budgets may be tailored to a particular level of sales or cost-driver activity—before or after the fact. They tell how much revenue and cost to expect for any level of activity.

Cost functions, or flexible-budget formulas, reflect fixed- and variable-cost behaviour and allow managers to compute budgets for any desired output or cost-driver activity level. The flexible-budget amounts are computed by multiplying the variable cost per unit of activity by the level of activity expected for the actual outputs achieved.

The evaluation of performance is aided by feedback that compares actual results with budgeted expectations. The flexible-budget approach helps managers explain why the master budget was not achieved. Master budget variances are divided into (sales) activity and flexible-budget variances. Activity variances reflect the organization's effectiveness in meeting financial plans. Flexible-budget variances reflect the organization's efficiency at actual levels of activity.

Expectations form the basis for budgeting and performance evaluation. Expectations may be formalized as standard costs and may be incorporated into standard cost systems, but only expectations (which may be called standards) are required for master and flexible budgets. The most commonly used standards are those considered to be attainable with reasonable effort.

Flexible-budget variances for variable inputs can be further broken down into price (or spending) and usage (or efficiency) variances. Price variances reflect the effects of changing input prices, holding usage of inputs constant at actual use. Usage variances reflect the effects of different levels of input usage, holding prices constant at expected prices.

SUMMARY PROBLEMS FOR YOUR REVIEW

Problem One

Refer to the data contained in Exhibits 13-1 and 13-2. Suppose actual production and sales were 8,500 units instead of 7,000 units; actual variable costs were $188,800; and actual fixed costs were $71,200.

1. Compute the master budget variance. What does this tell you about the efficiency of operations? The effectiveness of operations?
2. Compute the sales activity variance. Is the performance of the marketing function the sole explanation for this variance? Why?
3. Using a flexible budget, compute the budgeted contribution margin, budgeted operating income, and flexible-budget variance. What do you learn from this variance?

Solution

1. actual operating income = $(8,500 \times \$31) - \$188,800 - \$71,200 = \$3,500$

   master budget operating income = $\$12,800$ (from Exhibit 13-1)

   master budget variance = $\$12,800 - \$3,500 = \$9,300$ U

Three factors affect the master budget variance: sales activity, efficiency, and price changes. There is no way to tell from the master budget variance alone how much of the $9,300 U was caused by any of these factors alone.

2. sales activity variance = budgeted unit contribution margin × difference between the master budget unit sales and the actual unit sales
   = $\$9.20$ per unit CM × $(9,000 - 8,500)$
   = $\$4,600$ U

This variance is labelled as a sales activity variance because it quantifies the effect on operating income of the deviation from an original sales target while holding price and efficiency factors constant. This is a measure of the effectiveness of the operations—Dominion was ineffective in meeting its sales objective. Of course, the failure to reach target sales may be traced to a number of causes beyond the control of marketing personnel, including material shortages, factory breakdowns, and so on.

3. The budget formulas in Exhibit 13-2 are the basis for the following answers:

   flexible-budget contribution margin = $\$9.20 \times 8,500 = \$78,200$
   flexible-budget operating income = $\$78,200 - \$70,000 = \$8,200$
   actual operating income = $\$3,500$
   flexible-budget variance = $\$8,200 - \$3,500 = \$4,700$ U

The flexible-budget variance shows that the company spent $4,700 more to produce and sell the 8,500 units than it should have if operations had been efficient and unit costs had not changed. Note that this variance plus the $4,600 U sales activity variance total the $9,300 U master budget variance.

Problem Two

The following questions are based on the data contained in the Dominion Company illustration used on page 565.

- Direct materials: standard, 5 kilograms per unit @ $2 per kilogram
- Direct labour: standard, one-half hour @ $16 per hour

Suppose the following were the actual results for production of 8,500 units:

1. Direct material: 46,000 kilograms purchased and used at an actual unit price of $1.85 per kilogram for an actual total cost of $85,100.
2. Direct labour: 4,125 hours of labour used at an actual hourly rate of $16.80, for a total actual cost of $69,300.

1. Compute the flexible-budget and the price and usage variances for direct labour and direct material.
2. Suppose the company is organized so that the purchasing manager bears the primary responsibility for purchasing materials, and the production manager is responsible for the use of materials. Assume that the purchasing manager bought 60,000 kilograms of material. This means that there is an ending inventory of 14,000 kilograms of material. Recompute the materials variances.

Solution

1. The variances are as follows:

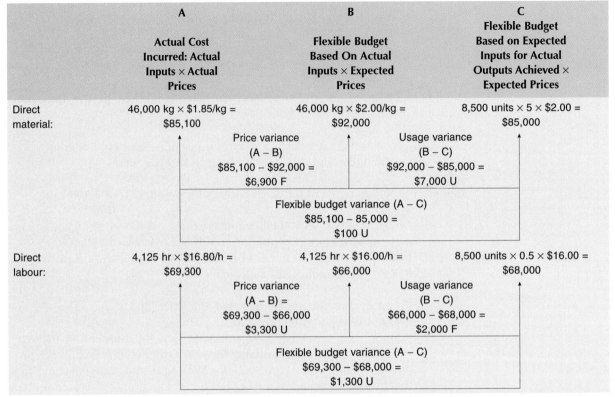

	A Actual Cost Incurred: Actual Inputs × Actual Prices	B Flexible Budget Based On Actual Inputs × Expected Prices	C Flexible Budget Based on Expected Inputs for Actual Outputs Achieved × Expected Prices
Direct material:	46,000 kg × $1.85/kg = $85,100	46,000 kg × $2.00/kg = $92,000	8,500 units × 5 × $2.00 = $85,000

Price variance
(A – B)
$85,100 – $92,000 =
$6,900 F

Usage variance
(B – C)
$92,000 – $85,000 =
$7,000 U

Flexible budget variance (A – C)
$85,100 – 85,000 =
$100 U

Direct labour:	4,125 hr × $16.80/h = $69,300	4,125 hr × $16.00/h = $66,000	8,500 units × 0.5 × $16.00 = $68,000

Price variance
(A – B) =
$69,300 – $66,000
$3,300 U

Usage variance
(B – C)
$66,000 – $68,000 =
$2,000 F

Flexible budget variance (A – C)
$69,300 – $68,000 =
$1,300 U

2. Price variances are isolated at the most logical control point—time of purchase rather than time of use. In turn, the operating departments that later use the materials are generally charged at some predetermined budget, expected or standard price rather than actual prices. This represents a slight modification of the approach in part 1 as follows:

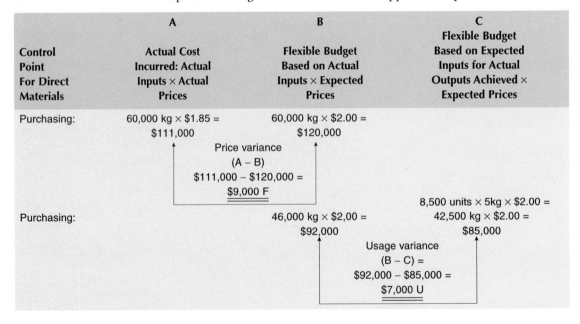

Control Point For Direct Materials	A Actual Cost Incurred: Actual Inputs × Actual Prices	B Flexible Budget Based on Actual Inputs × Expected Prices	C Flexible Budget Based on Expected Inputs for Actual Outputs Achieved × Expected Prices
Purchasing:	60,000 kg × $1.85 = $111,000	60,000 kg × $2.00 = $120,000	

Price variance
(A – B)
$111,000 – $120,000 =
$9,000 F

Purchasing:		46,000 kg × $2,00 = $92,000	8,500 units × 5kg × $2.00 = 42,500 kg × $2.00 = $85,000

Usage variance
(B – C) =
$92,000 – $85,000 =
$7,000 U

Note that this favourable price variance on balance may not be a good outcome—Dominion Company may not desire the extra inventory in excess of its immediate needs, and the favourable price variance may reflect that quality of the material is lower than planned. Note also that the usage variance is the same in parts 1 and 2. Typically, the price and usage variances for materials would now be reported separately and not added together because they are based on different measures of volume. The price variance is based on inputs *purchased*, but the usage variance is based on inputs *used*.

Problem Three

The Singapore Company makes a variety of leather goods. It uses standard costs and a flexible budget to aid planning and control. Budgeted variable overhead at a 60,000-direct-labour-hour level is $36,000.

During April the company had an unfavourable variable overhead efficiency variance of $1,200. Material purchases were $322,500. Actual direct-labour costs incurred were $187,600. The direct labour efficiency variance was $6,000 unfavourable. The actual average wage rate was $.20 lower than the average standard wage rate.

The company uses a variable overhead rate of 20 percent of standard direct-labour *cost* for flexible-budgeting purposes. Actual variable overhead for the month was $41,000.

Compute the following amounts and use U or F to indicate whether requested variances are unfavourable or favourable.

1. Standard direct labour cost per hour.
2. Actual direct labour hours worked.
3. Total direct labour price variance.
4. Total flexible budget for direct labour costs.
5. Total direct labour variance.
6. Variable overhead spending variance in total.

Solution

1. $3. The variable overhead rate is $.60, obtained by dividing $36,000 by 60,000 hours. Therefore the direct labour rate must be $.60 ÷ .20 = $3.
2. 67,000 hours. Actual costs, $187,600 ÷ ($3 − $.20) = 67,000 hours.
3. $13,400 F. 67,000 actual hours × $.20 = $13,400.
4. $195,000. Efficiency variance was $6,000 unfavourable. Therefore excess hours must have been $6,000 ÷ $3 = 2,000. Consequently, standard hours allowed must be 67,000 − 2,000 = 65,000. Flexible budget = 65,000 × $3 = $195,000.
5. $7,400 F. $195,000 − $187,600 = $7,400 F; or $13,400 F − $6,000 U = $7,400 F.
6. $800 U. Flexible budget = 65,000 × $.60 = $39,000. Total variance = $41,000 − $39,000 = $2,000 U. Price variance = $2,000 − $1,200 efficiency variance = $800 U.

ACCOUNTING VOCABULARY

activity-based flexible budget *p. 568*
activity-level variance *p. 569*
currently attainable standards *p. 576*
effectiveness *p. 569*
efficiency *p. 569*
efficiency variances *pp. 569, 581*
favourable expense variances *p. 565*
flexible budget *p. 565*
flexible-budget variances *p. 569*
master (static) budget variances *p. 565*
normal costing *p. 588*
perfection standards *p. 576*
practical capacity *p. 588*
price variance *p. 580*
production-volume variance *p. 586*

prorating the variances *p. 591*
quantity variance *p. 581*
sales-activity variances *p. 573*
sales volume variances *p. 569*
standard cost *p. 575*
standard cost systems *p. 575*
unfavourable expense variances *p. 565*
usage variance *p. 581*
variable budget *p. 565*
variable overhead efficiency
    variance *p. 585*
variable overhead spending
    variance *p. 585*
volume variance *p. 586*

ASSIGNMENT MATERIAL

QUESTIONS

Q13-1   Distinguish between favourable and unfavourable variances.

Q13-2   "The flex in the flexible budget relates solely to variable costs." Do you agree? Explain.

Q13-3   "We want a flexible budget because costs are hard to predict. We need the flexibility to change budgeted costs as input prices change." Does a flexible budget serve this purpose? Explain.

Q13-4   Explain the role of understanding cost behaviour and cost-driver activities for flexible budgeting.

Q13-5   "An activity-based flexible budget has a "flex" for every activity." Do you agree? Explain.

Q13-6   "Effectiveness and efficiency go hand in hand. You can't have one without the other." Do you agree? Explain.

Q13-7   Differentiate between a master budget variance and a flexible-budget variance.

Q13-8   "Managers should be rewarded for favourable variances and punished for unfavourable variances." Do you agree? Explain.

Q13-9   "A good control system places the blame for every unfavourable variance on someone in the organization. Without affixing blame, no one will take responsibility for cost control." Do you agree? Explain.

Q13-10   Who is usually responsible for sales activity variances? Why?

Q13-11   Differentiate between perfection standards and currently attainable standards.

Q13-12   What are two possible interpretations of "currently attainable standards?"

Q13-13   "A standard is one point in a band or range of acceptable outcomes." Criticize.

Q13-14   "Price variances should be computed even if prices are regarded as being outside of company control." Do you agree? Explain.

Q13-15   What are some common causes of usage variances?

Q13-16 "Failure to meet price standards is the responsibility of the purchasing officer." Do you agree? Explain.

Q13-17 Are direct material price variances generally recognized when the materials are purchased or when they are used? Why?

Q13-18 Why do the techniques for controlling overhead differ from those for controlling direct materials?

Q13-19 How does the variable overhead spending variance differ from the direct labour price variance?

Q13-20 When should managers investigate variances?

Q13-21 "In a standard absorption-costing system, the amount of fixed manufacturing overhead applied to the products rarely equals the budgeted fixed manufacturing overhead." Do you agree? Explain.

Q13-22 "The dollar amount of the production-volume variance depends on what expected volume of production was chosen to determine the fixed-overhead rate." Explain.

Q13-23 Why is there no production-volume variance for direct labour?

Q13-24 "An unfavourable production-volume variance means that fixed manufacturing costs have not been well controlled." Do you agree? Explain.

Q13-25 "Production-volume variances arise with normal-absorption and standard-absorption costing, but not with actual costing." Explain.

Q13-26 "Overhead variances arise only with absorption costing systems." Do you agree?

PROBLEMS

P13-1 FLEXIBLE BUDGET. Ralston Sports Company made 20,000 leather basketballs in a given year. Its total manufacturing costs were $170,000 variable and $70,000 fixed. Assume that no price changes will occur in the following year and that no changes in production methods are applicable. Compute the budgeted cost for producing 25,000 basketballs in the following year.

P13-2 BASIC FLEXIBLE BUDGET. The superintendent of police of Calgary is attempting to predict the costs of operating a fleet of police cars. Among the items of concern are fuel, $.15 per kilometre, and amortization, $6,000 per car per year.

The manager is preparing a flexible budget for the coming year. Prepare the flexible-budget amounts for fuel and amortization for each car at a level of 30,000, 40,000, and 50,000 kilometres.

P13-3 FLEXIBLE BUDGET. Consider the following data for the Boulder Delivery Service for a given month:

	BUDGET FORMULA PER UNIT	VARIOUS LEVELS OF OUTPUT		
Units	—	6,000	7,000	8,000
Sales	$18	$?	$?	$?
Variable costs:				
Direct material	?	48,000	?	?
Fuel	2	?	?	?
Fixed costs:				
Amortization		?	15,000	?
Salaries		?	?	40,000

Fill in the unknowns.

P13-4 BASIC FLEXIBLE BUDGET. The budgeted prices for materials and direct labour per unit of finished product are $12 and $5, respectively. The production manager is delighted about the following data:

	STATIC (MASTER) BUDGET	ACTUAL COSTS	VARIANCE
Direct materials	$96,000	$90,000	$6,000 F
Direct labour	40,000	37,600	2,400 F

Is the manager's happiness justified? Prepare a report that might provide a more detailed explanation of why the static (master) budget was not achieved. Good output was 6,800 units.

P13-5 MATERIAL AND LABOUR VARIANCES. Consider the following data.

	DIRECT MATERIAL	DIRECT LABOUR
Costs incurred: actual inputs × actual prices incurred	$153,000	$79,000
Actual inputs × standard prices	165,000	74,000
Standard inputs allowed for actual	172,500	71,300

Compute the price, usage, and flexible-budget variances for direct material and direct labour. Use U or F to indicate whether the variances are unfavourable or favourable.

P13-6 USAGE VARIANCES. Pacific Toy Company produced 9,000 stuffed bears. Suppose the standard direct material allowance is two kilograms per bear, at a cost per kilogram of $3. Actually, 17,000 kilograms of materials (input) were used to produce the 9,000 bears (output).

Similarly, assume that it is supposed to take five direct labour hours to produce one bear, and that the standard hourly labour cost is $3. But 46,500 hours (input) were used to produce the 9,000 bears in this Hong Kong factory.

Compute the usage variances for direct material and direct labour.

P13-7 DIRECT MATERIAL VARIANCES. Tailored Shirt Company (TSC) uses a special fabric in the production of dress shirts. During August TSC purchased 10,000 square metres of the fabric @ $6.90 per metre and used 7,900 square metres in the production of 3,800 jackets. The standard allows 2 metres @ $7.10 per metre for each jacket.

Calculate the material price variance and the material efficiency variance.

P13-8 LABOUR VARIANCES. The city of Halifax has a sign shop where street signs of all kinds are manufactured and repaired. The manager of the shop uses standards to judge performance. However, because a clerk mistakenly discarded some labour records, the manager has only partial data for April. She knows that the total direct labour variance was $1,855 favourable, and that the standard labour price was $12 per hour. Moreover, a recent pay raise produced an unfavourable labour price variance for April of $945. The actual hours of input were 1,750.

1. Find the actual labour price per hour.
2. Determine the standard hours allowed for the output achieved.

P13-9   VARIABLE OVERHEAD VARIANCES.   Materials support cost for the Industrial Equipment Manufacturing Company depends on the weight of material (plate steel, castings, etc.) moved. For the current budget period and based on scheduled production, Industrial expected to move 750,000 kilograms of material at a cost of $.20 per kilogram. Several orders were cancelled by customers and Industrial moved only 650,000 kilograms of material. Total materials support costs for the period were $175,000.

Compute materials support static and flexible-budget variances.

P13-10   LABOUR AND MATERIAL VARIANCES.

1. Information on Li Company's direct labour and direct material costs is as follows:

Standard direct labour rate	$ 13.50
Actual direct labour rate	$ 12.20
Standard direct labour hours	12,000
Direct labour, efficiency variance—unfavourable	$14,500

Complete the actual hours worked, rounded to the nearest hour.

2. Information on Oseok Kwon Company's direct material costs is as follows:

Standard unit price	$ 4.50
Actual quantity purchased	1,800
Standard quantity allowed for actual production	1,650
Materials purchase price variance—favourable	$ 288

Compute the actual purchase price per unit, rounded to the nearest penny.

P13-11   PARKS CANADA.   Parks Canada prepared the following budget for one of its national parks for 2002:

Revenue from fees	$5,000,000
Variable costs (miscellaneous)	500,000
Contribution margin	$4,500,000
Fixed costs (miscellaneous)	4,500,000
Operating income	$ 0

The fees were based on an average of 50,000 vehicle-admission days (vehicles multiplied by number of days in park) per week for the 20-week session, multiplied by average entry and other fees of $10 per vehicle-admission day.

The season was booming for the first four weeks. However, there were major forest fires during the fifth week. A large percentage of the park was scarred by the fires. As a result, the number of visitors dropped sharply during the remainder of the season.

Total revenue fell $1 million short of the original budget. Moreover, extra firefighters had to be hired at a cost of $360,000. The latter was regarded as a fixed cost.

Prepare a columnar summary of performance, showing the original (static) budget, sales volume variances, flexible budget, flexible-budget variances, and actual results.

P13-12 **SIMILARITY OF DIRECT LABOUR AND VARIABLE OVERHEAD VARIANCES.** The L. Ming Company has had great difficulty controlling costs in Singapore during the past three years. Last month a standard cost and flexible-budget system was installed. A condensation of results for a department follows.

	EXPECTED COST PER STANDARD DIRECT-LABOUR-HOUR	FLEXIBLE-BUDGET VARIANCE
Lubricants	$ .60	$300 F
Other supplies	.30	225 U
Rework	.60	450 U
Other indirect labour	1.50	450 U
Total variable overhead	$3.00	$825 U

F = Favourable   U = Unfavourable

The department initially planned to manufacture 9,000 audio-speaker assemblies in 6,000 standard direct labour hours allowed. However, material shortages and a heat wave resulted in the production of 8,100 units in 5,700 actual direct labour hours. The standard wage rate is $5.25 per hour, which is 20 cents higher than the actual average hourly rate.

1. Prepare a detailed performance report with two major sections: direct labour and variable overhead.
2. Prepare a summary analysis of price and efficiency variances for direct labour and spending and variances for variable overhead.
3. Explain the similarities and differences between the direct labour and variable overhead variances. What are some of the likely causes of the overhead variances?

P13-13 **ACTIVITY-BASED FLEXIBLE BUDGET.** Cost-behaviour analysis for the four activity centres in the Billing Department of Pacific Power Company is as follows:

ACTIVITY CENTRE	TRACEABLE COSTS		COST DRIVER ACTIVITY
	VARIABLE	FIXED	
Account Inquiry	$ 79,910	$ 155,270	3,300 Labour Hours
Correspondence	$ 9,800	$ 25,584	2,800 Letters
Account Billing	$ 156,377	$ 81,400	2,440,000 Lines
Account Verification	$ 10,797	$ 78,050	20,000 Accounts

The Billing Department constructs a flexible budget for each activity centre, based on the following ranges of cost-driver activity:

ACTIVITY CENTRE	COST-DRIVER	RELEVANT RANGE	
Account Inquiry	Labour Hours	3,000	5,000
Correspondence	Letters	2,500	3,500
Account Billing	Lines	2,000,000	3,000,000
Account Verification	Accounts	15,000	25,000

1. Develop flexible budget formulas for each of the four activity centres. Use the same format illustrated in Exhibit 13-4.
2. Compute the budgeted total cost in each activity centre for each of these levels of cost-driver activity: a) the smallest activity in the relevant range, b) the midpoint of the relevant range, and c) the highest activity in the relevant range.
3. Determine the total cost function for the Billing Department.
4. The following table gives the actual results for the Billing Department. Prepare a cost-control performance report comparing the flexible budget to actual results for each activity centre. Compute flexible budget variances.

ACTIVITY CENTRE	COST-DRIVER LEVEL (ACTUAL)	ACTUAL COST
Account Inquiry	4,400 Labour Hours	$229,890
Correspondence	3,250 Letters	$38,020
Account Billing	2,900,000 Lines	$285,000
Account Verification	22,500 Accounts	$105,320

P13-14 **VARIANCE ANALYSES.**   The Geneva Chocolate Company uses standard costs and a flexible budget to control its manufacture of fine chocolate. The purchasing agent is responsible for material price variances, and the production manager is responsible for all other variances. Operating data for the past week are summarized as follows:

1. Finished units produced: 4,000 boxes of chocolates.
2. Direct material: Purchases, 6,400 kilograms of chocolate @ 15.5 Swiss francs (SF) per kilogram; standard price is 16 SF per kilogram. Used, 4,300 kilograms. Standard allowed of 1 kilogram per box.
3. Direct labour. Actual costs, 6,400 hours @ 30.5 SF, or 195,200 SF. Standard allowed per box produced, 1.5 hours. Standard price per direct labour hour, 30 SF.
4. Variable manufacturing overhead: Actual costs, 69,500 SF. Budget formula is 10 SF per standard direct labour hour.
1. Compute the following variances
   a. Material purchase price variance
   b. Material efficiency variance
   c. Direct labour price variance
   d. Direct labour efficiency variance
   e. Variable manufacturing overhead spending variance
   f. Variable manufacturing overhead efficiency variance

Hint: For format, see the solution to the second Summary Problem, pages 595 to 598.

2. a. What is the budget allowance for direct labour?
   b. Would it be any different if production were 5,000 boxes?

P13-15 **SUMMARY EXPLANATION.** Wilcox Company produced 80,000 units, 8,000 more units than budgeted. Production data are as follows. Except for physical units, all quantities are in dollars:

	ACTUAL RESULTS AT ACTUAL PRICES	FLEXIBLE-BUDGET VARIANCES	FLEXIBLE BUDGET	SALES VOLUME VARIANCES	STATIC (MASTER) BUDGET
Physical units	80,000	—	?	?	72,000
Sales	?	6,400 F	?	?	720,000
Variable costs	492,000	?	480,000	?	?
Contribution margin	?	?	?	?	?
Fixed costs	?	8,000 U	?	?	195,000
Operating income	?	?	?	?	?

1. Fill in the unknowns.
2. Briefly explain why the original target operating income was not attained.

P13-16 **EXPLANATION OF VARIANCE IN INCOME.** Diaz Credit Services produces reports for consumers about their credit ratings. The company's standard contribution margins average 70 percent of dollar sales and average selling prices are $50 per report. Average productivity is four reports per hour. Some preparers work for sales commissions and others for an hourly rate. The master budget for 2002 had predicted sales of 800,000 reports, but only 700,000 reports were processed.

Fixed costs of rent, supervision, advertising, and other items were budgeted at $21.5 million, but the budget was exceeded by $700,000 because of extra advertising in an attempt to boost revenue.

There were no variances from the average selling prices, but the actual commissions paid to preparers and the actual productivity per hour resulted in flexible-budget variances (that is, total price and efficiency variances) for variable costs of $900,000 unfavourable.

The president was unhappy because the budgeted operating income of $6.5 million was not achieved. He said, "Sure, we had unfavourable variable cost variances, but our operating income was down far more than that. Please explain why."

Explain why the budgeted operating income was not attained. Use a presentation similar to Exhibit 13-5. Enough data have been given to permit you to construct the complete exhibit by filling in the known items and then computing the unknown. Complete your explanation by briefly summarizing what happened.

P13-17 **OVERHEAD VARIANCES.** Consider these data:

	FACTORY OVERHEAD	
	FIXED	VARIABLE
Actual incurred	$ 14,200	$13,300
Budget for standard hours allowed for output achieved	12,500	11,000
Applied	11,600	11,000
Budget for actual hours of input	12,500	11,400

From the information given, fill in the blanks below:

The flexible-budget variance is $ _____	Fixed $ _____ Variable $ _____
The production-volume variance is $ _____	Fixed $ _____ Variable $ _____
The spending variance is $ _____	Fixed $ _____ Variable $ _____
The efficiency variance is $ _____	Fixed $ _____ Variable $ _____

Mark your variances *F* for favourable and *U* for unfavourable.

P13-18 VARIANCES. Consider the following data regarding factory overhead:

	VARIABLE	FIXED
Budget for actual hours of input	45,000	70,000
Applied	41,000	64,800
Budget for standard hours allowed for output achieved	?	?
Actual incurred	$ 48,500	$68,500

Using the above data, fill in the blanks in the following table. Use *F* for favourable or *U* for unfavourable for each variance.

	TOTAL OVERHEAD	VARIABLE	FIXED
1. Spending variance	_____	_____	_____
2. Efficiency variance	_____	_____	_____
3. Production-volume variance	_____	_____	_____
4. Flexible-budget variance	_____	_____	_____
5. Underapplied overhead	_____	_____	_____

P13-19 SUMMARY OF AIRLINE PERFORMANCE. Consider the performance (in thousands of dollars) of Economy Airlines for a given year in the table below.

    The static (master) budget had been based on a budget of $.20 per revenue passenger kilometre. A revenue passenger kilometre is one paying passenger who has flown one kilometre. An average airfare decrease of 8 percent helped to generate an increase in passenger kilometres flown that exceeded the static budget for the year by 10 percent.

    The price per litre of jet fuel rose above the price used to formulate the static budget. The average price increase for the year was 12 percent.

	ACTUAL RESULTS AT ACTUAL PRICES	STATIC (MASTER) BUDGET	VARIANCE
Revenue	$?	$300,000	$?
Variable expenses	200,000	195,000 *	5,000 U
Contribution margin	?	105,000	?
Fixed expenses	77,000	75,000	2,000 U
Operating income	$?	$ 30,000	$?

* Includes the $90,000 cost of jet fuel.

1. Prepare a summary performance report for the president that is similar to Exhibit 13-5.
2. Assume that jet fuel costs are purely variable and the use of fuel was at the same level of efficiency as predicted in the static budget. What portion of the flexible-budget variance for variable expenses is attributable to jet fuel expenses? Explain.

P13-20 **ACTIVITY AND FLEXIBLE-BUDGET VARIANCES AT McDONALD'S.** Suppose a McDonald's franchise in Bangkok had budgeted sales for 2002 of B7.5 million (where B stands for baht, the Thai unit of currency). Cost of goods sold and other variable costs were expected to be 70 percent of sales. Budgeted annual fixed costs were B1.8 million. A booming Thai economy caused actual 2002 sales to soar to B 9.3 million and actual profits to increase to B 600,000. Fixed costs in 2002 were as budgeted. The franchisee was pleased with the increase in profit.

1. Compute the sales activity variance and the flexible budget variance for 2002. What can the franchisee learn from these variances?
2. In 2003 the Thai economy plummeted, and the franchise's sales fell back to the B7.5 million level. Given what happened in 2002, what do you expect to happen to profits in 2003?

P13-21 **FLEXIBLE AND STATIC BUDGETS.** Beta Alpha Psi, the accounting fraternity, recently held a dinner dance. The original (static) budget and actual results were as follows:

	BUDGET	ACTUAL	VARIANCE
Attendees	75	90	
Revenue	$2,625	$3,255	$630 F
Chicken dinners @ $17.60	1,320	1,668	348 U
Beverages: $6 per person	450	466	16 U
Club rental, $75 plus 8% tax	81	81	0
Music, 3 hours @ $240			
per hour	720	840	120 U
Profit	$ 54	$ 200	$ 146 F

1. Subdivide each variance into a sales activity variance portion and a flexible-budget variance portion. Use the format of Exhibit 13-5.
2. Provide possible explanations for the variances.

P13-22 **UNIVERSITY FLEXIBLE BUDGETING.** (CMA, adapted) The University of Liverpool offers an extensive continuing education program in many cities throughout Britain. For the convenience of its faculty and administrative staff and also to save costs, the university operates a motor pool. The motor pool operated with 25 vehicles until February of this year, when an additional automobile was acquired. The motor pool furnishes gasoline, oil, and other supplies for the cars and hires one mechanic who does routine maintenance and minor repairs. Major repairs are done at a nearby commercial garage. A supervisor manages the operations.

Each year the supervisor prepares an operating budget, informing university management of the funds needed to operate the pool. Depreciation on the automobiles is recorded in the budget in order to determine the cost per kilometre.

The schedule below presents the annual budget approved by the university. The actual costs for March are compared with one-twelfth of the annual budget.

University Motor Pool
Budget Report for
March

	ANNUAL BUDGET	ONE-MONTH BUDGET	MARCH ACTUAL	OVER (UNDER)
Gasoline	£ 75,000	£ 6,250	£ 7,500	£ 1,250
Oil, minor repairs, parts, and supplies	15,000	1,250	1,300	50
Outside repairs	2,700	225	50	(175)
Insurance	4,800	400	416	16
Salaries and benefits	21,600	1,800	1,800	—
Amortization	22,800	1,900	1,976	76
	£141,900	£ 11,825	£13,042	£ 1,217
Total kilometres	1,500,000	125,000	140,000	
Cost per kilometres	£ .0946	£ .0946	£ .0932	
Number of automobiles	25	25	26	

The annual budget was constructed upon the following assumptions:

1. 25 automobiles in the pool
2. 60,000 kilometres per year per automobile
3. 8 kilometres per litre per automobile
4. £0.40 per litre of gas
5. £.01 per kilometre for oil, minor repairs, parts, and supplies
6. £108 per automobile in outside repairs

The supervisor is unhappy with the monthly report comparing budget and actual costs for March; he claims it presents his performance unfairly. His previous employer used flexible budgeting to compare actual costs with budgeted amounts.

1. Employing flexible-budgeting techniques, prepare a report that shows budgeted amounts, actual costs, and monthly variation for March.
2. Briefly explain the basis of your budget figure for outside repairs.

P13-23 **STRAIGHTFORWARD VARIANCE ANALYSIS.** Beringer Metals Inc. uses a standard cost system. The month's data regarding its cast iron vats follow:

- Material purchased and used, 3,400 kilograms
- Direct-labour costs incurred, 5,500 hours, $20,900

- Variable overhead costs incurred, $4,780
- Finished units produced, 1,000
- Actual material cost, $.95 per kilogram
- Variable overhead rate, $.80 per hour
- Standard direct labour cost, $4 per hour
- Standard material cost, $1 per kilogram
- Standard kilograms of material in a finished unit, 3
- Standard direct labour hours per finished unit, 5

Prepare schedules of all variances, using the format of Exhibit 13-8.

P13-24 STANDARD MATERIAL ALLOWANCES. Geiger Company is a chemical manufacturer that supplies industrial users. The company plans to introduce a new solution and needs to develop a standard product cost for this new solution.

The new chemical solution is made by combining altium and bollium, boiling the mixture, adding a second compound (credix), and bottling the resulting solution in 20-litre containers. The initial mix, which is 20 litres in volume, consists of 24 kilograms of altium and 19.2 litres of bollium. A 20 percent reduction in volume occurs during the boiling process. The solution is then cooled slightly before 10 kilograms of credix are added; the addition of credix does not affect the total liquid volume.

The purchase prices of the raw materials used in the manufacture of this new chemical solution are as follows:

Altium	$1.50 per kilogram
Bollium	2.10 per litre
Credix	2.80 per kilogram

Determine the standard quantity for each of the raw materials needed to produce a 20-litre container of Geiger Company's new chemical solution and the standard materials cost of a 20-litre container of the new product.

P13-25 FLEXIBLE AND STATIC BUDGETS. Coast-to-Coast Shipping Company's general manager reports quarterly to the company's president on the firm's operating performance. The company has used a budget based on detailed expectations for the forthcoming quarter. For example, the condensed performance report for a recent quarter was (in dollars):

Although the general manager was upset about not obtaining enough revenue, she was happy that her cost performance was favourable; otherwise her net operating income would be even worse.

The president was totally unhappy and remarked: "I can see some merit in comparing actual performance with budgeted performance because we can see whether actual revenue coincided with our best guess for budget purposes. But I can't see how this performance report helps me evaluate cost-control performance."

	BUDGET	ACTUAL	VARIANCE
Net revenue	$8,000,000	$7,600,000	$400,000U
Fuel	160,000	$ 157,000	$ 3,000F
Repairs and maintenance	80,000	78,000	2,000F
Supplies and miscellaneous	800,000	788,000	12,000F
Variable payroll	5,360,000	5,200,000	160,000F
Total variable costs*	$ 6,400,000	$6,223,000	$177,000F
Supervision	$ 160,000	$ 164,000	4,000U
Rent	160,000	160,000	—
Amortization	480,000	480,000	—
Other fixed costs	160,000	158,000	2,000F
Total fixed costs	$ 960,000	$ 962,000	2,000U
Total costs charged against revenue	$7,360,000	$7,185,000	$175,000F
Operating income	$ 640,000	$ 415,000	$225,000U

U = Unfavourable   F = Favourable

* For purposes of this analysis, assume that these costs are totally variable with respect to sales revenue. In practice, many are mixed and have to be subdivided into variable and fixed components before a meaningful analysis can be made. Also assume that the prices and mix of services sold remain unchanged.

1. Prepare a columnar flexible budget for Coast-to-Coast Shipping at revenue levels of $7,000,000, $8,000,000, and $9,000,000. Use the format of the last three columns of Exhibit 13-2. Assume that the prices and mix of products sold are equal to the budgeted prices and mix.
2. Express the flexible budget for costs in formula form.
3. Prepare a condensed table showing the static (master) budget variance, the sales activity variance, and the flexible-budget variance. Use the format of Exhibit 13-5.

P13-26 DIRECT MATERIAL AND DIRECT LABOUR VARIANCES. Artistic Metalworks Company manufactures sculptured metal ornaments that are shaped and finished by hand. The following standards were developed for a line of lampposts:

During April, 550 lampposts were scheduled for production. However, only 525 were actually produced.

Direct materials purchased and used amounted to 5,500 kilograms at a unit price of $4.25 per kilogram. Direct labour was actually paid $26 per hour, and 2,850 hours were used.

	STANDARD INPUTS EXPECTED FOR EACH UNIT OF OUTPUT ACHIEVED	STANDARD PRICE PER UNIT OF INPUT
Direct materials	10 kilograms	$5 per kilogram
Direct labour	5 hours	$25 per hour

1. Compute the standard cost per lamppost for direct materials and direct labour.
2. Compute the price variances and usage variances for direct materials and direct labour.

3. Based on these sketchy data, what clues for investigation are provided by the variances?

P13-27 **FUNDAMENTALS OF OVERHEAD VARIANCES.** The Mendoza Company is installing an absorption standard-costing system and a flexible-overhead budget. Standard costs have recently been developed for its only product and are as follows:

Direct material, 3 kilograms @ $20	$60
Direct labour, 2 hours @ $14	28
Variable overhead, 2 hours @ $5	10
Fixed overhead	?
Standard cost per unit of finished product	$?

Expected production activity is expressed as 7,500 standard direct labour hours per month. Fixed overhead is expected to be $60,000 per month. The predetermined fixed-overhead rate for product costing is not changed from month to month.

1. Calculate the proper fixed-overhead rate per standard direct labour hour and per unit.
2. Graph the following for activity from zero to 10,000 hours:
   a. Budgeted variable overhead
   b. Variable overhead applied to product
3. Graph the following for activity from zero to 10,000 hours:
   a. Budgeted fixed overhead
   b. Fixed overhead applied to product
4. Assume that 6,000 standard direct labour hours are allowed for the output achieved during a given month. Actual variable overhead of $30,600 was incurred: actual fixed overhead amounted to $62,000. Calculate the
   a. Fixed-overhead flexible-budget variance
   b. Fixed-overhead production-volume variance
   c. Variable-overhead flexible-budget variance
5. Assume that 7,800 standard direct labour hours are allowed for the output achieved during a given month. Actual overhead incurred amounted to $99,700, $62,200 of which was fixed. Calculate the
   a. Fixed-overhead flexible-budget variance
   b. Fixed-overhead production-volume variance
   c. Variable-overhead flexible-budget variance

P13-28 **FIXED OVERHEAD AND PRACTICAL CAPACITY.** The expected activity of the paper-making plant of Leventhal Paper Company was 45,000 machine-hours per month. Practical capacity was 60,000 machine-hours per month. The standard machine-hours allowed for the actual output achieved in January were 54,000. The budgeted fixed-factory-overhead items were as follows:

Amortization, equipment	$340,000
Amortization, factory building	64,000
Supervision	47,000
Indirect labour	234,000
Insurance	18,000
Property taxes	17,000
Total	$720,000

Because of unanticipated scheduling difficulties and the need for more indirect labour, the actual fixed factory overhead was $751,000.

1. Using practical capacity as the denominator for applying fixed factory overhead, prepare a summary analysis of fixed-overhead variances for January.
2. Using expected activity as the denominator for applying fixed factory overhead, prepare a summary analysis of fixed-overhead variances for January.
3. Explain why some of your variances in requirements 1 and 2 are the same and why some differ.

P13-29 **VARIANCE ANALYSIS.** Study the format of the analysis of variances in Exhibit 13-12. Suppose production is 156,000 units. Also assume the following:

Standard direct labour hours allowed per unit produced	.25
Standard direct labour rate per hour	$6.00
Actual direct labour hours of input	42,000
Actual direct labour rate per hour	$6.15
Variable manufacturing overhead actually incurred	$36,000
Fixed manufacturing overhead actually incurred	$154,000

Other data are as shown in Exhibit 13-12.
Prepare an analysis of variances similar to that shown in Exhibit 13-12.

P13-30 **ROLE OF DEFECTIVE UNITS AND NONPRODUCTIVE TIME IN SETTING STANDARDS.** Sung Park owns and operates Transpac Machining, a subcontractor to several aerospace-industry contractors. When Mr. Park wins a bid to produce a piece of equipment, he sets standard costs for the production of the item. He then compares actual manufacturing costs with the standards to judge the efficiency of production.

In April 2002 Transpac won a bid to produce 15,000 units of a shielded component used in a navigation device. Specifications for the components were very tight, and Mr. Park expected that 20 percent of the components would fail his final inspection, even if every care was exercised in production. There was no way to identify defective items before production was complete. Therefore, 18,750 units had to be produced to get 15,000 good components. Standards were set to include an allowance for the expected number of defective items.

Each final component contained 2.8 kilograms of direct materials, and normal scrap from production was expected to average an additional .4 kilograms per unit. The direct material was expected to cost $11.25 per kilogram plus $.75 per kilogram for shipping and handling.

Machining of the components required close attention by skilled machinists. Each component required five hours of machining time. The machinists were paid $22 per hour and worked 40-hour weeks. Of the 40 hours, an average of 32 hours was spent directly on production. The other eight hours consisted of time for breaks and waiting time when machines were broken down or there was no work to be done. Nevertheless, all payments to machinists were considered direct labour, whether or not they were for time spent directly on production. In addition to the basic wage rate, Transpac paid fringe benefits averaging $5 per hour and payroll taxes of 10 percent of the basic wages.

Determine the standard cost of direct materials and direct labour for each good unit of output.

P13-31 AUTOMATION AND DIRECT LABOUR AS OVERHEAD. Precision Machining Company has a highly automated manufacturing process for producing a variety of auto parts. Through the use of computer-aided manufacturing and robotics, the company has reduced its labour costs to only 5 percent of total manufacturing costs. Consequently, labour is not accounted for as a separate item but is considered part of overhead.

The static budget for producing 750 units of part Z624 in March 2002 is

Direct materials	$18,000*
Overhead:	
Supplies	1,875
Power	1,310
Rent and other building services	2,815
Factory labour	1,500
Amortization	4,500
Total manufacturing costs	$30,000

* 3 kilograms per unit × $8 per kilogram × 750 units

Supplies and power are considered to be variable overhead. The other overhead items are fixed costs.

Actual costs in March 2002 for producing 900 units of Z624 were

Direct materials	$21,645*
Overhead:	
Supplies	2,125
Power	1,612
Rent and other building services	2,775
Factory labour	1,625
Amortization	4,500
Total manufacturing costs	$34,282

* 2,775 kilograms purchased and used @ $7.80 per kilogram

1. Compute (a) the direct-materials price and efficiency variances and (b) the flexible-budget variance for each overhead item.
2. Comment on the way Precision Machining Company accounts for and controls factory labour.

P13-32 REVIEW OF MAJOR POINTS IN CHAPTER. The following questions are based on the data contained in Exhibit 13-8.

1. Suppose actual production and sales were 8,000 units instead of 7,000 units. (a) Compute the sales-volume variance. Is the performance of the marketing function the sole explanation for this variance? Why? (b) Using a flexible budget, compute the budgeted contribution margin, the budgeted operating income, budgeted direct material, and budgeted direct labour.
2. Suppose the following were the actual results for the production of 8,000 units:

Direct material: 42,000 kilograms were used at an actual unit price of $1.85, for a total actual cost of $77,700.

Direct labour: 4,125 hours were used at an actual hourly rate of $16.40, for a total actual cost of $67,650.

Compute the flexible-budget variance and the price and usage variances for direct materials and direct labour. Present your answers in the form shown in Exhibit 13-5.

3. Suppose the company is organized so that the purchasing manager bears the primary responsibility for the acquisition prices of materials, and the production manager bears the primary responsibility for efficiency but no responsibility for unit prices. Assume the same facts as in requirement 2 except that the purchasing manager acquired 60,000 kilograms of materials at $1.85 per kilogram. This means that there is an ending inventory of 18,000 kilograms. Would your variance analysis of materials in requirement 2 change? Why? Show computations.

P13-33 **HOSPITAL COSTS AND EXPLANATION OF VARIANCES.** The emergency room at University Hospital uses a flexible budget based on patients seen as a measure of volume. An adequate staff of attending and on-call physicians must be maintained at all times, so physician scheduling is unaffected by volume. However, nurse scheduling varies as volume changes. A standard of .5 nurse hours per patient visit was set. Average hourly pay for nurses is $14, ranging from $8 to $17 per hour. All materials are considered to be supplies, which are a part of overhead; there are no direct materials. A statistical study showed that the cost of supplies and other variable overhead is more closely associated with nurse-hours than with patient visits. The standard for supplies and other variable overhead is $10 per nursing hour.

The head physician of the emergency room unit, Sandy Cox, is responsible for control of costs. During October the emergency room unit treated 4,000 patients. The budget and actual costs were as follows:

	BUDGET	ACTUAL	VARIANCE
Patient visits	3,800	4,000	200
Nursing hours	1,900	2,075	175
Nursing cost	$ 26,600	$ 31,050	$4,450
Supplies and other			
variable overhead	$ 19,000	$ 21,320	$2,320
Fixed costs	$ 92,600	$ 92,600	0
Total cost	$138,200	$144,970	$6,770

1. Calculate price and usage variances for nursing costs.
2. Calculate spending and usage variances for supplies and other variable overhead.
3. Dr. Cox has been asked to explain the variances to the chief of staff. Provide possible explanations.

P13-34 **MATERIAL, LABOUR, AND OVERHEAD VARIANCES.** Belfair Kayak Company makes molded plastic kayaks. Standards costs for an entry-level whitewater kayak are:

Direct materials, 60 kilograms @ $5.50 per kilogram	$330
Direct labour, 1.5 hours @ $16 per hour	24
Overhead, @ $12 per kayak	12
Total	$366

The overhead rate assumes production of 450 kayaks per month. The overhead cost function is $2.808 + $5.76 × number of kayaks.

During March, Belfair produced 430 kayaks and had the following actual results:

Direct materials purchased:	28,000 kilograms @ $5.30/kg
Direct materials used	27,000 kilograms
Direct labour	660 hours @ $15.90/hour
Actual overhead	$5,320

1. Compute material, labour, and overhead variances.
2. Interpret the variances.
3. Suppose variable overhead was $3.84 per labour hour instead of $5.76 per kayak. Compute the variable overhead efficiency variance and the total overhead spending variance. Would these variances lead you to a different interpretation of the overhead variances from the interpretation in requirement 2? Explain.

P13-35 ACTIVITY-BASED COSTING AND FLEXIBLE BUDGETING. The new printing department of Shark Advertising Inc. provides printing services to the other departments. Prior to the establishment of the in-house printing department, the departments contracted with external printers for their printing work. The Shark printing policy is to charge those departments using variable printing on the basis of number of pages printed. Fixed costs are recovered in pricing of external jobs.

The first year's budget for the printing department was based on the department's expected total costs divided by the planned number of pages to be printed.

The annual number of pages to be printed was 420,000 and total variable costs were budgeted to be $420,000. Most government accounts and all internal jobs were expected to use only single-colour printing. Commercial accounts were primarily colour printing. Variable costs were estimated based on the average variable cost of printing a two-colour page that is one-fourth graphics and three-fourths text. The expected annual costs for each division were as follows:

DEPARTMENT	PLANNED PAGES PRINTED	VARIABLE COST PER PAGE	BUDGETED CHARGES
Government accounts	120,000	$1.00	$90,000
Commercial accounts	250,000	$1.00	$300,000
Central administration total	50,000	$1.00	$ 30,000
	420,000		$420,000

After the first month of using the internal printing department, the printing department announced that its variable cost estimate of $1 per page was too low. The first month's actual costs were $50,000 to print 40,000 pages:

Government accounts	9,000 pages
Commercial accounts	27,500 pages
Central administration	3,500 pages

Three reasons were cited for higher-than-expected costs: all departments were using more printing services than planned and government and internal jobs were using more four-colour printing and more graphics than expected. The printing department also argued that additional four-colour printing equipment would have to be purchased if demand for four-colour printing continued to grow.

1. Compare the printing department actual results, static budget, and flexible budget for the month just completed.
2. Discuss possible reasons why the printing department static budget was inaccurate.
3. An activity-based costing (ABC) study completed by a consultant indicated that printing costs is to be driven by number of pages (@ $.30 per page) and use of colours (@ $1 extra per page).
   a. Discuss the likely effects of using the ABC results for budgeting and control of printing department use.
   b. Discuss the assumptions regarding cost behaviour implied in the ABC study results.
   c. Commercial accounts during the first month (27,500 pages) used four colours per page. Compare the cost of the commercial accounts under the old and the proposed ABC system.

P13-36 **PERFORMANCE EVALUATION.** Imperial Mills is a small flour company in the West. Lloyd Vineland became president in 2001. He is concerned with the ability of his production manager to control costs. To aid his evaluation, Vineland set up a standard-cost system.

Standard costs were based on 2001 costs in several categories. Each 2001 cost was divided by 1,520,000 cwt, the volume of 2001 production, to determine a standard for 2002 (cwt. means hundredweight, or 100 pounds):

	2001 COST (IN THOUSANDS)	2002 STANDARD (PER HUNDREDWEIGHT)
Direct materials	$1,824	$1.20
Direct labour	836	.55
Variable overhead	1,596	1.05
Fixed overhead	2,432	1.60
Total	$6,688	$4.40

At the end of 2002, Vineland compared actual results with the standards he established. Production was 1,360,000 cwt, and variances were as follows:

	ACTUAL	STANDARD	VARIANCE
Direct materials	$1,802	$1,632	$170 U
Direct labour	735	748	13 F
Variable overhead	1,422	1,428	6 F
Fixed overhead	2,418	2,176	242 U
Total	$6,377	$5,984	$393 U

Vineland was not surprised by the unfavourable variance in direct materials. After all, wheat prices in 2002 averaged 10 percent above those in 2001. But he was disturbed by the lack of control of fixed overhead. He called in the production manager and demanded an explanation.

1. Prepare an explanation for the large unfavourable fixed-overhead variance.
2. Discuss the appropriateness of using one year's costs as the next year's standards.

P13-37   COLLABORATIVE LEARNING EXERCISE: SETTING STANDARDS.   Form groups of two to six persons each. The groups should each select a simple product or service. Be creative, but do not pick a product or service that is too complex. For those having difficulty choosing a product or product or service, some possibilities are:

- One dozen chocolate-chip cookies
- A ten-kilometre taxi ride
- One copy of a 100-page course syllabus
- A machine-knit wool sweater
- A hand-knit wool sweater
- One hour of lawn mowing and fertilizing
- A hammer

1. Each student should individually estimate the direct materials and direct labour inputs needed to produce the product or service. For each type of direct material and direct labour, determine the standard quantity and standard price. Also, identify the overhead support needed, and determine the standard overhead cost of the product or service. The result should be a total standard cost for the product or service.
2. Each group should compare the estimate of its members. Where estimates differ, determine why there were differences. Did some members have more knowledge about the produce or service than others? Form a group estimate of the standard cost of the product or service.
3. After the group has agreed on a standard cost, discuss the process used to arrive at the cost. What assumptions did the group make? Is the standard cost an "ideal" standard or a "currently attainable" standard? Note how widely standard costs can vary depending on assumptions and knowledge of the production process.

CASES

C13-1   ANALYSIS OF OPERATING RESULTS.   Manchester Machining Company (MMC) produces and sells three main product lines. The company employs a standard cost-accounting system for record-keeping purposes.

At the beginning of 2003, the president of MMC presented the budget to the parent company and accepted a commitment to earn a profit of £16,400 in 2003. The president has been confident that the year's profit would exceed the budget target, since the monthly sales reports that he has been receiving have shown that sales for the year will exceed budget by 10 percent. The president is both disturbed and confused when the controller presents an adjusted forecast as of November 30, 2003, indicating that profit will be 14 percent under budget:

MMC Forecasts of Operating Results	**FORECASTS AS OF**	
	1/1/03	**11/30/03**
Sales	£156,000	£171,600
Cost of sales at standard	108,000*	118,800
Gross margin at standard	£ 48,000	£ 52,800
Over- (Under-) absorbed fixed manufacturing overhead		(6,000)
Actual gross margin	£ 48,000	£ 46,800
Selling expenses	£ 11,200	£ 12,320
Administrative expenses	20,400	20,400
Total operating expenses	£ 31,600	£ 32,720
Earnings before tax	£ 16,400	£ 14,080

*Includes fixed manufacturing overhead of £36,000.

There have been no sales price changes or product-mix shifts since the 1/1/03 forecast. The only cost variance on the income statement is the underabsorbed manufacturing overhead. This arose because the company produced only 16,000 standard machine-hours (budgeted machine-hours were 20,000) during 2003 as a result of a shortage of raw materials while its principal supplier was closed by a strike. Fortunately, MMC's finished-goods inventory was large enough to fill all sales orders received.

Required:

1. Analyze and explain why the profit has declined in spite of increased sales and good control over costs. Show computations.
2. What plan, if any, could MMC adopt during December to improve its reported profit at year-end? Explain your answer.
3. Illustrate and explain how MMC could adopt an alternative internal cost-reporting procedure that would avoid the confusing effect of the present procedure. Show the revised forecasts under your alternative.
4. Would the alternative procedure described in requirement 3 be acceptable to MMC for financial-reporting purposes? Explain.

C13-2 VARIANCE ANALYSIS MANUFACTURING. (CICA)   Pitfall Industries manufactures an industrial detergent called SCRAM. On November 15, 2002, Ezra Trump, the president of the company, met with his Executive Committee and stated:

I have reviewed the Company's preliminary operating results for the year ended September 30, 2002. Notwithstanding that the results are subject to audit, it is evident that we failed to achieve planned profits. A shortfall in net income before taxes for the year in the amount of $63,800 is indicated.

In view of the significant accumulated losses to the end of the Company's 2002 fiscal year, I have requested our controller, Cathy Collins, to prepare an analysis of the current year's results, together with her recommendations for corrective action, which, if adopted, would enhance future performance. That analysis should consider both short- and long-run considerations.

I am requesting that you cooperate fully with Cathy in the preparation of her report. In particular, John and Mark, our vice presidents of manufacturing and marketing respectively, will be expected to "open their books," so to speak.

At the conclusion of the meeting, Mr. Trump tabled the following condensed Statement of Income:

Pitfall Industries
Statement of Income
Year Ended
September 30, 2002

	ACTUAL 2001	ACTUAL 2002	BUDGET 2002	BUDGET VARIANCE*
Sales	$910,000	$880,000	$1,000,000	$(120,000)
Cost of Sales	837,200	809,800	860,000	50,200
Gross Profit	72,800	70,200	140,000	(69,800)
Selling and administration				
expenses	120,000	132,000	138,000	6,000
Net income (loss) before taxes	$ (47,200)	$ (61,800)	$ 2,000	$ (63,800)

* ( ) Denote unfavourable variances.

With the assistance of John and Mark, Cathy extracted the additional data outlined below from various records maintained independent of the Accounting Department.

1. A publication dated October 2002, containing marketing statistics for industrial detergents similar to SCRAM, revealed the following, relative to the years ending September 30th:

	2000	2001	2002
Industry (including Pitfall):			
Sales — Dollars	$6,100,000	$6,500,000	$6,970,000
— Units	610,000	650,000	689,000
Pitfall's Comparable Performance:			
Sales — Dollars	$ 820,000	$ 910,000	$ 880,000
— Units	82,000	91,000	80,000

In August 2001, the Economic Council of Canada forecast a 5 percent rate of growth in the economy for the ensuing year. At that time, the Company had planned to market 100,000 units of product during fiscal 2002, at a selling price of $10 per unit.

2. Marketing instituted a selling price increase of $1 per unit in late September 2001. Severe cost pressures resulting from labour contract settlements, coupled with a deterioration in manufacturing efficiency, were cited as the reasons for the price increase. Marketing believes that the Company could have maintained its increasing share of total industry sales had a price increase not been implemented.

3. Inventories of work-in-process and finished goods have remained virtually unchanged during the past four years. Inventories are costed at "standard" and all manufacturing cost variances are charged to Cost of Sales at the end of each year.

An analysis of Cost of Sales revealed the following for the years ended September 30th:

	2001 ACTUAL	2002 ACTUAL	2002 PLAN
Direct Materials	$445,900	$408,000	$460,000
Direct Labour	191,100	201,600	200,000
Variable Overhead	100,100	88,200	100,000
Fixed Overhead	100,100	112,000	100,000
	$837,200	$809,800	$860,000

Included in the above analysis is a write-off of $10,100 during 2002 as a result of spring flood damage. This charge was allocated to materials ($2,100) and fixed overhead ($8,000).

4. During 2002, 82,000 kilograms of materials and 42,000 direct labour hours were consumed in the manufacturing process. Eighty thousand (80,000) units of good product were produced and sold during the year. The standard cost of SCRAM is determined to be as follows:

Direct Material—1 kilogram	$4.60
Direct Labour—1/2 hour	2.00
Variable Overhead @ $2.00 per direct labour hour	1.00
Fixed Overhead	1.00
Total Standard Cost Per Unit	$8.60

Combined variable and fixed overhead are applied to product on the basis of $2 per unit, based on a normal activity of 100,000 units that represents 80 percent of the Company's manufacturing capacity.

For the previous year, 2001, manufacturing records revealed a net unfavourable cost variance from standard of approximately 7 percent. Direct material variances are not recognized until after the manufacturing process commences.

John maintained that Pitfall's product was superior in quality to that of similar industrial detergents presently being marketed by competition.

5. Selling and administrative expenses are fixed with the exception of sales staff's commissions, which are paid on the basis of $.70 per unit of SCRAM sold. During the year, there was an unplanned addition to the administrative clerical staff.

6. Of the $188,000 of fixed costs recorded by the organization in 2002, $90,000 are considered "sunk." Management does not attach any scrap value to plant equipment due to the unique attributes of the manufacturing process.

Upon receipt of the above information, Cathy proceeded with her analysis and report. Throughout this period, a "strained" atmosphere prevailed among manufacturing, marketing, and accounting.

Required: Write Cathy's report to the president presenting adequate analysis to support your recommendations.

C13-3 VARIANCE ANALYSIS—SERVICE. (ICAO) The Holcomb Hotel is a 200-room hotel located in a residential section of Kingston. It is an older hotel of distinction that is very popular with those who appreciate the amenities of the older style of service.

While the Holcomb is a respected hotel, it has not always been a profitable one. Competition from newer hotels and motels in the area, plus the simple inefficiencies of running a hotel in the "old style" has placed pressure on management to improve efficiency without impairing service. As a result, the newly appointed general manager of the Holcomb is attempting to tighten cost control.

The Holcomb operates its own laundry facilities instead of contracting with a laundry service as most modern hotels do. The general manager has been examining the operating results of the laundry for June, the month just ended. The budget for the laundry called for operating expenses of $5,310 at an occupancy rate of 70 percent for all types of rooms. The actual occupancy rate for the 30-day month was 75 percent, or 4,500 room-days instead of the 4,200 room-days budgeted. The higher-than-expected occupancy rate would, of course, cause proportionately higher costs in the laundry, but the actual expenses of $6,213 were higher than expected. The budgeted and actual expenses were as follows:

	BUDGET	ACTUAL
Labour	$2,230	$2,599
Soap and supplies	1,596	1,898
Supervision	480	520
Maintenance and repairs	500	656
Space charge	504	540
Total	$5,310	$6,213

To help her understand the reasons for the deviations from budget, the general manager assembled the following information from several sources within the hotel:

1. The hotel has two types of rooms. Standard rooms have one queen-size and one double bed. Standard rooms are expected to average six kilograms of laundry (bed linen and towels) per day, while superior rooms are expected to generate an average of 10 kilograms per day.
2. In June, the 120 standard rooms had 65 percent occupancy, while the 80 superior rooms had 90 percent occupancy.
3. In June, the laundry washed 38,760 kilograms of bed linen and towels. The laundry can process 70 kilograms of laundry per hour.
4. The laundry is staffed by one permanent full-time employee who is paid $5.60 per hour (including fringe benefits) for 7.5 hours a day for six days a week. On Sundays, the full-time person is replaced by a local university student who is paid the same rate for the same number of hours. In total, the full-time employee and his Sunday replacement receive $1,260 for a 30 day-month. Hourly employees are also retained, at a cost of $4.20 per hour.
5. The laundry is supervised by the assistant housekeeper. One-third of her salary is allocated to the laundry. In May, the assistant housekeeper received a raise from $1,440 per month to $1,560 per month.
6. Routine maintenance on the washers and dryers is covered by a maintenance contract. In June, a motor on one of the washing machines burned out and had to be replaced.
7. The space charge allocates the hotel's total variable costs of electricity and water to user departments. The allocation to the laundry is $.12 per room-day of occupancy.

Required: Prepare an analysis of the difference between the budgeted and actual expenses of the laundry department that explains the reasons for the variances.

C13-4 **FLEXIBLE BUDGETS AND VARIANCES ANALYSIS.** (SMAC) Sam Leaf, the president of Ginkgo Manufacturing Limited (Ginkgo), was very pleased but puzzled by the 2001 operating results (Exhibit 13A-1). He knew that both manufacturing and marketing had problems during the year and he had not anticipated that the actual income from operations would exceed budget. Sam placed a lot of importance on his managers' staying within the budget to ensure that the target profit was attained.

Ginkgo manufactured two product line—chlorine and bromine pellets—for home swimming pools. Production and sales were measured in kilograms, with the bromine being more expensive. The controller prepared a budget each December for the following year, but it was difficult to forecast sales, which were largely determined by the weather. As well, the mix of sales was difficult to forecast because of unpredictable switching of demand from one product to the other. In consultation with the sales manager, an estimate was made of total market sales in kilograms and the share each of Ginkgo's two products would achieve. From the resulting sales forecast, the budget was prepared. The fixed and variable cost elements in the budget were based on adjustments to the current year's figures to reflect the best estimates for the following year.

During 2001, the production schedule had to be changed numerous times to match sales demand. This had resulted in production problems and waste. The sales manager had attempted to stimulate sales of the higher-priced bromine and was pleased with the excess sales over budget.

EXHIBIT 13A-1

Ginkgo Manufacturing Limited
Operating Results for the Year Ended December 31, 2001

	STATIC BUDGET	ACTUAL
Sales in units (kilograms)	1,425,000	1,920,000
Sales in dollars	$17,575,000	$24,672,000
Variable costs:		
Manufacturing	10,022,500	13,440,000
Selling	4,560,000	7,968,000
Total variable costs	14,582,500	21,408,000
Contribution margin	2,992,500	3,264,000
Fixed costs:		
Manufacturing	550,000	565,000
Selling	345,000	370,000
Administration	150,000	140,000
Total fixed costs	1,045,000	1,075,000
Income from operations	$ 1,947,500	$ 2,189,000

EXHIBIT 13A-2

Ginkgo Manufacturing Limited
2001 Sales, Cost, and Market Data

	STATIC BUDGET		ACTUAL	
	CHLORINE	BROMINE	CHLORINE	BROMINE
Variable costs per kilogram:				
Manufacturing	$ 5.75	$ 8.50	$ 6.25	$ 7.50
Selling	2.50	4.00	2.50	5.25
Selling price per kilogram:	$10.00	$15.00	$10.00	$14.75

	SALES AND MARKET VOLUMES (MARKET SHARE)	
	BUDGETED KILOGRAMS	ACTUAL KILOGRAMS
Ginkgo's sales volume:		
Chlorine	760,000 (8%)	768,000 (8%)
Bromine	665,000 (7%)	1,152,000 (12%)
Total market volume	9,500,000 (100%)	9,600,000 (100%)

Sam asked his controller to provide him with a detailed analysis of operating results and a recommendation for awarding bonuses to the sales and production managers. As a first step, the controller put together the original underlying budget cost and revenue estimates, and the actual 2001 data, which he obtained from the cost records and trade statistics (Exhibit 13A-2).

Required:

1. Prepare a 2001 flexible budget for Ginkgo based on the data in the two exhibits. Your flexible budget should include columns for the two product lines as well as for the company overall.

2. Prepare a profit variance analysis. Explain the causes of the variances, identifying the effect of market factors as well as responsibility for variances between marketing and production.

C13-5 DETAILED VARIANCE ANALYSIS.   (SMAC) Ron Blacklock, President of Blacklock's Sporting Goods (BSG), was concerned about the profits earned by BSG during the fiscal year ending July 31, 2002. He had expected to sell 4,400 ski packages and earn $143,250 before taxes; actual profits earned were only $36,950.

The market for ski equipment is large and competitive. Ron had established a successful operation by specializing in low-cost mail-order ski packages. By offering only two packages, Ron was able to keep overhead costs to a minimum and negotiate favourable discounts from the ski equipment manufacturers. Both the downhill and cross-country ski packages contained skis, boots, poles, and a waxing kit.

Ron hired a consultant, Sam Wilson, CMA, to analyze the last fiscal year's results. "I just don't understand what went wrong," said Ron. "Things just did not happen the way I thought they would. For example, I was forced to cut our prices midway through the season because one of the big chain stores cut their prices. But I bargained with our suppliers and they gave us a break, which I thought would keep us on target. Then we had to spend a bit more on advertising to let everybody know about our new prices and another clerk had to be hired to speed up the order processing. Still, these two changes account for only $40,000. To top it all off, the Ski Retailers Association magazine just reported that more Canadians bought ski packages this past season than ever before. Early estimates were that 44,000 ski packages would be sold and it ended up that 48,000 packages were sold in Canada last season. My bookkeeper, Teresa, has put together these numbers." (See Exhibits 13A-3 and 13A-4.) "Please conduct a detailed analysis of last year's results. Prepare a report that explains why we did not realize our expected profits and include a recommended strategy, detailing information required, which will bring our profits back up."

EXHIBIT 13A-3

Blacklock's Sporting Goods
Master Budget for the Year Ended July 31, 2002

	CROSS-COUNTRY PACKAGE	DOWNHILL PACKAGE	TOTAL
Sales volume	3,100	1,300	4,400
Total sales revenue	$542,500	$455,000	$997,500
Cost of goods sold	263,500	221,000	484,500
Shipping	54,250	45,500	99,750
Total variable costs	317,750	266,500	584,250
Contribution margin	$224,750	$188,500	413,250
Fixed costs: Advertising & promotion			210,000
Administration			60,000
Net income before taxes			$143,250

BUDGETED DATA PER PACKAGE:	CROSS-COUNTRY	DOWNHILL
Selling price	$175.000	$350.00
Cost of goods sold	$ 85.00	$170.00
Shipping	17.50	35.00
Total variable costs per package	$ 102.50	$205.00

EXHIBIT 13A-4

Blacklock's Sporting Goods
Actual Results
for the Year Ended
July 31, 2002

	CROSS-COUNTRY PACKAGE	DOWNHILL PACKAGE	TOTAL
Sales volume	3,100	980	4,080
Total sales revenue	$511,500	$333,200	$844,700
Cost of goods sold	257,300	151,900	409,200
Shipping	54,250	34,300	88,550
Total variable costs	311,550	186,200	497,750
Contribution margin	$199,950	$147,000	346,950
Fixed costs: Advertising & promotion			230,000
Administration			80,000
Net income before taxes			$ 36,950

ACTUAL DATA PER PACKAGE:	CROSS-COUNTRY	DOWNHILL
Average Selling price	$165.00	$340.00
Average cost of goods sold	$83.00	$155.00
Shipping	17.50	35.00
Total average variable costs per package	$100.50	$190.00

Required: Prepare the analysis and the report requested by Ron Blacklock.

C13-6 CONTRIBUTION MARGIN AND VARIANCE ANALYSIS. (SMAC) Mark Ferguson, the President of Ferguson Foundry Limited (FFL), sat in his office early on June 2, 2002, reviewing the financial statements of FFL for the fiscal year ended May 31, 2002. The results for the year were both a shock and a disappointment.

Mr. Ferguson called Carl Holitzner, an independent consultant, to meet him in his office. When Carl arrived, Mr. Ferguson described his concerns.

I don't know what went wrong last year. Everybody kept telling me that we were selling more woodstoves than we thought we would and I knew from attending the trade shows that the sale of woodstoves throughout the province was rising. When I saw the statements for last year, I couldn't believe the drop in profits.

This company began in 1905. My grandfather used to make farm implements and sled runners; my father produced mostly trailers. I've dabbled in a few product lines like sewer grates and staircase railings, but, for the last five years, we've concentrated solely on woodstoves. Sales were slow at first and there were many producers in the market. But we have a good sales force and things have been steadily improving for the last two years. In 2001, we achieved record profits.

In addition to profits dropping, we have lost our management team. The sales manager took early retirement last month, the production manager is in the hospital for major surgery, and the accountant quit after we discussed the kind of information I felt he should be providing. He kept telling me that everything was running smoothly. Boy, was he wrong!

I called you here this morning because I need some help in understanding what went wrong last year. I want to be sure that similar mistakes are not made in the future. I'll be hiring some new people, but I need some answers quickly. Here is the statement of budgeted and actual results (Exhibit 13A-5). I was also able to dig up a statement of standard costs (Exhibit 13A-6) that was prepared last year plus some market and cost data that the accountant had prepared before he left (Exhibit 13A-7).

The standard costs are an accurate reflection of what it should cost to make either of the woodstove models.

Required:

Assume the role of Carl Holitzner and provide an explanation for FFL's lower-than-budgeted profit for the fiscal year ended May 31, 2002. Support your explanation with a detailed variance analysis.

EXHIBIT 13A-5

Ferguson Foundry Limited
Static Budget and Actual Results for the Year Ended May 31, 2002

| | STATIC BUDGET | | |
	BASIC	DELUXE	TOTAL
Sales volume (in units)	4,500	5,500	10,000
Sales revenue	$1,350,000	$4,400,000	$5,750,000
Variable costs:			
Direct materials	315,000	1,045,000	1,360,000
Direct labour	405,000	1,320,000	1,725,000
Overhead	202,500	660,000	862,500
Selling and administration	67,500	220,000	287,500
Total variable costs	990,000	3,245,000	4,235,000
Contribution margin	$ 360,000	$1,155,000	1,515,000
Fixed costs:			
Manufacturing			750,000
Selling and administration			132,500
Total fixed costs			882,500
Operating income			$ 632,500

| | ACTUAL RESULTS | | |
	BASIC	DELUXE	TOTAL
Sales volume (in units)	7,200	4,800	12,000
Sales revenue	$2,340,000	$3,360,000	$5,700,000
Variable costs:			
Direct materials	486,000	820,800	1,306,800
Direct labour	748,800	1,190,400	1,939,200
Overhead	374,400	595,200	969,600
Selling and administration	108,000	192,000	300,000
Total variable costs	1,717,200	2,798,400	4,515,600
Contribution margin	$ 622,800	$ 561,600	$1,184,400
Fixed costs:			
Manufacturing			780,000
Selling and administration			139,500
Total fixed costs			919,500
Operating income			$ 264,900

	BASIC WOODSTOVE	DELUXE WOODSTOVE
Direct materials:		
Standard quantity per unit	70 kg	190 kg
Standard price per kilogram	$ 1.00	$ 1.00
Direct labour:		
Standard quantity per unit	6 hrs.	16 hrs.
Standard rate per hour	$15.00	$15.00
Variable overhead:		
Standard quantity per unit	6 hrs.	16 hrs.
Standard rate per hour	$ 7.50	$ 7.50
Variable selling and		
administration rate per unit	$15.00	$40.00

Market Data:

Expected total market sales of woodstoves		100,000 units
Actual total market sales of woodstoves		133,333 units

Summary of Cost Sheets:

	BASIC	DELUXE	TOTAL
Units of woodstoves produced	7,200	4,800	12,000
Direct materials:			
Actual quantity used in kilograms	540,000	912,000	1,452,000
Actual price per kilogram			$0.90
Direct labour:			
Actual direct labour hours worked	46,800	74,400	121,200
Actual rate per hour			$16.00
Actual variable overhead allocated			
on the basis of direct labour hours	$374,400	$595,200	$ 969,600

Management Control Systems and Responsibility Accounting

LEARNING OBJECTIVES

After studying this chapter, you will be able to

1. Describe the relationship of management control systems to organizational goals and subgoals.

2. Use responsibility accounting to define an organizational subunit as a cost centre, expense centre, revenue centre, profit centre, or investment centre.

3. Explain the importance of evaluating performance and how it affects motivation, goal congruence, and employee effort.

4. Compare financial and nonfinancial performance, and explain why planning and control systems should consider both.

5. Prepare segment income statements for evaluating profit and investment centres using the contribution margin and controllable cost concepts.

6. Measure performance against quality, cycle time, and productivity objectives.

7. Describe the difficulties of management control in service and non-profit organizations.

8. Explain how management control systems must evolve with changing times.

The previous chapters have presented many important tools of management accounting. Tools such as activity-based costing, relevant costing, budgeting, and variance analysis are each useful by themselves. They are most useful, however, when they are parts of an integrated *system*—an orderly, logical plan to coordinate and evaluate all the activities of the organization, from the long-range planning of the chief executive officer, to the individual responses to customer or client inquiries, to the maintenance of physical assets. Managers of most organizations today, for example, realize that long-run success depends on focusing on efficiency and quality. This chapter considers how management accounting tools combined into a management control system focus resources and talents of the individuals in the organization on such goals as efficiency and quality. As you will see, no single system is inherently superior to another. The "best" system is the one that consistently leads to decisions that meet the organization's goals and objectives.

This chapter builds on previous chapters to describe how the individual tools of management accounting are blended systematically in order to help achieve organizational goals.

MANAGEMENT CONTROL SYSTEMS

OBJECTIVE 1

Describe the relationship of management control systems to organizational goals and subgoals.

Management Control System. A logical integration of management accounting tools to gather and report data and to evaluate performance.

A **management control system** is a logical integration of management accounting tools to gather and report data and to evaluate performance. The purposes of a management control system are to:

- clearly communicate the organization's goals
- ensure that every manager and employee understands the specific actions required of him/her to achieve organizational goals
- communicate results of actions across the organization
- ensure that the management control system adjusts to changes in the environment.

Exhibit 14-1 shows the components of a management control system. We will refer to Exhibit 14-1 often in this chapter as we consider the design and operation of management control systems.

Management Control Systems and Organizational Goals

A well-designed management control system aids and coordinates the process of making decisions and motivates individuals throughout the organization to work toward the same goals. It also coordinates forecasting revenue- and cost-driver levels, budgeting, measuring, and evaluating performance.

The first and most important component in a management control system is the organization's goals. Why? Because the focus of the management control system is on internal management decision making and evaluation of performance consistent with the organization's goals. As shown in Exhibit 14-2, setting goals, objectives, and performance measures involves managers at all levels.

Exhibit 14-2 shows that organization-wide (overall company) goals, performance measures, and targets are set by top management. Although these goals are not changed often, they are reviewed on a periodic basic, usually once a year. They are specific results that are desired in the future, and they spell out how an

EXHIBIT 14-1

The Management
Control System

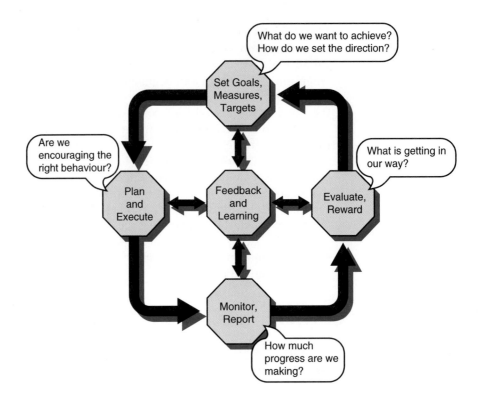

EXHIBIT 14-2

Setting Goals,
Objectives, and
Performance Measures

Top management develops organization-wide goals, measures, and targets. They also identify the critical processes.

Top management and critical process managers develop critical success factors and performance measures. They also identify specific objectives.

Critical process managers and lower-level managers develop performance measures for objectives.

organization will form its comprehensive plan for positioning itself in the market. As shown in Exhibit 14-1, goals answer the question, "What do we want to achieve?" However, goals without performance measures do not motivate managers.

The purpose of performance measures is to motivate managers to achieve organizational goals. In other words, they give managers a more specific idea of how to achieve a better goal. For example, a major luxury hotel chain, Luxury Suites, has the following goals and related performance measures:

ORGANIZATIONAL GOALS	PERFORMANCE MEASURES
Exceed Guest Expectations	• Satisfaction Index • # Repeat Stays
Maximize Revenue Yield	• Occupancy Rate • Room Rate • Income Before Fixed Costs
Focus on Innovation	• New Products/Services Implemented Per Year • # Employee Suggestions

Targets for goals are specific quantified levels of the measures. For example, a target for the performance measure *occupancy rate* might be "at least 70 percent."

As you can see, goals and performance measures are very broad. In fact, they are often too vague to guide managers and employees. As a result, top managers also identify critical processes and critical (key) success factors. A **critical process** is as series of related activities that directly impact the achievement of organizational goals. For example, the organizational goal "exceed guest expectations" would have "produce and deliver services" as a critical process. The next

Critical Process. An activity that directly impacts on the achievement of organizational goals.

COMPANY ⓢ STRATEGIES

ATTAINING GOAL CONGRUENCE AT IMPERIAL OIL RESOURCES DIVISION

Imperial Oil
www.imperialoil.com

Departments at Imperial Oil–Resources Division were given considerable latitude in carrying out their mandate. Although this management process was viewed as highly positive, particularly from a workforce motivation standpoint, it made overall goal congruence much more difficult to achieve. With the downturn in the economy and resulting substantial decline in earnings, the urgency of the need to assure corporate goal congruence was more readily apparent and became a key result area. The challenge was how to maintain the positive aspects of divisional/departmental latitude in performing management roles and at the same time introduce a mechanism to ensure overall coordination.

Two years ago the company introduced what is termed the "Board Concept" (see accompanying diagrams). The Senior Board consisted of the senior vice president and director of Imperial Oil and the vice presidents of Oil Sands and Production. Each of the vice presidents in turn had their own boards. Membership in each of the Vice Presidential Boards consisted of the senior vice president and director of Imperial Oil, the vice president and the Direct Reports to the Vice President. Again each of the Direct Reports had their own boards—membership included the Vice President, the Direct Reports and the immediate supervisors.

The Senior Board is responsible for setting corporate policies, goals, and strategies. The Vice Presidential Boards are similarly responsible for establishing their divisional policies, goals, and strategies. To ensure congruence with corporate objectives, the senior vice president is a member of each of these boards. Again, the Direct Report Boards set policies, goals, and strategies for their departments and the vice president to whom they report is a member to ensure congruence for his entire division.

Each board is required to meet at least monthly with more frequent meetings occurring on an as-needed basis. No board below the senior level may establish policies, goals, or strategies that impacted other boards without their consent. Disputes that could not be resolved were taken to the Senior Board for resolution. As deemed appropriate, members of one board could attend another board's meeting.

In addition to helping achieve goal congruence, these meetings are an excellent communication vehicle. Although still in its infancy, the board concept is proving to be very effective.

continued

Senior Board

```
        ┌─────────────────────────┐
        │ Senior Vice President and│
        │ Director, Imperial Oil   │
        │ (Chairperson)            │
        └────────────┬────────────┘
         ┌───────────┴───────────┐
┌────────┴────────┐     ┌────────┴────────┐
│ V.P. and G.M.,  │     │ V.P. and G.M.,  │
│ Oil Sands       │     │ Production      │
└─────────────────┘     └─────────────────┘
```

Vice Presidential Board

```
              ┌─────────────────────────┐
              │ Senior Vice President and│
              │ Director, Imperial Oil   │
              │ (Chairperson)            │
              │ V.P. and G.M., Production │
              └────────────┬────────────┘
```

Direct Reports →

Business Manager, Conventional Oil	Manager, Northern Operations	Manager, Natural Gas	Manager, Property Rationalization

Manager, Southern Operations	Manager, Technical Services	Project Manager, Operations Integrity

Direct Report Board

```
        ┌─────────────────────────┐
        │ V.P. and G.M., Production│
        │ Manager, Southern        │
        │ Operations (Chairperson) │
        └────────────┬────────────┘
```

Area Manager, Battle River	Area Manager, Quirk Creek	Area Manager, Cynthia	Business Analysis Leader

Area Manager, Medicine Hat	Technical Manager

Source: Written by John Baeck, Former Comptroller, Imperial Oil – Resources Division (formerly Esso Resources Canada Limited).

step in goal setting is for both top managers and the managers of the critical processes to develop subgoals or critical success factors and related performance measures. **Critical success factors** are activities that must be managed well in order to drive the organization toward its goals. An example of a critical success factor for the *produce and deliver services* process is *timeliness*. Performance measures for timeliness would include *check-in time, check-out time,* and *response time to guest requests (number of rings before pickup).*

Although critical success factors and related performance measures give managers more focus than do overall, organization-wide goals, they still do not give lower-level managers and employees the direction they need to guide their daily actions. As shown in Exhibit 14-2, to set this direction, critical-process managers work with lower-level managers within the appropriate business unit to establish objectives—specific tangible actions (or activities) that can be observed on a short-term basis. An example of a specific action related to timeliness for luxury suites is tracking travel details of arriving/departing guests.

Balancing the various objectives is a critical part of management control. Sometimes the management control system ignores critical success factors or inadvertently emphasizes the wrong factors. Managers often face trade-off decisions. For example, a sales manager can increase the "employee satisfaction" measure (a survey of employees) by setting lower standards for responding to customer inquires. This action may improve the employee satisfaction measure of the manager, but result in unsatisfied customers.

DESIGNING MANAGEMENT CONTROL SYSTEMS

To create a management control system that meets the organization's needs, designers need to recognize existing constraints, identify responsibility centres, weigh costs and benefits, provide motivations to achieve goal congruence and managerial effort, and install internal controls.

Organizational Structure

Every management control system needs to fit the organization's goals. (Though it is theoretically possible to persuade top management to change these goals, such alterations by designers of management control systems are very rare.) As shown in Exhibit 14-1, developing plans and then executing them is the second major function of a management control system. One of the primary purposes of planning (budgeting) is to encourage managers throughout the organization to act in congruence with overall goals. As a result, specifying how the organization will be structured is an important part of the planning process and the control system. Some firms are organized primarily by *functions* such as manufacturing, sales, and service. Others are organized by *divisions* bearing profit responsibility along product or geographical lines. Still others may be organized by some hybrid arrangement, such as a matrix structure. Exhibit 14-3 depicts an example of functional, divisional, and matrix structures.

Most of the time, changes in control systems are piecemeal improvements rather than complete replacements. Occasionally, however, the management control system designer is able to persuade top management to change the organization structure before redesigning the system. Large companies may use an

Crayola
www.crayola.com

autonomous division to experiment with changes in organization structure and/or management control systems before implementing wholesale changes throughout the organization.

Birney & Smith (Canada), a manufacturer of Crayola crayons, seized the U.S. parent's interest in a leaner corporate and work team structure. The Lindsay, Ontario, plant was reorganized into 10 teams, with only one layer of management—the team leaders—between the operations director and the factory workers.

By moving managers and workers closer together, and by letting each team take responsibility for the entire manufacturing process, from scheduling to customer service, improvements realized have been substantial. In about one year, costs have been reduced 9 percent, inventory levels have been reduced 75 percent, and profits are up 140 percent. As a result of these increases in efficiency and profitability, Birney & Smith International has shifted production to the plant so that production has now doubled and a third shift has become necessary.[1]

EXHIBIT 14-3

Alternative
Organizational
Structures

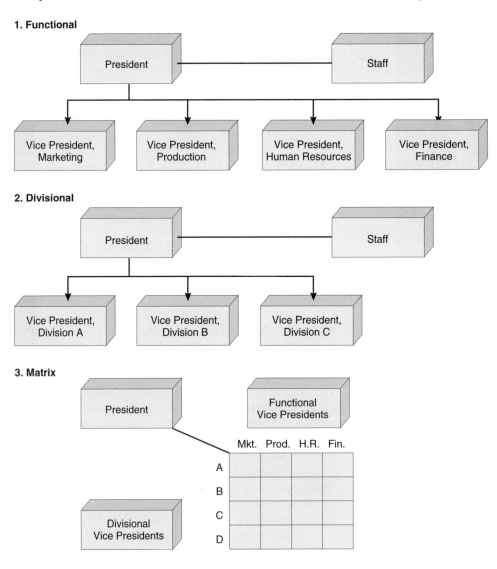

---

[1] "Crayon plant a brighter place," *The Globe and Mail*, June 18, 1992.

Responsibility Centres

Responsibility Centre. A set of activities assigned to a manager, a group of managers, or a group of employees.

Responsibility Accounting. Identifying what parts of the organization have primary responsibility for each objective, developing measures of achievement and objectives, and creating reports of these measures by organization subunit or responsibility centre.

In addition to organizational structures, designers of management control systems must consider the desired *responsibility centres* in an organization. A **responsibility centre** is defined as a set of activities assigned to a manager, a group of managers, or a group of employees. A set of machines and machining tasks, for example, may be a responsibility centre for a production supervisor; the full production department may be a responsibility centre for the department head; and the entire organization may be a responsibility centre for the president. In some organizations, management responsibility is shared by groups of employees in order to create wide "ownership" of management decisions, allow creative decision-making, and prevent one person's concern (or lack of concern) of the risk of failure to dominate decisions.

An effective management control system gives each lower-level manager responsibility for a group of activities and objectives and then reports on (1) the results of the activities, (2) the manager's influence on those results, and (3) effects of uncontrollable events. Such a system has innate appeal for most top managers because it helps them delegate decision making and gives them the freedom to plan and control. Lower-level managers appreciate the autonomy of decision making they inherit. Thus, system designers apply **responsibility accounting** to identify what parts of the organization have primary responsibility for each objective, develop measures and targets to achieve objectives, and design reports of these measures by organization subunit, or responsibility centre. Responsibility centres usually have multiple objectives that the management control system monitors. Responsibility centres are usually classified according to their *financial* responsibility, as cost centres, expense centres, revenue centres, profit centres, or investment centres.

Cost centres

Cost Centre. A responsibility centre for which costs are to be managed efficiently.

A **cost centre** is a responsibility centre in which a manager is accountable only for costs. Its financial responsibilities are to control and report costs only. An entire department may be considered a single cost centre, or a department may contain several cost centres. For example, although an assembly department may be supervised by one manager, it may contain several assembly lines and regard each assembly line as a separate cost centre. Likewise, within each line, separate machines or test equipment may be regarded as separate cost centres. The determination of the number of cost centres depends on cost-benefit considerations— do the benefits of smaller cost centres (for planning, control, and evaluation) exceed the higher costs of reporting?

Expense centres

Expense Centre. A responsibility centre for which the objective is to spend the budget but maximize the specific service objective of the centre.

An **expense centre**, sometimes referred to as a *discretionary cost centre*, must attain its objectives and spend its budget. For example, a training and development department may have a budget of $250,000 and have as its objective to maximize the value of the training and development that can be attained for an expenditure of $250,000.

Revenue centres

A **revenue centre** has a responsibility to maximize the total revenues. While frequently constrained by an expense budget, the revenue centre focuses on maximizing factors such as volume, price, and market share to maximize the revenues.

Profit centres

A **profit centre** is responsible for controlling costs (or expenses) as well as revenues—that is, profitability. Despite the name, a profit centre can exist in nonprofit organizations (though it may not be referred to as such) when a responsibility centre receives revenues for its services. All profit centre managers are responsible for both revenues and costs, but they may not be expected to maximize profits.

Investment centres

An **investment centre** goes a step further. Its success is measured not only by its income, but also by relating that income to its invested capital—as in a ratio of income to the value of the capital employed. In practice, the term investment centre is not widely used. Instead, the term profit centre is used indiscriminately to describe centres that are always assigned responsibility for revenues and expenses, but may or may not be assigned responsibility for the capital investment.

EXHIBIT 14-4

Responsibility Centres

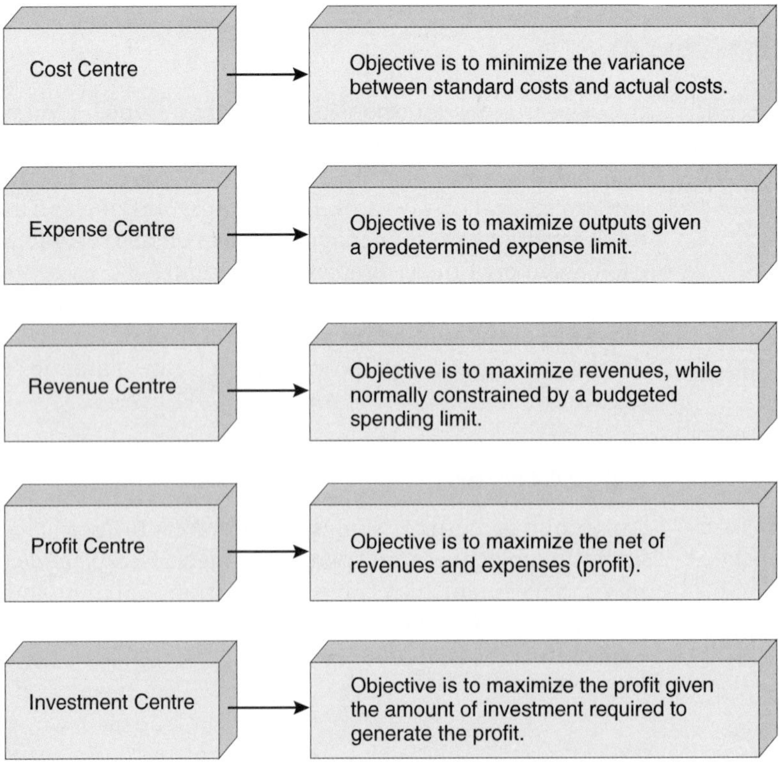

Cost Centre	Objective is to minimize the variance between standard costs and actual costs.
Expense Centre	Objective is to maximize outputs given a predetermined expense limit.
Revenue Centre	Objective is to maximize revenues, while normally constrained by a budgeted spending limit.
Profit Centre	Objective is to maximize the net of revenues and expenses (profit).
Investment Centre	Objective is to maximize the profit given the amount of investment required to generate the profit.

Exhibit 14-4 provides a summary of the objective of each of the five types of responsibility centres.

Weighing Costs and Benefits

The designer of the management control system must also weigh the costs and benefits of various alternatives, given the organization's needs. No system is perfect, but one system may be better than another if it can improve operating decisions at a reasonable cost.

Both benefits and costs of management control systems are often difficult to measure, and may become apparent only after experimentation or use. For example, the director of accounting policy of Citicorp has stated that, after several years of experience with a very detailed management control system, the system has proved to be too costly to administer relative to the perceived benefits. Accordingly, Citicorp plans to return to a simpler, less costly—though less precise—management control system.

MOTIVATING EMPLOYEES TO ACHIEVE GOAL CONGRUENCE AND TO EXERT MANAGERIAL EFFORT

Goal Congruence. Exists when individuals and groups aim at the same organizational goals.

Managerial Effort. Exertion toward a goal or objective, including all the conscious actions (such as supervising, planning, and thinking) that result in more efficiency and effectiveness.

To achieve maximum benefits at minimum cost, a management control system must foster *goal congruence* and *managerial effort*. **Goal congruence** exists when individuals and groups aim for the same organizational goals. Goal congruence is achieved when employees, working in their own perceived best interests, make decisions that meet the overall goals of the organization. **Managerial effort** is defined as exertion toward a goal or objective. Effort here means not merely working faster, but also working *better*. Effort includes all conscious actions (such as supervising, planning, thinking) that result in more efficiency and effectiveness. Effort is a matter of degree—it is optimized when individuals and groups *strive* for their objectives.

Goal congruence can exist with little accompanying managerial effort, and vice versa, but *incentives* are necessary for both to be achieved. The challenge of a management-control-system design is to specify objectives and rewards that induce (or at least do not discourage) employee decisions that will achieve organizational goals. For example, an organization may specify one of its subgoals to be continuous improvement in employee efficiency and effectiveness. Employees, however, might perceive that continuous improvements will result in tighter standards, faster pace of work, and loss of jobs. Even though they may agree with management that continuous improvements are competitively necessary, they should not be expected to exert effort for continuous improvements unless incentives are in place to make this effort in their own best interests. One may be pleasantly surprised that some individuals will act selflessly, but management control systems should be designed to take advantage of more typical human behaviour. Be aware that self-interest may be perceived differently in different cultures.

As another example, students may enrol in a university course because their goal is to learn about management accounting. The faculty and the students share the same goal, but goal congruence is not enough. Faculty also introduce rewards in the form of a grading system to spur student effort. Grading is a form of *performance evaluation*, as is the use of management control reports for raises,

promotions, and other forms of rewards in other settings. Performance evaluation is a widely used means of improving congruence and effort because most individuals tend to perform better when they receive feedback that is tied to their own self-interest. Thus Allen-Bradley Co., Corning, and other manufacturers that set quality improvements as critical subgoals, put quality objectives into the bonus plans of top managers. Corning has quality incentives for factory workers as well. In the Birney & Smith (Canada) plant described earlier, management is considering the "pay-of-knowledge system," which would compensate team members based on their skills.

In addition to incentives and performance evaluation, goal congruence can only be attained if the management control system is fair. *Fairness*[2] is achieved if the employees understand how the incentives and performance evaluation are measured and used. Employees must also understand how they may make decisions and change their behaviour to influence the performance evaluation and ultimately the incentives.

Continuing with the example of university students, if a professor desires to achieve a better learning experience in a course through class participation then a participation grade would likely be included in the grading system. However, to effectively achieve the goal of increased classroom participation and discussion, the professor should clearly explain how participation will be graded and provide some indication of the grade that could be expected with certain levels of participation.

To achieve goal congruence and managerial effort, designers of management control systems focus on motivating employees. **Motivation** has been defined as an aim for some selected goal together with the resulting drive (effort) that creates action toward that goal. Yet employees differ widely in their motivations. The system designer's task is more complex, ill-structured, and more affected by human behaviour than many people believe at first. The system designer must align individuals' self-interest with the goals of the organization. Thus the designer must focus on the different motivational impact—how each system will cause people to respond—of one management control system versus another.

To see how failure to anticipate motivational impact can cause problems, consider that some years ago in Russia, managers of the Moscow Cable Company decided to reduce copper wastage and actually slashed it by 60 percent that year. As a result they had only $40,000 worth of scrap instead of the $100,000 originally budgeted. Top management in the central government then fined the plant $45,000 for not meeting its scrap budget. What do you think this did to the cable company managers' motivation to control waste?

Responsibility accounting, budgets, variances, and the entire inventory of management control tools should constructively influence behaviour. However, they may be misused as weapons to punish, place blame, or find fault. They pose a threat to managers, who will resist and undermine the use of such techniques. Viewed positively, they assist managers to improve decisions.

OBJECTIVE 3

Explain the importance of evaluating performance and how it affects motivation, goal congruence, and employee effort.

Motivation. The drive for some selected goal that creates effort and action toward that goal.

---

[2] Richard F. Vancil, "What kind of management control do you need?" *Harvard Business Review*, March-April, 1973, p. 76.

A Measure of Their Worth

No longer simply scorekeepers, senior financial managers offer their organizations insightful analysis and assessment of information, both financial and otherwise. Seldom is this transition from statistician to business partner more evident than in a company's strategic planning process and especially in tying that process to an efficient, effective performance measurement system. Here's how the management team at BC Rail linked performance measurement and strategic plan goals to help senior managers sharpen focus, gain alignment, and raise accountability throughout the organization.

During the early 1990s, BC Rail had developed business unit scorecards containing financial and productivity information. The scorecards summarized the measures available from existing information systems; little emphasis was placed on establishing new measures. The scorecards were incorporated only into the monthly corporate financial statement package. Although business managers initially viewed them as useful tools for consolidating information, the scorecards never came to be considered integral to the management process. Why not?

A major flaw was the lack of a direct link between the performance scorecards and corporate goals. Although BC Rail had completed a strategic plan in 1990–91, the company had failed to recognize the significance of the plan to the development of performance metrics. When it updated its strategic plan last year, the company needed to re-think how it used and communicated its metrics. Most important, the performance measures had to become a direct outcome of the strategic plan.

In order to connect performance measures and its strategic plan, BC Rail underwent the following process:
- involved a broad senior management team;
- revisited the corporate mission statement, vision and values that had been established during previous planning sessions;
- analyzed strengths, weaknesses, opportunities and threats;
- reviewed the achievements and shortcomings of the previous five-year strategic plan;
- defined the company's three critical goals;
- established core strategies to achieve each goal;
- identified key metrics to measure progress toward each goal;
- established clear definitions, responsibilities, and annual targets for each metric;
- identified and scheduled current-year action plans in order to implement the strategies and achieve the metric targets; and
- established annual objectives for individual managers based on the action plans and metric targets, and linked these objectives to incentive compensation.

As it worked through this process, the company established consensus on each component necessary to achieve its strategies and goals. Strong CEO leadership created an environment that encouraged innovation and creative thinking throughout the planning process.

Source: Reprinted from an article appearing in *CMA Management* by Alan Qwen, July-August 1997, with permission of the Society of Management Accountants of Canada.

BC Rail
www.bcrail.com

Designing Internal Controls

Internal Control System. Methods and procedures to prevent errors and irregularities, detect errors and irregularities, and promote operating efficiency.

It is common in Canadian companies to ensure that an *internal controls system* is in place. Both managers and accountants are responsible for developing, maintaining, and evaluating internal control systems. An **internal control system** consists of methods and procedures to:

1. Prevent errors and irregularities by a system of authorization for transactions, accurate recording of transactions, and safeguarding of assets;

2. Detect errors and irregularities by reconciling accounting records with independently kept records and physical counts and reviewing accounts for possible reductions of values;
3. Promote operating efficiency by examining policies and procedures for possible improvements.

A management control system encompasses *administrative controls* (such as budgets for planning, controlling, and evaluating operations) and *accounting controls* (such as the common internal control procedure of separating the duties of the person who counts cash from the duties of the person who has access to the accounts receivable records). This text concentrates on the administrative control aspects of the management control system.

Developing Measures of Performance

OBJECTIVE 4

Compare financial and nonfinancial performance, and explain why planning and control systems should consider both.

Since most responsibility centres have multiple objectives, only some of these objectives are expressed in financial terms, such as operations budgets, profit targets, or required return on investment, depending on the financial classification of the centre. Other objectives, which are to be achieved concurrently, are nonfinancial in nature. For example, some companies list environmental stewardship and social responsibility as key objectives. The well-designed management control system functions alike for both financial and nonfinancial objectives to develop and report measures of performance. Good performance measures will

1. Relate to the goals of the organization
2. Balance long-term and short-term concerns
3. Reflect the management of key decisions and activities
4. Be affected by actions of managers and employees
5. Be readily understood by managers and employees
6. Be used in evaluating and rewarding employees
7. Be reasonably objective and easily measured
8. Be used consistently and regularly

Both financial and nonfinancial performance measures are important. Sometimes accountants and managers focus too much on financial measures such as profit or cost variances because they are readily available from the accounting system. However, managers can improve operational control by also considering nonfinancial measures of performance. Such measures may be more timely and more closely affected by employees at lower levels of the organization, where the product is made or the service is rendered.

Nonfinancial measures are often easier to quantify and understand. Hence, employees can be easily motivated toward achieving performance goals. For example, AT&T Universal Card Services, which was awarded the prestigious Baldrige National Quality Award (presented by the U.S. Department of Commerce), uses 18 performance measures for its customer inquiries process. Examples include average speed of answer, abandon rate, and application processing time (three days compared to the industry average of 24 days).

Often the effects of poor nonfinancial performance (quality, productivity, and customer satisfaction) do not show up in the financial measures until considerable ground has been lost. Financial measures are lagging indicators that may arrive too

Baldrige National Quality Award
www.software.org/
quagmire/descriptions/
baldrige.asp

late to help prevent problems and issues that affect the organization's wealth. What is needed are leading indicators. As a result, many companies now stress management of the *activities* that drive revenues and costs rather than waiting to explain the revenues or costs themselves after the activities have taken place. Superior financial performance usually follows from superior nonfinancial performance.

CONTROLLABILITY AND MEASURING FINANCIAL PERFORMANCE

Management control systems often distinguish between controllable and uncontrollable events and between controllable and uncontrollable costs. Usually, responsibility centre managers are in the best position to explain their centre's results even if the managers had little influence over them. For example, an importer of grapes from Chile to the United States suffered a sudden loss of sales several years ago after a few of the grapes were found to contain cyanide. The tampering was beyond the importer's control, and the importer's management control system compared actual profits to flexible-budgeted profits (see Chapter 13), given that actual sales were unusually depressed. This comparison separated the effects of activity volume—sales levels—from effects of efficiency—and reported the importer's profitability given the uncontrollable drop in sales.

Uncontrollable Cost. Any cost that cannot be affected by the management of a responsibility centre within a given time span.

An **uncontrollable cost** is any cost that cannot be affected by the management of a responsibility centre within a given time span. For example, a mail-order supervisor may only be responsible for costs of labour, shipping costs, ordering errors and adjustments, and customer satisfaction. The supervisor would not be responsible for costs of the supporting information system since the supervisor cannot control that cost.

Controllable Costs. Any costs that are influenced by a manager's decisions and actions.

Controllable costs should include all costs that are *influenced* by a manager's decisions and actions. For example, the costs of the mail-order information system, though uncontrollable by the mail-order supervisor, are controllable by the manager in charge of information systems.

In a sense, the term "controllable" is a misnomer because no cost is completely under the control of a manager. But the term is widely used to refer to any cost that is affected by a manager's decisions. Thus, the cost of operating the mail order information system may be affected by equipment or software failures that are not completely—but are partially—under the control of the information systems manager, who would be held responsible for all of the costs of the information system, even the costs of downtime.

The distinction between controllable and uncontrollable costs serves an information purpose. Costs that are completely uncontrollable tell nothing about a manager's decisions and actions because, by definition, nothing the manager does will affect the costs. Such costs should be ignored in evaluating the responsibility centre manager's performance. In contrast, reporting controllable costs provides evidence about a manager's performance.

Procter & Gamble
www.pg.com

Pharmacia
www.upjohn.com

Because responsibility for costs may be widespread, systems designers must depend on understanding cost behaviour to help identify controllable costs. This understanding is increasingly gained through activity-based costing (see Chapter 5). Both Procter & Gamble and Upjohn, Inc., for example, are experimenting with activity-based costing systems in some divisions. Procter & Gamble credits its experimental activity-based management control system for identifying controllable costs in one of its detergent divisions, which led to major strategic changes.

Contribution Margin

OBJECTIVE 5

Prepare segment income statements for evaluating profit and investment centres using the contribution margin and controllable cost concepts.

Many organizations combine the contribution approach to measuring income with responsibility accounting—that is, they report by cost behaviour as well as by degrees of controllability.

Exhibit 14-5 displays the contribution approach to measuring the financial performance of a retail food company. Study this exhibit carefully. It provides perspective on how a management control system can be designed to stress cost behaviour, controllability, manager performance, and responsibility centre performance simultaneously.

Line (a) in Exhibit 14-5 shows the contribution margin, sales revenue less all variable expenses. The contribution margin is especially helpful for predicting the effect on income of short-run changes in activity volume. Managers may quickly calculate any expected changes in income by multiplying increases in dollar sales by the contribution margin ratio (see Chapter 2). The contribution margin ratio for meats in Branch B is 0.20. Thus, a $1,000 increase in sales of meats in Branch B should produce a $200 increase income (0.20 × $1,000 = $200) if there are no changes in selling prices, operating expenses, or mix of sales between Stores 1 and 2.

Contribution Controllable by Segment Managers

Lines (b) and (c) in Exhibit 14-5 separate the contribution that is controllable by segment managers (b) and the overall segment contribution (c). The manager of Store 1 may have influence over some local advertising, but not other advertising, some fixed salaries but not other salaries, and so forth. Moreover, the meat manager at both the branch and store levels may have no influence over store depreciation or the president's salary. Therefore, Exhibit 14-5 separates costs by controllability. Managers on all levels are asked to explain the total segment contribution but are held responsible only for the controllable contribution.

Note that fixed costs controllable by the segment managers are deducted from the contribution margin to obtain the *contribution* controllable by segment managers. (This is very similar to the relevant costing analysis covered in Chapters 8 and 9.) These controllable costs are usually discretionary fixed costs such as local advertising and some salaries, but not the manager's own salary. Other, noncontrollable, fixed costs (shown between lines (a) and (b)) are not allocated in the breakdown because they are not considered controllable this far down in the organization. That is, of the $160,000 fixed cost that is controllable by the manager of Branch B, $140,000 is also controllable by subordinates (grocery, produce, and meat managers), but $20,000 is not. The latter are controllable by the Branch B manager, but not by lower managers. Similarly, the $30,000 in that same line are costs that are attributable to the meat department of Branch B, but not to individual stores.

In many organizations, managers have latitude to trade off some variable costs for fixed costs. To save variable material and labour costs, managers might make heavier outlays for automation, quality management and employee training programs, and so on. Moreover, decisions on advertising, research, and sales promotion affect sales activity and hence contribution margins. The controllable contribution includes these expenses and attempts to capture the results of these tradeoffs.

EXHIBIT 14-5

The Contribution Approach: Model Income Statement, by Segments*
(in thousands of dollars)

	RETAIL FOOD COMPANY AS A WHOLE	COMPANY BREAKDOWN INTO TWO DIVISIONS		POSSIBLE BREAKDOWN OF BRANCH B ONLY				POSSIBLE BREAKDOWN OF BRANCH B, MEATS ONLY		
		BRANCH A	BRANCH B	NOT ALLOCATED†	GROCERIES	PRODUCE	MEATS	NOT ALLOCATED†	STORE 1	STORE 2
Net sales	$4,000	$1,500	$2,500	—	$1,300	$300	$900	—	$600	$300
Variable costs:										
Cost of merchandise sold	$3,000	$1,100	$1,900	—	$1,000	$230	$670	—	$450	$220
Variable operating expenses	260	100	160	—	100	10	50	—	35	15
Total variable costs	$3,260	$1,200	$2,060	—	$1,100	$240	$720	—	$485	$235
(a) Contribution margin	$ 740	$ 300	$ 440	—	$ 200	$ 60	$180	—	$115	$ 65
Less: Fixed costs controllable by segment managers††	260	100	160	$ 20	40	10	90	$ 30	35	25
(b) Contribution controllable by segment managers	$ 480	$ 200	$ 280	$(20)	$ 160	$ 50	$ 90	$(30)	$ 80	$ 40
Less: Fixed costs controllable by others§	200	90	110	20	40	10	40	10	22	8
(c) Contribution by segments	$ 280	$ 110	$ 170	$(40)	$ 120	$ 40	$ 50	$(40)	$ 58	$ 32
Less: Unallocated costs¶	100									
(d) Income before income taxes	$ 180									

* Three different types of segments are illustrated here: branches, product lines, and stores. As you read across, note that the focus becomes narrower: from Branch A and B, to Branch B only, to meats in Branch B only.

† Only those costs clearly indentifiable to a product line should be allocated.

†† Examples are certain advertising, sales promotion, salespersons' salaries, management consulting, training and supervision costs.

§ Examples are amortization, property taxes, insurance, and perhaps the segment manager's salary.

¶ These costs are not clearly or practically allocable to any segment except by some highly questionable allocation base.

The distinctions in Exhibit 14-5 among which items belong in what cost classification are inevitably not clear-cut. For example, determining controllability is always a problem when service department costs are allocated to other departments. Should the store manager bear a part of the division headquarters costs? If so, how much and on what basis? How much, if any, store depreciation or lease rentals should be deducted in computing the controllable contribution? There are no easy answers to these questions. Each organization chooses ways that benefit it most with the lowest relative cost.

Contribution by Segments

The *contribution by segments*, line (c) in Exhibit 14-5, is an attempt to approximate the financial performance of the *segment*, as distinguished from the financial performance of its *manager*, which is measured in line (b). The "fixed costs controllable by others" typically include committed costs (such as depreciation and property taxes) and discretionary costs (such as the segment manager's salary). These costs are attributable to the segment but primarily are controllable only at higher levels of management.

Unallocated Costs

Exhibit 14-5 shows "unallocated costs" immediately before line (d). They might include central corporate costs such as the costs of top management and some corporate-level services (e.g., legal and taxation). When a persuasive cause-and-effect, or activity-based justification for assigning such costs cannot be found, many organizations favour not allocating them to segments.

The contribution approach highlights the relative objectivity of various means of measuring financial performance. The contribution margin itself tends to be the most objective. As you read downward in the report, the assignments become more subjective, and the resulting measures of contributions or income become more subject to dispute. Though such disputes may not be a productive use of management time, the analysis directs managers' attention to the costs of the entire organization and lead to organizational cost control. These issues are covered in more detail in Chapter 15.

Champion International
www.champint.com

NONFINANCIAL MEASURES OF PERFORMANCE

OBJECTIVE 6

Measure performance against quality, cycle time, and productivity objectives.

For many years, organizations have monitored their nonfinancial performance. For example, sales organizations have followed up on customers to assure their satisfaction. Manufacturers have tracked manufacturing defects and product performance. Government health organizations have kept meticulous statistics on disease incidence and reduction, which indicates the effectiveness of disease control efforts such as education, sanitation, and inoculation. In recent years, most organizations have developed a new awareness of the importance of controlling such nonfinancial performance as quality, cycle time, and productivity.

For example, Champion International Corporation's mill in Hamilton, Ohio, which produces for the premium paper market, changed its organizational structure when it implemented flexible manufacturing and just-in-time production. Newly adopted goals such as reduced cycle time and first-pass yield (the percentage of product flowing directly without rework to its intended destination) resulted in new demands on the accounting function. Accountants now include nonfinancial performance measures along with financial results and work with production management as "business partners."

Quality Control. The effort to ensure that products and services perform to customer requirements.

Quality control is the effort to ensure that products and services perform to customer requirements. Organizations around the globe have adopted formal quality management programs. It has also become apparent that increasing quality can be achieved by reducing the cycle time of delivering a product or service. Improvements in quality (from inception of the product to delivery and after-sales service) lead to reduced cycle time and increased productivity.

Since these factors are closely related, it is not coincidental that all types of organizations are concerned about quality, cycle time, and productivity. They are key subgoals that lead to long-term profitability for companies and are increasingly important in nonprofit and government organizations, where tighter appropriations and increasing demands for services are facts of life.

Control of Quality

In essence, customers or clients define quality by comparing their needs and expectations to the attributes of the product or service. For example, buyers judge the quality of an automobile based on reliability, performance, styling, safety, and image relative to their needs, budget, and the alternatives. Defining quality in terms of customer requirements is only half the battle, though. There remains the problem of reaching and maintaining the desired level of quality. There are many approaches to controlling quality. The traditional approach was to inspect products after they were completed and reject or rework those that failed the inspections. Because testing is expensive, often only a sample of products were inspected. The process was judged to be in control as long as the number of defective products did not exceed an *acceptable quality level.* This meant that some defective products could still make their way to customers.

In recent years, however, North American companies, confronted with the success of Japanese products, have learned that this is a very costly way to control quality. All the resources consumed to make a defective product and to detect it are wasted, or considerable rework may be necessary to correct the defects. In addition it is very costly to repair products in use by a customer or to win back a dissatisfied customer. IBM's CEO John Akers was quoted in *The Wall Street Journal* as saying, "I am sick and tired of visiting plants to hear nothing but great things about quality and cycle time—and then to visit customers who tell me of problems." The high costs of achieving quality by "inspecting it in" are evident in a **quality cost report**, which displays the financial impact of quality. The quality cost report shown in Exhibit 14-6 on the previous page measures four categories of quality costs:

Quality Cost Report. A report that displays the financial impact of quality.

1. Prevention—costs incurred to prevent the production of defective products or delivery of substandard services, including engineering analyses to improve product design for better manufacturing, improvements in production processes, increased quality of material inputs, and programs to train personnel.

Implementing Quality Programs at Grand Rapids Spring & Wire

Grand Rapids Spring & Wire Products, Inc. (GRSW) manufactures a variety of products for the automotive, appliance, furniture, and electronic industries. GRSW products include compression, extension, and torsion springs; stampings from progressive dies and four-slide stampings; roll forming; wire and grommet moulding and various assembly processes. In the mid-1980s, GRSW began an aggressive quality program designed to create a "quality culture." Various quality theories were carefully studied by management and employees.

GRSW restructured its organization into divisional mini-companies—cross-functional, self-directed units that would enhance continuous improvement. The four mini-companies are Small Metal Stamping, Four-Slide Stamping, Spring Torsion, and Secondary. Each mini-company was assigned support personnel, including accounting, engineering, and quality experts. This new organization has created a much flatter organizational structure and has improved communications. Each mini-company develops its own mission statement and plans. For example, the mission of the Secondary mini-company is, "Boosting our attendance and participation while maintaining/increasing quality and delivery levels will lead to the continuous improvement of Quality (Q), Cost (C), Delivery (D), Safety (S), Morale (M), and ultimate customer satisfaction."

Performance indicators have been developed to measure quality, cost, delivery, safety, and morale. Examples of performance indicators include the following:

MISSION COMPONENT	PERFORMANCE INDICATOR	GOAL
QUALITY	Defective Parts Per Million	<200
	Returns and Allowances	<.5%
	Customer Concerns	<3 per month
COST	Sales: Sales/Payroll	Increase
	Finished Goods Inventory as a % of Sales	<.15
DELIVERY	Percent on Time	>97%
SAFETY	Reported Accidents	0
	Outside Medical Aid Required	0
MORALE	Tardy, Leave Early, Absences	<12 per month
	Implemented Suggestions	>11 per month

Any time a process fails to achieve a performance goal, a team is formed to define and solve the problem. Each week, employees meet with the support people to review progress on each mission component (QCDSM). Twice a year the company holds a stakeholders' meeting for all employees to review how the mini-company is progressing toward its mission and goals.

Source: H. Roehm, Klein, D., and Castellano, J., "Blending Quality Theories for Continuous Improvement," *Management Accounting* (February 1995), pp. 26–32.

EXHIBIT 14-6

Eastside Manufacturing Company Quality Cost Report* (thousands of dollars)

MONTH			QUALITY COST AREA	YEAR-TO-DATE		
ACTUAL	PLAN	VARIANCE		ACTUAL	PLAN	VARIANCE
			1. Prevention Cost			
3	2	1	A. Quality—Administration	5	4	1
16	18	(2)	B. Quality—Engineering	37	38	(1)
7	6	1	C. Quality—Planning by Others	14	12	2
5	7	(2)	D. Supplier Assurance	13	14	(1)
31	33	(2)	Total Prevention Cost	69	68	1
5.5%	6.1%		% of Total Quality Cost	6.3%	6.3%	
			2. Appraisal Cost			
31	26	5	A. Inspection	55	52	3
12	14	(2)	B. Test	24	28	(4)
7	6	1	C. Insp. & Test of Purchased Mat.	15	12	3
11	11	0	D. Product Quality Audits	23	22	1
3	2	1	E. Maint of Insp. & Test Equip.	4	4	0
2	2	0	F. Mat. Consumed in Insp. & Test	5	4	1
66	61	5	Total Appraisal Cost	126	122	4
11.8%	11.3%		% of Total Quality Cost	11.4%	11.3%	
			3. Internal Failure Cost			
144	140	4	A. Scrap & Rework—Manuf.	295	280	15
55	53	2	B. Scrap & Rework—Engineering	103	106	(3)
28	30	(2)	C. Scrap & Rework—Supplier	55	60	(5)
21	22	(1)	D. Failure Investigation	44	44	0
248	245	3	Total Internal Failure Cost	497	490	7
44.3%	45.4%		% of Total Quality Cost	44.9%	45.3%	
345	339	6	Total Internal Quality Cost (1 + 2 + 3)	692	680	12
61.6%	62.8%		% of Total Quality Cost	62.6%	62.9%	
			4. External Failure Quality Cost			
75	66	9	A. Warranty Exp.—Manuf.	141	132	9
41	40	1	B. Warranty Exp—Engineering	84	80	4
35	35	0	C. Warranty Exp.—Sales	69	70	(1)
46	40	6	D. Field Warranty Cost	83	80	3
18	20	(2)	E. Failure Investigation	37	40	(3)
215	201	14	Total External Failure Cost	414	402	12
38.4%	37.2%		% of Total Quality Cost	37.4%	37.1%	
560	540	20	Total Quality Cost	1,106	1,082	24
9,872	9,800		Total Product Cost	20,170	19,600	
5.7%	5.5%		% Tol. Qual. Cost to Tot. Prod. Cost	5.5%	5.5%	

* Adapted from Allen H. Seed III, *Adapting Management Accounting Practice to an Advanced Manufacturing Environment* (National Association of Accountants, 1988) Table 5-2, p. 76. Institute of Management Accountants.

2. Appraisal—costs incurred to identify defective products or services, including inspection and testing.
3. Internal failure—costs of defective components and final products or services that are scrapped or reworked, also costs of delays caused by defective products or services
4. External failure—costs caused by delivery of defective products or services to customers, such as field repairs, returns, and warranty expenses.

This report shows that the great majority of costs spent by Eastside Manufacturing Company are due to internal or external failures. But these costs are almost certainly understated. Poor quality can result in large opportunity costs due to internal delays and lost sales. For example, quality problems in North American-built automobiles in the 1970s and 1980s probably caused foregone sales that were significantly more costly than the tangible costs measured in any quality cost report.

In recent years, more and more North American companies have been rethinking this approach to quality control. Instead, they have adopted an approach first espoused by an American, William Deming, and embraced by Japanese companies decades ago: *total quality management*. Following the old adage, "an ounce of prevention is worth a pound of cure," it focuses on *prevention* of defects and on customer satisfaction. The TQM approach is based on the assumption that the cost of quality is minimized when a company achieves high-quality levels. **Total quality management (TQM)** is the application of quality principles to *all* of the organization's endeavours to satisfy customers. TQM has significant implications for organization goals, structure, and management control systems. A complete discussion of TQM is beyond the scope of this text, but it includes delegating responsibility for many management functions to employees. For TQM to work, though, employees must be very well trained in the process, the product or service, and the use of quality control information.

To implement TQM, employees are trained to prepare, interpret, and act on quality control charts, like that shown in Exhibit 14-7. The most common form of quality control information that is used by employees is the *quality control chart*. The **quality control chart** is a statistical plot of measures of various product dimensions or attributes. This plot helps detect process deviations before the process generates defects. These plots also identify excessive variation in product dimensions or attributes that should be addressed by process or design engineers. Exhibit 14-7 shows that the Eastside Manufacturing Company generally is not meeting its defects objective of 0.5 percent defects (which is a relatively high defect rate). A manager looking at this chart would know that corrective action must be taken.

Total Quality Management (TQM). The application of quality principles to all of the organization's endeavours to satisfy customers.

Quality Control Chart. The statistical plot of measures of various product dimensions or attributes.

EXHIBIT 14-7

Eastside Manufacturing Company Quality Control Chart

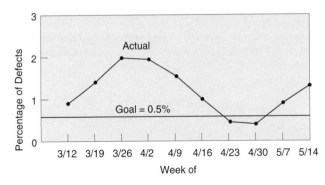

Control of Cycle Time

Cycle Time. The time taken to complete a product or service, or any of the components of a product or service.

One key to improving quality is to reduce *cycle time*. **Cycle time** or throughput time is the time taken to complete a product or service from initiation of the order by the customer to the receipt of the product or service. It is a summary measure of manufacturing or service efficiency and effectiveness, and an important cost driver. The longer a product or service is in process, the more costs are consumed. Low cycle time means quick completion of a product or service (without defects). Lowering cycle time requires smooth-running processes and high quality, and also creates increased flexibility and quicker reactions to customer needs. As cycle time is decreased, quality problems become apparent throughout the process and must be solved if quality is to be improved. Decreasing cycle time also results in bringing products or services more quickly to customers—a service that customers value.

Firms measure cycle time for the important stages of a process and for the process as a whole. An effective means of measuring cycle time is to use *barcoding*, where a barcode (similar to symbols on most grocery products) is attached to each component or product and read at the end of each stage of completion. Cycle time is measured for each stage as the time between readings of barcodes. Barcoding also permits effective tracking of materials and products for inventories, scheduling, and delivery.

Exhibit 14-8 shows a sample cycle time report. (Cycle time can also be displayed on a control chart.) This report shows that Eastside Manufacturing Company is meeting its cycle time objectives at two of its five production process stages. This report is similar to the flexible budget reports of Chapter 13. Explanations of the variances indicate that poor-quality materials and poor design led to extensive rework and retesting.

EXHIBIT 14-8

Eastside Manufacturing Company
Cycle Time Report for the Second Week of May

PROCESS STAGE	ACTUAL CYCLE TIME*	STANDARD CYCLE TIME	VARIANCE	EXPLANATION
Materials processing	2.1	2.5	0.4 F	
Circuit board	44.7	28.8	15.9 U	Poor quality materials caused rework
Power unit	59.6	36.2	23.4 U	Engineering change required rebuild of all power units
Assembly	14.6	14.7	0.1 F	
Functional and environmental test	53.3	32.0	21.3 U	Software failure in test procedures required retesting

* Average time per stage over the week.

Penril DataComm
www.compexch.com/
Penril/penril%20main.htm

Poor Quality Nearly Short-Circuits Electronics Company

Penril DataComm, a Maryland designer and maker of data communications equipment, was on the brink of financial disaster resulting from the cost of poor quality. Penril was performing 100 percent inspection in many of its manufacturing processes and reworking or scrapping one-third of everything it produced. Penril turned its financial fortunes around based on a total quality effort. The results of a customized quality program included:

1. Twelve-hundred and sixty-six percent increase in profits per employee;
2. Ninety-five percent increase in revenues;
3. Eighty-one percent decrease in defects per unit;
4. Eighty-three percent decrease in out-of-box failures (failures during the first three months in the field);
5. Seventy-three percent decrease in first-year warranty service repairs;
6. Reduced response time to customer's orders from 10 weeks to three days.

Penril's new mission is "to build an environment where internal and external customer expectations are met in every transaction." Penril supports this mission by following six principles:

1. Quality is the number-one priority. This requires a shift from short-term to long-term thinking. Resources are allocated for quality efforts, and quality teams are rewarded for improvements.
2. Customer focus. Customers and suppliers serve on concurrent engineering teams to "build the voice of the customer into all aspects of the business."
3. Emphasize prevention and continuous improvement. "Inspection only maintains the status quo." Total quality means reforming designs, modifying policies and procedures, and training people in correct practices.
4. Manage by data—Statistical analysis is used for control of processes.
5. Total employee involvement. According to Penril, the most important measure in the race for quality leadership is the rate of improvement, and this rate is maximized by involving everyone on a team. The team concept at Penril unleased employee energy that improved morale, communication, respect, and trust. Training includes job skills, TQM concepts, statistics, statistical process control, problem-solving skills, presentation skills, and communication skills.
6. Cross-functional management. Processes cross departments so each cross-functional team includes members from all areas involved in the process. Communication is enhanced by frequent meetings and newsletters. Employees present quality reports that document improvement efforts.

Perhaps the best measure of the success of Penril's new quality focus is in customer reaction—business has doubled in the three years since the program began. "We know of no greater testimony to a company's quality than to have another company ask it to design a product for them, build it for them, and put the customer's name on it."

Source: Productivity (February 1993), pp. 1–3.

Control of Productivity

Productivity. A measure of outputs divided by inputs.

Most companies in North America manage productivity as part of the effort to improve their competitiveness. **Productivity** is a measure of outputs divided by inputs. The fewer inputs needed to produce a given output, the more productive the organization. But this simple definition raises difficult measurement questions. How should outputs and inputs be measured? Specific management control problems usually determine the most appropriate measures of inputs and outputs. Labour-intensive (especially service) organizations are concerned with increasing the productivity of labour, so labour-based measures are appropriate.

Highly automated companies are concerned with machine utilization and productivity of capital investments, so capacity-based measures, such as the percentage of time machines are available, may be most important to them. Manufacturing companies in general are concerned with the efficient use of materials, and so for them measures of material *yield* (a ratio of material outputs over material inputs) may be useful indicators of productivity. In all cases of productivity ratios, a measure of the resource that management wishes to control is in the denominator (the input) and some measure of the objective of using the resource is in the numerator (the output).

Exhibit 14-9 shows 10 possible productivity measures. As you can see, they vary widely according to the type of resource with which management is concerned.

EXHIBIT 14-9

Measures of Productivity

RESOURCE (DENOMINATOR)	POSSIBLE OUTPUTS (NUMERATOR)	POSSIBLE INPUTS
1. Labour	a. Expected direct labour hours for good output ÷	Actual direct labour hours used
	b. Sales revenue ÷	Number of employees
	c. Bank deposit/loan activity (by a bank) ÷	Number of employees
	d. Service calls ÷	Number of employees
	e. Customer orders ÷	Number of employees
2. Materials	a. Weight of output ÷	Weight of input
	b. Number of good units ÷	Total number of units
3. Equipment, capital, physical capacity	a. Time (e.g., hours) utilized ÷	Time available for use
	b. Time available for use ÷	Time (e.g., 24 hours per day)
	c. Expected machine hours for good output ÷	Actual machine hours

Choosing Productivity Measures

Which productivity measures should a company choose to manage? The choice depends on the behaviours desired. Managers generally concentrate on achieving the performance levels desired by their superiors. Thus, if top management evaluates subordinates' performance based on direct labour productivity, lower-level managers will focus on improving that specific measure.

The challenge in choosing productivity measures is that a manager may be able to improve a single measure but hurt performance elsewhere in the organization. For example, long production runs may improve machine productivity, but result in excessive inventories. Or, improved labour productivity in the short run may be accompanied by a high rate of product defects.

Use of a single measure of productivity is unlikely to result in overall improvements in performance. The choice of management controls requires balancing expected tradeoffs that employees can be expected to make to improve their performance evaluations. Many organizations focus management control on more fundamental activities, such as control of quality and service, and use productivity measures to monitor the actual benefits of improvements in these activities.

It is necessary to consider the many dimensions of productivity. When assessing labour productivity, the Productivity Improvement Service of the federal department of Industry, Science and Technology Canada uses a number of measures before making any decisions, such as those listed below. They all add to the understanding of changes in labour productivity:

**Industry Canada
(Strategis)
www.strategis.ic.gc.ca**

- labour costs as a percentage of sales dollars
- sales per employee
- direct labour wage rate
- total labour cost per hour
- investment in machinery and equipment per production employee.

**SBC Communications
www.sbc.com**

Also be careful about comparing productivity measures over time. Changes in the process or in the rate of inflation can prove misleading. For example, consider labour productivity at SBC Communications. One measure of productivity tracked by SBC is *sales revenue per employee*:

	1999	1995	PERCENT CHANGE
Total revenue ($ millions)	$ 49,489	$ 37,134	+33.3%
Employees	204,530	182,610	+12.0%
Revenue per employee (unadjusted for inflation)	$241,695	$203,351	+18.9%

By this measure, SBC appears to have achieved an 18.9 percent increase in the productivity of labour. However, total revenue has not been adjusted for the effects of inflation. Because of inflation, each 1995 dollar was equivalent to 1.0909 1999 dollars. Therefore, SBC's 1995 sales revenue, expressed in 1999 dollars (to be equivalent with 1999 sales revenue) is $37,134 × 1.0909 = $40,509. The adjusted 1995 sales revenue per employee is as follows:

	1999	1995 (ADJUSTED)	PERCENT CHANGE
Total revenue ($ millions)	$ 49,489	$ 40,509	+22.2%
Employees	204,530	182,610	+12.0%
Revenue per employee (adjusted for inflation)	$241,965	$221,790	+9.0%

Adjusting for the effects of inflation reveals that SBC's labour productivity has increased only 9 percent not 18.9 percent. This is a signal to management that corrective action should be taken to reverse this slide—such as raise prices or reduce the number of employees.

Organizational Learning and Financial Results

Exhibit 14-1, on page 628 has feedback and learning at the centre of the management control system, since at all points in the planning and control process, it is vital that effective communications exist among all levels of management and employees. In fact, organization-wide learning is a foundation for gaining and maintaining financial strength. Rich Teerlink, former CEO of Harley Davidson said, "If you empower dummies, they make dumb decisions faster." Harley Davidson spends $1,000 per year per employee on training. Harley had 1999 sales of nearly $2.5 billion, one-year sales growth of 19 percent, one-year earnings growth of 25 percent.

It has also been said that the only sustainable competitive advantage is the rate at which a company's managers learn. However, even this powerful competitive edge can be overcome by competitors who develop or hire intellectual capital faster. Once a company has superior intellectual capital, how can it best maintain its leadership? Exhibit 14-10 shows how organizational learning leads to financial strength.

Organizational learning is monitored by measures such as training time, employee turnover, and staff satisfaction scores on employee surveys. The result of learning is continuous process improvement that is monitored by measures such as cycle time, number of defects (quality), and activity cost. Customers will value improved response (lower cycle time), higher quality, and lower prices, and thus increase their demand for products and services. Increased demand, combined with lower costs in making and delivering products and services, results in financial strength as monitored by such measures as product profitability and earnings before interest and taxes (EBIT).

EXHIBIT 14-10

The Components of a Successful Organization and Measures of Achievement

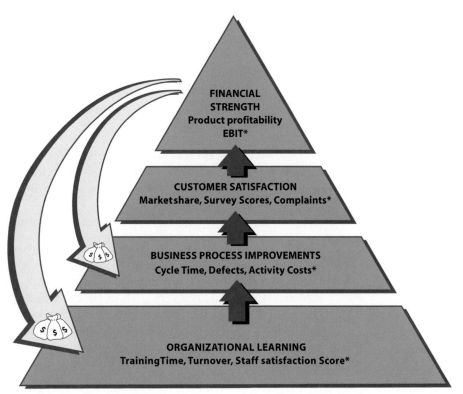

FINANCIAL STRENGTH
Product profitability
EBIT*

CUSTOMER SATISFACTION
Market share, Survey Scores, Complaints*

BUSINESS PROCESS IMPROVEMENTS
Cycle Time, Defects, Activity Costs*

ORGANIZATIONAL LEARNING
Training Time, Turnover, Staff satisfaction Score*

*Examples of performance measures used to monitor the achievement of the component.

It is important to note that the successful organization does not stop with one cycle of learning, process improvement, increased customer satisfaction, and improved financial strength. The benefits of improved financial strength, excess financial resources, must be reinvested within the organization by supporting both continuous learning and continuous process improvement. A key driver of enterprise performance is the culture within the company that fosters continual learning and growth at all levels of management. It is not enough to throw money at managers in order to train them if the resulting learning does not translate into improved processes, products, and services. It requires a culture of learning so that managers are motivated to translate learning into growth.

There are no guarantees that each of the components will "automatically" follow from success at the previous component. If there is no improvement in one or more core business processes, the cause-effect chain can be broken. For example, a lack of improvement in marketing and distribution techniques can lead to failure due to the inability to place the "new and improved" products or services at the location desired by the customer. E-commerce is a good example of this. The point is that improvement in business processes must take place across all parts of the value chain.

A good example of the application of an enterprise learning culture is General Electric Company (GE). With sales of more than $100 billion, GE has demonstrated a remarkable ability to generate formidable profits in a wide range of industries, including broadcasting (NBC), transportation equipment, aircraft engines, appliances, lighting, electric distribution and control equipment, generators and turbines, nuclear reactors, medical imaging equipment, plastics, and financial services. In 1999, GE was named *Fortune* magazine's "Most Admired Company in America."

CEO John Welch claims GE's success is due to "...a General Electric culture that values the contributions of every individual, thrives on learning, thirsts for the better idea, and has the flexibility and speed to put the better idea into action every day. We are a learning company, a company that studies its own successes and failures and those of others — a company that has the self-confidence and the resources to take big swings and pursue numerous opportunities based on winning ideas and insights, regardless of their source. That appetite for learning, and the ability to act quickly on that learning, will provide GE with what we believe is an insurmountable and sustainable competitive advantage."[3]

Removal of Boundaries.

Exactly what does John Welch mean by the "ability to act quickly on that learning?" He refers to a management leadership philosophy that ignores organizational boundaries when implementing learning. According to Welch, "These new leaders are changing the very DNA of GE culture. Work-Out, in the 80s, opened our culture up to ideas from everyone, everywhere, killed NIH (Not Invented Here) thinking, decimated the bureaucracy, and made boundaryless behavior a reflexive and natural part of our culture, thereby creating the learning culture..."[4]

---

[3] *Source:* General Electric's 1998 Annual Report.
[4] The term Work-Out refers to a process at GE where groups of employees meet at regular intervals to think of ways to improve GE. Then leadership comes in and listens to their ideas.

As shown in Exhibit 14-1, monitoring and reporting the results of business activities is a key component of a management control system. Exhibit 14-2 indicates that managers identify actions and related performance measures that are linked to the achievement of goals and objectives. Once these performance measures and actions are identified, an organization must obtain information on the achievement of desired outcomes. This is done through the performance reporting system. Effective performance reports align results with managers' goals and objectives, provide guidance to managers, communicate goals and their level of attainment throughout the organization, and enable organizations to anticipate and respond to change in a timely manner.

The Balanced Scorecard

Balanced Scorecard.
A performance measurement system that strikes a balance between financial and operating measures, links performance to rewards, and gives explicit recognition to the diversity of stakeholder interests.

There are several approaches to performance reporting. Each approach attempts to link organizational strategy to actions of managers and employees. One popular approach to performance reporting is the balanced scorecard. A **balanced scorecard** is a performance measurement and reporting system that strikes a balance between financial and operating measures, links performance to rewards, and gives explicit recognition to the diversity of organizational goals. Companies such as Champion International, Nova Chemical, Bank of Montreal, AT&T, Allstate, and Apple Computer use the balanced scorecard to focus management's attention on items subject to action on a month-by-month and day-to-day basis.

One advantage of the balanced scorecard approach is that line managers can see the relationship between nonfinancial measures, which they often can relate more easily to their own actions, and the financial measures that relate to organizational goals. Another advantage of the balanced scorecard is its focus on performance measures from each of the four components of the successful organization shown in Exhibit 14-10. This enhances the learning process because managers learn the results of their actions and how these actions are linked to the organizational goals.[5]

Apple
www.apple.com

EXHIBIT 14-11

Balanced Scorecard for
Luxury Suites Hotels

COMPONENT AND MEASURES	TARGET	RESULT
Financial Strength		
Revenue (millions of dollars) per new service	$50	$58
Revenue per arrival	$75	$81
Customer Satisfaction		
Customer satisfaction index	95	88
Brand loyalty index	60	40
Business Process Improvement		
Number of improvements	8	8
Average cycle time (minutes) for checkin and checkout	15	15
Organizational Learning		
Percent of staff re-trained	80	85
Training hours per employee	30	25

[5] For a more detailed discussion, see Anthony Atkinson and Marc Epstein, "Measure for Measure: Realizing the Power of the Balanced Scorecard," *Management*, September 2000, pp. 23–28.

What does a balanced scorecard look like? Exhibit 14-11 shows a balanced scorecard for the Luxury Suites hotel chain. This scorecard is for the organization as a whole. It has performance measures for all four components of organizational success. There are many scorecards within an organization. In fact, each area of responsibility will have its own scorecard. Scorecards for some lower-level responsibility centres that are focused strictly on day-to-day operations may be totally focused on only one of the four components. We should also note that not all performance measures appear on scorecards. Managers of responsibility centres include only those measures that are key performance indicators—measures that drive the organization to achieve its goals. For example, top management at Luxury Suites set "exceed guest expectations" as one organizational goal. The balanced scorecard should have at least one key performance indicator that is linked to this goal. The customer satisfaction index, brand loyalty index, number of improvements, and average cycle time for checkin and checkout measures all are linked to this goal.

MANAGEMENT CONTROL SYSTEMS IN SERVICE GOVERNMENT, AND NON-PROFIT ORGANIZATIONS

OBJECTIVE 7

Describe the difficulties of management control in service and non-profit organizations.

MBNA America
www.mbna.com

CUSO
www.cuso.org

Most service, government, and non-profit organizations have more difficulty implementing management control systems than do manufacturing firms. The main problem is that the outputs of service and non-profit organizations are harder to measure than the cars or computers that are produced by manufacturers. As a result, it may be more difficult to know whether the service provided is, for example, of top quality until (long) after the service has already been delivered.

The key to successful management control in any organization is proper training and motivation of employees to achieve goal congruence and effort, followed by consistent monitoring of objectives set in accordance with critical processes and success factors. This is even more important in service-oriented organizations. For example, MBNA America, a large issuer of bank credit cards, identifies customer retention as its primary critical success factor. MBNA trains its customer representatives carefully, measures and reports performance on 14 objectives consistent with customer retention (such as answering every call by the second ring, keeping the computer up 100 percent of the time, processing credit-line requests within one hour) each day, and rewards every employee based on those 14 objectives. Employees have earned bonuses as high as 20 percent of their annual salaries by meeting those objectives.

Non-profit and government organizations also have additional problems designing and implementing an objective that is similar to the financial "bottom line" that so often serves as a powerful incentive in private industry. Furthermore, many people seek positions in non-profit organizations primarily for other than monetary rewards. For example, volunteers in CUSO receive very little pay but derive much satisfaction from helping to improve conditions in under-developed countries. Thus, monetary incentives are generally less effective in non-profit organizations. Control systems in non-profit organizations probably will never be as highly developed as are those in profit-seeking firms because:

1. Organizational goals and objectives are less clear. Moreover, they are often multiple, requiring difficult tradeoffs.

2. Professionals (for example, teachers, lawyers, physicians, scientists, economists) tend to dominate non-profit organizations. Because of their perceived professional status, they have been less receptive to the installation or improvement of formal control systems.

3. Measurements are more difficult because:
   a. There is no profit measure.
   b. There are heavy amounts of discretionary fixed costs, which makes the relationships of inputs to outputs difficult to specify and to measure.

4. There is less competitive pressure from other organizations or from "owners" to improve management control systems. As a result, for example, many cities are "privatizing" some essential services such as sanitation by contracting with private firms.

5. The role of budgeting is often more a matter of playing bargaining games with sources of funding to get the largest possible authorization than it is rigorous planning.

6. Motivations and incentives of individuals may differ from those in for-profit organizations.

THE FUTURE OF MANAGEMENT CONTROL SYSTEMS

OBJECTIVE 8

Explain how management control systems must evolve with changing times.

As organizations mature and as environments change, managers cope with their responsibilities by expanding and refining their management control tools. The management control techniques that were quite satisfactory 10 or 20 years ago may not be adequate for many organizations today. One often hears accounting systems criticized for being especially slow to adapt to organizational change.

A changing environment often means that organizations must set different critical success factors. Different critical success factors create different objectives to be used as targets and create different benchmarks for evaluating performance. Obviously, the management control system must evolve, too, or the organization may not manage its resources effectively or efficiently. Thus, the management control tools presented in this text may not be adequate even a short time from now.

Does this mean that the time spent studying this material has been wasted? No. Certain management control principles will always be important and can guide the redesign of systems to meet new management needs:

1. Always expect that individuals will be pulled in the direction of their own self-interest. One may be pleasantly surprised that some individuals will act selflessly, but management control systems should be designed to take advantage of more typical human behaviour. Be aware that self-interest may be perceived differently in different cultures.

2. Design incentives so that individuals who pursue their own self-interest are also achieving the organization's objectives. If there are multiple objectives (as is usually the case), then multiple incentives are appropriate. Do not underestimate the difficulty of balancing these incentives—some experimentation may be necessary to achieve multiple objectives.

3. The best benchmark for evaluating actual performance is expected or planned performance, revised, if possible, for actual output achieved.

The concept of flexible budgeting can be applied to most subgoals and objectives, both financial and nonfinancial.

4. Nonfinancial performance is just as important as financial performance. In the short run, a manager may be able to generate good financial performance while neglecting nonfinancial performance, but it is not likely over a longer haul.

5. Establish performance measures across the entire value chain of the company. Recall that the value chain is the sequence of functions that adds value to the company's products or services. These functions include research and development, product and process design, production marketing, distribution, and customer service. This ensures that all activities that are critical to the long-run success of the company are integrated into the management control system.

6. Periodically review the success of the management control system. Are objectives being met? Does meeting the objectives mean that subgoals and goals are being met, too? Do individuals have, understand, and use the management control information effectively?

7. Learn from the management control successes (and failures) of competitors around the world. Despite cultural differences, human behaviour is remarkably similar. Successful applications of new technology and management controls may be observed in the performance of others.

How does a manager decide if the management control system requires a change or alteration? Exhibit 14-12 provides a method to answer this question.

First, ask what the critical success factors of the organization are and what key management decisions are required by managers in order for the organization to attain its goals. Second, evaluate the management control systems and consider the actual management decisions that managers are motivated to make given the existing control systems. If the actual management decisions fit (i.e., are goal-congruent) with the desired key management decisions, then no change is necessary. If, however, goal congruence does not exist, then change may be necessary.

EXHIBIT 14-12

Do You Have a Management Control System Problem?

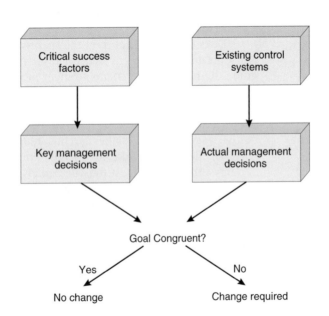

The essence of an effective management control system is the fit between four key factors that have been discussed in this chapter: the organizational goals, the organizational structure, the responsibility centres, and the selection of performance measures. Exhibit 14-13 illustrates the interrelationship of these factors. If a management control system is in need of change, and assuming that management has clearly defined appropriate organization goals, managers should consider alternative structures, responsibility centres, and performance measures in their decision to change to a better management control system. A better management control system will more effectively motivate employees to work toward achieving the organization's goals.

EXHIBIT 14-13

Effective Management
Control Systems[6]

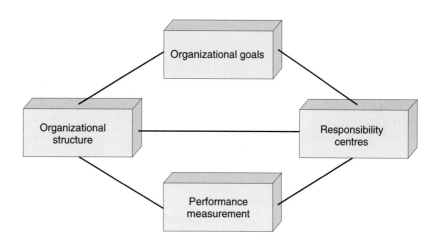

HIGHLIGHTS TO REMEMBER

The starting point for designing and evaluating a management control system is identifying organizational goals, subgoals, and objectives as specified by top management. Systems are typically designed within the constraints of a given set of goals and a given organizational structure.

The evolutionary design of management control systems depends on criteria of cost-benefit, goal congruence, and employee effort. The design should be the one that is expected to produce the best decisions at a reasonable cost.

The way performance is measured and evaluated affects individuals' behaviour. Measuring performance in areas such as quality and productivity causes employees to direct attention to those areas. The more rewards are tied to performance measures, the more incentive there is to improve the measures.

Measures of performance must be carefully thought-out for their behavioural effects. Improving the measures should improve organizational performance toward achieving its goals. Poorly designed or balanced measures may actually work against the organization's goals.

Responsibility accounting assigns particular revenue and/or cost objectives to the management of the subunit that has the greatest influence over them. The

[6] For a more detailed explanation of this framework see Howard Teall, "Strategic Management Control Systems," *CMA Management Magazine*, February 1992.

contribution approach to measuring income aids performance evaluation by separating a segment's costs into those controllable by the segment management and those beyond management's control.

Nonfinancial performance is as important as financial performance. In fact, nonfinancial performance usually leads to financial performance in time. Many companies focus on short-term nonfinancial performance measures, knowing that financial results will follow.

Management control in service, government, and nonprofit organizations is difficult because of a number of factors—chief of which is a relative lack of clearly observable outcomes. Systems designers in these organizations must contend with particularly difficult tradeoffs among objectives.

Management control systems must evolve with changing economic and organizational conditions if the systems are to continue to assist managers in their decision-making, controlling, and evaluation tasks.

SUMMARY PROBLEMS FOR YOUR REVIEW

Problem One

The Book & Game Company has bookstores in two locations: Auntie's and Merlin's. Each location has a manager who has a great deal of decision authority over the individual stores. However, advertising, market research, acquisition of books, legal services, and other staff functions are handled by a central office. The Book & Game Company's current accounting system allocates all costs to the stores. Results for 2001 were:

ITEM	TOTAL COMPANY	AUNTIE'S	MERLIN'S
Sales revenue	$700,000	$350,000	$350,000
Cost of merchandise sold	450,000	225,000	225,000
Gross margin	250,000	125,000	125,000
Operating expenses:			
Salaries and wages	63,000	30,000	33,000
Supplies	45,000	22,500	22,500
Rent and utilities	60,000	40,000	20,000
Amortization	15,000	7,000	8,000
Allocated staff costs	60,000	30,000	30,000
Total operating expenses	243,000	129,500	113,500
Operating income (loss)	$ 7,000	$ (4,500)	$ 11,500

Each bookstore manager makes decisions that affect salaries and wages, supplies, and amortization. In contrast, rent and utilities are beyond the managers' control because the managers did not choose the location or the size of the store.

Supplies are variable costs. Variable salaries and wages are equal to 8 percent of the cost of merchandise sold; the remainder of salaries and wages is a fixed cost. Rent, utilities, and amortization also are fixed costs. Allocated staff costs are unaffected by any events at the bookstores, but they are allocated as a proportion of sales revenue.

1. Using the contribution approach, prepare a performance report that distinguishes the performance of each bookstore from that of the bookstore manager.
2. Evaluate the financial performance of each bookstore.
3. Evaluate the financial performance of each manager.

Solution

1.

ITEM	TOTAL COMPANY	AUNTIE'S	MERLIN'S
Sales revenue	$700,000	$350,000	$350,000
Variable costs:			
Cost of merchandise sold	450,000	225,000	225,000
Salaries and wages	36,000	18,000	18,000
Supplies	45,000	22,500	22,500
Total variable costs	531,000	265,500	265,500
Contribution margin	169,000	84,500	84,500
Less: Fixed costs controllable by bookstore managers			
Salaries and wages	27,000	12,000	15,000
Amortization	15,000	7,000	8,000
Total controllable fixed costs	42,000	19,000	23,000
Contribution controllable by bookstore managers	127,000	65,500	61,500
Less: Fixed costs controllable by others			
Rent and utilities	60,000	40,000	20,000
Contribution by bookstore	$ 67,000	$ 25,500	$ 41,500
Unallocated costs	60,000		
Operating income	$ 7,000		

2. The financial performance of the bookstores (i.e., segments of the company) are best evaluated by the line "Contribution by bookstores." Merlin's has a substantially higher contribution, despite equal levels of sales revenues in the two stores. The major reason for this advantage is the lower rent and utilities paid by Merlin's.
3. The financial performance by managers is best judged by the line "Contribution controllable by bookstore managers." By this measure, the performance of Auntie's manager is better than that of Merlin's. The contribution margin is the same for each store, but Merlin's manager paid $4,000 more in controllable fixed costs than did Auntie's manager. Of course, this decision could be beneficial in the long run. What is missing from each of these segment reports is the year's master budget and a flexible budget, which would be the best benchmark for evaluating both the bookstore and bookstore manager.

Problem Two

Consider our example, the Luxury Suites hotel chain. As we have noted, top management established *"exceed guest expectations"* as one organization-wide goal. The critical process for this goal is *produce and deliver services*. Critical success factors for this critical process have also been identified as *quality and timeliness of the customer service department and personalized service*. Susan Pierce, the vice president of sales, is the manager responsible for the *produce and deliver services* critical process. She has already identified one action—upgrade customer service department capabilities.

1. Identify several possible performance measures for the *personalized service* critical success factor.
2. Recommend several specific actions or activities associated with upgrading customer service department capabilities that would drive Luxury Suites toward its goal of exceeding customer expectations.

Solution

1. Performance measures for the personalized service critical success factor include number of changes to registration, rating on "friendly, knowledgeable staff" question on guest survey, and percent of customers with completed profile.
2. Specific actions or activities include training employees, implementing a call checklist and monitoring compliance with the list, developing a customer satisfaction survey, and reengineering the order taking process.

ACCOUNTING VOCABULARY

balanced scorecard *p. 653*
controllable cost *p. 639*
cost centre *p. 633*
critical process *p. 629*
critical success factors *p. 631*
cycle time *p. 647*
expense centre *p. 633*
goal congruence *p. 635*
internal control system *p. 637*
investment centre *p. 634*
management control system *p. 627*
managerial effort *p. 635*

motivation *p. 636*
productivity *p. 648*
profit centre *p. 634*
quality control *p. 643*
quality control chart *p. 646*
quality cost report *p. 643*
responsibility accounting *p. 633*
responsibility centre *p. 633*
revenue centre *p. 634*
total quality management (TQM) *p. 646*
uncontrollable cost *p. 639*

ASSIGNMENT MATERIAL

QUESTIONS

Q14-1 What is the purpose of a management control system?
Q14-2 "Goals are useless without performance measures." Do you agree? Explain.

Q14-3   "There are corporate objectives other than profit." Name four.

Q14-4   How does management determine its critical (key) success factors?

Q14-5   Give three examples of how managers may improve short-run performance to the detriment of long-run results.

Q14-6   Name five kinds of responsibility centre.

Q14-7   How do profit centres and investment centres differ?

Q14-8   "Performance evaluation seeks to achieve *goal congruence* and *managerial effort*." Describe what is meant by this statement.

Q14-9   Why do accountants need to consider behavioural factors when designing a management control system?

Q14-10 List five characteristics of a good performance measure.

Q14-11 "Managers of profit centres should be held responsible for the centre's entire profit. They are responsible for profit even if they cannot control all factors affecting it." Discuss.

Q14-12 What is a balanced scorecard and why are more and more companies using one?

Q14-13 What are four nonfinancial measures of performance that managers find useful?

Q14-14 "Variable costs are controllable and fixed costs are uncontrollable." Do you agree? Explain.

Q14-15 "The contribution margin is the best measure of short-run performance." Do you agree? Explain.

Q14-16 Give four examples of segments.

Q14-17 "Always try to distinguish between the performance of a segment and its manager." Why?

Q14-18 "The contribution margin approach to performance evaluation is flawed because focusing on only the contribution margin ignores important aspects of performance." Do you agree? Explain.

Q14-19 There are four categories of cost in the quality cost report. Explain them.

Q14-20 Why are companies increasing their quality control emphasis on the prevention of defects?

Q14-21 Discuss how quality, cycle time, and productivity are related.

Q14-22 "Nonfinancial measures of performance can be controlled just like financial measures." Do you agree? Explain.

Q14-23 Identify three measures of labour productivity, one using all physical measures, one using all financial measures, and one that mixes physical and financial measures.

Q14-24 Discuss the difficulties of comparing productivity over time.

Q14-25 "Control systems in nonprofit organizations will never be as highly developed as in profit-seeking organizations." Do you agree? Explain.

PROBLEMS

P14-1   **MANAGEMENT CONTROL SYSTEMS AND INNOVATION.** The president of a fast-growing high-tech firm remarked, "Developing budgets and comparing performance with the budgets may be fine for some firms. But we want to encourage innovations and entrepreneurship. Budgets go with bureaucracy, not innovation." Do you agree? How can a management control system encourage innovation and entrepreneurship?

P14-2   MULTIPLE GOALS AND PROFITABILITY.   The following multiple goals were identified by the General Electric company:

Profitability   Employee attitudes
Market position   Public responsibility
Productivity   Balance between short-range and
Product leadership   long-range goals
Personnel development

**General Electric
www.ge.com**

General Electric is a huge, highly decentralized corporation. It has approximately 170 responsibility centres called "departments," but that is a deceiving term. In most other companies, these departments would be called divisions. For example, some GE departments have sales of over $500 million.

Each department manager's performance is evaluated annually in relation to the specified multiple goals. A special measurements group was set up to devise ways of quantifying accomplishments in each of the areas. In this way, the evaluation of performance would become more objective as the various measures were developed and improved.

1. How would you measure performance in each of these areas? Be specific.
2. Can the other goals be encompassed as ingredients of a formal measure of profitability? In other words, can profitability *per se* be defined to include the other goals?

P14-3   MUNICIPAL RESPONSIBILITY ACCOUNTING.   In 1975, New York City barely avoided bankruptcy. By the 1990s it had one of the most sophisticated budgeting and reporting systems of any municipality, and its budgetary problems had nearly disappeared. The Integrated Financial Management System (IFMS) "clearly identifies managers in line agencies, and correlates allocations and expenditures with organizational structure ... In addition, managers have more time to take corrective measures when variances between budgeted and actual expenditures start to develop" (*FE - The Magazine for Financial Executives*, Vol. 1, No. 8, p. 26).

Discuss how a responsibility accounting system such as IFMS can help manage a municipality such as New York City.

P14-4   RESPONSIBILITY FOR A STABLE EMPLOYMENT POLICY.   The Sargent Metal Fabricators has been manufacturing machine tools for a number of years and has an industrywide reputation for high-quality work. The company has been faced with irregularity of output over the years. It has been company policy to lay off welders as soon as there was insufficient work to keep them busy and to rehire them when demand warranted. The company, however, now has poor labour relations and finds it very difficult to hire good welders because of its layoff policy. Consequently, the quality of the work has been declining steadily.

The plant manager has proposed that the welders, who earn $20 per hour, be retained during slow periods to do plant maintenance work that is normally performed by workers earning $13 per hour in the plant maintenance department.

You, as a controller, must decide the most appropriate accounting procedure to handle the wages of the welders doing plant maintenance work. What department or departments should be charged with this work, and at what rate? Discuss the implications of your plan.

P14-5 SALES CLERK'S COMPENSATION PLAN.   You are manager of a department store in Kyoto. Sales are subject to month-to-month variations, depending on the individual salesclerk's efforts. A new salary-plus-bonus plan has been in effect for four months, and you are reviewing a sales performance report. The plan provides for a base salary of ¥45,000 per month, a ¥58,000 bonus each month if the monthly sales quota is met, and an additional commission of 5 percent of all sales over the monthly quota. The quota is set approximately 3 percent above the previous month's sales to motivate clerks toward increasing sales (in thousands):

		SALESCLERK A	SALESCLERK B	SALESCLERK C
January	Quota	¥4,500	¥1,500	¥7,500
	Actual	1,500	1,500	9,000
February	Quota	¥1,545	¥1,545	¥9,270
	Actual	3,000	1,545	3,000
March	Quota	¥3,090	¥1,590	¥3,090
	Actual	5,250	750	9,000
April	Quota	¥5,400	¥ 775	¥9,270
	Actual	1,500	780	4,050

1. Compute the compensation for each sales clerk for each month.
2. Evaluate the compensation plan. Be specific. What changes would you recommend?

P14-6 RESPONSIBILITY OF PURCHASING AGENT.   GL Interiors, Inc., a privately held enterprise has a subcontract to produce overhead storage bins for a Boeing airplane. Although GL was a low bidder, Boeing was reluctant to award the business to GL, a newcomer to this kind of activity. Consequently, GL assured Boeing of its financial strength by submitting its audited financial statements. Moreover, GL agreed to a penalty clause of $5,000 per day to be paid by GL for each day of late delivery for whatever reason.

Leesa Marinson, the GL purchasing agent, is responsible for acquiring materials and parts in time to meet production schedules. She placed an order with a GL supplier for a critical manufactured component. The supplier, who had a reliable record for meeting schedules, gave Martinson an acceptable delivery date. Martinson checked up several times and was assured that the component would arrive at GL on schedule.

On the date specified by the supplier for shipment to GL, Martinson was informed that the component had been damaged during final inspection. It was delivered 10 days late. Martinson had allowed four extra days for possible delays, but GL was six days late in delivering to Boeing and so had to pay a penalty of $30,000.

What department should bear the penalty? Why?

P14-7 PERFORMANCE EVALUATION.   Lynch, Barney, and Schwab is a stock brokerage firm that evaluates its employees on sales activity generated. Recently the firm also began evaluating its stockbrokers on the number of new accounts generated.

Discuss how these two performance measures are consistent, and how they may conflict. Do you believe that these measures are appropriate for the long-term goal of profitability?

P14-8 PRODUCTIVITY.   In early 2001, Global Telecom, a telephone communications company, purchased the controlling interest in Eurotel in an eastern European country. A key productivity measure monitored by Global Telecom is the number of customer telephone lines per employee. Consider the following data:

	2001 (without Eurotel)	2001* (with Eurotel)	2000
Customer lines	15,054,000	19,994,000	14,315,000
Employees	74,520	114,590	70,866
Lines per employee	202	174	202
Normal growth in lines and employees (prior to purchase of Eurotel)		3% per year	

* Includes customer lines and employees of Eurotel

1. Compute Global Telecom's 2001 productivity without Eurotel.
2. Compute Eurotel's 2000 productivity.
3. What difficulties do you foresee if Global Telecom brings Eurotel's productivity in line?

P14-9 CYCLE TIME REPORTING.   Digital Processors Ltd. monitors its cycle time closely in order to prevent schedule delays and excessive costs. The standard cycle time for the manufacture of printed circuit boards for one of its computers is 26.4 hours. Consider the following cycle time data from the past six weeks of circuit board production:

WEEK	UNITS COMPLETED	TOTAL CYCLE TIME
1	564	14,108 hours
2	544	14,592 hours
3	553	15,152 hours
4	571	16,598 hours
5	547	17,104 hours
6	552	16,673 hours

Analyze circuit-board cycle-time performance in light of the 26.4-hour objective.

P14-10 INCENTIVES IN THE FORMER SOVIET UNION.   Officials in what was the Soviet Union had been rewarding managers for exceeding a five-year-plan target for production quantities. But a problem arose because managers naturally tended to predict low volumes so that the targets would be set low. This hindered planning; good information about production possibilities was lacking.

The Soviets then devised a new performance evaluation measure. Suppose F is the forecast of production, A is actual production, and X, Y, and Z are positive constants set by top officials, with $X < Y < Z$.

$$\text{performance} = \begin{cases} (Y \times F) + X \times (A - F) & \text{if } F \leq A \\ (Y \times F) - Z \times (F - A) & \text{if } F > A \end{cases}$$

This performance measure was designed to motivate both high production and accurate forecasts.

Consider the Moscow Automotive Factory. During 1997, the factory manager, Nicolai Konstantin, had to predict the number of automobiles that could be produced during the next year. He was confident that at least 700,000 autos could be produced in 1998, and most likely they could produce 800,000 autos. With good luck, they might even produce 900,000. Government officials told him that the new performance evaluation measure would be used, and that X = .50, Y = .80, and Z = 1.00 for 1998 and 1999.

1. Suppose Konstantin predicted production of 800,000 autos and 800,000 were produced. Calculate the performance measure.
2. Suppose again that 800,000 autos were produced. Calculate the performance measure if Konstantin had been conservative and predicted only 700,000 autos. Also calculate the performance measure if he had predicted 900,000 autos.
3. Now suppose it is November 1998 and it is clear that the 800,000 target cannot be achieved. Does the performance measure motivate continued efforts to increase production? Suppose it is clear that the 800,000 target will be met easily. Will the system motivate continued effort to increase production?

P14-11 RESPONSIBILITY ACCOUNTING, PROFIT CENTRES, AND THE CONTRIBUTION APPROACH.
Consider the following data for the year's operations of an automobile dealer:

Sales of vehicles	$ 2,600,000
Sales of parts and service	600,000
Cost of vehicle sales	2,120,000
Parts and service materials	180,000
Parts and service labour	240,000
Parts and service overhead	60,000
General dealership overhead	120,000
Advertising of vehicles	120,000
Sales commissions, vehicles	48,000
Sales salaries, vehicles	60,000

The president of the dealership has long regarded the markup on material and labour for the parts and service activity as the amount that is supposed to cover all parts and service overhead plus all general overhead of the dealership. In other words, the parts and service department is viewed as a cost-recovery operation, and the sales of vehicles as the income-producing activity.

1. Prepare a departmentalized operating statement that harmonizes with the views of the president.
2. Prepare an alternative operating statement that would reflect a different view of the dealership operations. Assume that $15,000 and $60,000 of the $120,000 general overhead can be allocated with confidence to the parts and service department and to sales of vehicles, respectively. The remaining $45,000 cannot be allocated except in some highly arbitrary manner.
3. Comment on the relative merits of requirements 1 and 2.

P14-12 PRODUCTIVITY MEASUREMENT. Crystal Cleaners had the following results in 1999 and 2002:

	1999	2002
Kilograms of laundry processed	680,000 kilograms	762,500 kilograms
Sales revenue	$360,000	$697,000
Direct labour hours worked	22,550 hours	23,325 hours
Direct labour cost	$158,000	$249,000

Crystal used the same facilities in 2002 as in 1999. However, over the past four years the company put more effort into training its employees. The manager of Crystal was curious about whether the training had increased labour productivity.

1. Compute a measure of labour productivity for 2002 based entirely on physical measures. Do the same for 1999. That is, from the data given, choose measures of physical output and physical input, and use them to compare the physical productivity of labour in 2002 with that in 1999.
2. Compute a measure of labour productivity for 2002 based entirely on financial measures. Do the same for 1999. That is, from the data given, choose measures of financial output and financial input, and use them to compare the financial productivity of labour in 2002 with that in 1999.
3. Suppose the following productivity measure were used:

$$\text{productivity} = \frac{\text{sales revenue}}{\text{direct labour hours worked}}$$

Because of inflation, each 1999 dollar is equivalent to 1.4 2002 dollars. Compute appropriate productivity numbers for comparing 2002 productivity with 1999 productivity.

P14-13 TRADEOFFS AMONG OBJECTIVES. Computer Data Services (CDS) performs routine and custom information systems services for many other companies in a large metropolitan area. CDS has built a reputation for high-quality customer service and job security for its employees. Quality service and customer satisfaction have been CDS's primary subgoals—retaining a skilled and motivated workforce has been an important factor in achieving those goals. In the past, temporary downturns in business did not mean layoffs of employees, though some employees were required to perform other than their usual tasks. Three months ago, a new competitor began offering the same services to CDS's customers at prices averaging 20 percent lower than CDS. Rico Estrada, the company founder and president, believes that a significant price reduction is necessary in order to maintain the company's market share and avoid financial ruin, but is puzzled about how to achieve it without compromising quality, service, and the goodwill of his workforce.

CDS has a productivity objective of 20 accounts per employee. Estrada does not believe that he can increase this productivity and still maintain both quality and flexibility to customer needs. CDS also monitors average cost per account and the number of customer satisfaction adjustments (resolutions of complaints). The average billing markup rate is 25 percent. Consider the following data from the past six months:

	JUNE	JULY	AUGUST	SEPTEMBER	OCTOBER	NOVEMBER
Number of accounts	797	803	869	784	723	680
Number of employees	40	41	44	43	43	41
Average cost per account	$153	$153	$158	$173	$187	$191
Additions to long-term lease commitments for equipment				$10,000 per month		
Average salary per employee	$3,000	$3,000	$3,000	$3,000	$3,000	$3,000

1. Discuss the tradeoffs facing Rico Estrada.
2. Can you suggest solutions to his tradeoff dilemma?

P14-14 **CONTRIBUTION APPROACH TO RESPONSIBILITY ACCOUNTING.** George McBee owns a small chain of specialty toy stores in Edmonton and Calgary. The company's organization chart follows:

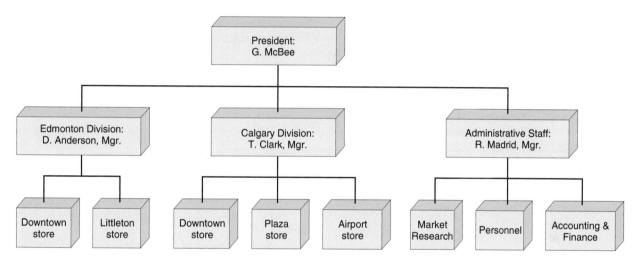

Financial results for 2001 were:

Sales revenue	$8,000,000
Cost of merchandise sold	5,000,000
Gross margin	3,000,000
Operating expenses	2,200,000
Income before income taxes	$ 800,000

The following data about 2001 operations were also available:

1. All five stores used the same pricing formula; therefore all had the same gross margin percentage.
2. Sales were largest in the two Downtown stores, with 30 percent of the total sales volume in each. The Plaza and Airport stores each provided 15 percent of total sales volume, and the Litteton store provided 10 percent.
3. Variable operating costs at the stores were 10 percent of revenue for the Downtown stores. The other stores had lower variable and higher fixed costs. Their variable operating costs were only 5 percent of sales revenue.

4. The fixed costs over which the store managers had control were $125,000 in each of the Downtown stores, $160,000 at Plaza and Airport, and $80,000 at Litteton.
5. The remaining $910,000 of operating costs consisted of
   a. $180,0000 controllable by the Calgary division manager, but not by individual stores
   b. $130,000 controllable by the Edmonton division manager, but not by individual stores
   c. $600,000 controllable by the administrative staff
6. Of the $600,000 spent by the administrative staff, $350,000 directly supported the Calgary division, with 20 percent for the Downtown store, 30 percent for each of the Plaza and Airport stores, and 20 percent for Calgary operations in general. Another $150,000 supported the Edmonton division, 50 percent for the Downtown store, 25 percent for the Littleton store, and 25 percent supporting Edmonton operations in general. The other $100,000 was for general corporate expenses.

   Prepare an income statement by segments using the contribution approach to responsibility accounting. Use the format of Exhibit 14-5. Column headings should be

	BREAKDOWN INTO TWO DIVISIONS			BREAKDOWN OF EDMONTON DIVISION			BREAKDOWN OF CALGARY DIVISION		
COMPANY AS A WHOLE	Edmonton Division	Calgary Division	Not Allocated	Down-town	Littleton	Not Allocated	Down-town	Plaza	Airport

P14-15 RESPONSIBILITY ACCOUNTING. The LaCrosse Manufacturing Company produces precision parts. LaCrosse uses a standard cost system, calculating variances for each department and reporting them to the department managers. Managers are supposed to use the information to improve their operations. Superiors use the same information to evaluate managers' performance.

Robert Dahl was recently appointed manager of the assembly department of the company. He has complained that the system as designed is disadvantageous to his department. Included among the variances charged to the departments is one for rejected units. The inspection occurs at the end of the assembly department. The inspectors attempt to identify the cause of the rejection so that the department where the error occurred can be charged with it. But not all errors can easily be identified with a department. The nonidentified units are totalled and apportioned to the departments according to the number of identified errors. The variance for rejected units in each department is a combination of the errors caused by the department plus a portion of the unidentified causes of rejects.

1. Is Dahl's complaint valid? Explain the reason(s) for your answer.
2. What would you recommend that the company do to solve its problem with Dahl and his complaint?

P14-16 DIVISIONAL CONTRIBUTION, PERFORMANCE, AND SEGMENT MARGINS. The Board of Directors of Atlantic Coast Railroad wants to obtain an overview of the company's operations, particularly with respect to comparing freight and passenger business. The Board Chair has heard about some new "contribution" approaches to cost allocations that emphasize cost behaviour patterns and so-called *contribution margins, contributions controllable by segment managers, and contributions by segments.* The Board has hired you as a consultant and has provided you with the following information.

Total revenue in 2001 was $80 million, of which $72 million was freight traffic and $8 million was passenger traffic. Fifty percent of the latter was generated by Division 1; 40 percent by Division 2; and 10 percent by Division 3.

Total variable costs were $45 million, of which $36 million was freight traffic. Of the $9 million allocable to passenger traffic, $3.3, $2.8, and $2.9 million could be allocated to Divisions 1, 2, and 3, respectively.

Total separable discretionary fixed costs were $8 million, of which $7.6 million applied to freight traffic. Of the remainder, $800,000 could not be allocated to specific divisions, although it was clearly traceable to passenger traffic in general. Divisions 1, 2, and 3 should be allocated $240,000, $60,000, and $20,000, respectively.

Total separable committed costs, which were not regarded as being controllable by segment managers, were $25 million, of which 90 percent was allocable to freight traffic. Of the 10 percent traceable to passenger traffic, Divisions 1, 2, and 3 should be allocated $1.5 million, $350,000, and $150,000, respectively; the balance was unallocable to a specific division.

The common fixed costs not clearly allocable to any part of the company amounted to $750,000.

1. The Board asks you to prepare statements, dividing the data for the company as a whole between the freight and passenger traffic and then subdividing the passenger traffic into three divisions.
2. Some competing railroads actively promote a series of one-day sightseeing tours on summer weekends. Most often, these tours are timed so that the cars with the tourists are hitched to regularly scheduled passenger trains. What costs are relevant for making decisions to run such tours? Other railroads, facing the same general cost picture, refuse to conduct such sightseeing tours. Why?
3. For the purposes of this analysis, even though the numbers may be unrealistic, suppose that Divisions 2's figures represented a specific run for a train instead of a division. Suppose further that the railroad has petitioned government authorities for permission to drop Division 2. What would be the effect on overall company net income for 2002, assuming that the figures are accurate and that 2002 operations are in all other respects a duplication of 2001 operations?

P14-17 **QUALITY COST REPORT.** Green River Manufacturing Division makes a variety of home furnishings. In 2000 the company installed a system to report on quality costs. At the end of 2002 the division general manager wanted an assessment of whether quality costs in 2002 differed from those in 2000. Each month the actual costs had been compared with the plan, but at this time the manager wanted to see only total annual numbers for 2002 compared with 2000. The production supervisor prepared the following report.

QUALITY COST AREA	2000 COST	2002 COST
1. Prevention Cost	45	107
% of Total Quality Cost	3.3%	12.3%
2. Appraisal Cost	124	132
% of Total Quality Cost	9.1%	15.2%
3. Internal Failure Cost	503	368
% of Total Quality Cost	36.9%	42.5%
Total Internal Quality Cost (1 + 2 + 3)	672	607
% of Total Quality Cost	49.3%	70.0%
4. External Failure Cost	691	259
% of Total Quality Cost	50.7%	29.9%
Total Quality Cost	1,363	866
Total Product Cost	22,168	23,462
% Total Quality Cost to Total Product Cost	6.1%	3.7%

Green River Manufacturing Division
Quality Cost Report (in thousands of dollars)

1. For each of the four quality cost areas, explain what types of costs are included and how those costs have changed between 2000 and 2002.
2. Assess overall quality performance in 2002 compared with 2000. What do you suppose has caused the changes observed in quality costs?

P14-18 INVENTORY MEASURES, PRODUCTION SCHEDULING, AND EVALUATING DIVISIONAL PERFORMANCE. The Paul Company stresses competition between the heads of its various divisions, and it rewards stellar performance with year-end bonuses that vary between 5 and 10 percent of division net operating income (before considering the bonus or income taxes). The divisional managers have great discretion in setting production schedules.

The Normandy Division produces and sells a product for which there is a long-standing demand but which can have marked seasonal and year-to-year fluctuations. On November 30, 2001, Byron LeDoux, the Normandy Division manager, is preparing a production schedule for December. The following data are available for January 1 through November 30 (FF means French franc):

Beginning inventory, January 1, in units	10,000
Sales price, per unit	FF400
Total fixed costs incurred for manufacturing	FF9,350,000
Total fixed costs: other (not inventoriable)	FF9,350,000
Total variable costs for manufacturing	FF18,150,000
Total other variable costs (fluctuate with units sold)	FF4,000,000
Units produced	110,000
Units sold	100,000
Variances	None

Production in October and November was 10,000 units each month. Practical capacity is 12,000 units per month. Maximum available storage space for inventory is 25,000 units. The sales outlook, for December through February, is 6,000 units monthly. To retain a core of key employees, monthly production cannot be scheduled at less than 4,000 units without special permission from the president. Inventory is never to be less than 10,000 units.

The denominator for applying fixed factory overhead is regarded as 120,000 units annually. The company uses a standard absorption-costing system. All variances are disposed of at year-end as an adjustment to standard cost of goods sold.

1. Given the restrictions as stated, and assuming that the manager wants to maximize the company's net income for 2001:
   a. How many units should be scheduled for production in December?
   b. What net operating income will be reported for 2001 as a whole, assuming that the implied cost-behaviour patterns will continue in December as they did throughout the year to date? Show your computations.
   c. If December production is scheduled at 4,000 units, what would reported net income be?
2. Assume that standard variable costing is used rather than standard absorption costing:
   a. What would net income for 2001 be, assuming that the December production schedule is the one in requirement 1, part (a)?
   b. Assuming that December production was 4,000 units?
   c. Reconcile the net incomes in this requirement with those in requirement 1.
3. From the viewpoint of the long-run interests of the company as a whole, what production schedule should the division manager set? Explain fully. Include in your explanation a comparison of the motivating influence of absorption and variable costing in this situation.
4. Assume standard absorption costing. The manager wants to maximize his after-income-tax performance over the long run. Given the data at the beginning of the problem, assume that income tax rates will be halved in 2002. Assume also that year-end write-offs of variances are acceptable for income tax purposes. How many units should be scheduled for production in December? Why?

P14-19 COMPARISON OF PRODUCTIVITY. Lakeland Foods and National Food and Beverage are consumer products companies. Comparative data for 1995 and 2001 are

		LAKELAND FOODS	NATIONAL FOOD AND BEVERAGE
Sales revenue	1995	$5,924,000,000	$7,658,000,000
	2001	$6,764,000,000	$9,667,000,000
Number of employees	1995	56,600	75,900
	2001	54,800	76,200

Assume that each 1995 dollar is equivalent to 1.2 2001 dollars, owing to inflation.

1. Compute 1995 and 2001 productivity measures in terms of revenue per employee for Lakeland Foods and National Food and Beverage.
2. Compare the change in productivity between 1995 and 2001 for Lakeland Foods with that for National Food and Beverage.

P14-20 QUALITY THEORIES COMPARED. Sketch the two graphs as they appear below. Compare the total quality management approach to the traditional theory of quality. Which theory do you believe represents the current realities of today's global competitive environment? Explain.

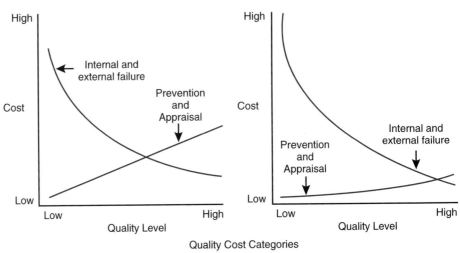

(a) Traditional Approach (b) Total Quality Management Approach

Quality Cost Categories
• Prevention
• Internal failure
• Appraisal
• External failure

P14-21 **QUALITY CONTROL CHART.** Baffin Manufacturing Company was concerned about a growing number of defective units being produced. At one time the company had the percentage of defective units down to less than fifty per thousand, but recently rates of defects have been near, or even above, 1 percent. The company decided to graph its defects for the last 8 weeks (40 working days), beginning Monday, September 1 through Friday, October 31. The graph follows:

Baffin Manfacturing Company
Quality Control Chart
September 1 through
October 31

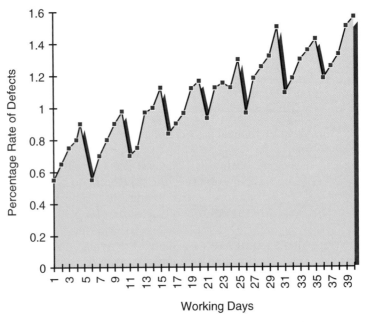

1. Identify two important trends evident in the quality control chart.
2. What might management of Baffin do to deal with each trend?

P14-22 REVIEW. As you are about to depart on a business trip, your accountant hands you the following information about your Thailand division:

1. Master budget for the fiscal year just ended on June 30, 2001:

Sales	$850,000
Manufacturing cost of goods sold	670,000
Manufacturing margin	$180,000
Selling and administrative expenses	120,000
Operating income	$ 60,000

2. Budgeted sales and production mix:

Product A	50,000 units
Product B	70,000 units

3. Standard variable manufacturing cost per unit:

Product A	Direct materials	10 pieces	@ $0.25	$2.50
	Direct labour	1 hour	@ $3.00	3.00
	Variable overhead	1 hour	@ $2.00	2.00
				$7.50
Product B	Direct materials	5 kilograms	@ $0.10	$0.50
	Direct labour	.3 hours	@ $2.50	0.75
	Variable overhead	.3 hours	@ $2.50	0.75
				$2.00

4. All budgeted selling and administrative expenses are common, fixed expenses; 60 percent are discretionary expenses.

5. Actual income statement for the fiscal year ended June 30, 2001:

Sales	$850,000
Manufacturing cost of goods sold	685,200
Manufacturing margin	$164,800
Selling and administrative expenses	116,000
Operating income	$ 48,800

6. Actual sales and production mix:

Product A	53,000 units
Product B	64,000 units

7. Budgeted and actual sales prices:

Product A	$10
Product B	5

8. Schedule of the actual variable manufacturing cost of goods sold by product; actual quantities in parentheses:

Product A: Material	$134,500	(538,000 pieces)
Labour	156,350	(53,000 hours)
Overhead	108,650	(53,000 hours)
Product B: Material	38,400	(320,000 kilograms)
Labour	50,000	(20,000 hours)
Overhead	50,000	(20,000 hours)
	$537,900	

9. Products A and B are manufactured in separate facilities. Of the *budgeted* fixed manufacturing cost, $130,000 is separable as follows: $45,000 to product A and $85,000 to product B. Ten percent of these separate costs is discretionary. All other budgeted fixed manufacturing expenses, separable and common, are committed.

The purpose of your business trip is a Board of Directors meeting. During the meeting it is quite likely that some of the information from your accountant will be discussed. In anticipation, you set out to prepare answers to possible questions. (There are no beginning or ending inventories.)

1. Determine the firm's *budgeted* break-even point in dollars, overall contribution-margin ratio, and contribution margins per unit by product.
2. Considering products A and B as segments of the firm, find the *budgeted* "contribution by segments" for each.
3. It is decided to allocate the *budgeted* selling and administrative expenses to the segments (in requirement 2) as follows: committed costs on the basis of budgeted unit sales mix and discretionary costs on the basis of actual unit sales mix. What are the final expense allocations? Briefly appraise the allocation method.
4. How would you respond to a proposal to base commissions to salespersons on the sales (revenue) value of orders received? Assume all salespersons have the opportunity to sell both products.
5. Determine the firm's *actual* "contribution margin" and "contribution controllable by segment managers" for the fiscal year ended June 30, 2001. Assume no variances in committed fixed costs.
6. Determine the "sales-volume variance" for each product for the fiscal year ended June 30, 2001.
7. Determine and identify all variances in *variable* manufacturing costs by product for the fiscal year ended June 30, 2001.

P14-23 **BALANCED SCORECARD.** Zenon Medical Instruments Company (ZMIC) recently revised its performance evaluation system. The company identified four major goals and several objectives required to meet each goal. Ruth Sanchez, Controller of ZMIC, suggested that a balanced scorecard be used to report on progress toward meeting the objectives. At a recent meeting, she told the managers of ZIMC listing the objectives was only the first step in installing a new performance measurement system. Each objective has to be accomplished by one or more measures to monitor progress toward achieving the objectives. She asked the help of the managers in identifying appropriate measures.

The goals and objectives determined by the top management of ZMIC are:

1. Maintain strong financial health
   a. Keep sufficient cash balances to assure financial survival
   b. Achieve consistent growth in sales and income
   c. Provide excellent returns to shareholders
2. Provide excellent service to customers
   a. Provide products that meet the needs of customers
   b. Meet customer needs on a timely basis
   c. Meet customer quality requirements
   d. Be the preferred supplier to customers
3. Be among the industry leaders in product and process innovations
   a. Bring new products to market before competition
   b. Lead competition in production process innovation
4. Develop and maintain efficient, state-of-the-art productions processes
   a. Excel in manufacturing efficiency
   b. Design products efficiently and quickly
   c. Meet or beat product introduction schedules

Propose at least one measure of performance for each of the objectives of ZMIC.

P14-24 QUALITY PROGRAMS, STRATEGIC INITIATIVES, GENERAL ELECTRIC. One of three major strategic initiatives of General Electric Company in 1998 was Six Sigma quality. The following comments were made by John Welch, Jr., CEO of GE in the 1998 Annual Report.

"Six Sigma quality, our third growth initiative, is, in itself, a product of learning. After observing the transformational effects this science, this way of life and work, had on the few companies that pursued it, we plunged into Six Sigma with a company-consuming vengeance just over three years ago. We have invested more than a billion dollars in the effort, and the financial returns have now entered the exponential phase — more than three quarters of a billion dollars in savings beyond our investment in 1998, with a billion and a half in sight for 1999."

"The Six Sigma-driven savings are impressive, but it is the radical change in the overall measures of operating efficiency that excite us most. For years — decades — we have been straining to improve operating margin and working capital turns. Our progress was typically measured in basis points for margins and decimal points in working capital turns. Six Sigma came along in 1995 when our margins were in the 13.6 percent range and turns at 5.8. At the end of 1998, margins hit 16.7 percent and turns hit 9.2. These numbers are an indicator of the progress and momentum in our Six Sigma journey.

"The ratio of plant and equipment expenditures to depreciation is another measure of asset efficiency. This number in 1998 dropped to 1.2 and will be in the .7 to .8 range in the future, as 'hidden factory' after 'hidden factory'— literally 'free capacity' — is uncovered by Six Sigma process improvements."

"Yes, we've had some early product successes, and those customers who have been touched by them understand what this Six Sigma they've heard so much about really means. But, as we celebrate our progress and count our financial gain, we need to focus on the most powerful piece of learning we have been given in 1998, summarized perfectly in the form of what most of our customers must be thinking, which is: 'When do I get the benefits of Six Sigma?' 'When does my company get to experience the GE I read about in the GE Annual Report?'"

"Questions like these are being asked because, up to now, our Six Sigma process improvements have concentrated primarily on our own internal processes and on internal measurements such as 'order-to-delivery' or 'shop turnaround time.' And in focusing that way — inwardly on our processes — we have tended to use all our energy and Six Sigma science to 'move the mean' to, for example, reduce order-to-delivery times from an average of, say, 17 days to 12 days, as reflected in the example below. We've repeated this type of improvement over and over again in thousands of GE processes and have been rewarded for it with less 'rework' and greater cash flow."

Order by Order Deliver Times (Days)	
Starting Point	After Project
29	11
18	24
7	10
19	6
6	12
8	8
16	15
19	10
33	4
15	20
Mean 17	Mean 12

Compute a measure of the variability in the data above. From a customer's perspective how would you view the results of Six Sigma as depicted in the example given by CEO Welch?

P14-25 **COLLABORATIVE LEARNING EXERCISE: GOALS, OBJECTIVES, AND PERFORMANCE MEASURES.** There is increasing pressure on colleges and universities to develop measures of accountability. The objective is to specify goals and objectives and to develop measures to assess the achievement of those goals and objectives.

Form a group of four to six students to be a consulting team to the accounting department at your college or university. (If you are not using this book as part of a course in an accounting department, select any department at a local college or university.) Based on your collective knowledge of the department, its mission, and its activities, formulate a statement of goals for the department. From that statement, develop several specific objectives, each of which can be measured. Then develop one or more measures of performance for each objective.

An optional second step in this exercise is to meet with a faculty member from the department, and ask him or her to critique your objectives and measures. As a member of the department, do the objectives make sense? Are the proposed measures feasible, and will they correctly measure attainment of the objectives? Will they provide proper incentives to the faculty? If the department has created objectives and performance measures, compare them to those your group developed.

CASES

C14-1 ORGANIZATION STRUCTURE.   (SMAC) Harold Mover has been the president of Newprod Ltd. (Newprod) for a little over six months. He had been brought in by the Board of Directors to reverse the trend of falling profits. He had told the Board that it would take him a while to get a thorough understanding of how things worked at Newprod.

Newprod is a multi-product manufacturer (see Exhibit 14A-1) that supplies various wholesalers and distributors across Canada. Newprod services its customers from one centrally located production plant just north of Toronto. Sales offices are located across the country.

Within the operations of the plant there are some sequential inter-departmental transfers, since several products may be incorporated into the production process of other departments in addition to being sold directly to consumers.

At Newprod, there is a very clear separation among the production equipment in each production department. However, there are also significant costs related to the plant facilities such as heat, light, etc., that are not easily segregated. This is partly due to the fact that some product lines depend on other departments within Newprod to manufacture component parts and partly because independent facilities, by product, are not economically feasible.

During his initial months at Newprod, Mover has found that Newprod operates under a strong central management structure, with almost everything flowing to the president for decisions. He has noticed that there is little motivation on the part of senior and middle managers, as they have only minimal participation in management decision-making other than those decisions relating to their direct responsibilities. Furthermore, there is no system of performance measurement.

In his spare moments, Mover has been reviewing some prior correspondence and has noticed that the internal auditors have frequently suggested that some type of integrated planning structure should be put in place and that a divisional management performance system would be appropriate for Newprod.

Using this as a basis for discussion, Mover has had various meetings with his vice presidents and other supervisory personnel.

With the vision of a "light at the end of the tunnel," the managers were more than willing to contribute their ideas and their preferences. However, while some were in favour of implementing a divisional structure, others were not. One important issue that was raised for discussion was the matter of performance measurement. All managers were in favour of some form of performance measurement, but they were undecided as to what would be best. Each wanted a chance to prove that he or she was performing well but feared a measurement that would be unfair in its application.

The managers also expressed a desire to participate in corporate planning and budgeting.

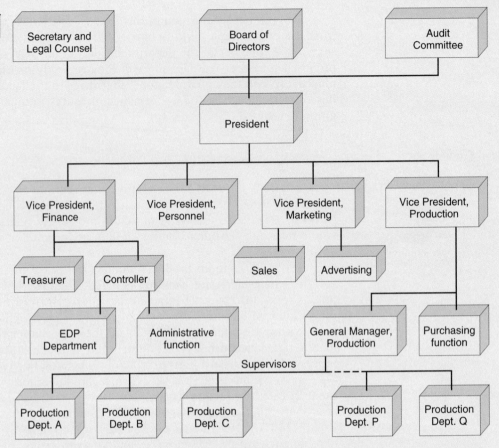

As a result of these meetings, Mover has had some serious discussion with Jill Adams, the corporate controller, about how best to proceed. It was generally felt that a good planning system in conjunction with a divisional management structure may be appropriate for Newprod. However, a concern was expressed that any such changes should be implemented only if the major corporate objectives of increased profits and improved employee motivation and morale could be achieved.

Jill Adams has asked you, the assistant controller, to prepare a report and provide a recommended plan of action to address the various concerns raised throughout the consultation process.

Required:

Prepare the report requested by Jill Adams. Be sure to discuss all of the issues raised above.

C14-2 **MANAGEMENT CONTROL IN A SERVICE DEPARTMENT.** (SMAC) Homestead Foods Limited is a large processor and distributor of packaged foods. Its product lines include soups, vegetables, potatoes, fruits, pasta, TV dinners, juices, and bread. In addition, it has three restaurant chains serving pizza, fish, and hamburgers.

Homestead originally started with canned soups 70 years ago. Management is proud of its past traditions. Success is attributed to the firm's good products and satisfied customers. Accordingly, the key success factors identified and upheld at Homestead are high product quality and customer research. This operating philosophy has been dominant in shaping the organization.

There is a high degree of decentralized decision-making at the operating-division level. The operating divisions (called product group divisions) are responsible for production and marketing of their products and are considered to be profit centres. Performance assessment is based on profitability plus product quality and customer satisfaction. There are eight product group divisions: soups, vegetables and potatoes, fruit, pasta, TV dinners, juices, bread, and restaurants. The head office is small and its activities are limited to preparation of financial statements, marketing research, treasury and legal activities, performance monitoring, and the approval of plans and budgets. The costs of these activities are not charged to operating divisions; they are controlled through a master budget and are reported only in the overall company statements.

Management has become concerned about the increasing costs of the market research department at the head office. Three main types of work are performed by this department: gathering regular market data, testing new product markets, and handling special research requests made by the operating divisions. Because of the emphasis that management has put on customer satisfaction as a key success factor, a wide range of standard data is produced by the market research department. Management originally felt that regularly producing market research data, which are gathered in a carefully planned and controlled manner, and making them available to the divisions would result in cost efficiencies. However, the divisions frequently make special requests for data not routinely gathered.

The market research department is considered to be highly successful and the operating divisions are happy with the service provided. The professional members of the market research department are well respected by their colleagues, and a number of them have taken part-time teaching assignments at universities and have had numerous articles and studies published in reputable journals.

Until now, there has been no attempt to measure the efficiency and effectiveness of the market research department. The president suspects that costs of Homestead's market research are up to double the amount incurred by similar firms for their in-house market research or, alternatively, for contracting with professional market research firms. He wonders whether the benefits of Homestead's market research activities exceed their costs and has asked you, as assistant controller, to analyze Homestead's situation and to give recommendations.

Required: | Respond to the president's request.

C14-3 **MANAGEMENT CONTROL-SERVICE SECTOR.** (ICAO) Lynda Carson is the recently appointed general manager of Crichton General Assurance Corporation (CGAC). She has been appointed to help the company regain profitability after several years of near-break-even operations.

CGAC is a general casualty insurance company, with its primary business in automobile, home-owner, and personal property insurance. The casualty insurance industry has been under severe profit pressure in recent years due to increasing claims. Political pressure has kept the industry from passing on the full cost of high damage settlements as quickly or completely as the industry would like. In addition, CGAC is a relatively small company in an industry dominated by several larger companies, some of which are controlled by major Canadian financial conglomerates. Its relatively minor position makes it more difficult to maintain a wide agent base and to advertise effectively. Therefore there is much pressure on Lynda to make the internal operations of the company more efficient.

One of the many areas that Lynda has been exploring to increase efficiency is that of budgeting. In the past, the company has attempted to plan and control operations by means of a fixed master budget for the company as a whole. Most of the administrative responsibility centres are cost centres, and departmental managers have been evaluated on the basis of variance from budget, on a line-by-line basis.

Lynda is considering using other means and bases of budgeting, including, but not restricted to, flexible budgets, performance budgets, and zero-based budgeting. In particular, she would like to have budgets that help her to better evaluate departmental efficiency. She has engaged you as a consultant to advise her on what the most appropriate budgeting approach(es) may be, and has asked that you formulate your recommendations on the basis of the underwriting department.

The underwriting department is responsible for compiling the new initial files and drawing up the insurance contracts for new clients, including assessing the premium. It also maintains the client base by monitoring client performance and drawing up renewal policies and premiums based on the client's performance. The premiums (per $1,000 of coverage) are assessed on the basis of various factors for each client, depending on the nature of the policy. For example, fire insurance premiums on building are determined by factors such as type of construction, use of premises, contents of premises, quality of fire protection and detection, distance from hydrants, accessibility by fire-fighting equipment and so forth. It is the responsibility of the underwriting department to assess experience factors and to recommend to the CGAC Executive Committee increases and decreases in premiums at least once every six months. The underwriting department does not have responsibility for sales; the sales department is a separate revenue centre.

The direct costs of the underwriting department are largely staff costs. There are several components or sections within the department. One such section is the investigative section, which assesses new insurance applications and recommends approval or rejection of coverage. Response time is very important both for competitive reasons and because the company is liable for coverage as soon as the insurance agent accepts the application. When surges in the volume of new policies occur, some of the policy investigation is contracted out to independent investigators in order to avoid delays.

Another section is the processing section. This group does the actual policy preparation, including the building and maintenance of the customer's computer file and the preparation of premium notices and renewals. Except for the initial inputting of the application information and sending the application to the investigation section, time constraints are not severe. In busy periods, the lag in the paper work and computer file maintenance will get larger, but without significant adverse consequences.

A third section of the underwriting department is the actuarial staff. The actuaries and their support staff are responsible for the monitoring and analysis of underwriting and claims experience in order to recommend new premium levels. Since the analysis underlying their recommendations is computerized, the level of activity in this section is not responsive to changes in underwriting volume.

The underwriting department makes extensive use of CGAC computer facilities in all aspects of its work. Many staff members work directly at computer terminals that can also function as stand-alone work stations for routine tasks such as letter-writing. The main-frame computer itself is operated and maintained by the data processing department, which is part of general administration and not a part of the underwriting department. Batch processing tasks such as premium reminder and renewal notices are performed by the data processing department and then routed through printers located in the underwriting department. In the past, there has been no charge made to user departments for the services of the data processing department.

Required:

Write a report to Lynda Carson in which you discuss the specific budget approach(es) that seems to be the most appropriate for the underwriting department and explain why it is appropriate. Also, briefly indicate the general circumstances in which the recommended approach(es) may not be appropriate for other departments in the company.

C14-4 MANAGEMENT CONTROL—GOVERNMENT SECTOR. (SMAC) The discovery of vast petroleum reserves in the country of Adanak has led to massive expenditures on government services. Several years ago, the Minister of Communications had automated the Adanak post office, but despite the latest equipment, the delivery of mail remained slow and unpredictable. Considerable pressure to improve the mail system was exerted on the Adanak government by business leaders claiming that it was essential for continued economic growth. A Canadian management consulting firm was commissioned by the Adanak Minister of Communications to recommend improvements in the mail service. Alex Peach, CMA, was sent to Adanak to analyze the situation.

In his initial self-familiarization of Adanak, Alex noted many similarities to Canada: size of population, large cities separated by long distances, and remote regions with poor communication systems and small populations. In recent years, since the automation of the post office, deliveries that had previously taken several weeks were now taking several days. Alex reviewed the seven organizational departments and decided to do a preliminary investigation of each.

The general manager of the post office told Alex that she wondered whether it would be feasible to use a profit-based management control system. Currently, the operating departments are organized as cost centres, except the marketing department, which is a revenue centre. The general manager's office prepares annual departmental budgets by applying a growth factor to the previous year's budgets.

Alex's investigation of the seven departments revealed the following information.

1. Transportation Department: The department manager is responsible for the domestic and international movement of bulk mail. He is evaluated on a two-part budget: fixed costs and variable operating costs. The variable portion is based on total weight moved times an average cost factor.

   The transportation manager complains that his equipment is old and always breaking down. His requests for repairs to the maintenance department are always turned down with the explanation that the equipment needs to be replaced. However, the general manager refuses equipment replacement requests from the transportation department because of a long-standing clash of personalities between the two managers.

   Another complaint of the transportation department manager is that the sorting department increases transportation costs by sorting at the source post office and shipping small bags of mail to many destinations. He also resents political interference in the awarding of international mail contracts to airlines, usually favouring Adanak Airlines at higher rates.

2. Sorting Department: In all postal stations, sorting is performed using modern equipment. Incoming mail is first sorted into three categories: parcels, commercial, and first class. Then, the mail is sorted according to final destination. The shift supervisors tend to select commercial mail first since it includes junk mail, which is easily and quickly sorted. The sorting department manager is evaluated on a flexible budget based on the actual number of pieces sorted in the year.

   The sorting department manager is very dissatisfied with the organization system. Since the sorters are unionized, he feels that he can do very little to improve their productivity. Furthermore, the marketing department encourages high-volume junk mail, which delays the sorting of first-class mail and increases the frequency of equipment breakdowns.

3. Delivery Department: The department budget is composed of a fixed amount plus a variable cost based on the number of pieces delivered. The manager can best meet the budget in commercial areas, where whole bags are delivered to large clients. In new suburban areas, he favours central customer mail boxes, but customers and the union demand home delivery.

4. Maintenance Department: In an attempt to keep maintenance costs down, the department is on a fixed budget. There is a tendency by the department manager to recommend replacement of post office equipment rather than incurring the expense of repairing equipment, since the replacement costs are the responsibility of the administration department.

5. Marketing Department: The department is evaluated as a revenue centre, with a budget based on annual sales increases over the prior year. The manager confided that she encourages expansion in commercial junk mail and home first-class letters. The commercial market is one where promotion has produced tangible results and the home market is growing rapidly with the suburban population explosion.

6. Administration Department: The general manager is convinced that the only practical way to control administration expenses is by fixed budgets. The department manager complains that his budget is typically exceeded because, with the exception of requests from the transportation department, the general manager seldom refuses requests for capital expenditures.

7. Personnel Department: This department is also on a fixed budget that it is not allowed to exceed. The manager confided that he often had to lay off some of his own staff for a month or two at the end of each year in order to stay within the budget. Moreover, selection criteria for post office personnel are poorly defined and the manager is often pressured to hire friends and relatives of politicians.

Required: | Analyze the management control system of the Adanak post office. Recommend, with reasons, possible improvements and discuss anticipated behavioural consequences.

C14-5 **NONFINANCIAL PERFORMANCE MEASURES.** (McCutcheon) Current River is a medium-sized city that has experienced rapid growth in the last two decades. For several of those years the city had the highest growth rate in the country. Much of the growth has occurred in the suburbs that now have full commercial facilities that are at least equal to those in the core area. Meanwhile, the core area has stagnated with many vacant stores and an increase in the numbers of businesses such as tattoo parlours, video arcades, and second-hand stores. The core area has numerous bars and other facilities that are attractive to younger people and those of lower socio-economic profiles. The Downtown Business Association and its members have made numerous requests that the police "clean up downtown" as they believe that customers are afraid to venture downtown. The downtown area and its problems have been the subject of many articles in the local paper. The City Council seems to be strongly supportive of the Downtown Business Association. It is noteworthy that the Mayor is an influential member of the Police Services Board.

In response to these pressures, the Police Services Board two years ago approved an experimental plan for extra policing in the core. Five officers were reassigned on a permanent basis from normal duties to the area. No particular instructions were given by the Board but there seemed to be an expectation that use would be made of foot and perhaps bicycle patrols. The Board now wishes to review the success of this project. Your role is to determine how to measure the performance of this experiment.

Required: Prepare a report to the Board with your recommendations of assessing the performance of this project.

C14-6 COMPARING THE PERFORMANCE OF TWO PLANTS. On your first day as assistant to the president of Harold Systems, Inc. (HSI), your in-box contains the following memo:

- To: Assistant to the President
- From: The President
- Subject: Mickey Mouse Watch Situation
- This note is to bring you up-to-date on one of our acquisition problem areas. Market research detected the current nostalgia wave almost a year ago and concluded that HSI should acquire a position in this market. Research data showed that Mickey Mouse Watches could become profitable ($5 contribution margin on $12 sales price) at a volume of 40,000 units per plant if they became popular again. Consequently, we picked up closed-down facilities on each coast, staffed them, and asked them to keep us posted on operations.
- Friday I got preliminary information from accounting that is unclear. I want you to find out why their costs of goods sold are far apart and how we should have them report in the future to avoid confusion. This is particularly important in the Mickey Mouse case, as market projections look bad and we may have to close one plant. I guess we'll close the West Coast plant unless you can show otherwise.

	EAST	WEST
Sales	$480,000	$480,000
Cost of goods sold	280,000	450,000
Gross margin	$200,000	$ 30,000
Administration costs		
(fixed)	30,000	30,000
Net income	$170,000	$ 0
Production	80,000 units	40,000 units
Variances (included		
in cost of goods sold)	$170,000 favourable	$ 85,000 unfavourable

Required: | As the assistant to the president, what is your response to the president's memo?

C14-7 **ABSORPTION COSTING AND INCENTIVE TO PRODUCE.** Allan McDonald is manager of the Pacific Division of Zenna Inc. His division makes a single product that is sold to industrial customers. Demand is seasonable but is readily predictable. The division's budget for 2002 called for production and sales of 120,000 units, with production of 10,000 units each month and sales varying between 8,000 and 13,000 units a month. The division's budget for 2002 had an operating income of $780,000:

Sales (120,000 × $50)	$6,000,000
Cost of goods sold (120,000 × $40)	4,800,000
Gross margin	$1,200,000
Selling and administrative expenses (all fixed)	420,000
Operating income	$ 780,000

By the end of November, sales lagged projections, with only 105,000 units sold. Sales of 9,000 units were originally budgeted and are still expected in December. Production had remained stable at 10,000 units per month, and the cost of production had been exactly as budgeted:

Direct materials, 110,000 × $9	$ 990,000
Direct labour, 110,000 × $10	1,100,000
Variable overhead, 110 × $8	880,000
Fixed overhead	1,430,000
Total production cost	$4,400,000

The division's operating income for the first 11 months of 2002 was

Sales (105,000 × $50)	$5,250,000
Cost of goods sold (105,000 × $40)	4,200,000
Gross margin	$1,050,000
Selling and administrative expenses (all fixed)	385,000
Operating income	$ 665,000

McDonald receives an annual bonus only if his division's operating income exceeds the budget. He sees no way to increase sales beyond 9,000 units in December.

Required:

1. From the budgeted and actual income statements shown, determine whether Zenna used variable or absorption costing.
2. Suppose Zenna uses a standard absorption-costing system. (a) Compute the 2002 operating income if 10,000 units are produced and 9,000 units are sold in December. (b) How could McDonald achieve his budgeted operating income for 2002?
3. Suppose Zenna uses a standard variable-costing system. (a) Compute the 2002 operating income if 10,000 units are produced and 9,000 units are sold in December. (b) How could McDonald achieve his budgeted operating income for 2002?
4. Which system motivates McDonald to make the decision that is in the best interests of Zenna? Explain.

Management Control in Decentralized Organizations

LEARNING OBJECTIVES

After studying this chapter, you will be able to

1. Define decentralization and identify its expected benefits and costs.

2. Distinguish between profit centres and decentralization.

3. Define transfer prices and state their purpose.

4. Identify the relative advantages and disadvantages of basing transfer prices on total costs, variable costs, and market prices.

5. Identify the factors affecting multinational transfer prices.

6. Explain how linking rewards to responsibility centre results affects incentives and risk.

7. Compute return on investment (ROI), residual income (RI), and economic value added (EVA) and contrast them as criteria for judging the performance of organization segments.

8. Compare the advantages and disadvantages of various bases for measuring the invested capital used by organization segments.

Decentralization. The delegation of freedom to make decisions. The lower in the organization that this freedom exists, the greater the decentralization.

As organizations grow and undertake more diverse and complex activities, many elect to delegate decision-making authority to managers throughout the organization. This delegation of the freedom to make decisions is called **decentralization**. The lower in the organization that this freedom exists, the greater the decentralization. Decentralization is a matter of degree along a continuum:

Centralization   Decentralization

Maximum constraints, minimum freedom   Minimum constraints, maximum freedom

    This chapter focuses on the role of management control systems in decentralized organizations. After providing an overview of decentralization, the chapter addresses the special problems created when one segment of an organization charges another for providing goods or services. Then it discusses how performance measures can be used to motivate managers in a decentralized company. Finally, measures used to assess the profitability of decentralized units are introduced and compared.

CENTRALIZATION VERSUS DECENTRALIZATION

OBJECTIVE 1

Define decentralization and identify its expected benefits and costs.

At any time, some firms will see advantages in decentralization and some in centralization. Consider the international airline industry in the 1990s. Most airlines, such as South China Airlines, Iberia Airlines, and Air France, were decentralizing. In contrast, at the same time Sabena, Belgium's state-owned airline, was reorganizing to *reverse* its trend toward decentralization. In the insurance industry, Aetna was decentralizing at the same time Equitable was centralizing. Even the Department of National Defence, a very centralized organization, has started some decentralization in recent years.

Costs and Benefits

Iberia
www.iberia.com

Air France
www.airfrance.com

Aetna
www.aetna.com

Equitable Life
www.equitable.com

There are many benefits of at least some decentralization for most organizations. First, lower-level managers have the best information concerning local conditions and therefore may be able to make better decisions than their superiors. Second, managers acquire decision-making ability and other management skills that help them move upward in the organization, assuring continuity of leadership. In addition, managers enjoy higher status from being independent and thus are better motivated.

    Of course, decentralization has its costs. Managers may make decisions that are not in the organization's best interests, either because they act to improve their own segment's performance at the expense of the organization's or because they are not aware of relevant facts from other segments. Managers in decentralized organizations also tend to duplicate services that might be less expensive if centralized (accounting, advertising, and personnel are examples). Furthermore, under decentralization, costs of accumulating and processing information frequently rise because responsibility accounting reports are needed for top management to learn about and evaluate decentralized units and their managers. Finally, managers in decentralized units may waste time negotiating with other units about goods or services one unit provides to the other.

Decentralization is more popular in profit-seeking organizations (where outputs and inputs can be measured) than in non-profit organizations. Managers can be given freedom when their results are measurable so that they can be held accountable for them. Poor decisions in a profit-seeking firm become apparent from the inadequate profit generated. Most non-profit organizations lack such a reliable performance indicator, so granting managerial freedom is more risky.

Middle Ground

Philosophies of decentralization differ considerably. Cost-benefit considerations usually require that some management decisions be highly decentralized and others centralized. To illustrate, much of the controller's problem-solving and attention-directing functions may be found at the lower levels, whereas income tax planning and mass scorekeeping such as payroll may be highly centralized.

Decentralization is most successful when an organization's segments are relatively independent of one another—that is, the decisions of one manager will not affect the fortunes of another manager. If segments do a lot of internal buying or selling, buying from the same outside suppliers, or selling to the same outside markets, they are candidates for heavier centralization.

Segment Autonomy. The delegation of decision-making power to segment managers.

In Chapter 14 we stressed that cost-benefit tests, goal congruence, and managerial effort must all be considered when designing a control system. If management has decided in favour of heavy decentralization, **segment autonomy**, the delegation of decision-making power to managers of segments of an organization, is also crucial. For decentralization to work, however, this autonomy must be real, not just lip-service. In most circumstances, top managers must be willing to abide by decisions made by managers.

Profit Centres and Decentralization

OBJECTIVE 2

Distinguish between profit centres and decentralization.

Do not confuse *profit centres* (accountability for revenue and expenses) with *decentralization* (freedom to make decisions). They are entirely separate concepts, although profit centres clearly are accounting devices that can aid decentralization. One can exist without the other. Some profit centre managers possess vast freedom to make decisions concerning labour contracts, supplier choices, equipment purchases, personnel decisions, and so on. In contrast, other profit centre managers may need top-management approval for almost all the decisions just mentioned. Indeed, cost centres may be more heavily decentralized than profit centres if cost centre managers have more freedom to make decisions.

There are many criticisms of profit centres on the grounds that managers are given profit responsibility without commensurate authority. Therefore, the criticism continues, the profit centre is "artificial" because the manager is not free to make a sufficient number of the decisions that affect profit.

Such criticisms confuse profit centres and decentralization. The fundamental question in deciding between using a cost centre or a profit centre for a given segment is not whether heavy decentralization exists. Instead, the fundamental question is, Will a profit centre better solve the problems of goal congruence and management effort than a cost centre? In other words, does one predict that a profit centre will induce managers to make a better collective set of decisions from the viewpoint of the organization as a whole?

All control systems are imperfect. Judgments about their merits should concentrate on which alternative system will bring more of the actions top management seeks. For example, a plant may seem to be a "natural" cost centre because the plant manager has no influence over decisions concerning the marketing of its products. Still, some companies evaluate a plant manager by the plant's profitability. Why? Because this broader evaluation base will affect the plant manager's behaviour. Instead of being concerned solely with running an efficient cost centre, the plant manager now "naturally" considers quality control more carefully and reacts to customers' special requests more sympathetically. A profit centre may thus obtain the desired plant-manager behaviour more than a cost centre.

From the viewpoint of top management, plant managers often have more influence on sales than is apparent at first glance. This is an example of how systems may evolve from cost centres to profit centres and an example of the first-line importance of predicting behavioural effects when an accounting control system is designed.

TRANSFER PRICING

OBJECTIVE 3

Define transfer prices and state their purpose.

Transfer Prices. The amounts charged by one segment of an organization for a product or service that it supplies to another segment of the same organization.

Very few problems arise in decentralized organizations when all the segments are independent of one another. Segment managers can then focus only on their own segments without hurting the organization as a whole. In contrast, when segments interact greatly, there is an increased possibility that what is best for one segment hurts another segment enough to have a negative impact on the entire organization. Such a situation may occur when one segment provides products or services to another segment and charges them a *transfer price*. **Transfer prices** are the amounts charged by one segment of an organization for a product or service that it supplies to another segment of the same organization. Most often, the term is associated with materials, parts, or finished goods. The transfer price is revenue to the segment producing the product or service, and it is a cost to the acquiring department.

Purposes of Transfer Pricing

Why do transfer-pricing systems exist? The principal reason is to communicate data that will lead to goal-congruent decisions. For example, transfer prices should guide managers to make the best possible decisions regarding whether to buy or sell products and services inside or outside the total organization. Another important reason is to evaluate segment performance and thus motivate both the selling manager and the buying manager toward goal-congruent decisions. Multinational companies also use transfer pricing to minimize their worldwide taxes, duties, and tariffs. These are easy aims to describe, but they are difficult aims to achieve.

Whenever there is a lull in a conversation with a manager, try asking, "Do you have any transfer-pricing problems?" The response is usually, "Let me tell you about the peculiar transfer-pricing difficulties in my organization." A manager in a large wood-products firm called transfer pricing his firm's most troublesome management control issue.

Decentralization in the 1990s

Pepsi
www.pepsiworld.com

IBM
www.ibm.com

Johnson & Johnson
www.jnj.com

Many companies moved to decentralize their operations in one way or another during the 1990s, among them PepsiCo, Dupont, and Procter & Gamble. But the two companies that stood out in their efforts to decentralize were IBM and Johnson & Johnson. The two companies approached decentralization from very different perspectives.

Johnson & Johnson (J & J), maker of Tylenol, Band-Aids, Johnson's Baby Powder, Ortho birth-control pills, and many other products, has a long history of decentralization, beginning in the 1930s. Its 166 separately chartered companies are empowered to act independently. Although ultimately accountable to executives at J & J headquarters in New Brunswick, New Jersey, some segment presidents see their bosses as few as four times a year. An article in *Business Week* called J & J "a model of how to make decentralization work." CEO Ralph Larson says that decentralization "provides a sense of ownership and responsibility for a business that you simply cannot get any other way." Larson sees his role as providing direction but giving managers creative freedom.

J & J spent the early 1990s fine-tuning its decentralization system to erase costly mistakes that could have been avoided with more guidance from top management. Also, J & J had incurred high overhead costs as independent units duplicated many functions. Larson introduced methods of coordinating the independent units while still preserving the basics of decentralization. Although perhaps toning down the

degree of decentralization, Larson vows that J & J "will never give up the principle of decentralization, which is to give our operating executives ownership of a business. They are ultimately responsible."

IBM, in contrast, entered the 1990s a highly centralized firm. Its growth, though, had stalled, and it lost money in 1991 for the first time in its history. Chairman John Akers instituted a vast reorganization that granted managers great autonomy but also put pressure on them to perform. The plan is to make IBM a set of "wholly owned but more or less autonomous marketing, service, product development, and manufacturing companies." Segment managers will have far more decision-making freedom, but they will also have to show results on the bottom line.

IBM's new structure includes 13 distinct businesses, nine in manufacturing and development, and four in marketing and services. Each of the 13 managers will be measured against targets in seven areas: revenue growth, profit, return on assets, cash flow, customer satisfaction, quality, and employee morale. Heavy incentives are tied to making performance targets. Akers hopes the reorganization will unleash the energy and creativity that were part of IBM's past but have been lacking in recent years.

Sources: D. Kirkpatrick, "Breaking Up IBM," July 27, 1992, *Fortune* Magazine, pp. 44–58; "A Big Company That Works," *Business Week*, May 4, 1992, pp. 124–130, reprinted by special permission © 1992 by McGraw-Hill Companies.

Organizations may use one or a combination of alternative transfer prices. Some alternatives are cost-based, some are market-based, and some rely on negotiated settlements.

Cost-Based Transfer Prices

Approximately half of the major companies in the world transfer items at cost. However, there are many possible definitions of cost. Some companies use only variable cost, others use full cost where fixed costs may be a lump sum or a permit charge, and still others use full cost plus a profit markup. Some use standard costs and some use actual costs.

When the transfer price is some version of cost, transfer pricing is nearly identical to cost allocation (see Chapters 4 through 7), where costs are accumulated in one segment and then assigned to (or transferred to) another segment. However two important points deserve mention here.

First, transferring or allocating costs can disguise a cost's behaviour pattern. Consider a computer manufacturer that makes keyboards in one division and transfers them to another division for assembly into personal computers. The manager of the keyboard division may have good knowledge of the cost drivers affecting the costs of keyboards. But if a single transfer price per unit is charged when transferring the keyboards to the assembly division, the only cost driver affecting the cost to the assembly division is "units of keyboards." Cost drivers other than units produced are ignored, and distinctions between fixed and variable costs are blurred. The assembly division manager sees the entire cost of keyboards as a variable cost, regardless of what the true cost behaviour is.

Other problems arise if actual cost is used as a transfer price. Because actual cost cannot be known in advance, the buying segment will not be able to plan its costs. More important, because inefficiencies are merely passed along to the buying division, the supplying division lacks incentive to control its costs. Thus, using budgeted or standard costs instead of actual costs is recommended for both cost allocation and transfer pricing.

Market-Based Transfer Prices

If there is a competitive market for the product or service being transferred internally, using the market price as a transfer price will generally lead to the desired goal congruence and managerial effort. The market price may come from published price lists for similar products or services, or it may be the price charged by the producing division to its external customers. If the latter, the internal transfer price may be the external market price less the selling and delivery expenses that are not incurred on internal business. The major drawbacks to market-based prices are that market prices are not always available for items transferred internally and that such a transfer may reduce the possibility of generating benefits through cooperation.

Consider a major outdoor-equipment manufacturer that makes clothing and gear for all kinds of outdoor activities. One division of the company makes fabrics that are used in many final products as well as being sold directly to external customers, and another division makes tents. A particular tent requires five square metres of a special waterproof fabric. Should the Tent Division obtain the fabric from the Fabric Division of the company or purchase it from an external supplier?

Suppose the market price of the fabric is $10 per square metre, or $50 per tent, and assume for the moment that the Fabric Division can sell its entire production to external customers without incurring any marketing or shipping costs. The Tent Division manager will refuse to pay a transfer price greater than $50 for the fabric for each tent. Why? Because if the transfer price is greater than $50, she will purchase the fabric from the external supplier in order to maximize her division's profit.

Furthermore, the manager of the Fabric Division will not sell five square metres of fabric for less than $50. Why? Because he can sell it on the market for $50, so any lower price will reduce his division's profit. The only transfer price that allows both managers to maximize their division's profit is $50, the market price. If the managers had autonomy to make decisions, one of them would decline the internal production of fabric at any transfer price other than $50.

Now suppose the Fabric Division incurs a $1 per square metre marketing and shipping cost that can be avoided by transferring the fabric to the Tent Division instead of marketing it to outside customers. Most companies would then use a transfer price of $9 per square metre, or $45 per tent, often called a "market-price-minus" transfer price. The Fabric Division would get the same net amount from the transfer ($45 with no marketing or shipping costs) as from an external sale ($50 less $5 marketing and shipping costs), while the Tent Division saves $5 per tent. Thus the overall organization benefits.

Variable Cost Pricing

Market prices have innate appeal in a profit-centre context, but they are not cure-all answers to transfer-pricing problems. Sometimes market prices do not exist, are inapplicable, or are impossible to determine. For example, no intermediate markets may exist for specialized parts, or markets may be too thin or scattered to permit the determination of a credible price. In these instances, versions of "cost-plus-a-profit" are often used in an attempt to provide a "fair" or "equitable" substitute for regular market prices.

To illustrate, consider again the outdoor equipment manufacturer. Exhibit 15-1 shows its selling prices and variable costs per unit. In this example the Fabric Division's variable costs of $8 per metre are the only costs affected by producing the additional fabric for transfer to the Tent Division. Upon receiving five metres of fabric, the Tent Division spends an additional $53 to process and sell each tent. Whether the fabric should be manufactured and transferred to the Tent Division depends on the existence of idle capacity in the Fabric Division (insufficient demand from outside customers).

As Exhibit 15-1 shows, if there were no idle capacity in the Fabric Division, the optimum action for the company as a whole would be for the Fabric Division to sell outside at $50, because the Tent Division would incur $53 of additional variable costs but add only $50 of additional revenue ($100–$50). Using market price would provide the correct motivation for such a decision because, if the fabric were transferred, the Tent Division's cost would be $50 plus $53 or $103, which would be $3 higher than its prospective revenue of $100 per unit. So the Tent Division would choose not to buy from the Fabric Division at the $50 market price. Of course, the Tent Division also would not buy from outside suppliers at a price of $50. If fabric is not available at less than $50 per tent, this particular tent will not be produced.

EXHIBIT 15-1	SELL FABRIC OUTSIDE		USE FABRIC TO MAKE TENT		
Analysis of Market Prices	Market price per metre of fabric		Sales price of finished tent		$100
	to outsiders	$10	Variable Costs:		
	Variable costs per metre of fabric	8	Fabric division		
	Contribution margin	$ 2	(5 metres @ $8)	$40	
	Total contribution for		Tent division:		
	50,000 metres	$100,000	Processing	$41	
			Selling	12	53	93
			Contribution margin		$ 7
			Total contribution for 10,000 tents		$70,000

What if the Fabric Division has idle capacity sufficient to meet all the Tent Division's requirements? The optimum action would be to produce the fabric and transfer it to the Tent Division. If there were no production and transfer, the Tent Division and the company as a whole would forego a total contribution of $70,000. In this situation, variable cost would be the better basis for transfer pricing and would lead to the optimum decision for the firm as a whole. To be more precise, the transfer price should be all additional costs that will be incurred by the production of the fabric to be transferred. For example, if a lump-sum setup cost is required to produce the 50,000 square metres of fabric required, the setup cost should be added to the variable cost in calculating the appropriate transfer price. (In the example there is no such cost.)

Teva Marion
www.tevamarion.com

PERSPECTIVES ON P O D M DECISION-MAKING

Activity-Based Costing and Transfer Pricing

Teva Pharmaceutical Industries Ltd. is a worldwide manufacturer of proprietary drugs. It is headquartered in Israel and had 1996 sales of $954 million. Teva entered the lucrative generic drug market in the mid-1980s. As part of its strategy, the company decentralized its pharmaceutical business into cost and profit centres as shown below.

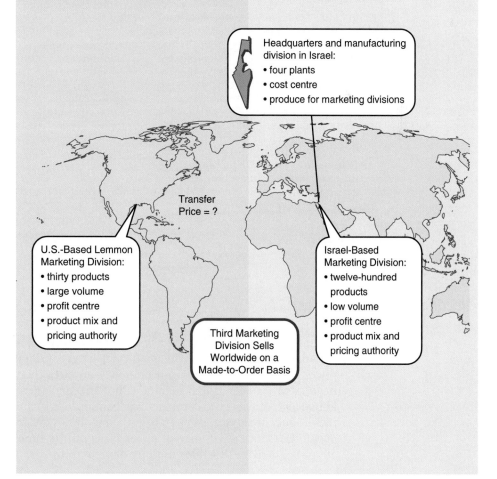

Each of the marketing divisions purchase generic drugs from the manufacturing division. Prior to decentralization, each marketing division was a revenue centre. With the new organization structure, management had to decide how to measure marketing division costs because profits were now the key financial performance measure.

A key cost to marketing divisions is the transfer price paid for drugs purchased from the manufacturing division. Management considered several alternative bases for the company's transfer prices. Market price was rejected because there was not a ready market. Negotiated price was rejected because management believed that the resulting debates over the proper price would be lengthy and disruptive. Variable cost (raw material and packaging costs) was adopted for a short time. Eventually, however, it was rejected because it did not lead to congruent decisions—products using many scarce resources were not differentiated from those using few. Further, when a local source for the drug did exist, the market price was always above the variable cost transfer price. Thus, managers in Teva's manufacturing division had little incentive to keep costs low.

Full cost was rejected because the traditional costing system did not capture the actual cost structure of the manufacturing division. Specifically, the system undercosted the low volume products and overcosted the large volume products. The system traced only raw materials directly to products. The remaining manufacturing costs were divided into two cost pools and allocated based on labour hours and machine hours. One problem with the traditional system was its inability to capture and correctly allocate the non-value-added cost of setup activity. The size of the errors in product cost was not known, but the lack of confidence in the traditional cost system led to full cost being rejected as the transfer-price base.

Teva's management adopted an activity-based costing system to improve the accuracy of its product costs. The ABC system had five activity centres and related cost pools: receiving, manufacturing, packaging, quality assurance, and shipping. Because of the dramatic increase in costing accuracy, management was able to adopt full activity-based cost as the transfer price.

Teva's managers are pleased with their transfer pricing system. The benefits include increased confidence that the costs being transferred are closely aligned with the actual short- and long-run costs being incurred, increased communication between divisions, and an increased awareness of the costs of low-volume products and the costs of capacity required to support these products.

Source: Robert Kaplan, Dan Weiss, and Eyal Desheh, "Transfer Pricing with ABC," *Management Accounting*, May, 1997, pp. 20–28.

Negotiated Transfer Prices

Companies heavily committed to segment autonomy often allow managers to negotiate transfer prices. The managers may consider both costs and market prices in their negotiations, but no policy requires them to do so. Supporters of negotiated transfer prices maintain that the managers involved have the best knowledge of what the company will gain or lose by producing and transferring the product or service, so open negotiation allows the managers to make optimal decisions. Critics of negotiated prices focus on the time and effort spent negotiating—an activity that adds nothing directly to the profits of the company.

Dysfunctional Behaviour

Dysfunctional Behaviour.
Any action taken in conflict with organizational goals.

Virtually any type of transfer pricing policy can lead to **dysfunctional behaviour**—actions taken in conflict with organizational goals. Gulf Oil provides a clear example:

> Segments tried to make their results look good at each other's expense. One widespread result: Inflated transfer payments among the Gulf segments as each one vied to boost its own bottom line. A top manager, quoted in *Business Week*, commented, "Gulf doesn't ring the cash register until we've made an outside sale."

What prompts such behaviour? Reconsider the situation depicted in Exhibit 15-1. Suppose the Fabric Division *has idle capacity*. As we saw earlier, when there is idle capacity, the optimal transfer price is the variable cost of $40 (that is, $8 per metre). As long as the fabric is worth at least $40 to the Tent Division, the company as a whole is better off with the transfer. Nevertheless, in a decentralized company, the Fabric Division manager, working in the division's best interests, may argue that the transfer price should be based on the market price instead of variable cost. If the division is a profit centre, the objective is to obtain as high a price as possible because such a price maximizes the contribution to the division's profit. (This strategy assumes that the number of units transferred will be unaffected by the transfer price—an assumption that is often shaky.)

If the company uses a market-based transfer pricing policy when the Fabric Division has idle capacity, dysfunctional behaviour can occur. At a $50 transfer price, the Tent Division manager will not purchase the fabric and make the tent. Why? Because at a transfer price of $50 and with additional processing costs of $53, the division's cost of $103 will exceed the tent's $100 selling price. Because the true *additional* cost of the fabric to the company is $40, the company foregoes a contribution of $100 − ($40 + $53) = $7 per tent.

Now suppose the Fabric Division has *no idle capacity*. A variable-cost transfer pricing policy can lead to dysfunctional decisions. The Tent Division manager might argue for a variable-cost-based transfer price. After all, the lowest possible transfer price will maximize the Tent Division's profit. But such a policy will not motivate the Fabric Division to produce fabric for the Tent Division. As long as output can be sold on the outside market for any price above the variable cost, the Fabric Division will use its capacity to produce for the market, regardless of how valuable the fabric might be to the Tent Division.

How are such dilemmas resolved? One possibility is for top management to impose a "fair" transfer price and insist that a transfer be made. But managers in a decentralized company often regard such orders as undermining their autonomy.

Alternatively, managers might be given the freedom to negotiate transfer prices on their own. The Tent Division manager might look at the selling price of the tent, $100, less the additional cost the division incurs in making it, $53, and decide to purchase fabric at any transfer price less than $47 ($100 − $53). The Tent Division will add to its profit by making the tent if the transfer price is below $47.

Similarly, the Fabric Division manager will look at what it costs to produce and transfer the fabric. If there is idle capacity, any transfer price above $40 will increase the Fabric Division's profit. However, if there is no idle capacity, so that transferring a unit causes the division to give up an external sale at $50, the minimum transfer price acceptable to the Fabric Division is $50.

Negotiation will result in a transfer if the maximum transfer price the Tent Division is willing to pay is greater than the minimum transfer price the Fabric

Division is willing to accept. When the Fabric Division has idle capacity, a transfer at a price between $40 and $47 will occur. The exact transfer price may depend on the negotiating ability of the two division managers. However, if the Fabric Division has no idle capacity, a transfer will not occur.

Use of Incentives

What should top management of a decentralized organization do if it sees segment managers making dysfunctional decisions? As usual, the answer is, "It depends." Top management can step in and force transfers, but doing so undermines segment managers' autonomy and the overall notion of decentralization. Frequent intervention results in a return to centralization. Indeed, if more centralization is desired, the organization could be redesigned by combining segments.

Top managers who wish to encourage decentralization will often make sure that both producing and purchasing division managers understand all the facts and then allow the managers to negotiate a transfer price. Even when top managers suspect that a dysfunctional decision might be made, they may swallow hard and accept the segment manager's judgment as a cost of decentralization. (Of course, repeated dysfunctional decision making may be a reason to change the organizational design or to change managers.)

Well-trained and informed segment managers who understand opportunity costs and fixed and variable costs will often make better decisions than will top managers. The producing division manager knows best the various uses of its capacity, and the purchasing division manager knows best what profit can be made on the items to be transferred. In addition, negotiation allows segments to respond flexibly to changing market conditions when setting transfer prices. One transfer price may be appropriate in a time of idle capacity and another when demand increases and operations approach full capacity.

To increase segment managers' willingness to accommodate one another's needs and benefit the organization as a whole, top managers rely on both formal and informal communications. They may informally ask segment managers to be good company citizens and to sacrifice results for the good of the organization. They may also formalize this communication by basing performance evaluation and rewards on company-wide as well as segment results. In the case of our outdoor equipment maker, the contribution to the company as a whole, $70,000 in the idle capacity case, could be split between the Fabric and Tent Divisions, perhaps equally, perhaps in proportion to the variable costs of each, or perhaps via negotiation.

Previous sections have pointed out that there is seldom a single transfer price that will ensure the desired decisions. The "correct" transfer price depends on the economic and legal circumstances and the decision at hand. We may want one transfer for goal congruence and a second to spur managerial effort. Furthermore, the optimal price for either may differ from that employed for tax reporting or for other external needs.

Income taxes, property taxes, and tariffs often influence the setting of transfer prices so that the firm as a whole will benefit, even though the performance of a segment may suffer. For example, to maximize tax deductions for percentage depletion allowances, which are based on revenue, a petroleum company may want to transfer crude oil to other segments at as high a price as legally possible.

Transfer pricing is also influenced in some situations by fair-trade and antitrust laws. Because of the differences in national tax structures around the world or because of the differences in the incomes of various divisions and subsidiaries, the firm may wish to shift profits and "dump" goods, if legally possible.

These considerations further illustrate the limits of decentralization where heavy interdependencies exist and explain why the same company may use different transfer prices for different purposes.

Multinational Transfer Pricing

Transfer-pricing policies of domestic companies focus on goal congruence and motivation. In multinational companies, other factors may dominate. For example, multinational companies use transfer prices to minimize worldwide income taxes, import duties, and tariffs.

Suppose a division in a high-income-tax-rate country produces a subcomponent for another division in a low-income-tax-rate country. By setting a low transfer price, most of the profit from the production can be recognized in the low-income-tax-rate country, thereby minimizing taxes. Likewise, items produced by divisions in a low-income-tax-rate country and transferred to a division in a high-income-tax-rate country should have a high transfer price to minimize taxes.

Sometimes income-tax effects are offset by import duties. Usually import duties are based on the price paid for an item, whether bought from an outside company or transferred from another division. Therefore, low transfer prices generally lead to low import duties.

Of course, tax authorities recognize the incentive to set transfer prices to minimize taxes and import duties. Therefore, most countries have restrictions on allowable transfer prices.

Consider an item produced by Division A in a country with a 25 percent income tax rate and transferred to Division B in a country with a 50 percent income tax rate. In addition, an import duty equal to 20 percent of the price of the item is assessed. Suppose the full unit cost of the item is $100 and the variable cost is $60.

PERSPECTIVES ON **DECISION-MAKING**

E-Accountibility

The days are over when technology shopping lists and three-page security policies were a good enough network security planning method for almost any medium to large size corporation.

It used to be that IT management would seek funding approval for a list of the usual appliances, such as firewalls and anti-virus tools, and the computers to run them on. Then the contest began to decide exactly how much money was appropriate for the security technology, with no formal means of cost justification. The IT group was really on its own to select and implement the technology. Unfortunately, most IT people in most companies are not security specialists and only have a cursory understanding of the needs and methodology to properly secure a company's assets. Executives, including board members, really only approved dollars and did not get involved with security any further,

This model is completely outdated. Executives must take an active, ongoing roll in the security process within their company. There are four compelling reasons why executives nee to take on this responsibility:

1. Avoidance of revenue losses.
2. Executives are held accountable for the costs and resulting liability of security breaches.
3. It is now recognized that network security is a mainstream business process, which can only be man dated and directed by senior management.
4. Trading partners sharing important information, or who are depending on accuracy of e-transactions, are demanding to see their e-partners' network security audits and policies.

For your eyes only

A recent example of new legal obligations in network security is the enactment of Bill C-6, the Personal Information Protection and Electronic Documents Act, which provides that:

4.1.3 An organization is responsible for personal information in its possession or custody, including information that has been transferred to a third party for processing. The organization shall use contractual or other means to provide a comparable level of protection while the information is being processed by a third party.

4.1.4 Organizations shall implement policies and practices to give effect to the principles, including:

    a. implementing procedures to protect personal information;

b. establishing procedures to receive and respond to complaints and inquiries;

c. training staff and communicating to staff information about the organization's policies and practices; and

d. developing information to explain the organization's policies and procedures.

4.7.1 Personal information shall be protected by security safeguards and appropriate to the sensitivity of the information. The security safeguards shall protect personal information against loss or theft, as well as unauthorized access, disclosure, copying, use, or modification.

Source: Ron Lepofsky and Thomas Adler, "E-Accountability: Why network security is an executive function," *CMA Management*, November 2000, pp. 38–40.

If tax authorities allow either variable or full-cost transfer prices, which should be chosen? By transferring at $100 rather than $60, the company gains $2 per unit:

Effect of transferring at $100 instead of at $60:	
Income of A is $40 higher; therefore A pays	
25% × $40 more income taxes	$(10)
Income of B is $40 lower; therefore B pays	
50% × $40 less income taxes	20
Import duty is paid by B on an additional $100 - $60 = $40;	
therefore B pays 20% × $40 more duty	(8)
Net savings from transferring at $100 instead of $60	$ 2

Companies may also use transfer prices to avoid financial restrictions imposed by some governments. For example, a country might restrict the amount of dividends paid to foreign owners. It may be easier for a company to get cash from a foreign division as payment for items transferred than as cash dividends.

In summary, transfer pricing is more complex in a multinational company than it is in a domestic company. Multinational companies have more objectives to be achieved through transfer-pricing policies, and some of the objectives often conflict with one another. In fact, companies use a variety of transfer-price methods and may also use different methods for their domestic transfers versus international transfers. The following table provides the results of a recent survey that demonstrates this point.

SUMMARY PROBLEM FOR YOUR REVIEW

Problem One

Examine Exhibit 15-1. In addition to the data there, suppose the Fabric Division has annual fixed manufacturing costs of $800,000 and expected annual production of 500,000 square metres. The "fully allocated cost" per square metre was computed as follows:

Variable costs per square metre	$8.00
Fixed costs, $800,000 ÷ 500,000 square metres	1.60
Fully allocated cost per square metre	$9.60

Therefore, the "fully allocated cost" of the five square metres required for one tent is 5 × $9.60 = $48.

Assume that the Fabric Division has idle capacity. The Tent Division is considering whether to buy enough fabric for 10,000 tents. Each tent will be sold for $100. The additional costs shown in Exhibit 15-1 for the Tent Division would prevail. If transfers were based on fully allocated cost, would the Tent Division manager buy? Explain. Would the company as a whole benefit if the Tent Division manager decided to buy? Explain.

Solution

The Tent Division manager would not buy. Fully allocated costing may occasionally lead to dysfunctional decisions. The resulting transfer price of $48 would make the acquisition of the fabric unattractive to the Tent Division. As Exhibit 15-1 shows, the company as a whole would benefit by $70,000 (10,000 tents × $7) if the fabric were transferred.

The major lesson here is that, when idle capacity exists in the supplier division, transfer prices based on fully allocated costs may induce the wrong decisions. Working in her own best interests, the Tent Division manager has no incentive to buy from the Fabric Division.

Tent Division:			
Sales price of final product			$100
Deduct costs:			
Transfer price paid to the Fabric Division			
(fully allocated cost)		$48	
Additional costs (from Exhibit 10-1):			
Processing	$41		
Selling	12	53	
Total costs to the Tent Division			101
Contribution to profit of the Tent Division			$ −1
Contribution to company as a whole			
(from Exhibit 10-1)			$ 7

PERFORMANCE MEASURES AND MANAGEMENT CONTROL

Transfer pricing affects responsibility centre reporting, thereby affecting the performance measures of responsibility. This section looks more generally at how performance measures affect managers' incentives.

Motivation, Performance, Rewards

Exhibit 15-2 shows the criteria and choices faced by top management when designing a management control system. Using the criterion of cost-benefit and the motivational criteria of goal congruence and effort, top management chooses responsibility centres (e.g., cost centre versus profit centre), performance measures, and rewards. As used in this context, **incentives** are defined as those informal and formal performance measures and rewards that enhance goal congruence and managerial effort. For example, how the $70,000 contribution in Exhibit 15-1 is split between the Fabric and Tent Divisions affects the measures of their performance. In turn, the performance measures may affect the managers' rewards.

Numerous performance measurement choices have been described in this book. Examples include whether to use tight or loose standards, whether to measure divisional performance by contribution margins or operating incomes, and whether to use both financial and nonfinancial measures of performance.

Research about rewards has generated a basic principle that is simple and important: managers tend to focus their efforts in areas where performance is measured and where their performance affects rewards. Research also shows that the more objective the measures of performance, the more likely the manager will provide effort. Thus accounting measures, which provide relatively objective evaluations of performance, are important. Moreover, if individuals believe that there is no connection between their behaviour and their measure of performance, they will not see how to alter their performance to affect their rewards.

The choice of rewards clearly belongs with an overall system of management control. Rewards may be both monetary and nonmonetary. Examples include pay raises, bonuses, promotion, praise, self-satisfaction, elaborate offices, and private dining rooms. However, the design of a reward system is mainly the concern of top managers, who frequently get advice from many sources besides accountants.

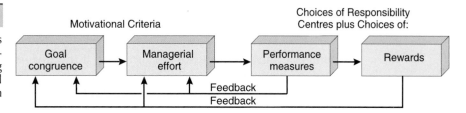

Agency Theory, Performance, Rewards, and Risk

Agency Theory. A theory used to describe the formal choices of performance measures and rewards.

Linking rewards to performance is desirable. But often a manager's performance cannot be measured directly. For example, responsibility centre results may be measured easily, but a manager's effect on those results (that is, managerial performance) may not. Ideally, rewards should be based on managerial performance, but in practice the rewards usually depend on the financial results in the manager's responsibility centre. Managerial performance and responsibility centre results are certainly related, but factors beyond a manager's control also affect results. The greater the influence of noncontrollable factors on responsibility centre results, the more problems there are in using the results to represent a manager's performance.

Economists describe the formal choices of performance measures and rewards as **agency theory**. For top management to hire a manager, both need to agree to an employment contract that includes specification of a performance measure and how it will affect rewards.[1] For example, a manager might receive a bonus of 15 percent of her salary if her responsibility centre achieves its budgeted profit. According to agency theory, employment contracts will trade off three factors:

1. *Incentive.* The more a manager's reward depends on a performance measure, the more incentive the manager has to take actions that maximize that measure. Top management should define the performance measure to promote *goal congruence* and base enough reward on it to achieve *managerial effort*.
2. *Risk.* The greater the influence of uncontrollable factors on a manager's reward, the more risk the manager bears. People generally avoid risk, so managers must be paid more if they are expected to bear more risk. Creating incentive by linking rewards to responsibility centre results,

---

[1] Often performance measures and rewards are implicit. For example, promotion is a reward, but usually the requirements for promotion are not explicit.

which is generally desirable, has the undesirable effect of imposing risk on managers.

3. *Cost of measuring performance.* The incentive versus risk trade-off is not necessary if a manager's performance is perfectly measured. Why? Because then a manager could be paid a fixed amount if he or she performs as expected and nothing if not. Whether to perform or not is completely controllable by the manager and observation of the level of performance is all that is necessary to determine the compensation earned. But directly measuring a manager's performance is usually expensive and sometimes infeasible. Responsibility centre results are more readily available. The cost-benefit criterion usually indicates that perfect measurement of a manager's performance is not worth its cost.

Consider a concert manager hired by a group of investors to promote and administer an outdoor rock performance. If the investors cannot directly measure the manager's effort and judgment, they would probably pay a bonus that depended on the economic success of the concert. The bonus would motivate the manager to put his effort toward generating a profit. On the other hand, it creates risk. Factors such as bad weather could also affect the concert's economic success. The manager might do an outstanding job and still not receive a bonus. Suppose the investors offer a contract with part guaranteed pay and part bonus. A larger bonus portion compared with the guaranteed portion creates more incentive, but it also means a larger expected total payment to compensate the manager for the added risk.

MEASURES OF PROFITABILITY

Return on Investment (ROI)

OBJECTIVE 7

Compute return on investment (ROI), residual income (RI), and economic value added (EVA) and contrast them as criteria for judging the performance of organization segments.

Return on Investment (ROI). A measure of income or profit divided by the investment required to obtain that income or profit.

A favourite objective of top management is to maximize profitability. Segment managers are often evaluated based on their segment's profitability. The trouble is that profitability does not mean the same thing to all people. Is it net income? Income before taxes? Net income percentage based on revenue? Is it an absolute amount? A percentage? In this section we consider the strengths and weaknesses of several commonly used measures.

Too often, managers stress net income or income percentages without tying the measure into the investment associated with generating the income. To say that Project A has an income of $200,000 and Project B has an income of $150,000 is an insufficient statement about profitability. A better test of profitability is the rate of **return on investment (ROI)**—income or profit divided by the investment required to obtain that income or profit. Given the same risks, for any given amount of resources required, the investor wants the maximum income. If Project A requires an investment of $500,000, while Project B requires only $150,000, all other things being equal, where would you put your money?

$$\text{ROI} = \frac{\text{income}}{\text{investment}}$$

$$\text{ROI Project A} = \frac{\$200,000}{\$500,000} = 40\%$$

$$\text{ROI Project B} = \frac{\$150,000}{\$150,000} = 100\%$$

ROI is a useful common denominator. It can be compared with rates inside and outside the organization and with opportunities in other projects and industries. It is affected by two major ingredients:

$$\text{ROI} = \frac{\text{income}}{\text{invested capital}}$$

$$= \frac{\text{income}}{\text{revenue}} \times \frac{\text{revenue}}{\text{invested capital}}$$

$$= \text{income percentage of revenue} \times \text{capital turnover}$$

Income Percentage of Revenue. Income divided by revenue.

Capital Turnover. Revenue divided by invested capital.

The terms of this equation are deliberately vague at this point because various versions of income, revenue, and invested capital are possible. As you can see, the rate of return is the result of combining two items, **income percentage of revenue**—income divided by revenue—and **capital turnover**—revenue divided by invested capital. An improvement in either without changing the other will improve the rate of return on invested capital.

Consider an example of these relationships:

	Rate of Return On Invested Capital	=	Income Revenue	x	Revenue Invested Capital
Present Outlook	20%	=	$\frac{16}{100}$	x	$\frac{100}{80}$
Alternatives:					
1. Increase income percentage by reducing expenses	25%	=	$\frac{20}{100}$	x	$\frac{100}{80}$
2. Increase turnover by decreasing investment in inventories	25%	=	$\frac{16}{100}$	x	$\frac{100}{64}$

Alternative 1 is a popular way to improve performance. Alert managers try to decrease expenses without reducing sales or to boost sales without increasing related expenses. Alternative 2 is less obvious, but it may be a quicker way to improve performance. Increasing the turnover of invested capital means generating higher revenue for each dollar invested in such assets as cash, receivables, inventories, or equipment. There is an optimal level of investment in these assets. Having too much is wasteful, but having too little may hurt credit standing and the ability to compete for sales. Increasing turnover is one of the advantages of implementing the just-in-time philosophy.

Residual Income (RI) and Economic Value Added (EVA)

Residual Income. Net income less "imputed" interest.

Cost of Capital. What a firm must pay to acquire more capital, whether or not it actually has to acquire more capital to take on a project.

Most managers agree that measuring return in relation to investment provides the ultimate test of profitability. ROI is one such comparison. However, some companies favour emphasizing an absolute amount of income rather than a percentage rate of return. They use **residual income (RI)**, defined as net income less "imputed" interest. "Imputed" interest refers to the **cost of capital**—what the firm must pay to acquire more capital—whether or not it actually has to acquire more capital to take on this project. In short, RI tells you how much your company's operating income exceeds what it is paying for capital. For example, suppose a division's net income was $900,000, the average invested capital in the division for the year was $10 million, and the corporate headquarters assessed an imputed interest charge of 8 percent:

Divisional net income after taxes	$900,000
Minus imputed interest on average invested	
capital (.08 x $10,000,000)	800,000
Equals residual income	$100,000

Economic Value Added (EVA). Net operating income minus the after-tax weighted-average cost of capital times the sum of the long-term liabilities and shareholders' equity.

There are several different ways to calculate residual income depending on how we choose to define the terms used. For example, some companies define "average invested capital" as funds provided by long-term creditors and shareholders (that is, long-term liabilities plus shareholders' equity). This variant of residual income is called economic value added (EVA), a term coined and marketed by Stern Stewart & Co. **Economic value added (EVA)** equals net operating income minus the after-tax weighted-average cost of capital multiplied by the sum of long-term liabilities and shareholders' equity.

$$\begin{pmatrix} \text{Economic value} \\ \text{added (EVA)} \end{pmatrix} = \begin{pmatrix} \text{Net operating} \\ \text{income} \end{pmatrix} - \left[\begin{pmatrix} \text{Weighted-average} \\ \text{cost of capital} \end{pmatrix} \times \begin{pmatrix} \text{Long-term} \\ \text{liabilities} \end{pmatrix} + \begin{pmatrix} \text{Shareholders'} \\ \text{equity} \end{pmatrix} \right]$$

AT&T
www.att.com

Coca-Cola
www.cocacola.com

CSX Corporation
www.csx.com

FMC Corporation
www.fmc.com

The weighted-average cost of capital is the cost of long-term liabilities and shareholders' equity weighted by their relative size for the company or division. RI and EVA have received much attention recently as scores of companies are adopting them as financial performance measures. AT & T, Coca-Cola, CSX, FMC, and Quaker Oats claim that EVA-motivated decisions have increased shareholder value. All these companies are successful. Why? Because they do a better job than their competitors at allocating, managing, and redeploying scarce capital resources (fixed assets such as heavy equipment, computers, real estate, and working capital). For example, the following data compare PepsiCo and Coca-Cola.

	PEPSICO.	COCA-COLA
1988 Sales revenue ($billions)	$12	$ 8
1997 Sales revenue ($billions)	$21	$19
Invested capital ($billions)	$20.1	$17.5

PepsiCo. had revenue growth of 75 percent compared to 138 percent for Coca-Cola. But both companies are in business to create wealth for their shareholders. So, which company created more value for its shareholders? PepsiCo.'s market value in 1999 was $48 billion but Coca-Cola's market value was

$144 billion. Thus, compared to PepsiCo, Coca-Cola created over three times the market value for its shareholders with less than half the invested capital. Coca-Cola began practising EVA in the early 1980s.

ROI or Residual Income?

Why do some companies prefer residual income (or EVA) to ROI? The ROI approach shows

Divisional net income after taxes	$ 900,000
Average invested capital	$10,000,000
Return on investment	9%

Under ROI, the basic message is, "Go forth and maximize your rate of return, a percentage." Thus, if performance is measured by ROI, managers of divisions currently earning 20 percent may be reluctant to invest in projects at 15 percent because doing so would reduce their average ROI.

However, from the viewpoint of the company as a whole, top management may want this division manager to accept projects that earn 15 percent. Why? Suppose the company's cost of capital is 8 percent. Investing in projects earning 15 percent will increase the company's profitability. When performance is measured by residual income, managers tend to invest in any project earning more than the imputed interest rate and thus raise the firm's profits. That is, the residual income approach fosters goal congruence and managerial effort. Its basic message is, "Go forth and maximize residual income, an absolute amount."

General Electric was one of the first companies to adopt a residual income approach. Consider two divisions of GE as an example. Division A has net income of $200,000; Division B has $50,000. Both have average invested capital of $1 million. Suppose a project is proposed that can be undertaken by either A or B. The project will earn 15 percent annually on a $500,000 investment, or $75,000 a year. The cost of capital for the project is 8 percent. ROI and residual income with and without the project are shown next.

Suppose you were the manager of Division A. If your evaluation were based on ROI, would you invest in the project? No. It would decrease your ROI from 20 percent to 18.3 percent. But suppose you were in Division B. Would you invest? Yes, because ROI increases from 5 percent to 8.3 percent. In general, in companies using ROI the least profitable divisions have more incentive to invest in new projects than do the most profitable divisions.

	WITHOUT PROJECT		WITH PROJECT	
	A	**B**	**A**	**B**
Net income	$ 200,000	$ 50,000	$ 275,000	$ 125,000
Invested capital	$1,000,000	$1,000,000	$1,500,000	$1,500,000
ROI (net income ÷ invested capital)	20%	5%	18.3%	8.3%
Capital charge (8% × invested capital)	$ 80,000	$ 80,000	$ 120,000	$ 120,000
Residual income (net income – capital charge)	$ 120,000	$ (30,000)	$ 155,000	$ 5,000

Now suppose you are evaluated using residual income. The project would be equally attractive to either division. Residual income increases by $35,000 for each division, $155,000 − $120,000 for A and $5,000 − ($30,000) for B. Both divisions have the same incentive to invest in the project, and the incentive depends on the profitability of the project compared with the cost of the capital used by the project.

In general, use of residual income will promote goal congruence and lead to better decisions than using ROI. Still, a majority of companies use ROI. Why? Probably because it is easier for managers to understand and facilitates comparison across divisions. Furthermore, combining ROI with appropriate growth and profit targets can minimize its dysfunctional motivations.

PERSPECTIVES ON **P O D M** DECISION-MAKING

Aligning IT Investment with Business Strategy

To align investments for success, introduce a prioritization process that looks at more than simple return on investment. Focus on key strategic alignment dimensions in each of the following areas:

- **Customer benefit** — Assign value to investments that bring value to your customers. Improving service times, providing information where and when it's expected, and adding new locations for the use of your most valued customers will improve the health of the firm.
- **Return on investment** — You shouldn't look at just this issue, but you should make a positive ROI with a specific hurdle rate one criterion you give weight to. ROI is still important, because it supports short-term shareholder value. But, it isn't everything.
- **Business partner benefit** — Give weight to the investment's adding value for distributors, suppliers, and other businesses you collaborate with. These partners are generally critical to our success in the marketplace. Be sure that you've accounted for them in your strategy, and your weighting scheme.
- **Employee benefit** — Our employees provide the brains and the means for implementing our business strategies. Give appropriate weighting to the impact of an investment on their satisfaction and effectiveness.
- **Competitive strategy alignment** — Above all else, be clear about your competitive strategy, and provide significant weighting to alignment of investments with this strategy. If you strive to compete through price, then focus on being the low-cost provider of a good or service. If you want brand allegiance, then focus on real and perceived quality that will keep customers with you for a long time. Whether you are going global, or going for a niche with less competition, use alignment with your strategy to weight IT investments.

The following table shows how a company pursuing a high-quality, customer-driven growth strategy might prioritize several different IT investments. Clearly, if we pursue different strategies, we would adjust our weightings, and alter our investment patterns. Still, if customer retention and satisfaction are paramount, customer-oriented investments would come out as important investments.

continued

Potential investment	Customer benefit	Return on investment	Business partner benefit	Employee benefit	Competitive strategy	Total
Weight	20%	20%	10%	10%	40%	100%
Interactive customer service	100	30	10	80	80	67
Direct marketing	30	100	30	10	40	46
Direct customer reporting	80	10	20	70	90	63
New general ledger system	10	20	30	30	20	20

Source: Reprinted from an article appearing in *CMA Management* by Ron Shelby, November 1997, with permission of the Society of Management Accountants of Canada.

A CLOSER LOOK AT INVESTED CAPITAL

OBJECTIVE 8

Compare the advantages and disadvantages of various bases for measuring the invested capital used by organization segments.

To apply either ROI or residual income, both income and invested capital must be measured. However, there are many different interpretations of these concepts. To understand what ROI or residual income figures really mean, you must first determine how invested capital and income are being defined and measured. We discussed various definitions of income in Chapter 14, so we will not repeat them here. We will, however, explore various definitions of invested capital.

Defining Invested Capital

Consider the following balance sheet classifications:

Current assets	$ 400,000	Current liabilities	$ 200,000
Property, plant, and equipment	800,000	Long-term liabilities	400,000
Construction in progress	100,000	Shareholders' equity	700,000
Total assets	$1,300,000	Total liab. and shr. eq.	$1,300,000

Possible definitions of invested capital include

1. *Total assets.* All assets are included, $1,300,000.
2. *Total assets employed.* All assets except agreed-upon exclusions of vacant land or construction in progress, $1,300,000 – $100,000 = $1,200,000.
3. *Total assets less current liabilities.* All assets except that portion supplied by short-term creditors, $1,300,000 – $200,000 = $1,100,000. This is sometimes expressed as *long-term invested capital*; note that it can also be

computed by adding the long-term liabilities and the shareholders' equity, $400,000 + $700,000 = $1,100,000, which is the definition for EVA.

4. *Shareholders' equity.* Focuses on the investment of the owners of the business, $700,000.

All the above may be computed as averages for the period under review. These averages may be based simply on the beginning and ending balances or on more complicated averages that weigh changes in investments through the months.

For measuring the performance of division managers, any of the three asset definitions is recommended rather than shareholders' equity. If the division manager's mission is to put *all* assets to their best use without regard to their financing, then total assets is best. If top management directs the manager to carry extra assets that are not currently productive, then total assets employed is best. If the manager has direct control over obtaining short-term credit and bank loans, then total assets less current liabilities is best. A key behavioural factor in choosing an investment definition is that *managers will focus attention on reducing those assets and increasing those liabilities that are included in the definition.* In practice, most companies using ROI or residual income include all assets in invested capital, and about half deduct some portion of current liabilities.

A few companies allocate long-term debt to their divisions and thus have an approximation of the shareholders' equity in each division. However, this practice has doubtful merit. Division managers typically have little responsibility for the long-term *financial* management of their divisions, as distinguished from *operating* management. The investment bases of division managers from two companies could differ radically if one company has heavy long-term debt and the other is debt-free.

Asset Allocation to Divisions

Just as cost allocations affect income, asset allocations affect the invested capital of particular divisions. The aim is to allocate this capital in a manner that will be goal-congruent, will spur managerial effort, and will recognize segment autonomy insofar as possible. (As long as the managers feel that they are being treated uniformly, though, they tend to be more tolerant of the imperfections of the allocation.)

A frequent criterion for asset allocation is avoidability. That is, the amount allowable to any given segment for the purpose of evaluating the division's performance is the amount that the corporation as a whole could avoid by not having that segment. Commonly used bases for allocation, when assets are not directly identifiable with a specific division, include the following:

ASSET CLASS	POSSIBLE ALLOCATION BASE
Corporate cash	Budgeted cash needs, as discussed shortly
Receivables	Sales weighted by payment terms
Inventories	Budgeted sales or usage
Plant and equipment	Usage of services in terms of long-run forecasts of demand or area occupied

The allocation base should be the activity that caused the asset to be acquired. Where the allocation of an asset would indeed be arbitrary (that is, no causal activity can be identified), many managers feel that it is better not to allocate.

Should cash be included in a division's investment if the cash balances are strictly controlled by corporate headquarters? Arguments can be made for both sides, but the manager is usually regarded as being responsible for the volume of business generated by the division. In turn, this volume is likely to have a direct effect on the overall cash needs of the corporation.

A popular allocation base for cash is sales dollars. However, the allocation of cash on the basis of sales dollars seldom gets at the economic rationale of cash holdings. As Chapter 12 explains, cash needs are influenced by a host of factors, including payment terms of customers and creditors.

Central control of cash is usually undertaken to reduce the holdings from what would be used if each division had a separate account. Fluctuations in cash needs of each division offset one another somewhat. For example, Division A might have a cash deficiency of $1 million in February, but Division B might have an offsetting cash excess of $1 million. Taken together for the year, Divisions A, B, C, D, and E might require a combined investment in cash of, say, $16 million if each were independent entities, but only $8 million if cash were controlled centrally. Hence, if Division C would ordinarily require a $4-million investment in cash as a separate entity, it would be allocated an investment of only $2 million as a segment of a company where cash was controlled centrally.

Valuation of Assets

Whatever assets are included in a division's invested capital must be measured in some way. Should the assets contained in the investment base be valued at *gross book value* (original cost) or *net book value* (original cost less accumulated amortization)? Should values be based on historical cost or some version of current value? Practice is overwhelmingly in favour of using net book value based on historical cost. Very few firms use replacement cost or any other type of current value. Historical cost has been widely criticized for many years as providing a faulty basis for decision making and performance evaluation. As previously pointed out, historical costs *per se* are irrelevant for making economic decisions. Despite these criticisms, managers have been slow to depart from historical cost.

Why is historical cost so widely used? Some critics would say that sheer ignorance is the explanation. But a more persuasive answer comes from cost-benefit analysis. Accounting systems are costly. Historical records must be kept for many legal purposes, so they are already in place. No additional money must be spent to evaluate performance based on historical costs. Furthermore, many top managers believe that such a system provides the desired goal congruence and managerial effort and that a more sophisticated system will not radically improve collective operating decisions. Some believe, in fact, that using current values would cause confusion unless huge sums were spent educating personnel.

Historical costs may even improve some decisions because they are more objective than current costs. Moreover, managers can better predict the historical-cost effects of their decisions, so their decisions may be more influenced by the control system. Furthermore, the uncertainty involved with current-cost measures may impose undesirable risks on the managers. In short, the historical-cost system may be superior for the *routine* evaluation of performance. In nonroutine instances, such as replacing equipment or deleting a product line, managers should conduct special studies to gather any current valuations that seem relevant.

Finally, while historical-cost systems are common, most well-managed organizations do not use historical-cost systems alone. The alternatives available to managers are not

```
┌──────────┐              ┌──────────┐
│ Current- │              │Historical-│
│  value   │   versus     │   cost    │
│  system  │              │  system   │
└──────────┘              └──────────┘
```

More accurately stated, the alternatives are

```
┌──────────────────────┐              ┌──────────────────────┐
│ Historical Cost:     │   versus     │ Current Value:       │
│ budget versus actual │              │ budget versus actual │
└──────────────────────┘              └──────────────────────┘
```

A budget system, whether based on historical cost or current value, causes managers to worry about inflation. Most managers seem to prefer to concentrate on improving their existing historical-cost budget system.

In sum, our cost-benefit approach provides no universal answers with respect to such controversial issues as historical values versus current values or return on investment versus residual income. Instead, using a cost-benefit test, each organization must judge for itself whether an alternative control system or accounting technique will improve collective decision making. The latter is the primary criterion.

Too often, there are pro-and-con discussions about which alternative is closer to perfection or truer than another in some logical sense. The cost-benefit approach is not concerned with "truth" or "perfection" by itself. Instead it asks, "Do you think your perceived 'truer' or 'more logical' system is worth its added cost? Or will our existing imperfect system provide about the same set of decisions if it is skillfully administered?"

Plant and Equipment: Gross or Net?

Net Book Value. The original cost of an asset less any accumulated amortization.

Gross Book Value. The original cost of an asset before deducting accumulated amortization.

In valuing assets, it is important to distinguish between net and gross book values. **Net book value** is the original cost of an asset less any accumulated amortization. **Gross book value** is the original cost of an asset before deducting accumulated amortization. Most companies use net book value in calculating their investment base. However, according to a recent survey, a significant minority use gross book value. The proponents of gross book value maintain that it facilitates comparisons between years and between plants or divisions.

Consider an example of a $600,000 piece of equipment with a three-year life and no residual value.

The rate of return on net book value goes up as the equipment ages. It could increase even if operating income gradually declined through the years. In contrast, the rate of return on gross book value is unchanged if operating income does not change. The rate would decrease if operating income gradually declined through the years.

	OPERATING INCOME BEFORE AMORTIZATION	AMORTIZATION	OPERATING INCOME	AVERAGE INVESTMENT			
YEAR				NET BOOK VALUE*	RATE OF RETURN	GROSS BOOK VALUE	RATE OF RETURN
1	$260,000	$200,000	$60,000	$500,000	12%	$600,000	10%
2	260,000	200,000	60,000	300,000	20%	600,000	10%
3	260,000	200,000	60,000	100,000	60%	600,000	10%

* ($600,000 − [1/2 × 200,000]); ($400,000 − [1/2 × 200,000]); etc.

The advocates of using net book value maintain that

1. It is less confusing because it is consistent with the assets shown on the conventional balance sheet and with the net income computations.
2. The major criticism of net book value is not peculiar to its use for ROI purposes. It is really a criticism of using historical cost as a basis for evaluation.

The effect on motivation should be considered when choosing between net and gross book value. Managers evaluated using gross book value will tend to replace assets sooner than will managers in firms using net book value. Consider a four-year-old machine with an original cost of $1,000 and net book value of $200. It can be replaced by a new machine that costs $1,500. The choice of net or gross book value does not affect net income. However, the investment base increases from $200 to $1,500 in a net-book-value firm, but it increases only $500 to $1,500 in a gross-book-value firm. To maximize ROI or residual income, managers want a low investment base. Managers in firms using net book value will tend to keep old assets with their low book value. Those in firms using gross book value will have less incentive to keep old assets. Therefore, to motivate managers to use state-of-the-art production technology, gross asset value is preferred. Net asset value promotes a more conservative approach to asset replacement.

KEYS TO SUCCESSFUL PERFORMANCE MEASURES

Successful management control systems have several key factors in addition to appropriate measures of profitability. We next explore some of these factors.

Focus on Controllability

As Chapter 14 explained, a distinction should be made between the performance of the division manager and the performance of the division as an investment by the corporation. Managers should be evaluated on the basis of their controllable performance (in many cases some controllable contribution in relation to controllable investment). However, decisions such as increasing or decreasing investment in a division are based on the economic viability of the *division*, not the performance of its *managers*.

This distinction helps to clarify some vexing difficulties. For example, top management may want to use an investment base to gauge the economic performance of a retail store, but the *manager* may best be judged by focusing on income and forgetting about any investment allocations. If investment is assigned to the manager, the aim should be to assign only that investment the manager can control. Controllability depends on what *decisions* managers can make regarding the size of the investment base. In a highly decentralized company, for instance, managers can influence the size of these assets and can exercise judgment regarding the appropriate amount of short-term credit and perhaps some long-term credit.

Management by Objectives (MBO). The joint formulation by a manager and his/her superior of a set of goals and plans for achieving the goals for a forthcoming period.

Management by objectives (MBO) describes the joint formulation by a manager and his or her superior of a set of goals and of plans for achieving the goals for a forthcoming period. For our purposes here, the terms *goals* and *objectives* are synonyms. The plans often take the form of a responsibility accounting budget (together with supplementary goals such as levels of management training and safety that may not be incorporated into the accounting budget). The manager's performance is then evaluated in relation to these agreed-upon budgeted objectives.

Regardless of whether it is so labelled, a management-by-objectives approach lessens the complaints about lack of controllability because of its stress on *budgeted results*. That is, a budget is negotiated between a particular manager and his or her superior for a *particular* time period and a *particular* set of expected outside and inside influences. In this way, a manager may more readily accept an assignment to a less successful segment. This is preferable to a system that emphasizes absolute profitability for its own sake. Unless focus is placed on currently attainable results, able managers will be reluctant to accept responsibility for segments that are in economic trouble.

Thus, skillful budgeting and intelligent performance evaluation will go a long way toward overcoming the common lament: "I'm being held responsible for items beyond my control."

Tailoring Budgets for Managers

Many of the troublesome motivational effects of performance evaluation systems can be minimized by the astute use of budgets. The importance of tailoring a budget to particular managers cannot be overemphasized. For example, either an ROI or a residual income system can promote goal congruence and managerial effort if top management gets everybody to focus on what is currently attainable in the forthcoming budget period. Typically, divisional managers do not have complete freedom to make major investment decisions without checking with senior management.

HIGHLIGHTS TO REMEMBER

As organizations grow, decentralization of some management functions becomes desirable. Decentralization immediately raises problems of obtaining decisions that are coordinated with the objectives of the organization as a whole. Ideally, planning and control systems should provide information that (a) aims managers toward decisions that are goal-congruent, (b) provides feedback (evaluation of performance) that improves managerial effort, and (c) preserves segment autonomy. Note that the common thread of these problems is motivation.

Profit centres are usually associated with heavily decentralized organizations, whereas cost centres are usually associated with heavily centralized organizations. However, profit centres and decentralization are separate ideas; one can exist without the other.

Transfer-pricing systems are often used as a means of communicating information among segments and of measuring their performance. Problems of transfer pricing and cost allocations are similar. Proper choices vary from situation to situation. Multinational companies use transfer prices to minimize worldwide income taxes and import duties, in addition to achieving goal congruence and motivation. Transfer prices can be based on costs, on market prices, or on negotiation. If the item can be sold to external customers, a transfer price based on market price is usually preferrable.

Choices of performance measures (such as return on investment and residual income) and rewards (such as bonuses and increases in salaries) can heavily affect goal congruence and managerial effort. To affect managerial behaviour, strong links must exist between effort, performance, and rewards.

ROI and residual income are measures of investment centre performance. Theorists tend to prefer residual income. Why? Because it focuses on an absolute amount of income after paying for the capital used. In practice,

ROI is more popular. Why? Probably because it is easier to understand and, though imperfect, leads to reasonably good motivations.

Both ROI and residual income require measures of income and invested capital. The way these items are measured can greatly affect managers' incentives.

SUMMARY PROBLEM FOR YOUR REVIEW

Problem One

Problem One appeared earlier in the chapter.

Problem Two

A division has assets of $200,000, current liabilities of $20,000, and net operating income of $60,000.

1. What is the division's ROI?
2. If interest is imputed at 14 percent, what is the residual income?
3. The weighted average cost of capital is 14 percent, what is the EVA?
4. What effects on management behaviour can be expected if ROI is used to gauge performance?
5. What effects on management behaviour can be expected if residual income is used to gauge performance?

Solution

1. $60,000 ÷ $200,000 = 30 percent.
2. $60,000 − .14 ($200,000) = $60,000 − $28,000 = $32,000.
3. EVA = $60,000 − .14($200,000 − $20,000)
            = $60,000 − $25,200
            = $34,800.
4. If ROI is used, the manager is prone to reject projects that do not earn a ROI of at least 30 percent. From the viewpoint of the organization as a whole, this may be undesirable because its best investment opportunities may lie in that division at a rate of, say, 22 percent. If a division is enjoying a high ROI, it is less likely to expand if it is judged via ROI than if it is judged via residual income or EVA.
5. If residual income or EVA is used, the manager is inclined to accept all projects whose expected rate of return exceeds the minimum desired rate. The manager's division is more likely to expand because his or her goal is to maximize a dollar amount rather than a rate.

ACCOUNTING VOCABULARY

agency theory *p. 701*
capital turnover *p. 703*
cost of capital *p. 704*
decentralization *p. 687*
dysfunctional behaviour *p. 695*
economic value added (EVA) *p. 704*
gross book value *p. 710*
incentives *p. 700*

income percentage of revenue *p. 703*
management by objectives (MBO) *p. 711*
net book value *p. 710*
residual income (RI) *p. 704*
return on investment (ROI) *p. 702*
segment autonomy *p. 688*
transfer prices *p. 689*

ASSIGNMENT MATERIAL

QUESTIONS

Q15-1 "Decentralization has benefits and costs." Name three of each.

Q15-2 Sophisticated accounting and communications systems aid decentralization. Explain how they accomplish this.

Q15-3 "The essence of decentralization is the use of profit centres." Do you agree? Explain.

Q15-4 Why is decentralization more popular in profit-seeking organizations than in nonprofit organizations?

Q15-5 What kinds of organizations find decentralization to be preferable to centralization?

Q15-6 Why are transfer-pricing systems needed?

Q15-7 Describe two problems that can arise when using actual full cost as a transfer price.

Q15-8 How does the presence or absence of idle capacity affect the optimal transfer-pricing policy?

Q15-9 "We use variable-cost transfer prices to ensure that no dysfunctional decisions are made." Discuss.

Q15-10 What is the major advantage of negotiated transfer prices? What is the major disadvantage?

Q15-11 Why does top management sometimes accept division managers' judgments, even if the division manager appears to be wrong?

Q15-12 Discuss two factors that affect multinational transfer prices but have little effect on purely domestic transfers.

Q15-13 According to agency theory, employment contracts trade off three factors. Name the three.

Q15-14 What is the major benefit of the ROI technique for measuring performance?

Q15-15 What two major items affect ROI?

Q15-16 "Both ROI and residual income use profit and invested capital to measure performance. Therefore, it really doesn't matter which we use." Do you agree? Explain.

Q15-17 Division A's ROI is 20 percent, and B's is 10 percent. Each manager is paid a bonus based on his or her division's ROI. Discuss whether each division manager would accept or reject a proposed project with a rate of return of 15 percent. Would either of them make a different decision if managers were evaluated using residual income with an imputed interest rate of 11 percent? Explain.

Q15-18 Give four possible definitions of invested capital that can be used in measuring ROI or residual income.

Q15-19 "Managers who use a historical-cost accounting system look backward at what something cost yesterday, instead of forward to what it will cost tomorrow." Do you agree? Why?

Q15-20 Company X uses net book value as a measure of invested capital when computing ROI. A division manager has suggested that the company change to using gross book value instead. What difference in motivation of division managers might result from such a change? Do you suppose most of the assets in the division of the manager proposing the change are relatively new or old? Why?

Q15-21 Describe management by objectives (MBO).

PROBLEMS

P15-1 VARIABLE COST AS TRANSFER PRICE. A desk calendar's variable cost is $5 and its market value is $6.25 at a transfer point from the Printing Division to the Binding Division. The Binding Division's variable cost of adding a simulated leather cover is $2.80, and the selling price of the final calendar is $8.50.

1. Prepare a tabulation of the contribution margin per unit for the Binding Division's performance and overall company performance under the two alternatives of (a) selling to outsiders at the transfer point and (b) adding the cover and then selling to outsiders.
2. As Binding Division manager, which alternative would you choose? Explain.

P15-2 MAXIMUM AND MINIMUM TRANSFER PRICE. Northland Company makes bicycles. Components are made in various divisions and transferred to the Western Division for assembly into final products. The Western Division can also buy components from external suppliers. The wheels are made in the Eastern Division, which also sells wheels to external customers. All divisions are profit centres and managers are free to negotiate transfer prices. Prices and costs for the Eastern and Western Divisions are

EASTERN DIVISION	
Sales price to external customers	$14
Internal transfer price	?
Costs:	
Variable costs per wheel	$9
Total fixed costs	$320,000
Budgeted production	64,000 wheels*
*Includes production for transfer to Western.	

WESTERN DIVISION	
Sales price to external customers	$175
Costs:	
Wheels, per bicycle	?
Other components, per bicycle	$90
Other variable costs, per bicycle	$20
Total fixed costs	$640,000
Budgeted production	16,000 bicycles

Fixed costs in both divisions will be unaffected by the transfer of wheels from the Eastern to the Western Division.

1. Compute the maximum transfer price per wheel the Western Division would be willing to pay to buy wheels from the Eastern Division.
2. Compute the minimum transfer price per wheel at which the Eastern Division would be willing to produce and sell wheels to the Western Division. Assume that Eastern has excess capacity.

P15-3   SIMPLE ROI CALCULATIONS.   Given the following data, compute

Sales	$140,000
Invested capital	$50,000
Return on investment	10%

1. Turnover of capital.
2. Net income.
3. Net income as a percentage of sales.

P15-4   SIMPLE ROI CALCULATIONS.   Fill in the blanks:

	DIVISION		
	A	**B**	**C**
Income percentage of revenue	7%	3%	%
Capital turnover	3		5
Rate of return on invested capital	%	24%	20%

P15-5   SIMPLE ROI AND RESIDUAL INCOME CALCULATIONS.   Consider the following data:

	DIVISION		
	X	**Y**	**Z**
Invested capital	$2,000,000	$ _____	$1,250,000
Income	$ _____	$ 182,000	$ 125,000
Revenue	$4,000,000	$3,640,000	$ _____
Income percentage of revenue	2.5%	%	%
Capital turnover	_____	_____	3
Rate of return on invested capital	%	14%	%

1. Prepare a similar tabular presentation, filling in all blanks.
2. Which division is the best performer? Explain.
3. Suppose each division is assessed an imputed interest rate of 10 percent on invested capital. Compute the residual income for each division.

P15-6   COMPARISON OF ASSET AND EQUITY BASES.   Alamo Footwear has assets of $2 million and a long-term, 10 percent debt of $800,000. Shirley Shoes has assets of $2 million and no long-term debt. The annual operating income (before interest) of both companies is $500,000.

1. Compute the rate of return on
   a. Assets available
   b. Shareholders' equity
2. Evaluate the relative merits of each base for appraising operating management.

P15-7 RATE OF RETURN AND TRANSFER PRICING. Consider the following data regarding budgeted operations of the Winnipeg Division of Yoshita Custom Signs:

Average available assets	
Receivables	$200,000
Inventories	250,000
Plant and equipment, net	450,000
Total	$900,000
Fixed overhead	$300,000
Variable costs	$2 per unit
Desired rate of return on	
average available assets	25 percent
Expected volume	75,000 units

1. **a.** What average unit sales price is needed to obtain the desired rate of return on average available assets?
   b. What would be the expected asset turnover?
   c. What would be the operating income percentage on dollar sales?
2. **a.** If the selling price is as computed above, what rate of return will be earned on available assets if sales volume is 90,000 units.
   b. If sales volume is 60,000 units?
3. Assume that 22,500 units are to be sold to another division of the same company and that only 52,500 units can be sold to outside customers. The other division manager has balked at a tentative selling price of $8. She has offered $4.50, claiming that she can manufacture the units herself for that price. The manager of the selling division has examined his own data. He had decided that he could eliminate $60,000 of inventories, $90,000 of plant and equipment, and $22,500 of fixed overhead if he did not sell to the other division and sold only 52,500 units to outside customers. Should he sell for $4.50? Show computations to support your answer.

P15-8 FINDING UNKNOWNS. Consider the following data:

	DIVISION		
	J	K	L
Income	$140,000	$	$
Revenue	$	$	$
Invested capital	$	$4,000,000	$16,000,000
Income percentage of revenue	7%	4%	%
Capital turnover	4		3
Rate of return on invested capital	%	20%	15%
Imputed interest rate on			
invested capital	20%	12%	%
Residual income	$	$	$ 480,000

1. Prepare a similar tabular presentation, filling in all blanks.
2. Which division is the best performer? Explain.

P15-9 PROFIT CENTRES AND TRANSFER PRICING IN AN AUTOMOBILE DEALERSHIP. A large automobile dealership is installing a responsibility accounting system and three profit centres: parts and service; new vehicles; and used vehicles. The department managers have been told to run their shop as if they were in business themselves.

However, there are interdepartmental dealings. For example:

    a. The parts and service department prepares new cars for final delivery and repairs used cars prior to resale.

    b. The used-car department's major source of inventory has been cars traded in as partial payment for new cars.

The owner of the dealership has asked you to draft a company policy statement on transfer pricing, together with specific rules to be applied to the examples cited. He has told you that clarity is of paramount importance because your statement will be relied upon for settling transfer-pricing disputes.

P15-10 ROLE OF ECONOMIC VALUE AND REPLACEMENT VALUE. "To me, economic value is the only justifiable basis for measuring plant assets for purposes of evaluating performance. By economic value, I mean the present value of expected future services. Still, we do not even do this upon acquisition of new assets—that is, we may compute a positive net present value, using discounted cash flow, but we record the asset at no more than its cost. In this way, the excess present value is not shown in the initial balance sheet. Moreover, the use of replacement costs in subsequent years is also unlikely to result in showing economic values; the replacement cost will probably be less than the economic value at any given instant of an asset's life.

Market values are totally unappealing to me because they represent a second-best alternative value—that is, they ordinarily represent the maximum amount obtainable from an alternative that has been rejected. Obviously, if the market value exceeds the economic value of the assets in use, they should be sold. However, in most instances, the opposite is true; market values of individual assets are far below their economic value in use.

Obtaining and recording total present values of individual assets based on discounted-cash-flow techniques is an infeasible alternative. I therefore conclude that replacement cost (less accumulated depreciation) of similar assets producing similar services is the best practical approximation of the economic value of the assets in use. Of course, it is more appropriate for the evaluation of the division's performance than the division manager's performance."

Critically evaluate these comments. Please do not wander; concentrate on the issues described by the quotation.

P15-11 TRANSFER PRICING. The Propellers Division of Jacksonville Sports Company produces propellers for outboard motors. It has been the sole supplier of propellers to the Outboard Motor Division and charges $32 per unit—the current market price for very large wholesale lots. The Pump Division also sells to outside retail outlets, at $40 per unit. Normally, outside sales amount to 25 percent of a total sales volume of one-million pumps per year. Typical combined annual data for the division follows:

Sales	$ 34,000,000
Variable costs, @ $26 per pump	$ 26,000,000
Fixed costs	3,000,000
Total costs	$ 29,000,000
Gross margin	$ 5,000,000

The Birmingham Fabricators Company, an entirely separate entity, has offered the Outboard Motor Division comparable propellers at a firm price of $30 per unit. The Propeller Division claims that it cannot possibly match this price because it could not earn any margin at $30.

1. Assume that you are the manager of the Outboard Motor Division. Comment on the Propeller Division's claim. Assume that normal outside volume cannot be increased.
2. Propeller Division believes that it can increase outside sales by 750,000 million propellers per year by increasing fixed costs by $2 million and variable costs by $3 per unit while reducing the selling price to $38. Assume that maximum capacity is one-million propellers per year. Should the division reject intracompany business and concentrate on outside sales?

P15-12   **TRANSFER PRICING CONCESSION.**   The Moncton Division of Glencoe Corporation, operating at capacity, has been asked by the Antigonish Division of Glencoe to supply it with Electrical Fitting No. LX29. Moncton sells this part to its regular customers for $10 each. Antigonish, which is operating at 50 percent capacity, is willing to pay $6.90 each for the fitting. Antigonish will put the fitting into a brake unit that it is manufacturing on essentially a cost-plus basis for a commercial airplane manufacturer.

Moncton has a variable cost of producing fitting No. LX29 of $6. The cost of the brake unit being built by Antigonish is as follows:

Purchased parts—outside vendors	$28.10
Moncton fitting No. LX29	6.90
Other variable costs	17.50
Fixed overhead and administration	10.00
	$62.50

Antigonish believes the price concession is necessary to get the job.

The company uses return on investment and dollar profits in the measurement of division and division-manager performance.

1. Consider that you are the division controller of Moncton. Would you recommend that Moncton supply fitting No. LX29 to Antigonish? Why or why not? (Ignore any income-tax issues.)
2. Would it be to the short-run economic advantage of the Glencoe Corporation for the Moncton Division to supply the Antigonish Division with fitting No. LX29 at $6.90 each? (Ignore any income-tax issues.) Explain your answer.
3. Discuss the organizational and manager-behaviour difficulties, if any, inherent in this situation. As the Glencoe controller, what would you advise the Glencoe Corporation president to do in this situation?

P15-13   **TRANSFER PRICES AND IDLE CAPACITY.**   The Furniture Division of Washington Woodcraft purchases lumber, which it uses to fabricate tables, chairs, and other wood furniture. Most of the lumber is purchased from the Southshore Mill, also a division of Washington Woodcraft. Both the Furniture Division and Southshore Mill are profit centres.

The Furniture Division proposes to produce a new Danish-designed chair that will sell for $92. The manager is exploring the possibility of purchasing the required lumber from the Southshore Mill. Production of 800 chairs is planned, using capacity in the Furniture Division that is currently idle.

The Furniture Division can purchase the lumber from an outside supplier for $72. Washington Woodcraft has a policy that internal transfers are priced at *fully allocated cost.*

Assume the following costs for the production of one chair and the lumber required for the chair:

SOUTHSHORE MILL		FURNITURE DIVISION		
Variable cost	$48	Variable costs:		
Allocated fixed cost	22	Lumber from Southshore Mill		$70
Fully allocated cost	$70	Furniture Division variable costs:		
		Manufacturing	$21	
		Selling	6	27
		Total cost		$97

1. Assume that the Southshore Mill has idle capacity and therefore would incur no additional fixed costs to produce the required lumber. Would the Furniture Division manager buy the lumber for the chair from the Southshore Mill, given the existing transfer-pricing policy? Why or why not? Would the company as a whole benefit if the manager decides to buy from the Southshore Mill? Explain.

2. Assume that there is no idle capacity at the Southshore Mill and the lumber required for one chair can be sold to outside customers for $70. Would the company as a whole benefit if the manager decides to buy? Explain.

P15-14 RATE OF RETURN AND TRANSFER PRICING. The Seoul division of Global Toy Company manufactures chess boards and sells them in the Korean market for KRW 30,000 each. (KRW is the Korean won.) The following data are from the Seoul Division's 2001 budget:

Variable cost	KRW 19,000 per unit
Fixed overhead	KRW 30,400,000
Total assets	KRW 62,500,000

Global Toy has instructed the Seoul Division to budget a rate of return on total assets (before taxes) of 20 percent.

1. Suppose the Seoul Division expects to sell 3,400 chess boards during 2001:
   a. What rate of return will be earned on total assets?
   b. What would be the expected capital turnover?
   c. What would be the operating income percentage of sales?
2. The Seoul Division is considering adjustments in the budget to reach the desired 20 percent rate of return on total assets.
   a. How many units must be sold to obtain the desired return in no other part of the budget is changed?
   b. Suppose sales cannot be increased beyond 3,400 units. How much must total assets be reduced to obtain the desired return? Assume

that for every KRW 1,000 decrease in total assets, fixed costs decrease by KRW 100.

3. Assume that only 2,400 units can be sold in the Korean market. However, another 1,400 units can be sold to the North American Marketing Division of Global Toy. The Seoul manager has offered to sell the 1,400 units for KRW 27,500 each. The North American Marketing Division manager has countered with an offer to pay KRW 25,000 per unit, claiming she can subcontract production to a North American producer at a cost equivalent to KRW 25,000. The Seoul manager knows that if his production falls to 2,400 units, he could eliminate some assets, reducing total assets to KRW 50 million and annual fixed overhead to KRW 24.5 million. Should the Seoul manager sell for KRW 25,000 per unit? Support your answer with the relevant computations. Ignore the effects of income taxes and import duties.

P15-15 ROI OR RESIDUAL INCOME. Keyworth Co. is a large integrated conglomerate with shipping, metals, and mining operations throughout the world. The general manager of the Shipbuilding Division plans to submit a proposed capital budget for 2001 for inclusion in the companywide budget.

The division manager has for consideration the following projects, all of which require an outlay of capital. All projects have equal risk.

PROJECT	INVESTMENT REQUIRED	RETURN
1	$4,800,000	$1,200,000
2	1,900,000	627,000
3	1,400,000	182,000
4	950,000	152,000
5	650,000	136,000
6	300,000	90,000

The division manager must decide which of the projects to take. The company has a cost of capital of 15 percent. An amount of $12 million is available to the division for investment purposes.

1. What will be the total investment, total return, return on capital invested, and residual income of the rational division manager if:
   a. The company has a rule that all projects promising at least 20 percent or more should be taken.
   b. The division manager is evaluated on his ability to maximize his return on capital invested (assume that this is a new division with no invested capital).
   c. The division manager is expected to maximize residual income as computed by using the 15 percent cost of capital.
2. Which of the three approaches will induce the most effective investment policy for the company as a whole? Explain.

P15-16 TRANSFER-PRICING PRINCIPLES. A consulting firm, TAC, is decentralized with 25 offices around the country. The headquarters is based in Vancouver, British Columbia. Another operating division is located in Calgary, a subsidiary printing operation, Kwik Print, is located in the headquarters building. Top management has indicated that they would like the Calgary office to use Kwik Print for printing reports. All charges are eventually billed to the client, but TAC was concerned about keeping such charges competitive.

Kwik Print charges the Calgary office the following:

Photographing page for offset printing (a setup cost)	$.25
Printing cost per page	.014

At this rate, Kwik Print sales have a 60 percent contribution margin to fixed overhead.

Outside bids for 100 copies of a 120-page report needed immediately have been

Print 4V	$204.00
Jiffy Press	180.25
Kustom Print	186.00

These three printers are located within a five-kilometre radius of TAC Calgary and can have the reports ready in two days. A messenger would have to be sent to drop off the original and pick up the copies. The messenger usually goes to headquarters, but in the past, special trips have been required to deliver the original or pick up the copies. It takes three to four days to get the copies from Kwik Print (because of the extra scheduling difficulties in delivery and pickup).

Quality control of Kwik Print is poor. Reports received in the past have had wrinkled pages and have occasionally been miscollated or had pages deleted. (In one circumstance an intracompany memorandum indicating TAC's economic straits was inserted in a report. Fortunately, the Calgary office detected the error before the report was distributed to the clients.) The degree of quality control in the three outside print shops is unknown.

(Although the differences in costs may seem immaterial in this case, regard the numbers as significant for purposes of focusing on the key issues.)

1. If you were the decision maker at TAC Calgary, to which print shop would you give the business? Is this an optimal economic decision from the entire corporation's point of view?
2. What would be the ideal transfer price in this case, if based only on economic considerations?
3. Time is an important factor in maintaining the goodwill of the client. There is potential return business from this client. Given this perspective, what might be the optimal decision for the company?
4. Comment on the wisdom of top management in indicating that Kwik Print should be used.

P15-17 **MULTINATIONAL TRANSFER PRICES.** Medical Instruments, Inc., produces a variety of medical products at its plant in Halifax, Nova Scotia. The company has sales divisions worldwide. One of these sales divisions is located in Oslo, Norway. Assume that the Canadian income tax rate is 34 percent, the Norwegian rate is 60 percent, and a 15 percent import duty is imposed on medical supplies brought into Norway.

One product produced in Halifax and shipped to Norway is a heart monitor. The variable cost of production is $350 per unit, and the fully allocated cost is $600 per unit.

1. Suppose the Norwegian government allows either the variable or fully allocated cost to be used as a transfer price. Which should Medical Instruments, Inc. choose to minimize the total of income taxes and import duties? Compute the amount the company saves if it uses your suggested transfer price instead of the alternative.
2. Suppose the Norwegian parliament passed a law decreasing the income tax rate to 50 percent and increasing the duty on heart monitors to 20 percent. Repeat requirement 1, using these new facts.

P15-18 AGENCY THEORY. The London Trading Company plans to hire a manager for its division in Kenya. London Trading's president and vice president/personnel are trying to decide on an appropriate incentive employment contract. The manager will operate far from the London corporate headquarters, so evaluation by personal observation will be limited. The president insists that a large incentive to produce profits is necessary; he favours a salary of £12,000 and a bonus of 10 percent of the profits above £120,000. If operations proceed as expected, profits will be £480,000, and the manager will receive £50,000. But both profits and compensation might be more or less than planned.

The vice president/personnel responds that £50,000 is more than most of London Trading's division managers make. She is sure that a competent manager can be hired for a guaranteed salary of £38,000. "Why pay £48,000 when we can probably hire the same person for £38,000?" she argued.

1. What factors would affect London Trading's choice of employment contract? Include a discussion of the pros and cons of each proposed contract.
2. Why is the expected compensation more with the bonus plan than with the straight salary?

P15-19 MARGINS AND TURNOVER. Return on investment is often expressed as the product of two components capital turnover and margin on sales. You are considering investing in one of three companies, all in the same industry, and are given the following information:

	COMPANY		
	X	Y	Z
Sales	$9,000,000	$2,500,000	$37,500,000
Income	1,350,000	375,000	375,000
Capital	4,500,000	12,500,000	12,500,000

1. Why would you desire the breakdown of return on investment into margin on sales and turnover on capital?
2. Compute the margin on sales, turnover on capital, and return on investment for the three companies, and comment on the relative performance of the companies as thoroughly as the data permit.

P15-20 ROI BY BUSINESS SEGMENT. Rupert Inc. does business in three different business segments: (1) Entertainment, (2) Publishing/Information, and (3) Consumer/Commercial Finance. Results for a recent year were (in millions):

	REVENUES	OPERATING INCOME	TOTAL ASSETS
Entertainment	$1,272.2	$223.0	$1,120.1
Publishing/Information	705.5	120.4	1,308.7
Consumer/Commercial Finance	1,235.0	244.6	924.4

1. Compute the following for each business segment:
   a. Income percentage of revenue
   b. Capital turnover
   c. Return on investment (ROI)
2. Comment on the differences in return on investment among the business segments. Include reasons for the differences.

P15-21 MULTINATIONAL TRANSFER PRICES.   Global Enterprises, Inc. has production and marketing divisions throughout the world. One particular product is produced in Japan, where the income tax rate 30 percent, and transferred to a marketing division is Sweden, where the income tax rate is 60 percent. Assume that Sweden places an import tax of 10 percent on the product.

The variable cost of the product is $200 and the full cost is $400. Suppose the company can legally select a transfer price anywhere between the variable and full cost.

1. What transfer price should Global Enterprise use to minimize taxes? Explain why this is the tax-minimizing transfer price.
2. Compute the amount of taxes saved by using the transfer price in requirement 1 instead of the transfer price that would result in the highest taxes.

P15-22 EVALUATING DIVISIONAL PERFORMANCE.   As the chief executive officer of Tiger Shoe Company, you examined the following measures of the performance of three divisions (in thousands of dollars):

	NET ASSETS BASED ON		OPERATING INCOME BASED ON*	
DIVISION	HISTORICAL COST	REPLACEMENT COST	HISTORICAL COST	REPLACEMENT COST
Shoes	$15,000	$15,000	$2,700	$2,700
Clothing	45,000	55,000	6,750	6,150
Accessories	30,000	48,000	4,800	3,900

*The differences in operating income between historical and replacement cost are attributable to the differences in depreciation expenses.

1. Calculate for each division the rate of return on net assets and the residual income based on historical cost and on replacement cost. For purposes of calculating residual income, use 10 percent as the minimum desired rate of return.
2. Rank the performance of each division under each of the four different measures computed above.
3. What do these measures indicate about the performance of the divisions? Of the division managers? Which measure do you prefer? Why?

P15-23 USING GROSS OR NET BOOK VALUE OF FIXED ASSETS.   Assume that a particular plant acquires $800,000 of fixed assets with a useful life of four years and no residual value. Straight-line amortization will be used. The plant manager is judged on income in relation to these fixed assets. Annual net income, after deducting amortization, is $80,000.

Assume that sales and all expenses except amortization are on a cash basis. Dividends equal net income. Thus, cash in the amount of the amortization charge will accumulate each year. The plant manager's performance is judged in relation to fixed assets because all current assets, including cash, are considered under central-company control.

1. Prepare a comparative tabulation of the plant's rate of return and the company's overall rate of return based on
   a. gross (i.e., original cost) assets.
   b. net book value of assets. Assume (unrealistically) that any cash accumulated remains idle.
2. Evaluate the relative merits of gross assets and net book value of assets as investment bases.

P15-24 NEGOTIATED TRANSFER PRICES. The Assembly Division of Office Furniture, Inc. needs 1,200 units of a subassembly from the Fabricating Division. The company has a policy of negotiated transfer prices. The Fabricating Division has enough excess capacity to produce 2,000 units of the subassembly. Its variable cost of production is $20. The market price of the subassembly is $50.

What is the natural bargaining range for a transfer price between the two divisions? Explain why no price below your range would be acceptable. Also explain why no price above your range would be acceptable.

P15-25 ECONOMIC VALUE ADDED. The Coca-Cola Company uses economic value added (EVA) to evaluate top management performance. In 1996 Coca-Cola had net operating income of $3,915 million, income taxes of $1,104 million, and long-term debt plus shareholders' equity of $8,755 million. The company's capital is about 30 percent long-term debt and 70 percent equity. Assume that the after-tax cost of debt is 5 percent and the cost of equity is 12 percent.

1. Compute Coca-Cola's economic value added (EVA).
2. Explain what EVA tells you about the performance of the top management of Coca-Cola in 1996.

P15-26 TRANSFER-PRICING DISPUTE. A transportation-equipment manufacturer, Mason Corporation, is heavily decentralized. Each division head has full authority on all decisions regarding sales to internal or external customers. The Pacific Division has always acquired a certain equipment component from the Southern Division. However, when informed that the Southern Division was increasing its unit price to $330, the Pacific Division's management decided to purchase the component from outside suppliers at a price of $300.

The Southern Division had recently acquired some specialized equipment that was used primarily to make this component. The manager cited the resulting high amortization charges as the justification for the price boost. He asked the president of the company to instruct the Pacific Division to buy from Southern at the $330 price. He supplied the following data to back his request:

Pacific's annual purchases of component	3,000 units
Southern's variable costs per unit	$285
Southern's fixed costs per unit	$30

1. Suppose there are no alternative uses of the Southern facilities. Will the company as a whole benefit if Pacific buys from the outside suppliers for $300 per unit? Show computations to support your answer.
2. Suppose internal facilities of Southern would not otherwise be idle. The equipment and other facilities would be assigned to other production operations that would otherwise require an additional annual outlay of $60,000. Should Pacific purchase from outsiders at $300 per unit?
3. Suppose there are no alternative uses for Southern's internal facilities and that the selling price of outsiders drops by $30. Should Pacific purchase from outsiders?
4. As the president, how would you respond to the request of the manager of Southern? Would your response differ, depending on the specific situations described in requirements 1 throught 3 above? Why?

P15-27 TRANSFER PRICING. Burger-Rama Enterprises runs a chain of drive-in hamburger stands on Cape Cod during the 10-week summer season. Managers of all stands are told to act as if they owned the stand and are judged on their profit performance. Burger-Rama Enterprises has rented an ice-cream machine for the summer to supply its stands with ice cream. Rent for the machine is $1,800. Burger-Rama is not allowed to sell ice cream to other dealers because it cannot obtain a dairy licence. The manager of the ice-cream machine charges the stands $4 per four-litres. Operating figures for the machine for the summer are as follows:

Sales to the stands (8,000 four-litres at $4)		$32,000
Variable costs (@ $2.10 per four-litre)	16,800	
Fixed costs		
Rental of machine	1,800	
Other fixed costs	5,000	23,600
Operating margin		$ 8,400

The manager of the Cape Drive-In, one of the Burger-Rama drive-ins, is seeking permission to sign a contract to buy ice cream from an outside supplier at $3.30 a four-litre. The Cape Drive-In uses 1,500 four-litres of ice cream during the summer. Linda Garton, controller of Burger-Rama, refers this request to you. You determine that the other fixed costs of operating the machine will decrease by $480 if the Cape Drive-In purchases from an outside supplier. Garton wants an analysis of the request in terms of overall company objectives and an explanation of your conclusion. What is the appropriate transfer price?

P15-28 REVIEW OF MAJOR POINTS IN CHAPTER. The Antonio Company uses the decentralized form of organizational structure and considers each of its divisions as an investment centre. Division L is currently selling 15,000 air filters annually, although it has sufficient productive capacity to produce 21,000 units per year. Variable manufacturing costs amount to $17 per unit, while the total fixed costs amount to $90,000. These 15,000 air filters are sold to outside customers at $37 per unit.

Division M, also part of the Antonio Company, has indicated that it would like to buy 1,500 air filters from Division L, but at a price of $36 per unit. This is the price that Division M is currently paying an outside supplier.

1. Compute the effect on the operating income of the company as a whole if Division M purchases 1,500 air filters from Division L.
2. What is the minimum price that Division L should be willing to accept for the air filters?
3. What is the maximum price that Division M should be willing to pay for the air filters?
4. Suppose instead that Division L is currently producing and selling 21,000 air filters annually to outside customers. What is the effect on the overall Antonio Company operating income if Division L is required by top management to sell 1,500 air filters to Division M at (a) $18 per unit and (b) $37 per unit?
5. For this question only, assume that Division L is currently earning an annual operating income of $36,000, and the division's average invested capital is $300,000. The division manager has an opportunity to invest in a proposal that will require an additional investment of $20,000 and will increase annual operating income by $2,200. (a) Should the division manager accept this proposal if the Antonio Company uses ROI in evaluating the performance of its divisional managers? (b) If the company uses residual income? (Assume an "imputed interest" charge of 9 percent.)

P15-29 **MANAGEMENT BY OBJECTIVES.** Tom Clay is the chief executive officer of Mayberry Company. Clay has a financial management background and is known throughout the organization as a "no-nonsense" executive. When Clay became chief executive officer, he emphasized cost reduction and savings and introduced a comprehensive cost-control and budget system. The company goals and budget plans were established by Clay and given to his subordinates for implementation. Some of the company's key executives were dismissed or demoted for failing to meet projected budget plans. Under the leadership of Tom Clay, Mayberry has once again become financially stable and profitable after several years of poor performance.

Recently, Clay has become concerned with the human side of the organization and has become interested in the management technique referred to as "management by objectives (MBO)." If there are enough positive benefits of MBO, he plans to implement the system throughout the company. However, he realizes that he does not fully understand MBO because he does not understand how it differs from the current system of establishing firm objectives and budget plans.

1. Briefly explain what "management by objectives" entails and identify its advantages and disadvantages.
2. Does the management style of Tom Clay incorporate the human value premises and goals of MBO? Explain your answer.

P15-30 **COLLABORATIVE LEARNING EXERCISE: RETURN ON INVESTMENT.** Form groups of three to six students. Each student should select a company. Coordinate the selection of companies so that each group has companies from a wide variety of industries. For example, a good mix of industries for a group of five students would be a retail company, a basic manufacturing company, a computer software company, a bank, and an electric utility.

1. Each student should find the latest report for his or her company (the Internet is a good source) and find the following metrics.
   a. Income percentage of revenue (return on sales)
   b. Capital turnover
   c. Return on investment (ROI)
2. As a group, compare these performance measures for the chosen companies. Why do they differ across companies? What characteristic of the company and its industry might explain the differences in the measures?

CASES

C15-1 PROFIT CENTRES AND CENTRAL SERVICES.   EZtronics, a manufacturer of small appliances, has an Engineering Consulting Department (ECD). The department's major task has been to help the production departments improve their operating methods and processes.

For several years the consulting services have been charged to the production departments based on a signed agreement between the managers involved. The agreement specifies the scope of the project, the predicted savings, and the number of consulting hours required. The charge to the production departments is based on the costs to the Engineering Department of the services rendered. For example, senior engineer hours cost more per hour than junior engineer hours. An overhead cost is included. The agreement is really a "fixed-price" contract. That is, the production manager knows the total cost of the project in advance. A recent survey revealed that production managers have a high level of confidence in the engineers.

The ECD department manager oversees the work of about 40 engineers and 10 draftsmen. She reports to the engineering manager, who reports to the vice-president of manufacturing. The ECD manager has the freedom to increase or decrease the number of engineers under her supervision. The ECD manager's performance evaluation is based on many factors, including the annual incremental savings to the company in excess of the costs of operating the ECD department.

The production departments are profit centres. Their goods are transferred to subsequent departments, such as a sales department or sales division, at prices that approximate market prices for similar products.

Top management is seriously considering a "no-charge" plan. That is, engineering services would be rendered to the production departments at absolutely no cost. Proponents of the new plan maintain that it would motivate the production managers to take keener advantage of engineering talent. In all other respects, the new system would be unchanged from the present system.

Required:
1. Compare the present and proposed plans. What are their strong and weak points? In particular, will the ECD manager tend to hire the "optimal" amount of engineering talent?
2. Which plan do you favour? Why?

C15-2 CONTRIBUTION MARGIN AND TRANSFER PRICES.   (SMAC) The Whole Company is an integrated multidivisional manufacturing firm. Two of its divisions, Rod and Champ, are profit centres and their division managers have full responsibility for production and sales (both internal and external). Both the Rod and Champ division managers are evaluated by top management on the basis of total profit.

Rod Division is the exclusive producer of a special equipment component called Q-32. The Rod Division manager used the results of a market study to set the price at $450 per unit of Q-32. At this price, the normal sales and production volume is 21,000 units per year; however, production capacity is 26,000 units per year. Standard production costs for one unit of Q-32 based on normal production volume are as follows:

Direct materials	$175.00
Direct labour	75.00
Variable overhead	50.00
Fixed overhead	90.00
Total unit production costs	$390.00

Champ Division produces machinery for several large customers on a contractual basis. It has recently been approached by a potential customer to produce a specially designed machine that would require one unit of Q-32 as its main component. The potential customer has indicated that it would be willing to sign a long-term contract for 10,400 units of the machine per year at a maximum price of $650 per unit. Although Champ Division has sufficient idle capacity to accommodate the production of this special machine, the division manager is not willing to accept the contract unless he can negotiate a reasonable transfer price with the Rod Division manager for Q-32. He has calculated that the unit costs to produce the special machine are as follows:

Direct material other than Q-32	$100.00
Direct labour	50.00
Variable overhead	35.00
Fixed overhead	50.00
Total unit production costs before transfer of Q-32	$235.00

Required:

1. What is the maximum unit transfer price that the Champ Division manager should be willing to accept for Q-32 if he wishes to accept the contract for the special machine? Support your answer.

2. What is the minimum unit transfer price that the Rod Division manager should be willing to accept for Q-32? Support your answer.

3. Assume that Rod Division would be able to sell its capacity of 26,000 units of Q-32 per year in the outside market if the selling price was reduced by 5 percent. From top management's point of view, evaluate, considering both quantitative and qualitative factors, whether Rod Division should lower its market price or transfer the required units of Q-32 to Champ Division. What would you recommend? Why?

C15-3 **COMPENSATION PLAN.** (CGAC) Riverside Mining and Manufacturing is a vertically integrated company that mines, processes, and finishes various non-precious metals and minerals. Riverside has decentralized both on a geographical and on an operational basis. For example, Exploration and Development, which includes all mining operations, has been designated a strategic business unit (SBU). There are multiple divisions within this SBU, such as the North American Exploration and Development Division, the South American Exploration and Development Division, and other divisions. Similarly, Refining, which has often been located near the mines, is another SBU and is divisionalized by geographical region.

Riverside has a clearly stated management control system that includes longstanding policies on transfer pricing, performance evaluation, and management compensation. Transfers are made at full cost plus a markup to approximate net realizable value. Riverside's primary operating divisions (such as mining) are required to fill internal orders before servicing outside orders. Each division has full responsibility over setting prices and sales targets as well as monitoring costs. Also, divisional managers have decision-making authority over fixed investments (capital equipment) up to $0.5 million as long as the investments can be internally financed. For any investment exceeding $0.5 million, final approval must be given by the SBU and head office.

For performance-evaluation purposes, Riverside uses two basic measures to evaluate managers. First, it uses budgeted income and second, return on investment (ROI). Divisional managers develop their budgets in line with goals set centrally for the organization. All budgets must be approved by the SBU and central executive before their final acceptance. Net income includes headquarters' allocations based on a percentage of divisional sales. ROI is calculated as net income divided by total assets. As with the budget target, the ROI target has to be approved. Although the weighted average cost of capital for the company is 12 percent, each division negotiates its target ROI based on past performance and perceived risks and uncertainty in the environment. Progress toward the budgeted income and ROI targets are evaluated on a quarterly basis.

Riverside's bonus compensation scheme was extended to its divisional managers last year. The bonus consists of a 50/50 cash plus deferred payment scheme that is measured each quarter. For example, if a division manager exceeds budgeted income and ROI targets for the division, then the manager is awarded a bonus, 50 percent of which is paid immediately in cash and 50 percent of which is invested in "phantom shares" that can be redeemed three years hence, given continued good performance. The total value of the bonuses range from 10 percent to 100 percent of regular salary, depending on how well managers did and their level in the organization. Actual amounts of bonuses earned in any given year depend on the centrally calculated bonus pool, which is defined as a percentage of overall company income.

Some of the divisional managers have been unhappy with the bonus compensation scheme. They felt they were at a disadvantage because of their lack of control over their prices (due to the nature of the external market), and their inability to achieve the growth in the ROI required by central headquarters. The division managers believed that a shift to residual income would help, but Riverside's CEO rejected this, feeling that residual income would not allow comparison of divisional results. The results of three of these divisions are shown in Exhibit 15A-1.

EXHIBIT 15A-1		Division A	Division B	Division C
Riverside Mining and Manufacturing—Selected divisional results for the most recent quarter (in thousands)	Budgeted net income	$ 185	$1,964	$895
	Actual net income	148	1,968	1,020
	Budgeted total assets	1,310	8,755	6,978
	Actual total assets	1,109	8,811	6,955
	Target ROI	14.12%	22.4%	12.8%
	Actual ROI	13.3%	22.3%	14.7%

As well, the managers of the Primary Operating Divisions wanted the restrictions on the internal versus external sales lifted so that they could achieve better results than they were currently experiencing.

Required:

1. **a.** Calculate the residual income figure for each of the three divisions.
   b. In point form, list the advantages and disadvantages that residual income might have over the use of ROI at Riverside.
2. Evaluate the management control system currently in place at Riverside, outlining its strengths and weaknesses and make recommendations for any changes you feel are necessary.

C15-4 TRANSFER PRICE ALTERNATIVES.   (SMAC) On your first day on the job as controller of XYZ Corporation, you, C.M. Anderson, are asked to participate in the weekly 9:00 a.m. management meeting. The organizational chart (Exhibit 15A-2) represents the extent of your knowledge of the company.

After appropriate introductions and greeting, the following exchange takes place:

Mr. Smith: I, for one, am glad to see someone with your qualifications as our controller, Anderson. Maybe now we can finally introduce an element of sanity to this transfer pricing problem we've been wrestling with...

Ms. Walters: Smith, transfer pricing was settled two years ago. You're the only one who's wrestling with anything.

Mr. Davis: That's not entirely true. Smith and I have been talking, and I'm beginning to think that our cost-based pricing formula isn't as effective as it was supposed to be when we set it up. In fact, last month's statements convinced me that my department is being taken advantage of worse than ever!

Ms. Walters: You feel that way for two reasons. First, no one has ever explained transfer pricing properly to you, and second, Smith doesn't know what he's talking about.

Mr. McLaren: This is embarrassing. We're bickering like children in front of the newest member of our management team. Let's at least fill Anderson in on the issue. Perhaps we can all benefit from the infusion of new ideas. Smith, you start.

Mr. Smith: My division manufactures primary components for our electronics division products. Davis and his people take my parts, plus many others from various subcontractors and small, specialized manufacturers, and basically just assemble them and ship them out. All he has to do is perform one or two technical procedures besides assembly to get things working. That's why we call his operation "second stage" manufacturing.

Anyway, things worked fine until about two years ago. At that time, I had completed a major expansion, doubling my production facilities, in response to a forecast by Walters' marketing people. Only a fraction of the new markets materialized, however, and I was strapped with 40 percent underutilized capacity. To maximize profits, I developed a market for our circuit boards myself, and soon I had

EXHIBIT 15A-2

**XYZ Corporation—
Electronics Division**

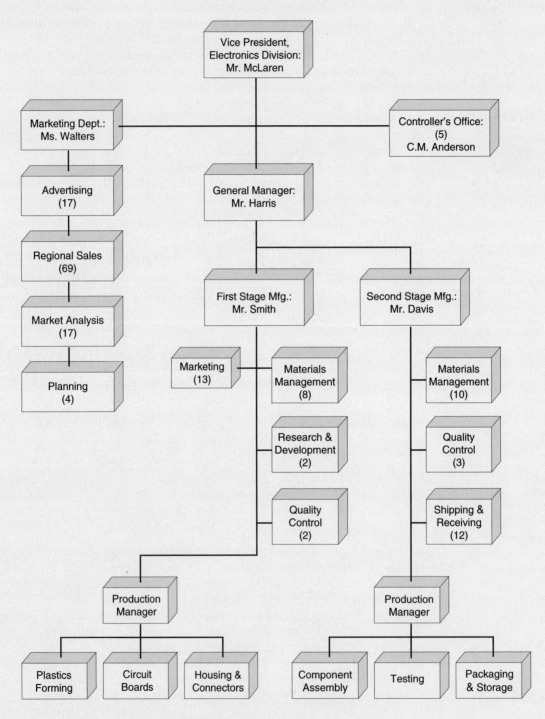

Note: Numbers in parentheses indicate number of staff in the area.

boosted production up to 90 percent of capacity. Since that time, my market has grown and I'm now running at about 110 percent of capacity with half of my product going to outside sales.

But as soon as I received one dollar in revenue, I became a profit centre. It was either that, they told me, or leave the sales end to Walters. For obvious reasons, I chose to become a profit centre.

So our controller at the time imposed what he called "a negotiated cost-based transfer price" on me. In reality, it's a dictated marginal-cost transfer price, but for appearance's sake, it has 12 percent thrown in to cover my overhead. Standard full costing would result in a markup of at least 20 percent over standard direct costs.

Ms. Walters: You haven't much reason to complain. Regardless of how you work the percentages, you've shown a profit in each of the last two years.

Mr. Smith: How would you like your annual bonus to be based on a $5,000 profit when you produce $15 million of circuit boards a year? Of course, I'm making a profit—that's what I'm paid to do. But to do it, I've had to pare costs below the minimum in dozens of areas. My circuit boards are twice as expensive as some of our competitors'. To turn a $5,000 profit, I've delivered to Katmandu at three o'clock in the morning, worked my staff to the breaking point, and given 10-year no-fault guarantees.

Let me warn you, no one can know what profit I've really made until two or three more years have passed. So far we've been lucky—warranty returns have been less than 0.5 percent. But if I have to honour 10 percent of my warranties, at least 20 percent of my annual production will be eaten up.

Mr. Davis: That's where the trouble is! In the last two years, your circuit boards have gone from 1 percent defective to almost 15 percent. In fact, Anderson, the situation is so serious that I now have three people on input quality control full-time, using $250,000 of testing equipment. Because of the tremendous workload in Smith's department, my department reworks all of the rejects that can be salvaged. Only about 10 percent of the rejects have to be scrapped.

Mr. Smith: Our production control standards haven't fallen one bit in the past five years!

Mr. Davis: But the standards of five years ago aren't very applicable in today's markets. Walters' market research staff has raised our minimum standards three times in the last two years alone. Surely you were advised?

That brings up another problem. Although Smith is working miracles flogging his boards outside at a premium price, I've been approached by two suppliers who could supply me with an identical product for even less than Smith's variable cost. And they would guarantee reject rates of less than 5 percent. If I were allowed to buy outside, I could probably reduce my costs by 2 or 3 percent. That would translate into a 5 percent increase in profits. As it is, I'm constantly running over budget and not just for circuit boards. Lately our plastics, housings, and connectors have shown signs of alarmingly high variances from minimum quality standards. We all appreciate the pressures Smith is under, but I can't help but wonder if anyone is benefitting from transfer pricing. That's where all these problems stem from—we didn't have any of them before this transfer pricing thing came up.

Mr. Smith: Your outside suppliers are manufacturers from Hong Kong and Taiwan. They both approached my biggest client, and he ran tests on their products. The defects ranged from 1 to 20 percent consistently. Needless to say, I didn't lose my client. My defects still have a range of less than 1 percent.

Ms. Walters: You're both neglecting the corporate view of the situation. Sure, you have problems, Smith. Your cost overruns are upsetting to you, Davis, but they are neither significant nor serious. Your total cost overruns are $500,000. That's about 1 percent and it's adequately covered by our margin, which is a direct result of our determination to maintain our image of high quality. During the past two years, while our competitors have had to cut their prices by as much as 20 percent, our prices have held firm, at least in most cases. Our profit may not have grown, but it certainly hasn't fallen by as much as our competitors'.

Even Smith's marketing strategy should get some credit because it fits hand-in-glove with our corporate strategy. And the fact that our major competitors either use our boards or make their own to our standards prevents them from reducing their cost base.

My key marketing tool is the way XYZ sets the standard for quality in the industry. If the second-stage manufacturing division were allowed to save a nickel by buying boards from other suppliers, Smith would have more of his production to sell. He might even increase his profits a bit. But if word got out that the XYZ unit doesn't use XYZ circuits, I'd be the laughingstock of the industry.

Trust me, the way we're running now, the entire company makes money. And, after all, gentlemen, what else are we employed for?

Mr. McLaren: There you have it, Anderson. I don't mean to put undue pressure on you. Maybe you can just identify the key elements that we will have to take into consideration in coming up with some kind of solution.

After the meeting, Mr. McLaren expressed his personal dissatisfaction with the entire situation. He suggested that a hard-hitting, comprehensive report might be the best way to redirect his managers and solve the problems quickly.

Required: Prepare a report addressed to the vice president of the Electronics Division, analyzing the issues brought to light at the meeting, together with a recommended plan of action.

C15-5 TRANSFER PRICING. (CGAC) Greg Soames, manager of the Pharon Division of Juneau Chemicals was studying his most recent quarterly results (shown in Exhibit 15A-3). Because of a recent economic downturn in the industry, Soames's division had not met its projected earnings, and there was no hope of meeting its annual ROI target of 18 percent.

Soames believed the problem to be compounded by the rigidity of the transfer pricing policy imposed by Juneau Chemicals. In spite of an open market price of $85 for the major raw material, Litaline, Pharon had to pay $105 per litre to a sister division—a price set, by company policy, as full standard cost plus a 15 percent markup. Having worked in the Litaline Division before moving to Pharon, Soames knew that the variable cost of producing Litaline was considerably less than $105, probably only 70 percent of the full standard cost. With this knowledge, Soames had tried to negotiate (which is permitted under company policy) a lower price so as to improve Pharon's return. His suggestion had been rejected by the Litaline manager, and Soames suspected that the reason for rejecting it stemmed from the Litaline manager's desire to achieve its ROI and income targets for the period, which would not happen if it had to meet the $85 market price.

EXHIBIT 15A-3		Budget	Actual
Pharon Division—	Sales	$3,525	$3,200
Statement of income for		2,000	1,920
the quarter ending	Cost of goods sold:		
September 30, 2001	Materials	900	925
(in thousands)	Labour	600	520
	Overhead	500	475
		2,000	1,920
	Gross Margin	$1,525	$1,280
	Other expenses:		
	Marketing	504	400
	Administration[1]	751	750
	Net Income	$ 270	$ 130
	Net assets	$1,500	$1,500
	ROI	18%	8.67%

[1] 50% of adminstration cost is allocated from central headquarters.

Soames feared that his compensation would suffer heavily in the period. Juneau paid its managers a base salary plus a bonus based on quarterly results and annual ROI targets. Bonuses were calculated on a sliding scale that ranged from 10 percent to 50 percent of salary and were paid in cash. For the past three years Soames, as manager of Pharon, had earned a bonus equal to 40 percent of his salary. But this year he felt either he would have to take drastic action or he would lose his bonus altogether and, perhaps, face even more severe consequences.

With this in mind, Soames approached his liaison on the Juneau Executive Committee, the vice president of operations, with a proposal to purchase Litaline on the external market. Without that option he felt that there was no way Pharon could salvage its current year's projections.

Required:

1. Evaluate Soames's proposal to purchase Litaline on the external market after calculating
   a. The per-unit profit effect on the firm; and
   b. The per-unit profit effect on the Pharon Division.

Required:

2. Discuss the strengths and weaknesses of the management control system in operation at Juneau Chemicals, and make any recommendations for change that you feel are necessary.

C15-6 INTERNATIONAL TRANSFER PRICING. (CICA) Durst Industries Inc. (Durst), a multinational company, has its head office in western Canada. Shares are listed on Canadian stock exchanges and on several foreign exchanges. For the fiscal year ended June 30, 1994, consolidated net sales amounted to $1.2 billion and net income was $45 million.

The company manufactures and markets heavy-construction and farm equipment at its 22 separate manufacturing facilities located in Canada, the United States, South America, Europe, and Asia. In this highly competitive, price-sensitive industry, Durst has maintained a reputation for high-quality, durable products. However, it recently lost several major contracts for farm tractors and combines.

While there is head office control of Durst's marketing and manufacturing strategies, the company's 22 manufacturing plants are treated as separate profit centres. Most of the subassembly and component parts are produced for internal use in the assembly of end products. There is no external market for most of these intermediate items. Those that are sold externally now generate approximately 2 percent of consolidated net sales. Selling prices to outsiders for subassembly and component parts have usually been determined at the plant level.

The following policy applies to transfers of goods between various Durst profit centres:

> Although it is necessary to have centralized control over the development and implementation of company marketing and manufacturing strategies, senior management needs to evaluate decentralized operations using a profit-centre concept. This is very important because the company's main production activity is focused on manufacturing subcomponents and subassemblies used exclusively for internal assembly of end products for consumers. Accordingly, there is a need for an appropriate pricing structure for interplant transfers.
>
> For guidance in determining transfer prices, plant managers should first refer to prices already established for outside sales. When there is no outside market, or when outside prices are not readily determinable, transfer prices are to be based on laid-down cost to the producing plant, plus a reasonable profit. This latter approach to arriving at a fair transfer price is consistent with the concept of "value-added pricing."

Thomas Smith, president and chief executive officer of Durst, received the following memorandum dated September 1, 2001 from Jim Brown, plant manager in Tulsa, Oklahoma.

> I have done everything I can to negotiate a fair price for our modified X-30 carburettor used in the assembly of the DXL 1300 tractor at our plant in eastern Canada. Roger Bertrand, the manager of this plant, has been most unreasonable, given that my modified X-30 is manufactured exclusively for installation in his DXL 1300 tractors.
>
> As you know, we still manufacture the unmodified version of the X-30, and its sales to our customers are substantial throughout the West. Unless you can convince Bertrand to be more reasonable, I shall cease

736 PART THREE MANAGEMENT ACCOUNTING FOR PLANNING AND CONTROL

production of the modified X-30 and concentrate our efforts on manufacturing the unmodified carburettor.

I expect you to let me know within ten days whether you have been able to convince Bertrand on this issue. Advise him that my last offer remains at $575 U.S., F.O.B. Tulsa.

Smith immediately called in Jean Talbot, CMA, vice president, finance, to discuss Brown's memo. Smith then asked Talbot to investigate the dispute. Talbot obtained the following information, which she related to Smith:

1. Unmodified X-30s were currently priced at $365.00 U.S., F.O.B. Tulsa.
2. Sales volume of the unmodified X-30 had dropped significantly during the last three years, and during this time its market price had similarly declined.
3. The modified X-30 represented a significant advance in carburettor technology.
4. To date, corporate management has not permitted production of the modified version for sale on the open market.
5. Tulsa's pricing of the modified X-30 was found to be in accord with company policy. The difference in price between these models is attributed to the additional cost of production plus the recovery of related development costs, overhead, and provision for "normal profit margin."
6. Costs incurred in the manufacture of carburettors at Tulsa are considered to be 60 percent variable and 40 percent fixed. Tulsa's gross margin on the carburettors has declined in recent years and is currently 35 percent.
7. When approached by Talbot, Bertrand would not reconsider his position. He contended that the Tulsa price was unacceptable, because of the duty and excise taxes he would necessarily incur to import the modified X-30 from the United States. He mentioned the availability of a less expensive but clearly inferior carburettor manufactured by a local competitor.

In discussions with Smith, Talbot emphasized that, while this dispute must be resolved, other problems existed. The present transfer pricing policy appears to have broader, long-range implications and the system might not be properly serving Durst's overall needs. At the conclusion of their discussion, Smith asked Talbot to prepare a report on the matter.

Required:

Assume the role of Jean Talbot and prepare the report to Thomas Smith. Recommend a solution to the current dispute, evaluate the present transfer pricing policy and recommend improvements. Support your recommendations.

Analyzing Financial Statements

LEARNING OBJECTIVES

After studying this chapter, you will be able to

1. Identify the meanings and interrelationships of the principal elements of financial statements: assets, liabilities, owners' equity, revenues, expenses, dividends,and others.

2. Analyze typical business transactions to determine their effects on the principal elements of financial statements.

3. Distinguish between the accrual basis of accounting and the cash basis of accounting.

4. Perform comparisons between companies within an industry and between companies from different industries.

5. Analyze a company's financial statements to assess its liquidity, profitability, stability, and growth.

6. Evaluate the sources and uses of cash that a company has employed in its financing and investing activities.

LINAMAR CORPORATION: REPORT TO SHAREHOLDERS

Linamar Corporation
www.linamar.com

Linamar Corporation is a global manufacturer of precision-machined components, assemblies and castings primarily for the automotive industry.

The company is focused on maintaining the low cost, high quality, on-time reputation for manufacturing that has facilitated its growth. With sales revenue for the year ended December 31, 1999 of $1.2 billion, Linamar has come a long way from the one-man operation started by the current chairman of the board and ceo, Frank Hasenfratz, in the basement of his home in Ariss, Ontario 34 years ago. In 1986, Mr. Hasenfratz further ensured the success and growth of Linamar by taking the Company public. Linamar has successfully traded on The Toronto Stock Exchange since that time. Linamar utilizes a strategy of balancing customer, employee, and financial satisfaction as the basic premise of running the business. This strategy permeates every business decision in every department, driving operations systems and even compensation systems

Though the Company was founded on machining for the defence, aerospace, and automotive industries, a decision was made in the mid-1980's to focus primarily on the automotive sector. As the automotive industry's requirements for high precision machining grew during the 1980's, Linamar became an established supplier. In 1999, the automotive industry accounted for over 86 percent of the Company's total sales. The Company's expertise in the machining and assembly of various automotive systems and components—engine, transmission, drivelines, steering, suspension and brake components — its solid, lean, entrepreneurial-management organizational structure and its dedication to leading edge technology are all key ingredients in what makes Linamar so successful.

Linamar's technical strength across a wide range of precision-machined components within the vehicle's highly engineered systems is a key competitive advantage. Particular attention has been given over the past few years to gaining product expertise in areas of the market which are currently expanding. With the majority of precision machined components in the vehicle still not available to the supply base, it is very important to be able to demonstrate capability and competency on those components next in line for outsourcing. Linamar has been very successful in this regard with acknowledged expertise in the manufacturing of several critical complex components

Linamar has recently taken the Company's precision machining core and enhanced it by the establishment of several facilities dedicated to complementary processes. Two foundries, one lost foam and one grey and ductile iron, are currently in operation in North America, with a third foundry planned to be constructed in Hungary with Joint Venture partner Wescast Industries Inc. within the next two years. As well, two facilities in North America are primarily focused on assembly operations, expanding on the many subassemblies most facilities produce. These moves have established Linamar more firmly as the full service supplier our customers are looking for.

Source: 1999 Annual Report for Linamar Corporation.

The objective of this chapter is to provide exposure to the accounting process, fundamental accounting terminology and concepts, and the means by which a company's financial statements can be analyzed. The primary purpose of financial statements is to provide users with information about the past that will improve their ability to make decisions about the future. For example, an analyst will evaluate a company's financial statements as part of an attempt to predict the future changes in a company's share price. A bank credit manager will use financial statements to assess a company's ability to first pay interest on a loan and second, if necessary, to provide sufficient security for a loan in the event of any defaults in payments. The list of potential users and the specific reasons for analyzing a company's financial statements is endless. Thus it is impossible to provide a list of techniques that are universally complete for all situations. This chapter will provide the basis for an evaluation of a company's financial statements, upon which a user can develop their own specific analysis. The range of possible techniques is limited only by the creativity of the user.

ENTITIES AND ACCOUNTING TRANSACTIONS

Managers, investors, and other interested groups usually want the answers to two important questions about an organization: How well did the organization perform for a given period of time? and, Where does the organization stand at a given point in time? The accountant answers these questions using two major financial statements: an income statement and a balance sheet. To create these statements, accountants continually record the history of an organization. Through the *financial accounting* process, the accountant accumulates, analyzes, quantifies, classifies, summarizes, and reports the seemingly countless events that take place in an organization and their effects on the entity. An *entity* is a specific area of accountability, a clearcut boundary for reporting. The entity concept is important because accounting usually focuses on the financial impact of events as they affect a particular entity. An example of an entity is a university, which encompasses many smaller entities such as the school of Law and the school of Engineering.

Corporations are the principal form of entity in terms of their financial impact on economies throughout the world. Corporations are organizations created by individual laws whose owners are identified as shareholders (also called stockholders). When approved, the corporation becomes a separate entity, an "artificial person" that conducts its business completely apart from its owners.

Transaction. Any event that affects the financial position of an organization and requires recording.

The accounting process focuses on transactions. A **transaction** is any event that affects the financial position of an entity and requires recording. Through the years, many concepts, conventions, and rules have been developed regarding what events are to be recorded as *accounting transactions* and how their financial impact is measured. These concepts will be introduced gradually over this last chapter.

FINANCIAL STATEMENTS

OBJECTIVE 1

Identify the meanings and interrelationships of the principal elements of financial statements: assets, liabilities, owners' equity, revenues, expenses, dividends, and others.

Financial statements are summarized reports of accounting transactions. They can apply to any point in time and to any span of time.

An efficient way to learn about accounting is to study a specific illustration. Suppose Retailer No. 1 began business as a corporation on March 1. An opening balance sheet (more accurately called statement of financial position or statement of financial condition) follows:

RETAILER NO. 1 Balance Sheet (Statement of Financial Position) As of March 1, 2001	**ASSETS**		**EQUITIES**	
	Cash	$100,000	Paid-in capital	$100,000

Assets. Economic resources that are expected to benefit future activities.
Equities. The claims against, or interests in, the assets.

The balance sheet is a photograph of financial status at an instant of time. It has two counterbalancing sections: assets and equities. **Assets** are economic resources that are expected to benefit future activities. **Equities** are the claims against, or interests in, the assets.

The accountant sees the balance sheet as an equation:

$$\text{assets} = \text{equities}$$

The equities side of this fundamental equation is often divided as follows:

$$\text{assets} = \text{liabilities} + \text{owners' equity}$$

The **liabilities** are the entity's economic obligations to nonowners. The **owners' equity** is the excess of the assets over the liabilities. For a corporation, the owners' equity is called **shareholders' equity**. In turn, the shareholders' equity is composed of the ownership claim against, or interest in, the total assets arising from any investments received, plus the ownership claim arising as a result of profitable operations (**retained income** or **retained earnings**).

Consider a summary of the *transactions* that occurred in March:

1. Initial investment by owners, $100,000 cash.
2. Acquisition of inventory for $75,000 cash.
3. Acquisition of inventory for $35,000 on open account. A purchase (or a sale) on open account is an agreement whereby the buyer pays cash some time after the date of sale, often in 30 days. Amounts owed on open accounts are usually called **accounts payable**, which are liabilities of the purchasing entity.
4. Merchandise carried in inventory at a cost of $100,000 was sold on open account for $120,000. These open customer accounts are called **accounts receivable**, which are assets of the selling entity.
5. Cash collections of accounts receivable, $30,000.
6. Cash payments of accounts payable, $10,000.
7. On March 1, $3,000 cash was disbursed for store rent for March, April, and May. Rent is $1,000 per month, payable quarterly in advance, beginning in March.

Note that these are summarized transactions. For example, all the sales will not take place at once, nor will purchases of inventory, collections from customers, or disbursements to suppliers. A vast number of repetitive transactions occur in practice, and specialized data collection techniques are used to measure their effects on the entity.

The foregoing transactions can be analyzed using the balance sheet equation, as shown in Exhibit 16-1. Explanations of Exhibit 16-1 follow:

Transaction 1, the initial investment by owners, increases assets and equities. That is, cash increases and share capital increases. Note, in this illustration, that share capital represents the claim arising from the owners' total initial investment in the corporation.

Transactions 2 and 3, the purchases of inventory, are steps toward the ultimate goal—earning a profit. But shareholders' equity is unaffected. That is, no profit is recorded until a sale is made.

Transaction 4 is the sale of $100,000 of inventory for $120,000. Two things happen simultaneously: a new asset, accounts receivable, is acquired (4a) in exchange for giving up inventory (4b), and shareholders' equity is increased by the amount of the asset received ($120,000) and decreased by the amount of the asset given up ($100,000).

Transaction 5, cash collections of accounts receivable, are examples of events that have no impact on shareholders' equity. Collections are merely the transformation of one asset (accounts receivable) into another (cash).

Transaction 6, cash payments of accounts payable, affect assets and liabilities only; they do not affect shareholders' equity. In general, collections from customers and payments to suppliers of the *principal* amounts of debt have no direct impact on shareholders' equity. Of course, as we will learn in a subsequent section, *interest* on debt does affect shareholders' equity as an item of expense.

EXHIBIT 16-1

RETAILER NO. 1
Analysis of Transactions (in dollars) For March 2001

TRANSACTIONS	ASSETS				=	LIABILITIES	+	SHAREHOLDERS' EQUITY	
	CASH	+ ACCOUNTS RECEIVABLE	+ INVENTORY	+ PREPAID RENT	=	ACCOUNTS PAYABLE	+	SHARE CAPITAL	+ RETAINED EARNINGS
1. Initial investment	+100,000				=			+100,000	
2. Acquire inventory for cash	–75,000		+75,000		=				
3. Acquire inventory for credit			+35,000		=	+35,000			
4a. Sales on credit		+120,000			=				+120,000 (revenue)
4b. Cost of inventory sold			–100,000		=				–100,000 (expense)
5. Collect from customers	+30,000	–30,000			=				
6. Pay accounts of suppliers	–10,000				=	–10,000			
7a. Pay rent in advance	–3,000			+3,000	=				
7b. Recognize expiration of rental services				–1,000	=				–1,000 (expense)
Balance, 3/31/01	+42,000	+90,000	+10,000	+2,000	=	+25,000		+100,000	+19,000
			144,000					144,000	

Transaction 7, the cash disbursement for rent, is made to acquire the right to use store facilities for the next three months. At March 1, the $3,000 measures the future benefit from these services, so the asset *Prepaid Rent* is created (7a). Assets are defined as economic resources. They are not confined to items that you can see or touch, such as cash or inventory. Assets also include legal rights to future services such as the use of facilities.

Transaction 7b recognizes that one-third of the rental services has expired during March, so the asset is reduced and shareholders' equity is also reduced by $1,000 as rent expense for March. This recognition of rent expense means that $1,000 of the asset Prepaid Rent has been "used up" (or has flowed out of the entity) in the conduct of operations during March.

For simplicity, we have assumed no expenses other than *costs of goods sold* and *rent*. The accountant would ordinarily prepare at least two financial statements: the balance sheet and the income statement.

RETAILER NO. 1
Income Statement
For the Month Ended
March 31, 2001

Sales (revenue)		$120,000
Expenses:		
Cost of goods sold	$100,000	
Rent	1,000	
Total expenses		101,000
Net income		$ 19,000

RETAILER NO. 1
Balance Sheet
As of March 31, 2001

ASSETS		LIABILITIES AND SHAREHOLDERS' EQUITY		
Cash	$ 42,000	Liabilities:		
Accounts receivable	90,000	Accounts payable		$ 25,000
Inventory	10,000	Shareholders' equity:		
Prepaid rent	2,000	Share capital	$100,000	
		Retained income	19,000	119,000
Total	$144,000	Total		$144,000

RELATIONSHIP OF BALANCE SHEET AND INCOME STATEMENT

Income Statement. A statement that measures the operating performance of the corporation by matching its accomplishments (revenue from customers, usually called sales) and its efforts (cost of goods sold and other expenses).

Balance Sheet. A statement of assets, liabilities, and equities.

The **income statement** measures the operating performance of the corporation by matching its accomplishments (revenue from customers, which is usually called *sales*) and its efforts (*cost of goods sold* and other expenses). The **balance sheet** shows the financial position at that time, but the income statement measures performance for a span of time, whether it be a month, a quarter, or longer. The income statement is the major link between balance sheets as shown below.

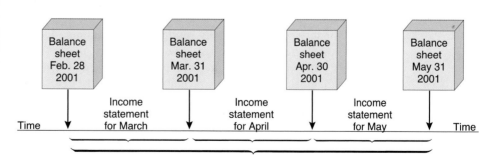

Income statement for quarter ended May 31, 2001

Examine the changes in shareholders' equity in Exhibit 16-1. The accountant records revenue and expense so that they represent increases (revenues) and decreases (expenses) in the owners' claims. At the end of a given period, these items are summarized in the form of an income statement. The heading of a balance sheet indicates a single date. The heading of an income statement indicates a specific period of time. The balance sheet is a photograph; the income statement is a motion picture.

Each item in a financial statement is frequently called an account, so that term will be used in the remaining chapters of this book. In the example Income Statement and Balance Sheet above, the outflows of assets are represented by decreases in the Inventory and Prepaid Rent accounts and corresponding decreases in shareholders' equity in the form of Cost of Goods Sold and Rent Expense. Expense accounts are basically negative elements of shareholders' equity. Similarly, the sales (revenue) account is a positive element of shareholders' equity.

REVENUES AND EXPENSES

Review Transaction 4. As Exhibit 16-1 shows, this transaction has two phases, a revenue phase (4a) and an expense phase (4b) (dollar signs omitted):

DESCRIPTION OF TRANSACTIONS		ASSETS	=	EQUITIES	
Balances after Transaction 3 in Exhibit 16-1*		$135,000	=		$135,000
4a. Sales on account (inflow)	Accounts receivable	+120,000	=	Shareholders' equity	+120,000
4b. Cost of Inventory sold (outflow)	Inventory	– 100,000	=	Shareholders' equity	– 100,000
Balances, after Transaction 4		$155,000			$155,000
* Cash of $100,000 – $75,000		= $ 25,000		Accounts payable	$ 35,000
Inventory of $75,000 + $35,000		= 110,000		Share capital	100,000
		$135,000			$135,000

Revenues. Increases in assets from delivering goods or services.

Transaction 4a illustrates the realization of *revenue*. **Revenues** generally arise from gross increases in assets from delivering goods or services. To be *realized* (that is, formally recognized in the accounting records as revenue earned during the current period), revenue must ordinarily meet three criteria. First, the goods or services must be fully rendered (for example, delivery to customers). Second, an exchange of resources evidenced by a market transaction must occur (for example, the buyer pays or promises to pay cash and the seller delivers merchandise). Third, the collectability of the asset (for example, an account receivable) must be reasonably assured.

Expenses. Decreases in assets from delivering goods or services.

Transaction 4b illustrates the incurrence of an expense. **Expenses** generally arise from gross decreases in assets from delivering goods or services.

Transactions 4a and 4b also illustrate the fundamental meaning of *profits* or *earnings* or *income*, which is defined as the excess of revenues over expenses.

As the Retained Earnings (Income) column in Exhibit 16-1 shows, increases in revenues increase shareholders' equity. In contrast, increases in expenses decrease shareholders' equity. So, expenses are negative shareholders' equity accounts.

Transactions 2 and 3 were purchases of merchandise inventory. They were steps toward the ultimate goal of earning a profit. Purchases cannot earn a profit by themselves; no profit is realized until a sale is actually made to customers (remember that shareholders' equity was unaffected by the inventory acquisitions in transactions 2 and 3).

Transaction 4 is the $120,000 sales on open account of inventory that cost $100,000. Two things happen simultaneously: a $120,000 inflow of assets in the form of accounts receivable (4a) in exchange for a $100,000 outflow of assets in the form of inventory (4b). Liabilities are completely unaffected, so owners' equity increases by $120,000 − $100,000, or $20,000.

Users of financial statements often ask, How well did the organization perform for a given period of time? The income statement helps answer this question. For Retailer No. 1, there has been a change in shareholders' equity attributable solely to operations. This change is measured by the revenue and expenses for the specific period.

THE ANALYTICAL POWER OF THE BALANCE SHEET EQUATION

As you study Exhibit 16-1, consider how accountants use the fundamental balance sheet equation as their framework for analyzing and reporting the effects of transactions:

$$\text{assets (A)} = \text{liabilities (L)} + \text{shareholders' equity (SE)} \qquad (1)$$

SE equals original ownership claim plus the increase in ownership claim because of profitable operations. That is, SE equals the claim arising from share capital plus the claim arising from retained earnings. Therefore:

$$A = L + \text{share capital} + \text{retained earnings} \qquad (2)$$

But, in our illustration, Retained Earnings equals Revenue minus Expenses. Therefore:

$$A = L + \text{share capital} + \text{revenue} - \text{expenses} \qquad (3)$$

Revenue and *expense accounts* are nothing more than subdivisions of shareholders' equity—they are temporary shareholders' equity accounts. Their purpose is to summarize the volume of sales and the various expenses so that management is kept informed of the reasons for the continual increases and decreases in shareholders' equity in the course of ordinary operations. In this way comparisons can be made, standards or goals can be set, and control can be better exercised.

The entire accounting system is based on the simple balance sheet equation. As you know, equations in general possess enormous analytical potential because of the dual algebraic manipulations that they permit. The equation is always kept in balance because of this duality.

Exhibit 16-1 illustrates the dual nature of the accountant's analysis. For each transaction, the equation is *always* kept in balance. If the items affected are confined to one side of the equation, you will find the total amount added equal to the total amount subtracted on that side. If the items affected are on both sides, then equal amounts are simultaneously added or subtracted on each side.

The striking feature of the balance sheet equation is its universal applicability. No transaction has ever been conceived, no matter how simple or complex, that cannot be analyzed via the equation. The top technical partners in the world's largest professional accounting firms, when confronted with the most intricate transactions of multinational companies, will inevitably discuss and think about their analysis in terms of the balance sheet equation. The partners focus on its major components: assets, liabilities, and owners' equity (including the explanations of changes in owners' equity that most often take the form of revenues and expenses in an income statement).

ACCRUAL BASIS AND CASH BASIS

OBJECTIVE 3

Distinguish between the accrual basis of accounting and the cash basis of accounting.

Accrual Basis. A process of accounting that recognizes the impact of transactions on the financial statements in the time periods when revenues and expenses occur instead of when cash is received or disbursed.

Cash Basis. A process of accounting where revenue and expense recognition would depend solely on the timing of various cash receipts and disbursements.

Measuring income and financial position is anchored to the accrual basis of accounting, as distinguished from the cash basis. The **accrual basis** is the process whereby the impact of transactions on the income statement and balance sheet is recognized as it is earned. Expenses are recognized as they are incurred—not when cash changes hands.

Transaction 4a in Exhibit 16-1, shows an example of the accrual basis. Revenue is recognized when sales are made on credit, not when cash is received. Similarly, Transactions 4b and 7b (for cost of goods sold and rent) show that expenses are recognized as efforts are expended or services are used to obtain the revenue (regardless of when cash is disbursed). Therefore income is often affected by measurements of noncash resources and obligations. The accrual basis is the principal conceptual framework for relating accomplishments (revenues) with efforts (expenses).

If the **cash basis** of accounting were used instead of the accrual basis, revenue and expense recognition would depend solely on the timing of various cash receipts and disbursements. Our Retailer example for March would show $30,000 of revenue, the amount of cash collected from customers. Similarly, rent expense would be $3,000 (the cash disbursed for rent) rather than the $1,000 rent applicable to March. A cash measurement of net income or net loss is not used in this case because it could mislead those unacquainted with the fundamentals of accounting.

Consider the rent example. Under the cash basis, March must bear expenses for the entire quarters' rent of $3,000 merely because cash outflows occurred then. In contrast, the accrual basis measures performance more sharply by allocating the rental expenses to the operations of each of the three months that benefitted from the use of the facilities. In this way, the economic performance of each month will be comparable. Most accountants maintain that it is nonsense to say that March's rent expense was $3,000 and April's and May's was zero.

The biggest problem with the cash basis of accounting is that it is incomplete. It fails to *match* efforts and accomplishments (expenses and revenues) in a manner that properly measures economic performance and financial position. Moreover, it omits key assets (such as accounts receivable and prepaid rent) and key liabilities (such as accounts payable) from balance sheets.

Despite the incompleteness of the cash basis of accounting, it is used widely by individuals when they measure their income for personal income-tax purposes. Also, many government and not-for-profit organizations also use the cash basis of accounting. For these purposes, the cash basis often provides a good approximation of the net financial impact of their activities. However, accountants and managers found cash-basis financial statements to be unsatisfactory as a measure of both performance and position. Today, more than 95 percent of all business is conducted on a credit basis; cash receipts and disbursements are not the critical transactions as far as the recognition of revenue and expense is concerned. Thus, the accrual basis evolved in response to desire for a more complete and, therefore, more accurate report of the financial impact of various events.

DIVIDENDS AND RETAINED EARNINGS

Dividends Are Not Expenses

Dividends. Distributions to shareholders of assets that reduce retained earnings.

Cash **dividends** are not expenses like rent and wages. They should not be deducted from revenues because dividends are not directly related to the generation of sales or the conduct of operations. Cash dividends are distributions of assets to shareholders that reduce retained earnings. The ability to pay dividends is fundamentally caused by profitable operations. Retained earnings increases as profits accumulate and decreases as dividends occur.

The entire right-hand side of the balance sheet can be thought of as claims against the total assets. The liabilities are the claims of creditors. The shareholders' equity represents the claims of owners arising out of their initial investment (share capital) and subsequent profitable operations (retained earnings). As a company grows, this account can become enormous if dividends are not paid. Retained earnings is frequently the largest shareholders' equity account.

Retained Earnings Is Not Cash

Retained earnings is *not* a pot of cash awaiting distribution to shareholders. Consider the following illustration:

Step 1. Assume an opening balance sheet of:

Cash	$100	Share capital	$100

Step 2. Purchase inventory for $50 cash. The balance sheet now reads:

Cash	$ 50	Share capital	$100
Inventory	50		
	$100		

Steps 1 and 2 demonstrate a fundamental point. Ownership equity is an undivided claim against the total assets (in the aggregate). For example, half the shareholders do not have a specific claim on cash, and the other half do not have a specific claim on inventory. Instead, all the shareholders have an undivided claim against (or, if you prefer, an undivided interest in) all the assets.

Step 3. Now sell the inventory for $80, which produces a retained earnings of $80 − $50 = $30:

Cash	$130	Share capital	$100
		Retained earnings	30
		Total equities	$130

At this stage, the retained earnings might be related to a $30 increase in cash. But the $30 in retained earnings connotes only a *general* claim against *total* assets. This may be clarified by the transaction that follows.

Step 4. Purchase equipment and inventory, in the amounts of $70 and $50, respectively. Now cash is $130 – $70 – $50 = $10:

Cash	$ 10	Share capital	$100
Inventory	50	Retained income	30
Equipment	70		
Total assets	$130	Total equities	$130

To what assets is the $30 in retained earnings related? Is it linked to Cash, to Inventory, or to Equipment? The answer is indeterminate. This example helps to explain the nature of the Retained Earnings account. It is a claim, not a pot of gold. You cannot buy a loaf of bread with retained earnings.

Retained earnings is increased by profitable operations, but the cash inflow from sales is an increment in assets (see Step 3). When the cash inflow takes place, management will use the cash, most often to buy more inventory or equipment (Step 4). Retained earnings (and also share capital) is a general claim against, or undivided interest in, total assets, not a specific claim against cash or against any other particular asset. Do not confuse the assets themselves with the claims against the assets.

RATIO ANALYSIS

OBJECTIVE 4

Perform comparisons between companies within an industry and between companies from different industries.

Time-Series Analysis. Comparison of a company's financial ratios with its own historical ratios.

Ratios form the basis of most financial statement analysis, which fundamentally involves the comparison of a ratio. Ratios for a company can be compared in three ways: (1) with its own ratios of a previous time period (called time-series analysis), (2) with other companies' ratios (called cross-sectional analysis), and (3) with rules of thumb or objectives (sometimes referred to as benchmarks).

Time-series analysis attempts to indicate changes in certain characteristics of a particular company. For example, a company may have tried to improve its cost efficiency in an effort to improve its overall returns. A time-series analysis will provide indications as to whether the company has been successful in this strategy. It is important though in analyzing a ratio over time, to also consider any other changes that may have also occurred over the same time period. While the ratios may indicate the extent that a cost efficiency strategy is working, other factors may also produce a change in the ratios (which can be unrelated to management's efforts). For example, increased competition among suppliers may reduce costs, which in turn would indicate improved efficiency. However, the improvements may not be the result of specific decisions taken within the company. Other changes such as changes in accounting policies, changes in the company's operations, etc. may also limit the ability of an analyst to accept a ratio at face value.

Cross-Sectional Analysis. Comparison of a company's financial ratios with ratios of other companies or with industry averages.

Cross-sectional analysis provides a comparison of a company to other companies either in the same industry or in another industry. While cross-sectional analysis can be performed at different times, each comparison is generally performed at about the same time in order to be as comparable as possible. However, an analyst must be aware that certain limitations do exist in order to draw comparisons between companies. For example, it is rare to find two companies in exactly the same industry producing exactly the same products. In fact in Canada, limitations in the market tend to require each company to specialize in a specific niche. As a result many Canadian managers will say that "there is no other company exactly like us." Furthermore, there are differences in terms of year-ends, the classification of accounts, and accounting policies. All of these potential differences require the analyst to consider the possible effects of the difference on the cross-sectional comparison.

Benchmarks provide useful objectives or rules of thumb by which an analyst can assess the relative merits of a particular ratio. For example, a company may have improved its overall return over the previous five years to the point where it now has the highest return of any company in the industry. Thus both the time-series and the cross-sectional analysis are very positive. However, if the company's return of 5 percent is compared to a benchmark of 8 percent for a relatively low-risk investment, it would indicate that both the company and its industry are performing at a level of low returns. It is sometimes difficult to obtain benchmarks and thus many analysts use rules of thumb based upon their experience. Some industry associations attempt to provide industry means, which are computed from information obtained from their members. Industry ratios are also provided by sources such as *Dun and Bradstreet Key Business Ratios, Financial Post Industry Reports, Investors Digest of Canada* and *Polymetric Report.*

Benchmarks can also be obtained by examining the ratios of specific companies. Annual reports of public companies can be obtained by contacting the company directly, through *The Globe And Mail's* annual report service, and through the Canadian Securities Administrators' service called SEDAR®, which is available at "www.sedar.com".

We will next discuss specific ratios that can be analyzed for most companies. The ratios will be organized into the four categories of: (1) profitability ratios, (2) liquidity ratios, (3) stability ratios, and (4) growth ratios. It is important to remember that any one ratio only provides a piece of the picture. To build a total picture of the financial strengths and weaknesses of a company, the analysis of each ratio should be considered with each other. Furthermore, it is common for an analyst to produce additional ratios beyond those listed in this chapter to examine a specific issue that may be unique to the company or its industry.

Exhibit 16-2 provides a summary of the ratios that will now be discussed. To assist in the discussion of the ratios, the 1998 and 1999 balance sheets and income statements of Linamar Corporation, a Canadian automobile parts manufacturer, are provided in Exhibit 16-3 and Exhibit 16-4 respectively.

Profitability Ratios

Profitability ratios examine the company's profits from different perspectives, in order to explain the reasons underlying the level of profits. *Return on assets* measures the overall profits on the assets that the company has used to generate the profits. For Linamar, the return on assets of 7.9 percent ($65,647/$827,063) means that the company earned 7.9 cents on every dollar of assets. The return on assets can be further segregated into the ratios of net income margin and asset turnover. Net income margin indicates the amount of income that remains from each dollar of sales after all expenses have been covered. The asset turnover ratio computes the number of sales dollars generated for each dollar of assets employed in the company. In 1999, Linamar's net income margin was

Benchmarks. General rules specifying appropriate levels for financial ratios.

Industry Canada
www.ic.gc.ca

Sedar
www.sedar.com

Profitability Ratios. Ratios that examine an organization's degree of profitability.

Analyze a company's
financial statements to
assess its liquidity,
profitability, stability,
and growth.

5.2 percent ($65,647/$1,252,115) and its asset turnover was 1.5 times ($1,252,115/$827,063). It is useful to note that the product of the *net income margin* and the *asset turnover* is the return of assets, i.e., 7.9 percent = 5.2 percent times 1.5 (with rounding). In other words, a company can improve its return on assets by maximizing its net income margin or its asset turnover or a combination of the two.

For a more detailed analysis of the return on assets ratio and thus a closer look at a company's profitability, it is possible to analyze the components of the net income margin further. For example, it is common to compute an operating earnings margin, which in Linamar's case was 8.5 percent ($106,802/$1,252,115). Likewise, any line on the income statement could be analyzed as a percentage of sales. Further it is also common to examine the *return on shareholders' equity*, which for Linamar was 14.0 percent in 1999 ($65,647/$469,545). The return on equity or any other component of the balance sheet merely provides another measure of returns that is more focused on a portion of the total assets.

Liquidity Ratios

Liquidity ratios tell whether a company is able to meet its short-term financial obligations. Generally, short term means any financial obligations due within one

EXHIBIT 16-2

Ratio Formulas

Liquidity Ratios
Ratios that examine an
organization's ability
to meet its short-term
finanical obligations.

PROFITABILITY RATIOS:

Return on Assets	=	Net Income/Total Assets
Net Income Margin	=	Net Income/Sales
Asset Turnover	=	Sales/Assets
Return on Shareholders' Equity	=	Net Income/Shareholders' Equity

LIQUIDITY RATIOS:

Current Ratio	=	Current Assets/Current Liabilities
Quick Ratio	=	(Cash + Accounts Receivable)/Current Liabilities
Working Capital	=	Current Assets − Current Liabilities
Age of Receivables	=	Accounts Receivable/(Sales ÷ No. of days)
Age of Inventory	=	Inventory/(Cost of Goods Sold ÷ No. of days)
Age of Payables	=	Accounts Payable/(Purchases* ÷ No. of days)
Inventory Turnover	=	Costs of Goods Sold/Inventory

STABILITY RATIOS:

Debt to Assets	=	Debt/Assets
Equity to Assets	=	Equity/Assets
Times Interest Earned	=	(Net Income before taxes + Interest)/Interest

GROWTH RATIOS:

Sales	=	(Current Year's Sales − Last Year's Sales)/ Last Year's Sales
Profit	=	(Current Year's Profit − Last Year's Profit)/ Last Year's Profit
Assets	=	(Current Year's Assets − Last Year's Assets)/ Last Year's Assets
Equity	=	(Current Year's Equity − Last Year's Equity)/ Last Year's Equity

* When purchases is not reported, cost of goods sold may be used.

Current Assets. Cash and all other assets that are reasonably expected to be converted to cash or sold or consumed during the coming year

Current Liabilites. An organization's debts that fall due within the coming year.

year. Normally assets and liabilities are segregated to distinguish the current assets and liabilities from other capital assets and liabilities. **Current assets** are those that are expected to be realized in the form of cash or could be turned into a cash receipt within one year. Similarly, **current liabilities** are debts that are due within one year.

The *current ratio* is computed by dividing the current assets by the current liabilities. In 1999, Linamar current ratio was 1.1 ($353,953/$318,948). This result would indicate that Linamar would be able to cover its current liabilities 1.1 times. However, for some companies there may be sufficient uncertainty concerning the company's ability to sell its inventories or to convert its pre-paid expenses into cash. Thus a more conservative test of its liquidity is war-ranted. The *quick ratio* or *acid test* refines the current ratio by including only cash and accounts receivable in the numerator. For Linamar, the quick ratio is .74 ([$14,451 + $222,281]/$318,948) which indicates that 74 percent of the current liabilities can be covered with cash and term deposits and the collection of the accounts receivable. Both of these ratios provide a comparison of the rel-ative size of the liquid assets and liabilities while the working capital provides in dollars the amount of the current assets that is available to a company after

EXHIBIT 16-3

LINAMAR CORPORATION. Consolidated Balance Sheets December 31, 1999 and 1998 (millions of dollars)

	Decmber 31 1999	December 31 1998
Assets		
Current Assets		
Cash and short-term investments	$ 14,451	$ 25,199
Accounts receivable	222,281	163,102
Inventories	101,082	91,998
Prepaid expenses	15,620	1,155
Other assets	-	862
Income taxes recoverable	519	3,194
	353,953	285,431
Investment in Preference Shares, at cost	686	914
Capital Assets	472,424	400,155
	$ $827,063	$ 686,579
Liabilities		
Current Liabilities		
Short-term bank borrowings	$ 129,897	$ 46,152
Accounts payable and accrued liabilities	182,458	161,485
Current portion of long-term debt	1,539	2,761
Advance payment from customers	5,054	3,840
	318,948	214,238
Accounts Payable not due in Current Year	-	5,840
Long-Term Debt	2,508	3,024
Future Income Taxes	14,515	16,080
Non-Controlling Interests	21,547	24,107
	357,489	263,289
Shareholders' Equity		
Share Capital	83,381	81,669
Retained Earnings	386,164	341,621
	469,545	423,290
	$ 827,063	$ 686,579

EXHIBIT 16-4

LINAMAR
CORPORATION
Consolidated
Statements of Income
Years ended
December 31, 1999
and 1998
(thousands of dollars)

	Decmber 31 1999	December 31 1998
Sales	$1,252,115	$ 998,312
Cost of Sales and Operating Expenses Before the Following	1,000,261	766,034
Amortization	84,771	58,465
Selling, general and administrative	60,281	46,093
	1,145,313	870,592
Operating Earnings	106,802	127,720
Other Income (Expense)		
Interest earned	1,882	4,585
Other income	36	882
Interest on long-term debt	(63)	(169)
Other interest expense	(5,164)	(1,407)
	(3,309)	3,891
	103,493	131,611
Provision for (Recovery of) Income Taxes		
Current	41,871	38,568
Future	(1,565)	4,758
	40,306	43,326
	63,187	88,285
Non-Controlling interests	(2,460)	3,900
Net Earnings for the Year	$ 65,647	$ 84,385

covering its current liabilities. In the case of Linamar, the *working capital* for 1999 was $35,005 thousands ($353,953 – $318,948).

For the above liquidity analysis, it is recognized that the current assets and liabilities will be converted into cash receipts or payments within one year. It would, however, be useful to know how long it actually takes within a company for these events to occur. The next three ratios are commonly used to evaluate this issue. The *age of receivables ratio* measures the average length of time that is required from the recording of the sale until the cash is collected. By dividing the accounts receivable balance by the average day's sales, it can be determined that Linamar's customers paid their invoices on average in about 65 days ($222,281/[$1,252,115/365]). The *age of inventory* of 37 days ($101,082/[$1,000,261/365]) indicates that from the time of the purchase of materials through to the production of its products and then to the point of sale of the finished product required 75 days for Linamar in 1999. By dividing the 75 days into 365 days in a year, an inventory turnover ratio of 9.9 provides the same information. The *age of payables* measures the average length of time that a company takes to pay its suppliers of goods and services. In 1999, Linamar paid their bills in about 67 days ($182,458/[$1,000,261/365]), using cost of sales and operating expenses of $1,000,261 thousands in place of purchases.

Stability Ratios

Stability Ratios. Ratios that examine an organization's degree of debt financing in comparison to its equity financing.

Stability ratios provide a measure of the long-term financial strength of the company, particularly in terms of its ability to carry its debt load. For most companies it is financially advisable to finance a portion of its assets with debt financing as opposed to a form of equity financing. However, given the requirement to pay interest on debts, it is a company's inability to meet its interest obligations that can result in its bankruptcy. For this reason it is important to assess the reasonableness of a company's debt load and its ability to cover its interest expenses. The *debt to assets ratio* is a measure of the extent to which a company has financed its assets with liabilities. For Linamar, its debt to assets of 43 percent ($357,518/$827,063) means that on average 43 cents of each dollar of assets is financed with debt. The *times interest earned ratio or interest coverage ratio* indicates the number of times that the company's interest expense could have been increased before a net loss would have been reported. Linamar's interest coverage was 3.2 times ($106,802/$3,309) in 1999.

Growth Ratios

Growth Ratios. Ratios that examine the areas of growth or decline within an organization over time.

Growth ratios provide a means of showing the areas in which a company has increased or decreased in size over the previous year. The areas of sales, income or profit, assets, and equity are commonly used growth ratios. However, an analyst would not limit the analysis to these areas if other segments of the company such as inventory were of greater concern. For Linamar, its sales grew by 25.4 percent from the 1998 sales of $998,312 to $1,252,115 in 1999. However, over the same period, the profits declined by 22.2% and assets and shareholders' equity grew by 28.5 percent, 20.5 percent, and 10.9 percent, respectively.

CASH-FLOW ANALYSIS

OBJECTIVE 6

Evaluate the sources and uses of cash that a company has employed in its financing and investing activities.

Statement of Cash Flows. A statement that reports the cash receipts and cash payments of an organization during a particular period.

A critical dimension to analyzing the financial aspects of a company is to understand the *sources and uses* of its cash. Much of the ratio analysis, and in particular the profitability analysis, focuses on the operating success of the company. However, a company without sufficient cash to fund its activities will eventually go bankrupt.

The objective of the **statement of cash flows**, is to provide information on the sources of cash generated by the company and on the activities that required use of its cash. Exhibit 16-5 provides the statement of changes in financial position for Linamar Corporation for the years 1998 and 1999. While much of the detailed terminology in this statement requires more than an introductory knowledge of financial accounting, the essence of the statement can be quickly appreciated.

The statement of cash flows is normally divided into three parts. The first part adjusts net income for any non-cash expenses and for changes in working capital to generate cash provided (used in) operating activities. In 1999, Linamar experienced a net source of cash of $91,901 thousands within its operating activities. The second part identifies the cash provided by financing activities that, in Linamar's case, raised $62,615 thousand during the year. The third part lists the investment activities in which Linamar used $165,264 thousand, primarily in the acquisition of capital assets. The net effect of these three components of operating activities, investing activities and financing activities will indicate the net change in cash or near-cash assets. For Linamar, the sum of these three areas of activities resulted in an decrease of $10,748 thousands of its available cash that left the company in a cash position of $14,451 thousands by year-end.

EXHIBIT 16-5

LINAMAR CORPORATION.
Consolidated Statement of Cash Flows
Years Ended December 31, 1999 and 1998 (thousands of dollars)

	December 31 1999	December 31 1998
Cash Provided by (Used in) Operating Activities		
Net Earnings for the year	$ 65,647	$ 84,385
Charges (credits) to earnings not involving cash:		
Amortization	84,771	58,465
Future income taxes	(1,565)	4,758
Non-controlling interests	(2,460)	3,900
Loss (gain) on disposal of captial assets	282	(75)
Government subsidy	–	(579)
	146,675	150,854
Changes in non-cash working capital (net of effects of acquisitions):		
Increase in accounts receivable	(59,179)	(45,248)
Increase in inventories	(9,084)	(18,942)
Decrease (increase) in prepaid expenses	(14,465)	139
Decrease (increase) in other assets	862	(862)
Decrease (increase) in income taxes recoverable	2,675	(3,194)
Increase (decrease) in accounts payable and accrued liabilities	23,203	(1,514)
Decrease in income taxes payable	–	(14,967)
Increase in advanced payments from customers	1,214	1,370
	91,901	67,636
Financing Activities		
Proceeds from short-term bank borrowings	83,745	46,152
Proceeds from long-term debt	1,209	–
Repayment of long-term debt	(2,947)	(2,023)
Proceeds from common share issuance	2,873	11,064
Repurchase of shares	(11,000)	(9,107)
Dividends to shareholders	(11,265)	(9,639)
Dividends by subsidaries to non-controlling interests		(288)
	62,615	36,159
Investing Activities		
Purchase of capital assets	(168,460)	(171,247)
Proceeds from disposal of capital assets	3,068	6,803
Proceeds on redemption of preference shares	228	229
Increase (decrease) in investment by a non- controlling interest	(100)	850
Business acquisitions		(24,981)
	(165,264)	(188,346)
Decrease in Cash and Short-Term Investments	(10,748)	(84,551)
Cash and Short-Term Investments—Beginning of Year	25,199	109,750
Cash and Short-Term Investments—End of Year	$ 14,451	$ 25,199

In management accounting, we recognize the importance of distinguishing accounting expenses from cash expenditures. This distinction is equally relevant in analyzing the financial strengths and weaknesses of a company from its published financial statements.

SUMMARY

This chapter provides an introduction to financial statement analysis by focusing on ratios and the statement of changes in financial position that are commonly examined by analysts. While a more thorough study of this subject does not necessarily require a detailed understanding of financial accounting, an analyst's ability to understand the intricacies of interpreting certain ratios would definitely be improved with a thorough grounding in financial accounting. For our purposes, these ratios provide a useful complement to an understanding of the possible impacts of management accounting decisions on the financial statements of a company.

HIGHLIGHTS TO REMEMBER

1. Ratio analysis involves the comparison of ratios over time, across companies, or against benchmarks.
2. To obtain a more thorough understanding of the liquidity, profitability, stability, and growth for a company, each ratio should not be evaluated independently from the other ratios. Rather the analysis of each ratio should be viewed as part of the total analysis of the company.
3. A statement of changes in financial position provides information concerning the sources and uses of cash in the operating, financing, and investing activities of a company.

SUMMARY PROBLEMS FOR YOUR REVIEW

Problem One

	2002	2001	2000
Annual amounts:			
Net income	Nkr. 100*	Nkr. 60	Nkr. 25
Gross profit on sales	525	380	200
Cost of goods sold	975	620	300
Operating expenses	380	295	165
Income tax expense	45	25	10
End-of-year amounts:			
Capital assets	Nkr. 250	Nkr. 220	Nkr. 180
Long-term debt	80	65	40
Current liabilities	70	55	35
Cash	10	5	10
Accounts receivable	95	70	40
Merchandise inventory	125	85	60
Share capital	205	205	205
Retained earnings	125	55	10
Dividends	30	15	15

* Nkr. is Norwegian kroner.

1. Compute the following for each of the last two years, 2001 and 2000:
   a. Net income margin
   b. Return on shareholders' equity
   c. Inventory turnover
   d. Current ratio
   e. Ratio of debt to assets
   f. Ratio of current debt to assets
   g. Gross income margin
   h. Average collection period for accounts receivable
   i. Sales growth
2. Answer yes or no to each of these questions and indicate which of the computations in requirement 1 support your answer:
   a. Has the merchandise become more saleable?
   b. Is there a decrease in the effectiveness of accounts receivable collection efforts?
   c. Has gross income margin improved?
   d. Has the net income margin improved?
   e. Has the rate of return on owners' investment increased?
   f. Have the risks of insolvency changed significantly?
   g. Have business operations margins improved?
   h. Has there been a worsening of the company's ability to pay current debts on time?
3. Basing your observations on only the available data and the ratios you computed, prepare some brief comments on the company's operations and financial changes during the three years.

Solution

1. (a) Net income margin:
   (Sales: (2000: 200+300 = 500; 2001: 380+620 = 1,000; 2002: 525+975 = 1,500)
   2001: 60 ÷ 1,000 = 6.0%
   2002: 100 ÷ 1,500 = 6.7%
   (b) Return on shareholders' equity:
   2001: 60 ÷ (205+55) = 23.1%
   2002: 100 ÷ (205+125) = 30.3%
   (c) Inventory turnover:
   2001: 620 ÷ 85 = 7.3 times
   2002: 975 ÷ 125 = 7.8 times
   (d) Current ratio:
   2001: (5+70+85) ÷ 55 = 2.9 to 1
   2002: (10+95+125) ÷ 70 = 3.3 to 1
   (e) Ratio of debt to assets:
   2001: (65+55) ÷ (220+5+70+85) = 31.6%
   2002: (80+70) ÷ (250+10+95+125) = 31.3%
   (f) Ratio of current debt to assets:
   2001: 55 ÷ (220+5+70+85) = 14.5%
   2002: 70 ÷ (250+10+95+125) = 14.6%
   (g) Gross profit margin:
   2001: 380 ÷ 1,000 = 38%
   2002: 525 ÷ 1,500 = 35%

(h) Average collection period for accounts receivable:
    2001: 70 ÷ (1000 ÷ 365) = 25.6 days
    2002: 95 ÷ (1500 ÷ 365) = 23.1 days

(i) Sales growth:
    2001: (1000-500) ÷ 500 = 100%
    2002: (1500-1000) ÷ 1000 = 50%

2. **(a)** Yes, c   **(c)** No, g   **(e)** Yes, b   **(g)** No, g
   (b) No, h   **(d)** Yes, a   **(f)** No, e, f   **(h)** No, d

3. The company has grown rapidly and profitably (ratios a, b and i). Moreover, the large increase in retained income indicates that the expansion has been financed largely by internally generated funds. The expansion has been accompanied by increased liquidity of current assets (ratios c and d).

Problem Two

The Buretta Company has prepared the following data. In December 2001, Buretta paid $54 million cash for a new building acquired to accommodate an expansion of operations. This was financed partly by a new issue of long-term debt for $40 million cash. During 2001 the company also sold fixed assets for $5 million cash that was equal to their book value. All sales and purchases of merchandise were on credit.

BURETTA COMPANY
Statement of Cash Flows
For the Year Ended
December 31, 2001
(in millions)

CASH FLOWS FROM OPERATING ACTIVITIES:		
Cash collection from customers		$ 85
Cash payments:		
Cash paid to suppliers	$(79)	
General expenses	(10)	
Interest paid	(3)	
Property taxes	(2)	(94)
Net cash used by operating activities		$ (9)
CASH FLOWS FROM INVESTING ACTIVITIES:		
Purchase of capital assets (building)	$(54)	
Proceeds from sale of capital assets	5	
Net cash used by investing activities		(49)
CASH FLOWS FROM FINANCING ACTIVITIES:		
Long-term debt issued	$ 40	
Dividends paid	(1)	
Net cash provided by financial activities		39
Net decrease in cash		$(19)
Cash balance, December 31, 19X1		20
Cash balance, December 31, 19X2		$ 1

BURETTA COMPANY
Supporting Schedule to
Statement of Cash Flows
Reconciliation of Net
Income to Net Cash
Provided by Operating
Activities
For the Year Ended
December 31, 2001
(in millions)

Net income (from income statement)	$ 4
Adjustments to reconcile net income to net cash provided	
by operating activities:	
Add: Amortization which was deducted in the computation	
of net income but does not decrease cash	8
Deduct: Increase in accounts receivable	(15)
Deduct: Increase in inventory	(31)
Deduct: Increase in prepaid general expenses	(2)
Add: Increase in accounts payable	25
Add: Increase in accrued property tax payable	2
Net cash provided by operating activities	$(9)

Because the net income of $4 million was the highest in the company's history, Mr. Buretta, the chairman of the board, was perplexed by the company's extremely low cash balance.

What is revealed by the statement of cash flows? Does it help you reduce Mr. Buretta's puzzlement? Why?

Solution

The statement of cash flows shows where cash has come from and where it has gone. Operations used $9 million of cash. Why? The statement shows that large increases in accounts receivable ($15 million) and inventory ($31 million), plus a $2-million increase in prepaid expenses, used $48 million of cash. In contrast, only $39 million (that is, $4 + $8 + $25 + $2 million) was generated. It also shows the $9 million use of cash slightly differently; the $85 million of cash receipts and $94 million in disbursements are shown directly. Investing activities also consumed cash because $54 million was invested in building, and only $5 million was received from sales of fixed assets. Financing activities generated $39 million cash, which was $19 million less than the $58 million used by operating and investing activities.

Mr. Buretta should no longer be puzzled. The statement of cash flows shows where cash has come from and where it has gone. Either operations must be changed so that they do not require so much cash, or investment must be curtailed, or more long-term debt or ownership equity must be raised. Otherwise Buretta Company will soon run out of cash.

ACCOUNTING VOCABULARY

accounts payable *p. 741*
accounts receivable *p. 741*
accrual basis *p. 746*
assets *p. 740*
balance sheet *p. 743*
benchmarks *p. 749*
cash basis *p. 746*
cross-sectional analysis *p. 748*
current assets *p. 751*
current liabilities *p. 751*

income statement *p. 743*
liabilities *p. 741*
liquidity ratios *p. 750*
owners' equity *p. 741*
profitability ratios *p. 749*
retained earnings *p. 741*
retained income *p. 741*
revenues *p. 744*
shareholders' equity *p.741*
stability ratios *p. 752*

ASSIGNMENT MATERIAL

QUESTIONS

Q16-1 Criticize: "Assets are things of value owned by the entity."

Q16-2 Criticize: "Net income is the difference in the ownership capital account balances at two points in time."

Q16-3 Distinguish between the accrual basis and the cash basis.

Q16-4 Name the three types of comparisons made with ratios.

Q16-5 Why is it useful to analyze income statements and balance sheets by component percentages?

Q16-6 What two ratios are multiplied to give the return on assets?

Q16-7 "The statement of cash flows is an optional statement included by most companies in their annual reports." Do you agree? Explain.

Q16-8 What are the purposes of a statement of cash flows?

Q16-9 What three types of activities are summarized in the statement of cash flows?

PROBLEMS

P16-1 **ANALYSIS OF TRANSACTIONS, PREPARATION OF STATEMENTS.** The Ekern Company was incorporated on April 1, 2000. Ekern had ten holders of common shares. Elke Ekern, who was the president and chief executive officer, held 51 percent of the shares. The company rented space in chain discount stores and specialized in selling ladies' shoes. Ekern's first location was in a store owned by Nordic Market Centres, Inc.

The following events occurred in April:

a. The company was incorporated. Common shareholders invested $90,000 cash.

b. Purchased merchandise inventory for cash, $35,000.

c. Purchased merchandise inventory on open account, $25,000.

d. Merchandise carried in inventory at a cost of $37,000 was sold for cash for $25,000 and on open account for $65,000, a grand total of $90,000. Ekern (not Nordic) carries and collects these accounts receivable.

e. Collection of the above accounts receivable, $15,000.

f. Payments of accounts payable, $18,000. See transaction C.

g. Special display equipment and fixtures were acquired on April 1 for $36,000. Their expected useful life was 36 months with no terminal scrap value. Straightline amortization was adopted. This equipment was removable. Ekern paid $12,000 as a down payment and signed a promissory note for $24,000.

h. On April 1, Ekern signed a rental agreement with Nordic. The agreement called for a flat $2,000 per month, payable quarterly in advance. Therefore Ekern paid $6,000 cash on April 1.

i. The rental agreement also called for a payment of 10 percent of all sales. This payment was in addition to the flat $2,000 per month. In this way, Nordic would share in any success of the venture and be compensated for general services such as cleaning and utilities. This payment was to be made in cash on the last day of each month as soon as the sales for the month were tabulated. Ekern made the payment on April 30.

j. Wages, salaries, and sales commissions were paid in cash for all earnings by employees. The amount was $38,000.

k. Amortization expense was recognized. See Transaction (g).

l. The expiration of an appropriate amount of prepaid rental services was recognized. See Transaction (h).

1. Prepare an analysis of Ekern Company's transactions, employing the equation approach demonstrated in Exhibit 16-1. Two additional columns will be needed: Equipment and Fixtures and Note Payable. Show all amounts in thousands.

2. Prepare a balance sheet as of April 30, 2000, and an income statement for the month of April. Ignore income taxes.

3. Given these sparse facts, analyze Ekern's performance for April and its financial position as of April 30, 2000.

P16-2 CASH BASIS VERSUS ACCRUAL BASIS. Refer to the preceding problem. If Ekern company measured income on the cash basis, what revenue would be reported for April? Which basis (accrual or cash) provides a better measure of revenue? Why?

P16-3 BALANCE SHEET EFFECTS. A bank showed the following items (among others) on its balance sheet at January 1, 2000:

Cash	$ 2,644,000,000
Total deposits	$41,644,000,000

1. Suppose you made a bank deposit of $1,000. How would each of the bank assets and equities be affected? How much would each of your personal assets and equities be affected? Be specific.

2. Suppose a branch makes a $900,000 loan to a local hospital for remodeling. What would be the effect on each of the branch's assets and equities immediately after the loan is made? Be specific.

3. Suppose you borrowed $10,000 from a trust company on a personal loan. How would such a transaction affect your personal assets and equities?

P16-4 BALANCE SHEET EQUATION. Micra Technology is one of the leading producers of semiconductor components. Its revenue grew from $506 million in 1992 to more than $3.8 billion in 1999. The company's actual data (in millions of dollars) follow for its fiscal year ended September 2, 1999.

Assets, beginning of period	$4,551.4
Assets, end of period	E
Liabilities, beginning of period	A
Liabilities, end of period	2,832.8
Share capital, beginning of period	587.0
Share capital, end of period	D
Retained earnings, beginning of period	2,114.3
Retained earnings, end of period	C
Revenues	3,764.0
Costs and expenses	B
Net income (loss)	(68.9)
Dividends	0.0
Additional investments by shareholders	1,331.7

Find the unknowns (in millions), showing computations to support your answers.

P16-5 ANALYSIS OF TRANSACTIONS, PREPARATION OF STATEMENTS. PACCAR has maintained its top position in the sales of medium- and heavy-duty diesel trucks in Japan since 1973. The company's actual condensed balance sheet data for January 1, 2000 follows (in millions):

ASSETS		EQUITIES	
Cash	$1,042	Accounts payable	$1,734
Accounts receivable	570	Other liabilities	4,088
Inventory	385		
Property, plant, and equipment	875	Shareholders' Equity	2,111
Prepaid expenses and other assets	5,061		
Total	$7,933	Total	$7,933

Suppose the following summarizes some major transactions during January (in millions):

1. Trucks carried in inventory at a cost of $400, were sold for cash of $150 and on open account of $500, a grand total of $650.
2. Acquired inventory on account, $500.
3. Collected receivables, $300.
4. On April 2, used $250 cash to prepay some rent and insurance for 2000.
5. Payments on accounts payable (for inventories), $450.
6. Paid selling and administrative expenses in cash, $100.
7. A total of $90 of prepaid expenses for rent and insurance expired in January 2000.
8. Depreciation expense of $20 was recognized for January.

1. Prepare an analysis of the PACCAR transactions, employing the equation approach demonstrated in Exhibit 16-1, p. 742. Show all amounts in millions of dollars (for simplicity, only a few major transactions are illustrated here.)
2. Prepare an income statement for the month ended January 31 and a balance sheet as of January 31. Ignore income taxes

P16-6 CASH BASIS VERSUS ACCRUAL BASIS. Refer to the preceding problem. If PACCAR measured income on the cash basis, what revenue would be exported for April? Which basis (accrual or cash) provides a better measure of revenue? Why?

EXHIBIT 16A-1	Net sales	¥6,099
	Cost of sales	4,206
HONDA MOTOR COMPANY	Gross profit	¥1,893
Income Statement for the Year Ended March 31, 2000 (billions except per share information)	Selling and administrative	1,133
	Research and development	334
	Operating income	¥ 426
	Other income (expenses)	
	Interest income	¥ 11
	Interest expense	(19)
	Other	14
	Total	6
	Income before income taxes	¥ 432
	Income taxes	(170)
	Net income	¥ 262
	Amounts per share	
	Net income	¥ 269
	Cash dividends	¥ 21

EXHIBIT 16A-2	**Assets**	
	Current assets	
HONDA MOTOR COMPANY	Cash and marketable securities	¥ 431
Balance Sheet March 31, 2000 (billions)	Receivables	1,122
	Inventories	568
	Other	335
	Total current assets	¥2,456
	Property, plant, and equipment, net	1,121
	Investments	389
	Other assets	932
	Total assets	¥4,898
	Liabilities and Shareholders' Equity	
	Current liabilities	
	Bank loans	¥ 496
	Payables	697
	Accrued expenses	484
	Current portion of long-term debt	343
	Other	182
	Total current liabilities	¥2,202
	Long-term liabilities	
	Long-term debt	¥ 575
	Other	191
	Total long-term liabilities	¥ 766
	Shareholders' equity	
	Common shares (974,414,215 shares outstanding)	¥ 86
	Additional share capital	172
	Retained earnings	2,219
	Other	(547)
	Total shareholders' equity	¥1,930
	Total liabilities and shareholders' equity	¥4,898

Canadian Company Percentages

BALANCE SHEET PERCENTAGES	A	B	C	D	E	F	G	H
Cash and Equivalents	4.8	9.5	2.5	1.5	3.3	1.1	2.4	8.9
Receivables	11.9	4.9	10.3	7.9	4.4	3.5	3.7	0.0
Inventories	10.5	16.1	1.9	2.3	0.0	6.4	1.2	0.0
Investments	47.7	1.9	0.0	0.0	0.0	0.0	35.0	78.3
Property, Plant & Equipment	22.0	45.0	11.8	85.7	90.5	85.0	50.1	1.0
Other Assets	3.2	22.6	73.6	2.6	1.7	3.9	7.6	11.8
TOTAL ASSETS	100.0	100.0	100.0	100.0	100.0	100.0	100.0	100.0
Current Liabilities	14.1	41.6	16.7	8.3	7.1	7.6	10.8	64.7
Long-term Debt	0.0	19.2	19.3	33.3	12.6	19.8	36.9	30.5
Other Liabilities	0.2	2.7	9.8	28.3	6.6	13.2	12.8	0.0
Shareholders' Equity	85.8	36.5	54.2	30.1	73.7	59.4	39.5	4.8
TOTAL LIABILITY & SHAREHOLDERS' EQUITY	100.0	100.0	100.0	100.0	100.0	100.0	100.0	100.0

RATIO ANALYSIS

PROFITABILITY

	A	B	C	D	E	F	G	H
Return on Investment (%)	0.13	0.10	0.07	0.15	-0.04	-0.02	0.03	0.13
Return on Assets (%)	0.11	0.04	0.04	0.05	-0.03	-0.01	0.01	0.01
Operating income Margin (%)	0.19	0.04	0.13	0.21	0.08	0.14	-0.03	0.23
Net Profit Margin (%)	0.14	0.02	0.08	0.10	-0.15	-0.04	0.03	0.08
LIQUIDITY								
Current Ratio (x:1)	5.47	0.76	1.01	1.47	1.11	1.56	0.89	0.30
Quick Ratio (x:1)	3.73	0.23	0.24	0.18	0.47	0.15	0.22	0.44
Age of Receivables (days)	53.73	9.94	73.27	65.15	81.97	52.19	35.10	n/a
Age of Inventory (days)	122.03	28.23	19.29	58.86	n/a	131.65	14.44	n/a
Age of Payables (days)	124.58	53.21	97.57	155.55	88.71	35.69	120.86	n/a
Inventory Turnover (times)	2.95	12.75	18.67	6.12	n/a	2.73	24.93	n/a
Fixed Asset Turnover (times)	3.61	3.91	4.28	0.51	0.21	0.28	0.76	7.46
Asset Turnover (times)	0.80	1.76	0.50	0.44	0.19	0.24	0.38	0.08
STABILITY								
Debt to Assets	0.00	0.19	0.19	0.33	0.13	0.20	0.37	0.31
Equity to Assets	0.86	0.37	0.54	0.30	0.74	0.59	0.39	0.05
Times Interest Earned	n/a	4.84	2.99	8.51	-19.72	0.12	1.45	1.13

n/a: not applicable or immaterial.

P16-7 COLLABORATIVE LEARNING EXERCISE: FINANCIAL RATIOS. Form groups of four to six persons each. Each member of the group should pick a different company and find the most recent annual report for that company. (If you do not have printed annual reports, try searching the Internet for one.)

1. Each member should compute the ratios listed in Exhibit 16-2.
2. As a group, list two possible reasons that each ratio differs across the selected companies. Focus on comparing the companies with the highest and lowest values for each ratio, and explain how the nature of the company might be the reason for the differences in ratios.

CASES

C16-1 **FINANCIAL RATIOS.** Honda Motor Company is a Japanese automobile company with sales equivalent to $80 billion. The company's income statement and balance sheet for the year ended March 31, 2000, are shown in Exhibits 16A-1 and 16A-2. Monetary amounts are in Japanese yen (¥).

1. Prepare a common-size income statement, that is, one showing component percentages.
2. Compute the following ratios:
   a. Current ratio
   b. Total debt to equity
   c. Gross profit margin
   d. Return on shareholders' equity (1999 shareholders' equity was ¥1,764 billion)
3. What additional information would help you interpret the percentages and ratios you calculated?

C16-2 **UNIDENTIFIED CANADIAN INDUSTRIES.** Within an industry, operating policies and practices may vary between companies. However, the underlying nature of that industry greatly affects the firms' needs for funds, how the firms meet these needs, and also the firms' financial results.

Presented in Exhibit 16A-3 are: Balance sheets, given in percentage form; Selected ratios, categorized as profitability, liquidity and stability ratios.

These percentages and ratios are derived from the balance sheets and income statements of eight firms from different industries. Although it is known that certain differences between firms in the same industry exist, each firm whose figures are summarized is typical of those in its industry.

Required:

Identify each of the eight industries listed below from the data given in Exhibit 16A-3. Be prepared to explain the distinctive asset structures and ratios for each:

1. Grocery Chain
2. Mining
3. Utility
4. Bank
5. Oil and Gas
6. Newspaper
7. Railway
8. High Technology

C16-3 **STRATEGIC ANALYSIS.** (SMAC) You have been recently recruited to the newly created position of financial analyst with a large firm. Two years ago, this firm completed its fourth consecutive year of record profits and was among the top 10 firms traded on the Toronto Stock Exchange in terms of return on equity. Although the stock was widely held, the directors at that time became increasingly concerned about the possibility of an unfriendly takeover bid by larger firms seeking access to the firm's growing cash surplus. In response to this situation, the Board of Directors authorized an expansion strategy for your firm to diversify and grow by acquiring other businesses. The relevant guidelines for this strategy are as follows:

- The cost of a single acquisition is not to exceed $10 million.
- Target firms must be in the top quartile in their own industries as demonstrated by "key" financial ratios. In other words, no "sick-company turnarounds."

- Target firms must be sufficiently well organized, staffed, and managed to continue operations independently after the acquisition, so as not to place a burden on your firm's already lean, but efficient, management team that includes its engineers.

In the two years since its inception, this program has been a remarkably effective method of reducing cash surpluses. Three of the four firms acquired have been severely affected by the recent recession and have required massive infusions of cash to continue operations. Despite these setbacks, the program continues. Your position was created because of a need for a skilled financial professional to evaluate and monitor such acquisitions.

On your first day on the job, the financial statements for Great White North Co. Ltd. (GWNCL), a potential acquisition, have been given to you by the vice president in charge of the program. (See Exhibit 16A-4). Also provided were the industry statistics in Exhibit 16A-5.

The engineering department at your firm has analyzed GWNCL's operations and estimates that with an investment of $2,000,000 by GWNCL in robotic fabricating equipment (with a useful life of 10 years), production costs would be changed as follows:

- materials would be reduced by 8 percent due to reduced scrap and rework
- direct labour would be reduced by 10 percent due to increased automation
- overhead would be increased by 20 percent due to increased maintenance and greater levels of expertise in supervisory staff.

The new robotic equipment could be installed and would be operational almost immediately. Your firm's engineering department has developed considerable expertise in this field and is one of the few groups in the country capable of successfully implementing such changes. Although the cost reductions could make GWNCL more price competitive, price competition is not a primary characteristic of the custom manufacturing industry. (Assume capital cost allowance rates of 30 percent declining balance for robotic equipment.)

The purchase price for the 2,000,000 outstanding shares of GWNCL has been estimated at $8,000,000, which is a premium over its current net worth. However, the market value of GWNCL is expected to be equal to its net worth at the end of the tenth year.

The question was also raised as to how the additional $2,000,000 capital expenditure will affect the ROI calculation.

Current market borrowing costs range from 12 percent to 15 percent depending on the risk.

Required: | Identify and evaluate the issues associated with the proposed acquisition and make appropriate recommendations.

GREAT WHITE NORTH
COMPANY LIMITED
Statement of Income
and Retained Earnings
For the Year Ended
June 30, 2000 (000s)

Sales		$10,000
Cost of goods sold:		
Materials	$4,500	
Labour	1,300	
Plant overhead	300	6,100
Gross margin		3,900
Expenses:		
Marketing	1,400	
Administration & Amortization	1,400	
Interest	150	2,950
Income before tax and extraordinary item		950
Income taxes		380
Income before extraordinary item		570
Extraordinary item		380
Net income		950
Retained earnings, beginning of year		3,100
Total		4,050
Less: Dividends paid		500
Retained earnings, end of year		$ 3,550

ASSETS

Current assets:	
Cash	$ 400
Accounts receivable	1,500
Inventories	1,900
Total current assets	3,800
Fixed assets (net)	2,200
Total assets	$6,000

LIABILITIES AND SHAREHOLDERS' EQUITY

Current liabilities:	
Accounts payable	$1,250
Long-term debt	1,000
Total liabilities	2,250
Common shares (2,000,000 shares issued and outstanding)	200
Retained earnings	3,550
Total liabilities and shareholders' equity	$6,000

The following statistics have been compiled from a survey of the financial statements of the top quartile of the firms in GWNCL's industry, as determined by profitability. Projected sales in this industry will remain constant in real terms for the foreseeable future. The following ratios represent the mean levels of the financial statistics of these profitable firms.

Industry Statistics:

Current Ratio	1.5:1	Return on Total Assets	12.5%
Debt Equity Ratio	1.7:1	Net Return on Sales	6.0%
Price Earnings Ratio	14.0:1	Return on Equity	20.0%
Inventory Turnover	4 times	Equity to Total Assets	23.0%
Receivables Turnover	45 days		

Recommended Readings

The following resources will aid readers who want to pursue some topics with more depth than is possible in this book. There is a hazard in compiling a group of recommended readings. Inevitably, some worthwhile books or periodicals are omitted. Moreover, such a list cannot include books published subsequent to the compilation date. This list is not comprehensive, but it suggests many excellent readings.

PERIODICALS

Professional Journals

The following professional journals are typically available in university libraries and include articles on the application of management accounting:

- *Accounting Horizons*. Published by the American Accounting Association; stresses current practice-oriented articles in all areas of accounting.
- *CMA Management (*formerly the *CMA Magazine)*. Published by The Society of Management Accountants of Canada; includes much practice-oriented research in management accounting.
- *Financial Executive*. Published by the Financial Executives Institute; emphasizes general policy issues for accounting and finance executives.
- *GAO Journal*. Covers managerial accounting issues of interest to the General Accounting Office of the U.S. government.
- *Harvard Business Review*. Published by Harvard Business School; directed to general managers, but contains excellent articles on applications of management accounting.
- *Journal of Accountancy*. Published by the American Institute of CPAs; emphasizes financial accounting and is directed at the practicing CPA.
- *Management Accounting*. Published by the Institute of Management Accountants; many articles on actual applications by individual organizations.
- *Planning Review*. Published by the Planning Executives Institute; a journal designed for business planners.
- *Canadian Business, Report on Business Magazine, Business Week, Forbes, Fortune, The Economist, The Wall Street Journal*. Popular publications that cover a variety of business and economics topics; often their articles relate to management accounting.

Academic Journals

The academic journal that focuses most directly on current management and cost accounting research is the *Journal of Management Accounting Research*, published by the Management Accounting section of the American Accounting Association. *The Accounting Review*, the general research publication of the American Accounting Association, *Journal of Accounting Research*, published at the University of Chicago, and *Contemporary Accounting Research*, published by the Canadian Academic Accounting Association cover all accounting topics at a more theoretical level. *Accounting, Organizations and Society*, a British journal, publishes much research on behavioural aspects of management accounting. The *Journal of Accounting and Economics* covers economics-based accounting research.

BOOKS IN MANAGEMENT ACCOUNTING

Most of the topics in this text are covered in more detail in the many books entitled *Cost Accounting* including *Cost Accounting: A Managerial Emphasis* by Charles T. Horngren, George Foster, Srikant M. Datar, and Howard D. Teall (Prentice Hall, 2000). You can find more advanced coverage in *Advanced Managerial Accounting*, 3rd ed. by R. S. Kaplan and Anthony A. Atkinson (Prentice Hall, 1998), and in *Management Accounting* by Anthony A. Atkinson, Rajiv D. Bankor, Robert S. Kaplan and S. Mark Young (Prentice Hall, 1997).

Handbooks and General Texts, Readings, and Case Books

The books in this list have wide application to management accounting issues. The handbooks are basic references. The textbooks are designed for classroom use but may be useful for self-study. Readings books are collections of some of the better periodical articles. The case books present applications from real companies.

- BIERMAN, H., JR., AND S. SMIDT, *The Capital Budgeting Decision*, 7th ed. New York: Macmillan, 1992. Expands the capital budgeting discussion in Chapters 11–12.
- BINKER, B., ed., *Handbook of Cost Management*. New York: Warren, Gorham and Lamont, 1994.
- COOPER, D., R. SCAPENS, AND J. ARNOLD, eds., *Management Accounting Research and Practice*. London: Institute of Cost and Management Accountants, 1983.
- COOPER, R., AND R. KAPLAN, *The Design of Cost Management Systems: Text, Cases and Readings*. Englewood Cliffs, NJ: Prentice Hall, 1991.
- DAVIDSON, S., AND R. WEIL, eds., *Handbook of Modern Accounting*. New York: McGraw-Hill, 1989.
- KAPLAN, R. AND W. BRUNS, eds., *Accounting and Management: Field Study Perspectives*. Boston, MA: Harvard Business School Press, 1987.
- PRYOR, T., et al., *Activity Dictionary: A Comprehensive Reference Tool for ABM and ABC*, ICMS, Inc., 1992.
- ROSEN, L., ed., *Topics in Management Accounting*. Toronto: McGraw-Hill, 1984.
- ROTCH, W., B. ALLEN, AND C. SMITH, *Cases in Management Accounting and Control Systems* 3rd ed. Upper Saddle River, NJ: Prentice Hall, 1995.

- SHANK, J., *Cases in Cost Management: A Strategic Emphasis*. Cincinnati, South-Western, 1995.

Strategic Nature of Management Accounting

Management accountants realize that cost and performance information is most useful to organizations when it helps define strategic alternatives and helps in the management of resources to achieve strategic objectives. The books in this list, though not necessarily accounting books, provide valuable foundation to the interaction of strategy and accounting information.

- KAPLAN, R. AND H. T. JOHNSON, *Relevance Lost: The Rise and Fall of Management Accounting*. Boston, MA: Harvard Business School Press, 1987.
- PORTER, M., *Competitive Strategy*. New York: Free Press, 1980.
- PORTER, M., *Competitive Advantage*. New York: Free Press, 1985.
- RAPPAPORT, A., *Creating Shareholder Value: The New Standard for Business Performance*. New York: Free Press, 1986.
- SHANK, J., AND V. GOVIDARAJAN, *Strategic Cost Analysis: The Evolution from Managerial to Strategic Accounting*. Homewood, IL: Irwin, 1989.

Modern Manufacturing

The following books provide background on the nature of modern manufacturing.

- CHASE, R. AND N. AQUILANO, *Production and Operation Management*. Homewood, IL: Irwin, 1989.
- HAYES, R., S. WHEELRIGHT, AND K. CLARK, *Dynamic Manufacturing*. New York, Free Press, 1988.
- SCHONBERGER, R., *World Class Manufacturing*. New York, Free Press, 1986.
- TEECE, P., *The Competitive Challenge: Strategies for Industrial Innovation and Renewal*. Cambridge, MA: Ballinger, 1987.
- ZUBOFF, S., *In the Age of the Smart Machine*. New York: Basic Books, 1984.

Management Accounting in Modern Manufacturing Settings

These books present relatively recent responses of management accountants to changes in manufacturing methods and practices.

- BENNETT, E., B. FOSSUM, R. HARRIS, D. ROBERTSON, AND F. SKIPPER, *Financial Practices in a Computer Integrated System (CIS) Environment*. Morristown, NJ: Financial Executives Research Foundation, 1987.
- BENNETT, R., J. HENDRICKS, D. KEYS, AND E. RUDNICKI, *Cost Accounting for Factory Automation*. Montvale, NJ: National Association of Accountants, 1987.
- GOLDRATT, E. AND J. COX, *The Goal*. Croton-On-Hudson, NY: North River Press, Inc., 1992. A novel illustrating the new manufacturing environment.
- HOWELL, R., J. BROWN, S. SOUCY, AND A. SEED, *Management Accounting in the New Manufacturing Environment*. Montvale, NJ: National Association of Accountants, 1987.

- HOWELL, R. AND S. SOUCY, *Factory 2000+*. Montvale, NJ: National Association of Accountants, 1988. A collection of five articles by the authors originally published in *Management Accounting*.
- KAPLAN, R., ed., *Measuring Manufacturing Performance*: Boston, MA: Harvard University Press, 1990.
- LEE, J., *Managerial Accounting Changes for the 1990s*. Artesia, CA: McKay Business Systems, 1987.

Management Control Systems

The topics covered in Chapters 12 to 15 can be explored further in several books, including:

- ANTHONY, R N., J. DEARDEN, AND V. GOVINDARAJAN, *Management Control Systems*. Homewood IL: Irwin, 1994. A popular textbook that includes many cases.
- ARROW, K. J., *The Limits of Organization*. New York: Norton, 1974. A readable classic by the Nobel laureate.
- EMMANUEL, C. AND D. OTLEY, *Accounting for Management Control*. Berkshire, England: Van Nostrand Reinhold (UK), 1990.
- KAPLAN, R. AND D. NORTON, *The Balanced Scorecard*. Boston: Harvard Business School Press, 1996.
- MACIARIELLO, J. A., *Management Control Systems*. Englewood Cliffs, NJ: Prentice Hall, 1984.
- MERCHANT, K., *Control in Business Organizations*. Boston: Pitman, 1984.
- SOLOMONS, D., *Divisional Performance: Measurement and Control*. New York: Markus Wiener, 1983. A reprint of a 1965 classic that is still relevant.
- VANCIL, R. R., *Decentralization: Managerial Ambiguity by Design*. Homewood, IL: Dow Jones-Irwin, 1979.

Management Accounting in Not-for-Profit Organizations

Many books discuss management accounting in not-for-profit organizations. Four examples are

- ANTHONY, R. N., AND D. YOUNG, *Management Control in Nonprofit Organizations*, 5th ed. Homewood, IL: Irwin, 1994.
- BRIMSON, J., AND J. ANTOS, *Activity Based Management for Service Industries, Government Entities, and Non-Profit Organizations*. New York: Wiley, 1994.
- HERZLINGER, R. AND D. NITTERHOUSE, *Financial Accounting and Managerial Control for Non-profit Organizations*. Cincinnati, OH: Soutwestern Publishing Co., 1994.
- NEUMAN, B., AND K. BOLES, *Management Accounting for Healthcare Organizations*, 5th ed. Bonus Books, 1998.

APPENDIX

Fundamentals of Compound Interest and the Use of Present-Value Tables

NATURE OF INTEREST

Interest is the cost of using money. It is the rental charge for cash, just as rental charges are often made for the use of automobiles or boats.

Interest does not always entail an outlay of cash. The concept of interest applies to ownership funds as well as to borrowed funds. The reason why interest must be considered on *all* funds in use, regardless of their source, is that the selection of one alternative necessarily commits funds that could otherwise be invested in some other opportunity. The measure of the interest in such cases is the return foregone by rejecting the alternative use. For instance, a wholly owned home or business asset is not cost free. The funds so invested could alternatively be invested in government bonds or in some other venture. The measure of this opportunity cost depends on what alternative incomes are available.

Newspapers often contain advertisements of financial institutions citing interest rates that are "compounded." This appendix explains compound interest, including the use of present-value tables.

Simple interest is calculated by multiplying an interest rate by an unchanging principal amount. In contrast, *compound interest* is calculated by multiplying an interest rate by a principal amount that is increased each interest period by the previously accumulated (unpaid) interest. The accumulated interest is added to the principal to become the principal for the new period. For example, suppose you deposited $10,000 in a financial institution that promised to pay 10 percent interest per annum. You then let the amount accumulate for three years before withdrawing the full balance of the deposit. The *simple-interest* deposit would accumulate to $13,000 at the end of three years:

	PRINCIPAL	SIMPLE INTEREST	BALANCE, END OF YEAR
Year 1	$10,000	$10,000 × 0.10 = $1,000	$11,000
Year 2	10,000	10,000 × 0.10 = 1,000	12,000
Year 3	10,000	10,000 × 0.10 = 1,000	13,000

Compound interest provides interest on interest. That is, the principal changes from period to period. The deposit would accumulate to $10,000 \times (1.10)^3 = $10,000 \times 1.331 = $13,310$:

	PRINCIPAL	COMPOUND INTEREST	BALANCE, END OF YEAR
Year 1	$10,000	$10,000 × 0.10 = $1,000	$11,000
Year 2	11,000	11,000 × 0.10 = 1,100	12,100
Year 3	12,100	12,100 × 0.10 = 1,210	13,310

The "force" of compound interest can be staggering. For example, the same deposit would accumulate as follows:

	AT END OF		
	10 Years	20 Years	40 Years
Simple interest			
$10,000 + 10 ($1,000) =	$20,000		
10,000 + 20 ($1,000) =		$30,000	
10,000 + 40 ($1,000) =			$ 50,000
Compound interest			
$10,000 × (1.10)^{10} = $10,000 × 2.5937 =	$25,937		
$10,000 × (1.10)^{20} = $10,000 × 6.7275 =		$67,275	
$10,000 × (1.10)^{40} = $10,000 × 45.2593 =			$452,593

Hand calculations of compound interest quickly become burdensome. Therefore compound interest tables have been constructed to ease computations. (Indeed, many hand-held calculators contain programs that provide speedy answers.) Hundreds of tables are available, but we will use only the two most useful for capital budgeting.[1]

TABLE 1: PRESENT VALUE OF $1

How shall we express a future cash inflow or outflow in terms of its equivalent today (at time zero)? Table 1, page 776, provides factors that give the *present value* of a single, lump-sum cash flow to be received or paid at the *end* of a future period.[2]

Suppose you invest $1 today. It will grow to $1.06 in one year at 6 percent interest; that is, $1 \times 1.06 = 1.06. At the end of the second year its value is ($1 \times 1.06) \times 1.06 = $1 \times (1.06)^2 = 1.124, and at the end of the third year it is $1 \times (1.06)^3 = 1.191. In general, $1 grows to $(1 + i)^n$ in n years at i percent interest.

To determine the *present value*, you reverse this accumulation process. If $1.00 is to be received in one year, it is worth $1 \div 1.06 = 0.9434 today at an interest rate of 6 percent. Suppose you invest $0.9434 today. In one year you will

---

[1] For additional tables, see R. Vichas, *Handbook of Financial Mathematics, Formulas and Tables.* Englewood Cliffs, NJ: Prentice Hall, 1979.

[2] The factors are rounded to four decimal places. The examples in this text use these rounded factors. If you use tables with different rounding, or if you use a calculator or personal computer, your answers may differ from those given because of a small rounding error.

have $0.9434 × 1.06 = $1. Thus, $0.9434 is the *present value* of $1 a year, hence at 6 percent. If the dollar will be received in two years, its present value is $1 ÷ (1.06)^2 = $0.8900. The general formula for the present value (*PV*) of an amount *S* to be received or paid in *n* periods at an interest rate of *i* percent per period is

$$PV + \frac{S}{(1 + i)^n}$$

Table 1 gives factors for the present value of $1 at various interest rates over several different periods. Present values are also called *discounted* values, and the process of finding the present value is *discounting*. You can think of this as discounting (decreasing) the value of a future cash inflow or outflow. Why is the value discounted? Because the cash is to be received or paid in the future, not today.

Assume that a prominent city is issuing a three-year non-interest-bearing note payable that promises to pay a lump sum of $1,000 exactly three years from now. You desire a rate of return of exactly 6 percent, compounded annually. How much would you be willing to pay now for the three-year note? The situation is sketched as follows:

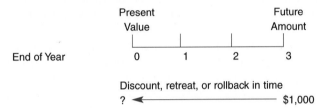

The factor in the period 3 row and 6 percent column of Table 1 is 0.8396. The present value of the $1,000 payment is $1,000 × 0.8396 = $839.60. You would be willing to pay $839.60 for the $1,000 to be received in three years.

Suppose interest is compounded semiannually rather than annually. How much would you be willing to pay? The three years become six interest payment periods. The rate per period is half the annual rate, or 6% ÷ 2 = 3%. The factor in the period 6 row and 3% column of Table 1 is 0.8375. You would be willing to pay $1,000 × 0.8375 or only $837.50 rather than $839.60.

As a further check on your understanding, review the earlier example of compound interest. Suppose the financial institution promised to pay $13,310 at the end of three years. How much would you be willing to deposit at time zero if you desired a 10 percent rate of return compounded annually? Using Table 1, the period 3 row and the 10% column show a factor of 0.7513. Multiply this factor by the future amount:

$$PV = 0.7513 × $13,310 = $10,000$$

A diagram of this computation follows:

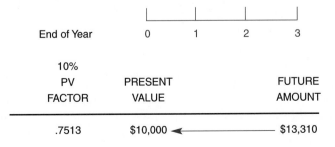

Pause for a moment. Use Table 1 to obtain the present values of

1. $1,600, at 20%, at the end of 20 years
2. $8,300, at 10%, at the end of 12 years
3. $8,000, at 4%, at the end of 4 years

Answers:

1. $1,600 (0.0261) = $41.76
2. $8,300 (0.3186) = $2,644.38
3. $8,000 (0.8548) = $6,838.40

TABLE 2: PRESENT VALUE OF AN ORDINARY ANNUITY OF $1

An *ordinary annuity* is a series of equal cash flows to take place at the *end* of successive periods of equal length. Its present value is denoted PV_A. Assume that you buy a note from a municipality that promises to pay $1,000 at the end of *each* of three years. How much should you be willing to pay if you desire a rate of return of 6 percent, compounded annually?

You could solve this problem using Table 1. First, find the present value of each payment, and then add the present values as in Exhibit B-1. You would be willing to pay $943.40 for the first payment, $890.00 for the second, and $839.60 for the third, a total of $2,673.00.

Since each cash payment is $1,000 with equal one-year periods between them, the note is an *ordinary annuity*. Table 2, page 777, provides a shortcut method. The present value in Exhibit B-1 can be expressed as

$$PV_A = \$1,000 \times \frac{1}{1.06} + \$1,000 \times \frac{1}{(1.06)^2} + \$1,000 \times \frac{1}{(1.06)^3}$$

$$= \$1,000 \left[\frac{1}{1.06} + \frac{1}{(1.06)^2} + \frac{1}{(1.06)^3} \right]$$

The three terms in brackets are the first three numbers from the 6% column of Table 1, and their sum is in the third row of the 6% column of Table 2: .9434 + .8900 + .8396 = 2.6730. Instead of calculating three present values and adding them, you can simply multiply the PV factor from Table 2 by the cash payment: $2.6730 \times \$1,000 = \$2,673$.

EXHIBIT B-1		END OF YEAR	0	1	2	3
	PAYMENT	TABLE ONE FACTOR	PRESENT VALUE			
	1	$\frac{1}{1.06} = .9434$	$ 943.40	$1,000		
	2	$\frac{1}{(1.06)^2} = .8900$	890.00		$1,000	
	3	$\frac{1}{(1.06)^3} = .8396$	839.60			$1,000
	Total		$2,673.00			

This shortcut is especially valuable if the cash payments or receipts extend over many periods. Consider an annual cash payment of $1,000 for 20 years at 6 percent. The present value, calculated from Table 2, is $1,000 × 11. 4699 = $11,469.90.

To use Table 1 for this calculation, you would perform 20 multiplications and then add the twenty products.

The factors in Table 2 can be calculated using the following general formula:

$$PV_A = \frac{1}{i} \left[1 - \frac{1}{(1+i)^n} \right]$$

Applied to our illustration:

$$PV_A = \frac{1}{.06} \left[1 - \frac{1}{(1.06)^3} \right] = \frac{1}{.06} (1 - .8396) = \frac{.1604}{.06} = 2.6730$$

Use Table 2 to obtain the present values of the following ordinary annuities:

1. $1,600 at 20% for 20 years
2. $8,300 at 10% for 12 years
3. $8,000 at 4% for 4 years

Answers:

1. $1,600 (4.8696) = $7,791.36
2. $8,300 (6.8137) = $56,553.71
3. $8,000 (3.6299) = $29,039.20

In particular, note that the higher the interest rate, the lower the present value.

TABLE 1

(Put a clip on this page for easy reference.)

Present Value of $1

$$PV = \frac{1}{(1 + i)^n}$$

PERIODS	3%	4%	5%	6%	7%	8%	10%	12%	14%	16%	18%	20%	22%	24%	25%	26%	28%	30%	40%
1	.9709	.9615	.9524	.9434	.9346	.9259	.9091	.8929	.8772	.8621	.8475	.8333	.8197	.8065	.8000	.7937	.7813	.7692	.7143
2	.9426	.9246	.9070	.8900	.8734	.8573	.8264	.7972	.7695	.7432	.7182	.6944	.6719	.6504	.6400	.6299	.6104	.5917	.5102
3	.9151	.8890	.8638	.8396	.8163	.7938	.7513	.7118	.6750	.6407	.6086	.5787	.5507	.5245	.5120	.4999	.4768	.4552	.3644
4	.8885	.8548	.8227	.7921	.7629	.7350	.6830	.6355	.5921	.5523	.5158	.4823	.4514	.4230	.4096	.3968	.3725	.3501	.2603
5	.8626	.8219	.7835	.7473	.7130	.6806	.6209	.5674	.5194	.4761	.4371	.4019	.3700	.3411	.3277	.3149	.2910	.2693	.1859
6	.8375	.7903	.7462	.7050	.6663	.6302	.5645	.5066	.4556	.4104	.3704	.3349	.3033	.2751	.2621	.2499	.2274	.2072	.1328
7	.8131	.7599	.7107	.6651	.6227	.5835	.5132	.4523	.3996	.3538	.3139	.2791	.2486	.2218	.2097	.1983	.1776	.1594	.0949
8	.7894	.7307	.6768	.6274	.5820	.5403	.4665	.4039	.3506	.3050	.2660	.2326	.2038	.1789	.1678	.1574	.1388	.1226	.0678
9	.7664	.7026	.6446	.5919	.5439	.5002	.4241	.3606	.3075	.2630	.2255	.1938	.1670	.1433	.1342	.1249	.1084	.0943	.0484
10	.7441	.6756	.6139	.5584	.5083	.4632	.3855	.3220	.2697	.2267	.1911	.1615	.1369	.1164	.1074	.0992	.0847	.0725	.0346
11	.7224	.6496	.5847	.5268	.4751	.4289	.3505	.2875	.2366	.1954	.1619	.1346	.1122	.0938	.0859	.0787	.0662	.0558	.0247
12	.7014	.6246	.5568	.4970	.4440	.3971	.3186	.2567	.2076	.1685	.1372	.1122	.0920	.0757	.0687	.0625	.0517	.0429	.0176
13	.6810	.6006	.5303	.4688	.4150	.3677	.2897	.2292	.1821	.1452	.1163	.0935	.0754	.0610	.0550	.0496	.0404	.0330	.0126
14	.6611	.5775	.5051	.4423	.3878	.3405	.2633	.2046	.1597	.1252	.0985	.0779	.0618	.0492	.0440	.0393	.0316	.0254	.0090
15	.6419	.5553	.4810	.4173	.3624	.3152	.2394	.1827	.1401	.1079	.0835	.0649	.0507	.0397	.0352	.0312	.0247	.0195	.0064
16	.6232	.5339	.4581	.3936	.3387	.2919	.2176	.1631	.1229	.0930	.0708	.0541	.0415	.0320	.0281	.0248	.0193	.0150	.0046
17	.6050	.5134	.4363	.3714	.3166	.2703	.1978	.1456	.1078	.0802	.0600	.0451	.0340	.0258	.0225	.0197	.0150	.0116	.0033
18	.5874	.4936	.4155	.3503	.2959	.2502	.1799	.1300	.0946	.0691	.0508	.0376	.0279	.0208	.0180	.0156	.0118	.0089	.0023
19	.5703	.4746	.3957	.3305	.2765	.2317	.1635	.1161	.0829	.0596	.0431	.0313	.0229	.0168	.0144	.0124	.0092	.0068	.0017
20	.5537	.4564	.3769	.3118	.2584	.2145	.1486	.1037	.0728	.0514	.0365	.0261	.0187	.0135	.0115	.0098	.0072	.0053	.0012
21	.5375	.4388	.3589	.2942	.2415	.1987	.1351	.0926	.0638	.0443	.0309	.0217	.0154	.0109	.0092	.0078	.0056	.0040	.0009
22	.5219	.4220	.3418	.2775	.2257	.1839	.1228	.0826	.0560	.0382	.0262	.0181	.0126	.0088	.0074	.0062	.0044	.0031	.0006
23	.5067	.4057	.3256	.2618	.2109	.1703	.1117	.0738	.0491	.0329	.0222	.0151	.0103	.0071	.0059	.0049	.0034	.0024	.0004
24	.4919	.3901	.3101	.2470	.1971	.1577	.1015	.0659	.0431	.0284	.0188	.0126	.0085	.0057	.0047	.0039	.0027	.0018	.0003
25	.4776	.3751	.2953	.2330	.1842	.1460	.0923	.0588	.0378	.0245	.0160	.0105	.0069	.0046	.0038	.0031	.0021	.0014	.0002
26	.4637	.3607	.2812	.2198	.1722	.1352	.0839	.0525	.0331	.0211	.0135	.0087	.0057	.0037	.0030	.0025	.0016	.0011	.0002
27	.4502	.3468	.2678	.2074	.1609	.1252	.0763	.0469	.0291	.0182	.0115	.0073	.0047	.0030	.0024	.0019	.0013	.0008	.0001
28	.4371	.3335	.2551	.1956	.1504	.1159	.0693	.0419	.0255	.0157	.0097	.0061	.0038	.0024	.0019	.0015	.0010	.0006	.0001
29	.4243	.3207	.2429	.1846	.1406	.1073	.0630	.0374	.0224	.0135	.0082	.0051	.0031	.0020	.0015	.0012	.0008	.0005	.0001
30	.4120	.3083	.2314	.1741	.1314	.0994	.0573	.0334	.0196	.0116	.0070	.0042	.0026	.0016	.0012	.0010	.0006	.0004	.0000
40	.3066	.2083	.1420	.0972	.0668	.0460	.0221	.0107	.0053	.0026	.0013	.0007	.0004	.0002	.0001	.0001	.0001	.0000	.0000

TABLE 2

Present Value of Ordinary Annuity of $1

$$PV_A = \frac{1}{i}\left[1 - \frac{1}{(1+i)^n}\right]$$

PERIODS	3%	4%	5%	6%	7%	8%	10%	12%	14%	16%	18%	20%	22%	24%	25%	26%	28%	30%	40%
1	.9709	.9615	.9524	.9434	.9346	.9259	.9091	.8929	.8772	.8621	.8475	.8333	.8197	.8065	.8000	.7937	.7813	.7692	.7143
2	1.9135	1.8861	1.8594	1.8334	1.8080	1.7833	1.7355	1.6901	1.6467	1.6052	1.5656	1.5278	1.4915	1.4568	1.4400	1.4235	1.3916	1.3609	1.2245
3	2.8286	2.7751	2.7232	2.6730	2.6243	2.5771	2.4869	2.4018	2.3216	2.2459	2.1743	2.1065	2.0422	1.9813	1.9520	1.9234	1.8684	1.8161	1.5889
4	3.7171	3.6299	3.5460	3.4651	3.3872	3.3121	3.1699	3.0373	2.9137	2.7982	2.6901	2.5887	2.4936	2.4043	2.3616	2.3202	2.2410	2.1662	1.8492
5	4.5797	4.4518	4.3295	4.2124	4.1002	3.9927	3.7908	3.6048	3.4331	3.2743	3.1272	2.9906	2.8636	2.7454	2.6893	2.6351	2.5320	2.4356	2.0352
6	5.4172	5.2421	5.0757	4.9173	4.7665	4.6229	4.3553	4.1114	3.8887	3.6847	3.4976	3.3255	3.1669	3.0205	2.9514	2.8850	2.7594	2.6427	2.1680
7	6.2303	6.0021	5.7864	5.5824	5.3893	5.2064	4.8684	4.5638	4.2883	4.0386	3.8115	3.6046	3.4155	3.2423	3.1611	3.0833	2.9370	2.8021	2.2628
8	7.0197	6.7327	6.4632	6.2098	5.9713	5.7466	5.3349	4.9676	4.6389	4.3436	4.0776	3.8372	3.6193	3.4212	3.3289	3.2407	3.0758	2.9247	2.3306
9	7.7861	7.4353	7.1078	6.8017	6.5152	6.2469	5.7590	5.3282	4.9464	4.6065	4.3030	4.0310	3.7863	3.5655	3.4631	3.3657	3.1842	3.0190	2.3790
10	8.5302	8.1109	7.7217	7.3601	7.0236	6.7101	6.1446	5.6502	5.2161	4.8332	4.4941	4.1925	3.9232	3.6819	3.5705	3.4648	3.2689	3.0915	2.4136
11	9.2526	8.7605	8.3064	7.8869	7.4987	7.1390	6.4951	5.9377	5.4527	5.0286	4.6560	4.3271	4.0354	3.7757	3.6564	3.5435	3.3351	3.1473	2.4383
12	9.9540	9.3851	8.8633	8.3838	7.9427	7.5361	6.8137	6.1944	5.6603	5.1971	4.7932	4.4392	4.1274	3.8514	3.7251	3.6059	3.3868	3.1903	2.4559
13	10.6350	9.9856	9.3936	8.8527	8.3577	7.9038	7.1034	6.4235	5.8424	5.3423	4.9095	4.5327	4.2028	3.9124	3.7801	3.6555	3.4272	3.2233	2.4685
14	11.2961	10.5631	9.8986	9.2950	8.7455	8.2442	7.3667	6.6282	6.0021	5.4675	5.0081	4.6106	4.2646	3.9616	3.8241	3.6949	3.4587	3.2487	2.4775
15	11.9379	11.1184	10.3797	9.7122	9.1079	8.5595	7.6061	6.8109	6.1422	5.5755	5.0916	4.6755	4.3152	4.0013	3.8593	3.7261	3.4834	3.2682	2.4839
16	12.5611	11.6523	10.8378	10.1059	9.4466	8.8514	7.8237	6.9740	6.2651	5.6685	5.1624	4.7296	4.3567	4.0333	3.8874	3.7509	3.5026	3.2832	2.4885
17	13.1661	12.1657	11.2741	10.4773	9.7632	9.1216	8.0216	7.1196	6.3729	5.7487	5.2223	4.7746	4.3908	4.0591	3.9099	3.7705	3.5177	3.2948	2.4918
18	13.7535	12.6593	11.6896	10.8276	10.0591	9.3719	8.2014	7.2497	6.4674	5.8178	5.2732	4.8122	4.4187	4.0799	3.9279	3.7861	3.5294	3.3037	2.4941
19	14.3238	13.1339	12.0853	11.1581	10.3356	9.6036	8.3649	7.3658	6.5504	5.8775	5.3162	4.8435	4.4415	4.0967	3.9424	3.7985	3.5386	3.3105	2.4958
20	14.8775	13.5903	12.4622	11.4699	10.5940	9.8181	8.5136	7.4694	6.6231	5.9288	5.3527	4.8696	4.4603	4.1103	3.9539	3.8083	3.5458	3.3158	2.4970
21	15.4150	14.0292	12.8212	11.7641	10.8355	10.0168	8.6487	7.5620	6.6870	5.9731	5.3837	4.8913	4.4756	4.1212	3.9631	3.8161	3.5514	3.3198	2.4979
22	15.9369	14.4511	13.1630	12.0416	11.0612	10.2007	8.7715	7.6446	6.7429	6.0113	5.4099	4.9094	4.4882	4.1300	3.9705	3.8223	3.5558	3.3230	2.4985
23	16.4436	14.8568	13.4886	12.3034	11.2722	10.3711	8.8832	7.7184	6.7921	6.0442	5.4321	4.9245	4.4985	4.1371	3.9764	3.8273	3.5592	3.3254	2.4989
24	16.9355	15.2470	13.7986	12.5504	11.4693	10.5288	8.9847	7.7843	6.8351	6.0726	5.4509	4.9371	4.5070	4.1428	3.9811	3.8312	3.5619	3.3272	2.4992
25	17.4131	15.6221	14.0939	12.7834	11.6536	10.6748	9.0770	7.8431	6.8729	6.0971	5.4669	4.9476	4.5139	4.1474	3.9849	3.8342	3.5640	3.3286	2.4994
26	17.8768	15.9828	14.3752	13.0032	11.8258	10.8100	9.1609	7.8957	6.9061	6.1182	5.4804	4.9563	4.5196	4.1511	3.9879	3.8367	3.5656	3.3297	2.4996
27	18.3270	16.3296	14.6430	13.2105	11.9867	10.9352	9.2372	7.9426	6.9352	6.1364	5.4919	4.9636	4.5243	4.1542	3.9903	3.8387	3.5669	3.3305	2.4997
28	18.7641	16.6631	14.8981	13.4062	12.1371	11.0511	9.3066	7.9844	6.9607	6.1520	5.5016	4.9697	4.5281	4.1566	3.9923	3.8402	3.5679	3.3312	2.4998
29	19.1885	16.9837	15.1411	13.5907	12.2777	11.1584	9.3696	8.0218	6.9830	6.1656	5.5098	4.9747	4.5312	4.1585	3.9938	3.8414	3.5687	3.3317	2.4999
30	19.6004	17.2920	15.3725	13.7648	12.4090	11.2578	9.4269	8.0552	7.0027	6.1772	5.5168	4.9789	4.5338	4.1601	3.9950	3.8424	3.5693	3.3321	2.4999
40	23.1148	19.7928	17.1591	15.0463	13.3317	11.9246	9.7791	8.2438	7.1050	6.2335	5.5482	4.9966	4.5439	4.1659	3.9995	3.8458	3.5712	3.3332	2.5000

COMPANY AND ORGANIZATION INDEX

SUBJECT INDEX

Key terms and the pages on which they are defined are printed in bold.